Scottish Footb
2017 / 18

Edited by Andy McGregor

Rel8 Media

SCOTTISH FOOTBALL ALMANAC 2017/18

Published by Rel8 Media
Unit 7, Woodend Business Centre, Cowdenbeath, Fife, KY4 8HG.

A great deal of effort has been made to ensure that the information in this book is as accurate as possible. However, in a work of this nature there will inevitably be some inaccuracies. Neither the publishers nor the author can accept responsibility for any consequences arising from using this book.

Sources used have been acknowledged where appropriate. The author has tried to clear all copyright permissions but where this has not been possible and where amendments are required, then the publisher will be pleased to make any necessary arrangements at the earliest opportunity.

British Library in Publication Data.
A catalogue record for this volume is available from the British Library.

ISBN 978-0-9574645-8-2

CONTENTS

SOURCES / ACKNOWLEDGEMENTS

Most of the information for this book has been culled from media sources. The websites of the SFA and SPFL have been most informative, as have official club websites. "Unofficial" web sources, including the mine of information that is Pie and Bovril, have also been useful in clarifying certain points.

Club match programmes have also been useful. Those that provide a "record" of club news and events are particularly helpful when putting together a project of this nature.

Historical records have come mainly from Rothmans and Sky Sports Year Books. For football outwith the Scottish Professional Football League extensive use was made of back issues of the invaluable Scottish Non League Review, published annually by Stewart Davidson since the late 1980s.

Thanks also to John Litster who has double-checked the stats and pointed out a number of errors and omissions from the original draft.

Others who have provided specific information are acknowledged in the body of the book.

My thanks go to everyone who takes the time to update and disseminate information about football, via websites, Twitter, Facebook and printed media.

Errors and Omissions
Inevitable in a work of this size there will be errors and omissions. We would be pleased to be informed of any, so that we can rectify these in any future edition.
rel8med@btinternet.com

INTRODUCTION

Welcome to the Fourth Edition of the Scottish Football Almanac. We believe that this is the most comprehensive record and guide available for Scottish football and the contents have again been expanded.

I doubt if there is any country in the world where sporting life is so dominated by one particular sport. Football is everything in Scotland. OK, we get quite excited about Andy Murray but it doesn't turn us into tennis fans. And we're actually just as interested that he's a Hibs fan as that he's the top tennis player in the world. By head of population more people watch football in Scotland than virtually any other country in the world. So why are our results on the international stage so bad?

Writing this in early July, with two Scottish teams already eliminated from Europe, it is impossible to explain how Rangers contrived to lose to Progres Niedercorn. But they did. St Johnstone went out to Lithuanian opposition. Goodness knows how our co-efficient will look like in a year's time as one of the best years of recent times "drops off" the calculation. Our teams will soon be unseeded against opponents that would once have been regarded as a bye.

Then international team's World Cup qualifying campaign has been unimpressive. Our chances of reaching the Finals are slim.

Celtic's achievement in going undefeated during 2016/17 was remarkable. Hoops fans will revel in it but the more intelligent amongst them must also see that it is concerning. The gap between Celtic and the rest of Scottish football is a chasm, yet Celtic view merely qualifying for the Champions League as a huge success. They are right to do so - just look at the teams who fail to qualify for evidence of that. Celtic's performances in the Champions League last season were a reality check - they were rightly lauded for two draws against Manchester City but the rest of the campaign is best forgotten.

The SPFL will benefit from the return of a rejuvenated Hibernian. Their journey from relegation under Terry Butcher via a Scottish Cup win to promotion is a reminder that fortunes change quickly for most teams in Scottish football. Inverness Caley Thistle, Cup winners two years ago, now find themselves relegated.

Outside of the SPFL there is a busy football scene. I would hesitate to say vibrant because at adult grass roots level the game is struggling. Saturday afternoon Amateur football has been decimated by the closure of many clubs. Sunday League football has contracted. Many Junior clubs face a problem of ageing committees and a lack of younger people to help. The evolution model employed by the SFA in developing a Pyramid system needs to be re-examined, and quickly. The SFA need to take a firm grip of football outside the SPFL and provide some direction and leadership before it is too late.

The purpose of this Almanac remains unchanged. It exists to record and hopefully preserve the minutiae of Scottish football. Today's results are tomorrow's history. With newspapers providing poorer coverage of the facts than ever before, and the ephemeral nature of internet resources, the need for a record book has never been greater.

Some new features have been added. In a year's time we aim to publish a companion volume with more detailed information about every player to turn out in the SPFL - full career stats and so on.

Hopefully the readers will enjoy the book and enjoy season 2017/18 whatever it may bring for their particular clubs.

Andy McGregor
July 2017

SCOTTISH FOOTBALL ASSOCIATION

SFA STRUCTURE 2016/17 (Source SFA Handbook and Website)

CONGRESS
The SFA Congress is theoretically the governing body for football in Scotland.

PATRON – HER MAJESTY THE QUEEN

Office Bearers

President - Alan McRae (Cove Rangers FC)
Vice-President - Rod Petrie (Hibernian FC)
Hon. Vice-Presidents - Jack McGinn, John McBeth, George W. Peat, R. Campbell Ogilvie

League Representatives

SCOTTISH PROFESSIONAL FOOTBALL LEAGUE
Andrew Dickson (Rangers), Malky Mackay (Queen's Park), Justine Mitchell (Dundee United), Mike Mulraney (Alloa Athletic), John Nelms (Dundee), David Reid (Stenhousemuir)

EAST OF SCOTLAND FOOTBALL LEAGUE
Thomas Brown

SCOTTISH HIGHLAND FOOTBALL LEAGUE
Finlay Noble

SCOTTISH LOWLAND FOOTBALL LEAGUE
John McCabe

SOUTH OF SCOTLAND FOOTBALL LEAGUE
R.W. Shaw M.B.E.

Affiliated National Association Representatives

SCOTTISH AMATEUR F.A.
Charles Rex Gallacher

SCOTTISH JUNIOR F.A.
Tom A. Johnston

SCOTTISH SCHOOLS' F.A.
John Watson

SCOTTISH WELFARE F.A.
Callum Shanks

SCOTTISH WOMEN'S FOOTBALL
Fiona Cardwell

SCOTTISH YOUTH F.A.
David Little

Football Family Representatives

PFA SCOTLAND
Fraser Wishart

MANAGERS' AND COACHES' ASSOCIATION
Walter Macadam

SCOTTISH SENIOR FOOTBALL REFEREES' ASSOCIATION
Crawford Allan

SPORTSCOTLAND
Louise Martin C.B.E.

MEDIA
Tba

SUPPORTERS
Supporters Direct Scotland

BOARD
The main Board consists of eight members: the Scottish FA Office Bearers (Alan McRae, President; Stewart Regan, Chief Executive; and Rod Petrie, Vice-President), plus Ralph Topping (SPFL), Michael Mulraney (SPFL), Tom Johnston (Scottish Junior FA) and independent non-executive directors, Barrie Jackson and Gary Hughes.

The Board focusses on corporate strategy and top-line decision-making, with the operational Professional and Non-Professional Boards representing their respective parts of the game.

SUB-BOARD/COMMITTEES

PROFESSIONAL GAME BOARD
Chairman: Rod Petrie (Scottish FA)
Members: Alan McRae (Scottish FA), Stewart Regan (Scottish FA), Andrew McKinlay (Scottish FA)*, Neil Doncaster (SPFL), Ralph Topping (SPFL), Duncan Fraser (SPFL), Michael Mulraney (SPFL), Stewart Robertson (SPFL), Sandy Stables (SHFL) and Andrew Waddell (SLFL)

NON-PROFESSIONAL GAME BOARD
Chairman: Alan McRae (Scottish FA)
Members: Rod Petrie (Scottish FA), Stewart Regan (Scottish FA), John Campbell (Scottish Welfare FA), Fiona Cardwell (Scottish Women's Football), John Gold (Scottish Schools FA), John Greenhorn (East of Scotland Football League), Colin Holden (South of Scotland Football League), Tom Johnston (Scottish Junior FA), Thomas McKeown (Scottish Amateur FA), David Little (Scottish Youth FA)

LICENSING COMMITTEE
(Chairman) Allan Cowan *
(Vice-Chairman) Ewen Cameron*
(Members) Finlay Noble, John McCabe, Anne McKeown, Craig Paterson* and Richard Shaw
*Co-opted member

REFEREE COMMITTEE
(Chairman) Alan McRae
(Vice-Chairwoman) Anne McKeown
(Members) Iain Brines*, Alan Freeland*, Ian Fyfe*, Calum Murray*, Tom Murphy*, Eddie Smith* and William Young*

*Co-opted member

SFA FOOTBALL REGULATORY ADVISORY GROUP
Anne Budge (Hearts), Brian Caldwell (St Mirren), Andrew Dickson (Rangers), Henry McClelland (Annan Athletic) Michael Nicholson (Celtic), Rod McKenzie (Harper McLeod Solicitors), Iain Blair (SPFL Company Secretary).

ASSOCIATIONS AND LEAGUES 2016/2017

Affiliated Associations
ABERDEENSHIRE AND DISTRICT F.A.
Secretary Brian Christie
Email adfa7@hotmail.co.uk

EAST OF SCOTLAND F.A.
Secretary John Greenhorn
Email secretary@eastofscotlandfa.co.uk www.eosfl.com

FIFE F. A .
Secretary James Stevenson
Email office@eastfifefc.info

FORFARSHIRE F.A.

Secretary Ken Ferguson
Email Chairman@brechincityfc.com

GLASGOW F.A .
Secretary Allison More
Email amore@celticfc.co.uk

NORTH OF SCOTLAND F.A.
Secretary Kenneth Houston
Email ken@kenhouston.f9.co.uk

SOUTHERN COUNTIES F.A.
Secretary Richard Osborne
Email richard.osborne1962@googlemail.com

STIRLINGSHIRE F.A.
Secretary Terry Bulloch
Email Terry.Bulloch@stenhousemuirfc.com

WEST OF SCOTLAND F.A.
Secretary Tracy McTrusty
Email tracy@ayrunitedfc.co.uk

Affiliated National Associations

SCOTTISH AMATEUR F.A.
Secretary Thomas McKeown, Hampden Park, Glasgow G42 9DB
Email SAFA@scottish-football.com
www.scottishamateurfa.co.uk

SCOTTISH JUNIOR F.A.
Secretary
Tom Johnston, Hampden Park, Glasgow G42 9DD
Email scottishjuniorfa@scottish-football.com
www.scottishjuniorfa.com

SCOTTISH SCHOOLS F.A.
Secretary John Watson, Hampden Park, Glasgow G42 9AZ
Email jcwatson@scottish-football.com
www.scottishschoolsfa.com

SCOTTISH WELFARE F.A.
Secretary John Campbell, 61 High Street, Rothes AB38 7AY
Telephone
Email johncampbell@mdwfa.co.uk

SCOTTISH WOMEN'S FOOTBALL
Administrator Gillian Graham, Hampden Park, Glasgow G42 9DF
Email swf@scottish-football.com
www.scottishwomensfootball.com

SCOTTISH YOUTH FOOTBALL ASSOCIATION
Secretary David Little, Hampden Park, Glasgow G42 9BF
Email syfa@scottish-football.com
www.scottishyouthfa.co.uk

Recognised Leagues

THE SCOTTISH PROFESSIONAL FOOTBALL LEAGUE
Secretary
Iain Blair, Hampden Park, Glasgow G42 9DE
Telephone(s)
(B) 0141 620 4140; (M) 07775 877234; (F) 0141 620 4141
Email iainblair@spfl.co.uk www.spfl.co.uk

THE SCOTTISH HIGHLAND FOOTBALL LEAGUE
Secretary
Roderick Houston
Email secretary@highlandleague.com
www.highlandfootballleague.com

THE SCOTTISH LOWLAND FOOTBALL LEAGUE
Secretary David Baxter,
Email secretary@slfl.co.uk

THE EAST OF SCOTLAND FOOTBALL LEAGUE
Secretary David Baxter
Email leaguesecretary@eastofscotlandfa.co.uk

THE SOUTH OF SCOTLAND FOOTBALL LEAGUE
Secretary Richard Osborne
Email richard.osborne1962@googlemail.com

REGISTER OF COMPETITIONS 2016/2017

The following is a list of competitions approved by the Scottish Football Association.

Affiliated Associations
Aberdeenshire & District F.A.
Aberdeenshire & District F.A. Challenge Cup
Aberdeenshire & District F.A. Shield

East of Scotland F.A.
East of Scotland Cup
East of Scotland Shield
King Cup
East of Scotland Qualifying Cup
Alex Jack Cup

Fife F.A.
The Fife Cup

Forfarshire F.A.
Forfarshire F.A. Challenge Cup

Glasgow F. A .
The City of Glasgow Cup

North of Scotland F.A
North of Scotland FA Cup
North of Scotland U20 League

Southern Counties F.A.
Southern Counties FA Challenge Cup
J Haig Gordon Memorial Trophy
Potts Cup
Southern Counties FA Alternate Cup
South Region Challenge Cup

Stirlingshire F.A.
Stirlingshire Cup

West of Scotland F.A.
Renfrewshire Cup
Renfrewshire Victoria Cup

Leagues
Aberdeenshire & District League
Aberdeenshire & District FA League

East of Scotland League
East of Scotland Football League Championship
East of Scotland Football Qualifying League
East of Scotland Football League Cup

Scottish Highland Football League
SHFL Championship
SHFL (Morganti) Cup
SHFL Under 17 League Championship

North Caledonian League
North Caledonian League

Scottish Professional Football League
Ladbrokes Premiership
Ladbrokes Championship
Ladbrokes League 1
Ladbrokes League 2
The Betfred Cup

IRN BRU Cup
SPFL Development League Division 1
SPFL Development League Division 2

South of Scotland Football League
South of Scotland Football League
South of Scotland Football League Cup

Scottish Lowland League
League Championship
League Cup
Lowland and East of Scotland Under 20 Development League
Knock Out Cup
Lowland and East of Scotland Under 20 Development League
Cup
Lowland and East of Scotland Under 20 Development League Championship
Lowland and East of Scotland Under 20 Development League Challenge Cup

North Caledonian F.A.
North Caledonian Cup
Football Times Cup
Jock Mackay Cup
Ness Cup
SWL Cup

Wigtownshire & District F.A.
Cree Lodge Cup
Tweedie Cup

SFA REGIONAL STRUCTURE

NORTH (Shetland, Orkney, Western Isles, Highland, Moray, Aberdeenshire and Aberdeen City)
Regional Office: Forres House Community Centre, High Street, Forres, IV36 1BU
Regional Administrator : Brent Bruce
Club Development Manager: Mark Slater
Player & Coach Development Officer: Calum MacDonald
Community Coaches: Claire Garrett (Aberdeen FC), Robbie Hedderman (Aberdeen FC)
Football Development Officers: Peter Budge (Highland Football Academy), Joanne Murphy (Girls & Womens Football)

EAST (Fife, Perth and Kinross, Dundee, Angus)
Regional Office: SFA East Region Office, Unit 6, Manhattan Works, Dundonald Street, Dundee, DD3 7PY.
Regional Manager: Kevin Lee
Office & Events Coordinator: Jo Whittet
Club Development Manager: Gavin Tinley
Girls & Womens Club Development Officer: Samantha Milne
Player & Coach Development Officer: Gavin Beith
Football Development Officer (Angus Council): Ross Smith
Football Development Officer (Dundee): Niall Nicolson
Football Development Officer (Perth & Kinross): Atholl Henderson
Football Development Officers (Fife): David Honeyman, Lee Bailey

CENTRAL (Clackmannanshire, East Dunbartonshire, North Lanarkshire, Stirling, West Dunbartonshire)
Regional Office: SFA Central Region Office, University of Stirling, Stirling, FK9 4LA
Regional Manager: Andrew Gilchrist
Office & Events Coordinator: Gillian Parry
Football Development Manager: Alan Taylor
Girls & Womens Club Development Officer: Kerry Kennedy
Player & Coach Development Officer: Jimmy Bone
Equity Officer: Atta Yaqub
Football Development Officer (N Lanarkshire): Steven Hamilton
Football Development Officer (W Dunbartonshire): Kenny McComish
Football Development Officer (Clackmannanshire): Martin Buckie
Football Development Officer (E Dunbartonshire):
Football Development Officer (N Lanarkshire): Craig Dargo
Club Development Officer): Alan Morgan
Football Development Officer (Active Stirling): Scott Kinross

SOUTH EAST (Borders, Lothians and Edinburgh)
Regional Office: SFA, McArthur Pavilion, 42 Peffermill Road, Edinburgh, EH16 5LL
Regional Manager: David Drummond
Regional Administrator: Lisa McKenzie
Player & Coach Development Officer: Chris Smith
Football Development Officer (Hearts): Alan White
Football Development Officer (Edinburgh):Chris Roberts
Football Development Officer (Borders): Drew Kelly
Football Development Officer (E Lothian) Sean McAuley
Football Development Officer (Midlothian): Keith Wright
Football Development Officer (Hibernian Community Foundation): Gary Hocknull
Girls & Womens Club Development Officer: Karen McConnell

SOUTH WEST (Dumfries & Galloway, S Lanarkshire, Ayrshire)
Regional Office: SFA South West Region, Magnum Leisure Centre, Irvine, KA12 8PP
Regional Manager: John Brown
Office & Events Coordinator: Andrew Jubb
Club Development Manager:David Sheldon
Girls & Womens Club Development Officer: Shirley Martin
Player & Coach Development Officer: Garry Hay
Football Development Officer (North Ayrshire) : Craig Hamilton
Football Development Officer (Dumfries & Galloway): Robbie Totten
Football Development Officer (Ayr United FC): Shaun Ferrie
Football Development Officer (S Lanarkshire): Colin McKendrick
Community Engagement Manager (Kilmarnock FC): Paul Di Giacomo

WEST (Glasgow, E Renfrewshire, Argyll and Bute, Renfrewshire, Inverclyde)
Regional Office: SFA West Region, Engage Renfrewshire, 10 Falcon Street, Paisley, PA3 1NS
Regional Manager: Paul McNeill
Regional Administrator: Craig Joyce
Club Development Manager: Corrie Campbell
Player & Coach Development Officer: Scott Chaplain
Football Development Officer (Argyll & Bute): Martin Rae
Football Development Officer (Renfrewshire): Chris Hendry
Football Development Officer (Glasgow): Gary Doctor
Football Development Officer (Glasgow): Stuart Smith
Football Development Officer (St Mirren FC): Fiona Dainty
Football Development Officer (Inverclyde): Stuart Rafferty
Football Development Officer (Glasgow): Stephen Clarke
Football Development Officer (E Renfrewshire) John Gervaise
Football Development Officer (Morton In The Community): Brian McLaughlin
Assistant Football Development Officer: Kenny McComish
Diversity and Inclusion Officer: Gary McDonald

INTERNATIONAL FOOTBALL

Scotland's chances of qualifying for the 2018 World Cup hang by the slenderest of threads. The 1-1 draw with Lithuiania at Hampden could prove to be fatal to Scotland's prospects. Going into the Autimn series of fixtures it looks as if nothing less than 4 wins from 4 games will suffice.

The national team continue to enthral and infuriate with equal measure. The match against England at Hampden in June summed it up—enthralling goals from Leigh Griffiths and infuriatingly poor defending to throw away two vital points.

Manager Gordon Strachan has been under pressure more or less from the start of the campaign. Before the England game rumours abounded that David Moyes was waiting in the wings to step in when Strachan resigned after the inevitable defeat. It didn't happen but Moyes is still in the reckoning. With his club management stock at a low ebb after three dreadful tenues at Manchester United, Real Sociedad and Sunderland, the time may be right for him to be given the Scotland job.

On the field a number of players must be reaching the end of their Scotland careers. It would be easy to say that the serial failures should be axed but the truth is that there are precious few players around to replace them. Many of the Scotland squad are but bit part players at their clubs in the lower reaches of the English Premiership or in the Championship.

When the fringe players were given a chance in the friendly against Canada at Easter Road, few did themselves any favours. Cairney of Fulham looked like a decent find but beyond that there was nothing to set the pulses racing.

The task of developing young Scottish talent is not easy. Promising players at any club other than Celtic are likely to be transferred South and disappear from first team action. Yet the progress of Kieran Tierney at Celtic shows what is possible when a young player is given extended first team action at a decent level. Hopefully he does not follow the same path as many into relative obscurity whilst pocketing an exorbitant wage.

Finally, the SFA should pay attention to the fact they struggled to sell-out the England game at Hampden. Ticket prices are too high, the stadium is far from brilliant,and the long-suffering fans have been taken for mugs for far too long.

World Cup 2018 - Russia

GROUP STAGES June 14- June 28								
GROUP	A	B	C	D	E	F	G	H
Venues	Moscow (Luzhniki)	St Petersburg	Kazan	Moscow (Otkryite)	Samara	Moscow (Luzhniki)	Sochi	Moscow (Otkryite)
	Yekaterinburg	Sochi	Saransk	Kaliningrad	Rostov	Nizhy Novgorod	Volgograd	Saransk
	St Petersburg	Moscow (Luzhniki)	Yekaterinburg	Nizhy Novgorod	St Petersburg	Sochi	Moscow (Otkryite)	Yekaterinburg
	Rostov	Kazan	Samara	Volgograd	Kaliningrad	Rostov	Nizhy Novgorod	Kazan
	Samara	Saransk	Moscow (Luzhniki)	St Petersburg	Moscow (Otkryite)	Kazan	Kaliningrad	Volgograd
	Volgograd	Kaliningrad	Sochi	Rostov	Nizhy Novgorod	Yekaterinburg	Saransk	Samara
KO Stages								
Rd 1	June 30-July 3	Sochi	Kazan	Samara	Rostov			
		Moscow (Luzhniki)	Nizhy Novgorod	St Petersburg	Moscow (Otkryite)			
QF	July 6-7	Nizhy Novgorod	Kazan	Sochi	Samara			
SF	July 10-11	St Petersburg	Moscow (Luzhniki)					
PO	July 14	St Petersburg						
F	July 15	Moscow (Luzhniki)						

FULL INTERNATIONALS 2016/17

Manager: Gordon Strachan

Assistants: Mark McGhee, Andy Watson, Tony Docherty, Callum Davidson

					Sep 4	Oct 8	Oct 11	Nov 11	Mar 22	Mar 26	Jun 10
					A	H	A	A	H	H	H
					Malta	Lithuania	Slovakia	England	Canada	Slovenia	England
					WC	WC	WC	WC	Fr	WC	WC
				Total	5-1	1-1	0-3	0-3	1-1	1-0	2-2
				Caps	15069	35966	11098	87258	9158	20435	48520
		Born			Ta Qali	Hampden	Trnava	Wembley	Easter Rd	Hampden	Hampden
Anya	Ikechi	Glasgow	Derby County	27	15&	Un	12*	10+	2	14+	11&
Armstrong	Stuart	Inverness	Celtic	2					Sq	6	10
Bannan	Barry	Airdrie	Sheffield Wednesday	25	6	8	9	Un	14+	Un	Un
Berra	Christophe	Edinburgh	Ipswich Town	36	Un	Un	Un	2	3	Un	2
Brown	Scott	Dunfermline	Celtic	53				5	Sq	7	6
Burke	Oliver	Kirkcaldy	RB Leipzig	5	7*	10+	Sq	Un	6+	Sq	
Cairney	Tom	Nottingham	Fulham	1					7<	Un	Un
Cooper	Liam	Hull	Leeds United	0					Un	Sq	
Fletcher	Darren	Dalkeith	West Bromwich Albion	78	8	6*	6+	7	8	Un	Un
Fletcher	Steven	Shrewsbury	Sheffield Wednesday	30	14+G	Un	11&	Un	Un	Sq	X
Forrest	James	Prestwick	Celtic	17	12*	14+	Un	9	Sq	9	Un
Fraser	Ryan	Aberdeen	Bournemouth	1					Sq	Sq	14+
Gordon	Craig	Edinburgh	Celtic	47	Un	Un	Un	1	Un	1	1
Greer	Gordon	Glasgow	Blackburn Rovers	11	Un	Sq	Sq	Sq			
Griffiths	Leigh	Edinburgh	Celtic	13	W	15&	14+	11	15&	10*	9GG
Hamilton	Jack	Denny	Hearts	0	Un	Un	Un	Un		Un	Un
Hanley	Grant	Dumfries	Newcastle United	27	3	3	3	4	W	W	
Hutton	Alan	Glasgow	Aston Villa	50	Un	W	W				
Kingsley	Stephen	Stirling	Swansea City	1				Un			Sq
Maloney	Shaun	Sarawak	Hull City	47		Un	Un				
Marshall	David	Glasgow	Cardiff City	27	1	1	1	Un	Sq	W	Un
Martin	Russell	Brighton	Norwich City	29	4	2	2	Un	Un	5	Un
Martin	Chris	Beccles	Derby County (OL to Fulham)	13	11+G	11	Un	Un	11&	15&G	15&
McArthur	James	Glasgow	Crystal Palace	28	W	12*G	8	12*	W	W	12*
McDonald	Kevin	Carnoustie	Fulham	0	W						
McGinn	John	Glasgow	Hibernian	3	Un	Sq	15&	Sq	17<	Un	X
McGregor	Allan	Edinburgh	Hull City (OL to Cardiff C)	36					1	Un	W
McKay	Barrie	Paisley	Rangers	1	Un	Sq	Sq				
McLean	Kenny	Rutherglen	Aberdeen	1							X
Morrison	James	Darlington	West Bromwich Albion	44	Un	Un	Un	6*	Sq	8&	7*
Mulgrew	Charlie	Glasgow	Blackburn Rovers	27				Sq	4	4	3
Murphy	Jamie	Glasgow	Brighton	0							X
Naismith	Steven	Irvine	Norwich City	45	Un	Sq	Sq	Un	9>G	12*	Un
Paterson	Callum	London	Hearts	5	2	5	4	14+			
Phillips	Matt	Aylesbury	West Bromwich Albion	4					W	W	
Reynolds	Mark	Motherwell	Aberdeen	0							Un
Rhodes	Jordan	Oldham	Middlesbrough (OL to Sheffield Wed)	14					16>	Un	
Ritchie	Matt	Gosport	Newcastle United	14	9&	9&	10*	15&	Sq	Un	
Robertson	Andrew	Glasgow	Hull City	15	5	4	Un		12*	2	4
Snodgrass	Robert	Glasgow	Hull City	24	10GGG	7	7	8&	10	11+	8+
Tierney	Kieran	Douglas, IOM	Celtic	4	W	Un	5		Sq	3	5
Wallace	Lee	Edinburgh	Rangers	10	W	Un	Un	3	5*	Sq	
Watt	Tony	Coatbridge	Charlton Athletic (OL to Hearts)	1	Sq						

X = Originally named in squad, later culled

WORLD CUP QUALIFYING STANDINGS - JULY 2017

		P	W	D	L	GF	GA	GD	Pts	Qualification	ENG	SVK	SVE	SCO	LIT	MAL
1	England	6	4	2	0	10	2	+8	14	Qualification to 2018 FIFA World Cup	—	4 Sep	5 Oct	3–0	2–0	2–0
2	Slovakia	6	4	0	2	12	4	+8	12	Possible second round[a]	0–1	—	1 Sep	3–0	4–0	8 Oct
3	Slovenia	6	3	2	1	6	3	+3	11		0–0	1–0	—	8 Oct	4 Sep	2–0
4	Scotland	6	2	2	2	9	10	-1	8		2–2	5 Oct	1–0	—	1–1	4 Sep
5	Lithuania	6	1	2	3	6	11	-5	5		8 Oct	1–2	2–2	1 Sep	—	2–0
6	Malta (E)	6	0	0	6	2	15	-13	0		1 Sep	1–3	0–1	1–5	5 Oct	—

Remaining Fixtures

Sep 1 A v Lithuania, Sep 4 H v Malta, Oct 5 H v Slovakia, Oct 8 A v Slovenia

FIFA WORLD RANKINGS	
Published June 2017	
1	Brazil
2	Argentina
3	Germany
4	Chile
5	Colombia
6	France
7	Belgium
8	Portugal
9	Switzerland
10	Spain
11	Poland
12	Italy
13	Wales
14	England
15	Peru
16	Uruguay
17	mexico
18	Croatia
19	Costa Rica
20	Egypt
21	Slovakia
22	Iceland
23	USA
24	Ecuador
25	Turkey
26	Republic of Ireland
27	Senegal
28	Northern Ireland
29	Bosnia & Herzegovina
30	iran
31	Netherlands
32	Cameroon
33	Hungary
34	Sweden
35	Austria
36	Pataguay
37	Ukraine
38	Nigeria
39	Congo DR
40	Greece
41	Tunisia
42	Burkina Faso
43	Korea Republic
44	Czech Republic
45	Japan
46	Romania
47	Cote d'Ivoire
48	Australia
49	Ghana
50	Serbia
51	Denmark
52	Montenegro
53	Algeria
54	Saudi Arabia
55	israel
56	Morocco
57	Slovenia
58	Venzuela
59	Panama
60	Bulgaria
61	Scotland
62	Uzbekistan
63	Russia
64	Haiti
65	South Africa
66	Mali
67	Albania
68	Armenia
69	Honduras
70	Curacao

SCOTLAND'S RECENT INTERNATIONAL RECORD

Date	Comp	Opponents	V	Location	Score	Res
08/10/2011	EU	Liechtenstein	A	Vaduz	1-0	Won
11/10/2011	EU	Spain	A	Alicante	1-3	Lost
11/11/2011	Fr	Cyprus	A	Larnaca	2-1	Won
29/02/2012	Fr	Slovenina	A	Koper	1-1	Drew
26/05/2012	Fr	USA	A	Jacksonville	1-5	Lost
15/08/2012	Fr	Australia	H	Easter Road	3-1	Won
08/09/2012	WC	Serbia	H	Hampden	0-0	Drew
11/09/2012	WC	FYR Macedonia	H	Hampden	1-1	Drew
12/10/2012	WC	Wales	A	Cardiff	1-2	Lost
16/10/2012	WC	Belgium	A	Brussels	0-2	Lost
14/11/2012	Fr	Luxembourg	A	Luxembourg	2-1	Won
06/02/2013	Fr	Estonia	H	Pittodrie	1-0	Won
22/03/2013	WC	Wales	H	Hampden	1-2	Lost
26/03/2013	WC	Serbia	A	Novi Sad	0-2	Lost
07/06/2013	WC	Croatia	A	Zagreb	1-0	Won
14/08/2013	WC	England	A	Wembley	2-3	Lost
06/09/2013	WC	Belgium	H	Hampden	0-2	Lost
10/09/2013	WC	FYR Macedonia	A	Skopje	2-1	Won
15/10/2013	WC	Croatia	H	Hampden	2-0	Won
15/11/2013	Fr	USA	H	Hampden	0-0	Drew
19/11/2013	Fr	Norway	A	Molde	1-0	Won
05/03/2014	Fr	Poland	A	Warsaw	1-0	Won
28/05/2014	Fr	Nigeria	N	Fulham	2-2	Drew
07/09/2014	EU	Germany	A	Dortmund	1-2	Lost
11/10/2014	EU	Georgia	H	Ibrox	1-0	Won
14/10/2014	EU	Poland	A	Warsaw	2-2	Drew
14/11/2014	EU	Republic of Ireland	H	Celtic Park	1-0	Won
18/11/2014	EU	England	H	Celtic Park	1-3	Lost
25/03/2015	Fr	Northern Ireland	H	Hampden	1-0	Won
29/03/2015	EU	Gibraltar	H	Hampden	6-1	Won
05/06/2015	Fr	Qatar	H	Easter Road	1-0	Won
13/06/2015	EU	Republic of Ireland	A	Dublin	1-1	Drew
04/09/2015	EU	Goergia	A	Tbilisi	0-1	Lost
07/09/2015	EU	Germany	H	Hampden	2-3	Lost
08/10/2015	EU	Poland	H	Hampden	2-2	Drew
11/10/2015	EU	Gibraltar	A	Faro	6-0	Won
24/03/2016	Fr	Czech Republic	A	Prague	0-1	Lost
29/03/2016	Fr	Denmark	H	Hampden	1-0	Won
29/05/2016	Fr	Italy	N	Ta Qali	0-1	Lost
04/06/2016	Fr	France	A	Metz	0-3	Lost
04/09/2016	WC	Malta	A	Ta Qali	5-1	Won
08/10/2016	WC	Lithuania	H	Hampden	1-1	Drew
11/10/2016	WC	Slovakia	A	Trnava	0-3	Lost
11/11/2016	WC	England	A	Wembley	0-3	Lost
22/03/2017	Fr	Canada	H	Easter Road	1-1	Drew
26/03/2017	WC	Slovenia	H	Hampden	1-0	Won
10/06/2017	WC	England	H	Hampden	2-2	Drew

U21 INTERNATIONALS 2016/17			Sep 2	Sep 6	Oct 5	Oct 11	Nov 9	Mar 28	May-31	Jun 3	Jun 6	Jun 8	Jun 10
Coach			H	A	A	A	A	H	N	N	N	N	N
Ricky Sbragia (until Sep 2016)			Macedonia	Ukraine	Iceland	Macedonia	Slovakia	Estonia	Czech Rep	Brazil	Indonesia	England	Czech Rep
replaced by Scott Gemmill			EC	EC	EC	EC	Fr	Fr	Toulon	Toulon	Toulon	Toulon	Toulon
Assistant Peter Grant			0-1	0-0	0-2	0-2	0-4	0-0	2-3	1-0	2-1	0-3	3-0
			4557	2150	332	12000		1271					
			Tynecastle	Kiev	Reykjavik	Skopje	Myjava	Paisley	Salon	Fos-Sur-Mer	Vitrolles	Fos-sur-Mer	Aubagne
Archibald	Theo	Brentford							W	W	W		
Ballantyne	Cammy	Dundee United						Un					
Bransgrove	James	Colchester United	Sq	Sq									
Brophy	Eamonn	Hamilton Accies					10^						
Burke	Oliver	Red Bull Leipzig							7&	11&	Un	11	11>
Burt	Liam	Rangers			12*	7							
Cadden	Chris	Motherwell	Un	8	W	W	8<	Un					
Cameron	Kyle	Newcastle United (OL to Newport County)			3	3	3+						
Chalmers	Joe	Motherwell		3									
Christie	Ryan	Celtic	10	Un									
Cummings	Jason	Hibernian	9	12*									
Docherty	Greg	Hamilton Accies			11*	Un	11%						
Doohan	Ross	Celtic					Un		Un	Un	Un	Un	1
Forrest	Alan	Ayr United					19%						
Fraser	Ryan	AFC Bournemouth	7&	Sq									
Frizzell	Adam	Kilmarnock							12*	9>	9+	8	14+
Fulton	Ryan	Liverpool (OL Chesterfield)			1	1	1	1*					
Gauld	Ryan	SC de Portugal (OL to Vitoria Setubal)	8	7&									
Hardie	Ryan	Rangers (OL to St Mirren, Raith R)			8	11+	18^	17<	14+	15&	10>GG	14+	10
Harper	Jack	Malaga CF						Sq					
Henderson	Liam	Celtic	11	6	4	6	7>	6					
Hendrie	Stephen	West Ham United (OL to Blackburn Rov)	Sq	Sq									
Holsgrove	Jordan	Reading							15&	14+	12*	9	12*
Hurst	Mark	St Johnstone (OL to East Fife)	Un	Un	Un	Un							
Hyam	Dominic	Reading	Un	5									
Iacovitti	Alex	Nottingham Forest (OL to Mansfield Town)			5	4	5	14+	4	3	3	3	3*
Jones	James	Crewe Alexandra			10	8&	9	8>					
Jules	Zak	Reading			6	5	6&	Sq	5	Un	16>	Un	4
Kelly	Liam	Rangers (OL to East Fife)	1	1									
Kiltie	Greg	Kilmarnock							W	W	W		
King	Billy	Hearts (OL to ICT)	15&	9									
Kingsley	Stephen	Swansea City	3	Sq									
Love	Donald	Sunderland	Sq	Sq									
MacLeod	Lewis	Brentford	W	W									
Magennis	Josh	St Mirren							6	8+	Un	15&	9
Mallan	Steven	St Mirren						9^					
McBurnie	Oliver	Swansea City	12*	11	9&	10		10<					
McCart	Jamie	Celtic (OL to Inverness CT)						5	Un	4	4	4	16>
McCrorie	Robbie	Rangers			Sq	12*							
McCrorie	Ross	Rangers							Un	12*	7	7*	
McDonald	Calum	Derby County			Un	14+	14+						
McFadzean	Callum	Kilmarnock	W	W									
McGhee	Jordan	Hearts (OL to Middlesbrough)	5	2+	2	Sq		4+					
McKay	Devlin	Kilmarnock (OL to Berwick R)						Un					
McMullan	Paul	Celtic (OL to Dunfermline Ath)						7&					
Morgan	Lewis	St Mirren						11					
Mutch	Robbie	Aberdeen (OL Arbroath)					Sq						
Nesbitt	Aiden	Celtic (OL to Morton)			7+	Un	17<		9>	Un	8*	Un	6&
Nicholson	Sam	Hearts	14+	10*									
O'Hara	Mark	Dundee	Un	15&									
Quitongo	Jai	Morton					16>						
Ralston	Anthony	Celtic							2	2	2	2	2+
Ruddy	Jack	Wolves						12*	1	1	1	1	Un
Sammut	Reuben	Chelsea			14+	15&	15&	Un	11	7*	15&	12*&	
Sheppard	Jake	Reading			Un	2*	12*						
Slater	Craig	Colchester United	6*	Un									
Smith	Liam	Hearts (OL to Raith Rovers)	2+	Un	W	W	2*	2					
Souttar	Jordan	Hearts	4	4			4						
Storie	Craig	Aberdeen	Sq	14+	Un	Un							
Taylor	Greg	Kilmarnock						3	3	5G	5	5	5
Thomas	Dominic	Motherwell (OL to QOS)						15&					
Thomson	Joe	Celtic (OL to QOS)						16>	10+	16>	14+	Un	8
Wardrop	Sam	Celtic							Sq	Sq	Sq	Un	
Wighton	Craig	Dundee			15&	9		18^	16>	10	11&	10+	15&
Wilson	Iain	Kilmarnock							Un	6	6	6	7
Wright	Scott	Aberdeen							8*	Un	Un	Un	

Ricky Sbragia was replaced as Manager early in the season after a poor run of results. Scott Gemmill stepped up from his role with the Under 19 squad to take over. Scotland failed to score in six successive games at this level, breaking their duck in the Toulon Tournament. Superficially the results in Toulon look very promising although it is not entirely clear how strong the opposition was. England, for example, fielded their Under 19sm who comfortably defeated the Scottish side. The win over Brazil generated some excitement and publicity which can hopefully be carried forward into the 2019 UEFA Qualifying campaign.

There was a huge turnover of players including many adopted Scots of English birth. How many of the 66 players used will progress to the full international squad?

2017 UEFA QUALIFYING		P	W	D	L	GF	GA	GD	Pts	Qualification	MAC	FRA	ICE	UKR	SCO	NIR
1	Macedonia	10	6	3	1	13	7	+6	21	Final tournament	—	2–2	0–0	1–0	2–0	2–0
2	France	10	6	2	2	17	8	+9	20		1–1	—	2–0	2–0	2–0	1–0
3	Iceland	10	5	3	2	13	9	+4	18		3–0	3–2	—	2–4	2–0	1–1
4	Ukraine	10	4	2	4	14	12	+2	14		0–2	1–0	0–1	—	4–0	1–1
5	Scotland	10	2	2	6	8	17	-9	8		0–1	1–2	0–0	2–2	—	3–1
6	Northern Ireland	10	0	2	8	6	18	-12	2		1–2	0–3	0–1	1–2	1–2	—

2019 Qualifying Fixtures (Host Italy)		
05/09/2017	H	Netherlands
06/10/2017	A	England
10/10/2017	A	Latvia
10/11/2017	H	Latvia
14/11/2017	H	Ukraine
23/03/2018	A	Andorra
6/9/2018	H	Andorra
11/09/2018	A	Netherlands
12/10/2018	A	Ukraine
16/10/2018	H	England

SCOTLAND UNDER 19 2016/17			Oct 4	Oct 6	Oct 25	Oct 27	Oct 30	Mar 22	Mar 24	Mar 27
			H	H	N	A	N	N	A	N
Coach			Sweden U18	Sweden U18	Liechtenstein	Andorra	Israel	Austria	Czech Rep	Hungary
Scott Gemmill			Fr	Fr	UEFA Q	UEFA Q	UEFA Q	UEFA El	UEFA El	UEFA El
			2-0	1-2	1-0	1-0	0-1	0-3	0-1	1-2
			Att	Att	50	280	60	154	1394	69
			Oriam	Oriam	Andorra	Andorra	Santa Coloma	Zlin	Zlin	Zlin
Allardice	Scott	Dundee United						15&	9	Sq
Archibald	Theo	Celtic (OL Albion Rovers)						8+	Un	8*
Burt	Liam	Rangers			6	7	Sq	5	12*	Sq
Coote	Ali	Dundee United		8*						
Crossan	Paul Joseph	Celtic	9+							
Doohan	Ross	Celtic	1		Un	Un	Sq	Un	1	Un
Frizzell	Adam	Kilmarnock		7&						
Gallacher	Tony	Falkirk	3<		3	3	2	Un	3	3
Gallacher	Owen	Newcastle United			Un	12*	11*			
Hamilton	Ethan	Manchester United			14+	10	8	6	6	6
Harvie	Daniel	Aberdeen (lOL to Dumbarton)	17<	2G				9	Un	10
Hendry	Regan	Celtic	7&	16>	9+	Un	15&			
Hill	Mark	Celtic	11G	12*	5	14+	14+	10*	Un	11
Hornby	Fraser	Everton	4	6	Sq	6G	5	Sq	Sq	Sq
Johnston	Mikey	Celtic						14+	5	5G
McCrorie	Ross	Rangers	6	3	4	4	3	3	4	4
McCrorie	Robbie	Rangers			1	1	1	1	Un	1
McIntyre	Tom	Reading			15&	5	4			
Miller	Calvin	Celtic	8		Un	9*				
Morrison	Stuart	Dunfermline Athletic	10	4						
Morrison	Greg	Ross County			W	W	W	Sq	Sq	Sq
Morrison	Lewis	Kilmarnock			W	W	W			
Mutch	Robbie	Aberdeen (OL Arbroath)		1						
O'Hara	Kevin	Falkirk (OL East Fife)	14+	14+	8*	Un	6&	Un	7*	12*
Porteous	Ryan	Hibernian (OL Edinburgh City)						Un	8+	Sq
Preston	Fraser	Sheffield Wednesday						12*	10	Un
Ralston	Anthony	Celtic	2		2	2	Sq	2	2	2
Ross	Frank	Aberdeen	16>	5+	10&	Un	7			
Shaw	Oli	Hibernian (OL Stenhousemuir)	12*G	11	7G	8	12*	7	14+	7
Souttar	Harry	Stoke City		9	11	Un	9	4	Sq	Sq
St Clair	Harvey	Chelsea	15&	10>	12*	11+	10+			
Wilson	Iain	Kilmarnock	5>	15&	Sq	Sq	Sq	11&	11	Sq

QUALIFICATION ROUND										
Pos	Team	Pld	W	D	L	GF	GA	GD	Pts	Qualification
1	Israel	3	3	0	0	9	2	7	9	Elite round
2	Scotland	3	2	0	1	2	1	1	6	Elite round
3	Andorra (H)	3	1	0	2	6	6	0	3	
4	Liechtenstein	3	0	0	3	2	10	-8	0	
ELITE ROUND										
1	Czech Republic (H)	3	3	0	0	6	1	5	9	Final tournament
2	Hungary	3	2	0	1	6	4	2	6	
3	Austria	3	1	0	2	4	6	-2	3	
4	Scotland	3	0	0	3	1	6	-5	0	

Scotland's U19 squad have been relatively successful in recent years. In 2016/17 they finished second in their UEFA Qualifying Group but failed to pick up a single point in their elite group matches.

At the end of the season quite a few players were promoted to the U20 / U21 age group with a view to the next UEFA Under 21 qualifying campaign.

SCOTLAND SCHOOLS UNDER 18			Jan 25	Mar 3	Mar 17	Mar 31	Apr 6
2016/17			H	H	A	A	H
			Australia	England	Wales	N Ireland	Rep Ireland
			Fr	CS	CS	CS	CS
			3-3	1-5	5-1	1-2	1-0
			Renfrew	Cappielow	Newtown	Cliftonville	Forthbank
Ballantyne	Cameron	The Glasgow Academy / St Johnstone	16>	15	8	8	8
Banner	Kyle	Graeme HS / Stirling Albion	4	4	2G	2	5G
Bollan	Luc	Monifieth HS / Dundee United	14+G	13	4G	4	4
Brown	Adam	Grove Academy, Dundee / Carnoustie Panmure	9^	18	9G	9G	9
Brown	Nathan	Stewart's Melville College /St Johnstone	5+	14G	5	5	Sub
Bruce	Robbie	Buckie HS / Elgin City	6	6	14+	Sub	Sub
Chapman	Jamie	Edinburgh College / Berwick Rangers	19%	8	12*	Sub	10
Connelly	Ross	Graeme HS / Hamilton Accies	1*	1	1	Sub	Sub
Dunne	Cieran	Stewart's Melville College / Falkirk	15&GG	11	15&	11	Sub
Fallans	Ronan	St Modans HS / Stirling Albion	12*	12	Sub	1	1
Glass	Declan	Ross HS / Dundee United	10%	10	10G+		
Kelly	John	Trinity HS, Rutherglen / Partick Thistle	17<	5	Sub	3	3
Kirkwood	Adam	Stranraer Academy / Creetown / Stranraer	2>	3	3		Sub
McGrory	Calvin	Eastwood HS / Queen's Park	8&	16	6*	7	6
O'Reilly	Euan	CS Auchterarder / St Johnstone	7	17	7&	6	
Reilly	Matthew	St Ninian's HS / St Mirren	11<	7	11G	10	11
Stanger	George	Dunblane HS / Stirling Albion	3	2	Sub	Sub	2
Sweeney	Kieran	St Kentigern's Acad, Blackburn	18^	9	Sub		7

In addition, the following warm-up matches were played:

27/12/16 v Alloa Athletic (at Toryglen), 1-1
14/2/17 v Sporting Futures USA (at Toryglen), 5-0
21/2/17 v Stirling University U20 (at Stirling Uni), 1-0

CENTENARY SHIELD							
Teams	P	W	D	L	F	A	PTS
England	4	3	0	1	16	9	9
Northern Ireland	4	3	0	1	10	4	9
Republic of Ireland	4	2	0	2	6	8	6
Scotland	4	2	0	2	8	8	6
Wales	4	0	0	4	4	15	0

The Under 18 Schools squad is something of an anomaly in the international structure. The best players at this age group are full-time footballers - those who are still at school are likely to progress to part time professional football at best.

Scotland's performance in the Centenary Shield was markedly better than 2015/16 when they failed to gather a single point.

U17 INTERNATIONALS 2016/17			Jul 30	Aug 1	Aug 3	Sep-16	Sep 18	Sep 21	Feb 24	Feb 26	Mar 17	Mar 19	Mar 22	May 3	May 6	May 9
			A	N	N	N	N	A	N	N	H	H	H	N	N	N
Coach			Hungary	Serbia	Czech Rep	Malta	Wales	Portugal	Japan	Japan	Montenegro	Serbia	Switzerland	Faroes	Hungary	France
Scott Gemmill			Tnt	Tnt	Tnt	UEFA Q	UEFA Q	UEFA Q	Fr	Fr	UEFA El	UEFA El	UEFA El	UEFA F	UEFA F	UEFA F
			1-5	2-1	1-0	6-0	1-0	1-0	0-0	0-0, 4-3p	6-1	1-0	1-0	2-0	1-1	1-2
						200	120	290			357	511	345	511	677	511
			Dabas	Telki	Telki	Febres	Pampilhosa	Coimbra	Spain	Spain	Paisley	Paisley	Paisley	Lucko	Lukco	Velika Gorica
Aitchison	Jack	Celtic				9*	9	9	Sq	Sq	6*GG	6&	6	6G	6	6
Antionazzi	Christian	Aberdeen	Sq	Sq	Sq											
Cameron	Innes	Kilmarnock							Sq	Sq	12*	Un	Un	12*G	14+	14+
Chalmers	Logan	Dundee United	Sq	Sq	Sq											
Church	Daniel	Celtic	Sq	G	Sq	3	3	3	Sq	Sq	2	2	2	3	3	3
Deas	Robbie	Celtic	Sq	Sq	Sq	4	4	4	Sq	Sq	4+	4	4	Sq	12*	15&
Donaldson	Josh	Dundee United							Sq	Sq	1	1	1			
Freeman	Kieran	Southampton	Sq	Sq	Sq	Sq	Sq	Sq								
Hamilton	Chris	Hearts				Un	15&	Un								
Henderson	Ewan	Celtic	Sq	Sq	Sq											
Houston	Jordan	Rangers				6	6	6	Sq	Sq	11	11	11	11	11	11
Hutchison	Lewis	Aberdeen	Sq	Sq	G	Sq	Sq	Sq	Sq	Sq	Un	Un	14+	14+	Un	Un
Irving	Andrew	Hearts	Sq	Sq	Sq	15&	Un	Un	Sq	Sq						
Kelly	Stephen	Rangers				14+	Un	14+	Sq	Sq						
Lyons	Luke	Leeds United	Sq	Sq	Sq											
Mair	Archie	Aberdeen	Sq	Sq	Sq											
Mayo	Lewis	Rangers	Sq	Sq	Sq				Sq	Sq	14+	14+	Un	2	2	2
Mayuba	Kris	Birmingham City							Sq	Sq						
McCracken	Joe	Hamilton Accies / Norwich City	Sq	Sq	Sq	1	1	1			Un	Un	Un	1	1	1
McDonald	Anthony	Hearts	Sq	Sq	Sq											
McInroy	Kerr	Celtic	Sq	Sq	Sq	5	5	5G	Sq	Sq	10G	10*	10*	Sq	10	10*
McPherson	Joe	Aberdeen				Un	14+	12*								
Middleton	Glenn	Norwich City	Sq	Sq	Sq	10	10+	10*	Sq	Sq	8GG	9G	8&G	8&	8*	9&
Mitchell	Jonny	Forth Valley Elite Academy							Sq	Sq	5	5+	5	5	5	5
Muir	Lewis	Rangers				Un	Un	Un								
Mullen	Ryan	Celtic							Sq	Sq				Un	Un	Un
Own Goal				G												
Palmer	Cameron	Rangers	Sq	Sq	Sq											
Reid	Aaron	Hearts	Sq	Sq	Sq	Un	12*	Un	Sq	Sq	15&	15&	Un	15&	Un	Un
Ross	Seb	Aberdeen				7	7G	8	Sq	Sq	9	12*	9	9+	9&	12*G
Rudden	Zak	Rangers				11&	11*	11	Sq	Sq	7G	8	7+	Sq	7+G	8+
Shiels	Matthew	Rangers	Sq	Sq	Sq											
Smith	Lewis	Hamilton Accies				12*	Un	Un	Sq	Sq	Un	Un	15&	10*	Un	Un
Thomson	Jack	Rangers							Sq	Sq	Sq	Sq	Sq			
Watt	Elliot	Wolves	Sq	Sq	Sq	8+	8&	7+	Sq	Sq	Sq	7	12*	7	15&	7
Welsh	Stephen	Celtic	Sq	Sq	Sq	2	2	2	Sq	Sq	3	3	3	4	4	4

QUALIFICATION ROUND

Pos	Team	Pld	W	D	L	GF	GA	GD	Pts	Qualification
1	Scotland	3	3	0	0	8	0	8	9	Elite round
2	Portugal (H)	3	2	0	1	7	1	6	6	Elite round
3	Wales	3	1	0	2	3	3	0	3	
4	Malta	3	0	0	3	0	14	-14	0	

ELITE ROUND

Pos	Team	Pld	W	D	L	GF	GA	GD	Pts	Qualification
1	Scotland (H)	3	3	0	0	8	1	7	9	Final tournament
2	Serbia	3	2	0	1	3	2	1	6	
3	Switzerland	3	1	0	2	4	4	0	3	
4	Montenegro	3	0	0	3	2	10	-8	0	

FINALS GROUP B

Pos	Team	Pld	W	D	L	GF	GA	GD	Pts	Qualification
1	Hungary	3	2	1	0	8	3	5	7	Knockout stage
2	France	3	2	0	1	11	4	7	6	Knockout stage
3	Scotland	3	1	1	1	4	3	1	4	
4	Faroe Islands	3	0	0	3	0	13	-13	0	

The Under 17 youth squad were once again the most successful of the Scotland sides. They came through their Preliminary and Elite Qualifying Rounds to reach the Finals, held in Croatia. Following a win over the Faroes and draw with Hungary, the Scots were desperately unlucky to lose to France, narrowly missing out on a Sem I Final place.

The challenge for these players is to maintain their levels and status at the Under 19 and Under 21 age groups. Some should be pushing at the door for first team football at their clubs - hopefully they will be given an opportunity as this will surely help their development.

SCOTLAND UNDER 16 INTERNATIONALS 2016/17

			Sep 27	Oct 30	Nov 1	Nov 4	Feb 27	Mar 1	Mar 3
			H	H	H	H	H	H	H
			France	N Ireland	Wales	Rep Ireland	Croatia	Iceland	Austria
			Fr	VS	VS	VS	UEFA Dev	UEFA Dev	UEFA Dev
			0-4	2-0	2-2	0-3	1-0	2-1	2-2 wop
			ORIAM	ORIAM	ORIAM	ORIAM	ORIAM	ORIAM	ORIAM
				300	300	500	150	200	200
Armer	Jack	Preston North End					Sq	Sq	Sq
Bagan	Joel	Southampton						SqG	
Binks	Luis	Tottenham Hotspur		5	4<	4	Sq	Sq	Sq
Butterworth	Zac	Rangers	Sq	14+G	8+	12*	Sq	Sq	Sq
Campbell	Dean	Aberdeen	Sq	10	15&	10	Sq	Sq	Sq
Cochrane	Harry	Hearts	Sq	11+	10	11*			
Dembele	Karamoko	Celtic		Un	14+	16>	Sq	Sq	Sq
Erhahon	Ethan	St Mirren	Sq	12*	3*	14+	Sq	Sq	Sq
Gilmour	Billy	Rangers	Sq	8	6	7<	Sq	Sq	Sq
Hamilton	Chris	Hearts	Sq	2	2	2^	Sq	Sq	SqG
Kerr	Andrew	Celtic	Sq	Un	11&	Un			
Kettings	Adam	Motherwell					Sq	Sq	Sq
Kinnear	Brian	Rangers					Sq	Sq	Sq
Leonard	Marc	Hearts	Sq	6>	Un	5>	Sq	Sq	Sq
Mair	Archie	Aberdeen	Sq	Un	Un	1	Sq	Sq	Sq
McBride	Connor	Forth Valley Elite Acad					SqG	Sq	Sq
McDonald	Anthony	Hearts	Sq	9*	Un	8+	Sq	Sq	Sq
McGrath	Kieran	Celtic	Sq	15&	9^	15&			
McKay	David	Celtic					Sq	Sq	Sq
McPake	Joshua	Rangers	Sq	Un	Sq	Sq			
Mebude	Adedapo	Rangers					Sq	SqG	Sq
Mullen	Ryan	Celtic	Sq	1	1	Un			
O'Connor	Kane	Hibernian	Sq	Un	7	Un	Sq	Sq	SqG
O'Connor	Harris	Rangers		Un	Un	9&			
Patterson	Nathan	Rangers	Sq	Sq	16>	17<	Sq	Sq	Sq
Pressley	Aaron	Aston Villa		15>	18^	Sq			
Semple	Jamie	Motherwell	Sq	7&	5GG>	6	Sq	Sq	Sq
Taylor	Terry	Aberdeen	Sq						
Walker	Jamie	Rangers		3	12*	18^			
Walker	Josh			Un	Un				
Wilson	Taylor	Hamilton Accies	Sq	4G	17<	3	Sq	Sq	Sq

VICTORY SHIELD 2016/17

	P	W	D	L	F	A	PTS
Republic of Ireland	3	3	0	0	9	1	9
Scotland	3	1	1	1	4	5	4
Wales	3	1	1	1	5	8	4
Northern Ireland	3	0	0	3	3	7	0

	ROI	Scot	Wales	NI
ROI				2-1
Scotland	0-3		2-2	2-0
Wales	0-4			3-2
N ireland				

The Victory Shield was played off over a single week at the ORIAM and the Scots finished second. Sadly England no longer see fit to enter the tournament. The Scots also won a UEFA Development Tournament, remaining undefeated in three games against varied opposition.

Unfortunately the SFA decreed that these games should be "closed doors" with no pre-publicity nor accredited access for the media. The SFA then had the temerity to criticise the media for not playing-up Scotland's success!

INTERNATIONAL FUTSAL

The international side played its first games in 2014/15, failing to qualify for the Euros.

During 2016/17 the following internationals were played:

2/12/06	v England	House of Sport Cardiff	0-9	Home Internationals
3/12/06	v Wales	House of Sport Cardiff	2-5	Home Internationals
4/12/16	v Northern Ireland	House of Sport Cardiff	8-2	Home Internationals
24/1/17	v Switzerland	Tbilisi	2-6	UEFA 2018 Qual
25/1/17	v Georgia	Tbilisi	0-11	UEFA 2018 Qual
26/1/17	v Israel	Tbilisi	2-6	UEFA 2018 Qual

Scotland Squad for UEFA Qualifiers in Georgia:	
Gordon McGillivray	Fair City Santos Futsal Club
Ben Tough	Fair City Santos Futsal Club
Scott Mollison	Fair City Santos Futsal Club
James Yates	Fair City Santos Futsal Club
Craig Holmes	Fair City Santos Futsal Club
Craig McLeish	Wattcell Futsal Club
Scott Chaplain	Adventure Kick Futsal Club
Jack Guthrie	Wattcell Futsal Club
Mark Caldow	Fair City Santos Futsal Club
Ryan Robb	Fair City Santos Futsal Club
Fraser Smith	Oakbank Futsal Club
Dayle Robertson	Fair City Santos Futsal Club
Andrew McCulloch	Fair City Santos Futsal Club
Ben Carswell	Fair City Santos Futsal Club

Women's International Football

At the time of going to press the Scotland Women's international team were tasking part in the UEFA Championships in the Netherlands. Securing a place at the Finals for the first time was a huge achievement and a testament to hard work by a lot of people. Much of the credit must go to Team Manager Anna Signeul who developed the squad from one with potential to genuine international class. Anna will leave after the Euros to be replaced by Shelley Kerr.

Unfortunately Scotland travelled to the Netherlands without two of their best players - both Kim Little and Jennifer Beattie were missing through injury.

WOMENS FULL INTERNATIONALS 2016/17															
				Sep 20	Oct 20	Jan 20	Jan 23	Mar 1	Mar 3	Mar 6	Mar 8	Apr 12	Jun 9	Jun 13
				A	H	N	N	N	N	N	N	A	H	A
				Iceland	Netherlands	Denmark	Denmark	N Zealand	S Korea	Austria	Wales	Belgium	Romania	Sweden
				UEFA	Fr	Fr	Fr	CypC	CypC	CypC	CypC	Fr	Fr	Fr
				2-1	0-7	2-2	1-1	3-2	0-2	3-1	0-0, 6-5p	0-5	2-0	0-1
				Reykjavik	Livingston	Larnaca	Parlamini	Larnaca	Nicosia	Nicosia	Parlamini	Leuven	Falkirk	Vaxjo
			Caps	6468	1326								1877	4622
Alexander	Lee	Glasgow City	0					Un	Un	Un		Sq	Un	Un
Arnot	Lizzie	Hibernian	13	Un	Un	14+	9>	16<	15&	9	9	8		
Arthur	Chloe	Bristol City	6		Un								Un	15&
Barsley	Vaila	Eskilstuna United	3									3	4	4
Beattie	Jennifer	Manchester City	107	2	Sq	4	12*	4	4	Sq			Sq	Sq
Brown	Fiona	Glasgow City / Eskilstuna Utd	18	Un	12*	10^	14+	18^	11^	10<	12*	11	10^	10&
Brown	Frankie	Bristol City	87		17<	3	2*	2	2*	2+	14+	5	2	2
Brownlie	Emma	Hibernian	0	Un										
Clark	Kelly	Celtic	0									Sq		
Clelland	Lana	UCP Tavagnacco	14	Un	Sq	Un	17<	W	W	W		16&	18^	Un
Corsie	Rachel	Seattle Reign	88			15&	4	W	W	W			Un	6+
Crichton	Leanne	Notts County	51	12*	14+	17<	16>	7&	16<	8	7	6	9	8
Cuthbert	Erin	Glasgow City / Chelsea	8		15&	16>G	11^	17>G	10>	Un	11^		17<	Un
Dieke	Ifeoma	Vittsjo GIK	119	Sq	3	5&	3	Sq	3	3	3	4	3*	Un
Docherty	Nicola	Glasgow City	12	Sq	W							2		
Emslie	Claire	Bristol City	2			18^	Un					Sq		
Evans	Lisa	Bayern Munchen	60	10	8	Un	6+	6+	14+	6G	15&	9	6&G	7
Fay	Gemma	Celtic / Glasgow City / Stjarnan	199	1	Sq	1*	Sq	Un	Un	1*		Sq	1	1
Graham	Lucy	Hibernian	0									Sq		
Harrison	Abigail	Hibernian	0	Sq										
Harrison	Rachel	Fortuna Hjorring	0			Un	Un							
Howard	Sophie	TSG Hoffenheim	2									14+		12*
Lauder	Hayley	Glasgow City	84	9	6&	9	Un	9<	Un	5&			5+	5
Little	Kim	Seattle Reign / Arsenal	121	Sq		7	8	8G	8	Sq				
Love	Joanne	Glasgow City	177	5	5+	Un	7&	14+	9<	Sq			8<	14+
Lynn	Shannon	Vittsjo GIK	24	Un	1	12*	1	1	1	12*	1	1	Un	Un
McLauchlan	Rachel	Hibernian	3		16>	Un	Un		Un	14+	2		Un	Un
Mitchell	Emma	Arsenal	51	3	2	2+	5	5	5	Sq				
Murray	Christie	Doncaster Rovers	47	Un	Un	Un	18^	11^	18^	Un	10&	15&	16>	Un
Murray	Joelle	Hibernian	43	4	11<	W	W	3*	Sq	4	4+		12*	3*
Ness	Zoe	Mallbackens IF	0	Sq	Un									
Ross	Jane	Vittsjo GIK / Manchester City	105	8GG	9	11>G	10<	10>G	17>	11G	16^	10	11G	11
Ross	Leanne	Glasgow City	131	6*	4*	6>	15&	Un	6+	16<G	6*	7	15&	Un
Smith	Kirsty	Hibernian	23	7	10>			12*	12*	15&	5	12*	14+	Un
Weir	Caroline	Liverpool	37	11	7	8<	Un	15&	7&	7	8		7>	9

Qualifying	P	W	D	L	F	A	GD	PTS
Group 1	8	7	0	1	34	2	32	21
Scotland	8	7	0	1	30	7	23	21
Slovenia	8	3	0	5	21	19	2	9
Belarus	8	3	0	5	10	20	-10	9
FYR Macedonia	8	0	0	8	4	51	-47	0

WOMENS UNDER 19 INTERNATIONALS 2016/17

			Aug 9	Aug 11	Sep 14	Sep 16	Sep 19	Mar 3	Mar 5	Mar 7	Apr 4	Apr 6	Apr 9
			A	A	A	N	N	N	N	N	A	N	N
Coach			Hungary	Hungary	Albania	Cyprus	Serbia	Italy	France	Germany	R of Ireland	Finland	Ukraine
Gareth Evans			Fr	Fr	UEFA	UEFA	UEFA	Tnt	Tnt	Tnt	UEFA	UEFA	UEFA
			0-0	2-1	11-0	8-0	PPD**	1-2	0-0	0-3	2-1	2-1	5-0
			Buk	Buk	Tirana	Durres	Durres	La Manga	La Manga	La Manga	Limerick	Limerick	Limerick
											455	80	75
Adams-Mullen	Claire	Rangers	7>	15&	11G	10	Sq	9	9&	9	10*	9*	12*
Boyce	Carla	Glasgow City	12*	9&	14+G	12*G	Sq	11<	14+	Sub	12*	11&G	11GG
Brown	Chantelle	Rangers	10	8+	9	9+G	Sq	8	8*	Sq			
Clachers	Erin	Glasgow City						Sub	Sq	Sub	UN	UN	UN
Cornet	Chelsea	Hibernian	2	6	11G	11G	Sq	10	Sq	11	11	10	10G
Cummings	Eartha	Spartans	Sq	1	Sq	Un	Sq						
Cunningham	Murron	Glasgow City	16>	17^									
Cuthbert	Erin	Glasgow City	6	14+G	7&GGGGG	7&	Sq				8GG	8G	6GG
Dalgliesh	Ellis	Celtic	4+	12*	Sq	14+	Sq	16<	3	3	3	3	3
Doran-Barr	Lauren	Rangers						Sub	Sq	Sub	UN	UN	15&
Flaherty	Rebecca	Aberdeen / Liverpool	1	Sq	1	1	Sq	1	1	1	1	1	1
Gallacher	Amy	Forfar Farmington / Hibernian	9	10G^	6*	6GG	Sq	6+	7+	7	7+	7+	UN
Hanson	Kirsty	Sheffield / Doncaster	8&	16>	8+GG	8*	Sq	7*	Sq	8	9&	UN	UN
Hay	Brogan	Glasgow City	5*	16<	12*	Un	Sq	15&	Sq	Sub	UN	15&	7*
Kerr	Samantha	Glasgow City	Sq	Sq	5G	5G	Sq	5&	6	6	6	6	UN
McGregor	Shannon	Aberdeen	15&	5>	15&	Un	Sq	12*	12*	Sub	14+	12*	8+
McLintock	Jordan	Rangers	Sq	2	Sq	15&	Sq	Sub	Sq	Sq	UN	UN	14+
Michie	Cailin	Hibernian	14+	4	2	2	Sq	2	2	2	2	2	2
Notley	Ellis	Hibernian		7<	Sq	Un	Sq	14+	15&	10	15&	14+	9&
Paterson	Donna	Aberdeen	3	3	3	3	Sq	3	4	4	4	4	4
Whyte	Courtney	Celtic	11	11*	4	4GG	Sq	4G	5	5	5	5	5

** Match Awarded 3-0 to Serbia, Scotland unable to play due to illness

QUALIFYING ROUND									
Pos	Team	Pld	W	D	L	GF	GA	GD	Pts	Qualification
1	Serbia	3	3	0	0	15	0	+15	9	Elite round
2	Scotland	3	2	0	1	19	3	+16	6	Elite round
3	Albania (H)	3	1	0	2	2	20	-18	3	
4	Cyprus	3	0	0	3	0	13	-13	0	

ELITE ROUND										
Pos	Team	Pld	W	D	L	GF	GA	GD	Pts	Qualification
1	Scotland	3	3	0	0	9	2	+7	9	Final tournament
2	Finland	3	2	0	1	9	3	+6	6	
3	Republic of Ireland (H)	3	1	0	2	4	5	-1	3	
4	Ukraine	3	0	0	3	0	12	-12	0	

The Finals take place in August 2017 in Northern Ireland.

Group A: Northern Ireland (hosts), Germany, Scotland, Spain
Group B: Italy, Netherlands, France, England

Scotland's fixtures are:

August 8	Scotland v Germany	Windsor Pk
August 11	Northern Ireland v Scotland	Lurgan
August 14	Spain v Scotland	Lurgan

Reaching the Euro 2017 Finals was a magnificent achievement for a squad that have done brilliantly over the past few years.

WOMENS UNDER 17 INTERNATIONALS 2016/17			Oct 10	Oct 12	Oct 15	Jan 29	Jan 31	Mar 13	Mar 15	Mar 18
Coach			H	H	H	a	A	N	N	A
Pauline Hamill			Croatia	Kazakhstan	France	N Ireland	N Ireland	Hungary	Rep of Ireland	Serbia
			UEFA	UEFA	UEFA	Fr	Fr	UEFA Q	UEFA Q	UEFA Q
			4-0	8-0	0-4	2-0	2-2	1-1	0-0	2-1
			Att	Att	Att					
			Oriam	Oriam	Spartans	Ballymoney	Jordanstown	Belgrade	Belgrade	Stara Pazova
				200						
Adderley	Georgia	Spartans	Un	12*	10+			2	2	3
Baillie	Jade	Celtic	Un	1	Un	Sq	Sq	1	1	1
Blues	Lindsay	Celtic	9&	14+	Un					
Callaghan	Abby	Celtic	12*	10GGG	12*	SqG				
Cameron	Nicole	Celtic	2	4*	4	Sq	Sq	3	3	4
Clark	Jenna	Rangers				Sq	Sq	Un	Un	Un
Cross	Morgan	Central Girls Academy	7GGG	9&	9	SqG	Sq	8G	8	9*
Davidson	Lauren	Glasgow City				Sq	Sq	11	11*	12*G
Eddie	Leah	Central Girls Academy	3	5	5	Sq	Sq	4	4	5
Gibson	Kiera	Celtic	1	Un	1	Sq	Sq	Un	Un	Un
Laing	Kirsten	Hibernian Development						10	10+	14+
Marriott	Jemma	Glasgow City	15&	2	2	Sq	Sq	Un	Un	2+
McAlonie	Michaela	Hearts	4	6G	6	Sq	SqG	5	5	6G
McAlpine	Kimberley	Central Girls Academy	8+G	Un	Un	Sq	Sq			
McCabe	Shaney	Central Girls Academy	Un	3+	3	Sq	Sq			
McDonald-Nguah	Kaela	Celtic	6	8GG	8			7*	7&	8
McIntosh	Kristie	Central Girls Academy	10	Un	14+	Sq	Sq	12*	12*	Un
McWhirter	Sarah	Celtic						Un	Un	Un
Muir	Amy	Rangers	5	7G	7	Sq	Sq	6	6	7
Napier	Jamie-Lee	Celtic	W	W		Sq	Sq	9	9	10
Robb	Megan	Dundee United	11*	15&	Un	Sq	Sq			
Santoyo-Brown	Elena	Boroughmuir Thistle	14+	11G	11*	Sq	SqG	Un	14+	Un
Welch	Naomi	Central Girls Academy				Sq	Sq	Un	15&	11

QUALIFYING ROUND

Pos	Team	Pld	W	D	L	GF	GA	GD	Pts	Qualification
1	France	3	3	0	0	25	0	+25	9	Elite round
2	Scotland (HOST)	3	2	0	1	12	4	+8	6	Elite round
3	Croatia	3	1	0	2	3	8	-5	3	
4	Kazakhstan	3	0	0	3	0	28	-28	0	

ELITE ROUND

Pos	Team	Pld	W	D	L	GF	GA	GD	Pts	Qualification
1	Republic of Ireland	3	2	1	0	2	0	+2	7	Final tournament
2	Scotland	3	1	2	0	3	2	+1	5	
3	Hungary	3	1	1	1	2	2	0	4	
4	Serbia (H)	3	0	0	3	1	4	-3	0	

Scotland's Under 17 Women were very unlucky not to make it to the Euro Finals, finishing second in their Elite Group qualifying round. However, it was still a very successful season for this talented squad.

Defender Georgia Adderley, a key player, has dediced to give up football to concentrate on Squash - a sport in which she is already ranked number 150 in the World, aged just 16.

WOMENS UNDER 16 INTERNATIONALS 2016/17			Sep 19	Sep 21	Feb 20	Feb 22	Feb 24
			A	A	H	H	H
			Finland	Finland	Austria	Iceland	Czech Rep
			Fr	Fr	UEFADev	UEFADev	UEFADev
			0-0	0-0	1-2	3-0	2-0
			Hameenlinna	Helsinki	Oriam	Oriam	Oriam
Allison	Sophie	Glasgow City	Sq	Sq	Sq	Sq	Sq
Baillie	Jade	Celtic	Sq	Sq			
Adderley	Georgie	Spartans	Sq	Sq	Sq	Sq	Sq
Fleming	Leah	Jeanfield Swifts	Sq	Sq	Sq	Sq	Sq
Laing	Kirsten	Celtic	Sq	Sq	Sq	Sq	Sq
McCallum	Philippa	Forfar Farmington	Sq	Sq	Sq	Sq	Sq
McGonigle	Tara	Celtic	Sq	Sq	Sq	Sq	SqG
McWhirter	Sara	Celtic	Sq	Sq	Sq	Sq	Sq
Clark	Jenna	Rangers	Sq	Sq	Sq	Sq	Sq
Craig	Emma	Celtic	Sq	Sq	Sq	Sq	Sq
Gibson	Kelsey	Chelsea	Sq	Sq			
McCartney	Laura	Glasgow City	Sq	Sq	Sq	Sq	Sq
McGowan	Rebecca	Raith Rovers	Sq	Sq	Sq	Sq	Sq
McGovern	Kathleen	Celtic	Sq	Sq	Sq	Sq	Sq
Morrison	Kirsty	Hibernian	Sq	Sq	Sq	Sq	Sq
Davidson	Lauren	Glasgow City	Sq	Sq		SqGG	Sq
Welch	Naomi	Central Girls Academy	Sq	Sq	Sq	Sq	Sq
Mutch	Emily	Aberdeen			Sq	Sq	Sq
Eddie	Leah	Central Girls Academy			Sq	Sq	Sq
Johnston	Cameron	Washington Spirit			Sq	Sq	Sq
McAlonie	Michaela	Hearts			Sq	SqGG	Sq
McIntosh	Kirstie	Central Girls Academy			Sq	Sq	SqG

UEFA DEVELOPMENT TOURNAMENT

	SCO	AUS	ICE	CZE
SCO		1-2	3-0	2-0
AUS			2-2 (4-3p)	2-1
ICE				
CZECH			1-0	

	P	W	D	L	F	A	PTS
Austria	3	2	1	0	6	4	7
Scotland	3	2	0	1	6	2	6
Czech Rep	3	1	0	2	2	4	3
Iceland	3	0	1	2	2	6	1

One defeat from five games was a good performance from an inexperienced side. Star player was Michaela McAlonie, then of Hearts and now of Spartans - a name to watch out for in future.

WOMENS UNDER 15 INTERNATIONALS 2016/17			Feb	Feb	Apr 10	Apr 11	Apr 12
			A	A	A	N	N
			Jersey	Jersey	Rep Ireland	Wales	England
			Fr	Fr	BDT	BDT	BDT
			10-1	4-0	3-4	0-0, 1-4p	1-1, 7-6p
			Sprinfield Stad	Springfield Stad	Clonhaugh	Clonhaugh	Clonhaugh
Crooks	Georgia	High School of Glasgow	7	16	Sq	Sq	Sq
Crooks	Mhairi	High School of Glasgow	9G	7G	Sq	Sq	Sq
Cunningham	Hannah	St Ambrose HS, Coatbridge	5	5	Sq	Sq	Sq
Girasoli	Carly	Lourdes Sec, Glasgow	4	4	Sq	Sq	Sq
Henderson	Cara	Mearns Castle HS, Newton Mearns	3	3	Sq	Sq	Sq
Maughan	Aisha	Broughton HS, Edinburgh	16	9G	Sq	Sq	Sq
McAllister	Rebecca	Our Lady and St Patricks HS, Dumbarton	2	2	Sq	Sq	Sq
McCartney	Laura	Lenzie Academy	6G	8	Sq	Sq	Sq
McCallum	Philippa	St John's HS, Dundee	11	9	Sq	Sq	Sq
McEarchan	Chelsea	St Mungo's HS, Falkirk	12GG	10	Sq	Sq	Sq
McGlinchey	Karsey	Govan HS, Glasgow	Sq	11	Sq	Sq	Sq
McGovern	Kathleen	Holy Cross HS, Hamilton	10GGGG	12	SqGGG	Sq	SqG
McQuilan	Rosie	St Peter the Apostle HS, Cludebank	15	6G	Sq	Sq	Sq
Meach	Aaliyah Jay	Monifieth HS	1	13	Sq	Sq	Sq
Scott	Hannah	St John Ogilvie HS, Hamilton	14G	14	Sq	Sq	Sq
Shore	Eilidh	Oldmachar Academy, Aberdeen	16	10G	Sq	Sq	Sq
Strachan	Jodie	Banff Academy	8G	15	Sq	Sq	Sq
Yates	Alicia	Dunfermline HS	18	1	Sq	Sq	Sq

Bob Docherty Cup Group Stages | U15 Girls' International Tournament
Republic of Ireland 1 (1) Wales 1 (3)
Shelbourne 0 (2) England 0 (4)

Republic of Ireland 4 Scotland 3
Shelbourne 1 Northern Ireland 3

Bob Docherty Cup Group Stages | U15 Girls' International Tournament
Wales 0 (4) Scotland 0 (1)
Northern Ireland 1 England 0

Bob Docherty Cup Play-offs | U15 Girls' International Tournament
Scotland 1 (7) England 1 (6) - for 5th and 6th place
Republic of Ireland A 9 Republic of Ireland B 0 - for 3rd and 4th place

Bob Docherty Cup Final | U15 Girls' International Tournament
Wales 2 Northern Ireland 0 for 1st and 2nd place

Bob Docherty Cup | Roll of Honour

YEAR	WINNER	VENUE
2002	Republic of Ireland	Ballymena, Northern Ireland
2003	Scotland	Edinburgh, Scotland
2004	Scotland	Clare, Republic of Ireland
2005	Republic of Ireland	Ballymena, Northern Ireland
2006	Scotland	Dumfries, Scotland
2007	Republic of Ireland	Wrexham, Wales
2008	Republic of Ireland	Salthill Devon, Galway
2009	Scotland	Belfast, Northern Ireland
2010	Republic of Ireland	Glasgow, Scotland
2011	Northern Ireland	Cardiff, Wales
2012	Northern Ireland	AUL Complex, Dublin
2013	Scotland	Shaws Bridge, Belfast
2014	England	Repton School, Derbyshire
2015	Scotland	Toryglen, Glasgow
2016	England	Dragon Park, Wales
2017	Wales	AUL Complex, Dublin

SCOTTISH AMATEUR FA			Sep 4	Oct 5	Oct 7	Oct 9	Apr 1	May 15
2016/17			H	A	N	N	A	H
			England	Malta	Ukraine	France	Rep Ireland	N Ireland
			Fr	UEFA Int	UEFA Int	UEFA Int	GHT	JBR
			3-1	5-0	0-3	0-4	0-2	4-1
			Lesser Hampden	Gozo	Gozo	Gozo	Dublin	Lesser Hampden
Brannan	Kieran	Larkhall Thistle AFC					11	16
Bruce	Harry	Bannockburn Ams	2+	4	4	3	2	3
Butler	Graham	Craigshill Thistle	14+	15&G	10*	Un		
Craig	Chris	Colville Park					10	
Currie	Gary	Bannockburn Ams		10&	Un	Un		
Drummond	Grant	Larkhall Thistle AFC					12	
Duffy	Andrew	Hamilton FPs		Un	Un	10		15
Feaks	Kenny	Doune Castle	4	2	2	15&		
Finnegan	Daniel	St Patrick's FP					9	17
Greenlees	Steven	Colville Park					4	
Heaver	Sean	Doune Castle	11	8	9			12G
Jaconelli	Tony	Craigshill Thistle	15&G					5
Kneale	David	Giffnock North	17^	6+	15&	6+		
Lafferty	Kris	Possil YM					16	
Malone	Chris	Southside					3	
Martin	Shaun	Craigshill Thistle					7	8G
Matthews	David	Drumchapel	6&		6+	7		
McAulay	Paul	Larkhall Thistle AFC	16>					
McClure	Niall	Doune Castle	10	7G	8	12*	15	10
McCracken	Paul	Craigshill Thistle	Un					
McCRum	Allan	Larkhall Thistle AFC					8	7
McGown	Andrew	Bannockburn Ams	5	5	5	4&	5	6G
McLay	Andrew	Glasgow Harp		Un	12*	5*		
Mclean	Kevin	East Kilbride	7>					
McLellan	Kenny	Bannockburn Ams	9^	11	11	14+	14	9
McPherson	Allan	Haldane United		9*	14+	9		
Methven	Scott	Leven United	3	4	3&	2		4
Millar	Darren	Colville Park					6	
Miller	Scott	Tollcross Thistle						1
Mitchell	Sami	Bowhill Rovers						18G
Moore	Nicky	Larkhall Thistle AFC	8<GG	12*GGG	7	8		11
Smith	Sean	Linlithgow Thistle	16<	14+	Un	11		
Tait	David	Bannockburn Ams					17	2
Walker	Scott	Fernieside	12*	Un	Un	1		
Wilson	Stuart	Gartcosh United	1*	1	1	Un	1	14

GHT = Graeme Harkness Trophy

JBR = Jack Britton Rosebowl

Group 1(Host country: Malta)									
	Teams	P	W	D	L	F	A	+/-	Pts
1	Ukraine Ingulec	3	3	0	0	8	2	6	9
2	France Ligue Paris Ile de France	3	1	1	1	5	2	3	4
3	Scotland East West Central Scotland	3	1	0	2	5	7	-2	3
4	Malta Gozo Region	3	0	1	2	1	8	-7	1

The UEFA Regions Cup

The biennial tournament is open to all 54 of UEFA's member associations, provided they run a domestic championship. Generally, teams are put forward via a domestic qualifying competition on a regional basis – hence the name, Regions' Cup – although smaller associations are allowed to submit a national representative team. The first UEFA Regions Cup was played in 1999. After a qualifying round involving 32 teams, the eight mini-tournament winners met in Veneto, in northern Italy, where the host team won the trophy by defeating Madrid 3-2 in the final. The format of the competition has remained relatively stable since then, with a series of qualifying mini-tournaments being held to provide enough teams for an eight-team final round. With rising interest in the tournament, a preliminary round was introduced for the 2005 tournament. The end result is an eight-team final round which is divided up into two groups. The four teams in each group play each other once in a league format with the teams that finish top of the two tables after the third and final game of the group stage taking each other on in the final.

In early years the Scottish Amateur FA have entered one of their Amateur Associations into this tournament, often represented by a single club. Results were poor. In 2013/14 a Scottish Amateur FA Select team was entered and won through the qualifying rounds - winning a group that included San Marino, Slovenia and Greece. This meant that they took part in the second stage held during September 2014. Unfortunately they were eliminated. In 2015/16 Scotland won their Qualifying Group, played in Lithuania. This meant they were through to the last 32. Eight groups of four were drawn with the winners of each progressing to the Finals - Scotland finished third in their group, hosted by Malta.

SPFL FOOTBALL

SCOTTISH PROFESSIONAL FOOTBALL LEAGUE

The Scottish Professional Football League was formed on June 27, 2013 when The Scottish Football League and The Scottish Premier League merged to create a single body to govern the 42 league clubs in Scotland. Most observers felt this was a long overdue development.

For 2016/17 the SPFL Board comprised Neil Doncaster, Ralph Topping, Karyn McCluskey (Non Executive Director), Peter Lawwell (Celtic), Anne Budge (Hearts), Ian Maxwell (Partick Thistle), Leeann Dempster (Hibernbian), Eric Drysdale (Raith Rovers) and Ken Ferguson (Brechin City).

The League structure is as follows:

Premiership
12 clubs. Play each other three times before split into top six and bottom six. Each group then plays each other once more - where possible maintaining an even split of home and away games. Bottom club relegated, 11th club goes into Play Off.

Championship
10 clubs. Play each other four times. Top team promoted. 4th plays 3rd in Round 1 of Play Off. Winner Plays 2nd in Play Off Semi Final. Winner of that then plays Premiership 11th in the Play Off Final. Bottom team relegated. 9th goes into relegation Play Off.

League One
10 clubs. Play each other four times. Top team promoted. Teams 2, 3 and 4 go into Play Off with 9th in Championship. One team relegated, 9th goes into relegation Play Off.

League Two
10 clubs. Play each other four times. Top team promoted. Teams 2, 3 and 4 go into Play Off with 9th in League One. Bottom team goes into Play off against winners of Highland League / Lowland League Play Off.

LEAGUE STRUCTURE 2017/18

PREMIERSHIP
Aberdeen
Celtic
Dundee
Hamilton Accies
Heart of Midlothian
Hibernian
Kilmarnock
Motherwell
Partick Thistle
Rangers
Ross County
St Johnstone

CHAMPIONSHIP
Brechin City
Dumbarton
Dundee United
Dunfermline Athletic
Falkirk
Inverness Caledonian Thistle
Livingston
Morton
Queen of the South
St Mirren

LEAGUE ONE
Airdrieonians
Albion Rovers
Alloa Athletic
Arbroath
Ayr United
East Fife
Forfar Athletic
Queen's Park
Raith Rovers
Stranraer

LEAGUE TWO
Annan Athletic
Berwick Rangers
Clyde
Cowdenbeath
Edinburgh City
Elgin City
Montrose
Peterhead
Stenhousemuir
Stirling Albion

NOTES ON THE CLUB INFORMATION SECTION

DATES OF BIRTH
The published information on player's dates of birth is very inaccurate. We have trawled many websites for information and find the same mistakes repeated over and over. In fact, the most accurate source of information has been player's own twitter feeds which frequently indicate their birthdays! Information for anyone born after 1994 is likely to be inaccurate - online databases seem to apply default birthdates to these players. Some club websites copy the inaccurate information. Presumably the SFA and SPFL are unwilling to provide this information to outside agencies.

APPEARANCES
Information refers to Appearances (A), Used Substitute Appearances (S) and Goals (G) in League (L), Scottish Cup (SC), League Cup (LC), Ramsdens Cup (RC) and European Ties (UC), The UNS column refers to Unused substitute appearances in all competitions.

Most media sources use information from a single reporter at matches via an Agency. Sometimes it is clear that mistakes have been made and I have corrected these. Where possible I have cross-referenced media reports with club sources such as websites and programmes and clarified any discrepancies.

CONTRACT
The information given is for guidance only. It has been gleaned primarily from club websites and newspapers.

SCORERS
Where possible these have been double checked but there may still be disputed goals. The information on the SPFL website is sometimes updated and changed following such instances.

ATTENDANCES
Most clubs publish accurate attendances for games. In some cases, notably Celtic and Rangers, these include all tickets sold, including season tickets. Matchday attendances are, in some cases, much less than the published figure.

PLAYER NUMBERING
Numbers 1-11 refer to players who started the match but bear no relation to actual numbers worn. Used substitutes are listed as 12,14 and 15, again regardless of actual numbers worn. Press Agencies ask for teams to provided in "formation" rather than numerical order which causes problems for reporters unfamiliar with the teams. Squad numbering is mandatory in the Premiership and the Championship but was optional in the other divisions for 2013/14.

TRIALISTS
In most cases trialists have been identified and are entered under their correct names.

FRIENDLY MATCHES
The lists of Friendly games may not be 100% comprehensive. Some clubs are very good at detailing games. Others publish details of matches which are really closed-door "joint training sessions" rather than proper matches.

Nationalities of Players with SPFL Clubs 2016/17

ALB	Albania	FRA	France	ROI	Republic of Ireland
ANG	Angola	GER	Germany	ROM	Romania
ANG	Angola	GHA	Ghana	RSA	South Africa
ANT	Antigua & Barbuda	GRE	Grenada	SCO	Scotland
ARG	Argentina	GUA	Guadeloupe	SEN	Senegal
AUS	Australia	GUI	Guinea	SER	Serbia
BEL	Belgium	HON	Honduras	SIE	Sierra Leone
BRA	Brazil	IRQ	Iraq	SKN	St Kitts & Nevis
BUL	Bulgaria	ITA	Italy	SPA	Spain
CAM	Cameroon	JAP	Japan	SVK	Slovakia
CAN	Canada	MAR	Martinique	SWE	Sweden
CDI	Cote D'Ivoire	MOR	Morocco	SWI	Switzerland
CDR	Congo Democratic Republic	NET	Netherlands	THA	Thailand
CRO	Croatia	NEZ	New Zealand	TRI	Trinidad & Tobago
CUR	Curacao	NIG	Nigeria	TUR	Turkey
CZR	Czech Republic	NIR	Northern Ireland	USA	United States of America
EGY	Egypt	NOR	Norway	WAL	Wales
ENG	England	OST	Austria		
EST	Estonia	POL	Poland		
FIN	Finland	POR	Portugal		

WORK PERMITS
Any player who is over 16 years old and is not from the European Economic Area, which covers 32 countries aside from the UK requires a work permit to play for a British club.
A Commonwealth citizen with at least one grandparent who was born in the UK does not need to apply through the points based system. Such players will still require a work permit but go through a different process.

When a club signs a player who requires a work permit, they agree to sponsor the player to be in the UK, meaning they will provide the funds for his time in the country. A certificate of sponsorship is then produced by the club, which is then submitted to the relevant FA for them to consider an endorsement.

The Scottish FA's rules on work permit endorsements follow the same guidelines as previously outlined by the UK Government. For the Scottish FA to give their approval, the player in question must have played 75 per cent of his nation's competitive games – excluding friendlies – in the two years prior to the date of application. Furthermore, the country the player is coming from must be in the top 70 of the FIFA rankings.

Failure to meet these requirements, unless it can be proven a player was unavailable for selection for a period of time, results in an automatic rejection of any application for an Scottish FA endorsement for a work permit certificate of sponsorship.

If an application is rejected, a club can then appeal to the SFA. An appeals panel will ultimately weigh up whether or not the player is, in their view, of the highest calibre and whether they would contribute significantly to the development of the game at the top level in the country. That appeals panel typically sits within three to five working days of an appeal submission, although urgent hearings can be convened.

The panel is made up of three representatives from the relevant football bodies, typically officials from the league, the association and the player's union. Up to three independent football experts, made up typically of former professionals, also sit on the panel.

The length of time a player can remain in the UK as a player depends on his grasp of the English language. There are two immigration statuses available to a player applying for a work permit: tier two and tier five.

Under tier two, a player can remain in the UK for an initial three years, with the possibility for an extension for a further two years. To qualify, the player must accrue 70 immigration points under the UK Government's system. 50 are given for getting an FA endorsement, with 10 more given for being able to prove sufficient funding to remain in the country.

The final 10 are awarded on the basis of the player's English. If the applicant comes from a predominantly English-speaking country, or has a degree from a course which was taught in English, the 10 points are subsequently awarded. Additionally, a player can sit an approved English language test upon their arrival in the UK to obtain tier two status.

IMPACT OF BREXIT
At this point it is not clear if EU citizens, currently working in the UK, will have to apply for a work permit under the rules described above. If Scotland were to remain in the EU but the rest of the UK was to leave, this could open up all sorts of issues regarding the status of English, Welsh and Northern Irish (i.e. non EU) citizens within Scotland.

Loan / Temporary Transfers

Loan transfers are very common these days, and the rules governing them are far from simple.

There are three types of temporary transfer:

Standard
Emergency
Development

Standard Temporary Transfers
Must be at least 28 days
Must be until the first day of the immediately succeeding transfer period

Emergency Temporary Transfers
Must be at least 28 days but no more than 93 days
Not allowed for Premiership clubs – only lower leagues

General
Maximum of 4 players on Standard / Emergency Temporary Transfers at any time
Maximum of ONE player on Standard / Emergency Temporary Transfer may be over 21 at any given time
Maximum of TWO players on Standard / Emergency temporary Transfer may be over 21 during one season
Maximum of ONE player on Standard / Emergency Temporary Transfer from a club in the same division at any one time
Maximum of TWO players on Standard / Emergency Temporary Transfer from a club in a different division at any one time
Maximum of THREE players on Standard / Emergency / Development Temporary Transfers from any one club at any one time
Maximum of FIVE players per season on Standard / Emergency Temporary Transfers
Maximum of FOUR Development loans at any one time

Goalkeepers
The League Management Committee can, in exceptional circumstances and on cause shown, sanction the Standard Temporary Transfer to a Premiership club, or an Emergency temporary Transfer to a Championship, league One or League Two side, of a goalkeeper, in addition to the above.

Playing Against Own Club
Players on Temporary Transfers may not play against their parent club. No other stipulations about opponents are permitted.

Development Temporary Transfers
Players can play in Development League games and Challenge Cup ties for their parent club. If they do not play in Challenge Cup for parent club then they can play in Challenge Cup for their loan club.

There must be one clear day between a player playing for his parent club and his loan club. If there is a "clash" then the loan club takes priority unless they have agreed in writing to waive priority.

A Development Loan must terminate at the latest on the first day of the Registration Period immediately following the date on which the Player ceases to qualify as an Under 20 Player
or, where such a Player will cease to so qualify during a Registration Period, the term of his Development Temporary Transfer must terminate not later than the date when he so ceases to so qualify as an Under 20 Player. Notwithstanding that a Player who is the subject of a Development
Temporary Transfer has ceased to qualify as an Under 20 Player on a date which is not within a Registration Period he shall, subject to compliance with this Regulation, be deemed for all purposes to continue to qualify as an Under 20 Player until the earlier of the first day of the next Registration Period and the expiry of the term of his Development Temporary Transfer.

.

REGISTRATION PERIODS

Registration Periods will apply to Professional Players who compete in football at Scottish Professional Football League level.

To those Clubs to which Registration Periods apply, a Professional Player may only be registered to play with such a Club during one of two Registration Periods per year as determined by the Board from time to time. Notwithstanding the foregoing provision, and subject to what follows, a Professional Player who at the conclusion of a Registration Period is not registered to a Club, may sign and be registered for a Club outwith the Registration Period.

Internationally and Domestically, a Professional Player may be registered with a maximum of three Clubs to which Registration Periods apply during one Season. Notwithstanding the foregoing the Professional Player is only eligible to play Official Matches for two Clubs, to which Registration Periods apply, in any
one Season.

The Scottish FA may in its absolute discretion, in exceptional circumstances, sanction an application for registration of a Professional Player outwith the Registration Periods subject to specific conditions, Board approval and, where required, approval of FIFA.

Current Registration Periods in Scotland are:

June 9 – September 1
January 1 – February 1

Aberdeen FC 2016/17

Founded	1903
Ground	Pittodrie Stadium
Capacity	20961
Postcode	AB24 5QH
Tel	01224 650400
Closest Railway Station	Aberdeen
Record Attendance	45061 v Hearts, SC, 1953/4
Record Win	13-0 v Peterhead, SC, 10/2/1923
Record Defeat	0-9, v Celtic, Lge, 6/11/2010
Most League Goals in a Season	38, Benny Yorston, 1929/30
Most Goals in Career	199, Joe Harper
Chairman	Stewart Milne
Chief Executive	Duncan Fraser
Football Operations Manager	Steven Gunn
Manager	Derek McInnes
Assistant Manager	Tony Docherty
Colours 2016/17 Top	Red / White Pinstripe
Shorts	Red
Sponsor	Saltire Energy
Manufacturer	Adidas
Change Colours 2016/17 Top	Black / red trim
Shorts	Black
Nicknames	Dons, Dandies, Sheep
Web	www.afc.co.uk
E Tickets	www.afc.co.uk/etickets
Match Programme 2015/16	Red Match Day £3
Theme Song	Northern Lights of Old Aberdeen

Aberdeen's Manager Derek McInnes's football background is well-known; Less well-known is his Assistant Tony Docherty. Doc, from East Kilbride, joined Dunfermline Athletic in 1990. He played in midfield but was released in 1991. He had a spell with Cambridge United before coming back to Scotland in October 1991. He signed for Stirling Albion and played 47 first team games, many as a substitute. He then played a few games for Shire and Albion Rovers. Off the field he studied for a degree in Sports Management and took his coaching badges. After a spell working for Glasgow City Council in Sports Development he became Football Development Officer at Falkirk FC. Tony was appointed Assistant Manager by Ian McCall, who then took him to Tannadice in the same role. He left Tannadice in 2007 to work with Derek McInnes at St Johnstone, and subsequently at Bristol City and Aberdeen.

Strange as it may seem, Aberdeen can take some satisfaction from finishing second in everything. They were the best of the rest in the Premiership - a mile behind Celtic, but comfortably clear of Rangers. They reached both Cup Finals, and lost both to Celtic. For the League Cup Final the Dons basically failed to turn up. For the Scottish Cup Final they produced an excellent display, took the game to Celtic, and made a big contribution to one of the best Scottish Cup Finals in years.

The biggest disappointment for the Dons was probably in Europe. Reaching the 3rd Qualifying Round is no mean achievement for a Scottish club, but the manner of their defeat to Maribor left everyone thinking about what might have been. Aberdeen had a great chance to progress but failed to do so.

Manager Derek McInnes could have left in the Summer to take up the Sunderland job if he had wanted. He has chosen to remain at Pittodrie and hopefully the Dons fans will remember that loyalty if and when things start to go wrong.

The club have lost several prominent players. Jonny Hayes and Niall McGinn will be big misses up front. Ryan Jack and Peter Pawlett have both been decent servants to the club but have chosen to move on. Jack will no doubt get a warm reception when he returns to Pittodrie in the colours of Rangers.

Dean Campbell became the youngest first team player in Aberdeen's history when he made his debut against Celtic aged 16 years, one month and 23 days. Earlier in the day he had sat his National 5 English exam.

PREDICTION 2017/18

Could well be second best again although unlikely to reach both Cup Finals.

Dons Stalwart

Andrew Considine		L			LC			SC			OC			Total		
Season	Club	A	S	G	A	S	G	A	S	G	A	S	G	A	S	G
2003/4	Aberdeen	1												1	0	0
2004/5	Aberdeen	1												1	0	0
2005/6	Aberdeen	8	4		1				1					9	5	0
2006/7	Aberdeen	23	9	2	2			2						27	9	2
2007/8	Aberdeen	2	1		2	1	2	5		2	7		1	16	2	5
2008/9	Aberdeen	17	3	1	1				2					18	5	1
2009/10	Aberdeen	15	1	1	1						2			18	1	1
2010/11	Aberdeen	26	1		3			4						33	1	0
2011/2	Aberdeen	36		3	2			4		1				42	0	4
2012/3	Aberdeen	17	1		2			2						21	1	0
2013/4	Aberdeen	21			2	1	1	4		1				27	1	2
2014/5	Aberdeen	35	1	2	2	1		1			3	1		41	3	2
2015/6	Aberdeen	26	6	2	1			1			6		1	34	6	3
2016/7	Aberdeen	36		6	5			4			5			50	0	6

Date	Comp	H/A	Opponents	F	A		HT			Crowd	Scorers
30/06/2015	UEFA	H	Fola Esch	3	1		0	0	M Kristoffersen	12570	Logan, McGinn, Rooney
07/07/2016	UEFA	A	Fola Esch	0	1		0	1	O Nilsen	1789	
14/07/2016	UEFA	H	Ventspils	3	0		0	0	J P Pinheiro	10672	Stockley, Rooney, Burns
21/07/2016	UEFA	A	Ventspils	1	0		0	0	D Grujic	2100	Rooney
28/07/2016	UEFA	H	Maribor	1	1		0	0	T Hansen	17105	Hayes
04/08/2016	UEFA	A	Maribor	0	1		0	0	T Hansen	9796	
07/08/2016	L	A	St Johnstone	0	0		0	0	W Collum	5728	
10/08/2016	LC1	A	Ayr United	2	1		2	1	A Muir	2653	Meggatt og, McGinn
13/08/2016	L	H	Hearts	0	0		0	0	K Clancy	13559	
20/08/2016	L	H	Partick Thistle	2	1		1	0	J Beaton	11049	McGinn, Storey
27/08/2016	L	A	Celtic	1	4		1	2	R Madden	57758	Rooney
10/09/2016	L	H	Inverness CT	1	1		0	0	C Allan	11356	McGinn
18/09/2016	L	A	Dundee	3	1		1	1	S McLean	6321	Maddison, Stockley, McLean
22/09/2016	LC2	H	St Johnstone	1	0		0	0	C Thomson	8829	Rooney
25/09/2016	L	H	Rangers	2	1		0	0	J Beaton	19263	Hayes, Maddison
01/10/2016	L	A	Kilmarnock	4	0		1	0	W Collum	4592	Rooney 2, Considine, Taylor
15/10/2016	L	H	Ross County	4	0		2	0	C Thomson	10091	Hayes, Logan, McGinn, Stockley
22/10/2016	LCSF	N	Morton	2	0	*	0	0	K Clancy	16183	Rooney, McLean
25/10/2016	L	A	Hamilton Accies	0	1		0	1	W Collum	2315	
29/10/2016	L	H	Celtic	0	1		0	1	S McLean	17105	
04/11/2016	L	A	Partick Thistle	2	1		1	0	B Madden	3974	O'Connor, Stockley
19/11/2016	L	A	Inverness CT	3	1		2	1	K Clancy	4867	McLean 2, Rooney
27/11/2016	LCF	N	Celtic	0	3		0	2	J Beaton	49629	
03/12/2016	L	A	Rangers	1	2		0	0	S McLean	50003	Considine
06/12/2016	L	H	Kilmarnock	5	1		3	0	S Finnie	8195	Hayes 2, McGinn, O'Connor, Pawlett
10/12/2016	L	H	St Johnstone	0	0		0	0	K Clancy	11501	
17/12/2016	L	A	Ross County	1	2		0	1	C Thomson	4467	McGinn
23/12/2016	L	A	Motherwell	3	1		2	1	B Madden	3428	Shinnie, McGinn, Rooney
27/12/2016	L	H	Hamilton Accies	2	1		1	1	A Dallas	13131	Taylor, Rooney
30/12/2016	L	A	Hearts	1	0		0	0	W Collum	16630	
21/01/2017	SC	H	Stranraer	4	0		2	0	D Robertson	8960	Rooney 2, McGinn 2
27/01/2017	L	H	Dundee	3	0		2	0	K Clancy	10512	Jack, McGinn 2
01/02/2017	L	A	Celtic	0	1		0	0	J Beaton	53958	
04/02/2017	L	H	Partick Thistle	2	0		0	0	G Aitken	10094	Stockley, Christie
11/02/2017	SC5	A	Ross County	1	0		0	0	B Madden	4671	Logan
15/02/2017	L	H	Motherwell	7	2		4	0	A Muir	10384	Rooney 3, Christie, Pawlett, Considine, Hayes
19/02/2017	L	A	Kilmarnock	2	1		0	1	A Dallas	3972	Stockley, Pawlett
25/02/2017	L	H	Ross County	1	0		0	0	W Collum	11774	Rooney
28/02/2017	L	A	Hamilton Accies	0	1		0	1	S McLean	2006	
05/03/2017	SC6	H	Partick Thistle	1	0		1	0	C Thomson	11333	Shinnie
11/03/2017	L	H	Motherwell	1	0		0	0	E Anderson	12524	McGinn
18/03/2017	L	H	Hearts	2	0		1	0	S McLean	12178	Logan, Hayes
31/03/2017	L	A	Dundee	7	0		4	0	A Muir	7324	Considine 3, Rooney, McLean, Jack, McGinn
04/04/2017	L	H	Inverness CT	1	0		1	0	A Dallas	11507	Taylor
09/04/2017	L	H	Rangers	0	3		0	0	K Clancy	19332	
15/04/2017	L	A	St Johnstone	2	1		2	0	B Madden	5132	Christie, Scobbie og
22/04/2017	SCSF	N	Hibernian	3	2		2	1	J Beaton	31969	Rooney, Christie, McGregor og
29/04/2017	L	H	St Johnstone	0	2		0	0	A Muir	10606	
07/05/2017	L	A	Hearts	2	1		1	0	W Collum	16552	O'Connor, Rooney
12/05/2017	L	H	Celtic	1	3		1	3	S McLean	16015	Hayes
17/05/2017	L	A	Rangers	2	1		1	0	J Beaton	48289	Shinnie, Christie
21/05/2017	L	A	Partick Thistle	6	0		5	0	E Anderson	3924	Wright 3, Christie 2, Hayes
27/05/2017	SCF	N	Celtic	1	2		1	2	J Beaton	48713	Hayes
ABD											
13/12/2016	L	H	Motherwell	0	0				A Muir		Floodlight Failure, 7 mins

FRIENDLIES / OTHER GAMES

20/06/2016	N	TNS	3	0				at St Andrews
23/06/2016	N	Hearts	1	0				at St Andrews
26/06/2016	A	Brechin City	3	0				
10/07/2016	A	East Fife	4	2				
16/07/2016	A	Inverurie Locos	3	0		U20		
19/07/2016	A	Deveronvale	0	1		U20		
23/07/2016	A	Arbroath	4	1				
25/07/2018	A	Kirkwall Thorfinn	5	2		U20		
16/02/2017	A	Buckie Thistle	2	1		U20		

Date	Comp	H/A	Opponents	F	A	1	2	3	4	5	6	7	8	9	10	11	12	13	14	15	16	17	18
30/06/2015	UEFA	H	Fola Esch	3	1	Lewis	Considine	Logan	Shinnie	Taylor	Flood*	Hayes	Jack	McGinn	McLean	Stockley	Rooney*	O'Connor	Pawlett	Reynolds	Wright	Smith	Alexander
07/07/2016	UEFA	A	Fola Esch	0	1	Lewis	Considine	Logan	Shinnie	Taylor	O'Connor*	Hayes	Jack	Pawlett+	McLean	Stockley&	Reynolds*	Flood+	Rooney&	Shankland	Wright	Smith	Alexander
14/07/2016	UEFA	H	Ventspils	3	0	Lewis	Considine	Logan	Shinnie	Taylor	Reynolds	Hayes	Jack	McGinn	McLean*	Rooney+	Stockley*	Burns+	Pawlett	McKenna	Storey	O'Connor	Alexander
21/07/2016	UEFA	A	Ventspils	1	0	Lewis	Considine	Logan	Shinnie	Taylor	Reynolds	Hayes&	Jack	McGinn*	McLean	Rooney+	Stockley*	Burns+	Storey&	McKenna	Wright	O'Connor	Alexander
28/07/2016	UEFA	H	Maribor	1	1	Lewis	Considine	Logan	Shinnie+	Taylor	Reynolds	Hayes	Jack	McGinn	Stockley*	Rooney	McLean*	Burns+	Pawlett	Storey	Wright	O'Connor	Alexander
04/08/2016	UEFA	A	Maribor	0	1	Lewis	Considine	Logan	Shinnie	Taylor	Reynolds	Burns*	Jack	McGinn&	McLean+	Rooney	Stockley*	Storey+	Wright&	Pawlett	Storie	O'Connor	Alexander
07/08/2016	L	A	St Johnstone	0	0	Lewis	Considine	Logan	Shinnie	O'Connor	Reynolds	Burns+	Jack	Stockley	McLean	Storey*	Rooney*	McGinn+	McKenna	Morris	Storie	Wright	Alexander
10/08/2016	LC1	A	Ayr United	2	1	Lewis	Considine	Logan	Shinnie	O'Connor	Reynolds	Burns	Jack	McGinn	McLean+	Rooney*	Stockley*	McKenna+	Nuttall	Storey	Storie	Wright	Alexander
13/08/2016	L	H	Hearts	0	0	Lewis	Taylor	Logan	Shinnie	O'Connor	Reynolds	Burns*	Jack	McGinn	Pawlett&	Stockley+	McLean*	Rooney+	Storey&	Considine	Storie	Wright	Alexander
20/08/2016	L	H	Partick Thistle	2	1	Lewis	Considine	Logan	Shinnie	O'Connor	Reynolds	McLean	Rooney&	McGinn	Pawlett*	Storey+	Burns*	Taylor+	Stockley&	McKenna	Storie	F Ross	Alexander
27/08/2016	L	A	Celtic	1	4	Lewis	Considine	Logan	Shinnie	O'Connor+	Reynolds	McLean	Rooney*	McGinn&	Taylor	Burns	Stockley*	Storey+	Storie&	McKenna	Morris	Wright	Alexander
10/09/2016	L	H	Inverness CT	1	1	Lewis	Considine	Logan	Shinnie*	O'Connor	Taylor	McLean	Rooney	McGinn	Hayes&	Burns+	Maddison*	Pawlett+	Stockley&	McKenna	Storie	Storey	Alexander
18/09/2016	L	A	Dundee	3	1	Lewis	Considine	Logan	Shinnie	O'Connor	Taylor	McLean	Rooney*	McGinn+	Hayes	Maddison&	Stockley*	Burns+	Storie&	Reynolds	Pawlett	Storey	Alexander
22/09/2016	LC2	H	St Johnstone	1	0	Lewis	Considine	Logan	Shinnie	O'Connor	Taylor	McLean	Burns*	McGinn	Stockley+	Maddison&	Pawlett*	Rooney+	Reynolds&	Storie	Wright	Storey	Alexander
25/09/2016	L	H	Rangers	2	1	Lewis	Considine	Logan	Shinnie	O'Connor	Reynolds	McLean	Rooney&	McGinn+	Hayes	Pawlett*	Maddison*	Burns+	Taylor&	Storie	Stockley	Storey	Alexander
01/10/2016	L	A	Kilmarnock	4	0	Lewis	Considine	Logan	Shinnie	O'Connor	Taylor	McLean	Rooney&	McGinn*	Hayes+	Maddison	Burns*	Stockley+	Storey&	Storie	Reynolds	Morris	Alexander
15/10/2016	L	H	Ross County	4	0	Lewis	Considine	Logan	Shinnie	O'Connor	Taylor*	McLean	Rooney+	McGinn&	Hayes	Maddison	Reynolds*	Stockley+	Pawlett&	Storie	Storey	Burns	Alexander
22/10/2016	LCSF	N	Morton	2	0 *	Lewis	Considine	Logan	Shinnie+	O'Connor	Reynolds	McLean	Rooney	McGinn&	Hayes	Maddison*	Jack*	Burns+	Storey&	Pawlett	Stockley	Morris	Alexander
25/10/2016	L	A	Hamilton Accies	0	1	Lewis	Considine	Logan	Shinnie	O'Connor	Reynolds+	McLean	Rooney	Burns*	Hayes	Maddison&	McGinn*	Pawlett+	Storey&	Storie	Jack	McKenna	Alexander
29/10/2016	L	H	Celtic	0	1	Lewis	Considine	Logan	Shinnie	O'Connor	Reynolds	McLean	McGinn+	Burns&	Hayes	Jack*	Rooney*	Maddison+	Stockley&	Storie	Pawlett	McKenna	Alexander
04/11/2016	L	A	Partick Thistle	2	1	Lewis	Considine	Logan	Shinnie	O'Connor	Maddison*	McLean	Rooney	Stockley+	Hayes	Jack	McGinn*	Reynolds+	Burns	Pawlett	Morris	Storey	Alexander
19/11/2016	L	A	Inverness CT	3	1	Lewis	Considine	Logan	Shinnie&	O'Connor	Maddison+	McLean	Rooney	Stockley*	Hayes	Jack	McGinn*	Taylor+	Reynolds&	Pawlett	Morris	Storey	Alexander
27/11/2016	LCF	N	Celtic	0	3	Lewis	Considine	Logan	Shinnie	O'Connor*	Maddison	McLean	Rooney&	Taylor	Hayes+	Jack	Stockley*	McGinn+	Burns&	Pawlett	Reynolds	Storey	Alexander
03/12/2016	L	A	Rangers	1	2	Lewis	Considine	Logan	Shinnie+	Reynolds	Maddison	McLean&	Stockley*	Taylor	Hayes	Jack	Rooney*	McGinn+	Pawlett&	Burns	O'Connor	Storey	Alexander
06/12/2016	L	H	Kilmarnock	5	1	Lewis	Considine	Logan	Shinnie	O'Connor	Maddison*	McLean	McGinn	Pawlett+	Hayes	Rooney&	Reynolds*	Burns+	Stockley&	Taylor	Storie	Storey	Alexander
10/12/2016	L	H	St Johnstone	0	0	Lewis	Considine	Jack	Shinnie&	O'Connor	Maddison	McLean	McGinn*	Pawlett+	Hayes	Rooney	Logan*	Stockley+	Burns&	Taylor	Reynolds	Storey	Alexander
17/12/2016	L	A	Ross County	1	2	Lewis	Considine	Logan	Shinnie	O'Connor	Maddison	McLean	Jack&	Burns*	Hayes	Stockley+	McGinn*	Rooney+	Storey&	Taylor	Reynolds	Pawlett	Alexander
23/12/2016	L	A	Motherwell	3	1	Lewis	Considine	Logan	Shinnie	Reynolds	Taylor	McLean	Jack	McGinn	Hayes*	Rooney	O'Connor*	Burns	Storey	Pawlett	Maddison	Stockley	Alexander
27/12/2016	L	H	Hamilton Accies	2	1	Lewis	Considine*	Logan	Shinnie	Reynolds	Taylor	McLean	Jack	McGinn+	Hayes	Rooney	Maddison*	O'Connor+	Burns	Pawlett	Storey	Stockley	Alexander
30/12/2016	L	A	Hearts	1	0	Lewis	Considine	Logan	Shinnie	Reynolds	Taylor	McLean	Jack	McGinn*	Hayes	Rooney	O'Connor*	Burns	Stockley	Pawlett	Storey	Maddison	Alexander
21/01/2017	SC	H	Stranraer	4	0	Lewis	Considine+	Logan	Shinnie	Reynolds	Taylor	McLean&	Jack	McGinn	Hayes*	Rooney	Pawlett*	Wright+	F Ross&	O'Connor	Storey	Stockley	Alexander
27/01/2017	L	H	Dundee	3	0	Lewis	Considine	Logan	Shinnie	Reynolds	Taylor	McLean	Jack	McGinn&	Hayes*	Rooney+	Christie*	Storey+	Wright&	O'Connor	Pawlett	Stockley	Alexander
01/02/2017	L	A	Celtic	0	1	Lewis	Considine	Logan&	Shinnie	Reynolds+	Taylor	McLean	Jack	McGinn	Hayes	Rooney*	Storey*	Stockley+	Pawlett&	O'Connor	Wright	F Ross	Alexander
04/02/2017	L	H	Partick Thistle	2	0	Lewis	Considine	Logan*	Shinnie	Reynolds+	Taylor	McLean	Jack	McGinn	Hayes	Rooney&	Christie*	Stockley+	O'Connor&	Pawlett	Wright	Storey	Alexander
11/02/2017	SC5	A	Ross County	1	0	Lewis	Considine	Logan	Shinnie	Reynolds*	Taylor	McLean	Jack	McGinn	Hayes	Rooney+	O'Connor*	Stockley+	Christie	Pawlett	Wright	Storey	Alexander
15/02/2017	L	H	Motherwell	7	2	Lewis	Considine	Logan	Christie&	Reynolds	Taylor	McLean	Jack	McGinn+	Hayes	Rooney*	Stockley*	Pawlett+	Storey&	O'Connor	Wright	F Ross	Alexander
19/02/2017	L	A	Kilmarnock	2	1	Lewis	Considine+	Logan	Christie&	Reynolds*	Taylor	McLean	Jack	McGinn	Hayes	Rooney	Shinnie*	Pawlett+	Stockley&	O'Connor	Wright	Storey	Alexander
25/02/2017	L	H	Ross County	1	0	Lewis	Considine	Logan	Shinnie	Reynolds*	Taylor	McLean	Jack	McGinn+	Hayes&	Rooney	Storey*	O'Connor+	Pawlett&	Christie	Wright	F Ross	Alexander
28/02/2017	L	A	Hamilton Accies	0	1	Lewis	Considine	Logan	Shinnie	Reynolds*	Taylor	McLean	Jack&	McGinn	Christie+	Rooney	Pawlett*	Storey+	O'Connor&	McLennan	Wright	F Ross	Alexander
05/03/2017	SC6	H	Partick Thistle	1	0	Lewis	Considine	Logan	Shinnie	Pawlett*	Taylor	McLean	Stockley	McGinn&	Hayes	Rooney+	O'Connor*	Storey+	Christie&	McLennan	Wright	F Ross	Alexander
11/03/2017	L	H	Motherwell	1	0	Lewis	O'Connor+	Logan	Shinnie	Jack	Taylor	McLean	Stockley	McGinn	Hayes	Rooney*	Christie*	Storey+	Pawlett	McLennan	Wright	F Ross	Alexander
18/03/2017	L	H	Hearts	2	0	Lewis	Considine	Logan	Shinnie	O'Connor	Taylor	McLean	Jack	McGinn&	Hayes+	Rooney*	Stockley*	Christie+	F Ross&	Pawlett	Wright	Rooney	Alexander
31/03/2017	L	A	Dundee	7	0	Lewis	Considine	Logan	Shinnie	O'Connor	Taylor	McLean*	Jack	McGinn&	Hayes+	Rooney	Christie*	Wright+	F Ross&	Pawlett	B Anderson	Storey	Alexander
04/04/2017	L	H	Inverness CT	1	0	Lewis	Considine	Logan	Shinnie	O'Connor	Taylor	McLean	Jack	McGinn+	Hayes	Rooney*	Storey*	Christie+	F Ross	Pawlett	B Anderson	Wright	Alexander
09/04/2017	L	H	Rangers	0	3	Lewis	Considine	Logan	Shinnie	O'Connor*	Taylor	McLean	Jack	McGinn	Hayes	Rooney	Stockley*	Christie	F Ross	Pawlett	Storey	Wright	Alexander
15/04/2017	L	A	St Johnstone	2	1	Lewis	Considine	Logan	Shinnie	O'Connor	Taylor	McLean	Jack	Christie*	Hayes+	Rooney	Pawlett*	Stockley+	F Ross	Reynolds	Storey	Wright	Alexander
22/04/2017	SCSF	N	Hibernian	3	2	Lewis	Considine	Logan	Shinnie	Reynolds+	Taylor	McLean	Jack	Christie*	Hayes	Rooney	O'Connor*	McGinn+	Pawlett	Stockley	Storey	Wright	Alexander
29/04/2017	L	H	St Johnstone	0	2	Lewis	Considine	Logan	Shinnie	McGinn	Taylor	McLean	Jack	Christie*	Hayes&	Rooney+	Stockley*	Pawlett+	Wright&	O'Connor	Storey	Reynolds	Alexander
07/05/2017	L	A	Hearts	2	1	Lewis	Considine	Logan	Shinnie	Reynolds	Taylor	McLean	Pawlett*	McGinn	Hayes	Rooney+	O'Connor*	Stockley+	Wright	F Ross	Storey	Christie	Alexander
12/05/2017	L	H	Celtic	1	3	Lewis	Considine	Logan	Shinnie	Reynolds+	Taylor	McLean	McGinn&	McGinn	Hayes	Stockley*	Rooney*	Wright+	Campbell&	F Ross	S Ross	Storey	Alexander
17/05/2017	L	A	Rangers	2	1	Lewis	Considine	Logan	Shinnie	Reynolds	Taylor	McLean	O'Connor	McGinn	Christie	Rooney*	Stockley*	Wright	Campbell	F Ross	S Ross	Storey	Alexander
21/05/2017	L	A	Partick Thistle	6	0	Lewis	Considine	Logan	Hayes&	Reynolds+	Taylor	McLean*	O'Connor	Wright	Christie	Rooney	Pawlett*	Jack+	F Ross&	Shinnie	McGinn	Storey	Alexander
27/05/2017	SCF	N	Celtic	1	2	Lewis	Considine	Logan	Shinnie	Reynolds	Taylor	McLean	Jack&	McGinn+	Hayes	Stockley*	Rooney*	O'Connor+	Wright&	F Ross	Pawlett	Storey	Alexander

						L			SC			LC			EUL							
			SQ	Nat	Pos	A	S	G	A	S	G	A	S	G	A	S	G	UNS				
Surname	First Name	DOB																	Signed	Previous Club	Notes	Contract
Alexander	Neil	10/03/1978	25	SCO	G													53	2016	Hearts		OOC
Anderson	Bruce	23/09/1998	34	SCO	M													2	2013	Dyce BC		
Antoniazzi	Chris	01/05/2000	45	SCO	F														2016	Celtic U17		
Burns	Wes	13/11/1994	8	WAL	F	7	6					2	2		1	3	1	6	2016	Bristol City (OL)	OL Aug 2016-Jan 2017	[redacted]
Campbell	Dean	19/03/2001	47	SCO			1											1	2016	Aberdeen Youths		
Christie	Ryan	22/02/1995	8	SCO	M	7	6	6	1	1	1							4	2017	Celtic (OL)	Jan-May 2017	[redacted]
Considine	Andrew	01/04/1987	4	SCO	D	36		6	5			4			6			1	2003	Aberdeen Youths		End 2018/19
Craddock	David	30/01/1998	50	ROI	GK														2015	Shelbourne		
Dangana	David	01/04/2000	38	SCO/NIG	F														2013	Lewis United		
Flood	Willo	10/04/1985	8	ROI	M										1	1			2013	Dundee United	Freed July 2016, joined Dundee Utd	[redacted]
Harvie	Daniel	14/07/1998	28	SCO	D														2016	Aberdeen Youths	OL to Dumbarton Aug-May	
Hayes	Jonny	09/07/1987	11	ROI	F	32		9	5		1	2			5		1		2012	Inverness CT	Transferred to Celtic, June 2017	[redacted]
Henry	Jamie	17/02/1997	31	SCO	F														2015	Aberdeen Youths	Freed May 2017	
Hutchison	Lewis	19/02/2000	42	SCO	F														2016	Aberdeen Youths		
Jack	Ryan	27/02/1992	22	SCO	M	25	1	2	4			2	1		6			1	2008	Aberdeen Youths	OOC, joined Rangers June 2017	[redacted]
Lennox	Aaron	19/02/1993	40	AUS	G														2015	Hayes & Yeading	OL to Raith R Aug-May, Freed June 2017 and joined Raith Rovers	
Lewis	Joe	06/10/1987	1	ENG	G	38			5			4			6				2016	Cardiff City		End 2019/20
Logan	Shaleum	29/01/1988	2	ENG	D	37	1	2	5		1	4			6		1		2014	Brentford		End 2017/18
Maddison	James	23/11/1996	23	ENG	F	10	4	2				3						2	2016	Norwich City LOAN	OL Aug-Dec 2016	[redacted]
Mbayo	Harlain	14/03/1998	35	ENG / DRC	D														2015	Oxford United U18		
McGinn	Niall	20/07/1987	10	NIR	F	31	6	10	4	1	2	3	1	1	5		1	1	2012	Celtic	OOC June 2017, joined Gwangju (S Korea)	[redacted]
McKenna	Scott	12/11/1996	24	SCO	D								1					8	2013	Aberdeen Youths	OL to Ayr United Nov-Dec	End 2017/18
McLean	Kenneth	08/01/1992	7	SCO	M	37	1	4	5			4		1	5	1			2015	St Mirren		End 2017/18
McLennan	Connor	05/10/1999	29	SCO	F													3	2015	Aberdeen Youths	OL to Brechin C Dec-Jan	
MacPherson	Joe	04/09/2000	37	SCO	D														2016	Aberdeen Youths		
Morris	Callum	03/02/1990	22	ENG	D													6	2016	Dundee United	Freed Jan 2017 joined Dunfemline Ath	[redacted]
Mutch	Robbie	20/08/1998	50	SCO	G														2015	Aberdeen Youths	OL to Arbroath Aug-Jan, Freed May 2017	
Norris	Aaron	04/02/1998	32	SCO	F														2015	Aberdeen Youths	Freed June 2017	
Nuttall	Joe	27/01/1997	20	ENG	F													1	2015	Manchester City	OL to Stranraer Nov-Jan, Dumbarton Mar-May, Freed May 2017	
O'Connor	Anthony	25/10/1992	15	ROI	D	24	7	3		4		4			1			12	2016	Burton Albion		
Omolukun	Kesiolu	05/12/1997	49	ENG	D														2016	Bradford City Youth	Freed Jan 2017	[redacted]
Pawlett	Peter	03/02/1991	16	SCO	M	6	12	3	1	1			1		1			24	2008	Aberdeen Youths	OOC June 2017, joined MK Dons	
Reynolds	Mark	07/05/1987	6	SCO	D	22	4		4			2	1		4	1		8	2013	Sheffield Wednesday		End 2017/18
Robertson	Sam	21/07/1999	41	SCO	D														2016	Aberdeen Youths		
Rogers	Danny	23/03/1994	30	ROI	GK														2011	Belvedere	OL to Falkirk Aug-May	End 2017/18
Rooney	Adam	21/04/1988	9	ROI	F	32	6	12	4	1	3	3	1	2	4	2	3	1	2014	Oldham Athletic		End 2019/20
Roscoe	Sam	16/06/1998		ENG	D														2016	Blackpool U18		
Ross	Sebastian	20/01/2000	36	SCO	F													2	2016	Aberdeen Youths		
Ross	Frank	18/02/1998	27	SCO	F		3			1								14	2014	Aberdeen Youths		End 2017/18
Shankland	Lawrence	10/08/1995	21	SCO	F													1	2013	Queen's Park	OL to St Mirren Jul-May, Freed May 2017	[redacted]
Shinnie	Graeme	04/08/1991	3	SCO	D	35	1	2	5		1	4			6			1	2015	Inverness CT		End 2018/19
Smith	Cammy	24/08/1995	14	SCO	M													2	2011	Aberdeen Youths	OL to Dundee Utd, Jul-Dec, St Mirren Jan-May. Released, joined St Mirren May 2017	[redacted]
Stockley	Jayden	15/09/1993	17	ENG	F	8	19	5	2	1		1	2		3	3	1	8	2016	AFC Bournemouth		
Storey	Miles	04/01/1994	39	ENG	F	2	12	1		1			1			2		31	2016	Swindon Town		End 2017/18
Storie	Craig	13/01/1996	19	SCO	M		2											13	2012	Aberdeen Youths		End 2017/18
Taylor	Ashton	02/09/1990	5	WAL	D	28	3	3	5			2			6			3	2014	Tranmere Rovers	OOC June 2017, left club	[redacted]
Thomas	Dylan	10/02/1997		WAL	M														2015	Swansea City U18	OL to Montrose Jan-May, Freed May 2017	
Wells	Toby	02/01/1998		ENG	D														2016	Stoke City Youths		
Wright	Scott	08/08/1997	26	SCO	F	1	4	3		2						1		25	2014	Aberdeen Youths		End 2018/19
Own Goals								1			1			1								
Source for Birthdates : Aberdeen FC Website																						
NEW SIGNINGS																						
Christie	Ryan				M														2017	Celtic (OL)	June 2017-May 2018	
Tansey	Greg				M														2017	Inverness CT		
Stewart	Greg				F														2017	Birmingham City	Jul-May	

Airdrieonians FC 2016/17

Founded	2002 (as Airdrie United)
Ground	Excelsior Stadium
Postcode	ML6 8QZ
Capacity	10101
Tel	07710 230775 (Club Office) 01236 622000 (Ground)
Closest Railway Station	Drumgelloch
Record Attendance	9044, 23/8/2013 v Rangers
Ground Record	9612, 6/11/05, Chall Cup F, Hamilton v St Mirren
Record Win	11-0, v Gala Fairydean, 19/11/2011
Record Defeat	0-6, v Rangers, Lge, 23/8/2013
Most Goals in a Season	19, Alan Russell, 2007/8
Chairman	Jim Ballantyne
Secretary	Anne Marie Ballantyne
Manager	Mark Wilson (until June) Vacant
Assistant Manager	Kevin McBride
Colours 2016/17 Top	White with red diamond
Shorts	White
Sponsor	Airdrie Supporters Trust
Manufacturer	Under Armour
Change Colours 2016/17 Top	Black with red diamond
Shorts	Black
Nicknames	Diamonds, Waysiders
Web	www.airdriefc.com
Match Programme 2015/16	Diamonds At Heart, £2
Theme Song	Only the Lonely

Airdrie gambled with full-time football last season but it did not pay off. They reached the Play Offs but were far from convincing in so doing. Their mix of youth and experience proved too inconsistent - capable of excellent results but also producing some horror shows. The crowds simply did not justify the full time set-up.

Airdrie have never recovered from their long spell away from the town. Support drifted away and the Excelsior Stadium has never held the same attraction for people as Broomfield did. It's too big, it's out of town and it lacks atmosphere.

Over the Summer there have been off-field issues to deal with. Chairman and major investor Tom Wotherspoon quit the club. Manager Mark Wilson decided to leave the day before pre-season was due to begin. Talismanic striker Iain Russell retired. Rumours linked his strike partner Andy Ryan with a transfer elsewhere.

PREDICTION 2017/18

Hard to see Airdrie doing any better than last season. Indeed, they are more likely to be flirting with the wrong end of the table.

						L			SC			LC			CC							
			SQ	Nat	Pos	A	S	G	A	S	G	A	S	G	A	S	G	UNS				
Surname	**First Name**	**DOB**																	**Signed**	**Previous Club**	**Notes**	**Contract**
Bell	Conor	15/01/1998		SCO	D													1	2016	Airdrieonians Youth		
Boateng	Daniel	02/09/1992		ENG	D	19	2		1						2			11	2016	Sodertalje FK	Ex Arsenal, Hibernian	OOC
Brown	Adam	09/06/1995		SCO	M	31	7	3	1			4		3	1				2016	St Mirren		OOC
Cairns	Dean	31/07/1997		SCO	D	1	1						1					26	2015	Airdrieonians Youth		
Conroy	Ryan	28/04/1987		SCO	M	39		3	1			3			2		1		2016	Queen of the South		End 2017/18
Cowie	Calvin	21/06/1998		SCO	M														2016	Airdrieonians Youth		
Daly	James	09/01/1995		ROI	M		2					1	2			2		13	2016	Athlone Town		
Duncan	Jordan	22/05/1999		SCO	F														2016	Airdrieonians Youth		
Ferguson	Rohan	06/12/1997		SCO	GK	38			1			4			2				2014	Airdrieonians Youth		End 2017/18
Fitzpatrick	Marc	11/05/1986		SCO	M	14		1				3			2				2014	Morton		End 2017/18
Gorman	Joe	01/09/1994		ROI	D	24	3	1	1			4				1		9	2016	Maidenhead United		End 2017/18
Higgins	John	11/02/1996		SCO	D								1					12	2015	Falkirk Youth	OL to Cumbernauld Utd Sep-Dec	End 2017/18
Hutton	Kyle	05/02/1991		SCO	M	22													2016	St Mirren (OL)	Nov 2016-May 2017	[redacted]
Kerr	Matthew	15/02/1998		SCO	GK													41	2015	Airdrieonians Youth		
Kinvig	Calum	17/08/1999		SCO	GK													3	2016	Airdrieonians Youth		
Leighton	Robbie	06/12/1998		SCO	M		8									1		17	2015	Airdrieonians Youth		
Leitch	Jack	17/07/1995		SCO	M	29	4	2	1						1				2016	Motherwell	On trial with Inverness CT, July 2017	OOC
Loudon	Murray	12/11/1996		SCO	M		7											13	2015	Airdrieonians Youth	OL to Cumbernauld Utd Sep-Dec	End 2017/18
MacDonald	Kieran	21/07/1993		SCO	D	37		1	1			4			2				2016	East Fife		End 2017/18
McGee	Michael				GK													1	2017	Airdrieonians Youth		
McGregor	Jordan	18/03/1997		SCO	D	7	1											1	2017	Hamilton Accies (OL)	Jan-May 2017	[redacted]
McIntosh	Sean	10/01/1997		SCO	M	27	3	3	1			4			2			6	2016	Celtic Youth		End 2017/18
McKay	Jack	19/11/1996		SCO	F	7	9	1										2	2017	Leeds United (OL)	Jan-May 2017	[redacted]
McLaughlin	Conor	22/01/1997		SCO	M	2	3					4				1		22	2015	Airdrieonians Youth		
Mensing	Simon	27/06/1982		ENG	D	17													2017	Carolina Railhawks		OOC
Pires Fa	Hugo Faria	15/02/1983		POR	M							1	1						2016	Livingston	Freed Dec 2016	[redacted]
Reilly	Ciaran	17/01/1997		SCO	F														2016	Airdrieonians Youth		
Ross	Arran	25/08/2000		SCO	D														2016	Airdrieonians Youth		
Russell	Iain	14/11/1982		SCO	F	34	1	18	1			4		1	2		1		2016	Queen of the South	Retired June 2017	[redacted]
Russell	Cammy	10/02/1998		SCO	F													2	2016	Airdrieonians Youth		
Ryan	Andy	29/09/1994		SCO	F	34		24	1		1	4		1	2		1	1	2016	Forfar Athletic		End 2017/18
Schmidt	Kevin	03/02/1994		NET	F	5	9			1			4		1			2	2016	East Kilbride FC	Freed Jan 2017, joined Vestri (Iceland)	[redacted]
Sculliion	Conor	20/03/1999		SCO	M	1	8			1					1			11	2016	Hamilton Accies (OL)	Jul-Dec 2016	[redacted]
Stewart	Scott	29/04/1996		SCO	D	30	2	3	1			4			2				2016	Airdrieonians Youth		OOC
Thomson	Scott	27/07/1997		SCO	F		1											5	2016	Airdrieonians Youth		
Truesdale	Craig	31/12/1999		SCO	M								2					13	2016	Airdrieonians Youth		
Own Goals								1									1					

Source of Birthdates is Airdrieonians FC website

Date	Comp	H/A	Opponents	F	A		HT		Referee	Crowd	Scorers
15/07/2016	LC	H	Partick Thistle	0	1		0	0	K Clancy	1632	
19/07/2016	LC	A	Queen of the South	0	2		0	2	N Walsh	1036	
23/07/2016	LC	H	Stenhousemuir	2	1		1	0	G Duncan	532	Brown 2
26/07/2016	LC	A	Queen's Park	3	3	8-7p	3	1	D Munro	553	Ryan, Brown, Russell
06/08/2016	L	A	Queen's Park	3	1		1	0	D Lowe	957	Russell, Fitzpatrick, Brown
13/08/2016	L	H	Livingston	2	4		0	2	M Northcroft	1048	Ryan 2
16/08/2016	CC2	A	Motherwell U20	2	1		1	0	M Taylor	1007	Russell, Ryan
20/08/2016	L	H	Stranraer	1	0		1	0	C Charleston	812	Ryan
27/08/2016	L	A	Stenhousemuir	2	2		0	1	G Ross	597	Russell, Brown
04/09/2016	CC3	A	Ayr United	2	3	AET	1	2	B Cook	1135	Conroy, Balatoni og
10/09/2016	L	A	Brechin City	2	3		1	1	G Duncan	466	Ryan, Stewart
17/09/2016	L	H	East Fife	1	1		0	1	G Beaton	814	Russell
24/09/2016	L	H	Albion Rovers	0	2		0	2	C Allan	972	
01/10/2016	L	A	Alloa Athletic	2	1		1	0	E Anderson	644	Conroy, Ryan
15/10/2016	L	H	Peterhead	1	3		0	0	A Muir	482	Russell
22/10/2016	L	H	Queen's Park	4	1		3	1	G Aitken	702	Russell 3, Stewart
29/10/2016	L	A	East Fife	1	0		1	0	G Ross	706	Ryan
05/11/2016	L	A	Albion Rovers	2	1		2	0	G Duncan	1199	Ryan, Russell
12/11/2016	L	H	Brechin City	1	0		0	0	C Napier	739	Russell
19/11/2016	L	H	Alloa Athletic	2	1		2	0	M Roncone	790	Goodwin og, Ryan
26/11/2016	SC3	H	Livingston	1	2		1	1	B Cook	780	Ryan
03/12/2016	L	A	Peterhead	4	2		3	1	A Newlands	475	Ryan 2, McIntosh, Russell
10/12/2016	L	H	Stenhousemuir	0	5		0	3	M Northcroft	791	
17/12/2016	L	A	Livingston	0	2		0	1	S Reid	989	
24/12/2016	L	A	Stranraer	2	1		1	1	G Ross	317	Brown, Ryan
02/01/2017	L	H	Albion Rovers	1	2		1	2	M Roncone	1633	Brown
07/01/2017	L	A	Queen's Park	1	2		1	1	G Beaton	922	Russell
14/01/2017	L	H	East Fife	2	2		1	1	A Newlands	833	Ryan, Leitch
28/01/2017	L	A	Stenhousemuir	2	4		1	1	C Napier	604	Ryan, Gorman
04/02/2017	L	H	Peterhead	4	1		0	1	C Charleston	599	McKay, Conroy, Ryan, Stewart
18/02/2017	L	H	Livingston	0	4		0	1	S Finnie	1012	
25/02/2017	L	A	Alloa Athletic	1	2		1	2	G Aitken	540	Russell
04/03/2017	L	H	Stranraer	1	2		0	0	C Charleston	706	Ryan
11/03/2017	L	A	Albion Rovers	4	3		1	0	C Steven	873	Russell, McIntosh, Leitch, Ryan
14/03/2017	L	A	Brechin City	0	3		0	1	D Lowe	346	
18/03/2017	L	H	Stenhousemuir	1	0		0	0	S Kirkland	568	Russell
25/03/2017	L	A	Livingston	2	4		1	2	C Allan	832	Conroy, Ryan
01/04/2017	L	A	Peterhead	1	1		1	1	E Anderson	524	McIntosh
08/04/2017	L	H	Brechin City	3	1		2	1	G Beaton	676	Russell 2, MacDonald
15/04/2017	L	A	Stranraer	1	2		0	1	S Finnie	489	Ryan
22/04/2017	L	H	Alloa Athletic	0	1		0	0	D Lowe	757	
29/04/2017	L	A	East Fife	4	0		1	0	S Millar	918	Ryan 3, Russell
06/05/2017	L	H	Queen's Park	3	2		1	1	J McKendrick	1011	Ryan 2, Russell
10/05/2017	PO	H	Alloa Athletic	1	0		0	0	S Finnie	1199	Ryan
13/05/2017	PO	A	Alloa Athletic	0	1	aet, 3-4p	0	0	B Cook	1181	

FRIENDLIES / OTHER GAMES				
16/06/2016	A	Gala Fairydean Rovers	3	1
02/07/2016	A	Clyde	4	1
05/07/2016	A	Spartans	0	0
06/07/2016	H	BSC Glasgow	2	0
09/07/2016	A	Annan Athletic	3	2

Date	Comp	H/A	Opponents	F A		1	2	3	4	5	6	7	8	9	10	11	12	13	14	15	16	17	18
15/07/2016	LC	H	Partick Thistle	0 1		Ferguson	Stewart	McIntosh	Gorman	MacDonald	Conroy	Brown&	Fitzpatrick*	I Russell	Ryan	McLaughlin+	Pires Fa*	Schmidt+	Truesdale&	*Daly*	*Higgins*	*Kerr*	*Cairns*
19/07/2016	LC	A	Queen of the South	0 2		Ferguson	Stewart	McIntosh	Gorman&	MacDonald	Conroy	Brown	Pires Fa*	I Russell	Ryan	McLaughlin+	Schmidt*	Daly+	Cairns&	*Truesdale*	*Higgins*	*Kerr*	*Loudon*
23/07/2016	LC	H	Stenhousemuir	2 1		Ferguson	Stewart	McIntosh	Gorman	MacDonald	Conroy	Brown+	Fitzpatrick	I Russell	Ryan	McLaughlin*	Daly*	Schmidt+	*Cairns*	*Truesdale*	*Higgins*	*Kerr*	*Loudon*
26/07/2016	LC	A	Queen's Park	3 3	8-7p	Ferguson	Stewart	McIntosh	Gorman	MacDonald&	Daly+	Brown	Fitzpatrick	I Russell	Ryan*	McLaughlin	Schmidt*	Higgins+	Truesdale&	*Cairns*	*C Russell*	*Kerr*	*Loudon*
06/08/2016	L	A	Queen's Park	3 1		Ferguson	Stewart	McIntosh	Gorman	MacDonald	Conroy	Brown	Fitzpatrick	I Russell+	Leitch	Schmidt*	Loudon*	Scullion+	*Truesdale*	*McLaughlin*	*Daly*	*Kerr*	*Higgins*
13/08/2016	L	H	Livingston	2 4		Ferguson	Stewart	McIntosh	Boateng	MacDonald	Conroy*	Brown+	Fitzpatrick	I Russell	Ryan	Leitch	Schmidt*	Daly+	*Gorman*	*McLaughlin*	*Scullion*	*Kerr*	*Higgins*
16/08/2016	CC2	A	Motherwell U20	2 1		Ferguson	Stewart	McIntosh	Boateng*	MacDonald	Conroy	Brown	Fitzpatrick	I Russell	Ryan	Schmidt+	Gorman*	Daly+	*Truesdale*	*McLaughlin*	*Scullion*	*Kerr*	*Higgins*
20/08/2016	L	H	Stranraer	1 0		Ferguson	Stewart	Leitch	Boateng	MacDonald	Conroy	Brown	Fitzpatrick	I Russell	Ryan	Schmidt*	Scullion*	*Daly*	*Truesdale*	*McLaughlin*	*Gorman*	*Kerr*	*Higgins*
27/08/2016	L	A	Stenhousemuir	2 2		Ferguson	Stewart	McIntosh	Boateng	MacDonald	Conroy	Brown	Fitzpatrick	I Russell	Ryan	Scullion*	Loudon*	*Daly*	*Truesdale*	*McLaughlin*	*Gorman*	*Kerr*	*Higgins*
04/09/2016	CC3	A	Ayr United	2 3	AET	Ferguson	Stewart	McIntosh	Boateng	MacDonald	Conroy	Leitch+	Fitzpatrick	I Russell	Ryan&	Scullion*	Daly*	McLaughlin+	Leighton&	*Truesdale*	*Gorman*	*Kerr*	*Cairns*
10/09/2016	L	A	Brechin City	2 3		Ferguson	Stewart	Brown	Boateng	MacDonald	Conroy	Leitch	Fitzpatrick	McLaughlin+	Ryan	Schmidt*	Scullion*	Leighton+	*Daly*	*McIntosh*	*Gorman*	*Kerr*	*Cairns*
17/09/2016	L	H	East Fife	1 1		Ferguson	Stewart	Brown+	Boateng	MacDonald	Conroy	Leitch	Fitzpatrick	McLaughlin*	Ryan	Russell	Schmidt*	Scullion+	*Daly*	*McIntosh*	*Gorman*	*Kerr*	*Leighton*
24/09/2016	L	H	Albion Rovers	0 2		Ferguson	Stewart	Brown	Boateng	MacDonald	Conroy+	Leitch	Fitzpatrick	McIntosh*	Ryan	Russell	Gorman*	Schmidt+	*Daly*	*Truesdale*	*Scullion*	*Kerr*	*McLaughlin*
01/10/2016	L	A	Alloa Athletic	2 1		Ferguson	Stewart	Gorman	Boateng	MacDonald	Conroy&	Leitch	Fitzpatrick	Brown	Ryan+	Schmidt*	Leighton*	Scullion+	Daly&	*Truesdale*	*McIntosh*	*McLaughlin*	*Kinvig*
15/10/2016	L	H	Peterhead	1 3		Ferguson	Stewart	Gorman	Boateng	MacDonald	Conroy	Leitch+	Fitzpatrick	Brown*	Ryan	Russell	Schmidt*	McLaughlin+	McGee	*Truesdale*	*McIntosh*	*Scullion*	*Cairns*
22/10/2016	L	H	Queen's Park	4 1		Ferguson	Stewart	Gorman	Boateng	MacDonald	Conroy	Leitch&	Fitzpatrick	Brown	Ryan*	Russell+	Schmidt*	Scullion+	McLaughlin&	*Truesdale*	*McIntosh*	*Kerr*	*Cairns*
29/10/2016	L	A	East Fife	1 0		Ferguson	Stewart*	Gorman	Boateng	MacDonald	Conroy	Leitch	Fitzpatrick	Brown	Ryan+	Russell	McIntosh*	Leighton+	*McLaughlin*	*Scullion*	*Russell*	*Kerr*	*Cairns*
05/11/2016	L	A	Albion Rovers	2 1		Ferguson	McIntosh	Gorman	Boateng	MacDonald	Conroy	Leitch	Fitzpatrick	Brown	Ryan*	Russell	Leighton*	*Cairns*	*Scullion*	*Daly*	*Truesdale*	*Kerr*	*McLaughlin*
12/11/2016	L	H	Brechin City	1 0		Ferguson	McIntosh	Gorman	Boateng	MacDonald	Conroy	Leitch	Fitzpatrick	Brown	Ryan+	Russell*	Scullion*	Schmidt+	*Leighton*	*Daly*	*Truesdale*	*Kerr*	*McLaughlin*
19/11/2016	L	H	Alloa Athletic	2 1		Ferguson	Stewart	Gorman	Boateng	MacDonald	Conroy	Leitch	Fitzpatrick*	Brown	Ryan	Russell	McLaughlin*	*Schmidt*	*Leighton*	*Daly*	*Scullion*	*Kinvig*	*Cairns*
26/11/2016	SC3	H	Livingston	1 2		Ferguson	Stewart*	Gorman	Boateng	MacDonald	Conroy	Leitch	McIntosh	Brown	Ryan	Russell+	Scullion*	Schmidt+	*Leighton*	*Daly*	*McLaughlin*	*Kinvig*	*Cairns*
03/12/2016	L	A	Peterhead	4 2		Ferguson	Hutton	Gorman	Boateng	MacDonald	Conroy	Leitch	McIntosh	Brown*	Ryan	Russell	Schmidt*	*Scullion*	*Leighton*	*Daly*	*McLaughlin*	*Kerr*	*Cairns*
10/12/2016	L	H	Stenhousemuir	0 5		Ferguson	Hutton	Gorman	Boateng	MacDonald	Conroy	Leitch*	McIntosh	Brown&	Ryan	Russell+	Scullion*	Cairns+	Leighton&	*Daly*	*McLaughlin*	*Kerr*	*Bell*
17/12/2016	L	A	Livingston	0 2		Ferguson	Hutton	Gorman	Stewart	MacDonald	Conroy	Leitch*	McIntosh	Brown	Schmidt+	Russell	Loudon*	Leighton+	*Scullion*	*Higgins*	*McLaughlin*	*Kerr*	*Cairns*
24/12/2016	L	A	Stranraer	2 1		Ferguson	Hutton	Gorman	Boateng	MacDonald	Conroy	Leitch	McIntosh	Brown	Ryan*	Stewart	Schmidt*	*Leighton*	*Scullion*	*Louden*	*McLaughlin*	*Kerr*	*Cairns*
02/01/2017	L	H	Albion Rovers	1 2		Ferguson	Cairns	Gorman	Boateng	MacDonald	Conroy	McKay+	McIntosh	Brown	Ryan	Russell*	Schmidt*	Loudon+	*Scullion*	*Higgins*	*McLaughlin*	*Kerr*	*Leighton*
07/01/2017	L	A	Queen's Park	1 2		Ferguson	Hutton	Gorman	Boateng+	MacDonald	Conroy	Leitch*	McIntosh	Brown	Ryan	Russell	McKay*	Louden+	*Schmidt*	*Higgins*	*McLaughlin*	*Kerr*	*Cairns*
14/01/2017	L	H	East Fife	2 2		Ferguson	Hutton	Gorman	Boateng+	MacDonald	Conroy	Leitch	McIntosh	Brown*	Ryan	Stewart	Russell*	McKay+	*Thomson*	*Higgins*	*Loudon*	*Kerr*	*Cairns*
28/01/2017	L	A	Stenhousemuir	2 4		Ferguson	Hutton	Gorman	Mensing	Stewart*	Conroy	Leitch	McIntosh	Brown	Ryan	Russell	McKay*	*Cairns*	*Thomson*	*Leighton*	*McLaughlin*	*Kerr*	
04/02/2017	L	H	Peterhead	4 1		Ferguson	Hutton	McGregor*	Mensing	MacDonald	Conroy	McKay	McIntosh	Brown	Ryan&	Russell+	Gorman*	Stewart+	Leighton&	*Thomson*	*McLaughlin*	*Kerr*	
18/02/2017	L	H	Livingston	0 4		Ferguson	Hutton	Gorman*	Mensing	MacDonald	Conroy	McKay	McIntosh	Brown+	Ryan	Russell	Stewart	Thomson+	*Leighton*	*Cairns*	*McLaughlin*	*Kerr*	
25/02/2017	L	A	Alloa Athletic	1 2		Ferguson	Hutton	McGregor	Mensing	MacDonald	Stewart+	Leitch	McIntosh	Brown*	Ryan	Russell	McKay*	Leighton+	*Gorman*	*Boateng*	*McLaughlin*	*Kerr*	*Thomson*
04/03/2017	L	H	Stranraer	1 2		Ferguson	Hutton	McGregor	Mensing	MacDonald	Stewart	Leitch	McIntosh	McKay	Ryan	Russell*	Brown*	Leighton	*Gorman*	*Boateng*	*Cairns*	*Kerr*	*Thomson*
11/03/2017	L	A	Albion Rovers	4 3		Ferguson	Hutton	McGregor&	Mensing	MacDonald	Stewart	Leitch+	Conroy	McKay*	Ryan	Russell	Brown*	McIntosh+	Gorman&	*Boateng*	*Cairns*	*Kerr*	*Leighton*
14/03/2017	L	A	Brechin City	0 3		Ferguson	Conroy	McGregor	Mensing	MacDonald+	Stewart	Leitch	McIntosh	McKay*	Ryan	Russell	Brown*	Boateng+	*Gorman*	*Leighton*	*Cairns*	*Kerr*	
18/03/2017	L	H	Stenhousemuir	1 0		Ferguson	Conroy	McGregor	Mensing	MacDonald	Stewart	Leitch	Gorman	Hutton	Brown	Russell	*McIntosh*	*Boateng*	*Ryan*	*Leighton*	*Cairns*	*Kerr*	*Louden*
25/03/2017	L	A	Livingston	2 4		Ferguson	Conroy	McGregor	Mensing	MacDonald	Stewart	Ryan	Gorman	Hutton	Brown*	Russell	McIntosh*	*Boateng*	*McLaughlin*	*Leighton*	*Cairns*	*Kerr*	*Louden*
01/04/2017	L	A	Peterhead	1 1		Ferguson	McIntosh	Conroy	Mensing	MacDonald	Stewart	Leitch	Gorman	Hutton	McKay*	Russell	Brown*	*Boateng*	*McGregor*	*Leighton*	*Cairns*	*Kerr*	*Louden*
08/04/2017	L	H	Brechin City	3 1		Ferguson	McIntosh*	Conroy	Mensing	MacDonald	Stewart	Leitch	Gorman	Hutton	Ryan+	Russell&	McGregor*	Brown+	McKay&	*Leighton*	*Cairns*	*Kerr*	*Louden*
15/04/2017	L	A	Stranraer	1 2		Ferguson	McIntosh	Conroy	Mensing	MacDonald	Stewart	Leitch+	Gorman*	Hutton	Ryan	Russell	Brown*	McKay+	*Boateng*	*Leighton*	*Cairns*	*Kerr*	*Louden*
22/04/2017	L	H	Alloa Athletic	0 1		Ferguson	McIntosh	Conroy	Mensing	MacDonald	Stewart+	Leitch*	Gorman	Hutton	Ryan	Russell	Brown*	McKay+	*Boateng*	*Loudon*	*Kerr*		
29/04/2017	L	A	East Fife	4 0		Ferguson	McIntosh	Conroy	Mensing	MacDonald	Stewart	Brown	Gorman	Hutton*	Ryan+	Russell&	Leitch*	McKay+	Loudon&	*Boateng*	*Kerr*		
06/05/2017	L	H	Queen's Park	3 2		Ferguson	McIntosh	Conroy	Mensing	MacDonald	Stewart	Brown	Gorman	Hutton	Ryan	Russell*	Leitch*	*McKay*	*Loudon*	*Boateng*	*Kerr*		
10/05/2017	PO	H	Alloa Athletic	1 0		Ferguson	McIntosh	Conroy	Mensing	MacDonald	Stewart	Brown	Gorman	Hutton	Ryan+	Russell*	Leitch*	McKay+	*Loudon*	*Boateng*	*Kerr*		
13/05/2017	PO	A	Alloa Athletic	0 1	aet, 3-4p	Ferguson	McIntosh	Conroy&	Mensing+	MacDonald	Stewart	Brown*	Gorman	Hutton	Ryan	Russell	Leitch*	Boateng+	Loudon&	*McKay*	*Kerr*		

Albion Rovers FC 2016/17

Founded	1882
Ground	Cliftonhill Stadium
Postcode	ML5 3RB
Tel	01236 606334
Capacity	1238
Closest Railway Station	Coatdyke
Record Attendance	27381, SC, v Rangers 8/2/36
Record Win	12-0, v Airdriehill, 3/9/1887
Record Defeat	1-11, v Partick Thistle, LC, 11/8/1993
Most League Goals in a Season	John Renwick, 41, 1932/3
Most Goals in Career	105, Bunty Weir
Chairman	Ronnie Boyd
Secretary	Paul Reilly
General Manager	Stevie Kirk
Manager	Brian Kerr
Assistant Manager	Stuart Malcolm
Colours 2016/17 Top	Yellow with White trim
Shorts	Red
Sponsor	Reigart Demolition
Manufacturer	Adidas
Change Colours 2016/17 Top	Red or Black
Shorts	Black
Nicknames	Wee Rovers
Web	www.albionroversfc.com
Match Programme 2015/16	£2

Rovers deserve credit for their achievements on limited resources. For spells last season they were on the fringe of the promotion play offs but they lacked the consistency to get there in the end. A Scottish Cup tie against Celtic, played at Airdrie in front of over 8000, provided a welcome financial boost to the club although a fair bit must have been spent on the hospitality provided to Rod Stewart. His performance at the subsequent draw for the next round was comedy gold.

It came as a bit of a surprise when it was announced that manager Darren Young's contract was not being renewed. The departure of the Dunlop brothers and the two Ross Stewart's during the Summer must also raise some alarm bells for Rovers supporters. Their line up had been very settled for several years and that has now been blown apart.

PREDICTION 2017/18

With so many changes in personnel, the new season will be a bit of an unknown. The new signings do not seem to match the quality of the players who have left, so Rovers could find themselves in a fight against relegation in the coming season.

						L			SC			LC			CC							
			SQ	Nat	Pos	A	S	G	A	S	G	A	S	G	A	S	G	UNS				
Surname	First Name	DOB																	Signed	Previous Club	Notes	Contract
Archibald	Paul	24/11/1998		SCO	F		2											23	2016	Albion Rovers Youth		OOC
Archibald	Theo	05/03/1998		SCO	F	11	3												2017	Celtic (OL)	Jan-May 2017	[redacted]
Boyd	Steven	12/04/1997		SCO	F	15		5	1										2016	Hamilton Accies (OL)	Aug 2016-Jan 2017	[redacted]
Cappie	Ben	26/04/1997		SCO	M													6	2015	Albion Rovers Youth		OOC
Davidson	Ross	28/10/1993		SCO	M	24	2	1	2			4		1					2014	Kilmarnock		End 2017/18
Dunlop	Ross	23/07/1988		SCO	D	36			2			4			2		3		2013	Pollok	OOC May 2017, joined Stenhousemuir	[redacted]
Dunlop	Michael	05/11/1982		SCO	D	35		2	2		1	4			2		1		2013	Stranraer	OOC May 2017, joined Stenhousemuir	[redacted]
Ferguson	Calum	12/02/1995		SCO / CAN	F	6	15	1		2	1	4			1			4	2016	Inverness CT	OOC May 2017, joined Elgin City	[redacted]
Ferry	Mark	19/01/1984		SCO	M	29	2	1	1			4			2		1	6	2015	Unattached	OOC May 2017, joined Stenhousemuir	[redacted]
Fisher	Gary	06/07/1992		SCO	M	26	6		2			4			2			1	2014	East Fife		End 2017/18
Fraser	Colin																		2015	Albion Rovers Youth		
Gallagher	Jaime	11/08/1997		SCO	M		1											6	2016	Queen's Park		
Gilmour	Ross	05/07/1994		SCO	D	10	15			2		1	1			1		10	2016	East Stirlingshire		OOC
Gray	Aaron																		2016	Albion Rovers BC		
Guthrie	John																	3	2016	Albion Rovers Youth		
Johnston	Daniel	08/07/1997		SCO	M													3	2016	Albion Rovers Youth		OOC
Lightbody	Daniel	27/03/1997		SCO	D	1	7									1		15	2016	Dumbarton		End 2017/18
McBride	Scott	19/09/1989		SCO	M	24	5	1	2			2	1		2				2015	Arbroath	OOC June 2017, joined Forfar Athletic	[redacted]
McCann	Kevin	11/09/1987		SCO	D	13	5		1	1								6	2016	Falkirk		OOC
McGlone	Antony																		2016	Albion Rovers BC		
McGuigan	Liam																	1	2016	Albion Rovers Youth		
McManus	Ryan	01/01/1999		SCO	F											2		9				
Munro	Jamie						1												2016	Albion Rovers Youths		
O'Kane	Anthony	01/01/1998		SCO	M													4				
Potts	Daniel	01/07/1999		SCO	GK		1											41	2016	Albion Rovers Youths		
Reid	Alan	12/07/1998		SCO	D	32			2			3			2			1	2007	Hamilton Accies		End 2017/18
Robertson	Mitchell																	1	2016	Albion Rovers Youths		
Shields	Connor	01/01/1999		SCO	F	6	12						1					9	2016	Albion Rovers Youths		
Smith	Bradley	23/04/1997		SCO	M		2											2	2017	Dundee United (OL)	Feb-May 2017	[redacted]
Stewart	Ross	16/04/1995		SCO	GK	36		12	2			4			2				2015	Motherwell	OOC May 2017, joined St Mirren	[redacted]
Stewart	Ross	01/09/1996		SCO	F	21	4		2				3		2			1	2016	Kilwinning Rangers	OOC May 2017, joined St Mirren	[redacted]
Turnbull	Kyle	22/01/1995		SCO	D	16	9		1			4			2			11	2014	Falkirk		OOC
Wallace	Ryan	30/07/1990		SCO	F	27		11	1			2			1				2016	Dunfermline Athletic	OOC May 2017, joined Stranraer	[redacted]
Whyte	James																		2016	Albion Rovers BC		
Willis	Paul	21/08/1991		SCO	M	28	4	5	1	1		4			2			1	2015	Berwick Rangers	OOC May 2017, joined East Fife	[redacted]
Young	Darren	13/10/1978		SCO	M											2		8	2014	Alloa Athletic	Contracted not renewed May 2017	[redacted]
Own Goals								2														
NEW SIGNINGS																						
Victroia	Joao				F														2017	East Kilbride		
Higgins	Sean				F														2017	Clyde		
Marr	Jason				M														2017	Alloa Athletic		
Holmes	Graham				M														2017	Alloa Athletic		
Bowman	Graham				GK														2017	Stenhousemuir		
Trouten	Alan				F														2017	Brechin City		

Date	Comp	H/A	Opponents	F	A		HT			Crowd	Scorers
16/07/2016	LC	H	Morton	0	0	3-4p	0	0	C Napier	431	
19/07/2016	LC	A	Berwick Rangers	0	0	5-4p	0	0	G Irvine	323	
26/07/2016	LC	H	Clyde	1	2		0	0	G Ross	377	Davidson
30/07/2016	LC	A	Kilmarnock	0	0	5-3p	0	0	A Newlands	2219	
06/08/2016	L	A	East Fife	2	2		1	2	M Roncone	682	Ferguson, Wallace
13/08/2016	L	H	Brechin City	0	2		0	1	G Aitken	228	
16/08/2016	CC2	H	Hamilton Accies U20	2	0		1	0	S Millar	114	R Dunlop, Ferry
20/08/2016	L	A	Peterhead	2	2		0	1	G Irvine	503	Stewart 2
27/08/2016	L	H	Alloa	0	4		0	0	S Kirkland	411	
03/09/2016	CC3	H	St Mirren	3	4	AET	3	3	M Roncone	711	R Dunlop 2, M Dunlop
10/09/2016	L	H	Stenhousemuir	4	0		0	0	S Millar	301	Boyd, Willis, Wallace, Hamilton og
17/09/2016	L	A	Stranraer	2	3		0	2	K Graham	402	Stewart, Willis
24/09/2016	L	A	Airdrieonians	2	0		2	0	C Allan	972	Willis, Ferry
01/10/2016	L	H	Queen's Park	2	0		1	0	A Newlands	444	Boyd, Wallace
15/10/2016	L	A	Livingston	2	1		1	0	C Charleston	702	Boyd, Wallace
22/10/2016	L	H	Peterhead	0	1		0	0	D Lowe	360	
29/10/2016	L	A	Alloa	0	0		0	0	K Graham	453	
05/11/2016	L	H	Airdrieonians	1	2		0	2	G Duncan	1199	Stewart
12/11/2016	L	H	Stranraer	3	2		2	1	A Muir	321	Stewart, Wallace 2
29/11/2016	SC3	H	Queen of the S(2)h	2	1		1	0	A Newlands	387	M Dunlop, Ferguson
03/12/2016	L	H	Livingston	0	1		0	0	D Munro	413	
06/12/2016	L	A	Brechin City	2	1		1	1	S Reid	283	Stewart 2
10/12/2016	L	A	Queen's Park	1	2		1	2	C Charleston	662	Stewart
17/12/2016	L	A	Stenhousemuir	0	1		0	0	G Beaton	371	
02/01/2017	L	A	Airdrieonians	2	1		2	1	M Roncone	1633	Boyd 2
07/01/2017	L	H	Brechin City	1	0		0	0	G Duncan	332	M Dunlop
22/01/2017	SC4	H	Celtic	0	3		0	1	W Collum	8319	
28/01/2017	L	H	Alloa	1	1		0	1	S Reid	348	Stewart
04/02/2017	L	A	Stranraer	0	3		0	1	G Duncan	364	
11/02/2017	L	A	Peterhead	1	1		0	1	M Roncone	423	Stewart
18/02/2017	L	H	Stenhousemuir	1	1		1	0	B Cook	327	M Dunlop
04/03/2017	L	A	East Fife	0	2		0	0	D Lowe	539	
07/03/2017	L	A	Livingston	0	3		0	1	N Walsh	548	
11/03/2017	L	H	Airdrieonians	3	4		0	1	C Steven	873	Davidson, Wallace 2
18/03/2017	L	H	Peterhead	0	0		0	0	S Finnie	285	
25/03/2017	L	A	Stenhousemuir	3	0		0	0	A Newlands	433	Stewart 2, McBride
28/03/2017	L	H	East Fife	1	0		0	0	K Graham	419	Wallace
01/04/2017	L	A	Alloa	1	1		1	1	C Allan	606	Willis
04/04/2017	L	H	Queen's Park	1	1		1	0	S Reid	512	Wallace
08/04/2017	L	H	Stranraer	3	0		1	0	G Irvine	377	Willis, Wallace, Neill og
15/04/2017	L	A	Queen's Park	0	2		0	1	L McGarry	677	
22/04/2017	L	H	East Fife	0	1		0	0	A Newlands	488	
29/04/2017	L	A	Brechin City	0	1		0	0	D Lowe	422	
06/05/2017	L	H	Livingston	0	2		0	2	S Kirkland	454	

FRIENDLIES / OTHER GAMES							
02/07/2016	H	Motherwell	1	3			445
09/07/2016	H	Falkirk	2	4			268
29/07/2016	A	Gartcairn	2	1		U20	
09/08/2016	H	Celtic XI	0	1			

Date	Comp	H/A	Opponents	F A		1	2	3	4	5	6	7	8	9	10	11	12	13	14	15	16	17	18
16/07/2016	LC	H	Morton	0 0	3-4p	Ross Stewart (1)	Reid	Turnbull	R Dunlop	M Dunlop	Fisher	Ferry*	Davidson	Willis	McBride	Ferguson	Shields*	*Gilmour*	*Young*	*Cappie*	*Johnston*	*Potts*	
19/07/2016	LC	A	Berwick Rangers	0 0	5-4p	Ross Stewart (1)	Gilmour	Turnbull	R Dunlop	M Dunlop	Fisher	Ferry	Davidson	Willis	McBride	Ferguson*	Ross Stewart (2)*	*Reid*	*Young*	*Cappie*	*Shields*	*Potts*	
26/07/2016	LC	H	Clyde	1 2		Ross Stewart (1)	Reid	Turnbull	R Dunlop	M Dunlop	Fisher	Ferry	Davidson	Willis	Wallace	Ferguson*	Ross Stewart (2)*	*Gilmour*	*Young*	*Cappie*	*Shields*		
30/07/2016	LC	A	Kilmarnock	0 0	5-3p	Ross Stewart (1)	Reid	Turnbull	R Dunlop	M Dunlop	Fisher	Ferry*	Davidson	Willis	Wallace&	Ferguson+	McBride*	Ross Stewart (2)+	Gilmour&	*Cappie*	*Shields*	*Potts*	*Young*
06/08/2016	L	A	East Fife	2 2		Ross Stewart (1)	Reid	Turnbull	R Dunlop	M Dunlop	Fisher	Ferry*	Davidson	Willis	Wallace	Ferguson+	McBride*	Ross Stewart (2)+	*Gilmour*	*Cappie*	*Shields*	*Potts*	*Young*
13/08/2016	L	H	Brechin City	0 2		Ross Stewart (1)	Reid	Turnbull	R Dunlop	M Dunlop	Fisher	Ferry	Davidson+	Willis	Wallace	Ferguson*	Lightbody*	Gilmour+	*Stewart*	*McManus*	*O'Kane*	*Potts*	*Young*
16/08/2016	CC2	H	Hamilton Accies U20	2 0		Ross Stewart (1)	Reid	Turnbull	R Dunlop	M Dunlop	Fisher	Ferry+	McBride&	Willis	Ross Stewart (2)	Ferguson*	McManus*	Young+	Lightbody&	*Cappie*	*O'Kane*	*Potts*	
20/08/2016	L	A	Peterhead	2 2		Ross Stewart (1)	Reid	Turnbull	R Dunlop	M Dunlop	Fisher	Ferry+	McBride	Willis	Ross Stewart (2)	Boyd*	Ferguson*	Gilmour+	*Lightbody*	*McManus*	*Young*	*Potts*	
27/08/2016	L	H	Alloa	0 4		Ross Stewart (1)	Reid	Turnbull	R Dunlop	M Dunlop	Fisher+	Ferry	McBride	Willis*	Ross Stewart (2)&	Boyd	Gilmour*	Ferguson+	Lightbody&	*O'Kane*	*Young*	*Potts*	*Robertson*
03/09/2016	CC3	H	St Mirren	3 4	AET	Ross Stewart (1)	Reid	Turnbull	R Dunlop	M Dunlop	Fisher	Ferry	McBride*	Willis	Ross Stewart (2)&	Wallace+	Young*	Gilmour+	McManus&	*O'Kane*	*Lightbody*	*Potts*	*Johnston*
10/09/2016	L	H	Stenhousemuir	4 0		Ross Stewart (1)	Reid	Turnbull	R Dunlop	M Dunlop	Ross Stewart (2)+	Ferry	McBride	Willis*	Boyd	Wallace+	Gilmour*	Shields+	*McManus*	*Young*	*Lightbody*	*Potts*	
17/09/2016	L	A	Stranraer	2 3		Ross Stewart (1)	Reid	Turnbull+	R Dunlop	M Dunlop	Ross Stewart (2)	Ferry*	McBride	Willis	Boyd	Wallace+	Gilmour*	P Archibald+	*McManus*	*Young*	*Lightbody*	*Potts*	
24/09/2016	L	A	Airdrieonians	2 0		Ross Stewart (1)	Reid	Davidson	R Dunlop	M Dunlop	Gilmour*	Ferry	McBride	Willis	Boyd+	Wallace&	Ross Stewart (2)*	Fisher+	Potts&	*Turnbull*	*McCann*		
01/10/2016	L	H	Queen's Park	2 0		Ross Stewart (1)	Reid	Davidson	R Dunlop	M Dunlop	Gilmour*	Ferry+	McBride	Willis	Boyd&	Wallace	Fisher*	McCann+	Ross Stewart (2)&	*Turnbull*	*P Archibald*	*Potts*	
15/10/2016	L	A	Livingston	2 1		Ross Stewart (1)	Reid	Davidson	R Dunlop	M Dunlop	Ross Stewart (2)*	Ferry	McBride	Willis	Boyd+	Wallace&	Turnbull*	Fisher+	Shields&	*McCann*	*P Archibald*	*Potts*	*Gilmour*
22/10/2016	L	H	Peterhead	0 1		Ross Stewart (1)	Reid+	Davidson	R Dunlop	M Dunlop	Ross Stewart (2)*	Ferry&	McBride	Willis	Boyd	Wallace	Shields*	Turnbull+	McCann&	*Fisher*	*P Archibald*	*Potts*	
29/10/2016	L	A	Alloa	0 0		Ross Stewart (1)	Reid	Davidson	R Dunlop	M Dunlop	Shields	Ferry+	McBride	Willis&	Ross Stewart (2)*	Wallace	Fisher*	Turnbull+	McCann&	*Gilmour*	*P Archibald*	*Potts*	*Ferguson*
05/11/2016	L	H	Airdrieonians	1 2		Ross Stewart (1)	Reid	Davidson	R Dunlop	M Dunlop	Shields+	Ferry*	McBride	Willis	Ross Stewart (2)	Boyd&	Fisher*	Turnbull+	Ferguson&	*Gilmour*	*P Archibald*	*Potts*	*McCann*
12/11/2016	L	H	Stranraer	3 2		Ross Stewart (1)	Reid	Davidson	R Dunlop	M Dunlop	Fisher	Wallace+	McBride	Willis*	Ross Stewart (2)	Boyd&	McCann*	Turnbull+	Ferguson&	*Gilmour*	*Ferry*	*Potts*	*Shields*
29/11/2016	SC3	H	Queen of the S(2)h	2 1		Ross Stewart (1)	Reid	Davidson	R Dunlop	M Dunlop	Fisher+	Wallace+	McBride	McCann&	Ross Stewart (2)	Boyd*	Gilmour*	Ferguson+	Willis&	*P Archibald*	*Ferry*	*Potts*	*Turnbull*
03/12/2016	L	H	Livingston	0 1		Ross Stewart (1)	Reid	Davidson	R Dunlop	M Dunlop	Fisher	Wallace+	McBride	Gilmour*	Willis	Boyd+	Ferguson*	Ross Stewart (2)+	*P Archibald*	*McCann*	*Ferry*	*Potts*	*Lightbody*
06/12/2016	L	A	Brechin City	2 1		Ross Stewart (1)	McCann+	Davidson*	R Dunlop	M Dunlop	Fisher	Wallace&	McBride	Ferry	Ross Stewart (2)	Boyd	Gilmour*	Willis+	Ferguson&	*Lightbody*	*P Archibald*		
10/12/2016	L	A	Queen's Park	1 2		Ross Stewart (1)	Reid	Gilmour	R Dunlop	M Dunlop	Fisher	Wallace	McBride	Ferry&	Ross Stewart (2)*	Boyd+	Ferguson*	Willis+	Gallagher&	*Lightbody*	*P Archibald*	*Potts*	
17/12/2016	L	A	Stenhousemuir	0 1		Ross Stewart (1)	Reid	Gilmour	R Dunlop	M Dunlop	Fisher	Turnbull	McBride	Ferry*	Shields	Boyd	P Archibald*	*Young*	*Gallagher*	*Lightbody*	*McManus*	*Potts*	*McGuigan*
02/01/2017	L	A	Airdrieonians	2 1		Ross Stewart (1)	Reid	Turnbull	R Dunlop	M Dunlop	Fisher	Davidson	McBride+	Willis&	Shields*	Boyd	Gilmour*	Ferry+	Ferguson&	*Gallagher*	*P Archibald*	*Potts*	*McManus*
07/01/2017	L	H	Brechin City	1 0		Ross Stewart (1)	Reid	Turnbull	R Dunlop	M Dunlop	Fisher&	Davidson	McBride+	Willis	Shields*	Ferry	Ferguson*	Gilmour+	Lightbody&	*Gallagher*	*P Archibald*	*Potts*	*McGuigan*
22/01/2017	SC4	H	Celtic	0 3		Ross Stewart (1)	Reid	Turnbull&	R Dunlop	M Dunlop	Fisher	Davidson	McBride	Willis	Ross Stewart (2)*	Ferry+	Ferguson*	Gilmour+	McCann&	*Lightbody*	*P Archibald*	*Potts*	*Shields*
28/01/2017	L	H	Alloa	1 1		Ross Stewart (1)	Reid	Turnbull	R Dunlop	M Dunlop	Fisher	Davidson&	McBride*	Willis+	Ross Stewart (2)	T Archibald	Ferguson*	McCann+	Gilmour&	*Ferry*	*P Archibald*	*Potts*	
04/02/2017	L	A	Stranraer	0 3		Ross Stewart (1)	Reid	Turnbull	R Dunlop	M Dunlop	Fisher*	Davidson&	McCann+	Willis	Ross Stewart (2)	T Archibald	Ferguson*	McBride+	Gilmour&	*Ferry*	*P Archibald*	*Potts*	*Shields*
11/02/2017	L	A	Peterhead	1 1		Ross Stewart (1)	McCann*	Turnbull	R Dunlop	M Dunlop	Fisher	Davidson	Gilmour	Ferguson+	Ross Stewart (2)	T Archibald	Ferry*	Shields+	*Gallagher*	*Lightbody*	*P Archibald*	*Potts*	
18/02/2017	L	H	Stenhousemuir	1 1		Ross Stewart (1)	Reid	Ferry	R Dunlop	M Dunlop	Fisher	Davidson	Gilmour	Ferguson*	Ross Stewart (2)	Wallace+	Shields*	T Archibald+	*Gallagher*	*Lightbody*	*P Archibald*	*Potts*	*Turnbull*
04/03/2017	L	A	East Fife	0 2		Ross Stewart (1)	Reid	T Archibald	R Dunlop	M Dunlop	Fisher+	Davidson	Gilmour&	Ferguson*	Ross Stewart (2)	Wallace	Smith*	Shields+	Turnbull&	*McCann*	*Ferry*	*Potts*	*Willis*
07/03/2017	L	A	Livingston	0 3		Ross Stewart (1)	Reid	Turnbull	R Dunlop	M Dunlop	Fisher*	Ferry	McCann+	T Archibald	Ross Stewart (2)	Wallace&	Davidson*	Willis+	Ferguson&	*Gilmour*	*Smith*	*Potts*	
11/03/2017	L	H	Airdrieonians	3 4		Ross Stewart (1)	Reid	Turnbull*	R Dunlop	M Dunlop	Fisher&	Ferry	McCann	T Archibald	Ross Stewart (2)+	Wallace	Davidson*	Willis+	Ferguson&	*Gilmour*	*Smith*	*Potts*	*Shields*
18/03/2017	L	H	Peterhead	0 0		Ross Stewart (1)	Reid	McCann*	R Dunlop	M Dunlop	Fisher+	Ferry	Davidson	T Archibald&	Willis	Wallace	Gilmour*	McBride+	Smith&	*Guthrie*	*McManus*	*Potts*	*Lightbody*
25/03/2017	L	A	Stenhousemuir	3 0		Ross Stewart (1)	Reid	McCann	R Dunlop	M Dunlop	Fisher	Ferry	Davidson	Willis*	Ross Stewart (2)&	Wallace+	Gilmour*	McBride+	Turnbull&	*Shields*	*McManus*	*Potts*	*Lightbody*
28/03/2017	L	H	East Fife	1 0		Ross Stewart (1)	Reid	McCann*	R Dunlop	M Dunlop	Fisher&	Ferry	McBride	Willis	Ross Stewart (2)	Wallace+	Turnbull*	Gilmour+	Lightbody&	*Ferguson*	*McManus*	*Potts*	
01/04/2017	L	A	Alloa	1 1		Ross Stewart (1)	Reid	Turnbull&	R Dunlop	M Dunlop	Gilmour+	Ferry	McBride	Willis	Ross Stewart (2)*	Wallace	Shields*	Fisher+	T Archibald&	*Ferguson*	*P Archibald*	*Potts*	*Lightbody*
04/04/2017	L	H	Queen's Park	1 1		Ross Stewart (1)	Reid	Davidson	R Dunlop	M Dunlop	Fisher+	Ferry	McBride	Willis	T Archibald*	Wallace	Shields*	Gilmour+	*Turnbull*	*Ferguson*	*P Archibald*	*Potts*	*McCann*
08/04/2017	L	H	Stranraer	3 0		Ross Stewart (1)	McCann	Davidson&	R Dunlop	M Dunlop	Fisher	Ferry	McBride+	Willis	T Archibald*	Wallace	Ferguson*	Turnbull+	Shields&	*Gilmour*	*P Archibald*	*Potts*	*Lightbody*
15/04/2017	L	A	Queen's Park	0 2		Ross Stewart (1)	McCann	Davidson	R Dunlop	Gilmour	Fisher	Ferry&	McBride*	Willis	T Archibald+	Wallace	Ferguson*	Shields+	Lightbody&	*Turnbull*	*P Archibald*	*Potts*	*Gallagher*
22/04/2017	L	H	East Fife	0 1		Ross Stewart (1)	McCann	Reid	R Dunlop	M Dunlop	Fisher	Ferry&	Shields*	Willis	Ferguson+	Wallace	McBride*	T Archibald+	Lightbody&	*Turnbull*	*P Archibald*	*Potts*	
29/04/2017	L	A	Brechin City	0 1		Ross Stewart (1)	McCann	Reid	R Dunlop	M Dunlop	Fisher	Ferry+	Davidson*	Willis	T Archibald	Wallace	Shields*	Lightbody+	*Guthrie*	*Turnbull*	*P Archibald*	*Potts*	
06/05/2017	L	H	Livingston	0 2		Ross Stewart (1)	McCann	Reid&	R Dunlop	M Dunlop	Turnbull*	Ferry	Lightbody	Willis	McBride+	Wallace	Gilmour*	Shields+	Munro&	*Guthrie*	*P Archibald*	*Potts*	

Alloa Athletic FC 2016/17

Founded	1878
Ground	Recreation Park (aka Indodrill Stadium)
Postcode	FK10 1RY
Tel	01259 722695
Capacity	3100
Closest Railway Station	Alloa
Record Attendance	15467 v Celtic, Scottish Cup, 1954/5
Record Win	9-0 v Selkirk, SC, 28/1/2005
Record Defeat	0-10 v Dundee, Lge, 82/47; v T Lanark, LC, 8/8/53
Most League Goals in a Season	49, Willie Crilley, 1921/2
Chairman	Mike Mulraney
Secretary	Ewan Cameron
Manager	Danny Lennon (until Jan), Jack Ross (from Jan)
Assistant Manager	Paddy Connolly
Colours 2016/17 Top	Black and Gold Hoops
Shorts	Black
Sponsor	Chrystal and Hill
Manufacturer	Pendle
Change Colours 2016/17 Top	Blue
Shorts	Blue
Nicknames	Wasps
Web	www.alloaathletic.co.uk
Match Programme 2016/17	The Wasp £2

Having come down from the Championship, Alloa had to adapt their game plan on a week-to-week basis. In 2015/16 it was backs to the wall and hit on the break. From the outset of 2016/17 Alloa were on the front foot. They made a fantastic start to the season under the management of Jack Ross, embarking on a long unbeaten run.

Ross's success earned him the St Mirren job, with Jim Goodwin taking over at the Recs. The team were not quite so consistent and they relinquished the league leaders place to Livingston. However, finishing second was a decent achievement and Alloa went into the play offs confident that they could go up. Airdrie were defeated but Alloa let themselves down badly in the Final against Brechin City and lost out to a team that finished well adrift of them during the regular season.

PREDICTION FOR 2017/18

Alloa will start off as one of the favourites for promotion. They will be up against full-time opposition in the shape of Raith and Ayr but it will be a major surprise if they do not reach the play-offs, at least.

Lower Leagues Stalwart

Andrew Graham		L			LC			SC			OC			Total		
Season	Club	A	S	G	A	S	G	A	S	G	A	S	G	A	S	G
2005/6	Stirling Albion	30		2	2			3			2			37	0	2
2006/7	Stirling Albion	14	1		1			2			1			18	1	0
2007/8	Stirling Albion	26			2			1						29	0	0
2008/9	Stirling Albion	25	1	2	1		1	1			1			28	1	3
2009/10	Stirling Albion	36		6	1			4			3		1	44	0	7
2010/11	Hamilton Accie:	10	5					2						12	5	0
2011/2	Morton	25	2					3			1			29	2	0
2012/3	Dumbarton	30		2	2			2		1	1			35	0	3
2013/4	Dumbarton	36		2	2			4			1			43	0	2
2014/5	Dumbarton	34		2	2		1	1			1			38	0	3
2015/6	Dumbarton	1	1		1						1			3	1	0
2015/6	Ayr United	23	4	2				1						24	4	2
2016/7	Alloa	38		4	6		1	2			2			48	0	5
														0	0	0
Total		328	14	22	20	0	3	26	0	1	14	0	1	388	14	27

The origins of football in Alloa can be traced back to 1878. However, the usual assumption that the present Alloa FC date from 1878, must be contested. In 1878 A Mr Goodyear, native of Birmingham, was a teacher at St John's School in Alloa. He organised a football match in the town's West End Park. Some 20 locals took part and formed the Clackmannan County Football Club. After about one year there was disagreement amongst the players and a breakaway club was formed called Alloa Football Club in 1879. Within one month they expanded their name to Alloa Association Football Club. Their first game was a 6-0 home defeat from King's Park. The leading light in this club was a James Rigg who played for King's Park in Stirling, but worked in Alloa. He organised a meeting in McGechan's Hall in Alloa and a new club was formed in opposition to Clackmannan County.

There was great rivalry between Alloa and Clackmannan County with both teams having spells when they outshone the other. However, within a couple of years County had been eclipsed and Alloa Association FC were the prime team in the town. Clackmannan County disbanded with some of their members joining Alloa Association FC.

Alloa Association FC became known as Alloa Athletic FC through a misunderstanding. The team wore the legend AAFC on their blue jerseys and the Secretary of Dunfermline FC assumed this meant Alloa Athletic FC and advertised a game between the clubs using this name. The Committee at Alloa preferred the new name and stuck with it from 1881 onwards.

Surname	First Name	DOB	SQ	Nat	Pos	L A	L S	L G	SC A	SC S	SC G	LC A	LC S	LC G	CC A	CC S	CC G	UNS	Signed	Previous Club	Notes	Contract
Allison	Kieran	09/04/1998			D														2016	Rossvale JFC		
Bamba	Yusuf	06/07/1999			F														2016	Rutherglen Glencairn		
Burns	Niall	05/01/2002			M														2016	Syngenta		
Carrick	Paul	20/02/1997			M														2016	Dundee United		
Cawley	Kevin	17/03/1989		SCO	F	36	3	6	2			3	3		3		1		2016	Dumbarton		End 2017/18
Crumlish	Jack	01/11/1998			D														2016	Rossvale JFC		
Cunningham	John	22/04/1998		SCO	F													3	2016	Dumbarton Youths		
Donnelly	Luke	20/01/1996		SCO	F		6	1								3		3	2016	Celtic (OL)	Aug 16-Jan 17	[redacted]
Flannigan	Iain	15/01/1988		SCO	M	26	6	8	2			6			2			1	2013	Falkirk		OOC
Forrest	Greg	25/01/1999			D														2016	Dundee United		
Goodwin	Jim	20/11/1981		ROI	M	14		1	1			5			2			4	2016	St Mirren	Player Manager	
Gordon	Ben	07/10/1985		SCO	D	3						1			1			1	2016	St Mirren (OL)	Sep-Oct 2016	
Graham	Andrew	22/09/1983		SCO	D	38		4	2			6		1	2				2016	Ayr United		End 2017/18
Greene	Mark	23/02/2000			F														2016	Alloa FC Youths		
Hariri	Caleb	18/09/1999			D														2016	FC Kirkwood		
Hetherington	Steven	03/03/1993		ENG	M	13	11		1			1						9	2014	Motherwell		End 2017/18
Hoggan	Ryan	19/06/1998		SCO	D	1	5		1							1		33	2016	Hearts		OOC
Holmes	Graeme	26/03/1984		SCO	M	20	9		1			1	5		2	1		6	2011	Morton	Released May 2017, joined Albion Rovers	[redacted]
Hutchison	Callum	20/03/1998			D														2016	Alloa FC Youths		
Hynd	Scott	10/08/1997		SCO	F		4	1										20	2014	Alloa FC Youths	OL to Montrose Aug-Nov, Released May 2017	[redacted]
Kearney	Ronan	22/08/1999			F														2016	Hamilton Caledonian Th	OL to Lanark Utd, Aug-May	
Kirkpatrick	Jordan	06/03/1992		SCO	M	36	2	14	2			5	1	2	3		1	1	2016	Dumbarton	OOC May 2017, joined St Mirren	[redacted]
Layne	Isaac	16/05/1995		ENG	F		6	1				1	4	2				2	2015	Southend United	OL to Stirling Alb, Freed Jan 2017 joined Billericay T	[redacted]
Longworth	Jamie	03/08/1987		SCO	F	8	23	3		2	1	2	4		1	2		6	2016	Stranraer	Released May 2017	OOC
Mackin	Dylan	15/01/1997		SCO	F	15	1	4											2017	Motherwell (OL)	Jan-May 2017	[redacted]
Marr	Jason	23/02/1989		SCO	D	24	1	2				5		1	2			16	2012	Clyde	Released May 2017, joined Albion Rovers	[redacted]
Martin	Adam	29/05/1998		SCO	F	2	7	1								2		19	2016	Rossvale JFC		
McCluskey	Stefan	22/08/1990		SCO	F	7	9	1		1	1							2	2017	Ex Peterhead		OOC
McDonald	Declan	13/01/2001		SCO	F													3	2016	Alloa FC Youths		
McDowall	Craig	24/08/1990		SCO	GK	6												43	2016	Unattached	Ex Livingston	OOC
McKeown	Frank	18/08/1986		SCO	D	15	1		1										2017	Stranraer		End 2017/18
McNeill	Aiden	07/06/1998			M														2016	Alloa FC Youths		
Monaghan	Dylan	23/11/1999			M														2016	Partick Thistle		
Parry	Neil	08/11/1985		SCO	GK	33			2			6			3			1	2016	Airdrieonians		End 2017/18
Robertson	Jon	25/04/1989		SCO	M	26	8	2	1			6		1	3		1	4	2016	Stenhousemuir		OOC
Scullion	Pat	02/03/1986		SCO	M		1											15	2016	Cowdenbeath	OL to Berwick R Dec-Jan, Freed Jan and joined Berwick	[redacted]
Sinclair	Scott	13/12/2000			F														2016	Alloa Wasps		
Smith	Christopher	20/06/2001		SCO	GK														2016	Calderbraes BC		
Smith	Stephen	27/05/1997			D														2016	Kilsyth Athletic		
Spence	Greig	06/07/1992		SCO	F	36	3	19	2		1	6		3	3		3	1	2016	Cowdenbeath	OOC May 2017, joined Raith Rovers	[redacted]
Stone	Corin	09/02/1999			M														2016	Falkirk		
Taggart	Scott	27/12/1991		SCO	D	40		3	2			6			3				2016	Dumbarton		OOC
Waters	Calum	10/03/1996		SCO	D	40		1	2			6		1	3		1		2016	Celtic		OOC
Williamson	Rhys	28/08/1999			M														2016	Falkirk		
Wilson	Andrew	22/04/1998		SCO	GK	1												6	2016	Dundee United		
Wilson	Lewis	01/08/1996		SCO	D													23	2015	Alloa FC Youths	OL to Cumbernauld Colts Jan-May, Released May 2017	[redacted]
Own Goals								2														

Source of Birthdates is Alloa Athletic Fc Match Programme

New Signings						Signed	Previous Club
Cook	Alan				F	2017	Stenhousemuir
Meggatt	Daryll				D	2017	Ayr United
Malcolm	Craig				F	2017	Stranraer
Renton	Kris				F	2017	Cowdenbeath
Fleming	Gary				F	2017	Dumbarton
Grant	Thomas				M	2017	Stenhousemuir

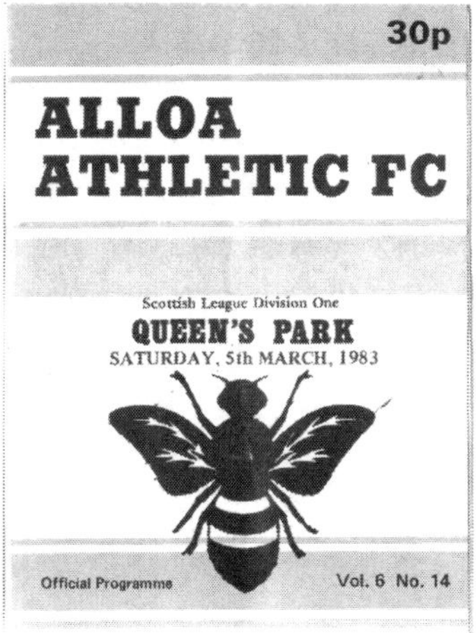

Date	Comp	H/A	Opponents	F	A		HT		Referee	Crowd	Scorers
19/07/2016	LC	H	Cove Rangers	4	0		1	0	S Reid	213	Spence, Graham, Kirkpatrick, Layne
23/07/2016	LC	A	Montrose	2	0		1	0	G irvine	358	Spence, Layne
26/07/2016	LC	H	Ross County	3	2		2	2	S Finnie	319	Kirkpatrick, Robertson, Waters
30/07/2016	LC	A	Raith Rovers	1	0		1	0	K Clancy	1674	Spence
06/08/2016	L	H	Peterhead	4	0		3	0	A Newlands	504	Kirkptrick 2, Cawley, Layne
09/08/2016	LC1	H	Inverness CT	1	0		1	0	D Robertson	613	Marr
13/08/2016	L	A	Stranraer	5	2		5	1	G Ross	448	Spence 2, Kirkpatrick 2, Flannigan
20/08/2016	L	H	East Fife	2	1		2	0	D Lowe	652	Flannigan, Spence
27/08/2016	L	A	Albion Rovers	4	0		0	0	S Kirkland	411	Kirkpatrick, Watters, Donnelly, M Dunlop og
03/09/2016	CC3	H	East Fife	3	0		3	0	K Graham	444	Kirkpatrick, Watters, Spence
10/09/2016	L	H	Livingston	1	3		0	3	C Charleston	712	Spence
17/09/2016	L	A	Queen's Park	2	1		0	0	B Cook	664	Spence, Flannigan
21/09/2016	LC2	A	Celtic	0	2		0	0	A Muir	15900	
24/09/2016	L	A	Stenhousemuir	2	2		1	0	C Napier	466	Kerr og, Goodwin
01/10/2016	L	H	Airdrieonians	1	2		0	1	E Anderson	644	Spence
08/10/2016	CC4	A	Bala Town	4	2		3	0	S Taylor (NI)	591	Spence 2, Robertson, Cawley
15/10/2016	L	A	Brechin City	1	0		0	0	J McKendrick	413	Marr
22/10/2016	L	A	Livingston	1	3		0	0	S Finnie	977	Spence
29/10/2016	L	H	Albion Rovers	0	0		0	0	K Graham	453	
05/11/2016	L	H	Stenhousemuir	4	1		3	1	S Reid	458	Spence, Graham, Longworth, Cawley
12/11/2016	CC4	A	Queen of the South	0	2		0	1	E Anderson	1180	
15/11/2016	L	A	East Fife	2	2		0	1	A Newlands	412	Longworth, Hynd
19/11/2016	L	A	Airdrieonians	1	2		0	2	M Roncone	790	Taggart
26/11/2016	SC3	A	Peterhead	1	0		0	0	E Anderson	563	Longworth
10/12/2016	L	A	Peterhead	1	1		0	0	G Ross	365	Kirkpatrick
13/12/2016	L	H	Stranraer	2	2		1	1	G Irvine	309	Kirkpatrick, Spence
17/12/2016	L	H	Queen's Park	1	1		0	0	G Duncan	442	Spence
24/12/2016	L	H	Brechin City	1	2		0	1	D Munro	386	Kirkpatrick
31/12/2016	L	A	Stenhousemuir	4	2		3	1	D Lowe	335	Cawley, Spence, Kirkpatrick 2
07/01/2017	L	A	Stranraer	2	1		0	1	C Napier	383	Flannigan, Robertson
14/01/2017	L	H	Peterhead	0	1		0	0	C Steven	504	
21/01/2017	SC4	H	Dunfermline Athletic	2	3		0	2	A Newlands	1871	McCluskey, Spence
28/01/2017	L	A	Albion Rovers	1	1		1	0	S Reid	348	Taggart
04/02/2017	L	H	Livingston	2	2		1	1	K Graham	565	Kirkaptrick, Mackin
18/02/2017	L	A	Queen's Park	2	0		1	0	A Muir	657	Spence, Kirkpatrick
25/02/2017	L	H	Airdrieonians	2	1		2	1	G Aitken	540	Graham 2
28/02/2017	L	H	East Fife	3	0		2	0	B Cook	436	Spence, Cawley, Longworth
11/03/2017	L	H	Stenhousemuir	2	1		1	0	D Lowe	508	Mackin, Spence
18/03/2017	L	A	East Fife	0	0		0	0	C Steven	612	
21/03/2017	L	A	Brechin City	2	1		1	0	C Napier	372	Cawley, Graham
25/03/2017	L	H	Queen's Park	2	2		1	1	M Roncone	675	Flannigan, Taggart
01/04/2017	L	H	Albion Rovers	1	1		1	1	C Allan	606	Kirkpatrick
08/04/2017	L	A	Livingston	1	2		0	1	G Aitken	1099	Mackin
15/04/2017	L	H	Brechin City	6	1		2	1	S Kirkland	662	McCluskey, Spence 2, Flanagan 2, Marr
22/04/2017	L	A	Airdrieonians	1	0		0	0	D Lowe	757	Kirkpatrick
29/04/2017	L	H	Stranraer	1	0		0	0	M Northcroft	507	Cawley
06/05/2017	L	A	Peterhead	2	3		1	0	C Charleston	681	Flannigan, Martin
10/05/2017	PO	A	Airdrieonians	0	1		0	1	S Finnie	1199	
13/05/2017	PO	H	Airdrieonians	1	0	aet, 4-3p	0	0	B Cook	1181	Robertson
17/05/2017	PO	A	Brechin City	0	1		0	0	E Anderson	702	
20/05/2017	PO	H	Brechin City	4	3	aet, 4-5p	2	1	N Walsh	1204	Spence 3, Mackin

FRIENDLIES / OTHER GAMES						
25/06/2016	H	Fort William	3	0		
29/06/2016	H	Dunfermline Athletic	1	1		600
01/07/2016	H	Dundee	1	1		
09/07/2016	A	Cowdenbeath	2	1		
09/07/2016	A	St Rochs	0	6	U20	
16/07/2016	H	Berwick Rangers	1	0		

Date	Comp	H/A	Opponents	F A		1	2	3	4	5	6	7	8	9	10	11	12	13	14	15	16	17	18
19/07/2016	LC	H	Cove Rangers	4 0		Parry	Taggart	Waters	Graham	Marr	Goodwin	Cawley*	Robertson+	Kikpatrick	Flannigan	Spence&	Layne*	Holmes+	Longworth&	*McDowall*	*Hoggan*	*Hetherington*	*L Wilson*
23/07/2016	LC	A	Montrose	2 0		Parry	Taggart	Waters	Graham	Marr	Hetherington+	Holmes	Robertson	Layne*	Flannigan	Spence&	Longworth*	Kirkpatrick+	Cawley&	*McDowall*	*Hoggan*	*Goodwin*	*L Wilson*
26/07/2016	LC	H	Ross County	3 2		Parry	Taggart	Waters	Graham	Marr	Goodwin	Cawley+	Robertson	Kikpatrick*	Flannigan	Spence&	Holmes*	Layne+	Longworth&	*McDowall*	*Hoggan*	*Hetherington*	*L Wilson*
30/07/2016	LC	A	Raith Rovers	1 0		Parry	Taggart	Waters	Graham	Marr	Goodwin&	Longworth*	Robertson	Kirkpatrick+	Flannigan	Spence	Layne*	Cawley+	Holmes&	*McDowall*	*Hoggan*	*Hetherington*	*L Wilson*
06/08/2016	L	H	Peterhead	4 0		Parry	Taggart	Waters	Graham	Marr	Holmes	Cawley	Robertson	Kirkpatrick*	Flannigan&	Spence+	Layne*	Hetherington+	Longworth&	*McDowall*	*Hoggan*	*Hynd*	*L Wilson*
09/08/2016	LC1	H	Inverness CT	1 0		Parry	Taggart	Waters	Graham	Marr	Goodwin	Longworth*	Robertson	Kirkpatrick+	Flannigan	Spence&	Cawley*	Holmes+	Layne&	*McDowall*	*Hoggan*	*Hetherington*	*L Wilson*
13/08/2016	L	A	Stranraer	5 2		Parry	Taggart	Waters	Graham	Marr	Goodwin*	Cawley&	Robertson+	Kirkpatrick	Flannigan	Spence	Holmes*	Hetherington+	Layne&	*McDowall*	*Hoggan*	*Hynd*	*L Wilson*
20/08/2016	L	H	East Fife	2 1		Parry	Taggart	Waters	Graham	Marr	Goodwin	Cawley	Holmes*	Kirkpatrick	Flannigan+	Spence&	Layne*	Hetherington+	Hoggan&	*McDowall*	*Scullion*	*Hynd*	*L Wilson*
27/08/2016	L	A	Albion Rovers	4 0		Parry	Taggart	Waters	Graham	Marr*	Goodwin	Cawley&	Holmes	Kirkpatrick+	Flannigan	Spence	Robertson*	Donnelly+	Hetherington&	*McDowall*	*Hoggan*	*Hynd*	*L Wilson*
03/09/2016	CC3	H	East Fife	3 0		Parry	Taggart	Waters	Graham	Robertson	Goodwin	Cawley*	Holmes&	Kirkpatrick	Flannigan	Spence+	Donnelly*	Longworth+	Hoggan&	*McDowall*	*Scullion*	*Martin*	*L Wilson*
10/09/2016	L	H	Livingston	1 3		Parry	Taggart	Waters	Graham	Marr*	Goodwin	Cawley	Holmes+	Kirkpatrick	Robertson	Spence	Longworth*	Donnelly+	*Hoggan*	*McDowall*	*Scullion*	*Martin*	*L Wilson*
17/09/2016	L	A	Queen's Park	2 1		Parry	Taggart	Waters	Graham	Gordon	Goodwin	Cawley	Flannigan	Kirkpatrick*	Robertson	Spence&	Longworth*+	Donnelly+	Holmes&	*McDowall*	*Scullion*	*Hoggan*	*L Wilson*
21/09/2016	LC2	A	Celtic	0 2		Parry	Taggart	Waters	Graham	Gordon	Goodwin+	Cawley*	Flannigan	Kirkpatrick	Robertson	Spence	Holmes*	Longworth+	*Marr*	*McDowall*	*Scullion*	*Hoggan*	*L Wilson*
24/09/2016	L	A	Stenhousemuir	2 2		Parry	Taggart	Waters	Graham	Gordon	Goodwin	Cawley+	Flannigan	Kirkpatrick*	Robertson	Spence&	Holmes*	Longworth+	Marr&	*McDowall*	*Donnelly*	*Hoggan*	*L Wilson*
01/10/2016	L	H	Airdrieonians	1 2		Parry	Taggart	Waters	Marr&	Gordon	Holmes	Cawley+	Flannigan	Kirkpatrick*	Robertson	Spence	Longworth*	Donnelly+	Hoggan&	*McDowall*	*Scullion*	*Martin*	*L Wilson*
08/10/2016	CC4	A	Bala Town	4 2		Parry	Taggart	Waters	Marr	Gordon	Holmes	Cawley*	Flannigan&	Kirkpatrick+	Robertson	Spence	Donnelly*	Longworth+	Martin&	*McDowall*	*Scullion*	*Cunningham*	*L Wilson*
15/10/2016	L	A	Brechin City	1 0		Parry	Taggart	Waters	Marr	Graham	Goodwin*	Cawley	Flannigan	Kirkpatrick+	Robertson	Spence	Holmes*	Martin+	*Gordon*	*McDowall*	*Longworth*	*Hoggan*	*Donnelly*
22/10/2016	L	A	Livingston	1 3		Parry	Taggart	Waters	Marr	Graham	Goodwin	Cawley	Martin	Kirkpatrick	Robertson	Spence	Scullion*	Longworth+	Donnelly&	*McDowall*	*L Wilson*	*Hoggan*	*Holmes*
29/10/2016	L	H	Albion Rovers	0 0		Parry	Taggart	Waters	Marr	Graham	Goodwin	Cawley	Flannigan	Kirkpatrick*	Robertson	Spence	Longworth*	*Holmes*	*Hoggan*	*McDowall*	*Martin*	*Scullion*	*Donnelly*
05/11/2016	L	H	Stenhousemuir	4 1		Parry	Taggart	Waters	Marr	Graham	Goodwin*	Cawley	Longworth	Kirkpatrick&	Robertson	Spence+	Holmes*	Donnelly+	Martin&	*McDowall*	*Hoggan*	*Scullion*	*L Wilson*
12/11/2016	CC4	A	Queen of the South	0 2		Parry	Taggart	Waters	Marr	Graham	Goodwin*	Cawley	Longworth+	Kirkpatrick	Robertson&	Spence	Holmes*	Donnelly+	Martin&	*McDowall*	*Hoggan*	*Scullion*	*L Wilson*
15/11/2016	L	A	East Fife	2 2		Parry	Taggart	Waters	Marr	Graham	Holmes+	Cawley	Longworth*	Flannigan	Robertson	Spence	Kirkpatrick*	Hynd+	*Goodwin*	*A Wilson*	*Hoggan*	*Scullion*	*L Wilson*
19/11/2016	L	A	Airdrieonians	1 2		Parry	Taggart	Waters	Marr*	Graham	Goodwin	Cawley+	Flannigan&	Kirkpatrick	Robertson	Spence	Hoggan*	Longworth+	Hynd&	*Martin*	*McDowell*	*Scullion*	*Layne*
26/11/2016	SC3	A	Peterhead	1 0		Parry	Taggart	Waters	Hoggan	Graham	Goodwin	Cawley	Flannigan	Kirkpatrick*	Robertson	Spence	Longworth*	*Layne*	*Hynd*	*Martin*	*McDowell*	*Scullion*	*L Wilson*
10/12/2016	L	A	Peterhead	1 1		Parry	Taggart	Waters	Hoggan*	Graham	Marr	Holmes	Flannigan+	Longworth	Robertson	Spence	Kirkpatrick*	Layne+	*Hetherington*	*Martin*	*McDowell*	*Scullion*	*L Wilson*
13/12/2016	L	H	Stranraer	2 2		Parry	Taggart	Waters	Cawley	Graham	Marr	Holmes*	Kirkpatrick	Longworth	Robertson	Spence	Layne*	*Hynd*	*Hetherington*	*Martin*	*McDowell*	*Scullion*	*Hoggan*
17/12/2016	L	H	Queen's Park	1 1		Parry	Taggart	Waters	Cawley	Graham	Marr	Goodwin	Kirkpatrick	Longworth*	Robertson	Spence	Layne*	*Hynd*	*Hetherington*	*Martin*	*McDowell*	*Hoggan*	*L Wilson*
24/12/2016	L	H	Brechin City	1 2		Parry	Taggart	Waters	Cawley	Graham	Marr	Flannigan	Kirkpatrick+	Hetherington*	Robertson	Spence	Longworth*	Hynd+	*Holmes*	*Martin*	*McDowell*	*Hoggan*	*Goodwin*
31/12/2016	L	A	Stenhousemuir	4 2		Parry	Taggart	Waters	Cawley&	Graham	Marr	Goodwin	Kirkpatrick	Hetherington+	Robertson	Spence*	Longworth*	Flannigan+	Holmes&	*Martin*	*McDowell*	*Hoggan*	*Hynd*
07/01/2017	L	A	Stranraer	2 1		Parry	Taggart	Waters	Cawley	Graham	Marr	Goodwin*	Kirkpatrick&	Hetherington+	Robertson	Spence	Flannigan*	Holmes+	Longworth&	*Martin*	*McDowell*	*Hoggan*	*Hynd*
14/01/2017	L	H	Peterhead	0 1		Parry	Taggart	Waters	Cawley	Graham	Marr+	Flannigan	Kirkpatrick	Hetherington*	Robertson	Spence	Longworth*	McKeown+	*Holmes*	*Martin*	*McDowell*	*Hoggan*	*Hynd*
21/01/2017	SC4	H	Dunfermline Athletic	2 3		Parry	Taggart	Waters	Cawley	Graham	McKeown	Flannigan*	Kirkpatrick	Hetherington+	Holmes	Spence	Longworth*	McCluskey+	Goodwin	*Martin*	*McDowell*	*Hoggan*	*Marr*
28/01/2017	L	A	Albion Rovers	1 1		A Wilson	Taggart	Waters	Cawley	Graham	McKeown	McCluskey+	Kirkpatrick	Longworth*	Holmes&	Spence	Hetherington*	Mackin+	Robertson&	*Flannigan*	*Hynd*	*Hoggan*	*Marr*
04/02/2017	L	H	Livingston	2 2		McDowell	Taggart	Waters	Cawley&	Graham	McKeown	McCluskey+	Kirkpatrick	Hetherington*	Holmes	Mackin	Spence*	Flannigan+	Longworth&	*Robertson*	*Marr*	*Hoggan*	*A Wilson*
18/02/2017	L	A	Queen's Park	2 0		McDowell	Taggart	Waters	Robertson	Graham	McKeown	Spence+	Kirkpatrick&	Hetherington*	Holmes	Mackin	Flannigan*	*Cawley+*	*Longworth&*	*Hynd*	*Marr*	*McCluskey*	*A Wilson*
25/02/2017	L	H	Airdrieonians	2 1		McDowell	Taggart	Waters	Cawley	Graham	McKeown	McCluskey+	Kirkpatrick	Spence*	Holmes&	Mackin	Hetherington*	Flannigan+	Robertson&	*Hynd*	*Longworth*	*Hoggan*	*A Wilson*
28/02/2017	L	H	East Fife	3 0		McDowell	Taggart	Waters	Cawley+	Graham	McKeown	Hetherington	Kirkpatrick	Spence&	Flannigan	Mackin*	Longworth*	Robertson+	Holmes&	*Hynd*	*Hoggan*	*Marr*	*A Wilson*
11/03/2017	L	H	Stenhousemuir	2 1		Parry	Taggart	Waters	Cawley+	Graham	McKeown	Holmes	Kirkpatrick	Spence&	Flannigan*	Mackin	McCluskey*	Longworth+	Hoggan&	*Marr*	*Martin*	*McDonald*	*McDowell*
18/03/2017	L	A	East Fife	0 0		Parry	Taggart	Waters	Cawley+	Graham	McKeown	Holmes	Kirkpatrick	Spence*	Flannigan	Mackin&	Hetherington*	McCluskey+	Longworth&	*Marr*	*Robertson*	*Hynd*	*McDowell*
21/03/2017	L	A	Brechin City	2 1		McDowell	Taggart	Waters	Cawley	Graham	McKeown	Hetherington&	Kirkpatrick	McCluskey*	Robertson	Mackin+	Flannigan*	Longworth+	Spence&	*Marr*	*Holmes*	*Hynd*	*A Wilson*
25/03/2017	L	H	Queen's Park	2 2		Parry	Taggart	Waters	Cawley	Graham	McKeown	Holmes	Kirkpatrick*	Spence+	Flannigan	Mackin	Longworth*	Hetherington+	*Robertson*	*Marr*	*McCluskey*	*Hynd*	*McDowell*
01/04/2017	L	H	Albion Rovers	1 1		Parry	Taggart	Waters	Cawley	Graham	McKeown	Holmes+	Kirkpatrick*	Spence	Flannigan	Hetherington	McCluskey*	Longworth+	*Robertson*	*Marr*	*Martin*	*Hynd*	*McDowell*
08/04/2017	L	A	Livingston	1 2		Parry	Taggart	Waters	Marr	Graham	Cawley+	Holmes	Kirkpatrick*	Spence&	Mackin	Hetherington	Robertson*	McCluskey+	Longworth&	*Marr*	*Martin*	*McDonald*	*McDowell*
15/04/2017	L	H	Brechin City	6 1		Parry	Taggart	Waters	Marr	Graham	Cawley	Holmes+	McCluskey*	Spence	Mackin&	Flanagan	Martin*	Robertson+	Longworth&	*Hetherington*	*Hoggan*	*McDonald*	*McDowell*
22/04/2017	L	A	Airdrieonians	1 0		Parry	Taggart	Waters	Marr	Graham	Robertson	Hetherington+	Kirkpatrick	Spence	Mackin&	Flanagan*	Cawley*	McCluskey+	Longworth&	*Holmes*	*Hoggan*	*Martin*	*McDowell*
29/04/2017	L	H	Stranraer	1 0		Parry	Taggart	Waters	Marr	Graham	Cawley	Holmes*	Kirkpatrick	Spence+	McCluskey&	Longworth	Hetherington*	Robertson+	Martin&	*Hynd*	*Hoggan*	*Cunningham*	*McDowell*
06/05/2017	L	A	Peterhead	2 3		McDowell	Taggart	Waters+	Marr	McKeown	Robertson	Hetherington	Martin	Flannigan*	McCluskey&	Longworth	Cawley*	Hoggan+	Hynd&	*Spence*	*Kirkpatrick*	*Cunningham*	*Parry*
10/05/2017	PO	A	Airdrieonians	0 1		Parry	Taggart	Waters	McKeown	Graham	Cawley	Holmes+	Kirkpatrick&	Flannigan	Mackin*	Spence	Hetherington*	Robertson+	McCluskey&	*Marr*	*Martin*	*Longworth*	*McDowell*
13/05/2017	PO	H	Airdrieonians	1 0	aet, 4-3p	Parry	Taggart	Waters	McKeown	Graham	Cawley&	Robertson	Kirkpatrick	Flannigan+	Mackin	Spence*	Hetherington*	McCluskey+	Martin&	*Marr*	*Hynd*	*Longworth*	*McDowell*
17/05/2017	PO	A	Brechin City	0 1		Parry	Taggart	Waters	McKeown	Graham	Cawley*	Robertson	Kirkpatrick&	Flannigan	Mackin	Hetherington+	Spence*	McCluskey+	Martin&	*Marr*	*Hoggan*	*Longworth*	*McDowell*
20/05/2017	PO	H	Brechin City	4 3	aet, 4-5p	Parry	Taggart	Waters	McKeown	Graham	Cawley*	Robertson+	Kirkpatrick	Flannigan	Mackin&	Spence	McCluskey*	Holmes+	Martin&	*Hetherington*	*Marr*	*Longworth*	*McDowell*

Annan Athletic FC 2016/17

Founded	1942
Ground	Galabank
Postcode	DG12 5DQ
Tel	01461 204108
Capacity	2514
Closest Railway Station	Annan
Record Attendance	2517 v Rangers, Sep 2013
Record Win	Annan Athletic 6 Elgin City 0, 07.03.2009
Record Defeat	Inverness CT 8 Annan Athletic 1, 24.01.1998
Most League Goals in a Season	22, Peter Weatherston, 2014/15
Chairman	Henry McClelland
Secretary	Alan Irving
Manager	Jim Chapman (until May), Peter Murphy
Assistant Manager	John Joyce (until May), Kevin Rutkiewicz
Colours 2016/17 Top	Gold with Black Flashes
Shorts	Black
Sponsor	M and S Engineering
Manufacturer	Stanno
Change Colours 2016/17 Top	Grey
Shorts	Grey
Nicknames	Galabankies
Web	www.annanathleticfc.co.uk
Match Programme 2016/17	£2

2016/17 was another season of comparative success for Annan Athletic. Once again they reached the promotion play offs but as in previous seasons they failed at that hurdle. Still, on limited resources and a geographical handicap for player recruitment, their final position was still quite an achievement. Credit must go to two veterans who pulled them together during the second half of the season. Gavin Skelton demonstrated just how good a player he is and Peter Weatherson returned from a spell in the Juniors to lead the line with aplomb.

One result stands out from 2016/17 for all the wrong reasons - a 0-4 thumping from Formartine United in the Scottish Cup. That must have been a sore one.

PREDICTION FOR 2017/18

Annan without Jim Chapman is like Pie without Bovril. Chapman worked wonders at Galabank but has now moved on to take over at Clyde. His replacement, Peter Murphy may have hero status in Carlisle but he is unproven at managerial level. If he can steer them to a play off spot again then that will be real success - but it may be a case of mid-table for Annan in the coming season.

223 Senior Goals

Peter Weatherson		L			LC			SC			OC			Total		
Season	Club	A	S	G	A	S	G	A	S	G	A	S	G	A	S	G
2000/1	QOS	31	3	16	2		1	3		3	1			37	3	20
2001/2	QOS	26	7	15	2			2						30	7	15
2002/3	QOS	29	4	6	2		1	1	1	1	5		2	37	5	10
2003/4	Morton	31		14	2		1	2		1	2		3	37	0	19
2004/5	Morton	26	6	11	1	1		3		3	1			31	7	14
2005/6	Morton	37		10	1			2		1	4			44	0	11
2006/7	Morton	34		15	1			3		1	4		2	42	0	18
2007/8	Morton	33	2	9	1			4		2	4			42	2	11
2008/9	Morton	31	3	9	1	2		1				3	1	33	8	10
2009/10	Morton	31	2	10	2		2	3			1	1		37	3	12
2010/11	Morton	19	12	6	1	1	2		4		1	1		21	18	8
2011/2	Morton	19	12	3		2	1		3	1	1	1	1	20	18	6
2012/3	Morton	18	10	6	2		1	4	1	5	2			26	11	12
2013/4	Annan Athletic	11		2	1			4			4		1	20	0	3
2014/5	Annan Athletic	26	2	22				4		3				30	2	25
2015/6	Annan Athletic	24	2	15	1		2	4		5	2		1	31	2	23
2016/7	Shettleston													0	0	0
2016/7	Annan Athletic	16	2	6										16	2	6
														0	0	0
TOTAL		442	67	175	20	6	11	40	9	26	32	6	11	534	88	223

The club initially played in the wartime welfare league but turned junior in 1945. Between 1945 and 1951 they had some conparative success in the Scottish Junior Cup – once reaching the Fifth Round before losing 2-1 to Jeanfield Swifts in Perth.

Annan competed with considerable success in the Carlisle and District League and Cumberland FA competitions between 1952 and 1977. At that point they decided to switch to Scottish football and joined the South of Scotland League and FA. From 1978 they were eligible to play in the Scottish Qualifying Cup.

			SQ	Nat	Pos	L			SC			LC			CC							
Surname	First Name	DOB				A	S	G	A	S	G	A	S	G	A	S	G	UNS	Signed	Previous Club	Notes	Contract
Ashgar	Adam	26/07/1994		SCO	M	3	4			2	1	1	3					13	2016	Alloa Athletic		OOC
Black	Steven	17/06/1992		SCO	D	12			1			3			1			2	2013	Queen of the South		OOC
Bradbury	Aaron	01/01/1997		ENG	F		2			1		1			1			7	2016	Carlisle United		
Bronsky	Stephen	16/06/1994		SCO	D	10	1		1									11	2016	BSC Glasgow	Ex Clyde	
Cuddihy	Barry	19/12/1996		SCO	M	21	3	2	3			4						4	2016	St Mirren		OOC
Currie	Blair	19/02/1994		SCO	GK	37			3			4						2	2015	Hamilton Accies	OOC June 2017, joined Clyde	
Dachnowicz	Przemyslaw	12/04/1999		SCO	M	1	6			1			4	1				16	2016	Rangers	OL to St Rochs Mar-May 2017	OOC
Finnie	Ryan	19/02/1995		SCO	D	12			2	1			1	1	1				2016	Alloa Athletic	Freed Jan 2017	
Flanagan	Nathan	04/05/1997		SCO	M	22	2											1	2016	St Mirren (OL)	Dec 2016-May 2017	
Fry	Tom	31/05/1997		WAL	M		3											8	2017	Motherwell (OL)	Jan-May 2017	
Gibson	Liam	01/01/1999			M													3	2016	Annan Athletic Youths		
Home	Callum			SCO	D	13	5											13	2016	BSC Glasgow	Ex East Kilbride FC	
Jaekel	Ben	01/01/1999			F													1	2016	Annan Athletic Youths		
Krissian	Raffi			FRA/LEB	D	24	2	2	2	1		4			1			11	2016	Edusport Academy		End 2017/
Liddell	Connor	09/02/1998			F													3	2016	Annan Athletic Youths		
Lucas	Jean Guy	27/05/1994		FRA	D	31	3		3			4			1			4	2016	Edusport Academy	Ex Vannes	
McKenna	David	18/09/1986		SCO	F	24	11	11	3		1	4			1			3	2016	East Stirlingshire	OOC May 2017, joined Beith Juniors	
Mitchell	Alex	21/03/1991		ENG	GK	1									1			42	2016	Workington		End 2017/
Nade	Christian	18/09/1984		FRA	F	3														Trialist, ex Stranraer		
Norman	Scott	02/01/1998		SCO	M		1						1			1		4	2016	Annan Athletic Youths		
Omar	Rabin	21/07/1997		IRQ/NET	F	25	8	4	3			3		1	1		1		2014	Thistle Weir Academy		End 2017/
Osadolor	Smart	26/03/1991		NIG	F	5	7	4										6	2017	Rossvale JFC		OOC
Park	Liam	31/05/1995		SCO	M		4						3			1		2	2015	Dalbeattie Star	Freed Jan 2017	
Pearson	Ellis	19/10/1997		ENG	D		1											5	2016	Carlisle United		
Ramsay	Darren	21/08/1995		SCO	M	29	3	9	3										2016	Rangers		OOC
Ribeiro	Tony	04/02/1991		FRA	M		1					3				1		13	2016	Edusport Academy	Ex Cormontreuil, AS Taissy	
Robertson	William	14/04/1993		SCO	M	2	3					2							2016	Stirling Albion	Freed Nov 2016, rejoined Stirling Albion	[redacted]
Sharkey	Stewart	05/01/1991		SCO	D							1						4	2016	Yoker Athletic		OOC
Sinnamon	Ryan	22/07/1996		SCO	D	8	1		3									1	2015	Rangers (OL)	Oct 2016-Jan 2017	
Skelton	Gavin	27/03/1981		ENG	M	21													2016	Appleby, ex QOS	Joined Carlisle Utd as Academy Coach May 2017	
Smith	Aidan	11/05/1997		SCO	F	16	18	9										2	2016	Queen of the South (OL)	Aug-May	
Stewart	Jordan	05/03/1996		SCO	M	10		1											2017	St Mirren (OL)	Jan-May 2017	
Swinglehurst	Steven	23/10/1992		ENG	D	27	1	4	3			4			1			2	2012	Carlisle United		End 2017/
Watson	Peter	20/08/1986		SCO	D	19	3	2	2			2			1			4	2008	Albion Rovers		OOC
Weatherson	Peter	29/05/1980		ENG	F	16	2	6											2017	Shettleston JFC	Retired at end of 2016/17	
Wright	Max	21/08/1995		SCO	M	26	9	9	1	2		4		1	1			3	2016	East Stirlingshire	OOC May 2017, joined Clyde	
Own Goals								2														
NEW SIGNINGS																						
Hooper	Scott				D														2017	QOS		
Smith	Aiden				F														2017	QOS		
Murphy	Peter				D														2017	Ayr United	Player Manager	
Rutkiewicz	Kevin				D														2017	Clyde	Player Assistant Manager	
Stevenson	Ryan				F														2017	Peninsula Strikers	Ex Hearts, Aye etc	
Orsi	Dan				M														2017	Glenafton Athletic		
Moxon	Owen				M														2017	QOS		

Source of Birthdates is transfermarkt.com

The main stand at Galabank, 2002.

Date	Comp	H/A	Opponents	F	A	HT		Referee	Crowd	Scorers
16/07/2016	LC	H	Stranraer	1	2	0	0	S Reid	418	Dachnowicz
19/07/2016	LC	A	Rangers	0	2	0	1	E Anderson	31628	
23/07/2016	LC	H	Motherwell	1	3	1	1	N Walsh	956	Omar
30/07/2016	LC	A	East Stirlingshire	2	0	0	0	M Roncone	134	Finnie, Wright
02/08/2016	PC	A*	Celtic U20	1	5	1	3	D Dickinson	216	Omar
06/08/2016	L	H	Stirling Albion	3	2	3	1	G Irvine	421	Forsyth og, McKenna, Smith
13/08/2016	L	A	Berwick Rangers	0	2	0	1	C Steven	366	
20/08/2016	L	H	Clyde	3	2	1	0	C Napier	421	McKenna, Ramsay, Omar
27/08/2016	L	A	Montrose	2	2	2	0	S Millar	340	Ramsay, Wright
10/09/2016	L	H	Forfar Athletic	1	2	1	0	D Munro	403	Wright
17/09/2016	L	A	Arbroath	1	1	0	0	G Ross	482	McKenna
24/09/2016	L	H	Edinburgh City	1	1	1	0	M Roncone	351	McKenna
01/10/2016	L	A	Elgin City	2	0	1	0	K Graham	583	Ramsay, McKenna
15/10/2016	L	A	Cowdenbeath	2	2	2	0	M Northcroft	331	Cuddihy, McKenna
22/10/2016	SC2	H	East Stirlingshire	0	0	0	0	A Newlands	302	
29/10/2016	SC2R	A	East Stirlingshire	2	1	1	1	A Newlands	304	McKenna, Ashgar
05/11/2016	L	H	Arbroath	1	2	1	0	D Lowe	326	Swinglehurst
08/11/2016	L	H	Montrose	2	3	1	2	G Duncan	289	Ramsay, I Campbell og
12/11/2016	L	A	Edinburgh City	0	1	0	0	G Irvine	246	
19/11/2016	L	H	Elgin City	1	0	1	0	J McKendrick	353	McKenna
03/12/2016	SC3	A	Formartine United	0	4	0	0	C Steven	345	
10/12/2016	L	H	Cowdenbeath	2	0	1	0	D Munro	241	Ramsay, Swingleshurst
13/12/2016	L	A	Forfar Athletic	1	5	0	3	S Reid	337	Smith
17/12/2016	L	A	Stirling Albion	1	3	1	2	C Napier	694	Wright
24/12/2016	L	H	Berwick Rangers	3	1	3	1	D Lowe	430	McKenna, Watson, Omar
31/12/2016	L	A	Clyde	3	2	0	1	S Millar	467	McKenna 2, Smith
07/01/2017	L	H	Forfar Athletic	1	2	1	1	C Charleston	432	Wright
14/01/2017	L	A	Elgin City	2	3	0	3	M Roncone	638	Weatherson, Osadolor
21/01/2017	L	A	Arbroath	2	1	1	1	S Millar	566	Ramsay, Krissian
28/01/2017	L	H	Stirling Albion	4	1	1	1	G Irvine	420	Osadolor 2, Wright 2
04/02/2017	L	A	Berwick Rangers	1	4	1	2	D Lowe	355	Weatherson
11/02/2017	L	H	Edinburgh City	1	0	1	0	S Reid	379	Weatherson
18/02/2017	L	A	Cowdenbeath	1	0	0	0	C Napier	258	Ramsay
25/02/2017	L	H	Clyde	1	0	0	0	A Newlands	398	Wright
04/03/2017	L	A	Montrose	3	2	3	1	G Ross	384	Omar, Wright, Swinglehurst
11/03/2017	L	H	Elgin City	1	0	1	0	G Aitken	328	McKenna
18/03/2017	L	A	Stirling Albion	0	1	0	0	D Munro	531	
25/03/2017	L	H	Cowdenbeath	1	0	0	0	C Napier	386	Smith
01/04/2017	L	H	Arbroath	2	5	2	2	C Charleston	456	Weatherson, Stewart
08/04/2017	L	A	Clyde	1	2	1	1	D Lowe	462	Smith
15/04/2017	L	H	Berwick Rangers	2	1	0	0	J Mckendrick	460	Ramsay, Smith
22/04/2017	L	A	Edinburgh City	0	2	0	1	G Beaton	378	
29/04/2017	L	H	Montrose	5	1	4	0	S Reid	461	Omar, Cuddihy, Swingleshurst, Krissian, Weatherson
06/05/2017	L	A	Forfar Athletic	4	2	3	1	G Irvine	917	Watson, Osadolor, Wright, Smith
10/05/2017	PO	H	Forfar Athletic	2	2	2	0	C Allan	629	Weatherson, Smith
13/05/2017	PO	A	Forfar Athletic	2	4	0	3	J McKendrick	665	Smith, Ramsay

* at Cappielow

FRIENDLIES / OTHER GAMES				
02/07/2016	A	Crusaders	2	2
09/07/2016	H	Airdrieonians	2	3
12/07/2016	H	QOTS	0	4

Date	Comp	H/A	Opponents	F	A	1	2	3	4	5	6	7	8	9	10	11	12	13	14	15	16	17	18
16/07/2016	LC	H	Stranraer	1	2	Currie	Lucas	Sharkey*	Swinglehurst	Krissian	Ashgar	Robertson	Cuddihy	Wright	McKenna+	Ribeiro&	Norman*	Park+	Dachnowicz&	Liddell	Jaekel	Gibson	Mitchell
19/07/2016	LC	A	Rangers	0	2	Currie	Lucas	Black	Swinglehurst	Krissian	Omar&	Robertson+	Cuddihy	Wright	McKenna	Ribeiro*	Park*	Ashgar+	Dachnowicz&	Liddell	Norman	Watson	Mitchell
23/07/2016	LC	H	Motherwell	1	3	Currie	Lucas	Black	Swinglehurst&	Krissian	Omar	Watson	Cuddihy*	Wright	McKenna	Ribeiro+	Park*	Dachnowicz+	Ashgar&	Liddell	Norman	Gibson	Mitchell
30/07/2016	LC	A	East Stirlingshire	2	0	Currie	Lucas	Black	Swingelhurst	Krissian&	Omar	Watson	Cuddihy*	Wright	McKenna+	Bradbury	Finnie*	Dachnowicz+	Ashgar&	Ribeiro	Norman	Gibson	Mitchell
02/08/2016	PC	A*	Celtic U20	1	5	Mitchell	Lucas	Black	Swinglehurst&	Krissian	Omar	Watson	Finnie	Wright	McKenna*	Bradbury+	Ribeiro*	Park+	Norman&	Ashgar	Dachnowicz	Sharkey	Currie
06/08/2016	L	H	Stirling Albion	3	2	Currie	Lucas	Black	Ramsay	Krissian	Omar+	Watson	Finnie	Wright	McKenna*	Smith	Park*	Dachnowicz+	Ribeiro	Ashgar	Norman	Sharkey	Mitchell
13/08/2016	L	A	Berwick Rangers	0	2	Currie	Lucas+	Black	Ramsay	Krissian	Robertson	Watson	Finnie	Wright	McKenna*	Smith&	Bradbury*	Norman+	Dachnowicz&	Ashgar	Ribeiro	Sharkey	Mitchell
20/08/2016	L	H	Clyde	3	2	Currie	Lucas	Black	Ramsay	Krissian	Omar	Watson	Finnie	Wright	McKenna+	Cuddihy*	Asgar*	Park+	Dachnowicz	Bradbury	Ribeiro	Sharkey	Mitchell
27/08/2016	L	A	Montrose	2	2	Currie	Lucas	Black	Ramsay	Krissian	Omar	Watson	Finnie	Wright	McKenna*	Cuddihy	Smith*	Park	Dachnowicz	Bradbury	Swinglehurst	Ashgar	Mitchell
10/09/2016	L	H	Forfar Athletic	1	2	Currie	Swinglehurst+	Black	Ramsay	Krissian	Omar	Watson	Finnie&	Wright	McKenna*	Cuddihy	Smith*	Lucas+	Robertson&	Ashgar	Ribeiro	Park	Mitchell
17/09/2016	L	A	Arbroath	1	1	Currie	Swinglehurst	Black	Ramsay&	Krissian+	Omar	Watson	Finnie	Wright	McKenna*	Cuddihy	Smith*	Robertson+	Park&	Ashgar	Ribeiro	Lucas	Mitchell
24/09/2016	L	H	Edinburgh City	1	1	Currie	Swinglehurst	Black	Ramsay&	Krissian	Robertson	Watson	Finnie	Wright*	McKenna+	Cuddihy	Smith*	Park+	Dachnowicz&	Ashgar	Ribeiro	Lucas	Mitchell
01/10/2016	L	A	Elgin City	2	0	Currie	Swinglehurst	Black	Ramsay*	Sinnamon	Omar	Watson	Finnie	Smith	McKenna+	Cuddihy	Robertson*	Wright+	Bradbury	Ashgar	Krissian	Lucas	Mitchell
15/10/2016	L	A	Cowdenbeath	2	2	Currie	Swinglehurst	Black	Ramsay*	Sinnamon	Omar	Watson	Finnie	Smith	McKenna+	Cuddihy	Wright*	Lucas+	Bradbury	Ashgar	Krissian	Bronsky	Mitchell
22/10/2016	SC2	H	East Stirlingshire	0	0	Currie	Swinglehurst	Black*	Ramsay	Sinnamon	Omar+	Watson	Finnie	Lucas	McKenna	Cuddihy	Krissian*	Wright+	Bradbury	Ashgar	Home	Bronsky	Mitchell
29/10/2016	SC2R	A	East Stirlingshire	2	1	Currie	Swinglehgurst	Krissian	Ramsay	Sinnamon	Omar+	Watson	Finnie&	Lucas	McKenna*	Cuddihy	Wright*	Ashgar+	Dachnowicz&	Bradbury	Home	Bronsky	Mitchell
05/11/2016	L	H	Arbroath	1	2	Currie	Swinglehurst	Smith	Ramsay&	Sinnamon	Wright	Watson	Finnie+	Lucas	McKenna	Cuddihy*	Dachnowicz*	Omar+	Ashgar&	Krissian	Home	Bronsky	Mitchell
08/11/2016	L	H	Montrose	2	3	Currie	Swinglehurst&	Bronsky	Ashgar	Sinnamon	Wright*	Ramsay+	Finnie	Lucas	Omar	Smith	Watson*	McKenna+	Home&	Krissian	Dachnowicz	Ribeiro	Mitchell
12/11/2016	L	A	Edinburgh City	0	1	Currie	Krissian	Bronsky	Cuddihy	Sinnamon*	McKenna	Ramsay&	Finnie+	Lucas	Omar	Smith	Wright*	Pearson+	Dachnowicz&	Bradbury	Home	Ribeiro	Mitchell
19/11/2016	L	H	Elgin City	1	0	Currie	Swinglehurst	Bronsky	Cuddihy	Sinnamon	McKenna&	Ramsay	Nade+	Lucas	Omar	Wright*	Bradbury*	Krissian+	Home&	Pearson	Dachnowicz	Ribeiro	Mitchell
03/12/2016	SC3	A	Formartine United	0	4	Currie	Swinglehurst	Bronsky	Krissian+	Sinnamon*	McKenna	Ramsay&	Cuddihy	Lucas	Omar	Wright*	Bradbury*	Ashgar+	Dachnowicz&	Pearson	Home	Ribeiro	Mitchell
10/12/2016	L	H	Cowdenbeath	2	0	Currie	Swinglehurst	Bronsky	Ashgar	Sinnamon	McKenna&	Ramsay	Cuddihy	Lucas	Nade+	Home*	Watson*	Smith+	Flanagan&	Pearson	Wright	Krissian	Mitchell
13/12/2016	L	A	Forfar Athletic	1	5	Currie	Swinglehurst	Bronsky*	Ashgar+	Sinnamon	McKenna&	Ramsay	Cuddihy	Lucas	Watson	Smith	Wright*	Flanagan+	Ribeiro&	Krissian	Dachnowicz	Home	
17/12/2016	L	A	Stirling Albion	1	3	Currie	Swinglehurst	Bronsky	Home	Flanagan	Wright+	Ramsay*	Cuddihy	Lucas	Nade&	Smith	Omar*	Watson	McKenna&	Krissian	Dachnowicz	Ashgar	Mitchell
24/12/2016	L	H	Berwick Rangers	3	1	Currie	Swinglehurst	Watson	Home	Flanagan	Wright&	Ramsay*	Cuddihy	Lucas	Omar	McKenna+	Smith*	Sinnamon+	Ashgar&	Krissian	Pearson	Mitchell	
31/12/2016	L	A	Clyde	3	2	Currie	Swinglehurst	Watson	Home	Flanagan	Wright	Skelton	Cuddihy	Lucas	Omar*	McKenna+	Smith*	Ramsay+	Ashgar	Krissian	Dachnowicz	Sinnamon	Mitchell
07/01/2017	L	H	Forfar Athletic	1	2	Currie	Krissian	Watson	Home	Flanagan	Wright+	Skelton	Osadolor	Lucas&	Omar	McKenna*	Smith*	Dachnowicz+	Ashgar&	Bronsky	Ribeiro	Pearson	
14/01/2017	L	A	Elgin City	2	3	Currie	Swinglehurst*	Watson	Home	Flanagan	Wright+	Skelton	Weatherson	Lucas	Omar	McKenna&	Krissian*	Ramsay+	Osadolor&	Ashgar	Dachnowicz	Smith	Mitchell
21/01/2017	L	A	Arbroath	2	1	Currie	Krissian	Watson	Home	Flanagan&	Ramsay	Skelton	Weatherson	Lucas*	Omar	Osadolor+	Smith*	Wright+	McKenna&	Ribeiro	Dachnowicz	Mitchell	
28/01/2017	L	H	Stirling Albion	4	1	Currie	Krissian	Watson	Home	Flanagan&	Ramsay*	Skelton	Weatherson	Lucas	Omar	Osadolor+	Wright*	Swinglehurst+	McKenna&	Black	Dachnowicz	Smith	Mitchell
04/02/2017	L	A	Berwick Rangers	1	4	Currie	Swinglehurst	Watson	Horne	Flanagan	Ramsay	Skelton&	Weatherson	Lucas	Omar+	Osadolor*	Smith*	McKenna+	Wright&	Fry	Dachnowicz	Bronsky	Mitchell
11/02/2017	L	H	Edinburgh City	1	0	Currie	Swinglehurst	Stewart	Black	Flanagan*	Ramsey	Skelton	Weatherson&	Lucas	Wright	McKenna+	Omar*	Smith+	Osadolor&	Krissian	Dachnowicz	Fry	Mitchell
18/02/2017	L	A	Cowdenbeath	1	0	Currie	Swinglehurst	Stewart	Krissian+	Flanagan+	Ramsey	Skelton	Weatherson	Lucas*	Wright	McKenna&	Home*	Omar+	Smith&	Osadolor	Dachnowicz	Fry	Mitchell
25/02/2017	L	H	Clyde	1	0	Currie	Swinglehurst	Stewart	Krissian	Flanagan+	Ramsey	Skelton	Weatherson	Lucas	Wright	McKenna*	Smith*	Omar+	Cuddihy	Osadolor	Home	Fry	Mitchell
04/03/2017	L	A	Montrose	3	2	Currie	Swinglehurst	Stewart	Krissian	Flanagan&	Ramsey	Skelton	Omar	Lucas	Wright+	McKenna*	Fry*	Smith+	Cuddihy&	Osadolor	Home	Bronsky	Mitchell
11/03/2017	L	H	Elgin City	1	0	Currie	Swingelhurst	Stewart	Krissian	Flanagan	Cuddihy	Skelton	Omar+	Lucas	Wright	McKenna*	Weatherson*	Smith+	Bronsky	Black	Home	Fry	Mitchell
18/03/2017	L	A	Stirling Albion	0	1	Currie	Swingelhurst	Stewart	Krissian	Flanagan	Cuddihy*	Skelton+	Omar	Lucas	Wright&	Weatherson	Fry*	Smith+	McKenna&	Bronsky	Dachnowicz	Home	Mitchell
25/03/2017	L	H	Cowdenbeath	1	0	Currie	Swinglehurst	Stewart	Krissian	Flanagan	Ramsey	Skelton	Omar*	Lucas	Wright+	Weatherson	Smith*	Cuddihy+	McKenna	Osadolor	Fry	Home	Mitchell
01/04/2017	L	H	Arbroath	2	5	Currie	Swinglehurst	Stewart	Krissian	Flanagan*	Ramsey+	Skelton	Smith	Lucas&	Wright	Weatherson	Fry*	Osadolor+	Home&	McKenna	Cuddihy	Bronsky	Mitchell
08/04/2017	L	A	Clyde	1	2	Currie	Bronsky	Stewart*	Krissian	Flanagan&	Ramsey+	Skelton	Smith	Lucas	Wright	Weatherson	Home*	Cuddihy+	Omar&	Osadolor	Fry	McKenna	Mitchell
15/04/2017	L	H	Berwick Rangers	2	1	Currie	Bronsky	Black	Krissian	Flanagan*	Ramsey	Skelton	Smith	Lucas	Wright+	Weatherson&	Omar*	McKenna+	Osadolor&	Cuddihy	Fry	Home	Mitchell
22/04/2017	L	A	Edinburgh City	0	2	Currie	Swinglehurst	Black	Krissian	Flanagan+	Ramsey	Skelton&	Smith	Omar	Bronsky*	Weatherson	Lucas*	McKenna+	Osadolor&	Cuddihy	Home	Wright	Mitchell
29/04/2017	L	H	Montrose	5	1	Currie	Swinglehurst	Home	Krissian	Flanagan*	Cuddihy&	Skelton	Smith	Lucas	Omar	Weatherson+	McKenna*	Osadolor+	Bronsky&	Wright	Watson	Mitchell	
06/05/2017	L	A	Forfar Athletic	4	2	Mitchell	Bronsky	Home	Watson	Wright+	Cuddihy	Skelton	Dachnowicz*	Lucas	McKenna	Osadolor&	Omar*	Weatherson+	Smith&	Krissian	Swinglehurst	Flanagan	Currie
10/05/2017	PO	H	Forfar Athletic	2	2	Currie	Swinglehurst	Home	Krissian	Flanagan&	Cuddihy	Skelton*	Smith	Lucas	Omar	Weatherson+	Wright*	Osadolor+	McKenna&	Bronsky	Dachnowicz	Watson	Mitchell
13/05/2017	PO	A	Forfar Athletic	2	4	Currie	Swinglehurst	Home	Krissian	Flanagan*	Cuddihy	Skelton&	Smith	Stewart+	Omar	Weatherson	Ramsay*	McKenna+	Wright&	Osadolor	Lucas	Watson	Mitchell

* at Cappielow

Arbroath FC 2016/17

Founded	1878
Ground	Gayfield Park
Postcode	DD11 1QB
Tel	01241 872157
Capacity	6600
Closest Railway Station	Arbroath
Record Attendance	13510, v Rangers, SC, 23/2/1952
Record Win	36-0 v Bon Accord, SC, 12/9/1885
Record Defeat	1-9 v Celtic, LC, 25/8/1993
Most League Goals in a Season	45, Dave Easson, 1958/9
Most Goals in Career	120, Jimmy Jack
Chairman	Mike Caird
Secretary	Gary Callon
Manager	Dick Campbell
Assistant Manager	Ian Campbell
Colours 2016/17 Top	Maroon
Shorts	Maroon
Sponsor	Megatech Projects
Manufacturer	Pendle
Change Colours 2016/17 Top	Navy, Yellow Trim
Shorts	Navy, Yellow Trim
Nicknames	Red Lichties
Web	www.arbroathfc.co.uk
Match Programme	The Red Lichties £2 (JJ Sports Promotions)

For much of the season Arbroath lagged behind county rivals Forfar Athletic in the promotion race. However, they came good at the right time and, as Forfar faltered, it was Arbroath who clinched the automatic promotion place. Over 1000 Arbroath fans travelled to Stirling to see them clinch the title with a 1-1 draw on the last day. The single inexplicable result of the season was a 0-5 defeat to Clyde in the Scottish Cup - no idea at all where that one came from.

Manager Dick Campbell deserves a lot of credit for the success. His experience and no-nonsense approach paid dividends and many players seem to thrive under his management style. He's a strong tactician and one of the most successful lower league managers of all time. Those of us who remember him cutting his managerial teeth at Cowdenbeath might confess to being a little surprised.

PREDICTION FOR 2017/18

There's no reason why Arbroath shouldn't match the majority of League One clubs. They have strengthened their squad with some decent signings which should ensure another decent campaign. A promotion play off place will not be beyond them.

						L			SC			LC			CC							
Surname	First Name	DOB	SQ	Nat	Pos	A	S	G	A	S	G	A	S	G	A	S	G	UNS	Signed	Previous Club	Notes	Contract
Brown	Jason	07/07/1996		SCO	M	3	1											0	2016	Inverness CT (OL)	Sep-Oct 2016	[redacted]
Callaghan	Liam	10/10/1994		SCO	M	2	4			1		1	3		1	1		14	2016	Cowdenbeath	Freed Jan 2017 joined Montrose	
Doris	Steven	09/08/1988		SCO	F	30	6	12	2		1	4			2			0	2016	Stirling Albion		End 2017/18
Douglas	Rab	24/04/1972		SCO	GK													10	2016	Forfar Athletic	Goalkeeping Coach	OOC
Dunlop	Michael	11/01/1993		SCO	D	3	3					1	1		1	1		9	2016	Forfar Athletic	Freed Jan 2017, joined Berwick R	[redacted]
Ferns	Eddie	18/04/1991		SCO	M	5	7	1										3	2017	Stirling Albion	OOC May 2017 joined Stenhousemuir	
Gill	Cammy	07/04/1998		SCO	GK													7	2017	Dunfermline Ath (OL)	Jan-Mar 2017	
Gold	David	01/01/1993		SCO	M	28	4	1	2			1	2		1			5	2015	Berwick Rangers		End 2017/18
Gomes	Ricky	19/07/1993		CAN/POR	GK	28	1		2						1			12	2016	AC Malveira		End 2017/18
Hamilton	Colin	07/05/1992		SCO	D	36		1	2		1	4		1	2		1	0	2016	Alloa Athletic		End 2017/18
Hester	Kane	12/07/1995		SCO	F	1	8						2		1	1	1	6	2015	Arbroath Vics		End 2017/18
Hodge	Bryan	23/09/1987		SCO	M	14												1	2017	Stirling Albion		OOC
Kader	Omar	29/04/1986		SCO	M	20	13	5	2			4			1		1	3	2016	Forfar Athletic		End 2017/18
Linn	Bobby	10/10/1985		SCO	F	36		5	2		1	4			1	1		0	2013	Ballingry Rovers		End 2017/18
Little	Ricky	20/05/1989		SCO	D	34		2	2			2			2		1	0	2013	Queen's Park		End 2017/18
Malin	Gavin	25/08/1988		ENG	M	3	12	2		1			1					21	2016	Forfar Athletic		OOC
McCallum	Donald	27/09/1996		SCO	F		5											11	2017	Dumbarton (OL)	Jan-May 2017	[redacted]
McCord	Ryan	21/03/1989		SCO	M	30	1	13	2			3			1	1		2	2016	Raith Rovers		OOC
Mutch	Robbie	20/08/1998		SCO	GK	8						4			1	1		7	2016	Aberdeen (OL)	Aug 2016-Jan 2017	[redacted]
Phillips	Gary	01/05/1988		SCO		7	1		1	1		4			1			11	2016	Largs Thistle	Freed Jan 2017, joined Berwick R	
Prunty	Bryan	12/01/1983		SCO	F	11	16	2		1		4			1			11	2016	Airdrieonians		End 2017/18
Scott	Martin	15/02/1986		SCO	M	22	4	9	2			2			2		1	1	2016	Salgaocar	OOC May 2017 joined Stenhousemuir	[redacted]
Skelly	Josh	11/04/1997		SCO	F	13	9	5		2								0	2016	Dundee (OL)	Aug 2016-May 2017	
Smyth	Matt	08/05/1998		NIR	D	4	4	1										6	2017	Dundee (OL)	Jan-May 2017	
Stewart	Ryan	01/01/1999		SCO	GK													6	2016		OL to Luncarty Mar-Apr 2017	
Sukar	Jassem	11/09/1996		ENG/EGY	D	23	3		1						1			5	2016	Dundee United (OL)	Aug 2016-Jan 2017	[redacted]
Thomson	Josh	14/04/1997		SCO	D							2	2					14	2016	Cowdenbeath	OL to Dundonald BB Feb-May	OOC
Whatley	Mark	11/07/1990		SCO	M	35		2	2			4			2			0	2014	Spartans		End 2017/18
Own Goals								2														
NEW SIGNINGS																						
Skelly	Josh			SCO	F														2017	Dundee		End 2017/18
O'Brien	Thomas			SCO	D														2017	Forfar Athletic		End 2018/19
Denholm	Danny			SCO	M														2017	Forfar Athletic		End 2018/19
Yule	Blair			SCO	M														2017	Cove Rangers		End 2018/19

Source of Birthdates : Arbroath FC website and transfermarkt.com

Date	Comp	H/A	Opponents	F	A		HT		Referee	Crowd	Scorers
15/07/2016	LC	H	Dundee United	1	1	3-5p	0	0	D Robertson	3124	Hamilton
19/07/2016	LC	A	Dunfermline Athletic	0	3		0	1	D Munro	1974	
27/07/2016	LC	H	Cowdenbeath	0	2		0	2	M Roncone	421	
30/07/2016	LC	A	Inverness CT	0	7		0	4	G Aitken	1316	
02/08/2016	PC	A	Inverness CT U20	3	0		2	0	A Shepherd	296	Kader, Hamilton, Scott
06/08/2016	L	H	Berwick Rangers	1	1		0	0	S Millar	502	Scott
13/08/2016	L	A	Montrose	1	1		1	0	S Kirkland	794	McCord
17/08/2016	CC	H	East Fife	2	3		1	0	G Duncan	335	Little, Hester
20/08/2016	L	A	Elgin City	1	0		0	0	A Newlands	519	Skelly
27/08/2016	L	H	Stirling Albion	5	3		1	1	G Beaton	601	Linn 3, Skelly, Kader
10/09/2016	L	A	Clyde	2	3		2	2	S Reid	559	Skelly, Linn
17/09/2016	L	H	Annan Athletic	1	1		0	0	G Ross	482	McCord
24/09/2016	L	H	Cowdenbeath	0	0		0	0	M Taylor	588	
01/10/2016	L	A	Edinburgh City	3	3		1	1	S Millar	590	Kader, Little, Scott
15/10/2016	L	H	Forfar Athletic	2	0		0	0	C Napier	862	Cox og, Scott
22/10/2016	SC2	H	Stirling University	3	1		3	1	G Beaton	412	Hamilton, Linn, Doris
29/10/2016	L	A	Berwick Rangers	1`	1		1	0	G Irvine	390	Gold
05/11/2016	L	A	Annan Athletic	2	1		0	1	D Lowe	326	Whatley, Skelly
12/11/2016	L	H	Clyde	4	0		1	0	C Steven	615	Linn, Scott 2, McCord
19/11/2016	L	A	Stirling Albion	2	2		1	0	D Munro	605	Doris, Kader
03/12/2016	L	H	Edinburgh City	0	1		0	0	K Graham	582	
06/12/2016	SC3	A	Clyde	0	5		0	3	G Duncan	390	
10/12/2016	L	A	Forfar Athletic	1	0		0	0	D Lowe	786	McCord
17/12/2016	L	H	Elgin City	3	2		0	1	M Roncone	584	Prunty, Doris 2
24/12/2016	L	A	Cowdenbeath	2	0		0	0	A Newlands	317	Skelly, Doris
02/01/2017	L	H	Montrose	0	0		0	0	S Reid	1731	
07/01/2017	L	A	Edinburgh City	2	0		1	0	G Ross	481	Ferns, Kader
14/01/2017	L	H	Berwick Rangers	4	1		0	1	D Munro	539	McCord 2, Scott, Malin
21/01/2017	L	H	Annan Athletic	1	2		1	1	S Millar	566	Doris
28/01/2017	L	A	Clyde	2	1		1	0	D Lowe	465	Hamilton, Little
04/02/2017	L	H	Forfar Athletic	0	1		0	1	J McKendrick	1008	
11/02/2017	L	A	Montrose	3	1		0	1	C Napier	1002	Smyth, McCord, Kader
18/02/2017	L	H	Stirling Albion	1	1		0	0	R Milne	625	Doris
25/02/2017	L	H	Cowdenbeath	4	1		2	0	M Roncone	519	Scott, Doris, Henderson og, Malin
04/03/2017	L	A	Elgin City	0	0		0	0	M Northcroft	640	
11/03/2017	L	H	Clyde	1	0		1	0	K Graham	566	Whatley
18/03/2017	L	A	Berwick Rangers	2	0		1	0	S Millar	425	Doris, Scott
25/03/2017	L	H	Montrose	0	1		0	0	S Reid	1156	
01/04/2017	L	A	Annan Athletic	5	2		2	2	C Charleston	456	McCord, Doris 3, Prunty
08/04/2017	L	A	Forfar Athletic	1	1		0	0	G Ross	1564	McCord
15/04/2017	L	H	Edinburgh City	0	1		0	0	M Roncone	775	
22/04/2017	L	A	Cowdenbeath	2	1		1	0	D Munro	501	Doris, McCord
29/04/2017	L	H	Elgin City	3	2		1	0	G Irvine	807	McCord 3
06/05/2017	L	A	Stirling Albion	1	1		1	0	K Graham	1748	Scott

FRIENDLIES / OTHER GAMES							
03/07/2016	H	Motherwell	1	0			
05/07/2016	H	Turriff United	2	2			
09/07/2016	H	Raith Rovers	0	4			
23/07/2016	H	Aberdeen	1	4			
10/01/2017	H	Dundee	0	2			749

Date	Comp	H/A	Opponents	F	A		1	2	3	4	5	6	7	8	9	10	11	12	13	14	15	16	17	18
15/07/2016	LC	H	Dundee United	1	1	3-5p	Mutch	Whatley	Phillips	Little	Hamilton	McCord*	Kader	Scott	Linn&	Prunty+	Doris	Thomson*	Gold+	Callaghan&	*Malin*	*Dunlop*	*Hester*	*Gomes*
19/07/2016	LC	A	Dunfermline Athletic	0	3		Mutch	Whatley	Phillips*	Little	Hamilton	McCord+	Kader	Scott	Linn&	Prunty	Doris	Thomson*	Malin+	Callaghan&	*Gold*	*Dunlop*	*Hester*	*Gomes*
27/07/2016	LC	H	Cowdenbeath	0	2		Mutch	Whatley	Phillips	Dunlop*	Hamilton	McCord	Kader	Thomson+	Linn	Prunty	Doris&	Gold*	Callaghan+	Hester&	*Malin*	*Gomes*		
30/07/2016	LC	A	Inverness CT	0	7		Mutch	Whatley	Phillips	Callaghan	Hamilton	Gold	Kader	Thomson*	Linn	Prunty+	Doris	Dunlop*	Hester+	*Gomes*				
02/08/2016	PC	A	Inverness CT U20	3	0		Gomes*	Whatley	Little	Dunlop	Hamilton	McCord	Kader	Scott	Linn+	Prunty	Doris&	Mutch*	Callaghan+	Hester&	*Phillips*	*Gold*		
06/08/2016	L	H	Berwick Rangers	1	1		Mutch	Whatley	Little	Dunlop	Hamilton	McCord	Kader	Scott	Linn	Prunty+	Doris*	Hester*	Gold+	*Malin*	*Phillips*	*Callaghan*	*Gomes*	
13/08/2016	L	A	Montrose	1	1		Mutch	Whatley	Little	Dunlop	Hamilton	McCord	Kader	Sukar	Linn+	Prunty*	Doris&	Gold*	Skelly+	Hester&	*Phillips*	*Callaghan*	*Malin*	*Gomes*
17/08/2016	CC	H	East Fife	2	3		Mutch	Whatley	Little	Phillips	Hamilton	Scott*	Gold+	Sukar	Callaghan	Hester&	Doris	McCord*	Linn+	Dunlop&	*Prunty*	*Thomson*	*Gomes*	
20/08/2016	L	A	Elgin City	1	0		Mutch	Whatley	Little	Phillips*	Hamilton	Callaghan	Gold	Sukar	Linn&	Hester+	Skelly	Doris*	Kader+	Dunlop&	*Prunty*	*Thomson*	*Malin*	*Gomes*
27/08/2016	L	H	Stirling Albion	5	3		Mutch	Whatley	Little	Phillips*	Hamilton	Kader	Gold	Sukar	Linn	Skelly&	Doris+	Brown*	Hester+	Prunty&	*Callaghan*	*McCord*	*Malin*	*Gomes*
10/09/2016	L	A	Clyde	2	3		Mutch	Whatley*	Little	Brown	Hamilton	Kader	Scott	Sukar	Linn	Skelly&	Doris+	Gold*	Prunty+	Hester&	*Callaghan*	*McCord*	*Phillips*	*Gomes*
17/09/2016	L	H	Annan Athletic	1	1		Mutch	Phillips	Little	Brown	Hamilton	Kader+	Scott	McCord	Linn	Skelly*	Prunty&	Gold*	Doris+	Hester&	*Callaghan*	*Malin*	*Dunlop*	*Gomes*
24/09/2016	L	H	Cowdenbeath	0	0		Mutch	Whatley&	Little	Brown	Hamilton	Sukar	Scott	McCord	Linn	Skelly+	Callaghan*	Kader*	Hester+	Doris&	*Prunty*	*Gold*	*Phillips*	*Gomes*
01/10/2016	L	A	Edinburgh City	3	3		Mutch*	Whatley	Little	Kader	Hamilton	Sukar	Scott	McCord	Linn	Skelly&	Prunty+	Gomes*	Doris+	Hester&	*Callaghan*	*Gold*	*Phillips*	*Malin*
15/10/2016	L	H	Forfar Athletic	2	0		Gomes	Whatley	Little	Kader	Hamilton	Phillips	Scott	McCord*	Linn&	Gold	Doris+	Malin*	Skelly+	Prunty&	*Callaghan*	*Dunlop*	*Thomson*	*Mutch*
22/10/2016	SC2	H	Stirling University	3	1		Gomes	Whatley	Little	Kader*	Hamilton	Phillips	Scott	McCord&	Linn	Gold	Doris+	Callaghan*	Skelly+	Malin&	*Dunlop*	*Prunty*	*Thomson*	*Douglas*
29/10/2016	L	A	Berwick Rangers	1`	1		Gomes	Whatley&	Little	Kader	Hamilton	Phillips	Scott	McCord	Linn+	Gold	Doris*	Hester*	Prunty+	Callaghan&	*Malin*	*Sukar*	*Thomson*	*Mutch*
05/11/2016	L	A	Annan Athletic	2	1		Gomes	Whatley	Little	Kader	Hamilton	Sukar	Scott	McCord	Linn	Gold	Prunty	Callaghan*	Doris+	Skelly&	*Malin*	*Phillips*	*Thomson*	*Mutch*
12/11/2016	L	H	Clyde	4	0		Gomes	Whatley	Little	Kader	Hamilton	Sukar	Scott&	McCord	Linn+	Gold	Prunty*	Doris*	Skelly+	Malin&	*Callaghan*	*Philips*	*Thomson*	*Stewart*
19/11/2016	L	A	Stirling Albion	2	2		Gomes	Whatley	Little	Kader+	Hamilton	Sukar	Scott	McCord&	Linn*	Gold	Doris	Malin*	Callaghan+	Phillips&	*Dunlop*	*Prunty*	*Mutch*	
03/12/2016	L	H	Edinburgh City	0	1		Gomes	Whatley	Dunlop	Kader+	Hamilton	Sukar	Scott	McCord*	Linn	Gold	Doris&	Skelly*	Malin+	Prunty&	*Phillips*	*Callaghan*	*Thomson*	*Mutch*
06/12/2016	SC3	A	Clyde	0	5		Gomes	Whatley	Little	Kader&	Hamilton	Sukar	Scott	McCord*	Linn	Gold	Doris+	Phillips*	Skelly+	Prunty&	*Malin*	*Callaghan*	*Dunlop*	*Douglas*
10/12/2016	L	A	Forfar Athletic	1	0		Gomes	Whatley	Little	Skelly	Hamilton	Sukar	Scott*	McCord	Linn&	Gold+	Doris	Kader*	Dunlop+	Prunty&	*Malin*	*Callaghan*	*Phillips*	*Mutch*
17/12/2016	L	H	Elgin City	3	2		Gomes	Whatley	Little	Skelly	Hamilton	Sukar	Prunty+	McCord*	Linn&	Gold	Doris	Malin*	Kader+	Dunlop&	*Thomson*	*Callaghan*	*Phillips*	*Mutch*
24/12/2016	L	A	Cowdenbeath	2	0		Gomes	Whatley	Little	Skelly	Hamilton	Phillips	Prunty*	McCord+	Linn&	Gold	Doris	Kader*	Callaghan+	Malin&	*Thomson*	*Hester*	*Dunlop*	*Douglas*
02/01/2017	L	H	Montrose	0	0		Gomes	Whatley	Little	Skelly+	Hamilton	Phillips	Prunty*	McCord&	Linn	Gold	Doris	Kader*	Malin+	Scott&	*Hester*	*Callaghan*	*Dunlop*	*Douglas*
07/01/2017	L	A	Edinburgh City	2	0		Gomes	Whatley	Little	Kader	Hamilton	Sukar	Ferns&	McCord*	Linn	Gold	Doris+	Malin*	Prunty+	Scott&	*Callaghan*	*Thomson*	*Stewart*	
14/01/2017	L	H	Berwick Rangers	4	1		Gomes	Whatley	Little	Kader*	Hamilton	Sukar	Ferns+	McCord&	Linn	Gold	Doris	Skelly*	Scott+	Malin&	*Prunty*	*Thomson*	*Stewart*	
21/01/2017	L	H	Annan Athletic	1	2		Gomes	Whatley	Little	Kader+	Hamilton	Sukar&	Ferns*	McCord	Linn	Gold	Doris	Scott*	Skelly+	McCallum&	*Hodge*	*Malin*	*Prunty*	*Gill*
28/01/2017	L	A	Clyde	2	1		Gomes	Whatley	Little	Hodge	Hamilton	Sukar	Skelly	Scott*	Linn+	Gold	Doris&	Prunty*	Kader+	Malin&	*Thomson*	*McCallum*	*Gill*	
04/02/2017	L	H	Forfar Athletic	0	1		Gomes	Whatley	Little	Hodge	Hamilton	Sukar	Skelly*	Ferns+	Linn	Gold	Doris	McCallum*	Kader+	*Prunty*	*Thomson*	*Malin*	*Smyth*	*Gill*
11/02/2017	L	A	Montrose	3	1		Gomes	Whatley	Smyth	Hodge	Hamilton	Sukar+	Skelly	Ferns*	Linn&	Gold	Doris	Prunty*	McCord+	Kader&	*Hester*	*Malin*	*McCallum*	*Gill*
18/02/2017	L	H	Stirling Albion	1	1		Gomes	Whatley	Little	Hodge	Hamilton	Kader	Prunty+	McCord	Linn&	Gold*	Doris	Smyth*	Ferns+	Skelly&	*Sukar*	*Malin*	*McCallum*	*Gill*
25/02/2017	L	H	Cowdenbeath	4	1		Gomes	Whatley	Little	Hodge*	Hamilton	Sukar	Malin	McCord&	Linn	Scott+	Doris	Skelly*	McCallum+	Smyth&	*Kader*	*Prunty*	*Ferns*	*Gill*
04/03/2017	L	A	Elgin City	0	0		Gomes	Whatley	Little	Hodge	Hamilton	Sukar	Malin*	McCord	Linn	Scott+	Doris&	Kader*	Smyth+	Ferns&	*McCallum*	*Prunty*	*Gold*	*Gill*
11/03/2017	L	H	Clyde	1	0		Gomes	Whatley	Little	Hodge&	Hamilton	Sukar	Gold	McCord	Linn*	Scott+	Doris	Kader*	Prunty+	Ferns&	*McCallum*	*Malin*	*Smyth*	*Stewart*
18/03/2017	L	A	Berwick Rangers	2	0		Gomes	Whatley	Little	Hodge	Hamilton	Malin+	Gold	McCord*	Linn	Scott	Doris	Smyth*	Kader+	*Prunty*	*McCallum*	*Sukar*	*Stewart*	
25/03/2017	L	H	Montrose	0	1		Gomes	Whatley	Little	Hodge*	Hamilton	Sukar	Gold	McCord	Linn&	Kader+	Doris	Prunty*	McCallum+	Ferns&	*Malin*	*Smyth*	*Douglas*	
01/04/2017	L	A	Annan Athletic	5	2		Gomes	Whatley	Little	Hodge*	Hamilton	Prunty&	Gold	McCord	Linn+	Kader+	Doris	Sukar*	Ferns+	McCallum&	*Hester*	*Smyth*	*Douglas*	*Scott*
08/04/2017	L	A	Forfar Athletic	1	1		Gomes	Whatley	Little	Hodge	Hamilton	Scott*	Gold	McCord&	Linn	Kader+	Doris	Prunty*	Ferns+	Malin&	*Sukar*	*Smyth*	*Douglas*	*McCallum*
15/04/2017	L	H	Edinburgh City	0	1		Gomes	Whatley	Little	Scott*	Hamilton	Sukar	Gold	McCord	Linn	Kader	Doris	Prunty*	*Smyth*	*Malin*	*McCallum*	*Stewart*		
22/04/2017	L	A	Cowdenbeath	2	1		Gomes	Whatley	Little	Hodge	Hamilton	Smyth	Gold	McCord+	Linn*	Scott&	Doris	Ferns*	Malin+	Prunty&	*McCallum*	*Sukar*	*Kader*	*Douglas*
29/04/2017	L	H	Elgin City	3	2		Gomes	Whatley	Little	Hodge	Hamilton	Smyth	Gold	McCord+	Linn	Scott	Doris*	Prunty*	Sukar+	*Kader*	*Malin*	*Ferns*	*McCallum*	*Douglas*
06/05/2017	L	A	Stirling Albion	1	1		Gomes	Whatley	Little	Hodge*	Hamilton	Smyth	Gold	McCord	Linn+	Scott&	Doris	Sukar*	Kader+	Prunty&	*Malin*	*Ferns*	*McCallum*	*Douglas*

Ayr United FC 2016/17

Founded	1910
Ground	Somerset Park
Postcode	KA8 9NB
Capacity	10185
Tel	01292 263435
Closest Railway Station	Ayr
Record Attendance	25225, v Rangers, Lge, 13/9/1969
Record Win	11-1 v Dumbarton, LC 13/8/1952
Record Defeat	0-9, v Rangers 1929, v Hearts 1931, v Third Lanark 1954
Most Goals in a Season	66 Jimmy Smith, 1927/8
Most Goals in Career	213 Peter Price
Chairman	Lachlan Cameron
Managing Director	Lewis Grant
Operations Manager	Tracy McTrusty
Manager	Ian McCall
Assistant Manager	Neil Scally
Colours 2016/17 Top	Black and White Hoops
Shorts	Black
Sponsor	Bodog
Manufacturer	Adidas
Change Colours 2016/17 Top	Red with Black flash
Shorts	Black
Nicknames	Honest Men
Web	www.ayrunitedfc.co.uk
Match Programme 2016/17	£2 (Garthland)

Having gone up through the play offs, Ayr were always considered a possibility for the drop. However, in the early part of the season they looked to have put enough distance between themselves and St Mirren to ensure safety. What followed was more of a massive improvement by the Paisley side rather than a drastic slump by Ayr - but the final tables doe not lie. The outcome will be a bitter disappointment to Ayr's loyal fans who believe that their club should be higher than tier three of Scottish football. It's difficult to pinpoi8nt but there certainly seems to have been a malaise of some sort at Somerset Park for a long time now.

Ayr failed to win in their last seven games of the season. A 2-6 defeat at the hands of St Mirren in April was probably the key result. That handed the psychological advantage to a St Mirren team that showed more fight at the important times.

PREDICTION FOR 2017/18

Ayr are gambling on remaining full time in League One. Some of their higher earners have been moved on and they will focus on a smaller group of players, hoping that the right blend of youth and experience will seem them through. On paper they should be promotion challengers - anything less than a play off spot will be abject failure.

Surname	First Name	DOB	SQ	Nat	Pos	L			SC			LC			CC			UNS	Signed	Previous Club	Notes	Contract
						A	S	G	A	S	G	A	S	G	A	S	G					
Adams	Jamie	26/08/1987	16	SCO	M	16	2	2	2	1		4						3	2015	Wigtown & Bladnoch		End 2017/18
Avci	Lyall	01/01/1999		SCO / TUR	GK													1	2016	Ayr United Youths		End 2017/18
Balatoni	Konrad	27/01/1991	22	SCO / ENG	D	30		1	6		1				3		1		2016	Kilmarnock	Released June 2017	[redacted]
Balfour	Kieran	27/09/1999		SCO	M													1	2016	Rangers U20		End 2017/18
Boyle	Paddy	20/03/1987	3	SCO	D	26	3		5			5			2			6	2015	Airdrieonians		End 2017/18
Cairney	Paul	29/08/1997	14	SCO	M	27	3	5	3	1	1	4	1		2	1		3	2016	Stranraer		OOC
Crawford	Robbie	22/01/1994	8	SCO	M	24	3	2	3			5		1	1	1		3	2010	Ayr United Youths		End 2017/18
Devlin	Nicky	17/10/1993	2	SCO	D	34			6			5			3				2014	Stenhousemuir	OOC June 2017, joined Walsall	[redacted]
Docherty	Ross	23/01/1993	23	SCO	M	29		2	6			4			3				2015	Airdrieonians		End 2017/18
Donald	Michael	20/01/1989	11	SCO	M	1	5		1			2	1			3		13	2013	Maybole	Freed Jan 2017, joined Stranraer	[redacted]
El Alagui	Farid	10/02/1985	15	FRA / MOR	F	8	3	3										2	2017	Dunfermline Athletic	Freed May 2017	
Fleming	Greg	27/09/1986	1	SCO	GK	36			6			4			3			1	2015	Stenhousemuir	Transferred to Peterhead July 2017	
Forrest	Alan	09/09/1996	10	SCO	F	24	10	6	1	5		2		2	3		1	1	2013	Ayr United Youth		End 2017/18
Gilmour	Brian	08/05/1987	4	SCO	M	19	6	1	4	2		2	2	1	2			7	2013	AK Akureyri		End 2017/18
Harkins	Gary	02/01/1985	12	SCO	M	30	2	5	6						2		1	3	2016	Dundee	Transferred to Morton June 2017	[redacted]
Hart	Jordan	22/01/1996	19	SCO	GK		1					1						47	2016	Annan Athletic		End 2017/18
Johnstone	Andrew	30/09/1998		SCO	D								2					2	2016	Ayr United Youths	Freed Dec 2016, joined Kirkintilloch RR	[redacted]
McCracken	Craig	22/03/1996		SCO	D													5	2015	Ayr United Youths	Freed Aug 2016 joined Auchinleck Talbot	
McDaid	Declan	22/11/1995	11	SCO	F	2	5		2		1							1	2017	Partick Thistle		End 2017/18
McGuffie	Craig	15/12/1997	21	SCO	M	6	20		3	3	1	2	3	1	3		1	7	2015	Glenafton Athletic		End 2017/18
McKenna	Scott	12/11/1996	26	SCO	D	11		1	2						1			6	2016	Aberdeen (OL)	Nov 2016-Jan 2017	[redacted]
McKenzie	Sean	26/09/1997	17	SC)	F					1								5	2017	Cumnock	Freed May 2017, rejoined Cumnock	
Meggatt	Darryl	20/10/1990	18	SCO	D	31			4			5			2	1		4	2016	Dundee	Freed May 2017	
Moore	Craig	16/08/1994	9	SCO	F	9	4	2	3		1	1						1	2016	Motherwell (OL)	Aug 2016-May 2017	
Murphy	Peter	27/10/1980	6	ROI	D	9			2	1		5		1	1			24	2014	Celtic Nation	Appointed Manager Annan Ath June 2017	
Murphy	Leon	18/04/1999		SCO	M													1	2016	Ayr United Youths		End 2017/18
Nisbet	Kevin	08/03/1997	17	SCO	F	11	9	2											2016	Partick Thistle (OL)	Aug 2016-Jan 2017	[redacted]
O'Connell	Andy	09/03/1993		ROI	F	1	7		1		1	1	2			3	1	7	2016	Cobh Ramblers	Freed Jan 2017	
Rose	Michael	11/10/1995	5	SCO	D	10	10	1		4								15	2016	Aberdeen		End 2017/18
Thomas	Jamie	10/01/1997		WAL / ENG	F		3					3			1			5	2016	Burnley (OL)	Jul-Oct 2016	[redacted]
Wardrope	Michael	17/12/1996	20	SCO	M	2	3			2	1		3		1			20	2013	Ayr United Youths	Freed May 2017	
NEW SIGNINGS																						
Moore	Craig	16/08/1994		SCO	F														2017	Motherwell		End 2017/18
Moffat	Michael	17/01/1984			F														2017	Dunfermline Ath		End 2018/19
Geggan	Andy	08/05/1987			M														2017	Dunfermline Ath		End 2018/19
Higgins	Chris	04/07/1985			D														2017	Queen of the South		End 2017/18
Reid	Craig				D														2017	Peterhead		

Source of Birthdates: Ayr United website and transfermarkt.com

Date	Comp	H/A	Opponents	F	A		HT		Referee	Crowd	Scorers
16/07/2016	LC	H	Hamilton Accies	2	1		1	0	W Collum	994	Forrest, Crawford
19/07/2016	LC	H	St Mirren	0	1		0	0	J Beaton	2098	
23/07/2016	LC	H	Edinburgh City	1	0		1	0	B Cook	862	Gilmour
26/07/2016	LC	A	Livingston	2	0		1	0	D Lowe	643	Murphy, McGuffie
06/08/2016	L	H	Raith Rovers	0	2		0	1	E Anderson	1550	
10/08/2016	LC1	H	Aberdeen	1	2		1	2	A Muir	2653	Forrest
13/08/2016	L	A	Queen of the South	1	4		0	2	S Finnie	1982	Nisbet
20/08/2016	L	A	Dundee United	0	3		0	2	G Aitken	6427	
27/08/2016	L	H	St Mirren	1	1		1	0	C Allan	2165	Adams
04/09/2016	CC3	H	Airdrieonians	3	2	AET	2	1	B Cook	1135	McGuffie, Forrest, Balatoni
10/09/2016	L	H	Morton	2	1		0	0	J McKendrick	1441	Cairney, Forrest
17/09/2016	L	A	Hibernian	2	1		0	0	N Walsh	15056	Balatoni, Gilmour
24/09/2016	L	A	Falkirk	0	2		0	0	W Collum	4345	
01/10/2016	L	H	Dunfermline Athletic	0	0		0	0	D Robertson	2883	
07/10/2016	CC4	H	Falkirk	1	0	AET	0	0	A Muir	1247	Harkins
15/10/2016	L	A	Dumbarton	3	0		1	0	G Duncan	1005	Forrest 3
22/10/2016	L	H	Queen of the South	1	0		0	0	J Beaton	1842	Cairney
29/10/2016	L	A	Morton	1	2		1	0	M Northcroft	1859	Nisbet
05/11/2016	L	H	Hibernian	0	3		0	1	K Clancy	3100	
13/11/2016	CC4	A	St Mirren	1	2		0	0	C Allan	2199	O'Connell
19/11/2016	L	H	Falkirk	0	1		0	1	G Duncan	1414	
22/11/2016	L	A	Raith Rovers	1	1		0	1	C Charleston	1241	Harkins
29/11/2016	SC3	A	Brechin City	1	0		0	0	A Muir	308	O'Connell
03/12/2016	L	A	Dunfermline Athletic	1	1		0	1	B Cook	3250	Forrest
10/12/2016	L	H	Dundee United	0	1		0	1	W Collum	2049	
17/12/2016	L	A	St Mirren	1	1		0	0	G Aitken	3124	Cairney
24/12/2016	L	H	Dumbarton	4	4		2	1	C Charleston	1441	McKenna, Harkins, Forrest, Cairney
31/12/2016	L	A	Queen of the South	0	0		0	0	S Kirkland	1594	
07/01/2017	L	H	Dunfermline Athletic	0	2		0	2	C Thomson	2261	
14/01/2017	L	A	Falkirk	1	1		1	1	B Madden	5038	Harkins
21/01/2017	SC4	H	Queen's Park	0	0		0	0	B Cook	1326	
24/01/2017	SC4R	A	Queen's Park	2	2	aet, 5-4p	1	2	B Cook	1026	Moore, Balatoni
28/01/2017	L	H	Morton	1	4		1	3	D Robertson	1576	Adams
04/02/2017	L	A	Hibernian	1	1		1	0	C Allan	14349	Crawford
11/02/2017	SC5R	H	Clyde	1	1		0	0	S Finnie	1554	Cairney
14/02/2017	SC5R	A	Clyde	2	1	aet	1	0	S Finnie	965	McDaid, Wardrope
18/02/2017	L	A	Dumbarton	2	2		0	0	J McKendrick	1198	Moore, Rose
25/02/2017	L	H	St Mirren	0	2		0	0	C Thomson	2712	
28/02/2017	L	H	Raith Rovers	1	0		0	0	W Collum	1103	El Alagui
04/03/2017	SC6	A	Hibernian	1	3		1	2	N Walsh	13602	McGuffie
11/03/2017	L	H	Falkirk	1	4		0	1	S McLean	1614	Harkins
18/03/2017	L	A	Dunfermline Athletic	1	0		0	0	B Madden	3276	Docherty
25/03/2017	L	H	Dumbarton	2	1		1	1	C Charleston	1608	El Alagui, Crawford
28/03/2017	L	A	Dundee United	1	2		0	1	B Cook	4661	Harkins
01/04/2017	L	A	St Mirren	2	6		0	4	G Duncan	4620	Cairney, El Alagui
08/04/2017	L	H	Queen of the South	0	2		0	0	A Newlands	1476	
15/04/2017	L	H	Dundee United	0	0		0	0	C Allan*	1205	* replaced by G Irvine 30 mins
22/04/2017	L	A	Morton	1	1		1	1	S Kirkland	2390	Moore
29/04/2017	L	H	Hibernian	0	4		0	2	S Finnie	2152	
06/05/2017	L	A	Raith Rovers	1	2		0	0	S McLean	3064	Docherty

FRIENDLIES / OTHER GAMES					
02/07/2016	A	Stenhousemuir	2	0	
09/07/2016	N	South Shields	0	2	Gretna Tnt
10/07/2016	A	Gretna	8	0	Gretna Tnt
11/07/2016	A	Upper Annandale	4	0	U20
25/07/2016	A	Muirkirk	2	0	U20
27/07/2016	A	Maybole	2	2	U20

Date	Comp	H/A	Opponents	F	A		1	2	3	4	5	6	7	8	9	10	11	12	13	14	15	16	17	18
16/07/2016	LC	H	Hamilton Accies	2	1		Fleming	Devlin	Boyle	Murphy	Meggatt	Gilmour&	Crawford	Cairney*	Docherty	Forrest	Adams+	McGuffie*	Wardrope+	Johnston&	*McCracken*	*Hart*		
19/07/2016	LC	H	St Mirren	0	1		Fleming	Devlin	Boyle	Murphy	Meggatt	Donald+	Crawford	Cairney	Docherty	Moore	Adams*	Gilmour*	McGuffie+	*Johnston*	*McCracken*	*Wardrope*	*Hart*	
23/07/2016	LC	H	Edinburgh City	1	0		Hart	Devlin	Boyle	Murphy	Meggatt	Gilmour*	Crawford	McGuffie&	Docherty	Thomas	O'Connell+	Cairney*	Donald+	Wardrope&	*McCracken*	*Johnston*	*Fleming*	
26/07/2016	LC	A	Livingston	2	0		Fleming	Devlin	Boyle	Murphy*	Meggatt	Donald	Crawford	Cairney	Docherty+	Thomas&	Adams	McGuffie*	Wardrope+	O'Connell&	*McCracken*	*Rose*	*Hart*	
06/08/2016	L	H	Raith Rovers	0	2		Fleming	Devlin	Boyle	Murphy	Meggatt	Donald*	Crawford+	Cairney	Docherty	Forrest	Adams&	McGuffie*	Thomas+	O'Connell&	*McCracken*	*Rose*	*Hart*	*Wardrope*
10/08/2016	LC1	H	Aberdeen	1	2		Fleming	Devlin	Boyle	Murphy	Meggatt	Thomas*	Crawford&	Cairney	McGuffie+	Forrest	Adams	Gilmour*	O'Connell+	Johnston&	*Donald*	*Rose*	*Hart*	*Wardrope*
13/08/2016	L	A	Queen of the South	1	4		Fleming	Devlin	Boyle	Rose	Meggatt	Harkins&	Crawford+	Cairney*	Gilmour	Docherty	Nisbet	Forrest*	Adams+	McGuffie&	*Donald*	*Thomas*	*Hart*	*O'Connell*
20/08/2016	L	A	Dundee United	0	3		Fleming	Devlin	Boyle	Murphy	Docherty	Harkins	Crawford*	Cairney	Adams	Forrest+	Nisbet&	Gilmour*	Thomas+	McGuffie&	*Meggatt*	*Rose*	*Hart*	*O'Connell*
27/08/2016	L	H	St Mirren	1	1		Fleming	Devlin	Boyle	Murphy	Meggatt	Harkins	Gilmour	Cairney+	Adams	Docherty	Nisbet*	Forrest*	Crawford+	*McGuffie*	*Thomas*	*Rose*	*Hart*	*O'Connell*
04/09/2016	CC3	H	Airdrieonians	3	2	AET	Fleming	Devlin	Boyle	Balatoni	Meggatt	Wardrope*	Gilmour	McGuffie&	Thomas+	Docherty	Forrest	Cairney*	O'Connell+	Donald&	*Murphy*	*Rose*	*Hart*	*Crawford*
10/09/2016	L	H	Morton	2	1		Fleming	Devlin	Boyle	Balatoni	Meggatt	Harkins+	Gilmour&	Cairney*	Adams	Docherty	Forrest	Nisbet*	McGuffie+	O'Connell&	*Murphy*	*Thomas*	*Hart*	*Crawford*
17/09/2016	L	A	Hibernian	2	1		Fleming	Devlin	Boyle	Balatoni	Meggatt	Harkins+	Gilmour	Cairney*	Adams	Docherty	Forrest&	Nisbet*	McGuffie+	Crawford&	*Murphy*	*Thomas*	*Hart*	*Donald*
24/09/2016	L	A	Falkirk	0	2		Fleming	Devlin	Boyle	Balatoni	Meggatt	Harkins+	Gilmour	Crawford	Nisbet&	Docherty	Forrest*	Cairney*	Thomas+	McGuffie&	*Rose*	*Murphy*	*Hart*	*Donald*
01/10/2016	L	H	Dunfermline Athletic	0	0		Fleming	Devlin	Boyle	Balatoni	Meggatt	Harkins	Gilmour	Crawford&	Adams+	Docherty	Forrest*	Nisbet*	McGuffie+	Cairney&	*Murphy*	*Thomas*	*Hart*	*Donald*
07/10/2016	CC4	H	Falkirk	1	0	AET	Fleming	Devlin	Murphy	Balatoni	Meggatt	Harkins	Gilmour+	Cairney&	McGuffie*	Docherty	Forrest	Donald*	O'Connell+	Crawford&	*Rose*	*Wardrope*	*Hart*	
15/10/2016	L	A	Dumbarton	3	0		Fleming	Devlin	Murphy	Balatoni	Meggatt	Harkins&	Gilmour	Cairney*	Crawford	Docherty	Forrest+	Nisbet*	Donald+	McGuffie&	*Boyle*	*O'Connell*	*Hart*	
22/10/2016	L	H	Queen of the South	1	0		Fleming	Devlin	Murphy	Balatoni	Meggatt	Harkins	Gilmour	Cairney&	Crawford*	Docherty	Forrest+	Nisbet*	Donald+	Adams&	*Boyle*	*O'Connell*	*Hart*	*McGuffie*
29/10/2016	L	A	Morton	1	2		Fleming	Devlin	Murphy	Balatoni	Meggatt	Harkins	Gilmour	Cairney+	Adams*	Docherty	Nisbet&	Crawford*	Donald+	Forrest&	*Boyle*	*O'Connell*	*Hart*	*McGuffie*
05/11/2016	L	H	Hibernian	0	3		Fleming	Devlin	Boyle	Balatoni	Meggatt	Harkins&	Gilmour*	Cairney	Adams+	Docherty	Forrest	McGuffie*	Nisbet+	O'Connell&	*Murphy*	*Crawford*	*Hart*	*Donald*
13/11/2016	CC4	A	St Mirren	1	2		Fleming	Devlin	Boyle*	Balatoni	McKenna	Crawford	McGuffie&	Cairney	Harkins	Docherty	Forrest+	Meggatt*	O'Connell+	Donald&	*Murphy*	*Rose*	*Hart*	*Wardrope*
19/11/2016	L	H	Falkirk	0	1		Fleming	Devlin	Boyle	Balatoni	McKenna	Crawford+	McGuffie	Cairney	Harkins	Nisbet	Forrest*	O'Connell*	Rose+	*Donald*	*Murphy*	*Meggatt*	*Hart*	*Wardrope*
22/11/2016	L	A	Raith Rovers	1	1		Fleming	Devlin	Meggatt	Balatoni	McKenna	Crawford	McGuffie+	Cairney	Harkins	Nisbet&	Wardrope*	Forrest*	Rose+	O'Connell&	*Donald*	*Boyle*	*Hart*	
29/11/2016	SC3	A	Brechin City	1	0		Fleming	Devlin	Meggatt	Balatoni	Boyle	Crawford	McGuffie+	Adams*	Harkins	O'Connell&	Docherty	Forrest*	Gilmour+	Rose&	*Donald*	*Wardrope*	*Avci*	
03/12/2016	L	A	Dunfermline Athletic	1	1		Fleming	Devlin	McKenna	Balatoni	Boyle	Crawford	Forrest	Adams*	Harkins	Nisbet+	Docherty	Gilmour*	O'Connell+	*Rose*	*Donald*	*Wardrope*	*Meggatt*	*Hart*
10/12/2016	L	H	Dundee United	0	1		Fleming	Devlin	Meggatt	Balatoni	McKenna	Crawford&	Forrest	Adams*	Harkins	Cairney+	Docherty	O'Connell*	Nisbet+	Gilmour&	*Boyle*	*Rose*	*McGuffie*	*Hart*
17/12/2016	L	A	St Mirren	1	1		Fleming	Devlin	Meggatt*	Balatoni	McKenna	Crawford	Forrest+	Adams	Harkins&	Cairney	Docherty	Boyle*	Nisbet+	Rose&	*Gilmour*	*O'Connell*	*McGuffie*	*Hart*
24/12/2016	L	H	Dumbarton	4	4		Fleming	Rose	Meggatt	Balatoni	McKenna	Crawford	O'Connell+	Nisbet*	Harkins	Cairney	Docherty	Boyle*	Forrest+	*Murphy*	*Gilmour*	*Donald*	*McGuffie*	*Hart*
31/12/2016	L	A	Queen of the South	0	0		Fleming	Boyle	Meggatt	Balatoni	McKenna	Crawford	Forrest&	Gilmour*	Harkins	Cairney+	Docherty	Nisbet*	McGuffie+	Donald&	*Rose*	*Murphy*	*Wardrope*	*Hart*
07/01/2017	L	H	Dunfermline Athletic	0	2		Fleming	Boyle	Devlin	Balatoni	McKenna	Crawford	Forrest&	Adams+	Harkins	Cairney	Nisbet*	Gilmour*	Rose+	Donald&	*Meggatt*	*Murphy*	*Wardrope*	*Hart*
14/01/2017	L	A	Falkirk	1	1		Fleming	Boyle	Devlin	Balatoni	McKenna	Crawford	Gilmour*	Docherty	Harkins	Cairney	Nisbet+	Rose*	Forrest+	*Donald*	*Wardrope*	*Murphy*	*Hart*	
21/01/2017	SC4	H	Queen's Park	0	0		Fleming	Boyle	Devlin	Balatoni	McKenna	Crawford	Gilmour*	Docherty	Harkins	Cairney+	Moore&	Forrest*	Adams+	McGuffie&	*Rose*	*Murphy*	*Hart*	*Donald*
24/01/2017	SC4R	A	Queen's Park	2	2	aet, 5-4p	Fleming	Boyle	Devlin^	Balatoni	Murphy	Crawford	Gilmour*	Docherty	Harkins	Donald+	Moore&	Cairney*	Forrest+	McGuffie&	*Rose^*	*McKenna*	*Hart*	*Adams*
28/01/2017	L	H	Morton	1	4		Fleming	Rose*	Devlin	Balatoni	Meggatt	Crawford+	McKenna	Cairney&	Harkins	Adams	Moore	McGuffie*	Forrest+	Wardrope&	*Boyle*	*Gilmour*	*Hart*	*Murphy*
04/02/2017	L	A	Hibernian	1	1		Fleming	Boyle	Devlin	Balatoni	Meggatt	Crawford	McDaid	Cairney+	Harkins&	Adams*	Docherty	Gilmour*	McGuffie+	Rose&	*Wardrope*	*Forrest*	*Hart*	*Murphy*
11/02/2017	SC5R	H	Clyde	1	1		Fleming	Boyle*	Devlin	Balatoni	Meggatt	McGuffie&	McDaid	Cairney	Harkins	Adams+	Docherty	Murphy*	Gilmour+	Forrest&	*Wardrope*	*Rose*	*Hart*	*McKenna*
14/02/2017	SC5R	A	Clyde	2	1	aet	Fleming	Murphy	Devlin	Balatoni	Meggatt	Gilmour&	McDaid	Cairney^	Harkins+	Forrest*	Docherty	Rose*	McGuffie+	McKenzie&	*Wardrope^*	*Adams*	*Hart*	*McKenna*
18/02/2017	L	A	Dumbarton	2	2		Fleming	Boyle	Devlin	Balatoni	Meggatt	Adams	McDaid*	Cairney	Harkins&	El Alagui+	Docherty	Moore*	Rose+	McGuffie&	*Wardrope*	*Murphy*	*Hart*	*McKenna*
25/02/2017	L	H	St Mirren	0	2		Fleming	Murphy&	Devlin	Balatoni	Meggatt	Adams*	Boyle+	Cairney	Harkins	El Alagui	Moore	Rose*	Wardrope+	Forrest&	*Gilmour*	*McGuffie*	*Hart*	*McKenna*
28/02/2017	L	H	Raith Rovers	1	0		Fleming	McKenna	Devlin	Balatoni	Meggatt	Wardrope+	Gilmour	Cairney*	McGuffie&	El Alagui	Forrest	Rose*	Moore+	Boyle&	*Harkins*	*McKenzie*	*Hart*	
04/03/2017	SC6	A	Hibernian	1	3		Fleming	McKenna	Devlin	Balatoni	Meggatt	Boyle	Gilmour	Docherty+	Harkins	McGuffie&	Moore*	Forrest*	Rose+	Wardrope&	*Balfour*	*McKenzie*	*Hart*	*Murphy*
11/03/2017	L	H	Falkirk	1	4		Fleming	Crawford	Devlin	Balatoni	Meggatt	Boyle	Gilmour*	El Alagui	Harkins	McGuffie&	Moore+	Rose*	Forrest+	McDaid&	*Wardrope*	*McKenzie*	*Hart*	*Murphy*
18/03/2017	L	A	Dunfermline Athletic	1	0		Fleming	Crawford	Devlin	Balatoni	Meggatt	Boyle	Gilmour	El Alagui+	Rose	Docherty*	Forrest&	McGuffie*	Moore+	Harkins&	*Wardrope*	*McKenzie*	*Hart*	*McKenna*
25/03/2017	L	H	Dumbarton	2	1		Fleming	Crawford	Devlin	Balatoni	Meggatt	Boyle	Gilmour	El Alagui	Rose	Docherty*	Forrest+	McGuffie*	Moore+	*Harkins*	*Wardrope*	*Murphy*	*Hart*	*Cairney*
28/03/2017	L	A	Dundee United	1	2		Fleming	Crawford&	Devlin	Balatoni	Meggatt	Boyle	Gilmour	Moore+	Rose	Docherty	Harkins*	El Alagui*	Forrest+	McGuffie&	*Wardrope*	*Murphy*	*Hart*	*Cairney*
01/04/2017	L	A	St Mirren	2	6		Fleming	Crawford&	Devlin	Balatoni*	Meggatt	Boyle	Gilmour+	Forrest	Rose	Docherty	El Alagui	McGuffie*	Cairney+	Wardrope&	*Harkins*	*Murphy*	*Hart*	*Moore*
08/04/2017	L	H	Queen of the South	0	2		Fleming	Crawford	Devlin	Murphy	Meggatt	Boyle	Cairney+	Forrest&	Moore	Docherty	El Alagui*	Harkins*	McGuffie+	McDaid&	*Gilmour*	*Rose*	*Hart*	*Wardrope*
15/04/2017	L	H	Dundee United	0	0		Fleming	Rose	Devlin	Murphy	Meggatt	McGuffie*	Cairney+	Forrest	Moore	Docherty	Harkins	McDaid*	*El Alagui*	*McKenzie*	*Gilmour*	*Wardrope*	*Hart*	*L Murphy*
22/04/2017	L	A	Morton	1	1		Fleming	Rose	Devlin	Balatoni	Meggatt	Boyle	Cairney*	Forrest+	Moore	Docherty	Harkins	McGuffie*	McDaid+	*Murphy*	*Gilmour*	*El Alagui*	*Hart*	
29/04/2017	L	H	Hibernian	0	4		Fleming	Rose*	Devlin	Balatoni	Meggatt	Boyle	Cairney+	Forrest&	Moore	Docherty	Harkins	McGuffie*	El Alagui+	Gilmour&	*Murphy*	*McDaid*	*Hart*	
06/05/2017	L	A	Raith Rovers	1	2		Fleming&	McGuffie+	Devlin	Balatoni	Meggatt	Boyle	Gilmour	Forrest	Moore*	Docherty	Harkins	McDaid*	El Alagui+	Hart&	*Murphy*	*Cairney*	*Adams*	

Berwick Rangers FC 2016/17

Founded	1884
Ground	Shielfield Park
Postcode	TD12 2EF
Tel	01289 307424
Capacity	4131
Closest Railway Station	Berwick-upon-Tweed
Record Attendance	13283, v Rangers, SC 28/1/1967
Record Win	8-1 v Forfar, Lge, 25/12/1965;
	v Vale of Leithen, SC, 1966/7
Record Defeat	1-9 v Hamilton Accies, Lge 9/8/1980
Most League Goals in a Season	33 Ken Bowron, 1963/4
Most Appearances Career	439 Eric Tait
Chairman	Len Eyre
Football Secretary	Dennis McCleary
Manager	John Coughlin
Assistant Manager	Myles Allan
Colours 2016/17 Top	Black and Gold stripes
Shorts	Black
Sponsor	Implenergy
Manufacturer	Zoo Sport
Change Colours 2016/17 Top	Sky Blue
Shorts	Sky Blue
Nicknames	Borderers, Wee Rangers, Black & Gold
Web	www.berwickrangersfc.co.uk
Match Programme 2016/17	The Black and Gold £2.50

Berwick are one of the clubs who have had to come to terms with the prospect of relegation from the SPFL. The advent of the Pyramid Play Off has injected urgency and tension to the lower reaches of League Two. Had it not been for the inadequacies of Cowdenbeath, then it could well have been Berwick facing the prospect of relegation from the SPFL at the end of last season.

Despite that, John Coughlin does a decent job in difficult circumstances. Resources are scarce but the club does its best to compete and to operate a decent youth policy.

The Cup competitions, sometimes a source of welcome income, proved disastrous. Berwick were knocked out at home by Spartans in the Challenge Cup and by Hawick Royal Albert in the Scottish Cup. At the same time they were capable of beating the promotion contenders.

PREDICTION FOR 2017/18

Hard to see anything but more of the same inconsistency at Berwick. More likely to be near the foot of the table than the top but unlikely to finish bottom.

Stamford Bridge to Shielfield

Kevin McKinlay, who belongs to Stirling, was signed up by Chelsea as a youth player. He was a regular in their youth team during 2002/3 and 2003/4 - his team mates included Carlton Cole, Filipe Morias and Yves Makalambay.

Kevin McKinlay		L			LC			SC			OC			Total		
Season	Club	A	S	G	A	S	G	A	S	G	A	S	G	A	S	G
ex Hutcheson Vale																
2003/4	Ross County													0	0	0
2004/5	Ross County	1	3											1	3	0
2005/6	Ross County	14	13	1	1	1		3		1		2		18	16	2
2006/7	Ross County	27	3	5	1		1	1			5		3	34	3	9
2007/8	Ross County													0	0	0
2007/8	Partick Thistle	18	8	3	1			2	3		1	1		22	12	3
2008/9	Partick Thistle	12	17	2	2	1		2			2	2		18	20	2
2009/10	Morton	7	1											7	1	0
2010/11	Morton	23	2		1			4			2			30	2	0
2011/2	Stenhousemuir	26	3		1			2			1			30	3	0
2012/3	Stenhousemuir	25	1	2	3			2			1			31	1	2
2013/4	Stenhousemuir	25	3	1	1			4			3			33	3	1
2014/5	Ayr United	13	1		2							1		15	2	0
2014/5	Stirling Albion	10												10	0	0
2015/6	Stirling Albion	13	3	1				4						17	3	1
2016/7	Berwick Rangers	25	2		3						1			29	2	0
														0	0	0
		239	60	15	16	2	1	24	3	1	16	6	3	295	71	20

An exhibition match between a team of North Eastern Railway Clerks from Newcastle and the Tynefield Club of Dunbar, held in Berwick towards the end of 1881, was the impetus for local youths to form their own football club. A group of young men approached Canon Baldwin and asked him if they could hold a meeting in the Parade School for the purposes of forming a football team.

The headquarters for the team were established in an old shed owned by Peter Cowe, a local fish merchant and football enthusiast.

Willie Bald was one of the most influential early players. He owned a rule book and had experience of the game from when he lived in Dunfermline.

Date	Comp	H/A	Opponents	F	A		HT		Referee	Crowd	Scorers
19/07/2016	LC	H	Albion Rovers	0	0	4-5p	0	0	G Irvine	323	
23/07/2016	LC	A	Clyde	1	1	5-6p	0	0	G Beaton	397	Sheerin
26/07/2016	LC	H	Kilmarnock	2	3		1	0	G Duncan	609	Fairbairn, Mackie
30/07/2016	LC	A	Morton	0	2		0	2	R Madden	1044	
02/08/2016	CC1	H	Spartans	0	3		0	2	D Smith	302	
06/08/2016	L	A	Arbroath	1	1		0	0	S Millar	502	Thomson
13/08/2016	L	H	Annan Athletic	2	0		1	0	C Steven	366	Thomson, McKenna
20/08/2016	L	H	Forfar Athletic	1	2		0	1	S Reid	421	Sheerin
27/08/2016	L	A	Edinburgh City	2	1		0	0	C Napier	419	Sheerin 2
10/09/2016	L	H	Elgin City	2	4		1	2	G Irvine	407	Hurst 2
17/09/2016	L	A	Cowdenbeath	2	0		2	0	S Millar	327	Thomson 2
24/09/2016	L	A	Montrose	0	0		0	0	G Beaton	283	
01/10/2016	L	H	Clyde	1	1		1	1	G Aitken	469	Thomson
15/10/2016	L	A	Stirling Albion	0	0		0	0	M Taylor	517	
22/10/2016	SC2	H	Hawick Royal Albert	2	3		1	3	M Roncone	477	McKenna, Rutherford
29/10/2016	L	H	Arbroath	1	1		0	1	G Irvine	390	Thomson
05/11/2016	l	H	Cowdenbeath	1	1		1	0	K Graham	454	Rutherford
12/11/2015	L	A	Forfar Athletic	0	2		0	1	B Cook	477	
19/11/2016	L	A	Clyde	2	3		0	1	C Napier	546	Rutherford, Hurst
06/12/2016	L	H	Stirling Albion	3	2		2	2	G Ross	302	Hurst, Sheerin 2
10/12/2016	L	A	Elgin City	0	6		0	2	G Beaton	535	
17/12/2016	L	H	Montrose	1	2		0	0	C Allan	361	McKenna
24/12/2016	L	A	Annan Athletic	1	3		1	3	D Lowe	430	Scullion
31/12/2016	L	H	Edinburgh City	1	3		0	2	K Graham	515	Sheerin
07/01/2017	L	A	Cowdenbeath	1	0		0	0	R Milne	343	Thomson
14/01/2017	L	A	Arbroath	1	4		1	0	D Munro	539	McKenna
28/01/2017	L	A	Montrose	1	2		0	0	M Roncone	1222	McKenna
04/02/2017	L	H	Annan Athletic	4	1		2	1	D Lowe	355	Thomson 3, Orru
11/02/2017	L	A	Stirling Albion	2	2		2	0	D Dickinson	515	Hamilton, Murrell
18/02/2017	L	H	Forfar Athletic	3	2		1	2	L Wilson	480	Lavery, Bain og, Phillips
25/02/2017	L	H	Elgin City	0	1		0	1	C Steven	403	
07/03/2017	L	H	Clyde	4	3		3	2	G Duncan	336	Phillips, Rutherford 2, Thomson
11/03/2017	L	H	Cowdenbeath	1	3		0	1	S Reid	408	Rutherford
15/03/2017	L	A	Edinburgh City	2	2		1	0	G Irvine	423	Rutherford, Thomson
18/03/2017	L	H	Arbroath	0	2		0	1	S Millar	425	
25/03/2017	L	A	Forfar Athletic	3	2		1	1	R Milne	477	Scullion, Murrell, Rutherford
01/04/2017	L	A	Elgin City	2	2		2	1	K Graham	588	Rutherford, Murrell
08/04/2017	L	H	Stirling Albion	0	1		0	1	C Napier	440	
15/04/2017	L	A	Annan Athletic	1	2		0	0	J McKendrick	460	Thomson
22/04/2017	L	H	Montrose	0	1		0	1	L Wilson	452	
29/04/2017	L	A	Clyde	1	1		0	1	M Roncone	710	Fairbairn
06/05/2017	L	H	Edinburgh City	3	2		2	0	D Lowe	695	Lavery, Rutherford, Verlaque

FRIENDLIES / OTHER GAMES							
02/07/2016	A	Consett	1	2			250
03/07/2016	A	Ryton & Crawcrook Albion	2	0			
05/07/2016	H	Hibernian	1	1			
06/07/2016	A	Gala Fairydean Rovers	1	3		U20	
11/07/2016	A	Whitehill Welfare	0	1		U20	
12/07/2016	H	Gateshead	0	4			240
16/07/2016	A	Alloa Athletic	0	1			
16/07/2016	N	Tynecastle	0	2		U20 Rosyth Tnt	
16/07/2016	N	Crossgates Primrose	3	2		U20 Tranent Tnt	
17/07/2016	A	Tranent	1	1	3-5p	U20 Tranent Tnt	
23/07/2016	A	Blackburn United	3	3		U20	
26/07/2016	A	Scone Thistle	1	2		U20	
02/08/2016	A	Penicuik Athletic	0	4		U20	

Date	Comp	H/A	Opponents	F	A		1	2	3	4	5	6	7	8	9	10	11	12	13	14	15	16	17	18
19/07/2016	LC	H	Albion Rovers	0	0	4-5p	KWalker	Wilson&	Fairbairn	Martin	Hamilton	McKinlay	Notman	A Walker+	Thomson	Lavery*	Sheerin	McKenna*	Bauld+	Beveridge&	Ingram	K Scott	S Scott	Brennan
23/07/2016	LC	A	Clyde	1	1	5-6p	Brennan	Wilson	Fairbairn	Martin	Hamilton	McKinlay*	Beveridge	A Walker	Thomson	McKenna	Sheerin	Orru*	Ingram	K Scott	S Scott	K Walker		
26/07/2016	LC	H	Kilmarnock	2	3		KWalker	Wilson	Fairbairn	Martin	Hamilton	Mackie	Stirling*	A Walker+	Thomson	McKenna&	Sheerin	Beveridge*	Ingram+	Orru&	Graham	Brennan		
30/07/2016	LC	A	Morton	0	2		Brennan	McKinlay*	Fairbairn	Martin	Hamilton	Mackie	Notman	A Walker+	Thomson	McKenna	Sheerin&	Orru*	Lavery+	McDonald&	Hogg	Wilson	Swanney	K Walker
02/08/2016	CC1	H	Spartans	0	3		KWalker	Wilson*	Fairbairn	Martin	Bauld+	McKinlay	Notman	Lavery	Thomson	McKenna&	Sheerin	A Walker*	Hamilton+	Hogg&	Orru	Ingram	Brennan	
06/08/2016	L	A	Arbroath	1	1		KWalker	Stirling	Fairbairn	Martin	Hamilton	McKinlay	Notman*	A Walker	Thomson	Lavery*	Sheerin	Beveridge*	Wilson	Hogg	Orru	Bauld	Brennan	
13/08/2016	L	H	Annan Athletic	2	0		KWalker	Stirling	Fairbairn	Martin	Hamilton	McKinlay	Notman	A Walker*	Thomson+	McKenna	Sheerin&	Wilson*	Orru+	Lavery&	Hogg	Beveridge	Brennan	
20/08/2016	L	H	Forfar Athletic	1	2		KWalker	Stirling	Wilson	Martin	Hamilton*	McKinlay	Notman	A Walker+	Thomson	McKenna	Sheerin	Lavery*	Hogg+	Orru	Brennan	Beveridge		
27/08/2016	L	A	Edinburgh City	2	1		KWalker	Stirling*	Wilson	Martin	Hamilton&	McKinlay	Notman	Lavery	Thomson	Hurst+	Sheerin	A Walker*	Orru+	Bauld&	Hogg	Brennan		
10/09/2016	L	H	Elgin City	2	4		KWalker	Stirling	Fairbairn	Martin	Lavery	McKinlay+	Notman	A Walker&	Thomson*	Hurst	Sheerin	Wilson*	Beveridge+	Orru&	Hamilton	Brennan		
17/09/2016	L	A	Cowdenbeath	2	0		KWalker	Wilson	Fairbairn	Martin	Beveridge	McKinlay	Notman	McKenna+	Thomson	Hurst*	Sheerin	Lavery*	Orru+	Hamilton	Brennan			
24/09/2016	L	A	Montrose	0	0		KWalker	Wilson	Fairbairn	Martin	Beveridge	McKinlay	Lavery	McKenna	Thomson	Hurst	Sheerin	Hogg	MacDonald	Dolan	Hamilton	Orru	Notman	Brennan
01/10/2016	L	H	Clyde	1	1		KWalker*	Wilson	Fairbairn	Lavery	Beveridge	McKinlay	Notman	McKenna	Thomson	Hurst+	Sheerin	Brennan*	Orru+	Dolan	Hamilton	Hogg	McDonald	
15/10/2016	L	A	Stirling Albion	0	0		KWalker	Wilson	Fairbairn	Lavery	Beveridge	McKinlay	Notman	Martin	Thomson	Hurst*	Sheerin	Watt*	Hogg	Dolan	Orru	Hamilton	Brennan	
22/10/2016	SC2	H	Hawick Royal Albert	2	3		KWalker	Wilson	Stirling*	Lavery	Beveridge	Orru+	Notman	Martin	Thomson	McKenna	Sheerin&	Hamilton*	Rutherford+	Watt&	Jones	Watters	Brennan	Hogg
29/10/2016	L	H	Arbroath	1	1		KWalker	Wilson	Fairbairn	Lavery	Beveridge	Hamilton&	Notman+	Martin	Thomson	Rutherford	Sheerin*	Hurst*	Stirling+	Orru&	Jones	Watt	Brennan	Hogg
05/11/2016	l	H	Cowdenbeath	1	1		KWalker	McKinlay	Fairbairn	Lavery	McKenna*	Hamilton	Notman	Martin	Thomson	Rutherford	Sheerin+	Beveridge*	Hogg+	Orru	Jones	Watt	Brennan	MacDonald
12/11/2015	L	A	Forfar Athletic	0	2		KWalker	McKinlay*	Fairbairn	Stirling	Beveridge	Hamilton+	Hurst	Martin	McKenna	Rutherford	Sheerin&	Orru*	Hogg+	Watt&	McDonald	Watt	Brennan	
19/11/2016	L	A	Clyde	2	3		KWalker	Martin	Fairbairn	Stirling	Beveridge*	Hamilton	Hurst&	Lavery	Thomson	Rutherford	Sheerin+	Hogg*	Watt+	Orru&	McDonald	Jones	Brennan	
06/12/2016	L	H	Stirling Albion	3	2		KWalker	McKinlay	Fairbairn	Notman	Beveridge	Hamilton	Hurst*	McKenna&	Thomson	Rutherford	Sheerin+	Perez*	Hogg+	Watt&	Orru	Bauld	Ingram	Brennan
10/12/2016	L	A	Elgin City	0	6		KWalker	McKinlay	Fairbairn	Notman	Martin	Hamilton	Mackie&	McKenna	Thomson*	Perez+	Sheerin	Beveridge*	Watt+	Orru&	Hogg	Hurst	Brennan	
17/12/2016	L	H	Montrose	1	2		KWalker	McKinlay	Scullion	Notman	Martin	Hamilton*	Lavery+	McKenna	Thomson	Rutherford	Sheerin	Beveridge*	Perez+	Orru	Hogg	Watt	Mackie	Brennan
24/12/2016	L	A	Annan Athletic	1	3		Brennan	McKinlay	Scullion	Notman*	Martin	Hamilton	Lavery	McKenna	Thomson+	Rutherford	Sheerin&	Stirling*	Mackie+	Perez&	Beveridge	Watt	Bauld	K Walker
31/12/2016	L	H	Edinburgh City	1	3		KWalker	Martin*	Sullion	Fairbairn	Stirling	Hamilton&	Lavery	McKenna	Thomson+	Rutherford	Mackie	Notman*	Sheerin+	Perez&	Beveridge	Watt	Orru	Brennan
07/01/2017	L	A	Cowdenbeath	1	0		KWalker	McKinlay+	Scullion	Fairbairn	Phillips	Hamilton	Lavery	McKenna	Thomson&	Rutherford*	Notman	Sheerin*	Stirling+	Orru&	Perez	Watt	Martin	Brennan
14/01/2017	L	A	Arbroath	1	4		Brennan	McKinlay	Scullion	Dunlop*	Phillips	Martin	Lavery	McKenna	Thomson	Rutherford+	Notman	Perez*	Watt+	Orru	Fairbairn	Cook	Sheerin	Kwalker
28/01/2017	L	A	Montrose	1	2		Brennan	McKinlay	Scullion	Spark	Phillips	Martin*	Lavery	McKenna	Thomson+	Rutherford&	Notman	Hamilton*	Murrell+	Perez&	Orru	Cook	Watt	Goodfellow
04/02/2017	L	H	Annan Athletic	4	1		MacKay	McKinlay*	Scullion	Spark	Phillips	Hamilton	Lavery	McKenna	Thomson	Rutherford&	Sheerin+	Orru*	Murrell+	Kessels&	Watt	Cook	Donkor	Brennan
11/02/2017	L	A	Stirling Albion	2	2		MacKay	Orru+	Scullion	Spark	Phillips	Hamilton	Lavery	McKenna	Thomson	Rutherford	Murrell*	Bauld*	Kessels+	Watt	Donkor	Cook	KWalker	
18/02/2017	L	H	Forfar Athletic	3	2		MacKay	Donkor*	Scullion	Spark	Phillips	Hamilton	Lavery	McKirdy&	Thomson	McKenna	Murrell+	Rutherford*	Verlaque+	McKinlay&	Watt	Orru	KWalker	Kessels
25/02/2017	L	H	Elgin City	0	1		MacKay	Notman	Scullion	Spark	Phillips	Hamilton*	Lavery	Rutherford	Thomson&	McKenna	Murrell+	McKinlay*	Orru+	Kessels&	Watt	McKirdy	KWalker	Donkor
07/03/2017	L	H	Clyde	4	3		KWalker	Notman&	Scullion	Spark	Phillips	Hamilton	Lavery	Rutherford	Thomson*	McKinlay	Murrell+	Orru*	Watt+	McKirdy&	Kessels	Donkor	Fairbairn	
11/03/2017	L	H	Cowdenbeath	1	3		Brennan	Notman	Scullion+	Spark	Phillips&	Hamilton	Lavery	Rutherford	Thomson	McKirdy	Kessells*	Murrell*	Verlaque+	Fairbairn&	Orru	Donkor	Watt	Goodfellow
15/03/2017	L	A	Edinburgh City	2	2		Brennan	Verlaque*	Scullion	Spark	McKinley	Hamilton	Lavery	Rutherford	Thomson	McKirdy+	Murrell	Phillips*	Notman+	Kessels	Orru	Fairbairn	Watt	Goodfellow
18/03/2017	L	H	Arbroath	0	2		Brennan	Notman	Scullion	Spark+	McKinley	Hamilton*	Lavery	Rutherford	Thomson	McKenna	Murrell&	Fairbairn*	Verlaque+	Phillips&	Kessels	Donkor	McKirdy	Goodfellow
25/03/2017	L	A	Forfar Athletic	3	2		Brennan	Notman	Scullion	Spark	McKinley	McKirdy*	Lavery+	Rutherford	Phillips	McKenna	Murrell&	Orru*	Verlaque+	Kessells&	Watt	Helm	Donkor	Goodfellow
01/04/2017	L	A	Elgin City	2	2		Brennan	Notman	Scullion*	Spark	McKinley+	McKirdy&	Verlaque	Rutherford	Phillips	McKenna	Murrell	Fairbairn*	Page+	Thomson&	Watt	Kessels	Donkor	Goodfellow
08/04/2017	L	H	Stirling Albion	0	1		Brennan	Notman	Scullion	Spark	Page	McKirdy*	Verlaque	Rutherford	Thomson&	McKenna	Murrell+	Lavery*	Hamilton+	Watt&	McKinlay	Kessels	Fairbairn	Goodfellow
15/04/2017	L	A	Annan Athletic	1	2		Brennan	Notman	Scullion	Spark	McKinley+	Hamilton	Lavery	Rutherford	Thomson	McKirdy*	Phillips&	McKenna*	Verlaque+	Murrell&	Watt	Kessels	Donkor	Goodfellow
22/04/2017	L	H	Montrose	0	1		Brennan	Notman*	Scullion	Spark	Fairbairn	Hamilton&	Lavery	Rutherford	Thomson+	McKenna	Phillips	Murrell*	Kessels+	Verlaque&	Watt	Donkor	Bauld	Goodfellow
29/04/2017	L	A	Clyde	1	1		Brennan	Notman	Scullion	Spark	Fairbairn	Phillips	Lavery	Rutherford	Thomson	McKenna	Murrell	Watt	Orru	Hamilton	Kessels	Donkor	Verlaque	K Walker
06/05/2017	L	H	Edinburgh City	3	2		Brennan	Notman	Scullion	Spark	Fairbairn	Phillips	Lavery	Rutherford*	Thomson&	McKenna	Murrell+	Hamilton*	Verlaque+	McKirdy&	Kessels	Donkor	Watt	K Walker

Surname	First Name	DOB	SQ	Nat	Pos	L			SC			LC			CC			UNS	Signed	Previous Club	Notes	Contract
						A	S	G	A	S	G	A	S	G	A	S	G					
Allan	Stuart				D														2016	Berwick Rangers Youth	OL to Crossgates Primrose Sep-Dec	
Anderson	Ethan	23/10/96		SCO	F														2015	Burntisland Shipyard	OL to Crossgates Primrose Sep-Dec	
Bauld	Euan	13/01/1997		SCO	D		2						1		1			4	2014	Hibernian	OL to Haddington Ath, Freed May 2017	[redacted]
Beveridge	Graeme	07/10/1990		SCO	M	8	5		1			1	2					4	2015	Elgin City	Freed Jan 2017	[redacted]
Brennan	Sean	17/02/1997		SCO	GK	13	1					2						22	2016	Hibernian	OL to Bonnyrigg Rose Feb-May	End 2017/18
Chapman	Jamie	16/11/1998			M														2016	Berwick Rangers Youth	OL to Whitehill Welfare	
Cook	Jack	26/01/1998			D													4	2016	Berwick Rangers Youth	OL to Newtongrange Star	End 2017/18
Dickson	Cameron				D														2016	Berwick Rangers Youth	OL to Craigroyston	
Dolan	Gary	25/07/1998		SCO	M													3	2016	Berwick Rangers Youth	OL to Craigroyston	
Donkor	Renne	30/03/1997		NET	D	1												12	2017	Nieuw Utrecht	Freed May 2017	[redacted]
Dunlop	Michael	11/01/1993		SCO	D	1													2017	Arbroath	Freed May 2017	[redacted]
Fairbairn	Jonny	10/01/1990		ENG	D	18	3	1				4		1	1			4	2012	Mississippi Stars		End 2017/18
Goodfellow	Grant	04/02/99		SCO	GK													9	2016	Hibernian U17	OL to Haddington Ath Nov -Dec	
Graham	Regan	04/01/1996		ENG	M													1	2013	Berwick Rangers Youth		
Hamilton	Lee	15/09/1995		SCO	D	24	3	1		1		4				1		6	2016	Stirling Albion	On trial with Stirling Albion July 2017	OOC
Helm	Calum	02/03/1996			F													1	2015	Hutchison Vale		OOC
Herriot	Ewan	24/06/1997																	2016	Berwick Rangers Youth	OL to Blackburn Utd	
Hogg	Barry	27/01/1997		SCO	M		5									1		11	2015	Tynecastle FC	Freed Dec 2016, joined Musselburgh Ath	[redacted]
Hurst	Greg	08/04/1997		SCO	F	9	1	4										1	2016	St Johnstone (OL)	Sep-Jan	[redacted]
Ingram	Kieran	01/01/1997		ENG	M								1					4	2016	FMU Patriots	OL to Haddington Ath Aug-Jan, to Dunbar Utd Feb-May	
Jones	Sam				M													4	2016	Berwick Rangers Youth	OL to Penicuik Ath	
Kessels	Ricardo Leao	17/06/1997		BRA / SCO	F	1	5											9	2017	Wilhelmina 08	Freed May 2017	[redacted]
Lavery	Darren	13/12/1991		SCO	F	28	4	2	1			1	1		1				2011	Leith Athletic		End 2017/18
MacDonald	Alistair	21/05/1997		SCO	D								1					5	2015	Cowdenbeath Youth	OL to Oakley United	
Mackay	Devlin					4													2016	Kilmarnock (OL)	Jan-May 2017	[redacted]
Mackie	Sean	04/11/1998		SCO	D	2	1					2		1				1	2016	Hibernian (OL)	Aug-Jan	[redacted]
Martin	Brian	14/05/1985		SCO	D	18			1			4			1			1	2016	Musselburgh Athletic	Freed Feb 17 after receiving Football Banning Order	[redacted]
McKenna	Michael	04/01/1991		SCO	M	26	1	4	1		1	3	1		1				2015	Livingston		End 2017/18
McKinlay	Kevin	28/02/1986		SCO	D	25	2					3			1			1	2016	Stirling Albion		End 2017/18
McKirdy	Sean	12/04/1998		SCO	M	7	2											2	2017	Hamilton Accies (OL)	Feb-May 2017	[redacted]
Murrell	Aaron	23/09/1997		SCO	F	11	5	3											2017	Dundee United (OL)	Jan-May 2017	[redacted]
Notman	Steven	21/08/1986		SCO	M	28	2		1			2			1			1	2007	Hibernian		End 2017/18
Orru	Jordan	17/08/1997		SCO	D	1	14	1	1				3					15	2016	Dunfermline Athletic	OL to Bonnyrigg Rose	OOC
Page	Greg				D	1	1												2017	St Johnstone (OL)	Mar-May 2017	[redacted]
Perez	Samuel	23/03/1990		SPA	F	1	6											1	2016	Ex Team Northumbria	Freed Feb 2017	[redacted]
Phillips	Gary	01/05/1988		SCO	M	15	2	2											2017	Arbroath		End 2017/18
Porteous	Ryan				F														2016	Berwick Rangers Youth	OL to Arniston Rangers	
Rutherford	Greg	17/05/1994		ENG	F	25	1	9		1	1								2016	Ex Alloa, Arbroath		End 2017/18
Scott	Kyle	01/10/1998		SCO	M													2	2016	Berwick Rangers Youth	OL to Penicuik Ath Aug-Jan	
Scott	Stephen	01/10/1998		SCO	F													2	2016	Berwick Rangers Youth	OL to Penicuik Ath Aug-Jan	
Scullion	Pat	02/03/1986		SCO	M	21		2											2016	Alloa (OL)	OL Dec-Jan, signed permanently Jan 2017	End 2017/18
Sheerin	Jordyn	18/08/1989		SCO	F	18	2	6	1			4		1	1			1	2015	Livingston	Freed Jan 2017, joined Kelty Hearts	[redacted]
Spark	Euan				D	16													2017	Dunfermline Athletic (OL)	Jan-May 2017	[redacted]
Stirling	Ben	16/08/1998		SCO	M	8	3		1			1							2016	Hibernian (OL)	Aug-Jan	[redacted]
Sutherland	Scott	13/02/1999																	2017	Cowdenbeath Youth	OL to Jeanfield Swifts	
Swanney	Lewis	01/01/1998		SCO	D													1	2016	Berwick Rangers Youth	OL to Newtongrange Star Aug-Dec	
Thomson	Steven	21/03/1985		SCO	F	33	1	13	1			4			1				2016	Musselburgh Athletic		End 2017/18
Verlaque	David	11/08/1995		SCO	M	3	7	1										1	2017	Stirling Albion	Freed May 2017	[redacted]
Walker	Kevin	12/09/1991		SCO	GK	19			1			2			1			9	2015	Livingston	Freed May 2017	[redacted]
Walker	Allan	03/01/1986		SCO	M	4	1					4				1			2016	East Fife	Freed Sep 2016	[redacted]
Watt	Daniel	24/02/1996		SCO	F		8			1								20	2016	Berwick Rangers Youth		OOC
Watters	Ross				D													1	2016	Berwick Rangers Youth		
Wilson	Robert	29/01/1995		SCO	D	7	2		1			3			1			2	2016	Musselburgh Athletic		End 2017/18
Own Goal								1														
NEW SIGNINGS																						
Fleming	Oliver			SCO	D														2017	Sauchie Juniors		End 2017/18
McCrorie	Robbie			SCO	GK														2017	Rangers (OL)	Jul-May	
Irving	Andrew																		2017	Hearts (OL)	Jul-May	
Donaldson	Callum																		2017	Hibernian (OL)	Jul-Dec	
Waugh	Kevin																		2017	Hibernian (OL)	Jul-Dec	
Stewart	Keiran	20/05/1994		SCO	M														2017	Elgin City		

Source of Birthdates: transfermarkt.com

Brechin City FC 2016/17

Founded	1906
Ground	Glebe Park
Postcode	DD9 6BJ
Tel	01356 622856
Capacity	3960
Closest Railway Station	Montrose
Record Attendance	8122 v Aberdeen, SC 3/2/1973
Record Win	12-1 v Thornhill, SC, 28/1/1926
Record Defeat	0-10, v Airdrieonians, Albion
	Rovers & Cowdenbeath, 1937/8
Most League Goals in a Season	26 Ronald McIntosh, 1959/60
Most Goals in Career	131 Ian Campbell
Chairman	Ken Ferguson
Secretary	Angus Fairlie
Manager	Darren Dods
Assistant Manager	Lee Bailey
Colours 2016/17 Top	Red
Shorts	Black
Sponsor	Delson
Manufacturer	Pendle
Change Colours 2016/17 Top	Gold
Shorts	Dark Blue
Nicknames	City
Web	www.brechincity.com
Match Programme 2016/17	No programmes issued

At the midway point of 2015/16 Brechin looked certainties for relegation to League Two. Daren Dods must have been aware that his job was on the line. They performed a miracle escape from relegation and continued the good work in 2016/17.

Nobody would have thought promotion was likely, even when Brechin scraped into the play offs. Yet wins over Raith Rovers and Alloa demonstrate that timing is everything. Brechin became the first club to be promoted having lost more games than they won, and conceding more goals than they scored.

The club operated with a very small squad of players. The outstanding individual was probably James Dale but this was a team effort rather than a product of individual brilliance. Definitely a case of the whole being better than the sum of the parts.

PREDICTION FOR 2017/18

Brechin will struggle badly in the Championship. Being rea;listic the besty theyc an jope for is second bottom and a place in the Play Offs.

						L			SC			LC			CC							
			SQ	Nat	Pos	A	S	G	A	S	G	A	S	G	A	S	G	UNS				
Surname	**First Name**	**DOB**																	**Signed**	**Previous Club**	**Notes**	**Contract**
Buchanan	Robbie	23/02/1996		SCO	F	3	1		1									1	2016	Hearts (OL)	Nov-Dec 2016	[redacted]
Caldwell	Ross	26/10/1993		SCO	F	15	15	7	1			2	2		2		1	10	2016	Cowdenbeath	Freed May 2017	
Costello	Scott	01/01/2001		SCO	GK													8	2016	Burntisland Shipyard	OL to Glenrothes JFC Aug-Jan	
Dale	James	01/01/1990		ENG	M	32	1	1				3			2			0	2015	Forfar Athletic		End 2017/18
Dods	Daren	07/01/1975		SCO	D	0	1											39	2015	Forfar Athletic		End 2017/18
Dyer	Willie	25/02/1987		SCO	D	32		1	1			3		1	2			4	2015	Dundee		End 2017/18
Ford	Elliot	26/05/1996		SCO	D	12	9	1	1			1	1		1	1		19	2016	Raith Rovers		End 2017/18
Fusco	Gary	01/06/1982		SCO	M	22	3		1									17	2014	Forfar Athletic		End 2017/18
Graham	Finn	05/06/1996		SCO	M	31	4	1				3	1		2		1	4	2016	Berwick Rangers		End 2017/18
Hill	Dougie	16/01/1985		SCO	D	32	1	3	1			4			1			1	2016	Alloa Athletic	Freed May 2017	[redacted]
Jackson	Andy	09/01/1988		SCO/ROI	F	32	1	13				3	1	1	1		2	0	2012	Morton		End 2018/19
Love	Ally	22/08/1991		SCO	M	31	6	8	1			4		1	2		1	1	2016	Albion Rovers		End 2017/18
Lynas	Aaron	19/04/1996		SCO	M	21	9		1				2		1	1		12	2016	Alloa Athletic		End 2017/18
McCormack	Darren	29/09/1988		SCO	D	5	5	1		1		4				1		18	2014	Airdrieonians	Freed May 2017	[redacted]
McLean	Paul	02/02/1990		SCO	D	31	2	3							2			3	2009	Falkirk		End 2017/18
McLennan	Connor	05/10/1999		SCO	F	3		1										0	2016	Aberdeen (OL)	Dec 2016-Jan 2017	[redacted]
O'Neill	Chris	22/08/1995		SCO	D	19	1					4						9	2016	Airdrieonians		OOC
O'Neill	Patrick	31/03/1992		SCO	GK	2	3											41	2014	Northwood Univ Seahawks		OOC
Rodger	Gareth	22/02/1994		SCO	D	13	6		1			4			2			11	2016	Forfar Athletic	Freed May 2017 joined Edinburgh City	[redacted]
Smith	Graeme	08/06/1983		SCO	GK	38			1			4			2			0	2013	Ayr United		End 2017/18
Smith	Euan	29/01/1994		SCO	M	18			1			2	1		2			0	2015	Kilmarnock		OOC
Spence	Lewis	28/01/1996		SCO	M	7												0	2016	Dunfermline Athletic (OL)	Sep-Nov 2016	[redacted]
Trouten	Alan	08/11/1985		SCO	M	20	8	6				3	1	2				4	2016	Ayr United	Freed May 2017 joined Albion Rovers	
Watt	Liam	21/01/1994		SCO	M	21		3										0	2017	Livingston		End 2017/18
Trialist																		2				
Own Goals								2														
NEW SIGNINGS																						
McGeever	Ryan				D														2017	Queen's Park		End 2017/18
Layne	Isaac				F														2017	Grays Athletic		
Spark	Euan				M														2017	Dunfermline Athletic		

Source of Birthdates: Brechin City website

Date	Comp	H/A	Opponents	F	A		HT			Crowd	Scorers
19/07/2016	LC	H	Stirling Albion	2	1		1	1	G Beaton	362	Love, Trouten
23/07/2016	LC	A	Elgin City	2	4		1	2	C Napier	506	Dyer, Trouten
26/07/2016	LC	H	St Johnstone	1	1	4-2p	1	0	J McKendrick	912	Jackson
30/07/2016	LC	A	Falkirk	0	2		0	0	S McLean	1073	
06/08/2016	L	H	Stenhousemuir	2	1		1	0	D Munro	402	Trouten, Caldwell
13/08/2016	L	A	Albion Rovers	2	0		1	0	G Aitken	228	Trouten, Jackson
16/08/2016	CC	H	Cove Rangers	4	1		2	1	G Ross	242	Graham, Jackson 2, Caldwell
20/08/2016	L	H	Queen's Park	0	0		0	0	M Roncone	447	
27/08/2016	L	A	East Fife	2	1		1	1	G Irvine	609	Caldwell, Graham
03/09/2016	CC3	H	Dunfermline Athletic	1	5		1	2	C Allan	577	Love
10/09/2016	L	H	Airdrieonians	3	2		1	1	G Duncan	466	Love, Jackson, Hill
17/09/2016	L	A	Livingston	1	2		0	1	A Newlands	858	Trouten
24/09/2016	L	H	Peterhead	2	1		1	1	C Charleston	431	Love, Jackson
01/10/2016	L	A	Stranraer	1	0		0	0	D Munro	402	Jackson
15/10/2016	L	H	Alloa	0	1		0	0	J McKendrick	413	
22/10/2016	L	A	Stenhousemuir	3	1		0	0	C Steven	352	Love, McLean, McCormack
29/10/2016	L	H	Livingston	0	3		0	0	B Madden	517	
05/11/2016	L	A	Peterhead	3	1		1	0	S Kirkland	621	Caldwell 3
12/11/2016	L	A	Airdrieonians	0	1		0	0	C Napier	739	
29/11/2016	SC3	H	Ayr United	0	1		0	0	A Muir	308	
03/12/2016	L	A	Queen's Park	0	2		0	1	M Roncone	632	
06/12/2016	L	H	Albion Rovers	1	2		1	1	S Reid	283	Stewart og
10/12/2016	L	H	East Fife	0	1		0	1	S Kirkland	414	
17/12/2016	L	H	Stranraer	2	0		2	0	K Graham	402	Love, McLennan
24/12/2016	L	A	Alloa	2	1		1	0	D Munro	386	Trouten, Love
02/01/2017	L	H	Peterhead	0	1		0	0	G Irvine	553	
07/01/2017	L	A	Albion Rovers	0	1		0	0	G Duncan	332	
28/01/2017	L	A	Livingston	0	3		0	2	A Newlands	746	
04/02/2017	L	H	Stenhousemuir	2	2		1	2	S Millar	403	Jackson, Hill
18/02/2017	L	A	East Fife	2	3		1	2	D Munro	642	Jackson, Dyer
25/02/1987	L	A	Stranraer	0	2		0	1	S Reid	340	
28/02/2017	L	H	Queen's Park	3	1		2	1	J McKendrick	393	Love, Hill, Jackson
11/03/2017	L	A	Peterhead	1	0		0	0	M Northcroft	483	Jackson
14/03/2017	L	H	Airdrieonians	3	0		1	0	D Lowe	346	Love 2, Jackson
18/03/2017	L	A	Queen's Park	1	1		0	0	R Milne	481	Jackson
21/03/2017	L	H	Alloa	1	2		0	1	C Napier	372	Jackson
25/03/2017	L	H	East Fife	2	1		1	0	A Muir	525	Watt, Jackson
01/04/2017	L	H	Livingston	0	2		0	1	S Millar	523	
08/04/2017	L	A	Airdrieonians	1	3		1	2	G Beaton	676	Leitch og
15/04/2017	L	A	Alloa	1	6		1	2	S Kirkland	662	Jackson
22/04/2017	L	H	Stranraer	0	0		0	0	G Ross	403	
29/04/2017	L	H	Albion Rovers	1	0		0	0	D Lowe	422	McLean
06/05/2017	L	A	Stenhousemuir	1	1		1	0	G Aitken	557	Trouten
10/05/2017	PO	H	Raith Rovers	1	1		1	0	D Robertson	1022	Caldwell
13/05/2017	PO	A	Raith Rovers	3	3	aet 4-3p	0	0	A Muir	1932	Caldwell, Trouten, Watt
17/05/2017	PO	H	Alloa	1	0		0	0	E Anderson	702	Ford
20/05/2017	PO	A	Alloa	3	4	aet 5-4p	1	2	N Walsh	1204	Dale, McLean, Watt

FRIENDLIES / OTHER GAMES							
26/06/2016	H	Aberdeen	0	3			
02/07/2016	H	Raith Rovers	0	2			207
05/07/2016	H	Hearts XI	3	1			
09/07/2016	H	Dundee United	0	5		Forfarshire Cup	
12/07/2016	H	Dundee XI	1	0			
30/07/2016	A	Brechin Vics	2	4		U19	

Date	Comp	H/A	Opponents	F	A		1	2	3	4	5	6	7	8	9	10	11	12	13	14	15	16	17	18
19/07/2016	LC	H	Stirling Albion	2	1		G Smith	C O'Neill	Dyer	McCormack	Hill	Rodger	Trouten	E Smith+	Graham	Love	Caldwell*	Jackson*	Lynas+	*Ford*	*Fusco*	*Dods*	*P O'Neill*	
23/07/2016	LC	A	Elgin City	2	4		G Smith	C O'Neill	Dyer+	McCormack	Hill	Rodger	Trouten	E Smith&	Dale	Love*	Jackson	Caldwell*	Ford+	Graham&	*Fusco*	*Dods*	*P O'Neill*	*Lynas*
26/07/2016	LC	H	St Johnstone	1	1	4-2p	G Smith	C O'Neill	Dyer	McCormack	Hill	Rodger	Graham	Caldwell*	Dale	Love	Jackson	Trouten*	*Ford*	*Lynas*	*Fusco*	*Dods*	*P O'Neill*	
30/07/2016	LC	A	Falkirk	0	2		G Smith	C O'Neill	Ford	McCormack*	Hill	Rodger	Trouten	Graham+	Dale	Love&	Jackson	E Smith*	Caldwell+	Lynas&	*Fusco*	*Dods*	*P O'Neill*	
06/08/2016	L	H	Stenhousemuir	2	1		G Smith	C O'Neill	Dyer	E Smith	Hill	Rodger	Trouten	Graham	Dale	Love*	Jackson	Caldwell*	*Ford*	*Lynas*	*McLean*	*Dods*	*P O'Neill*	
13/08/2016	L	A	Albion Rovers	2	0		G Smith	C O'Neill+	Dyer	E Smith	Hill&	Rodger	Trouten	Graham	Dale	Love*	Jackson	Caldwell*	McLean+	Fusco&	*Ford*	*Dods*	*P O'Neill*	*Lynas*
16/08/2016	CC	H	Cove Rangers	4	1		G Smith	McLean	Dyer+	E Smith	Ford	Rodger	Caldwell	Graham	Dale	Love*	Jackson	Lynas*	McCormack+	*Fusco*	*C O'Neill*	*Dods*	*P O'Neill*	
20/08/2016	L	H	Queen's Park	0	0		G Smith	C O'Neill	Dyer	E Smith	Hill	Rodger	Trouten	Graham	Dale	Love*	Jackson	Caldwell*	*McCormack*	*Lynas*	*Ford*	*McLean*	*P O'Neill*	*Fusco*
27/08/2016	L	A	East Fife	2	1		G Smith	C O'Neill*	Dyer	E Smith	Hill	Rodger	Caldwell	Graham+	Dale	Love	Jackson	McLean*	Lynas+	*Fusco*	*Ford*	*Dods*	*P O'Neill*	*McCormack*
03/09/2016	CC3	H	Dunfermline Athletic	1	5		G Smith	McLean	Dyer*	E Smith	Hill	Rodger	Caldwell	Graham	Dale	Love	Lynas	Ford*	*McCormack*	*Dods*	*C O'Neill*	*P O'Neill*		
10/09/2016	L	H	Airdrieonians	3	2		G Smith*	McLean	Dyer+	E Smith	Hill	C O'Neill&	Caldwell	Graham	Dale	Love	Jackson	P O'Neill*	Ford+	Rodger&	*Lynas*	*Dods*	*Fusco*	*McCormack*
17/09/2016	L	A	Livingston	1	2		G Smith	McLean	Dyer	E Smith	Hill&	C O'Neill*	Caldwell	Graham+	Dale	Love	Jackson	Ford*	Trouten+	McCormack&	*Lynas*	*Rodger*	*P O'Neill*	*Fusco*
24/09/2016	L	H	Peterhead	2	1		G Smith	McLean	Dyer	E Smith	Hill*	Ford	Trouten	Spence+	Dale	Love&	Jackson	McCormack*	Graham+	Lynas&	*Caldwell*	*Rodger*	*P O'Neill*	*Fusco*
01/10/2016	L	A	Stranraer	1	0		G Smith	McLean	Dyer	E Smith	Hill	Ford*	Trouten+	Spence	Dale	Love&	Jackson	McCormack*	Caldwell+	Lynas&	*Graham*	*Rodger*	*P O'Neill*	*Fusco*
15/10/2016	L	H	Alloa	0	1		G Smith	McLean	Dyer	E Smith	Hill	Ford	Trouten	Spence+	Dale	Love*	Jackson	Caldwell*	Graham+	*Lynas*	*Dods*	*Rodger*	*P O'Neill*	*McCormack*
22/10/2016	L	A	Stenhousemuir	3	1		G Smith	McLean	Dyer	E Smith&	Hill	McCormack	Trouten	Spence*	Dale	Love+	Jackson	Graham*	Caldwell+	Ford&	*Fusco*	*Rodger*	*P O'Neill*	*Lynas*
29/10/2016	L	H	Livingston	0	3		G Smith	McCormack	Dyer	E Smith	Hill	Ford*	Trouten	Spence	Dale	Love	Jackson	Caldwell*	*Graham*	*Lynas*	*Fusco*	*Rodger*	*P O'Neill*	*Dods*
05/11/2016	L	A	Peterhead	3	1		G Smith	McCormack*	Dyer	E Smith	Hill	Graham	Trouten	Spence	Dale	Love	Caldwell+	Rodger*	Lynas+	*Fusco*	*Ford*	*Dods*	*P O'Neill*	
12/11/2016	L	A	Airdrieonians	0	1		G Smith	McLean	Dyer	E Smith	Hill	Rodger	Trouten*	Spence	Dale	Love	Caldwell	Lynas*	*Dods*	*Fusco*	*Ford*	*P O'Neill*		
29/11/2016	SC3	H	Ayr United	0	1		G Smith	Ford	Dyer	E Smith	Hill	Rodger	Fusco	Lynas	Buchanan*	Love	Caldwell	McCormack*	*Graham*	*Dods*	*P O'Neill*			
03/12/2016	L	A	Queen's Park	0	2		G Smith	Ford	Dyer	E Smith	Hill	Rodger	Fusco+	Lynas	Buchanan*	Love*	Caldwell&	Trouten*	Graham+	Jackson&	*McCormack*	*Dods*	*P O'Neill*	
06/12/2016	L	H	Albion Rovers	1	2		G Smith	Ford	Dyer	E Smith	McCormack	Rodger	Graham&	Lynas	Buchanan+	Jackson	Trouten*	Love*	Caldwell+	Fusco&	*Dods*	*P O'Neill*		
10/12/2016	L	H	East Fife	0	1		G Smith	Ford	Dyer	E Smith	Hill	Rodger*	Graham	Lynas	Buchanan+	Caldwell	Trouten	McCormack*	Love+	*McLean*	*Dods*	*P O'Neill*		
17/12/2016	L	H	Stranraer	2	0		G Smith+	McCormack*	Dyer	E Smith	Hill	McLean	Fusco	Graham	Love&	McLennan	Trouten	Lynas*	P O'Neill+	Buchanan&	*Dods*	*Caldwell*		
24/12/2016	L	A	Alloa	2	1		G Smith	Lynas	Dyer	E Smith*	Hill	McLean	Fusco	Graham	Love&	McLennan+	Trouten	Rodger*	Caldwell+	*Buchanan*	*Dods*	*Costello*	*P O'Neill*	
02/01/2017	L	H	Peterhead	0	1		G Smith	Lynas	Dyer	Rodger	Hill	McLean	Fusco	Graham*	Love	McLennan+	Trouten	Ford*	Caldwell+	*Dods*	*Costello*	*P O'Neill*		
07/01/2017	L	A	Albion Rovers	0	1		G Smith	Lynas	Dyer	Rodger	Watt	McLean	Fusco	Graham*	Love	Caldwell	Trouten	Dods*	*Ford*	*C O'Neill*	*Trialist*	*Trialist*	*P O'Neill*	
28/01/2017	L	A	Livingston	0	3		G Smith	Lynas	C O'Neill*	Rodger	Hill	McLean	Fusco	Graham	Love	Watt	Jackson+	Dale*	Caldwell+	*Ford*	*McCormack*	*Dods*	*P O'Neill*	
04/02/2017	L	H	Stenhousemuir	2	2		G Smith	Lynas	C O'Neill	Rodger	Hill	McLean	Fusco*	Dale	Love	Watt	Jackson	Trouten*	Caldwell	*Ford*	*McCormack*	*Graham*	*P O'Neill*	*Dyer*
18/02/2017	L	A	East Fife	2	3		G Smith	Dyer	C O'Neill+	Rodger	Hill	McLean	Graham	Dale	Trouten	Watt*	Jackson	Caldwell*	Ford+	*Fusco*	*McCormack*	*Lynas*	*P O'Neill*	*Dods*
25/02/1987	L	A	Stranraer	0	2		G Smith	Dyer	C O'Neill+	Love	Hill	McLean	Fusco	Dale*	Graham	Watt	Jackson	Rodger*	Lynas+	*Caldwell*	*McCormack*	*Ford*	*P O'Neill*	*Dods*
28/02/2017	L	H	Queen's Park	3	1		G Smith	Dyer	C O'Neill	Love*	Hill	McLean	Fusco	Dale	Graham	Watt	Jackson	Lynas*	*Rodger*	*Caldwell*	*McCormack*	*Ford*	*P O'Neill*	*Dods*
11/03/2017	L	A	Peterhead	1	0		G Smith	Dyer	C O'Neill	Love	Hill*	McLean	Fusco	Dale	Graham+	Watt	Jackson	Rodger*	Lynas+	*Caldwell*	*McCormack*	*Ford*	*P O'Neill*	*Dods*
14/03/2017	L	H	Airdrieonians	3	0		G Smith	Lynas	C O'Neill	Love*	Hill	McLean	Fusco	Dale	Graham	Watt	Jackson	Ford*	*Rodger*	*Caldwell*	*McCormack*	*Dods*	*Costello*	
18/03/2017	L	A	Queen's Park	1	1		G Smith	Lynas	C O'Neill	Love	Hill	McLean	Fusco*	Dale	Graham	Watt	Jackson	Ford*	*Rodger*	*Caldwell*	*McCormack*	*Dods*	*P O'Neill*	*Trouten*
21/03/2017	L	H	Alloa	1	2		G Smith	Lynas	C O'Neill	Love*	Hill	McLean	Fusco	Dale	Graham+	Watt	Jackson	Caldwell*	Ford+	Rodger&	*McCormack*	*Dods*	*P O'Neill*	*Trouten*
25/03/2017	L	H	East Fife	2	1		G Smith	Lynas	C O'Neill	Caldwell	Hill	McLean	Fusco	Dale	Graham	Watt	Jackson	*Dyer*	*Ford*	*Rodger*	*McCormack*	*Dods*	*P O'Neill*	*Trouten*
01/04/2017	L	H	Livingston	0	2		G Smith	Lynas	C O'Neill	Caldwell+	Hill	McLean	Fusco*	Dale	Graham	Watt	Jackson	Trouten*	Love+	*Rodger*	*McCormack*	*Ford*	*P O'Neill*	*Dyer*
08/04/2017	L	A	Airdrieonians	1	3		G Smith	Dyer	C O'Neill	Love*	Hill	McLean	Fusco+	Dale	Graham	Watt	Jackson	Caldwell*	Trouten+	*Lynas*	*McCormack*	*Ford*	*P O'Neill*	*Dods*
15/04/2017	L	A	Alloa	1	6		G Smith	Lynas	C O'Neill*	Love	Hill	McLean	Caldwell&	Dale	Graham+	Watt	Jackson	McCormack*	P O'Neill+	Trouten&	*Fusco*	*Ford*	*Dyer*	*Dods*
22/04/2017	L	H	Stranraer	0	0		P O'Neill	Lynas	Dyer	Love	Trouten	McLean	Fusco	Dale	Graham	Watt	Jackson	*Caldwell*	*Ford*	*C O'Neill*	*Dods*			
29/04/2017	L	H	Albion Rovers	1	0		P O'Neill	Lynas	Dyer	Love*	Trouten	McLean	Fusco	Dale	Ford	Watt	Jackson	Caldwell*	*Costello*	*C O'Neill*	*Dods*			
06/05/2017	L	A	Stenhousemuir	1	1		G Smith	Lynas	Dyer	Love+	Hill	McLean	Graham	Dale	Trouten*	Watt	Jackson	Ford*	Fusco+	*C O'Neill*	*Dods*	*Caldwell*	*P O'Neill*	
10/05/2017	PO	H	Raith Rovers	1	1		G Smith	Lynas	Dyer	Ford	Fusco	McLean	Graham	Dale	Caldwell	Watt	Jackson	*Costello*	*Love*	*C O'Neill*	*Dods*	*P O'Neill*		
13/05/2017	PO	A	Raith Rovers	3	3	aet 4-3p	G Smith	Lynas	Dyer	Ford*	Fusco	McLean	Graham&	Dale	Caldwell+	Watt	Jackson	C O'Neill*	Trouten+	Love&	*Dods*	*P O'Neill*	*Costello*	
17/05/2017	PO	H	Alloa	1	0		G Smith	Lynas	Dyer	Ford	Fusco	McLean	Graham	Dale	Caldwell*	Watt	Jackson	Love*	*Trouten*	*C O'Neill*	*Dods*	*P O'Neill*	*Costello*	*Hill*
20/05/2017	PO	A	Alloa	3	4	aet 5-4p	G Smith	Lynas	Dyer	Ford*	Fusco	McLean	Graham&	Dale	Caldwell+	Watt	Jackson	Trouten*	Hill+	Love&	*Dods*	*P O'Neill*	*Costello*	*C O'Neill*

Celtic FC 2016/17

Founded	1888
Ground	Celtic Park
Postcode	G40 3RE
Tel	0871 226 1888
Capacity	60355
Closest Railway Station	Duke Street
Record Attendance	92000 v Rangers, Lge, 1/1/1938
Record Win	11-0 v Dundee, Lge, 26/10/1895
Record Defeat	0-8 v Motherwell, Lge, 30/4/1937
Most League Goals in a Season	50 Jimmy McGrory, 1935/6
Most Goals in Career	397 Jimmy McGrory
Chairman	Ian Bankier
Chief Executive	Peter Lawwell
Secretary	Michael Nicholson
Manager	Brendan Rodgers
Assistant Manager	Chris Davies
Colours 2016/17 Top	Green and White Hoops
Shorts	White
Sponsor	Dafabet
Manufacturer	New Balance
Change Colours 2016/17 Top	Black / Gold
Shorts	Black / Gold
3rd Choice 2016/17 Top	Fluorescent Green
Shorts	Fluorescent Green
Nicknames	Tic, Bhoys, Invincibles
Web	www.celticfc.net
Match Programme 2016/17	£3
E-Ticketing	www.eticketing.co.uk/celtic

Celtic invincible. Winners of both Cups, and League Champions by a ridiculous margin. Sounds like a dull season?

Well, no. It began with defeat from Lincoln Red Imps in Gibraltar. Some had the knives out for Brendan Rodgers at that stage. But once that hurdle was overcome in the second leg, Celtic went on to produce some fantastic football. Rodgers showed that he could re-invigorate players who had been coasting for years - Brown, Forrest and Armstrong had their best seasons for a long time. His signings, particularly, Dembele and Sinclair, brought a breath of fresh air to the Scottish game. Unlike under Ronnie Deila, Celtic were good to watch and attacked with style. Furthermore, Rodgers showed that he was prepared to give youth a chance as Kieran Tierney developed into a player of talent rather than just a prospect.

Reality check time - 0-7 to Barcelona. Celtic may be top dogs in Scotland and better than they have been for a long time, but they are still a mile off the pace in Europe. Borussia Moenchengladbach were also a cut above Celtic, although credit must be given for two draws against Manchester City.

PREDICTION FOR 2017/18

Of course a domestic defeat is inevitable (I reckon Hibs will break their run), but a repeat domestic treble is a very realistic possibility.

Broonie Fae Hill of Beath

Scott Brown		L			LC			SC			OC			Total		
Season	Club	A	S	G	A	S	G	A	S	G	A	S	G	A	S	G
2002/3	Hibernian	3	1	3										3	1	3
2003/4	Hibernian	34	2	3	3	1	1	1						38	3	4
2004/5	Hibernian	18	2	1				2		1	2			22	2	2
2005/6	Hibernian	16	3	1	1			2		2	1			20	3	3
2006/7	Hibernian	30		5	5		2	5			2			42	0	7
2007/8	Celtic	31	4	3	2			3			9			45	4	3
2008/9	Celtic	36		5	3	1	1	2		1	6			47	1	7
2009/10	Celtic	19	2	1				3			5	1		27	3	1
2010/1	Celtic	26	2	2	2			4	1	2	4			36	3	4
2011/2	Celtic	20	2	3	2		1	4		2	3	1		29	3	6
2012/3	Celtic	14	3	3	2			3	1		10			29	4	3
2013/4	Celtic	37	1	2	1			2		2	9			49	1	4
2014/5	Celtic	31	1	5	4			5			7		1	47	1	6
2015/6	Celtic	22		1	1	1		3			9			35	1	1
2016/7	Celtic	34		1	4			5		1	12		1	55	0	3
														0	0	0
Total		371	23	39	30	3	5	44	2	11	79	2	2	524	30	57

Date	Comp	H/A	Opponents	F	A	HT		Referee	Crowd	Scorers
12/07/2016	UCL	A	Lincoln Red Imps	0	1	1	0	A Ekberg	1632	
20/07/2016	UCL	H	Lincoln Red Imps	3	0	3	0	B Frankowski	55632	Lustig, Griffiths, Roberts
27/07/2016	UCL	A	FC Astana	1	1	0	1	P Mazzoleni		Griffiths
03/08/2016	UCL	H	FC Astana	2	1	2	1	I Kovacs	52952	Griffiths, Dembele
07/08/2016	L	A	Hearts	2	1	1	1	J Beaton	16777	Forrest, Sinclair
10/08/2016	LC1	H	Motherwell	5	0	2	0	K Clancy	20165	Rogic 2, Dembele 2, Sinclair
17/08/2016	UCL	H	Hapoel Be'er Sheva	5	2	3	0	D Skomina	52659	Rogic, Griffiths 2, Dembele, Brown
20/08/2016	L	A	St Johnstone	4	3	3	0	C Thomson	6823	Griffiths, Forrest, Christie, Sinclair
23/08/2016	UCL	A	Hapoel Be'er Sheva	0	2	0	1	B Nijhuis	15383	
27/08/2016	L	H	Aberdeen	4	1	2	1	B Madden	57758	Griffiths, Forrest, Sinclair, Rogic
10/09/2016	L	H	Rangers	5	1	2	1	W Collum	58348	Dembele 3, Sinclair, Armstrong
13/09/2016	UCL	A	CF Barcelona	0	7	0	2	O Hategan	73290	
18/09/2016	L	A	Inverness CT	2	2	2	1	D Robertson	6061	Rogic, Sinclair
21/09/2016	LC2	H	Alloa	2	0	0	0	A Muir	15900	Forrest, Dembele
24/09/2016	L	H	Kilmarnock	6	1	2	1	N Walsh	53532	Dembele 2, Forrest, Griffiths, Sinclair, Rogic
28/10/2016	UCL	H	Manchester City	3	3	2	2	N Rizzoli	57592	Dembele 2, Stirling og
01/10/2016	L	A	Dundee	1	0	0	0	A Dallas	8827	Brown
15/10/2016	L	H	Motherwell	2	0	1	0	J Beaton	54159	Sinclair, Dembele
19/10/2016	UCL	H	Borussia Moenchengladbach	0	2	0	0	A Sidiropolous	57814	
23/10/2016	LCSF	N	Rangers	1	0	0	0	C Thomson	50697	Dembele
26/10/2016	L	A	Ross County	4	0	1	0	A Muir	6290	Roberts, Armstrong, Sinclair, Dembele
29/10/2016	L	A	Aberdeen	1	0	1	0	S McLean	17105	Rogic
01/11/2016	UCL	A	Borussia Moenchengladbach	1	1	0	1	J De Sousa	46283	Dembele
05/11/2016	L	H	Inverness CT	3	0	0	0	C Allan	54152	Sinclair, Griffiths, Rogic
18/11/2016	L	A	Kilmarnock	1	0	1	0	D Robertson	10962	Armstrong
23/11/2016	UCL	H	CF Barcelona	0	2	0	1	D Orsato	57937	
27/11/2016	LCF	N	Aberdeen	3	0	2	0	J Beaton	49626	Rogic, Dembele, Forrest
03/12/2016	L	A	Motherwell	4	3	0	2	K Clancy	8535	McGregor, Roberts, Armstrong, Rogic
06/12/2016	UCL	A	Manchester City	1	1	1	1	S Vincic	51927	Roberts
09/12/2016	L	A	Partick Thistle	4	1	1	0	C Thomson	7609	Armstrong 2, Griffiths, McGregor
13/12/2016	L	H	Hamilton Accies	1	0	1	0	C Allan	55076	Griffiths
17/12/2016	L	H	Dundee	2	1	1	0	B Madden	53589	Griffiths, Biton
20/12/2016	L	H	Partick Thistle	1	0	1	0	E Anderson	55733	Sinclair
24/12/2016	L	A	Hamilton Accies	3	0	1	0	W Collum	5003	Griffiths, Armstrong, Dembele
28/12/2016	L	H	Ross County	2	0	2	0	N Walsh	55355	Armstrong, Sviatchenko
31/12/2016	L	A	Rangers	2	1	1	1	S McLean	50126	Dembele, Sinclair
22/01/2017	SC4	A	Albion Rovers	3	0	1	0	W Collum	8319	Sinclair, Dembele, Armstrong
25/01/2017	L	H	St Johnstone	1	0	0	0	A Dallas	51057	Boyata
29/01/2017	L	H	Hearts	4	0	1	0	B Madden	58247	McGregor, Sinclair 2, Roberts
01/02/2017	L	H	Aberdeen	1	0	0	0	J Beaton	53958	Boyata
05/02/2017	L	A	St Johnstone	5	2	1	2	C Thomson	6548	Henderson, Sinclair, Dembele 3
11/02/2017	SC5	H	Inverness CT	6	0	2	0	K Clancy	25557	Dembele 3, Lustig, Tierney, Brown
18/02/2017	L	H	Motherwell	2	0	2	0	D Robertson	56366	Dembele, Forrest
25/02/2017	L	H	Hamilton Accies	2	0	1	0	C Allan	54685	Dembele 2
01/03/2017	L	A	Inverness CT	4	0	1	0	A Dallas	5948	Dembele 2, Armstrong, Sinclair
05/03/2017	SC6	H	St Mirren	4	1	0	1	S McLean	27455	Dembele, Lustig, Sinclair, Griffiths
12/03/2017	L	H	Rangers	1	1	1	0	B Madden	58545	Armstrong
19/03/2017	L	A	Dundee	2	1	1	0	W Collum	8968	Simunovic, Armstrong
02/04/2017	L	A	Hearts	5	0	2	0	K Clancy	16539	Sinclair 3, Armstrong, Roberts
05/04/2017	L	H	Partick Thistle	1	1	0	0	G Aitken	54047	Sinclair
08/04/2017	L	H	Kilmarnock	3	1	1	0	C Thomson	57679	Armstrong, Sinclair, Forrest
16/04/2017	L	A	Ross County	2	2	1	0	D Robertson	6205	Tierney, Roberts
23/04/2017	SCSF	N	Rangers	2	0	1	0	W Collum	49645	McGregor, Sinclair
29/04/2017	L	A	Rangers	5	1	2	0	J Beaton	49822	Sinclair, Griffiths, McGregor, Boyata, Lustig
06/05/2017	L	H	St Johnstone	4	1	0	0	N Walsh	52796	Roberts 2, Boyata, McGregor
12/05/2017	L	A	Aberdeen	3	1	3	1	S McLean	16015	Boyata, Armstrong, Griffiths
18/05/2017	L	A	Partick Thistle	5	0	3	0	A Dallas	7847	Griffiths, Rogic, Roberts 2, McGregor
21/05/2017	L	H	Hearts	2	0	0	0	J Beaton	58967	Griffiths, Armstrong
27/05/2017	SCF	N	Aberdeen	2	1	2	1	J Beaton	48713	Armstrong, Rogic

FRIENDLIES / OTHER GAMES				
30/06/2016	A	Celje	2 2	
03/07/2016	A	Sturm Graz	1 0	
06/07/2016	A	Olimpia Lubljana	2 1	
09/07/2016	A	Clyde	2 2	U20
09/07/2016	A	Maribor	0 0	
13/07/2016	A	Dalbeattie Star	4 0	U20
16/07/2016	H	VfL Wolfsburg	2 1	
16/07/2016	A	Whitehill Welfare	0 0	U20
23/07/2016	H	Leicester City	1 1	
24/07/2016	A	Vale of Leithen	4 2	U20
30/07/2016	N	CF Barcelona	1 3	in Dublin
09/08/2016	A	Albion Rovers	1 0	U20
13/08/2016	N	Inter Milan	0 2	in Limerick

Surname	First Name	DOB	SQ	Nat	Pos	L A	L S	L G	SC A	SC S	SC G	LC A	LC S	LC G	UC A	UC S	UC G	UNS	Signed	Previous Club	Notes	Contract
Aitchison	Jack	05/03/2000	76	SCO	F		2											2	2015	Celtic Youths		End 2018/19
Ajer	Kristoffer	17/04/1998	35	NOR	D											1			2016	IK Start	OL to Kilmarnock Jan-May	End 2019/20
Allan	Scott	28/11/1991	19	SCO	M														2015	Hibernian	OL to Rotherham U Aug-May, OL to Dundee 2017/18	End 2018/19
Ambrose	Efe	18/10/1988	4	NIG	D	4									2				2012	FC Ashdod	OL to Hibs Mar-May, Joined permanently June 2017	[redacted]
Armstrong	Stuart	30/03/1992	14	SCO	M	25	6	15	4		2	2	1		6	3		4	2015	Dundee United		End 2017/18
Bailly	Logan	27/12/1985	26	BEL	GK													6	2015	OH Leuven		End 2017/18
Biton	Nir	30/10/1991	6	ISR	M	16	10	1	3			1	1		5	3		13	2013	FC Ashdod		End 2019/20
Boyata	Dedryck	28/11/1990	20	BEL	D	17		5	5									3	2015	Manchester City		End 2018/19
Brown	Scott	25/06/1985	8	SCO	M	34		1	5		1	4			12		1		2007	Hibernian		End 2017/18
Christie	Ryan	22/02/1995	17	SCO	F	3	2	1					1		1			12	2015	Inverness CT	OL to Aberdeen Jan 2016-May 2018	End 2018/19
Ciftci	Nadir	12/02/1992	7	TUR	F		1			1						2		6	2015	Dundee United	OL to Pogon Szczecin Feb-May	End 2018/19
Commons	Kris	30/08/1983	15	SCO	M														2011	Derby County	OL to Hibernian Dec-Jan, Freed May 2017	[redacted]
De Vries	Dorus	29/12/1980	24	NET	GK	4									1			39	2016	Nottingham Forest		End 2017/18
Dembele	Moussa	12/07/1996	10	FRA	F	20	9	17	4		5	4		5	9	3	5	1	2016	Fulham		End 2019/20
Donnelly	Luke	20/01/1996		SCO	M														2013	Celtic Youths	OL to Alloa Aug-Jan, Morton Feb-May	
Doohan	Ross	29/03/1998	67	SCO	GK														2015	Celtic Youths		
Fasan	Leonardo	04/01/1994	38	ITA	GK													8	2011	Celtic Youths	OL to Port Vale Jan-May	OOC
Forrest	James	07/07/1991	49	SCO	M	23	5	6	2	1		4		2	8	3		6	2009	Celtic Youths		End 2018/19
Gamboa	Cristian	24/10/1989	12	CRC	D	13	4		1				1		2			26	2016	West Bromwich Albion		End 2018/19
Gordon	Craig	31/12/1982	1	SCO	GK	34	1		5			4			11			4	2014	Unattached		End 2019/20
Griffiths	Leigh	20/08/1990	9	SCO	F	15	8	12	1	2	1		2		6	3	5	4	2014	Wolves		End 2020/21
Hazard	Conor	05/03/1998		NIR	GK													1	2015	Cliftonville		End 2018/19
Henderson	Liam	25/04/1996	53	SCO	M	5	5	1	1				1			1		8	2008	Celtic Youths		End 2017/18
Hendry	Regan	21/01/1998		SCO	M														2010	Hutchison Vale		End 2018/19
Hill	Mark	10/07/1998		SCO	F														2012	Hamilton Accies		End 2019/20
Izaguirre	Emilio	10/05/1986	3	HON	D	10	2					2			3	1		22	2010	Montagua FC		End 2017/18
Janko	Saidy	22/10/1995	22	SWI / GAM	D	1	1					1			3	1		3	2015	Manchester United	OL to Barnsley Aug-June	End 2018/19
Johansen	Stefan	08/01/1991	25	NOR	M											1		1	2014	Stromsgodset	Transferred to Fulham Aug 2016	[redacted]
Johnston	Michael	19/04/1999		SCO	F	1													2016	Celtic Youths		End 2019/20
Kelleher	Fiacre	10/03/1996		ROI	D														2013	Celtic Youths	OL to Peterhead Jul 2016-Jan 2017,	[redacted]
																					Freed June 2017 joined Oxford Utd	
Kouassi	Eboue	13/12/1997		CIV	M	1	3			1								7	2017	Krasnodar		End 2020/21
Lindsay	Jamie	11/10/1995		SCO	M														2014	Celtic Youths	OL to Morton Jul-May, OL to Ross Co 2017/18	End 2017/18
Lustig	Mikael	13/12/1986	23	SWE	D	28	1	1	5		2	4			11		1	2	2011	Rosenborg Trondheim		End 2018/19
Mackay-Steven	Gary	31/08/1990	16	SCO	M	4	4		1							1		9	2015	Dundee United		End 2018/19
McAdams	Aidan	23/03/1999		SCO	GK														2015	Celtic Youths		
McCart	Jamie	20/06/1997		SCO	D								1						2014	Celtic Youths		
McGregor	Callum	14/06/1993	42	SCO	M	20	11	6	2	2	1	1	1		6	3		11	2009	Celtic Youths		End 2018/19
McManus	Conor	29/02/1996		SCO	M														2015	Celtic Youths	OL to QOS Mar-May	OOC
McMullan	Paul	25/02/1996		SCO	F														2014	Celtic Youths	OL to Dunfermline Ath Jul-May,	[redacted]
																					Freed June joined Dundee U	
Miller	Calvin	09/01/1998		SCO	F	1													2015	Celtic Youths		End 2018/19
Nesbitt	Aiden	05/02/1997	55	SCO	F														2015	Celtic Youths	OL to Morton Aug-May	End 2018/19
O'Connell	Eoghan	13/08/1995	34	ROI	D	2						1			3	1		2	2013	Celtic Youths	OL to Walsall Jan-May 2016,	OOC
Ralston	Anthony	16/11/1998	51	SCO	D	1							1					1	2015	Celtic Youths	Freed June 2016 joined Bury	End 2018/19
Roberts	Patrick	05/02/1997	27	ENG	F	20	12	9	2	2		2			5	4	2	4	2016	Manchester City (OL)	Jan 2016-May 2017	[redacted]
Rogic	Tom	16/12/092	18	AUS	M	14	7	7		2	1	4		3	7	2	1	4	2013	Central Coast Mariners		End 2018/19
Simunovic	Jozo	04/08/1994	5	CRO	D	24	1	1	2	1		3			2			5	2015	Dinamo Zagreb		End 2019/20
Sinclair	Scott	25/03/1989	11	ENG	M	30	5	21	5		3	2	1	1	7				2016	Manchester City		End 2019/20
Sviatchenko	Erik	04/10/1991	28	DEN	D	23	6	1	2	1		2	1		8	1		7	2016	Midtylland		End 2019/20
Thomson	Joseph	14/01/1997	51	SCO	M														2014	Celtic Youths	OL to Dumbarton Aug-Dec ,OL to QOS Jan-May	End 2017/18
Tierney	Kieran	05/06/1997	63	SCO	D	24		1	5		1	2			9			2	2014	Celtic Youths		End 2020/21
Toure	Kolo	19/03/1981	2	CIV	D	1	4			1		1			5	1		19	2016	Liverpool		OOC
Own Goal																	1					
NEW SIGNINGS																						
Hayes	Johnny																		2017	Aberdeen		End 2019/2
Benyu	Kundai			ENG / ZIM															2017	Ipswich Town		End 2020/2

Source of Birthdates: www.uefa.com / transfermarkt.com

Date	Comp	H/A	Opponents	F	A	1	2	3	4	5	6	7	8	9	10	11	12	13	14	15	16	17	18
12/07/2016	UCL	A	Lincoln Red Imps	0	1	Gordon	Janko	Ambrose	Sviatchenko	Tierney	Brown	Biton	Rogic+	Christie*	Dembele&	Griffiths	Forrest*	Armstrong+	Ciftci&	*Lustig*	*Roberts*	*McGregor*	*Fasan*
20/07/2016	UCL	H	Lincoln Red Imps	3	0	Gordon	Lustig	Forrest+	Sviatchenko	Tierney*	Brown	Armstrong	McGregor	Roberts	Dembele&	Griffiths	Ajer*	Izaguirre+	Ciftci&	*Christie*	*Rogic*	*Janko*	*Fasan*
27/07/2016	UCL	A	FC Astana	1	1	Gordon	Lustig	Ambrose	O'Connell	Tierney	Brown	Armstrong+	McGregor&	Roberts	Dembele*	Griffiths	Biton*	Forrest+	Rogic&	*Izaguirre*	*Ciftci*	*Janko*	*Fasan*
03/08/2016	UCL	H	FC Astana	2	1	Gordon	Lustig	Janko	O'Connell	Tierney	Brown	Armstrong+	McGregor	Roberts*	Forrest&	Griffiths	Johansen*	Toure+	Dembele&	*Izaguirre*	*Ciftci*	*Rogic*	*Fasan*
07/08/2016	L	A	Hearts	2	1	Gordon	Lustig	Toure	O'Connell+	Tierney	Brown	Armstrong*	McGregor	Dembele	Forrest&	Griffiths&	Sinclair*	Rogic+	Janko&	*Izaguirre*	*Ciftci*	*Johansen*	*Fasan*
10/08/2016	LC1	H	Motherwell	5	0	Gordon	Lustig*	Janko&	O'Connell	Izaguirre	Brown+	Rogic	McGregor	Dembele	Forrest	Sinclair	McCart*	Henderson+	Ralston&	*Armstrong*	*Ciftci*	*Christie*	*Fasan*
17/08/2016	UCL	H	Hapoel Be'er Sheva	5	2	Gordon	Lustig+	Toure	O'Connell	Tierney	Brown	Rogic&	McGregor*	Sinclair	Forrest	Griffiths	Biton*	Janko+	Dembele&	*Henderson*	*Christie*	*Sviatchenko*	*Fasan*
20/08/2016	L	A	St Johnstone	4	3	Gordon	Janko	Toure	O'Connell	Tierney	Brown	Rogic	Biton+	Sinclair	Forrest&	Griffiths*	Denbele*	Henderson+	Christie&	*Izaguirre*	*McGregor*	*Sviatchenko*	*Fasan*
23/08/2016	UCL	A	Hapoel Be'er Sheva	0	2	Gordon	Janko	Toure	Lustig	Tierney	Brown	McGregor&	Biton	Sinclair	Forrest*	Griffiths+	Rogic*	Dembele+	Sviatchenko&	*Izaguirre*	*Roberts*	*Armstrong*	*De Vries*
27/08/2016	L	H	Aberdeen	4	1	De Vries	Sviatchenko	Toure	Lustig	Tierney	Brown	Rogic	Biton&	Sinclair	Forrest*	Griffiths+	Roberts*	Dembele+	McGregor&	*Izaguirre*	*Christie*	*Janko*	*Gordon*
10/09/2016	L	H	Rangers	5	1	De Vries	Sviatchenko	Toure	Lustig	Tierney	Brown&	Rogic*	Biton	Sinclair	Forrest+	Dembele	Armstrong*	Roberts+	McGregor&	*Izaguirre*	*Ciftci*	*Gamboa*	*Gordon*
13/09/2016	UCL	A	CF Barcelona	0	7	De Vries	Sviatchenko+	Toure	Lustig	Tierney	Brown	Gamboa	Biton&	Sinclair	Roberts*	Dembele	Armstrong*	O'Connell+	McGregor&	*Izaguirre*	*Rogic*	*Forrest*	*Gordon*
18/09/2016	L	A	Inverness CT	2	2	De Vries	Sviatchenko	Gamboa*	Lustig	Tierney	Brown	Rogic&	McGregor	Sinclair	Roberts+	Dembele	Simunovic*	Forrest+	Armstrong&	*Izaguirre*	*Biton*	*Christie*	*Gordon*
21/09/2016	LC2	H	Alloa	2	0	Gordon	Simunovic+	Toure	Lustig	Tierney	Brown	Rogic&	Armstrong	Forrest	Roberts*	Dembele	Sinclair*	Christie+	Sviatchenko&	*Gamboa*	*Biton*	*Henderson*	*De Vries*
24/09/2016	L	H	Kilmarnock	6	1	De Vries*	Simunovic	Sviatchenko	Lustig	Tierney	Brown	Rogic	Biton	Sinclair&	Forrest	Dembele+	Gordon*	Griffiths+	Roberts&	*Gamboa*	*Toure*	*Armstrong*	*McGregor*
28/10/2016	UCL	H	Manchester City	3	3	Gordon	Sviatchenko	Toure	Lustig	Tierney	Brown	Rogic*	Biton&	Sinclair	Forrest+	Dembele	Armstrong*	Roberts+	Griffiths&	*Gamboa*	*Simunovic*	*McGregor*	*De Vries*
01/10/2016	L	A	Dundee	1	0	Gordon	Sviatchenko	Simunovic	Lustig	Tierney	Brown	Rogic*	Biton	Sinclair&	Forrest+	Dembele	Griffiths*	Roberts+	Armstrong&	*Gamboa*	*Toure*	*McGregor*	*De Vries*
15/10/2016	L	H	Motherwell	2	0	Gordon	Sviatchenko	Simunovic	Gamboa*	Tierney	Brown	Armstrong+	Henderson	Sinclair	Forrest&	Dembele	Griffiths*	Roberts+	Toure&	*Izaguirre*	*Christie*	*McGregor*	*De Vries*
19/10/2016	UCL	H	Borussia Moenchengladbach	0	2	Gordon	Sviatchenko	Toure	Lustig	Tierney	Brown	Rogic+	Biton*	Sinclair	Forrest&	Dembele	McGregor*	Griffiths+	Roberts&	*Izaguirre*	*Simunovic*	*Armstrong*	*De Vries*
23/10/2016	LCSF	N	Rangers	1	0	Gordon	Sviatchenko	Simunovic	Lustig	Tierney	Brown	Rogic+	Biton*	Sinclair	Forrest&	Dembele	Armstrong*	Griffiths+	Gamboa&	*Toure*	*Roberts*	*McGregor*	*De Vries*
26/10/2016	L	A	Ross County	4	0	Gordon	Sviatchenko	Gamboa	Lustig	Izaguirre	Henderson+	McGregor	Roberts	Christie*	Armstrong	Griffiths&	Dembele*	Sinclair+	Biton&	*O'Connell*	*Forrest*	*Rogic*	*De Vries*
29/10/2016	L	A	Aberdeen	1	0	Gordon	Sviatchenko	Simunovic	Lustig&	Izaguirre	Brown	Rogic*	Forrest+	Sinclair	Armstrong	Dembele	Biton*	Roberts+	Gamboa&	*O'Connell*	*Griffiths*	*McGregor*	*De Vries*
01/11/2016	UCL	A	Borussia Moenchengladbach	1	1	Gordon	Sviatchenko	Gamboa&	Lustig	Izaguirre	Brown	Rogic+	Forrest*	Sinclair	Armstrong	Dembele	Roberts*	McGregor+	Henderson&	*Biton*	*Ciftci*	*Boyata*	*De Vries*
05/11/2016	L	H	Inverness CT	3	0	Gordon	Sviatchenko	Simunovic	Lustig*	Roberts	Brown+	Griffiths	McGregor	Sinclair	Armstrong	Dembele&	Izaguirre*	Biton+	Rogic&	*Gamboa*	*Christie*	*Forrest*	*De Vries*
18/11/2016	L	A	Kilmarnock	1	0	Gordon	Sviatchenko	Boyata	Lustig	Roberts*	Brown	Forrest+	McGregor	Sinclair	Armstrong	Dembele	Rogic*	Biton+	*Toure*	*Gamboa*	*Christie*	*Izaguirre*	*De Vries*
23/11/2016	UCL	H	CF Barcelona	0	2	Gordon	Sviatchenko	Simunovic	Lustig	Izaguirre	Brown	Rogic+	McGregor&	Sinclair*	Armstrong	Dembele	Forrest*	Biton+	Roberts&	*Gamboa*	*Toure*	*Henderson*	*De Vries*
27/11/2016	LCF	N	Aberdeen	3	0	Gordon	Svaitchenko	Simunovic	Lustig	Izaguirre	Brown	Rogic+	Forrest&	Roberts*	Armstrong	Dembele	Biton*	McGregor+	Griffiths&	*Gamboa*	*Toure*	*Mackay-Steven*	*De Vries*
03/12/2016	L	A	Motherwell	4	3	Gordon	Toure	Simunovic	Lustig	Izaguirre*	Brown	Rogic	Forrest&	Roberts+	Armstrong	Dembele	McGregor*	Biton+	Gamboa&	*Christie*	*Boyata*	*Mackay-Steven*	*De Vries*
06/12/2016	UCL	A	Manchester City	1	1	Gordon	Sviatchenko	Simunovic	Lustig	Izaguirre	Brown	Rogic	Forrest*	Roberts	Armstrong	Dembele+	Mackay-Steven*	Griffiths+	Gamboa	*Toure*	*Biton*	*McGregor*	*De Vries*
09/12/2016	L	A	Partick Thistle	4	1	Gordon	Sviatchenko	Gamboa	Lustig	Izaguirre	Brown	Rogic+	Mackay-Steven*	Roberts&	Armstrong	Griffiths	Christie*	McGregor+	Dembele&	*Toure*	*Biton*	*Boyata*	*De Vries*
13/12/2016	L	H	Hamilton Accies	1	0	Gordon	Sviatchenko	Simunovic	Lustig	McGregor*	Brown	Rogic	Griffiths	Roberts	Armstrong	Dembele+	Mackay-Steven*	Biton+	*Izaguirre*	*Toure*	*Christie*	*Gamboa*	*De Vries*
17/12/2016	L	H	Dundee	2	1	Gordon	Sviatchenko	Simunovic	Gamboa	Izaguirre	Biton	Rogic*	Griffiths&	Christie	Armstrong	Mackay-Steven+	McGregor*	Sinclair+	Dembele&	*Toure*	*Lustig*	*Roberts*	*De Vries*
20/12/2016	L	H	Partick Thistle	1	0	Gordon	Lustig	Simunovic	Gamboa	Miller*	Brown	Roberts	McGregor	Sinclair+	Henderson	Dembele&	Izaguirre*	Armstrong+	Griffiths&	*Biton*	*Sviatchenko*	*Mackay-Steven*	*De Vries*
24/12/2016	L	A	Hamilton Accies	3	0	Gordon	Lustig	Sviatchenko	Gamboa	Izaguirre	Brown	Roberts+	McGregor	Sinclair&	Armstrong	Griffiths*	Dembele*	Biton+	Forrest&	*Toure*	*Christie*	*Henderson*	*De Vries*
28/12/2016	L	H	Ross County	2	0	Gordon	Lustig	Sviatchenko	Simunovic	Izaguirre	Brown	Christie*	Forrest&	Sinclair	Armstrong	Griffiths+	Henderson*	Dembele+	Roberts&	*Toure*	*Biton*	*Gamboa*	*De Vries*
31/12/2016	L	A	Rangers	2	1	Gordon	Lustig	Sviatchenko	Simunovic	Izaguirre	Brown	McGregor+	Forrest*	Sinclair	Armstrong	Dembele	Roberts*	Biton+	*Gamboa*	*Toure*	*Griffiths*	*Mackay-Steven*	*De Vries*
22/01/2017	SC4	A	Albion Rovers	3	0	Gordon	Lustig*	Boyata	Gamboa	Tierney+	Brown	Biton	Forrest&	Sinclair	Armstrong	Dembele	Simunovic*	McGregor+	Roberts&	*Christie*	*Henderson*	*Mackay-Steven*	*De Vries*
25/01/2017	L	H	St Johnstone	1	0	Gordon	Simunovic	Boyata	Gamboa&	Tierney	Brown	Biton	Forrest*	Sinclair	Armstrong	Dembele+	Roberts*	Griffiths+	Sviatchenko&	*Izaguirre*	*McGregor*	*Mackay-Steven*	*De Vries*
29/01/2017	L	H	Hearts	4	0	Gordon	Simunovic	Boyata	Gamboa+	Tierney	Brown	Biton	Forrest*	Sinclair	Roberts&	McGregor	Henderson*	Lustig+	Aitchison&	*Izaguirre*	*Sviatchenko*	*Mackay-Steven*	*De Vries*
01/02/2017	L	H	Aberdeen	1	0	Gordon	Simunovic	Boyata	Lustig	Tierney	Brown	Biton	Forrest*	Sinclair	Roberts&	McGregor+	Mackay-Steven*	Henderson+	Sviatchenko&	*Izaguirre*	*Gamboa*	*Aitchison*	*De Vries*
05/02/2017	L	A	St Johnstone	5	2	Gordon	Svatchenko	Boyata	Lustig	Tierney	Brown	Biton	Mackay-Steven*	Sinclair	Roberts&	Henderson+	Dembele*	McGregor+	Ciftci&	*Simunovic*	*Gamboa*	*Forrest*	*De Vries*
11/02/2017	SC5	H	Inverness CT	6	0	Gordon	Sviatchenko	Boyata&	Lustig	Tierney	Brown	Biton	Forrest	Sinclair	Dembele+	Henderson*	McGregor*	Ciftci+	Toure&	*Izaguirre*	*Gamboa*	*Mackay-Steven*	*De Vries*
18/02/2017	L	H	Motherwell	2	0	Gordon	Simunovic	Boyata	Lustig	Tierney	Brown	Biton+	Forrest	Sinclair	Dembele	Henderson*	Armstrong*	McGregor+	*Sviatchenko&*	*Izaguirre*	*Gamboa*	*Mackay-Steven*	*De Vries*
25/02/2017	L	H	Hamilton Accies	2	0	Gordon	Sviatchenko	Boyata	Gamboa	Tierney	Brown	Biton	Forrest*	Sinclair	Dembele+	Armstrong&	Mackay-Steven*	Griffiths+	McGregor&	*Izaguirre*	*Toure*	*Henderson*	*De Vries*
01/03/2017	L	A	Inverness CT	4	0	Gordon	Sviatchenko	Boyata	Lustig	Tierney	Brown+	Biton	Mackay-Steven*	Sinclair	Dembele	Armstrong	McGregor*	Henderson+	*Griffiths*	*Izaguirre*	*Toure*	*Gamboa*	*De Vries*
05/03/2017	SC6	H	St Mirren	4	1	Gordon	Sviatchenko	Boyata	Lustig	Tierney	Brown	Biton+	Mackay-Steven*	Sinclair	Dembele	Armstrong&	Roberts*	Griffiths+	Eboue&	*Simunovic*	*McGregor*	*Gamboa*	*De Vries*
12/03/2017	L	H	Rangers	1	1	Gordon	Sviatchenko	Boyata	Lustig	Tierney	Brown	Biton*	Forrest+	Sinclair	Dembele	Armstrong&	McGregor*	Roberts+	Griffiths&	*Simunovic*	*Eboue*	*Gamboa*	*De Vries*
19/03/2017	L	A	Dundee	2	1	Gordon	Simunovic	Boyata	Lustig	Tierney	Brown	McGregor*	Forrest+	Sinclair&	Dembele	Armstrong	Kouassi*	Roberts+	Sviatchenko&	*Biton*	*Griffiths*	*Gamboa*	*Bailly*
02/04/2017	L	A	Hearts	5	0	Gordon	Simunovic	Boyata&	Lustig+	Tierney	Brown	McGregor	Forrest	Sinclair	Roberts*	Armstrong	Mackay-Steven*	Gamboa+	Toure&	*Biton*	*Aitchison*	*Kouassi*	*Bailly*
05/04/2017	L	H	Partick Thistle	1	1	Gordon	Simunovic	Sviatchenko	Lustig	Izaguirre*	Biton	McGregor&	Gamboa	Sinclair	Roberts	Kouassi+	Armstrong*	Rogic+	Aitchison&	*Henderson*	*Tierney*	*Toure*	*Bailly*
08/04/2017	L	H	Kilmarnock	3	1	Gordon	Simunovic	Boyata	Lustig	Tierney	Brown	McGregor+	Forrest	Sinclair	Roberts*	Armstrong&	Dembele*	Rogic+	Kouassi&	*Izaguirre*	*Biton*	*Sviatchenko*	*Hazard*
16/04/2017	L	A	Ross County	2	2	Gordon	Simunovic	Sviatchenko	Rogic+	Tierney	Brown	McGregor	Forrest&	Sinclair	Dembele*	Armstrong	Griffiths*	Gamboa+	Roberts&	*Izaguirre*	*Toure*	*Kouassi*	*Bailly*
23/04/2017	SCSF	N	Rangers	2	0	Gordon	Simunovic	Boyata	Lustig	Tierney	Brown	McGregor+	Roberts&	Sinclair	Dembele*	Armstrong	Griffiths*	Rogic+	Forrest&	*Gamboa*	*Eboue*	*Sviatchenko*	*Bailly*
29/04/2017	L	A	Rangers	5	1	Gordon	Simunovic	Boyata	Lustig	Tierney	Brown&	McGregor	Roberts*	Sinclair	Griffiths	Armstrong+	Forrest*	Rogic+	Kouassi&	*Gamboa*	*Biton*	*Sviatchenko*	*De Vries*
06/05/2017	L	H	St Johnstone	4	1	Gordon	Simunovic	Boyata	Ralston	Tierney	Biton	Johnston*	Roberts&	Rogic+	Griffiths	Armstrong	Sinclair*	McGregor+	Forrest&	*Gamboa*	*Toure*	*Henderson*	*De Vries*
12/05/2017	L	A	Aberdeen	3	1	Gordon	Simunovic	Boyata	Lustig&	Tierney	Rogic*	McGregor	Roberts	Sinclair	Griffiths+	Armstrong	Biton*	Forrest+	Sviatchenko&	*Gamboa*	*Toure*	*Kouassi*	*De Vries*
18/05/2017	L	A	Partick Thistle	5	0	Gordon	Sviatechanko	Boyata*	Gamboa	Izaguirre	Brown	McGregor	Roberts	Rogic	Griffiths+	Forrest&	Toure*	Sinclair+	Biton&	*Ralston*	*Tierney*	*Kouassi*	*Bailly*
21/05/2017	L	H	Hearts	2	0	Gordon	Simunovic+	Boyata	Gamboa*	Tierney	Brown	McGregor	Roberts	Sinclair	Griffiths	Armstrong&	Rogic*	Toure+	Sviatchenko&	*Biton*	*Forrest*	*Kouassi*	*De Vries*
27/05/2017	SCF	N	Aberdeen	2	1	Gordon	Simunovic	Boyata	Lustig	Tierney*	Brown	McGregor	Roberts+	Sinclair	Griffiths	Armstrong	Rogic*	Sviatchenko+	*Dembele*	*Biton*	*Forrest*	*Gamboa*	*De Vries*

Clyde FC 2016/17

Founded	1877
Ground	Broadwood Stadium
Postcode	G69 9NE
Capacity	7936
Tel	01236 451511
Closest Railway Station	Croy
Record Attendance	52000 v Rangers, 21/1/1908
Record Win	11-1 v Cowdenbeath, 6/10/1951
Record Defeat	0-11, v Dumbarton, SC 22/11/1879,
	v Rangers SC, 13/11/1880
Most League Goals in a Season	32 Billy Boyd, 1932/3
Most Goals in Career	124 Tommy Ring
Chairman	Norrie Innes
Secretary	Gordon Thomson
Manager	Barry Ferguson (until Feb),
	Peter MacDonald / JP McGovern (Until May)
	Jim Chapman (from May)
Assistant Manager	Bob Malcolm (until Feb), John Joyce (from June)
Colours 2016/17 Top	White with redtrim
Shorts	Black
Sponsor	Advance Construction
Manufacturer	Hummel
Change Colours 2016/17 Top	Sky Blue
Shorts	Sky Blue
Sponsor	Heartfelt
Nicknames	Bully Wee
Web	www.clydefc.co.uk
Match Programme 2016/17	Clyde View £2.50

Under Barry Ferguson's management Clyde seemed to be heading in one direction only - destination Lowland League. Good Cup results couldn't disguise the fact that league results were awful. Barry's "Shuffle the pack" style of management wasn't working which was a shame - because he genuinely seemed to care about Clyde.

He was replaced in February and the caretaker duo of Peter MacDonald and John Paul McGoven did enough to ensure Clyde finished ahead of Cowdenbeath. Job done for them but with the talent in their squad they should not have been in that position in the first place.

Off-field issues seemed to be a problem at the fan-owned club. Hopefully for Clyde's sake these have been resolved and the club can focus on looking upwards in the near future.

PREDICTION FOR 2017/18

Jim Chapman did an admirable job as Annan manager. At Clyde he will find it easier to recruit players so he will have high expectations. Clyde fans expect their team to be challenging for promotion - they could be an outside bet for the title but more likely to qualify for the Play Offs.

Scott McLaughlin - Another Stalwart

Scott McLaughlin		L			LC			SC			OC			Total		
Season	Club	A	S	G	A	S	G	A	S	G	A	S	G	A	S	G
2001/2	Hamilton Accies		2											0	2	0
2002/3	Livingston	1												1	0	0
2003/4	Livingston	8	9	1		1		1	2					9	12	1
2004/5	Livingston	7	3			2								7	5	0
2004/5	Morton	14	1											14	1	0
2005/6	Livingston	2	2			1								2	3	0
2005/6	Morton	27	5	1				2				2	1	29	7	2
2006/7	Morton	28	1	2	1			2			4		1	35	1	3
2007/8	Morton	23	1					4		1	1			28	1	1
2008/9	Airdrie United	32	6	5	3			2		1	3	2		40	8	6
2009/10	Airdrie United													0	0	0
2009/10	Airdrie United	35		3	1			3			1			40	0	3
2010/11	Ayr United	37		5	1			4			3			45	0	5
2011/2	QOS	35		5	3			3		1	1			42	0	6
2012/3	Peterhead	26		3	1			1			1			29	0	3
2012/3	Ayr United	8		1										8	0	1
2013/4	Ayr United	37		1	1			3			2			43	0	1
2014/5	Ayr United	21	1	7	2		1	2			1			26	1	8
2014/5	Clyde	4												4	0	0
2015/6	Clyde	38	1	5	1			1			1			41	1	5
2016/7	Clyde	35	1		4			6		1				45	1	1
														0	0	0
TOTAL		418	33	39	18	4	1	34	2	4	18	4	2	488	43	46

Clyde were formed by a group of local boatmen who formed a football club in the banks of the Clyde at Flesher's Haugh in 1877. This was the same location and scenario that had led to the formation of Rangers a few years earlier.

In 1877 the Club Secretary John Graham lived at 24 Monteith Row, Glasgow.

The Daily Record of 29th August 1970 broke a story that caused shockwaves in Scottish football:

"Clyde and Hamilton Accies shocked football yesterday by merging to play First Division football at Douglas Park from September 19th. Hamilton die immediately leaving Raith Rovers without a Second Division match this afternoon. Clyde will play Falkirk at Brockville today, Celtic at home next week and then go to Motherwell in midweek before moving out of Shawfield for good.

The sudden decision to merge – it took only four days to decide – is the biggest upset in post-war Scottish football . . . So well kept in fact that the 16 £10 a week Hamilton players for whom the Scottish League will now try to find new clubs, will not be told officially about the change until they meet at 11 o'clock today for a game that won't be played.

Continued on next page . . .

					L			SC			LC			CC							
Surname	First Name	DOB	SQ Nat	Pos	A	S	G	A	S	G	A	S	G	A	S	G	UNS	Signed	Previous Club	Notes	Contract
Bain	Steven	11/07/1997	SCO	M													1	2016	Clyde Youths		
Barr	Kyle		SCO	F										1				2016	Celtic Youths		
Caddis	Dylan	18/02/1995	SCO	GK					1								9	2016	Ardrossan Winton Rovers	Freed Nov 2016 joined Ardrossan WR	[redacted]
Clark	Lewis	27/08/1998	SCO	D										1				2016	Clyde Youths		
Creechan	Matthew	17/03/1997	SCO	GK													2	2016	Clyde Youths		
Davidson	Robbie	25/01/1999	SCO	M										1			20	2016			
Easton	Dylan	06/04/1994	SCO	F	5		1				3	1	1					2016	Elgin City	OOC May 2017, joined Forfar Athletic	[redacted]
Edwards	Matthew	21/05/1998	SCO	M										1				2016	Clyde Youths		
Ferguson	Kyle	24/09/1999	SCO	M					1					1			20	2016	Blantyre Vics	Freed May 2017, joined Medaille Colllege	[redacted]
Ferguson	Scott	28/01/1995	SCO	M	7	17		3	3								5	2013	Clyde Youths		End 2017/18
Finnie	Ryan	19/02/1995	SCO	M	3	4											7	2017	Annan Athletic	OOC May 2017, joined Grange Thistle (Australia)	[redacted]
Flynn	Matt	15/05/1988	SCO	M	20	9	2	1	4	1	2				1		5	2016	Annan Athletic		End 2017/18
Gibson	John	31/01/1989	SCO	GK	25			4			4						10	2015	Alloa Athletic	Freed May 2017	[redacted]
Goodwillie	David	28/03/1989	SCO	F	5	1	4											2017	Doune Castle Amateurs		End 2018/19
Gormley	David	10/05/1988	SCO	F	28	7	8	6		8	1	3						2015	Auchinleck Talbot		End 2017/18
Gourlay	Kyle	24/09/1998	SCO	GK	6													2017	Dundee (OL)	Mar-May	[redacted]
Higgins	Sean	29/10/1984	SCO	F	24	7	7	6			3						4	2015	Cowdenbeath	Freed May 2017, joined Albion Rovers	
Johnston	Philip	19/09/1990	SCO	M	29	2		5			4							2016	Stirling Albion		End 2017/18
Kilpatrick	Robbie	09/02/1999	SCO	M										1				2016	Clyde Youths		
Linton	Scott	06/09/1989	SCO	D	21		1	2	1		4						1	2015	Dumbarton		OOC
Lochhead	Scott	23/01/1997	SCO	M	2	2											4	2017	Dunfermline Athletic (OL)	Jan-May	[redacted]
Long	Brett	11/04/1997	NIR	GK	1												1	2017	Dundee United (OL)	Jan 7-31 2017	
Lowdon	Jordan	24/06/1992	SCO	D	3						4							2016	Arbroath		End 2017/18
MacDonald	Peter	17/11/1980	SCO	F	30	1	17	6		4	3	1	1				5	2016	Dundee	OOC May 2017, joined Stirling Albion	[redacted]
Marsh	David	06/04/1990	SCO	M		1					1	1		1			3	2012	Cumbernauld United	Freed Aug 2016, joined Stenhousemuir	
McCardle	Connor	23/08/1998	SCO	F											1			2016	Clyde Youths		
McGinty	Michael	07/07/1999	SCO	M										1			7	2016	Airdrieonians Youth		
McGovern	John Paul	03/10/1980	SCOo	M	5				1								14	2015	Stirling Albion	Freed May 2017 joined Elgin City	[redacted]
McKenzie	Marc	11/07/1985	SCO	F	5	6											4	2017	Stirling Albion	Freed May 2017, joined Arthurlie	
McLaughlin	Scott	20/01/1984	SCO	M	35	1		6		1	4							2015	Peterhead	Freed May 2017	
McMillan	Jordan	16/10/1988	SCO	M	11			3									2	2017	Unattached	Ex Partick Th	OOC
McMillan	Mark	23/12/1998	SCO	GK	1									1			20	2015	Clyde Youths		OOC
McNeil	Ewan	04/10/1993	SCO	D	33		1	6			4		1					2016	Berwick Rangers		End 2017/18
McNiff	Martin	23/08/1991	SCO	D	30	1	1	5	1		4						2	2016	Annan Athletic		End 2017/18
McPhee	Jamie	18/10/1999	SCO	M													2	2016	Clyde Youths		
Miller	Aaron		SCO	F													2	2016	Clyde Youths		
Miller	Darren	04/08/1992	SCO	M	4	6		1	2								11	2016	Queen's Park (OL)	Nov 16-Jan 2017	[redacted]
Oliver	Michael	20/03/1990	SCO	D	4	1					2						11	2016	Cumbernauld Colts	OL to East Stirling Jan-May	OOC
Perry	Ross	07/02/1990	SCO	D	20	1		4	1								1	2016	Brechin City	Freed May 2017	[redacted]
Quinn	Craig	31/05/1997	SCO	M	3			2									3	2014	Hamilton Accies U17		OOC
Rutkewicz	Kevin	10/05/1980	SCO	D	2	1												2017	Unattached	Freed May 2017, joined Annan Ath	[redacted]
Shanganya	Divine	01/01/1998	ZIM	F													1	2016	St Catharine (USA)	OL to Camelon Jan-May 2016	
Smith	Christopher	31/08/1988	SCO	D	25	3	5	6						1			3	2015	Stirling Albion		OOC
Sweeney	Ronan	02/07/1998	SCO	M													6	2016	Clyde Youths		
Tiffoney	Scott	26/08/1998	SCO	F	3	3											1	2016	Morton (OL)	Nov 16-Jan 2017	[redacted]
Trella	Dustin	12/11/1999	SCO	F											1			2016	Clyde Youths		
Trialist						1															
Waddell	Kerr	14/06/1998	SCO	D	6													2017	Dundee (OL)	Mar-May	[redacted]
Watson	Jamie	06/03/1995	SCO	F		4			1		1	2	1	1			13	2016	Annan Athletic	OL to Shettleston Nov-Jan, Freed Feb joined Cumbernauld Utd	
Own Goals							2														
NEW SIGNINGS																					
Currie	Blair		SCO	GK														2017	Annan Athletic		
Miller	Darren	04/08/1992	SCO	M														2017	Colville Park		
Breslin	Jack																	2017	Hamilton Accies		
Stewart	Jordan																	2017	St Mirren		
Nicoll	Kevin			D														2017	Petershill		
Wright	Max			F														2017	Annan Athletic		

Source of Birthdates: Clyde FC Website

Last night these points were made clear: Dog racing at Shawfield will continue as usual; the name of the new club will continue to be Clyde – at least for the season – because of administrative difficulties. Several names have been considered such as Strathclyde Accies; Archie Robertson will manage the linked-up Clyde, and the players, all from Clyde, will continue as part-timers.

Clyde said they were moving out to the greater crowd potential of Hamilton to "avoid slow death". They need to earn £40,000 a year to exist. Hamilton explained that all their creditors would be paid (believed to amount to between £5000 and £6000) and that the move was 'for the benefit of both teams'. The link up between 101 year old Hamilton and Clyde was mooted in a phone chat between chairman Willie Dunn (Clyde) and John Crines (Hamilton) on Monday. Things moved swiftly from there with both boards – three strong Hamilton's and Clyde's seven – unanimous."

Within a few days a group of four former Hamilton Accies directors attempted to 'buy out' John Crines. They would have immediately reversed the merger decision. Other problems arose over the lease of the ground in Hamilton which was owned by the Town Council. Clyde were determined to go ahead despite the fact the move would cost up to £30,000 (paying off Accies debts and moving the floodlight system from Shawfield).

Hamilton Accies Supporters Club also applied for an interim interdict to prevent the move. Within a week the merger was off!

SOURCE: **Whatever Happened to Strathclyde Academicals**? – Unattributed article in SFH Number 60, February / March 1996

Date	Comp	H/A	Opponents	F	A		HT		Referee	Crowd	Scorers
16/07/2016	LC	H	Kilmarnock	1	2		0	0	J Beaton	1303	Watson
19/07/2016	LC	A	Morton	0	1		0	0	J McKendrick	931	
23/07/2016	LC	H	Berwick Rangers	1	1	6-5p	0	0	G Beaton	397	MacDonald
26/07/2016	LC	A	Albion Rovers	2	1		0	0	G Ross	377	McNeil, Easton
02/08/2016	CC	H	Partick Thistle U20	0	5		0	0	D Lowe	351	
06/08/2016	L	H	Montrose	2	1		1	0	K Graham	445	Easton, Flynn
13/08/2016	L	A	Stirling Albion	1	1		0	0	A Newlands	777	Higgins
20/08/2016	L	A	Annan Athletic	2	3		0	1	C Napier	421	MacDonald 2
27/08/2016	L	H	Cowdenbeath	5	3		3	2	D Munro	538	Smith 2, Higgins 2, Sives og
10/09/2016	L	H	Arbroath	3	2		2	2	S Reid	559	Linton, McNiff, MacDonald
17/09/2016	L	A	Elgin City	2	0		2	0	C Charleston	713	Higgins, MacDonald
24/09/2016	L	H	Forfar Athletic	0	1		0	1	G Ross	660	
01/10/2016	L	A	Berwick Rangers	1	1		1	1	G Aitken	469	Higgins
15/10/2016	L	A	Edinburgh City	1	0		0	0	G Beaton	432	Higgins
22/10/2016	SC2	A	Brora Rangers	2	0		0	0	S Lambie	350	Gormley, Flynn
29/10/2016	L	H	Stirling Albion	1	1		1	1	D Lowe	738	MacDonald
05/11/2016	L	H	Elgin City	2	1		2	0	M Roncone	616	Gormley, MacDonald
12/11/2016	L	A	Arbroath	0	4		0	1	C Steven	615	
19/11/2016	L	H	Berwick Rangers	3	2		1	0	C Napier	546	MacDonald, Gormley, Smith
03/12/2016	L	A	Cowdenbeath	0	1		0	0	S Reid	309	
06/12/2016	SC3	H	Arbroath	5	0		3	0	G Duncan	390	MacDonald 2, Gormley 2, McLaughlin
10/12/2016	L	A	Montrose	1	2		0	1	R Milne	396	MacDonald
17/12/2016	L	H	Edinburgh City	0	0		0	0	A Newlands	461	
26/12/2016	L	A	Forfar Athletic	3	4		2	1	M Northcroft	659	McNeil, Gormley, MacDonald
31/12/2016	L	H	Annan Athletic	2	3		1	0	S Millar	467	MacDonald 2
07/01/2017	L	A	Stirling Albion	0	3		0	1	S Reid	718	
21/01/2017	SC4R	A	Stirling Albion	2	2		1	1	M Northcroft	869	MacDonald 2
28/01/2017	L	H	Arbroath	1	2		0	1	D Lowe	465	MacDonald
31/01/2017	SC4R	H	Stirling Albion	3	2		3	1	M Northcroft	625	Gormley 3
04/02/2017	L	A	Edinburgh City	0	0		0	0	G Beaton	302	
11/02/2017	SC5	A	Ayr United	1	1		0	0	S Finnie	1554	Gormley
14/02/2017	SC5R	H	Ayr United	1	2	aet	1	1	S Finnie	965	Gormley
18/02/2017	L	A	Elgin City	1	4		0	1	G Ross	881	Higgins
25/02/2017	L	A	Annan Athletic	0	1		0	0	A Newlands	398	
28/02/2017	L	H	Montrose	1	2		0	2	G Irvine	365	MacDonald
04/03/2017	L	H	Forfar Athletic	2	2		0	1	S Millar	490	MacDonald, Gormley
07/03/2017	L	A	Berwick Rangers	3	4		2	3	G Duncan	336	Smith, Scullion og, Gormley
11/03/2017	L	A	Arbroath	0	1		0	1	K Graham	566	
18/03/2017	L	H	Edinburgh City	3	1		0	1	L Wilson	484	Flynn, MacDonald 2
21/03/2017	L	H	Cowdenbeath	0	2		0	1	C Steven	395	
25/03/2017	L	H	Stirling Albion	2	3		1	0	G Ross	606	MacDonald, Gormley
01/04/2017	L	A	Cowdenbeath	0	1		0	0	G Irvine	460	
08/04/2017	L	H	Annan Athletic	2	1		1	1	D Lowe	462	Smith, Gormley
15/04/2017	L	H	Elgin City	3	2		0	2	C Napier	465	Goodwillie 3
22/04/2017	L	A	Forfar Athletic	0	3		0	1	S Reid	741	
29/04/2017	L	H	Berwick Rangers	1	1		1	0	M Roncone	710	Gormley
06/05/2017	L	A	Montrose	1	1		1	0	G Beaton	1324	Goodwillie

FRIENDLIES / OTHER GAMES						
25/06/2016	A	Jersey XI	1	1		
02/07/2016	H	Airdrieonians	1	4		
05/07/2016	H	Dunfermline Athletic	0	1		
09/07/2016	H	Celtic XI	2	2		

16/07/2016	LC	H	Kilmarnock	1 2		Gibson	McNeil	Lowdon	McNiff	Johnston	Linton+	McLaughlin	Easton	Flynn	Higgins&	MacDonald*	Gormley*	Marsh+	Watson&	*Oliver*	*McMillan*	*K Ferguson*	
19/07/2016	LC	A	Morton	0 1		Gibson	McNeil	Lowdon	McNiff	Johnston	Linton	McLaughlin	Marsh+	Flynn	Higgins*	MacDonald&	Easton*	Gormley+	Watson&	*Oliver*	*McGinty*	*McMillan*	*K Ferguson*
23/07/2016	LC	H	Berwick Rangers	1 1	6-5p	Gibson	McNeil	Lowdon	McNiff	Johnston	Linton	McLaughlin	Easton	Oliver	Gormley	MacDonald	*Higgins*	*Davidson*	*Watson*	*K Ferguson*	*McGinty*	*McMillan*	
26/07/2016	LC	A	Albion Rovers	2 1		Gibson	McNeil	Lowdon	McNiff	Johnston	Linton	McLaughlin	Easton	Oliver	Higgins+	Watson*	Gormley*	MacDonald+	*Davidson*	*K Ferguson*	*McGinty*	*McMillan*	
02/08/2016	CC	H	Partick Thistle U20	0 5		M McMillan	Clark	Kilkpatrick&	Smith	Marsh	Edwards+	Watson	McGinty	K Ferguson	Barr*	Davidson	Flynn*	Trella+	McCardle&	*Sweeney*	*Bain*	*McPhee*	*Gibson*
06/08/2016	L	H	Montrose	2 1		Gibson	McNeil	Lowdon	McNiff	Johnston	Linton	McLaughlin	Easton	Oliver*	Gormley	MacDonald	Flynn*	*Smith*	*Watson*	*Marsh*	*McGinty*	*McMillan*	*K Ferguson*
13/08/2016	L	A	Stirling Albion	1 1		Gibson	McNeil	Lowdon	McNiff	Johnston	Linton	McLaughlin	Easton	Flynn	Gormley*	MacDonald	Higgins*	*Smith*	*Watson*	*Marsh*	*Oliver*	*McMillan*	*K Ferguson*
20/08/2016	L	A	Annan Athletic	2 3		Gibson	McNeil	Lowdon*	McNiff	Johnston	Linton	McLaughlin	Easton	Flynn&	Higgins+	MacDonald	Smith*	Gormley+	Marsh&	*Watson*	*Oliver*	*McGinty*	*Creechan*
27/08/2016	L	H	Cowdenbeath	5 3		Gibson	McNeil	Smith	McNiff	Oliver	Linton	McLaughlin	Easton	Flynn	Higgins*	MacDonald+	Watson*	Gormley+	*Marsh*	*Davidson*	*K Ferguson*	*McGinty*	*Creechan*
10/09/2016	L	H	Arbroath	3 2		Gibson	McNeil	Smith	McNiff	Johnston&	Linton	McLaughlin	Easton	Flynn*	Higgins+	MacDonald	Gormley*	S Ferguson+	Perry&	*Watson*	*Oliver*	*M McMillan*	*K Ferguson*
17/09/2016	L	A	Elgin City	2 0		Gibson	McNeil	Smith	McNiff	Johnston	Linton	McLaughlin	Perry	Flynn	Higgins+	MacDonald*	Gormley*	S Ferguson+	*Davidson*	*Watson*	*Oliver*	*M McMillan*	*K Ferguson*
24/09/2016	L	H	Forfar Athletic	0 1		Gibson	McNeil	Smith	Gormley*	Johnston	Linton	McLaughlin	Perry	Flynn+	Higgins	MacDonald	S Ferguson*	Watson+	*Davidson*	*McGinty*	*Oliver*	*Miller*	*K Ferguson*
01/10/2016	L	A	Berwick Rangers	1 1		Gibson	McNeil	Smith	McNiff	Johnston	Linton	McLaughlin	Perry	Flynn*	Higgins+	MacDonald	S Ferguson*	Gormley+	*Watson*	*Shanganya*	*Oliver*	*M McMillan*	*K Ferguson*
15/10/2016	L	A	Edinburgh City	1 0		Gibson	McNeil	Smith	McNiff	Johnston*	Linton	McLaughlin	Perry	Gormley+	Higgins	MacDonald	S Ferguson*	Flynn+	*Watson*	*Davidson*	*Oliver*	*M McMillan*	*K Ferguson*
22/10/2016	SC2	A	Brora Rangers	2 0		Gibson	McNeil	Smith	Gormley*	Johnston	Linton	McLaughlin	Perry	Flynn	Higgins&	MacDonald+	McNiff*	S Ferguson+	Watson&	*Davidson*	*McMillan*	*K Ferguson*	
29/10/2016	L	H	Stirling Albion	1 1		Gibson	McNeil	Smith	McNiff+	Johnston	Linton	McLaughlin	Perry	Flynn*	Higgins	MacDonald	Gormley*	S Ferguson+	*Watson*	*Oliver*	*Sweeney*	*M McMillan*	*K Ferguson*
05/11/2016	L	H	Elgin City	2 1		Gibson	McNeil	Smith	McNiff	Johnston	Linton	McLaughlin	Perry*	Gormley+	Higgins	MacDonald	S Ferguson*	Oliver+	*Watson*	*Davidson*	*Sweeney*	*M McMillan*	*K Ferguson*
12/11/2016	L	A	Arbroath	0 4		Gibson	McNeil	Smith	McNiff	Johnston	Linton	McLaughlin	Tiffoney+	Gormley *	Higgins	MacDonald&	Miller*	S Ferguson+	Flynn&	*M McMillan*			
19/11/2016	L	H	Berwick Rangers	3 2		Gibson	McNeil	D Miller	Perry	Johnston+	Linton	McLaughlin	Tiffoney*	Gormley&	Higgins	MacDonald	S Ferguson*	Smith+	Flynn&	*McNiff*	*McMillan*		
03/12/2016	L	A	Cowdenbeath	0 1		Gibson	McNeil	Smith	McNiff	Perry	D Miller	McLaughlin	Tiffoney*	Gormley	Higgins	MacDonald	S Ferguson*	*Flynn*	*McPhee*	*Caddis*			
06/12/2016	SC3	H	Arbroath	5 0		Gibson	McNeil	Smith	McNiff	Perry	Linton&	McLaughlin	D Miller*	Gormley	Higgins+	MacDonald	Flynn*	S Ferguson+	K Ferguson&	*Davidson*	*Caddis*		
10/12/2016	L	A	Montrose	1 2		Gibson	McNeil	Smith	McNiff	Perry	Linton+	McLaughlin	D Miller*	Gormley	Higgins	MacDonald	S Ferguson*	Tiffoney+	*Davidson*	*K Ferguson*	*Caddis*		
17/12/2016	L	H	Edinburgh City	0 0		Gibson	McNeil	Smith	McNiff	Perry	Linton	McLaughlin+	S Ferguson*	Gormley	Higgins&	MacDonald	Johnston*	Tiffoney+	Miller&	*Flynn*	*Caddis*	*Davidson*	*K Ferguson*
26/12/2016	L	A	Forfar Athletic	3 4		Gibson	McNeil	Smith	McNiff	Perry	Linton	McLaughlin	Johnston	Gormley	Flynn	MacDonald	*D Miller*	*Tiffoney*	*S Ferguson*	*Davidson*	*Caddis*	*A Millar*	*K Ferguson*
31/12/2016	L	H	Annan Athletic	2 3		Gibson	McNeil	Oliver	D Miller+	Perry	Linton	McLaughlin	Johnston	Gormley	Flynn*	MacDonald	Tiffoney*	S Ferguson+	*Higgins*	*Davidson*	*Caddis*	*A Millar*	
07/01/2017	L	A	Stirling Albion	0 3		Long	McNeil	Oliver	McNiff	Perry	Linton+	McLaughlin*	Johnston	Gormley	Higgins	MacDonald	Flynn*	Finnie+	*Millar*	*Caddis*	*K Ferguson*		
21/01/2017	SC4R	A	Stirling Albion	2 2		Gibson	McNeil	Smith	McNiff	Perry	J McMillan	McLaughlin	Johnston	Gormley*	Higgins	MacDonald	Ferguson+	*McGovern*	*Oliver*	*K Ferguson*	*Watson*	*Long*	
28/01/2017	L	H	Arbroath	1 2		Gibson	McNeil	Smith	McNiff	Finnie	J McMillan	McLaughlin	McKenzie	Gormley	Higgins*	MacDonald+	Ferguson+	Flynn+	*Davidson*	*Caddis*	*Watson*	*McGovern*	
31/01/2017	SC4R	H	Stirling Albion	3 2		Gibson	McNeil	Smith	McNiff	Johnston	J McMillan	McLaughlin	S Ferguson*	Gormley	Higgins	MacDonald+	Flynn*	Caddis+	*Watson*	*Miller*	*McGovern*	*Sweeney*	*Davidson*
04/02/2017	L	A	Edinburgh City	0 0		Gibson	McNeil	Smith	McNiff	Johnston	J McMillan	McLaughlin	McKenzie	Gormley	Higgins*	MacDonald&	Flynn*	Millar+	*Davidson*	*Sweeney*	*McGovern*	*Caddis*	
11/02/2017	SC5	A	Ayr United	1 1		Quinn	McNeil	Smith	McNiff	Johnston	J McMillan*	McLaughlin	S Ferguson+	Gormley	Higgins	MacDonald&	Perry*	Flynn+	Millar&	*Linton*	*Davidson*	*M McMillan*	*McGovern*
14/02/2017	SC5R	H	Ayr United	1 2	aet	Quinn	McNeil	Smith	McNiff*	Johnston	Perry	McLaughlin+	S Ferguson&	Gormley	Higgins^	MacDonald	Flynn*	Linton+	Millar&	*McGovern^*	*Davidson*	*Sweeney*	*Gibson*
18/02/2017	L	A	Elgin City	1 4		Quinn	Perry	Smith	McNiff	Johnston	J McMillan	Flynn+	McKenzie	Gormley&	Higgins	MacDonald	Linton*	S Ferguson+	McLaughlin&	*Finnie*	*Gibson*		
25/02/2017	L	A	Annan Athletic	0 1		Quinn	McNeil	Smith	S Ferguson	Johnston	Linton	McLaughlin	McKenzie	Gormley*	Higgins	MacDonald	Finnie*	*McNiff*	*Flynn*	*Millar*	*Gibson*	*Perry*	*McGovern*
28/02/2017	L	H	Montrose	1 2		Gibson	McNeil	Smith*	S Ferguson+	J McMillan	Linton	McLaughlin	McKenzie&	Perry	Higgins	MacDonald	McNiff*	Gormley+	Johnston&	*Flynn*	*Finnie*	*Quinn*	*McGovern*
04/03/2017	L	H	Forfar Athletic	2 2		Gibson	McNeil	McNiff	S Ferguson&	J McMillan+	Finnie*	McLaughlin	Johnston	Perry	Gormley	MacDonald	Flynn*	Smith+	Linton&	*Higgins*	*Millar*	*McGovern*	*Quinn*
07/03/2017	L	A	Berwick Rangers	3 4		Gibson	McNeil	McNiff	Smith	Linton*	Flynn	McLaughlin	Johnston	Perry	Gormley	Higgins+	McKenzie*	Millar+	*S Ferguson*	*Davidson*	*MacDonald*	*McGovern*	*M McMillan*
11/03/2017	L	A	Arbroath	0 1		Gibson	McNeil	McNiff	S Ferguson	J McMillan	Flynn+	McLaughlin	Johnston&	Perry	Gormley*	MacDonald	Higgins*	Lochhead+	McKenzie&	*Smith*	*Millar*	*McGovern*	*M McMillan*
18/03/2017	L	H	Edinburgh City	3 1		Quinn	McNeil	McNiff	Smith	J McMillan	Flynn	McLaughlin	Johnston	S Ferguson+	Gormley	MacDonald*	Higgins*	McKenzie+	*Finnie*	*Lochhead*	*Millar*	*McGovern*	*M McMillan*
21/03/2017	L	H	Cowdenbeath	0 2		M McMillan	McNeil	Finnie&	Smith	J McMillan+	Flynn	McLaughlin	Johnston*	S Ferguson	Higgins	MacDonald	McKenzie*	Rutkiewicz+	Millar&	*Lochhead*	*Davidson*	*McGovern*	*Quinn*
25/03/2017	L	H	Stirling Albion	2 3		Gibson	Perry*	Rutkiewicz	Smith	McNiff	Flynn&	McLaughlin	Johnston	Lochhead+	Gormley	MacDonald	Finnie*	Higgins+	Millar&	*McKenzie*	*S Ferguson*	*McGovern*	*M McMillan*
01/04/2017	L	A	Cowdenbeath	0 1		Gourlay	Waddell	Rutkiewicz	J McMillan	McNiff	Flynn&	McLaughlin	Johnston	Lochhead*	Gormley	MacDonald+	Finnie*	Goodwillie+	S Ferguson&	*McKenzie*	*Higgins*	*Miller*	*Gibson*
08/04/2017	L	H	Annan Athletic	2 1		Gourlay	Waddell	McNeil	Smith	McNiff	Flynn*	McLaughlin	Johnston	McGovern	Gormley	Goodwillie+	Lochhead*	Higgins+	*S Ferguson*	*McKenzie*	*Finnie*	*MacDonald*	*Gibson*
15/04/2017	L	H	Elgin City	3 2		Gourlay	Waddell	McNeil	Smith	McNiff	Flynn	McLaughlin	Johnston*	McGovern	Gormley	Goodwillie+	S Ferguson*	Higgins+	*Finnie*	*J McMillan*	*Lochhead*	*MacDonald*	*Gibson*
22/04/2017	L	A	Forfar Athletic	0 3		Gourlay	Waddell	McNeil+	Perry*	McNiff	Flynn	McLaughlin	J McMillan	McGovern	Gormley&	Goodwillie	S Ferguson*	Finnie+	Higgins&	*McKenzie*	*Millar*	*MacDonald*	*Gibson*
29/04/2017	L	H	Berwick Rangers	1 1		Gourlay	Waddell*	McNeil	Smith	McNiff	Higgins+	McLaughlin	Johnston	McGovern	Gormley&	Goodwillie	McKenzie*	Flynn+	MacDonald&	*Finnie*	*J McMillan*	*Lochhead*	*Gibson*
06/05/2017	L	A	Montrose	1 1		Gourlay	Waddell	McNeil	J McMillan	McNiff	Higgins+	McLaughlin	Johnston*	McGovern	Gormley	Goodwillie	McKenzie*	*Finnie*	*S Ferguson*	*MacDonald*	*Millar*	*Flynn*	*Gibson*

Cowdenbeath FC 2016/17

Founded	1882
Ground	Central Park
Postcode	KY4 9QQ
Tel	01383 610166
Capacity	4309
Closest Railway Station	Cowdenbeath
Record Attendance	25586 v Rangers, LC, 21/9/49
Record Win	12-0 v Johnstone, SC, 21/1/1928
Record Defeat	1-11, v Clyde, Lge, 6/10/51
Most League Goals in a Season	54, Rab Walls, 1938/9
Most Goals in Career	127 Willie Devlin
Chairman	Donald Findlay QC
Secretary	David Allan
Manager	Liam Fox (until Feb), Gary Locke
Assistant Manager	Jason Dair (until Feb), Billy Brown
Colours 2016/17 Top	Blue
Shorts	White
Sponsor	Subsea
Manufacturer	Uhlsport
Change Colours 2016/17 Top	Black
Shorts	Black
Nicknames	Blue Brasil, Miners
Web	www.cowdenbeathfc.com
Match Programme 2016/17	Blue Brazilian £2.50

Cowdenbeath were staring in the face of a third successive relegation. Stranded at the foot of the table for much of the season, they ended up surviving in the SPFL thanks to a penalty shoot-out win over Lowland League Champions East Kilbride.

The danger signs were there early on. Manager Liam Fox seemed to have a problem motivating experienced players and several vanished from the scene without explanation. Results were mixed to begin with, then bad. Surprisingly Fox was left in charge until February by which time it was too late to have much chance of avoiding bottom place. Garry Locke was brought in as a temporary replacement and brought about a significant improvement. Results were not always brilliant but at least the players looked like they wanted to win. They went into the Play Off on the back of some improved performances.

Off the field the club was rocked by revelations about gambling issues involving stalwart player Dean Brett. Cowden were left with little option but to sack him at a time when he was needed most.

PREDICTION FOR 2017/18

Will Cowden's "near death experience" have been enough of a fright to ensure it doesn't happen again? Competition at the foot of League Two is intense with the stakes so high. Cowden lack the resources to recruit in the same way as some other clubs can - it could be another uncomfortable season for the loyal supporters of this great club.

Date	Comp	H/A	Opponents	F	A		HT	Referee	Crowd	Scorers
16/07/2016	LC	H	Inverness CT	1	2		1 1	S Finnie	487	Brett
19/07/2016	LC	A	Dundee United	1	6		1 4	C Allan	3360	Turner
23/07/2016	LC	H	Dunfermline Athletic	0	3		0 0	C Steven	1481	
27/07/2016	LC	A	Arbroath	2	0		2 0	M Roncone	421	Johnston, Todorov
06/08/2016	L	H	Elgin City	0	1		0 0	S Reid	315	
13/08/2016	L	A	Forfar Athletic	3	4		1 2	C Charleston	516	Sives, Todorov, Moore
16/08/2016	CC	H	Celtic U20	1	2		1 0	S Kirkland	449	Todorov
20/08/2016	L	H	Edinburgh City	2	0		1 0	J McKendrick	325	Renton, Moore
27/08/2016	L	A	Clyde	3	5		2 3	D Munro	538	Brett,B Ross, Gormley og
10/09/2016	L	A	Montrose	2	1		1 1	D Lowe	393	Glen, Renton
17/09/2016	L	H	Berwick Rangers	0	2		0 2	S Millar	327	
24/09/2016	L	A	Arbroath	0	0		0 0	M Taylor	558	
01/10/2016	L	H	Stirling Albion	0	2		0 1	G Irvine	342	
15/10/2016	L	H	Annan Athletic	2	2		0 2	M Northcroft	331	Miller, Todorov
22/10/2016	SC2	H	East Kilbride	0	1		0 1	G Ross	286	
29/10/2016	L	A	Elgin City	1	3		0 2	S Reid	650	B Ross
05/11/2016	L	A	Berwick Rangers	1	1		0 1	K Graham	454	Muirhead
12/11/2016	L	H	Montrose	2	0		1 0	S Kirkland	270	Todorov, Renton
19/11/2016	L	A	Edinburgh City	1	1		1 0	G Beaton	382	Renton
03/12/2016	L	H	Clyde	1	0		0 0	S Reid	309	Renton
10/12/2016	L	A	Annan Athletic	0	2		0 1	D Munro	241	
17/12/2016	L	H	Forfar Athletic	3	4		1 2	G Irvine	277	Mullen 2, Renton
24/12/2016	L	H	Arbroath	0	2		0 2	A Newlands	317	
31/12/2016	L	A	Stirling Albion	2	1		0 0	A Muir	538	Renton, Moore
07/01/2017	L	H	Berwick Rangers	0	1		0 0	R Milne	343	
21/01/2017	L	A	Montrose	1	2		0 1	G Ross	432	Brett
28/01/2017	L	A	Forfar Athletic	1	3		1 0	C Steven	547	Carrick
18/02/2017	L	H	Annan Athletic	0	1		0 0	C Napier	258	
25/02/2017	L	A	Arbroath	1	4		0 2	M Roncone	519	Rumsby
28/02/2017	L	H	Edinburgh City	1	2		1 1	G Ross	309	Carrick
04/03/2017	L	H	Stirling Albion	0	2		0 1	G Beaton	381	
11/03/2017	L	A	Berwick Rangers	3	1		1 0	S Reid	408	Buchanan, B Ross, Renton
14/03/2017	L	H	Elgin City	1	1		0 1	D Munro	278	Carrick
18/03/2017	L	H	Montrose	0	2		0 1	J McKendrick	302	
21/03/2017	L	A	Clyde	2	0		1 0	C Steven	395	Miller, Syme
25/03/2017	L	A	Annan Athletic	0	1		0 0	C Napier	386	
01/04/2017	L	H	Clyde	1	0		0 0	G Irvine	460	Carrick
08/04/2017	L	A	Edinburgh City	1	1		0 1	C Charleston	577	Renton
15/04/2017	L	A	Stirling Albion	3	0		2 0	S Millar	638	Carrick 2, Renton
22/04/2017	L	H	Arbroath	1	2		0 1	D Munro	501	Rumsby
29/04/2017	L	H	Forfar Athletic	1	1		0 0	R Milne	571	Buchanan
06/05/2017	L	A	Elgin City	0	0		0 0	M Roncone	909	
13/05/2017	PO	A	East Kilbride	0	0		0 0	G Duncan	600	
20/05/2017	PO	H	East Kilbride	1	1	aet, 5-3p	1 0	C Charleston	1676	Mullen

FRIENDLIES / OTHER GAMES					
02/07/2016	H	Hearts XI	2	2	
05/07/2016	H	Motherwell	3	1	
09/07/2016	H	Alloa Athletic	1	2	
12/07/2016	A	Stenhousemuir	0	1	
16/07/2016	A	Kelty Hearts	1	6	U20 Kelty Tnt
17/07/2016	N	Dundonald Bluebell	4	1	U20 Kelty Tnt
23/07/2016	N	Arniston Rangers	2	5	U20 Preston Ath Tnt
24/07/2016	A	Preston Athletic	6	1	U20 Preston Ath Tnt
30/07/2016	A	East Fife	2	3	

Date	Comp	H/A	Opponents	F	A		1	2	3	4	5	6	7	8	9	10	11	12	13	14	15	16	17	18
16/07/2016	LC	H	Inverness CT	1	2		McGurn	Brett	Rutherford	G Ross	McLauchlan	Mullen	Moore	O'Brien&	Turner+	Glen*	Renton	Miller*	Robertson+	Johnston&	Swann	Creaney	Muirhead	Sneddon
19/07/2016	LC	A	Dundee United	1	6		McGurn	Brett	Rutherford	G Ross	McLauchlan*	Mullen	Moore	Sives	Turner&	Miller	Renton+	O'Brien*	Johnston+	Robertson&	Swann	Leslie	Sneddon	
23/07/2016	LC	H	Dunfermline Athletic	0	3		McGurn	Brett	O'Brien+	G Ross	McLauchlan	Mullen	B Ross	Sives	Turner*	Miller	Johnston	Robertson*	Muirhead+	Denton	Swann	Leslie	George	Sneddon
27/07/2016	LC	A	Arbroath	2	0		McGurn	Rutherford	O'Brien	G Ross	McLauchlan*	Mullen	B Ross&	Sives	Todorov	Miller	Johnston+	Robertson*	Muirhead+	Denton&	Swann	Leslie	Sneddon	
06/08/2016	L	H	Elgin City	0	1		McGurn	Rutherford	O'Brien&	G Ross	Brett	Mullen+	Turner*	Sives	Todorov	Miller	Glen	Moore*	B Ross+	Johnston&	Swann	Robertson	Creaney	Sneddon
13/08/2016	L	A	Forfar Athletic	3	4		McGurn	Rutherford	Moore	G Ross	Brett	Mullen	Turner	Sives	Todorov*	B Ross	Glen	Johnston*	Miller	O'Brien	Swann	Robertson	Creaney	Sneddon
16/08/2016	CC	H	Celtic U20	1	2		McGurn	Rutherford	Moore&	G Ross	Brett	O'Brien*	Turner	Sives	Todorov	B Ross+	Renton	Mullen*	Miller+	Glen&	Johnston	Robertson	Creaney	Sneddon
20/08/2016	L	H	Edinburgh City	2	0		McGurn	Rutherford	Moore	G Ross	Brett	Mullen	Turner	Sives	Todorov	B Ross*	Renton+	Miller*	Glen+	Leslie	Johnston	Robertson	Creaney	Sneddon
27/08/2016	L	A	Clyde	3	5		McGurn	Rutherford	Moore	G Ross	Brett	Mullen	Turner+	Sives	Glen*	B Ross	Renton	Todorov*	Miller+	McLaughlin	Muirhead	Robertson	Creaney	Sneddon
10/09/2016	L	A	Montrose	2	1		McGurn	Creaney	McLauchlan	Miller	Brett	Mullen	Robertson*	Todorov	Glen+	B Ross	Renton	Turner*	Murrell+	Sives	Moore	Rutherford	O'Brien	Sneddon
17/09/2016	L	H	Berwick Rangers	0	2		McGurn	Creaney	McLauchlan	Miller&	Brett	Mullen	Robertson+	Todorov	Glen	B Ross*	Renton	Moore*	Turner+	Murrell&	Sives	Rutherford	O'Brien	Sneddon
24/09/2016	L	A	Arbroath	0	0		McGurn	Creaney	McLauchlan	Moore	Brett	Mullen	Turner	Todorov*	Sives	B Ross	Renton	Glen*	Miller	O'Brien	Rutherford	Pyper	Murrell	Sneddon
01/10/2016	L	H	Stirling Albion	0	2		McGurn	Creaney	McLauchlan	Moore	Brett&	Mullen	Turner*	Todorov+	Sives	B Ross	Renton	Miller*	Glen+	Murrell&	Rutherford	Pyper	O'Brien	Sneddon
15/10/2016	L	H	Annan Athletic	2	2		McGurn	Rutherford	McLauchlan	Pyper	O'Brien	Mullen	Miller	Glen*	Sives	B Ross	Renton+	Murrell*	Todorov+	Brett	Robertson	Creaney	Muirhead	Sneddon
22/10/2016	SC2	H	East Kilbride	0	1		McGurn	Rutherford	McLauchlan+	Pyper	O'Brien	Mullen	Miller	Todorov*	Sives	B Ross&	Renton	Muirhead*	Robertson+	Turner&	Murrell	Creaney	Sneddon	
29/10/2016	L	A	Elgin City	1	3		McGurn	Moore*	Creaney	Pyper	O'Brien+	Mullen	Miller&	Todorov	Sives	Turner	Renton	Robertson*	B Ross+	Murrell&	Glen	Rutherford	McLauchlan	Sneddon
05/11/2016	L	A	Berwick Rangers	1	1		McGurn	Brett	McLauchlan	Pyper	O'Brien	Moore	Miller	Todorov+	Johnston	B Ross*	Renton	Robertson*	Muirhead+	Murrell	Mullen	Sives	Creaney	Sneddon
12/11/2016	L	H	Montrose	2	0		McGurn	Brett	McLauchlan	Pyper	O'Brien+	Moore&	Miller	Todorov	Johnston*	B Ross	Renton	Muirhead*	Mullen+	Creaney&	Turner	Sives	Murrell	Sneddon
19/11/2016	L	A	Edinburgh City	1	1		McGurn	Brett	McLauchlan	Pyper	O'Brien*	Moore	Miller	Todorov	Johnston+	B Ross	Renton	Mullen*	Muirhead+	Sives	Rutherford	Robertson	Murrell	Sneddon
03/12/2016	L	H	Clyde	1	0		McGurn	Brett	McLauchlan	Pyper	Mullen	Moore+	Miller	Todorov	Johnston*	B Ross	Renton	Muirhead*	Rutherford+	Sives	O'Brien	Robertson	Turner	Sneddon
10/12/2016	L	A	Annan Athletic	0	2		McGurn	Brett&	McLauchlan	Pyper	Mullen	Moore	Miller	Todorov	Johnston*	B Ross+	Renton	Muirhead*	Robertson+	Rutherford&	O'Brien	Sives	Turner	Sneddon
17/12/2016	L	H	Forfar Athletic	3	4		McGurn	Brett	McLauchlan	Pyper*	Mullen	Moore	Miller	Todorov	Muirhead+	B Ross	Renton	Rutherford*	Johnston+	Robertson	O'Brien	Glen	Turner	Sneddon
24/12/2016	L	H	Arbroath	0	2		McGurn	Brett	McLauchlan	Rutherford	Mullen	Moore	Miller	Todorov	Muirhead+	B Ross*	Renton	Robertson*	Johnston+	Pyper	O'Brien	Glen	Murrell	Sneddon
31/12/2016	L	A	Stirling Albion	2	1		McGurn	Brett	McLauchlan	Rutherford	Mullen	Moore	Miller	Todorov	Johnston*	B Ross	Renton	Robertson*	O'Brien	Glen	Pyper	Murrell	Muirhead	Sneddon
07/01/2017	L	H	Berwick Rangers	0	1		McGurn	Brett	McLauchlan	Rutherford	O'Brien*	Moore	Miller	Todorov	Johnston+	B Ross	Renton	Swann*	Muirhead+	Pyper	Robertson	Murrell	Thompson	Sneddon
21/01/2017	L	A	Montrose	1	2		McGurn	Rumsby	McLauchlan	Rutherford	Henderson	Moore	Miller	Brett	Johnston*	Mullen	Renton	Muirhead*	O'Brien	Swann	Pyper	B Ross	Sneddon	
28/01/2017	L	A	Forfar Athletic	1	3		McGurn	Rumsby	Pyper	Rutherford	Henderson	Moore	Miller	Brett*	Carrick	Mullen	Renton	O'Brien*	McLauchlan	Swann	Johnston	B Ross	Muirhead	Donoghue
18/02/2017	L	H	Annan Athletic	0	1		Sneddon	Rumsby	McLauchlan	Rutherford	Henderson+	Moore*	Miller	Mullen	Carrick	Buchanan	Renton	Rooney*	Ross+	O'Brien	Johnston	Pyper	Muirhead	McGurn
25/02/2017	L	A	Arbroath	1	4		Sneddon	Rumsby	McLauchlan	Rooney*	Henderson	Moore+	Miller	Mullen	Carrick	Buchanan	Renton&	B Ross*	O'Brien+	Muirhead&	Johnston	Pyper	Rutherford	McGurn
28/02/2017	L	H	Edinburgh City	1	2		Sneddon	Rumsby	McLauchlan	Rutherford	Henderson	Pyper	B Ross	Mullen	Carrick	Buchanan*	Renton	Moore*	Miller	O'Brien	Johnston	Muirhead	McGurn	
04/03/2017	L	H	Stirling Albion	0	2		Sneddon	Rumsby	McLauchlan	Rutherford	Henderson	Pyper	B Ross+	Moore*	Carrick	Buchanan	Renton	Miller*	Muirhead+	O'Brien	Johnston	Glen	McGurn	
11/03/2017	L	A	Berwick Rangers	3	1		Sneddon	Rumsby	McLauchlan	Rutherford	Henderson	Pyper	B Ross	Mullen	Carrick+	Buchanan*	Renton&	Johnston*	Moore+	Glen&	O'Brien	Muirhead	McGurn	
14/03/2017	L	H	Elgin City	1	1		Sneddon	Rumsby	McLauchlan	Rutherford	Henderson	Pyper	Syme	Mullen	Carrick	Buchanan*	Renton	Moore*	Miller	Glen	Johnston	Muirhead	McGurn	
18/03/2017	L	H	Montrose	0	2		Sneddon	Rumsby	McLauchlan	Rutherford	Henderson*	Pyper	Syme&	Mullen	Carrick	Buchanan+	Renton	Moore*	Johnston+	Miller&	Glen	B Ross	Muirhead	McGurn
21/03/2017	L	A	Clyde	2	0		Sneddon	Rumsby	McLauchlan	Rutherford	Henderson*	Pyper	Syme	Mullen	Carrick+	Miller	Renton	B Ross*	Muirhead+	O'Brien	Glen	Johnston	Buchanan	McGurn
25/03/2017	L	A	Annan Athletic	0	1		Sneddon	Rumsby	McLauchlan	Rutherford	Henderson+	Pyper	Syme	Mullen&	Carrick*	Miller	Renton	Glen*	Buchanan+	Moore&	B Ross	Johnston	Muirhead	McGurn
01/04/2017	L	H	Clyde	1	0		Sneddon	Rumsby	McLauchlan	Rutherford	Henderson	Pyper	Syme	Mullen	Carrick	Miller*	Renton	B Ross*	Buchanan	Moore	O'Brien	Johnston	Muirhead	McGurn
08/04/2017	L	A	Edinburgh City	1	1		Sneddon	Buchanan*	O'Brien&	Rutherford	Henderson+	Pyper	Syme	Mullen	Carrick	Miller	Renton	Moore*	Muirhead+	Johnston&	B Ross	McGurn		
15/04/2017	L	A	Stirling Albion	3	0		Sneddon	Rumsby	O'Brien	Rutherford	Henderson	Pyper	Syme	Mullen*	Carrick	Miller	Renton	Moore*	Muirhead	Johnston	B Ross	McLauchlan	Buchanan	McGurn
22/04/2017	L	H	Arbroath	1	2		Sneddon	Rumsby	O'Brien*	Rutherford	Henderson&	Pyper	Syme	Mullen	Carrick	Miller	Moore+	Johnston*	Buchanan+	Muirhead&	Rooney	McLauchlan	McGurn	
29/04/2017	L	H	Forfar Athletic	1	1		Sneddon	Rumsby	Buchanan	Rutherford	Henderson	Pyper	Syme*	Mullen	Carrick	Miller	Renton	Moore*	O'Brien	Rooney	Johnston	Muirhead	McGurn	
06/05/2017	L	A	Elgin City	0	0		Sneddon	Rumsby	Buchanan*	Rutherford	Henderson	Pyper	Syme	Mullen+	Carrick	Miller	Renton	Moore*	Muirhead+	Rooney	Johnston	O'Brien	McLauchlan	McGurn
13/05/2017	PO	A	East Kilbride	0	0		Sneddon	Rumsby	McLauchlan	Moore	Henderson*	Pyper	Syme	Mullen	Carrick	Miller	Renton	Buchanan*	O'Brien	Johnston	Rooney	Muirhead	McGurn	
20/05/2017	PO	H	East Kilbride	1	1	aet, 5-3p	Sneddon	Rumsby	McLauchlan	Buchanan*	Henderson	Pyper	Syme	Mullen	Carrick&	Miller+	Renton	Moore*	O'Brien+	Johnston&	Rooney	Muirhead	McGurn	

						L			SC			LC			CC							
			SQ	Nat	Pos	A	S	G	A	S	G	A	S	G	A	S	G	UNS				
umame	First Name	DOB																	Signed	Previous Club	Notes	Contract
damson	Kenny	21/08/1988		SCO	D														2007	Livingston	Freed May 2017, joined Kelty Hearts	[redacted]
rett	Dean	08/12/1992		SCO	D	19		2				3		1	1			10	2008	Cowdenbeath Youths	Sacked Mar 2017, joined Bonnyrigg Rose	[redacted]
uchanan	Robbie	23/02/1996		SCO	M	11	3	2										3	2017	Hearts (OL)	Jan-May	[redacted]
arrick	Dale	07/01/1994		SCO	F	18		6											2017	Livingston |(OL)	Jan-May	[redacted]
reaney	James	19/10/1988		SCO	D	5	1												2016	Hurlford United	Freed Jan 2017	[redacted]
enton	Charlie	03/03/1997		SCO	M								1					1	2016	Berwick Rangers	OL to Whitehill Welfare Aug-Jan	
onoghue	Shaun	14/07/1999		SCO	GK													1	2016	Cowdenbeath Youths	OL to Broxburn Ath Aug-Jan	
eorge	Rory	01/01/1998		SCO	M													1	2016	Cowdenbeath Youths	OL to Oakley Utd Sep-Jan	
len	Gary	22/03/1990		SCO	F	6	5	1				1				1		8	2016	Livingston	Freed May 2017	[redacted]
enderson	Liam	23/08/1996		SCO	M	19													2017	Falkirk (OL)	Jan-May	[redacted]
enderson	John-James	04/12/1999		SCO	M														2016	Dunfermline Ath U17		
ohnston	Craig	22/12/1994		SCO	F	8	9					2	2	1				15	2011	East Fife	OL to Spartans Sep-Nov 2016,	[redacted]
																					OOC May 2017, joined Montrose	
ellichan	Lyle	28/03/2000		SCO	D														2016	Lochgelly Colts	OL to Burntisland SY Aug-Sep, Oakley Utd Sep-Nov	
eslie	Jordan	26/12/1999		SCO	D													4	2016	Cowdenbeath Youths	OL to Jeanfield Swifts Sep-Jan	End 2017/18
McConnell	Dean	12/11/1998		SCO	D														2016	Berwick Rangers U20		
McGurn	David	14/09/1980		SCO	GK	21			1			4			1			17	2016	Raith Rovers		End 2017/18
McLauchlan	Gerry	08/03/1989		SCO	D	27			1			4						6	2016	Ayr United		OOC
McManus	Sean	16/04/1999		SCO															2016	Fife Elite FA	OL to Glenrothes Aug - Nov	End 2017/18
Miller	Kyle	08/08/1992		SCO	M	28	5	2	1			3	1			1		4	2015	Cowdenbeath Youths		End 2017/18
Moore	Lewis	04/06/1998		SCO	M	22	12	3				2			1			2	2016	Hearts (OL)	Jul 2016-May 2017	[redacted]
Muirhead	Cameron	18/05/1998		SCO	F	2	13	1		1			2					16	2015	Fife Elite FA		End 2017/18
Mullen	Fraser	08/11/1993		SCO	D	33	2	3	1			4				1		1	2016	East Fife		End 2017/18
Murrell	Aaron	23/09/1997		SCO	F		5											8	2016	Dundee United (OL)	Aug-Jan	[redacted]
O'Brien	Burton	10/06/1981		RSA/SCO	M	10	3		1			3	1		1			20	2016	Alloa Athletic	Retired May 2017	[redacted]
Pyper	Jamie	22/08/1993		SCO	D	24			1									8	2016	Gallivare MFF		End 2017/18
Renton	Kieran	12/07/1990		SCO	F	35		10	1			2			1				2016	Newtongrange Star	OOC May 2017, joined Alloa Athletic	[redacted]
Robertson	David	23/09/1986		SCO	M	2	5			1			4					10	2016	Selkirk	Retired Jan 2017	[redacted]
Rooney	Matthew	18/02/1990		NIR	F	1	1											5	2017	Portadown		
Ross	Greg	02/05/1987		SCO	M	4						4			1				2016	Penicuik Athletic	Freed Sep 2016, joined Tynecastle FC	[redacted]
Ross	Brian	08/05/1995		SCO	M	20	6	3	1			2			1			6	2016	Fauldhouse United	Freed April 2017	
Rumsby	Scott	01/01/1994		SCO	D	18		2											2017	Peterhead		End 2017/18
Rutherford	Shaun	03/10/1996		SCO	D	24	3		1			3			1			7	2016	Queen of the South		End 2017/18
ives	Craig	09/04/1986		SCO	D	8		1	1			3			1			7	2016	Livingston	Freed Jan 2017	[redacted]
neddon	Jamie	06/09/1997		SCO	GK	17												26	2014	Hearts	OOC June 2017, joined Partick Thistle	[redacted]
wann	Harvey	12/08/1997		ENG	M		1											8	2016	Cowdenbeath Youths	OL to Whitehill Welfare Sep-Dec 2016,	End 2017/18
																					Linlithgow Rose Jan-May	
yme	David	23/06/1997		SCO	D	12		1											2017	Raith Rovers (OL)	Mar-May	[redacted]
Thomson	Hamish	15/05/1998		SCO	D													1	2016	Cowdenbeath Youths	OL to Fauldhouse Utd Sep-Jan	
Todorov	Nikolai	24/08/1996		BUL	D	17	2	3	1			1		1	1		1		2016	Hearts (OL)	Jul-Jan	[redacted]
urnbull	Lewis	29/11/1999		SCO	M														2016	Fife Elite FA		End 2017/18
Turner	Chris	03/01/1987		NIR	M	7	2			1		3		1	1			4	2016	Hamilton Accies	Freed Feb 2017, joined Glenavon	[redacted]
Watt	Callum	14/05/1999		SCO	D														2016	Cowdenbeath Youths	OL to Burntisland SY Aug-Jan	
Wilson	Josh	25/09/1997		ENG															2015	Raith Rovers	OL to Glenrothes Aug-Sep, Oakley Utd Sep-Oct,	[redacted]
																					Freed Jan	
Own Goals								1														
NEW SIGNINGS																						
ack Whittaker					M														2017	Kilmarnock		End 2017/18
Robbie Buchanan					F														2017	Hearts		End 2017/18
osh Morris					F														2017	Hawick Royal Albert		End 2017/18
David Syme					D														2017	Raith Rovers		End 2017/18
oe McGovern					GK														2017	Forfar Athletic		End 2017/18

Source of Birthdates: Cowdenbeath FC Programme & transfermarkt.com

Dumbarton FC 2016/17

Founded	1872
Ground	Dumbarton Stadium
Postcode	G82 1JJ
Tel	01389 762569
Capacity	2020
Closest Railway Station	Dumbarton East
Record Attendance	18000 v Raith Rovers, SC, 2/3/57
Record Win	13-1 v Kirkintilloch Central, SC, 1/1/1888
Record Defeat	1-11 v Albion Rovers, Lge, 30/1/1926;
	v Ayr United, LC, 13/8/52
Most League Goals in a Season	38 Kenny Wilson, 1971/2
Most Goals in Career	202 Hughie Gallacher
Chairman	Alan Jardine
Manager	Steven Aitken
Assistant Manager	Ian Durrant
General Manager	Frank Meade
Colours 2016/17 Top	White with Black and Gold Chest Band
Shorts	White
Sponsor	Turnberry Homes
Manufacturer	Joma
Change Colours 2016/17 Top	Red and Black Stripes
Shorts	Black
Nicknames	Sons
Web	www.dumbartonfootballclub.com
Match Programme 2016/17	Sons View £2.50

Dumbarton were the choice of many as favourites fc relegation. After a season of some ups and downs the survived comfortably which was quite an achievemer against better-resourced clubs.

It all looked bleak at the turn of the year. Dumbarto had been emptied from the Scottish Cup by Bonnyrig Rose - the first time a Championship side had lost t Junior opponents. Calls were made for the head c manager Stevie Aitken. But Dumbarton kept a calr head, and soldiered on. The problem in the Cup ha partly been an over-reliance of loan players who we ineligible, as well as two below-par performances agains Bonnyrigg.

PREDICTION FOR 2017/18

Dumbarton's problem is that their best players wi always be enticed away by the prospect of full tim football. It has happened again in 2017 with several ke figures moving to other Championship sides. That mear another re-building job for manager Aitken. This seaso they are not the only part time side in the League, havin been joined by Brechin. Realistically second-bottom where they should finish, but it is quite possible that the will hoist themselves up to lower mid-table.

						L			SC			LC			CC							
			SQ	Nat	Pos	A	S	G	A	S	G	A	S	G	A	S	G	UNS				
Surname	First Name	DOB																	Signed	Previous Club	Notes	Con
Barclay	Jamie	29/09/1989	13	SCO	GK													6	2016	Stenhousemuir	Freed Aug 2016, joined E Stirlingshire	[redacted]
Barr	Darren	17/03/1985	14	SCO	D	31	1		2						1			4	2015	Ross County	OOC May 2017, joined Morton as Head of Youth	
Brown	Mark	28/02/1981	1	SCO	GK		1					4						10	2015	Ross County	Retired March 2017, joined Police	
Buchanan	Gregor	31/03/1990	5	SCO	D	33		1	2			4		1	1			1	2015	Dunfermline Athletic	OOC May 2017, joined St Mirren	
Cameron	Jay	07/04/1999		SCO	M														2016	Dumbarton Youths	OL to Newmains Utd Oct-Feb, Freed Feb 2017	
Carswell	Stuart	09/09/1993	6	SCO	M	16													2017	Keflavik		End
Clark	Ryan	01/08/1997	20	SCO	M													7	2016	Dumbarton Youths	OL to Kilwinning Rangers Aug-Dec 2016	
Crawford	Lewis	17/01/2000	24	SCO	D													5	2016	Dumbarton Youths		
Docherty	Mark	15/05/1988	3	SCO	D	23	6	4	2			4			1			2	2015	Alloa Athletic	Freed May 2017, joined East Fife	[redacted]
Ewings	Jamie	04/08/1984	19	SCO	GK													27	2011	Alloa Athletic		End
Fleming	Garry	17/05/1987	9	SCO		13	16	5	2			4		1		1		1	2012	Irvine Meadow	Freed May 2017, joined Alloa Athletic	
Gallagher	Grant	11/01/1991	8	SCO	M	6						2		1	1				2015	Stranraer		End
Gallagher	Callum	13/09/1994	7	SCO	M	3	4											8	2017	St Mirren		End
Harvie	Daniel	14/07/1998	12	SCO	D	34		3										0	2016	Aberdeen (OL)	Aug 16-May 2017	
Kassarate	Amadou	14/01/1996	21	ENG / SEN	F								2					10	2016	Dumbarton Youths	OL to Kirkintilloch RR Sep-Dec 2016, Stranraer Jan-May	
Lang	Thomas	12/07/1997	4	ENG	D	1	5											10	2017	Unattached	Ex Rangers, Freed May 2017, joined Stranraer	[redacted]
Lyden	Ross	13/04/2000	16	SCO	M		2											3	2016	Dumbarton Youths		
Martin	Alan	01/01/1989	27	SCO	GK	36			2						1				2016	Hamilton Accies	OOC May 20178, joined QOS	
McCallum	Donald	27/09/1996	15	SCO	F	1	6		1	1			2			1		16	2015	Dumbarton Youths	Freed May 2017	
McCrorie	Ross	18/03/1998	2	SCO	D	6	3											1	2017	Rangers (OL)	Jan-May 2017	
Nade	Christian	18/09/1984	72	FRA	F	10	5	4										1	2017	Stranraer		End
Nuttall	Joe	27/01/1997	25	ENG	F		2											4	2017	Aberdeen (OL)	Apr-May	
Pettigrew	Craig	25/11/1986	2	SCO	M	10	2		1	1		4			1			8	2016	Stranraer	Freed Jan 2017, joined Stranraer	
Prior	Kyle	30/08/1999	18	SCO	M		1											8	2016	Dumbarton Youths	OL to Vale of Clyde Aug-Jan	End
Smith	David	01/03/1993	17	SCO		34	2		2			4		1		1			2016	Falkirk		End
Stanton	Sam	19/04/1994	11	SCO	M	22	4	4							1				2016	Hibernian (OL)	Aug 16-May 2017	
Stevenson	Ryan	24/08/1984	6	SCO	M	9	8	3	2			4		1	1			2	2016	Ayr United	Freed Jan 2017 joined Raith Rovers	
Stirling	Andy	05/03/1990	22	SCO	M	26	8	3	2			4			1				2016	Stranraer	OOC May 2017, joined QOS	
Thomson	Robert	28/05/1993	10	SCO	F	35	1	12	1	1		4		1	1				2016	Brechin City	OOC May 2017, joined Morton	
Thomson	Joe	14/01/1997	4	SCO		18		2	1										2016	Celtic (OL)	Sep-Dec 2016	
Todd	Josh	11/06/1994	7	ENG		16	4		2			3	1		1				2016	Annan Athletic	Freed Jan 2017, joined St Mirren	
Vaughan	Lewis	19/12/1995	23	SCO	F	11	4	4											2017	Raith Rovers (OL)	Jan-May 2017	
Wright	Frazer	01/05/1979	18	SCO	D	2						3		1				9	2015	St Johnstone	Freed Jan 2017 joined Stirling Albion	
Own Goals								1														
NEW SIGNINGS																						
Dowie	Andy				M														2017	Queen of the South		End
Stewart	Mark				F														2017	Raith Rovers		End
Walsh	Tom				F														2017	Limerick		End
Gallagher	Scott				GK														2017	Hibernian		End
Barr	Craig				D														2017	Raith Rovers		End
Wilson	David				M														2017	Partick Thistle		End

Source of Birthdates: Dumbarton FC Website, transfermarkt.com

Date	Comp	H/A	Opponents	F	A		HT		Referee	Crowd	Scorers
16/07/2016	LC	A	Forfar Athletic	2	2	3-5p	0	1	D Lowe	426	Gallagher, Fleming
19/07/2016	LC	H	East Fife	0	2		0	2	C Charleston	452	
23/07/2016	LC	A	Dundee	2	6		2	1	K Clancy	2319	Wright, Buchanan
30/07/2016	LC	H	Peterhead	3	3	5-6p	2	1	A Muir	305	R Thomson, Smith, Stevenson
06/08/2016	L	A	Dunfermline Athletic	3	4		1	2	B Cook	3496	R Thomson, Docherty 2
13/08/2016	L	H	Dundee United	1	0		0	0	G Duncan	1475	Docherty
20/08/2016	L	A	Morton	1	1		1	0	M Northcroft	1586	Gaston og
27/08/2016	L	A	Falkirk	0	1		0	0	D Robertson	4311	
03/09/2016	CC3	A	Stranraer	0	1		0	0	J McKendrick	401	
10/09/2016	L	H	Hibernian	0	1		0	1	G Aitken	1339	
17/09/2016	L	H	St Mirren	1	1		1	1	S Finnie	1101	Stirling
24/09/2016	L	A	Raith Rovers	2	3		0	3	S Kirkland	1636	Stevenson, R Thomson
01/10/2016	L	H	Queen of the South	0	0		0	0	M Northcroft	840	
15/10/2016	L	H	Ayr United	0	3		0	1	G Duncan	1005	
22/10/2016	L	A	Dundee United	1	2		0	0	C Charleston	5979	R Thomson
29/10/2016	L	H	Dunfermline Athletic	2	2		1	0	S Kirkland	1018	J Thomson, Fleming
05/11/2016	L	A	St Mirren	1	0		0	0	J McKendrick	2758	Fleming
12/11/2016	L	H	Morton	0	2		0	0	D Robetson	1147	
19/11/2016	L	H	Raith Rovers	0	0		0	0	A Muir	600	
26/11/2016	SC3	A	Bonnyrigg Rose	0	0		0	0	S Finnie	1552	
03/12/2016	L	A	Queen of the South	2	1		2	0	G Duncan	1261	Stevenson, Fleming
06/12/2016	SC3R	H	Bonnyrigg Rose	0	1		0	0	G Aitken	632	
10/12/2016	L	A	Hibernian	0	2		0	1	J McKendrick	13881	
17/12/2016	L	H	Falkirk	2	1		1	0	M Northcroft	832	R Thomson, Fleming
24/12/2016	L	A	Ayr United	4	4		1	2	C Charleston	1441	R Thomson, J Thomson, Harvie, Stevenson
31/12/2016	L	H	Dundee United	1	0		1	0	S Finnie	1221	Docherty
07/01/2017	L	A	Morton	1	2		0	1	J Beaton	2094	Stirling
14/01/2017	L	H	Hibernian	0	1		0	1	N Walsh	1523	
21/01/2017	L	H	Queen of the South	1	2		0	1	S Kirkland	825	Nade
28/01/2017	L	A	Raith Rovers	3	1		0	1	M Northcroft	1413	Nade, Harvie, Buchanan
04/02/2017	L	H	St Mirren	2	2		0	1	J Beaton	1377	R Thomson, Nade
18/02/2017	L	H	Ayr United	2	2		0	0	J McKendrick	1198	Stanton 2
25/02/2017	L	A	Falkirk	2	2		1	1	M Northcroft	4160	Vaughan, Stirling
04/03/2017	L	A	Dunfermline Athletic	1	5		0	2	K Clancy	3320	Harvie
11/03/2017	L	H	Raith Rovers	4	0		2	0	A Newlands	719	R Thomson 2, Stanton, Fleming
18/03/2017	L	A	Hibernian	2	2		1	0	G Duncan	14093	Nade, Thomson
25/03/2017	L	A	Ayr United	1	2		1	1	C Charleston	1608	Thomson
01/04/2017	L	H	Morton	1	0		0	0	J Beaton	1323	Vaughan
08/04/2017	L	A	St Mirren	1	1		1	1	S Kirkland	3906	Vaughan
15/04/2017	L	H	Dunfermline Athletic	0	2		0	0	A Muir	1142	
22/04/2017	L	A	Queen of the South	2	1		2	1	J McKendrick	1289	Stanton, R Thomson
29/04/2007	L	A	Dundee United	2	2		1	1	N Walsh	5107	R Thomson, Vaughan
06/05/2017	L	H	Falkirk	0	1		0	0	D Robertson	1660	

FRIENDLIES / OTHER GAMES					
28/06/2016	H	Dundee	1	2	
04/07/2016	A	Cumbernauld Colts	3	0	
05/07/2016	N	Stranraer	1	2	at Benburb
09/07/2016	H	Motherwell	1	2	
02/08/2016	A	Clydebank	0	2	U20

Date	Comp	H/A	Opponents	F	A		1	2	3	4	5	6	7	8	9	10	11	12	13	14	15	16	17	18
16/07/2016	LC	A	Forfar Athletic	2	2	3-5p	Brown	Docherty	Pettigrew	Buchanan	Wright	Stevenson	G Gallagher	Smith*	Stirling	Fleming	R Thomson	Todd*	McCallum	Clark	Kassarte	Barclay		
19/07/2016	LC	H	East Fife	0	2		Brown	Docherty	Pettigrew	Buchanan	Todd	Stevenson	G Gallagher	Smith*	Stirling	Fleming	R Thomson	McCallum*	Barr	Clark	Kassarte	Barclay		
23/07/2016	LC	A	Dundee	2	6		Brown	Docherty	Pettigrew	Buchanan	Wright	Stevenson	Todd	Smith	Stirling	Fleming*	R Thomson	Kassarate*	Barr	Clark	McCallum	Barclay		
30/07/2016	LC	H	Peterhead	3	3	5-6p	Brown	Docherty	Pettigrew	Buchanan	Wright+	Stevenson	Todd	Smith	Stirling	Fleming*	R Thomson	McCallum*	Kassarte+	Clark	Barclay			
06/08/2016	L	A	Dunfermline Athletic	3	4		Martin	Harvie	Pettigrew	Buchanan	Wright+	Stevenson*	Todd	Smith	Stirling	J Thomson	R Thomson	McCallum*	Docherty+	Clark	Kassarte	Barr	Barclay	
13/08/2016	L	H	Dundee United	1	0		Martin	Harvie	Pettigrew	Buchanan	Docherty	Stevenson	Todd	G Gallagher*	Smith	J Thomson	R Thomson	Stirling*	McCallum	Clark	Kassarte	Barclay		
20/08/2016	L	A	Morton	1	1		Martin	Harvie	Pettigrew	Buchanan	Docherty	Stevenson	Todd	G Gallagher	Smith*	J Thomson	R Thomson	Stirling*	McCallum	Clark	Kassarte	Barr	Ewings	
27/08/2016	L	A	Falkirk	0	1		Martin	Harvie	Pettigrew	Buchanan	Docherty	Stevenson+	Todd	G Gallagher	Smith&	J Thomson*	R Thomson	Stirling*	Barr+	Fleming&	Kassarte	McCallum	Ewings	
03/09/2016	CC3	A	Stranraer	0	1		Martin	Barr	Pettigrew	Buchanan	Docherty	Stevenson+	Todd	G Gallagher	Stanton*	Stirling	R Thomson&	Fleming*	Smith+	McCallum&	Kassarte	Ewings		
10/09/2016	L	H	Hibernian	0	1		Martin	Barr	Pettigrew	Buchanan	Harvie	Stevenson*	Todd	G Gallagher+	Smith&	J Thomson	R Thomson	Fleming*	Docherty+	McCallum&	Kassarte	Ewings		
17/09/2016	L	H	St Mirren	1	1		Martin	Barr	Pettigrew	Buchanan	Harvie	Stirling+	Todd	G Gallagher	Smith*	J Thomson	R Thomson	Fleming*	Stanton+	McCallum	Kassarte	Ewings	Wright	Stevenson
24/09/2016	L	A	Raith Rovers	2	3		Martin	Barr	Pettigrew*	Buchanan	Harvie	Stirling+	Fleming&	G Gallagher	Smith	J Thomson	R Thomson	Stanton*	Todd+	Stevenson&	Kassarte	Ewings	Docherty	McCallum
01/10/2016	L	H	Queen of the South	0	0		Martin	Barr	Pettigrew	Docherty	Harvie	Stanton*	Todd	Stevenson	Smith	J Thomson+	R Thomson	Stirling*	Fleming+	McCallum	Ewings			
15/10/2016	L	H	Ayr United	0	3		Martin	Barr	Pettigrew	Docherty	Harvie	Stanton*	Todd+	Stevenson	Smith*	J Thomson&	R Thomson	Stirling*	Fleming+	McCallum&	Buchanan	Ewings	Wright	
22/10/2016	L	A	Dundee United	1	2		Martin	Barr	Buchanan	Docherty	Harvie	Stanton	Todd*	Fleming+	Smith	J Thopson&	R Thomson	Stirling*	Stevenson+	McCallum&	Pettigrew	Ewings	Wright	
29/10/2016	L	H	Dunfermline Athletic	2	2		Martin	Barr	Buchanan	Docherty	Harvie	Stanton*	Todd	Fleming	Smith	J Thomson	R Thomson+	Stirling*	Stevenson+	McCallum	Pettigrew	Ewings	Wright	
05/11/2016	L	A	St Mirren	1	0		Martin	Barr	Buchanan	Docherty	Harvie	Stanton	Stirling*	Fleming+	Smith	J Thomson	R Thomson	Todd*	Stevenson+	McCallum	Pettigrew	Ewings	Wright	
12/11/2016	L	H	Morton	0	2		Martin	Wright+	Buchanan	Docherty*	Harvie	Stanton	Stirling	Fleming	Smith	J Thomson&	R Thomson	Todd*	Pettigrew+	McCallum&	Stevenson	Ewings		
19/11/2016	L	H	Raith Rovers	0	0		Martin	Barr	Buchanan	Docherty	Harvie	Stanton	Todd	Stevenson	Smith	McCallum+	R Thomson*	Fleming*	Stirling+	Pettigrew	Lyden	Ewings		
26/11/2016	SC3	A	Bonnyrigg Rose	0	0		Martin	Barr	Buchanan	Docherty	Pettigrew	Stirling	Todd	Stevenson	Smith	McCallum*	Fleming	R Thomson*	Crawford	Lyden	Wright	Ewings		
03/12/2016	L	A	Queen of the South	2	1		Martin	Barr	Buchanan	Fleming*	Harvie	Stirling&	Todd	Stevenson+	Smith	J Thomson	R Thomson	Pettigrew*	McCallum+	Lyden&	Crawford	Brown		
06/12/2016	SC3R	H	Bonnyrigg Rose	0	1		Martin	Barr	Buchanan	Docherty	Fleming	Stirling	Todd	Stevenson*	Smith	J Thomson	R Thomson+	Pettigrew*	McCallum+	Crawford	Brown			
10/12/2016	L	A	Hibernian	0	2		Martin	Barr	Buchanan	Docherty	Harvie	Stirling	Todd	Fleming*	Smith	J Thomson	R Thomson	Stevenson*	McCallum	Crawford	Pettigrew	Lyden	Brown	
17/12/2016	L	H	Falkirk	2	1		Martin	Barr	Buchanan	Docherty	Harvie	Stirling*	Stanton	Fleming+	Smith	J Thomson	R Thomson	Todd*	Stevenson+	Wright	Pettigrew	McCallum	Brown	
24/12/2016	L	A	Ayr United	4	4		Martin	Barr	Buchanan	Docherty	Harvie	Stirling	Todd*	Fleming	Smith	J Thomson	R Thomson	Stevenson*	Crawford	Wright	Pettigrew	McCallum	Brown	
31/12/2016	L	H	Dundee United	1	0		Martin	Barr	Buchanan	Docherty	Harvie	Stanton	Todd	Fleming*	Smith	J Thomson	R Thomson	Stevenson*	Pettigrew	Wright	McCallum	Brown		
07/01/2017	L	A	Morton	1	2		Martin*	Barr	Buchanan	Docherty+	Pettigrew	Stanton	Todd	Fleming	Smith	Stirling	R Thomson&	Brown*	Nade+	Vaughan&	McCallum			
14/01/2017	L	H	Hibernian	0	1		Martin	Barr	Buchanan	Docherty	Harvie	Carswell+	Vaughan	Fleming	Smith	Stirling	R Thomson*	Nade*	Lang+	McCallum	Brown			
21/01/2017	L	H	Queen of the South	1	2		Martin	Barr	Buchanan	Docherty	Harvie	Carswell*	Vaughan	Stanton	Smith&	Stirling	Nade+	C Gallagher*	Fleming+	R Thomson&	Lang	Brown		
28/01/2017	L	A	Raith Rovers	3	1		Martin	Barr	Buchanan	Docherty	Harvie	Carswell	Nade*	Stanton+	Smith	Stirling&	R Thomson	C Gallagher*	McCrorie+	Lang&	Brown			
04/02/2017	L	H	St Mirren	2	2		Martin	Barr*	Buchanan	Docherty	Harvie	Carswell&	Nade	Stanton+	Smith	Stirling	R Thomson	Lang*	Fleming+	Vaughan&	C Gallagher	Brown		
18/02/2017	L	H	Ayr United	2	2		Martin	Barr	Buchanan	Docherty	Harvie	Carswell	Nade*	Stanton&	Smith+	Stirling	R Thomson	McCrorie*	Fleming+	Vaughan&	C Gallagher	Lang	Prior	Ewings
25/02/2017	L	A	Falkirk	2	2		Martin	Barr	Buchanan	Docherty	Harvie	Carswell	Nade+	Vaughan*	Smith	Stirling&	R Thomson	Stanton*	Fleming+	McCrorie&	C Gallagher	Lang	Prior	Ewings
04/03/2017	L	A	Dunfermline Athletic	1	5		Martin	Barr	Buchanan	Docherty+	Harvie	Carswell*	Nade&	Vaughan	Smith	Stirling	R Thomson	Stanton*	Fleming+	Lang&	C Gallagher	McCrorie	Prior	Ewings
11/03/2017	L	H	Raith Rovers	4	0		Martin	Barr	Lang	C Gallagher*	Harvie	Carswell	Nade+	Stanton	Smith	Stirling&	R Thomson	Fleming*	Prior+	Lyden&	Ewings			
18/03/2017	L	A	Hibernian	2	2		Martin	Barr	Buchanan	C Gallagher*	Harvie	Carswell	Nade+	McCrorie	Smith	Stirling	R Thomson	Vaughan*	Fleming+	Lang	Prior	Ewings		
25/03/2017	L	A	Ayr United	1	2		Martin	Barr+	Buchanan	Docherty	C Gallagher*	Carswell	Vaughan	Stanton	Smith	Stirling	R Thomson	Fleming*	Lang+	Nade	Prior	Ewings		
01/04/2017	L	H	Morton	1	0		Martin	Barr	Buchanan	Stanton+	Harvie	Carswell	Vaughan*	McCrorie	Smith	Stirling&	R Thomson	Nuttall*	C Gallagher+	Docherty&	Prior	Ewings	Lang	
08/04/2017	L	A	St Mirren	1	1		Martin	Barr	Buchanan	Stanton	Harvie	Carswell	Vaughan*	McCrorie	Smith	Stirling	R Thomson	Nade*	C Gallagher	Nuttall	Prior	Ewings	Lang	
15/04/2017	L	H	Dunfermline Athletic	0	2		Martin	Barr	Buchanan	Stanton	Harvie	Carswell+	Vaughan*	McCrorie	Smith	Stirling	R Thomson	Nade*	Nuttall+	Docherty	C Gallagher	Ewings	Lang	Fleming
22/04/2017	L	A	Queen of the South	2	1		Martin	Barr	Buchanan	Stanton	Harvie	Carswell	Vaughan+	McCrorie	Nade*	Stirling&	R Thomson	Docherty*	Fleming+	Smith&	C Gallagher	Ewings	Lang	Nuttall
29/04/2007	L	A	Dundee United	2	2		Martin	Barr	Buchanan	Stanton&	Harvie	Carswell	Vaughan*	McCrorie	Nade+	Stirling	R Thomson	Docherty*	Fleming+	Smith&	C Gallagher	Ewings	Lang	Nuttall
06/05/2017	L	H	Falkirk	0	1		Martin	Barr	Buchanan	Stanton	Harvie	Carswell&	Vaughan+	Fleming*	Smith	Stirling	R Thomson	Nade*	C Gallagher+	Docherty&	Prior	Ewings	Lang	Nuttall

ɔundee FC 2016/17

ɔunded	1893
round	Dens Park
ɔstcode	DD3 7JY
el	01382 889966
apacity	11506
osest Railway Station	Dundee
ecord Attendance	43024, SC, v Rangers 7/2/1953
ecord Win	10-0 v Alloa, Lge 9/3/47; v Dunfermline 22/3/47
ecord Defeat	0-11 v Celtic, Lge, 26/10/1895
nairman	Tim Keys
eneral Manager	Jim Thomson
lanager	Paul Hartley (until Feb), Neil McCann
ssistant Manager	Gerry McCabe (Until Feb), Graham Gartland
olours 2016/17 Top	Navy Blue
norts	White
ponsor	McEwan Fraser Legal
lanufacturer	Puma
hange Colours 2016/17 Top	White
norts	Navy Blue
icknames	Dee, Dark Blues
'eb	www.dundeefconline.co.uk
latch Programme 2016/17	The Dee £3

Dundee were plagued with inconsistency all season. In February they won 5-1 away to Motherwell (5-0 up at half time). A month later they lost 0-7 at home to Aberdeen. At that stage of the season they looked to be in danger of sliding into relegation trouble and Manager Paul Hartley was axed. Neil McCann came in and steered them out of trouble only to say he didn't want the job permanently. Dundee tried to recruit Jack Ross from St Mirren but he wasn't for moving, then McCann performed an about turn to take the job.

The Dens Park side have the city to themselves as far as Premiership football goes. This is their big chance to really gain some ground over United and re-establish themselves as the dominant team in Dundee. Will they take it? Perhaps they lack the finance to really drive forward and this time they will not be reckless enough to spend money they do not have.

PREDICTION FOR 2017/18

Neil McCann is untested at this level. Things seldom run smoothly at Dens Park - a place in the top half of the bottom six would be as much as they can hope for.

Date	Comp	H/A	Opponents	F	A		HT		Referee	Crowd	Scorers
16/07/2016	LC	A	East Fife	1	1	2-4p	1	0	B Cook	1407	Hemmings
23/07/2016	LC	H	Dumbarton	6	2		1	2	K Clancy	2319	Stewart 3, Hemmings 2, O'Dea
26/07/2016	LC	A	Peterhead	1	2		0	0	N Walsh	998	Stewart
30/07/2016	LC	H	Forfar Athletic	7	0		3	0	W Collum	2219	McGowan, Duffy, Stewart 2, Leanzibarrut, Loy, Tei
06/08/2016	L	A	Ross County	3	1		2	0	R Madden	3669	Loy 2, McGowan
13/08/2016	L	H	Rangers	1	2		1	2	C Thomson	9702	O'Hara
19/08/2016	L	H	Hamilton Accies	1	1		1	1	K Clancy	5287	O'Hara
27/08/2016	L	A	Motherwell	0	0		0	0	A Dallas	4078	
10/09/2016	L	H	Kilmarnock	1	1		1	1	D Robertson	5111	El Bakhtoui
18/09/2016	L	H	Aberdeen	1	3		1	1	S Mclean	6321	Holt
24/09/2016	L	A	Inverness CT	1	3		0	2	K Clancy	2884	Low
01/10/2016	L	H	Celtic	0	1		0	0	A Dallas	8827	
15/10/2016	L	A	Hearts	0	2		0	1	K Clancy	16512	
23/10/2016	L	A	St Johnstone	1	2		0	0	N Walsh	3646	Loy
26/10/2016	L	H	Partick Thistle	0	2		0	1	S McLean	4783	
29/10/2016	L	A	Hamilton Accies	1	0		0	0	S Finnie	1853	McGowan
05/11/2016	L	H	Motherwell	2	0		1	0	J Beaton	5471	Kerr, Haber
19/11/2016	L	A	Rangers	0	1		0	0	W Collum	48773	
26/11/2016	L	H	Inverness CT	2	1		1	0	A Dallas	5094	Wighton, Gadzhalov
03/12/2016	L	A	Kilmarnock	0	2		0	1	C Allan	3615	
10/12/2016	L	H	Ross County	0	0		0	0	E Anderson	4742	
17/12/2016	L	A	Celtic	1	2		0	1	B Madden	53589	Haber
23/12/2016	L	H	Hearts	3	2		0	1	K Clancy	6160	O'Dea, McGowan, Haber
28/12/2016	L	A	Partick Thistle	0	2		0	2	A Muir	3758	
31/12/2016	L	H	St Johnstone	3	0		2	0	D Robertson	6492	El Bakhtoui, Gadzhalov, Anderson og
21/01/2017	SC	H	St Mirren	0	2		0	1	B Madden	3622	
27/01/2017	L	A	Aberdeen	0	3		0	2	K Clancy	10512	
04/02/2017	L	A	Inverness CT	2	2		2	0	N Walsh	2606	Haber, O'Dea
11/02/2017	L	H	Kilmarnock	1	1		1	1	A Muir	4708	Holt
19/02/2017	L	H	Rangers	2	1		2	0	C Thomson	9017	O'Hara, Holt
25/02/2017	L	A	Motherwell	5	1		5	1	S Finnie	4002	Jules og, Haber 2, Wighton, O'Hara
01/03/2017	L	H	Partick Thistle	0	1		0	1	J Beaton	5328	
11/03/2017	L	A	St Johnstone	0	2		0	2	A Dallas	4195	
19/03/2017	L	H	Celtic	1	2		0	1	W Collum	8968	El Bakhtoui
31/03/2017	L	H	Aberdeen	0	7		0	4	A Muir	7314	
04/04/2017	L	A	Ross County	1	2		1	1	J Beaton	2819	O'Dea
08/04/2017	L	A	Hearts	0	1		0	1	C Allan	16304	
15/04/2017	L	H	Hamilton Accies	0	2		0	1	J Beaton	6489	
29/04/2017	L	A	Motherwell	3	2		1	0	S Mclean	4919	O'Hara 2, Haber
06/05/2017	L	A	Kilmarnock	1	0		0	0	C Thomson	4040	Haber
13/05/2017	L	H	Ross County	1	1		0	1	N Walsh	6812	O'Dea
17/05/2017	L	H	Inverness CT	0	2		0	2	K Clancy	5574	
20/05/2017	L	A	Hamilton Accies	0	4		0	2	C Allan	2616	

FRIENDLIES / OTHER GAMES								
28/06/2016	A	Dumbarton	2	1				
01/07/2016	A	Alloa Athletic	1	1				
12/07/2016	A	Brechin City	0	1				
14/07/2016	N	Fauldhouse United	3	0		U20 at Airdrie		
20/07/2016	A	East Kilbride	2	1		U20		
23/07/2016	A	Benburb	3	1		U20		
10/01/2017	A	Arbroath	2	0			749	

Date	Comp	H/A	Opponents	F	A		1	2	3	4	5	6	7	8	9	10	11	12	13	14	15	16	17	18
16/07/2016	LC	A	East Fife	1	1	2-4p	Mitchell	Holt	O'Dea	Leanzibarrut	Kerr	Duffy*	Williams	O'Hara	Ross	Wighton+	Hemmings	Vincent*	Loy+	Teijsse	A Black	Gourlay		
23/07/2016	LC	H	Dumbarton	6	2		Mitchell	Holt	O'Dea	Leanzibarrut	Kerr	Duffy+	Vincent*	Stewart	Ross	Loy&	Hemmings	O'Hara*	Williams+	Teijsse&	A Black	Wighton	Curran	Bain
26/07/2016	LC	A	Peterhead	1	2		Bain	Holt	O'Dea	Leanzibarrut	Kerr	Williams	Vincent	Stewart	Wighton+	Loy	O'Hara*	McGowan*	Duffy+	Curran	A Black	Mitchell		
30/07/2016	LC	H	Forfar Athletic	7	0		Bain	Holt	O'Dea	Leanzibarrut	Kerr	Williams+	Vincent&	Stewart	Teijsse*	McGowan	Duffy*	Loy*	Wighton+	Curran&	Gadzhalov	Mitchell		
06/08/2016	L	A	Ross County	3	1		Bain	Holt	O'Dea	Leanzibarrut	Kerr	Williams*	Vincent	O'Hara	Loy	McGowan	Duffy+	El Bakhtoui*	Ross+	Wighton	Teijsse	Gadzhalov	Curran	Mitchell
13/08/2016	L	H	Rangers	1	2		Bain	Holt	O'Dea	Leanzibarrut	Kerr	Williams	Vincent*	O'Hara	Loy&	McGowan	Duffy+	Ross*	Teijsse+	El Bakhtoui&	Wighton	Gadzhalov	Mitchell	
19/08/2016	L	H	Hamilton Accies	1	1		Bain	Holt	O'Dea	Leanzibarrut	Kerr	Williams	Vincent*	O'Hara	Loy	Ross	El Bakhtoui	Tejisse*	Gadzhalov	Curran	Quigley	Smyth	Mitchell	
27/08/2016	L	A	Motherwell	0	0		Bain	Holt	O'Dea	Gomis	Kerr	Williams*	Duffy	O'Hara	McGowan	Ross	El Bakhtoui	Loy*	Gadzhalov	Curran	Quigley	Smyth	Leanzibarrut	Mitchell
10/09/2016	L	H	Kilmarnock	1	1		Bain	Holt	O'Dea*	Gomis	Kerr	Hateley+	Wighton&	O'Hara	McGowan	Ross	El Bakhtoui	Leanzibarrut*	Teijsse+	Loy&	Low	Williams	Smith	Mitchell
18/09/2016	L	H	Aberdeen	1	3		Bain	Holt	O'Dea	Leanzibarrut	Kerr	Hateley&	Williams*	O'Hara	McGowan	Ross+	El Bakhtoui	Wighton*	Duffy+	Loy&	Low	Vincent	Gadzhalov	Mitchell
24/09/2016	L	A	Inverness CT	1	3		Bain	Holt	O'Dea	Leanzibarrut	Kerr	Hateley*	Low	Duffy+	McGowan	Ross&	El Bakhtoui	Loy*	Teijsse+	Williams&	Wighton	Vincent	Gadzhalov	Mitchell
01/10/2016	L	H	Celtic	0	1		Bain	Holt	O'Dea	Gomis	Kerr	Williams&	Low+	O'Hara	McGowan	Teijsse	El Bakhtoui*	Wighton*	Ross+	Loy&	Quigley	Vincent	Leanzibarrut	Mitchell
15/10/2016	L	A	Hearts	0	2		Bain	Holt	Gadzhalov&	Gomis	Vincent*	Williams	Hateley+	O'Hara	McGowan	Teijsse	El Bakhtoui	Duffy*	Kerr+	Loy&	Ross	Wighton	Leanzibarrut	Gourlay
23/10/2016	L	A	St Johnstone	1	2		Bain	Holt	O'Dea	Gomis	Vincent	Williams	Hateley&	Ross+	McGowan	Teijsse	El Bakhtoui*	Duffy*	Wighton+	Loy&	Kerr	Gadzhalov	Leanzibarrut	Mitchell
26/10/2016	L	H	Partick Thistle	0	2		Bain	Holt	O'Dea	Gomis*	Kerr	Williams&	Hateley	Wighton	McGowan	Loy+	Haber	Gadzhalov*	Duffy+	Teijsse&	Ross	Vincent	Leanzibarrut	Mitchell
29/10/2016	L	A	Hamilton Accies	1	0		Mitchell	Holt	O'Dea	Leanzibarrut	Kerr	Gadzhalov	Hateley	Vincent	McGowan*	Wighton	Haber+	Ross*	Teijsse+	Loy	Duffy	Williams	Smith	Gourlay
05/11/2016	L	H	Motherwell	2	0		Mitchell	Holt	O'Dea	Gomis*	Kerr	Gadzhalov	Hateley	Vincent	McGowan	Wighton	Haber	Williams*	Low	Loy	Duffy	Ross	Teijsse	Bain
19/11/2016	L	A	Rangers	0	1		Bain	Holt	O'Dea	Gomis	Kerr	Gadzhalov	Hateley	Vincent	McGowan	Wighton*	Haber+	El Bakhtoui*	Williams+	Loy	Duffy	Ross	Leanzibarrut	Mitchell
26/11/2016	L	H	Inverness CT	2	1		Bain	Holt	O'Dea	Gomis	Kerr	Gadzhalov	Hateley	Vincent*	McGowan	Wighton	Haber+	Williams*	Leanzibarrut+	Loy	Duffy	El Bakhtoui	Curran	Mitchell
03/12/2016	L	A	Kilmarnock	0	2		Bain	Holt	O'Dea	Leanzibarrut	Kerr	Gadzhalov&	Hateley	Vincent*	McGowan	Wighton+	Haber	Williams*	El Bakhtoui+	Loy&	Duffy	Ross	Curran	Mitchell
10/12/2016	L	H	Ross County	0	0		Bain	Holt	O'Dea	Gomis	Kerr	Gadzhalov	Hateley+	Curran*	McGowan	Wighton	Haber	El Bakhtoui*	Vincent+	Loy	Duffy	Ross	Williams	Mitchell
17/12/2016	L	A	Celtic	1	2		Bain	Holt	O'Dea	Gomis	Kerr	Gadzhalov	Hateley+	Vincent	Williams*	Wighton	Haber	O'Hara*	El Bakhtoui+	Loy	Curran	Ross	Leanzibarrut	Mitchell
23/12/2016	L	H	Hearts	3	2		Bain	Holt	O'Dea	Gomis*	Kerr	Gadzhalov	Hateley	Vincent	O'Hara+	Wighton	Haber	Leanzibarrut*	McGowan+	Loy	Williams	Ross	El Bakhtoui	Mitchell
28/12/2016	L	A	Partick Thistle	0	2		Bain	Holt	O'Dea	Leanzibarrut+	Kerr	Gadzhalov	Hateley	Vincent*	McGowan	Wighton	Haber	El Bakhtoui*	Loy+	Curran	Williams	Ross	Gomis	Mitchell
31/12/2016	L	H	St Johnstone	3	0		Bain	Holt	O'Hara*	Leanzibarrut	Kerr	Gadzhalov	Hateley	El Bakhtoui+	McGowan	Wighton	Haber	Ross*	Williams+	Loy	Duffy	Curran	Waddell	Mitchell
21/01/2017	SC	H	St Mirren	0	2		Bain	Holt	O'Hara	Leanzibarrut	Kerr	Gadzhalov	Hateley+	El Bakhtoui*	McGowan	Wighton	Haber	Williams*	Duffy+	Ross	Vincent	Gomis	Curran	Mitchell
27/01/2017	L	A	Aberdeen	0	3		Bain	Gomis	O'Hara	Leanzibarrut*	Kerr	Gadzhalov	Hateley	Ross	McGowan	Wighton	Haber	El Bakhtoui*	Duffy	Williams	Waddell	Mitchell		
04/02/2017	L	A	Inverness CT	2	2		Bain	Gomis	O'Hara	Leanzibarrut	Holt	O'Dea	Hateley*	Kerr	McGowan	Ojamaa+	Haber	Klok*	El Bakhtoui+	Williams	Vincent	Ross	Wighton	Mitchell
11/02/2017	L	H	Kilmarnock	1	1		Bain	Gomis+	O'Hara	Gadzhalov	Holt	O'Dea	Hateley*	Kerr	McGowan	Ojamaa&	Haber	Klok*	Wighton+	El Bakhtoui&	Vincent	Ross	Williams	Ferrie
19/02/2017	L	H	Rangers	2	1		Bain	Vincent	O'Hara	Leanzibarrut	Holt	O'Dea	Wighton	Kerr	McGowan	Ojamaa*	Haber	Williams*	Hateley	El Bakhtoui	Gadzhalov	Ross	Gomis	Gourlay
25/02/2017	L	A	Motherwell	5	1		Bain	Vincent	O'Hara*	Leanzibarrut	Holt	O'Dea	Wighton&	Kerr	McGowan	Ojamaa+	Haber	Williams*	Hateley+	El Bakhtoui&	Gadzhalov	Ross	Gomis	Ferrie
01/03/2017	L	H	Partick Thistle	0	1		Bain	Vincent	O'Hara	Leanzibarrut&	Holt	O'Dea	Wighton+	Kerr	McGowan	Ojamaa*	Haber	El Bakhtoui*	Williams+	Gadzhalov&	Hateley	Ross	Gomis	Gourlay
11/03/2017	L	A	St Johnstone	0	2		Bain	Vincent	O'Hara	Gadzhalov	Holt	O'Dea	Wighton+	Kerr	McGowan	Ojamaa*	Haber	El Bakhtoui*	Williams+	Klok	Hateley	Ross	Gomis	Ferrie
19/03/2017	L	H	Celtic	1	2		Bain	Vincent*	O'Hara	Gomis	Holt	O'Dea	Hateley+	Kerr	McGowan	Ojamaa&	Haber	Wighton*	Ross+	El Bakhtoui&	Williams	Klok	Gadzhalov	Mitchell
31/03/2017	L	H	Aberdeen	0	7		Bain	Vincent	O'Hara	Gomis	Holt	O'Dea	Hateley+	Kerr	McGowan	Ross*	El Bakhtoui	Ojamaa*	Wighton+	Higgins	Williams	Klok	Mitchell	
04/04/2017	L	A	Ross County	1	2		Bain	Vincent	O'Hara	Gomis	Holt	O'Dea	Williams	Kerr	McGowan	Ojamaa*	Haber	Wighton*	Hateley	Higgins	Klok	Ross	Mitchell	
08/04/2017	L	A	Hearts	0	1		Bain	Vincent	O'Hara	Higgins	Holt	O'Dea	Hateley	Kerr	McGowan	Ojamaa*	Haber	Wighton*	Ross	Dryden	I Smith	Gomis	Mitchell	
15/04/2017	L	H	Hamilton Accies	0	2		Bain	Vincent+	Wighton	Higgins	Holt	O'Dea	Hateley	Kerr*	McGowan	El Bakhtoui	Haber	O'Hara*	Ojamaa+	Ross	I Smith	Gomis	Gadzhalov	Mitchell
29/04/2017	L	A	Motherwell	3	2		Bain	Vincent	O'Hara+	Gomis	Holt	O'Dea	Hateley	Ross&	McGowan	Wighton*	Haber	Williams*	Higgins+	El Bakhtoui&	Ojamaa	I Smith	Gadzhalov	Mitchell
06/05/2017	L	A	Kilmarnock	1	0		Bain	Vincent	O'Hara	Gomis	Holt	O'Dea	Hateley	Kerr	McGowan+	El Bakhtoui*	Haber&	Wighton*	Ross+	Ojamaa&	Williams	Higgins	Gadzhalov	Ferrie
13/05/2017	L	H	Ross County	1	1		Bain	Vincent	O'Hara	Gomis+	Holt	O'Dea	Hateley*	Kerr	McGowan	El Bakhtoui&	Haber	Ross*	Gadzhalov+	Wighton&	Williams	Ojamaa	Higgins	Ferrie
17/05/2017	L	H	Inverness CT	0	2		Bain	Vincent	O'Hara	Gomis*	Holt	O'Dea	Ross	Kerr	McGowan	El Bakhtoui&	Haber+	Higgins*	Ojamaa+	Wighton&	Williams	Dryden	Smith	Ferrie
20/05/2017	L	A	Hamilton Accies	0	4		Bain	Vincent	O'Hara&	Gadzhalov	Holt	O'Dea	Ross*	Kerr	McGowan	El Bakhtoui	Haber+	Wighton*	Ojamaa+	Williams&	Higgins	Dryden	Smith	Ferrie

Surname	First Name	DOB	SQ	Nat	Pos	L A	L S	L G	SC A	SC S	SC G	LC A	LC S	LC G	CC A	CC S	CC G	UNS	Signed	Previous Club	Notes	Contra
Allan	Matty	17/01/1996	34	SCO	D														2015	Dundee FC Youths	OL to Montrose Jan-May, Freed May and joined Montrose	
Bain	Scott	22/11/1991	1	SCO	GK	36			1			2						2	2014	Alloa Athletic		End 20
Berry	Taylor	17/01/2000		**SCO**	M														2016	Dundee FC Youths		
Black	Andy	20/09/1995		SCO	D													3	2015	Dundee FC Youths	Freed September 2016, joined Fauldhouse United	
Colquhoun	Calvin	25/07/1996	35	SCO	M														2014	Dundee FC Youths	OL to Stirling Albion Nov-May, Freed May 2017	
Coupe	Conor	27/09/1999		SCO	M														2016	Dundee FC Youths		
Curran	Jesse	16/07/1996	27	AUS	M	1							1					11	2015	Central Coast Mariners	OL to East Fife Feb-May	End 20
Dryden	Sam	12/09/1996	25	ENG	D													3	2015	Derby County		End 20
Duffy	Michael	28/07/1994	10	NIR	F	4	4			1		3	1	1				8	2016	Celtic (OL)	Aug-May	
El Bakhtoui	Faisal	08/11/1992	20	FRA	F	15	15	3	1									3	2016	Dunfermline Athletic		End 20
Ferrie	Calum	16/06/1998		ENG	GK													7	2016	Port Vale		End 20
Gadzhalov	Kostadin	20/06/1989	26	BUL	D	15	3	2	1									14	2015	Dobrudzha Dobrich		End 20
Gomis	Kevin	20/01/1989	55	FRA	D	22												8	2016	OGC Nice		OOC
Gourlay	Kyle	24/08/1998		SCO	GK													5	2014	Dundee FC Youths	OL to Clyde Mar-May	End 20
Haber	Marcus	11/01/1989	21	CAN	F	27		8	1										2016	Crewe Alexandra		End 20
Hateley	Tom	12/09/1989	7	ENG	M	26	1		1									4	2016	Slask Wroclaw		End 20
Hemmings	Kane	08/04/1991		ENG	F							2		3					2014	Cowdenbeath	Transferred to Oxford United Aug 2016	
Higgins	Daniel	08/04/1998	45	SCO	D	2	2											5	2017	Celtic	Freed June 2017, joined Kilmarnock	
Holt	Kevin	25/01/1993	2	SCO	D	37		3	1			4							2015	Queen of the South		End 20
Kerr	Cammy	10/09/1995	30	SCO	D	35	1	1	1			4						1	2012	Dundee FC Youths		End 20
Klok	Marc	20/04/1993		NET	M		2											4	2017	Oldham Athletic	Freed Apr 2017, joined PSM Makassar	
Leanzibarrut	Julen Extaberugan	07/03/1991	16	SPA	D	14	3		1			4		1				7	2015	East Fife		End 20
Low	Nicky	06/01/1992	8	SCO	M	2		1										2	2015	Aberdeen	OL to Derry City Jan-June	End 20
Loy	Rory	19/03/1988	9	SCO	F	4	9	3				2	2	1				9	2015	Falkirk	OL to St Mirren Jan-May	End 20
McGowan	Paul	07/10/1987	18	SCO	M	35	1	3	1			1	1	1					2014	St Mirren		End 20
McPake	James	25/06/1984	5	SCO/NIR	D														2014	Hibernian		OOC
Mitchell	David	04/04/1990	12	SCO	GK	2						2						29	2015	Stranraer	OOC June 2017, joined Falkirk	
O'Dea	Darren	04/02/1987	6	ROI	D	35		4				4		1					2016	Mumbai City		End 20
O'Hara	Mark	12/12/1995	14	SCO	M	26	2	6	1			2	1					3	2016	Kilmarnock		End 20
Ojamaa	Henrik	20/05/1991	22	EST	F	9	5											2	2017	Go Ahead Eagles (OL)	Jan-Jun	
Quigley	Conor	04/12/1997	49	NIR	D														2016	Swansea City	OL to Stirling Albion	End 20
Ross	Nick	11/11/1991	17	SCO	M	11	8					2						19	2015	Inverness CT	Released June 2017	
Skelly	Josh	11/04/1997		SCO	F														2015	Dundee FC Youths	OL to Arbroath Aug-May, Freed May joined Arbroath	
Smith	Ian	08/05/1998		SCO	F													7	2016	Hearts		End 2
Smyth	Matty	08/05/1998	50	NIR	D													2	2016	Stevenage	OL to Arbroath Jan-May, Freed May 2017	
Stewart	Greg	17/03/1990		SCO	F							3		6					2014	Cowdenbeath	Transferred to Birmingham City Aug 2016	
Teijsse	Yordi	19/07/1992	19	NET	F	3	6					1	1	1				3	2016	Quick Boys	OL to Wuppertaler SV Jan-May, Freed May 2017	
Vincent	James	27/09/1989	4	ENG	M	27	1					3	1					7	2016	Inverness CT		End 20
Waddell	Kerr	14/06/1998		SCO	D													2	2015	Dundee FC Youths	OL to Clyde Mar-May	End 20
Warwick	Greg	25/02/1998		SCO	D														2015	Dundee FC Youths	OL to Forfar Ath Oct-Jan, East Craigie Jan-May	
Wighton	Craig	27/07/1997	33	SCO	F	19	10	2	1			2	1					6	2013	Dundee FC Youths		End 20
Williams	Danny	25/01/1988	11	ENG	M	11	14			1		3	1					13	2016	Inverness CT		End 20
Own Goals								2														
NEW SIGNINGS																						
Deacon	Roarie				F														2017	Sutton United		End 20
Allan	Scott				M														2017	Celtic (OL)	Jul-May	
Spence	Lewis																		2017	Dunfermline Athletic		End 20
Wolters	Randy																		2017	Go Ahead Eagles		End 20

Source of Birthdates: Dundee FC Website and transfermakt.com

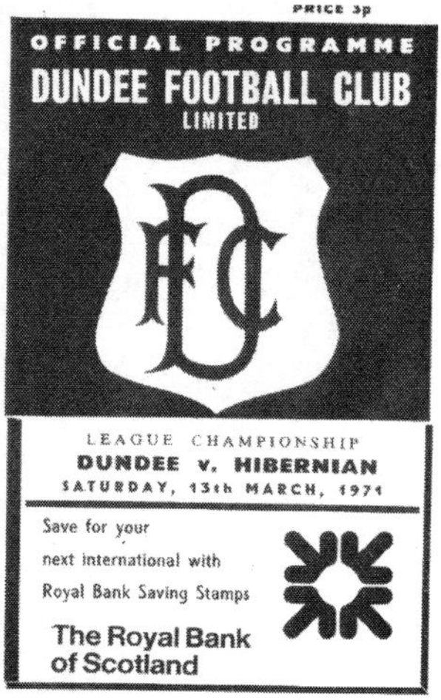

Season 1978-79 Price 12p
DUNDEE F.C.
Official Programme and Club News
DUNDEE FOOTBALL CLUB LIMITED
LEAGUE CHAMPIONSHIP
DENS PARK, SATURDAY, 16th DECEMBER, 1978
KICK-OFF 3.00 P.M.
DUNDEE
STIRLING ALBION
THE LINE-UP
1 ALLY DONALDSON
2 LES BARR
3 BILLY WILLIAMSON
4 STEWART McLAREN
5 BOBBY GLENNIE
6 WILLIE WATSON
7 ALAN LAMB
8 IAN REDFORD
9 BILLY PIRIE
10 JIM SHIRRA
11 ALEC McGHEE
Substitutes
12 JOCKY SCOTT
14 ALEC CALDWELL
1 GORDON ARTHUR
2 GEORGE NICOL
3 JIM BURNS
4 GEORGE WATSON
5 JOHN KENNEDY
6 ALLAN MOFFAT
7 MATT McPHEE
8 BOBBY GRAY
9 BILLY STEELE
10 GRAEME ARMSTRONG
11 JIM BROWN
Substitutes
12 STUART HEGGIE
14 IAN BROWNING
Referee — B. R. McGinlay, Glasgow

The BOBBY GLENNIE Testimonial Match
DUNDEE F.C.
v
MANCHESTER CITY
Sunday, April 6. Kick-off 3 p.m.
50

Dundee United FC 2016/17

Founded	1909
Ground	Tannadice Park
Capacity	14229
Postcode	DD3 7JW
Tel	01382 833166
Closest Railway Station	Dundee
Record Attendance	28000 v Barcelona, Fairs Cup, 16/11/1966
Record Win	14-0 v Nithsdale Wanderers, SC, 17/1/1931
Record Defeat	1-12 v Motherwell, Lge, 23/1/1954
Most League Goals in a Season	40 John Coyle, 1955/6
Chairman	Stephen Thompson
General Manager	David Southern
Manager	Ray McKinnon
Assistant Manager	Laurie Ellis
Colours 2016/17 Top	Tangerine with Black Trim
Shorts	Tangerine
Sponsor	McEwan Fraser Legal
Manufacturer	Nike
Change Colours 2016/17 Top	White with Black Trim
Shorts	Black
Nicknames	United, Terrors, Arabs
Web	www.dundeeunitedfc.co.uk
Match Programme 2016/17	United Review £2.50 (Curtis Sport
Theme Song	Beautiful Sunday

Relegation has hit hard at Tannadice. Whilst the club's support at home remained loyal throughout the season, the numbers travelling away have plummeted.

Few United fans expected an automatic return to the Premiership at the first attempt. They knew that Hibs would be the strong favourites and so it proved. However, most expected that they would mount a strong challenge and that did not really happen. United, Falkirk and Morton were much of a muchness and all three lacked the quality to challenge Hibs on a consistent basis.

Ray McKinnon seemed to take a while to decide on his best team. The line up and formation was chopped and changed with some of the players being brought in clearly sub-standard. Some of the promising youngsters from previous seasons failed to kick on in the way that had been hoped for.

Victory in the Challenge Cup was scant consolation for a club who have achieved so much more in the past - this was the 30th Anniversary of their UEFA Cup Final and a run that saw them beat Barcelona and Borussia Moenchengladbach. Next year it's Brechin they will be playing.

PROSPECTS FOR 2017/18

A make or break season looms for United. Either they get back up in 2017/18 or they could have a long stay in the Championship. A Play Off spot is probably most likeely.

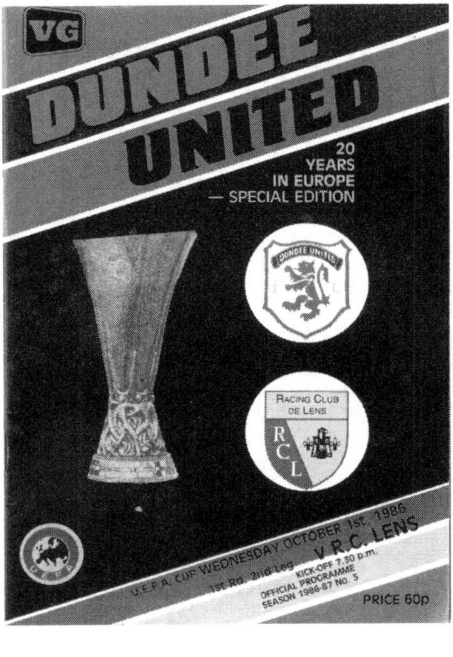

Date	Comp	H/A	Opponents	F	A		HT		Referee	Crowd	Scorers
15/07/2016	LC	A	Arbroath	1	1	5-3p	0	0	D Robertson	3124	Anier
19/07/2016	LC	H	Cowdenbeath	6	1		4	1	C Allan	3360	Murray 3, Toshney, C Smith, Anier
23/07/2016	LC	A	Inverness CT	1	1		0	1	E Anderson	1839	Murdoch
30/07/2016	LC	H	Dunfermline Athletic	2	0		0	0	J McKendrick	4951	Murray, Fraser
06/08/2016	L	H	Queen of the South	1	1		0	1	A Dallas	7058	Van der Velden
09/08/2016	LC1	H	Partick Thistle	3	1		3	0	S McLean	5036	C Smith 3
13/08/2016	L	A	Dumbarton	0	1		0	0	G Duncan	1475	
20/08/2016	L	H	Ayr United	3	0		2	0	G Aitken	6427	Murray, Robson, Flood
27/08/2016	L	H	Raith Rovers	2	2		2	1	C Thomson	7434	Flood, C Smith
03/09/2016	CC3	H	Peterhead	3	2	AET	2	2	N Walsh	3520	Telfer, Van der Velden, Andreu
10/09/2016	L	A	Dunfermline Athletic	3	1		1	0	J Beaton	5563	Murray, Andreu 2
17/09/2016	L	A	Falkirk	1	3		1	1	C Allan	5488	Obadeyi
20/09/2016	LC2	A	Morton	1	2		0	2	A Dallas	2149	Van der Velden
24/09/2016	L	H	Morton	2	1		0	0	B Cook	5829	Andreu 2
02/10/2016	L	A	Hibernian	1	1		0	1	C Thomson	15492	Edjengeule
08/10/2016	CC4	A	Stranraer	1	0		0	0	G Aitken	629	Andreu
15/10/2016	L	A	St Mirren	2	0		1	0	N Walsh	3612	Fraser, Andreu
22/10/2016	L	H	Dumbarton	2	1		0	0	C Charleston	5979	Buchanan og, Edjenguele
29/10/2016	L	H	Falkirk	1	0		0	0	E Anderson	7046	Durnan
05/11/2016	L	A	Queen of the South	4	1		2	1	S McLean	2316	Durnan, Andreu, Fraser, Murray
08/11/2016	L	H	Dunfermline Athletic	1	0		0	0	D Robertson	5996	Murray
12/11/2016	CC4	A	Dunfermline Athletic	1	0		1	0	W Collum	2576	Durnan
19/11/2016	L	A	Morton	0	0		0	0	C Allan	2578	
02/12/2016	L	H	Hibernian	1	0		0	0	B Madden	10925	Andreu
10/12/2016	L	A	Ayr United	1	0		1	0	W Collum	2049	Obadeyi
17/12/2016	L	A	Raith Rovers	0	0		0	0	S Kirkland	4361	
24/12/2016	L	H	St Mirren	2	1		2	1	J McKendrick	7247	Fraser, Murray
31/12/2016	L	A	Dumbarton	0	1		0	1	S Finnie	1221	
06/01/2017	L	A	Hibernian	0	3		0	2	W Collum	18786	
14/01/2017	L	H	Queen of the South	3	3		1	1	A Muir	6136	Murray 2, Fraser
21/01/2017	SC	A	Ross County	2	6		2	4	K Clancy	2440	Andreu 2
28/01/2017	L	A	Dunfermline Athletic	1	1		1	1	A Dallas	4670	Andreu
04/02/2017	L	H	Raith Rovers	3	0		1	0	S Finnie	5232	Mikkelsen 2, Andreu
11/02/2017	L	A	Falkirk	0	3		0	1	E Anderson	5028	
18/02/2017	CCSF	A	Queen of the South	3	2		3	0	N Walsh	1526	Telfer, Fraser, Andreu
25/02/2017	L	H	Morton	1	1		0	1	K Clancy	6065	Durnan
10/03/2017	L	H	Hibernian	0	1		0	1	D Robertson	9532	
15/03/2017	L	A	St Mirren	2	3		1	2	G Aitken	2766	Andreu 2
18/03/2017	L	A	Raith Rovers	1	2		0	1	C Charleston	2192	Murray
25/03/2017	CCF	N	St Mirren	2	1		1	1	N Walsh	8089	Andreu, Mikkelsen
28/03/2017	L	H	Ayr United	2	1		1	0	B Cook	4661	Murray, Durnan
01/04/2017	L	A	Queen of the South	2	4		1	2	S Finnie	1514	Mikkelsen 2
08/04/2017	L	H	Falkirk	1	1		0	0	E Anderson	6313	Murray
11/04/2017	L	H	Dunfermline Athletic	1	0		1	0	W Collum	5304	Mikkelsen
15/04/2017	L	A	Ayr United	0	0		0	0	C Allan*	1205	* replaced by G Irvine 30 mins
22/04/2017	L	H	St Mirren	3	2		1	1	C Charleston	6225	Mikkelsen, Andreu, Spittal
29/04/2007	L	H	Dumbarton	2	2		1	1	N Walsh	5107	Andreu, Mikkelsen
06/05/2017	L	A	Morton	1	1		0	0	J Beaton	2158	Spittal
10/05/2017	PO	A	Morton	2	1		0	1	W Collum	3306	Murray, Spittal
13/05/2017	PO	H	Morton	3	0		0	0	A Dallas	6606	Murray, Kuate, Spittal
16/05/2017	PO	H	Falkirk	2	2		1	1	B Madden	7034	Murray, Spittal
19/05/2017	PO	A	Falkirk	2	1		0	1	K Clancy	7926	Murray, Dixon
25/05/2017	PO	H	Hamilton Accies	0	0		0	0	S McLean	9386	
28/05/2017	PO	A	Hamilton Accies	0	1		0	0	C Thomson	5027	

FRIENDLIES / OTHER GAMES							
02/07/2016	N	Cove Rangers	3	0		at St Andrews	
05/07/2016	A	Forfar Athletic	1	1			
09/07/2016	A	Brechin City	5	0		Forfarshire Cup	
12/07/2016	N	Blackpool	0	3		at St Andrews	
13/07/2016	A	Turriff United	4	2		U20	
28/07/2016	A	Dundee North End	4	2		U20	
21/03/2017	H	Hearts	2	2		Dillin Te	3260

Surname	First Name	DOB	SQ	Nat	Pos	L A	L S	L G	SC A	SC S	SC G	LC A	LC S	LC G	CC A	CC S	CC G	UNS	Signed	Previous Club	Notes	Contract
Allardice	Scott	31/03/1998	35	SCO	M	4	2											9	2010	Dundee FC Youths		End 2018/19
Andreu	Tony	22/05/1988	19	FRA	F	37	1	13	1		2				4		4		2016	Norwich City (OL)	Aug 2016-May 2017	[redacted]
Anier	Henri	17/12/1990		EST	F		1						4	2					2015	Erzgebirge Aue	Transferred to Kalmar FF Aug 16	
Appere	Louis	26/03/1999	47	SCO	F													1	2016	AM Soccer		
Ballantyne	Cammy	13/04/1997	26	SCO	D													1	2013	DundeeUnited Youth	OL to Montrose Aug-May	End 2017/18
Bell	Cammy	18/09/1986	1	SCO	GK	41			1			6			1				2016	Rangers		End 2017/18
Booth	Ryan	13/03/1998		SCO	GK														2014	Dundee United Youth	OL to Inverurie Locos Aug-Jan, F Freed Jan joined Inverurie	[redacted]
Chalmers	Logan	24/03/2000	42	SCO	F														2016	Dundee United Youth		
Coote	Ali	11/06/1998	22	ENG/SCO	M	2	9						1		1	3		9	2014	Tayport Thistle	Transferred to Brentford June 2017	[redacted]
Dailly	Harvey	01/01/1999	39	SCO	D														2016	Dundee United Youth		
Davie	Logan	11/08/1998	36	SCO	M														2015	Dundee United Youth		End 2018/19
Dillon	Sean	30/07/1983	2	ROI	D	9	5					1	1		3	1		22	2007	Shelbourne	Released June 2017, joined Montrose	[redacted]
Dixon	Paul	22/11/1986	3	SCO	D	20	1	1				4			3			13	2015	Huddersfield Town	Released June 2017	
Donaldson	Coll	09/04/1995	5	SCO	D	7	7					4	1		1	2		20	2015	QPR		End 2017/18
Donaldson	Josh	05/05/2000	46	SCO	GK													1	2015	Rangers Youths		
Durnan	Mark	24/11/1992	4	SCO	D	37		4	1			4	1		3		1	3	2015	Queen of the South		End 2017/18
Edjenguele	William	07/05/1987	14	FRA	D	35		2	1			2			4				2016	Veria FC		End 2018/19
Flood	Willo	10/04/1985	16	ROI	M	38		2		1		4			3				2016	Aberdeen		OOC
Fraser	Scott	30/03/1995	10	SCO	M	23	5	4	1			5		1	3		1	3	2014	Dundee United Youth		End 2017/18
Garden	Jordan	20/06/1997	33	SCO	F														2012	Dundee FC Youths	Freed May 2017	[redacted]
Hornby	Jordan	18/06/1998	38	SCO	D														2015	Dundee United Youth		End 2017/18
Johnson	Justin	27/08/1996	17	NET	F		1						1					2	2014	FC United of Manchester	OL to York City Aug-Jan, Freed Jan 2017	[redacted]
Kuate	Wato	19/09/1995	17	CAM / POR	M	7	2	1										3	2017	Unattached	Ex Asteras Tripoli, Freed May 2017	
Long	Brett	11/04/1997	31	NIR	GK													5	2016	Motherwell	OL to Clyde Jan 2017	End 2017/18
McMeekin	Dominic	16/03/1999	44	SCO	M														2016	Dundee United Youth		
Mikkelsen	Thomas	19/01/1990	18	DEN	F	20	3	7		1						2	1		2017	Odense BK (OL)	Jan-May 2017	[redacted]
Murdoch	Stewart	09/05/1990	8	SCO	M	19	2		1			5		1	1	1		8	2016	Ross County		End 2018/19
Murray	Simon	15/03/1992	9	SCO	F	30	8	14	1			4	2	4	4	1		1	2015	Arbroath	OOC June 2017, joined Hibernian	[redacted]
Murrell	Aaron	23/09/1997	34	SCO	F														2016	Spartans	OL to Cowdenbeath Aug-Jan, Berwick Jan-May	End 2017/18
Nicholls	Alex	09/12/1987	23	ENG	F	4	7								1	1		7	2017	Barnet (OL)	Jan-May 2017	[redacted]
Obadeyi	Topi	29/10/1989	11	ENG	M	11	7	2	1			5	1					4	2016	Kilmarnock	Freed Jan 2017, joined Oldham Athletic	
Reekie	Scott	28/01/2000	43	SCO	D														2016	Dundee United Youth		
Ritchie	Gavin	23/10/1999	41	SCO	D														2015	Dundee United Youth		
Robson	Jamie	19/12/1997	24	SCO	D	22	2	1	1			2			2			20	2014	Dundee United Youth		End 2017/18
Smith	Cammy	24/8/9i5	15	SCO	M	5	11	1				4	1	4	2			4	2016	Aberdeen (OL)	Jul 2016-Jan 2017	[redacted]
Smith	Bradley	23/04/1997	27	SCO	M										1			8	2013	Dundee United Youth	OL to Albion R Feb-May 2017	End 2017/18
Smith	Matthew	13/03/1997	28	SCO	F													3	2015	St Johnstone Youths	OL to Montrose Jan-May 2017	End 2018/19
Souttar	Harry	22/10/1998	32	SCO	D							1						5	2013	Celtic BC	Transferred to Stoke City Sep 2016	[redacted]
Spittal	Blair	19/12/1995	7	SCO	M	24	6	5		1		4	2		3			5	2014	Queen's Park	OOC June 2017, joined Partick Thistle	
Sukar	Jassem	11/10/1996	25	ENG	D													2	2015	Sunderland U21	OL to Arbroath Aug-May	End 2017/18
Taylor	Graham	19/03/1998	37	SCO	M											1		1	2007	Cowie Colts		End 2018/19
Telfer	Charlie	14/07/1995	12	SCO	M	18	12		1			1	2		4		2	13	2014	Rangers	Released June 2017	[redacted]
Toshney	Lewis	26/04/1992	6	SCO	D	18	2					6		1	2			8	2016	Raith Rovers		End 2018/19
Van der Struijk	Frank	28/03/1985	20	NET	D	16			1			1			2			3	2014	Willem II Tilburg	Freed June 2017	[redacted]
Van der Velden	Nick	16/12/1981	23	NET	F	14	10	1				3	1	1	3		1	9	2016	Willem II Tilburg	Freed Apr 2017, joined Bali United	
Zwick	Luis	14/11/1989	21	GER	GK	1	2								4			45	2014	Hertha Zehlendorf	Freed June 2017	
Own Goals								1														
NEW SIGNINGS																						
Keatings	James																		2017	Hibernian		End 2018/19
King	Billy																		2017	Hearts		End 2018/19
Scobbie	Tom																		2017	St Johnstone		End 2018/19
McMullan	Paul																		2017	Celtic		End 2018/19
N'Koyi	Patrick																		2017	MVV Maastricht		End 2017/18

Source of Birthdates: Dundee United FC Programme & Website

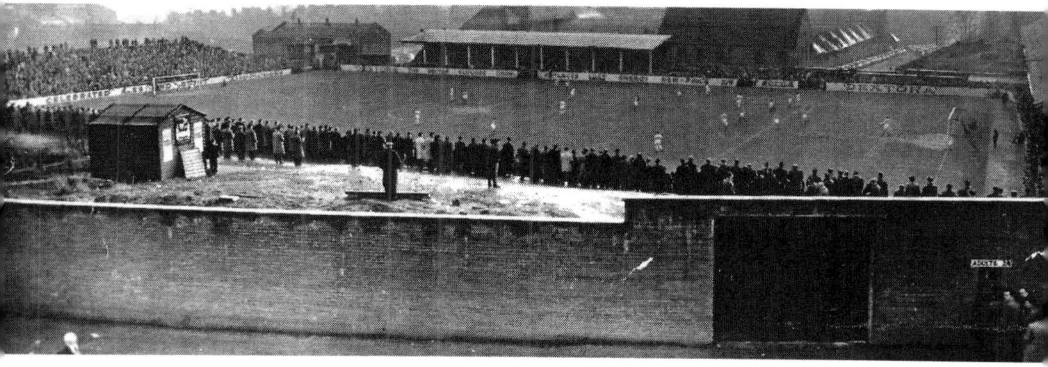

Date	Comp	H/A	Opponents	F	A		1	2	3	4	5	6	7	8	9	10	11	12	13	14	15	16	17	18
15/07/2016	LC	A	Arbroath	1	1	5-3p	Bell	Dixon	C Donaldson	Toshney	Souttar	Spittal*	Murdoch	Fraser	Obadeyi+	Telfer	Murray&	C Smith*	Johnson+	Anier&	Dillon	Coote	Robson	Zwick
19/07/2016	LC	H	Cowdenbeath	6	1		Bell	Dixon	Dillon	Toshney	Durnan	C Smith	Murdoch	Fraser*	Obadeyi+	Flood	Murray&	Spittal*	Van der Velden+	Anier&	C Donaldson	Telfer	Souttar	Zwick
23/07/2016	LC	A	Inverness CT	1	1		Bell	Dixon*	C Donaldson	Toshney	Durnan	Spittal+	Murdoch	Van der Velden&	C Smith	Flood	Murray	Dillon*	Obadeyi+	Anier&	Fraser	Telfer	Souttar	Zwick
30/07/2016	LC	H	Dunfermline Athletic	2	0		Bell	Fraser	C Donaldson	Toshney	Durnan	Robson	Murdoch	Van der Velden&	Obadeyi*	Flood	Murray+	Spittal*	Anier+	Telfer&	Dillon	Johnson	Souttar	Zwick
06/08/2016	L	H	Queen of the South	1	1		Bell	Dillon	C Donaldson	C Smith	Durnan	Robson	Murdoch	Van der Velden+	Obadeyi	Flood	Murray*	Anier*	Johnson+	Telfer	Spittal	Sukar	Souttar	Zwick
09/08/2016	LC1	H	Partick Thistle	3	1		Bell	Fraser&	C Donaldson	Toshney*	Durnan	Robson	Murdoch	Spittal	Obadeyi	Flood	C Smith+	Dillon*	Murray+	Telfer&	Coote	Sukar	Johnson	Zwick
13/08/2016	L	A	Dumbarton	0	1		Bell	Fraser	C Donaldson	Toshney	Durnan	Robson	Murdoch	Spittal*	Obadeyi+	Flood	C Smith&	Murray*	Van der Velden+	Telfer&	Coote	Dillon	Souttar	Zwick
20/08/2016	L	H	Ayr United	3	0		Bell	Fraser+	C Donaldson	Toshney	Dillon	Robson	Murdoch	Van der Velden	Murray	Flood&	C Smith*	Obadeyi*	Spittal+	Telfer&	Coote	Durnan	B Smith	Zwick
27/08/2016	L	H	Raith Rovers	2	2		Bell	Fraser+	C Donaldson	Toshney	Dillon	Robson	Murdoch	Van der Velden	Murray*	Flood	C Smith	Obadeyi*	Spittal+	Telfer	Ballantyne	M Smith	B Smith	Zwick
03/09/2016	CC3	H	Peterhead	3	2	AET	Zwick	Fraser*	Dixon	Toshney	Spittal	Van der Struijk+	Edjengeule&	Van der Velden	Andreu	Flood	Telfer	Murray*	Dillon+	C Donaldson&	J Donaldson	Robson	B Smith	Taylor
10/09/2016	L	A	Dunfermline Athletic	3	1		Bell	Edjengeule	Dixon	Toshney	Obadeyi*	Van der Struijk	Murray+	Van der Velden&	Andreu	Flood	Telfer	Robson*	C Smith+	C Donaldson&	Dillon	Fraser	Spittal	Zwick
17/09/2016	L	A	Falkirk	1	3		Bell	Edjengeule	Robson	Toshney*	Obadeyi	Van der Struijk	Murray	Van der Velden	Andreu&	Flood+	Telfer	Dillon*	Fraser+	C Smith&	C Donaldson	Durnan	Spittal	Zwick
20/09/2016	LC2	A	Morton	1	2		Bell	Edjengeule	Dixon	Toshney	Obadeyi&	Van der Struijk+	Murdoch	Van der Velden	Fraser*	Spittal	C Smith	Murray*	Donaldson+	Coote&	Robson	Dillon	B Smith	Zwick
24/09/2016	L	H	Morton	2	1		Bell	Edjengeule	Dixon	Toshney	Durnan	Van der Struijk	Murray	Van der Velden&	Andreu	Spittal*	C Smith+	Obadeyi*	Fraser+	Dillon&	C Donaldson	Robson	B Smith	Zwick
02/10/2016	L	A	Hibernian	1	1		Bell	Edjengeule	Dixon	Toshney*	Durnan	Van der Struijk	Murray&	Van der Velden+	Andreu	Spittal	Fraser	Telfer*	C Smith+	Obadeyi&	C Donaldson	Robson	Dillon	Zwick
08/10/2016	CC4	A	Stranraer	1	0		Zwick	Edjengeule	Dixon	Dillon	Durnan	Telfer	Murray	C Smith*	Andreu	Spittal	Fraser	Coote*	C Donaldson	Van der Struijk	Robson	B Smith	M Smith	Long
15/10/2016	L	A	St Mirren	2	0		Bell	Edjengeule	Dixon	Telfer	Durnan	Van der Struijk	Flood	Van der Velden*	Andreu&	Obadeyi+	Fraser	Spittal*	Murray+	C Donaldson&	Dillon	C Smith	Coote	Zwick
22/10/2016	L	H	Dumbarton	2	1		Bell	Edjengeule	Dixon	Telfer	Donaldson	Van der Struijk	Flood	Van der Velden	Andreu	Obadeyi*	Fraser	Coote*	Murray	Allardice	Dillon	C Smith	B Smith	Zwick
29/10/2016	L	H	Falkirk	1	0		Bell	Edjengeule	Dixon	Telfer	Durnan	Van der Struijk	Flood	Van der Velden+	Andreu	Obadeyi*	Fraser&	Murray*	C Smith+	C Donaldson&	Dillon	Spittal	Robson	Zwick
05/11/2016	L	A	Queen of the South	4	1		Bell+	Edjengeule	Dixon*	Telfer	Durnan&	Van der Struijk	Flood	Murray	Andreu	Obadeyi	Fraser	Robson*	Zwick+	C Donaldson&	Dillon	C Smith	Coote	Van der Velden
08/11/2016	L	H	Dunfermline Athletic	1	0		Bell	Edjengeule	Robson	Telfer*	Durnan	Van der Struijk	Flood	Murray&	Andreu	Obadeyi+	Fraser	C Smith*	Van der Velden+	Spittal&	C Donaldson	Dillon	Toshney	Zwick
12/11/2016	CC4	A	Dunfermline Athletic	1	0		Zwick	Dillon	Robson	Spittal	Durnan	C Donaldson	Toshney&	Murray*	B Smith	C Smith+	Van der Velden	Coote*	Taylor+	Murdoch&	M Smith	Allardice	Appere	Long
19/11/2016	L	A	Morton	0	0		Bell	Edjengeule	Robson	Spittal	Durnan	Van der Struijk*	Telfer	Murray+	Andreu&	Flood	Fraser	Toshney*	Van der Velden+	C Smith&	C Donaldson	Dillon	Obadeyi	Zwick
02/12/2016	L	H	Hibernian	1	0		Bell	Edjengeule	Robson	Spittal+	Durnan	Toshney	Telfer	Van der Velden*	Andreu&	Flood	Fraser	Murray*	Murdoch+	C Smith&	C Donaldson	Dillon	Obadeyi	Zwick
10/12/2016	L	A	Ayr United	1	0		Bell	Edjengeule	Robson	Spittal	Durnan	Toshney	Telfer	Obadeyi*	Andreu	Flood	Fraser+	C Smith*	Van der Velden&	Murdoch	C Donaldson	Allardice	Dillon	Zwick
17/12/2016	L	A	Raith Rovers	0	0		Bell	Edjengeule	Robson	Spittal	Durnan	Toshney	Telfer+	Obadeyi*	Andreu	Flood	Fraser	Dillon*	Murray+	Murdoch	C Donaldson	C Smith	Van der Velden	Zwick
24/12/2016	L	H	St Mirren	2	1		Bell	Edjengeule	Dillon	Spittal	Durnan*	Dixon	Telfer+	Murray&	Andreu	Flood	Fraser	C Donaldson*	Van der Velden+	C Smith&	Murdoch	Obadeyi	Robson	Zwick
31/12/2016	L	A	Dumbarton	0	1		Bell	Edjengeule	Dillon	Spittal+	Durnan	Dixon	Van der Velden	Murray*	Murdoch	Flood	Fraser&	C Smith*	Obadeyi+	C Donaldson&	Toshney	Telfer	Robson	Zwick
06/01/2017	L	A	Hibernian	0	3		Bell	Edjengeule	Toshney	Murdoch&	Durnan	Dixon	Van der Velden*	Telfer+	Andreu	Flood	Fraser	Obadeyi*	C Smith+	Mikkelsen&	Dillon	Spittal	Robson	Zwick
14/01/2017	L	H	Queen of the South	3	3		Bell	Edjengeule	Toshney	Murdoch&	Durnan	Dixon	Mikkelsen+	Murray	Andreu*	Flood	Fraser	Obadeyi*	Spittal+	Telfer&	Dillon	Robson	Van der Velden	Zwick
21/01/2017	SC	A	Ross County	2	6		Bell	Edjengeule	Van der Struijk	Murdoch*	Durnan	Robson	Telfer	Murray&	Andreu	Obadeyi+	Fraser	Flood*	Mikkelsen+	Spittal&	Toshney	Dixon	Van der Velden	Zwick
28/01/2017	L	A	Dunfermline Athletic	1	1		Bell*	Edjengeule	Van der Struijk	Toshney	Durnan	Dixon	Spittal	Mikkelsen+	Andreu	Flood	Fraser	Zwick*	Murray+	Obadeyi	Dillon	Telfer	Van der Velden	Robson
04/02/2017	L	H	Raith Rovers	3	0		Bell	Edjengeule	Van der Struijk	Toshney&	Durnan	Dixon	Spittal	Mikkelsen+	Andreu*	Murray	Fraser	Van der Velden*	Nicholls+	Telfer&	Dillon	Murdoch	Robson	Zwick
11/02/2017	L	A	Falkirk	0	3		Zwick	Flood	Van der Struijk	Toshney+	Durnan	Dixon	Spittal*	Mikkelsen	Andreu	Nicholls	Fraser&	Murray*	Dillon+	Murdoch&	Telfer	Robson	Van der Velden	Long
18/02/2017	CCSF	A	Queen of the South	3	2		Zwick	Edjengeule	Van der Struijk	Dillon	Telfer	Dixon	Flood	Murray*	Andreu	Nicholls+	Fraser	Mikkelsen*	Coote+	Durnan	Murdoch	B Smith	Allardice	Long
25/02/2017	L	H	Morton	1	1		Bell	Edjengeule	Van der Struijk	Telfer	Durnan	Dixon	Flood	Van der Velden*	Andreu	Mikkelsen+	Fraser	Murray*	Coote+	Nicholls	Murdoch	Robson	Dillon	Zwick
10/03/2017	L	H	Hibernian	0	1		Bell	Edjengeule	Van der Struijk	Toshney	Durnan	Dixon	Flood	Nicholls	Andreu*	Murray	Fraser+	Mikkelsen*	Van der Velden+	Telfer	Murdoch	Robson	Dillon	Zwick
15/03/2017	L	A	St Mirren	2	3		Bell	Edjengeule	Robson	Dillon	Durnan	Telfer	Flood	Nicholls+	Andreu	Murray&	Fraser*	Mikkelsen*	Coote+	Van der Velden&	Dixon	Murdoch	C Donaldson	Zwick
18/03/2017	L	A	Raith Rovers	1	2		Bell	Edjengeule	Robson	Toshney	Durnan	Murdoch&	Flood	Van der Struijk*	Andreu	Murray	Mikkelsen+	Nicholls8	Van der Velden+	Coote&	Dixon	Telfer	C Donaldson	Long
25/03/2017	CCF	N	St Mirren	2	1		Bell	Edjengeule	Robson	Telfer	Durnan	Murdoch	Flood	Van de Velden*	Andreu	Murray+	Coote&	Mikkelsen*	Nicholls+	C Donaldson&	Dixon	Toshney	Van der Struijk	Zwick
28/03/2017	L	H	Ayr United	2	1		Bell	Edjengeule	Robson	Telfer	Durnan	Murdoch	Flood	Nicholls*	Andreu	Murray+	Mikkelsen	Coote*	Kuate+	Van der Velden	C Donaldson	Dixon	Van der Struijk	Zwick
01/04/2017	L	A	Queen of the South	2	4		Bell+	Edjengeule	Dixon	Telfer	Durnan	Murdoch	Flood	Coote*	Andreu	Murray	Mikkelsen&	Spittal*	Zwick+	Nicholls&	C Donaldson	Toshney	Van der Velden	Robson
08/04/2017	L	H	Falkirk	1	1		Bell	Edjengeule	Spilttal*	Robson	Durnan	Murdoch	Flood	Allardice+	Andreu	Murray	Mikkelsen	Nicholls*	Telfer+	Dixon	Kuate	Toshney	Van der Velden	Zwick
11/04/2017	L	H	Dunfermline Athletic	1	0		Bell	Edjengeule	Spittal+	Robson	Durnan	Murdoch	Flood	Allardice*	Andreu	Murray	Mikkelsen&	Toshney*	Van der Velden+	Coote&	Kuate	Dixon	Telfer	Zwick
15/04/2017	L	A	Ayr United	0	0		Bell	Edjengeule	Spittal+	Robson	Durnan	Murdoch	Toshney*	Allardice	Andreu	Murray	Mikkelsen	Telfer*	C Donaldson	Coote	Kuate	Dixon	Nicholls	Zwick
22/04/2017	L	H	St Mirren	3	2		Bell	Edjengeule	Spittal+	Robson	Durnan	Murdoch	Flood	Allardice*	Andreu	Murray	Mikkelsen	Kuate*	C Donaldson+	Coote	Telfer	Dixon	Nicholls	Zwick
29/04/2007	L	H	Dumbarton	2	2		Bell	C Donaldson	Spittal	Robson	Durnan	Murdoch	Flood	Kuate*	Andreu	Murray	Mikkelsen	Coote*	Allardice	Dillon	Telfer	Dixon	Nicholls	Zwick
06/05/2017	L	A	Morton	1	1		Bell	C Donaldson	Spittal	Robson	Durnan	Murdoch	Flood&	Kuate+	Andreu	Coote*	Mikkelsen	Telfer*	Allardice+	Nicholls&	Dillon	Dixon	Zwick	
10/05/2017	PO	A	Morton	2	1		Bell	Edjengeule	Spittal	Robson	Durnan	Murdoch	Flood	Kuate	Andreu	Murray+	Mikkelsen*	Allardice*	Coote+	Nicholls	C Donaldson	Dixon	Telfer	Zwick
13/05/2017	PO	H	Morton	3	0		Bell	Edjengeule	Spittal	Robson	Durnan	Murdoch	Flood*	Kuate	Andreu	Murray+	Mikkelsen&	Telfer*	Fraser+	Coote&	C Donaldson	Dixon	Allardice	Zwick
16/05/2017	PO	H	Falkirk	2	2		Bell	Edjengeule	Spittal	Robson&	Durnan	Murdoch*	Flood	Kuate+	Andreu	Murray	Mikkelsen	Dillon*	Telfer+	Dixon&	Fraser	Nicholls	Allardice	Zwick
19/05/2017	PO	A	Falkirk	2	1		Bell	Edjengeule	Spittal	Dillon	Durnan	Dixon	Flood*	Kuate	Andreu	Murray	Mikkelsen+	Fraser*&	Telfer+	Nicholls&	C Donaldson	Robson	Allardice	Zwick
25/05/2017	PO	H	Hamilton Accies	0	0		Bell	Edjengeule	Spittal	Dillon	Durnan	Dixon	Flood	Kuate*	Andreu+	Murray	Mikkelsen	Telfer*	Nicholls+	Robson	C Donaldson	Toshney	Coote	Zwick
28/05/2017	PO	A	Hamilton Accies	0	1		Bell	Edjengeule	Spittal	Dillon	Durnan	Dixon	Flood	Telfer*	Andreu	Murray	Mikkelsen	Fraser*	Nicholls	Robson	C Donaldson	Toshney	Allardice	Zwick

Dunfermline Athletic FC 2016/17

Founded	1885
Ground	East End Park
Postcode	KY12 7RB
Tel	01383 724295
Capacity	11480
Closest Railway Station	Dunfermline Town
Record Attendance	27816, v Celtic, Lge, 30/4/68
Record Win	11-2 v Stenhousemuir, Lge 27/9/1930
Record Defeat	1-13 v St Bernards, SC, 15/9/1883
Most League Goals in a Season	53, Bobby Skinner, 1925/6
Chairman	Bob Garmary
General Manager	David McMorrine
Secretary	Shirley Forrester
Manager	Alan Johnson
Assistant Manager	Sandy Clark
Colours 2016/17 Top	Black and White Stripes
Shorts	Black
Sponsor	SRJ Windows
Manufacturer	Joma
Change Colours 2016/17 Top	Red with Black and White Band
Shorts	White
Nicknames	Pars
Web	www.dafc.co.uk
Match Programme 2016/17	Black and White £3
Theme Song	Into The Valley

Having come up fro League One it was always going to take time to adjust to Championship level. The Pars ended the season comfortable in mid table after a decent run after Christmas.

It took some time for Alan Johnson to bed in his new signings and to decide what his strongest line-up was. The addition of Nicky Clark was an inspired signing and his goals were crucial. However, the club struggled to replace the creativity of Faisal El Bakhtoui who left for Dundee at the end of 2015/16.

Some of the signings were disappointing. Gavin Reilly, on loan from Hearts, seldom featured after Christmas. Others such as Nat Wedderburn took a long time to find their best form. Some stalwarts of the League One campaign, such as Michael Moffat, didn't really cut it at Championship leveL.

PREDICTION FOR 2017/18

Logic would say that having established themselves in ten Championship, the Pars should kick on and challenge for promotion. But this is Dunfermline Athletic - anything could happen. Given the transfers in and out over the Summer we would expect a similar position to last season, possibly just pushing towards the promotion Play Off spots.

Dunfermline's first match was against Edinburgh Thistle at Ladysmill on 10/2/1877. This is thought to be the first proper football match in the town.

In 1877 the Club Secretary was William Sandilands of 26 Knabbie Street, Dunfermline. The club played home games at the Town Green on Appin Crescent until 1879 and then at McKane Park.

The club was really a part of the Cricket Club and disputes between the players led to a splinter group forming Dunfermline Athletic FC in 1885. This was the start of the end for Dunfermline FC. Dunfermline Cricket Club continue at McKane Park to this day.

Date	Comp	H/A	Opponents	F	A		HT	Referee	Crowd	Scorers
19/07/2016	LC	H	Arbroath	3	0		1 0	D Munro	1974	Moffat 2, Geggan
23/07/2016	LC	A	Cowdenbeath	3	0		0 0	C Steven	1481	Geggan 2, Ashcroft
26/07/2016	LC	H	Inverness CT	1	5		1 2	C Allan	2580	Geggan
30/07/2016	LC	A	Dundee United	0	2		0 0	J McKendrick	4951	
06/08/2016	L	H	Dumbarton	4	3		2 1	B Cook	3496	Cardle 3, Hopkirk
13/08/2016	L	A	Hibernian	1	2		0 1	W Collum	16477	Reilly
20/08/2016	L	A	Raith Rovers	0	2		0 0	A Muir	5114	
27/08/2016	L	H	Queen of the South	0	1		0 1	C Charleston	3973	
03/09/2016	CC3	A	Brechin City	5	1		2 1	C Allan	577	Ashcroft 2, McMullan, Reilly, Hill og
10/09/2016	L	H	Dundee United	1	3		0 1	J Beaton	5563	Paton
17/09/2016	L	A	Morton	1	2		1 1	K Clancy	1756	Clark
24/09/2016	L	H	St Mirren	4	3		1 2	G Aitken	2732	Clark 2, Webster og, El Alagui
01/10/2016	L	A	Ayr United	0	0		0 0	D Robertson	2883	
08/10/2016	CC4	H	Queen's Park	2	1		0 0	N Walsh	1930	El Alagui 2
15/10/2016	L	A	Falkirk	1	2		0 1	A Dallas	6377	El Alagui
22/10/2016	L	H	Hibernian	1	3		1 0	A Muir	7622	Higginbotham
29/10/2016	L	A	Dumbarton	2	2		0 1	S Kirkland	1018	Clark, Cardle
05/11/2016	L	H	Raith Rovers	0	0		0 0	C Thomson	5649	
08/11/2016	L	A	Dundee United	0	1		0 0	D Robertson	5996	
12/11/2015	CC4	H	Dundee United	0	1		0 1	W Collum	2576	
19/11/2016	L	A	St Mirren	1	0		1 0	N Walsh	2126	Clark
26/11/2016	SC3	A	Buckie Thistle	5	3		2 2	C Charleston		Munro og, Paton, Higginbotham, McMullan 2
03/12/2016	L	H	Ayr United	1	1		1 0	B Cook	3250	Clark
10/12/2016	L	H	Morton	2	1		2 1	S Finnie	3101	Moffat 2
17/12/2016	L	A	Queen of the South	2	2		0 1	J McKendrick	1561	Talbot, Higginbotham
26/12/2016	L	H	Falkirk	1	1		0 1	E Anderson	6134	McCabe
02/01/2017	L	A	Raith Rovers	2	0		1 0	D Robertson	5899	Clark, Ashcroft
07/01/2017	L	A	Ayr United	2	0		2 0	C Thomson	2261	Clark, Geggan
14/01/2017	L	H	St Mirren	1	1		1 0	W Collum	4108	Higginbotham
21/01/2017	SC4	A	Alloa	3	2		2 0	A Newlands	1871	Clark, McMullan, Cardle
28/01/2017	L	H	Dundee United	1	1		1 1	A Dallas	4670	Herron
04/02/2017	L	A	Falkirk	0	2		0 1	W Collum	5953	
11/02/2017	SC5	H	Hamilton Accies	1	1		1 0	C Thomson	2945	McMullan
14/02/2017	SC5R	A	Hamilton Accies	1	1	AET, 0-3p	1 0	C Thomson	1222	Morris
25/02/2017	L	A	Hibernian	2	2		1 2	J Beaton	14437	McMullan, Higginbotham
04/03/2017	L	H	Dumbarton	5	1		2 0	K Clancy	3320	Clark 4, McMullan
07/03/2017	L	H	Queen of the South	1	1		1 1	E Anderson	2653	Moffat
11/03/2017	L	A	St Mirren	0	0		0 0	S Finnie	4582	
18/03/2017	L	H	Ayr United	0	1		0 0	B Madden	3276	
25/03/2017	L	A	Morton	1	0		1 0	M Northcroft	2670	Wedderburn
01/04/2017	L	H	Hibernian	1	1		0 1	G Aitken	7058	Higginbotham
08/04/2017	L	H	Raith Rovers	1	0		0 0	A Dallas	4865	Higginbotham
11/04/2017	L	A	Dundee United	0	1		0 1	W Collum	5304	
15/04/2017	L	A	Dumbarton	2	0		0 0	A Muir	1142	McCabe, Hopkirk
22/04/2017	L	H	Falkirk	1	2		1 0	G Duncan	5076	Clark
29/04/2017	L	H	Morton	3	1		1 1	E Anderson	3339	Clark, Moffat, McCabe
06/05/2017	L	A	Queen of the South	1	0		0 0	A Newlands	1849	Clark

FRIENDLIES / OTHER GAMES						
29/06/2016	A	Alloa	1	1		600
02/07/2016	A	Livingston	5	1		
05/07/2016	A	Clyde	1	0		
08/07/2016	A	Civil Service Strollers	1	0		
09/07/2016	H	Hearts	3	1		2016
16/07/2016	N	Dundonald Bluebell	5	1	U20, Kelty Tnt	
17/07/2016	A	Kelty Hearts	0	2	U20, Kelty Tnt	
27/07/2016	A	Crossgates Primrose	8	0	U20	

Date	Comp	H/A	Opponents	F	A		1	2	3	4	5	6	7	8	9	10	11	12	13	14	15	16	17	18
19/07/2016	LC	H	Arbroath	3	0		Hutton	Williamson	Martin	Ashcroft	Richards-Everton	Geggan	McCabe+	Wedderburn&	Cardle	Reilly*	Moffat	McMullan*	Higginbotham+	Spence&	Talbot	Smith	Gill	
23/07/2016	LC	A	Cowdenbeath	3	0		Hutton	Williamson	Talbot	Ashcroft	Richards-Everton	Geggan	Higginbotham&	Wedderburn*	Cardle+	Reilly	Moffat	McCabe*	McMullan+	Spence&	Martin	Thomas	Gill	
26/07/2016	LC	H	Inverness CT	1	5		Hutton	Williamson	Talbot	Ashcroft	Richards-Everton	Geggan	Higginbotham*	Spence	Cardle&	McCabe	Moffat+	McMullan*	Smith+	Thomas&	Martin	Paton	Gill	
30/07/2016	LC	A	Dundee United	0	2		Hutton	Martin	Talbot	Ashcroft	Richards-Everton	Wedderburn+	Higginbotham	Spence	Cardle	McCabe*	Moffat	McMullan*	Thomas+&	Lochhead&	Smith	Paton	Fordyce	Gill
06/08/2016	L	H	Dumbarton	4	3		Hutton	Williamson	Martin	Ashcroft	Richards-Everton	Geggan	Higginbotham+	Reilly*	Cardle	McCabe	Moffat&	McMullan*	Paton+	Hopkirk&	Spence	Wedderburn	Fordyce	Gill
13/08/2016	L	A	Hibernian	1	2		Hutton	Williamson	Martin	Fordyce	Richards-Everton	Geggan	Higginbotham	Reilly	Cardle	McCabe	Moffat*	Hopkirk*	Paton	McMullan	Spence	Talbot	Lochhead	Gill
20/08/2016	L	A	Raith Rovers	0	2		Hutton	Williamson	Martin&	Ashcroft	Richards-Everton	Geggan	Higginbotham	Reilly	Cardle	McCabe+	Moffat*	Hopkirk*	Paton+	Talbot&	McMullan	Spence	Fordyce	Gill
27/08/2016	L	H	Queen of the South	0	1		Hutton	Williamson	Talbot	Ashcroft	Richards-Everton	Geggan	Higginbotham*	Reilly	Paton	McCabe&	Moffat+	McMullan*	Martin+	Spence&	Fordyce	Spark	Gill	
03/09/2016	CC3	A	Brechin City	5	1		Hutton	Williamson	Martin	Ashcroft	Fordyce	Geggan	McMullan	Reilly	Paton*	McCabe+	Clark&	Cardle*	Herron+	Higginbotham&	Moffat	Spence	Richards-Everton	Gill
10/09/2016	L	H	Dundee United	1	3		Hutton	Williamson*	Martin+	Ashcroft	Fordyce	Geggan	McMullan	Reilly	Paton	McCabe	Clark	El Alagui*	Cardle+	Higginbotham	Moffat	Herron	Richards-Everton	Gill
17/09/2016	L	A	Morton	1	2		Hutton	Fordyce	Martin	Ashcroft	Richards-Everton	Geggan	McMullan*	Reilly&	Paton+	McCabe	Clark	Cardle*	Higginbotham+	El Alagui&	Moffat	Herron	Williamson	Murdoch
24/09/2016	L	H	St Mirren	4	3		Murdoch	Fordyce*	Martin	Ashcroft	Talbot	Geggan	Herron	Reilly+	Paton	Cardle&	Clark	Williamson*	El Alagui+	McMullan&	Moffat	McCabe	Higginbotham	Hutton
01/10/2016	L	A	Ayr United	0	0		Murdoch	Williamson	Martin	Ashcroft	Talbot	Geggan	Herron*	Reilly&	Paton	Cardle	Clark+	McCabe*	El Alagui+	Moffat&	McMullan	Richards-Everton	Higginbotham	Hutton
08/10/2016	CC4	H	Queen's Park	2	1		Murdoch	Williamson	Martin	Ashcroft	Talbot	Geggan	McCabe+	Reilly*	Paton	Cardle	Clark&	El Alagui*	Higginbotham+	Hopkirk&	McMullan	Richards-Everton	Moffat	Hutton
15/10/2016	L	A	Falkirk	1	2		Murdoch	Williamson	Martin	Ashcroft	Talbot	Geggan	McCabe*	Higginbotham	Paton+	El Alagui	Clark	Hopkirk*	Reilly+	Moffat	McMullan	Richards-Everton	Spark	Hutton
22/10/2016	L	H	Hibernian	1	3		Murdoch	Richards-Everton	Martin	Ashcroft	Talbot	Geggan	Wedderburn	Higginbotham+	Paton&	El Alagui*	Reilly	Hopkirk*	Moffat+	McMullan&	Fordyce	Wedderburn	McCabe	Hutton
29/10/2016	L	A	Dumbarton	2	2		Murdoch	Williamson	Martin	Ashcroft	Talbot	Geggan	Wedderburn	Higginbotham	Paton*	Clark	Reilly+	Cardle*	Moffat+	McMullan	Fordyce	Galloway	McCabe	Hutton
05/11/2016	L	H	Raith Rovers	0	0		Murdoch	Herron	Martin	Ashcroft	Talbot	Geggan	Wedderburn	Higginbotham	El Alagui	Clark	Cardle	Williamson	Fordyce	Paton	McMullan	Moffat	McCabe	Hutton
08/11/2016	L	A	Dundee United	0	1		Murdoch	Herron	Martin	Ashcroft	Talbot	Geggan	Wedderburn	Higginbotham+	El Alagui	Clark	Cardle*	McCabe*	McMullan+	Paton	Fordyce	Moffat	Smith	Hutton
12/11/2015	CC4	H	Dundee United	0	1		Murdoch	Herron	Martin	Ashcroft	Talbot	Geggan	Moffat+	Higginbotham	McCabe	Clark&	Cardle*	Fordyce*	El Alagui+	McMullan&	Paton	Duthie	Smith	Hutton
19/11/2016	L	A	St Mirren	1	0		Murdoch	Fordyce	Martin	Ashcroft	Talbot	Herron	Paton*	Higginbotham	McCabe	Clark	El Alagui+	McMullan*	Moffat+	Cardle	Galloway	Duthie	Smith	Hutton
26/11/2016	SC3	A	Buckie Thistle	5	3		Murdoch	Fordyce	Martin	Ashcroft	Wedderburn	Duthie	Paton*	Moffat	McCabe&	Clark+	McMullan	Higginbotham*	El Alagui+	Herron&	Talbot	Cardle	Spence	Hutton
03/12/2016	L	H	Ayr United	1	1		Murdoch	Fordyce	Martin	Ashcroft	Talbot	Herron	El Alagui*	Higginbotham	McCabe	Clark+	McMullan	Duthie*	Moffat+	Wedderburn	Paton	Cardle	Spence	Hutton
10/12/2016	L	H	Morton	2	1		Murdoch	Fordyce	Herron*	Ashcroft	Talbot	Duthie+	Moffat	Higginbotham	McCabe	Clark&	McMullan	Wedderburn*	Williamson+	El Alagui&	Paton	Cardle	Reilly	Hutton
17/12/2016	L	A	Queen of the South	2	2		Murdoch	Fordyce	Martin	Ashcroft	Talbot	Wedderburn	Moffat	Higginbotham	McCabe	Clark	McMullan*	Cardle*	Williamson	Geggan	Hopkirk	Reilly	El Alagui	Hutton
26/12/2016	L	H	Falkirk	1	1		Murdoch	Herron	Martin	Ashcroft	Talbot	Geggan	Moffat*	Cardle+	McCabe	Clark&	McMullan	Reilly*	Paton+	El Alagui&	Williamson	Fordyce	Wedderburn	Hutton
02/01/2017	L	A	Raith Rovers	2	0		Murdoch	Fordyce	Herron*	Ashcroft	Talbot	Geggan	Wedderburn	Higginbotham	Moffat	Clark+	McMullan*	Cardle*	Reilly+	El Alagui	Williamson	Duthie	Paton	Hutton
07/01/2017	L	A	Ayr United	2	0		Murdoch	Fordyce	Herron	Ashcroft	Talbot	Geggan	Wedderburn	Higginbotham+	Moffat&	Clark*	McMullan	Reilly*	Cardle+	El Alagui&	Martin	McCabe	Paton	Hutton
14/01/2017	L	H	St Mirren	1	1		Murdoch	Fordyce	Herron	Ashcroft	Talbot	Geggan	Wedderburn	Higginbotham	Moffat	Clark	McMullan*	Cardle*	Reilly	El Alagui	Martin	McCabe	Morris	Hutton
21/01/2017	SC4	A	Alloa	3	2		Murdoch	Morris	Herron&	Ashcroft	Martin	Geggan	Wedderburn	Higginbotham*	Reilly	Clark+	McMullan	Cardle*	Moffat+	McCabe&	El Alagui	Talbot	Paton	Hutton
28/01/2017	L	H	Dundee United	1	1		Murdoch	Morris	Herron	Ashcroft	Talbot	Geggan	Wedderburn	Higginbotham&	Moffat+	Clark	McMullan*	Cardle*	Reilly+	Hopkirk&	Martin	Fordyce	McCabe	Hutton
04/02/2017	L	A	Falkirk	0	2		Murdoch	Morris	Herron&	Ashcroft	Talbot	Geggan	Wedderburn	Higginbotham	Moffat+	Clark	McMullan*	Reilly*	Hopkirk+	Cardle&	Martin	Paton	McCabe	Hutton
11/02/2017	SC5	H	Hamilton Accies	1	1		Murdoch	Morris	Herron	Ashcroft	Martin	Geggan*	Wedderburn	Higginbotham	Moffat+	Clark	McMullan	Talbot*	Hopkirk+	Cardle	Reilly	Paton	McCabe	Hutton
14/02/2017	SC5R	A	Hamilton Accies	1	1	AET, 0-3p	Murdoch	Morris	Herron	Ashcroft	Talbot	Martin	Wedderburn	Higginbotham^	Moffat+	Clark*	McMullan&	Reilly*	McCabe+	Paton&	Cardle^	Hopkirk	Morrison	Hutton
25/02/2017	L	A	Hibernian	2	2		Murdoch	Morris	Herron	Ashcroft	Talbot	Geggan	Wedderburn	Higginbotham	Moffat	Clark	McMullan	Fordyce	Paton	Hopkirk	Cardle	Reilly	McCabe	Hutton
04/03/2017	L	H	Dumbarton	5	1		Murdoch	Morris	Herron*	Ashcroft	Talbot	Geggan	Wedderburn+	Higginbotham	Moffat&	Clark	McMullan	McCabe*	Spence+	Reilly&	Fordyce	Paton	Cardle	Hutton
07/03/2017	L	H	Queen of the South	1	1		Murdoch	Morris	Herron	Ashcroft	Talbot	Geggan	Wedderburn	Higginbotham*	Moffat+	Clark	McMullan&	Cardle*	Paton+	Reilly&	Fordyce	Spence	McCabe	Gill
11/03/2017	L	A	St Mirren	0	0		Murdoch	Morris	Herron	Ashcroft	Talbot	Geggan	Wedderburn	Higginbotham*	Moffat	Clark	McMullan	Paton*	Cardle	Reilly	Fordyce	Spence	McCabe	Gill
18/03/2017	L	H	Ayr United	0	1		Murdoch	Morris	Herron	Ashcroft	Talbot	Williamson	Wedderburn	Higginbotham+	Moffat*	Clark	Cardle&	Hopkirk*	Paton+	Reilly&	Fordyce	Spence	McCabe	Hutton
25/03/2017	L	A	Morton	1	0		Murdoch	Morris	Herron*	Ashcroft	Talbot	Geggan	Wedderburn	Higginbotham	Moffat+	Clark	McMullan&	McCabe*	Hopkirk+	Cardle&	Williamson	Paton	Reilly	Gill
01/04/2017	L	H	Hibernian	1	1		Murdoch	Morris	Herron*	Ashcroft	Talbot	Geggan	Wedderburn	Higginbotham	Moffat	Clark	McMullan	McCabe*	Martin	Cardle	Williamson	Paton	Reilly	Gill
08/04/2017	L	H	Raith Rovers	1	0		Murdoch	Morris	McCabe	Ashcroft	Talbot	Geggan	Wedderburn	Higginbotham	Moffat	Clark	McMullan*	Cardle*	Martin	Spence	Williamson	Paton	Reilly	Gill
11/04/2017	L	A	Dundee United	0	1		Murdoch	Morris	McCabe	Ashcroft	Talbot	Geggan+	Wedderburn	Higginbotham	Moffat*	Clark	McMullan&	Reilly*	Williamson+	Cardle&	Martin	Paton	Spence	Hutton
15/04/2017	L	A	Dumbarton	2	0		Murdoch	Morris	McCabe	Ashcroft	Talbot	Geggan	Wedderburn	Higginbotham	Moffat+	Reilly*	McMullan	Hopkirk*	Paton+	Williamson	Martin	Cardle	Spence	Hutton
22/04/2017	L	H	Falkirk	1	2		Murdoch+	Morris*	McCabe	Ashcroft	Talbot	Geggan	Wedderburn	Higginbotham	Hopkirk	Clark	McMullan	Martin*	Hutton+	Williamson	Moffat	Cardle	Paton	Reilly
29/04/2017	L	H	Morton	3	1		Murdoch	Williamson	Fordyce	Ashcroft	Talbot	McCabe	Wedderburn	Higginbotham	Moffat&	Clark+	McMullan*	Paton*	Smith+	Reilly&	Morrison	Cardle	Spence	Hutton
06/05/2017	L	A	Queen of the South	1	0		Murdoch	Williamson	Fordyce	Ashcroft	Paton	McCabe	Wedderburn	Higginbotham	Moffat*	Clark	McMullan+	Cardle*	Smith+	Reilly	Morrison	Luke	Spence	Hutton

Surname	First Name	DOB	SQ	Nat	Pos	L A	L S	L G	SC A	SC S	SC G	LC A	LC S	LC G	CC A	CC S	CC G	UNS	Signed	Previous Club	Notes	Contract
Ashcroft	Lee	29/08/1993	12	SCO	D	35		1	4			4		1	3		2		2016	Kilmarnock		End 2017/18
Cardle	Joe	07/02/1987	11	SCO	F	9	14	4		1	1	4			2	1		12	2015	Ross County		End 2017/18
Clark	Nicky	03/06/1991	37	SCO	F	30		15	4		1				3				2016	Bury		End 2017/18
Crawford	Robbie	01/07/1998	29	SCO	F														2015	Fife Elite Academy	Freed May 2017	[redacted]
Duncan	Reece	16/07/1998	27	SCO	D														2015	Fife Elite Academy	Freed May 2017	
Duthie	Conner	02/02/1997		SCO	M	1	1		1									3	2016	Hibernian	OL to Stenhousemuir Jan-May	End 2017/18
El Alagui	Farid	28/08/1985	48	FRA/MOR	F	6	7	2		1						2	2	4	2016	Hibernian	Freed Jan 2017, joined Ayr United	[redacted]
Fordyce	Callum	23/06/1992	5	SCO	D	13			1						1	1		15	2015	Livingston	Released June 2017 joined QOS	
Galloway	Johnny	16/09/1998		SCO	M													2	2015	Fife Elite Academy	Freed May 2017	
Geggan	Andrew	08/05/1987	6	SCO	M	29		1	2			3		4	3			1	2012	Ayr United	OOC June 2017, joined Ayr United	
Gill	Cammy	07/04/1998	30	SCO	GK													15	2014	Dunfermline Athletic Youths	OL to Arbroath Jan-Mar	End 2018/19
Herron	John	01/02/1994	21	SCO	D	20		1	3	1					1	1		2	2016	Blackpool (OL)	Aug 2016-May 2017	[redacted]
Higginbotham	Kallum	15/06/1989	20	ENG	F	31	1	6	3	1	1	3	1		1	2		3	2016	Kilmarnock		End 2017/18
Hopkirk	David	17/01/1993	10	SCO	F	1	10	2		1						1		3	2015	Annan Athletic		End 2017/18
Horne	Evan	07/06/1998	25	SCO	M														2016	Dundee United	Freed May 2017	[redacted]
Hutton	David	18/05/1985	43	SCO	GK	6	1					4			1			30	2015	Ayr United	Released June 2017	
Lochhead	Scott	23/01/1997		SCO	F								1					1	2016	Dundee United Youths	OL to Clyde Jan-May	End 2017/18
Luke	Brandon	15/03/1999	32	SCO	M													1	2016	Dunfermline Athletic Youths		
Martin	Lewis	08/04/1996	4	SCO	D	16	2		4			2			3			10	2012	Dunfermline Athletic Youths		End 2017/18
McCabe	Rhys	24/07/1992	16	SCO	M	18	5	3	1	2		3	1		3			13	2015	Sheffield Wednesday	OOC June 2017, joined Sligo Rovers	[redacted]
McMullan	Paul	25/02/1996	18	SCO	F	23	6	2	4		4		4		1	1	1	7	2016	Celtic (OL)	Jul 2016-May 2017	
Moffat	Michael	15/02/1985	9	SCO	F	24	5	4	3	1		4		2	1			9	2014	Ayr United	OOC June 2017, joined Ayr United	
Morris	Callum	03/02/1990	22	NIR / ROI	D	13			3		1							1	2017	Aberdeen		End 2017/18
Morrison	Stuart	18/04/1999	31	SCO	D													3	2016	Dunfermline Athletic Youths		End 2018/19
Murdoch	Sean	31/07/1986	1	SCO	GK	30			4						2			1	2015	Rochester Rhinos		End 2017/18
Paton	Michael	25/03/1989	7	SCO	F	10	8	1	1	2	1				2			20	2015	Queen of the South	OOC	
Reilly	Gavin	10/05/1993	17	SCO	F	11	11	1	1	1		2			2		1	11	2016	Hearts (OL)	Jul 2016-May 2017	[redacted]
Richards-Everton	Ben	17/10/1992	14	ENG	D	6	0					4						5	2015	Partick Thistle	Released June 2017	
Smith	Callum	13/11/1999	33	SCO	F		2						1					5	2016	Fife Elite Academy		End 2017/18
Spark	Euan	29/11/1996		SCO	D													2	2016	Dundee United	OL to Berwick Rangers Jan-May, Freed June 2017, joined Brechin C	[redacted]
Spence	Lewis	28/01/1996	15	SCO	M		2					2	2					14	2012	Dunfermline Athletic Youths	OL to Brechin City Sep-Nov 2016, Freed June 2017 joined Dundee	
Talbot	Jason	30/09/1985	3	SCO	D	30	1	1	1	1		3			2			4	2015	Livingston		End 2017/18
Thomas	James	06/04/1997		SCO									2					1	2014	Dunfermline Athletic Youths	Freed Nov 2016	[redacted]
Wedderburn	Nat	30/06/1991	8	ENG	M	23	1	1	4			3						4	2016	Inverness CT		End 2017/18
Williamson	Ryan	28/01/1996	2	SCO	D	11	3					3			2			10	2012	Dunfermline Athletic Youths	OOC	End 2017/18
Own Goals								1			1						1					
NEW SIGNINGS																						
M'Voto	Jean-Yves			FRA	D														2017	Raith Rovers		End 2017/18
Allan	Paul			SCO															2017	Fife Elite Academy		End 2018/19
McManus	Declan			SCO	F														2017	Fleetwood Town		End 2017/18
Splaine	Aaron			SCO	M														2017	Kilmarnock		End 2017/18

Source of Birthdates: Dunfermline Athletic FC Programme & Website, transfermarkt.com

East Fife FC 2016/17

Founded	1903
Ground	Bayview Stadium
Postcode	KY8 3RW
Tel	01333 426323
Capacity	1980
Closest Railway Station	Kirkcaldy
Record Attendance	22515 v Raith Rovers, 2/1/1950
Record Win	13-2 v Edinburgh City, Lge, 11/12/1937
Record Defeat	0-9, v Hearts, Lge, 5/10/1957
Most League Goals in a Season	41 Jock Wood 1926/7; Henry Morris 1947/8
Chairman	Jim Stevenson
Secretary	Douglas Briggs
Manager	Gary Naymsith / Barry Smith / Darren Young
Assistant Manager	Tony McMinn
Colours 2016/17 Top	Gold with Black stripes and sleeves
Shorts	White
Sponsor	W Glendinning Haulage Contractors
Manufacturer	Joma
Change Colours 2016/17 Top	Purple with Black and White shoulders
Shorts	Black
Nicknames	Fifers
Web	www.eastfifefc.info
Match Programme	The Bayview £2
Theme Song	Telstar

Keeping a note of East Fife's appearances fo2 1016/17, they seldom seemed to have more than four substitutes. This was down to a combination of a very small squad and a horrendous injury list. In that context their performance over the season was pretty good. League One was very tight but East Fife ended up in mid-table which was about the best they could have hoped for.

Manager Garry Naysmith left in the early winter to take over at Queen of the South, with former Dundee, Alloa and Aldershot boss Barry Smith taking over. He too has now moved on, accepting the post at Raith Rovers who will be in the same division as East Fife next season.

PREDICTION FOR 2016/17

Darren Young's task as Manager is to improve on last season, presumably challenging for a promotion pay off spot. East Fife haven't been at tier two for 20 years and to get back there would be a huge achievement. Looking at their resouyrces and the quality of opposition, a mid table finish is the best that East Fife can hope for in 2017/18.

						L			SC			LC			CC							
			SQ	Nat	Pos	A	S	G	A	S	G	A	S	G	A	S	G	UNS				
Surname	First Name	DOB																	Signed	Previous Club	Notes	Contract
Austin	Jordan	03/10/1995		ENG	F	7	8			1		1	1			1		17	2016	Leven United	OL to Dundonald BB Aug 2016, OL to St Andrew's Utd Sep-Nov 2016	OOC
Brown	Ross	10/06/1993		SCO	M	32	1	2	4			1	3		1			3	2010	East Fife Youths	OOC May 2017, joined Livingston	[redacted]
Cooper	Alex	04/11/1991		SCO	M	3	3											4	2017	Cheltenham Town		OOC
Cordery	Tom	06/07/1995		SCO	GK													1	2017	Danderhall MW	Signed for 1 week, then released	[redacted]
Couser	Ryan			SCO	GK													3		Trialist, Fife Elite Academy		
Curran	Jesse	16/07/1996		NEW	M	11	1												2017	Dundee (OL)	Feb-May	[redacted]
Duffie	Kieran	04/03/1992		SCO	D	5	1												2017	Falkirk		OOC
Duggan	Chris	30/10/1994		AUS	F	13	3	5	1	1	2		2					1	2016	Partick Thistle		End 2017/18
Flockhart	Chris	12/04/1984		SCO	GK													1		Trialist	Ex Preston Athletic	[redacted]
Goodfellow	Ryan	26/05/1993		SCO	GK	10	1		4			2			2			14	2015	Dunfermline Athletic		End 2017/18
Gordon	Craig	20/12/1994		SCO	GK													10	2017	Unattached	Ex East Stirlingshire	OOC
Gray	Brodie	29/06/1997		SCO	M											1		4	2016	Kennoway Star Hearts	OL to Dundonald BB Aug-Sep 2016, Freed Sep 2016, joined Dundonald BB	[redacted]
Hurst	Mark	21/10/1995		SCO	GK	23	1											10	2015	St Johnstone (OL)	Sep 16-May 2017	[redacted]
Insall	Jamie	01/03/1992		ENG	F	12	12	6	3	1					1			2	2016	Hibernian (OL)	Aug 16-May 2017	[redacted]
Kane	Chris	31/05/1993		SCO	M	34		3	3	1	1	2	1		2			1	2016	Cowdenbeath		End 2018/19
Kerr	Jason	06/02/1997		SCO	D	31	2	7	3	1	1	4			2			3	2016	St Johnstone (OL)	Sep 16-May 2017	[redacted]
Lamont	Mark	04/02/1993		SCO	M	13	6	1	1	2		3	1		2			10	2016	Stirling Albion		End 2017/18
McManus	Paul	26/12/1982		SCO	F	4	5					3	1	2		1	1	3	2016	Arbroath	Freed Nov 2016, joined Cove Rangers	[redacted]
Mercer	Scott	18/06/1995		SCO	D	16	2		2			4			2				2015	Dunfermline Athletic	Transferred to QOS Jan 2017	[redacted]
Muir	William	16/03/1993		SCO	GK	3						2						3	2016	Queen's Park	Freed Sep 2016, rejoined Queen's Park	[redacted]
Mutch	Ross	15/01/1999		SCO	F		1											21	2016	AM Soccer	OL to Glenrothes JFC Sep-Dec 2016	End 2017/18
Naysmith	Gary	16/11/1978		SCO	D	10	2		1			4			1	1		1	2013	Aberdeen	Appointed QOS Manager Dec 2016	[redacted]
O'Hara	Kevin	11/08/1998		SCO	F	6	10	3				1	1		1			2	2016	Falkirk (OL)	Aug 16-Jan 2017	[redacted]
Page	Jonathan	08/02/1990		ENG	D	27			4			4		1	2		1		2015	Dunfermline Athletic		End 2018/19
Paterson	Nicki	19/07/1985		SCO	M	15			2		1								2017	Indy Eleven (Indianapolis)	Released May 2017	[redacted]
Penrice	James	22/12/1998		SCO	D	18			2										2017	Partick Thistle	Jan-May 2017	[redacted]
Reilly	Ben	20/08/1997		SCO	D	1	5											10	2017	Hamilton Accies		End 2017/18
Robinson	Scott	11/03/1992		SCO	M	22	1	5	4			3			1	1		1	2016	Dunfermline Athletic	OOC May 2017, joined Livingston	[redacted]
Slattery	Patrick	03/06/1993		SCO	M	29	1		3	1		3	1			1		2	2015	Queen of the South		End 2018/19
Smith	Kevin	20/03/1987		SCO	F	24	5	7	4			4		2	1		1	1	2014	Dumbarton		End 2018/19
Wallace	Tony	22/02/1991		SCO	F	7	9			2					2				2016	Nairn County		OOC
Watt	Luke	20/06/1997		SCO	D	2	1		1										2017	Motherwell (OL)	Jan-May 2017	[redacted]
Wilkie	Kyle	20/03/1991		SCO	M	18			2			3			2				2015	Berwick Rangers		End 2017/18
Own Goals								2														
NEW SIGNINGS																						
Miller	Kieran	14/10/1993		SCO	M														2017	Stenhousemuir		
Willis	Paul	21/08/1991		SCO	M														2017	Albion Rovers		
Wilson	Kyle																		2017	Kennoway Star Hearts		
Docherty	Mark																		2017	Dumbarton		

Source of Birthdates: East Fife FC Website and transfermarkt.com

Date	Comp	H/A	Opponents	F	A		HT		Referee	Crowd	Scorers
16/07/2016	LC	H	Dundee	1	1	4-2p	0	1	B Cook	1407	Smith
19/07/2016	LC	A	Dumbarton	2	0		2	0	C Charleston	452	Smith, McManus
23/07/2016	LC	H	Peterhead	2	1		1	1	K Graham	532	Page, McManus
26/07/2016	LC	A	Forfar Athletic	0	2		0	1	M Northcroft	565	
06/08/2016	L	H	Albion Rovers	2	2		2	1	M Roncone	682	Smith, R Dunlop og
13/08/2016	L	A	Peterhead	3	0		2	0	D Munro	492	Kerr, Smith, Lamont
17/08/2016	CC2	A	Arbroath	3	2		0	1	G Duncan	335	Page, Smith, McManus
20/08/2016	L	A	Alloa	1	2		0	2	D Lowe	652	O'Hara
27/08/2016	L	H	Brechin City	1	2		1	1	G Irvine	609	Robinson
03/09/2016	CC3	A	Alloa	0	3		0	3	K Graham	444	
10/09/2016	L	H	Stranraer	2	0		1	0	M Roncone	555	Insall 2
17/09/2016	L	A	Airdrieonians	1	1		1	0	G Beaton	814	Smith
24/09/2016	L	H	Livingston	3	1		3	0	D Lowe	784	Insall 2, Kane
01/10/2016	L	H	Stenhousemuir	0	1		0	0	S Reid	563	
15/10/2016	L	A	Queen's Park	0	1		0	1	S Millar	571	
22/10/2016	L	A	Stranraer	1	1		1	0	J McKendrick	428	Brown
29/10/2016	L	H	Airdrieonians	0	1		0	1	G Ross	706	
05/11/2016	L	A	Livingston	1	3		0	1	C Napier	907	Smith
15/11/2016	L	H	Alloa	2	2		1	0	A Newlands	412	Smith, Taggart og
19/11/2016	L	H	Queen's Park	1	2		1	1	M Northcroft	557	Insall
29/11/2016	SC3	H	Edinburgh City	1	1		0	1	D Lowe	339	Kerr
07/12/2016	SC3R	A	Edinburgh City	1	0		0	0	D Lowe	397	Kane
10/12/2016	L	A	Brechin City	1	0		1	0	S Kirkland	414	Robinson
17/12/2016	L	H	Peterhead	2	0		0	0	C Charleston	486	Kerr, O'Hara
20/12/2016	L	A	Stenhousemuir	1	0		1	0	M Roncone	356	O'Hara
31/12/2016	L	H	Livingston	2	1		0	1	G Duncan	661	Insall, Robinson
07/01/2017	L	H	Stenhousemuir	1	0		1	0	K Graham	635	Robinson
14/01/2017	L	A	Airdrieonians	2	2		1	1	A Newlands	833	Kerr, Brown
21/01/2017	SC4	A	Livingston	1	0		1	0	C Steven	726	Paterson
28/01/2017	L	H	Stranraer	0	0		0	0	S Millar	584	
04/02/2017	L	A	Queen's Park	2	2		0	2	G Ross	566	Duggan, Robinson
11/02/2017	SC5	H	St Mirren	2	3		0	1	D Robertson	1510	Duggan 2
18/02/2017	L	H	Brechin City	3	2		2	1	D Munro	642	Smith, Kane, Duggan
25/02/2017	L	A	Peterhead	1	1		0	0	G Duncan	495	Smith
28/02/2017	L	A	Alloa	0	3		0	2	B Cook	436	
04/03/2017	L	H	Albion Rovers	2	0		0	0	D Lowe	539	Duggan 2
11/03/2017	L	A	Livingston	1	0		0	0	G Irvine	773	Kerr
18/03/2017	L	H	Alloa	0	0		0	0	C Steven	612	
25/03/2017	L	A	Brechin City	1	2		0	1	A Muir	525	Duggan
28/03/2017	L	A	Albion Rovers	0	1		0	0	K Graham	419	
01/04/2017	L	H	Queen's Park	0	0		0	0	D Lowe	692	
08/04/2017	L	A	Stenhousemuir	1	3		0	1	J McKendrick	455	Kane
15/04/2017	L	H	Peterhead	1	2		1	1	M Northcroft	636	Kerr
22/04/2017	L	A	Albion Rovers	1	0		0	0	A Newlands	488	Kerr
29/04/2017	L	H	Airdrieonians	0	4		0	1	S Millar	908	
06/05/2017	L	A	Stranraer	1	2		0	0	S Reid	462	Kerr

FRIENDLIES / OTHER GAMES								
02/07/2016	H	Spartans	4	0			226	
05/07/2016	H	Edinburgh City	2	0			212	
10/07/2016	H	Aberdeen	2	4				
30/07/2016	H	Cowdenbeath	3	2				

Date	Comp	H/A	Opponents	F	A		1	2	3	4	5	6	7	8	9	10	11	12	13	14	15	16	17	18
16/07/2016	LC	H	Dundee	1	1	4-2p	Muir	Mercer	Page	Kerr	Naysmith	Slattery	Brown*	Wilkie&	Robinson	Smith	Austin+	Lamont*	Duggan+	McManus&	*Kane*	*Gray*	*Mutch*	*Goodfellow*
19/07/2016	LC	A	Dumbarton	2	0		Goodfellow	Mercer	Page	Kerr	Naysmith	Kane	Lamont+	Wilkie	Robinson	Smith	McManus*	Duggan*&	Brown+	Slattery&	*Austin*	*Gray*	*Mutch*	*Muir*
23/07/2016	LC	H	Peterhead	2	1		Muir	Mercer	Page	Kerr	Naysmith	Kane	Lamont	Wilkie*	Slattery	Smith+	McManus	Brown*	O'Hara+	*Gray*	*Mutch*	*Austin*	*Goodfellow*	
26/07/2016	LC	A	Forfar Athletic	0	2		Goodfellow	Mercer	Page	Kerr	Naysmith&	Slattery	Lamont	O'Hara*	Robinson	Smith	McManus+	Brown*	Austin+	Kane&	*Mutch*	*Gray*	*Muir*	
06/08/2016	L	H	Albion Rovers	2	2		Muir	Mercer	Page	Kerr	Kane	Slattery*	Lamont	Wilkie	Robinson	Smith	McManus+	Wallace*	O'Hara+	*Brown*	*Mutch*	*Goodfellow*		
13/08/2016	L	A	Peterhead	3	0		Muir	Mercer	Page	Kerr	Kane&	Brown	Lamont	Wilkie+	Robinson	Smith	McManus*	O'Hara*	Wallace+	Mutch&	*Naysmith*	*Goodfellow*		
17/08/2016	CC2	A	Arbroath	3	2		Goodfellow	Mercer	Page	Kerr	Kane	Brown*	Lamont	Wilkie	Wallace+	Smith	O'Hara&	Robinson*	Naysmith+	McManus&	*Mutch*	*Slattery*	*Muir*	
20/08/2016	L	A	Alloa	1	2		Muir	Mercer	Page	Kerr	Kane&	Brown*	Naysmith	Wilkie	Robinson	Smith	McManus+	Lamont*	O'Hara+	Wallace&	*Mutch*	*Goodfellow*		
27/08/2016	L	H	Brechin City	1	2		Goodfellow	Mercer	Page	Kerr	Kane+	Lamont	Naysmith	Wilkie	Robinson	O'Hara*	McManus	Wallace*	Austin+	*Brown*	*Mutch*	*Hurst*		
03/09/2016	CC3	A	Alloa	0	3		Goodfellow	Mercer	Page	Kerr	Kane	Lamont&	Naysmith	Wilkie	Robinson+	Wallace*	Insall	Slattery*	Austin+	Gray&	*McManus*			
10/09/2016	L	H	Stranraer	2	0		Hurst	Mercer	Page	Slattery	Kane	Lamont+	Naysmith	Wilkie	Robinson*	Smith	Insall&	Wallace*	Brown+	O'Hara&	*Kerr*	*Austin*	*McManus*	*Goodfellow*
17/09/2016	L	A	Airdrieonians	1	1		Hurst	Mercer	Page	Slattery	Kane	Lamont*	Naysmith	Wilkie	Brown	Smith+	Insall&	O'Hara*	Wallace+	McManus&	*Kerr*	*Goodfellow*		
24/09/2016	L	H	Livingston	3	1		Hurst	Mercer	Page	Slattery&	Kane	Lamont+	Naysmith	Wilkie	Brown	Smith*	Insall	O'Hara*	Wallace+	Kerr&	*Austin*	*McManus*	*Goodfellow*	
01/10/2016	L	H	Stenhousemuir	0	1		Hurst	Mercer	Page	Slattery&	Kane	Lamont+	Naysmith	Wilkie	Brown*	Smith	Insall	O'Hara*	McManus+	Wallace&	*Kerr*	*Robinson*	*Goodfellow*	
15/10/2016	L	A	Queen's Park	0	1		Hurst	Mercer*	Page	Slattery+	Kane	Wallace	Naysmith	Wilkie	Brown&	Smith	Insall	Kerr*	Robinson+	O'Hara&	*Lamont*	*Goodfellow*		
22/10/2016	L	A	Stranraer	1	1		Hurst	Mercer	Page	Slattery	Kane	Wallace*	Naysmith	Wilkie	Brown+	Smith	Kerr	Insall*	McManus+	*O'Hara*	*Goodfellow*			
29/10/2016	L	H	Airdrieonians	0	1		Hurst	Mercer&	Page	Slattery	Kane	Insall	Naysmith	Wilkie*	Brown+	Smith	Kerr	Lamont*	Wallace+	McManus&	*Goodfellow*			
05/11/2016	L	A	Livingston	1	3		Hurst	Mercer	O'Hara*	Slattery	Kane	Wallace&	Naysmith	Wilkie	Brown	Smith+	Kerr	Goodfellow*	McManus+	Insall&	*Lamont*	*Austin*		
15/11/2016	L	H	Alloa	2	2		Goodfellow	Insall&	Page	Slattery	Kane	Wallace*	Lamont+	Wilkie	Brown	Smith	Kerr	Mercer*	Naysmith+	Austin&	*O'Hara*			
19/11/2016	L	H	Queen's Park	1	2		Hurst	Insall	Page	Slattery+	Kane&	Wallace*	Lamont	Wilkie	Brown	Smith	Kerr	Mercer*	Naysmith+	O'Hara&	*Goodfellow*			
29/11/2016	SC3	H	Edinburgh City	1	1		Goodfellow	Mercer	Page	Robinson&	Kane	Naysmith	Lamont	Wilkie	Brown+	Smith	Insall*	Wallace*	Kerr+	Slattery&	*Austin*	*Hurst*		
07/12/2016	SC3R	A	Edinburgh City	1	0		Goodfellow	Mercer	Page	Robinson*	Kane	Slattery	Insall+	Wilkie	Brown	Smith	Kerr	Wallace*	Austin+	*Mutch*	*Hurst*			
10/12/2016	L	A	Brechin City	1	0		Goodfellow	Mercer	Page	Robinson	Kane	Slattery	Wallace	Wilkie	Brown+	Austin*	Kerr	Insall*	O'Hara+	*Smith*	*Mutch*	*Hurst*		
17/12/2016	L	H	Peterhead	2	0		Goodfellow	Mercer	Page	O'Hara	Kane	Slattery	Wallace*	Wilkie	Brown	Austin	Kerr	Insall*	*Lamont*	*Mutch*	*Hurst*			
20/12/2016	L	A	Stenhousemuir	1	0		Goodfellow	Mercer	Page	O'Hara	Kane	Slattery	Robinson+	Wilkie	Brown	Austin	Kerr	Hurst*	Insall+	*Mutch*	*Lamont*			
31/12/2016	L	H	Livingston	2	1		Hurst	Penrice	Page	O'Hara	Kane	Slattery	Robinson	Wilkie*	Brown	Austin+	Kerr	Lamont*	Insall+	*Mutch*	*Couser*			
07/01/2017	L	H	Stenhousemuir	1	0		Hurst	Penrice	Page	O'Hara*	Kane	Slattery	Robinson	Mercer	Brown	Insall+	Kerr	Smith*	Austin+	*Lamont*	*Duggan*	*Mutch*	*Couser*	
14/01/2017	L	A	Airdrieonians	2	2		Hurst	Penrice	Page	Paterson	Kane&	Slattery	Robinson	Lamont*	Brown	Insall+	Kerr	Smith*	Duggan+	Austin&	*Mutch*	*Couser*		
21/01/2017	SC4	A	Livingston	1	0		Goodfellow	Penrice	Page	Paterson	Kane	Slattery	Robinson	Smith	Brown*	Insall+	Kerr	Lamont*	Duggan+	*Austin*	*Mutch*	*Cordery*		
28/01/2017	L	H	Stranraer	0	0		Goodfellow	Penrice	Page	Paterson	Kane	Slattery	Robinson	Smith	Brown+	Insall*	Kerr	Duggan*	Lamont+	*Austin*	*Mutch*	*Hurst*	*Reillly*	
04/02/2017	L	A	Queen's Park	2	2		Goodfellow	Penrice	Page	Paterson	Watt	Slattery	Robinson	Smith+	Brown	Duggan*	Kerr	Insall*	Austin+	*Lamont*	*Reilly*	*Hurst*		
11/02/2017	SC5	H	St Mirren	2	3		Goodfellow	Penrice	Page	Paterson	Watt*	Slattery	Robinson	Smith+	Brown&	Duggan	Kerr	Kane*	Lamont+	Insall&	*Flockhart*	*Austin*		
18/02/2017	L	H	Brechin City	3	2		Goodfellow	Penrice	Page	Paterson	Kane	Slattery	Lamont*	Smith	Brown+	Duggan	Kerr	Insall*	Reilly+	*Austin*	*Hurst*			
25/02/2017	L	A	Peterhead	1	1		Goodfellow	Penrice	Page	Robinson	Kane	Slattery+	Lamont*	Smith	Brown	Duggan	Kerr	Reilly*	Insall+	*Austin*	*Hurst*			
28/02/2017	L	A	Alloa	0	3		Goodfellow	Penrice	Page	Robinson	Kane	Reilly+	Curran	Insall	Brown	Austin*	Kerr	Lamont*	Duggan+	*Mutch*	*Hurst*			
04/03/2017	L	H	Albion Rovers	2	0		Hurst	Penrice	Page	Robinson	Kane	Paterson	Curran*	Smith	Brown	Duggan	Kerr	Reilly*	*Lamont*	*Mutch*	*Insall*	*Austin*	*Goodfellow*	
11/03/2017	L	A	Livingston	1	0		Hurst	Penrice	Page	Robinson*	Kane	Paterson	Curran	Smith	Brown	Duggan+	Kerr	Slattery*	Insall+	*Cooper*	*Austin*	*Reilly*	*Gordon*	
18/03/2017	L	H	Alloa	0	0		Hurst	Penrice	Slattery	Robinson	Kane	Paterson	Curran	Smith*	Brown	Duggan	Kerr	Cooper*	*Reilly*	*Insall*	*Austin*	*Gordon*		
25/03/2017	L	A	Brechin City	1	2		Hurst	Penrice	Page*	Slattery	Kane	Paterson+	Robinson	Smith	Brown	Duggan&	Kerr	Curran*	Cooper+	Insall&	*Austin*	*Reilly*	*Gordon*	
28/03/2017	L	A	Albion Rovers	0	1		Hurst	Penrice	Curran	Slattery	Kane	Paterson	Robinson	Cooper+	Brown	Duggan*	Kerr	Insall*	Austin+	*Mutch*	*Reilly*	*Gordon*		
01/04/2017	L	H	Queen's Park	0	0		Hurst	Penrice*	Curran	Slattery	Kane	Paterson	Robinson	Smith+	Brown	Duggan	Kerr	Cooper*	Duffie+	*Austin*	*Reilly*	*Gordon*		
08/04/2017	L	A	Stenhousemuir	1	3		Hurst	Cooper	Curran	Duffie	Kane	Paterson	Robinson*	Smith+	Brown	Duggan	Kerr	Austin*	Lamont+	*Slattery*	*Reilly*	*Gordon*		
15/04/2017	L	H	Peterhead	1	2		Hurst	Cooper+	Curran	Duffie	Penrice	Paterson	Lamont*	Slattery	Brown	Duggan	Kerr	Smith*	Austin+	*Gordon*	*Reilly*			
22/04/2017	L	A	Albion Rovers	1	0		Hurst	Penrice	Curran	Duffie	Kane	Paterson	Austin*	Slattery	Brown	Duggan	Kerr	Smith*	*Lamont*	*Gordon*	*Reilly*	*Mutch*	*Cooper*	
29/04/2017	L	H	Airdrieonians	0	4		Hurst	Penrice	Curran	Duffie	Kane	Paterson	Austin	Slattery	Brown*	Smith+	Kerr	Watt*	Reilly+	*Gordon*	*Cooper*	*Lamont*		
06/05/2017	L	A	Stranraer	1	2		Hurst	Penrice	Curran	Duffie	Kane	Paterson+	Robinson	Slattery	Watt*	Duggan	Kerr	Reilly*	Smith+	*Gordon*	*Cooper*	*Lamont*	*Brown*	*Austin*

Edinburgh City FC 2016/17

Founded	1928
Ground	Ainslie Park (Spartans FC)
Postcode	EH5 2HF
Tel	Tel: 0845 463 1932 Club Office
Capacity	4625
Closest Railway Station	Edinburgh Waverley
Record Attendance	6000, H v St Bernards, Scottish Cup 1931/2
Record League Win	6-1 v Brechin City, 18/9/37
Record League Defeat	2-13, v East Fife, 11/12/37
Most League Goals in a Season	78, 1931/2
Chairman	Jim Brown
Secretary	Gavin Kennedy
Manager	Gary Jardine
Assistant Manager	Ross McNamara
Colours 2016/17 Top	White with Black Sash
Shorts	Black
Sponsor	Hutchinson Networks
Manufacturer	Joma
Change Colours 2016/17 Top	Yellow
Shorts	Black
Nicknames	City, Lilywhites, Citizens
Web	www.edinburghcityfc.com
Match Programme 2016/17	The Citizen, £2

It took several months for City to adjust to League Two football. Once they did get their first win, away to Forfar in the Cup, they didn't really look back. Of course they did have Cowdenbeath to thank for taking some of the pressure off them but their final position will have been hugely satisfying for those involved at the club. Over the course of the season they added to the quality of their squad with some judicious signings as they recognised some of the shortcomings of players who had served them well in the Lowland League.

PREDICTION FOR 2017/18

City are groundsharing at Spartans for the next three seasons which is bound to affect their crowds and income. They worked hard to attract a local support at Meadowbank but may have lost some of them now. However, their squad is much stronger than this time last year and they will not make such a bad start—a promotion play off place could be within grasp for City in the coming season.

						L			SC			LC			CC							
			SQ	Nat	Pos	A	S	G	A	S	G	A	S	G	A	S	G	UNS				
Surname	**First Name**	**DOB**																	**Signed**	**Previous Club**	**Notes**	**Contra**
Allan	Lewis	25/10/1996		SCO	F	13	1	4											2017	Hibernian (OL)	Jan-May	
Allum	Ross	07/10/1988		SCO	F	6	9	1	2	2	1	3	1	1				4	2014	Hill of Beath Hawthorn	Released Jan 2017, joined Spartans	
Amos	Gregor	18/02/1995		SCO	GK							1						4	2015	Falkirk	Freed Aug 2016, joined Selkirk	
Antell	Calum	13/06/1992		WAL	GK	13						1			1			27	2016	Nairn County		End 20
Beattie	Craig	16/01/1984		SCO	F	15	8	4	1			1						1	2016	Stirling Albion		End 20
Caddow	Jordan	27/09/1983		SCO	D	13	9	1	3	1		3				1		12	2013	Tynecastle		End 20
Carse	Dean	28/04/1994		SCO	F													1	2015	Berwick Rangers	Freed Jul 2016 joined Civil Service Strollers	
Cummings	Dean	29/03/1993		SCO	M	14	7		1	1		3	1		1		1	7	2016	Lothian Thistle HV		OOC
Deniran	Ortega	28/03/1986		NIG	M													4	2013	Port Harcourt Dolphins		OOC
Donaldson	Gordon	01/01/1991		SCO	D	13	5		1			4			1			13	2013	Edinburgh City Youths		OOC
Dunn	John	19/04/1987		SCO	M	22	3			1			1		1			7	2014	Craigroyston		End 20
Dunsmore	Aaron	24/07/1996		SCO	D	30	1		3									3	2016	Hibernian (OL)	Aug-May	
Gair	Douglas	11/10/1985		SCO	M	23	9	9	4			1						3	2004	Edinburgh City Youths	Retired May 2017	
Gibson	Dominico	09/06/1992		SCO	F	1	1					3	1		1			2	2013	Aberdeen		OOC
Guthrie	Ross	24/02/1990		SCO	M	11	12	1	4			1	3		1			7	2009	Edinburgh City Youths		OOC
Harrison	Shaun	01/01/1990		SCO	D	14	1		3				1		1			11	2009	Edinburgh City Youths		End 20
Hay	Scott	15/03/1998		SCO	M													1	2016	Tynecastle Colts		
Laird	Marc	23/01/1986		SCO	M	24		1	4									4	2016	Yeovil Town		End 20
MacDonald	John	02/01/1992		SCO	M		1					1	1		1			7	2014	Lothian Thistle HV	Freed Oct 2016, joined Penicuik Athletic	
Mafoko	Serge	03/09/1986		DRC	F		2											1	2017	Tooting & Mitcham United		OOC
Martyniuk	Neil	24/07/1996		SCO	D	2						3			1			5	2016	St Johnstone	OL to Newtongrange Star Oct-May 2016, Freed June 2017 joined Bonnyrigg R	
Mbu	Joe	14/02/1982		SCO/CAM	D	30			2	2		4						2	2014	East Fife	Retired May 2017	
McConnell	Mark	01/01/1994		SCO	M	13	15		2	1		2	2			1		7	2013	Edinburgh City Youths		OOC
McFarland	Ian	08/02/1991		SCO	M	24	4		3	1		3			1			6	2009	Edinburgh City Youths		OOC
McKee	Christopher	02/04/1990		SCO	D	29		1	3			3		1	1			1	2014	Stirling University		End 20
Muhsin	Sean	31/07/1988		SCO	M	2	5		2	1		3				1		9	2015	Spartans	Freed Jan 2017, joined Linlithgow Rose	
Paterson	Frazer	27/09/1990		SCO	D							1						6	2013	Heriot Watt University	OL to Broxburn Athletic Nov-Dec 2016, Freed Jan and joined Broxburn Ath	
Porteous	Ryan	01/03/1999		SCO	D	23		3	1									4	2016	Hibernian (OL)	Aug-Dec 2016	
Riordan	Derek	16/01/1983		SCO	F	7		3										3	2017	Unattached	Ex York City	OOC
See	Ousman	25/08/1994		SCO	F	15	5	6	1	2	1	1	1					2	2015	Selkirk	Out of Contract June 2017, joined Forfar Athlet	
Stobie	Andrew	19/12/1990		SCO	GK	23			4			2						14	2011	East Fife		OOC
Vanson	Grant			SCO	M														2010	Loughborough University	Freed Aug 2016	
Walker	Josh	21/02/1989		EBG	M	16		3											2017	Bengaluru		End 20
Own Goal								1														
NEW SIGNINGS																						
Grimes	Ashley																		2017	Southport		
Thomson	Craig				M														2017	Kelty Hearts		
Rodger	Gareth				D														2017	Brechin City		
Source of Birthdates: Transfermarkt.com																						

Date	Comp	H/A	Opponents	F	A	HT		Referee	Crowd	Scorers
20/07/2016	LC	H	Livingston	0	3	0	2	A Newlands	525	
23/07/2016	LC	A	Ayr United	0	1	0	1	B Cook	862	
27/07/2016	LC	H	Hamilton Accies	2	4	2	2	C Steven	459	McKee, Allum
30/07/2016	LC	A	St Mirren	0	3	0	3	S Kirkland	1800	
02/08/2016	CC1	A	Motherwell U20	1	2	0	1	L Wilson	402	Cummings
06/08/2016	L	H	Forfar Athletic	2	3	1	2	G Beaton	547	Beattie, Guthrie
13/08/2016	L	A	Elgin City	0	3	0	3	M Roncone	610	
20/08/2016	L	A	Cowdenbeath	0	2	0	1	J McKendrick	325	
27/08/2016	L	H	Berwick Rangers	1	2	0	0	C Napier	419	See
10/09/2016	L	A	Stirling Albion	1	1	0	0	C Steven	465	Allum
17/09/2016	L	H	Montrose	0	1	0	0	G Irvine	309	
24/09/2016	L	A	Annan Athletic	1	1	0	1	M Roncone	351	Swinglehurst og
01/10/2016	L	H	Arbroath	3	3	1	1	S Millar	495	Laird, See 2
08/10/2016	L	H	Elgin City	1	2	0	2	C Steven	352	Gair
15/10/2016	L	H	Clyde	0	1	0	0	G Beaton	432	
22/10/2016	SC2	H	Forfar Athletic	0	0	0	0	K Graham	328	
29/10/2016	L	A	Forfar Athletic	1	1	1	0	S Millar	491	See
01/11/2016	SC2	A	Forfar Athletic	1	0	0	0	C Charleston	388	Allum
05/11/2016	L	A	Montrose	1	0	0	0	D Munro	388	Gair
12/11/2016	L	H	Annan Athletic	1	0	0	0	G Irvine	246	Porteous
19/11/2016	L	H	Cowdenbeath	1	1	0	1	G Beaton	382	Gair
29/11/2016	SC3	A	East Fife	1	1	1	0	D Low	339	See
03/12/2016	L	A	Arbroath	1	0	0	0	K Graham	582	See
07/12/2016	SC3R	H	East Fife	0	1	0	0	D Low	397	
10/12/2016	L	H	Stirling Albion	2	0	1	0	M Roncone	368	See, Gair
17/12/2016	L	A	Clyde	0	0	0	0	A Newlands	461	
31/12/2016	L	A	Berwick Rangers	3	1	2	0	K Graham	515	McKee, Gair, Beattie
07/01/2017	L	H	Arbroath	0	2	0	1	G Ross	481	
21/01/2017	L	H	Forfar Athletic	0	1	0	1	C Napier	352	
28/01/2017	L	A	Elgin City	1	3	0	2	R Milne	563	Beattie
04/02/2017	L	H	Clyde	0	0	0	0	G Beaton	302	
11/02/2017	L	A	Annan Athletic	0	1	0	1	S Reid	379	
18/02/2017	L	H	Montrose	1	1	1	0	G Duncan	341	Walker
25/02/2017	L	A	Stirling Albion	0	1	0	1	K Graham	501	
28/02/2017	L	A	Cowdenbeath	2	1	1	1	G Ross	309	Walker, Gair
11/03/2017	L	A	Forfar Athletic	2	1	0	1	M Roncone	446	Riordan, Allan
15/03/2017	L	H	Berwick Rangers	2	2	0	1	G Irvine	423	Riordan, Gair
18/03/2017	L	A	Clyde	1	3	1	0	L Wilson	484	Allan
25/03/2017	L	H	Elgin City	3	0	1	0	J McKendrick	396	Gair 2, Caddow
01/04/2017	L	A	Montrose	0	3	0	1	D Dickinson	454	
08/04/2017	L	H	Cowdenbeath	1	1	1	0	C Charleston	577	Walker
15/04/2017	L	A	Arbroath	1	0	0	0	M Roncone	775	Porteous
22/04/2017	L	H	Annan Athletic	2	0	1	0	G Beaton	378	Beattie, Allan
29/04/2017	L	H	Stirling Albion	1	0	0	0	G Ross	388	Riordan
06/05/2017	L	A	Berwick Rangers	2	3	0	2	D Lowe	695	Allan, Porteous

FRIENDLIES / OTHER GAMES

05/07/2016	A	East Fife	0	2		212
07/07/2016	H	Hibernian	1	6		2522
29/07/2016	A	Pumpherston	4	8	U20	

Date	Comp	H/A	Opponents	F	A	1	2	3	4	5	6	7	8	9	10	11	12	13	14	15	16	17	18
20/07/2016	LC	H	Livingston	0	3	Amos	MacDonald	Donaldson	McKee	Mbu	Guthrie+	McFarland&	Gair	Martyniuk	Allum*	Cummings	Gibson*	See+	McConnell&	*Patterson*	*Caddow*	*Mushin*	*Stobie*
23/07/2016	LC	A	Ayr United	0	1	Stobie	Paterson	Donaldson	McKee	Mbu	Mushin	McFarland*	Caddow	Gibson	See*	Cummings&	Allum*	Guthrie+	McConnell&	*Carse*	*MacDonald*	*Martyniuk*	*Amos*
27/07/2016	LC	H	Hamilton Accies	2	4	Stobie	Martyniuk	Donaldson	McKee&	Mbu	Mushin	McFarland	Caddow	Gibson*	Allum	McConnell+	Guthrie*	Cummings+	Harrison&	*Gair*	*MacDonald*	*Dunn*	*Amos*
30/07/2016	LC	A	St Mirren	0	3	Antell	Martyniuk	Donaldson	Cummings&	Mbu	Mushin	Beattie+	Caddow	Gibson	Allum*	McConnell	Guthrie*	Dunn+	MacDonald&	*Harrison*	*Donaldson*	*Stobie*	
02/08/2016	CC1	A	Motherwell U20	1	2	Antell	Martyniuk	Donaldson	McKee	MacDonald	Harrison	Dunn+	McFarland	Gibson*	Guthrie&	Cummings	Mushin*	McConnell+	Caddow&	*See*	*Allum*	*Amos*	
06/08/2016	L	H	Forfar Athletic	2	3	Antell	Harrison	Donaldson	McKee	Mbu	Mushin&	Caddow	McFarland*	Gibson	Beattie+	McConnell	Cummings*	Guthrie+	Dunn&	*Martyniuk*	*MacDonald*	*Porteous*	*Amos*
13/08/2016	L	A	Elgin City	0	3	Antell	Martyniuk	Donaldson	McKee	Porteous*	Dunsmore	Cummings	McFarland+	Dunn	Beattie+	Guthrie&	Gibson*	Mushin+	Allum&	*Caddow*	*MacDonald*	*McConnell*	*Stobie*
20/08/2016	L	A	Cowdenbeath	0	2	Antell	Martyniuk+	Caddow	McKee	Porteous	Dunsmore	Cummings	McFarland&	Dunn	Allum	Guthrie*	See*	MacDonald+	McConnell&	*Donaldson*	*Mushin*	*Gair*	*Stobie*
27/08/2016	L	H	Berwick Rangers	1	2	Antell	Mbu	Caddow	McKee	Porteous	Dunsmore	Cummings*	McFarland+	Dunn	Allum	See	Gair*	McConnell+	*Paterson*	*Donaldson*	*MacDonald*	*Martyniuk*	*Stobie*
10/09/2016	L	A	Stirling Albion	1	1	Antell	Mbu	Caddow	McKee	Porteous	Dunsmore+	Cummings	McFarland*	Dunn	Allum	McConnell&	Gair*	Beattie+	See&	*Donaldson*	*MacDonald*	*Mushin*	*Stobie*
17/09/2016	L	H	Montrose	0	1	Antell	Mbu	Caddow	McKee	Porteous	Dunsmore*	Cummings	McFarland&	Dunn	Allum	McConnell+	Beattie*	See+	Muhsin&	*Donaldson*	*MacDonald*	*Gair*	*Stobie*
24/09/2016	L	A	Annan Athletic	1	1	Stobie	Mbu	Harrison	McKee	Muhsin	Dunsmore	Laird	See*	Dunn&	Beattie+	Gair	Allum*	Caddow+	McFarland&	*Donaldson*	*Cummings*	*Guthrie*	*Antell*
01/10/2016	L	H	Arbroath	3	3	Stobie	Mbu	Harrison	McKee	McFarland	Dunsmore	Laird+	See	Dunn	Beattie*	Gair	Allum*	McConnell+	*Porteous*	*Donaldson*	*Caddow*	*Guthrie*	*Antell*
08/10/2016	L	H	Elgin City	1	2	Stobie	Mbu*	Harrison	McKee	McFarland	Dunsmore	Guthrie&	See	Dunn	Beattie+	Gair	McConnell*	Caddow+	Allum&	*Donaldson*	*Martyniuk*	*Muhsin*	*Antell*
15/10/2016	L	H	Clyde	0	1	Stobie	Donaldson	Porteous	McKee&	McFarland+	Caddow	Guthrie*	See	Dunn	Laird	Gair	McConnell*	Beattie+	Allum&	*Dunsmore*	*Martyniuk*	*Patterson*	*Antell*
22/10/2016	SC2	H	Forfar Athletic	0	0	Stobie	Donaldson*	Porteous	McKee	McFarland	Caddow	Guthrie+	McConnell&	Beattie	Laird	Gair	Mbu*	Muhsin+	Allum&	*Dunsmore*	*See*	*Harrison*	*Antell*
29/10/2016	L	A	Forfar Athletic	1	1	Stobie	Mbu	Porteous	McKee	McFarland	Caddow	See&	McConnell*	Beattie+	Laird	Gair	Muhsin*	Allum+	Guthrie&	*Dunsmore*	*Patterson*	*Harrison*	*Antell*
01/11/2016	SC2	A	Forfar Athletic	1	0	Stobie	Harrison	Dunsmore	McKee	Muhsin	Caddow*	Guthrie	McConnell	Allum&	Laird+	Gair	Mbu*	McFarland+	See&	*Patterson*	*Hay*	*Antell*	
05/11/2016	L	A	Montrose	1	0	Stobie	Harrison	Dunsmore	McKee	Mbu	McFarland	Beattie*	McConnell+	See&	Laird	Gair	Allum*	Muhsin+	Guthrie&	*Patterson*	*Cummings*	*Caddow*	*Antell*
12/11/2016	L	H	Annan Athletic	1	0	Stobie	Harrison	Dunsmore	McKee	Mbu	McFarland	Porteous	Guthrie+	See*	Laird&	Allum	Cummings*	McConnell+	Gair&	*Muhsin*	*Gibson*	*Dunn*	*Antell*
19/11/2016	L	H	Cowdenbeath	1	1	Stobie	Harrison&	Dunsmore	Gair	Mbu	McFarland	Porteous	Guthrie*	McConnell+	Laird	Allum	See*	Cummings+	Caddow&	*Muhsin*	*Gibson*	*Dunn*	*Antell*
29/11/2016	SC3	A	East Fife	1	1	Stobie	Harrison	Dunsmore+	McKee	Mbu	McFarland&	Gair	Guthrie*	Cummings	Laird	See	Dunn*	Allum+	Caddow&	*Muhsin*	*McConnell*	*Antell*	
03/12/2016	L	A	Arbroath	1	0	Stobie	Caddow	Donaldson&	McKee	Mbu	McFarland+	McConnell*	Dunn	Cummings	Laird	See	Muhsin*	Allum+	Gair&	*Guthrie*	*Antell*		
07/12/2016	SC3R	H	East Fife	0	1	Stobie	Caddow	Dunsmore	Harrison	Mbu	McFarland&	Guthrie*	Gair	Muhsin+	Laird	Allum	See*	Cummings+	McConnell&	*Dunn*	*Porteous*	*Donaldson*	*Antell*
10/12/2016	L	H	Stirling Albion	2	0	Stobie	Donaldson	Dunsmore	Porteous	Mbu	McFarland	McConnell*	McKee	See	Laird	Cummings	Gair*	*Guthrie*	*Harrison*	*Muhsin*	*Caddow*	*Allum*	*Antell*
17/12/2016	L	A	Clyde	0	0	Stobie	Donaldson	Dunsmore	Porteous	Mbu	McFarland	McConnell*	McKee	See	Laird	Cummings+	Gair*	Guthrie+	*Harrison*	*Muhsin*	*Beattie*	*Dunn*	*Antell*
31/12/2016	L	A	Berwick Rangers	3	1	Stobie	Donaldson	Dunsmore	Porteous	Mbu	McFarland	McConnell+	McKee	See	Laird	Gair*	Beattie*	Dunn+	*Cummings*	*Caddow*	*Allum*	*Antell*	
07/01/2017	L	H	Arbroath	0	2	Stobie	Donaldson	Dunsmore	Porteous	Mbu	McFarland&	McConnell+	McKee*	See	Laird	Gair	Allum*	Beattie+	Cummings&	*Caddow*	*Harrison*	*Dunn*	*Antell*
21/01/2017	L	H	Forfar Athletic	0	1	Stobie	Donaldson+	Dunsmore	Harrison	Mbu	McFarland&	Dunn	McKee	See	Laird	Cummings*	Beattie*	Gair+	McConnell&	*Caddow*	*Guthrie*	*Allum*	*Antell*
28/01/2017	L	A	Elgin City	1	3	Stobie	Donaldson	Dunsmore	Harrison	Mbu	McFarland+	Dunn	Walker	Gair	Guthrie&	Cummings*	Beattie*	Caddow+	See&	*McConnell*	*Laird*	*Antell*	
04/02/2017	L	H	Clyde	0	0	Stobie	Caddow	Dunsmore	Harrison	Mbu*	McConnell	Dunn&	Walker	Gair	See+	Allan	Donaldson*	Guthrie+	McFarland&	*Cummings*	*Antell*		
11/02/2017	L	A	Annan Athletic	0	1	Stobie	Porteous	Dunsmore	Harrison	Guthrie+	McKee	Dunn	Walker	Gair*	Laird&	Allan	McConnell*	McFarland+	Caddow&	*Donaldson*	*Mbu*	*Antell*	
18/02/2017	L	H	Montrose	1	1	Stobie	Caddow	Dunsmore	Harrison	Guthrie*	McKee	Dunn	Walker	Gair	Laird&	Allan+	McConnell*	McFarland+	Cummings&	*Donaldson*	*Deniran*	*Antell*	
25/02/2017	L	A	Stirling Albion	0	1	Stobie	Porteous	Dunsmore&	Harrison+	Cummings	McKee	Donaldson	Walker	McFarland*	Laird	Allan	Guthrie*	Gair+	Caddow&	*McConnell*	*Dunn*	*Mbu*	*Antell*
28/02/2017	L	A	Cowdenbeath	2	1	Stobie	Porteous	Dunsmore+	Cummings*	Mbu	McKee	Dunn	Walker	Gair	Laird	Allan&	McConnell*	Caddow+	Donaldson&	*McFarland*	*Deniran*	*Riordan*	*Antell*
11/03/2017	L	A	Forfar Athletic	2	1	Stobie	Caddow	Donaldson	McConnell&	Mbu	McKee+	Dunn	Walker*	Cummings	Beattie	Riordan	Allan*	Gair+	Guthrie&	*Harrison*	*Deniran*	*Laird*	*Antell*
15/03/2017	L	H	Berwick Rangers	2	2	Stobie	Porteous	Donaldson	Dunsmore	Mbu	Allan	Gair	Walker	Laird	Beattie*	Riordan+	Dunn*	McConnell+	*Cummings*	*McFarland*	*Guthrie*	*Caddow*	*Antell*
18/03/2017	L	A	Clyde	1	3	Stobie	Caddow	Porteous	Dunsmore&	Mbu	Allan	Gair	Walker*	Laird	Dunn	Riordan+	Donaldson*	Beattie+	Guthrie&	*McFarland*	*Cummings*	*McConnell*	*Antell*
25/03/2017	L	H	Elgin City	3	0	Antell	McKee	McFarland+	Dunsmore	Mbu	Allan	Gair	Walker&	Laird	Dunn	Beattie*	Caddow*	McConnell+	Guthrie&	*Riordan*	*Cummings*	*Harrison*	*Stobie*
01/04/2017	L	A	Montrose	0	3	Antell	McKee	McFarland*	Dunsmore	Mbu	Allan	Gair+	Walker	Laird	Dunn	Beattie&	Guthrie*	Mafoko+	McConnell&	*Caddow*	*Porteous*	*Harrison*	*Stobie*
08/04/2017	L	H	Cowdenbeath	1	1	Antell	McKee*	Porteous	Dunsmore	Mbu	Allan&	Gair	Walker	Laird	Dunn+	Beattie	Cummings*	Harrison+	Caddow&	*McFarland*	*Guthrie*	*Riordan*	*Stobie*
15/04/2017	L	A	Arbroath	1	0	Antell	McKee	Porteous	Riordan*	Mbu	Allan	Gair	Walker	Laird	Dunn	Beattie+	Dunsmore*	Guthrie+	*McConnell*	*McFarland*	*Harrison*	*Donaldson*	*Stobie*
22/04/2017	L	H	Annan Athletic	2	0	Antell	McKee	Porteous	Riordan	Mbu	Allan	Gair	Walker	Laird	Dunsmore	Beattie*	Guthrie*	*Caddow*	*McConnell*	*McFarland*	*Harrison*	*Donaldson*	*Stobie*
29/04/2017	L	H	Stirling Albion	1	0	Antell	Harrison	Porteous	Dunsmore	Mbu	McFarland+	Gair	Walker	Guthrie&	Riordan	Beattie*	McConnell*	Cummings+	Donaldson&	*Caddow*	*Mafoko*	*Laird*	*Stobie*
06/05/2017	L	A	Berwick Rangers	2	3	Antell	Caddow	Porteous	Dunsmore*	Mbu	Allan	Gair	Walker	Guthrie&	Riordan	Cummings+	Donaldson*	McConnell+	Mafoko&	*Deniran*	*Laird*	*McKee*	*Stobie*

Elgin City FC 2016/17

Founded	1893
Ground	Boroughbriggs
Postcode	IV30 1AP
Tel	01343 551114
Capacity	4520
Closest Railway Station	Elgin
Record Attendance	12608 v Arbroath, SC, 17/2/1968
Record Win	18-1 v Brora Rangers, NOS Cup, 6/2/1960
Record Defeat	1-14 v Hearts, SC, 4/2/1939
Most League Goals in a Season	19 Martin Johnston 2005/6
Chairman	Graham Tatters
Secretary	Kate Taylor
Manager	Jim Weir
Assistant Manager	Gavin Price
Colours 2016/17 Top	Black and White Stripes
Shorts	Black
Sponsor	McDonald and Munro
Manufacturer	
Change Colours 2016/17 Top	Blue and Red Stripes
Shorts	Blue
Nicknames	City
Web	www.elgincity.com
Match Programme 2016/17	Black & White £2

Elgin had a very good first half of 2016/17 but fell away badly after New Year. Injury to top striker Shane Sutherland was a major blow and they lost other key players for spells as well. Even going into April a ppromotion play off place was within their grasp but they let that slip away in the final weeks.

Crowds at Borough Briggs are excellent and the home fans deserve a shot at a higher level of football. This will be their 18th season of Scottish league membership, all have been spent in the bottom tier.

Attracting players always poses a problem and Elgin frequently end up with a split squad. Some are based in Moray and some in the Central Belt. It's a difficult problem to overcome.

PREDICTION FOR 2017/18
Jim Weir must arrest the decline of the second half of last season. Perhaps if they make a decent start they will again challenge for promotion but a mid-table position looks more likely.

						L			SC			LC			CC							
Surname	**First Name**	**DOB**	**SQ**	**Nat**	**Pos**	**A**	**S**	**G**	**A**	**S**	**G**	**A**	**S**	**G**	**A**	**S**	**G**	**UNS**	**Signed**	**Previous Club**	**Notes**	**Contract**
Black	Stewart	15/05/1995		SCO	GK	3						4						5	2012	Elgin City Youths	Freed Oct 2016	[redacted]
Brownlie	David	22/03/1997		SCO	D	13												1	2017	Ross County (OL)	Jan-May	
Bruce	Robbie	01/06/1999		SCO	M		4					1	1			1		32	2015	Aberdeen	Released May 2017	
Cameron	Brian	19/12/1990		SCO	M	35		12	3		3	3	1		2				2008	Elgin City Youths		OOC
Cooper	Matthew	01/01/1994		SCO	D	28			2	1		3			2			3	2014	Inverness CT		End 2017/18
Crawford	David	30/06/1985		SCO	GK	1														Trialist	Ex Partick Thistle	[redacted]
Cullen	Ben	04/06/1991		ENG	F		1									1		8	2016	RAF Lossiemouth	OL to Rothes Jan-May	OOC
Dear	Trevor	01/01/2001		SCO	GK													3	2016	Elgin City Youths		End 2017/18
Dodd	Chris	28/02/1991		SCO	M	25	6	4	3				1		1	1		4	2016	Jeanfield Swifts		End 2017/18
Duff	Jamie	26/01/1989		SCO	D							2		1	2			10	2010	Inverness CT	Freed Nov 2016, joined Brora R	[redacted]
Dunn	Stevie	11/04/1971		SCO	GK													9	2016	Ex Lossiemouth		
Gunn	Craig	17/07/1987		SCO	F	12	22	5		3	1	3	1	2		1		3	2009	Ross County	Released May 2017, joined Brora R	[redacted]
Mackay	Cameron	09/12/1996		SCO	GK	18									2			4	2016	Inverness CT (OL)	Aug Sep, Dec-May	
MacLeod	Kyle	07/07/1995		SCO	D		12			1		2	1	1	1	1	1	7	2016	Ross County (OL)	Jul-Jan	
MacPhee	Archie	20/03/1993		SCO	D	34		3	3			4			2				2014	Nairn County		OOC
McHardy	Darryl	22/05/1995		SCO	D	32	2	6	3				1	1				2	2014	Elgin City Youths		End 2018/19
McLeish	Chris	12/08/1992		SCO	F	34	2	9	3		2	1	2		1			2	2016	Jeanfield Swifts		End 2017/18
Moore	Daniel	11/10/1988		SCO	M	22	11	1	2	1		3	1	1	1	1		2	2014	Nairn County	Released May 2017, joined Rothes	[redacted]
Nicholson	Mark	25/06/1988		SCO	D	31	1	1	3		1	4			2		1	1	2008	Ross County	Released May 2017, joined Brora R	
Reid	Jamie	11/01/1994		SCO	M	12	14	3	1	2		2	1		1			9	2016	Arbroath		End 2017/18
Reilly	Thomas	15/09/1994		SCO	M	35		2	2			4			1			1	2015	St Mirren		End 2017/18
Sinnamon	Ryan	22/07/1996		SCO	D	3												5	2017	Rangers	Released May 2017	[redacted]
Smith	Scott	21/07/1995		SCO	M	2	4					2	1					9	2016	Forfar Athletic		OOC
Stewart	Keiran	20/05/1994		SCO	M	14	12		2	1		3			2			9	2016	Arbroath	OOC May 2017, joined Berwick R	[redacted]
Sutherland	Shane	23/10/1990		SCO	F	23	1	19	3		5	3	1		2		1	1	2016	Peterhead		End 2018/19
Sutherland	Ali	19/09/1996		SCO	F	5	9											1	2017	Inverness CT		End 2017/18
Waters	Marc	30/03/1996		SCO	GK	14			3									10	2017	Queen's Park	OL from Q Park Oct-Jan	End 2017/18
Watson	Michael																	1				
Watson	Errol	04/09/1984		SCO	GK													14	2016	Clachnacuddin	Released May 2017	[redacted]
Wilson	David	01/01/2001		SCO	F													4	2016	Elgin City Youths		
Own Goals								2			1											
NEW SIGNINGS																						
McGovern	John Paul				M														2017	Clyde		
Ferguson	Callum				F														2017	Albion Rovers		

Source of Birthdates: Transfermarkt.com

Date	Comp	H/A	Opponents	F	A	HT		Referee	Crowd	Scorers
16/07/2016	LC	H	St Johnstone	1	3	0	1	A Muir	1046	Duff
19/07/2016	LC	A	Falkirk	0	3	0	2	K Graham	1278	
23/07/2016	LC	H	Brechin City	4	2	2	1	C Napier	506	Gunn 2, McHardy, Moore
26/07/2016	LC	A	Stirling Albion	1	4	1	1	S Millar	522	MacLeod
06/08/2016	L	A	Cowdenbeath	1	0	0	0	S Reid	315	McLeish
13/08/2016	L	H	Edinburgh City	3	0	3	0	M Roncone	610	Gunn, Sutherland 2
16/08/2016	CC	H	Hearts U20	2	0	1	0	G Beaton	350	Sutherland, MacLeod
20/08/2016	L	H	Arbroath	0	1	0	0	A Newlands	519	
27/08/2016	L	A	Forfar Athletic	2	3	2	1	D Lowe	537	McLeish 2
03/09/2016	CC3	A	Falkirk	1	6	1	3	M Northcroft	1591	Nicholson
10/09/2016	L	A	Berwick Rangers	4	2	2	1	G Irvine	407	Sutherland, Reid, Gunn 2
17/09/2016	L	H	Clyde	0	2	0	2	C Charleston	713	
24/09/2016	L	A	Stirling Albion	4	0	3	0	J McKendrick	457	Sutherland 2, Dodd, Gunn
01/10/2016	L	H	Annan Athletic	0	2	0	1	K Graham	583	
08/10/2016	L	A	Edinburgh City	2	1	2	0	C Steven	352	Dodd, Reilly
15/10/2016	L	A	Montrose	5	0	3	0	M Roncone	302	McHardy 2, Cameron 2, Sutherland
22/10/2016	SC2	A	Gala Fairydean Rovers	4	0	3	0	G Irvine	440	Sutehrland, Millar og, McLeish, Camerc
29/10/2016	L	H	Cowdenbeath	3	1	2	0	S Reid	650	Cameron, MacPhee, Sutherland
05/11/2016	L	A	Clyde	1	2	0	2	M Roncone	616	McHardy
12/11/2016	L	H	Stirling Albion	2	3	1	0	S Millar	585	McHardy, Cameron
19/11/2016	L	A	Annan Athletic	0	1	0	1	J McKendrick	363	
26/11/2016	SC3	H	Hawick Royal Albert	8	1	3	1	M Northcroft	549	Sutherland 4, Cameron 2, Gunn, McLei
03/12/2016	L	H	Montrose	4	1	0	0	D Lowe	586	McPhee, McLeish, Sutherland, Camero
10/12/2016	L	H	Berwick Rangers	6	0	2	0	G Beaton	535	Sutherland 3, Cameron 2, Moore
17/12/2016	L	A	Arbroath	2	3	1	0	M Roncone	584	Cameron, McLeish
02/01/2017	L	H	Forfar Athletic	2	2	2	1	G Ross	1091	McLeish, McHardy
07/01/2017	L	A	Montrose	3	0	2	0	S Millar	562	Dodd, Sutherland 2
14/01/2007	L	H	Annan Athletic	3	2	3	0	M Roncone	638	Cameron, McLeish, Sutherland
21/01/2017	SC4	H	Inverness CT	1	2	1	1	J McKendrick	3624	Nicolson
28/01/2017	L	H	Edinburgh City	3	1	2	0	R Milne	563	Sutherland 3
11/02/2017	L	A	Forfar Athletic	1	1	0	1	A Newlands	551	Sutherland
18/02/2017	L	H	Clyde	4	1	1	0	G Ross	881	Nicholson, Sutherland, Perry og, Gunn
25/02/2017	L	A	Berwick Rangers	1	0	1	0	C Steven	403	McLeish
28/02/2017	L	A	Stirling Albion	0	1	0	0	C Napier	412	
04/03/2017	L	H	Arbroath	0	0	0	0	M Northcroft	640	
11/03/2017	L	A	Annan Athletic	0	1	0	1	G Aitken	328	
14/03/2017	L	A	Cowdenbeath	1	1	1	0	D Munro	278	Cameron
18/03/2017	L	H	Forfar Athletic	1	1	0	0	G Beaton	709	McHardy
25/03/2017	L	A	Edinburgh City	0	3	0	1	J McKendrick	396	
01/04/2017	L	H	Berwick Rangers	2	2	1	2	K Graham	588	Reilly, Cameron
08/04/2017	L	H	Montrose	1	1	1	0	S Millar	781	Cameron
15/04/2017	L	A	Clyde	2	3	2	0	C Napier	465	McLeish, Dodd
22/04/2017	L	H	Stirling Albion	2	2	0	0	R Milne	785	Reid, MacPhee
29/04/2017	L	A	Arbroath	2	3	0	1	G Irvine	807	Reid, Sukar og
06/05/2017	L	H	Cowdenbeath	0	0	0	0	M Roncone	909	

FRIENDLIES / OTHER GAMES				
02/07/2016	A	Keith	8	2
09/07/2016	A	Lossiemouth	2	0
12/07/2016	H	Inverness CT	0	3

Date	Comp	H/A	Opponents	F	A	1	2	3	4	5	6	7	8	9	10	11	12	13	14	15	16	17	18
16/07/2016	LC	H	St Johnstone	1	3	Black	Cooper	MacPhee	Nicholson	Duff	Reilly+	Gunn	Cameron	Moore	MacLeod*	Sutherland&	Smith*	Dodd+	McLeish&	*Reid*	*Stewart*	*McHardy*	*Dunn*
19/07/2016	LC	A	Falkirk	0	3	Black	Cooper	MacPhee	Nicholson	Stewart	Reilly*	Smith&	Cameron	Moore	Reid+	Sutherland	Gunn*	McLeish+	Bruce&	*Duff*	*MacLeod*	*Dunn*	
23/07/2016	LC	H	Brechin City	4	2	Black	Cooper*	MacPhee	Nicholson	Stewart	Reilly	McLeish+	Cameron	Moore	Gunn&	Sutherland	McHardy*	MacLeod+	Reid&	*Duff*	*Smith*	*Dunn*	*Bruce*
26/07/2016	LC	A	Stirling Albion	1	4	Black	Duff	MacPhee	Nicholson	Stewart	Reilly	Bruce*	Smith&	Reid	Gunn+	MacLeod	Cameron*	Sutherland+	Moore&	*McLeish*	*Cullen*	*Dunn*	
06/08/2016	L	A	Cowdenbeath	1	0	Black	Cooper	MacPhee	Nicholson	Stewart	Reilly	McLeish+	Cameron	Moore&	Gunn*	Sutherland	MacLeod*	Smith+	Dodd&	*Bruce*	*Cullen*	*Dunn*	
13/08/2016	L	H	Edinburgh City	3	0	Mackay	Cooper	MacPhee	Nicholson	Stewart	Reilly	McLeish	Cameron*	Moore	Gunn+	Sutherland	Smith*&	MacLeod+	Dodd&	*McHardy*	*Duff*	*Reid*	*Black*
16/08/2016	CC	H	Hearts U20	2	0	Mackay	Cooper	MacPhee	Nicholson	Stewart*	Duff	Dodd&	Cameron	Reid+	MacLeod	Sutherland	Bruce*	Moore+	Cullen&	*Gunn*	*McLeish*	*Black*	
20/08/2016	L	H	Arbroath	0	1	Mackay	Cooper	MacPhee	Nicholson	Stewart	Reilly	McLeish	Cameron	Moore+	Gunn*	Sutherland	MacLeod*	McHardy+	*Dodd*	*Reid*	*Duff*	*Bruce*	*Black*
27/08/2016	L	A	Forfar Athletic	2	3	Mackay	Cooper	MacPhee	Nicholson	Stewart	Reilly+	McLeish	Cameron	Moore&	Gunn*	Sutherland	MacLeod*	McHardy+	Reid&	*Dodd*	*Duff*	*Bruce*	*Black*
03/09/2016	CC3	A	Falkirk	1	6	Mackay	Cooper	MacPhee	Nicholson	Stewart	Reilly	McLeish&	Cameron	Moore+	Duff*	S Sutherland	Gunn*	Dodd+	MacLeod&	*Reid*	*Cullen*	*Bruce*	*Black*
10/09/2016	L	A	Berwick Rangers	4	2	Black	Cooper	MacPhee	Nicholson	McHardy	Reilly	McLeish+	Cameron	Reid&	Dodd*	S Sutherland	Moore*	Gunn+	Stewart&	*MacLeod*	*Duff*	*Bruce*	*Dunn*
17/09/2016	L	H	Clyde	0	2	Black	Cooper	MacPhee	Nicholson	McHardy	Reilly	Moore+	Cameron	Reid*	Gunn&	S Sutherland	McLeish*	Stewart+	Dodd&	*MacLeod*	*Duff*	*Bruce*	*Dunn*
24/09/2016	L	A	Stirling Albion	4	0	Crawford	Cooper	MacPhee*	Nicholson	McHardy	Reilly	Dodd	Cameron	Reid&	McLeish+	S Sutherland	Moore*	Gunn+	MacLeod&	*Stewart*	*Bruce*	*E Watson*	
01/10/2016	L	H	Annan Athletic	0	2	Waters	Cooper	MacPhee	Nicholson	McHardy	Reilly	Dodd+	Cameron	Reid*	McLeish&	S Sutherland	Moore*	Gunn+	MacLeod&	*Stewart*	*E Watson*		
08/10/2016	L	A	Edinburgh City	2	1	Waters	Cooper	MacPhee	Nicholson	McHardy	Reilly	Dodd+	Cameron	Reid&	McLeish*	S Sutherland	Stewart*	Moore+	MacLeod&	*Gunn*	*Bruce*	*Dunn*	
15/10/2016	L	A	Montrose	5	0	Waters	Cooper	MacPhee	Nicholson	McHardy	Reilly*	Dodd&	Cameron	Reid	McLeish+	S Sutherland	Stewart*	Gunn+	Bruce&	*Moore*	*MacLeod*	*Duff*	*E Watson*
22/10/2016	SC2	A	Gala Fairydean Rovers	4	0	Waters	Cooper	MacPhee	Nicholson	McHardy	Stewart	Dodd	Cameron	Reid*	McLeish+	S Sutherland&	Moore*	Gunn+	McLeod&	*Bruce*	*Reilly*	*Duff*	*E Watson*
29/10/2016	L	H	Cowdenbeath	3	1	Waters	Cooper	MacPhee	Nicholson	McHardy	Reilly	Dodd*	Cameron	Reid&	McLeish+	S Sutherland	Moore*	Gunn+	Stewart&	*MacLeod*	*Bruce*	*Duff*	*E Watson*
05/11/2016	L	A	Clyde	1	2	Waters	Cooper	MacPhee	Stewart	McHardy	Reilly	Dodd&	Cameron	Reid*	McLeish+	S Sutherland	Moore*	MacLeod+	Gunn&	*Nicholson*	*Bruce*	*E Watson*	
12/11/2016	L	H	Stirling Albion	2	3	Waters	Cooper	MacPhee	Nicholson	McHardy	Reilly	Dodd&	Cameron	Reid*	McLeish+	S Sutherland	Gunn*	MacLeod+	Moore&	*Stewart*	*Bruce*	*Cullen*	*E Watson*
19/11/2016	L	A	Annan Athletic	0	1	Waters	Cooper	MacPhee	Stewart	McHardy	Reilly&	Moore	Cameron	Gunn*	McLeish+	S Sutherland	Dodd*	MacLeod+	Reid&	*Cullen*	*Bruce*	*E Watson*	
26/11/2016	SC3	H	Hawick Royal Albert	8	1	Waters	Stewart	MacPhee	Nicholson	McHardy	Reilly*	Moore&	Cameron	Dodd	McLeish+	S Sutherland	Cooper*	Gunn+	Reid&	*MacLeod*	*Bruce*	*E Watson*	
03/12/2016	L	H	Montrose	4	1	Mackay	Stewart	MacPhee	Nicholson	McHardy	Reilly	Moore	Cameron	Dodd+	McLeish*	S Sutherland&	Gunn*	Reid+	MacLeod&	*Cooper*	*Bruce*	*Dunn*	
10/12/2016	L	H	Berwick Rangers	6	0	Mackay	Stewart	MacPhee	Nicholson	McHardy	Reilly	Moore	Cameron	Dodd+	McLeish*	S Sutherland&	Gunn*	Reid+	MacLeod&	*Cooper*	*E Watson*		
17/12/2016	L	A	Arbroath	2	3	Mackay	Stewart	MacPhee+	Nicholson	McHardy	Reilly	Moore	Cameron	Dodd	McLeish*	S Sutherland	Gunn*	Reid+	*MacLeod*	*Cooper*	*Bruce*	*Cullen*	*Watson*
02/01/2017	L	H	Forfar Athletic	2	2	Mackay	Cooper	MacPhee	Nicholson	McHardy	Reid	Moore	Cameron	Dodd+	McLeish*	S Sutherland	Gunn*	Bruce+	Cullen&	*M Watson*	*E Watson*		
07/01/2017	L	A	Montrose	3	0	Mackay	Cooper	MacPhee	Nicholson	McHardy	Reilly	Moore*	Cameron	Dodd+	McLeish&	S Sutherland	Reid*	Stewart+	Gunn&	*Bruce*	*Cullen*	*Wilson*	*E Watson*
14/01/2007	L	H	Annan Athletic	3	2	Mackay	Cooper	MacPhee	Nicholson	McHardy	Reilly	Moore+	Cameron	Dodd*	McLeish&	S Sutherland	Reid*	Stewart+	Bruce&	*Gunn*	*Wilson*	*Waters*	
21/01/2017	SC4	H	Inverness CT	1	2	Waters	Cooper	MacPhee	Nicholson*	McHardy	Reilly	Moore&	Cameron	Dodd+	McLeish	S Sutherland	Stewart*	Reid+	Gunn&	*Bruce*	*Wilson*	*Cullen*	*E Watson*
28/01/2017	L	H	Edinburgh City	3	1	Mackay	Cooper	MacPhee	Brownlie	McHardy	Reilly	Moore&	Cameron	Dodd+	McLeish*	S Sutherland	Gunn*	Stewart+	Reid&	*Bruce*	*Wilson*	*Waters*	
11/02/2017	L	A	Forfar Athletic	1	1	Waters	Cooper	MacPhee	Brownlie	McHardy	Reilly	Moore	Cameron	Nicholson	McLeish*	S Sutherland	Gunn*	*Dodd*	*Reid*	*Stewart*	*A Sutherland*	*Bruce*	*Mackay*
18/02/2017	L	H	Clyde	4	1	Mackay	Cooper	MacPhee	Dodd+	McHardy	Reilly	Moore	Cameron	Nicholson	McLeish&	S Sutherland*	Gunn*	Reid+	A Sutherland&	*Stewart*	*Bruce*	*Waters*	
25/02/2017	L	A	Berwick Rangers	1	0	Mackay	Cooper	MacPhee	Brownlie	McHardy	Reilly	Moore&	Cameron	Dodd+	McLeish*	Gunn	Stewart*	A Sutherland+	Reid&	*Bruce*	*Waters*		
28/02/2017	L	A	Stirling Albion	0	1	Mackay	Cooper	MacPhee	Brownlie	McHardy	Reilly+	Moore&	Cameron	Dodd	Nicholson	Gunn*	McLeish*	A Sutherland+	*Stewart*	*Reid*	*Waters*	*Smith*	
04/03/2017	L	H	Arbroath	0	0	Mackay	Cooper	MacPhee	Brownlie	McHardy	Reilly	McLeish+	Cameron	Dodd*	Nicholson	Gunn	Moore*	A Sutherland+	*Stewart*	*Reid*	*Waters*	*Smith*	*Bruce*
11/03/2017	L	A	Annan Athletic	0	1	Mackay	Cooper	MacPhee	Brownlie	McHardy	Reilly	McLeish+	Cameron	Moore*	Nicholson	Gunn&	A Sutherland*	Stewart+	Bruce&	*S Sutherland*	*Waters*	*Smith*	
14/03/2017	L	A	Cowdenbeath	1	1	Mackay	Cooper*	MacPhee	Brownlie	McHardy	Reilly	McLeish	Cameron	Stewart	Dodd	A Sutherland+	Nicolson*	S Sutherland+&	Gunn&	*Reid*	*Waters*	*Smith*	*Moore*
18/03/2017	L	H	Forfar Athletic	1	1	Mackay	Nicholson	MacPhee	Brownlie	McHardy	Reilly	McLeish	Cameron	Stewart	Dodd+	Gunn*	A Sutherland*	Moore+	*Reid*	*Smith*	*Bruce*	*Sinnamon*	*Waters*
25/03/2017	L	A	Edinburgh City	0	3	Mackay	Nicholson	Sinammon	Brownlie	McHardy	Reilly	McLeish+	Cameron	Stewart*	Dodd	A Sutherland&	Moore*	Reid+	Gunn&	*Smith*	*Bruce*	*Waters*	
01/04/2017	L	H	Berwick Rangers	2	2	Waters	Nicholson	Sinammon*	Brownlie&	McHardy	Reilly	McLeish	Cameron	Reid+	Moore	MacPhee	Stewart*	A Sutherland+	Gunn&	*Smith*	*Dodd*	*Bruce*	*Dear*
08/04/2017	L	H	Montrose	1	1	Waters	Nicholson	MacPhee	Brownlie+	McHardy	Reilly	McLeish	Cameron	Stewart	Moore&	A Sutherland*	Dodd*	Gunn+	Reid&	*Smith*	*Sinnamon*	*Bruce*	*Dear*
15/04/2017	L	A	Clyde	2	3	Waters	Nicholson	Sinnamon+	Brownlie	McHardy	Reilly	McLeish	Dodd&	Stewart	Moore	A Sutherland*	Reid*	Gunn+	Smith&	*Bruce*	*Dear*		
22/04/2017	L	H	Stirling Albion	2	2	Waters	Cooper	MacPhee	Cameron	McHardy	Reilly	McLeish	Dodd&	Nicholson	Moore*	Gunn+	Reid*	A Sutherland+	Smith&	*Bruce*	*Sinnamon*	*Stewart*	*MacKay*
29/04/2017	L	A	Arbroath	2	3	Waters	Cooper	MacPhee	Brownlie+	McHardy	Reilly&	McLeish*	Cameron	Nicholson	Reid	Smith	Gunn*	A Sutherland+	Dodd&	*Bruce*	*Sinnamon*	*MacKay*	
06/05/2017	L	H	Cowdenbeath	0	0	Waters	Cooper	MacPhee	Cameron	McHardy	Reilly	McLeish+	Dodd&	Nicholson	A Sutherland*	Smith	Moore*	Gunn+	Stewart&	*Brownlie*	*Sinnamon*	*Bruce*	*Mackay*

Falkirk FC 2016/17

Founded	1876
Ground	Falkirk Stadium
Postcode	FK2 9DX
Tel	01324 624121
Capacity	8750
Closest Railway Station	Falkirk Grahamston
Record Attendance	23100 v Celtic, SC, 21/2/1953
Record Win	11-1 v Tillicoultry, SC, 7/9/1889
Record Defeat	1-1 v Airdrieonians, Lge, 28/4/51
Most League Goals in a Season	43 Evelyn Morrison, 1928/9
Chairman	Doug Henderson
Company Secretary	Ronnie Bateman
Head Coach	Peter Houston
Coaches	James McDonagh, Alan Maybury
Technical Director	Alex Smith MBE
Colours 2016/17 Top	Navy Blue with Red and White Stripe
Shorts	White
Sponsor	Central Demolition
Manufacturer	Puma
Change Colours 2016/17 Top	White
Shorts	Blue
Nicknames	Bairns
Web	www.falkirkfc.co.uk
Match Programme 2016/17	The Navy Blue £2.50 (Garthland)
Theme Song	Amarillo

As in 2015/16, Falkirk proved to be the "nearly men" of the Championship. More than good enough to secure a Play Off spot, they came up short at the death, partly due to a punishing programme of matches.

Falkirk's crowds and infrastructure merit Premiership football. But the structure of the promotion play offs is stacked against the Championship clubs. Winning the title has to be the goal but that was never really likely with Hibernian in the division.

Falkirk also tend to lose their better players to bigger clubs. Peter Houston and his coaching staff have a great reputation for recognising and developing young talent and other clubs know that. During 2016/17 Craig Sibbald reinforced his standing as one of the top players in the Championship—how he has not moved on to a higher level is a mystery.

PREDICTION FOR 2017/18

With Hibs out of the way the main challenge for promotion will come from Falkirk, Dundee United and possibly St Mirren. Falkirk are most likely to again occupy a Play off position making that dream of Premiership football so hard to achieve.

Lee Miller - 151 goals and counting

Lee Miller		L			LC			SC			OC			Total		
Season	Club	A	S	G	A	S	G	A	S	G	A	S	G	A	S	G
2000/1	Falkirk													0	0	0
2001/2	Falkirk	27		11				2						29	0	11
2002/3	Falkirk	34		17	3		1	4			3		2	44	0	20
2003/4	Bristol City	33	10	8	2	1	1	2						37	11	9
2004/5	Bristol City	2	5		1	1								3	6	0
2004/5	Hearts	17	1	8	1			4		3				22	1	11
2005/6	Dundee United	22	12	8	1				1		2			25	13	8
2006/7	Dundee United	1	2		1									2	2	0
2006/7	Aberdeen	25	7	4										25	7	4
2007/8	Aberdeen	32	4	12	3		1	6			7			48	4	13
2008/9	Aberdeen	34		10	1		1	2		1				37	0	12
2009/10	Aberdeen	18		3	1			1		1	2			22	0	4
2009/10	Middlesbrough	6	4											6	4	0
2010/11	Middlesbrough		1			1								0	2	0
2010/11	Notts County	5	1	2					1					5	2	2
2010/11	Scunthorpe Utd	12	5	1										12	5	1
2011/12	Carlisle United	33		14				2		1	1			36	0	15
2012/13	Carlisle United	23		9	1									24	0	9
2013/14	Carlisle United	28	6	5	1			2	1	3				31	7	8
2014/5	Kilmarnock	9	10	1		2		1						10	12	1
2015/6	Falkirk	17	15	7		1		1		3	1			19	16	10
2016/7	Falkirk	17	14	9	1	2	1	1			1	1		20	17	10
														0	0	0
TOTAL		395	97	129	17	8	5	28	3	12	17	1	2	457	109	148

Date	Comp	H/A	Opponents	F	A		HT		Referee	Crowd	Scorers
16/07/2016	LC	A	Stirling Albion	0	1		0	1	C Steven	1315	
19/07/2016	LC	H	Elgin City	3	0		2	0	K Graham	1278	Vaulks, Miller, McHugh
23/07/2016	LC	A	St Johnstone	0	3		0	2	R Madden	2725	
30/07/2016	LC	H	Brechin City	2	0		0	0	S McLean	1073	Gasparotto, Austin
06/08/2016	L	H	Hibernian	1	2		1	1	K Clancy	6458	Sibbald
13/08/2016	L	A	Morton	1	1		0	1	J Beaton	2079	Leahy
20/08/2016	L	A	Queen of the South	0	2		0	1	S Kirkland	1841	
27/08/2016	L	H	Dumbarton	1	0		0	0	D Robertson	4311	Miller
03/09/2016	CC3	H	Elgin City	6	1		3	1	M Northcroft	1591	McHugh 2, Baird 2, Hippolyte, McCracken
10/09/2016	L	A	Raith Rovers	2	0		1	0	E Anderson	2320	Baird, Taiwo
17/09/2016	L	H	Dundee United	3	1		1	1	C Allan	5488	Baird, Hippolyte, Miller
24/09/2016	L	H	Ayr United	2	0		0	0	W Collum	4345	Meggatt og, Miller
01/10/2016	L	A	St Mirren	1	1		1	0	J Beaton	2334	Sibbald
07/10/2016	CC4	A	Ayr United	0	1	AET	0	0	A Muir	1247	
15/10/2016	L	H	Dunfermline Athletic	2	1		1	0	A Dallas	6377	Sibbald, Hippolyte
22/10/2016	L	H	Raith Rovers	2	4		1	2	B Cook	4773	Baird, Miller
29/10/2016	L	A	Dundee United	0	1		0	0	E Anderson	7046	
05/11/2016	L	H	Morton	1	1		0	0	G Aitken	4432	Miller
12/11/2016	L	A	Hibernian	1	1		0	0	J Beaton	14551	Baird
19/11/2016	L	A	Ayr United	1	0		1	0	G Duncan	1414	Craigen
03/12/2016	L	H	St Mirren	3	1		0	1	C Thomson	4486	Miller, McHigh, Hippolyte
10/12/2016	L	H	Queen of the South	2	2		1	1	N Walsh	4170	Hippolyte 2
17/12/2016	L	A	Dumbarton	1	2		0	1	M Northcroft	832	Sibbald
26/12/2016	L	A	Dunfermline Athletic	1	1		1	0	E Anderson	6134	Hippolyte
31/12/2016	L	H	Hibernian	1	2		1	1	C Allan	6747	Sibbald
07/01/2017	L	A	Raith Rovers	4	1		3	1	A Dallas	2202	Hippolyte, McHugh, Sibbald 2
14/01/2017	L	H	Ayr United	1	1		1	1	B Madden	5038	Grant
21/01/2017	SC	A	Morton	0	2		0	1	G Aitken	2349	
28/01/2017	L	A	St Mirren	2	1		1	0	A Muir	3316	Baird 2
04/02/2017	L	H	Dunfermline Athletic	2	0		1	0	W Collum	5953	Baird, Miller
11/02/2017	L	H	Dundee United	3	0		1	0	E Anderson	5028	Baird, Muirhead, Craigen
18/02/2017	L	A	Morton	2	2		1	1	G Aitken	2397	Craigen, Muirhead
25/02/2017	L	H	Dumbarton	2	2		1	1	M Northcroft	4160	Leahy, Austin
04/03/2017	L	A	Queen of the South	2	0		1	0	G Duncan	1995	Kidd, Sibbald
11/03/2017	L	A	Ayr United	4	1		1	0	S McLean	1514	Austin 2, Sibbald Aird
18/03/2017	L	H	Morton	0	1		0	0	A Muir	4584	
25/03/2017	L	A	Hibernian	1	2		0	0	K Clancy	16140	Sibbald
01/04/2017	L	H	Raith Rovers	1	0		0	0	N Walsh	4823	Miller
08/04/2017	L	A	Dundee United	1	1		0	0	E Anderson	6313	Leahy
15/04/2017	L	H	St Mirren	2	2		1	1	C Thomson	4737	Miller, McHugh
22/04/2017	L	A	Dunfermline Athletic	2	1		0	1	G Duncan	5076	Muirhead, Austin
29/04/2017	L	H	Queen of the South	2	2		1	1	C Allan	4673	Austin, Muirhead
06/05/2017	L	A	Dumbarton	1	0		0	0	D Robertson	1660	Austin
16/05/2017	PO	A	Dundee United	2	2		1	1	B Madden	7034	McKee, Craigen
19/05/2017	PO	H	Dundee United	1	2		1	0	K Clancy	7926	Craigen

FRIENDLIES / OTHER GAMES							
29/06/2016	A	Bray Wanderers	0	1			
02/07/2016	A	Shelbourne	3	0			
05/07/2016	A	Stenhousemuir	3	2		U20	
09/07/2016	A	Albion Rovers	4	2			268
12/07/2016	H	Stirling University	3	1		U20	
25/07/2016	H	Musselburgh Athletic	3	0		U20	
28/07/2016	H	Swansea City U21	0	1			423

Date	Comp	H/A	Opponents	F	A	1	2	3	4	5	6	7	8	9	10	11	12	13	14	15	16	17	18
16/07/2016	LC	A	Stirling Albion	0	1	Rogers	Kidd	Leahy	Gasparotto	Watson	Kerr	Sibbald	Hippolyte*	Craigen&	Baird+	McHugh	Austin*	Miller+	Taiwo&	*Muirhead*	*McCracken*	*O'Hara*	*Mehmet*
19/07/2016	LC	H	Elgin City	3	0	Mehmet	Muirhead	Leahy	Gasparotto	Watson	Kerr	Sibbald&	Vaulks	Craigen	Austin+	Miller*	Baird*	McHugh+	Taiwo&	*Kidd*	*McCracken*	*Hippolyte*	*Rogers*
23/07/2016	LC	A	St Johnstone	0	3	Rogers	Muirhead	Leahy	Gasparotto	Watson	Kerr	Sibbald	Rankin	Craigen	Baird+	Taiwo*	Austin*	McHugh+	*Miller*	*Kidd*	*McCracken*	*Hippolyte*	*Mehmet*
30/07/2016	LC	H	Brechin City	2	0	Rogers	Kidd	Leahy	Gasparotto	Watson	Kerr+	Sibbald	Rankin	Craigen	Austin*	McHugh&	Miller*	Taiwo+	Baird&	*Muirhead*	*McCracken*	*Hippolyte*	*Mehmet*
06/08/2016	L	H	Hibernian	1	2	Rogers	Muirhead	Leahy	Gasparotto	Watson	Taiwo+	Sibbald&	Rankin	McCracken	Baird*	McHugh	Austin*	Craigen+	Miller&	*Kidd*	*Henderson*	*Hippolyte*	*Mehmet*
13/08/2016	L	A	Morton	1	1	Mehmet	Muirhead	Leahy	Gasparotto	Watson	Taiwo	Sibbald	Rankin	Craigen+	Miller*	McHugh&	Baird*	Hippolyte+	Austin&	*Kidd*	*McCracken*	*Kerr*	*McMinn*
20/08/2016	L	A	Queen of the South	0	2	Rogers	Muirhead	Leahy	Gasparotto	Watson	Taiwo+	Sibbald*	Rankin&	Kerr	Baird	McHugh	Hippolyte*	Craigen+	Austin&	*Kidd*	*McCracken*	*Miller*	*Mehmet*
27/08/2016	L	H	Dumbarton	1	0	Rogers	McCracken	Leahy	Gasparotto	Kidd&	Taiwo*	Sibbald	Hippolyte	Kerr	Baird+	McHugh	Craigen*	Miller+	Muirhead&	*Rankin*	*Shepherd*	*Watson*	*Mehmet*
03/09/2016	CC3	H	Elgin City	6	1	Mehmet	McCracken	Watson	Gallacher	Kidd	Taiwo	Sibbald&	Hippolyte	Kerr+	Baird	McHugh*	Miller*	Rankin+	Shepherd&	*Leahy*	*Gasparotto*	*Austin*	*Craigen*
10/09/2016	L	A	Raith Rovers	2	0	Rogers	McCracken	Leahy	Gasparotto	Kidd	Taiwo	Sibbald&	Hippolyte*	Kerr	Baird+	McHugh	Rankin*	Miller+	Craigen&	*Watson*	*Shepherd*	*Austin*	*McMinn*
17/09/2016	L	H	Dundee United	3	1	Rogers	McCracken	Leahy	Gasparotto	Kidd	Taiwo*	Sibbald+	Hippolyte	Kerr	Baird	McHugh&	Rankin*	Craigen+	Miller&	*Watson*	*Shepherd*	*Gallacher*	*McMinn*
24/09/2016	L	H	Ayr United	2	0	Rogers	McCracken	Leahy	Gasparotto	Kidd	Taiwo	Sibbald&	Hippolyte	Kerr*	Baird	McHugh+	Rankin*	Miller+	Shepherd&	*Watson*	*Henderson*	*Gallacher*	*Mehmet*
01/10/2016	L	A	St Mirren	1	1	Rogers	McCracken	Leahy	Gasparotto	Kidd	Taiwo*	Sibbald&	Rankin	Kerr	Baird	McHugh+	Miller*	Craigen+	Hippolyte&	*Watson*	*Shepherd*	*Austin*	*Mehmet*
07/10/2016	CC4	A	Ayr United	0	1 AET	Mehmet	Watson	Leahy	Gasparotto	Kidd	Hipployte	Shepherd+	Rankin	Kerr&	Miller	McHugh*	Sibbald*	Baird+	Blues&	*McCracken*	*Henderson*	*Gallacher*	*McMinn*
15/10/2016	L	H	Dunfermline Athletic	2	1	Rogers	McCracken	Leahy	Gasparotto	Kidd*	Taiwo+	Sibbald	Hippolyte&	Kerr	Baird	McHugh	Watson*	Shepherd+	Rankin&	*Miller*	*Gallacher*	*Blues*	*Mehmet*
22/10/2016	L	H	Raith Rovers	2	4	Rogers	McCracken	Leahy	Gasparotto	Watson	Taiwo+	Sibbald	Hippolyte&	Kerr	Baird	McHugh*	Miller*	Craigen+	Shepherd&	*Rankin*	*Gallacher*	*Grant*	*Mehmet*
29/10/2016	L	A	Dundee United	0	1	Rogers	McCracken	Leahy	Gasparotto	Muirhead	Taiwo	Sibbald*	Rankin&	Kerr	Baird+	Miller	Hippolyte*	McHugh+	Craigen&	*Grant*	*Shepherd*	*Watson*	*Mehmet*
05/11/2016	L	H	Morton	1	1	Rogers	McCracken	Leahy	Gasparotto	Muirhead	Taiwo*	Sibbald	Hippolyte	Kerr	Baird+	Miller	Craigen*	McHugh+	*Rankin*	*Grant*	*Shepherd*	*Watson*	*Mehmet*
12/11/2016	L	A	Hibernian	1	1	Rogers	McCracken	Leahy	Gasparotto	Muirhead	Taiwo	Sibbald*	Hippolyte&	Kerr	Baird	Miller+	Rankin*	McHugh+	Grant&	*Craigen*	*Shepherd*	*Watson*	*Mehmet*
19/11/2016	L	A	Ayr United	1	0	Rogers	McCracken	Leahy	Gasparotto	Muirhead	Rankin	Sibbald*	Craigen	Kerr	Baird+	Miller&	Hippolyte*	McHugh+	Austin&	*Kidd*	*Grant*	*Watson*	*Mehmet*
03/12/2016	L	H	St Mirren	3	1	Rogers	McCracken	Leahy	Gasparotto	Muirhead	Rankin*	Hippolyte	Craigen+	Kerr	Baird&	Miller	Sibbald*	McHugh+	Shepherd&	*Kidd*	*Grant*	*Watson*	*Mehmet*
10/12/2016	L	H	Queen of the South	2	2	Rogers	McCracken	Leahy	Gasparotto	Muirhead	Sibbald	Hippolyte	Craigen*	Kerr&	Baird+	Miller	McHugh*	Shepherd+	Taiwo&	*Rankin*	*Grant*	*Watson*	*Mehmet*
17/12/2016	L	A	Dumbarton	1	2	Rogers	McCracken	Taiwo*	Grant	Muirhead	Sibbald	Hippolyte	Gallacher	Kerr	Baird	Miller+	Craigen*	Shepherd+	*Leahy*	*Rankin*	*Gasparotto*	*Watson*	*Mehmet*
26/12/2016	L	A	Dunfermline Athletic	1	1	Rogers	Gasparotto	Taiwo&	Grant	Muirhead	Sibbald	Hippolyte*	Gallacher	Kerr	Baird	Shepherd+	McHugh*	Miller+	Rankin&	*Kidd*	*Leahy*	*Watson*	*Mehmet*
31/12/2016	L	H	Hibernian	1	2	Rogers	Gasparotto	Taiwo	Grant	Muirhead	Sibbald	Hippolyte	Gallacher	Kerr	Baird*	Shepherd+	McHugh*	Miller+	*Rankin*	*Kidd*	*Leahy*	*Craigen*	*Mehmet*
07/01/2017	L	A	Raith Rovers	4	1	Rogers	Watson+	Taiwo	Grant	Muirhead	Sibbald	Hippolyte	Gallacher	Kerr	Baird*	McHugh	Shepherd*	Gasparotto+	*Miller*	*Kidd*	*Leahy*	*Craigen*	*Thomson*
14/01/2017	L	H	Ayr United	1	1	Rogers	McCracken	Taiwo*	Grant	Muirhead	Sibbald	Hippolyte	Gallacher	Kerr	Baird&	McHugh+	Craigen*	Miller+	Shepherd&	*Kidd*	*Leahy*	*Gasparotto*	*Thomson*
21/01/2017	SC	A	Morton	0	2	Rogers	McCracken	Watson	Aird	Muirhead	Sibbald	Hippolyte+	Gallacher	Kerr	Craigen*	Miller	McHugh*	Baird+	*Grant*	*Kidd*	*Leahy*	*Gasparotto*	*Thomson*
28/01/2017	L	A	St Mirren	2	1	Rogers	Leahy	Watson	Grant	Muirhead	Sibbald	Hippolyte	Aird+	Kerr	Baird&	Miller*	McHugh*	Kidd+	Gasparotto&	*Shepherd*	*Gallacher*	*Craigen*	*Thomson*
04/02/2017	L	H	Dunfermline Athletic	2	0	Rogers	Leahy*	Watson	Grant	Muirhead	Sibbald	Hippolyte	McKee	Craigen	Baird+	Miller&	Gallacher*	McHugh+	Austin&	*Shepherd*	*Kidd*	*Gasparotto*	*Thomson*
11/02/2017	L	H	Dundee United	3	0	Rogers	Leahy	Watson	Grant	Muirhead	Sibbald	Hippolyte	Taiwo+	Craigen	Baird*	Miller&	Austin*	Kidd+	Aird&	*McHugh*	*Gallacher*	*Gasparotto*	*Thomson*
18/02/2017	L	A	Morton	2	2	Rogers	Leahy	Watson	Grant	Muirhead	Sibbald	Hippolyte+	Taiwo	Craigen&	Austin	Miller*	McHugh*	Kerr+	Aird&	*Kidd*	*Gallacher*	*Gasparotto*	*Thomson*
25/02/2017	L	H	Dumbarton	2	2	Rogers	Leahy	Watson	Grant	Muirhead	Sibbald	Hippolyte*	Taiwo	Craigen	Austin&	Miller+	Aird*	Baird+	McHugh&	*Kidd*	*Kerr*	*Gasparotto*	*Thomson*
04/03/2017	L	A	Queen of the South	2	0	Rogers	Leahy	Gasparotto	Grant	Kidd	Sibbald	Kerr	Taiwo	Craigen*	Austin&	Baird+	Aird*	McHugh+	Miller&	*Shepherd*	*Gallacher*	*Blues*	*Thomson*
11/03/2017	L	A	Ayr United	4	1	Rogers	Leahy	Gasparotto	Grant	Kidd	Sibbald	Kerr	Taiwo	Aird	Austin+	Baird*	Miller*	McHugh+	*Muirhead*	*Shepherd*	*Gallacher*	*Hippolyte*	*Thomson*
18/03/2017	L	H	Morton	0	1	Rogers	Leahy	Gasparotto	Grant	Kidd	Sibbald	Kerr*	Taiwo	Aird&	Austin	Baird+	Hippolyte*	McHugh+	Craigen&	*Shepherd*	*Muirhead*	*Miller*	*Thomson*
25/03/2017	L	A	Hibernian	1	2	Thomson	Leahy	Gasparotto	Grant	Kidd&	Sibbald	Kerr	Taiwo*	Aird	McHugh+	Baird	Hippolyte*	Austin+	Muirhead&	*Shepherd*	*Miller*	*Craigen*	*Rogers*
01/04/2017	L	H	Raith Rovers	1	0	Thomson	Leahy	Gasparotto	Grant	Kidd	Sibbald	Hippolyte	Taiwo	Aird*	McHugh+	Baird+	Miller*	Craigen+	*Muirhead*	*Shepherd*	*Kerr*	*Austin*	*McMinn*
08/04/2017	L	A	Dundee United	1	1	Thomson	Leahy	Gasparotto	Grant	Muirhead	Sibbald	Hippolyte*	Taiwo	Kerr	McHugh++	Baird&	Craigen*	Austin+	Shepherd&	*McCracken*	*O'Hara*	*Aird*	*McMinn*
15/04/2017	L	H	St Mirren	2	2	Thomson	Leahy	Gasparotto	Grant	Muirhead	Sibbald	Miller&	Taiwo	Kerr*	Craigen	Baird+	Austin*	Aird+	McHugh&	*Kidd*	*Shepherd*	*Gallacher*	*Rogers*
22/04/2017	L	A	Dunfermline Athletic	2	1	Thomson	Leahy	Gasparotto	Grant	Muirhead	Sibbald	Miller+	Taiwo&	Kerr*	Craigen	Baird	Hippolyte*	Austin+	McKee&	*Kidd*	*McHugh*	*Aird*	*Rogers*
29/04/2017	L	H	Queen of the South	2	2	Thomson	Leahy	Kidd*	Grant	Muirhead	Sibbald	Austin	Taiwo	Kerr	Craigen&	Baird+	McHugh*	Aird+	Miller&	*McCracken*	*McKee*	*Shepherd*	*Rogers*
06/05/2017	L	A	Dumbarton	1	0	Thomson	Leahy	Gasparotto	Grant	Muirhead	Sibbald	Austin+	McKee	Kerr	Craigen*	Miller	Aird*	McHugh+	*Baird*	*Kidd*	*Gallacher*	*Shepherd*	*Rogers*
16/05/2017	PO	A	Dundee United	2	2	Thomson	Leahy	Gasparotto	Grant	Muirhead	Sibbald+	Austin&	McKee	Kerr	Craigen	Miller*	Baird*	Taiwo+	McHugh&	*Aird*	*Hippolyte*	*Watson*	*Rogers*
19/05/2017	PO	H	Dundee United	1	2	Thomson	Leahy	Gasparotto	Watson	Muirhead	Sibbald	Austin	McKee*	Kerr	Craigen&	Baird+	Taiwo*	McHugh+	Hippolyte&	*Kidd*	*Miller*	*Aird*	*Rogers*

Surname	First Name	DOB	SQ	Nat	Pos	L A	L S	L G	SC A	SC S	SC G	LC A	LC S	LC G	CC A	CC S	CC G	UNS	Signed	Previous Club	Notes	Contract
Aird	Fraser	02/02/1995		CAN	F	5	7	1	1									4	2017	Rangers	Released June 2017	[redacted]
Austin	Nathan	15/02/1994	16	ENG	F	9	10	6				2	2	1				4	2016	East Fife		
Baird	John	22/08/1985	9	SCO	F	33	3	8		1		2	2		1	1	2	1	2015	Queen of the South	OOC June 2017, joined Inverness CT	[redacted]
Blues	Cameron	13/04/1998	31	SCO	M											1		2	2015	Falkirk FC Youths		
Craigen	James	28/03/1991	28	ENG	M	15	14	5	1			4						6	2016	Raith Rovers		OOC
Eadie	Cameron	27/02/1998	23	SCO	D														2015	Falkirk FC Youths	Released June 2017	
Finlayson	Mark	30/05/1998	36	SCO	D														2015	Forth Valley Elite Academy		End 2017/18
Gallacher	Tony	23/07/1999	33	SCO	D	5	1		1						1			12	2015	Forth Valley Elite Academy		
Gasparotto	Luca	09/03/1995	15	CAN	D	29	2					4		1	1			8	2016	Rangers		OOC
Grant	Peter	11/03/1994	14	SCO	D	21	1	1										7	2014	Peterborough United		End 2017/18
Henderson	Liam	23/08/1996	22	SCO	D													3	2016	Hearts	OL to Cowdenbeath Jan-May 2017	End 2017/18
Hippolyte	Myles	09/11/1994	11	ENG	M	22	9	7	1			1			2		1	6	2016	Livingston		OOC
Johnson	Kyle	07/03/1998	35	SCO	D														2015	Falkirk FC Youths	Released June 2017	[redacted]
Kerr	Mark	02/03/1982	8	SCO	M	31	1		1			4			2			3	2015	Queen of the South		End 2017/18
Kidd	Lewis	30/01/1995	2	SCO	D	12	2	1				2			2			19	2016	Queen of the South		OOC
Langton	Conor	26/11/1998	34	SCO	F														2015	Forth Valley Elite Academy		
Leahy	Luke	19/11/1992	3	ENG	D	33		3				4			1			7	2012	Rugby Town	Released June 2017, joined Walsall	[redacted]
McCracken	David	16/10/1981	5	SCO	D	16			1						1		1	9	2013	St Johnstone	Released June 2017, joined Peterhead	
McHugh	Bob	16/07/1991	19	SCO	F	15	20	3		1		2	2	1	2		2	2	2015	Motherwell	Released June 2017, joined Morton	
McKee	Joe	31/10/1992	6	SCO	M	4	1	1										1	2017	Carlisle United		End 2018/19
McMinn	Lewis	04/08/1997	26	SCO	GK													6	2015	Rangers	Released June 2017	[redacted]
Mehmet	Denez Dogan	19/09/1992		ENG/TUR	GK	1						1			2			19	2015	Kayserispor	Freed Jan 2017 joined Port Vale	
Miller	Lee	18/05/1983	18	SCO	F	17	14	9	1			1	2	1	1	1		7	2015	Kilmarnock		End 2017/18
Muirhead	Aaron	30/08/1990	4	SCO	D	26	2	4	1			2						5	2015	Partick Thistle		End 2017/18
O'Hara	Kevin	11/08/1998	20	SCO	F													2	2014	Forth Valley Elite Academy	OL to East Fife Aug-Dec 2016	End 2017/18
Rankin	John	27/06/1983		SCO	M	7	6					2			1	1		6	2016	Dundee Utd	Freed Jan 2017, joined QOS	[redacted]
Rogers	Danny	23/03/1994	1	ROI	GK	28			1			3						8	2015	Aberdeen (OL)	Aug 16-May 2017	
Shepherd	Scott	29/05/1996	23	SCO	F	2	9								1	1		17	2013	Falkirk FC Youths		End 2018/19
Sibbald	Craig	18/05/1995	10	SCO	M	37	1	10	1			4			1	1			2011	Falkirk FC Youths		OOC
Taiwo	Tom	27/02/1990	7	ENG	M	30	3	1				1	3		1				2014	Hibernian		End 2017/18
Thomson	Robbie	07/03/1993	24	SCO	GK	9												11	2017	Hamilton Accies		End 2017/18
Vaulks	Will	13/09/1993		ENG	D							1		1					2013	Workington	Transferred to Rotherham United Jul 2016	[redacted]
Watson	Paul	20/12/1990	44	SCO	D	11	1		1			4			2			14	2015	Raith Rovers		End 2017/18
Own Goal								1														
NEW SIGNINGS																						End 2018/19
Mitchell	David				GK														2017	Dundee		End 2018/19
Harris	Alex																		2017	Hibernian		
Girdwood	Harry				F														2017	Spartans		
McBride	Connor				F														2017	Forth Valley Elite Academy		
Munro	Marky				D														2017	Forth Valley Elite Academy		
Jarvis	Jason				M														2017	Forth Valley Elite Academy		
Sweeney	Kieran																		2017	Forth Valley Elite Academy		
Dunne	Ciaran				M														2017	Forth Valley Elite Academy		
Mitchell	Kyle				D														2017	Forth Valley Elite Academy		

Source of Birthdates: Falkirk FC website and Transfermarkt.com

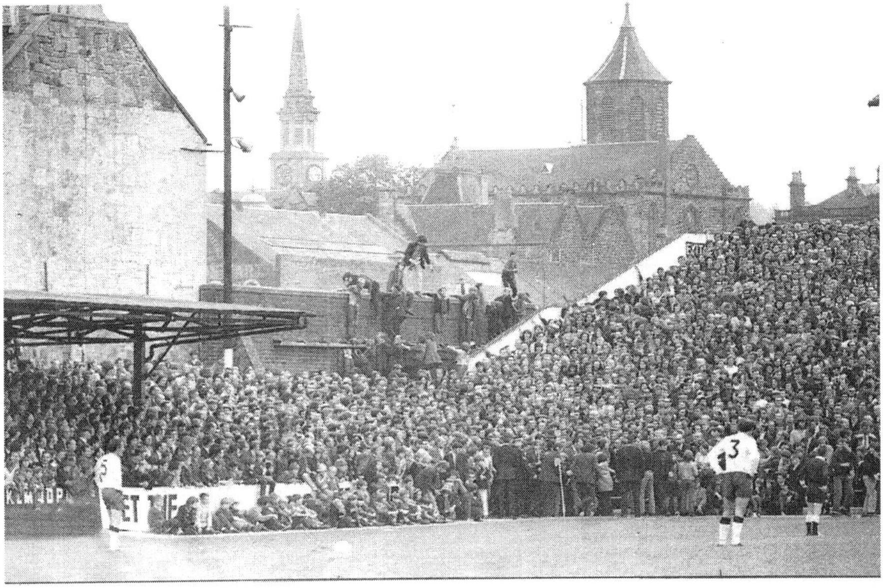

Forfar Athletic FC 2016/17

Founded	1885
Ground	Station Park
Postcode	DD8 3BT
Tel	01307 463576
Capacity	6777
Closest Railway Station	Dundee
Record Attendance	19780 v Rangers, SC, 2/2/1970
Record Win	14-1 v Lindertis, SC, 1/9/1888
Record Defeat	2-12 v King's Park, Lge, 2/1/1930
Most League Goals in a Season	46 David Kilgour, 1929/30
Chairman	Alasair Donald
Secretary	David McGregor
Manager	Dick Campbell (until Dec), Gary Bollan
Assistant Manager	John Young (until Dec), Stuart Balmer
Colours 2016/17 Top	Navy Blue with Sky Blue Band
Shorts	Navy Blue
Sponsor	Orchard Timber Products
Manufacturer	Pendle
Change Colours 2016/17 Top	White
Shorts	Sky Blue
Nicknames	Loons
Web	www.forfarathletic.co.uk
Match Programme 2016/17	The Loons £2

At one stage Forfar looked home and dry as Champions then they contrived to almost throw away promotion entirely. Going into the play offs on a stuttering run of form, they came good at the right time to breeze past Annan Athletic and Peterhead.

Gary Bollan's teams are always well organised and hard to beat. They win few friends for exciting football but they are difficult to play against.

They lacked a consistent striker and that is an area which they must address for 2017/18.

PREDICTION FOR 2017/18

Promoted teams usually survive at the higher level for at least one year. Bluntly, that is as much as Forfar can expect to do. They've lost some of their top players over the Summer so Gary Bollan has had to rebuild. A mid table finish would be an excellent result for Forfar in 2017/18.

						L			SC			LC			CC							
			SQ	Nat	Pos	A	S	G	A	S	G	A	S	G	A	S	G	UNS				
Surname	**First Name**	**DOB**																	**Signed**	**Previous Club**	**Notes**	**Contract**
Adam	Grant	16/04/1991		SCO	GK	39			2			4			3				2016	Cowdenbeath		End 2017/18
Aitken	Matthew	19/07/1997		SCO	F		1						2			1		19	2015	St Johnstone		OOC
Bain	Jamie	06/08/1991		SCO	M	37		1	2			3			3			1	2016	Airdieonians		End 2017/18
Cox	David	17/03/1989		SCO	F	37		12	2			4			1				2016	Airdieonians		End 2017/18
Denholm	Danny	26/08/1990		SCO	M	34	4	14	2			3			2	1		1	2014	Livingston	OOC May 2017, joined Arbroath	[redacted]
Devine	Frankie	17/07/1997		SCO	M													11	2015	Forfar Athletic Youths	OL to Downfield, Dundee NE	OOC
Fotheringham	Martyn	23/03/1983		SCO	M	15	4	3	1				2		1			23	2007	Cowdenbeath	Freed May 2017, joined Montrose	[redacted]
Gill	Jamie	01/01/1997		SCO	F													2	2016	Kinnoull		
Halliwell	Bryn	01/10/1980		ENG	GK	1														Trialist	from Gartcairn JFC	[redacted]
Hay	Kerr	16/01/1996		SCO	F								1			1		10	2014	Forfar Athletic Youths		
Hill	Darren	03/12/1981		SCO	GK													9	2016	Hamilton Accies	Freed Aug 2016, joined Linlithgow Rose	[redacted]
Kennedy	Michael	23/10/1996		SCO	D	9	1								2	1		24	2014	Forfar Athletic Youths		End 2017/18
King	Jason	14/03/1998		SCO	GK													9	2014	Forfar Athletic Youths		
Lister	Jim	26/02/1981		SCO	F	26	8	8	2			4		1	1			2	2016	Airdieonians		End 2017/18
Long	Brett	11/04/1997		NIR	GK													5	2016	Dundee United (OL)	Aug-Oct 2016	[redacted]
Mackintosh	Murray	08/08/1997		SCO	M	8			2			4			1			9	2015	Forfar Athletic Youths	OL to Carnoustie Panmure Jan-May 2017)	
Mailer	Angus	04/07/1998		SCO	D							1						5	2015	Forfar Athletic Youths		
Malcolm	Stuart	20/08/1979		SCO	D	19	1		2			4			3		1	10	2016	Stenhousemuir	OOC May 2017, joined Albion Rovers	[redacted]
Malone	Aiden	19/02/1992		SCO		1	10	1										3	2017	Unattached, Ex Q. Park		OOC
Malone	Eddie	06/04/1985		SCO	M	15												2	2017	Spartans		End 2017/18
McCawl	Eoghan	31/01/1996		NIR	M	4	7		1									12	2016	St Johnstone (OL)	Oct-May	[redacted]
McGovern	Joe	02/03/1994		NIR	GK													26	2016	Dundee United	Released May 2017, joined Cowdenbeath	
McLaughlin	Chris	22/03/1998		SCO	D	18													2017	Ross County (OL)	Jan-May	
Milne	Lewis	26/04/1994		SCO	M	30	4	9				2	2		1	1	1	6	2015	Cowdenbeath	Moved to Australia June 2017	OOC
Munro	Andy	05/11/1991		SCO	D	22	3	3	2			4		1	3			11	2016	Arbroath		End 2017/18
O'Brien	Thomas	07/08/1991		SCO	D	38		7	1			3		1	2				2015	Cowdenbeath	OOC May 2017, joined Arbroath	[redacted]
Peters	Josh	04/09/1996		SCO	F	21	11	12	2			4		1	3		4	5	2016	Hibernian	OOC June 2017, joined Livingston	
Scott	Marc	20/09/1996		SCO	M	8	24			1					3			11	2016	Carnoustie Panmure		End 2017/18
Smith	Allan	25/01/1994		ENG	F	1	8			2					1	1		8	2016	Stenhousemuir	Freed Jan 2017 joined Peterhead	[redacted]
Swankie	Gavin	22/11/1983		SCO	F	35		8	1	1		4			3		1		2012	Arbroath		End 2017/18
Travis	Michael	06/05/1993		RSA	D	21	1	3										4	2015	Arbroath		End 2017/18
Trialist																		1				
Warwick	Greg	25/02/1998		SCO	D	1													2016	Dundee (OL)	Oct-Jan	[redacted]
Yates	James	30/12/1996		SCO	D													2	2014	Forfar Athletic Youths		
Own Goals								1														
NEW SIGNINGS																						
McBride	Scott				M														2017	Albion Rovers		End 2017/18
Easton	Dylan																		2017	Clyde		End 2018/19
Millar	Mark																		2017	Livingston		End 2017/18
See	Ouzy																		2017	Edinburgh City		

Source of Birthdates: Forfar Athletic FC website and Transfermarkt.com

Date	Comp	H/A	Opponents	F	A		HT			Crowd	Scorers
16/07/2016	LC	H	Dumbarton	2	2	5-3p	1	0	D Lowe	426	Peters, O'Brien
19/07/2016	LC	A	Peterhead	0	2		0	2	G Ross	508	
26/07/2016	LC	H	East Fife	2	0		1	1	M Northcroft	565	Lister, Munro
30/07/2016	LC	A	Dundee	0	7		0	3	W Collum	2219	
06/08/2016	L	A	Edinburgh City	3	2		2	1	G Beaton	547	Cox, Milne, Lister
13/08/2016	L	H	Cowdenbeath	4	3		2	1	C Charleston	516	Lister, Denholm, Peters, Swankie
16/08/2016	CC	A*	Aberdeen U20	3	1		1	0	M Roncone	221	Peters 2, Smith
20/08/2016	L	A	Berwick Rangers	2	1		1	0	S Reid	421	Milne, Peters
27/08/2016	L	H	Elgin City	3	2		1	2	D Lowe	537	O'Brien 2, Peters
03/09/2016	CC3	H	Raith Rovers	3	2		2	1	A Newlands	690	Milne, Peters 2
10/09/2016	L	A	Annan Athletic	2	1		0	1	D Munro	403	Munro, Milne
17/09/2016	L	H	Stirling Albion	4	1		1	1	C Napier	635	Munro, Peters 2, Denholm
24/09/2016	L	A	Clyde	1	0		1	0	G Ross	660	O'Brien
01/10/2016	L	H	Montrose	1	3		0	1	C Steven	740	Denholm
08/10/2016	CC4	H	TNS	1	3		1	1	E Boyce (NI)	691	Malcolm
15/10/2016	L	A	Arbroath	0	2		0	0	C Napier	862	
22/10/2016	SC2	A	Edinburgh City	0	0		0	0	K Graham	328	
29/10/2016	L	H	Edinburgh City	1	1		0	1	S Millar	491	Denholm
01/11/2016	SC2R	H	Edinburgh City	0	1		0	0	C Charleston	388	
05/11/2016	L	A	Stirling Albion	3	0		1	0	G Beaton	663	Munro, Swankie, Cox
12/11/2016	L	H	Berwick Rangers	2	0		1	0	B Cook	477	Cox, Milne
19/11/2016	L	A	Montrose	1	1		1	1	G Ross	630	Denholm
10/12/2016	L	H	Arbroath	0	1		0	0	D Lowe	786	
13/12/2016	L	H	Annan Athletic	5	1		3	0	S Reid	337	Cox, O'Brien, Denholm, Milne 2
17/12/2016	L	A	Cowdenbeath	4	3		2	1	G Irvine	277	Milne, Swankie 2, Peters
26/12/2016	L	H	Clyde	4	3		1	2	M Northcroft	659	Swankie, Fotheringham, Lister, Cox
02/01/2017	L	A	Elgin City	2	2		1	2	G Ross	1091	Cox, Swankie
07/01/2017	L	A	Annan Athletic	2	1		1	1	C Charleston	432	Lister, Home og
14/01/2017	L	H	Stirling Albion	1	1		1	1	S Millar	632	Cox
21/01/2017	L	A	Edinburgh City	1	0		1	0	C Napier	352	Cox
28/01/2017	L	H	Cowdenbeath	3	1		0	1	C Steven	547	Peters, O'Brien, Milne
04/02/2017	L	A	Arbroath	1	0		1	0	J McKendrick	1008	Peters
11/02/2017	L	H	Elgin City	1	1		1	0	A Newlands	551	Peters
18/02/2017	L	A	Berwick Rangers	2	3		2	1	L Wilson	480	Cox, Peters
25/02/2017	L	H	Montrose	0	0		0	0	D Lowe	725	
04/03/2017	L	A	Clyde	2	2		1	0	S Millar	490	Denholm, Lister
11/03/2017	L	H	Edinburgh City	1	2		1	0	M Roncone	446	Lister
18/03/2017	L	A	Elgin City	1	1		0	0	G Beaton	709	Lister
25/03/2017	L	H	Berwick Rangers	2	3		1	1	R Milne	477	Denholm, Cox
01/04/2017	L	A	Stirling Albion	3	0		2	0	M Northcroft	738	Lister, Denholm 2
08/04/2017	L	H	Arbroath	1	1		0	0	G Ross	1564	Peters
15/04/2017	L	A	Montrose	0	1		0	1	D Munro	984	
22/04/2017	L	H	Clyde	3	0		1	0	S Reid	741	Denholm, Cox, O'Brien
29/04/2017	L	A	Cowdenbeath	1	1		0	0	R Milne	571	Denholm
06/05/2017	L	H	Annan Athletic	2	4		1	3	G Irvine	917	Travis, O'Brien
10/05/2017	PO	A	Annan Athletic	2	2		0	2	C Allan	629	Travis, Fotheringham
13/05/2017	PO	H	Annan Athletic	4	2		3	0	J McKendrick	665	Swankie 2, Denholm, Bain
17/05/2017	PO	H	Peterhead	2	1		0	1	S Finnie	958	Fotheringham, Travis
20/05/2017	PO	A	Peterhead	5	1		2	0	G Duncan	1084	Milne, Cox, Denholm, A Malone, Peters

* at Formartine United

FRIENDLIES / OTHER GAMES

28/06/2017	H	Raith Rovers	2	0		250
02/07/2016	H	Brora Ramgers	2	1		
05/07/2016	H	Dundee United XI	1	1		
09/07/2016	H	Inverurie Locos	1	0		
12/07/2016	H	Cove Rangers	3	3		
21/03/2017	H	Dundee	1	3	Fotheringham Test	

Date	Comp	H/A	Opponents	F	A		1	2	3	4	5	6	7	8	9	10	11	12	13	14	15	16	17	18
16/07/2016	LC	H	Dumbarton	2	2	5-3p	Adam	Bain	Mackintosh	Munro	Malcolm	O'Brien	Cox	Milne	Swankie	Lister	Peters	*Fotheringham*	*Hay*	*Yates*	*Mailer*	*Devine*	*Hill*	
19/07/2016	LC	A	Peterhead	0	2		Adam	Mailer	Mackintosh	Munro	Malcolm	Denholm	Cox	Milne*	Swankie	Lister	Peters+	Hay*	Fotheringham+	*Yates*	*Devine*	*Hill*		
26/07/2016	LC	H	East Fife	2	0		Adam	Bain	Mackintosh	Munro	Malcolm	O'Brien	Cox	Denholm+	Swankie	Lister	Peters*	Aitken*	Milne+	*Mailer*	*Devine*	*Fotheringham*	*Hay*	*Hill*
30/07/2016	LC	A	Dundee	0	7		Adam	Bain	Mackintosh	Munro	Malcolm	O'Brien	Cox	Denholm+	Swankie&	Lister	Peters*	Milne*	Aitken+	Fotheringham&	*Mailer*	*Devine*	*Hay*	*Hill*
06/08/2016	L	A	Edinburgh City	3	2		Adam	Bain	Mackintosh	Munro	Malcolm	O'Brien	Cox	Denholm	Swankie	Lister	Milne*	Scott*	*Aitken*	*Fotheringham*	*Mailer*	*Devine*	*Peters*	*Hill*
13/08/2016	L	H	Cowdenbeath	4	3		Adam	Bain	Mackintosh	Munro	Malcolm	O'Brien	Peters*	Denholm	Swankie	Lister	Milne+	Scott*	Smith+	*Fotheringham*	*Aitken*	*Kennedy*	*Hay*	*Hill*
16/08/2016	CC	A*	Aberdeen U20	3	1		Adam	Bain	Mackintosh	Munro*	Malcolm	O'Brien	Peters*	Denholm+	Swankie	Scott	Smith&	Milne*	Kennedy+	Hay&	*Aitken*	*Fotheringham*	*Mailer*	*Hill*
20/08/2016	L	A	Berwick Rangers	2	1		Adam	Bain	Mackintosh	Munro	Malcolm	O'Brien	Peters+	Cox	Swankie*	Lister	Milne	Scott*	Smith+	*Kennedy*	*Denholm*	*Fotheringham*	*Hay*	*Hill*
27/08/2016	L	H	Elgin City	3	2		Adam	Bain	Mackintosh	Munro	Malcolm	O'Brien	Peters*	Cox+	Swankie	Lister	Milne	Scott*	Denholm+	*Kennedy*	*Aitken*	*Fotheringham*	*Hay*	*Hill*
03/09/2016	CC3	H	Raith Rovers	3	2		Adam	Bain	Kennedy	Munro	Malcolm	O'Brien	Peters	Cox	Swankie*	Scott+	Milne	Denholm*	Aitken+	*MacKintosh*	*Devine*	*Fotheringham*	*Long*	
10/09/2016	L	A	Annan Athletic	2	1		Adam	Bain	Kennedy	Munro	Malcolm	O'Brien	Peters*	Cox	Denholm	Lister	Milne	Smith*	*Aitken*	*MacKintosh*	*Devine*	*Fotheringham*	*Long*	*Scott*
17/09/2016	L	H	Stirling Albion	4	1		Adam	Bain	Kennedy	Munro	Malcolm	O'Brien	Peters	Cox*	Swankie+	Lister	Milne	Denholm*	Scott+	*MacKintosh*	*Devine*	*Smith*	*Long*	*Aitken*
24/09/2016	L	A	Clyde	1	0		Adam	Bain	Kennedy	Munro	Malcolm	O'Brien	Peters*	Cox&	Swankie	Lister+	Milne	Scott*	Denholm+	Smith&	*MacKintosh*	*Fotheringham*	*Long*	*Aitken*
01/10/2016	L	H	Montrose	1	3		Adam	Bain	Kennedy	Munro	Malcolm	O'Brien	Denholm	Smith*	Swankie	Lister	Milne+	Scott*	Fotheringham+	*Devine*	*MacKintosh*	*Aitken*	*Long*	
08/10/2016	CC4	H	TNS	1	3		Adam	Bain	Kennedy	Munro	Malcolm	Scott*	Denholm	Fotheringham	Swankie	Lister	Peters	Smith*	*MacKintosh*	*Aitken*	*Devine*	*McGovern*		
15/10/2016	L	A	Arbroath	0	2		Adam	Bain	Kennedy	Munro	Malcolm	O'Brien*	Peters+	Cox	Swankie	Lister	Milne&	Denholm*	Scott+	Smith&	*MacKintosh*	*Fotheringham*	*Aitken*	*McGovern*
22/10/2016	SC2	A	Edinburgh City	0	0		Adam	Bain	Mackintosh	Munro	Malcolm	Fotheringham	Peters*	Cox	Swankie	Lister	Denholm	Smith*	*Scott*	*Aitken*	*Devine*	*Kennedy*	*McGovern*	
29/10/2016	L	H	Edinburgh City	1	1		Adam	Warwick*	O'Brien	Munro	Malcolm	Fotheringham	McCawl	Cox	Swankie	Lister	Denholm+	Peters*	Scott+	*Aitken*	*Smith*	*Milne*	*Kennedy*	*McGovern*
01/11/2016	SC2R	H	Edinburgh City	0	1		Adam	Bain	Mackintosh*	Munro	Malcolm	O'Brien	McCawl	Cox	Peters	Lister&	Denholm+	Scott*	Swankie+	Smith&	*Milne*	*Fotheringham*	*Kennedy*	*McGovern*
05/11/2016	L	A	Stirling Albion	3	0		Adam	Bain	Mackintosh	Munro*	Fotheringham	O'Brien	Milne	Cox	Scott	Swankie	Denholm+	Malcolm*	Smith+	*Lister*	*Peters*	*McCawl*	*Kennedy*	*McGovern*
12/11/2016	L	H	Berwick Rangers	2	0		Adam	Bain	Mackintosh	Fotheringham	Malcolm	O'Brien	Milne	Cox	Scott	Swankie*	Denholm&	Peters*	Lister+	*Aitken*	*Smith*	*McCawl*	*Kennedy*	*McGovern*
19/11/2016	L	A	Montrose	1	1		Adam	Bain	Mackintosh	Fotheringham+	Malcolm	O'Brien	Milne	Cox	Scott*	Swankie	Denholm	Lister*	Peters+	*Aitken*	*Smith*	*McCawl*	*Gill*	*McGovern*
10/12/2016	L	H	Arbroath	0	1		Adam	Bain	Mackintosh+	McCawl	Malcolm	O'Brien	Milne	Cox	Scott*	Swankie	Denholm	Peters*	Smith+	Aitken	*Munro*	*Travis*	*Kennedy*	*McGovern*
13/12/2016	L	H	Annan Athletic	5	1		Adam	Bain	Kennedy	Fotheringham	Malcolm	O'Brien	Milne&	Cox*	Peters	Swankie	Denholm+	Smith*	Scott+	Aitken&	*Munro*	*Travis*	*McCawl*	*McGovern*
17/12/2016	L	A	Cowdenbeath	4	3		Adam	Bain	Kennedy	Fotheringham	Malcolm	O'Brien	Milne*	Cox	Peters	Swankie	Denholm+	Scott*	McCawl+	*Aitken*	*Munro*	*Travis*	*Smith*	*McGovern*
26/12/2016	L	H	Clyde	4	3		Adam	Bain	Kennedy	Fotheringham	Malcolm	O'Brien	Milne*	Cox	Peters+	Swankie&	Denholm	McCawl*	Lister+	Scott&	*Munro*	*Travis*	*Smith*	*King*
02/01/2017	L	A	Elgin City	2	2		Adam	Bain	Kennedy	Fotheringham	Malcolm	Munro	McCawl	Cox	Peters+	Swankie*	Denholm	Travis*	Lister+	*Scott*	*McIntosh*	*Hay*	*Smith*	*McGovern*
07/01/2017	L	A	Annan Athletic	2	1		Adam	Bain	Travis	Fotheringham*	O'Brien	Munro	Milne+	Cox	Lister	Swankie	Denholm	McCawl*	Peters+	*Kennedy*	*Scott*	*Hay*	*Smith*	*McGovern*
14/01/2017	L	H	Stirling Albion	1	1		Adam	Bain	Travis	Peters	O'Brien	Munro	Milne	Cox	Lister*	Swankie	Denholm+	Scott*	McCawl+	*Kennedy*	*Fotheringham*	*Hay*	*Malcolm*	*McGovern*
21/01/2017	L	A	Edinburgh City	1	0		Adam	Bain	Travis	Peters+	O'Brien	Munro	Milne	Cox	E Malone	Swankie*	Denholm	Scott*	McCawl+	*Kennedy*	*Malcom*	*Hay*	*Aitken*	*McGovern*
28/01/2017	L	H	Cowdenbeath	3	1		Adam	Bain	Travis	Peters	O'Brien	Munro	Milne	Cox	E Malone	Scott*	Denholm	McCawl*	*Fotheringham*	*Kennedy*	*Malcom*	*Lister*	*Aitken*	*McGovern*
04/02/2017	L	A	Arbroath	1	0		Adam	Bain	Travis	McLaughlin	O'Brien	Peters*	Milne	Cox	E Malone	Swankie	Denholm	Lister*	Fotheringham	*Kennedy*	*McCawl*	*Munro*	*Scott*	*McGovern*
11/02/2017	L	H	Elgin City	1	1		Adam	Bain	Travis	McLaughlin	O'Brien	Peters+	Milne	Cox	E Malone	Swankie*	Denholm	Lister*	McCawl+	*Kennedy*	*Fotheringham*	*Munro*	*Scott*	*McGovern*
18/02/2017	L	A	Berwick Rangers	2	3		Adam	Bain	Travis	McLaughlin	O'Brien	Peters*	Milne&	Cox	Munro	Swankie+	Denholm	Scott*	A Malone+	Lister&	*Fotheringham*	*Malcolm*	*McCawl*	*McGovern*
25/02/2017	L	H	Montrose	0	0		Adam	Bain	Travis	Mclaughlin	O'Brien	Peters	Milne+	Cox	Fotheringham	Swankie	McCawl*	Lister*	Scott+	*Malcolm*	*Kennedy*	*A Malone*	*Gill*	*McGovern*
04/03/2017	L	A	Clyde	2	2		Adam	Bain	Travis	McLaughlin*	O'Brien	Peters+	Milne&	Cox	Malcolm	Denholm	Lister	Kennedy*	Scott+	Fotheringham&	*Munro*	*McCawl*	*Aitken*	*King*
11/03/2017	L	H	Edinburgh City	1	2		Halliwell	Bain	Travis	McLaughlin	O'Brien	Fotheringham+	E Malone&	Cox	Malcolm	Denholm	Lister*	Peters*	Scott+	Milne&	*Munro*	*Kennedy*	*Trialist*	*King*
18/03/2017	L	A	Elgin City	1	1		Adam	Bain	Travis	McLaughlin*	O'Brien	A Malone	Milne	Cox	Swankie	Denholm+	Lister	Munro*	Scott+	*Peters*	*Fotheringham*	*E Malone*	*McCawl*	*King*
25/03/2017	L	H	Berwick Rangers	2	3		Adam	Bain	Travis*	McLaughlin&	O'Brien	E Malone	Milne	Cox	Swankie	Denholm	Lister+	Munro*	Peters+	A Malone&	*Fotheringham*	*Scott*	*McCawl*	*King*
01/04/2017	L	A	Stirling Albion	3	0		Adam	Munro	Travis	McLaughlin	O'Brien	E Malone	Peters*	Cox	Swankie	Denholm+	Lister&	A Malone*	Scott+	Fotheringham&	*Milne*	*Kennedy*	*McIntosh*	*McGovern*
08/04/2017	L	H	Arbroath	1	1		Adam	Munro	Travis	McLaughlin	Bain	E Malone	Peters*	Scott	Swankie	Denholm	Lister	A Malone*	*Malcolm*	*Fotheringham*	*Milne*	*McCawl*	*Kennedy*	*KIng*
15/04/2017	L	A	Montrose	0	1		Adam	Munro	Travis	McLaughlin	O'Brien	E Malone&	Peters*	Cox	Swankie	Denholm+	Lister	A Malone*	Scott+	Milne&	*Bain*	*Fotheringham*	*Kennedy*	*King*
22/04/2017	L	H	Clyde	3	0		Adam	Bain	Travis	McLaughlin	O'Brien	E Malone	Milne*	Cox	Swankie	Denholm	Lister+	A Malone*	Peters+	*Malcolm*	*Scott*	*Fotheringham*	*Kennedy*	*King*
29/04/2017	L	A	Cowdenbeath	1	1		Adam	Bain+	Munro	McLaughlin	O'Brien	E Malone	Milne*	Cox	Swankie	Denholm	Lister	Peters*	A Malone+	*Malcolm*	*Scott*	*Fotheringham*	*Kennedy*	*King*
06/05/2017	L	H	Annan Athletic	2	4		Adam	Bain&	Travis	McLaughlin	O'Brien	E Malone+	Peters	Cox*	Swankie	Denholm	Lister	Munro*	Fotheringham+	Scott&	*A Malone*	*Milne*	*Kennedy*	*McGovern*
10/05/2017	PO	A	Annan Athletic	2	2		Adam	Bain	Travis	McLaughlin	O'Brien	Fotheringham	Munro	Cox	Swankie	Denholm	Lister	*Peters*	*Malcolm*	*E Malone*	*A Malone*	*Milne*	*Scott*	*McGovern*
13/05/2017	PO	H	Annan Athletic	4	2		Adam	Bain	Travis	McLaughlin	O'Brien	Fotheringham&	E Malone	Cox	Swankie	Denholm+	Lister*	Scott*	A Malone+	Milne&	*Munro*	*Peters*	*McCawl*	*McGovern*
17/05/2017	PO	H	Peterhead	2	1		Adam	Bain	Travis	McLaughlin	O'Brien	Fotheringham&	E Malone	Cox	Swankie*	Denholm	Lister+	A Malone*	Peters+	L Milne&	*Munro*	*Scott*	*Kennedy*	*McGovern*
20/05/2017	PO	A	Peterhead	5	1		Adam	Bain	Travis	McLaughlin	O'Brien	Fotheringham*	E Malone	Cox	Milne	Denholm+	Lister	A Malone*&	Scott+	Peters&	*Munro*	*Malcolm*	*McCawl*	*McGovern*

Hamilton Accies FC 2016/17

Founded	1874
Ground	New Douglas Park
Postcode	ML3 0FT
Tel	01698 368652
Capacity	6078
Closest Railway Station	Hamilton West
Record Attendance	28690 v Hearts, SC, 3/3/1937
Ground Record	5895 v Rangers, Lge, 28/2/2009
Record Win	9-0 v Gala Fairydean, SC, 28/1/1922
Record Defeat	1-1 v Hibernian, Lge, 6/11/1965
Most League Goals in a Season	35 David Wilson, 1936/7
Chairman	Les Gray
Secretary	
Manager	Martin Canning
Assistant Manager	Guilleme Beuzelin
Colours 2016/17 Top	Red and White Hoops
Shorts	White
Sponsor	Superseal
Manufacturer	Adidas
Change Colours 2016/17 Top	Sky Blue
Shorts	Navy Blue
Nicknames	Accies, Acas
Web	www.acciesfc.co.uk
Match Programme 2016/17	Academia £2.50

On paper Accies should always be favourite for relegation from the Premiership. Their crowds are small and they have limited potential for sponsorship compared to many of their rivals. But time and again the Accies defy the odds and survive. It was touch and go for spells during 2016/17 with an element of the Accies fans very unhappy with Manager Martin Canning at times. Quite what these fans expect I cannot fathom. Survival in the Premiership is some achievement for this club, evenif it was achieved through a win in the Play offs against Dundee United.

Their team comprises a mix of home-grown talent and exotic imports from around the world. Some of these work, and some don't.

PREDICTION FOR 2017/18

Hard to see anything other than another relegation battle for Accies. With Inverness gone, it's hard to see who the other strugglers might be—I suspect they could end up back in the Play offs this season/

Dougie Imrie - Accies Legend

Dougie Imrie		L			LC			SC			OC			Total		
Season	Club	A	S	G	A	S	G	A	S	G	A	S	G	A	S	G
2005/6	Clyde	8	3	2				1						9	3	2
2006/7	Clyde	34		6	1		1	1			3		1	39	0	8
2007/8	Clyde	19		4	1			2		1	2			24	0	5
2007/8	Inverness CT	12	3	2										12	3	2
2008/9	Inverness CT	33	5	4	2	1	2	2						37	6	6
2009/10	Inverness CT	8	5	1	1		1		1	1		1		9	7	3
2009/10	Hamilton Accies	16		2										16	0	2
2010/11	Hamilton Accies	35		4	1			2						38	0	4
2011/2	Hamilton Accies	18	1	5	1			2			3	1		24	2	5
2011/2	St Mirren	12	2											12	2	0
2012/13	St Mirren	13	14	3	1				1					14	15	3
2013/14	Morton	32		9	4		2	1			1			38	0	11
2014/5	Hamilton Accies	33	1	2	2	1	1	1						36	2	3
2015/6	Hamilton Accies	34	1	6		1								34	2	6
2016/7	Hamilton Accies	38	1	4	5		3	3	1					46	2	7
															0	0
		345	36	54	19	3	10	15	3	2	9	2	1	388	44	67

The date of foundation for the club has been disputed. Their first match appears to have been on 19/12 1874 against Hamilton FC Second Eleven. The first AGM of the club was held on 24/2/ 1875. In 1877 the club may have changed its name to Hamilton Athletic for a short spell. However, there is evidence that the club may have been a direct descendent of Hamilton Gymnasium FC. They were formed in 1866 and took up football in 1869. Their last recorded match was in 1872. Local newspapers record in detail the formation of Hamilton FC and Hamilton Gymnasium FC, but NOT Hamilton Academical FC. Several of the players who appeared for Hamilton Academical in 1874 had played for Hamilton Gymnasium until 1872. It is possible that Hamilton Academical are actually one year older than Queen's Park, who are generally accepted as the oldest football club in Scotland.

Date	Comp	H/A	Opponents	F	A		HT			Crowd	Scorers
16/07/2016	LC	A	Ayr United	1	2		0	1	W Collum	994	Longridge
23/07/2016	LC	H	St Mirren	3	0		1	0	D Robertson	1379	Crawford, Imrie, Donati
27/07/2016	LC	A	Edinburgh City	4	2		2	2	C Steven	459	Crawford, D'Acol, McGregor, Imrie
30/07/2016	LC	H	Livingston	2	1		1	1	E Anderson	764	D'Acol, Longridge
06/08/2016	L	A	Rangers	1	1		1	0	D Robertson	49125	Crawford
09/08/2016	LC1	H	Morton	1	2		1	0	S Finnie	1112	Imrie
13/08/2016	L	H	Kilmarnock	1	2		1	0	S McLean	2228	Longridge
19/08/2016	L	A	Dundee	1	1		1	1	K Clancy	5287	Lyon
27/08/2016	L	H	Ross County	1	0		0	0	G Aitken	1609	Imrie
10/09/2016	L	A	Hearts	1	3		0	0	C Thomson	15947	Crawford
17/09/2016	L	A	Motherwell	2	4		1	3	W Collum	4515	Crawford 2
25/09/2016	L	H	St Johnstone	1	1		1	0	E Anderson	1705	Docherty
01/10/2016	L	H	Inverness CT	1	1		1	0	B Cook	1611	D'Acol
15/10/2016	L	A	Partick Thistle	2	2		1	2	G Aitken	2843	Donati, Brophy
25/10/2016	L	H	Aberdeen	1	0		1	0	W Collum	2315	D'Acol
29/10/2016	L	H	Dundee	0	1		0	0	S Finnie	1853	
05/11/2016	L	A	Kilmarnock	0	0		0	0	E Anderson	3387	
21/11/2016	L	H	Hearts	3	3		1	1	S McLean	2339	Crawford, Bingham 2
26/11/2016	L	A	Ross County	1	1		0	1	C Thomson	3275	Crawford
03/12/2016	L	H	Partick Thistle	1	1		1	0	D Robertson	2210	D'Acol
10/12/2016	L	A	Inverness CT	1	1		1	0	G Aitken	2473	Crawford
13/12/2016	L	A	Celtic	0	1		0	1	C Allan	55076	
16/12/2016	L	H	Rangers	1	2		0	1	A Muir	5292	Imrie
24/12/2016	L	H	Celtic	0	3		0	1	W Collum	5003	
27/12/2016	L	A	Aberdeen	1	2		1	1	A Dallas	13131	Imrie
31/12/2016	L	H	Motherwell	1	1		0	0	E Anderson	3526	D'Acol
21/01/2017	SC	A	Kilmarnock	1	0		0	0	C Allan	2944	Bingham
28/01/2017	L	A	St Johnstone	0	3		0	0	N Walsh	3279	
31/01/2017	L	H	Inverness CT	3	0		1	0	E Anderson	1745	D'Acol, Gillespie, Bingham
04/02/2017	L	H	Kilmarnock	1	1		1	1	S McLean	2159	Brophy
11/02/2017	SC5	A	Dunfermline Athletic	1	1		0	1	C Thomson	2945	Redmond
14/02/2017	SC5R	H	Dunfermline Athletic	1	1	AET,3-0p	0	1	C Thomson	1222	Bingham
18/02/2017	L	A	Partick Thistle	0	2		0	0	W Collum	3057	
25/02/2017	L	A	Celtic	0	2		0	1	C Allan	54685	
28/02/2017	L	H	Aberdeen	1	0		1	0	S McLean	2006	Devlin
04/03/2017	SC6	A	Rangers	0	6		0	1	J Beaton	27287	
11/03/2017	L	A	Hearts	0	4		0	1	C Thomson	15881	
18/03/2017	L	A	Rangers	0	4		0	2	D Robertson	49090	
01/04/2017	L	H	St Johnstone	1	0		0	0	D Robertson	1662	D'Acol
05/04/2017	L	A	Motherwell	0	0		0	0	K Clancy	4644	
08/04/2017	L	H	Ross County	1	1		1	0	S McLean	1548	Donati
15/04/2017	L	A	Dundee	2	0		1	0	J Beaton	6489	D'Acol, Devlin
29/04/2017	L	H	Kilmarnock	0	2		0	2	W Collum	2482	
06/05/2017	L	A	Inverness CT	1	2		0	2	A Dallas	2478	Redmond
13/05/2017	L	H	Motherwell	0	1		0	0	K Clancy	4173	
16/05/2017	L	A	Ross County	2	3		1	1	A Muir	4871	Bingham, Templeton
20/05/2017	L	H	Dundee	4	0		2	0	C Allan	2616	Bingham, Skondras, Imrie, Crawfc
25/05/2017	PO	A	Dundee United	0	0		0	0	S McLean	9386	
28/05/2017	PO	H	Dundee United	1	0		0	0	C Thomson	5027	Docherty

FRIENDLIES / OTHER GAMES				
13/07/2016	H	Eastleigh	2	1
31/07/2016	H	Swansea City U21	1	1

Date	Comp	H/A	Opponents	F	A		1	2	3	4	5	6	7	8	9	10	11	12	13	14	15	16	17	18
16/07/2016	LC	A	Ayr United	1	2		Matthews	Kurakins	Devlin	Gillespie&	Garcia Tena+	Imrie	Docherty	Crawford	McKinnon	D'Acol*	Longridge	Redmond*	McMann+	Hughes&	*McGregor*	*Boyd*	*Tierney*	*Martin*
23/07/2016	LC	H	St Mirren	3	0		Matthews	McMann	Devlin	Gillespie	McGregor&	Imrie	Donati	Crawford	McKinnon*	D'Acol+	Longridge	Docherty*	Redmond+	Breslin&	*Boyd*	*Hughes*	*Tierney*	*Martin*
27/07/2016	LC	A	Edinburgh City	4	2		Matthews	Kurakins	Hughes	Gillespie	McGregor	Imrie	Donati&	Crawford	Docherty	D'Acol*	Longridge+	McKinnon*	Boyd+	Cunningham&	*Reilly*	*Breslin*	*Tierney*	*Woods*
30/07/2016	LC	H	Livingston	2	1		Matthews	Kurakins	Devlin	Gillespie	Sarris*	Imrie	Donati+	Crawford	Docherty	D'Acol&	Longridge	McGregor*	McKinnon+	Boyd&	*Cunningham*	*Hughes*	*Tierney*	*Woods*
06/08/2016	L	A	Rangers	1	1		Matthews	Kurakins	Devlin	Gillespie	Sarris	Imrie	Donati+	Crawford	Docherty&	D'Acol*	Longridge	Brophy*	Lyon+	Hughes&	*Cunningham*	*Want*	*Boyd*	*Woods*
09/08/2016	LC1	H	Morton	1	2		Matthews	Kurakins*	Devlin	Gillespie	Sarris	Imrie	McKinnon&	Crawford	Docherty	Boyd+	Longridge	Lyon*	Donati+	Roy&	*Cunningham*	*Want*	*Tierney*	*Woods*
13/08/2016	L	H	Kilmarnock	1	2		Matthews	Lyon	Devlin	Gillespie	Sarris	Imrie+	Donati	Crawford	Docherty	D'Acol*	Longridge	Brophy*	Roy+	*Boyd*	*McKinnon*	*Want*	*Hughes*	*Woods*
19/08/2016	L	A	Dundee	1	1		Matthews	Lyon	Devlin	Gillespie	Sarris	Imrie	Donati&	Crawford	McKinnon	D'Acol*	Longridge+	Brophy*	Kurtaj+	Docherty&	*Roy*	*Want*	*McMann*	*Woods*
27/08/2016	L	H	Ross County	1	0		Matthews	Lyon	Devlin	Gillespie	Sarris	Imrie	Donati	Docherty&	McKinnon	D'Acol+	Kurtaj*	Redmond*	Brophy+	Seabourne&	*Roy*	*Bingham*	*McMann*	*Woods*
10/09/2016	L	A	Hearts	1	3		Matthews	Lyon	Seaborne*	Gillespie	Sarris	Imrie	Donati	Docherty&	McKinnon	D'Acol+	Crawford	Want*	Bingham+	Redmond&	*Kurtaj*	*Longridge*	*Brophy*	*Thomson*
17/09/2016	L	A	Motherwell	2	4		Matthews	Lyon*	Devlin	Gillespie&	Sarris	Imrie	Donati	Longridge	McKinnon+	Brophy	Crawford	Bingham*	Redmond+	Kurtaj&	*Docherty*	*D'Acol*	*Want*	*Thomson*
25/09/2016	L	H	St Johnstone	1	1		Matthews	Brophy+	Seaborne	Gillespie	Sarris	Imrie	Donati	Docherty	McKinnon	D'Acol*	Crawford	Longridge*	Bingham+	*Redmond*	*Roy*	*McMann*	*Want*	*Thomson*
01/10/2016	L	H	Inverness CT	1	1		Matthews+	Lyon	Seaborne	Gillespie	Sarris	Imrie	Longridge&	Docherty	McKinnon	D'Acol*	Crawford	Bingham*	Thomson+	Want&	*Roy*	*Redmond*	*Tierney*	*Hughes*
15/10/2016	L	A	Partick Thistle	2	2		Woods	Sowah	Bingham*	Gillespie	Sarris	Imrie	Donati	Docherty+	McKinnon	D'Acol&	Crawford	Brophy*	McMann+	Kurtaj&	*Redmond*	*Longridge*	*Want*	*Thomson*
25/10/2016	L	H	Aberdeen	1	0		Woods	Sowah	Devlin	Gillespie	Sarris	Imrie	Brophy*	Docherty+	McKinnon	D'Acol	Crawford&	Kurtaj*	Redmond+	Longridge&	*McMann*	*Bingham*	*Want*	*Thomson*
29/10/2016	L	H	Dundee	0	1		Woods	Sowah	Devlin	Gillespie	Sarris	Imrie	Brophy+	Docherty&	McKinnon	D'Acol*	Crawford	Bingham*	Kurtaj+	Redmond&	*McMann*	*Longridge*	*Want*	*Thomson*
05/11/2016	L	A	Kilmarnock	0	0		Woods	Kurtaj+	Devlin	Gillespie	Sarris	Imrie&	Donati	Docherty	McKinnon	Bingham*	Crawford	Brophy*	Longridge+	McMann&	*Redmond*	*Lyon*	*Want*	*Thomson*
21/11/2016	L	H	Hearts	3	3		Woods	Seaborne	Devlin	Gillespie*	Sarris	Imrie&	Donati	Kurtaj	McKinnon	Bingham+	Crawford	Docherty*	D'Acol+	Sowah&	*Redmond*	*Brophy*	*Longridge*	*Thomson*
26/11/2016	L	A	Ross County	1	1		Woods	Seaborne+	Devlin	Gillespie	Sarris	Sowah	Donati*	Kurtaj&	McKinnon	Bingham	Crawford	Docherty*	Imrie+	D'Acol&	*Lyon*	*Brophy*	*Longridge*	*Thomson*
03/12/2016	L	H	Partick Thistle	1	1		Woods	Seaborne	Devlin	Gillespie	Sowah	Imrie	Donati*	D'Acol	McKinnon	Bingham+	Crawford	Docherty*	Brophy+	*Redmond*	*Lyon*	*Sarris*	*Longridge*	*Thomson*
10/12/2016	L	A	Inverness CT	1	1		Woods	Seaborne	McMann	Gillespie	Sarris	Imrie	Docherty	D'Acol*	McKinnon	Longridge+	Crawford	Redmond*	Bingham+	*Brophy*	*Donati*	*Cunningham*	*Hughes*	*Thomson*
13/12/2016	L	A	Celtic	0	1		Woods	Docherty	McMann	Gillespie	Sarris	Imrie	Donati	Redmond+	McKinnon	Bingham*	Crawford&	Brophy*	Longridge+	Cunningham&	*D'Acol*	*McGregor*	*Hughes*	*Thomson*
16/12/2016	L	H	Rangers	1	2		Woods	Docherty*	McMann	Gillespie	Sarris	Imrie	Devlin	Redmond&	McKinnon	D'Acol+	Crawford	Donati*	Bingham+	Brophy&	*Longridge*	*Cunningham*	*Hughes*	*Thomson*
24/12/2016	L	H	Celtic	0	3		Woods	Donati	McMann	Bingham+	Sarris	Imrie	Devlin	Redmond*	McKinnon	Longridge	Crawford	Brophy*	D'Acol+	*Breslin*	*Seabourne*	*Cunningham*	*Hughes*	*Thomson*
27/12/2016	L	A	Aberdeen	1	2		Woods	Bingham+	McMann	Gillespie	Sarris	Imrie	Devlin	Redmond	McKinnon&	Longridge*	Crawford	Brophy*	D'Acol+	Donati&	*Seabourne*	*Kurtaj*	*Sowah*	*Thomson*
31/12/2016	L	H	Motherwell	1	1		Woods	Seabourne	Sowah	Gillespie	Sarris+	Donati	Devlin	Redmond*	Brophy&	D'Acol	Crawford	Longridge*	Kurtaj+	McKinnon&	*Bingham*	*Cunningham*	*Hughes*	*Thomson*
21/01/2017	SC	A	Kilmarnock	1	0		Woods	McKinnon	McMann	Gillespie	Imrie	Donati	Devlin	Redmond	Brophy*	D'Acol+	Crawford	Bingham*	Longridge+	*Watson*	*Seabourne*	*Cunningham*	*Hughes*	*Matthews*
28/01/2017	L	A	St Johnstone	0	3		Woods	Seabourne	McMann	Gillespie	Imrie	Watson	McKinnon&	Redmond+	Bingham*	D'Acol	Crawford	Brophy*	Cunningham+	*Want*	*Boyd*	*Hughes*	*Adams*	*Matthews*
31/01/2017	L	H	Inverness CT	3	0		Woods	Devlin	McMann	Gillespie	Imrie	Donati	McKinnon&	Redmond	Bingham+	D'Acol&	Crawford*	Adams*	Boyd+	Brophy&	*Seabourne*	*Cunningham*	*Watson*	*Matthews*
04/02/2017	L	H	Kilmarnock	1	1		Woods	Devlin	Seabourne	Gillespie	Imrie	Donati+	McKinnon&	Redmond&	Bingham	D'Acol*	Adams	Brophy*	Hughes+	Boyd&	*Watson*	*Cunningham*	*McKirdy*	*Matthews*
11/02/2017	SC5	A	Dunfermline Athletic	1	1		Matthews	Devlin	Skondras+	Gillespie*	Seabourne	Donati	McKinnon&	Redmond	Bingham	Brophy&	Adams	Imrie*	McMann+	Kurtaj&	*Watson*	*Cunningham*	*Hughes*	*Woods*
14/02/2017	SC5R	H	Dunfermline Athletic	1	1	AET,3-0p	Matthews	Devlin	McMann	Gillespie&	Seabourne*	Watson	McKinnon	Redmond	Bingham^	Imrie	Kurtaj+	Donati*	Brophy+	Skondras&	*Cunningham^*	*Adams*	*Hughes*	*Woods*
18/02/2017	L	A	Partick Thistle	0	2		Woods	Devlin	McMann	Donati+	Skondras	Watson	McKinnon	Redmond*	Bingham	Imrie	Brophy&	Gillespie*	Kurtaj+	Adams&	*Cunningham*	*Seabourne*	*S Boyd*	*Matthews*
25/02/2017	L	A	Celtic	0	2		Woods	Devlin	McMann	Donati	Skondras	Gillespie	McKinnon	Redmond+	Bingham&	Imrie	S Boyd*	Docherty*	Kurtaj+	Brophy&	*Seabourne*	*Adams*	*Watson*	*Matthews*
28/02/2017	L	H	Aberdeen	1	0		Woods	Devlin	McMann	Sarris	Skondras	Gillespie	McKinnon	Redmond*	Bingham&	Imrie	Kurtaj+	Docherty*	Crawford+	Donati&	*Brophy*	*Adams*	*S Boyd*	*Matthews*
04/03/2017	SC6	A	Rangers	0	6		Matthews	Devlin	Adams+	Sarris*	Skondras	Gillespie	Donati	Crawford	Bingham	Imrie	Kurtaj&	Watson*	McMann+	Docherty&	*Gogic*	*Cunningham*	*Brophy*	*Woods*
11/03/2017	L	A	Hearts	0	4		Woods	Docherty	McMann	Sarris	Skondras	Crawford	Donati	Redmond	Bingham&	Imrie*	Brophy+	Gogic*	Gillespie+	Tierney&	*Kurtaj*	*Watson*	*S Boyd*	*Matthews*
18/03/2017	L	A	Rangers	0	4		Woods	Docherty*	McMann	Sarris	Gogic	Gillespie+	Donati	Redmond&	McKinnon	Imrie	Crawford	D'Acol*	Skondras+	Kurtaj&	*Bingham*	*Watson*	*Brophy*	*Matthews*
01/04/2017	L	H	St Johnstone	1	0		Matthews	Devlin	McMann	Sarris	Docherty+	Gillespie*	D'Acol	Bingham&	McKinnon	Imrie	Crawford	Skondras*	Brophy+	Redmond&	*Gogic*	*Donati*	*Adams*	*Jamieson*
05/04/2017	L	A	Motherwell	0	0		Matthews	Devlin	McMann	Sarris	Docherty	Skondras	D'Acol	Bingham*	McKinnon	Imrie&	Crawford+	Redmond*	Donati+	Gogic&	*Brophy*	*Boyd*	*Adams*	*Jamieson*
08/04/2017	L	H	Ross County	1	1		Matthews	Devlin	McMann	Sarris	Docherty	Skondras	D'Acol&	Bingham*	Donati	Imrie	Crawford+	Adams*	Gogic+	Brophy&	*Redmond*	*Boyd*	*Watson*	*Woods*
15/04/2017	L	A	Dundee	2	0		Matthews	Devlin	McMann	Sarris	Docherty+	Skondras	D'Acol&	Bingham*	Donati	Imrie	McKinnon	Redmond*	Gogic+	Brophy&	*Longridge*	*Templeton*	*Adams*	*Woods*
29/04/2017	L	H	Kilmarnock	0	2		Matthews	Devlin	McMann	Sarris	Docherty	Adams&	D'Acol	Bingham	Donati	Imrie+	Crawford*	Redmond*	Longridge+	Brophy&	*Gogic*	*Watson*	*S Boyd*	*Woods*
06/05/2017	L	A	Inverness CT	1	2		Matthews	Devlin	McMann	Sarris	Docherty&	Skondras	D'Acol	Bingham+	Donati*	Imrie	McKinnon	Redmond*	Crawford+	Brophy&	*Gillespie*	*Templeton*	*Adams*	*Woods*
13/05/2017	L	H	Motherwell	0	1		Matthews	Devlin	Skondras	Sarris	Docherty*	Skondras	D'Acol	Gillespie	Redmond+	Imrie	McKinnon	Brophy*	Templeton+	*Bingham*	*Gogic*	*Longridge*	*Donati*	*Woods*
16/05/2017	L	A	Ross County	2	3		Matthews	Gogic	Skondras	Longridge*	McMann	Crawford	Bingham+	Donati	Docherty&	Imrie	McKinnon	Templeton*	Tierney+	Redmond&	*Gillespie*	*Watson*	*Want*	*Woods*
20/05/2017	L	H	Dundee	4	0		Matthews	Gogic	Skondras	Devlin*	McMann	Crawford	Bingham	Redmond&	Templeton+	Imrie	McKinnon	Donati*	Longridge+	Gillespie&	*Docherty*	*D'Acol*	*Watson*	*Woods*
25/05/2017	PO	A	Dundee United	0	0		Matthews	Gogic	Skondras	Redmond+	McMann	Crawford	Bingham&	Donati	Templeton*	Imrie	McKinnon	Longridge*	Docherty+	D'Acol&	*Gillespie*	*Want*	*Watson*	*Woods*
28/05/2017	PO	H	Dundee United	1	0		Matthews	Gogic	Skondras	Redmond	McMann	Crawford	Bingham&	Gillespie	Templeton*	Imrie	Docherty+	Longridge*	Lyon+	Sarris&	*S Boyd*	*Cunningham*	*Watson*	*Jamieson*

						L			SC			LC			CC					
Surname	First Name	DOB	SQ	Nat	Pos	A	S	G	A	S	G	A	S	G	A	S	G	UNS	Signed	Previous Club
Adams	Blair	08/09/1991	39	ENG	D	2	3		2									8	2017	Cambridge United
Bingham	Rakish	25/10/1993	15	ENG	F	25	7	5	3	1	2							5	2016	Hartlepool United
Boyd	Steven	12/04/1997		SCO	M	1	2					1	2					12	2014	Celtic Youth
Breslin	Jack	06/04/1997	32	SCO	D								1					2	2016	Celtic
Brophy	Eamonn	10/03/1996	20	SCO	F	7	21	2	2	1								8	2013	Hamilton Accies You
Canning	Martin	03/12/1981	5	SCO	D														2008	Hibernian
Crawford	Ali	30/07/1991	11	SCO	M	32	2	8	2			5		2					2010	Hamilton Accies You
Cunningham	Ross	23/05/1998	28	SCO	M		2			1			1					14	2014	Hamilton Accies You
D'Acol	Alex	18/07/1996	9	ITA/BRA	F	24	6	7	1			4		2				3	2015	AEK Athens
Devlin	Michael	03/10/1993	4	SCO	D	28		2	4			4							2011	Hamilton Accies You
Docherty	Greg	10/09/1996	8	SCO	M	24	7	2		1		4	1					2	2012	Hamilton Accies You
Donati	Massimo	26/03/1981	21	ITA	M	27	5	2	3	1		3	1	1				3	2016	Bari
Garcia Tena	Jesus	07/06/1990	24	SPA	D							1							2013	Livingston
Gillespie	Grant	02/07/1991	6	SCO	M	29	3	1	4			5						3	2009	Hamilton Accies You
Gogic	Alex	13/04/1994	14	CYP / SER	D	5	4											4	2016	Swansea City
Hughes	Ronan	15/12/1998	33	SCO	M		2					1	1					13	2015	Hamilton Accies You
Imrie	Dougie	03/08/1983	7	SCO	M	38	1	4	3	1		5		3					2014	Morton
Jamieson	Darren	15/02/1991	19	SCO	GK													3	2016	Bo'ness United
Kurakins	Antons	01/01/1990		LAT	D	1						4							2015	Ventspils
Kurtaj	Gramoz	30/04/1991	12	GER/KOS	M	5	9		2	1								3	2015	FK Most
Longridge	Louis	03/07/1991	17	SCO	M	9	9	1		1		5		2				9	2012	Bo'ness United
Lyon	Darren	08/06/1995	22	SCO	M	6	2	1					1					3	2014	Hamilton Accies You
Marshall	Alex	15/02/1998	26	SCO	GK														2015	Hamilton Accies You
Martin	Alan	01/01/1989		SCO	GK													2	2015	Clyde
Matthews	Remi	10/02/1994	1	ENG	GK	19			3			5						9	2016	Norwich City (OL)
McGregor	Jordan	18/03/1997	29	SCO	D							2	1	1				2	2016	Hibernian
McKinnon	Darian	09/10/1985	18	SCO	M	33	1		3			3	2					1	2012	Clydebank
McKirdy	Sean	12/04/1998		SCO	M													1	2016	Hearts U20
McMann	Scott	09/07/1996	23	SCO	D	22	2		2	2		1	1					5	2013	Hamilton Accies You
Quitongo	Rico	15/07/1999		SCO/ANG	M														2015	Hamilton Accies You
Redmond	Danny	02/03/1991	10	ENG	M	17	12	1	3		1		2					7	2014	Wigan Athletic
Reilly	Ben	20/08/1997	25	SCO	D													1	2014	Rangers U20
Roy	Richard	10/10/1987	14	TRI	F		1						1					4	2016	Defence Force FC
Sarris	Georgios	08/09/1989	89	GRE	D	30	1		1			2						1	2016	Erciyesspor
Scullion	Conor	20/03/1999		SCO	M														2016	Hamilton Accies You
Seabourne	Dan	05/03/1983	2	ENG	D	10	1		2									6	2016	Partick Thistle
Skondras	Giannis	21/02/1990	3	GRE	D	14	2	1	2	1									2017	PAOK Salonika
Sowah	Lennard	23/08/1992	46	GER/GHA	D	6	1											1	2016	Hamburger SV II
Templeton	David	07/01/1989	37	SCO	F	3	2	1										2	2017	Unattached
Thomson	Robbie	07/03/1993	35	SCO	GK		1											16	2016	QOTS
Tierney	Ryan	30/01/1998	31	SCO	F		2											6	2015	Hamilton Accies You
Want	Shaun	09/02/1997	27	SCO	D		2											13	2014	Hamilton Accies You
Watson	Craig	13/02/1995	16	SCO	D	2			1	1								13	2012	Hamilton Accies You
Woods	Gary	01/01/1990	34	ENG	GK	21			1									18	2016	Leyton Orient

Source of Birthdates: Hamilton Accies FC website and Transfermarkt.com

Heart of Midlothian FC 2016/17

Founded	1874
Ground	Tynecastle Park
Postcode	EH11 2NL
Tel	0131 200 7207
Capacity	17529
Closest Railway Station	Haymarket
Record Attendance	57857 v Barcelona, Friendly, 28/7/2007
Ground Record	53396 v Rangers, SC, 13/2/1932
Record Win	21-0 v Anchor, East of Scotland Cup, 30/10/1880
Record Defeat	1-8, v Vale of Leven, Scottish Cup, 1882
Most League Goals in a Season	44 Barney Battles, 1930/1
Most League Goals in Career	214 John Robertson
Chairman / Chief Executive	Anne Budge
Operations Director	Eric Hogg
Secretary	David Southern
Manager	Robbie Neilson, then Ian Cathro
Assistant Manager	Stevie Crawford, then Austin McPhee
Colours 2016/17 Top	Maroon
Shorts	White
Sponsor	Save the Children
Manufacturer	Puma
Change Colours 2016/17 Top	Yellow and Pink Hoops
Shorts	Yellow
Nicknames	Jam Tarts, Jambos
Web	www.heartsfc.co.uk
Match Programme 2016/17	£3.50
Theme Song	The Hearts Song

2016/17 is a difficult season to sum up for Hearts. Twice they destroyed Rangers at Tynecastle and looked like world beaters. On other occasions they struggled badly and played like haddies. Under Robbie Neilson, during the first half of the season, they definitely under-performed. Defeat in Europe to Birkirkara was exceptionally poor but Hearts looked and played like they were on a pre-season warm-up.

Ian Cathro arrived to a mixed reception. Hailed as a guru by some and decried as an imposter by others, the jury remains out on the man with the lap top. His January signings were less than inspiring - most have been shipped out again but some remain on bizarrely lengthy contracts.

The Hearts fans remained steadfastly loyal to the club, if not to the Manager and to Director of Football Craig Levein. Defeat to Hibs in the Scottish Cup tried their patience as did seeing Celtic clinch the title at Tynecastle.

PREDICTION FOR 2017/18

The period up until the end of September is crucial. If Ian Cathro's methods do not start to produce results then the pressure on him will be unbearable. Being optimistic, the new signings will gel and the results will come together allowing Hearts to challenge again for a top four finish.

The club is named after a Dance Hall in Holyrood Square, itself named after the old Tolbooth Jail next to St Giles in Parliament Square. The name is also that of the Sir Walter Scott novel in which Jeanie Dean journeys to London to appeal on behalf of her sister who was accused of child murder. Jeanie Dean's Tavern was located in the St Leonards / Dumbiedykes area – a part of the town more associated with Hibernian supporters.

In their early days Hearts players were identified with the plumbing, roofing and chimney sweeping trades. Most came from the Gifford Park, Buccleugh Street and St Patrick Square areas.

When playing in the Meadows they used Mother Andersons pub at West Crosscauseway for changing

In 1877 the Club Secretary was Hugh Wylie of 7 Hill Place, Edinburgh.

In 1878/9 the club used the Anderson's Coffee Rooms and Tavern at 1 Patrick Street as their headquarters.

Grounds:
East Meadows (adjacent to Borough Loch)
Powburn (located where McDowall Road and West Savile Terrace now stand)
Powderhall (1878-1881)
Tynecastle Fields (1881-6)
Tynecastle Park (1886-)

In 1955/6 an 'Anglo Scottish Floodlit League' was inaugurated featuring Hearts, Hibernian, Partick Thistle, Manchester City, Newcastle Unitedand Tottenham. Hearts were to play their home games at Easter Road because they had no lights at that time. The SFA and FA banned the competition but the teams played a series of home and away friendlies.

Hearts floodlights vwere switched on for the first time for a match against Hibernian on 7/10/1957.

The second half of a First Round European Cup tie against Standard Liege at Tynecastle on 9/9/1958 was televised live – the first appearance by Hearts on live tv, and the first ever live transmission of a European Cup tie.

Date	Comp	H/A	Opponents	F	A		HT		Referee	Crowd	Scorers
30/06/2015	UEFA	H	FC Infonet	2	1		2	1	V Thorarinsson	14417	Buaben, Kalimullin og
06/07/2015	UEFA	A	FC Infonet	4	2		3	0	P Ardeleanu	1354	Rossi 2, Paterson, Ozturk
14/07/2015	UEFA	A	Birkirkara	0	0		0	0	I Stoyanov	1868	
21/07/2016	UEFA	H	Birkirkara	1	2		0	0	V Nevalainen	14301	Sammon
07/08/2016	L	H	Celtic	1	2		1	1	J Beaton	16777	Walker
10/08/2016	LC1	A	St Johnstone	2	3		2	1	C Allan	4314	Paterson, Walker
13/08/2016	L	A	Aberdeen	0	0		0	0	K Clancy	13559	
20/08/2016	L	H	Inverness CT	5	1		2	0	S McLean	15880	Nicholson 2, Sammon, Cowie 2
27/08/2016	L	A	Partick Thistle	2	1		1	0	W Collum	4919	Paterson, Watt
10/09/2016	L	H	Hamilton Accies	3	1		0	0	C Thomson	15947	Walker 2, Nicholson
17/09/2016	L	A	St Johnstone	0	1		0	0	J Beaton	5456	
24/09/2016	L	H	Ross County	0	0		0	0	A Muir	16321	
30/09/2016	L	A	Motherwell	3	1		1	0	S McLean	4666	Nicholson, Paterson, Djoum
15/10/2016	L	H	Dundee	2	0		0	0	K Clancy	16512	Paterson, Johnsen
26/10/2016	L	A	Kilmarnock	0	2		0	1	A Dallas	3917	
29/10/2016	L	A	Inverness CT	3	3		1	2	C Thomson	3565	Johnsen, Rherras, Djoum
05/11/2016	L	H	St Johnstone	2	2		1	1	D Robertson	16421	Buaben, Paterson
21/11/2016	L	A	Hamilton Accies	3	3		1	1	S McLean	2339	Walker 2, Paterson
26/11/2016	L	H	Motherwell	3	0		1	0	B Madden	16129	Johnsen 2, Walker
30/11/2016	L	H	Rangers	2	0		1	0	C Thomson	16803	Muirhead 2
03/12/2016	L	A	Ross County	2	2		0	1	W Collum	4042	Johnsen, Paterson
10/12/2016	L	A	Rangers	0	2		0	1	J Beaton	50039	
17/12/2016	L	H	Partick Thistle	1	1		1	0	D Robertson	16418	Johnsen
23/12/2016	L	A	Dundee	2	3		1	0	K Clancy	6160	Walker, Paterson
27/12/2016	L	H	Kilmarnock	4	0		2	0	C Thomson	16696	Walker 2, Paterson, Djoum
30/12/2016	L	H	Aberdeen	0	1		0	0	W Collum	16630	
22/01/2017	SC4	A	Raith Rovers	1	1		1	0	J Beaton	5036	Walker
25/01/2017	SC4R	H	Raith Rovers	4	2	AET	1	1	J Beaton	10740	Walker, Currie, Martin, Johnse
28/01/2017	L	A	Celtic	0	4		0	1	B Madden	58247	
01/02/2017	L	H	Rangers	4	1		1	1	K Clancy	16570	Nowak, Cowie, Walker 2
04/02/2017	L	A	Motherwell	3	0		0	0	A Dallas	4651	Tziolis, Goncalves 2
12/02/2017	SC5	H	Hibernian	0	0		0	0	W Collum	16971	
18/02/2017	L	H	Inverness CT	1	1		0	1	B Madden	16372	Djoum
22/02/2017	SC5R	A	Hibernian	1	3		0	2	S McLean	20205	Goncalves
25/02/2017	L	A	Partick Thistle	0	2		0	1	N Walsh	4143	
01/03/2017	L	H	Ross County	0	1		0	0	A Muir	15470	
11/03/2017	L	H	Hamilton Accies	4	0		1	0	C Thomson	15881	Djoum, Goncalves, Walker, M
18/03/2017	L	A	Aberdeen	0	2		0	1	S McLean	12178	
02/04/2017	L	H	Celtic	0	5		0	2	K Clancy	16539	
05/04/2017	L	A	St Johnstone	0	1		0	0	N Walsh	4197	
08/04/2017	L	H	Dundee	1	0		1	0	C Allan	16304	Goncalves
14/04/2017	L	A	Kilmarnock	0	0		0	0	E Anderson	4110	
29/04/2017	L	H	Partick Thistle	2	2		0	0	A Dallas	15930	Goncalves, Struna
07/05/2017	L	H	Aberdeen	1	2		0	1	W Collum	16552	Goncalves
13/05/2017	L	A	Rangers	1	2		0	1	B Madden	47809	Golcalves
17/05/2017	L	A	St Johnstone	0	1		0	1	D Robertson	3141	
21/05/2017	L	A	Celtic	0	2		0	0	J Beaton	58967	

FRIENDLIES / OTHER GAMES						
22/06/2016	N	TNS	3	0	at St Andrews	
23/06/2016	N	Aberdeen	0	1	at St Andrews	
25/06/2016	A	Gala Fairydean Rovers	0	2	U20	
28/06/2016	A	Stenhousemuir	1	2	U20	250
02/07/2016	A	Cowdenbeath	1	1		439
05/07/2016	A	Brechin City	1	3	U20	
09/07/2016	A	Dunfermline Athletic	1	3		2016
12/07/2016	A	Civil Service Strollers	4	0	U20	
19/07/2016	A	Kelty Hearts	0	2	U20	
26/07/2016	A	Dunbar United	5	3	U20	
21/03/2017	A	Dundee United	2	2	Dillon Testimonial	3260

						L			SC			LC			UC							
			SQ	Nat	Pos	A	S	G	A	S	G	A	S	G	A	S	G	UNS				
Surname	First Name	DOB																	Signed	Previous Club	Notes	Contract
Akers	Zidan	01/12/1998	45	ENG	F														2016	Reading Youths		End 2017/18
Avlonitis	Anastasios	01/01/1990	12	GRE	D	8	1		2									6	2017	Olympiakos	Freed June 2017	[redacted]
Baxter	Dale	28/02/1998	31	SCO	M														2015	Hearts Youths	OL to Selkirk Sep-Jan, Released June 2017	[redacted]
Baur	Daniel	06/05/1999	39	SCO	D														2015	Hearts Youths		OOC
Beith	Angus	22/02/1996	22	SCO	M		2											5	2013	Hearts Youths	OL to Stirling Albion Oct-Jan	End 2017/18
Bikey	Dylan Nguene	18/02/1995	23	FRA / CAM	F		2											1	2017	Stirling Albion	Released May 2017	[redacted]
Brandon	Jamie	05/02/1998	29	SCO		1												2	2016	Rangers		OOC
Buaben	Prince	23/04/1988	8	GHA	M	11	9	1	1			1			4		1	9	2014	Carlisle United		End 2017/18
Buchanan	Robbie	23/02/1996	21	SCO	F														2013	Hearts Youths	OL to Brechin Nov-Dec, Cowdenbeath Jan-May, Freed May 2017 joined Cowden	[redacted]
Cowie	Don	15/02/1983	15	SCO	M	34		3	2			1				2			2016	Wigan Athletic		End 2017/18
Currie	Rory	20/02/1998	30	SCO	F	1	8		1	1	1							12	2016	Rangers		End 2019/20
Djoum	Arnaud	02/05/1989	10	CAM	M	30	3	5	1	1		1			4				2015	Lech Poznan		End 2018/19
El Ouriachi	Moha Choulay	13/01/1996	16	MOR	M	3	8			1								6	2017	Stoke City (OL)	Jan-May	[redacted]
Gajda	Wojciech	21/10/1998		POL / USA	GK														2016	New York Bulls		End 2017/18
Gallacher	Paul	16/08/1979	51	SCO	GK													2	2016	Partick Thistle		End 2017/18
Godinho	Marcus	28/06/1997	28	CAN / POR	D													2	2016	Toronto FC II		End 2017/18
Gomis	Morgaro	14/07/1985	21	FRA / SEN	M													1	2014	Dundee United	Transferred to Kelantan FA Jul 2016	[redacted]
Goncalves	Esmael	25/06/1991	77	POR	F	15		7	2		1								2017	Anorthosis Famagusta		End 2019/20
Hamilton	Jack	22/03/1994	1	SCO	GK	35			4			1			4			3	2008	Stenhousemuir Youth		End 2019/20
Henderson	Euan	01/01/2001		SCO	F		1												2016	Hearts Youths		
Hughes	Aaron	08/11/1979	5	NIR	D	8			4									1	2017	Kerala Blasters		End 2017/18
Irving	Andy	13/05/2000	44	SCO	F														2016	Hearts Youths	OL to Berwick Rangers 2017/18	
Johnsen	Bjorn	06/11/1991	20	USA / NOR	F	22	12	6	2	1	1							2	2016	Litex Lovetch		End 2019/19
Jones	Leon	28/02/1998	32	SCO	D														2015	Hearts Youths		OOC
Juanma Delgado		17/11/1990	9	SPA	F										1	3			2015	AEL Kalloni	OL to Murcia Aug-Jan, Transferred to VV Nagasaki Jan 2017	[redacted]
King	Billy	12/05/1994		SCO	F											1			2011	Hearts Youths	OOC June 2017, joined Dundee United	[redacted]
Kitchen	Perry	29/02/1992	6	USA	M	26	3		3						2	1		9	2016	DC United		End 2017/18
Martin	Malaury	25/08/1988	88	FRA	M	5	8	1	4		1							4	2017	Lillestrom SK		End 2019/20
Mason	Kelby	16/10/1998	38	SCO	GK														2015	Hearts Youths	OL to Bonnyrigg Rose Jan-Feb	OOC
McGhee	Jordan	24/07/1996		SCO	D														2013	Hearts Youths	OL to Middlesbrough Jul-May	OOC
McLean	Russell	16/06/1998		SCO	F														2015	Alloa Athletic Youth	OL to Civil Service S Oct-Jan, Freed Jan joined East Kilbride	[redacted]
Moore	Lewis	04/06/1998	36	SCO	M														2015	Hearts Youths	OL to Cowdenbeath Aug-May	End 2018/19
Morrison	Callumn	05/07/1999	40	SCO	F														2015	Hearts Youths	OL to Stirling Albion Aug-May	OOC
Muirhead	Robbie	08/03/1996	23	SCO	F	6	12	2				1				1		4	2016	Dundee United	Transferred to MK Dons Jan 2017	[redacted]
Nicholson	Sam	20/01/1995	11	SCO	M	13	6	4	1	2			1		2	2		2	2013	Hearts Youths	OOC June 2017, joined Minnesota United	[redacted]
Noring	Viktor	03/02/1991	13	SWE	GK	3												42	2016	Lyngby BK		End 2017/18
Nowak	Krystian	01/04/1994	19	POL	D	17		1	1	1								15	2016	Podbeskidzie		End 2017/18
Oshinawa	Juwon	14/09/1990	17	NIG	D													9	2015	FC Ashdod	Contract Cancelled July 2017	[redacted]
Ozturk	Alim	17/11/1992	5	TUR	D	2	3					1			4		1	13	2014	Trabzonspor	Released Jan 2017, joined Boluspor	[redacted]
Paterson	Callum	13/10/1994	2	SCO	D	20		8				1		1	4		1		2010	Tynecastle Colts	OOC, joined Cardiff City July 2017	[redacted]
Paton	Harry	23/05/1998	35	CAN / ENG	M													1	2016	Fulham		
Petkov	Alex	25/07/1999	41	BUL	M														2016	Unknown		End 2018/19
Reid	Aaron	11/05/2000	42	SCO	D														2016	Hearts Youths		
Reilly	Gavin	10/05/1993		SCO	F														2015	Queen of the South	OL to Dunfermline Jan-May, Sold to St Mirren June 2017	[redacted]
Rherras	Faycal	07/04/1993	3	MOR / BEL	D	17	2	1							4			6	2016	St Truiden	Freed May 2017	[redacted]
Rossi	Igor	10/03/1989	4	BRA	D	20						1			3		2	1	2015	Maritimo Funchal B	Transferred to Al Faisaly Jan 2017	[redacted]
Roy	Alistair	26/07/1997	27	SCO	F														2014	Stirling Albion Youths	OL to Stenhousemuir Aug-May	End 2018/19
Sammon	Connor	06/11/1986	18	ROI	F	9	10	1		2		1			4		1	3	2016	Derby County	OL to Kilmarnock Jan-May	End 2018/19
Smith	Kyle	18/02/2000	43	SCO	D														2016	Hearts Youths		End 2017/18
Smith	Liam	10/04/1996	24	SCO	D	12	8			1			1		3			12	2013	Hearts Youths		End 2017/18
Souttar	John	25/09/1996	14	SCO	D	22			2			1			1	1		2	2016	Dundee United		End 2019/20
Sowah	Lennard	23/08/1992	46	GER	D	11			4									1	2017	Hamilton Accies	Released June 2017	[redacted]
Struna	Andraz	23/04/1989	27	SVE	D	13		1	4										2017	PAS Giannina	Released June 2017	[redacted]
Todorov	Nikolai	24/08/1996	25	BUL	F													2	2016	Nottingham Forest	OL to Cowdenbeath Aug-Dec, Livingston Jan 2017-May 2018	End 2017/18
Tziolis	Alexandros	13/02/1985	4	GRE	D	14	2	1	2										2017	PAOK Salonika	Released June 2017	[redacted]
Vladislav	Yves	12/05/1998		SWI	M														2016	Alshwil	Transferred to Teleoptik Zemun, Jan 2017	[redacted]
Walker	Jamie	25/06/1993	7	SCO	F	28	6	12	4		2	1		1	4				2011	Hearts Youths		End 2017/18
Watt	Tony	29/12/1993	32	SCO	F	12	4	1					1					4	2016	Charlton Athletic (OL)	Jul-Jan	[redacted]
Zanatta	Daro	24/05/1997	26	CAN	F		1			2								10	2015	Vancouver Whitecaps Residency	OL to Q Park Sep-May	End 2018/19
Own Goals																	1					
NEW SIGNINGS																						
Berra	Christophe																		2017	Ipswich Town		End 2019/20
Stockton	Cole																		2017	Tranmere Rovers		End 2018/19
Grzelak	Rafal																		2017	Korona Kielce		End 2018/19
Lafferty	Kyle																		2017	Norweich City		End 2018/19
Smith	Michael																		2017	Peterborough United		End 2018/19
Smith-Brown	Ashley																		2017	Manchester City (On Loan)		End 2017/18

Source of Birthdates: Hearts FC website and Transfermarkt.com

Date	Comp	H/A	Opponents	F	A		1	2	3	4	5	6	7	8	9	10	11	12	13	14	15	16	17	18
30/06/2015	UEFA	H	FC Infonet	2	1		Hamilton	Ozturk	Paterson	Souttar	Rherras	Djoum	Buaben+	Walker	Nicholson	Sammon	Juanma*	King*	Kitchen+	L Smith	Todorov	Zanatta	Rossi	Gallacher
06/07/2015	UEFA	A	FC Infonet	4	2		Hamilton	Ozturk	Paterson	Rossi	Rherras	Djoum&	Buaben+	Walker*	Kitchen	Sammon	L Smith	Nicholson*	Souttar+	Juanma&	Todorov	Zanatta	Gomis	Gallacher
14/07/2015	UEFA	A	Birkirkara	0	0		Hamilton	Ozturk	Paterson	Rossi	Rherras	Djoum	Buaben	Walker&	Kitchen*	Sammon+	L Smith	Cowie*	Juanma+	Nicholson&	Souttar	Zanatta	Muirhead	Noring
21/07/2016	UEFA	H	Birkirkara	1	2		Hamilton	Ozturk	Paterson	Rossi+	Rherras	Djoum	Buaben&	Walker	Nicholson	Sammon	L Smith*	Juanma*	Muirhead+	Cowie&	Souttar	Zanatta	Godinho	Noring
07/08/2016	L	H	Celtic	1	2		Hamilton	Souttar	Paterson	Rossi	Rherras	Djoum	Cowie	Walker	Nicholson	Sammon+	Watt*	Muirhead*	Buaben+	Oshinawa	L Smith	Zanatta	Paton	Noring
10/08/2016	LC1	A	St Johnstone	2	3		Hamilton	Souttar	Paterson	Rossi	Ozturk	Djoum	Cowie	Walker*	Buaben&	Sammon	Muirhead+	Watt*	Nicholson+	L Smith&	Oshinawa	Zanatta	Nowak	Noring
13/08/2016	L	A	Aberdeen	0	0		Hamilton	Souttar	Paterson	Rossi	Rherras+	Djoum	Cowie	Nicholson&	Buaben*	Sammon	Watt	Kitchen*	L Smith+	Muirhead&	Ozturk	Zanatta	Nowak	Noring
20/08/2016	L	H	Inverness CT	5	1		Hamilton	Souttar	Paterson	Rossi	Rherras	Djoum	Cowie&	Nicholson	Kitchen*	Sammon+	Watt	Buaben*	Johnsen+	Muirhead&	Ozturk	L Smith	Nowak	Noring
27/08/2016	L	A	Partick Thistle	2	1		Hamilton	Souttar	Paterson	Rossi	Rherras	Djoum	Cowie	Nicholson*	Kitchen	Sammon+	Watt&	Walker*	Johnsen+	L Smith&	Ozturk	Muirhead	Buaben	Noring
10/09/2016	L	H	Hamilton Accies	3	1		Hamilton	Souttar	Paterson	Rossi	Rherras	Djoum*	Cowie	Walker	Kitchen	Sammon+	Watt&	Nicholson*	Johnsen+	Muirhead&	Ozturk	L Smith	Buaben	Noring
17/09/2016	L	A	St Johnstone	0	1		Hamilton	Souttar	Paterson	Rossi	Rherras	Nicholson	Cowie&	Walker	Kitchen	Johnsen+	Watt*	Djoum*	Sammon+	Muirhead&	Ozturk	L Smith	Buaben	Noring
24/09/2016	L	H	Ross County	0	0		Hamilton	Souttar*	Paterson	Rossi	Rherras	Nicholson	Cowie+	Djoum	Kitchen	Sammon&	Watt	Ozturk*	Walker+	Johnsen&	Nowak	Muirhead	Buaben	Noring
30/09/2016	L	A	Motherwell	3	1		Hamilton	Souttar	Paterson	Rossi	Rherras	Nicholson+	Walker&	Djoum	Kitchen	Sammon*	Watt	Johnsen*	Buaben+	Muirhead&	Nowak	Currie	Ozturk	Noring
15/10/2016	L	H	Dundee	2	0		Hamilton	Souttar	Paterson	Rossi	Ozturk	Cowie&	Walker	Djoum	Kitchen	Sammon+	Watt*	Muirhead*	Johnsen+	Buaben&	Nowak	Currie	Oshinawa	Noring
26/10/2016	L	A	Kilmarnock	0	2		Hamilton	Souttar	Paterson	Rossi	Rherras	Cowie	Muirhead	Djoum	Kitchen&	Sammon*	Watt+	Walker*	Johnsen+	Buaben&	Nowak	Ozturk	Oshinawa	Noring
29/10/2016	L	A	Inverness CT	3	3		Hamilton	Souttar	Paterson	Rossi	Rherras+	Cowie	Muirhead*	Djoum	Kitchen	Walker	Johnsen&	Watt*	Ozturk+	Sammon&	Nowak	Buaben	Oshinawa	Noring
05/11/2016	L	H	St Johnstone	2	2		Hamilton	Souttar	Paterson	Rossi	L Smith	Cowie	Buaben*	Johnsen&	Kitchen	Walker	Watt+	Djoum*	Muirhead+	Sammon&	Rherras	Ozturk	Currie	Noring
21/11/2016	L	A	Hamilton Accies	3	3		Hamilton	Souttar	Paterson	Ozturk	L Smith	Cowie	Buaben*	Johnsen+	Kitchen	Walker	Watt&	Djoum*	Sammon+	Rherras&	Nowak	Muirhead	Currie	Noring
26/11/2016	L	H	Motherwell	3	0		Hamilton	Souttar	Paterson*	Rossi	Rherras	Cowie&	Djoum	Johnsen+	Kitchen	Walker	Muirhead	L Smith*	Sammon+	Currie&	Nowak	Buaben	Watt	Noring
30/11/2016	L	H	Rangers	2	0		Hamilton	Souttar	Paterson	Rossi	Rherras	Cowie+	Djoum	Johnsen&	Kitchen	Walker	Muirhead*	Buaben*	L Smith+	Sammon&	Nowak	Currie	Watt	Noring
03/12/2016	L	A	Ross County	2	2		Hamilton	Souttar	Paterson	Rossi+	Rherras	Cowie&	Djoum	Johnsen	Kitchen	Walker	Muirhead*	Sammon*	Ozturk+	Buaben&	L Smith	Currie	Watt	Noring
10/12/2016	L	A	Rangers	0	2		Hamilton	Souttar	Paterson	Rossi	Rherras	Cowie&	Djoum	Johnsen	Kitchen	Walker*	Muirhead+	Watt*	Sammon+	L Smith&	Ozturk	Buaben	Oshinawa	Noring
17/12/2016	L	H	Partick Thistle	1	1		Hamilton	Souttar	Paterson	Rossi	L Smith	Cowie	Djoum	Johnsen&	Kitchen	Walker+	Buaben*	Sammon*	Muirhead+	Watt&	Ozturk	Rherras	Nowak	Noring
23/12/2016	L	A	Dundee	2	3		Hamilton	Souttar	Paterson	Rossi	L Smith&	Cowie*	Djoum	Johnsen	Kitchen	Walker+	Nowak	Muirhead*	Watt+	Rherras&	Ozturk	Sammon	Zanatta	Noring
27/12/2016	L	H	Kilmarnock	4	0		Hamilton	Souttar	Paterson*	Rossi	Rherras	Buaben+	Djoum	Johnsen	Kitchen	Walker&	Nowak	L Smith*	Muirhead+	Zanatta&	Ozturk	Sammon	Watt	Noring
30/12/2016	L	H	Aberdeen	0	1		Hamilton	Souttar	L Smith	Rossi+	Rherras	Cowie	Djoum*	Johnsen	Kitchen	Walker	Nowak	Currie*	Muirhead+	Zanatta	Ozturk	Sammon	Oshinawa	Noring
22/01/2017	SC4	A	Raith Rovers	1	1		Hamilton	Souttar	Struna+	Sowah	Hughes	Cowie	Martin	Johnsen	Kitchen	Walker*	Nowak	Zanatta*	Sammon+	Beith	Currie	Godinho	L Smith	Noring
25/01/2017	SC4R	H	Raith Rovers	4	2	AET	Hamilton	Souttar	Struna+	Sowah	Hughes	Buaben*	Martin	Johnsen	Kitchen	Walker	Currie&	Nicholson*^	L Smith+	Zanatta&	Sammon^	Oshinawa	Beith	Noring
28/01/2017	L	A	Celtic	0	4		Hamilton	Souttar	L Smith	Sowah	Hughes	Cowie	Martin+	Johnsen	Kitchen&	Walker	Nicholson*	El Ouriachi*	Sammon+	Beith&	Zanatta	Oshinawa	Nguene Bikey	Noring
01/02/2017	L	H	Rangers	4	1		Hamilton	Nowak	Struna	Sowah	Hughes	Cowie	Martin*	Johnsen+	Kitchen	Walker	Goncalves&	Tziolis*	Nicholson+	Avlonitis&	El Ouriachi	Beith	L Smith	Noring
04/02/2017	L	A	Motherwell	3	0		Hamilton	Tziolis	Struna	Sowah	Hughes	Cowie	Martin+	Johnsen*	Avlonitis	Walker&	Goncalves	El Ouriachi*	Kitchen+	Nicholson&	Rherras	Nowak	Currie	Noring
12/02/2017	SC5	H	Hibernian	0	0		Hamilton	Tziolis	Struna	Sowah	Hughes	Cowie&	Martin*	Nicholson+	Avlonitis	Walker	Goncalves	Johnsen*	Djoum+	Nowak&	El Ouriachi	Kitchen	Currie	Noring
18/02/2017	L	H	Inverness CT	1	1		Hamilton	Tziolis	Struna	Sowah	Hughes	Kitchen&	Djoum	El Ouriachi+	Avlonitis	Johnsen*	Goncalves	Walker*	Currie+	Martin&	Nicholson	Nowak	L Smith	Noring
22/02/2017	SC5R	A	Hibernian	1	3		Hamilton	Tziolis	Struna&	Sowah	Hughes	Kitchen*	Djoum	Martin+	Avlonitis	Walker	Goncalves	Nicholson*	Currie+	El Ouriachi&	Rherras	Nowak	Johnsen	Noring
25/02/2017	L	A	Partick Thistle	0	2		Hamilton	Tziolas	Struna	Sowah	Rherras&	Nowak	Djoum	Currie+	Avlonitis	Walker*	Goncalves	Nicholson*	Nguene Bikey+	El Ouriachi&	Kitchen	L Smith	Martin	Noring
01/03/2017	L	H	Ross County	0	1		Hamilton	Tziolas	Struna	Sowah	Cowie&	Nowak	Djoum	El Ouriachi*	Avlonitis	Nicholson	Johnsen+	Currie*	Nguene Bikey+	Martin&	Kitchen	Rherras	Buaben	Noring
11/03/2017	L	H	Hamilton Accies	4	0		Hamilton	Tziolas	Struna	Sowah	Cowie&	Nowak	Djoum*	Nicholson+	Avlonitis	Walker&	Goncalves	Martin*	El Ouriachi+	Johnsen&	Kitchen	L Smith	Buaben	Noring
18/03/2017	L	A	Aberdeen	0	2		Hamilton	Tziolas+	Struna	Sowah	Cowie&	Nowak	Djoum*	Nicholson	Avlonitis	Walker&	Goncalves	Johnsen*	Kitchen+	Martin&	El Ouriachi	Rherras	Hughes	Noring
02/04/2017	L	H	Celtic	0	5		Hamilton	Tziolas*	Struna	Sowah	Cowie&	Nowak	Kitchen	Johnsen	Avlonitis	Walker+	Goncalves&	Buaben*	Martin+	Beith&	Nicholson	L Smith	Currie	Noring
05/04/2017	L	A	St Johnstone	0	1		Hamilton	Tziolas	Struna	Sowah&	Cowie	Nowak	Kitchen	Johnsen+	Avlonitis*	Walker	Goncalves	Buaben*	Nicholson+	L Smith&	El Ouriachi	Martin	Currie	Noring
08/04/2017	L	H	Dundee	1	0		Hamilton	Tziolas	Struna	L Smith	Cowie	Nowak	Kitchen	Djoum*	Buaben	Walker+	Goncalves&	Currie*	Martin+	Johnsen&	El Ouriachi	Avlonitis	Beith	Noring
14/04/2017	L	A	Kilmarnock	0	0		Hamilton	Tziolas	Struna	L Smith	Cowie+	Nowak	Kitchen	Djoum	Buaben*	Walker&	Goncalves	Currie*	El Ouriachi+	Martin&	Johnsen	Avlonitis	Beith	Noring
29/04/2017	L	H	Partick Thistle	2	2		Hamilton	Tziolis*	Struna	L Smith	Cowie	Nowak	El Ouriachi+	Djoum	Buaben	Walker	Goncalves	Nicholson*	Johnsen+	Kitchen	Sowah	Avlonitis	Martin	Noring
07/05/2017	L	H	Aberdeen	1	2		Hamilton	Tziolis	Struna*	Hughes	Cowie&	Nowak	Sowah+	Djoum	Buaben	Walker	Goncalves	L Smith*	El Ouriachi+	Johnsen&	Currie	Kitchen	Martin	Noring
13/05/2017	L	A	Rangers	1	2		Noring	Martin*	L Smith	Hughes	Cowie	Nowak	Nicholson&	Djoum	Buaben	Johnsen+	Goncalves	Tziolis*	Currie+	El Ouriachi&	Brandon	Kitchen	Avlonitis	Hamilton
17/05/2017	L	A	St Johnstone	0	1		Noring	Martin+	L Smith	Hughes	Cowie	Nowak	Nicholson&	Djoum	Tziolis	Johnsen*	Goncalves	Currie*	Walker+	El Ouriachi&	Brandon	Kitchen	Avlonitis	Hamilton
21/05/2017	L	A	Celtic	0	2		Noring	Brandon	L Smith	Hughes	Cowie	Nowak	Buaben+	Djoum	Tziolis&	Johnsen	Goncalves*	Martin*	Walker+	Henderson&	El Ouriachi	Kitchen	Avlonitis	Hamilton

Hibernian FC 2016/17

Founded	1875
Ground	Easter Road Stadium
Postcode	EH7 5QG
Tel	0131 661 2159
Capacity	20421
Closest Railway Station	Edinburgh Waverley
Record Attendance	65860 v Hearts, Lge, 2/1/1950
Record Win	15-1 v Peebles Rovers, SC, 11/2/1961
Record Defeat	0-10 v Rangers, Lge, 24/12/1898
Most League Goals in a Season	42 Joe Baker, 1959/60
Chairman	Rod Petrie
Chief Executive	Leanne Dempster
Manager	Neil Lennon
Assistant Manager	Gary Parker
Colours 2016/17 Top	Green with white sleeves
Shorts	White
Sponsor	Marathon Bet
Manufacturer	Nike
Change Colours 2016/17 Top	Bright yellow
Shorts	Black
Nicknames	Hibees, Cabbage
Web	www.hibernianfc.co.uk
Match Programme 2016/17	£3.00
Theme Song	Sunshine on Leith

Hibs brought a massive feelgood factor into 2016/17 off the back of their Scottish Cup win. Season ticket sales soared as two abortive promotion campaigns were forgotten. Neil Lennon his the ground running as Hibs manager and carried on where Alan Stubbs had left off. It wasn't always easy or pretty but Hibs had more than enough about hem to see off the opposition and landed the Championship title with something to spare.

Lennon proved to be an astute tactician, mixing things around depending no the opposition. That was never clearer than against Hearts in the Scottish Cup when Hibs outfought and outthought their city rivals. The fans hoped for "Two In A Row" but were generally content with a Semi Final place this season.

Lennon also used the transfer market effectively. Grant Holt was a worthwhile addition for one season. Kris Commons short stint added sparkle, and the arrival of Efe Ambrose stiffened up the defence.

Jason Cummings was dropped for a spell but came back a much better player—further testament to Lennon's ability as a Coach and Manager.

PREDICTION FOR 2017/18

Hib have shown in Cup ties that they are a match for Premiership sides. A top six finish is likely.

HIBERNIAN'S ORIGINS - SECTARIAN OR NOT?

Brown (1979) is blunt about the sectarian origins of the club. "Hibs were a sectarian club for the first 18 years of their existence, catering solely for Irish Catholics. But that policy chaNged once Celtic appeared on the scene, to start up in Glasgow with a nucleus of players lured from the Edinburgh club. Hibs resources were so drained that the club went defunct for a brief period before their re-birth as an 'open' organisation in 1891". The idea that the club was sectarian is repeated by Murray (19??). He said "Hibernian were the first sectarian team in Scotland being founded in 1875 by Canon Edward Hannan, who had it written into the constitution of the club that its players must be practicing Catholics." This differs slightly from the version given by Docherty and Thomson (1975) in the club's official centenary book. They said that the players had to be Catholic, but made no mention of them being practising.

Weir (1992) uncovered evidence from a letter that appeared in Scottish Sport magazine of 22nd January 1889:

"Permit me, as one of the patrons and founders of Hibernian FC, to correct an error into which you have fallen in your issue of Tuesday last. Neither the club, nor the team, are confined to the members of any religious persuasion. Apart from the fact that I am a Protestant myself, men like Brogan of Bolton and Higgins of Kilmarnock were Protestants and members of the team. No enquiry as to religion was ever made, but the fact of the club getting the use of the Catholic Institute in St Mary's Street, Edinburgh for their meetings, no doubt gave rise to the belief that only Catholics were admitted as members of the club."

This seems clear enough but the issue is further confused by statements made when the club was re-formed in 1892. A piece in The Scotsman, quoted by Weir (1992), says that those interested in the promotion of the club "wish it to be distinctly understood that it would be promoted on somewhat different lines from the old club. They desired it should be non-sectarian".

Perhaps the key issue is the definition of 'sectarian' in the context of late Victorian Scotland. Hibernian were probably deemed to be 'sectarian', not because their players were exclusively Catholic, practising or otherwise, but because the club was associated With the Nationalist movement in Ireland.

Weir (1992) also quotes the February 22nd 1884 issue of the Scottish Athletic Journal: "It is rumoured in Edinburgh that a club composed of Orangemen will be one of the features of next season's contests. The recent battle – for battle it was in the real meaning of the word – between the Hearts and the Hibs has set afloat the rumour. The Hibs are all Nationalists, and the Hearts have now become ardent believers in the principles advocated by Lord Rossmore".

Sources Quoted:

Brown, Stewart – **Hibernian**; in Soccer Monthly, July 1979; reproduced in SFH Number 49, January / February 1992
Docherty, G and Thomson, P – **100 Years of Hibs, 1875-1975**, 1975
Weir, John – **The Original Hibs** – in SFH, Number 50, March / April 1992

14/07/2016	UEFA	H	Brondby IF	0	1		0	1	J Martinez	13454	
21/07/2016	UEFA	A	Brondby IF	1	0	3-5p	0	0	M Avram	11548	Gray
06/08/2016	L	A	Falkirk	2	1		1	1	K Clancy	6458	Cummings 2
09/08/2016	LC1	H	Queen of the South	1	3		1	0	E Anderson	7647	Hanlon
13/08/2016	L	H	Dunfermline Athletic	2	1		1	0	W Collum	16477	Richards-Everton og, Cummings
20/08/2016	L	A	St Mirren	2	0		2	0	D Robertson	4517	Cummings 2
27/08/2016	L	H	Morton	4	0		2	0	A Muir	14508	Shinnie, Holt, Cummings, Graham
04/09/2016	CC3	A	Turriff United	3	0		2	0	E Anderson	1791	F Murray, Graham, Boyle
10/09/2016	L	A	Dumbarton	1	0		1	0	G Aitken	1339	Cummings
17/09/2016	L	H	Ayr United	1	2		0	0	N Walsh	15056	Cummings
24/09/2016	L	A	Queen of the South	0	0		0	0	S McLean	3703	
02/10/2016	L	H	Dundee United	1	1		1	0	C Thomson	15492	Keatings
08/10/2016	CC4	H	St Mirren	1	2		1	1	W Collum	4393	Harris
15/10/2016	L	A	Raith Rovers	0	0		0	0	S Finnie	3753	
22/10/2016	L	A	Dunfermline Athletic	3	1		0	1	A Muir	7622	Wedderburn og, Holt, Graham
29/10/2016	L	H	St Mirren	2	0		2	0	D Robertson	14485	Boyle, Holt
05/11/2016	L	A	Ayr United	3	0		1	0	K Clancy	3100	Boyle 2, McGinn
12/11/2016	L	H	Falkirk	1	1		0	0	J Beaton	14551	Hanlon
19/11/2016	L	H	Queen of the South	4	0		2	0	C Charleston	13861	Graham, Higgins og, Gray, Boyle
02/12/2016	L	A	Dundee United	0	1		0	0	B Madden	10925	
10/12/2016	L	H	Dumbarton	2	0		1	0	J McKendrick	13881	Hanlon, Graham
17/12/2016	L	A	Morton	1	1		0	0	S McLean	2156	Cummings
24/12/2016	L	H	Raith Rovers	1	1		0	0	G Aitken	15409	Boyle
31/12/2016	L	A	Falkirk	2	1		1	1	C Allan	6747	Cummings, Commons
06/01/2017	L	H	Dundee United	3	0		2	0	W Collum	18786	Cummings 2, McGinn
14/01/2017	L	A	Dumbarton	1	0		1	0	N Walsh	1523	Commons
21/01/2017	SC	A	Bonnyrigg Rose	8	1		3	1	A Muir		Cummings 2, Shinnie, Stevenson, Humphrey, Forster, Keatings 2
28/01/2017	L	A	Queen of the South	1	0		0	0	S McLean	3007	McGinn
04/02/2017	L	H	Ayr United	1	1		0	1	C Allan	14349	Cummings
11/02/2017	SC5	A	Hearts	0	0		0	0	W Collum	16971	
18/02/2017	L	A	Raith Rovers	1	1		0	0	C Charleston	4172	Cummings
22/02/2017	SC5R	H	Hearts	3	1		2	0	S McLean	20205	Cummings, Holt, Shinnie
25/02/2017	L	H	Dunfermline Athletic	2	2		2	1	J Beaton	14437	Cummings, Boyle
01/03/2017	L	A	St Mirren	0	2		0	1	E Anderson	3441	
04/03/2017	SC6	H	Ayr United	3	1		2	1	N Walsh	13602	McGinn, Cummings, Keatings
10/03/2017	L	A	Dundee United	1	0		1	0	D Robertson	9532	Cummings
18/03/2017	L	H	Dumbarton	2	2		0	1	G Duncan	14093	Harvie og, Boyle
25/03/2017	L	H	Falkirk	2	1		0	0	K Clancy	16140	Ambrose, Keatings
29/03/2017	L	H	Morton	0	0		0	0	N Walsh	15149	
01/04/2017	L	A	Dunfermline Athletic	1	1		1	0	G Aitken	7058	McGinn
08/04/2017	L	A	Morton	1	1		1	0	B Madden	4229	Cummings
15/04/2017	L	H	Queen of the South	3	0		2	0	B Cook	17054	McGregor 2, Gray
22/04/2017	SCSF	N	Aberdeen	2	3		1	2	J Beaton	31969	Holt, McGeouch
26/04/2017	L	H	Raith Rovers	3	2		1	0	G Aitken	13604	Keatings 2, Holt
29/04/2017	L	A	Ayr United	4	0		2	0	S Finnie	2152	Cummings 2, Boyle, Keatings
06/05/2017	L	H	St Mirren	1	1		0	0	A Muir	19764	Holt

FRIENDLIES / OTHER GAMES							
02/07/2016	A	Hawick Royal Albert	3	1		U20	400
05/07/2016	A	Berwick Rangers	1	1			
07/07/2016	A	Edinburgh City	6	1			2522
10/07/2016	H	Motherwell	4	1			
12/07/2016	A	Spartans	1	0		U20	
16/07/2016	A	Coldstream	8	1		U20	
19/07/2016	A	Selkirk	5	1		U20	
22/07/2016	A	Gala Fairydean Rovers	0	2		U20	
24/07/2016	H	Birmingham City	1	0			
31/07/2016	A	Shrewsbury Town	4	1			2007
02/08/2016	A	Tranent	3	1		U20	

Date	Comp	H/A	Opponents	F	A		1	2	3	4	5	6	7	8	9	10	11	12	13	14	15	16	17	18
14/07/2016	UEFA	H	Brondby IF	0	1		Virtanen	Gray	McGregor	Hanlon	Stevenson	Boyle&	McGinn	McGeouch+	Bartley*	Holt	Cummings	Fontaine*	Keatings+	Harris&	*Crane*	*Stanton*	*Handling*	*Laidlaw*
21/07/2016	UEFA	A	Brondby IF	1	0	3-5p	Laidlaw	Gray*	McGregor	Hanlon	Stevenson	Fontaine	McGinn	McGeouch	Bartley&	Holt	Cummings+	Boyle*	Keatings+	Forster&	*Crane*	*Stanton*	*Harris*	*Virtanen*
06/08/2016	L	A	Falkirk	2	1		Laidlaw	Gray	McGregor&	Hanlon	Stevenson	Fontaine	McGinn	Keatings+	Martin*	Holt	Cummings	Bartley*	Boyle+	Forster&	*Carmichael*	*Stanton*	*Harris*	*Virtanen*
09/08/2016	LC1	H	Queen of the South	1	3		Laidlaw	Gray	McGregor+	Hanlon	Stevenson	Fontaine	McGinn	Keatings	Bartley	Holt*	Cummings&	Boyle*	Harris+	Forster&	*Carmichael*	*Stanton*	*S Martin*	*Virtanen*
13/08/2016	L	H	Dunfermline Athletic	2	1		Laidlaw	Gray	McGregor	Hanlon	Stevenson	Fontaine+	McGinn	Keatings	Bartley&	Holt*	Cummings	Boyle*	McGeouch+	Forster&	*Harris*	*Crane*	*S Martin*	*Virtanen*
20/08/2016	L	A	St Mirren	2	0		Laidlaw	Gray	McGregor	Hanlon	Stevenson	McGeouch	McGinn	Keatings*	Bartley	Holt+	Cummings&	Shinnie*	Graham+	Boyle&	*Fyvie*	*Crane*	*Forster*	*Virtanen*
27/08/2016	L	H	Morton	4	0		Marciano	Gray	McGregor	Hanlon	Stevenson	Fyvie	McGinn	Shinnie	Bartley+	Holt*	Cummings&	Graham*	Keatings+	Boyle&	*Harris*	*Crane*	*Forster*	*Laidlaw*
04/09/2016	CC3	A	Turriff United	3	0		Marciano	Martin	Crane	Hanlon	Forster	Fyvie	F Murray	Boyle	McGeouch*	Harris	Graham	I Murray*	*O'Conner*	*Smith*	*Laidlaw*			
10/09/2016	L	A	Dumbarton	1	0		Marciano	Gray	McGregor	Hanlon	Stevenson	Fyvie	McGinn	Shinnie&	Bartley*	Holt	Cummings+	Graham*	McGeouch+	Forster&	*Boyle*	*Keatings*	*Harris*	*Laidlaw*
17/09/2016	L	H	Ayr United	1	2		Marciano	Gray	McGregor	Hanlon	Stevenson	Fyvie	McGinn	Shinnie&	Bartley	Holt*	Cummings+	Graham*	Boyle+	Keatings&	*McGeouch*	*Forster*	*Harris*	*Laidlaw*
24/09/2016	L	A	Queen of the South	0	0		Marciano	Gray	McGregor	Hanlon	Stevenson	McGeouch+	McGinn	Boyle&	Bartley	Graham	Cummings*	Fortester*	Fyvie+	Keatings&	*Holt*	*Shinnie*	*Harris*	*Laidlaw*
02/10/2016	L	H	Dundee United	1	1		Marciano	Gray*	McGregor	Hanlon	Forster	McGeouch	McGinn	Fyvie	Shinnie+	Keatings	Cummings&	Eardley*	Boyle+	Graham&	*Holt*	*Bartley*	*Harris*	*Laidlaw*
08/10/2016	CC4	H	St Mirren	1	2		Marciano	Gray	McGregor	Hanlon	Forster	McGeouch	Boyle*	Fyvie	Shinnie+	Keatings	Harris&	Cummings*	Bartley+	Holt&	*Stevenson*	*Eardley*	*Graham*	*Laidlaw*
15/10/2016	L	A	Raith Rovers	0	0		Marciano	Gray	McGregor	Hanlon	Stevenson	Bartley	McGinn	Fyvie	Holt+	Keatings*	Cummings	Boyle*	Graham+	*Shinnie*	*Forster*	*Eardley*	*Harris*	*Laidlaw*
22/10/2016	L	A	Dunfermline Athletic	3	1		Marciano	Gray	McGregor	Hanlon	Stevenson	Fontaine	McGinn	Fyvie	Holt+	Keatings*	Shinnie	Boyle*	Graham+	*Bartley*	*Forster*	*Cummings*	*Harris*	*Laidlaw*
29/10/2016	L	H	St Mirren	2	0		Marciano	Gray	McGregor	Hanlon	Stevenson	Fontaine	McGinn*	Fyvie	Holt+	Boyle&	Shinnie	Bartley*	Graham+	Harris&	*Forster*	*Cummings*	*S Martin*	*Laidlaw*
05/11/2016	L	A	Ayr United	3	0		Marciano	Gray	McGregor	Hanlon	Stevenson	Fontaine	McGinn&	Fyvie	Holt*	Boyle	Shinnie+	Graham*	Bartley+	Cummings&	*Forster*	*Harris*	*S Martin*	*Laidlaw*
12/11/2016	L	H	Falkirk	1	1		Laidlaw	Gray+	McGregor	Hanlon	Stevenson	Fontaine*	McGinn	Fyvie	Holt	Boyle	Shinnie&	Harris*	Cummings+	McGeouch&	*Forster*	*Bartley*	*Graham*	*Virtanen*
19/11/2016	L	H	Queen of the South	4	0		Marciano	Gray	McGregor	Hanlon	Stevenson	Fontaine	McGinn+	Fyvie*	Graham	Boyle&	Shinnie	McGeouch*	Cummings+	Bartley&	*Forster*	*Holt*	*Crane*	*Laidlaw*
02/12/2016	L	A	Dundee United	0	1		Marciano	Gray	McGregor	Hanlon	Stevenson	Fontaine&	McGeouch	Bartley+	Holt	Boyle*	Shinnie	Cummings*	Graham+	Eardley&	*Forster*	*S Martin*	*Crane*	*Laidlaw*
10/12/2016	L	H	Dumbarton	2	0		Laidlaw	Gray	McGregor	Hanlon	Stevenson	Fontaine	Graham	Bartley*	Cummings	Boyle	Shinnie	McGeouch*	*Holt*	*Eardley*	*Forster*	*S Martin*	*Crane*	*Virtanen*
17/12/2016	L	A	Morton	1	1		Laidlaw	Gray	McGregor	Hanlon	Stevenson	Fontaine+	Graham*	Bartley	Commons	Boyle&	Shinnie	Holt*	Cummings+	Forster&	*Keatings*	*Eardley*	*Crane*	*Virtanen*
24/12/2016	L	H	Raith Rovers	1	1		Laidlaw	Gray	McGregor	Hanlon	Stevenson	McGeouch&	S Martin	Holt	Commons*	Cummings+	Shinnie	Keatings*	Boyle+	Graham&	*Fontaine*	*Bartley*	*Crane*	*Virtanen*
31/12/2016	L	A	Falkirk	2	1		Laidlaw	Gray	McGregor	Hanlon	Stevenson	McGeouch	S Martin	Holt+	Commons&	Cummings*	Shinnie	Boyle*	Graham+	Forster&	*Fontaine*	*Bartley*	*Crane*	*Virtanen*
06/01/2017	L	H	Dundee United	3	0		Laidlaw	Gray	McGregor	Hanlon	Stevenson	McGeouch	Bartley	Boyle	Commons*	Cummings&	Humphrey+	McGinn*	Keatings+	Graham&	*Fontaine*	*Bartley*	*Keatings*	*Virtanen*
14/01/2017	L	A	Dumbarton	1	0		Laidlaw	Gray	McGregor	Fontaine	Stevenson	Fyvie	Bartley	Boyle	Commons&	Cummings+	Humphrey*	McGinn*	Holt+	Forster&	*Fontaine*	*Holt*	*Shinnie*	*Virtanen*
21/01/2017	SC	A	Bonnyrigg Rose	8	1		Marciano*	Forster	McGregor	Fontaine	Stevenson	Holt	McGinn+	Keatings	Shinnie	Cummings&	Humphrey	Laidlaw*	Fyvie+	Boyle&	*Keatings*	*Graham*	*Shinnie*	*Marciano*
28/01/2017	L	A	Queen of the South	1	0		Laidlaw	Gray	McGregor	Fontaine	Stevenson	Fyvie	McGinn	Keatings&	Shinnie	Cummings*	Holt+	Boyle*	Forster+	Graham&	*Bartley*	*Graham*	*Crane*	*P Martin*
04/02/2017	L	H	Ayr United	1	1		Laidlaw	Gray	McGregor	Fontaine	Stevenson	Fyvie	McGinn	Keatings	Shinnie+	Boyle&	Humphrey*	Holt*	Cummings+	Graham&	*McGeouch*	*Humphrey*	*Crane*	*Gallacher*
11/02/2017	SC5	A	Hearts	0	0		Marciano	Gray	McGregor	Forster*	Stevenson	Fyvie	McGinn	Keatings	Holt+	Cummings	Bartley	Fontaine*	Graham+	*Boyle*	*McGeouch*	*Bartley*	*Crane*	*Gallacher*
18/02/2017	L	A	Raith Rovers	1	1		Marciano	Gray	McGregor	Fontaine	Stevenson	Fyvie*	McGinn	Keatings+	Graham&	Cummings	Bartley	Humphrey*	Boyle+	Holt&	*McGeouch*	*Shinnie*	*Humphrey*	*Laidlaw*
22/02/2017	SC5R	H	Hearts	3	1		Marciano	Gray	McGregor	Fontaine	Stevenson	Boyle	McGinn	Bartley	Holt+	Cummings&	Humphrey*	Shinnie*	Graham+	Fyvie&	*Crane*	*S Martin*	*Donaldson*	*Laidlaw*
25/02/2017	L	H	Dunfermline Athletic	2	2		Marciano	Gray	McGregor	Fontaine*	Stevenson	Boyle	McGinn	Fyvie+	Holt	Cummings	Shinnie&	Bartley*	Crane+	Keatings&	*Keatings*	*Martin*	*Donaldson*	*Laidlaw*
01/03/2017	L	A	St Mirren	0	2		Marciano	Gray	McGregor	Ambrose	Stevenson	Boyle&	McGinn	Fyvie	Bartley*	Cummings	Shinnie+	Holt*	Keatings+	Graham&	*Graham*	*S Martin*	*Donaldson*	*Laidlaw*
04/03/2017	SC6	H	Ayr United	3	1		Marciano	Gray	Forster	Ambrose	Stevenson	Boyle	McGinn	Holt&	Bartley+	Cummings*	Shinnie	Keatings*	Fyvie+	Graham&	*McLean*	*S Martin*	*Crane*	*Laidlaw*
10/03/2017	L	A	Dundee United	1	0		Marciano	Gray	McGregor	Ambrose	Stevenson	Boyle&	McGinn	Holt+	Bartley*	Cummings	Shinnie	Fyvie*	Graham+	Forster&	*McLean*	*S Martin*	*Crane*	*Laidlaw*
18/03/2017	L	H	Dumbarton	2	2		Marciano	Gray+	McGregor	Ambrose	Stevenson	Boyle	McGinn	Holt	Bartley*	Keatings	Shinnie&	McGeouch*	Forster+	Graham&	*Keatings*	*S Martin*	*Crane*	*Laidlaw*
25/03/2017	L	H	Falkirk	2	1		Laidlaw	Forster&	McGregor	Ambrose	Stevenson	Boyle	McGeouch	Holt+	Bartley	Cummings	Shinnie*	Keatings*	Graham+	Hanlon&	*F Murray*	*S Martin*	*Crane*	*Laidlaw*
29/03/2017	L	H	Morton	0	0		Marciano	Hanlon&	McGregor	Ambrose	Stevenson	Boyle	McGinn	Holt*	Bartley	Cummings+	Keatings	Graham*	Forster+	McGeouch&	*Fyvie*	*Handling*	*S Martin*	*Gallacher*
01/04/2017	L	A	Dunfermline Athletic	1	1		Marciano	McLean	McGregor	Ambrose	Stevenson	Boyle*	McGinn	McGeouch	Bartley	Cummings&	Graham+	Keatings*	Holt+	Gray&	*Fyvie*	*McLean*	*S Martin*	*Laidlaw*
08/04/2017	L	A	Morton	1	1		Marciano	Gray	McGregor	Ambrose	Stevenson	Boyle+	McGinn	McGeouch&	Bartley	Cummings	Graham*	Holt*	Harris+	Shinnie&	*Fyvie*	*F Murray*	*S Martin*	*Laidlaw*
15/04/2017	L	H	Queen of the South	3	0		Marciano	Gray	McGregor	Ambrose	Stevenson	Boyle+	McGinn	McGeouch&	Fyvie	Cummings	Shinnie*	Harris*	Keatings+	Bartley&	*Fyvie*	*McLean*	*Keatings*	*Laidlaw*
22/04/2017	SCSF	N	Aberdeen	2	3		Marciano	Gray	McGregor	Ambrose&	Stevenson	Boyle	McGinn	McGeouch+	Fyvie*	Cummings	Bartley	Holt*	Shinnie+	Graham&	*Holt*	*Forster*	*Graham*	*Laidlaw*
26/04/2017	L	H	Raith Rovers	3	2		Laidlaw	Forster	McLean	Ambrose	Martin	F Murray&	Shinnie*	Humphrey	Harris	Keatings	Graham+	Bartley*	Holt+	Mackie&	*Keatings*	*Forster*	*Humphrey*	*Laidlaw*
29/04/2017	L	A	Ayr United	4	0		Laidlaw	Gray	McGregor	Forster	Stevenson	Boyle*	McGinn+	Humphrey&	Fyvie	Cummings	Holt	Keatings*	Shinnie+	F Murray&	*I Murray*	*Waugh*	*Donaldson*	*Dabrowski*
06/05/2017	L	H	St Mirren	1	1		Marciano	Gray+	McGregor	Ambrose	Stevenson	Boyle	McGinn	Bartley*	Shinnie&	Cummings	Holt	Forster*	Fyvie+	Keatings&	*Ambrose*	*S Martin*	*Graham*	*P Martin*

Surname	First Name	DOB	SQ	Nat	Pos	L			SC			LC			CC			UC			UNS	Signed	Previous Club	Notes	Contract
						A	S	G	A	S	G	A	S	G	A	S	G	A	S	G					
Allan	Lewis	25/10/1996	49	SCO	F																	2013	Hibernian Youths	OL to Livingston Sep-Oct 2016	End 2017/1
Ambrose	Efe	18/10/1988		NIG	D	10		1	2												1	2017	Celtic (OL)	Mar-May	[illegible]
Bartley	Marvin	04/07/1986	6	ENG/TRI	D	21	7		4			1				1		2			7	2015	Leyton Orient		End 2018/1
Boyle	Martin	25/04/1993	17	SCO	F	22	12	8	3	1			1		2		1	1	1		2	2015	Dundee		End 2018/1
Breen	Jack	11/06/1999		SCO	M																	2015	Hibernian Youths		
Carmichael	Danny	21/06/1990		SCO	M																2	2015	Queen of the South	Freed Oct 2016 joined Queen of the South	[redacted]
Commons	Kris	30/08/1983		SCO	M	5		2														2016	Celtic (OL)	Dec 16-Jan 2017	
Crane	Callum	08/03/1996	43	SCO	D		1								1						18	2012	AC Oxgangs		End 2017/
Cummings	Jason	01/08/1995	35	SCO	F	26	6	19	5		4	1				1		2			2	2013	Hutchison Vale		End 2019/2
Dabrowski	Maciej	09/06/1998		POL	GK																1	2017	Lech Poznan II		
Donaldson	Callum	22/10/1999	52	SCO	D																4	2015	Hibernian Youths		
Dunsmore	Aaron	24/07/1996	42	SCO	D																	2012	Hearts Youths	OL to Edinburgh C Aug 16-Jan 2017, Released May 2017	[illegible]
Eardley	Neil	06/11/1988		WAL	D		2														4	2016	Birmingham City	Freed Jan 2017 joined Northampton Town	[illegible]
Fontaine	Liam	07/01/1986	5	ENG	D	15			2	1		1						1	1		3	2014	Bristol City		End 2017/1
Forster	Jordan	23/09/1993	23	SCO	D	4	12		3		1		1		2				1		13	2010	Celtic Youths	Transferred to Cheltenham Town, July 2017	[illegible]
Fyvie	Fraser	27/03/1993	8	SCO	M	18	3		2	3					2						5	2015	Wigan Athletic		OOC
Gallacher	Scott	15/07/1989	32	SCO	GK																3	2017	St Mirren	Released May 2017, joined Dumbarton	[redacted]
Graham	Brian	23/11/1987	29	SCO	F	8	20	4		4					1		1				8	2016	Ross County		End 2017/1
Gray	David	04/05/1988	2	SCO	D	32	1	2	4			1			1			2		1		2014	Burton Albion		End 2018/1
Gullan	Jamie	02/07/1999		SCO	M																	2015	Hearts Youths		
Handling	Danny	06/02/1994	14	SCO	F																2	2010	Hibernian Youths	OL to Raith Rovers Mar-May	End 2017/1
Hanlon	Paul	20/01/1990	4	SCO	D	21	1	2				1		1	2			2				2007	Hibernian Youths		End 2018/1
Harris	Alex	31/08/1994	33	SCO	M	1	4						1		2		1		1		11	2012	Hibernian Youths	Released May 2017, joined Falkirk	[redacted]
Holt	Grant	12/04/1981	9	ENG	F	22	8	5	4	1	2	1				1		2			6	2016	Rochdale	Released May 2017	
Humphrey	Chris	19/09/1987	27	ENG/TRI	M	5	1		2		1										4	2017	Preston North End	Released May 2017	
Insall	Jamie	01/03/1992		ENG	F																	2015	Stourbridge	OL to East Fife Aug 16-May 2017, Freed May 2017, Failed Drugs Test May 2017	
Keatings	James	20/02/1992	19	SCO	F	12	12	5	2	1	3	1			1				2		8	2015	Hearts	OOC June 2017, joined Dundee United	
Laidlaw	Ross	12/07/1992	31	SCO	GK	15				1		1						1			28	2016	Raith Rovers		End 2018/1
Mackie	Sean	04/11/1988	53	SCO	D		1															2016	Raith Rovers	OL to Berwick Rangers Sep 16-Jan 2017	[redacted]
Marciano	Ofir	07/10/1989	1	ISR	GK	21			5						2						1	2016	FC Ashdod (OL)	Sep 16-May 2017	
Martin	Scott	01/04/1997	48	SCO	M	4									1						18	2013	Hibernian Youths		End 2017/
Martin	Patrick	01/01/1999	41	SCO	GK																2	2016	St Johnstone Youth		
McGeouch	Dylan	15/01/1993	10	SCO	M	11	7		1		1				2			2			4	2015	Celtic		End 2017/
McGinn	John	18/10/1994	7	SCO	M	27	2	4	5		1	1						2				2015	St Mirren		End 2018/
McGregor	Darren	07/08/1985	24	SCO	D	35		2	4			1			1			2				2015	Rangers		End 2018/
McLean	Brian	28/02/1985	15	SCO / NIR	D	2															4	2017	DPMM FC (Singapore)	Released June 2017	[redacted]
Murray	Fraser	07/05/1999	57	SCO	M	1	1								1		1				2	2015	Hibernian Youths		End 2017/
Murray	Innes	17/02/1998		SCO	M											1					1	2016	Celtic Youths		End 2017/
O'Connor	Kane	17/01/2001		SCO	D																1	2016	Hibernian Youths		
Paton	Ruari	09/08/2000		ROI	F																	2016	Belvedere Dublin		End 2018/
Porteous	Ryan	01/03/1999		SCO	D																	2016	Hibernian Youths	OL to Edinburgh City Aug 16-Jan 2017	End 2017/
Shaw	Oliver	12/09/1998		SCO	F																	2015	Hibernian Youths	OL to Stenhousemuir Sep 16-May 2017	
Shinnie	Andrew	17/07/1989	22	SCO	M	24	3	1	2	2	2				1						5	2016	Birmingham City (OL)	Sep 16-May 2017	[illegible]
Smith	Alisdair	13/04/1998	54	SCO	M	0															1	2015	Hibernian Youths	OL to Vale of Leithen Jan-May, Released May 2017	[illegible]
Stanton	Sam	19/04/1994		SCO	M	0															4	2011	Hibernian Youths	OL to Dumbarton Aug 16-May 2017	End 2017/
Stevenson	Lewis	05/01/1988	16	SCO	D	34			5		1	1						2			1	2005	Hibernian Youths		End 2018/
Stirling	Ben	16/08/1998	46	SCO	D																	2015	Hibernian Youths	OL to Berwick Rangers Sep 16-Jan 2017	
Virtanen	Otso	03/04/1994		FIN	GK													1			11	2016	IFK Marienhamn	Freed Jan 2017, joined KuPS	[illegible]
Watson	Adam	18/06/1998	52	SCO	M																	2015	Hibernian Youths	OL to Gala Fairydean Aug 16-May 2017	
Waugh	Kevin	29/04/1998	55	SCO	D																1	2015	Hibernian Youths	OL to Gala Fairydean Aug 16-May 2017	
Own Goals								4																	
NEW SIGNINGS																									
Swanson	Danny				M																	2017	St Johnstone		
Ambrose	Efe				D																	2017	Celtic		
Murray	Simon				F																	2017	Dundee United		
Marciano	Ofir				GK																	2017	FC Ashdod		
Source of Birthdates: Transfermarkt.com																									

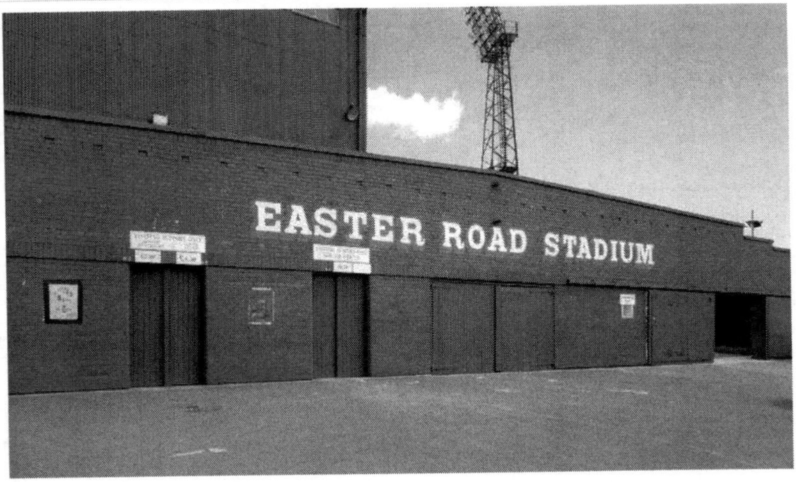

Inverness Caledonian Thistle FC 2016/17

Founded	1994
Ground	Caledonian Stadium
Postcode	IV1 1FF
Tel	01463 222880
Capacity	7800
Closest Railway Station	Inverness
Record Attendance	7753 v Rangers, Lge, 20/1/2008
Record Win	8-1 v Annan Athletic, SC 24/1/88
Record Defeat	0-6 v Airdrie Lge 21/9/2000; v Celtic LC 22/9/2010
Most League Goals in a Season	27 Iain Stewart 1996/7, Dennis Wyness 2002/3
Chairman	Willie Finlayson
Secretary	Ian MacDonald
Manager	Richie Foran (until May), John Robertson
Assistant Manager	Russell Latapy
Colours 2016/17 Top	Royal Blue / Red Stripes
Shorts	Royal Blue
Sponsor	McEwan Fraser Legal
Manufacturer	Carbrini
Change Colours 2016/17 Top	Cream
Shorts	Black
Nicknames	Caley, ICT
Web	www.ictfc.co.uk
Match Programme 2016/17	£3 (Curtis Sport)

Over the course of the season Inverness deserved to be relegated. Yes, there were occasional flashes of something better, but overall it was a poor season of disappointing performances.

In retrospect the appointment of Richie Foran as Manager was an error of judgement. He never seemed comfortable in the role and his lack of confidence transmitted itself onto the field. Players who had done well under previous managers regressed and the defeats racked up. Particularly dispiriting were results aginst local rivals Ross County who took 11 points out of a possible 12 against ICT.

PREDICTION FOR 2017/18

With John Robertson at the helm, anything is possible. He's been out of management for so long that he can only be described as an unknown quantity. Finances will be tight so ICT must again go down the route of a small squad. Next season is probably their best chance of getting back up—but I fear they will fall some way short.

Caledonian FC and Inverness Thistle FC were both represented at the meeting held on 31/5/1888 in the Glenalbyn Hotel Inverness, at which the North of Scotland Football Association was formed.

Both were founder members of the Highland League in 1893. Thistle were the first Highland League champions.

Thistle were the first Highland League club to meet an SFL club in the Scottish Cup, losing 9-3 away to Third Lanark in 1893/4.

Caley were traditionally the best-supported club, drawing patronage from outwith Inverness itself. Thistle were seen as the team of "Upper Inverness", the area South of the town centre. Of course, there were two other prominent Inverness sides. Clachnacuddin remain in the Highland League and are / were the team of the Merkinch district of the town. Inverness Citadel competed in the Highland League before World War Two - known as the Sheepbags, they played in the Harbour district.

With vacancies in the Scottish Football League, Caley and Thistle decided to promote a joint bid for the 1994/5 season. They presented a sound business case and were accepted into the League. Initially they played at Caley's old Telford Street ground until the new Caledonian Stadium was completed on the opposite side of the town.

On the field the club have enjoyed success, reaching the Premier Division and winning the Scottish Cup. Off the field they have found it hard to attract support - the location of their ground is not the handiest and there is still some residual resentment from hard-core Thistle and Caley fans against the merger.

Date	Comp	H/A	Opponents	F	A	HT	Referee	Crowd	Scorers
16/07/2016	LC	A	Cowdenbeath	2	1	1 1	S Finnie	487	Draper, Warren
23/07/2016	LC	H	Dundee United	1	1	1 0	E Anderson	1839	Boden
26/07/2016	LC	A	Dunfermline Athletic	5	1	2 1	C Allan	2580	Vigurs 3, King, Tremarco
30/07/2016	LC	H	Arbroath	7	0	4 0	G Aitken	1316	King, Boden 3, Tremarco 2, Vigurs
06/08/2016	L	A	Partick Thistle	0	2	0 1	N Walsh	2943	
09/08/2016	LC1	A	Alloa Athletic	0	1	0 1	D Robertson	613	
13/08/2016	L	H	Ross County	2	3	1 2	A Dallas	4204	Boden, Draper
20/08/2016	L	A	Hearts	1	5	0 2	S McLean	15880	Draper
27/08/2016	L	H	St Johnstone	2	1	0 0	S Finnie	2729	Draper, Meekings
10/09/2016	L	A	Aberdeen	1	1	0 0	C Allan	11356	Vigurs
18/09/2016	L	H	Celtic	2	2	1 2	D Robertson	6061	King, Fisher
24/09/2016	L	H	Dundee	3	1	2 0	K Clancy	2884	Doumbouya, Tansey, Polworth
01/10/2016	L	A	Hamilton Accies	1	1	0 1	Brad Cook	1611	Polworth
14/10/2016	L	H	Rangers	0	1	0 1	W Collum	7012	
22/10/2016	L	H	Kilmarnock	1	1	0 1	A Dallas	2591	Doumbouya
26/10/2016	L	A	Motherwell	3	0	0 0	D Robertson	3131	Tremarco, Doumbouya, Polworth
29/10/2016	L	H	Hearts	3	3	2 1	C Thomson	3565	Raven, Doumbouya, Doran
05/11/2016	L	A	Celtic	0	3	0 0	C Allan	54152	
19/11/2016	L	H	Aberdeen	1	3	1 2	K Clancy	4867	Doumbouya
26/11/2016	L	A	Dundee	1	2	0 1	A Dallas	5094	Tremarco
03/12/2016	L	A	St Johnstone	0	3	0 1	E Anderson	2549	
10/12/2016	L	H	Hamilton Accies	1	1	0 1	G Aitken	2473	Cole
17/12/2016	L	A	Kilmarnock	1	1	0 0	N Walsh	3294	Warren
24/12/2016	L	A	Rangers	0	1	0 1	D Robertson	48528	
28/12/2016	L	H	Motherwell	1	2	0 0	Brad Cook	3097	Tansey
31/12/2016	L	A	Ross County	2	3	1 2	Brad Madden	5111	Tremarco, Fisher
21/01/2017	SC	A	Elgin City	2	1	1 1	J McKenrick	3624	Cole, Doumbouya
28/01/2017	L	H	Partick Thistle	0	0	0 0	S Finnie	2823	
31/01/2017	L	A	Hamilton Accies	0	3	0 1	E Anderson	1745	
04/02/2017	L	H	Dundee	2	2	0 2	N Walsh	2606	W McKay, Tansey
11/02/2017	SC5	A	Celtic	0	6	0 2	K Clancy	25557	
18/02/2017	L	A	Hearts	1	1	1 0	B Madden	16372	Tremarco
24/02/2017	L	H	Rangers	2	1	1 0	S McLean	6415	Tansey, W McKay
01/03/2017	L	H	Celtic	0	4	0 1	A Dallas	5948	
11/03/2017	L	A	Partick Thistle	1	1	0 1	W Collum	3082	Warren
18/03/2017	L	H	Ross County	1	1	0 0	C Allan	4123	Tansey
01/04/2017	L	H	Kilmarnock	1	1	1 1	B Madden	2780	W McKay
04/04/2017	L	A	Aberdeen	0	1	0 1	A Dallas	11507	
08/04/2017	L	H	St Johnstone	0	3	0 1	S Finnie	2961	
15/04/2017	L	A	Motherwell	2	4	1 2	W Collum	3696	Fisher 2
28/04/2017	L	A	Ross County	0	4	0 2	C Thomson	4928	
06/05/2017	L	H	Hamilton Accies	2	1	2 0	A Dallas	2478	McKay, Tansey
13/05/2017	L	A	Kilmarnock	1	2	0 1	J Beaton	3137	Fisher
17/05/2017	L	A	Dundee	2	0	2 0	K Clancy	5574	W McKay, Fisher
20/05/2017	L	H	Motherwell	3	2	0 0	C Thomson	5351	Tansey, Fisher 2

FRIENDLIES / OTHER GAMES

Date	H/A	Opponents	F	A	
10/07/2016	A	Clachnacuddin	3	1	
12/07/2016	A	Elgin City	3	0	
13/07/2016	A	Strathspey Thistle	0	1	U20
19/07/2016	A	Forres Mechanics	3	1	
16/08/2016	A	Nairn County	5	1	

Date	Comp	H/A	Opponents	F	A	1	2	3	4	5	6	7	8	9	10	11	12	13	14	15	16	17	18
16/07/2016	LC	A	Cowdenbeath	2	1	Esson+	Tremarco	McNaughton	Polworth*	Warren	Draper	Vigurs	Tansey	King	Horner	Boden	Mulraney*	C Mackay+	*Brown*	*Fisher*	*Sutherland*		
23/07/2016	LC	H	Dundee United	1	1	C Mackay	Tremarco	McNaughton	Polworth	Warren	Draper	Vigurs*	Tansey	King	Raven	Boden+	Mulraney*	Fisher+	*Brown*	*Horner*	*Sutherland*	*Fon Williams*	
26/07/2016	LC	A	Dunfermline Athletic	5	1	C Mackay	Tremarco	McNaughton	Polworth	Warren	Mulraney*	Vigurs&	Tansey	King	Raven	Boden+	Draper*	Fisher+	Sutherland&	*Horner*	*Brown*	*Fon Williams*	
30/07/2016	LC	H	Arbroath	7	0	Fon Williams	Tremarco	McNaughton+	Polworth	Warren	Mulraney&	Vigurs	Tansey	King*	Raven	Boden	Draper*	Brown+	Fisher&	*Horner*	*Sutherland*	*Cogan*	*C Mackay*
06/08/2016	L	A	Partick Thistle	0	2	Fon Williams	Tremarco	McNaughton	Polworth	Warren	Mulraney*	Vigurs+	Tansey	King	Raven	Boden	Draper*	Fisher+	*Brown*	*Horner*	*Sutherland*	*Cogan*	*C Mackay*
09/08/2016	LC1	A	Alloa Athletic	0	1	Fon Williams	Tremarco	McNaughton	Polworth&	Warren	Mulraney*	Vigurs	Tansey	King	Raven	Boden+	Draper*	Fisher+	Cogan&	*Horner*	*Sutherland*	*Brown*	*C Mackay*
13/08/2016	L	H	Ross County	2	3	Fon Williams	Tremarco	McNaughton*	Polworth	Warren	Draper	Vigurs&	Tansey	King+	Raven	Boden	Horner*	Mulraney+	Cogan&	*Fisher*	*Sutherland*	*Brown*	*Esson*
20/08/2016	L	A	Hearts	1	5	Fon Williams	Tremarco	Meekings	Polworth	Warren	Draper	Vigurs	Tansey	Mulraney&	Raven+	Boden*	Fisher*	Horner+	Cogan&	*Brown*	*Esson*		
27/08/2016	L	H	St Johnstone	2	1	Fon Williams	Tremarco	Meekings	Poworth	Warren	Draper	Vigurs+	Tansey	Horner	King&	Fisher*	Doumbouya*	Boden+	Mulraney&	*Raven*	*Sutherland*	*Cogan*	*Esson*
10/09/2016	L	A	Aberdeen	1	1	Fon Williams	Tremarco	Meekings	Polworth	Warren	Draper	Vigurs+	Tansey	Brad McKay	King&	Fisher*	Doumbouya*	Cogan+	Horner&	*Raven*	*Mulraney*	*Boden*	*C MacKay*
18/09/2016	L	H	Celtic	2	2	Fon Williams	Tremarco	Meekings	Polworth+	Warren	Draper	Vigurs*	Tansey	Brad McKay	King	Doumbouya&	Cogan*	Mulraney+	Fisher&	*Raven*	*Boden*	*Cole*	*C Mackay*
24/09/2016	L	H	Dundee	3	1	Fon Williams	Tremarco	Meekings	Polworth	Warren	Draper	Mulraney&	Tansey	Brad McKay	King+	Doumbouya*	Fisher*	Cogan+	Cole&	*Vigurs*	*Boden*	*Sutherland*	*C Mackay*
01/10/2016	L	A	Hamilton Accies	1	1	Fon Williams	Tremarco	Meekings	Polworth	Warren	Draper	Vigurs&	Tansey*	Brad McKay	King+	Doumbouya	Boden*	Mulraney+	Cole&	*Cogan*	*Horner*	*Fisher*	*C Mackay*
14/10/2016	L	H	Rangers	0	1	Fon Williams	Tremarco	Raven	Polworth	Warren	Draper	Vigurs*	Tansey	Brad McKay	King+	Doumbouya&	Cogan*	Mulraney+	Fisher&	*Boden*	*Horner*	*Cole*	*C Mackay*
22/10/2016	L	H	Kilmarnock	1	1	Fon Williams	Tremarco	Meekings	Polworth	Warren	Draper*	Vigurs	Tansey	Brad McKay&	Mulraney+	Doumbouya	Cogan*	King+	Boden&	*Raven*	*Horner*	*Fisher*	*C Mackay*
26/10/2016	L	A	Motherwell	3	0	Fon Williams	Tremarco	Meekings+	Polworth	Warren	Draper	Vigurs	Tansey	Brad McKay	Cogan*	Doumbouya&	King*	Raven+	Boden&	*Mulraney*	*Horner*	*C Mackay*	
29/10/2016	L	H	Hearts	3	3	C Mackay	Tremarco*	Meekings	Polworth	Warren	Draper	Vigurs&	Tansey	Brad McKay	Cogan+	Doumbouya	Raven*	Mulraney+	Horner&	*Boden*	*Sutherland*	*Hoban*	
05/11/2016	L	A	Celtic	0	3	Fon Williams	Horner	Meekings	Polworth&	Warren	Draper	Vigurs	Tansey	Brad McKay	King*	Doumbouya+	Mulraney*	Fisher+	Cole&	*Boden*	*Sutherland*	*C Mackay*	
19/11/2016	L	H	Aberdeen	1	3	Fon Williams	Tremarco	Meekings	Cogan	Warren	Draper	Vigurs	Cole*	Brad McKay+	King&	Doumbouya	Mulraney*	Horner+	Fisher&	*Boden*	*Sutherland*	*Esson*	
26/11/2016	L	A	Dundee	1	2	Fon Williams	Tremarco	Meekings	Cogan+	Warren	Draper	Vigurs&	Tansey	Horner	King*	Doumbouya	Mulraney*	Boden+	Cole&	*MacRae*	*Sutherland*	*Esson*	
03/12/2016	L	A	St Johnstone	0	3	Fon Williams	Tremarco&	Meekings	Cogan*	Warren	Draper	Vigurs	Cole	Tansey	King	Doumbouya+	Mulraney*	Sutherland+	Gilchrist&	*Robertson*	*MacLennan*	*Esson*	
10/12/2016	L	H	Hamilton Accies	1	1	Fon Williams	Tremarco	Meekings	Horner*	Brad McKay	Draper	Vigurs	Cole	Tansey	Mulraney	Doumbouya	King*	*Cogan*	*Sutherland*	*Robertson*	*MacLennan*	*Gilchrist*	*Esson*
17/12/2016	L	A	Kilmarnock	1	1	Fon Williams	Tremarco	Meekings	Warren	Brad McKay+	Draper	Vigurs	Cole	Tansey	Horner&	Doumbouya*	Fisher*	Polworth+	King&	*Cogan*	*Mulraney*	*Boden*	*Esson*
24/12/2016	L	A	Rangers	0	1	Fon Williams	Tremarco	Meekings	Warren	Brad McKay	Draper	Vigurs*	Cole&	Tansey	Polworth	Doumbouya+	Cogan*	Fisher+	Boden&	*King*	*Mulraney*	*Sutherland*	*Esson*
28/12/2016	L	H	Motherwell	1	2	Fon Williams	Tremarco	Meekings	Warren	Brad McKay	Draper	Vigurs	Cole*	Tansey	Polworth&	Doumbouya+	Cogan*	Fisher+	Mulraney&	*King*	*Boden*	*Sutherland*	*Esson*
31/12/2016	L	A	Ross County	2	3	Fon Williams	Tremarco	Meekings	Warren	Brad McKay	Draper	Vigurs&	Cole*	Tansey	Cogan*	Doumbouya+	Fisher*	King+	Boden&	*Polworth*	*Mulraney*	*Sutherland*	*Esson*
21/01/2017	SC	A	Elgin City	2	1	Fon Williams	Tremarco	Cogan	Warren	Brad McKay	Polworth	Vigurs	Cole	Tansey	Boden*	Dounbouya	Anier*	*Gilchrist*	*McLennan*	*Ebbe*	*Brown*	*Sutherland*	*Esson*
28/01/2017	L	H	Partick Thistle	0	0	Fon Williams	Tremarco	Draper&	Warren	Brad McKay	Polworth	Raven	Cole+	Tansey	Anier	Doumbouya*	Vigurs*	Mulraney+	Cogan&	*Ebbe*	*Boden*	*Gilchrist*	*Esson*
31/01/2017	L	A	Hamilton Accies	0	3	Fon Williams	Tremarco	Draper*	Warren	Brad McKay	Polworth	Raven	Vigurs	Tansey	Anier+	Billy McKay	Cole*	Ebbe+	*McCart*	*Mulraney*	*Boden*	*Fisher*	*Esson*
04/02/2017	L	H	Dundee	2	2	Esson	Tremarco	Draper	Warren	McCart	King*	Raven	Vigurs+	Tansey	Anier	Billy McKay	Mulraney*	Polworth&	*Brad McKay*	*Ebbe*	*Boden*	*Cole*	*Fon Williams*
11/02/2017	SC5	A	Celtic	0	6	Fon Williams	Tremarco	Draper&	Warren	Brad McKay	King*	Raven	Vigurs	Tansey	Anier	Billy McKay+	Mulraney*	Ebbe+	Cole&	*Polworth*	*Boden*	*Fisher*	*Hoban*
18/02/2017	L	A	Hearts	1	1	Fon Williams	Tremarco	Draper	Laing	McCart	Polworth	Raven	Mulraney*	Tansey	Cole	Billy McKay+	Cogan*	Anier+	*Ebbe*	*Gilchrist*	*Boden*	*Fisher*	*Hoban*
24/02/2017	L	H	Rangers	2	1	Fon Williams	Tremarco*	Draper&	Laing	McCart	Polworth	Raven	Mulraney+	Tansey	Cole	Billy McKay	Brad McKay*	King+	Vigurs&	*Warren*	*Ebbe*	*Anier*	*Hoban*
01/03/2017	L	H	Celtic	0	4	Fon Williams	Warren	Draper	Laing	Brad McKay	Polworth	Raven	King	Tansey	Cole*	Billy McKay+	Vigurs*	Anier+	*McNaughton*	*Fisher*	*Ebbe*	*Boden*	*Hoban*
11/03/2017	L	A	Partick Thistle	1	1	Fon Williams	Warren	McCart	Laing	Brad McKay	Polworth*	Raven	Vigurs+	Tansey	Anier&	Billy McKay	King*	Cole+	Boden&	*McNaughton*	*Ebbe*	*Fisher*	*Hoban*
18/03/2017	L	H	Ross County	1	1	Fon Williams	Tremarco	McCart	Laing	Warren	Draper	Raven	Vigurs*	Tansey	Anier+	Billy McKay	Polworth*	Ebbe+	*Boden*	*Billy King*	*Brad McKay*	*Cole*	*Hoban*
01/04/2017	L	H	Kilmarnock	1	1	Fon Williams	Brad McKay*	McCart	Laing	Warren	Draper	Raven	King+	Tansey	Cole&	Billy McKay	McNaughton*	Mulraney+	Polworth&	*Ebbe*	*Boden*	*Anier*	*Esson*
04/04/2017	L	A	Aberdeen	0	1	Fon Williams	Tremarco	McNaughton&	Laing	Warren	Draper*	Raven	Polworth	Tansey	Anier+	Billy McKay	Cole*	Ebbe+	Fisher&	*McCart*	*Brad McKay*	*King*	*Esson*
08/04/2017	L	H	St Johnstone	0	3	Fon Williams	Tremarco	McCart&	Laing	Warren	Draper*	McNaughton+	Cole	Tansey	Fisher	Billy McKay	King*	Polworth+	Boden&	*Mulraney*	*Brad McKay*	*Anier*	*Esson*
15/04/2017	L	A	Motherwell	2	4	Fon Williams	Tremarco*	McCart	Laing	Brad McKay	Draper	Vigurs+	Polworth	Tansey	Fisher	King&	McNaughton*	Mulraney+	Anier&	*Ebbe*	*Horner*	*Boden*	*Esson*
28/04/2017	L	A	Ross County	0	4	Esson	McNaughton	McCart	Laing	Raven+	Mulraney	Vigurs&	Polworth	Tansey	Fisher	King*	Billy McKay*	Anier+	Draper&	*Horner*	*Brad McKay*	*Cole*	*Hoban*
06/05/2017	L	H	Hamilton Accies	2	1	Esson	Warren	Brad McKay+	Laing	Raven	Draper	Mulraney&	Anier	Tansey	Fisher*	Billy McKay	Boden*	McNaughton+	King&	*Horner*	*McCart*	*Cole*	*Hoban*
13/05/2017	L	A	Kilmarnock	1	2	Esson	Warren	Brad McKay	Laing	Raven	Draper&	Mulraney*	Anier+	Tansey	Fisher	Billy McKay	Vigurs*	Polworth+	Cole&	*McNaughton*	*Ebbe*	*McCart*	*Hoban*
17/05/2017	L	A	Dundee	2	0	Esson	Warren	Brad McKay	Laing	Raven	Draper	Polworth	Vigurs&	Tansey	Fisher+	Billy McKay*	Anier*	McNaughton+	McCart&	*Mulraney*	*Ebbe*	*Cole*	*Hoban*
20/05/2017	L	H	Motherwell	3	2	Esson	Warren	Brad McKay	Laing	Raven	Draper	Polworth*	Vigurs+	Tansey	Fisher	Billy McKay	Mulraney*	McCart+	*Anier*	*McNaughton*	*Boden*	*Cole*	*Hoban*

						L			SC			LC							
			SQ	Nat	Pos	A	S	G	A	S	G	A	S	G	UNS				
Surname	First Name	DOB														Signed	Previous Club	Notes	Con
Anier	Henri	17/12/1990	23	EST	F	8	5		1	1					4	2017	Kalmar FF	Released June 2017	
Boden	Scott	23/11/1989	19	ENG	F	3	10	1	1			5		4	19	2016	Newport County	Released June 2017	
Brown	Jason	07/07/1996	14	SCO	M								1		8	2014	ICT Youths	OL to Arbroath Aug-Oct 2016,	
																		Cove R Jan-May, Freed May	
Brown	Christopher	06/02/1997	32	SCO	D											2014	ICT Youths	OL to Rothes Feb-May	
Cole	Larnell	09/03/1993	29	ENG	M	13	8	1	1	1	1				8	2016	Fulham (OL)	Aug 16-May 2017	
Doran Cogan	Aaron	13/05/1991	10	ROI	M	6	11	1	1				1		6	2011	Blackburn Rovers		End
Doumbouya	Lonsana	26/09/1990	26	FRA/GUI	F	17	2	5	1		1					2016	Cercle Brugge	Freed Jan 2017, joined FC St Polten	
Draper	Ross	22/10/1988	8	ENG	M	35	2	3	1			2	3	1		2012	Macclesfield Town		End
Ebbe	Dean	16/07/1994	9	SCO	F		3								11	2017	Bluebell United	Released June 2017	
Esson	Ryan	19/03/1980	1	SCO	GK	6						1			18	2008	Hereford United		End
Fisher	Alex	30/06/1990	18	ENG	F	9	12	8		1			4		9	2016	Torquay United	OOC June 2017, joined Motherwell	
Fon Wiliams	Owain	17/03/1987	25	WAL	GK	31			2			2			3	2015	Tranmere Rovers		End
Foster	Stephen	29/08/1998	46	SCO	GK											2016	ICT Youths	OL to Fort William Jan-May	
Gilchrist	Cameron	29/09/1997	33	ENG	D		1								4	2015	Swansea City Youths		
Hoban	Daniel	05/04/1998	42	SCO	GK										12	2014	ICT Youths		
Horner	Lewis	01/02/1992	17	ENG	D	5	5					1			12	2014	Blyth Spartans	Released June 2017	
King	Billy	12/05/1994	20	SCO	F	17	9	1	1			5		2	4	2016	Hearts (OL)	Jul 16-May 2017	
Laing	Louis	06/03/1993	21	ENG	D	14										2017	Motherwell	Released June 2017	
MacArthur	Struan	04/04/1997	36	SCO	M											2014	ICT Youths	OL to Rothes Feb-May	
MacDonald	Liam	06/10/1999	44	SCO	M											2016	ICT Youths		
MacKay	Cammy	09/12/1996	31	SCO	GK	1						2	1		11	2015	ICT Youths	OL to Elgin City Aug-Sep, Dec-May	OOC
MacLennan	Blair	05/05/1997	38	SCO	M										3	2016	ICT Youths		
MacRae	Andrew	12/05/1998	43	SCO	F										1	2015	ICT Youths	OL to Forres Mechanics Feb-May	
McCart	Jamie	20/06/1997		SCO	D	9	2								4	2017	Celtic	Jan-May	
McKay	Brad	26/03/1993	22	SCO	D	25	1		2						5	2016	St Johnstone		End
McKay	Billy	22/10/1988		NIR	F	14	1	5	1							2017	Wigan Athletic (OL)	Jan-May	
McLennan	Blair	05/05/1997	38	SCO	M											2014	ICT Youths	OL to Brora R, Feb-May	
McNaughton	Kevin	28/08/1982	4	SCO	D	5	4					5			4	2016	Wigan Athletic	Released June 2017	
McRitchie	Ryan	05/06/1999	35	SCO	D											2016	ICT Youths	OL to Rothes Feb-May	
Meekings	Josh	02/09/1992	6	ENG	D	18		1								2011	Ipswich Town	Released June 2017	
Mulraney	Jake	05/04/1996	15	ROI	F	10	16			1		3	2		8	2016	QPR		End
Polworth	Liam	12/10/1994	7	SCO	M	26	6	3	1			5			2	2012	ICT Youths		End
Raven	David	10/03/1985	2	ENG	D	19	2	1	1			4			4	2012	Tranmere Rovers		End
Rennie	Stephen	31/03/1997	41	SCO	D											2014	ICT Youths	OL to Rothes Feb-May	
Robertson	Sam	04/07/1997	37	SCO	D										2	2016	Aberdeen Youth		
Smith	Keir	01/01/1999	39	SCO	M											2016	ICT Youths	OL to Rothes Feb-May	
Stark	Alasdair	03/01/1998	34	SCO	D											2015	ICT Youths	OL to Fort William Nov-May	
Sutherland	Ali	19/09/1996	21	SCO	F		1						1		17	2013	ICT Youths	Freed Feb 2017, joined Elgin City	
Tansey	Greg	21/11/1981	16	ENG	M	37		7	2			5				2014	Stevenage	OOC June 2017, joined Aberdeen	
Tremarco	Carl	11/10/1985	3	ENG	D	29		4	2			5		3		2013	Macclesfield Town		End
Vigurs	Iain	07/05/1988	11	SCO	M	28	4	1	2			5		4	1	2015	Motherwell		End
Warren	Gary	16/08/1984	5	ENG	D	33		2	2			5		1	1	2012	Newport County		End
Wilson	Jaime	13/12/1997	40	SCO	F											2014	ICT Youths	OL to Clach Jan-May	
NEW SIGNINGS																			
Baird	John				F											2017	Falkirk		
Ridgers	Mark				GK											2017	Partick Thistle		
Oakley	George				F											2017	AFC Wimbledon		

Kilmarnock FC 2016/17

Founded	1869
Ground	Rugby Park
Postcode	KA1 2DP
Tel	01563 545300
Capacity	18128
Closest Railway Station	Kilmarnock
Record Attendance	35995 v Rangers, SC, 10/3/1962
Record Win	11-1 v Paisley Academical, SC, 18/1/1930
Record Defeat	1-9 v Celtic, Lge 13/8/1938
Most League Goals in a Season	34 Harry Cunningham 1927/8, Andy Kerr 1960/1
Chairman	Jim Mann
Secretary	Pritti Trivedi
Manager	Lee Clark (until Jan), Lee McCulloch
Assistant Manager	Lee McCulloch (until Jan)
Colours 2016/17 Top	Blue and White Stripes
Shorts	Blue
Sponsor	QTS
Manufacturer	Nike
Change Colours 2016/17 Top	White with Red Diagonal Band
Shorts	Red
Nicknames	Killie
Web	www.kilmarnockfc.co.uk
Match Programme 2016/17	KTID £3
Theme Song	Paper Roses

Last year I commented that following Kilmarnock over recent years had not been easy. 2016/17 saw some signs of a possible improvement on the way.

The season began under Lee Clark with a wave of signings from the English lower leagues and abroad. Most proved to be duds but their were a few gems—Coulibaly being one. He was sold for big money in January then Clark himself moved on to take charge at Bury.

Lee McCulloch was placed in interim charge and that proved to be a good decision. Results stabilised and gradually Killie demonstrated that they were better than relegation contenders. Greatest satisfaction came from the emergence of several talented young Scots—Taylor, Wilson and Frizzell amongst others. Hopefully they will ge a chance to progress further at Killie in 2017/18.

Drawing crowds back to Rugby Park remains a problem. For a club that was so well supported 20 years ago, their fan-base has dwindled. The emty stands at Rugby Park are a sad sight but the prospect of them being filled is scarce.

PREDICTION FOR 2017/18
Lee McCulloch is now in full charge. Provided he ignores the urge to surround himself with former Ibrox team mates then Killie can progress upwards. The signing of Kirk Broadfoot does not bode well. Bottom six, probably bottom three.

Date	Comp	H/A	Opponents	F	A		HT		Referee	Crowd	Scorers
16/07/2016	LC	A	Clyde	2	1		0	0	J Beaton	1303	Coulibaly, Boyle
23/07/2016	LC	H	Morton	0	2		0	1	S McLean	3020	
26/07/2016	LC	A	Berwick Rangers	3	2		0	1	G Duncan	609	Coulibaly 2, McKenzie
30/07/2016	LC	H	Albion Rovers	0	0	3-5p	0	0	A Newlands	2219	
06/08/2016	L	H	Motherwell	1	2		0	1	C Thomson	4308	M Smith
13/08/2016	L	A	Hamilton Accies	2	1		0	1	S McLean	2228	K Boyd, Coulibaly
20/08/2016	L	A	Ross County	0	2		0	1	N Walsh	3263	
26/08/2016	L	H	Rangers	1	1		1	0	K Clancy	11800	K Boyd
10/09/2016	L	A	Dundee	1	1		1	1	D Robertson	5111	Coulibaly
17/09/2016	L	H	Partick Thistle	2	2		1	1	A Dallas	4169	K Boyd, Coulibaly
24/09/2016	L	A	Celtic	1	6		1	2	N Walsh	53532	Coulibaly
01/10/2016	L	H	Aberdeen	0	4		0	1	W Collum	4592	
15/10/2016	L	A	St Johnstone	1	0		0	0	S McLean	2930	S Boyd
22/10/2016	L	A	Inverness CT	1	1		1	0	A Dallas	2591	Coulibaly
26/10/2016	L	H	Hearts	2	0		1	0	A Dallas	3917	Coulibaly, S Smith
29/10/2016	L	A	Rangers	0	3		0	2	J Beaton	49302	
05/11/2016	L	H	Hamilton Accies	0	0		0	0	E Anderson	3387	
18/11/2016	L	H	Celtic	0	1		0	1	D Robertson	10962	
03/12/2016	L	H	Dundee	2	0		1	0	C Allan	3615	McKenzie, Coulibaly
06/12/2016	L	A	Aberdeen	1	5		0	3	S Finnie	8195	McKenzie
10/12/2016	L	A	Motherwell	0	0		0	0	S McLean	3684	
17/12/2016	L	H	Inverness CT	1	1		0	0	N Walsh	3294	Coulibaly
23/12/2016	L	H	St Johnstone	0	1		0	1	S Finnie	3056	
27/12/2016	L	A	Hearts	0	4		0	2	C Thomson	16696	
31/12/2016	L	A	Partick Thistle	0	0		0	0	K Clancy	3584	
21/01/2017	SC	H	Hamilton Accies	0	1		0	0	C Allan	2944	
28/01/2017	L	H	Ross County	3	2		1	2	B Cook	3207	K Boyd, Dicker, Longstaff
04/02/2017	L	A	Hamilton Accies	1	1		1	1	S McLean	2159	Longstaff
11/02/2017	L	A	Dundee	1	1		1	1	A Muir	4708	K Boyd
19/02/2017	L	H	Aberdeen	1	2		1	0	A Dallas	3972	McKenzie
25/02/2017	L	A	St Johnstone	2	0		1	0	D Robertson	2933	McKenzie, Sammon
04/03/2017	L	H	Motherwell	1	2		1	0	B Madden	4726	K Boyd
11/03/2017	L	A	Ross County	2	1		0	0	N Walsh	3380	Sammon, K Boyd
18/03/2017	L	H	Partick Thistle	1	1		0	0	J Beaton	4519	Sammon
01/04/2017	L	A	Inverness CT	1	1		1	1	B Madden	2780	K Boyd
05/04/2017	L	H	Rangers	0	0		0	0	A Muir	9548	
08/04/2017	L	A	Celtic	1	3		0	1	C Thomson	57679	Jones
14/04/2017	L	H	Hearts	0	0		0	0		4110	
29/04/2017	L	A	Hamilton Accies	2	0		2	0	W Collum	2482	Jones, Sammon
06/05/2017	L	H	Dundee	0	1		0	0	C Thomson	4040	
13/05/2017	L	H	Inverness CT	2	1		1	0	J Beaton	3137	Longstaff, Jones
16/05/2017	L	A	Motherwell	1	3		1	1	N Walsh	5246	Frizzell
20/05/2017	L	H	Ross County	1	2		1	1	B Madden	3951	Sammon

FRIENDLIES / OTHER GAMES						
09/07/2016	H	Morpeth Town	4	1	CD	
12/07/2016	H	East Kilbride U20	6	0	U20	
19/07/2016	A	Creetown	4	0	U20	
24/07/2016	A	Auchinleck Talbot	3	1	U20	
11/01/2017	A	Gateshead	1	1		141

Date	Comp	H/A	Opponents	F	A		1	2	3	4	5	6	7	8	9	10	11	12	13	14	15	16	17	18
16/07/2016	LC	A	Clyde	2	1		MacDonald	S Smith	Addison	Boyle	Cobain	McKenzie	Dicker	Kiltie	McFadzean+	Coulibaly	Bojaj*	Magennis*	Jones+	M Smith	Burn	Davies	Frizzell	Taylor
23/07/2016	LC	H	Morton	0	2		MacDonald	M Smith	Addison	Burn	Webb	Jones	Waddington*	Kiltie&	Taylor	K Boyd+	Magennis	Dicker*	Coulibably+	Frizzell&	S Smith	Davies	Boyle	McFadzean
26/07/2016	LC	A	Berwick Rangers	3	2		Davies	S Smith	Addison	Burn	Boyle	McKenzie	Dicker	Jones	Taylor*	Coulibaly	Magennis	Bojaj*	M Smith	Cobain	Hawkshaw	McFadzean	MacDonald	
30/07/2016	LC	H	Albion Rovers	0	0	3-5p	Davies	S Smith	Addison	Webb*	Boyle	McKenzie	Dicker	Jones+	M Smith	Coulibaly	Magennis	Taylor*	Bojaj+	Frizzell	Waddington	McFadzean	Burn	MacDonald
06/08/2016	L	H	Motherwell	1	2		MacDonald	S Smith	Addison	McFadzean	Boyle	McKenzie*	Dicker	Kiltie&	Taylor	Coulibaly	Hawkshaw+	K Boyd*	Jones+	M Smith&	Waddington	Davies	Burn	Cobain
13/08/2016	L	A	Hamilton Accies	2	1		MacDonald	S Smith	Addison	M Smith+	Boyle	McKenzie	Dicker	Jones&	Taylor	Green*	K Boyd	Coulibaly*	McFadzean+	Waddington&	Morrison	Davies	Burn	Cobain
20/08/2016	L	A	Ross County	0	2		MacDonald	S Smith	Addison*	M Smith	Boyle	Hendrie	Adams&	Jones	Coulibaly	Green+	K Boyd	Burn*	McFadzean+	Hawkshaw&	Dicker	Davies	Bojaj	Taylor
26/08/2016	L	H	Rangers	1	1		MacDonald	S Smith	Burn	Taylor	Boyle	Hendrie	Dicker	Kiltie+	Frizzell*	Hawkshaw	K Boyd&	Adams*	Green+	Coulibaly&	Jones	Kayode	Bojaj	MacKay
10/09/2016	L	A	Dundee	1	1		MacDonald	S Smith	Burn	S Boyd	McKenzie	Hendrie	Dicker	K Boyd	Frizzell*	Hawkshaw+	Coulibaly	Jones*	Adams+&	Green&	Boyle	Kayode	Morrison	MacKay
17/09/2016	L	H	Partick Thistle	2	2		MacDonald	S Smith*	Burn	S Boyd	McKenzie	Hendrie	Dicker	K Boyd	Frizzell+	Hawkshaw	Coulibaly	M Smith*&	Tyson+	Jones&	Boyle	Wilson	Morrison	MacKay
24/09/2016	L	A	Celtic	1	6		MacDonald	Taylor	Burn	S Boyd	McKenzie&	Hendrie	Dicker	K Boyd	Tyson+	Hawkshaw*	Coulibaly	Adams*	Jones+	Morrison&	Boyle	Frizzell	M Smith	MacKay
01/10/2016	L	H	Aberdeen	0	4		MacDonald	Taylor	Burn&	S Boyd	McKenzie	Hendrie	Dicker	K Boyd	Kiltie+	Adams*	Coulibaly	Tyson*	Jones+	Addison&	Kayode	Paterson	Morrison	MacKay
15/10/2016	L	A	St Johnstone	1	0		MacDonald	Taylor	Burn*	Addison	McKenzie	Hendrie	Dicker	Tyson	Jones	M Smith	Coulibaly+	S Boyd*	Adams+	Boyle	Bojaj	Frizzell	Wilson	MacKay
22/10/2016	L	A	Inverness CT	1	1		MacDonald	Taylor	S Boyd	Addison	McKenzie	Hendrie	Dicker	Tyson	Jones	M Smith*	Coulibaly+	S Smith*	K Boyd+	Boyle	Bojaj	Frizzell	Paterson	MacKay
26/10/2016	L	H	Hearts	2	0		MacDonald	Taylor	S Boyd	Addison	McKenzie	Hendrie	Dicker	Tyson*	Jones+	S Smith	Coulibaly	Frizzell*	K Boyd+	Boyle	Bojaj	M Smith	Wilson	MacKay
29/10/2016	L	A	Rangers	0	3		MacDonald	Taylor	S Boyd	Addison	McKenzie	Hendrie	Dicker	Tyson*	Jones	S Smith	Coulibaly	K Boyd*	Burn	Boyle	Bojaj	M Smith	Frizzell	MacKay
05/11/2016	L	H	Hamilton Accies	0	0		MacDonald	Taylor	S Boyd	Addison*	McKenzie	Hendrie	Dicker	K Boyd	Jones	S Smith+	Coulibaly	Burn*	Frizzell+	Boyle	Bojaj	M Smith	Tyson	MacKay
18/11/2016	L	H	Celtic	0	1		MacDonald	Taylor	S Boyd	Boyle	McKenzie	Hendrie	Dicker&	Frizzell	Jones+	S Smith	Bojaj*	Tyson*	Coulibably+	McFadzean&	Adams	M Smith	Wilson	MacKay
03/12/2016	L	H	Dundee	2	0		MacDonald	Taylor	S Boyd	Boyle	McKenzie	Hendrie	Dicker	Tyson	Jones*	S Smith	Coulibaly	Frizzell*	Bojaj	McFadzean	Adams	Wilson	Cameron	MacKay
06/12/2016	L	A	Aberdeen	1	5		MacDonald	Taylor	S Boyd	Boyle	McKenzie	Hendrie	Dicker	Frizzel+	Jones*	S Smith	Coulibaly&	I Wilson*	Tyson+	Adams&	McFadzean	Bojaj	Cameron	MacKay
10/12/2016	L	A	Motherwell	0	0		MacDonald	Taylor	S Boyd	Boyle	McKenzie	Hendrie	Dicker	Tyson	Jones*	S Smith	Coulibaly	Hawkshaw*	M Smith	Adams	Frizzell	Bojaj	I Wilson	MacKay
17/12/2016	L	H	Inverness CT	1	1		MacDonald	Taylor	I Wilson	Boyle	McKenzie	Hendrie	Dicker	Tyson	Jones	S Smith	Coulibaly	Hawkshaw	M Smith	Adams	Frizzell	Bojaj	Cameron	MacKay
23/12/2016	L	H	St Johnstone	0	1		MacDonald	Taylor	I Wilson	Boyle	McKenzie*	Hendrie	Dicker	Tyson+	Jones	S Smith&	Coulibaly	Hawkshaw*	K Boyd+	Cameron&	Frizzell	M Smith	Adams	MacKay
27/12/2016	L	A	Hearts	0	4		MacDonald	Taylor	I Wilson	Boyle&	M Smith*	Adams	Dicker	Tyson	K Boyd+	S Smith	Coulibaly	Jones*	Hawkshaw+	Webb&	Frizzell	Bojaj	Cameron	MacKay
31/12/2016	L	A	Partick Thistle	0	0		MacDonald	Taylor	I Wilson	Adams	Hawkshaw*	Hendrie	Dicker	Tyson+	Bojaj	S Smith	Coulibaly	Frizzell*	Jones+	Boyle	K Boyd	McLean	Cameron	MacKay
21/01/2017	SC	H	Hamilton Accies	0	1		Woodman	Osborne	Ajer	Taylor	Longstaff	Hendrie	Dicker	Tyson+	McKenzie*	Jones	Roberts&	S Smith*	K Boyd+	Coulibaly&	Hawkshaw	S Boyd	Frizzell	MacDonald
28/01/2017	L	H	Ross County	3	2		Woodman	Osborne*	Ajer	Taylor	S Smith	Hendrie	Dicker	K Boyd&	McKenzie	Longstaff	Roberts+	I Wilson*	Jones+	Tyson&	Hawkshaw	Cameron	Frizzell	MacDonald
04/02/2017	L	A	Hamilton Accies	1	1		Woodman	I Wilson	Ajer	Taylor	S Smith*	Hendrie	Dicker	K Boyd&	McKenzie	Longstaff	Jones+	Hawkshaw*	Umerah+	Sammon&	Tyson	S Boyd	Roberts	MacDonald
11/02/2017	L	A	Dundee	1	1		Woodman	I Wilson	Ajer	Taylor	Sammon	Hendrie*	Dicker	K Boyd+	McKenzie	Longstaff	Jones&	Addison*	Tyson+	Roberts&	M Smith	S Boyd	Umerah	MacDonald
19/02/2017	L	H	Aberdeen	1	2		Woodman	S Smith*	Ajer	Taylor	Sammon+	Hendrie	Dicker	K Boyd	McKenzie	Longstaff&	Jones	Addison*	I Wilson+	Umerah&	M Smith	S Boyd	Roberts	MacDonald
25/02/2017	L	A	St Johnstone	2	0		Woodman	S Boyd	Ajer	Taylor	Sammon	Hendrie	Dicker	K Boyd	Taylor	Longstaff*	Jones	M Smith*	I Wilson	Umerah	Roberts	Frizzell	Tyson	MacDonald
04/03/2017	L	H	Motherwell	1	2		Woodman	S Boyd	Ajer	Taylor	Sammon	Hendrie	Dicker	K Boyd	McKenzie	Longstaff*	Jones	Roberts*	I Wilson	Umerah	M Smith	Frizzell	Cameron	MacDonald
11/03/2017	L	A	Ross County	2	1		Woodman	S Boyd	Ajer	Taylor	Sammon	Hendrie	Roberts*	K Boyd+	I Wilson	Longstaff	Jones	Hawkshaw*	Umerah+	Osborne	M Smith	Frizzell	Cameron	MacDonald
18/03/2017	L	H	Partick Thistle	1	1		Woodman	S Boyd	Ajer	Taylor	Sammon	Hendrie	Dicker	K Boyd	McKenzie	Longstaff*	Jones+	I Wilson*	Umerah+	Osborne	M Smith	Frizzell	Roberts	MacDonald
01/04/2017	L	A	Inverness CT	1	1		Woodman	S Boyd	Ajer	Taylor	Sammon	I Wilson	Dicker	K Boyd	McKenzie*	Longstaff	Jones+	Kiltie*	Roberts+	Osborne	Hawkshaw	Frizzell	Cameron	MacDonald
05/04/2017	L	H	Rangers	0	0		Woodman	Kiltie*	Ajer	Taylor	Sammon	I Wilson	Dicker	K Boyd	Hendrie	Longstaff	Jones	Roberts*	M Smith	Osborne	S Boyd	Frizzell	Cameron	MacDonald
08/04/2017	L	A	Celtic	1	3		Woodman	S Boyd	M Smith	Taylor	Sammon	I Wilson	Dicker	Hendrie	Roberts+	Longstaff*	Jones&	Hawkshaw*	Frizzell+	Graham&	Osborne	K Boyd	Cameron	MacDonald
14/04/2017	L	H	Hearts	0	0		Woodman	M Smith*	Ajer	Taylor	K Boyd	I Wilson	Dicker	Hendrie	Roberts&	Longstaff+	Jones	Hawkshaw*	Kiltie+	Frizzell&	Osborne	Graham	Cameron	MacDonald
29/04/2017	L	A	Hamilton Accies	2	0		Woodman	S Smith	Ajer	Taylor	Sammon	I Wilson	Dicker	Hendrie	K Boyd	Longstaff*	Jones+	Kiltie*	Frizzell+	Roberts	Osborne	Graham	Cameron	MacDonald
06/05/2017	L	H	Dundee	0	1		Woodman	S Smith	Ajer	Taylor	Sammon	I Wilson*	Dicker	Hendrie	K Boyd	Longstaff	Jones+	Kiltie*	Roberts+	Frizzell	Osborne	Graham	Hawkshaw	MacDonald
13/05/2017	L	H	Inverness CT	2	1		MacDonald	S Smith	Ajer	Kiltie*	Sammon	I Wilson	Dicker	Hendrie	Frizzell	Longstaff	Jones	McKenzie*	Roberts	Cameron	Osborne	Graham	Hawkshaw	MacDonald
16/05/2017	L	A	Motherwell	1	3		MacDonald	S Smith	Ajer	Kiltie+	Sammon	I Wilson&	Dicker	Taylor	Frizzell	Hawkshaw*	Jones	Roberts*	McKenzie+	Graham&	Osborne	Queen	Cameron	Lyle
20/05/2017	L	H	Ross County	1	2		MacDonald	S Smith	Ajer	Kiltie*	Sammon	I Wilson&	Dicker	Taylor	Frizzell	Longstaff	Jones+	McKenzie*	Cameron+	Graham&	Osborne	Roberts	Hawkshaw	Lyle

						L			SC			LC							
Surname	First Name	DOB	SQ	Nat	Pos	A	S	G	A	S	G	A	S	G	UNS	Signed	Previous Club	Notes	Contract
Adams	Charlee	16/02/1995	18	ENG	M	4	5								5	2016	Birmingham City (OL)	Aug 16-Jan 2017	
Addison	Miles	07/01/1989	4	ENG	D	8	3					4				2016	Unattached		End 2018/
Ajer	Kristoffer	17/04/1998	20	NOR	M	16			1							2017	Celtic (OL)	Jan-May 2017	
Bojaj	Flo	13/04/1996	20	ALB	F	2						1	2		12	2016	Huddersfield Town (OL)	Jul 16-Jan 2017	
Boyd	Kris	18/08/1983	9	SCO	F	22	5	8		1		1			2	2015	Rangers		End 2017/
Boyd	Scott	04/06/1986	16	SCO	D	18	1	1							5	2016	Ross County (OL)	Sep 16-May 2017	End 2017/
Boyle	William	01/09/1995	5	ENG	D	11						3		1	10	2016	Huddersfield Town (OL)	Jul 16-May 2017	
Burn	Jonathan	01/08/1995	17	ENG	D	6	2					2			5	2016	Middlesbrough (OL)	Jul 16-Jan 2017	
Cameron	Innes	22/08/2000	44	SCO	M		2								15	2016	Kilmarnock Youths		
Clark	Lewis	12/02/1998	37	SCO	D											2015	Kilmarnock Youths		
Cobain	Jamie	11/11/1996	22	ENG	D							1			3	2016	Newcastle United	Released June 2017	
Coulibaly	Souleymane	26/12/1994	19	CDI/ROI	F	18	3	8		1		3	1	3		2016	Peterborough United	Transferred to Al Ahly Jan 2017	
Davies	Oliver	31/12/1994	12	WAL	GK							2			5	2015	Swansea City (OL)	Jul-Aug 2016	
Dempsie	Thomas	10/12/1999	39	SCO	M											2016	Kilmarnock Youths		
Dicker	Gary	31/07/1986	8	ROI	M	36		1	1			3	1		1	2016	Carlisle United		OOC
Frizzell	Adam	21/02/1998	21	SCO	M	8	7	1					1		19	2015	Kilmarnock Youths		End 2018
Graham	William	23/06/1999	40	SCO	F		3								4	2016	Kilmarnock Youths		End 2018
Green	George	02/01/1996	25	ENG	M	2	2									2016	Burnley (OL)	Aug-Sep 2016	
Hawkshaw	Dean	24/04/1997	33	SCO	M	7	8								8	2014	Kilmarnock Youths		
Hendrie	Luke	27/08/1994	27	ENG	D	32			1							2016	Burnley (OL)	Aug 16-May 2017	
Jones	Jordan	24/10/1994	11	ENG	F	29	8	3	1			3	1		1	2016	Middlesbrough		OOC
Kayode	Dapo	30/09/1992	15	ENG/NIG	D										3	2016	Dinamo Bucharest II	Released June 2017	
Kiltie	Greg	18/01/1997	10	SCO	F	7	4					2				2012	Kilmarnock Youths		End 2017
Lidington	Sam	04/03/1997	30	SCO	D											2015	Kilmarnock Youths		End 2018
Longstaff	Sean	30/10/1997	18	ENG	M	16		3	1							2017	Newcastle United (OL)	Jan-May 2017	[redacted]
Lyle	Curtis	08/09/1999	42	SCO	D										3	2016	Kilmarnock Youths		
MacDonald	Jamie	17/04/1986	1	SCO	GK	24						2			17	2015	Falkirk		End 2017
Mackay	Devlin	23/01/1997	31	SCO	GK										18	2015	Kilmarnock Youths	OL to Berwick R Jan-May	End 2018
Magennis	Josh	15/08/1990	28	NIR	F							3	1			2014	Aberdeen	Transferred to Charlton Athletic Aug 2016	[redacted]
McFadzean	Callum	16/01/1994	14	SCO/ENG	M	1	3					1			5	2016	Sheffield United		End 201
McKenzie	Rory	07/10/1993	7	SCO	F	24	3	4	1			3		1		2010	Kilmarnock Youths		End 201
McLean	Scott	30/08/1997	32	SCO	F										1	2015	Kilmarnock Youths		End 201
Morrison	Lewis	12/03/1999	35	SCO	F		1								4	2015	Kilmarnock Youths		
Osborne	Karleigh	19/03/1988	5	ENG	D	1			1						11	2017	Plymouth Argyle		End 201
Paterson	Jack	24/05/2000		SCO	M										2	2016	Kilmarnock Youths		
Queen	Taylor	24/09/1998	38	SCO	D										1	2016	Kilmarnock Youths		
Roberts	Callum	14/04/1997	25	ENG	F	4	6		1						7	2017	Newcastle United (OL)	Jan-May 2017	
Sammon	Conor	06/11/1986		ROI	F	14	1	5								2017	Hearts (OL)	Jan-May 2017	
Smith	Steven	30/03/1985	3	SCO	D	24	1	1		1		3			1	2015	Rangers		End 201
Smith	Martin	02/10/1995	6	ENG	M	7	3	1				2			16	2016	Sunderland		OOC
Taylor	Greg	05/11/1997	24	SCO	D	36			1			2	1		2	2014	Kilmarnock Youths		End 201
Tyson	Nathan	04/05/1982	12	ENG/BAR	F	11	6		1						3	2016	Doncaster Rovers		OOC
Umerah	Josh	01/04/1998		ENG / NIG	F		4								3	2017	Charlton Athletic (OL)	Jan-May 2017	[redacted]
Waddington	Mark	11/10/1996	16	ENG	M		1					1			2	2016	Stoke City (OL)	Jul-Aug 2016	
Webb	Josh	10/08/1995	2	ENG	D		1					2				2016	Aston Villa		OOC
Whittaker	Jack	08/09/1997	34	SCO	M											2015	Kilmarnock Youths	OL to Stranraer Jan-May 2017, Freed June joined Cowdenbeath	[redacted]
Wilson	Iain	15/12/1998	36	SCO	D	16	4								8	2015	Kilmarnock Youths		End 20
Wilson	Aidan	15/01/1999	41	SCO	D											2016	Kilmarnock Youths		
Woodman	Freddie	04/03/1997	17	ENG	GK	14			1							2017	Newcastle United (OL)	Jan-May 2017	
Wylie	Ross	01/01/1999		SCO	GK											2016	Kilmarnock Youths		
NEW SIGNINGS																			
Power	Alan															2017	Lincoln City		
Higgins	Daniel															2017	Dundee		
Waters	Callum															2017	Alloa Athletic		End 20
O'Donnell	Stephen															2017	Luton Town		

Source of Birthdates: Kilmarnock FC Programme and Transfermarkt.com

.ivingston FC 2016/17

unded	1943
ound	Almondvale Stadium
stcode	EH54 7DN
l	01506 417000
pacity	9865
osest Railway Station	Livingston North / Livingston South
cord Attendance	10024, Lge v Celtic, 18/8/2001
cord Win	8-0 v Stranraer, LC, 4/8/12
cord Defeat	0-8 v Hamilton Accies, Lge, 14/12/74
ost League Goals in a Season	22 Leigh Griffiths 2008/9 / Iain Russell 2010/11
airman	Robert Wilson
cretary	Brian Ewing
anager	David Hopkin
sistant Manager	Ian McCaldon
lours 2016/17 Top	Black
orts	Black
onsor	Tony Macaroni
anufacturer	Joma
ange Colours 2016/17 Top	Light Blue
orts	White
cknames	Lions, Livi
eb	www.livingstonfc.co.uk
atch Programme 2016/17	Roar £2.50

Livingston's gamble of full time football brought results and promotion was secured with plenty to spare. However, running a full-time operation with a home support reduced to fewer than 1000 must be very difficult.

Whoever works the financial magic behind the scenes at Almondvale deserves a medal more than any of the players. After a slightly indifferent start to the season when Alloa were leaders, Livingston quickly overtook them and never relinquished top spot. Veteran striker Liam Buchanan was their most consistent player and contributed a handsome goals tally.

PREDICTION FOR 2017/18

The jump from league One to Championship is quite a big one. Livi have the luxury of knowing part-time Brechin are odds-on to finish bottom. Keeping out of the Play off spot will be David Hopkin's primary objective but he should also have the likes of Dumbarton and Queen of the South in his sights.

Date	Comp	H/A	Opponents	F	A		HT	Referee	Crowd	Scorers
16/07/2016	LC	H	St Mirren	2	3		0 1	G Duncan		Cadden, Carrick
20/07/2016	LC	A	Edinburgh City	3	0		2 0	A Newlands	525	Mullin, Mullen, Buchanan
26/07/2016	LC	H	Ayr United	0	2		0 1	D Lowe	643	
30/07/2016	LC	A	Hamilton Accies	1	2		1 1	E Anderson	764	Matthews og
06/08/2016	L	H	Stranraer	5	1		2 0	C Steven	693	Pittman 2, Buchanan 2, Mullen
13/08/2016	L	A	Airdrieonians	4	2		2 0	M Northcroft	1048	Mullen, Buchanan, Boateng og, Mullin
20/08/2016	L	H	Stenhousemuir	4	1		2 0	G Duncan	769	Mullen 2, Pittman, Longridge
27/08/2016	L	A	Queen's Park	0	1		0 1	K Graham	698	
03/09/2016	CC3	H	Celtic U20	5	1		5 1	S Kirkland	1214	Buchanan 3, Crighton, Mullen
10/09/2016	L	A	Alloa	3	1		3 0	C Charleston	712	Pittman, Buchanan, Miller
17/09/2016	L	H	Brechin City	2	1		1 0	A Newlands	858	Mullen, Pittman
24/09/2016	L	A	East Fife	1	3		0 3	D Lowe	784	Mullin
01/10/2016	L	A	Peterhead	2	1		1 1	G Duncan	569	Mullen 2
07/10/2016	CC4	A	Crusaders	2	1	*	0 0	D Morgan (W)		Buchanan, Pittman
15/10/2016	L	H	Albion Rovers	1	2		0 1	C Charleston	702	Buchanan
22/10/2016	L	H	Alloa	3	1		0 0	S Finnie	977	Miller, Buchanan 2
29/10/2016	L	A	Brechin City	3	0		0 0	B Madden	517	Buchanan, Longridge, Byrne
01/11/2016	CC4	A	Crusaders	3	0		0 0	N Pratt (W)		Cadden, De Vita, Buchanan
05/11/2016	L	H	East Fife	3	1		1 0	C Napier	907	Buchanan 2, Miller
13/11/2016	CC5	H	TNS	0	3		0 1	R Crangle (NI)	733	
19/11/2016	L	H	Peterhead	1	2		0 1	G Aitken	712	Buchanan
26/11/2016	SC3	A	Airdrieonians	2	1		1 1	B Cook	780	Cadden, Mullen
03/12/2016	L	A	Albion Rovers	1	0		0 0	D Munro	413	Cadden
10/12/2016	L	A	Stranraer	2	1		0 1	C Steven	333	Carrick, De Vita
13/12/2016	L	A	Stenhousemuir	4	0		1 0	K Graham	334	Summers og, De Vita, Carrick, Buchanan
17/12/2016	L	H	Airdrieonians	2	0		1 0	S Reid	989	Carrick, Cadden
24/12/2016	L	H	Queen's Park	1	2		1 0	S Kirkland	819	Buchanan
31/12/2016	L	A	East Fife	1	2		1 0	G Duncan	661	Buchanan
07/12/2016	L	A	Peterhead	3	2		0 0	D Lowe	582	Gallagher, Buchanan, Byrne
21/01/2017	SC4	H	East Fife	0	1		0 1	C Steven	726	
28/01/2017	L	H	Brechin City	3	0		2 0	A Newlands	746	Buchanan, Halkett, Cadden
04/02/2017	L	A	Alloa	2	2		1 1	K Graham	565	Mullen, Buchanan
11/02/2017	L	H	Stranraer	0	0		0 0	G Beaton	677	
18/02/2017	L	A	Airdrieonians	4	0		1 0	S Finnie	1012	Crighton, Gorman og, Mullen, Cadden
04/03/2017	L	A	Queen's Park	1	1		1 1	A Newlands	701	Pittman
07/03/2017	L	H	Albion Rovers	3	0		1 0	N Walsh	548	Todorov 2, Mullen
11/03/2017	L	H	East Fife	0	1		0 0	G Irvine	773	
18/03/2017	L	A	Stranraer	1	0		0 0	C Napier	523	Buchanan
21/03/2017	L	H	Stenhousemuir	1	0		1 0	B Cook	531	Todorov
25/03/2017	L	H	Airdrieonians	4	2		2 1	C Allan	832	Mullen 2, Gallagher, Cadden
01/04/2017	L	A	Brechin City	2	0		1 0	S Millar	523	Buchanan 2
08/04/2017	L	H	Alloa	2	1		1 0	G Aitken	1099	Pittman, Longridge
15/04/2017	L	A	Stenhousemuir	1	0		0 0	C Steven	472	Buchanan
22/04/2017	L	H	Queen's Park	4	0		1 0	G Irvine	821	Todorov, Mullen, Mullin. Cadden
29/04/2017	L	H	Peterhead	4	1		3 0	K Graham	891	Buchanan, Pittman, Mullen, Mullin
06/05/2017	L	A	Albion Rovers	2	0		2 0	S Kirkland	454	Pittman, De Vita

* Replay ordered due to Livingston fielding suspended player (A Lithgow)

FRIENDLIES / OTHER GAMES				
02/07/2016	H	Dunfermline Athletic	1	5
05/07/2016	H	Morton	2	2
12/07/2016	H	St Johnstone	1	1
23/07/2016	H	Hartlepool United	0	0
27/07/2016	A	Bo'ness United	2	2

Date	Comp	H/A	Opponents	F	A	1	2	3	4	5	6	7	8	9	10	11	12	13	14	15	16	17	18
16/07/2016	LC	H	St Mirren	2	3	Kelly	Longridge	Lithgow	Crichton	Halkett	Miller	Mullin	Buchanan+	Cadden	Sinclair*	Mullen&	Pittman*	Carrick+	Orr&	Byrne	Knox	Watt	Jamieson
20/07/2016	LC	A	Edinburgh City	3	0	Kelly	Longridge	Lithgow	Crichton	Halkett	Miller	Byrne	Mullin	Cadden*	Carrick&	Mullen+	Knox*	Buchanan+	Watt&	Pittman	Orr	Sinclair	Jamieson
26/07/2016	LC	H	Ayr United	0	2	Kelly	Longridge	Lithgow	Crichton	Halkett	Miller	Sinclair+	Mullin	Buchanan	Carrick*	Mullen&	Cadden*	Byrne+	Knox&	Pittman	Orr	Watt	Jamieson
30/07/2016	LC	A	Hamilton Accies	1	2	Kelly	Longridge	Lithgow	Crichton	Halkett	Miller	Byrne&	Mullin*	Cadden	Pittman	Mullen+	Knox*	Orr+	Watt&	Reid	Sinclair	Ogilvie	Maley
06/08/2016	L	H	Stranraer	5	1	Kelly	Longridge	Lithgow	Crichton	Neill	Miller	Byrne*	Mullin+	Cadden	Pittman	Mullen&	Buchanan*	Sinclair+	Watt&	Knox	Orr	Maley	Smith
13/08/2016	L	A	Airdrieonians	4	2	Kelly	Longridge	Lithgow	Crichton	Halkett	Miller	Byrne*	Mullin	Cadden+	Pittman	Buchanan	Watt*	Mullin+	Neill	Knox	Orr	Maley	Allan
20/08/2016	L	H	Stenhousemuir	4	1	Kelly	Longridge	Lithgow	Crichton	Halkett	Miller	Byrne	Buchanan*	Cadden+	Pittman	Mullen&	Watt*	Allan+	Orr&	Mullin	Neill	Maley	Sinclair
27/08/2016	L	A	Queen's Park	0	1	Kelly	Longridge	Lithgow	Crichton	Halkett	Miller	Byrne&	Buchanan	Cadden*	Pittman	Mullen+	Mullin*	Neill+	Watt&	Sinclair	Orr	Maley	Allan
03/09/2016	CC3	H	Celtic U20	5	1	Maley	Longridge&	Lithgow	Crichton	Halkett	Miller	Byrne*	Buchanan+	Mullin	Pittman	Mullen	Sinclair*	Allan+	Neill&	Cadden	Carrick	Watt	Quinn
10/09/2016	L	A	Alloa	3	1	Kelly	Sinclair*	Lithgow	Crichton	Halkett	Michael Miller	Cadden	Buchanan+	Mullin&	Pittman	Mullen	Byrne*	Carrick+	Allan&	Knox	Currie	Maley	Smith
17/09/2016	L	H	Brechin City	2	1	Kelly	Cadden+	Lithgow	Crichton	Halkett	Michael Miller	Byrne	Buchanan&	Mullin*	Pittman	Mullen	Watt*	Sinclair+	Allan&	Knox	Currie	Maley	Carrick
24/09/2016	L	A	East Fife	1	3	Kelly	Cadden+	Lithgow	Crichton	Halkett	Michael Miller	Byrne*	Buchanan	Mullin	Pittman	Mullen	Carrick*	Longridge+	Watt	Knox	Currie	Maley	Sinclair
01/10/2016	L	A	Peterhead	2	1	Kelly	Cadden*	Longridge	Crichton	Halkett&	Michael Miller	Neill	Buchanan	Mullin+	Pittman	Mullen	Watt*	Carrick+	Sinclair&	Knox	Byrne	Maley	Allan
07/10/2016	CC4	A	Crusaders	2	1	* Maley	Lithgow	Longridge+	Crichton	Halkett	Michael Miller	Byrne*	Buchanan	Knox&	Pittman	Mullen	Cadden*	Mullin+	Watt&	Neill	Sinclair	Carrick	Kelly
15/10/2016	L	H	Albion Rovers	1	2	Kelly	Cadden*	Longridge	Crichton	Halkett	Michael Miller	Byrne	Buchanan	Mullin+	Pittman&	Mullen	Watt*	Knox+	Carrick&	Neill	Sinclair	Maley	Ogilvie
22/10/2016	L	H	Alloa	3	1	Kelly	Lithgow	Longridge	Crichton	Halkett	Michael Miller	Cadden*	Buchanan	De Vita&	Pittman	Mullen+	Mullin*	Watt+	Byrne&	Neill	Sinclair	Carrick	Knox
29/10/2016	L	A	Brechin City	3	0	Kelly	Lithgow	Longridge	Crichton	Halkett	Michael Miller*	Cadden+	Buchanan&	De Vita	Pittman	Mullen	Byrne*	Watt+	Carrick&	Neill	Sinclair	Maley	Mullin
01/11/2016	CC4	A	Crusaders	3	0	Maley	Lithgow	Neill	Crichton	Halkett	Mullin	Cadden+	Byrne	Sinclair&	Watt*	Carrick	Mullen*	De Vita+	Buchanan&	Longridge	Pittman	Currie	Kelly
05/11/2016	L	H	East Fife	3	1	Kelly	Neill	Longridge	Crichton	Halkett	Michael Miller	Cadden*	Buchanan&	De Vita+	Pittman	Mullen	Byrne*	Currie+	Carrick&	Mullin	Sinclair	Maley	Watt
13/11/2016	CC5	H	TNS	0	3	Maley	Lithgow	Longridge*	Crichton	Halkett	Michael Miller	Cadden+	Buchanan&	De Vita	Pittman	Mullen	Mullin*	Carrick+	Byrne&	Neill	Knox	Watt	Kelly
19/11/2016	L	H	Peterhead	1	2	Kelly	Lithgow	Longridge*	Crichton	Halkett	Michael Miller	Byrne+	Buchanan	Mullin&	Pittman	Mullen	Cadden*	Carrick+	Knox&	Neill	Currie	Watt	Maley
26/11/2016	SC3	A	Airdrieonians	2	1	Kelly	Lithgow	Longridge	Crichton	Halkett	Michael Miller*	Byrne	Buchanan+	Mullin	Pittman	Mullen	Cadden*	De Vita+	Knox	Neill	Currie	Carrick	Maley
03/12/2016	L	A	Albion Rovers	1	0	Kelly	Lithgow	Longridge	Crichton	Halkett	Watt*	Byrne	Buchanan+	De Vita	Pittman	Cadden	Carrick*	Neill+	Mullen	Knox	Currie	Ogilvie	Maley
10/12/2016	L	A	Stranraer	2	1	Kelly	Lithgow	Longridge	Crichton	Halkett	Watt*	Byrne	Buchanan&	De Vita	Pittman	Cadden+	Carrick*	Mullin+	Ogilvie&	Knox	Currie	Neill	Maley
13/12/2016	L	A	Stenhousemuir	4	0	Kelly	Lithgow	Longridge	Crichton	Halkett	Mullin&	Byrne	Knox*	De Vita+	Pittman	Carrick	Buchanan*	Cadden+	Currie&	Watt	Ogilvie	Neill	Maley
17/12/2016	L	H	Airdrieonians	2	0	Kelly	Lithgow	Longridge*	Crichton	Halkett	Mullin	Byrne	Buchanan&	De Vita	Pittman	Carrick+	Cadden*	Mullen+	Neill&	Knox	Currie	Ogilvie	Maley
24/12/2016	L	H	Queen's Park	1	2	Kelly	Lithgow	Cadden&	Crichton	Halkett	Mullin*	Byrne	Buchanan	De Vita	Pittman	Carrick+	Longridge*	Mullen+	Neill&	Knox	Currie	Sinclair	Maley
31/12/2016	L	A	East Fife	1	2	Kelly	Lithgow	Longridge	Crichton	Halkett	Mullen	Byrne	Buchanan	De Vita	Pittman	Carrick*	Mullin*	Ogilvie	Neill	Knox	Currie	Sinclair	Maley
07/12/2016	L	A	Peterhead	3	2	Kelly	Lithgow	Gallacher	Crichton	Halkett	Mullen&	Byrne	Buchanan+	De Vita*	Pittman	Michael Miller	Cadden*	Carrick+	Longridge&	Knox	Neill	Mullin	Maley
21/01/2017	SC4	H	East Fife	0	1	Kelly	Lithgow	Gallacher	Crichton	Halkett	Mullen	Byrne	Buchanan	De Vita*	Pittman	Cadden+	Mullin*	Carrick+	Sampson	Longridge	Ogilvie	Sinclair	Maley
28/01/2017	L	H	Brechin City	3	0	Kelly	Lithgow	Gallacher	Crichton	Halkett	Mullen+	Byrne	Buchanan*	Mark Miller	Pittman	Cadden&	Todorov*	De Vita+	Sinclair&	Longridge	Mullen	Knox	Maley
04/02/2017	L	A	Alloa	2	2	Kelly	Lithgow	Gallacher	Crichton	Halkett	Mullen+	Byrne	Buchanan&	Mark Millar	Pittman	Cadden*	De Vita*	Todorov+	Mullin&	Longridge	Sinclair	Knox	Maley
11/02/2017	L	H	Stranraer	0	0	Kelly	Lithgow	Gallacher	Crichton	Halkett	Mullen	Byrne	Buchanan	Mark Millar+	Pittman	Cadden*	De Vita*	Mullin+	Todorov	Longridge	Jacobs	Knox	Maley
18/02/2017	L	A	Airdrieonians	4	0	Kelly	Lithgow	Gallacher*	Crichton	Halkett	Mullen&	Byrne	Buchanan+	Mark Millar	Pittman	Longridge	De Vita*	Todorov+	Cadden&	Mullin	Sinclair	Knox	Maley
04/03/2017	L	A	Queen's Park	1	1	Kelly	Lithgow	De Vita&	Crichton	Halkett	Mullen	Byrne*	Buchanan+	Mark Millar	Pittman	Longridge	Mullin*	Todorov+	Cadden&	Gallacher	Sinclair	Knox	Maley
07/03/2017	L	H	Albion Rovers	3	0	Kelly	Lithgow	Gallacher	Crichton	Halkett	Cadden+	Byrne	Buchanan*	Mark Millar&	Pittman	Todorov	Mullen*	Longridge+	Mullin&	De Vita	Sinclair	Knox	Maley
11/03/2017	L	H	East Fife	0	1	Kelly	Longridge	Gallacher	Crichton	Halkett	Mullin	Byrne&	De Vita*	Mullen+	Pittman	Todorov	Cadden*	Mark Millar+	Buchanan&	Lithgow	Sinclair	Knox	Maley
18/03/2017	L	A	Stranraer	1	0	Kelly	Longridge	Gallacher	Lithgow	Halkett	Mullin	Mark Millar	Buchanan&	Mullen+	Pittman	Todorov*	Cadden*	Crichton+	Sampson&	Ogilvie	Sinclair	Knox	Maley
21/03/2017	L	H	Stenhousemuir	1	0	Kelly	Byrne	Gallacher	Lithgow	Halkett	Mullin	Mark Millar*	Buchanan&	De Vita	Pittman	Todorov+	Cadden*	Mullen+	Longridge&	Crichton	Sinclair	Knox	Maley
25/03/2017	L	H	Airdrieonians	4	2	Kelly	Longridge	Gallacher	Lithgow	Halkett	Mullin+	Byrne	Buchanan*	De Vita	Pittman	Mullen&	Todorov*	Cadden+	Knox&	Crichton	Sinclair	Mark Millar	Maley
01/04/2017	L	A	Brechin City	2	0	Kelly	Byrne	Gallacher	Lithgow	Halkett	Cadden&	Crichton	Buchanan	De Vita*	Pittman	Mullen+	Jacobs*	Todorov+	Longridge&	Mullin	Sinclair	Knox	Maley
08/04/2017	L	H	Alloa	2	1	Kelly	Byrne	Gallacher	Lithgow	Halkett	Mullin+	Longridge*	Buchanan	De Vita	Pittman	Mullen&	Crichton*	Cadden+	Todorov&	Jacobs	Sinclair	Knox	Maley
15/04/2017	L	A	Stenhousemuir	1	0	Kelly	Jacobs	Sinclair+	Lithgow	Knox*	Cadden	Longridge	Buchanan&	Mark Millar	Pittman	Todorov	Sampson*	De Vita+	Ogilvie&	Mullen	Reid	Halkett	Maley
22/04/2017	L	H	Queen's Park	4	0	Maley	Jacobs	Crichton*	Mullin	Halkett	Cadden	Longridge	Knox	Mullen&	Pittman	Todorov+	Gallacher*	Buchanan+	Ogilvie&	Lithgow	Mark Millar	De Vita	Kelly
29/04/2017	L	H	Peterhead	4	1	Kelly	Mullin*	Gallacher+	Lithgow	Halkett	De Vita	Longridge	Buchanan	Mark Millar	Pittman	Mullen	Crichton*	Cadden+&	Knox&	Todorov	Jacobs	Michael Miller	Maley
06/05/2017	L	A	Albion Rovers	2	0	Maley	Mullin	Gallacher	Lithgow	Jacobs	De Vita*	Todorov	Buchanan	Mark Millar&	Pittman	Mullen+	Knox*	Sampson+	Michael Miller&	Sinclair	Ogilvie	Kelly	

						L			SC			LC			CC			UC							
Surname	First Name	DOB	SQ	Nat	Pos	A	S	G	A	S	G	A	S	G	A	S	G	A	S	G	UNS	Signed	Previous Club	Notes	Contract
Allan	Lewis	25/10/1996	18	SCO	F		3									1					3	2016	Hibernian (OL)	Aug-Oct 2016	[redacted]
Buchanan	Liam	27/03/1985	9	SCO	F	32	4	22	2			2	1	1	3	1	5					2015	Alloa	OOC June 2017, joined Raith Rovers	
Byrne	Shaun	09/06/1993	6	SCO	M	26	4	2	2			2	1		3	1					2	2016	Dunfermline Athletic		End 2017/18
Cadden	Nicky	19/09/1996	11	SCO	M	22	12	6	1	1	1	3	1	1	2	1	1				1	2016	Airdrieonians		End 2017/18
Carrick	Dale	07/01/1994	19	SCO	F	4	10	3		1		2	1	1	1	1					5	2016	Kilmarnock	OL to Cowdenbeath Jan-May	End 2017/18
Crichton	Sean	26/03/1990	5	SCO	D	29	3	1	2			4			4		1				2	2016	Airdrieonians		End 2017/18
Currie	Ryan	07/11/1997	20	SCO	M		2														11	2014	Livingston Youths	Freed Jan 2017, joined East Kilbride	[redacted]
De Vita	Rafaelle	23/09/1987	23	ITA	F	18	9	3	1	1					1	1	1				2	2016	Ross County		End 2017/18
Gallacher	Declan	13/02/1991	31	SCO	D	14	1	2	1												1	2017	Ex Livingston		End 2017/18
Halkett	Craig	29/05/1995	26	SCO	D	33		1	2			4			4						1	2016	Rangers		End 2017/18
Jacobs	Keighan	09/09/1989	14	SCO/RSA	M	3	1														3	2017	Bidvest Wits		End 2017/18
Jamieson	Darren	15/12/1991	1	SCO	GK																3	2008	Livingston Youths	OL to Bo'ness Utd Aug 2016,	[redacted]
																								then freed and joined Bo'ness then Hamilton	
Kelly	Liam	23/01/1996	1	SCO	GK	34			2			4									5	2016	Rangers (OL)	Aug 16-May 2017	End 2018/19
Knox	Matthew	22/12/1999	16	SCO	F	3	5						3		1						27	2015	Livingston Youths		End 2017/18
Lithgow	Alan	12/03/1988	4	SCO	D	31	0		2			4			4						2	2016	Airdrieonians		End 2017/18
Longridge	Jackson	12/04/1995	3	SCO	D	24	6	3	1			4			3						5	2015	Stranraer		End 2017/18
Maley	Gary	03/08/1982	30	SCO	GK	2									4						36	2016	Broxburn Athletic		OOC
Miller	Michael	31/12/1994	2	SCO	D	14	1		1			4			3						1	2016	Morton		
Miller	Mark	23/02/1988	18	SCO	M	11	1	3													2	2017	Queen of the South	OOC June 2017, joined Forfar Athletic	[redacted]
Mullen	Danny	01/03/1995	10	SCO	F	27	4	14	2		1	4		1	3	1	1				3	2012	Livingston Youths		End 2017/18
Mullin	Josh	23/09/1992	7	SCO	M	19	9	4	1	1		4		1	2	2					6	2016	Albion Rovers		End 2017/18
Neill	Morgyn	10/03/1996	15	SCO	D	3									1	1					13	2015	Motherwell	OL to Stranraer Jan-May 2017,	
																								Freed May joined Stranraer	
Ogilvie	Jack	06/08/1999	38	SCO	M		3														9	2016	Livingston Youths		
Orr	Thomas	13/03/1997	14	SCO	F		1						2								5	2016	Morton (OL)	Jul-Aug 2016	
Pittman	Scott	09/07/1992	8	SCO / USA	M	36		9	2			1	1		3		1				3	2015	Bo'ness United		End 2017/18
Quinn	Connor	28/03/1998	35	SCO	GK																1	2015	Livingston Youths		
Reid	Craig	09/01/1999	39	SCO	D																2	2016	Livingston Youths		
Sampson	Kyle	30/06/2000	33	SCO	F		3														1	2016	Livingston Youths		End 2017/18
Sinclair	Jordan	11/07/1996	17	SCO	M	2	4					2			1	1					24	2016	Hibernian	Released May 2017	[redacted]
Smith	Darren	19/09/1997	36	SCO	M																2	2015	Livingston Youths		
Todorov	Nikolai	24/08/1996	22	BUL	F	1	7	4													2	2017	Hearts (OL)	Jan-May 2017	
Watt	Liam	21/01/1994	21	SCO	M	8	9						2		1	1					8	2016	Airdrieonians	Freed Jan 2017 joined Brechin City	
White	Cammy	05/02/1999	40	SCO	D																	2016	Livingston Youths		
Willis	Jay	19/07/1999	34	SCO	M																	2016	Livingston Youths		
Own Goals								3						1											
NEW SIGNINGS																									End 2017/1
Robinson	Scott	11/03/1992		SCO	M																	2017	East Fife		End 2017/1
Brown	Ross	10/06/1993		SCO	M																	2017	East Fife		End 2017/1
Peters	Josh	04/09/1996		SCO	F																	2017	Forfar Athletic		
Todorov	Nikolai																					2017	Hearts (OL)	July-May	
Mackin	Dylan	15/01/1997		SCO	F																	2017	Motherwell		End 2018/1

Includes first game v Crusaders

Source of Birthdates: Livingston FC website and transfermarkt.com

Livingston Football Club
The Lions
Official Match Day Programme
50p
Pre Season Tournament
Saturday 19th and Sunday 20th July 1997
Livingston • Heart of Midlothian • Ayr United • York City

Montrose FC 2016/17

Founded	1879
Ground	Links Park
Postcode	DD10 8QD
Tel	01674 673200
Capacity	3292
Closest Railway Station	Montrose
Record Attendance	8983 v Dundee, SC, 17/3/1973
Record Win	12-0 v Vale of Leithen, SC, 4/1/1975
Record Defeat	0-13 v Aberdeen, 17/3/1951
Most League Goals in a Season	28 Brian Third, 1972/3
Chairman	John Crawford
Secretary	Brian Petrie
Manager	Paul Hegarty, then Stuart Petrie
Assistant Manager	John Holt, then Ross Campbell
Colours 2016/17 Top	Blue
Shorts	Blue
Sponsor	Intervention rentals
Manufacturer	Nike
Change Colours 2016/17 Top	Red
Shorts	Red
Nicknames	Gable Endies, Mo
Web	www.montrosefc.co.uk
Match Programme 2016/17	The Gable Ender, £2
Theme Song	Links Park Dynamo

After decades of indifferent results Montrose finally hit a decent run and made it to the promotion Play offs. Few would have predicted this at the start of the season. Indeed, a few months in, with Paul Hegarty still at the helm, a relegation battle looked likely. However, the appointment of Stuart Petrie changed things. He brought new life to jaded players and added a few new signings to see the Links Park side climb the table. Top man was surely striker Chris Templeman, a veteran of many clubs and nearly 20 years in the game, yet still a potent goal threat at this level.

The Play Offs revealed some shortcominGs but Petrie has made a few new signings that will strengthen Montrose's squad for next season.

PREDICTION FOR 2017/18

Montrose will start the season well. Other teams will have a look at Stewart Petrie and he will take a job elsewhere (Forfar would be my bet). Montrose will hit a decline and finish mid-table.

Big Sanny - 681 games, 191 goals

Chris Templeman		League			LC			SC			OC			Total		
Season	*Club*	*A*	*S*	*G*	*A*	*S*	*G*	*A*	*S*	*G*	*A*	*S*	*G*	*A*	*S*	*G*
ex Rosyth Recreation Colts																
1997/8	Dunfermline Athletic													0	0	0
1998/9	Dunfermline Athletic	5	7											5	7	0
1999/0	Dunfermline Athletic		2											0	2	0
1999/0	Dumbarton (Loan)	3		3										3	0	3
2000/1	Dunfermline Athletic		1											0	1	0
2000/1	Stirling Albion	20	1	3				3		2				23	1	5
2001/2	Brechin City	34	1	15	1			1	1		4		1	40	2	16
2002/3	Brechin City	34	1	21				1			4	1	2	39	2	23
2003/4	Brechin City	22	11	5		3	1	1			4		2	27	14	8
2004/5	Brechin City	11	5	14	2		2	1		2		1		14	6	18
2004/5	Morton	18	1	6										18	1	6
2005/6	Morton	9	10	2	1				2	1	3		1	13	12	4
2005/6	Brechin City (Loan)	3	7											3	7	0
2006/7	Morton	23	12	12	1			3		2	1	3		28	15	14
2007/8	Morton	7	10		1				1	1	3		2	11	11	3
2007/8	East Fife	12	1	3										12	1	3
2008/9	East Fife	25	8	4		1		3			1	1	1	29	10	5
2009/10	Forfar Athletic	28	8	5	1			3		1	1		1	33	8	7
2010/1	Forfar Athletic	31	5	11	2		1	1			2		1	36	5	13
2011/2	Forfar Athletic	32	1	16	2		1	3		2	2			39	1	19
2012/3	Forfar Athletic	36	1	12	1			4		1	1	1		42	2	13
2013/4	Forfar Athletic	35	1	5	2			4		3		1		41	2	8
2014/5	Forfar Athletic	26	9	6	1				1			1		27	11	6
2015/6	Forfar Athletic	9	6	1	2		1	2			1	1		14	7	2
2015/6	Montrose	11	2	3										11	2	3
2016/7	Montrose	31	5	11	3			1	1	1	2			37	6	12
														0	0	0
														0	0	0
		465	116	158	20	4	6	31	6	16	29	10	11	545	136	191

Date	Comp	H/A	Opponents	F	A	HT	Referee	Crowd	Scorers
16/07/2016	LC	H	Ross County	0	1	0 0	C Charleston	557	
19/07/2016	LC	A	Raith Rovers	1	2	0 1	C Steven	1147	Bolochoweckyj
23/07/2016	LC	H	Alloa	0	2	0 1	G Irvine	358	
27/07/2016	LC	A*	Cove Rangers	0	3	0 1	M Taylor	189	
02/08/2016	CC	A	East Stirlingshire	3	0	1 0	C Napier	149	Masson, Webster, Ferguson
06/08/2016	L	A	Clyde	1	2	0 1	K Graham	445	Templeman
13/08/2016	L	H	Arbroath	1	1	0 1	S Kirkland	794	Templeman
17/08/2016	CC	A	Turriff United	0	1	0 0	G Duncan	180	
20/08/2016	L	A	Stirling Albion	0	2	0 0	G Ross	497	
27/08/2016	L	H	Annan Athletic	2	2	0 2	S Millar	340	MacDonald, Fraser
10/09/2016	L	H	Cowdenbeath	1	2	1 1	D Lowe	393	Fraser
17/09/2016	L	A	Edinburgh City	1	0	0 0	G irvine	309	Fraser
24/09/2016	L	H	Berwick Rangers	0	0	0 0	G Beaton	283	
01/10/2016	L	A	Forfar Athletic	3	1	1 0	C Steven	740	Fraser 2, Templeman
15/10/2016	L	H	Elgin City	0	5	0 3	M Roncone	302	
22/10/2016	SC2	A	Preston Athletic	3	0	0 0	C Napier	350	Fraser, Templeman, Court
05/11/2016	L	H	Edinburgh City	0	1	0 0	D Munro	388	
08/11/2016	L	A	Annan Athletic	3	2	2 1	G Duncan	289	I Campbell, Watson, Bolochowec
12/11/2016	L	A	Cowdenbeath	0	2	0 1	S Kirkland	270	
19/11/2016	L	H	Forfar Athletic	1	1	1 1	G Ross	630	Fraser
29/11/2016	SC3	A	Queen's Park	0	2	0 1	S Reid	348	
03/12/2016	L	A	Elgin City	1	4	0 0	D Lowe	586	Bolochoweckyj
10/12/2016	L	H	Clyde	2	1	1 0	R Milne	396	Fraser, Webster
17/12/2016	L	A	Berwick Rangers	2	1	0 0	C Allan	361	Ferguson, Court
24/12/2016	L	H	Stirling Albion	2	2	0 1	G Beaton	610	Masson, Fraser
02/01/2017	L	A	Arbroath	0	0	0 0	S Reid	1731	
07/01/2017	L	H	Elgin City	0	3	0 2	S Millar	562	
21/01/2017	L	H	Cowdenbeath	2	1	1 0	G Ross	432	McLauchlan og, Fraser
28/01/2017	L	H	Berwick Rangers	2	1	0 0	M Roncone	1222	Templeman, Ferguson
04/02/2017	L	A	Stirling Albion	2	1	0 1	S Kirkland	494	Templeman, Webster
11/02/2017	L	H	Arbroath	1	3	1 0	C Napier	1002	Smith
18/02/2017	L	A	Edinburgh City	1	1	0 1	G Duncan	341	Ballantyne
25/02/2017	L	A	Forfar Athletic	0	0	0 0	D Lowe	725	
28/02/2017	L	A	Clyde	2	1	2 2	G Irvine	365	Hay, Pascazio
04/03/2017	L	H	Annan Athletic	2	3	1 3	G Ross	384	Fraser, Hay
11/03/2017	L	H	Stirling Albion	1	3	0 1	S Kirkland	401	Hay
18/03/2017	L	A	Cowdenbeath	2	0	1 0	J McKendrick	302	Bolochoweckyj, Smith
25/03/2017	L	A	Arbroath	1	0	0 0	S Reid	1156	Fraser
01/04/2017	L	H	Edinburgh City	3	0	1 0	D Dickinson	454	Steeves, Watson, Templeman
08/04/2017	L	A	Elgin City	1	1	0 1	S Millar	781	Templeman
15/04/2017	L	H	Forfar Athletic	1	0	1 0	D Munro	984	Templeman
22/04/2017	L	A	Berwick Rangers	1	0	1 0	L Wilson	452	Templeman
29/04/2017	L	A	Annan Athletic	1	5	0 4	S Reid	461	Hay
06/05/2017	L	H	Clyde	1	1	0 1	G Beaton	1324	Templeman
10/05/2017	PO	H	Peterhead	1	1	1 1	M Northdroct	1251	Templeman
13/05/2017	PO	A	Peterhead	0	3	0 1	S Kirkland	1096	
* at Forfar									

FRIENDLIES / OTHER GAMES

01/07/2016	H	Deveronvale	1	0	
05/07/2016	H	Peterhead	0	2	

Date	Comp	H/A	Opponents	F	A	1	2	3	4	5	6	7	8	9	10	11	12	13	14	15	16	17	18
16/07/2016	LC	H	Ross County	0	1	Miller	Hegarty	Steeves	Pascazio	Bolochoweckyj	Masson	McWalter	Watson	R Campbell	Fraser	Templeman	Webster	Ferguson	McLeod	Lennie	Anderson	Harwood	Fleming
19/07/2016	LC	A	Raith Rovers	1	2	Miller	Hegarty	Steeves	Pascazio	Bolochoweckyj	Masson	McWalter+	Watson	R Campbell*	Fraser	Templeman	Webster*	Lennie+	McLeod	Ferguson	Anderson	Harwood	Fleming
23/07/2016	LC	H	Alloa	0	2	Fleming	Hegarty	Steeves	Pascazio	Bolochoweckyj	Masson	McWalter&	Watson*	R Campbell+	Fraser	Webster	Lennie*	Ferguson+	McLeod&	Hester	Anderson	Harwood	Miller
27/07/2016	LC	A*	Cove Rangers	0	3	Miller	Anderson	Steeves	Pascazio	R Campbell&	Masson	McWalter	Watson+	Templeman	Fraser*	Webster	Ferguson*	Lennie+	Harwood&	Hester	McLeod	Fleming	
02/08/2016	CC	A	East Stirlingshire	3	0	Fleming	Anderson	Steeves	Lennie	I Campbell	Masson+	McWalter	Ferguson&	Templeman*	Fraser	Webster	R Campbell*	Watson+	Willox&	Pascazio	McLeod	Harwood	Miller
06/08/2016	L	A	Clyde	1	2	Miller	McDonald	Steeves	Lennie	I Campbell	Watson+	McWalter	Ferguson*	Templeman	Fraser	Webster	R Campbell*	Anderson+	Willox	Pascazio	McLeod	Harwood	Fleming
13/08/2016	L	H	Arbroath	1	1	Miller	Anderson	Steeves	MacDonald	I Campbell	Masson	McWalter	Ferguson+	Templeman	Fraser*	Webster	R Campbell*	Lennie+	Willox	Pascazio	Watson	Harwood	Fleming
17/08/2016	CC	A	Turriff United	0	1	Fleming	Anderson&	Steeves	Willox	I Campbell	Masson	McWalter	Ferguson+	Templeman*	R Campbell	Webster	Milne*	Pascazio+	Lennie&	Bolochoweckyj	Watson	Harwood	Miller
20/08/2016	L	A	Stirling Albion	0	2	Miller	Anderson	Bolochoweckyj	Pascazio*	I Campbell	Masson	McWalter+	Watson	R Campbell	Fraser&	Webster	Lennie*	Ferguson+	Milne&	Willox	McLeod	Harwood	Fleming
27/08/2016	L	H	Annan Athletic	2	2	Fleming	Steeves*	Bolochoweckyj	MacDonald	I Campbell	Masson	McWalter	Watson	R Campbell+	Fraser	Webster	Lennie*	Ferguson	Anderson	Willox	McLeod	Pascazio	Miller
10/09/2016	L	H	Cowdenbeath	1	2	Fleming	Steeves	Bolochoweckyj	MacKay+	I Campbell	Masson	McWalter*	Ballantyne	Templeman	Fraser	Hynd	R Campbell*	Anderson+	Watson	Court	Ferguson	Pascazio	Miller
17/09/2016	L	A	Edinburgh City	1	0	Fleming	Steeves	Bolochoweckyj	R Campbell	I Campbell	Masson	McWalter	Ferguson*	Templeman	Fraser	Webster	Hynd*	Anderson	McKay	Court	Ballantyne	Pascazio	Miller
24/09/2016	L	H	Berwick Rangers	0	0	Fleming	Steeves	Bolochoweckyj*	R Campbell	I Campbell	Watson&	McWalter	Ferguson+	Templeman	Fraser	Webster	Anderson*	Hynd+	Ballantyne&	Court	MacKay	Pascazio	Miller
01/10/2016	L	A	Forfar Athletic	3	1	Fleming	McDonald*	Bolochoweckyj	Anderson	I Campbell	Masson	McWalter	Ferguson+	Templeman	Fraser&	Webster	Ballantyne*	Hynd+	Court&	Watson	MacKay	Pascazio	Miller
15/10/2016	L	H	Elgin City	0	5	Fleming	McDonald	Bolochoweckyj	Anderson	I Campbell	Masson*	McWalter	Ferguson&	Templeman+	Fraser	Webster	Ballantyne*	Court+	Hynd&	Watson	R Campbell	Pascazio	Miller
22/10/2016	SC2	A	Preston Athletic	3	0	Fleming	McDonald	Bolochoweckyj	Ballantyne	I Campbell	Masson+	McWalter	Ferguson*	Templeman&	Fraser	Webster	Court*	Hynd+	Watson&	Lennie	McKay	Pascazio	Miller
05/11/2016	L	H	Edinburgh City	0	1	Fleming	Anderson	Steeves	Ballantyne	I Campbell	Masson	McWalter	Ferguson+	Templeman*	Court	Webster&	R Campbell*	Hynd+	Watson&	Lennie	Pascazio	Miller	
08/11/2016	L	A	Annan Athletic	3	2	Fleming	Anderson	Steeves	Ballantyne	I Campbell	Masson	McWalter*	R Campbell+	Watson&	Fraser	Webster	Bolochoweckyj*	Templeman+	Court&	Lennie	Pascazio	Ferguson	Miller
12/11/2016	L	A	Cowdenbeath	0	2	Fleming	Bolochoweckyj	Steeves	Ballantyne	I Campbell	Masson	McWalter	R Campbell+	Watson&	Templeman*	Webster	Court*	Lennie+	Fraser&	Anderson	Pascazio	Ferguson	Miller
19/11/2016	L	H	Forfar Athletic	1	1	Fleming	Bolochoweckyj	Steeves	MacDonald	Anderson	Masson	McWalter*	Ferguson	Court	Fraser+	Webster	Lennie*	Templeman+	R Campbell	I Campbell	Pascazio	Watson	Miller
29/11/2016	SC3	A	Queen's Park	0	2	Fleming	Bolochoweckyj	Steeves	MacDonald	Anderson+	Masson	McWalter	Ferguson	Court*	Fraser	Webster&	Templeman*	Watson+	R Campbell&	I Campbell	Pascazio	Lennie	Miller
03/12/2016	L	A	Elgin City	1	4	Fleming	Bolochoweckyj	Steeves	MacDonald	Ballantyne	Masson	Watson*	Ferguson+	Templeman	Fraser	Webster	R Campbell*	McWalter+	Thomson	Anderson	Pascazio	Lennie	Miller
10/12/2016	L	H	Clyde	2	1	Miller	Bolochoweckyj	Steeves	MacDonald	Ballantyne+	Masson	Watson*	Ferguson	Templeman*	Fraser&	Webster	R Campbell*	Anderson+	Court&	McWalter	Pascazio	Lennie	Fleming
17/12/2016	L	A	Berwick Rangers	2	1	Miller	Bolochoweckyj	Steeves	MacDonald	Ballantyne	Masson	Watson	Ferguson	McWalter*	Fraser+	Webster	Court*	Templeman+	R Campbell	Anderson	Pascazio	Lennie	Fleming
24/12/2016	L	H	Stirling Albion	2	2	Miller	Bolochoweckyj	Steeves	MacDonald	Ballantyne	Masson	Watson	Ferguson	Templeman*	Fraser	Webster	Court*	McWalter	R Campbell	Anderson	Pascazio	Lennie	Fleming
02/01/2017	L	A	Arbroath	0	0	Miller	Bolochoweckyj*	Steeves	Anderson	Ballantyne	Masson	Watson	Ferguson	Templeman+	Fraser&	Webster	Pascazio*	R Campbell+	Court&	McWalter	Wallace	Lennie	Fleming
07/01/2017	L	H	Elgin City	0	3	Miller	Bolochoweckyj	Steeves	Anderson	Ballantyne	Masson	Watson+	Ferguson	Templeman*	Fraser&	Webster	R Campbell*	Thomas+	Court&	McWalter	Pascazio	Lennie	Fleming
21/01/2017	L	H	Cowdenbeath	2	1	Miller	Pascazio	Steeves	Anderson*	Ballantyne	Thomas+	McWalter	Ferguson	Templeman&	Smith	Webster	MacDonald*	Callaghan+	Fraser&	R Campbell	Gammie	Thomson	Fleming
28/01/2017	L	H	Berwick Rangers	2	1	Miller	Pascazio	Steeves	McDonald	Ballantyne	Masson	McWalter	Ferguson&	Callaghan+	R Campbell*	Webster	Templeman*	Anderson+	Thomas&	Thomson	Bridgeford	Fleming	
04/02/2017	L	A	Stirling Albion	2	1	Miller	Pascazio	Steeves	McDonald	Ballantyne	Masson	McWalter*	Ferguson	Callaghan+	Templeman&	Webster	Smith*	Hay+	Thomas&	Anderson	R Campbell	Allan	Fleming
11/02/2017	L	H	Arbroath	1	3	Miller	Pascazio	Steeves	McDonald	Ballantyne	Masson+	Allan	Ferguson*	Smith	Templeman	Webster	Hay*	Fraser+	McWalter	R Campbell	Callaghan	Bolochoweckyj	Fleming
18/02/2017	L	A	Edinburgh City	1	1	Miller	Pascazio&	Steeves	Bolochoweckyj	Ballantyne	Masson	Allan*	Callaghan	Smith	Fraser	Webster+	Templeman*	Ferguson+	Hay&	Thomas	Anderson	R Campbell	Fleming
25/02/2017	L	A	Forfar Athletic	0	0	Miller	Pascazio	Steeves*	Bolochoweckyj	Ballantyne	Masson	McWalter	Ferguson&	Templeman	Fraser	Webster+	Allan*	Hay+	Smith&	Thomas	Anderson	Callaghan	Fleming
28/02/2017	L	A	Clyde	2	1	Miller	Pascazio	Thomas&	Bolochoweckyj	Ballantyne	Masson	McWalter	Callaghan	Templeman+	Hay*	Smith	Webster*	Fraser+	McDonald&	Allan	R Campbell	Ferguson	Fleming
04/03/2017	L	H	Annan Athletic	2	3	Miller	Pascazio*	Steeves	Bolochoweckyj	Ballantyne	Masson	McWalter+	Fraser	Templeman	Hay	Smith&	McDonald*	Callaghan+	Webster&	Allan	R Campbell	Thomas	Fleming
11/03/2017	L	H	Stirling Albion	1	3	Fleming	Watson*	Steeves	Bolochoweckyj	Ballantyne	Masson	McDonald&	Fraser	Templeman	Hay	Smith+	Webster*	Callaghan+	McWalter&	Allan	I Campbell	Thomas	Miller
18/03/2017	L	A	Cowdenbeath	2	0	Fleming	Watson*	Steeves	Bolochoweckyj	Ballantyne	Masson&	McDonald	Fraser+	Templeman	Allan	Callaghan*	I Campbell*	Smith+	Thomas&	Webster	Hay	Pascazio	Miller
25/03/2017	L	A	Arbroath	1	0	Fleming	Watson	Steeves	Bolochoweckyj	Ballantyne*	Masson	McDonald	Fraser	Templeman&	Allan	I Campbell+	McWalter*	Thomas+	Smith&	Webster	Hay	Callaghan	Miller
01/04/2017	L	H	Edinburgh City	3	0	Fleming	Watson&	Steeves	Bolochoweckyj	Ballantyne	Masson	Webster	Fraser*	Templeman+	Allan	Hay	Smith*	I Campbell+	Callaghan&	McWalter	R Campbell	McDonald	Miller
08/04/2017	L	A	Elgin City	1	1	Fleming	Watson	Steeves	Bolochoweckyj	Ballantyne	McWalter*	Webster+	Fraser	Templeman	Allan	Smith	Thomas*	Hay+	Callaghan	Pascazio	R Campbell	I Campbell	Miller
15/04/2017	L	H	Forfar Athletic	1	0	Fleming	Watson	Steeves	Bolochoweckyj*	Ballantyne	Masson	Webster+	Fraser&	Templeman	Allan	Smith	I Campbell*	Hay+	Ferguson&	Callaghan	McWalter	Thomas	Miller
22/04/2017	L	A	Berwick Rangers	1	0	Fleming	Watson+	Steeves	I Campbell	Ballantyne	Masson&	Webster*	Fraser	Templeman	Allan	Smith	Ferguson*	Thomas+	McWalter&	Callaghan	Hay	Pascazio	Miller
29/04/2017	L	A	Annan Athletic	1	5	Fleming	Watson&	Steeves	I Campbell	Ballantyne	Masson*	Hay	Fraser+	Templeman	Allan	Smith	McWalter*	Callaghan+	Pascazio&	Webster	Ferguson	R Campbell	Miller
06/05/2017	L	H	Clyde	1	1	Fleming	Watson	Steeves	Pascazio	Ballantyne	Masson*	Hay+	Fraser&	Templeman	Allan	Smith	Ferguson*	Webster+	Callaghan&	McWalter	R Campbell	Miller	
10/05/2017	PO	H	Peterhead	1	1	Fleming	Watson&	Steeves	Pascazio	Ballantyne	Callaghan	Webster+	Fraser*	Templeman	Allan	Smith	Masson*	Hay+	I Campbell&	McWalter	R Campbell	Ferguson	Miller
13/05/2017	PO	A	Peterhead	0	3	Fleming	Watson	Steeves	Pascazio	Ballantyne	Masson	Webster+	Callaghan*	Templeman&	Allan	Smith	Ferguson*	McWalter+	Hay&	I Campbell	R Campbell	Miller	

						L			SC			LC			CC						
			SQ	Nat	Pos	A	S	G	A	S	G	A	S	G	A	S	G	UNS			
Surname	**First Name**	**DOB**																	**Signed**	**Previous Club**	**Notes**
Allan	Matthew	17/01/1996		SCO	M	12	1											4	2017	Dundee (OL)	Jan-May 2017
Anderson	Gregor	02/12/1994		SCO	D	10	5		1			1			2			12	2016	Tayport	OL to Tayport Mar-May, Freed May 2017
Ballantyne	Cammy	13/04/1997		SCO	M	29	3	1	1									1	2016	Dundee United (OL)	Aug 16-May 2017
Bolochoweckyj	Michael	04/05/1984		SCO	D	25	1	3	2			3		1				2	2016	Clyde	
Bridgeford	Stuart																	1			
Callaghan	Liam	10/10/1994		SCO	M	7	6											6	2017	Arbroath	
Campbell	Ross	17/03/1987		SCO	F	7	8			1		4			1	1		16	2015	East Fife	Retired May 2017
Campbell	Iain	28/06/1985		SCO	D	15	4	1	1						2			5	2016	Forfar Athletic	
Court	Jonny	30/03/1996		SCO	F	2	9	1	1	1	1						1	3	2016	Raith Rovers (OL)	Aug 16-May 2017
Ferguson	Ryan	15/01/1994		SCO	D	19	6	2	2				2		2			9	2015	Brechin City	
Fleming	Allan	06/03/1984		SCO	GK	22			2			1			2			19	2016	Arbroath	
Fraser	Gary	20/06/1986		SCO	F	30	4	11	2		1	4			1				2015	Jeanfield Swifts	
Gammie	Ryan																	1			
Harwood	Adam	17/01/1995		NIR	D								1					8	2015	Dundee United	OL to Carnoustie Panmure Sep-May
Hay	Kerr	16/01/1996		SCO	F	6	8	4										3	2017	Forfar Athletic	
Hegarty	Chris	24/07/1984		SCO	D							3							2016	Buckie Thistle	Freed May 2017
Hester	Lloyd	12/05/1998		SCO	F													2	2015	Montrose Youth	OL to Arbroath Vics Sep-Jan, Montrose Roselea
																					Jan-May, Freed May
Hynd	Scott	10/08/1997		SCO	F	1	5			1									2016	Alloa (OL)	Aug-Nov 2016
Lennie	Ross	10/11/1995		**SCO**	M	1	5						3		1	1		11	2016	Bathgate Thistle	Freed Jan 2017, joined Dundonald BB
Mackay	David	17/01/1998		SCO	D	1												4	2016	Raith Rovers (OL)	Aug-Oct 2016
Masson	Terry	03/07/1988		SCO	M	33	1	1	2			4			2		1		2010	Carnoustie Panmure	
McDonald	Callum	31/05/1983		SCO	D	16	3	1	2									1	2016	Gartcairn Juniors	
McLeod	Kyle	19/02/1997		SCO	F								1					7	2014	Montrose Youth	OL to Forfar Albion Sep-Oct Montrose
																					Roselea Oct-May, Freed May
McWalter	Kieran	06/10/1995		SCO	M	21	6		2			4			2			9	2016	Arbroath	Freed May 2017
Miller	Jordan	22/11/1996		SCO	GK	16						3						27	2016	St Johnstone	
Milne	Declan	06/11/1997		SCO	F		1									1			2014	Montrose Youth	OL to Buckie Thistle Nov-May, Freed May 2017
Pascazio	Greg	10/04/1996		SCO	D	12	2	1				4				1		23	2015	Rangers	
Smith	Matty	13/03/1997		SCO	F	13	5	2											2017	Dundee United (OL)	Jan-May 2017
Steeves	Andrew	25/07/1994		SCO	D	34		1	1			4			2				2015	Forfar Athletic	
Templeman	Chris	12/01/1980		SCO	F	31	5	11	1	1	1	3			2				2016	Forfar Athletic	
Thomas	Dylan	10/02/1997		WAL	M	2	7											5	2017	Aberdeen (OL)	Jan-May 2017
Thomson	Kieran																	3			
Wallace	Matthew	28/02/1998																1	2016	Montrose Youths	
Watson	Paul	22/11/1985		SCO	M	23	1	2		2		4				1		6	2012	St Andrews United	
Webster	Graham	15/05/1992		SCO	M	30	4	2	2			2	1		2		1	4	2012	Dundee	
Willox	Kyle	28/02/1998		SCO	F										1	1		4	2016	Aberdeen East End	OL to Inverurie L Oct-Jan, Deveronvale Jan-May
Own Goals								1													
NEW SIGNINGS																					
Redman	Jamie				M														2017	Peterhead	
Brett	Dean				D														2017	Bonnyrigg Rose	
Fotheringham	Martyn				M														2017	Forfar Athletic	
Cavanagh	Danny				F														2017	Broughty Athletic	
Allan	Matty				D														2017	Dundee	
Johnston	Craig				F														2017	Cowdenbeath	

Source of Birthdates: Montrose FC website / Transfermarkt.com

Morton FC 2016/17

Founded	1874
Ground	Cappielow Park
Postcode	PA15 2TY
Tel	01475 723571
Capacity	11589
Closest Railway Station	Cartsdyke
Record Attendance	23500 v Celtic, 29/4/1922
Record Win	11-0 v Carfin Shamrock, SC, 13/11/1886
Record Defeat	1-10 v Port Glasgow, Lge, 5/5/1894 /
	v St Bernards Lge 14/10/1933
Most League Goals in a Season	58 Allan McGraw, 1963/4
Chairman	Douglas Rae
Chief Executive	Gillian Donaldson
Manager	Jim Duffy
Assistant Manager	Craig McPherson
Colours 2016/17 Top	Blue and White Hoops
Shorts	White
Sponsor	Millions
Manufacturer	Nike
Change Colours 2016/17 Top	Yellow with blue check
Shorts	Yellow
Nicknames	Ton
Web	www.gmfc.net
Match Programme 2016/17	£2

Jim Duffy fully deserves the reputation as a "wily old fox" on the basis of Morton's results in recent seasons.

2016/17 saw them reach a national Cup Semi Final for the first time in donkey's years. They lost to Aberdeen but the status that goes with a Semi Final game at Hampden should not be underestimated.

The Cappielow club also made a genuine promotion bid. They were never likely to win the League but they had a Play Off place sewn up with something to spare. Fans who were unhappy at the outcome of the Play Offs would do well to remember where Morton were not that long ago—the transformation of the club, on and off the field, has been impressive.

Duffy's uses the transfer market and in particular the loan sector very well.

PREDICTION FOR 2017/18

It will be hard to match the levels of 2016/17. Morton may slip back a little buit will still be mid table.

The match against Port Glasgow Athletic at Cappielow on 8/4/1899, a Renfrewshire Cup tie, ended in one of the worst riots ever witnessed in Scottish football. The riot was recalled in an article in the Sunday Mail some 80 years later. Hundreds of spectators invaded the field and fought a bloody battle with police. There were 43 arrests, allegations of police brutality and a virtual state of war between the towns of Greenock and Port Glasgow. Contemporary reports suggest that the trouble started amongst the Port Glasgow supporters at the east (Sinclair Street) end of the ground. When Morton went 2-0 up they attempted to invade the field using bricks, bottles and wooden staves ripped from the fencing around the ground as weapons. The game ended in a 4-3 win for Morton. Only 5 arrests were made at the ground but dozens of police were injured. A posse of police officers headed out in cabs to Port Glasgow later that night. They arrested 18 suspected rioters. Similar night-time raids continued for the next week. None of the alleged rioters was allowed bail when they appeared in court. Both teams exacerbated the situation by issuing statements decrying the behaviour of the other's supporters. Ultimately 24 of the accused saw their charges dropped although the ringleaders of the rioting were jailed. One 14-year old, convicted of throwing a stone at the police was sentenced "to twelve stripes from the birching rod".

Morton have appeared in European competition on one occasion - in the Inter Cities Fairs Cup of 1968/9. They were drawn against and lost to Chelsea - so although they have played "in Europe" they have not actually played a competitive game outside the UK.

The Norseman pub at the bottom of Sinclair Street is so-named because of the influx of Scandinavian players to Cappielow in the 1960s and 1970s. Morton manager Hal Stewart was a pioneer in recruiting overseas players, many of whom were sold on at a considerable profit.

Date	Comp	H/A	Opponents	F	A		HT		Referee	Crowd	Scorers
16/07/2016	LC	A	Albion Rovers	0	0	4-3p	0	0	C Napier	461	
19/07/2016	LC	H	Clyde	1	0		0	0	J McKendrick	931	O'Ware
23/07/2016	LC	A	Kilmarnock	2	0		1	0	S McLean	3020	Oliver, Quitongo
30/07/2016	LC	H	Berwick Rangers	2	0		2	0	R Madden	1044	Lindsay, Quitongo
06/08/2016	L	A	St Mirren	1	1		1	0	S McLean	4997	O'Ware
09/08/2016	LC1	A	Hamilton Accies	2	1		0	1	S Finnie	1112	Forbes, Quitongo
13/08/2016	L	H	Falkirk	1	1		1	0	J Beaton	2079	Kilday
20/08/2016	L	H	Dumbarton	1	1		0	1	M Northcroft	1586	Oyenuga
27/08/2016	L	A	Hibernian	0	4		0	2	A Muir	14508	
03/09/2016	CC3	A	Queen's Park	0	2		0	1	G Duncan	1085	
10/09/2016	L	A	Ayr United	1	2		0	0	J McKendrick	1441	Forbes
17/09/2016	L	H	Dunfermline Athletic	2	1		1	1	K Clancy	1756	Oliver, Quitongo
20/09/2016	LC2	H	Dundee United	2	1		2	0	A Dallas	2149	Quitongo, O'Ware
24/09/2016	L	A	Dundee United	1	2		0	0	B Cook	5829	Dillon og
01/10/2016	L	H	Raith Rovers	1	0		1	0	C Charleston	1528	Forbes
15/10/2016	L	A	Queen of the South	5	0		3	0	S Kirkland	1695	Forbes, McDonagh, Oliver, Quitongo, O'Ware
22/10/2016	LCSF	N	Aberdeen	0	2	*	0	0	K Clancy	16183	
29/10/2016	L	H	Ayr United	2	1		0	1	M Northcroft	1859	O'Ware, Oliver
01/11/2016	L	H	St Mirren	3	1		2	0	W Collum	3378	O'Ware, Forbes, Oliver
05/11/2016	L	A	Falkirk	1	1		0	0	G Aitken	4432	KIlday
12/11/2016	L	A	Dumbarton	2	0		0	0	D Robertson	1147	Russell, Oyenuga
19/11/2016	L	H	Dundee United	0	0		0	0	C Allan	2578	
03/12/2016	SC3	A	Beith Juniors	6	0		3	0	J McKendrick	1693	Forbes, Tidser, McDonagh, Lindsay, O'Ware 2
10/12/2016	L	A	Dunfermline Athletic	1	2		1	2	S Finnie	3101	Nesbitt
17/12/2016	L	H	Hibernian	1	1		0	0	S McLean	2156	Oliver
24/12/2016	L	H	Queen of the South	1	0		1	0	B Cook	1628	O'Ware
31/12/2016	L	A	St Mirren	1	1		0	1	N Walsh	4902	Lamie
07/01/2016	L	H	Dumbarton	2	1		1	0	J Beaton	2094	Buchanan og, Tidser
14/01/2016	L	H	Raith Rovers	2	0		1	0	G Duncan	1957	Forbes, Shankland
21/01/2017	SC4	H	Falkirk	2	0		1	0	G Aitken	2439	Lindsay, Forbes
28/01/2017	L	A	Ayr United	4	1		3	1	D Robertson	1576	Forbes 2, Oliver 2
04/02/2017	L	A	Queen of the South	0	3		0	0	B Madden	1588	
07/02/2017	L	A	Raith Rovers	1	0		0	0	G Duncan	1161	Kilday
12/02/2017	SC5	A	Rangers	1	2		1	1	A Dallas	30295	Tidser
18/02/2017	L	H	Falkirk	2	2		1	1	G Aitken	2397	O'Ware, Forbes
25/02/2017	L	A	Dundee United	1	1		1	0	K Clancy	6065	Kilday
11/03/2017	L	H	Queen of the South	1	0		0	0	C Charleston	1451	Forbes
18/03/2017	L	A	Falkirk	1	0		0	0	A Muir	4584	Oyenuga
25/03/2017	L	H	Dunfermline Athletic	0	1		0	1	M Northcroft	2670	
29/03/2017	L	A	Hibernian	0	0		0	0	N Walsh	15149	
01/04/2017	L	A	Dumbarton	0	1		0	0	J Beaton	1323	
08/04/2017	L	H	Hibernian	1	1		0	1	B Madden	4229	Shankland
11/04/2017	L	H	St Mirren	1	4		1	1	S Finnie	4609	Murdoch
15/04/2017	L	A	Raith Rovers	0	2		0	1	A Newlands	1720	
22/04/2017	L	H	Ayr United	1	1		1	1	S Kirkland	2390	Shankland
29/04/2017	L	A	Dunfermline Athletic	1	3		1	1	E Anderson	3339	Shankland
06/05/2017	L	H	Dundee United	1	1		0	0	J Beaton	2158	Oyenuga
10/05/2017	PO	H	Dundee United	1	2		1	0	W Collum	3306	O'Ware
13/05/2017	PO	A	Dundee United	0	3		0	0	A Dallas	6606	

* at Hampden

FRIENDLIES / OTHER GAMES						
30/06/2016	A	Cumbernauld Colts	0	3		U20
05/07/2016	A	Livingston	2	2		
09/07/2016	H	Partick Thistle	1	2		
26/07/2016	H	Swansea City U21	1	2		
28/07/2016	A	Largs Thistle	1	4		U20

Surname	First Name	DOB	SQ	Nat	Pos	L A	L S	L G	SC A	SC S	SC G	LC A	LC S	LC G	CC A	CC S	CC G	UNS	Signed	Previous Club	Notes	Contract
Anderson	David	12/02/1999	13	SCO	M														2016	Morton Youths		
Armour	Ben	17/04/1998	23	SCO	F		1											1	2016	Queen's Park		End Dec 2017
Connor	Greig	10/11/1999		SCO	GK														2017	Morton Youths		
Docherty	Blair	23/06/1999	36	SCO	F														2016	Morton Youths		
Donnelly	Luke	20/01/1996		SCO		2	4			1								8	2017	Celtic (OL)	Feb-May	[redacted]
Doyle	Michael	01/08/1991	6	SCO	D	28	3		2			7			1			6	2016	St Johnstone		End 2017/18
Duffy	Mitchell	08/02/1999	34	SCO	D														2016	Morton Youths		
Eardley	Ben	19/12/1999	40	SCO	M														2016	Morton Youths		
Forbes	Ross	03/03/1989	8	SCO	M	35		9	3		2	6		1	1			1	2015	Dunfermline Athletic		End 2017/18
Gaston	Derek	18/04/1987	1	SCO	GK	30	1		3			2						8	2012	Albion Rovers		End 2017/18
Gunning	Gavin	26/01/1991	5	ROI	D	10						2						2	2016	Unattached	ex Dundee Utd, Freed Jan 2017 joined Grimsby T	[redacted]
Halliwell	Bryn	01/10/1980		ENG	GK	1													2017	Trialist	Gartcairn JFC	[redacted]
Hynes	Darren	12/01/1999	41	SCO	D														2016	Morton Youths		
Kilday	Lee	04/02/1992	2	SCO	D	18	4	4	3			3	2		1			7	2014	Hamilton Accies		End 2017/18
Lamie	Ricky	26/06/1993	3	SCO	D	25	4	1	3			4						4	2014	Airdrieonians		End 2017/18
Langan	Ruaridh	15/06/1998	33	SCO	M													2	2015	Morton Youths	OL to Neilston Jan 2017	End Dec 2017
Lindsay	Jamie	11/10/1995	10	SCO	M	31	2		3		2	4		1				2	2016	Celtic (OL)	Aug 16-May 2017	[redacted]
McAleer	Caolan	19/08/1993	16	NIR	F		6					2	3		1			6	2016	Airdrieonians	Freed Dec 2016, joined Finn Harps	[redacted]
McDonagh	Jamie	08/05/1996	18	ENG	D	21	7	1	1	3	1	5	2			1		6	2016	Sheffield United	Released May 2017	[redacted]
McGowan	Jamie	29/01/1997	30	SCO	GK	1	1											23	2015	Morton Youths		End 2017/18
McNeil	Andy	19/01/1987	19	SCO	GK	6	1					5			1			14	2016	Alloa	Freed Jan 2017 joined Guangzhou R and F	[redacted]
McWaters	Alex	22/02/1998	31	SCO	F														2015	Morton Youths	OL to Largs Thistle Aug-Jan, Freed May 2017	[redacted]
Miller	Scott	14/11/1999	35	SCO	F														2016	Morton Youths		
Mitchell	John	21/02/1998	32	SCO	D													2	2015	Morton Youths	Ol to Greenock Juniors Dec-Jan, Freed May 2017	[redacted]
Murdoch	Andy	30/09/1995	21	SCO	M	28	2	1	2			1						2	2016	Rangers		End 2017/18
Nesbitt	Aidan	05/02/1997	11	SCO		25	6	1	2			1	2					2	2016	Celtic (OL)	Aug 16-May 2017	[redacted]
Oliver	Gary	14/07/1995	7	SCO	F	31	1	7	2			7		1	1			2	2016	Queen of the South		End 2017/18
Orr	Thomas	13/01/1997	22	SCO	F		3											7	2014	Morton Youths	OL to Livingston Jul-Aug, BSC Glasgow Jan-May, Freed May	[redacted]
O'Ware	Thomas	20/03/1993	4	SCO	D	37		7	3		2	7		2	1				2011	Bonnyton Thistle		End 2017/18
Oyenuga	Kudus	18/03/1993	9	ENG/NIG	F	9	17	4				2			1			3	2016	Hartlepool United	Released May 2017 joined Chelmsford City	[redacted]
Pepper	Conor	04/05/1994	15	ROI	M														2014	Inverness CT	Released May 2017	[redacted]
Purdue	Jack	01/01/2000	38	SCO	M														2016	Morton Youths		
Quitongo	Jai	14/09/1997	24	SCO/ANG	F	14		2	1			5	2	4		1		1	2015	Aberdeen Youths		End 2017/18
Russell	Mark	22/03/1996	17	SCO	D	29	3	1	3			4	1					5	2013	Morton Youths		End 2017/18
Scullion	Jon	16/03/1995	14	SCO	F	1	9					1	2			1		31	2014	St Mirren	Released May 2017	[redacted]
Shankland	Lawrence	10/08/1995	16	SCO	F	14	4	4											2017	Aberdeen (OL)	Jan-May 2017	[redacted]
Stevenson	Dylan	17/02/1997	21	SCO	F							1	1					3	2014	Morton Youths	Freed Aug 2016 joined Auchinleck Talbot	[redacted]
Strapp	Lewis	26/11/1999	39	SCO	D	2						2			1			29	2015	Linwood Rangers		End 2017/18
Tennent	John	27/08/1997	23	SCO	D													5	2014	Morton Youths	OL to Cumbernauld Colts Aug-Nov, Freed Jan 2017	[redacted]
Tidser	Michael	15/01/1990	12	SCO	M	17	13	1	2		2	5			1			4	2015	Rotherham United		End 2018/19
Tiffoney	Scott	26/08/1998	37	SCO	F	3	6					1	6		1			16	2015	Morton Youths	OL to Clyde Dec-Jan	End 2017/18
Own Goals								2														
NEW SIGNINGS																						
Harkins	Gary				M														2017	Ayr United		End 2017/18
McHugh	Bob				F														2017	Falkirk		End 2018/19
Thomson	Robert																		2017	Dumbarton		End 2018/19
Barr	Darren																		2017	Dumbarton	Youth Team Manager	

Source of Birthdates: Morton Fc website and transfermarkt.com

Date	Comp	H/A	Opponents	F	A		1	2	3	4	5	6	7	8	9	10	11	12	13	14	15	16	17	18
16/07/2016	LC	A	Albion Rovers	0	0	4-3p	McNeil	Kilday	O'Ware	Forbes	Doyle	Strapp	Tidser	Stevenson*	Oliver	Scullion&	McDonagh+	McAleer*	Quitongo+	Tiffoney&	Lamie	Tennant	Gaston	
19/07/2016	LC	H	Clyde	1	0		McNeil	Lamie	O'Ware	Forbes	Doyle	Strapp+	Tidser&	McAleer*	Tiffoney	Oliver	McDonagh	Quitongo*	Russell+	Kilday&	Stevenson	Tennant	Scullion	Gaston
23/07/2016	LC	A	Kilmarnock	2	0		McNeil	Lamie	O'Ware	Forbes	Doyle	Kilday	Tidser	McAleer*	Russell	Oliver&	Quitongo+	Tiffoney*	McDonagh+	Scullion&	Stevenson	Tennant	Strapp	Gaston
30/07/2016	LC	H	Berwick Rangers	2	0		Gaston	Lamie	O'Ware	Forbes	Doyle	Lindsay+	Tidser	McDonagh*	Russell	Oliver&	Quitongo	Tiffoney*	Scullion+	Stevenson&	Kilday	McAleer	Strapp	McNeill
06/08/2016	L	A	St Mirren	1	1		Gaston	Lamie	O'Ware	Forbes	Doyle	Lindsay*	Tidser	McDonagh	Kilday	Oliver&	Quitongo+	Russell*	Tiffoney+	McAleer&	Stevenson	Scullion	Strapp	McNeill
09/08/2016	LC1	A	Hamilton Accies	2	1		Gaston	Lamie	O'Ware	Forbes	Doyle	Lindsay	Tidser	Nesbitt&	Kilday	Oliver+	Quitongo*	McDonagh*	McAleer+	Tiffoney&	Tennant	Scullion	Strapp	McNeill
13/08/2016	L	H	Falkirk	1	1		Gaston	Lamie	O'Ware	Forbes	Doyle	Lindsay*	Tidser	Nesbitt+	Kilday	Oliver	Quitongo&	Oyenuga*	McDonagh+	McAleer&	Tiffoney	Scullion	Strapp	McNeill
20/08/2016	L	H	Dumbarton	1	1		Gaston	Lamie	O'Ware	Forbes	Doyle	Lindsay*	Tidser	Tiffoney	Kilday	Oliver+	Quitongo	Oyenuga*	Scullion+	McAleer	Russell	McDonagh	Strapp	McNeill
27/08/2016	L	A	Hibernian	0	4		Gaston+	Russell	O'Ware	Forbes	Doyle	Lindsay	Tidser	Nesbitt	Kilday	Oliver&	Quitongo*	Oyenuga*	McNeill+	McAleer&	Tiffoney	McDonagh	Scullion	Tennant
03/09/2016	CC3	A	Queen's Park	0	2		McNeil	Strapp	O'Ware	Forbes	Doyle&	McAleer*	Tidser	Tiffoney+	Kilday	Oliver	Oyenuga	Scullion*	Quitongo+	McDonagh&	Lindsay	Russell	Orr	Gaston
10/09/2016	L	A	Ayr United	1	2		McNeil	Russell	O'Ware	Forbes	Doyle	Lindsay	Lamie*	Quitongo	Kilday	Oliver&	Oyenuga+	Nesbitt*	McDonagh+	Orr&	Scullion	McAleer	Tiffoney	McGowan
17/09/2016	L	H	Dunfermline Athletic	2	1		McNeil	Gunning	O'Ware	Forbes	Doyle	McDonagh	Nesbitt+	Quitongo	Kilday*	Oliver&	Oyenuga	Lindsay*	Tiffoney+	Orr&	Scullion	McAleer	Strapp	McGowan
20/09/2016	LC2	H	Dundee United	2	1		McNeil	Gunning	O'Ware	Forbes	Doyle	McDonagh	Russell	Quitongo+	Lindsay	Oliver&	Oyenuga*	McAleer*	Nesbitt+	Tiffoney&	Scullion	Strapp	Gaston	
24/09/2016	L	A	Dundee United	1	2		McNeil	Gunning	O'Ware	Forbes	Doyle	McDonagh	Russell	Quitongo	Lindsay*	Oliver	Nesbitt+	Tiffoney*	Murdoch+	Orr	Scullion	Strapp	Gaston	
01/10/2016	L	H	Raith Rovers	1	0		McNeil&	Gunning*	O'Ware	Forbes	Doyle	McDonagh	Russell	Quitongo	Lindsay	Oliver	Nesbitt+	Murdoch*	Tiffoney+	Gaston&	Scullion	Strapp	Orr	
15/10/2016	L	A	Queen of the South	5	0		Gaston	Murdoch	O'Ware	Forbes&	Doyle	McDonagh	Russell	Quitongo+	Lindsay	Oliver	Nesbitt*	Oyenuga*	Scullion+	Tiffoney&	McNeill	Mitchell	Orr	
22/10/2016	LCSF	N	Aberdeen	0	2	*	McNeil	Gunning	O'Ware	Oyenuga*	Doyle	McDonagh+	Russell	Quitongo	Lindsay&	Oliver	Murdoch	Nesbitt*	Tiffoney+	Kilday&	Lamie	Tidser	Scullion	Gaston
29/10/2016	L	H	Ayr United	2	1		McNeil	Lamie	O'Ware	Forbes	Nesbitt+	McDonagh	Russell	Quitongo	Lindsay	Oliver&	Murdoch*	Scullion*	Oyenuga+	Doyle&	McAleer	Orr	Strapp	McGowan
01/11/2016	L	H	St Mirren	3	1		Gaston	Lamie	O'Ware	Forbes+	Nesbitt	McDonagh	Russell	Quitongo*	Lindsay	Oliver	Murdoch	Oyenuga*	Tidser+	Doyle	Kilday	Gunning	Scullion	McNeill
05/11/2016	L	A	Falkirk	1	1		Gaston	Gunning	O'Ware	Forbes	Doyle	Oyenuga*	Russell	Quitongo&	Lindsay	Oliver	Murdoch+	Nesbitt*	Kilday+	Tidser&	Lamie	McDonagh	Scullion	McNeill
12/11/2016	L	A	Dumbarton	2	0		Gaston	Gunning	O'Ware	Forbes+	Lamie	McDonagh&	Russell	Oyenuga*	Lindsay	Oliver	Murdoch	McAleer*	Tidser+	Kilday&	Quitongo	Doyle	Scullion	McNeill
19/11/2016	L	H	Dundee United	0	0		Gaston	Gunning	O'Ware	Forbes	Lamie	Doyle	Russell	Quitongo*	Lindsay	Oliver	Murdoch+	Oyenuga*	Tidser+	Nesbitt	McAleer	Strapp	McNeill	
03/12/2016	SC3	A	Beith Juniors	6	0		Gaston	Kilday	O'Ware	Forbes+	Lamie	Tidser&	Russell	Quitongo*	Lindsay	Oliver	McDonagh	Oyenuga*	McAleer+	Nesbitt&	Gunning	Doyle	Murdoch	McNeill
10/12/2016	L	A	Dunfermline Athletic	1	2		Gaston	Gunning	O'Ware	Forbes	Murdoch&	Nesbitt	Russell	Quitongo+	Lindsay*	Oliver	McDonagh	Tidser*	Oyenuga+	McAleer&	Kilday	Doyle	Lamie	McNeill
17/12/2016	L	H	Hibernian	1	1		Gaston	Gunning	O'Ware	Forbes	Lamie	Tidser	Russell	Murdoch+	Oyenuga*	Oliver	McDonagh	Kilday*	Doyle+	Nesbitt	Scullion	Strapp	McNeill	
24/12/2016	L	H	Queen of the South	1	0		McNeill	Gunning	O'Ware	Forbes	Doyle	Lindsay	Russell	Murdoch+	Nesbit+	Oliver	McDonagh*	Lamie*	Tidser+	Kilday	Scullion	Strapp	McGowan	
31/12/2016	L	A	St Mirren	1	1		Gaston	Gunning	O'Ware	Forbes	Doyle	Lindsay+	Russell	Murdoch&	Lamie	Oliver*	McDonagh	Oyenuga*	Nesbitt+	Tidser&	Scullion	Strapp	Kilday	McNeill
07/01/2016	L	H	Dumbarton	2	1		Gaston	Kilday	O'Ware	Forbes	Doyle	Lindsay	Russell	Murdoch	Tidser	Nesbit+	Oyenuga*	Scullion*	Orr+	Oliver	Tiffoney	Strapp	McGowan	
14/01/2016	L	H	Raith Rovers	2	0		Gaston	Kilday	O'Ware	Forbes	Doyle	Lindsay	Russell	Murdoch	Oliver	Nesbit*	Shankland+	Tidser*	Lamie+	Scullion&	Tiffoney	Strapp	Orr	McGowan
21/01/2017	SC4	H	Falkirk	2	0		Gaston	Kilday	O'Ware	Forbes	Doyle	Lindsay	Russell	Murdoch	Oliver	Nesbit*	Lamie	McDonagh*	Tidser	Scullion	Tiffoney	Strapp	Orr	McGowan
28/01/2017	L	A	Ayr United	4	1		Gaston	Kilday	O'Ware	Forbes&	Doyle	Shankland+	Tidser	Murdoch	Oliver	Nesbit	Lamie*	Russell*	McDonagh+	Scullion&	Tiffoney	Strapp	McGowan	
04/02/2017	L	A	Queen of the South	0	3		Gaston	Lindsay	O'Ware	Forbes&	Doyle	Shankland	Russell+	Murdoch	Oliver*	Nesbit	Lamie	Kilday*	McDonagh+	Scullion&	Tiffoney	Strapp	Tidser	McGowan
07/02/2017	L	A	Raith Rovers	1	0		Gaston	Kilday	O'Ware	Lindsay	Doyle	Tidser	Russell	McDonagh	Donnelly*	Shankland	Lamie	Nesbitt*	Murdoch	Scullion	Tiffoney	Strapp	Forbes	McGowan
12/02/2017	SC5	A	Rangers	1	2		Gaston	Kilday	O'Ware	Forbes	Doyle*	Tidser	Russell	Murdoch	Lindsay	Nesbit	Lamie+	McDonagh*	Donnelly+	Scullion	Tiffoney	Strapp	Oyenuga	McGowan
18/02/2017	L	H	Falkirk	2	2		Gaston	Kilday	O'Ware	Forbes	Murdoch	Tidser	Russell	McDonagh*	Shankland	Nesbit+	Lamie	Donnelly*	Oyenuga+	Scullion	Tiffoney	Strapp	Langan	McGowan
25/02/2017	L	A	Dundee United	1	1		Gaston	Kilday	O'Ware	Forbes	Murdoch	Tidser	Russell+	McDonagh	Shankland*	Nesbit	Lamie	Donnelly*	Oyenuga+	Scullion	Tiffoney	Strapp	Doyle	McGowan
11/03/2017	L	H	Queen of the South	1	0		Gaston	Kilday	O'Ware	Forbes	Doyle	Tidser+	Murdoch	McDonagh*	Shankland	Nesbit	Lindsay	Lamie*	Oyenuga+	Scullion	Oilver	Russell	Donnelly	McGowan
18/03/2017	L	A	Falkirk	1	0		Gaston	Kilday	O'Ware	Forbes	Lamie	Russell	Murdoch	Oliver+	Shankland*	Nesbit	Lindsay	Oyenuga*	Donnelly+	Scullion	Tidser	McDonagh	McGowan	
25/03/2017	L	H	Dunfermline Athletic	0	1		Gaston	Kilday*	O'Ware	Forbes	Doyle	Russell	Murdoch	Oliver	Shankland&	Nesbit	Lindsay+	Lamie*	Tidser+	Oyenuga&	Scullion	Donnelly	McGowan	
29/03/2017	L	A	Hibernian	0	0		Gaston	Lamie	O'Ware	Forbes*	Doyle	Russell	Murdoch	Oliver+	Tidser	Nesbit	Lindsay	Oyenuga*	Shankland+	Tiffoney	Scullion	Donnelly	Strapp	McGowan
01/04/2017	L	A	Dumbarton	0	1		Gaston	Lamie	O'Ware	Donnelly&	Doyle	Russell	Murdoch	Shankland	Tidser+	Tiffoney*	Lindsay	Nesbitt*	Forbes+	Oliver&	Scullion	McDonagh	Strapp	McGowan
08/04/2017	L	H	Hibernian	1	1		Gaston	Lamie	O'Ware	Forbes	Doyle	Russell	Murdoch	Oliver*	Tidser+	Nesbitt	Lindsay	Shankland*	McDonagh+	Tiffoney	Scullion	Kilday	Donnelly	McGowan
11/04/2017	L	H	St Mirren	1	4		Gaston	Lamie	O'Ware	Forbes	Doyle	Russell	Murdoch	Oliver	Shankland+	Nesbitt	Lindsay*	Tidser*	Donnelly+	Oyenuga	Scullion	Kilday	McDonagh	McGowan
15/04/2017	L	A	Raith Rovers	0	2		Gaston	Lamie	O'Ware	Forbes	Kilday	McDonagh	Murdoch*	Oliver&	Oyenuga	Nesbitt	Lindsay+	Scullion*	Tidser+	Shankland&	Russell	Doyle	Donnelly	McGowan
22/04/2017	L	H	Ayr United	1	1		Gaston	Lamie	O'Ware	Forbes	Kilday	Doyle	Murdoch	Oliver	Tidser&	Nesbitt+	Shankland*	McDonagh*	Russell+	Lindsay&	Oyenuga	Donnelly	Strapp	Halliwell
29/04/2017	L	A	Dunfermline Athletic	1	3		Gaston	Lamie	Strapp	Lindsay	Kilday	Doyle*	McDonagh	Oliver+	Tidser	Tiffoney	Shankland&	Oyenuga*	Scullion+	Armour&	Russell	Donnelly	Mitchell	McGowan
06/05/2017	L	H	Dundee United	1	1		Halliwell+	Lamie	O'Ware	Forbes*	Strapp	Doyle	McDonagh	Russell	Murdoch	Oyenuga&	Scullion	Tidser*	McGowan+	Nesbit&	Lindsay	Donnelly	Tiffoney	Langan
10/05/2017	PO	H	Dundee United	1	2		Gaston	Lamie	O'Ware	Forbes*	Oliver	Tidser&	McDonagh	Russell	Murdoch	Shankland+	Lindsay	Doyle*	Oyenuga+	Tiffoney&	Scullion	Strapp	McGowan	
13/05/2017	PO	A	Dundee United	0	3		McGowan	Lamie	O'Ware	Forbes*	Oliver	Doyle	Nesbitt&	Russell	Murdoch	Oyenuga	Lindsay+	Tidser*	Shankland+	McDonagh&	Scullion	Strapp	Tiffoney	Gaston

* at Hampden

Motherwell FC 2016/17

unded	1886
ound	Fir Park
stcode	ML1 2QN
l	01698 333333
pacity	13677
osest Railway Station	Airbles
cord Attendance	35632, v Rangers SC, 12/3/1952
cord Win	12-1 v Dundee United, Lge, 23/1/1954
cord Defeat	0-8 v Aberdeen, Lge, 26/3/1979
ost League Goals in a Season	52 Willie McSpadyen, 1931/2
n President	John Chapman OBE
eneral Manager	Alan Burrows
anager	Mark McGhee
	(until Feb), Stephen Robinson
sistant Manager	Stephen Robinson / James McFadden
lours 2016/17 Top	Amber with Claret Chest Band
orts	Amber
onsor	Motorpoint
anufacturer	Macron
ange Colours 2016/17 Top	Grey
orts	Grey
cknames	Well, Steelmen
eb	www.motherwellfc.co.uk
atch Programme 2016/17	Steelmen £3 (Curtis Sport)

Inconsistency was Motherwell's down fall both under Mark McGhee in the early part of the season and Stephen Robinson later on. Some of McGhee's comments at the end of the season were bewildering, suggesting that he felt badly treated by the club.

I'm not sure the Motherwell fans would concur. The feeling seemed to be that under Robinson the style of play improved and provided greater entertainment.

Certainly Motherwell have relied heavily on veterans like Keith Lasley and Steve Hammell. They have been fantastic servants down the years but the time is right for young talent to be given a chance at Fir Park.

Top striker Louis Moult was reportedly on the radar of other clubs—he might be wise to stick with Motherwell as he seems to be a good fit there.

PREDICTION FOR 2017/18
Resource constraints mean Motherwell will not challenge at the top of the table but they should be in contention for a top six place this time round. They may just fall short of that.

Date	Comp	H/A	Opponents	F	A		HT		Referee	Crowd	Scorers
16/07/2016	LC	H	Rangers	0	2		0	0	S McLean	6951	
23/07/2016	LC	A	Annan Athletic	3	1		1	1	N Walsh	956	Johnson, Moult 2
26/07/2016	LC	H	East Stirlingshire	3	0		0	0	C Charleston	2503	Johnson, McDonald, Cadden
30/07/2016	LC	A	Stranraer	3	0		0	0	D Robertson	953	Cadden, Johnson, McDonald
06/08/2016	L	A	Kilmarnock	2	1		1	0	C Thomson	4308	Ainsworth, Johnson
10/08/2016	LC1	A	Celtic	0	5		0	2	K Clancy	20165	
13/08/2016	L	H	St Johnstone	1	2		0	0	E Anderson	3739	Cadden
20/08/2016	L	A	Rangers	1	2		1	0	B Madden	48716	McDonald
27/08/2016	L	H	Dundee	0	0		0	0	A Dallas	4078	
10/09/2016	L	A	Ross County	1	1		0	0	A Muir	3019	Moult
17/09/2016	L	H	Hamilton Accies	4	2		3	1	W Collum	4514	Moult 4
24/09/2016	L	A	Partick Thistle	1	1		0	1	C Thomson	3227	McDonald
30/09/2016	L	H	Hearts	1	3		0	1	S McLean	4666	McFadden
15/10/2016	L	A	Celtic	0	2		0	1	J Beaton	54159	
26/10/2016	L	H	Inverness CT	0	3		0	0	D Robertson	3131	
29/10/2016	L	H	Ross County	4	1		2	0	N Walsh	3177	McDonald, Van der Weg og, Tait, Ainswort
05/11/2016	L	A	Dundee	0	2		0	1	J Beaton	5471	
19/11/2016	L	H	Partick Thistle	2	0		2	0	A Dallas	3759	Moult, McDonald
26/11/2016	L	A	Hearts	0	3		0	1	B Madden	16199	
03/12/2016	L	H	Celtic	3	4		2	0	K Clancy	8535	Moult 2, Ainsworth
10/12/2016	L	H	Kilmarnock	0	0		0	0	S McLean	3684	
17/12/2016	L	A	St Johnstone	1	1		1	0	W Collum	2836	Clark og
23/12/2016	L	H	Aberdeen	1	3		1	2	B Madden	3428	McDonald
28/12/2016	L	A	Inverness CT	2	1		0	0	B Cook	3097	Clay, McDonald
31/12/2016	L	A	Hamilton Accies	1	1		0	1	E Anderson	3526	Moult
21/01/2017	SC	A	Rangers	1	2		0	0	C Thomson	31921	Moult
28/01/2017	L	H	Rangers	0	2		0	0	W Collum	7902	
31/01/2017	L	A	Ross County	2	1		1	1	S McLean	2511	McDonald, Moult
04/02/2017	L	H	Hearts	0	3		0	0	A Dallas	4651	
15/02/2017	L	A	Aberdeen	2	7		0	4	A Muir	10384	Bowman, Pearson
18/02/2017	L	A	Celtic	0	2		0	2	D Robertson	56366	
25/02/2017	L	H	Dundee	1	5		1	5	S Finnie	4002	Moult
04/03/2017	L	A	Kilmarnock	2	1		0	1	B Madden	4726	McHugh, Jules
11/03/2017	L	A	Aberdeen	0	1		0	0	E Anderson	12524	
18/03/2017	L	H	St Johnstone	1	2		1	1	G Aitken	3588	McDonald
01/04/2017	L	A	Rangers	1	1		1	0	S McLean	49198	Moult
05/04/2017	L	H	Hamilton Accies	0	0		0	0	K Clancy	4644	
08/04/2017	L	A	Partick Thistle	0	1		0	1	J Beaton	3920	
15/04/2017	L	H	Inverness CT	4	2		2	1	W Collum	3696	Cadden, Moult, McDonald, Campbell
29/04/2017	L	H	Dundee	2	3		0	1	S McLean	4919	Moult, Cadden
06/05/2017	L	H	Ross County	0	1		0	0	B Madden	3870	
13/05/2017	L	A	Hamilton Accies	1	0		0	0	K Clancy	4173	Moult
16/05/2017	L	H	Kilmarnock	3	1		1	1	N Walsh	5246	McHugh, Ainsworth, Frear
20/05/2017	L	A	Inverness CT	2	3		0	0	C Thomson	5351	McFadden, Bowman
ABD											
13/12/2016	L	A	Aberdeen	0	0				A Muir		Floodlight Failure, 7 mins

FRIENDLIES / OTHER GAMES							
02/07/2016	A	Albion Rovers	3	1			445
03/07/2016	A	Arbroath	0	1			
05/07/2016	A	Cowdenbeath	1	3		U20	287
09/07/2016	A	Dumbarton	2	1			
10/07/2016	A	Hibernian	1	4			

Date	Comp	H/A	Opponents	F	A	1	2	3	4	5	6	7	8	9	10	11	12	13	14	15	16	17	18
16/07/2016	LC	H	Rangers	0	2	Samson	Tait	Hammell	Heneghan	McManus	Ainsworth+	McHugh	Cadden&	Chalmers*	Johnson	McDonald	Moult*	Thomas+	Blyth&	Ferguson	Campbell	MacLean	Brill
23/07/2016	LC	A	Annan Athletic	3	1	Samson	Tait	Hammell	Heneghan	McManus	Ainsworth+	McHugh	Lasley	Lucas*	Johnson&	Moult	Cadden*	Thomas+	Mackin&	Laing	Chalmers	Turnbull	Brill
26/07/2016	LC	H	East Stirlingshire	3	0	Samson	Tait	Hammell*	Heneghan	McManus	Cadden	Thomas+	Lasley	Clay	Johnson	McDonald	Ainsworth*	Chalmers+	Mackin	Laing	MacLean	Turnbull	Brill
30/07/2016	LC	A	Stranraer	3	0	Samson	Tait	Hammell	Heneghan	McManus	Cadden+	Ainsworth*	Lasley	Clay	Johnson	McDonald&	Chalmers*	McLean+	Mackin&	Laing	McHugh	Thomas	Brill
06/08/2016	L	A	Kilmarnock	2	1	Samson	Tait	Hammell	Heneghan	McManus	Cadden	Ainsworth+	McHugh*	Clay	Johnson	McDonald	Chalmers*	McLean+	Mackin	Ferguson	Campbell	Thomas	Brill
10/08/2016	LC1	A	Celtic	0	5	Samson	Tait	Hammell*	Heneghan	McManus	Cadden	Chalmers	Lasley	Clay	Johnson	McDonald	Ainsworth*	Laing	Mackin	Ferguson	Lucas	Thomas	Brill
13/08/2016	L	H	St Johnstone	1	2	Samson	Tait	Ainsworth+	Heneghan	McManus	Cadden*	Chalmers	Lasley	Clay	Johnson	McDonald	Blyth*	Thomas+	McFadden	Ferguson	Lucas	McLean	Brill
20/08/2016	L	A	Rangers	1	2	Samson	Tait	Ainsworth	Heneghan	McManus	Cadden	Chalmers	Lasley	Clay*	Johnson	McDonald	Blyth*	Thomas	McFadden	Ferguson	Lucas	McLean	Brill
27/08/2016	L	H	Dundee	0	0	Samson	Tait	Ainsworth*	Heneghan	McManus	Cadden	Chalmers	Lasley	Clay	Johnson	McDonald	McFadden*	Thomas	Hammell	Ferguson	Lucas	Mclean	Brill
10/09/2016	L	A	Ross County	1	1	Samson	Tait	Hammell	Heneghan	McManus	Cadden	Chalmers&	Lasley*	Clay	Bowman+	McDonald	Ainsworth*	Moult+	McFadden&	Thomas	Fry	Ferguson	Brill
17/09/2016	L	H	Hamilton Accies	4	2	Samson	Tait	Hammell	Heneghan	McManus	Cadden	Moult*	Lasley	Clay	Bowman	McDonald	Ainsworth*	Lucas	McFadden	Thomas	McLean	Ferguson	Brill
24/09/2016	L	A	Partick Thistle	1	1	Samson	Tait	Hammell	Heneghan	McManus	Cadden	Moult*	Lasley+	Clay	Bowman	McDonald	McFadden*	Ainsworth+	Lucas	Mackin	Campbell	Ferguson	Brill
30/09/2016	L	H	Hearts	1	3	Samson	Tait	Hammell	Heneghan	McManus	Cadden*	Moult	Lasley+	Clay	Bowman&	McDonald	Lucas*	Ainsworth+	McFadden&	Ferguson	Thomas	McMillan	Brill
15/10/2016	L	A	Celtic	0	2	Samson	Tait	McMillan+	Heneghan	McManus	Cadden	Moult	Lasley	Clay	MacLean&	McDonald*	Bowman*	Ferguson+	Hastie&	Ainsworth	Kennedy	Campbell	Brill
26/10/2016	L	H	Inverness CT	0	3	Samson	Tait	McMillan	Heneghan	McManus	Cadden	Moult	Lasley	Clay+	MacLean&	Bowman*	McDonald*	McFadden+	Ainsworth&	Ferguson	Hastie	Lucas	Brill
29/10/2016	L	H	Ross County	4	1	Samson	Tait	McMillan	Heneghan	McManus	Cadden	Moult	Lucas*	Clay	Ainsworth+	McDonald	Campbell*	McLean+	Bowman	Ferguson	Kennedy	Blyth	Brill
05/11/2016	L	A	Dundee	0	2	Samson	Tait	Hammell*	Heneghan	McManus	Cadden	Moult	Lasley&	Clay	Ainsworth+	McDonald	McMillan*	Thomas+	MacLean&	Ferguson	Bowman	Campbell	Brill
19/11/2016	L	H	Partick Thistle	2	0	Samson	Tait	McMillan	Heneghan	McManus	Cadden	Moult	Lasley	Clay	Ferguson	McDonald	Ainsworth	Kennedy	MacLean	Hastie	Bowman	Campbell	Brill
26/11/2016	L	A	Hearts	0	3	Samson	Tait	McMillan+	Heneghan	McManus	Cadden&	Moult	Lasley	Clay	Ferguson*	McDonald	Hammell*	Ainsworth+	Hastie&	McLean	Bowman	Campbell	Brill
03/12/2016	L	H	Celtic	3	4	Samson	Tait&	Hammell	Heneghan	McManus	Cadden*	Moult	Lasley	Clay	McLean+	McDonald	Ainsworth*	McMillan+	Bowman&	Thomas	Ferguson	Campbell	Brill
10/12/2016	L	H	Kilmarnock	0	0	Samson	Tait	Hammell	Ferguson	McManus	Ainsworth+	Moult	Lasley&	Clay	McLean*	McDonald	Lucas*	Thomas+	Hastie&	Bowman	Campbell	Maguire	Brill
17/12/2016	L	A	St Johnstone	1	1	Samson	Tait	Ferguson*	Heneghan	McManus	Cadden	Moult	Lasley+	Clay	McMillan&	McDonald	Lucas*	Ainsworth+	Bowman&	Thomas	Turnbull	Maguire	Brill
23/12/2016	L	H	Aberdeen	1	3	Samson	Tait	Hammell	Heneghan	McManus&	Cadden+	Moult	Lasley*	Clay	Lucas	McDonald	Thomas*	Ainsworth+	Bowman&	Ferguson	Mackin	McMillan	Brill
28/12/2016	L	A	Inverness CT	2	1	Samson	Tait	Hammell+	Heneghan	McManus	Cadden*	Moult	McHugh	Clay	Lucas	McDonald	Ainsworth*	McMillan+	Bowman	Ferguson	Mackin	Campbell	Brill
31/12/2016	L	A	Hamilton Accies	1	1	Samson	Tait	Campbell	Heneghan	McManus	McMillan*	Moult	McHugh	Clay	Lucas	McDonald	Ainsworth*	McFadden+	Bowman	Ferguson	Mackin	Turnbull	Brill
21/01/2017	SC	A	Rangers	1	2	Samson	Tait	Hammell	Chalmers*	McManus	Lasley	Moult	McHugh	Clay	Cadden+	Heneghan	McDonald*	McMillan+	Bowman	Ferguson	Ainsworth	Campbell	Brill
28/01/2017	L	H	Rangers	0	2	Samson	Tait&	Hammell	Heneghan	McManus	Chalmers*	Moult	McHugh	Clay	Cadden+	McDonald	McMillan*	Frear+	Bowman&	Jules	Ainsworth	Lasley	Griffiths
31/01/2017	L	A	Ross County	2	1	Samson	Tait	Hammell+	Heneghan	McManus	Lasley	Moult&	McHugh	Lucas*	Cadden	McDonald	Clay*	Jules+	Ainsworth&	Bowman	Frear	McMillan	Griffiths
04/02/2017	L	H	Hearts	0	3	Samson	Tait*	Hammell+	Heneghan	McManus	Lasley	Moult	McHugh	Jules	Cadden	Ainsworth&	McMillan*	Lucas+	Pearson&	Bowman	Frear	Clay	Griffiths
15/02/2017	L	A	Aberdeen	2	7	Samson	Tait	Hammell	Heneghan	McManus	Lasley	Moult	Frear+	Lucas*	Cadden	Pearson	Bowman*	Clay+	Ainsworth	Jules	Campbell	McMillan	Griffiths
18/02/2017	L	A	Celtic	0	2	Samson	McMillan	Chalmers	Heneghan	McManus*	Lasley	Moult	McDonald	Clay	Cadden+	Pearson	Jules*	Bowman+	Ainsworth	Frear	Campbell	Lucas	Griffiths
25/02/2017	L	H	Dundee	1	5	Samson	McMillan	Chalmers*	Heneghan	Jules	McHugh	Moult	McDonald	Clay	Cadden	Pearson	Frear*	Bowman	Lasley	Hastie	Ferguson	Lucas	Griffiths
04/03/2017	L	A	Kilmarnock	2	1	Samson	Tait&	Hammell+	Heneghan	Jules	McHugh	Moult	McDonald	Lasley*	Cadden	Pearson	Bowman*	Frear+	Ferguson&	Ainsworth	Clay	Campbell	Griffiths
11/03/2017	L	A	Aberdeen	0	1	Samson	Ferguson	Hammell+	Heneghan	Jules	McHugh	Clay	McDonald	Bowman*	Cadden	Pearson	Blyth*	Frear+	Gordon	Ainsworth	Lasley	Campbell	Griffiths
18/03/2017	L	H	St Johnstone	1	2	Samson	Ferguson	Hammell*	Frear+	Jules	McHugh	Clay	McDonald	Moult	Cadden	Pearson	Bowman*	Ainsworth+	Blyth	McMillan	Lasley	Campbell	Griffiths
01/04/2017	L	A	Rangers	1	1	Samson	Bowman+	Hammell	Heneghan	Frear	McHugh	Clay*	McDonald	Moult&	Cadden	Pearson	Lasley*	Blyth+	Ainsworth&	McMillan	Jules	Gordon	Griffiths
05/04/2017	L	H	Hamilton Accies	0	0	Samson	Bowman+	Hammell	Heneghan	Frear&	McHugh	Clay*	McDonald	Blyth+	Cadden	Pearson	Lasley*	Gordon+	Ainsworth&	Campbell	Jules	Ferguson	Griffiths
08/04/2017	L	A	Partick Thistle	0	1	Samson	Bowman	Jules	Heneghan	Frear*	McHugh	Clay+	McDonald	Gordon&	Cadden	Pearson	Ainsworth*	Lasley+	Blyth&	Campbell	McMillan	Hammell	Griffiths
15/04/2017	L	H	Inverness CT	4	2	Samson	Bowman*	Hammell&	Heneghan	Frear	McHugh	Campbell	McDonald	Moult+	Cadden	Pearson	Ainsworth*	Blyth+	Jules&	Ferguson	Clay	Gordon	Griffiths
29/04/2017	L	H	Dundee	2	3	Samson	Bowman*	Hammell	Heneghan	Frear	McHugh	Campbell	McDonald&	Moult	Cadden	Lasley+	Ainsworth*	Gordon+	Clay&	Jules	McMillan	Turnbull	Griffiths
06/05/2017	L	H	Ross County	0	1	Griffiths	Lasley	Hammell*	Heneghan	Frear	McHugh	Campbell&	McDonald	Moult	Cadden	Ainsworth+	Jules*	Bowman+	Clay&	McFadden	Ferguson	Gordon	Samson
13/05/2017	L	A	Hamilton Accies	1	0	Griffiths	Lasley*	Hammell	Heneghan	Frear+	McHugh	Campbell	McDonald	Moult&	Cadden	Clay	Ainsworth*	Bowman+	Ferguson&	Jules	Livingstone	Gordon	Pain
16/05/2017	L	H	Kilmarnock	3	1	Griffiths	Lasley	Hammell	Heneghan	Frear	McHugh	Ferguson*	McDonald	Moult+	Cadden	Clay	Ainsworth*&	Bowman+	Livingstone&	Jules	McFadden	Campbell	Pain
20/05/2017	L	A	Inverness CT	2	3	Griffiths	Campbell	Hammell	Heneghan	Frear	McHugh	Ainsworth*	Gordon+	Moult&	Cadden	Clay	Livingstone*	Bowman+	McFadden&	Jules	Lasley	Turnbull	Pain

Surname	First Name	DOB	SQ	Nat	Pos	L A	L S	L G	SC A	SC S	SC G	LC A	LC S	LC G	UNS	Signed	Previous Club	Notes	Contract
Ainsworth	Lionel	01/10/1987	7	ENG	M	10	20	4				3	2		8	2014	Rotherham United		
Armstrong	Jordan	02/04/1999	37	SCO	M											2016	Motherwell Youths		End 2017/
Belic	Luca	18/04/1996	21	SER/BEL	F											2017	West Ham United (OL)	Jan-Jan 2017	
Blyth	Jacob	14/04/1992	19	ENG	F	1	6						1		2	2016	Leicester City		End 2017/
Bowman	Ryan	30/11/1991	11	ENG	F	11	13	2							11	2016	Gateshead		End 2017/
Brill	Dean	02/12/1985	13	ENG	GK										26	2016	Inverness CT	Freed Jan 2017, joined Colchester Utd	
Cadden	Chris	19/09/1996	12	SCO	M	36		3	1			4	1	2		2013	Motherwell Youths		End 2018/
Campbell	Allan	04/07/1998	26	SCO	M	6	1	1							19	2015	Motherwell Youths		End 2018/
Chalmers	Joe	03/01/1994	15	SCO	D	7	1		1			2	2		1	2015	Celtic		OOC
Clay	Craig	05/05/1992	20	ENG	M	31	4	1	1			3			3	2016	Grimsby Town		End 2017/
Falconer	Dylan	23/05/1999	35	SCO	F											2015	Motherwell Youths		End 2017/
Ferguson	David	24/03/1996	25	SCO	D	7	3								22	2013	Motherwell Youths	Released June 2017	
Frear	Elliot	11/09/1990	17	ENG	ENG	11	4	1							3	2017	Forest Green Rovers		End 2018/
Fry	Tom	31/03/1997		WAL	M										1	2016	Bristol City	Released June 2017	
Gordon	Shea	16/05/1998	36	NIR	M	2	2								5	2017	Sheffield United		End 2017/
Griffiths	Russell	13/04/1996	13	ENG	GK	4									14	2017	Everton (OL)	Jan-May 2017	[redacted]
Hammell	Stevie	18/02/1982	3	SCO	D	25	1		1			5			2	2008	Southend United		End 2017/
Hastie	Jake	18/03/1998	34	SCO	F		3								3	2015	Motherwell Youths		End 2017/
Heneghan	Ben	19/09/1993	4	ENG/ROI	D	36			1			5				2016	Chester		End 2017,
Johnson	Marvin	01/12/1990		ENG	F	4		1				5		3		2015	Kidderminster Harriers	Transferred to Oxford United Aug 2016	
Jules	Zak	02/07/1997	21	SCO	D	6	4	1							8	2017	Reading (OL)	Jan-May 2017	
Kennedy	Kieran	23/09/1993	16	ENG	D										3	2015	Leicester City		
Laing	Louis	06/03/1993	5	ENG	D										4	2015	Nottingham Forest	OL to Notts Co Aug 16-Jan 2017, Freed Jan 2017 joined ICT	
Lasley	Keith	21/09/1979	14	SCO	M	25	3		1			4			5	2006	Plymouth Argyle	Retired June 2017, appointed Assistant Manager	
Livingstone	Adam	22/02/1998	40	SCO	D		2								1	2013	Motherwell Youths		End 201.
Lucas	Lee	10/06/1992	18	WAL	M	6	4					1			9	2016	Swansea City	Released June 2017	
Mackin	Dylan	15/01/1997		SCO	F								2		7	2013	Motherwell Youths	OL to Alloa Jan-May 2017, freed June 2017 joined Livingston	
Maguire	Barry	27/04/1998	33	SCO	D										2	2015	Motherwell Youths		End 2017,
McDonald	Scott	21/08/1983	77	AUS	F	34	1	9		1		4		2		2015	Millwall	Left June 2017	
McFadden	James	14/04/1983	24	SCO	F		7	2							5	2015	St Johnstone	Released June 2017	
McHugh	Carl	05/02/1993	8	ROI	D	19		2	1			2			1	2016	Plymouth Argyle		End 2017
McLean	Ross	13/03/1997	27	SCO	F	4	3						1		8	2014	Motherwell Youths		End 2018
McManus	Stephen	10/09/1982	6	SCO	D	25			1			5				2013	Middlesbrough		End 2017
McMillan	Jack	18/12/1997	30	SCO	D	9	5			1					8	2014	Motherwell Youths		End 2018
Moore	Josh	26/03/1998	42	SCO	M											2015	Motherwell Youths		
Moore	Craig	16/08/1994		SCO	F											2009	Hearts Youths	OL to Ayr Jul 16-May 2017, released June 2017 joined Ayr	[redacted]
Morrison	PJ	27/02/1998	41	SCO	GK											2015	Motherwell Youths		End 2017
Moult	Louis	14/05/1992	9	ENG	F	30	1	15	1		1	1	1	2		2015	Wrexham		End 2017
Pain	Oliver	28/10/1997		AUS / ENG	GK										3	2017	Sunderland (OL)	Jan-May 2017	[redacted]
Pearson	Stephen	02/10/1982	88	SCO	M	10	1	1								2017	Atletico Kolkata	Released June 2017	[redacted]
Samson	Craig	24/08/1984	1	SCO	GK	34			1			5			1	2015	Kilmarnock	Released June 2017, joined St Mirren	[redacted]
Scott	James	30/08/2000	38	SCO	F											2016	Motherwell Youths		End 201
Stachini	Josh	19/12/1997	31	NIR	D											2016	Sheffield Wednesday	Freed Jan 2017 joined Ashton United	[redacted]
Tait	Richard	02/12/1989	2	SCO	D	25		1	1			5				2016	Grimsby Town		End 201
Thomas	Dom	14/02/1996	23	SCO	M		4					1	2		10	2013	Motherwell Youths	OL to QOS Jan-May 2017	End 201
Turnbull	David	10/07/1999	32	SCO	M										6	2015	Motherwell Youths		End 201
Watt	Luke	20/06/1997		SCO	D											2014	Motherwell Youths	OL to Stranraer Aug 16-Jan 2017	End 201
Watters	Ryan	12/05/1998	36	SCO	F			2								2014	Motherwell Youths	Freed Jan 2017, joined St Mirren	
Own Goals																			
NEW SIGNINGS																			
Carson	Trevor			NIR	GK											2017	Hartlepool United		End 201
Tanner	Craig			ENG	M											2017	Reading		End 201
Fisher	Alex			ENG	F											2017	Inverness CT		End 201
Bigirmana	Gael			BRU	M											2017	Coventry City		End 201
Rose	Andy				M											2017	Coventry City		End 201
Griffiths	Russell				GK											2017	Everton		End 201
Dunne	Charles				D											2017	Oldham Athletic		End 201

Source of Birthdates: Motherwell Fc website and transfermarkt.com

Partick Thistle FC 2016/17

Founded	1876
Ground	Firhill Stadium
Postcode	G20 7AL
Tel	0871 402 1971
Capacity	10102
Closest Railway Station	St Georges X / Kelvin Bridge (Subway)
Record Attendance	49838 v Rangers, Lge, 18/2/1922
Record Win	16-0 v Royal Albert, SC, 17/1/1931
Record Defeat	0-10 v Queen's Park, SC, 3/12/1881
Most League Goals in a Season	41 Alex Hair, 1926/7
Chairman	David Beattie
General Manager	Ian Maxwell
Manager	Alan Archibald
Assistant Manager	Scott Paterson
Colours 2016/17 Top	Yellow with Broad Red "Ajax" stripe
Shorts	Black
Sponsor	Kingsford Capital Management
Manufacturer	Joma
Change Colours 2016/17 Top	White
Shorts	White
Nicknames	Jags, Harry Wraggs
Web	www.ptfc.co.uk
Match Programme 2016/17	£3

Alan Archibald endeared himself to the Thistle fans with another season of over achievement. A top six place is more than can be expected from the Firhill club but a just reward for the hard work and ability of those in charge. That would include Chief Executive Ian Maxwell who looks to be one of the most talented administrators in the game these days.

Thistle's blend of Scottish talent and unusual imports provided bags of entertainment. It's pleasing to note that Scots lads like Lawless, Booth and Doolan were a big part of that. One stand out was defender Niall Keown who was on loan from Reading but has now signed permanently.

Thistle are long overdue a decent Cup run. Many fans will have never seen them in a major Semi Final and the club would benefit from the exposure that would bring.

PREDICTION FOR 2017/18

If Thistle could repeat their top six finish it would be amazing. I doubt if they will but they will be the best of the rest. And maybe this will be their year for a Cup run!

Date	Comp	H/A	Opponents	F	A	HT		Referee	Crowd	Scorers
15/07/2016	LC	A	Airdrieonians	1	0	0	0	K Clancy	1632	Doolan
23/07/2016	LC	H	Queen of the South	2	1	0	0	A Muir	2358	Erskine, Lawless
26/07/2016	LC	A	Stenhousemuir	4	1	2	0	D Robertson	1433	Pogba, Welsh, Amoo, Azeez
30/07/2016	LC	H	Queen's Park	2	0	1	0	A Dallas	2250	Erskine, Lindsay
06/08/2016	L	H	Inverness CT	2	0	1	0	N Walsh	2943	Erskine, Amoo
09/08/2016	LC1	A	Dundee United	1	3	0	3	S McLean	5036	Welsh
20/08/2016	L	A	Aberdeen	1	2	0	1	J Beaton	11049	Erskine
27/08/2016	L	H	Hearts	1	2	0	1	W Collum	4919	Lindsay
10/09/2016	L	H	St Johnstone	0	2	0	1	N Walsh	2885	
17/09/2016	L	A	Kilmarnock	2	2	1	1	A Dallas	4169	Lawless, Lindsay
24/09/2016	L	H	Motherwell	1	1	1	0	C Thomson	3227	Erskine
01/10/2016	L	A	Rangers	0	2	0	2	S Finnie	49680	
15/10/2016	L	H	Hamilton Accies	2	2	2	1	G Aitken	2843	Edwards, Lindsay
22/10/2016	L	H	Ross County	1	1	1	0	D Robertson	3777	Welsh
26/10/2016	L	A	Dundee	2	0	1	0	S McLean	4783	Azeez, Doolan
29/10/2016	L	A	St Johnstone	2	1	1	1	B Cook	3096	Doolan, Osman
04/11/2016	L	H	Aberdeen	1	2	0	1	B Madden	3974	Barton
19/11/2016	L	A	Motherwell	0	2	0	2	A Dallas	3759	
26/11/2016	L	H	Rangers	1	2	0	0	N Walsh	7951	Doolan
03/12/2016	L	A	Hamilton Accies	1	1	0	1	D Robertson	2210	Welsh
09/12/2016	L	H	Celtic	1	4	0	1	C Thomson	7609	Lindsay
17/12/2016	L	A	Hearts	1	1	0	1	D Robertson	16418	Welsh
20/12/2016	L	A	Celtic	0	1	0	1	E Anderson	55733	
23/12/2016	L	A	Ross County	3	1	0	0	J Beaton	2935	Lindsay, Dooian, Erskine
28/12/2016	L	H	Dundee	2	0	2	0	A Muir	3758	Booth, Doolan
31/12/2016	L	H	Kilmarnock	0	0	0	0	K Clancy	3584	
21/01/2017	SC	H	Formartine United	4	0	3	0	C Charleston	2782	Erskine 2, Lawless, Osman
28/01/2017	L	A	Inverness CT	0	0	0	0	S Finnie	2823	
01/02/2017	L	H	St Johnstone	0	1	0	1	C Allan	2257	
04/02/2017	L	A	Aberdeen	0	2	0	0	G Aitken	10094	
11/02/2017	SC5	A	St Johnstone	1	0	1	0	S McLean	2884	Barton
18/02/2017	L	H	Hamilton Accies	2	0	0	0	W Collum	3057	Doolan 2
25/02/2017	L	H	Hearts	2	0	1	0	N Walsh	4143	Doolan, Lindsay
01/03/2017	L	A	Dundee	1	0	1	0	J Beaton	5328	Leanzibarrut og
05/03/2017	SC6	A	Aberdeen	0	1	0	1	C Thomson	11333	
11/03/2017	L	H	Inverness CT	1	1	0	0	W Collum	3082	Doolan
18/03/2017	L	A	Kilmarnock	1	1	0	0	J Beaton	4519	Erskine
01/04/2017	L	H	Ross County	2	1	0	0	W Collum	3149	Doolan 2
05/04/2017	L	A	Celtic	1	1	0	0	G Aitken	54047	Azeez
08/04/2017	L	H	Motherwell	1	0	1	0	J Beaton	3920	Doolan
15/04/2017	L	A	Rangers	0	2	0	1	N Walsh	49748	
29/04/2017	L	A	Hearts	2	2	0	0	A Dallas	15930	Doolan, Lawless
07/05/2017	L	H	Rangers	1	2	1	0	C Allan	6799	Doolan
13/05/2017	L	A	St Johnstone	0	1	0	1	S Finnie	3630	
18/05/2017	L	H	Celtic	0	5	0	3	A Dallas	7847	
21/05/2017	L	H	Aberdeen	0	6	0	5	E Anderson	3924	

FRIENDLIES / OTHER GAMES					
29/06/2016	A	Cirencester Town	6	0	
02/07/2016	A	Bath City	0	4	
02/07/2016	A	Stranraer	2	4	U20
05/07/2016	A	Raith Rovers	0	0	
09/07/2016	A	Morton	2	1	
13/07/2016	A	East Kilbride	0	4	U20
21/07/2016	A	Ashfield	4	5	U20
13/01/2017	N	Lokeren	2	5	at La Manga

Date	Comp	H/A	Opponents	F	A	1	2	3	4	5	6	7	8	9	10	11	12	13	14	15	16	17	18
15/07/2016	LC	A	Airdrieonians	1	0	Crawford	Booth	Lindsay	Devine	Gordon	Welsh	Erskine+	Lawless	Wilson	McDaid*	Doolan	Azeez*	Edwards+	*Syme*	*Nisbet*	*Penrice*	*Pogba*	*Cullen*
23/07/2016	LC	H	Queen of the South	2	1	Crawford	Booth	Lindsay	Devine	Gordon	Welsh	Erskine	Lawless	Wilson&	Amoo+	Azeez*	Doolan*	Edwards+	Pogba&	*Nisbet*	*Syme*	*McDaid*	*Cerny*
26/07/2016	LC	A	Stenhousemuir	4	1	Crawford	Booth	Lindsay	Syme	Gordon	Welsh	Edwards	Lawless*	Pogba+	Amoo &	Doolan	Nisbet*	Azeez+	McDaid&	*Erskine*	*Penrice*	*Wilson*	*Cerny*
30/07/2016	LC	H	Queen's Park	2	0	Cerny	Booth	Lindsay	Devine	Gordon	Welsh	Erskine	Lawless+	Wilson	Edwards*	Doolan&	Amoo*	Azeez+	Pogba&	*Nisbet*	*Syme*	*McDaid*	*Crawford*
06/08/2016	L	H	Inverness CT	2	0	Cerny	Booth	Lindsay+	Devine	Gordon	Welsh	Erskine*	Lawless	Osman	Amoo	Doolan	Edwards*	Azeez+	Wilson	*Pogba*	*Syme*	*McDaid*	*Scully*
09/08/2016	LC1	A	Dundee United	1	3	Scully	Booth	Syme+	Devine	Gordon	Welsh	Erskine	Lawless	Osman	Amoo*	Doolan&	Azeez*	Edwards+	Pogba&	*Wilson*	*McDaid*	*Crawford*	
20/08/2016	L	A	Aberdeen	1	2	Cerny	Booth	Lindsay	Devine	Gordon	Welsh	Edwards*	Lawless	Osman	Amoo+	Azeez&	Erskine*	Doolan+	Pogba&	*Wilson*	*McDaid*	*Elliot*	*Scully*
27/08/2016	L	H	Hearts	1	2	Cerny	Booth	Lindsay	Devine	Gordon	Erskine	Edwards	Lawless	Osman	Doolan+	Azeez*	Amoo*	Pogba+	*Syme*	*Wilson*	*McDaid*	*Elliot*	*Scully*
10/09/2016	L	H	St Johnstone	0	2	Cerny*	Booth	Lindsay	Devine	Gordon	Welsh&	Erskine	Lawless	Osman	Doolan	Azeez+	Scully*	Edwards+	Amoo&	*Wilson*	*McDaid*	*Elliot*	*Barton*
17/09/2016	L	A	Kilmarnock	2	2	Scully	Booth	Lindsay	Devine	Gordon	Edwards	Erskine+	Lawless	Osman	Doolan&	Amoo*	Azeez*	Elliot+	Welsh&	*Wilson*	*McDaid*	*Stuckmann*	*Barton*
24/09/2016	L	H	Motherwell	1	1	Scully	Barton	Lindsay	Devine	Gordon	Edwards	Erskine*	Lawless+	Elliot	Azeez	Amoo	Welsh*	Doolan+	*Penrice*	*Wilson*	*McDaid*	*Stuckmann*	*Syme*
01/10/2016	L	A	Rangers	0	2	Scully	Booth	Lindsay	Devine	Gordon	Edwards	Erskine+	Lawless	Osman	Azeez&	Amoo*	Elliot*	Welsh+	McDaid&	*Wilson*	*Barton*	*Stuckmann*	*Fraser*
15/10/2016	L	H	Hamilton Accies	2	2	Scully	Booth	Lindsay	Devine	Gordon	Edwards	Erskine&	Lawless*	Osman	Barton	Doolan+	Amoo*	Azeez+	Elliot&	*Welsh*	*Wilson*	*Stuckmann*	*McDaid*
22/10/2016	L	H	Ross County	1	1	Scully	Booth	Lindsay+	Devine	Elliot	Edwards	Welsh	Azeez	Osman	Barton	Doolan*	Gordon*	Amoo+	*Syme*	*Penrice*	*Wilson*	*Stuckmann*	*McDaid*
26/10/2016	L	A	Dundee	2	0	Scully*	Booth	Lindsay	Devine	Elliot	Edwards	Welsh	Azeez	Osman+	Barton	Doolan	Stuckmann*	Wilson+	*Syme*	*Amoo*	*Erskine*	*Gordon*	*McDaid*
29/10/2016	L	A	St Johnstone	2	1	Stuckmann	Booth	Lindsay	Devine	Elliot	Edwards	Welsh	Azeez+	Osman	Barton	Doolan*	Erskine*	Amoo+	*Wilson*	*McDaid*	*Syme*	*Gordon*	*Cullen*
04/11/2016	L	H	Aberdeen	1	2	Stuckmann	Booth	Lindsay	Devine	Elliot	Edwards&	Welsh	Azeez+	Osman	Barton	Doolan*	Erskine*	Amoo+	McDaid&	*Wilson*	*Syme*	*Gordon*	*Cullen*
19/11/2016	L	A	Motherwell	0	2	Stuckmann	Booth	Lindsay	Devine	Elliot&	Edwards*	Welsh	Azeez	Osman	Barton	Erskine+	Doolan*	Lawless+	Amoo&	*Wilson*	*McDaid*	*Gordon*	*Cerny*
26/11/2016	L	H	Rangers	1	2	Stuckmann	Booth	Lindsay	Gordon	Elliot	Amoo+	Welsh	Doolan&	Osman	Barton	Erskine*	Edwards*	Lawless+	Azeez&	*Wilson*	*McDaid*	*Devine*	*Cerny*
03/12/2016	L	A	Hamilton Accies	1	1	Cerny	Booth	Lindsay	Gordon	Elliot	Azeez*	Welsh	Doolan&	Osman	Barton	Edwards	Erskine*	*Lawless*	*Amoo*	*Wilson*	*McDaid*	*Devine*	*Stuckmann*
09/12/2016	L	H	Celtic	1	4	Cerny	Booth	Lindsay	Gordon	Elliot	Amoo*	Welsh	Doolan&	Osman	Barton	Erskine+	Edwards*	Lawless+	Azeez&	*Wilson*	*McDaid*	*Devine*	*Stuckmann*
17/12/2016	L	A	Hearts	1	1	Cerny	Booth	Lindsay	Devine	Elliot	Edwards	Welsh	Doolan	Osman	Barton	Azeez*	Erskine*	*Lawless*	*Amoo*	*Wilson*	*McDaid*	*Gordon*	*Stuckmann*
20/12/2016	L	A	Celtic	0	1	Cerny	Booth	Lindsay	Devine	Gordon	Edwards	Welsh+	Amoo*	Osman	Lawless	Azeez&	Erskine*	Barton+	Doolan&	*Wilson*	*McDaid*	*Elliot*	*Stuckmann*
23/12/2016	L	A	Ross County	3	1	Cerny	Booth	Lindsay	Devine	Elliot	Edwards	Welsh	Doolan*	Osman	Lawless+	Erskine	Azeez*	Amoo+	*Barton*	*Wilson*	*McDaid*	*Gordon*	*Stuckmann*
28/12/2016	L	H	Dundee	2	0	Cerny	Booth	Lindsay*	Devine	Elliot	Edwards	Welsh	Doolan	Osman	Barton	Erskine+	Gordon*	Azeez+	*Lawless*	*Wilson*	*McDaid*	*Amoo*	*Stuckmann*
31/12/2016	L	H	Kilmarnock	0	0	Cerny	Booth	Lawless*	Devine	Elliot	Edwards+	Welsh	Doolan	Osman	Barton	Erskine&	Amoo*	Azeez+	McDaid&	*Wilson*	*Gordon*	*McCarthy*	*Stuckmann*
21/01/2017	SC	H	Formartine United	4	0	Cerny	Booth*	Lawless	Devine	Elliot	Amoo+	Welsh&	Doolan	Osman	Barton	Erskine	Dumbuya*	Azeez+	*McCarthy&*	*McDaid*	*Edwards*	*Gordon*	*Ridgers*
28/01/2017	L	A	Inverness CT	0	0	Cerny	Booth	Lawless	Keown	Elliot	Edwards	Welsh	Lindsay	Azeez*	Barton	Erskine	Doolan*	*Nisbet*	*Dumbuya*	*McDaid*	*Amoo*	*McCarthy*	*Ridgers*
01/02/2017	L	H	St Johnstone	0	1	Cerny	Booth	Lawless	Keown	Elliot	Edwards	Welsh+	Lindsay	Doolan&	Barton	Erskine*	Azeez*	Osman+	Amoo&	*Dumbuya*	*Devine*	*Nisbet*	*Ridgers*
04/02/2017	L	A	Aberdeen	0	2	Cerny	Dumbuya	Lawless	Devine	Elliot	Edwards&	Osman	Lindsay	Doolan*	Barton	Amoo+	Azeez*	Erskine+	Nisbet&	*Welsh*	*Keown*	*Banton*	*Ridgers*
11/02/2017	SC5	A	St Johnstone	1	0	Cerny	Keown	Lawless	Devine	Welsh	Edwards	Osman	Lindsay	Azeez*	Barton	Amoo	Doolan*	*Banton*	*Nisbet*	*Erskine*	*McCarthy*	*Ridgers*	
18/02/2017	L	H	Hamilton Accies	2	0	Cerny	Dumbuya	Lawless	Devine	Booth	Edwards	Osman	Lindsay	Azeez+	Barton	Amoo*	Doolan*	Erskine+	Nisbet	*Keown*	*McCarthy*	*Ridgers*	
25/02/2017	L	H	Hearts	2	0	Cerny	Dumbuya*	Keown	Devine	Booth	Edwards	Osman	Lindsay	Doolan&	Barton	Erskine+	Elliot*	Lawless+	Azeez&	*Amoo*	*Nisbet*	*McCarthy*	*Ridgers*
01/03/2017	L	A	Dundee	1	0	Cerny	Elliot	Keown	Devine	Booth	Edwards	Osman	Lindsay	Doolan+	Barton	Erskine*	Lawless*	Azeez+	*McCarthy*	*Amoo*	*Nisbet*	*Ridgers*	
05/03/2017	SC6	A	Aberdeen	0	1	Cerny	Elliot	Keown	Devine	Booth	Edwards	Osman	Lindsay	Doolan&	Barton*	Erskine+	Lawless*	Azeez+	Nisbet&	*Amoo*	*Dumbuya*	*Ridgers*	*McCarthy*
11/03/2017	L	H	Inverness CT	1	1	Cerny	Dumbuya	Keown	Lawless+	Booth	Edwards	Osman*	Lindsay	Doolan	Barton	Erskine&	Amoo*	Azeez+	Elliot&	*Nisbet*	*Lamont*	*Ridgers*	*McCarthy*
18/03/2017	L	A	Kilmarnock	1	1	Cerny	Dumbuya	Keown	Lawless*	Elliot	Edwards	Osman	Lindsay	Doolan	Barton	Erskine	Devine*	*Azeez*	*Booth*	*Amoo*	*Nisbet*	*Ridgers*	*McCarthy*
01/04/2017	L	H	Ross County	2	1	Cerny	Dumbuya	Keown	Lawless	Elliot	Edwards	Osman*	Lindsay	Doolan	Barton	Erskine+	Devine*	Azeez+	*Booth*	*Amoo*	*Nisbet*	*Ridgers*	*McCarthy*
05/04/2017	L	A	Celtic	1	1	Cerny	Booth	Keown	Devine	Elliot	Edwards	McCarthy+	Lindsay	Amoo*	Barton	Azeez	Doolan*	Erskine+	Dumbuya	*Lawless*	*Nisbet*	*Ridgers*	*McLaughlin*
08/04/2017	L	H	Motherwell	1	0	Cerny	Dumbuya	Keown	Devine	Elliot	Edwards	Erskine*	Lindsay	Doolan	Barton	Lawless+	Azeez*	McCarthy+	Booth	*Amoo*	*Nisbet*	*Ridgers*	*McLaughlin*
15/04/2017	L	A	Rangers	0	2	Cerny	Dumbuya	Keown	Devine	Elliot	Edwards	Amoo*	Lindsay	Azeez+	Barton	Lawless&	Erskine*	Doolan+	Nisbet&	*McCarthy*	*Lamont*	*Ridgers*	*McLaughlin*
29/04/2017	L	A	Hearts	2	2	Cerny	Booth	Keown	Devine	Elliot	Edwards	Erskine*	McCarthy	Doolan	Barton	Lawless	Azeez*	*Amoo*	*Nisbet*	*Lamont*	*McLaughlin*	*Ridgers*	
07/05/2017	L	H	Rangers	1	2	Cerny	Booth	Keown	Osman	Elliot	Edwards+	Erskine*	Lindsay	Doolan	Barton	Lawless	Azeez*	McCarthy+	*Dumbuya*	*Amoo*	*McLaughlin*	*Nisbet*	*Ridgers*
13/05/2017	L	A	St Johnstone	0	1	Cerny	Booth	Keown	Devine*	Elliot	Edwards&	Osman	Lindsay	Doolan	Barton	Azeez+	Erskine*	Lawless+	Nisbet&	*Amoo*	*McLaughlin*	*McCarthy*	*Ridgers*
18/05/2017	L	H	Celtic	0	5	Cerny+	Booth	Erskine&	Devine	Elliot	Amoo	Osman*	Lindsay	Doolan	Barton	Lawless	Edwards*	Ridgers+	Azeez&	*Keown*	*McLaughlin*	*McCarthy*	*Nisbet*
21/05/2017	L	H	Aberdeen	0	6	Ridgers	Edwards	Keown	Erskine	McCarthy&	Amoo*	Azeez	Lindsay	Doolan	Barton	Lawless+	Fleming*	Lamont+	McLaughlin&	*C Wilson*	*Scully*		

						L			SC			LC							
			SQ	Nat	Pos	A	S	G	A	S	G	A	S	G	UNS				
Surname	First Name	DOB														Signed	Previous Club	Notes	Cont
Amoo	David	13/04/1991	7	ENG/NIG	F	14	11	1	2			3	1	1	14	2015	Carlisle United	Freed May 2017, joined Cambridge United	
Azeez	Adebayo	08/01/1994	16	ENG/NIG	F	19	18	2	1	2		1	4	1	1	2016	AFC Wimbledon		End 2
Bannigan	Stuart	17/09/1992	8	SCO	M											2009	Partick Thistle Youth		End 2
Banton	Jason	15/12/1992		ENG / JAM	M										2	2017	Crawley Town (OL)	Jan-May 2017	
Barton	Adam	07/01/1991	13	ENG/NIR	D	30	1	1	3		1				4	2016	Portsmouth		End 2
Booth	Callum	30/05/1991	3	SCO	D	31		1	2			5			3	2015	Hibernian		End 2
Cerny	Tomas	10/04/1985	1	CZR	GK	27			3			1			4	2015	Hibernian		End 2
Crawford	David	30/06/1985	35	SCO	GK							3			2	2016	Alloa Athletic	Freed Sep 2016, joined Stenhousemuir	
Cullen	Conor	20/02/1997	33	SCO	GK										3	2014	Partick Thistle Youth	Freed June 2017	
Devine	Daniel	07/09/1992	15	ENG	D	28	2		3			4			4	2016	Inverness CT		End 2
Docherty	Dominic	22/03/1997	24	SCO	M											2014	Hibernian U17	OL to Queen's Park Jan-May, Freed June 2017	
Doolan	Kris	11/12/1986	9	SCO	F	29	8	14	2	1		4	1	1		2009	Auchinleck Talbot		End 2
Dumbuya	Mustapha	07/08/1987	2	SIE/ENG	D	8				1					5	2015	Notts County		End 2
Edwards	Ryan	17/11/1993	19	AUS/SCO	M	33	5	1	2			2	3		1	2015	Reading		End 2
Elliot	Christie	26/05/1991	14	ENG	F	26	5		2						4	2011	Whitley Bay		End 2
Erskine	Chris	08/02/1987	10	SCO	M	25	11	5	2		2	4		2	3	2016	Dundee United		End 2
Fleming	Ross	09/08/1999	38	SCO	D		1									2016	Partick Thistle Youth		End 2
Fraser	Gary	02/07/1994	22	SCO	M										1	2014	Bolton Wanderers		OOC
Gordon	Zygmunt	23/04/1993	23	SCO/POL	D	12	2					5			8	2016	Hamilton Accies	Transferred to J. Bialystok Jan 2017	
Hall	Jamie	29/10/1998	24	SCO	M											2016	Partick Thistle Youth	Freed June 2017	
Herd	Struan	01/10/1996		SCO	GK											2016	Mandurah City	Freed June 2017	
Higgins	Connor	22/11/1999	39	SCO	F											2016	Partick Thistle Youth		End 2
Keown	Niall	05/04/1995	17	ENG/ROI	D	14			2						3	2017	Reading (OL)	Jan-May 2017	
Lamont	Mark	25/02/1998	32	SCO	M		1								3	2015	Partick Thistle Youth		End 2
Lawless	Steven	12/04/1991	11	SCO	F	24	6	2	2	1	1	5		1	4	2012	Motherwell		End 2
Lindsay	Liam	12/10/1995	5	SCO	D	36		6	2			4		1		2012	Partick Thistle Youth		End 2
McCarthy	Andrew	20/10/1998	30	SCO	M	3	2			1					13	2015	Partick Thistle Youth		End 2
McDaid	Declan	22/11/1995	20	SCO	M		3					1	1		23	2013	Morton	Freed Jan 2017, joined Ayr	
McInally	Matthew	02/08/1997	25	SCO	D										0	2015	PT Weir Academy	Freed June 2017	
McLaughlin	Neil	06/11/1998	26	SCO	M		1								7	2014	PT Weir Academy		End 2
McMullin	Michael	10/02/1997		SCO	D											2014	PT Weir Academy	OL to Peterhead Jan-May, Freed June 2017	
Nisbet	Kevin	08/03/1997	27	SCO	F		3			1			1		17	2014	Partick Thistle Youth	OL to Ayr Uinited Aug-Jan	End 2
Osman	Abdul	27/02/1987	6	GHA/ENG	M	30	1	1	3		1	1				2014	Crewe Alexandra		End 2
Penrice	James	22/12/1998	29	SCO	D										4	2015	Partick Thistle Youth	OL to East Fife Jan-May 2017	End 2
Pogba	Mathias	19/08/1990	99	GUI	F		2					1	3	1	2	2015	Crawley Town	Transferred to Sparta Rotterdam Sep 2016	
Ridgers	Mark	09/08/1990	35	SCO	GK	1	1								18	2017	Orlando City B	Released June 2017, joined Inverness CT	
Scully	Ryan	29/10/1992	12	SCO	GK	6	1					1			4	2008	Partick Thistle Youth		End 2
Stokes	Ian	10/02/1999	37	SCO	D											2016	Partick Thistle Youth		End 2
Stokes	James	10/02/1999	40	SCO	F											2016	Partick Thistle Youth		End 2
Stuckmann	Thomas	17/03/1981		GER	GK	4	1								12	2016	Doncaster Rovers	Freed Jan 2017, joined Chesterfield	
Syme	David	23/06/1997	21	SCO	D	0						2			10	2016	Kilmarnock	Freed Jan 2017, joined Raith Rovers	
Welsh	Sean	15/03/1990	4	SCO	M	18	3	3	2			5		2	2	2012	Hibernian	Released June 2017	
Wilson	David	06/09/1994	18	SCO	M		1					3			22	2011	Raith Rovers BC	OL to Stranraer Jan-May 2017, Freed May 2017	
Wilson	Callum	23/06/1999	41	SCO	M										1	2016	Partick Thistle Youth		End 2
Own Goal								1											
NEW SIGNINGS																			
Spittal	Blair				M											2017	Dundee United		
Sneddon	Jamie				GK											2017	Cowdenbeath		
Keown	Neil				D											2017	Reading		

Source of Birthdates: transfermarkt.com

Peterhead FC 2016/17

Founded	1891
Ground	Balmoor Stadium
Postcode	AB42 1EU
Tel	01779 478256
Capacity	3150
Closest Railway Station	Aberdeen
Record Attendance	8643 v Raith Rovers, SC, 25/2/1987
Ground Record	4855 v Rangers, Lge, 19/1/2013
Record Win	8-0 v Forfar Athletic, Lge, 30/9/2006
Record Defeat	0-13 v Aberdeen, SC, 10/2/1923
Most League Goals in a Season	21 Iain Stewart 2002/3,
	Scott Michie 2004/5, Rory McAllister 2012/13
Chairman	Rodger Morrison
Secretary	Nat Porter
Manager	Jim McInally
Assistant Manager	David Nicholls
Colours 2016/17 Top	Blue
Shorts	Blue
Sponsor	LFH Engineering
Manufacturer	Adidas
Change Colours 2016/17 Top	White
Shorts	Blue
Nicknames	Blue Toon
Web	www.peterheadfc.co.uk
Match Programme 2016/17	Monthly Magazine only

Peterhead's a dour kind of place and Peterhead are a dour kind of team. Their luck ran out in 2016/17 as they finished second bottom and then lost the Play Off final to Forfar Athletic.

Jim McInally has a hard job recruiting players for what is a footballing outpost. Most never see Balmoor from one home game to the next which creates a further problem of alienation from their fan base.

Once again they relied heavily on Rory McCallister for goals. Once again he was suspended for a key play off game—that's why he's playing at this level and not further up the footballing ladder.

PREDICTION FOR 2017/18

Jim McInally has had a total clear out with most of last season's team departing. They need to get off to a good start. If they do, confidence in the newly-assembled squad will grow and they could be amongst the front runners. If they do not get a good start then it will be difficult. Overall I tend to think they will be nearer the top than the bottom, probably in the Play offs.

						L			SC			LC			CC							
			SQ	Nat	Pos	A	S	G	A	S	G	A	S	G	A	S	G	UNS				
Surname	First Name	DOB																	Signed	Previous Club	Notes	Contract
Adams	Scott	13/10/1996		SCO	M													7	2014	Arbroath Youths	OL to Banks o' De eFeb-May 2017	OOC
Anderson	Grant	20/08/1986		SCO	F	13	4	3										1	2017	Queen of the South	Released May 2017 joined Stranraer	[redacted]
Baptie	Ryan	18/03/1995		SCO	D	3	1	1							2			25	2015	Inverness CT	OL to Broxburn Ath Mar-May 2017	OOC
Blockley	Nathan	15/06/1992		SCO	D	8	6		1			2	3		1	1		10	2015	Airdrieonians	Released May 2017	[redacted]
Brown	Jordon	18/11/1992		SCO	M	19	17	5		1		2	2	1	1		1	6	2013	Aberdeen		OOC
Brown	Scott	25/11/1994		SCO	M	36		3	1						1				2016	St Johnstone		OOC
Comrie	Aaron	03/02/1997		SCO	D	14	2											4	2017	St Johnstone (OL)	Jan-May 2017	[redacted]
Dzierzawski	Kevin	28/06/1991		USA	M	10	10	1		1		4		1	1			14	2015	Queen of the South	Released May 2017	
Ferry	Simon	11/01/1988		SCO	M	28	2		1			3						3	2015	Dundee		OOC
Gordon	Liam	26/01/1996		SCO	D	10	1												2016	St Johnstone (OL)	Jan-May 2017	[redacted]
Hobday	Fraser	26/09/1995		SCO	GK	10									2			35	2016	Huntly (OL)	Jul-May 2017	
Jarvie	Paul	14/06/1982		SCO	GK													2	2008	Inverurie Locos		
Kelleher	Fiacre	10/03/1996		ROI	D	19		3	1			3			2				2016	Celtic (OL)	Aug-Dec 2016	[redacted]
Lawrence	Mark	11/08/1998		SCO	M														2015	Lewis United	OL to Fraserburgh Aug 16-May 2017	End 2017/18
McAllister	Rory	13/05/1987		SCO	F	36		19	1			5		4	1	1	3		2011	Brechin City		End 2018/19
McCluskey	Stefan	22/08/1990		SCO	F	8	2								1				2016	Morton	Freed Jan 2017, joined Alloa	[redacted]
McIntosh	Leighton	06/02/1993		SCO	F	7	24	4	1			1	4	1	2		1	7	2015	Montrose	Released May 2017	
McMullin	Michael	10/02/1997		SCO	D	11	3											3	2016	Partick Thistle (OL)	Jan-May 2017	
Nassor	Salim	07/07/1997		ENG/SOM	M		1					1	2		1			11	2016	Ternana Calcio	Freed Jan 2017 joined Leatherhead	
Noble	Steven	16/04/1988		SCO	D	28	1		1			5						8	2012	Stranraer	OOC May 2017, joined Stirling Albion	
Redman	Jamie	13/08/1986		SCO	M	21	9	4		1		3	1		1	1		4	2011	Brechin City	OOC May 2017, joined Montrose	
Reid	Craig	26/02/1986		SCO	D	11		1											2017	Keflavik IF	Freed May 2017	
Riley	Nicky	10/05/1986		SCO	M	25	10	4	1			2	2			2		2	2015	Dundee		OOC
Ross	Scott	19/04/1991		SCO	D	26	5		1			4			1			1	2011	Aberdeen		OOC
Rumsby	Scott	01/01/1994		SCO	D	4	6					5			2			11	2016	Stranraer	Freed Jan 2017, joined Cowdenbeath	[redacted]
Samuels	Hugh	09/05/1992		JAM	D								1		1			6	2016	Cobham	Freed Aug 2016	
Smith	Graeme	03/10/1982		SCO	GK	30			1			5						11	2012	Partick Thistle	Released May 2017	
Smith	Allan	25/01/1994		SCO	F		8											11	2017	Forfar Athletic		OOC
Sopel	Aidan	01/01/2000		SCO	M														2016	Inverness CT	OL to Banks o' Dee Sep 2016 -Jan 2017	OOC
Stevenson	Jamie	13/07/1984		SCO	M	32	2		1			5						2	2014	Cowdenbeath		OOC
Strachan	Ryan	01/08/1990		SCO	D	31	1	2				5			2			1	2009	Celtic	Released May 2017	[redacted]
Own Goals														1								
NEW SIGNINGS																						
Gibson	Willie			SCO	M														2017	Stranraer		End 2017/18
Robertson	Mason				M														2017	Stenhousemuir		End 2017/18
McLean	Russell				F														2017	East Kilbride		End 2017/18
Fleming	Greg				GK														2017	Ayr United		End 2017/18
McCracken	David				D														2017	Falkirk		End 2017/18
Hobday	Fraser				GK														2017	Huntly		End 2017/18

Source of Birthdates: transfermarkt.com

Date	Comp	H/A	Opponents	F	A		HT		Referee	Crowd	Scorers
19/07/2016	LC	H	Forfar Athletic	2	0		2	0	G Ross	508	Munro og, McAllister
23/07/2016	LC	A	East Fife	1	2		1	1	K Graham	532	J Brown
26/07/2016	LC	H	Dundee	2	1		0	0	N Walsh	998	McAllister 2
30/07/2016	LC	A	Dumbarton	3	3	6-5p	1	2	A Muir	305	Dzierzawski, McIntosh, McAllister
06/08/2016	L	A	Alloa	0	4		0	3	A Newlands	504	
09/08/2016	LC1	A	Rangers	0	5		0	2	A Dallas	27076	
13/08/2016	L	H	East Fife	0	3		0	2	D Munro	492	
16/08/2016	CC2	H	Brora Rangers	3	2		0	1	M Northcroft	399	J Brown, McAllister, McIntosh
20/08/2016	L	H	Albion Rovers	2	2		1	0	G Irvine	503	Baptie, McAllister
27/08/2016	L	A	Stranraer	0	1		0	1	E Anderson	376	
03/09/2016	CC3	A	Dundee United	2	3	AET	2	2	N Walsh	3520	McAllister 2
10/09/2016	L	H	Queen's Park	2	0		0	0	S Finnie	519	Redman, Riley
17/09/2016	L	A	Stenhousemuir	2	2		2	0	S Kirkland	331	Riley, Dzierzawski
24/09/2016	L	A	Brechin City	1	2		1	1	C Charleston	431	McAllister
01/10/2016	L	H	Livingston	1	2		1	1	G Duncan	569	Kelleher
15/10/2016	L	A	Airdrieonians	3	1		0	0	A Muir	482	Kelleher, McAllister, McIntosh
22/10/2016	L	A	Albion Rovers	1	0		0	0	D Lowe	360	J Brown
29/10/2016	L	H	Stranraer	2	0		0	0	C Steven	444	McAllister, S Brown
05/11/2016	L	H	Brechin City	1	3		0	1	S Kirkland	621	McAllister
12/11/2016	L	A	Queen's Park	0	0		0	0	N Walsh	524	
19/11/2016	L	A	Livingston	2	1		1	0	G Aitken	712	McIntosh, S Brown
26/11/2016	SC3	H	Alloa	0	1		0	0	E Anderson	563	
03/12/2016	L	H	Airdrieonians	2	4		1	3	A Newlands	475	Riley, McIntosh
10/12/2016	L	H	Alloa	1	1		0	0	G Ross	365	Kelleher
17/12/2016	L	A	East Fife	0	2		0	0	C Charleston	486	
26/12/2016	L	H	Stenhousemuir	0	2		0	0	C Napier	427	
02/01/2017	L	A	Brechin City	1	0		0	0	G Irvine	553	McAllister
07/01/2017	L	H	Livingston	2	3		0	0	D Lowe	582	Riley, McAllister
14/01/2017	L	A	Alloa	1	0		0	0	C Steven	504	McIntosh
28/01/2017	L	H	Queen's Park	4	0		3	0	K Graham	442	Strachan, Anderson, McAllister 2
04/02/2017	L	A	Airdrieonians	1	4		1	0	C Charleston	599	McAllister
11/02/2017	L	H	Albion Rovers	1	1		1	0	M Roncone	423	McAllister
18/02/2017	L	A	Stranraer	3	3		1	2	S Kirkland	459	McAllister 2, Anderson
25/02/2017	L	H	East Fife	1	1		0	0	G Duncan	495	J Brown
04/03/2017	L	A	Stenhousemuir	1	3		0	2	D Munro	362	J Brown
11/03/2017	L	H	Brechin City	0	1		0	0	M Northcroft	483	
18/03/2017	L	A	Albion Rovers	0	0		0	0	S Finnie	285	
25/03/2017	L	H	Stranraer	2	2		1	2	G Beaton	449	McAllister, Redman
01/04/2017	L	H	Airdrieonians	1	1		1	1	E Anderson	524	McAllister
08/04/2017	L	A	Queen's Park	0	2		0	1	B Cook	501	
15/04/2017	L	A	East Fife	2	1		1	1	M Northcroft	636	Redman, Reid
22/04/2017	L	H	Stenhousemuir	0	1		0	1	S Finnie	587	
29/04/2017	L	A	Livingston	1	4		0	3	K Graham	891	Redman
06/05/2017	L	H	Alloa	3	2		0	1	C Charleston	681	McAllister, Anderson, J Brown
10/05/2017	PO	A	Montrose	1	1		1	1	M Northcroft	1251	Strachan
13/05/2017	PO	H	Montrose	3	0		1	0	S Kirkland	1096	McAllister 2, J Brown
17/05/2017	PO	A	Forfar Athletic	1	2		1	0	S Finnie	958	McAllister
20/05/2017	PO	H	Forfar Athletic	1	5		0	2	G Duncan	1084	S Brown

FRIENDLIES / OTHER GAMES						
05/07/2016	A	Montrose	2	0		
09/07/2016	A	Fraserburgh	1	0		
10/07/2016	A	Formartine United	6	1		

Date	Comp	H/A	Opponents	F	A		1	2	3	4	5	6	7	8	9	10	11	12	13	14	15	16	17	18
19/07/2016	LC	H	Forfar Athletic	2	0		G Smith	Blockley	Noble	Strachan	Rumsby	Dzierzawski	Stevenson&	Redman	Ferry	McAllister+	Riley*	McIntosh*	J Brown+	Samuels&	Baptie	Hobday		
23/07/2016	LC	A	East Fife	1	2		G Smith	Ross	Noble	Strachan	Rumsby	Dzierzawski&	Stevenson	J Brown	Ferry*	McAllister	Riley+	Redman*	McIntosh+	Blockley&	Baptie	Hobday	Samuels	Adams
26/07/2016	LC	H	Dundee	2	1		G Smith	Ross	Noble	Strachan	Rumsby	Kelleher	Stevenson+	Redman	Dzierzawski*	McAllister	J Brown&	McIntosh*	Nassor+	Blockley&	Baptie	Hobday	Samuels	Adams
30/07/2016	LC	A	Dumbarton	3	3	6-5p	G Smith	Ross&	Noble	Strachan	Rumsby	Kelleher	Stevenson	Nassor*	Dzierzawski	McAllister	McIntosh+	J Brown*	Riley+	Blockley&	Baptie	Hobday	Samuels	Adams
06/08/2016	L	A	Alloa	0	4		G Smith	Ross	Noble	Strachan+	Rumsby	Kelleher	Stevenson	Redman&	Dzierzawski*	McAllister	J Brown	McIntosh*	Riley+	Blockley&	Baptie	Hobday	Samuels	Nassor
09/08/2016	LC1	A	Rangers	0	5		G Smith	Ross+	Noble	Strachan	Rumsby	Kelleher	Stevenson*	Redman&	Ferry	McAllister	Blockley	Riley*	McIntosh+	Nassor&	J Brown	Hobday	Samuels	Dzierzawski
13/08/2016	L	H	East Fife	0	3		G Smith	Ross	Noble	Strachan	Dzierzawski	Kelleher	Stevenson*	Redman+	Ferry	McAllister	Riley&	McIntosh*	J Brown+	Nassor&	Rumsby	Hobday	Samuels	Baptie
16/08/2016	CC2	H	Brora Rangers	3	2		Hobday	Samuels*	Nassor+	Strachan	Rumsby	Kelleher	Baptie	Redman	Blockley	McIntosh	J Brown	McAllister*	Riley+	Ferry	Jarvie			
20/08/2016	L	H	Albion Rovers	2	2		Hobday	Ross	Ferry	Strachan	Rumsby*	Kelleher	Baptie	J Brown&	Dzierzawski	McIntosh+	McAllister	McCluskey*	Redman+	Riley&	Noble	Blockley	Nassor	G Smith
27/08/2016	L	A	Stranraer	0	1		Hobday	Ross	Ferry*	Strachan	McCluskey	Kelleher	Baptie	S Brown	J Brown&	Blockley+	McAllister	Dzierzawski*	Riley+	McIntosh&	Redman	Rumsby	Noble	G Smith
03/09/2016	CC3	A	Dundee United	2	3	AET	Hobday	Ross	Rumsby*	Strachan+	McCluskey	Kelleher	Baptie	S Brown	Dzierzawski	McIntosh&	McAllister	Blockley*	Redman+	Riley&	J Brown	Noble	Nassor	G Smith
10/09/2016	L	H	Queen's Park	2	0		Hobday	Ross*	Noble	Strachan	McCluskey	Kelleher	Riley&	S Brown	Dzierzawski	Redman	McAllister+	Rumsby*	McIntosh+	J Brown&	Baptie	Blockley	Nassor	G Smith
17/09/2016	L	A	Stenhousemuir	2	2		Hobday	Rumsby	Noble	Strachan	McCluskey*	Kelleher	Riley+	S Brown	Dzierzawski	Redman&	McAllister	McIntosh*	Ferry+	Stevenson&	J Brown	Baptie	Nassor	G Smith
24/09/2016	L	A	Brechin City	1	2		G Smith	Stevenson	Noble	Strachan	Ferry	Kelleher	Riley+	S Brown	Dzierzawski&	Redman*	McAllister	McIntosh*	McCluskey+	J Brown&	Rumsby	Baptie	Nassor	G Smith
01/10/2016	L	H	Livingston	1	2		G Smith	Stevenson	Noble	Strachan&	Ferry	Kelleher	Riley*	S Brown	Dzierzawski	McCluskey+	McAllister	McIntosh*	J Brown+	Redman&	Rumsby	Baptie	Blockley	Hobday
15/10/2016	L	A	Airdrieonians	3	1		G Smith	Stevenson	Noble	Strachan	Ferry	Kelleher	Riley*	S Brown	Dzierzawski+	McCluskey&	McAllister	J Brown*	Redman+	McIntosh&	Rumsby	Baptie	Blockley	Hobday
22/10/2016	L	A	Albion Rovers	1	0		G Smith	Stevenson	Noble	Strachan	Ferry	Kelleher	Redman+	S Brown	J Brown&	McCluskey*	McAllister	Riley*	Dzierzawski+	Rumsby&	McIntosh	Baptie	Blockley	Hobday
29/10/2016	L	H	Stranraer	2	0		G Smith	Stevenson	Noble*	Strachan	Ferry&	Kelleher	Riley+	S Brown	J Brown	McCluskey	McAllister	Ross*	McIntosh+	Dzierzawski&	Rumsby	Baptie	Blockley	Hobday
05/11/2016	L	H	Brechin City	1	3		G Smith	Stevenson	Noble	Strachan	Ferry	Kelleher	Riley+	S Brown	J Brown&	McCluskey*	McAllister	McIntosh*	Ross+	Blockley&	Rumsby	Baptie	Dzierzawski	Hobday
12/11/2016	L	A	Queen's Park	0	0		G Smith	Stevenson	Noble	Ross*	Ferry	Kelleher	Riley+	S Brown	J Brown*	McIntosh	Blockley	Strachan*	Dzierzawski+	Rumsby&	Nassor	Baptie	Hobday	
19/11/2016	L	A	Livingston	2	1		G Smith	Stevenson+	Noble	Ross	Strachan	Kelleher	Blockley	S Brown	J Brown*	McIntosh	McAllister&	Dzierzawski*	Riley+	Rumsby&	Nassor	Baptie	Hobday	
26/11/2016	SC3	H	Alloa	0	1		G Smith	Stevenson+	Noble	Ross	Ferry	Kelleher	Blockley	S Brown&	Riley*	McIntosh	McAllister	J Brown*	Dzierzawski+	Redman&	Nassor	Baptie	Jarvie	Rumsby
03/12/2016	L	H	Airdrieonians	2	4		G Smith	Stevenson*	Noble	Ross	Ferry+	Kelleher	Blockley	S Brown	J Brown&	McIntosh	Riley	Dzierzawski*	Redman+	Rumsby&	Nassor	Baptie	Hobday	
10/12/2016	L	H	Alloa	1	1		G Smith	Dzierzawski	Noble	Ross	Ferry	Kelleher	Redman*	S Brown	McAllister	McIntosh	Riley+	J Brown*	Baptie+	Rumsby	Blockley	Hobday		
17/12/2016	L	A	East Fife	0	2		Hobday	Dzierzawski*	Noble	Ross	Ferry	Kelleher	Redman&	S Brown	J Brown+	McAllister	Riley	Blockley*	McIntosh+	Rumsby&	Stevenson	Baptie	Nassor	G Smith
26/12/2016	L	H	Stenhousemuir	0	2		Hobday	Stevenson	Noble	Ross	Ferry	Kelleher	Redman*	S Brown	Baptie+	McAllister	Riley	McIntosh*	J Brown+	Rumsby	Nassor	Dzierzawski	G Smith	
02/01/2017	L	A	Brechin City	1	0		G Smith	Stevenson	Noble	Ross	Ferry	Kelleher	Comrie	S Brown	J Brown+	McAllister&	Riley*	McIntosh*	Redman+	Dzierzawski&	Baptie	Rumsby	Adams	Hobday
07/01/2017	L	H	Livingston	2	3		G Smith	Stevenson	Noble	Ross	Ferry	Rumsby	Comrie	S Brown	J Brown*	McAllister	Riley+	McIntosh*	Blockley+	Dzierzawski	Baptie	Adams	Hobday	
14/01/2017	L	A	Alloa	1	0		G Smith	Stevenson	Noble	Ross	Ferry	McMullin	Comrie	S Brown	Blockley+	McAllister*	Riley&	McIntosh*	Dzierzawski+	J Brown&	Baptie	Adams	Hobday	
28/01/2017	L	H	Queen's Park	4	0		G Smith	Strachan	Noble	Anderson	Ferry*	McMullin	Comrie	S Brown	Blockley+	McAllister	Stevenson&	A Smith*	J Brown+	Redman&	Baptie	Adams	Dzierzawski	Hobday
04/02/2017	L	A	Airdrieonians	1	4		G Smith	Strachan	Noble	Anderson	Ferry+	McMullin	Comrie	S Brown	Blockley&	McAllister	Stevenson*	McIntosh*	Ross+	J Brown&	A Smith	Redman	Dzierzawski	Hobday
11/02/2017	L	H	Albion Rovers	1	1		G Smith	Strachan	Noble+	Anderson	Ross&	McMullin	Gordon	S Brown	Blockley*	McAllister	Stevenson	Comrie*	McIntosh+	A Smith&	J Brown	Redman	Dzierzawski	Hobday
18/02/2017	L	A	Stranraer	3	3		G Smith	Strachan&	Riley*	Anderson	Ross	McMullin	Gordon	S Brown	Comrie	McAllister	Stevenson+	McIntosh*	Redman+	Dzierzawski&	J Brown	A Smith	Baptie	Hobday
25/02/2017	L	H	East Fife	1	1		G Smith	Strachan	Riley*	Anderson	Ferry&	McMullin	Gordon	S Brown	Comrie	McAllister	Stevenson+	J Brown*	A Smith+	Dzierzawski&	Redman	McIntosh	Baptie	Hobday
04/03/2017	L	A	Stenhousemuir	1	3		G Smith	Strachan	J Brown	Anderson	Ferry*	McMullin	Gordon	Ross+	Comrie	McAllister	Stevenson&	Noble*	McIntosh+	Redman&	Riley	Dzierzawski	Smith	Hobday
11/03/2017	L	H	Brechin City	0	1		G Smith	Noble*	J Brown	Anderson	Reid	Redman&	Gordon	S Brown	Comrie	Riley	Stevenson+	McMullin*	McIntosh+	A Smith&	Strachan	Dzierzawski	Ross	Hobday
18/03/2017	L	A	Albion Rovers	0	0		G Smith	Strachan&	McMullin*	Anderson	Reid	Redman	Gordon	S Brown	Comrie	McAllister	Stevenson+	Ross*	J Brown+	Riley&	A Smith	Dzierzawski	McIntosh	Hobday
25/03/2017	L	H	Stranraer	2	2		G Smith	Strachan	Ross	Anderson	Reid	Redman	Gordon*	S Brown	Comrie&	McAllister	Riley	McMullin*+	Ferry+	J Brown&	A Smith	Stevenson	Noble	Hobday
01/04/2017	L	H	Airdrieonians	1	1		G Smith	Strachan	Noble	Anderson	Reid*	Redman+	Ferry	S Brown	Comrie	McAllister	Riley&	McMullin*	J Brown+	Stevenson&	A Smith	Dzierzawski	McIntosh	Hobday
08/04/2017	L	A	Queen's Park	0	2		Hobday	Strachan	Noble	Anderson&	Ross	Redman+	Ferry	S Brown	Stevenson	McAllister	J Brown*	Riley*	Comrie+	A Smith&	McMullin	Dzierzawski	McIntosh	G Smith
15/04/2017	L	A	East Fife	2	1		Hobday	Strachan	Reid	Comrie	Ross	Redman	Ferry	S Brown	Stevenson+	McAllister&	Riley*	Anderson*	J Brown+	A Smith&	Noble	McMullin	McIntosh	G Smith
22/04/2017	L	H	Stenhousemuir	0	1		Hobday	Strachan	Reid	Comrie*	Ross	Redman	Ferry	S Brown+	Stevenson	McAllister	Anderson&	Riley*	J Brown+	A Smith&	Noble	McMullin	McIntosh	G Smith
29/04/2017	L	A	Livingston	1	4		Hobday	Strachan	Reid	Noble	Ross	Redman	Ferry*	S Brown	Stevenson	McAllister	Riley+	McIntosh*	J Brown+	A Smith	Anderson	Comrie	Blockley	G Smith
06/05/2017	L	H	Alloa	3	2		G Smith	Strachan	Reid	Noble*	Ross	Redman	J Brown	S Brown	Stevenson	McAllister	McIntosh+	Riley*	Anderson+	A Smith	Dzierzawski	Comrie	Blockley	Hobday
10/05/2017	PO	A	Montrose	1	1		G Smith	Strachan	Reid	Noble	Ross+	Redman	J Brown*	S Brown	Stevenson	McAllister	Anderson&	Riley*	Gordon+	McIntosh&	Ferry	A Smith	Comrie	Hobday
13/05/2017	PO	H	Montrose	3	0		G Smith	Strachan	Reid	Gordon	Ferry&	McMullin	J Brown	S Brown*	Stevenson	McAllister	Riley+	Redman*	McIntosh+	Anderson&	Comrie	A Smith	Noble	Hobday
17/05/2017	PO	A	Forfar Athletic	1	2		G Smith	Strachan	Reid+	Gordon	Redman	McMullin&	J Brown*	S Brown	Stevenson	McAllister	Anderson	Ross*	McIntosh+	Blockley&	Riley	A Smith	Ferry	Hobday
20/05/2017	PO	H	Forfar Athletic	1	5		G Smith	Strachan&	Ross	Gordon	Redman+	McMullin*	Ferry	S Brown	Stevenson	Riley	McIntosh	Anderson*	A Smith+	Blockley&	Dzierzawski	J Brown	Noble	Hobday

Queen of the South FC 2016/17

Founded	1919
Ground	Palmerston Park
Postcode	DG2 9BA
Tel	01387 254853
Capacity	7620
Closest Railway Station	Dumfries
Record Attendance	26552 v Hearts, SC, 23/2/1952
Record Win	11-1 v Stranraer, SC, 16/1/1932
Record Defeat	2-10 v Dundee, Lge 1/12/1962
Most League Goals in a Season	37 Jimmy Gray 1927/8
Chairman	Billy Hewitson
Secretary	Craig Paterson
Manager	Gavin Skelton , then Gary Naysmith
Assistant Manager	Dougie Anderson
Colours 2016/17 Top	Blue
Shorts	White
Sponsor	KBT Pharmacy Kirkcudbright
Manufacturer	Macron
Change Colours 2014/15 Top	Red
Shorts	Red
Nicknames	Doonhamers, Queens
Web	www.qosfc.com
Match Programme 2016/17	The Queens £2.50

Since achieving the heights in 2014/15 it has been downhill for the Doonhamers. Although never seriously troubled by relegation they also never challenged for the promotion play offs. A season of consistent inconsistency would be the way to put it.

Gavin Skelton left the club after only a few months in charge and Garry Naysmith came in to replace him. It was unfair to judge Naysmith on a squad that was not really his own—2017/18 will be different as he has had time to bring in more of the players he wants.

Queens last played in the top flight of Scottish football more than 50 years ago. Given that towns such as Perth, Falkirk, Dunfermline etc have sustained top level football for long spells in that time, there is no reason why Queens should not aspire to this. In 2016/17 there was no prospect of it happening despite the ebst efforts of Stephen Dobbie, who looks a class above Championship level.

PREDICTION FOR 2017/18

Same old, same old. Mid table with something to spare at either end of the table.

THE ORIGINS OF QUEEN OF THE SOUTH

Formed by the amalgamation of 5th KOSB, Dumfries and Arrol-Johnston FC. A meeting was held in Dumfries Town Hall on 21st March 1919 to establish a club to represent the 'twin burghs' of Dumfries and Maxwelltown.

According to Allan (1996) a Mr McGeorge of Nunfield chaired the meeting and he hoped that "in place of the former divided support and the jealousies which they used to have locally with two or three teams in the district, one strong club would be created".

The intention was that four clubs (the three named above plus Dumfries Amateurs) would merge to form a new club. However, Dumfries Amateurs wanted no part of the plan.

Allan (1996) quotes a number of names that were debated for the club before Queen of the South was chosen: Nithvale, Vale of Nith, Dumfries United, Southern Wanderers, Southern United, Riverburn and Dumfries and Maxwelltown United.

Queen of the South was chosen both for its Burns connection and because it did not identify specifically with either Dumfries or Maxwelltown. Palmerston Park was adopted as a home ground and the club chose to continue with the old 5th KRV and Max-welltown Volunteers colours of blue and white.

Allan, David A – **The Birth of the Queens**, in SFH Number 60, February / March 1996

And yes, they are **THE ONLY TEAM IN THE BIBLE** . . .

Matthew 12:42

"The queen of the south will rise at the judgment with this generation and condemn it; for she came from the ends of the earth to hear the wisdom of Solomon, and now One greater than Solomon is here."

Date	Comp	H/A	Opponents	F	A		HT		Referee	Crowd	Scorers
16/07/2016	LC	A*	Queen's Park	2	0		2	0	A Newlands	410	Pickard, Dowie
19/07/2016	LC	H	Airdrie	2	0		2	0	N Walsh	1036	Lyle 2
23/07/2016	LC	A	Partick Thistle	1	2		0	0	A Muir	2358	Hilson
30/07/2016	LC	H	Stenhousemuir	1	0		0	0	K Graham	1013	Hamill
06/08/2016	L	A	Dundee United	1	1		1	0	A Dallas	7058	Millar
09/08/2016	LC1	A	Hibernian	3	1		0	1	E Anderson	7646	Dobbie, Anderson, Dykes
13/08/2016	L	H	Ayr United	4	1		2	0	S Finnie	1982	Lyle 2, Dobbie, Dykes
20/08/2016	L	H	Falkirk	2	0		1	0	S Kirkland	1841	Dobbie 2
27/08/2016	L	A	Dunfermline Athletic	1	0		1	0	C Charleston	3973	Lyle
03/09/2016	CC3	H	Stenhousemuir	7	1		4	0	G Aitken	1158	Dobbie 2, Rigg 2, Hilson, Anderson, Lyle
10/09/2016	L	A	St Mirren	3	1		2	1	B Cook	3102	Lyle 2, Dobbie
17/09/2016	L	H	Raith Rovers	3	1		0	0	G Duncan	1864	Dobbie 2, Brotherston
20/09/2016	LC2	A	Rangers	0	5		0	1	D Robertson	26079	
24/09/2016	L	H	Hibernian	0	0		0	0	S McLean	3703	
01/10/2016	L	A	Dumbarton	0	0		0	0	M Northcroft	840	
09/10/2016	CC4	H	Linfield	2	0	AET	0	0	I Griffiths (W)	2358	Dykes, Dobbie
15/10/2016	L	H	Morton	0	5		0	3	S Kirkland	1695	
22/10/2016	L	A	Ayr United	0	1		0	0	J McKendrick	1842	
29/10/2016	L	A	Raith Rovers	0	1		0	0	C Allan	1244	
05/11/2016	L	H	Dundee United	1	4		1	2	S McLean	2316	Anderson
12/11/2016	CC5	H	Alloa	2	0		1	0	E Anderson	1180	Dobbie 2
19/11/2016	L	A	Hibernian	0	4		0	2	C Charleston	13861	
29/11/2016	SC3	A	Albion Rovers	1	2		0	1	A Newlands	387	Hamill
03/12/2016	L	H	Dumbarton	1	2		0	2	G Duncan	1261	Lyle
06/12/2016	L	H	St Mirren	2	3		2	1	C Allan	1147	Dobbie 2
10/12/2016	L	A	Falkirk	2	2		1	1	N Walsh	4170	Dobbie, Lyle
17/12/2016	L	H	Dunfermline Athletic	2	2		1	0	J McKendrick	1561	Brownlie, Dobbie
24/12/2016	L	A	Morton	0	1		0	1	B Cook	1638	
31/12/2016	L	H	Ayr United	0	0		0	0	S Kirkland	1594	
07/01/2017	L	A	St Mirren	3	0		1	0	M Northcroft	3105	Dobbie, Thomson, McKenzie og
14/01/2017	L	A	Dundee United	3	3		1	1	A Muir	6136	Dobbie, Thomson, Thomas
21/01/2017	L	A	Dumbarton	2	1		1	0	S Kirkland	825	Thomas 2
28/01/2017	L	H	Hibernian	0	1		0	0	S McLean	3007	
04/02/2017	L	H	Morton	3	0		0	0	B Madden	1588	Lyle, Jacobs, Thomson
18/02/2017	CCSF	H	Dundee United	2	3		0	3	N Walsh	1526	Dobbie, Lyle
25/02/2017	L	H	Raith Rovers	2	1		2	0	B Cook	1484	Rankin, Lyle
04/03/2017	L	H	Falkirk	0	2		0	1	G Duncan	1995	Kidd, Sibbald
07/03/2017	L	A	Dunfermline Athletic	1	1		1	1	E Anderson	2635	Thomson
11/03/2017	L	A	Morton	0	1		0	0	C Charleston	1451	
18/03/2017	L	H	St Mirren	0	2		0	1	A Dallas	1728	
25/03/2017	L	A	Raith Rovers	1	1		1	1	C Steven	1609	Dobbie
01/04/2017	L	H	Dundee United	4	2		2	1	S Finnie	1514	Lyle, Dobbie, Dykes, Hilson
08/04/2017	L	A	Ayr United	2	0		0	0	A Newlands	1476	Dobbie 2
15/04/2017	L	A	Hibernian	0	3		0	2	B Cook	17054	
22/04/2017	L	H	Dumbarton	1	2		1	2	J McKendrick	1289	Dobbie
29/04/2017	L	A	Falkirk	2	2		1	1	C Allan	4673	Dobbie 2
06/05/2017	L	H	Dunfermline Athletic	0	1		0	0	A Newlands	1849	

FRIENDLIES / OTHER GAMES					
01/07/2016	A	Dalbeattie Star	4	0	
05/07/2016	A	Carlisle United	3	2	CD
09/07/2016	A	Gretna	6	1	Tnt
10/07/2016	N	South Shields	3	1	at Gretna Tnt
12/07/2016	A	Annan Athletic	4	0	
13/07/2016	A	Penrith	4	3	
26/07/2016	A	Workington	2	1	
28/07/2016	A	Cumnock	0	3	U20

Date	Comp	H/A	Opponents	F	A		1	2	3	4	5	6	7	8	9	10	11	12	13	14	15	16	17	18
16/07/2016	LC	A*	Queen's Park	2	0		Robinson	Hamill	Marshall	Dowie	Higgins	Anderson	Pickard&	Tapping	Dykes+	Hilson	Rigg*	Lyle*	Brotherston+	Jacobs&	*Brownlie*	*Smith*	*Moxon*	*Atkinson*
19/07/2016	LC	H	Airdrie	2	0		Robinson	Hamill	Marshall	Dowie	Higgins	Anderson	Pickard*	Tapping	Dykes	Hilson+	Lyle&	Jacobs*	Smith+	Rigg&	*Brownlie*	*Brotherston*	*Moxon*	*Atkinson*
23/07/2016	LC	A	Partick Thistle	1	2		Robinson	Hamill	Marshall	Dowie	Higgins	Anderson*	Millar	Tapping+	Jacobs	Hilson	Lyle&	Dykes*	Moxon+	Rigg&	*Brownlie*	*Brotherston*	*Smith*	*Atkinson*
30/07/2016	LC	H	Stenhousemuir	1	0		Robinson	Hamill	Marshall	Dowie	Higgins	Anderson	Millar	Pickard	Dykes	Smith+	Lyle*	Hilson*	Brotherston+	*Jacobs*	*Brownlie*	*Hooper*	*Moxon*	*Thomson*
06/08/2016	L	A	Dundee United	1	1		Robinson	Hamill	Marshall	Dowie	Higgins*	Anderson	Millar	Jacobs	Dykes	Hilson&	Lyle+	Brownlie*	Dobbie+	Tapping&	*Rigg*	*Brotherston*	*Pickard*	*Thomson*
09/08/2016	LC1	A	Hibernian	3	1		Robinson	Hamill+	Brownlie	Dowie	Hooper	Anderson	Millar	Jacobs	Dykes	Hilson*	Lyle&	Dobbie*	Brotherston+	Rigg&	*Moxon*	*Tapping*	*Pickard*	*Thomson*
13/08/2016	L	H	Ayr United	4	1		Robinson	Hamill	Brownlie	Dowie	Marshall	Anderson	Tapping+	Jacobs	Dykes	Dobbie&	Lyle*	Brotherston*	Pickard+	Rigg&	*Moxon*	*Murray*	*Moxon*	*Thomson*
20/08/2016	L	H	Falkirk	2	0		Robinson	Hamill	Brownlie	Dowie	Marshall	Anderson	Millar+	Jacobs	Dykes	Dobbie&	Lyle*	Hilson*	Pickard+	Moxon&	*Rigg*	*Hooper*	*Tapping*	*Thomson*
27/08/2016	L	A	Dunfermline Athletic	1	0		Robinson	Hamill	Brownlie	Dowie	Marshall	Anderson	Millar&	Jacobs	Dykes+	Dobbie&	Lyle*	Hilson*	Rigg+	Tapping&	*Higgins*	*Pickard*	*Moxon*	*Thomson*
03/09/2016	CC3	H	Stenhousemuir	7	1		Robinson	Hamill	Brownlie	Dowie	Marshall	Anderson*	Millar	Jacobs+	Hilson	Dobbie	Lyle&	Moxon*	Pickard+	Rigg&	*Higgins*	*Tapping*	*Brotherston*	*Atkinson*
10/09/2016	L	A	St Mirren	3	1		Robinson	Hamill	Brownlie	Dowie	Marshall	Anderson&	Millar*	Jacobs	Hilson	Dobbie	Lyle+	Pickard*	Rigg+	Brotherston&	*Higgins*	*Tapping*	*Moxon*	*Atkinson*
17/09/2016	L	H	Raith Rovers	3	1		Robinson	Hamill	Brownlie	Dowie	Marshall	Anderson*	Millar	Jacobs	Hilson&	Dobbie	Lyle+	Dykes*	Brotherston+	Rigg&	*Higgins*	*Pickard*	*Moxon*	*Atkinson*
20/09/2016	LC2	A	Rangers	0	5		Robinson	Hamill	Brownlie	Dowie	Marshall	Anderson*	Millar	Jacobs+	Hilson	Dobbie	Lyle&	Dykes*	Pickard+	Brotherston&	*Higgins*	*Rigg*	*Moxon*	*Atkinson*
24/09/2016	L	H	Hibernian	0	0		Robinson	Hamill	Brownlie	Dowie	Higgins	Dykes	Millar	Jacobs*	Hilson	Dobbie	Lyle+	Pickard*	Anderson+	*Hooper*	*Higgins*	*Rigg*	*Moxon*	*Atkinson*
01/10/2016	L	A	Dumbarton	0	0		Robinson	Hamill	Brownlie	Dowie	Higgins	Anderson*	Millar	Jacobs	Dykes	Dobbie	Rigg+	Brotherston*	Pickard+	*Hooper*	*Marshall*	*Moxon*	*Leighfield*	
09/10/2016	CC4	H	Linfield	2	0	AET	Robinson	Hamill	Brownlie	Dowie	Marshall	Anderson+	Pickard	Jacobs*	Dykes	Dobbie	Rigg&	Millar*	Brotherston+	Moxon&	*Higgins*	*Hooper*	*Nelson*	*Leighfield*
15/10/2016	L	H	Morton	0	5		Robinson	Hamill	Brownlie	Dowie	Marshall	Anderson*	Millar+	Pickard	Dykes	Dobbie	Rigg&	Hooper*	Brotherston+	Fergusson&	*Moxon*	*Bell*	*Nelson*	*Leighfield*
22/10/2016	L	A	Ayr United	0	1		Robinson	Higgins	Brownlie	Dowie	Marshall	Brotherston+	Millar	Jacobs	Dykes	Dobbie	Pickard*	Anderson*	Rigg+	*Moxon*	*Ferguson*	*Nelson*	*Leighfield*	
29/10/2016	L	A	Raith Rovers	0	1		Robinson	Higgins	Brownlie	Dowie	Marshall	Anderson*	Rigg	Jacobs	Dykes	Dobbie	Pickard+	Brotherston*	Millar+	*Moxon*	*Ferguson*	*Nelson*	*Bell*	*Atkinson*
05/11/2016	L	H	Dundee United	1	4		Robinson	Higgins	Brownlie	Dowie	Marshall	Anderson+	Millar	Jacobs&	Dykes	Dobbie	Lyle*	Rigg*	Brotherston+	Hamill&	*Hooper*	*Pickard*	*Moxon*	*Atkinson*
12/11/2016	CC5	H	Alloa	2	0		Robinson	Hamill	Brownlie	Dowie	Marshall	Anderson	Millar+	Jacobs	Dykes	Dobbie	Lyle*	Brotherston*	Pickard+	*Moxon*	*Hooper*	*Rigg*	*Higgins*	*Atkinson*
19/11/2016	L	A	Hibernian	0	4		Robinson	Higgins	Brownlie	Dowie	Marshall	Anderson*	Millar	Jacobs	Dykes	Pickard	Lyle+	Brotherston*	Rigg+	*Fergusson*	*Hooper*	*Moxon*	*Bell*	*Atkinson*
29/11/2016	SC3	A	Albion Rovers	1	2		Robinson	Higgins	Brownlie	Dowie*	Marshall	Anderson	Millar	Pickard+	Dykes	Dobbie	Lyle	Hamill*	Carmichael+	*Moxon*	*Hooper*	*Brotherston*	*Atkinson*	
03/12/2016	L	H	Dumbarton	1	2		Robinson	Hamill	Brownlie	Dowie	Marshall	Anderson*	Millar+	Pickard	Dykes	Dobbie	Carmichael	Lyle*	Moxon+	*Higgins*	*Hooper*	*Brotherston*	*Bell*	*Atkinson*
06/12/2016	L	H	St Mirren	2	3		Robinson	Hamill	Brownlie	Dowie	Marshall	Anderson+	Millar	Higgins	Dykes*	Dobbie	Lyle	Pickard*&	Carmichael+	Brotherston&	*Hooper*	*Moxon*	*Bell*	*Atkinson*
10/12/2016	L	A	Falkirk	2	2		Robinson	Hamill	Brownlie	Dowie	Marshall	Anderson*	Millar&	Higgins	Jacobs	Dobbie	Lyle+	Carmichael*	Fergusson+	Moxon&	*Hooper*	*Brotherston*	*Nelson*	*Atkinson*
17/12/2016	L	H	Dunfermline Athletic	2	2		Robinson	Hamill	Brownlie	Dowie	Marshall	Anderson+	Millar	Higgins	Jacobs*	Dobbie	Lyle&	Carmichael*	Moxon+	Fergusson&	*Hooper*	*Bell*	*Nelson*	*Atkinson*
24/12/2016	L	A	Morton	0	1		Robinson	Hamill	Brownlie	Dowie	Marshall	Anderson+	Millar&	Higgins*	Jacobs	Dobbie	Lyle	Bell*	Carmichael+	Fergusson&	*Hooper*	*Moxon*	*Nelson*	*Atkinson*
31/12/2016	L	H	Ayr United	0	0		Robinson	Hamill	Brownlie	Dowie	Marshall	Bell*	Millar+	Carmichael	Jacobs	Dobbie&	Lyle	Moxon*	Fergusson+	Anderson&	*Hooper*	*Higgins*	*Nelson*	*Atkinson*
07/01/2017	L	A	St Mirren	3	0		Robinson	Hamill	Brownlie	Dowie	Marshall	Rankin	Thomson	Carmichael*	Jacobs	Dobbie+	Thomas&	Dykes*	Lyle+	Murray&	*Moxon*	*Higgins*	*Fergusson*	*Atkinson*
14/01/2017	L	A	Dundee United	3	3		Robinson	Mercer	Brownlie	Dowie	Marshall	Rankin	Thomson	Carmichael*	Jacobs	Dobbie+	Thomas	Dykes*	Hamill+	*C Murray*	*Bell*	*Higgins*	*Lyle*	*Atkinson*
21/01/2017	L	A	Dumbarton	2	1		Robinson	Mercer	Brownlie	Dowie	Higgins	Rankin	Thomson	Carmichael*	Jacobs	Dobbie	Thomas	Lyle*	*Hooper*	*C Murray*	*Bell*	*Dykes*	*Atkinson*	
28/01/2017	L	H	Hibernian	0	1		Robinson	Mercer	Brownlie	Dowie	Marshall	Rankin	Thomson	Carmichae*	Jacobs+	Dobbie	Thomas	Lyle*	Dykes+	*C Murray*	*Bell*	*Higgins*	*Hamill*	*Atkinson*
04/02/2017	L	H	Morton	3	0		Robinson	Mercer	Brownlie	Higgins	Marshall	Rankin	Thomson	Thomas&	Jacobs	Dobbie*	Lyle+	Dykes*	Murray+	Hamill&	*Bell*	*Carmichael*	*Atkinson*	
18/02/2017	CCSF	H	Dundee United	2	3		Robinson	Hamill+	Brownlie	Higgins	Marshall	Dowie	Murray*	Thomas	Jacobs	Dobbie	Lyle	Dykes*	Carmichael+	*Hooper*	*Bell*	*Fergusson*	*Atkinson*	
25/02/2017	L	H	Raith Rovers	2	1		Robinson	Mercer	Brownlie	Rankin	Marshall	Dowie	Thomson	Thomas+	Jacobs	Dobbie&	Lyle*	Dykes*	Carmichael+	Ferguson&	*Hamill*	*Higgins*	*Murray*	*Atkinson*
04/03/2017	L	H	Falkirk	0	2		Robinson	Mercer	Brownlie	Rankin*	Marshall	Dowie	Thomson	Thomas	Jacobs	Dobbie&	Lyle+	Dykes*	Hilson+	Carmichael&	*Hamill*	*Higgins*	*Murray*	*Atkinson*
07/03/2017	L	A	Dunfermline Athletic	1	1		Robinson	Mercer	Brownlie	Rankin	Hamill	Higgins	Thomson&	Thomas	Jacobs	Dobbie*	Dykes+	Lyle*	Hilson+	Bell&	*Dowie*	*Carmichael*	*Murray*	*Atkinson*
11/03/2017	L	A	Morton	0	1		Robinson	Mercer	Brownlie	Rankin	Hamill	Higgins	Thomson	Thomas	Jacobs*	Dobbie+	Dykes&	Hilson*	Lyle+	Carmichael&	*Marshall*	*Sonkur*	*Murray*	*Atkinson*
18/03/2017	L	H	St Mirren	0	2		Atkinson	Mercer	Marshall	Dowie	Rankin+	Higgins	Thomson	Thomas&	Jacobs	Dobbie	Dykes*	Lyle*	Hilson+	Murray&	*Hamill*	*Ferguson*	*Carmichael*	*Copland*
25/03/2017	L	A	Raith Rovers	1	1		Robinson	Mercer*	Brownlie	Dowie	Rankin+	Higgins	Thomson+	Marshall	Jacobs	Dobbie	Lyle&	Thomas*	McManus+	Dykes&	*Murray*	*Bell*	*Carmichael*	*Atkinson*
01/04/2017	L	H	Dundee United	4	2		Robinson	Thomas&	Brownlie	Carmichael+	Rankin+	Higgins	Thomson	Marshall	Jacobs	Dobbie	Lyle*	Dykes*	Murray+	Hilson&	*Dowie*	*McManus*	*Mercer*	*Atkinson*
08/04/2017	L	A	Ayr United	2	0		Robinson	Thomas*	Brownlie	Carmichael+	Rankin	Higgins	Thomson	Marshall	Jacobs	Dobbie	Dykes&	Murray*	Hilson+	McManus&	*Dowie*	*Mercer*	*Atkinson*	
15/04/2017	L	A	Hibernian	0	3		Robinson	Thomas*	Brownlie	Carmichael+	Rankin	Higgins	Thomson	Marshall	Jacobs	Dobbie	Dykes&	McManus*	Murray+	Hilson&	*Dowie*	*Mercer*	*Bell*	*Leighfield*
22/04/2017	L	H	Dumbarton	1	2		Robinson	McManus	Brownlie	Murray+	Rankin	Higgins	Thomson*	Marshall	Jacobs	Dobbie	Hilson&	Dykes*	Thomas+	Carmichael&	*Tapping*	*Mercer*	*Atkinson*	
29/04/2017	L	A	Falkirk	2	2		Robinson	Mercer+	Brownlie	Carmichael	Rankin	Higgins	Thomson*	Marshall	Jacobs	Dobbie	Dykes	Thomas*	Tapping+	*Dowie*	*Hilson*	*McManus*	*Murray*	*Atkinson*
06/05/2017	L	H	Dunfermline Athletic	0	1		Robinson	Thomas	Brownlie	Carmichael&	Rankin	Higgins	Tapping*	Marshall	Jacobs	Dobbie	Dykes+	Thomson*	Lyle+	Murray&	*Dowie*	*Hilson*	*Mercer*	*Atkinson*

urname	First Name	DOB	SQ	Nat	Pos	A	S	G	A	S	G	A	S	G	A	S	G	A	S	G	UNS	Signed	Previous Club	Notes	Contract
kubuine	Jesse	08/03/1998		ENG / NIG	M																	2016	Brentford Youth	OL to Dalbeattie Star Jan-May	End 2017/18
nderson	Grant	20/08/1986	7	SCO	M	16	3	1	1			6		1	3		1					2016	Raith Rovers	Freed Jan 2017, joined Peterhead	[redacted]
tkinson	Jim	06/01/1995	20	ENG	GK	1															35	2008	Gretna	Released May 2017	
ell	Owen	15/01/1999	29	SCO	M	1	2														13	2012	Lochar Youths		End 2017/18
rannan	Jack	27/01/1998	26	ENG	D																	2016	QOS Youth	OL to Gretna Aug-Jan, Freed Jan joined Gretna	[redacted]
rotherston	Dean	01/09/1997	35	SCO	F	1	9	1					4			2					7	2009	Lochar Youths	OL to Dalbeattie Star, Jan-May, Released May 2017	
rownlie	Darren	10/04/1994	5	SCO	D	34	1	1	1			2			4						4	2015	Cowdenbeath		End 2017/18
armichael	Daniel	21/06/1990	39	SCO	M	11	8			1						1					4	2016	Hibernian		End 2017/18
opland	Cameron	05/09/1998		ENG	GK																1	2015	Carlisle United	Released May 2017	[redacted]
obbie	Stephen	05/12/1982	11	SCO	F	34	1	19	1			1	1	1	4		6					2016	Bolton Wanderers		End 2017/18
owie	Andy	25/03/1983	4	SCO	M	27			1			6		1	4						6	2013	Partick Thistle	Released May 2017, joined Dumbarton	[redacted]
ykes	Lyndon	07/10/1995	25	AUS	F	20	10	2	1			4	2	1	2	1	1				1	2016	SP Apollo		End 2017/18
ergusson	Ross	01/04/1997	32				6														6	2009	Heston Rovers		End 2017/18
lean	Shane	23/06/1997		ENG / USA	D																	2016	Prescot Cables	Freed June 2017	[redacted]
ourlay	Ewan	29/03/1999		SCO	D																	2016	QOS Youth	OL to Upper Annandale Aug-Jan	
amill	Jamie	29/07/1986	2	SCO	D	18	3			1	1	6		1	4						4	2016	Kilmarnock	Released May 2017, joined Stranraer	[redacted]
enderson	Sam	19/01/1999		SCO	GK																	2016	QOS Youth	OL to St Cuthbert Wanderers Aug-Jan, Freed May 2017	
iggins	Chris	04/07/1985	6	SCO	D	23			1			4			1						15	2011	Dunfermline Athletic	Released May 2017	
ilson	Dale	23/12/1992	10	SCO	F	5	9	1				5	1	1	1		1				2	2015	Forfar Athletic	Released May 2017, joined St Mirren	
ooper	Scott	14/01/1995	16	SCO	D		1					1									17	2006	Unattached	Released May 2017, joined Annan Athletic	
acobs	Kyle	14/06/1991	14	RSA	M	33		1				3	2		4						1	2015	Livingston		End 2017/18
eighfield	Jack	23/03/1998	21	SCO	GK																5	2016	Upper Annandale	OL to Gretna Aug-Nov	End 2017/18
yle	Derek	13/02/1981	9	SCO	F	19	8	10	1			5	1	2	3		2				1	2012	Cowdenbeath		End 2017/18
arshall	Jordan	27/10/1996	3	ENG	D	31			1			5			4						2	2015	Carlisle United		End 2017/18
cManus	Conor	29/02/1996		SCO	M	1	3														2	2017	Celtic (OL)	Mar-May 2017	[redacted]
ercer	Scott	18/06/1995		SCO	D	11															5	2017	East Fife		End 2017/18
illar	Mark	23/02/1988	8	SCO	M	17	1	1	1			4			2	1						2015	Peterhead	Freed Jan 2017, joined Livingston	[redacted]
oxon	Owen	17/01/1998	19	ENG	M		5						1			2					22	2014	Carlisle United	Ol to Gretna Jan-May, Freed May 2017	
urray	Connor	24/04/1997	27	SCO	F	1	7								1						10	2015	St Mirren	OL to Gretna Aug-Jan	End 2017/18
urray	Robert	04/03/1997	28	SCO																		2016	QOS Youth	OL to Gretna Aug-Jan, Dalbeattie Jan-May, Freed May 2017	[redacted]
elson	Ryan	14/10/1997	31	ENG																	8	2015	Shildon		
ickard	Jake	14/03/1997	17	ENG		5	6		1			3	1	1	1	2					5	2013	Sunderland	Freed Jan 2017, joined Washington FC	[redacted]
ankin	John	27/06/1983		SCO	M	16		1														2017	Falkirk		End 2017/18
igg	Steven	30/06/1992	12	ENG	F	3	7					1	3		1	1	2				5	2016	Carlisle United	Released May 2017	[redacted]
obertson	Liam	02/03/1999		SCO	F																	2016	QOS Youth	OL to Upper Annandale Aug-Jan	
obinson	Lee	02/07/1986	1	ENG	GK	35			1			6			4							2016	Rangers		End 2017/18
mith	Aidan	11/05/1997	18	SCO	F							1	1								2	2008	Greystone Rovers	OL to Annan Athletic Aug-May, Freed May 2017 joined Annan	[redacted]
onkur	Ayrton	02/06/1998		SCO	M																1	2016	QOS Youth	OL to Hawick RA Aug-Jan, Freed May 2017	
apping	Callum	05/06/1993	22	ENG	D	3	3					3									5	2015	Brechin City		End 2017/18
homas	Dom	14/02/1996		SCO	M	14	3	3							1							2017	Motherwell (OL)	Jan-May 2017	[redacted]
hompson	Jake	08/12/1999		ENG	D																	2016	QOS Youth	OL to Dalbeattie Star Nov-Jan	
homson	Joseph	14/01/1997		SCO	M	16	1	4														2017	Celtic (OL)	Jan-May 2017	[redacted]
homson	Robbie	07/03/1993	21	SCO	GK																6	2015	Cowdenbeath		
remble	Declan	20/04/1999		SCO	F																	2016	QOS Youth	OL to Heston Rovers Aug-Jan	
phill	Adam	30/07/1998		SCO	D																	2016	QOS Youth	OL to Upper Annandale Aug-Jan	
hite	Bailey	17/07/1999		SCO	F																	2016	QOS Youth	OL to Upper Annandale Aug-Jan	
illiams	Callum	04/07/1999		ENG	M																	2016	QOS Youth	OL to Upper Annandale Aug-Jan	
wn Goals								1																	
EW SIGNINGS																									
ooney	Shaun			SCO	D																	2017	York City		End 2017/18
artin	Alan			SCO	GK																	2017	Dumbarton		End 2018/19
ordyce	Calum				D																	2017	Dunfermline Athletic		End 2017/18
tirling	Andy			SCO	F																	2017	Dumbarton		

ource of Birthdates: QOS Match Programme

Queen's Park FC 2016/17

Founded	1867
Ground	Hampden Park
Postcode	G42 9BA
Tel	0141 620 4000
Capacity	52025
Closest Railway Station	Mount Florida
Record Attendance	95772 v Rangers, SC, 18/1/1930
Ground Record	149547, Scotland v England, 1937
Record Win	16-0 v St Peters, SC, 12/9/1885
Record Defeat	0-9 v Motherwell, Lge, 26/4/1930
Most League Goals in a Season	30 William Martin, 1937/8
President	Alan Hutchinson
Secretary	Christine Wright
Manager	Gus McPherson
Assistant Manager	Chris Hillcoat
Colours 2016/17 Top	Blue
Shorts	Grey
Sponsor	Irn Bru
Manufacturer	Underarmour
Change Colours 2016/17 Top	Black and White Hoops
Shorts	White
Nicknames	Spiders
Web	www.queensparkfc.co.uk
Match Programme 2016/17	None issued

Robertson and Ross (2003) quote some interesting figures from the immediate post-Second World War period. In the Summer of 1947 the Glasgow Weekly News reported that during 1946/7 Hampden Park had admitted 1,423,127 spectators to all the sporting occasions it hosted:

Queen's Park League Games (15)	163,014
Third Lanark League Games (15)	194,717
QP League Cup Games (3)	55,901
Thirds League Cup Games (3)	52,009
QP Scottish Cup Game	10,207
Thirds Scottish Cup Game	17,211
QP Friendly v St Johnstone	2,737
Thirds / QP Friendly v Silesia	14,557
Glasgow Cup Final	29,680
Glasgow Charity Cup Tie	16,511
League Cup Semi Final and Final	207,938
Scottish Cup Semi Final and Final	130,160
Great Britain v Rest of Europe	130,617
Scotland v Ireland	98,144
Scottish League v English League	86,917
2nd XI Cup Final	13,953
Schools and Youth Matches	25,880
Junior Cup Ties	136,344
SAAA Championships	11,245
Boxing, Paterson v Medina	25,358

Robertson, Forrest and Ross, David – **The First 100 Years of Hampden**; First Press Publishing, 2003

Gus McPherson continues to do a great job at Hamp consolidating Queens in league One after promotion at end of 2015/16. Indeed, for a spell it looked as i Amateurs could challenge for a play off spot but in the they finished mid table.

2017 marks the 150th Anniversary of this vene institution. In some ways it is a miracle that they survived that long. After dominating the early year Scottish football they have carved out a niche for themse helped by the ownership of Hampden. If the SFA carry their threat to abandon Hampden as their home venue Queens could face a real battle for survival.

PREDICTION FOR 2017/18

As always happens several of the key players have move for greater reward elsewhere. Queens have a fine y policy that will generate replacements but whether or they are ready for the first team is open to debate. Qu might struggle this season and find themselves in the bo two.

Middlesex Wanderers 2016/17

Middlesex Wanderers are a Touring Amateur side – a throwback to a bye-gone age. Over the years many Que Park players have worn their colours, touring all parts of world. Nowadays their tours are more restricted and the choice of Amateur players much more limited.

Middlesex Wanderers – Great War Memorial Tour to France, 2017

26/6/17 US Boulogne Sur Mer v Middlesex Wanderers,
28/6/17 AS Marck V Middlesex Wanderers, 2-5

Queen's Park personnel involved

Ryan McGeever (Tour Captain)
John Manderson (Player)
Ali Miller (Player)
Grant Houghton (Player)
Tony Quinn (Tour Assistant Manager)
Andy Harrison (Tour Physio)

Date	Comp	H/A	Opponents	F	A		HT		Referee	Crowd	Scorers
16/07/2016	LC	H*	Queen of the South	0	2		0	2	A Newlands	410	
19/07/2016	LC	A	Stenhousemuir	2	0		1	0	C Napier	273	Burns, McVey
26/07/2016	LC	H*	Airdrieonians	3	3	7-8p	1	3	D Munro	553	Cummins, Malone, Burns
30/07/2016	LC	A	Partick Thistle	0	2		0	1	A Dallas	2250	
02/08/2016	CC1	H	Kilmarnock U20	5	2		3	2	G Aitken	299	Brown, Wharton, McGeever, Galt, MacPherson
06/08/2016	L	H	Airdrieonians	1	3		0	1	D Lowe	957	Fitzpatrick og
13/08/2016	L	A	Stenhousemuir	2	1		0	1	J McKendrick	534	Miller, Watt
16/08/2016	CC2	A	Partick Thistle U20	1	1	AET, 6-5p	0	0	D Munro	436	Carter
20/08/2016	L	A	Brechin City	0	0		0	0	M Roncone	447	
27/08/2016	L	H	Livingston	1	0		1	0	K Graham	698	Malone
03/09/2016	CC3	H	Morton	2	0		1	0	G Duncan	1085	Cummins, Galt
10/09/2016	L	A	Peterhead	0	2		0	0	S Finnie	519	
17/09/2016	L	H	Alloa	1	2		0	0	B Cook	664	Millen
24/09/2016	L	H	Stranraer	0	2		0	1	C Steven	534	
01/10/2016	L	A	Albion Rovers	0	2		0	1	A Newlands	444	
08/10/2016	CC4	A	Dunfermline	1	2		0	0	N Walsh	1930	El Alagui og
15/10/2016	L	H	East Fife	1	0		1	0	S Millar	571	Fotheringham
22/10/2016	L	A	Airdrieonians	1	4		1	3	G Aitken	702	Millen
29/10/2016	L	H	Stenhousemuir	0	3		0	1	D Munro	538	
05/11/2016	L	A	Stranraer	2	0		1	0	G Ross	466	Zanatta, Brady
12/11/2016	L	H	Peterhead	0	0		0	0	N Walsh	524	
19/11/2016	L	A	East Fife	2	1		1	1	M Northcroft	557	Cummins, Millen
29/11/2016	SC3	H	Montrose	2	0		1	0	S Reid	348	Galt, Woods
03/12/2016	L	H	Brechin City	2	0		1	0	M Roncone	632	Millen, McGeever
10/12/2016	L	H	Albion Rovers	2	1		2	1	C Charleston	662	Millen, Woods
17/12/2016	L	A	Alloa	1	1		0	0	G Duncan	442	Millen
24/12/2016	L	A	Livingston	2	1		0	1	S Kirkland	819	McKernon, Cummins
31/12/2016	L	H	Stranraer	0	1		0	0	D Munro	556	
07/01/2017	L	H	Airdrieonians	2	1		1	1	G Beaton	922	Fotheringham, McGeever
21/01/2017	SC3	A	Ayr United	0	0		0	0	B Cook	1326	
24/01/2017	SC3R	H	Ayr United	2	2	aet, 4-5p	2	1	B Cook	1026	Woods, Wharton
28/01/2017	L	A	Peterhead	0	4		0	3	K Graham	442	
04/02/2017	L	H	East Fife	2	2		2	0	G Ross	566	Zanatta, Brady
11/02/2017	L	A	Stenhousemuir	2	0		1	0	G Irvine	423	Zanatta, Brady
18/02/2017	L	H	Alloa	0	2		0	1	A Muir	657	
28/02/2017	L	A	Brechin City	1	3		1	2	J McKendrick	393	Wharton
04/03/2017	L	H	Livingston	1	1		1	1	A Newlands	701	Zanatta
11/03/2017	L	A	Stranraer	1	1		1	0	G Ross	434	Millen
18/03/2017	L	H	Brechin City	1	1		0	0	R Milne	481	McGeever
25/03/2017	L	A	Alloa	2	2		1	1	M Roncone	675	Galt, MacPherson
01/04/2017	L	A	East Fife	0	0		0	0	D Lowe	692	
04/04/2017	L	A	Albion Rovers	1	1		0	1	S Reid	512	Brady
08/04/2017	L	H	Peterhead	2	0		1	0	B Cook	501	Zanatta, McGeever
15/04/2017	L	H	Albion Rovers	2	0		1	0	L McGarry	677	MacPherson, Galt
22/04/2017	L	A	Livingston	0	4		0	1	G Irvine	821	
29/04/2017	L	H	Stenhousemuir	0	2		0	1	C Napier	764	
06/05/2017	L	A	Airdrieonians	2	3		1	1	J McKendrick	1011	Zanatta, Orsi

FRIENDLIES / OTHER GAMES					
05/07/2016	H	East Stirlingshire	3	0	at New Lesser Hampden
30/07/2016	A	Maryhill	2	3	U20
03/08/2016	A	Neilston	1	3	U20

Date	Comp	H/A	Opponents	F	A		1	2	3	4	5	6	7	8	9	10	11	12	13	14	15	16	17	18
16/07/2016	LC	H*	Queen of the South	0	2		Murphy	Millen	Burns	Wharton	McGeever	Fotheringham*	Miller	Brown+	Woods&	Malone	Galt	Williams*	Brady+	MacPherson&	Watt	McLeish	Mitchell	Bradley
19/07/2016	LC	A	Stenhousemuir	2	0		Murphy	Gibson	Cummins	Millen	McGeever	Brady	Miller	Brown*	Burns	Malone&	Bradley+	McVey*	Galt+	MacPherson&	Watt	Wharton	Woods	Williams
26/07/2016	LC	H*	Airdrieonians	3	3	7-8p	Murphy	Gibson	Cummins	Millen	McGeever	Woods	Miller	Brown*	Burns	Malone&	Bradley +	McVey*	Galt+	MacPherson&	Watt	Wharton	Williams	Fotheringham
30/07/2016	LC	A	Partick Thistle	0	2		Murphy	Brady	Cummins	Millen	McGeever	Watt*	Miller	McVey	Burns	Malone&	Galt+	Bradley*	Woods+	MacPherson&	Gibson	Wharton	Williams	Brown
02/08/2016	CC1	H	Kilmarnock U20	5	2		Murphy	Wharton	Cummins	Williams	McGeever	McLeish	Miller+	Fotheringham	Brown	Malone&	Bradley*	Galt*	Millen+	MacPherson&	Burns	Foy	Brady	Watt
06/08/2016	L	H	Airdrieonians	1	3		Murphy	Millen	Cummins	Gibson&	McGeever	Woods+	Miller	McVey	Brady	Malone	Galt*	MacPherson*	Brown+	Watt&	Bradley	Wharton	Williams	Fotheringham
13/08/2016	L	A	Stenhousemuir	2	1		Murphy	Millen	Cummins	Gibson	McGeever	Woods&	Miller	Brown*	Brady	Burns+	Galt	MacPherson*	Watt+	Carter&	McVey	Wharton	Williams	Fotheringham
16/08/2016	CC2	A	Partick Thistle U20	1	1	AET, 6-5p	Waters	Gibson	Cummins	Wharton	Williams+	Fotheringham	Miller	Brown	McLeish*	Malone&	McPherson	Galt*	Watt+	Carter&	McVey	Millen	Brady	Foy
20/08/2016	L	A	Brechin City	0	0		Murphy	Millen	Cummins	Gibson	McGeever	Watt	Miller	McVey	Woods	Burns*	Carter+	Galt*	Malone+	MacPherson	Williams	Wharton	Brady	Fotheringham
27/08/2016	L	H	Livingston	1	0		Murphy	Millen	Cummins	Gibson	McGeever	Watt*	Miller	McVey	Woods&	Burns	Malone+	Galt*	Carter+	Brady&	Brown	Wharton	MacPherson	Fotheringham
03/09/2016	CC3	H	Morton	2	0		Murphy	Millen	Cummins	Gibson	McGeever	Fotheringham	Miller	Brady	Galt+	Burns	Malone*	Carter*	Woods+	McVey	McLeish	Wharton	MacPherson	Waters
10/09/2016	L	A	Peterhead	0	2		Murphy	Millen	Cummins+	Gibson	McGeever	McVey	Miller	Woods*	Galt	Burns	Malone&	Brady*	Carter+	MacPherson&	McLeish	Wharton	Muir	Fotheringham
17/09/2016	L	H	Alloa	1	2		Muir	Millen	Cummins	Gibson*	McGeever	Fotheringham+	Miller	Brady	Woods	Burns&	Carter	Wharton*	McVey+	Galt&	McLeish	Malone	MacPherson	Murphy
24/09/2016	L	H	Stranraer	0	2		Muir	Millen	Cummins	Gibson*	McGeever	Fotheringham	Miller	Brady&	Galt+	Burns	Zanatta	Malone*	Brown+	Woods&	McLeish	Carter	McVey	Murphy
01/10/2016	L	A	Albion Rovers	0	2		Muir	Millen	Cummins	Gibson	McGeever	Fotheringham&	Woods	Brady+	Carter*	McLeish	Zanatta	Malone*	Brown+	MacPherson&	Burns	McVey	Murphy	
08/10/2016	CC4	A	Dunfermline	1	2		Muir	Millen	Cummins	Miller	McGeever	Fotheringham&	Woods	Brady+	Carter*	McLeish	Burns	Malone*	Brown+	MacPherson&	Gibson	McVey	Murphy	Wharton
15/10/2016	L	H	East Fife	1	0		Muir	Millen	Cummins	Miller	McGeever	Fotheringham	Woods	Brown*	Malone+	McLeish	Zanatta&	Burns*	Carter+	Brady&	Gibson	Watt	Murphy	Wharton
22/10/2016	L	A	Airdrieonians	1	4		Muir	Millen	Cummins	Miller	McGeever	Fotheringham	Woods	Brown*	Malone+	McLeish+	Zanatta	Watt*	Brady+	Wharton	Gibson	McVey	Mortimer	McGorry
29/10/2016	L	H	Stenhousemuir	0	3		Muir	Millen	Cummins	Miller&	McGeever	Fotheringham	Woods+	Brown	Malone*	McLeish	Zanatta	McKernon*	Watt+	Brady&	Gibson	McVey	Wharton	MacPherson
05/11/2016	L	A	Stranraer	2	0		Muir	Millen	Cummins	Gibson	McGeever	Fotheringham*	Woods+	Brady	Burns	McKernon	Zanatta	McVey*	Carter+&	Malone&	McLeish	Brown	Wharton	MacPherson
12/11/2016	L	H	Peterhead	0	0		Muir	Millen	Cummins	Gibson	McGeever	Fotheringham&	Woods+	Brady	Burns	McKernon	Malone*	Carter*	Galt+	Brown&	McLeish	McVey	Wharton	MacPherson
19/11/2016	L	A	East Fife	2	1		Muir	Millen	Cummins	Gibson	McGeever	Fotheringham	Woods*	Brady+	Burns	McKernon	Zanatta&	Galt*	McVey+	Carter&	Malone	Brown	Wharton	MacPherson
29/11/2016	SC3	H	Montrose	2	0		Muir	Millen	Cummins	Gibson	McGeever	Galt&	Woods	Brady+	Burns	McKernon	Carter*	Malone*	Brown+	Fotheringham&	Stott	McVey	Wharton	MacPherson
03/12/2016	L	H	Brechin City	2	0		Muir	Millen	Cummins	Gibson	McGeever	Fotheringham	Woods	Galt*	Burns	McKernon+	Zanatta&	Brady*	McVey+	Carter&	Malone	Brown	Wharton	MacPherson
10/12/2016	L	H	Albion Rovers	2	1		Muir	Millen	Cummins	Wharton	McGeever	Fotheringham	Woods&	Galt*	Burns	McKernon	Zanatta+	Brady*	Carter+	McVey&	Malone	McLeish	Mortimer	MacPherson
17/12/2016	L	A	Alloa	1	1		Muir	Millen	Cummins	Wharton	Gibson	Fotheringham	Woods	Brady*	Burns	McKernon	Zanatta	Malone*	Carter	McVey	Brown	McLeish	Mortimer	MacPherson
24/12/2016	L	A	Livingston	2	1		Muir	McGeever	Cummins	Wharton	Gibson	McVey	Woods	Brady	Burns	McKernon	Malone*	Galt*	Stott	Foy	Brown	McLeish	Mortimer	MacPherson
31/12/2016	L	H	Stranraer	0	1		Muir	McGeever	Cummins	Wharton	Gibson+	Galt	Woods	Brady	Burns	McKernon	Malone*	MacPherson*	Brown+	Foy	McVey	McLeish	Mortimer	Stott
07/01/2017	L	H	Airdrieonians	2	1		Muir	McGeever	Millen	Wharton	Gibson*	Fotheringham	Woods	Brady	Burns	McKernon	MacPherson+	Cummins*	Malone+	Brown	McVey	McLeish	Mortimer	Mitchell
21/01/2017	SC3	A	Ayr United	0	0		Muir	McGeever	Millen	Wharton	Cummins	Fotheringham	Woods*	Brady	Burns	McKernon	MacPherson+	Malone*	Galt+	Brown	McVey	Stott	Mortimer	Mitchell
24/01/2017	SC3R	H	Ayr United	2	2	aet, 4-5p	Muir	McGeever	Millen	Wharton	Cummins	Fotheringham	Woods&	Brady+	Burns	McKernon	MacPherson*	Malone*	McVey+	Galt&	Brown	Stott	Mortimer	Mitchell
28/01/2017	L	A	Peterhead	0	4		Muir	McGeever	Millen	Wharton	Cummins	Fotheringham+	Woods	McVey	Burns*	McKernon&	Galt	Mitchell*	Mortimer+	Brown&	Malone	MacPherson	Docherty	Foy
04/02/2017	L	H	East Fife	2	2		Muir	Mitchell+	Millen	Wharton	Cummins	Brown	Woods	Brady*	McIlduff	McKernon	Zanatta&	Docherty*	Galt+	Orsi&	Fotheringham	MacPherson	Burns	McVey
11/02/2017	L	A	Stenhousemuir	2	0		Muir	McGeever	Millen	Wharton	Cummins	Docherty*	Woods+	Brady	McIlduff	McKernon	Zanatta&	Fotheringham*	Mitchell+	Orsi&	Galt	Brown	Burns	McVey
18/02/2017	L	H	Alloa	0	2		Muir	McGeever	Mitchell	Wharton	Burns	Docherty	Woods*	Brady	Galt	McKernon	Orsi+	Brown*	MacPherson+	Gibson	Mortimer	Foy	Miller	McVey
28/02/2017	L	A	Brechin City	1	3		Muir	McGeever	Millen&	Wharton	Burns	Docherty	Woods+	Brady*	Cummins	McKernon	Zanatta	Orsi*	Galt+	McIlduff&	Mitchell	Brown	Stott	McVey
04/03/2017	L	H	Livingston	1	1		Muir	McGeever	Millen	Wharton	Burns	McVey	Orsi*	Brady	Cummins	McKernon	Zanatta	Galt*	Docherty	McIlduff	Mitchell	Brown	Mortimer	
11/03/2017	L	A	Stranraer	1	1		Muir	McGeever	Millen*	Wharton	Burns	McVey	Galt+	Brady	Cummins	McKernon	Zanatta	McIlduff*	MacPherson+	Docherty	Foy	Brown	Mortimer	
18/03/2017	L	H	Brechin City	1	1		Muir	McGeever	Foy&	Wharton	Burns	McVey	Galt*	Brady	McIlduff	McKernon	Zanatta+	Orsi*	MacPherson+	Docherty&	Stott	Brown	Mortimer	
25/03/2017	L	A	Alloa	2	2		Muir	McGeever	Foy*	Millen	Cummins	McVey	Galt&	Docherty+	Burns	McKernon	Zanatta	Brown*	Mortimer+	MacPherson&	Wharton	Gibson	McIlduff	Mitchell
01/04/2017	L	A	East Fife	0	0		Muir	McGeever	Foy	Millen	Cummins	McVey	Galt	Brady	Burns	McKernon	Zanatta	Brown	Mortimer	MacPherson	Wharton	Docherty	McIlduff	Mitchell
04/04/2017	L	A	Albion Rovers	1	1		Muir	McGeever	Foy	Millen*	Cummins	McVey+	Galt	Brady	Burns&	McKernon	Zanatta	Mitchell*	MacPherson+	Brown&	Wharton	Docherty	Mortimer	Stott
08/04/2017	L	H	Peterhead	2	0		Muir	McGeever	Foy	Mitchell	Cummins	Docherty	Galt	Brady	Burns	MacPherson*	Zanatta	Orsi*	McIlduff	Brown	Wharton	McGrory	Mortimer	Stott
15/04/2017	L	H	Albion Rovers	2	0		Muir	McGeever	Foy	Mitchell	Cummins	McKernon	Galt	Brady	Burns	MacPherson*	Zanatta+	Orsi*	Mortimer+	Docherty	Wharrton	McVey	McIlduff	Brown
22/04/2017	L	A	Livingston	0	4		Muir	McGeever	Foy*	Mitchell+	Cummins	McKernon	Galt	Brady	Burns&	McVey	Zanatta	MacPherson*	McIlduff+	Orsi&	Wharton	Docherty	Mortimer	Brown
29/04/2017	L	H	Stenhousemuir	0	2		Muir	McGeever	Wharton	McIlduff	Gibson+	McKernon	Galt	Brady	Burns	MacPherson*	Zanatta&	Orsi*	Brown+	Docherty&	Mortimer	McVey	Foy	Stott
06/05/2017	L	A	Airdrieonians	2	3		Muir	McGeever	Wharton*	Docherty	Cummins	Orsi+	Galt	Brady	Burns	McVey&	Zanatta	Miller*	Brown+	MacPherson&	Mortimer	Gibson	Foy	Stott

						L			SC			LC			CC							
Surname	First Name	DOB	SQ	Nat	Pos	A	S	G	A	S	G	A	S	G	A	S	G	UNS	Signed	Previous Club	Notes	Contrac
Bradley	Joe	02/03/1990		SCO	M							2	1		1			2	2015	Beith Juniors	OL to Beith Dec-May	OOC
Brady	Anton	07/02/1994		SCO	M	26		4	3			2	1		2			3	2016	East Kilbride FC		OOC
Brennan	Grant	04/01/1998		SCO	M														2015	Q Park Youth		OOC
Brown	Liam	06/04/1999		SCO	M	5	11			1		3			2	1		19	2015	Q Park Youth	OOC June 2017, joined Motherwell	
Burns	Sean	06/10/1991		SCO	D	29	1		3			4		2	2		1	4	2011	St Mirren		OOC
Carter	John	14/02/1987		SCO	F	3	9		1						1	2	1	2	2014	Greenock Juniors	Freed Jan 2017, joined Glenafton Athletic	
Cummins	Adam	03/03/1993		ENG	D	32	1	2	3			3		1	4		1		2016	Bangor City		OOC
Devlin	Jonny			SCO	D		7												2016	Queen's Park Youth		OOC
Docherty	Dominic	22/05/1997		SCO	F	6	3											7	2017	Partick Thistle (OL)	Jan-May	
Fotheringham	Gregor	09/06/1994		SCO	M	14	1	2	2	1		1			4			7	2016	Camelon Juniors		OOC
Foy	Cammy	01/05/1998		SCO	D	7												9	2015	Q Park Youth		OOC
Galt	David	07/11/1990		SCO	M	19	9	2	1	2	1	2	2		1	2	2	1	2015	Blantyre Vics		OOC
Gibson	Scott	10/11/1993		SCO	D	17			1			2			2			8	2014	Q Park Youth		OOC
Henderson	Andrew			SCO	M														2016	Queen's Park Youth		OOC
MacPherson	Ewan	26/02/1999		SCO	F	4	12	2	2				4		1	2	1	16	2015	Q Park Youth		OOC
Malone	Aiden	19/02/1992		SCO	F	9	6	1		3		4		1	3	1		5	2016	Cumnock Juniors	Freed Jan 2017, joined Forfar Athletic	
Manderson	Joseph	06/06/1999		SCO	F														2016	Q Park Youth		OOC
McDonald	Ross			SCO	D														2016	Queen's Park Youth		OOC
McGeever	Ryan	30/04/1994		SCO	D	34		4	3			4			3		1		2015	Falkirk	OOC May 2017, joined Brechin City	[redacted]
McGrory	Calvin	09/08/1999		SCO	M													2	2016	Q. Park Youth		OOC
McIlduff	Aidan	20/04/1997		SCO	D	4	3											5	2017	Celtic (OL)	Jan-May	[redacted]
McKenzie	Sam			SCO	M		1												2016	Queen's Park Youth		OOC
McKernon	Jamie	01/04/1992		SCO	M	23	1	1	3										2015	Glenafton Athletic		OOC
McLeish	Craig	27/03/1990		SCO	M	4									3			12	2015	Clyde	OL to East Kilbride Jan-May	OOC
McVey	Conor	15/04/1994		SCO	M	14	5			1		1	2	1				20	2013	Q Park Youth		OOC
Millen	Ross	28/09/1994		SCO	D	27		7	3			4			2	1		1	2016	Clyde		OOC
Miller	Darren	04/08/1992		SCO	M	10	1	1				4			4			1	2016	Kilbirnie Ladeside	OL to Clyde Nov-Jan, Freed Mar 2017 joined Colville Park	[redacted]
Miller	Ali			SCO	M														2016	Queen's Park Youth		OOC
Mitchell	Gavin	31/12/1995		SCO	D	5	3											8	2013	Q Park Youth		OOC
Mortimer	Billy	09/01/1997		SCO	F		3											18	2015	Q Park Youth		OOC
Muir	William	16/03/1993		SCO	GK	31			3						1			1	2016	East Fife		OOC
Murphy	Andrew	30/05/1993		SCO	GK	5						4			2			5	2016	Fauldhouse United		OOC
Orsi	Kalvin	15/04/1997		SCO	F	3	8	1											2017	St Mirren (OL)	Jan-May	[redacted]
Stott	Owen	01/01/1999		SCO	GK													11	2016	Q Park Youth		OOC
Waters	Marc	30/03/1996		SCO	GK										1			1	2016	Partick Thistle	OL to Elgin City Oct-Jan, Freed Jan 2017 joined Elgin C	[redacted]
Watt	Josh	31/08/1993		SCO	M	2	4	1				1				1		5	2016	Cumnock Juniors	OL to Cumnock Nov-May	OOC
Wharton	Bryan	08/06/1990		SCO	D	15	1	1	2		1	1			2		1	24	2014	Shotts Bon Accord		OOC
Williams	Mark	15/05/1995		SCO	M								1		2			6	2016	Alloa	Freed Sep 2016 joined Cumnock	[redacted]
Woods	Paul	18/09/1986		SCO	M	24		1	3		2	2	1		1	1		1	2014	Petershill	Freed Mar 2017, joined East Kilbride	
Zanatta	Dario	24/05/1997		CAN	F	24		6											2016	Hearts (OL)	Oct-May	OOC
Own Goals								1									1					

Source of Birthdates: Queen's Park FC website

Raith Rovers FC 2016/17

Founded	1883
Ground	Stark's Park, Pratt Street
Postcode	KY1 1SA
Tel	01592 263514
Capacity	8473
Closest Railway Station	Kirkcaldy
Record Attendance	31306 v Hearts, SC, 7/2/1953
Record Win	10-1 v Coldstream, SC, 13/2/1954
Record Defeat	2-11 v Morton, Lge, 18/3/1936
Most League Goals in a Season	38 Norman Haywood, 1937/8
Chairman	Alan Young
Chief Executive / Secretary	Eric Drysdale
Manager	Gary Locke (until Feb), John Hughes (until May),
	Barry Smith
Assistant Manager	Darren Jackson (until Feb), Kevin McBride
	Gordon Young
Colours 2016/17 Top	Navy Blue with white sleeves
Shorts	White
Sponsor	valmcdermid.com
Manufacturer	Puma
Change Colours 2016/17 Top	Whit and red fade
Shorts	Blue
Nicknames	Rovers
Web	www.raithrovers.net
Match Programme 2016/17	Rovers Review £2
Theme Song	Geordie Munro

Given the strength of their squad Raith's relegatior inexcusable. Yet there was something of inevitability about it from the early part of the seas Gary Locke was never convincing as Manag especially when he brought in so many ex Hea players. Skacel was a waste of a wage and Stevens a waste of a jersey.

John Hughes came in with time to turn things arou Yet within weeks he found himself fielding a te with an outfield player in goals for a League matc that reveals a staggering level of incompetence beh the scenes at Stark's Park despite the excuses t were forthcoming.

Hughes never seemed comfortable ni his role a some of his comments were counter productive. I ahd hoped to enhance his reputation by taking this then it backfired spectacularly.

Relegation came with a loss to Brechin in the Play c Some might say losing on penalties is unlucky. Otl would say not beating Brechin over 210 minutes open play is negligent.

PREDICTION FOR 2017/18
Barry Smith is in charge and expectations are h Raith will challenge for promotion but they are by means certainties. More disappointment could b the cards for the Kirkcaldy fans.

Robert Stark was a local councillor and rope manufacturer who had a licensed business at the West Bridge. In November 1881 he presented some grazing land to local youths seeking a football field – it was referred to as Mr Stark's Park, and the team were Kirk dy Wanderers. They moved on to Newton Park in 1884.

Raith Rovers moved to Stark's Park in 1891 bringing with them the pavilion they had installed at Robbie's Park. Their first game o the ground was in the Midland League against Grangemouth on 15/8/1891.

The L-Shaped grandstand was built in 1922. In 1954 a covered enclosure was built at the west end of the ground. Floodlights we added in 1960 with a special match against Aston Villa on 27/9/60 – the lights had actually been used before then.

Date	Comp	H/A	Opponents	F	A		HT		Referee	Crowd	Scorers
15/07/2016	LC	A	Cove Rangers*	2	1		1	1	G Beaton	362	Benedictus, Vaughan
19/07/2016	LC	H	Montrose	2	1		1	0	C Steven	1147	Johnston, Vaughan
23/07/2016	LC	A	Ross County	1	1	4-3p	1	0	J McKendrick	1173	Cikos og
30/07/2016	LC	H	Alloa	0	1		0	1	K Clancy	1674	
06/08/2016	L	A	Ayr United	2	0		1	0	E Anderson	1550	Callachan, Matthews
13/08/2016	L	H	St Mirren	3	1		1	0	K Graham	2140	McManus 2, Callachan
20/08/2016	L	H	Dunfermline Athletic	2	0		0	0	A Muir	5114	Barr, Stewart
27/08/2016	L	A	Dundee United	2	2		1	2	C Thomson	7434	Thompson, McHattie
03/09/2016	CC3	A	Forfar Athletic	2	3		1	2	A Newlands	690	Stewart, McManus
10/09/2016	L	H	Falkirk	0	2		0	1	E Anderson	2320	
17/09/2016	L	A	Queen of the South	1	3		0	0	G Duncan	1864	Mvoto
24/09/2016	L	H	Dumbarton	3	2		3	0	S Kirkland	1636	McHattie, Callachan, Roberts
01/10/2016	L	A	Morton	0	1		0	1	C Charleston	1528	
15/10/2016	L	H	Hibernian	0	0		0	0	S Finnie	3753	
22/10/2016	L	A	Falkirk	4	2		2	1	B Cook	4773	Davidson, Stewart 2, McManus
29/10/2016	L	H	Queen of the South	1	0		0	0	C Allan	1244	Stewart
05/11/2016	L	A	Dunfermline Athletic	0	0		0	0	C Thomson	5649	
19/11/2016	L	A	Dumbarton	0	0		0	0	A Muir	600	
22/11/2016	L	H	Ayr United	1	1		1	0	C Charleston	1241	Coustrain
10/12/2016	L	A	St Mirren	0	1		0	0	B Cook	2630	
17/12/2016	L	H	Dundee United	0	0		0	0	S Kirkland	4361	
24/12/2016	L	A	Hibernian	1	1		0	0	G Aitken	15409	Mvoto
02/01/2017	L	H	Dunfermline Athletic	0	2		0	1	D Robertson	5899	
07/01/2017	L	H	Falkirk	1	4		1	3	A Dallas	2202	Johnston
14/01/2017	L	A	Morton	0	2		0	1	G Duncan	1957	
22/01/2017	SC4	H	Hearts	1	1		0	1	J Beaton	5036	McManus
25/01/2017	SC4R	A	Hearts	2	4	AET	1	1	J Beaton	10740	Barr, Hardie
28/01/2017	L	H	Dumbarton	1	3		1	0	M Northcroft	1413	Hardie
04/02/2017	L	A	Dundee United	0	3		0	1	S Finnie	5232	
07/02/2017	L	H	Morton	0	1		0	0	G Duncan	1161	
18/02/2017	L	H	Hibernian	1	1		0	0	C Charleston	4172	Stevenson(a)
25/02/2017	L	A	Queen of the South	1	2		0	2	B Cook	1484	Mvoto
28/02/2017	L	A	Ayr United	0	1		0	0	W Collum	1103	
08/03/2017	L	H	St Mirren	2	0		0	0	C Allan	2124	Hardie 2
11/03/2017	L	A	Dumbarton	0	4		0	2	A Newlands	719	
18/03/2017	L	H	Dundee United	2	1		1	0	C Charleston	2192	Barr, Hardie
25/03/2017	L	H	Queen of the South	1	1		1	1	C Steven	1609	Hardie
01/04/2017	L	A	Falkirk	0	1		0	0	N Walsh	4823	
08/04/2017	L	A	Dunfermline Athletic	0	1		0	0	A Dallas	4865	
15/04/2017	L	H	Morton	2	0		1	0	A Newlands	1720	C Barr, Matthews
26/04/2017	L	A	Hibernian	2	3		0	1	G Aitken	13604	McManus, Hardie
29/04/2017	L	A	St Mirren	0	5		0	2	K Clancy	4937	
06/05/2017	L	H	Ayr United	2	1		1	0	S Mclean	3064	Court, McManus
10/05/2017	PO	A	Brechin City	1	1		0	1	D Robertson	1022	McManus
13/05/2017	PO	H	Brechin City	3	3	aet, 3-4p	0	0	A Muir	2932	Mvoto, McManus, Hardie

* at Forfar

19/11/2016	L	A	Dumbarton	0	0		0	0	A Muir	600	
22/11/2016	L	H	Ayr United	1	1		1	0	C Charleston	1241	Coustrain
10/12/2016	L	A	St Mirren	0	1		0	0	B Cook	2630	
17/12/2016	L	H	Dundee United	0	0		0	0	S Kirkland	4361	
24/12/2016	L	A	Hibernian	1	1		0	0	G Aitken	15409	Mvoto
02/01/2017	L	H	Dunfermline Athletic	0	2		0	1	D Robertson	5899	
07/01/2017	L	H	Falkirk	1	4		1	3	A Dallas	2202	Johnston
14/01/2017	L	A	Morton	0	2		0	1	G Duncan	1957	
22/01/2017	SC4	H	Hearts	1	1		0	1	J Beaton	5036	McManus
25/01/2017	SC4R	A	Hearts	2	4	AET	1	1	J Beaton	10740	Barr, Hardie
28/01/2017	L	H	Dumbarton	1	3		1	0	M Northcroft	1413	Hardie
04/02/2017	L	A	Dundee United	0	3		0	1	S Finnie	5232	

Date	Comp	H/A	Opponents	F	A		1	2	3	4	5	6	7	8	9	10	11	12	13	14	15	16	17	18
15/07/2016	LC	A	Cove Rangers*	2	1		Cuthbert	Jas Thomson	McHattie	Benedictus	Davidson	Callachan	Johnston*	R Barr	Matthews	Stewart+	Vaughan	Osei-Oopuku*	Coustrain+	*Bates*	*Berry*	*McKay*	*Lennox*	
19/07/2016	LC	H	Montrose	2	1		Cuthbert	Jas Thomson	McHattie	Benedictus	Davidson	Callachan	Johnston*	R Barr	Matthews	Osei-Opuku+	Vaughan	Stewart*	Robertson+	*Bates*	*Court*	*McKay*	*Lennox*	*Mvoto*
23/07/2016	LC	A	Ross County	1	1	4-3p	Cuthbert	Jas Thomson	McHattie	Benedictus	Davidson	Callachan	Mvoto	R Barr	Matthews&	McManus	Vaughan*	Stewart*	Johnston+	Roberts&	*Osei-Opuku*	*Court*	*Lennox*	*Bates*
30/07/2016	LC	H	Alloa	0	1		Cuthbert	Jas Thomson	McHattie&	Benedictus	Davidson	Callachan	Mvoto	R Barr	Johnston*	McManus	Vaughan+	Coustrain*	Skacel+	Stewart&	*Osei-Opuku*	*Matthews*	*Lennox*	*Roberts*
06/08/2016	L	A	Ayr United	2	0		Cuthbert	Jas Thomson	McHattie	Benedictus	Jor Thompson	Callachan	Mvoto	R Barr&	Matthews	McManus+	Vaughan*	Skacel*	Stewart+	Robertson&	*Osei-Opuku*	*Coustrain*	*Lennox*	*Johnston*
13/08/2016	L	H	St Mirren	3	1		Lennox	Jas Thomson	McHattie	Benedictus	Jor Thompson&	Callachan	Mvoto	R Barr	Matthews	McManus+	Vaughan*	Skacel*	Stewart+	Roberts&	*Osei-Opuku*	*Coustrain*	*Cuthbert*	*Johnston*
20/08/2016	L	H	Dunfermline Athletic	2	0		Lennox	Jas Thomson	McHattie	Benedictus	Jor Thompson*	Callachan	Mvoto	R Barr	Matthews	McManus&	Vaughan+	Skacel*	Stewart+	Roberts&	*Osei-Opuku*	*Coustrain*	*Cuthbert*	
27/08/2016	L	A	Dundee United	2	2		Brennan	Jas Thomson	McHattie	Benedictus	Jor Thompson*	Callachan	Mvoto	R Barr	Matthews	McManus&	Vaughan+	Skacel*	Stewart+	Davidson&	*Osei-Opuku*	*Roberts*	*Court*	*Cuthbert*
03/09/2016	CC3	A	Forfar Athletic	2	3		Brennan	Davidson+	McHattie	Benedictus	Stewart*	Callachan	Mvoto	R Barr	Matthews	McManus	Skacel	Vaughan*	Coustrain+	*Berry*	*Thorsen*	*Cuthbert*		
10/09/2016	L	H	Falkirk	0	2		Brennan	Jas Thomson	McHattie	Benedictus	Davidson	Callachan	Jor Thompson*	R Barr	Matthews&	McManus	Vaughan+	Roberts*	Skacel+	Coustrain&	*Thorsen*	*Stevenson*	*Cuthbert*	
17/09/2016	L	A	Queen of the South	1	3		Brennan	Mvoto	McHattie	Benedictus	Davidson	Callachan	Jor Thompson*	R Barr	Matthews	McManus&	Roberts+	Stewart*	Vaughan+	Skacel&	*Johnston*	*Coustrain*	*Cuthbert*	
24/09/2016	L	H	Dumbarton	3	2		Cuthbert	Mvoto	McHattie	Benedictus	Davidson	Callachan	L Smith	R Barr	Skacel*	McManus&	Roberts+	Stewart*	Johnston+	Jor Thompson&	*Matthews*	*Brennan*		
01/10/2016	L	A	Morton	0	1		Cuthbert	Mvoto	McHattie	Benedictus	Davidson	Callachan	L Smith&	R Barr	Skacel*	McManus	Roberts+	Stewart*	Johnston+	Jor Thompson&	*Matthews*	*Coustrain*	*Brennan*	
15/10/2016	L	H	Hibernian	0	0		Cuthbert	Mvoto	McHattie	Benedictus	Davidson	Callachan	Matthews	R Barr	Skacel*	McManus+	Jor Thompson&	Vaughan*	Stewart+	Johnston&	*Coustrain*	*Roberts*	*Brennan*	
22/10/2016	L	A	Falkirk	4	2		Cuthbert	Mvoto	McHattie	Benedictus	Davidson	Callachan	Matthews	R Barr*	Stewart+	McManus&	Jor Thompson	Johnston*	Roberts+	Vaughan&	*Coustrain*	*Skacel*	*Lennox*	
29/10/2016	L	H	Queen of the South	1	0		Cuthbert	Mvoto	McHattie	Benedictus	Davidson	Callachan	Matthews	Johnson+	Stewart	McManus*	Jor Thompson&	Vaughan*	Roberts+	Skacel&	*Coustrain*	*C Brennan*	*Smith*	*Lennox*
05/11/2016	L	A	Dunfermline Athletic	0	0		Cuthbert	Mvoto	McHattie	Benedictus	Davidson	Callachan	Matthews	Johnson*	Stewart+	McManus	Jor Thompson	Roberts*	Skacel+	*Vaughan*	*Coustrain*	*C Brennan*	*Crawford*	*Lennox*
19/11/2016	L	A	Dumbarton	0	0		Cuthbert	Mvoto	McHattie	Benedictus	Davidson	Callachan	Matthews	Johnson+	Stewart&	McManus	Jor Thompson*	Roberts*	Coustrain+	Vaughan&	*Osei-Opuku*	*Skacel*	*Crawford*	*Lennox*
22/11/2016	L	H	Ayr United	1	1		Cuthbert	Mvoto	McHattie	Benedictus	Davidson	Callachan	Matthews	Coustrain+	Stewart*	McManus	Roberts&	Jor Thompson*	Skacel+	Johnston&	*Osei-Opuku*	*Vaughan*	*Crawford*	*Brennan*
10/12/2016	L	A	St Mirren	0	1		Cuthbert	Mvoto	McHattie	Roberts*	Davidson	Callachan	Matthews+	Johnson	Stewart&	McManus	Jor Thompson	R Barr*	Skacel+	Vaughan&	*Osei-Opuku*	*Coustrain*	*Crawford*	*Lennox*
17/12/2016	L	H	Dundee United	0	0		Cuthbert	Mvoto	McHattie	Benedictus	Davidson	Callachan	Skacel*	Johnson	R Barr&	McManus+	Jor Thompson	Stewart*	Vaughan+	Coustrain&	*Matthews*	*Roberts*	*Crawford*	*Brennan*
24/12/2016	L	A	Hibernian	1	1		Cuthbert	Mvoto	Jas Thomson	Benedictus	Davidson	Matthews	Skacel*	Johnson	R Barr	McManus	Jor Thompson+	Stewart*	C Barr+	*Vaughan*	*Osei-Opuku*	*Coustrain*	*Roberts*	*Lennox*
02/01/2017	L	H	Dunfermline Athletic	0	2		Cuthbert	Mvoto	Jas Thomson	McHattie	Davidson	Callachan	Skacel*	Johnson&	R Barr	McManus+	Jor Thompson	Hardie*	Stewart+	Stevenson(a)&	*C Barr*	*Coustrain*	*Roberts*	*Lennox*
07/01/2017	L	H	Falkirk	1	4		Cuthbert	Benedictus	Jas Thomson	McHattie+	Davidson	Callachan	Hardie	Johnson	R Barr	Stevenson(a)*	Jor Thompson	McManus*	Stewart+	*Coustrain*	*Roberts*	*Skacel*	*Lennox*	
14/01/2017	L	A	Morton	0	2		Cuthbert	Benedictus	Mvoto	McHattie	Davidson	Callachan	Hardie+	Johnson*	R Barr	Stevenson(a)&	Jor Thompson	Stewart*	Roberts+	McManus&	*Jas Thomson*	*Skacel*	*C Barr*	*Brennan*
22/01/2017	SC4	H	Hearts	1	1		Cuthbert	Benedictus	Mvoto	McHattie	Davidson	Callachan	Matthews	Johnson*	R Barr	Stewart+	Jor Thompson&	Hardie*	McManus+	Skacel&	*C Barr*	*Jas Thomson*	*Roberts*	*Brennan*
25/01/2017	SC4R	A	Hearts	2	4	AET	Cuthbert	Benedictus	Mvoto	McHattie	Davidson*	Callachan	Matthews	McManus&	R Barr^	Stewart	Jor Thompson+	Jas Thomson*	Hardie+	Johnson&	*Skacel^*	*C Barr*	*Roberts*	*Brennan*
28/01/2017	L	H	Dumbarton	1	3		Cuthbert	Benedictus	Mvoto	McHattie	Jas Thomson&	Callachan	Matthews	Johnson*	R Barr+	Stewart	Hardie	Stevenson(a)*	Roberts+	Skacel&	*C Barr*	*Jor Thompson*	*Bell*	*Brennan*
04/02/2017	L	A	Dundee United	0	3		Cuthbert*	Benedictus	Mvoto	McHattie	Jas Thomson	Callachan	Matthews+	Davidson	R Barr	Stewart	McManus&	Brennan*	Hardie+	Stevenson(a)&	*C Barr*	*Jor Thompson*	*Skacel*	*Johnston*
07/02/2017	L	H	Morton	0	1		Brennan	Benedictus	Mvoto	C Barr	Jas Thomson&	Callachan+	Stevenson(a)*	Davidson	R Barr	Hardie	Jor Thompson	Stewart*	McManus+	Skacel&	*Matthews*	*McHattie*	*Johnston*	*Roberts*
18/02/2017	L	H	Hibernian	1	1		Brennan	Benedictus&	Mvoto	C Barr	Jas Thomson	Callachan	Stevenson(a)*	Matthews	R Barr	Stewart+	Jor Thompson	Johnston*	McManus+	Coustrain&	*Roberts*	*Skacel*	*Hardie*	*Stevenson(b)*
25/02/2017	L	A	Queen of the South	1	2		Brennan	Benedictus	Mvoto	C Barr	Jas Thomson	Callachan	Stevenson(a)&	Davidson	R Barr*	Stewart	Jor Thompson+	Hardie*	McManus+	Johnston&	*Roberts*	*Skacel*	*McHattie*	*Matthews*
28/02/2017	L	A	Ayr United	0	1		Stevenson (a)	Benedictus*	Mvoto	C Barr	Jas Thomson	Callachan	McHattie	Davidson	Johnson+	McManus&	Hardie	Coustrain*	Stewart+	R Barr&	*Roberts*	*Skacel*	*Matthews*	*Jor Thompson*
08/03/2017	L	H	St Mirren	2	0		Penksa	Benedictus	Mvoto	C Barr	Jas Thomson	Callachan	R Barr	Davidson+	Johnson	McManus	Stewart*	Matthews*	Hardie+	*Stevenson(a)*	*Roberts*	*Skacel*	*Coustrain*	*Jor Thompson*
11/03/2017	L	A	Dumbarton	0	4		Penksa	Benedictus	Mvoto	C Barr	Jas Thomson	Callachan	R Barr	Matthews&	Johnson+	McManus	Hardie*	Skacel*	*Osei-Opuku+*	*Roberts&*	*Syme*	*Court*	*Coustrain*	*Jor Thompson*
18/03/2017	L	H	Dundee United	2	1		Penksa	Benedictus	Mvoto	C Barr	Jas Thomson	Callachan	Jor Thompson*	Matthews	Johnson	McManus	Hardie	*Skacel*	*R Barr*	*Roberts*	*McHattie*	*Court*	*McKay*	
25/03/2017	L	H	Queen of the South	1	1		Penksa	Benedictus+	Mvoto	C Barr	Jas Thomson	Callachan	Jor Thompson	Matthews	Johnson*	McManus&	Hardie	Skacel*	R Barr+	Roberts&	*McHattie*	*Court*	*Davidson*	*Brennan*
01/04/2017	L	A	Falkirk	0	1		Penksa	Benedictus+	Mvoto	C Barr	McHattie	Callachan*	Jor Thompson	Davidson	Johnson	McManus	Hardie	Handling*	Roberts+	*R Barr*	*Skacel*	*Court*	*Brennan*	
08/04/2017	L	A	Dunfermline Athletic	0	1		Penksa	McHattie	Mvoto	C Barr	Jas Thomson	Skacel+	Jor Thompson*	Davidson	Johnson	Handling	Hardie	R Barr*	Court+	*Roberts*	*McManus*	*McKay*	*Brennan*	
15/04/2017	L	H	Morton	2	0		Penksa	McHattie	Mvoto	C Barr	Jas Thomson	Skacel	Matthews	Davidson	Johnson*	Handling&	Hardie+	R Barr*	McManus+	Stewart&	*Benedictus*	*Jor Thompson*	*Court*	*Brennan*
26/04/2017	L	A	Hibernian	2	3		Penksa	McHattie	Mvoto	C Barr	Jas Thomson	R Barr	Matthews	Stewart*	Johnson+	McManus	Jor Thompson	Court*	Hardie+	*Roberts*	*Benedictus*	*Brennan*		
29/04/2017	L	A	St Mirren	0	5		Penksa	McHatte	Mvoto	C Barr	Jas Thomson	R Barr&	Skacel*	Handling	Johnson+	McManus	Jor Thompson	Stewart*	Court+	Hardie&	*Benedictus*	*Roberts*	*Brennan*	
06/05/2017	L	H	Ayr United	2	1		Penksa	Benedictus	Mvoto	C Barr	Jas Thomson+	Matthews	Skacel*	Handling	Davidson	McManus	Court	Brennan*	Hardie+	*McHattie*	*Stewart*	*Jor Thompson*	*Johnston*	*R Barr*
10/05/2017	PO	A	Brechin City	1	1		Brennan	Benedictus	Mvoto	C Barr	Jas Thomson	Matthews	Skacel*	Handling	Davidson	McManus	Court+	Hardie*	Johnston+	*Robertson*	*Stewart*	*Roberts*	*Brian*	*R Barr*
13/05/2017	PO	H	Brechin City	3	3	aet, 3-4p	Brennan	Benedictus+	Mvoto	C Barr	Jas Thomson	Matthews&	Hardie	Handling	Davidson	McManus	Court*	R Barr*	Robertson+	Jor Thompson&	*Stewart*	*Roberts*	*Brian*	*Skacel*

ame	First Name	DOB	SQ	Nat	Pos	L A	L S	L G	SC A	SC S	SC G	LC A	LC S	LC G	CC A	CC S	CC G	UNS	Signed	Previous Club	Notes	Contract
	Robert	23/06/1988	11	SCO	M	24	6	2	2		1	4			1			4	2016	Morton		End 2017/18
	Craig	29/03/1987	55	SCO	D	16	1	1										6	2014	Airdrieonians	Released June 2017, joined Dumbarton	[redacted]
es	David	05/10/1996		SCO	D													3	2014	Raith Rovers Youth	OL to Rangers Aug 16-Jan 2017, sold to Rangers Jan 2017	[redacted]
	Kyle	17/10/1999		SCO	M													1	2016	AM Soccer		End 2017/18
edictus	Kyle	07/12/1991	6	SCO	D	32			2			4		1	1			3	2015	Dundee		End 2017/18
y	James	11/06/1999	27	SCO	M													2	2016	Fife Elite Football Academy		End 2017/18
nnan	Connor	30/03/2004	23	NIR	GK	8	2								1			17	2016	Kilmarnock	Released May 2017	[redacted]
n	Rory	01/02/1999		AUS	GK													2	2017	South Melbourne		End 2017/18
achan	Ross	04/09/1993	4	SCO	M	30		3	2			4			1				2010	Raith Rovers Youth		End 2017/18
ins	James	26/04/2009		SCO	M														2016	Dundee United Youth		
rt	Jonny	30/03/1996	26	SCO	F	3	3	1										8	2014	Raith Rovers Youth	OL to Montrose Aug 16-Jan 2017	End 2017/18
strain	Joel	22/01/1996	16	ROI	F	1	5	1					2			1		15	2016	Sheffield United	Released May 2017	[redacted]
wford	Robbie	19/03/1993		SCO	M													5	2016	Unattached	Ex Rangers, Freed Jan 2017 joined East Kilbride	[redacted]
nbert	Kevin	08/09/1982	1	SCO	GK	17			2			4						6	2014	Hamilton Accies		End 2017/18
idson	Iain	14/01/1984	14	SCO	M	27	1	1	2			4			1			1	2015	Dundee		End 2017/18
dling	Danny	06/02/1994		SCO	F	6	1												2017	Hibernian (OL)	Mar-May 2017	[redacted]
die	Ryan	17/03/1997	52	SCO	F	12	8	7		2	1							1	2017	Rangers (OL)	Jan-May 2017	[redacted]
nston	Chris	03/09/1994	7	SCO	M	20	8	1	1	1		3	1	1				6	2016	Kilmarnock	Released May 2017	[redacted]
nox	Aaron	19/02/1993	17	AUS	GK	2												13	2016	Aberdeen (OL)	Aug 16-May 2017	[redacted]
thews	Ross	23/01/1996	12	SCO	M	23	1	2	2			3			1			7	2015	Raith Rovers Youth		End 2018/19
Cann	Lewis	07/06/1999		SCO	M														2016	Raith Rovers Youth		
Donald	Josh	05/06/1998		SCO	D														2016	East Kilbride		
Hattie	Kevin	15/07/1993	3	SCO	D	27		2	2			4			1			5	2016	Kilmarnock	Released May 2017	[redacted]
Kay	David	17/06/1998	29	SCO	D													4	2015	Hibernian Youth	OL to Montrose Aug-Oct 2016	
eod Kay	Fionn	02/08/1999		SCO	M														2016	Raith Rovers Youth	OL to Glenrothes JFC Aug-Dec	End 2017/18
Manus	Declan	03/08/1994	20	SCO	F	30	6	7	1	1	1	2			1		1	1	2016	Fleetwood Town (OL)	Aug 16-May 2017	[redacted]
oto	Jean-Yves	06/09/1988	5	FRA/CAM	D	36		4	2			2			1			1	2016	Zawisza Bydgoszcz	OOC May 2017, joined Dunfermline Athletic	[redacted]
i-Opuku	Yaw	19/02/1998	15	SWA/GHA	F		1					1	1					10	2016	Chalfont St Peter		OOC
ska	Pavol	07/11/1985	36	SVK	GK	10												1	2017	Tatran Presov		OOC
erts	Scott	15/03/1996	18	SCO	F	5	12	1					1					20	2016	Rangers	OL Aug-Jan, then permanent, Released May 2017	[redacted]
ertson	Scott	07/04/1985	8	SCO	M		2						1					1	2015	FC Botosani		End 2017/18
cel	Rudi	17/07/1979	19	CZR	M	11	14			2			1		1			12	2016	Unattached	Ex Mlada Boleslav, Released May 2017	[redacted]
th	Liam	10/04/1996		SCO	D	4												1	2016	Hearts (OL)	Sep-Oct 2016	[redacted]
venson	Ryan	24/08/1984	66	SCO	M	6	3	1										2	2016	Dumbarton	Freed Feb 2017, joined Troon JFC	[redacted]
venson	Ryan (b)	18/01/1999		SCO	M													1	2016	Fife Elite Football Academy		End 2017/18
wart	Mark	22/06/1988	9	SCO	F	12	17	4	2			1	3		1		1	3	2014	Derry City	Released May 2017, joined Dumbarton	[redacted]
ne	David	23/06/1997		SCO	D													1	2017	Partick Thistle	OL to Cowdenbeath Mar-May, Freed May Joined Cowden	[redacted]
mpson	Jordan	03/01/1997	21	NIR	M	26	4	1	2									7	2016	Rangers (OL)	Aug 16-May 2017	[redacted]
mson	Jason	26/07/1987	2	SCO	D	25				1		4						2	2012	Hearts		End 2017/18
rsen	Andreas	17/12/1997	30	DEN	M													2	2016	Hong Kong FC		OOC
ghan	Lewis	19/12/1995		SCO	F	5	7					4		2		1		2	2012	Raith Rovers Youth	OL to Dumbarton Jan-May 2017	End 2017/18
tson	Jamie	17/06/1999		SCO	D																	End 2017/18
n Goals														1								
W SIGNINGS																						
hanan	Liam			SCO	F														2017	Livingston		
nce	Greig			SCO	F														2017	Alloa Athletic		
rray	Euan			SCO	D														2017	Southport		
nox	Aaron			AUS	GK														2017	Aberdeen		

rce of Birthdates: Raith Rovers Match Programme and transfermarkt.com

Rangers FC 2016/17

Founded	1872
Ground	Ibrox Stadium
Postcode	G51 2XD
Tel	0141 580 8647
Capacity	50987
Closest Railway Station	Ibrox (Subway)
Record Attendance	118567 v Celtic, Lge, 2/1/1939
Record Win	14-2 v Blairgowrie, SC, 20/1/1934
Record Defeat	1-7 v Celtic, LC Final, 19/10/1957
Most League Goals in a Season	44 Sam English, 1931/2
Chairman	Dave King
Chief Executive	Stewart Robertson
Manager	Mark Warburton (until Feb), Pedro Caixinha
Assistant Manager	David Weir (until Feb), Helder Baptista
Colours 2016/17 Top	Blue
Shorts	White
Sponsor	32 Red
Manufacturer	Puma
Change Colours 2016/17 Top	Red and white quarters
Shorts	Red
Nicknames	Gers, Teddy Bears
Web	www.rangers.co.uk
Match Programme 2016/17	£3
Theme Song	Follow Follow

"Oh what a Circus, Oh What a Show . . ." At the end fo Rangers finished third in the Premiership on their re from lower league exile. For many clubs that would h been satisfactory but it was never going to be enough the Ibrox side.

Mixed results resulted in growing disenchantment for M Warburton amongst the fans. It was easy to de disenchantment from Warburton as well, perh frustrated at the level of investment which restricted quality of his signings. The parting of the ways inevitable but in true Rangers fashion had an elemen pantomime about it.

Graeme Murty took over and made some improveme He was then moved aside as Pedro Caixinha was unve as the new manager. Elements of the media and within Rangers support slavered over "The new Mourin Others were more sceptical.

In the closing stages of the season Caixinha presided ov 5-1 home drubbing from Celtic and a first home de from Aberdeen in living memory. On the plus side he introduce some decent looking youngsters to the te 2017/18 would see his own players brought in and allo proper verdict to be reached.

PREDICTION FOR 2017/18

The new signings have flooded into Ibrox, most of th unknown quantities. Bruno Alves has the credentials will he have the legs for the SPFL? Dorrans looks lik great capture. But even as these words are writ Rangers are reeling from defeat to progress Niedercorn the Europa League. The only prediction that is possibl that it will be another rollercoaster of a season.

Date	Comp	H/A	Opponents	F	A	HT		Referee	Crowd	Scorers
16/07/2016	LC	A	Motherwell	2	0	0	0	S McLean	6951	Tavernier, Waghorn
19/07/2016	LC	H	Annan Athletic	2	0	1	0	E Anderson	31628	McKay, Waghorn
23/07/2016	LC	A	East Stirlingshire	3	0	2	0	C Allan	2246	Halliday, Windass, Dodoo
25/07/2016	LC	H	Stranraer	3	0	2	0	J Beaton	29575	Waghorn 2, Kranjcar
06/08/2016	L	H	Hamilton Accies	1	1	0	1	D Robertson	49125	Waghorn
09/08/2016	LC1	H	Peterhead	5	0	2	0	A Dallas	27076	Kranjcar, Hill 2, Kelleher og, Dodoo
13/08/2016	L	A	Dundee	2	1	2	1	C Thomson	9702	Forrester, Miller
20/08/2016	L	H	Motherwell	2	1	0	1	B Madden	48716	Forrester, Miller
26/08/2016	L	A	Kilmarnock	1	1	0	1	K Clancy	11800	Tavernier
10/09/2016	L	A	Celtic	1	5	1	2	W Collum	58348	Garner
17/09/2016	L	H	Ross County	0	0	0	0	G Aitken	47935	
20/09/2016	LC2	H	Queen of the South	5	0	1	0	D Robertson	26079	Waghorn 3, Holt, Halliday
25/09/2016	L	A	Aberdeen	1	2	0	0	J Beaton	19263	Halliday
01/10/2016	L	H	Partick Thistle	2	0	2	0	S Finnie	49680	Krajncar, Halliday
14/10/2016	L	A	Inverness CT	1	0	1	0	W Collum	7012	Miller
23/10/2016	LCSF	N	Celtic	0	1	0	0	C Thomson	50697	
26/10/2016	L	H	St Johnstone	1	1	1	1	K Clancy	46563	Garner
29/10/2016	L	H	Kilmarnock	3	0	2	0	J Beaton	49302	Halliday, Wallace, Garner
06/11/2016	L	A	Ross County	1	1	1	1	A Dallas	6590	Hill
19/11/2016	L	H	Dundee	1	0	0	0	W Collum	48773	Forrester
26/11/2016	L	A	Partick Thistle	2	1	0	0	N Walsh	7951	Dodoo 2
30/11/2016	L	A	Rangers	0	2	0	1	C Thomson	16803	
03/12/2016	L	H	Aberdeen	2	1	0	0	S McLean	50003	Miller, Hodson
10/12/2016	L	H	Hearts	2	0	1	0	J Beaton	50039	Kiernan, McKay
16/12/2016	L	A	Hamilton Accies	2	1	1	0	A Muir	5292	Waghorn 2
24/12/2016	L	H	Inverness CT	1	0	1	0	D Robertson	48528	Waghorn
28/12/2016	L	A	St Johnstone	1	1	1	1	C Allan	7979	McKay
31/12/2016	L	H	Celtic	1	2	1	1	S McLean	50126	Miller
21/01/2017	SC4	H	Motherwell	2	1	0	0	C Thomson	31921	Miller 2
28/01/2017	L	A	Motherwell	2	0	0	0	W Collum	7902	Miller, Hyndman
01/02/2017	L	A	Hearts	1	4	1	1	K Clancy	16570	Hyndman
04/02/2017	L	H	Ross County	1	1	0	1	D Robertson	49428	Wallace
12/02/2017	SC5	H	Morton	2	1	1	1	A Dallas	30295	Miller, Waghorn
19/02/2017	L	A	Dundee	1	2	0	2	C Thomson	9017	Garner
24/02/2017	L	A	Inverness CT	1	2	0	1	S McLean	6415	Waghorn
01/03/2017	L	H	St Johnstone	3	2	1	0	K Clancy	46800	McKay, Waghorn, Hyndman
04/03/2017	SC6	H	Hamilton Accies	6	0	1	0	J Beaton	27287	Garner 3, Waghorn, Toral, Hill
12/03/2017	L	A	Celtic	1	1	0	1	B Madden	58545	Hill
18/03/2017	L	H	Hamilton Accies	4	0	2	0	D Robertson	49090	Hyndman, Hill, Waghorn, Wallace
01/04/2017	L	H	Motherwell	1	1	0	1	S McLean	49198	Garner
05/04/2017	L	A	Kilmarnock	0	0	0	0	A Muir	9548	
09/04/2017	L	A	Aberdeen	3	0	0	0	K Clancy	19332	Miller 2, Dodoo
15/04/2017	L	H	Partick Thistle	2	0	1	0	N Walsh	49748	Miller, Toral
23/04/2017	SCSF	N	Celtic	0	2	0	1	W Collum	49645	
29/04/2017	L	H	Celtic	1	5	0	2	J Beaton	49822	Miller
07/05/2017	L	A	Partick Thistle	2	1	0	1	C Allan	6799	McKay, Garner
13/05/2017	L	H	Hearts	2	1	1	0	B Madden	47809	McKay, Garner
17/05/2017	L	H	Aberdeen	1	2	0	1	J Beaton	48289	Waghorn
21/05/2017	L	A	St Johnstone	2	1	1	0	A Dallas	6799	Miller, Toral

FRIENDLIES / OTHER GAMES

06/07/2016	A	Charleston Battery	2	1	
13/07/2016	H	Tynecastle	6	0	U2o, at Murray Park
30/07/2016	H	Burnley	1	3	
03/09/2016	A	Linfield	7	0	Testimonial
15/01/2017	A	RB Leipzig	0	4	

Date	Comp	H/A	Opponents	F A	1	2	3	4	5	6	7	8	9	10	11	12	13	14	15	16	17	18
16/07/2016	LC	A	Motherwell	2 0	Foderingham	Tavernier	Kiernan	Wallace	Wilson	McKay	Halliday	Holt&	Miller*	Forrester+	Waghorn	Kranjcar*	O'Halloran+	Windass&	Hill	Hodson	Thompson	Gilks
19/07/2016	LC	H	Annan Athletic	2 0	Gilks	Hill	Kiernan	Wallace	Hodson	McKay&	Halliday	Windass*	Kranjcar+	O'Halloran	Waghorn	Barton*	Miller+	Forrester&	Tavernier	Wilson	Holt	Foderingham
23/07/2016	LC	A	East Stirlingshire	3 0	Gilks	Hill	Wilson	Wallace	Hodson	McKay	Halliday	Windass*	Miller	O'Halloran+	Forrester&	Kranjcar*	Dodoo+	Thompson&	Hardie	Waghorn	Kiernan	Foderingham
25/07/2016	LC	H	Stranraer	3 0	Foderingham	Tavernier	Kiernan	Wallace	Wilson	McKay&	Halliday+	Barton*	Waghorn	Kranjcar	Forrester	Miller*	Dodoo+	Rossiter&	Hill	Hodson	O'Halloran	Gilks
06/08/2016	L	H	Hamilton Accies	1 1	Foderingham	Tavernier	Kiernan	Wallace	Hill	McKay	Halliday&	Barton	Waghorn	Kranjcar*	Miller+	Forrester*	O'Halloran+	Rossiter&	Dodoo	Hodson	Holt	Gilks
09/08/2016	LC1	H	Peterhead	5 0	Gilks	Tavernier	Kiernan	Hodson	Hill	Rossiter+	Dodoo	Barton*	O'Halloran	Kranjcar&	Forrester	McKay*	Halliday+	Holt&	Bates	Miller	Foderingham	
13/08/2016	L	A	Dundee	2 1	Foderingham	Tavernier	Kiernan	Wallace	Wilson	Rossiter	Halliday+	Barton	Miller*	McKay	Forrester&	Dodoo*	Krajncar+	O'Halloran&	Bates	Hill	Hodson	Gilks
20/08/2016	L	H	Motherwell	2 1	Foderingham	Tavernier	Kiernan	Wallace	Wilson	Rossiter	Halliday*	Barton	Miller	McKay+	Forrester&	Dodoo*	Krajncar+	O'Halloran&	Bates	Hill	Hodson	Gilks
26/08/2016	L	A	Kilmarnock	1 1	Foderingham	Tavernier	Kiernan	Wallace	Hill	Rossiter+	Dodoo*	Barton&	Miller	McKay	Forrester	Garner*	Krajncar+	Halliday&	Hodson	O'Halloran	Gilks	
10/09/2016	L	A	Celtic	1 5	Foderingham	Tavernier	Kiernan&	Wallace	Senderos	Windass	Kranjcar*	Barton	Miller+	McKay	Garner	Halliday*	Waghorn+	Forrester&	Hodson	O'Halloran	Hill	Gilks
17/09/2016	L	H	Ross County	0 0	Foderingham	Tavernier	Wilson	Wallace	Hill	Windass	Halliday	Holt&	Waghorn+	McKay	Garner*	Miller*	O'Halloran+	Kranjcar&	Hodson	Forrester	Crooks	Gilks
20/09/2016	LC2	H	Queen of the South	5 0	Gilks	Tavernier	Wilson	Hodson	Hill	Kranjcar	Halliday	Holt*	Waghorn	O'Halloran&	Forrester+	McKay*	Crooks+	Miller&	Senderos	Garner	Foderingham	
25/09/2016	L	A	Aberdeen	1 2	Foderingham	Tavernier	Wilson	Wallace	Hill	Forrester*	Halliday	Holt	Waghorn+	McKay	Garner&	Kranjcar*	O'Halloran+	Miller&	Senderos	Hodson	Dodoo	Gilks
01/10/2016	L	H	Partick Thistle	2 0	Foderingham	Tavernier	Wilson	Wallace	Senderos	Kranjcar&	Halliday	Holt	Waghorn+	McKay*	Miller	Garner*	Dodoo+	Forrester&	Kiernan	Hodson	O'Halloran	Gilks
14/10/2016	L	A	Inverness CT	1 0	Foderingham	Tavernier	Kiernan	Wallace	Hill	Krajncar&	Halliday	Holt	Waghorn+	McKay*	Miller	Garner*	Dodoo+	Windass&	Forrester	Hodson	Senderos	Gilks
23/10/2016	LCSF	N	Celtic	0 1	Gilks	Tavernier	Kiernan	Wallace	Hill	Hodson	Halliday	Holt	Windass+	McKay&	Miller*	Garner*	Waghorn+	Dodoo&	Crooks	Senderos	O'Halloran	Foderingham
26/10/2016	L	H	St Johnstone	1 1	Foderingham	Hodson	Kiernan	Wallace	Hill	Garner&	Halliday	Holt	Windass*	Forrester+	O'Halloran	Miller*	McKay+	Waghorn&	Crooks	Tavernier	Dodoo	Gilks
29/10/2016	L	H	Kilmarnock	3 0	Foderingham	Tavernier	Kiernan	Wallace	Hill	Garner*	Halliday	Holt	Windass&	Miller+	O'Halloran	Dodoo*	Waghorn+	Crooks&	McKay	Forrester	Hodson	Gilks
06/11/2016	L	A	Ross County	1 1	Foderingham	Tavernier	Kiernan	Wallace	Hill	Garner*	Halliday	Holt	Windass	Miller+	O'Halloran&	Waghorn*	McKay+	Dodoo&	Crooks	Hodson	Wilson	Gilks
19/11/2016	L	H	Dundee	1 0	Foderingham	Tavernier	Kiernan	Wallace	Hill	Garner	Halliday	Holt	Windass*	Miller&	O'Halloran+	McKay*	Doddoo+	Forrester&	Crooks	Hodson	Wilson	Gilks
26/11/2016	L	A	Partick Thistle	2 1	Foderingham	Tavernier	Kiernan	Wallace	Wilson	Garner+	Halliday	Holt	Windass*	Miller	Forrester&	McKay*	Dodoo+	O'Halloran&	Senderos	Hodson	Waghorn	Gilks
30/11/2016	L	A	Rangers	0 2	Foderingham	Tavernier	Kiernan	Wallace	Wilson	Dodoo+	Halliday	Holt	Crooks&	Miller	Forrester*	O'Halloran*	Garner+	McKay&	Senderos	Hodson	Waghorn	Gilks
03/12/2016	L	H	Aberdeen	2 1	Foderingham	Hodson	Kiernan	Wallace	Hill	Garner	Halliday	Holt	McKay&	Miller*	O'Halloran+	Tavernier*	Waghorn+	Forrester&	Wilson	Dodoo	Crooks	Gilks
10/12/2016	L	H	Hearts	2 0	Foderingham	Hodson	Kiernan	Wallace	Wilson	Garner+	Halliday	Holt	McKay&	Miller*	Tavernier	Waghorn*	Dodoo+	Burt&	Senderos	O'Halloran	Crooks	Gilks
16/12/2016	L	A	Hamilton Accies	2 1	Foderingham	Hodson	Kiernan	Wallace	Wilson	Garner	Halliday	Holt	McKay	Waghorn*	Tavernier	Forrester*	Dodoo	Hill	Senderos	O'Halloran	Miller	Gilks
24/12/2016	L	H	Inverness CT	1 0	Foderingham	Hodson	Kiernan	Wallace	Hill	Garner	Halliday	Holt	McKay*	Waghorn&	Tavernier+	Miller*	Windass+	Forrester&	Dodoo	O'Halloran	Wilson	Gilks
28/12/2016	L	A	St Johnstone	1 1	Foderingham	Tavernier	Kiernan	Wilson	Hill+	Garner*	Halliday	Holt	McKay	Windass	Miller&	Waghorn*	Hodson+	O'Halloran&	Senderos	Forrester	Crooks	Gilks
31/12/2016	L	H	Celtic	1 2	Foderingham	Tavernier	Kiernan	Wilson	Hill	Garner*	Halliday	Holt&	McKay	Windass+	Miller	Waghorn*	Dodoo+	Forrester&	Hodson	O'Halloran	Crooks	Gilks
21/01/2017	SC4	H	Motherwell	2 1	Foderingham	Hodson	Kiernan	Wallace	Hill	Toral*	Halliday	Holt&	McKay	O'Halloran+	Miller	Windass*	Waghorn+	Hyndman&	Bates	Forrester	Senderos	Gilks
28/01/2017	L	A	Motherwell	2 0	Foderingham	Tavernier	Kiernan	Wallace	Hill	Toral*	Halliday	Hyndman	McKay+	O'Halloran	Miller&	Waghorn*	Forrester+	Windass&	Dodoo	Holt	Senderos	Gilks
01/02/2017	L	A	Hearts	1 4	Foderingham	Tavernier	Kiernan	Wallace	Hill	Toral&	Halliday	Hyndman+	McKay	Waghorn*	Miller	Forrester*	Windass+	Holt&	Dodoo	Hodson	Senderos	Alnwick
04/02/2017	L	H	Ross County	1 1	Foderingham	Tavernier	Senderos	Wallace	Hill	Toral	Holt	Hyndman	McKay*	Garner+	Miller	Forrester*	Waghorn+	Wilson	Dodoo	Hodson	Halliday	Alnwick
12/02/2017	SC5	H	Morton	2 1	Foderingham	Tavernier	Senderos	Wallace&	Hill	Holt*	Halliday	Hyndman+	McKay	Waghorn	Miller	O'Halloran*	Toral+	Hodson&	Wilson	Garner	Forrester	Alnwick
19/02/2017	L	A	Dundee	1 2	Foderingham	Tavernier	Kiernan	Hodson	Hill*	Garner	Halliday&	Hyndman	McKay+	Waghorn	Miller	Wilson*	Forrester+	Holt&	Dodoo	O'Halloran	Houston	Alnwick
24/02/2017	L	A	Inverness CT	1 2	Foderingham	Tavernier	Kiernan	Wallace	Wilson	Toral+	Halliday*	Hyndman	McKay	Waghorn	Miller	Holt*	Garner+	Hodson	Dodoo	Forrester	Windass	Alnwick
01/03/2017	L	H	St Johnstone	3 2	Foderingham	Tavernier	Kiernan	Wallace	Hill	Toral&	Holt	Hyndman	McKay	Waghorn+	Miller*	Garner*	Wilson+	Halliday&	Hodson	Forrester	O'Halloran	Alnwick
04/03/2017	SC6	H	Hamilton Accies	6 0	Foderingham	Tavernier	Kiernain	Wallace	Hill	Toral	Holt	Hyndman&	McKay	Waghorn+	Miller*	Garner*	O'Halloran+	Forrester&	Hodson	Halliday	Wilson	Alnwick
12/03/2017	L	A	Celtic	1 1	Foderingham	Tavernier	Hodson	Wallace	Hill	Wilson	Holt+	Hyndman	McKay*	Waghorn&	Miller	Windass*	Forrester+	O'Halloran&	Dodoo	Senderos	Bates	Alnwick
18/03/2017	L	H	Hamilton Accies	4 0	Foderingham	Tavernier	Toral	Wallace	Hill	Wilson	Holt	Hyndman	McKay*	Waghorn+	Miller&	Garner*	Dodoo+	Forrester&	Wilson	Senderos	Hodson	Alnwick
01/04/2017	L	H	Motherwell	1 1	Foderingham	Kiernan	Toral	Wallace+	Hill*	Hodson&	Holt	Hyndman	McKay	Waghorn	Miller	Garner*	Halliday+	O'Halloran&	Windass	Senderos	Dodoo	Alnwick
05/04/2017	L	A	Kilmarnock	0 0	Foderingham	Tavernier	Wilson	Beerman	Bates	Halliday	Holt	Hyndman*	McKay	Waghorn&	Garner+	Miller*	Dodoo+	Windass&	Toral	O'Halloran	A Wilson	Alnwick
09/04/2017	L	A	Aberdeen	3 0	Foderingham	Tavernier	Wilson	Beerman	Bates	Toral	Holt	Hyndman*	Miller	Waghorn&	Garner+	Windass*	Dodoo+	Halliday&	McKay	Hodson	A Wilson	Alnwick
15/04/2017	L	H	Partick Thistle	2 0	Foderingham	Tavernier	Wilson	Beerman	Bates	Toral&	Holt	Hyndman	Miller	Waghorn+	McKay*	Dodoo*	Garner+	Halliday&	Windass	Hodson	A Wilson	Alnwick
23/04/2017	SCSF	N	Celtic	0 2	Foderingham	Tavernier	Wilson	Beerman	Bates	Halliday*	Holt	Hyndman&	Miller	Waghorn	Garner+	McKay*	Dodoo+	Windass&	Hill	Hodson	Toral	Alnwick
29/04/2017	L	H	Celtic	1 5	Foderingham	Tavernier	Wilson	Beerman	Hill	Windass	Holt	Hyndman+	Miller	Waghorn	Dodoo*	Halliday*	Garner+	McKay	Forrester	Bates	O'Halloran	Alnwick
07/05/2017	L	A	Partick Thistle	2 1	Foderingham	Tavernier	Wilson	Beerman	Bates	Windass+	Holt&	Garner	Miller	Waghorn*	Dodoo	Hill*	Barjonas+	McKay&	Halliday	Dallas	Atakayi	Alnwick
13/05/2017	L	H	Hearts	2 1	Foderingham	Tavernier	Hill	Hodson	Bates	Windass*	Holt+	Garner	Miller	Toral&	McKay	Dodoo*	Barjonas+	Waghorn&	Halliday	Beerman	AWilson	Alnwick
17/05/2017	L	H	Aberdeen	1 2	Foderingham	Tavernier	A Wilson	Hodson*	Bates	Windass	Dodoo+	Garner	Miller	Toral&	McKay	Beerman*	Waghorn+	Barjonas&	Halliday	Holt	Atakayi	Alnwick
21/05/2017	L	A	St Johnstone	2 1	Alnwick	Tavernier	A Wilson	Beerman	Bates	Windass	Holt	Waghorn+	Miller	Toral*	Barjonas&	McKay*	Bradley+	Halliday&	Dodoo	Lyon	Atakayi	Foderingham

Surname	First Name	DOB	SQ	Nat	Pos	L A	L S	L G	SC A	SC S	SC G	LC A	LC S	LC G	UNS	Signed	Previous Club	Notes	Contract
Abaradan Bouzaig	Amin	01/06/1997		MOR/SPA	F											2016	Alhaurin		OOC
Adamson	Jack	07/01/1999		SCO	M											2016	Rangers Youths		OOC
Alnwick	Jak	17/06/1993	25	ENG	GK	1									18	2017	Port Vale		End 2019/2
Ashmore	Max	26/05/1998	49	SCO	M											2015	Rangers Youths		OOC
Atakayi	Serge	30/01/1999		FIN/CDR	F										3	2016	FF Jaro		End 2018/1
Barjonas	Jamie	24/01/1999	65	SCO	M	1	3									2016	Rangers Youths		End 2017/1
Barton	Joey	02/09/1982	8	ENG	M	5						2	1			2016	Burnley	Freed Nov 2016, joined Burnley	
Bates	David	05/10/1996	27	SCO	D	7			1						6	2017	Raith Rovers		End 2017/1
Beerman	Myles	13/03/1999		MAL	D	6	1		1						1	2016	Manchester City Youths		End 2017/1
Bradley	Kyle	14/02/1999	63	SCO	D		1									2016	Rangers Youths	OL to Clyde July 2017-May 2018	End 2017/1
Burt	Liam	01/02/1999	62	SCO	F		1									2015	Rangers Youths		End 2017/1
Crooks	Matt	20/01/1994	21	ENG	M	1	1						1		9	2016	Accrington Stanley	OL to Scunthorpe United Jan-May 2017	End 2019/2
Dallas	Andrew	22/07/1999		SCO	F										1	2016	Rangers Youths		
Dodoo	Joe	29/06/1995	14	ENG/GHA		5	15	3		1		1	3	2	14	2016	Leicester City		End 2019/2
Foderingham	Wes	14/01/1991	1	ENG	GK	37			4			2			6	2015	Swindon Town		End 2018/1
Forrester	Harry	02/01/1991	15	ENG	F	7	14	3		1		5	1		9	2016	Doncaster Rovers		End 2018/1
Garner	Joe	12/04/1988	7	ENG	F	21	10	7	1	1	3		1		2	2016	Preston North End	Transferred to Ipswich Town June 2017	[redacted]
Gibson	Jordan	26/02/1998	55	ENG	M											2016	Rangers Youths		OOC
Gilks	Matt	04/06/1982	25	SCO/ENG	GK							5			25	2016	Burnley	Freed Jan 2017, joined Wigan Athletic	
Halliday	Andrew	11/10/1991	16	SCO	M	24	8	3	3			6	1	2	5	2015	Bradford City	OL to FK Gabala July 2017-May 2018	End 2019/2
Hardie	Ryan	17/03/1997	42	SCO	F										1	2014	Rangers Youths	OL to St Mirren Jul-Dec, to Raith Rovers Jan-May	End 2017/18
Hill	Clint	19/10/1978	3	ENG	D	23	1	3	3		1	5		2	7	2016	QPR	Freed June 2017	
Hodson	Lee	02/10/1991	17	NIR	D	10	1	1	1	1		5			26	2016	MK Dons		End 2018/1
Holt	Jason	19/02/1993	23	SCO	M	28	3		4			3	1	1	4	2015	Hearts		End 2019/20
Houston	Jordan	20/01/2000		SCO	D										1	2016	Rangers Youths		
Hyndman	Emerson	09/04/1996	20	USA	M	13		4	3	1						2017	AFC Bournemouth (OL)	Jan-May	
Jamieson	Sam	14/03/1999	66	SCO	F											2016	Rangers Youths	OL to Stirling University Aug-May	OOC
Jeffries	Josh	13/01/1998	45	SCO	M											2015	Rangers Youths	OL to Stirling Albion Jan-May, Freed June 2017	
Kelly	Liam	23/01/1996	32	SCO	GK											2012	Rangers Youths	OL to Livingston Jul 16-May 2017	End 2018/19
Kiernan	Rob	13/01/1991	4	ROI	D	24		1	2			5			2	2015	Wigan Athletic		End 2017/18
Kranjcar	Niko	13/08/1984	19	CRO	M	4	5	1				4	2	2		2016	New York Cosmos		End 2017/18
Krones	Jason	25/01/1999	61	SCO	D											2016	Rangers Youths	OL to Gala Fairydean Rovers Jan-May	End 2017/18
Lyon	Ross	26/03/1998	52	SCO	D										1	2015	Rangers Youths		
McCrorie	Robby	18/03/1998	61	SCO	GK											2015	Rangers Youths	OL to Berwick Rangfers July 2017-May 2018	End 2018/19
McCrorie	Ross	18/03/1998	50	SCO	D											2015	Rangers Youths	OL to Dumbarton Jan-May	End 2018/19
McKay	Barrie	30/12/1994	10	SCO	F	28	7	5	3	1		5	2	1	3	2011	Kilmarnock Youths		End 2017/18
Miller	Kenny	23/12/1979	9	SCO	F	32	5	11	4		3	3	3		2	2014	Vancouver Whitecaps		End 2017/18
Mounada	Ursene	02/08/1998		ENG/CDI	M											2016	Hartley Juniors		OOC
Nelson	Grant	15/01/1999	60		F											2016	Rangers Youths		OOC
O'Halloran	Michael	06/01/1991	29	SCO	F	6	10		1	2		4	1		13	2016	St Johnstone		End 2019/20
Roberts	Scott	15/03/1996		SCO	F											2016	Rangers Youths	OL to Raith Jul-Jan, Freed Jan 2017 joined Raith	[redacted]
Rossiter	Jordan	24/03/1997	18	ENG	M	3	1					1	1			2016	Liverpool		End 2019/20
Senderos	Philippe	14/02/1985	24	SWI	D	3			1						15	2016	Grasshoppers Zurich	Freed June 2017	[redacted]
Sinnamon	Ryan	22/07/1996		SCO	D											2013	Rangers Youth	OL to Annan Ath Oct-Dec, Freed Jan 2017	
Tavernier	James	31/10/1991	2	ENG	D	35	1	1	3			5		1	2	2015	Wigan Athletic		End 2018/19
Thompson	Jordan	03/01/1997	45	NIR	M								1		1	2015	Manchester United	OL to Raith Rovers Aug 16-May 2017	End 2017/18
Toral	Jon-Miquel	05/02/1995	8	SPA	M	12		2	2	1	1				2	2017	Arsenal (OL)	Jan-May	[redacted]
Waghorn	Martyn	23/10/1990	33	ENG	F	20	12	8	3	1	2	4	1	7	3	2015	Wigan Athletic		End 2017/18
Wallace	Lee	01/08/1987	5	SCO	D	27		3	3			5				2011	Hearts		End 2018/19
Walsh	Tom	11/07/1996		SCO	F											2013	Rangers Youths	OL to St Mirren Jul-Jan, Freed joined Limerick	[redacted]
White	Lewis	15/01/1998	56	SCO	D											2015	Rangers Youths	Freed Jan 2017	
Wilson	Danny	27/12/1991	6	SCO	D	19	2		1			4			9	2015	Hearts		End 2017/18
Wilson	Aidan	02/01/1999	64	SCO	D	2									4	2016	Rangers Youth		End 2018/19
Windass	Josh	09/01/1994	11	ENG	M	14	7			2		3	1	1	3	2016	Accrington Stanley		End 2019/20
Wright	Kieran	01/04/2000	67	SCO	GK											2016	Rangers Youth	OL to Gala Fairydean Rovers Aug-May	End 2017/18
Own Goal														1					
NEW SIGNINGS																			
Cardoso	Fabio	19/04/1994		POR	D											2017	Vitoria Setubal		End 2019/20
Alves	Bruno	27/11/1981		POR	D											2017	Cagliari		End 2018/19
Morelos	Alfredo	21/06/1996		COL	F											2017	HJK Helsinki		End 2019/20
Jack	Ryan	27/02/1992		SCO	M											2017	Aberdeen		End 2019/20
Dalcio	22/5/96	22/05/1996		POR	M											2017	Benfica "B" (OL)	Jun 2017-May 2018	End 2017/18
Candeias	Daniel	25/02/1988		POR	M											2017	Benfica		End 2018/19
Herrera	Eduardo	25/07/1988		MEX	F											2017	Pumas		End 2019/20
Pena	Carlos	29/03/1990		MEX	M											2017	Guadalajara		End 2019/20

Source of Birthdates: Rangers Match Programme / transfermarkt.com

Ross County FC 2016/17

Founded	1929
Ground	Victoria Park
Postcode	IN15 9QZ
Tel	01349 860860
Capacity	6541
Closest Railway Station	Dingwall
Record Attendance	6110 v Celtic, Lge, 18/8/2012
Record Win	11-0 v St Cuthbert Wanderers, SC, 1/12/1993
Record Defeat	0-7 v Kilmarnock, SC, 17/2/1962
Most League Goals in a Season	24 Andy Barrowman, 2007/8
Chairman	Roy McGregor
Secretary	Donnie McBean
Manager	Jim McIntyre
Assistant Manager	Billy Dodds
Colours 2016/17 Top	Navy Blue with white "Ajax" stripe
Shorts	Navy Blue
Sponsor	CRC Evans Offshore
Manufacturer	Macron
Change Colours 2016/17 Top	White with red pin stripe
Shorts	White
Nicknames	Staggies
Web	www.rosscountyfootballclub.co.uk
Match Programme 2016/17	3 (Curtis Sport)

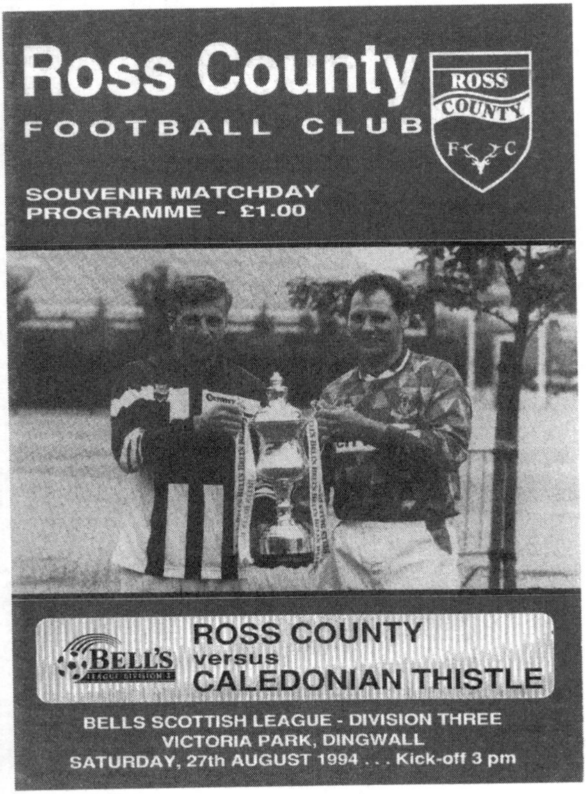

Liam Boyce's goals helped County to secure their SPFL status as fellow Highlanders ICT bit the dust.

Jim McIntyre deserves great praise for the way he got things together at County. He knitted together a good team with a superb work ethic that fully deserved to retain their place ibn the top flight.

He will be disappointed at how easily they surrendered the League Cup. Having won it in February they were out by the end of July, suffering defeat to Alloa.

PREDICTION FOR 2017/18

Boyce has departed for the English Championship and his will be a difficult jersey to fill. However, McIntyre has a track record of unearthing gems from obscure areas of the transfer market. It's a cliche but nobody likes going to Dingwall and that alone should ensure County hang on again in the SPFL. Will finish in the bottom four but safe enough.

HISTORICAL SNIPPETS

Ross County were represented at the meeting held on 31/5/1888 in the Glenalbyn Hotel Inverness, at which the North of Scotland Football Association was formed.

The club declined an invitation to be founder members of the Highland League in 1893. They eventually joined the Highland League in 1929.

County played Manchester United in a friendly at Dingwall on 11/8/1973. The English side fielded the likes of Stepney, Holton, Buchan, Mrgan, Kidd, Macari and Greenhoff. They won 2-0 in front of a crowd of 4000 with goals by Gerry Daly and Brian Kidd.

Honours:
Highland League Champions 1966/7, 1990/1, 1991/2
Highland League Cup 1949/50, 1968/9, 1978/9, 1991/2
Scottish Qualifying Cup (North) Winners 1973/4, 1993/4
North of Scotland Cup Winners 1929/30, 1969/70, 1971/2, 1991/2
Inverness Cup Winners 1930/1, 1959/60, 1964/5, 1966/7, 1978/9, 1979/80, 1991/2, 1992/3

Date	Comp	H/A	Opponents	F	A		HT		Referee	Crowd	Scorers
16/07/2016	LC	A	Montrose	1	0		0	0	C Charleston	557	Graham
23/07/2016	LC	H	Raith Rovers	1	1	3-4p	0	1	J McKendrick	1173	Graham
26/07/2016	LC	A	Alloa	2	3		2	2	S Finnie	319	Graham, Schalk
30/07/2016	LC	H	Cove Rangers	7	0		1	0	M Northcroft	722	Schalk 2, Graham 3, Curran 2
06/08/2016	L	H	Dundee	1	3		0	2	R Madden	3669	Curran
13/08/2016	L	A	Inverness CT	3	2		2	1	A Dallas	4202	Boyce 3
20/08/2016	L	H	Kilmarnock	2	0		1	0	N Walsh	3263	Boyce 2
27/08/2016	L	A	Hamilton Accies	0	1		0	0	G Aitken	1609	
10/09/2016	L	H	Motherwell	1	1		0	0	A Muir	3019	Boyce
17/09/2016	L	A	Rangers	0	0		0	0	G Aitken	47935	
24/09/2016	L	A	Hearts	0	0		0	0	A Muir	16321	
01/10/2016	L	H	St Johnstone	0	2		0	1	C Allan	3299	
15/10/2016	L	A	Aberdeen	0	4		0	2	C Thomson	10091	
22/10/2016	L	A	Partick Thistle	1	1		0	1	D Robertson	3777	Burke
26/10/2016	L	H	Celtic	0	4		0	1	A Muir	6290	
29/10/2016	L	A	Motherwell	1	4		0	2	N Walsh	3177	Schalk
06/11/2016	L	H	Rangers	1	1		1	1	A Dallas	6590	Davies
19/11/2016	L	A	St Johnstone	4	2		2	0	J Beaton	2554	McEveley, Routis, Curran, Boyce
26/11/2016	L	H	Hamilton Accies	1	1		1	0	C Thomson	3275	Boyce
03/12/2016	L	H	Hearts	2	2		1	0	W Collum	4042	McEveley, Boyce
10/12/2016	L	A	Dundee	0	0		0	0	E Anderson	4742	
17/12/2016	L	H	Aberdeen	2	1		1	0	C Thomson	4467	Boyce, Dow
23/12/2016	L	H	Partick Thistle	1	3		0	0	J Beaton	2935	Boyce
28/12/2016	L	A	Celtic	0	2		0	2	N Walsh	55355	
31/12/2016	L	H	Inverness CT	3	2		2	1	B Madden	5111	Boyce 2, Woods
21/01/2017	SC4	H	Dundee United	6	2		4	2	K Clancy	2440	Routis 2, Quinn, Chow, Boyce, O'Brien
28/01/2017	L	A	Kilmarnock	2	3		2	1	B Cook	3207	Routis, Schalk
31/01/2017	L	H	Motherwell	1	2		1	1	S Mclean	2511	McEveley
04/02/2017	L	A	Rangers	1	1		1	0	D Robertson	49428	Schalk
11/02/2017	SC5	H	Aberdeen	0	1		0	0	B Madden	4671	
18/02/2017	L	H	St Johnstone	1	2		0	1	J Beaton	3187	Curran
25/02/2017	L	A	Aberdeen	0	1		0	0	W Collum	11774	
01/03/2017	L	A	Hearts	1	0		0	0	A Muir	15470	Schalk
11/03/2017	L	H	Kilmarnock	1	2		0	0	N Walsh	3380	Boyce
18/03/2017	L	A	Inverness CT	1	1		0	0	C Allan	4123	Schalk
01/04/2017	L	A	Partick Thistle	1	2		0	0	W Collum	3149	Curran
04/04/2017	L	H	Dundee	2	1		1	1	J Beaton	2819	Chow, Boyce
08/04/2017	L	A	Hamilton Accies	1	1		0	1	S McLean	1548	Curran
16/04/2017	L	H	Celtic	2	2		0	1	D Robertson	6205	Gardyne, Boyce
28/04/2017	L	H	Inverness CT	4	0		2	0	C Thomson	4928	Boyce 4
06/05/2017	L	A	Motherwell	1	0		0	0	B Madden	3870	Routis
13/05/2017	L	A	Dundee	1	1		1	0	N Walsh	6812	Boyce
16/05/2017	L	H	Hamilton Accies	3	2		1	1	A Muir	4871	Gardyne, O'Brien, Franks
20/05/2017	L	A	Kilmarnock	2	1		1	1	B Madden	3951	Boyce 2

FRIENDLIES / OTHER GAMES					
05/07/2016	A	Paksi	3	1	
06/07/2016	H	Wick Academy	2	1	U20, at HFA
08/07/2016	A	Soroksar	1	1	
12/07/2016	A	Buckie Thistle	2	5	U20
26/07/2016	A	Alness	3	1	U17

Date	Comp	H/A	Opponents	F	A		1	2	3	4	5	6	7	8	9	10	11	12	13	14	15	16	17	18
16/07/2016	LC	A	Montrose	1	0		Fox	Cikos	McEveley	Davies*	Van Der Weg	Gardyne	Woods	Franks	McShane	Boyce&	Schalk+	Robertson*	Curran+	Graham&	*Routis*	*Foster*	*T Dingwall*	*McCarey*
23/07/2016	LC	H	Raith Rovers	1	1	3-4p	Fox	Cikos	McEveley	Robertson	Van Der Weg	Gardyne	Woods*	Foster	McShane	Boyce&	Curran+	Routis*	Schalk+	Graham&	*Franks*	*Quinn*	*T Dingwall*	*McCarey*
26/07/2016	LC	A	Alloa	2	3		Fox	Quinn	McEveley	Robertson	Routis	Gardyne&	Woods	Foster+	Graham	Boyce	Schalk*	Curran*	Franks+	T Dingwall&	*McShane*	*Van der Weg*	*R Dingwall*	*McCarey*
30/07/2016	LC	H	Cove Rangers	7	0		McCarey	Quinn	McEveley	Davies	Routis	Gardyne*	Woods+	Van der Weg	Graham	Boyce	Schalk&	T Dingwall*	McShane+	Curran&	*Franks*	*McLaughlin*	*R Dingwall*	*Fox*
06/08/2016	L	H	Dundee	1	3		Fox	Quinn	McEveley	Davies	Routis	Gardyne	Woods*	Van der Weg+	Graham&	Boyce	Schalk	McShane*	Franks+	Curran&	*Cikos*	*Foster*	*T Dingwall*	*McCarey*
13/08/2016	L	A	Inverness CT	3	2		Fox	Quinn	McEveley	Davies	Routis	Gardyne&	Woods	Foster	Cikos	Boyce+	Curran*	Schalk*	McShane+	Franks&	*Van der Weg*	*Graham*	*T Dingwall*	*McCarey*
20/08/2016	L	H	Kilmarnock	2	0		Fox	Quinn	McEveley	Davies	Routis	Gardyne&	Woods	Franks+	Cikos	Boyce	Curran*	Schalk*	T Dingwall+	Morrison&	*Van der Weg*	*Fraser*	*McShane*	*McCarey*
27/08/2016	L	A	Hamilton Accies	0	1		Fox	Quinn	McEveley	Davies	Routis+	Gardyne	Woods	Franks&	Cikos	Boyce	Curran*	Schalk*	Chow+	T Dingwall&	*Van der Weg*	*G Morrison*	*McShane*	*McCarey*
10/09/2016	L	H	Motherwell	1	1		Fox	Quinn	McEveley	Davies	Routis	Gardyne&	Woods	Franks+	Cikos	Boyce	Schalk*	Van der Weg*	Curran+	Chow&	*Fraser*	*G Morrison*	*McShane*	*McCarey*
17/09/2016	L	A	Rangers	0	0		Fox	Quinn	Fraser	Davies	Routis	Gardyne	Woods	Franks*	Van Der Weg	Curran&	Schalk+	Chow*	T Dingwall+	Morrison&	*Cikos*	*McShane*	*McCarey*	
24/09/2016	L	A	Hearts	0	0		Fox	Quinn	Fraser	Davies&	Routis	Gardyne	Woods	Franks*	Van Der Weg	McShane	Boyce+	T Dingwall*	Curran+	McEveley&	*Cikos*	*Chow*	*G Morrison*	*McCarey*
01/10/2016	L	H	St Johnstone	0	2		Fox	Quinn	Fraser	McEveley	Routis&	Gardyne	Woods	Franks*	Van Der Weg	Morrison+	Boyce	Dow*	Burke+	Chow&	*Cikos*	*T Dingwall*	*R Dingwall*	*McCarey*
15/10/2016	L	A	Aberdeen	0	4		Fox	Quinn	Fraser	Davies	Chow	Gardyne	Woods	Franks*	Van Der Weg	McShane+	Curran&	T Dingwall*	Routis+	Dow&	*McEveley*	*Burk*	*G Morrison*	*McCarey*
22/10/2016	L	A	Partick Thistle	1	1		Fox	Quinn	Fraser+	Davies	Dow	Gardyne	Woods	Schalk*	Van Der Weg	McShane	Curran&	G Morrison*	Burke+	T Dingwall&	*McEveley*	*Routis*	*Cikos*	*McCarey*
26/10/2016	L	H	Celtic	0	4		Fox	Quinn*	Fraser&	Davies	Dow	Gardyne	Woods	Burke+	Van Der Weg	McShane	Boyce	McEveley*	T Dingwall+	Schalk&	*G Morrison*	*Routis*	*Cikos*	*McCarey*
29/10/2016	L	A	Motherwell	1	4		Fox	Quinn	Fraser	Davies	Dow	Gardyne*	Woods	Burke	Van Der Weg	McShane	Boyce+	Curran*	Schalk+	*McEveley*	*Chow*	*Routis*	*Cikos*	*McCarey*
06/11/2016	L	H	Rangers	1	1		Fox	Cikos*	Fraser	Davies	Dow&	Routis	McEveley	Burke	Curran+	Chow	Boyce	Van der Weg*	Schalk+	T Dingwall&	*Franks*	*McShane*	*G Morrison*	*McCarey*
19/11/2016	L	A	St Johnstone	4	2		Fox*	Gardyne	Fraser	Davies	Van der Weg	Routis	McEveley	Burke&	Curran+	Chow	Boyce	McCarey*	Schalk+	Dow&	*Cikos*	*McShane*	*G Morrison*	*T Dingwall*
26/11/2016	L	H	Hamilton Accies	1	1		Fox	Gardyne&	Fraser	Davies	Van Der Weg	Routis	McEveley	Dow+	Curran*	Chow	Boyce	Schalk*	Franks+	T Dingwall&	*Cikos*	*McShane*	*G Morrison*	*McCarey*
03/12/2016	L	H	Hearts	2	2		Fox	Gardyne	Fraser	Davies	Van Der Weg	Routis	McEveley	T Dingwall&	Curran*	Chow+	Boyce	Schalk*	Woods+	Dow&	*Cikos*	*McShane*	*Franks*	*McCarey*
10/12/2016	L	A	Dundee	0	0		Fox	Gardyne+	Fraser	Davies	Van Der Weg	Routis	McEveley	T Dingwall&	Curran*	Chow	Boyce	Schalk*	Dow+	Franks&	*Quinn*	*McShane*	*Dykes*	*McCarey*
17/12/2016	L	H	Aberdeen	2	1		Fox	Gardyne+	Fraser	Davies	Van Der Weg	Routis	Quinn	T Dingwall*	Curran&	Chow	Boyce	Dow*	Franks+	Schalk&	*Cikos*	*McShane*	*Woods*	*McCarey*
23/12/2016	L	H	Partick Thistle	1	3		Fox	Dow+	Fraser	Davies	McEveley	Routis	Quinn	T Dingwall&	Curran*	Chow	Boyce	Schalk*	Franks+	McLaughlin&	*Cikos*	*McShane*	*G Morrison*	*McCarey*
28/12/2016	L	A	Celtic	0	2		Fox	Woods	Fraser	Davies	McEveley	Routis+	Quinn	Schalk*	Curran	Chow	Boyce&	Tumilty*	McShane+	G Morrison&	*Dow*	*T Dingwall*	*McLaughlin*	*McCarey*
31/12/2016	L	H	Inverness CT	3	2		Fox	Van der Weg	Fraser	Davies	McEveley	Routis	Woods+	Schalk*	Dow&	Chow	Boyce	Curran*	Franks+	T Dingwall&	*Quinn*	*Tumilty*	*McLaughlin*	*McCarey*
21/01/2017	SC4	H	Dundee United	6	2		Fox	Van der Weg	Fraser	Woods+	McEveley*	Routis	Quinn	Schalk&	Dow	Chow	Boyce	Tumilty*	O'Brien+	Lalkovic&	*Gobern*	*Dykes*	*Curran*	*McCarey*
28/01/2017	L	A	Kilmarnock	2	3		Fox	Van der Weg	Fraser	Woods	McEveley	Routis+	Quinn	Schalk*	Dow&	Chow	Boyce	O'Brien*	Curran+	Gardyne&	*Gobern*	*Naismith*	*Lalkovic*	*McCarey*
31/01/2017	L	H	Motherwell	1	2		Fox	Van der Weg	Fraser	Woods	McEveley+	Routis*	Quinn	Schalk	O'Brien&	Chow	Boyce	Naismith*	Lalkovic+	Gardyne&	*Gobern*	*Dow*	*Curran*	*McCarey*
04/02/2017	L	A	Rangers	1	1		Fox	Van der Weg	Fraser	Woods	Davies	Naismith	Lalkovic+	Schalk&	O'Brien*	Chow	Boyce	Gardyne*	Dow+	Curran&	*Gobern*	*Tumilty*	*Dykes*	*McCarey*
11/02/2017	SC5	H	Aberdeen	0	1		Fox	Van der Weg	Fraser	Woods	Davies	McEveley	Gardyne+	Schalk&	O'Brien	Chow*	Boyce	Gobern*	Lalkovic+	Curran&	*Dow*	*Tumilty*	*Quinn*	*McCarey*
18/02/2017	L	H	St Johnstone	1	2		Fox	Van der Weg*	Fraser	Woods	Davies	McEveley	Gardyne&	Lalkovic	Curran	Chow+	Boyce	Naismith*	O'Brien+	Schalk&	*Dow*	*Gobern*	*Quinn*	*McCarey*
25/02/2017	L	A	Aberdeen	0	1		Fox	Naismith	Fraser	Woods	Davies	Quinn*	Gardyne	Schalk	Curran&	Chow+	Boyce	Van der Weg*	O'Brien+	Lalkovic&	*Dow*	*Gobern*	*Tumilty*	*McCarey*
01/03/2017	L	A	Hearts	1	0		Fox	Van der Weg	Fraser	Woods*	Davies	McEveley+	Naismith	Schalk&	Curran	Chow	Boyce	O'Brien*	Tumilty+	Gardyne&	*Dow*	*Lalkovic*	*Dykes*	*McCarey*
11/03/2017	L	H	Kilmarnock	1	2		McCarey	Van der Weg	Fraser	Woods*	Quinn	Gardyne+	Naismith	Schalk	Curran&	Chow	Boyce	Routis*	O'Brien+	Dow&	*Gobern*	*Lalkovic*	*Tumilty*	*Foden*
18/03/2017	L	A	Inverness CT	1	1		McCarey	Van der Weg	Fraser	Routis*	Davies	Gardyne+	Naismith	Schalk	Curran&	Chow	Boyce	O'Brien*	Lalkovic+	Dow&	*Gobern*	*Dykes*	*Tumilty*	*Foden*
01/04/2017	L	A	Partick Thistle	1	2		Fox	Van der Weg	Fraser	Routis+	Davies	McEveley*	Naismith	Schalk	Curran&	Woods	Boyce	Gardyne*	O'Brien+	Dow&	*Lalkovic*	*Dykes*	*Tumilty*	*McCarey*
04/04/2017	L	H	Dundee	2	1		Fox	Van der Weg	Fraser	O'Brien	Davies+	Gardyne	Naismith	Chow	Curran	Woods*	Boyce	Routis*	McEveley+&	Tumilty&	*Lalkovic*	*Dow*	*Schalk*	*McCarey*
08/04/2017	L	A	Hamilton Accies	1	1		Fox	Van der Weg	Fraser	Dow&	Davies	Gardyne	Naismith	Chow+	Curran*	Woods	Boyce	Schalk*	Routis+	Lalkovic&	*Gobern*	*Tumilty*	*Dykes*	*McCarey*
16/04/2017	L	H	Celtic	2	2		Fox	Van der Weg	Fraser	Dow	Davies	Gardyne&	Naismith	Chow	O'Brien+	Tumilty*	Boyce	Schalk*	Routis+	Franks&	*Curran*	*Lalkovic*	*Dykes*	*McCarey*
28/04/2017	L	H	Inverness CT	4	0		Fox	Van der Weg	Fraser	Dow	Woods+	Gardyne	Naismith	Chow&	O'Brien	Curran	Boyce*	Routis*	Tumilty+	Dykes&	*Franks*	*Gobern*	*Malcolm*	*McCarey*
06/05/2017	L	A	Motherwell	1	0		Fox	Van der Weg+	Fraser	Dow*	Davies	Gardyne	Naismith	Chow	O'Brien&	Woods	Curran	Routis*	Tumilty+	Franks&	*Dykes*	*Gobern*	*Malcolm*	*McCarey*
13/05/2017	L	A	Dundee	1	1		Fox	Woods	Fraser	Dow*	Davies	Gardyne	Naismith	Chow	O'Brien+	Boyce	Curran&	Van der Weg*	Tumilty+	Schalk&	*Dykes*	*Franks*	*Routis*	*McCarey*
16/05/2017	L	H	Hamilton Accies	3	2		Fox	Van der Weg	Fraser	Tumilty	Routis	Gardyne*	Naismith	Chow	Franks	Boyce	Schalk&	Woods*+	O'Brien+	Curran&	*Keillor-Dunn*	*Malcolm*	*Dykes*	*McCarey*
20/05/2017	L	A	Kilmarnock	2	1		McCarey	Van der Weg	Fraser	Malcolm	Routis	Franks	Naismith	Chow*	O'Brien&	Boyce	Curran+	Dykes*	Schalk+	R Dingwall&	*Keillor-Dunn*	*Tumilty*	*McShane*	*Fox*

						L			SC			LC							
Surname	First Name	DOB	SQ	Nat	Pos	A	S	G	A	S	G	A	S	G	UNS	Signed	Previous Club	Notes	Contract
Boyce	Liam	08/04/1991	10	NIR	F	34		23	2		1	4				2014	Cliftonville	Transferred to Burton Albion June 2017	[redacted]
Boyd	Scott	04/08/1986	14	SCO	D											2008	Partick Thistle	OL to Kilmarnock Aug-Jan, signed for Killie Jan 2017	
Brownlie	David	22/03/1997		SCO	D											2016	Rangers	OL to Elgin City Jan-May 2017	OOC
Burke	Chris	02/12/1983	22	SCO	M	4	2	1							1	2016	Unattached	Ex Nottingham Forest	OOC
Chow	Tim	18/06/1994	12	ENG	M	26	4	1	2		1				2	2016	Wigan Athletic		End 2017/18
Cikos	Erik	01/07/1988	3	SVK	D	5						2			12	2016	Slovan Bratislava	Freed Jan 2017, joined SS Monopoli 1966	[redacted]
Curran	Craig	23/08/1989	11	ENG	F	26	8	5		1		1	3	2	3	2015	Nuneaton Town		End 2017/18
Davies	Andrew	17/12/1984	15	ENG	D	31		1	1			2				2015	Bradford City		End 2018/19
Dingwall	Tony	25/07/1994	16	SCO	F	4	10						2		7	2014	Ross County Youth		OOC
Dingwall	Russell	26/06/1997	58	SCO	F		1								3	2015	Ross County Youth		End 2017/18
Dow	Ryan	07/06/1991	9	SCO	F	13	10	1	1						7	2016	Dundee United		End 2018/19
Dykes	Dylan	14/03/1996		SCO	M		2								11	2016	Rangers		End 2017/18
Foden	Mark	19/03/1996	41	ENG	GK										2	2015	St Mirren Youths		End 2017/18
Foster	Richard	31/07/1985	12	SCO	D	1						2			2	2015	Rangers	Freed Jul 2016, joined St Johnstone	[redacted]
Fox	Scott	28/06/1987	1	SCO	GK	35			2			3			2	2015	Partick Thistle		End 2018/19
Franks	Jonathan	08/04/1990	17	ENG	F	9	9	1				1	1		6	2015	Hartlepool United	Released June 2017	[redacted]
Fraser	Marcus	23/06/1994	2	SCO	D	33			2						2	2015	Celtic		End 2017/18
Gardyne	Michael	23/01/1986	7	SCO	M	28	5	2	1			4				2015	Dundee United		End 2017/18
Gobern	Oscar	26/01/1991	19	ENG	M					1					11	2017	Mansfield Town	Released June 2017	[redacted]
Graham	Brian	23/11/1987	19	SCO	F	1						2	2	6	1	2015	Dundee United	Tranhsferred to Hibernian Aug 2016	
Hall	Matthew	06/01/1997		ENG	D											2016	Watford	Freed June 2017	
Keillor-Dunn	Davis	02/11/1997		ENG	F										2	2016	Chesterfield		End 2017/18
Lalkovic	Milan	09/12/1992	27	SVK	F	2	4			2					6	2017	Portsmouth (OL)	Jan-May 2017	[redacted]
Malcolm	Blair	03/02/1997		SCO	M	1									3	2015	Partick Thistle Youth		End 2017/18
McCarey	Aaron	14/01/1992	31	ROI	GK	3	1					1			39	2016	Wolves		End 2017/18
McEveley	Jay	11/02/1985	5	SCO/ENG	D	19	3	3	2			4			3	2016	Sheffield United		End 2017/18
McIver	Ross	28/02/1999		SCO	M											2016	Ross County Youth	OL to Wick Academy Jan-May 2017	End 2017/18
McLaughlin	Christopher	05/03/1996	44	SCO	D		1								3	2015	Dundee United Youth	OL to Forfar Athletic Jan-May 2017	OOC
McLennan	Tom	27/01/1997		SCO	M											2014	Ross County Youth		OOC
McLeod	Kyle	07/06/1995		SCO	F											2015	Ross County Youth	OL to Elgin City Aug 16-Jan 2017,	[redacted]
																		Freed Jan 2017 joined Brora Rangers	
McShane	Ian	20/12/1992	18	SCO	M	5	3					2	1		13	2015	Queen of the South		End 2017/18
Morrison	Greg	19/02/1998	53	SCO	F	1	4								9	2015	Ross County Youth		End 2018/19
Morrison	Sam	09/09/1998		SCO	D											2015	Ross County Youth		End 2017/18
Munro	Ross	01/04/2000		SCO	GK											2016	Ross County Youth	OL to Brora Rangers Dec 16-May 2017	End 2017/18
Naismith	Jason	25/06/1994	3	SCO	D	14	2								1	2017	St Mirren		
O'Brien	Jim	28/09/1987	6	SCO/ROI	M	8	8	1	1	1	1					2017	Shrewsbury Town (OL)	Jan-May 2017	[redacted]
Quinn	Paul	21/07/1985	43	SCO	D	19			1		1	2			5	2016	Aberdeen	Released June 2017	
Robertson	Chris	11/10/1986	6	SCO	D							2	1			2015	Port Vale	Freed Sep 2016, joined AFC Wimbledon	
Routis	Chris	03/03/1990	4	GFRA/SWI	D	23	7	3	1		2	2	1		5	2016	Bradford City		End 2017/18
Schalk	Alex	07/08/1992	23	NET	F	15	17	5	2			3	1	3	1	2015	Go Ahead Eagles		End 2017/18
Tumilty	Reghan	26/02/1997		SCO	D	2	6			1					9	2016	Dundee United		End 2017/18
Van der Weg	Kenny	19/02/1991	28	NET	D	29	4		2			3			4	2016	NAC Breda		End 2017/18
Wallace	James	29/08/2000		SCO	F											2016	Ross County Youth		End 2017/18
Woods	Martin	01/01/1986	8	SCO	M	27	2	1	2			4			1	2014	Barnsley		End 2017/18
NEW SIGNINGS																			
Kelly	Sean	01/11/1993		SCO	D											2017	AFC Wimbledon		End 2018/19
Limdsay	Jamie	11/10/1995		SCO	M											2017	Celtic (OL)	July-May	End 2017/18
Mikkelsen	Thomas	19/01/1990		DAN	F											2017	OB Odense		End 2018/19

Source of Birthdates: transfermarkt.com

St Johnstone FC 2016/17

Founded	1884
Ground	McDiarmid Park
Postcode	PH1 2SJ
Tel	01738 459096
Capacity	10696
Closest Railway Station	Perth
Record Attendance	29972 v Dundee, SC, 10/2/1951
Ground Record	10545 v Dundee, Lge, 23/5/99
Record Win	9-0 v Albion Rovers, LC, 9/3/1946
Record Defeat	1-10 v Third Lanark, SC, 24/1/1903
Most League Goals in a Season	36 Jimmy Benson, 1931/2
Chairman	Steve Brown
General Manager	Dave Ryan
Secretary	Paul Smith
Manager	Tommy Wright
Assistant Manager	Callum Davidson
Colours 2016/17 Top	Light Blue with White diagonal flashes
Shorts	White
Sponsor	Alan Storrar Cars
Manufacturer	Joma
Change Colours 2015/146Top	Yellow
Shorts	Yellow
Nicknames	Saints, Sainties
Web	www.perthstjohnstonefc.co.uk
Match Programme 2016/17	£2
Theme Song	The Saints Are Coming

St Johnstone were promoted to the SPFL nine years ago u Derek Mcinnes. Since then they have produced a remar level of consistency and once again achieved a top six finish

Manager Tommy Wright has a tremendous ability to un good players and to mould them into a side that is very di to beat. Brendan Rodgers paid them quite a complimen season when he said that playing against St Johnstone playing "proper men's football", implying that professionalism and attitude of Saints was second to none.

Despite their success it still proves difficult to motivate cr into McDiarmid Park. It is just as well that the club mak use of the facilities at their ground to generate revnue on match days.

PREDICTION FOR 2017/18

No doubt Saints will again e hard to beat and they could ac a top six finish. Much depends on holding on to Tommy W as Manager—the time may come when he wants to test hi with greater resources and a higher profile.

The origins of St Johnstone were recorded in Peter Baxter's "Football in Perthshire, past and Present", published in 1898. However, Blair and Doyle (1997) disagree with many of his dates and facts. Their research was based on painstaking examination of contemporary sources and should be taker more reliable.

Baxter's version has a man called John Colborn as central to the formation of St Johnstone. He was a fishing tackle expert and moved from Edinburgh Dunkeld to work in a fishing shop owned by a Mr R Anderson. In 1884 he was a member of the St Johnstone Cricket Club, and along with a number o other members, decided to form a football team to keep them occupied in the winter months.

However. Blair and Doyle's research finds no trace of a St Johnstone game until 1885. In fact, their research shows that at the AGM of the St Johnstor Cricket Club, on 6th February 1885, it was proposed to start an Association Football Club. A meeting to that effect was held on the 24th of February 18 It is likely that some of the members had informal football practices in 1884 but the real date of formation of the club is 24/2/1885. The first match t place on 7/3/1885, on the South Inch, against the Caledonian Railway.

Baxter's version has John Colburn at the centre of the club and taking on the role of captain. Contemporary newspaper reports do not bear this out – Daniel Scott is named in the local press as the first captain of the club.

By 1886 the Saints had 90 members – more than any other club in Perth – which may explain why they flourished when others went under.

The 20 original members of the club each subscribed a pound in the summer of 1885 to secure the lease of a piece of land called Craigie Haugh from landowner, Sir Robert Moncrieffe. They developed the land into the Recreation Grounds. It is located behind the current petrol station on and occup by AJ Stephen Builders in 2006. The pitch always suffered from poor drainage throughout its use.

In the early 1920s the club embarked on a fund-raising scheme to finance improvements to the Recreation Grounds. Their target was to raise £5000. However, it became clear that this was not a sufficient sum to modernise the ground. Consequently, the prospect of moving to a new ground was cor ered. In February 1924 the Earl of Mansfield asked for a meeting with the club and offered them seven acres of land at Muirton on the northern outs of Perth.

Work on Muirton Park began quickly and it was opened on Christmas Day 1924. The last match at the Recreation Grounds was on 13/12/1924. St Joh stone defeated Kilmarnock 4-2.

Blair, A and Doyle, B - **Bristling with Possibilities, The Official History of St Johnstone FC**, Perth, 1997

Date	Comp	H/A	Opponents	F	A		HT		Referee	Crowd	Scorers
16/07/2016	LC	A	Elgin City	3	1		1	0	A Muir	1046	Swanson, Cummins, MacLean
23/07/2016	LC	H	Falkirk	3	0		2	0	R Madden	2725	Swanson 2, MacLean
26/07/2016	LC	A	Brechin City	1	1	2-4p	0	1	J McKendrick	912	Kane
30/07/2016	LC	H	Stirling Albion	4	0		3	9	B Cook	2858	Anderson, MacLean, Craig, Wotherspoon
07/08/2016	L	H	Aberdeen	0	0		0	0	W Collum	5728	
10/08/2016	LC1	H	Hearts	3	2		1	2	C Allan	4214	Swanson 2, B McKay
13/08/2016	L	A	Motherwell	2	1		0	0	E Anderson	3739	Swanson, MacLean
20/08/2016	L	H	Celtic	2	4		0	3	C Thomson	6823	Swanson, McLean
27/08/2016	L	A	Inverness CT	1	2		0	0	S Finnie	2729	Foster
10/09/2016	L	A	Partick Thistle	2	0		1	0	N Ross	2885	Anderson, MacLean
17/09/2016	L	H	Hearts	1	0		0	0	J Beaton	5456	Cummins
22/09/2016	LC2	A	Aberdeen	0	1		0	0	C Thomson	8829	
25/09/2016	L	A	Hamilton Accies	1	1		0	1	E Anderson	1705	Craig
01/10/2016	L	A	Ross County	2	0		1	0	C Allan	3299	Swanson, Kane
15/10/2016	L	H	Kilmarnock	0	1		0	0	S McLean	2930	
23/10/2016	L	H	Dundee	2	1		0	0	N Walsh	3646	Anderson, Swanson
26/10/2016	L	A	Rangers	1	1		1	1	K Clancy	46563	Alston
29/10/2016	L	H	Partick Thistle	1	2		1	1	B Cook	3096	MacLean
05/11/2016	L	A	Hearts	2	2		1	1	D Robertson	16421	Swanson, Kane
19/11/2016	L	H	Ross County	2	4		0	2	J Beaton	2554	Swanson, MacLean
03/12/2016	L	H	Inverness CT	3	0		1	0	E Anderson	2549	Craig, Swanson, Davidson
10/12/2016	L	A	Aberdeen	0	0		0	0	K Clancy	11501	
17/12/2016	L	H	Motherwell	1	1		0	1	W Collum	2836	Kane
23/12/2016	L	A	Kilmarnock	1	0		1	0	S Finnie	3056	Davidson
28/12/2016	L	H	Rangers	1	1		1	1	C Allan	7979	MacLean
31/12/2016	L	A	Dundee	0	3		0	2	D Robertson	6492	
21/01/2017	SC4	H	Stenhousemuir	2	0		2	0	E Anderson	2441	Maclean, Alston
25/01/2017	L	A	Celtic	0	1		0	0	A Dallas	51057	
28/01/2017	L	H	Hamilton Accies	3	0		0	0	N Walsh	3279	Cummins 2, Davidson
01/02/2017	L	A	Partick Thistle	1	0		1	0	C Allan	2257	MacLean
05/02/2017	L	H	Celtic	2	5		2	1	C Thomson	6548	Watson, Boyata og
11/02/2017	SC5	H	Partick Thistle	0	1		0	1	S McLean	2884	
18/02/2017	L	A	Ross County	2	1		1	0	J Beaton	3187	MacLean, Kane
25/02/2017	L	H	Kilmarnock	0	2		0	1	D Robertson	2933	
01/03/2017	L	A	Rangers	2	3		0	1	K Clancy	46800	Wotherspoon, Anderson
11/03/2017	L	H	Dundee	2	0		2	0	A Dallas	4195	Paton, Alston
18/03/2017	L	A	Motherwell	2	1		1	1	G Aitken	3588	Craig 2
01/04/2017	L	A	Hamilton Accies	0	1		0	0	D Robertson	1662	
05/04/2017	L	H	Hearts	1	0		0	0	N Walsh	4197	Shaughnessy
08/04/2017	L	A	Inverness CT	3	0		1	0	S Finnie	2961	MacLean, Craig, Cummins
15/04/2017	L	H	Aberdeen	1	2		0	2	B Madden	5132	Swanson
29/04/2017	L	A	Aberdeen	2	0		0	0	A Muir	10606	Swanson, Thomson
06/05/2017	L	A	Celtic	1	4		0	0	N Walsh	52796	MacLean
13/05/2017	L	H	Partick Thistle	1	0		1	0	S Finnie	3630	Swanson
17/05/2017	L	H	Hearts	1	0		1	0	D Robertson	3141	Kane
21/05/2017	L	H	Rangers	1	2		0	1	A Dallas	6799	Cummins

FRIENDLIES / OTHER GAMES

09/07/2016	A	Glentoran	2	1		
12/07/2016	A	Livingston	1	1		
15/07/2016	A	Turriff United	2	2		U20
19/07/2016	A	Spartans	1	3		U20
19/07/2016	H	Bradford City	2	0		
23/07/2016	A	Luncarty	4	1		U20, Luncarty Tnt
24/07/2016	N	Camelon	3	3	wop	U20, Luncarty Tnt
03/08/2016	A	Manchester City				CD

Date	Comp	H/A	Opponents	F	A		1	2	3	4	5	6	7	8	9	10	11	12	13	14	15	16	17	18
16/07/2016	LC	A	Elgin City	3	1		Clark	Anderson	Shaughnessy	Watson	Easton	Alston&	Miller	Swanson+	Craig	MacLean	Cummins*	Kane*	Paton+	Craig Thomson&	*Scobbie*	*Mackay*	*G Hurst*	*Mannus*
23/07/2016	LC	H	Falkirk	3	0		Mannus	Anderson	Shaughnessy	Scobbie	Easton	Alston&	Miller	Swanson+	Craig	MacLean	Cummins*	Kane*	Coulson+	Paton&	*Craig Thomson*	*Comrie*	*B McKay*	*Clark*
26/07/2016	LC	A	Brechin City	1	1	2-4p	Clark	Anderson	Shaughnessy&	Scobbie	Easton	Davidson	Paton	Craig Thomson*	Craig+	Coulson	Kane	Alston*	Swanson+	Cummins&	*MacLean*	*Comrie*	*B McKay*	*Mannus*
30/07/2016	LC	H	Stirling Albion	4	0		Mannus	Anderson	Shaughnessy	Scobbie	Easton+	Alston	Miller*	Swanson&	Craig	MacLean	Cummins	Paton*	Wotherspoon+	Coulson&	*Davidson*	*Kane*	*B McKay*	*Clark*
07/08/2016	L	H	Aberdeen	0	0		Mannus	Anderson	Shaughnessy	Scobbie	Easton	Alston+	Davidson	Swanson	Craig	MacLean&	Cummins*	Kane*	Wotherspoon+	Coulson&	*Paton*	*Comrie*	*B McKay*	*Clark*
10/08/2016	LC1	H	Hearts	3	2		Mannus	Anderson	Shaughnessy	Scobbie*	Easton	Alston	Wotherspoon	Swanson	Craig+	Kane	Paton	B McKay*	MacLean+	*Coulson*	*Millar*	*Comrie*	*G Hurst*	*Clark*
13/08/2016	L	A	Motherwell	2	1		Mannus	Anderson	Shaughnessy	B McKay	Easton	Alston*	Davidson	Swanson&	McLean	Kane	Miller+	Wotherspoon*	Paton+	Craig&	*Gordon*	*Comrie*	*Cummins*	*Clark*
20/08/2016	L	H	Celtic	2	4		Mannus	Foster	Shaughnessy	B McKay&	Easton	Alston*	Davidson	Swanson	McLean	Wotherspoon+	Paton	Craig*	Kane+	Cummins&	*Gordon*	*Comrie*	*McLaren*	*Clark*
27/08/2016	L	A	Inverness CT	1	2		Mannus	Anderson	Shaughnessy	Foster	Easton	Alston*	Kane+	Swanson	McLean	Wotherspoon	Paton&	Davidson*	Cummins+	Craig&	*Millar*	*Gordon*	*Coulson*	*Clark*
10/09/2016	L	A	Partick Thistle	2	0		Clark	Anderson	Shaughnessy	Foster	Easton	Miller	Kane*	Swanson+	McLean	Craig	Paton	Cummins*	Wotherspoon+	Alston	*Comrie*	*Gormley*	*Coulson*	*Mannus*
17/09/2016	L	H	Hearts	1	0		Clark	Anderson	Shaughnessy	Foster	Easton	Davidson	Coulson*	Cummins+	McLean&	Craig	Paton	Wotherspoon*	Kane+	Alston&	*Comrie*	*Gormley*	*Cam Thomson*	*Mannus*
22/09/2016	LC2	A	Aberdeen	0	1		Clark	Anderson	Shaughnessy	Gordon	Easton	Davidson	Wotherspoon	Swanson+	McLean	Gormley*	Paton&	Coulson*	Craig+	Kane&	*Comrie*	*Alston*	*Cummins*	*Mannus*
25/09/2016	L	A	Hamilton Accies	1	1		Clark	Anderson	Shaughnessy	Foster*	Easton	Davidson	Alston	Swanson	Craig	Coulson+	Cummins&	Comrie*	Gormley+	Kane&	*Wotherspoon*	*Paton*	*Gordon*	*Mannus*
01/10/2016	L	A	Ross County	2	0		Clark	Anderson	Shaughnessy	Foster	Easton	Davidson	Alston*	Swanson+	Craig	MacLean	Kane	Wotherspoon*	Paton+	*Coulson*	*Gordon*	*Gormley*	*Cummins*	*Mannus*
15/10/2016	L	H	Kilmarnock	0	1		Clark	Anderson	Shaughnessy	Foster	Easton	Davidson	Alston*	Swanson	Craig&	MacLean	Kane+	Wotherspoon*	Cummins+	Coulson&	*Miller*	*Paton*	*Gordon*	*Mannus*
23/10/2016	L	H	Dundee	2	1		Clark	Anderson	Shaughnessy	Foster	Easton	Davidson	Wotherspoon	Swanson+	Craig	MacLean	Kane*	Coulston*	Paton+	*Alston*	*Miller*	*Cummins*	*Gordon*	*Mannus*
26/10/2016	L	A	Rangers	1	1		Clark	Anderson	Shaughnessy	Foster	Easton	Miller+	Alston	Swanson	Craig	Paton	Kane*	Cummins*	Wotherspoon+	MacLean	*Coulson*	*Comrie*	*Gordon*	*Mannus*
29/10/2016	L	H	Partick Thistle	1	2		Clark	Anderson	Shaughnessy	Foster	Easton	MacLean	Wotherspoon&	Swanson+	Craig	Paton	Cummins*	Kane*	Coulson+	Alston&	*Miller*	*Comrie*	*Gordon*	*Mannus*
05/11/2016	L	A	Hearts	2	2		Clark	Anderson	Shaughnessy	Foster	Easton	MacLean	Wotherspoon	Swanson+	Miller*	Paton	Alston	Craig*	Kane+	*Scobbie*	*Coulson*	*Cummins*	*Gordon*	*Mannus*
19/11/2016	L	H	Ross County	2	4		Clark&	Anderson	Shaughnessy*	Foster	Easton	MacLean	Wotherspoon	Swanson	Craig+	Paton	Alston	Kane*	Scobbie+	Mannus&	*Coulson*	*Cummins*	*Gordon*	*McLaren*
03/12/2016	L	H	Inverness CT	3	0		Clark	Anderson	Shaughnessy	Foster	Easton	MacLean+	Wotherspoon	Swanson&	Craig	Davidson	Coulson*	Alston*	Cummins+	Kane&	*Scobbie*	*Millar*	*Gordon*	*Mannus*
10/12/2016	L	A	Aberdeen	0	0		Clark	Anderson	Shaughnessy	Foster	Easton	MacLean	Wotherspoon	Kane+	Craig	Davidson	Coulson*	Alston*	Cummins+	*McLaren*	*Scobbie*	*Millar*	*Watson*	*Mannus*
17/12/2016	L	H	Motherwell	1	1		Clark	Scobbie	Shaughnessy	Foster	Easton	MacLean	Wotherspoon	Kane&	Miller+	Davidson	Coulson*	Alston*	Paton+	Cummins&	*Hunter*	*Gordon*	*Watson*	*Mannus*
23/12/2016	L	A	Kilmarnock	1	0		Clark	Anderson	Shaughnessy	Foster	Easton	Alston	Wotherspoon	Kane*	Miller	Davidson	Swanson+	Cummins*	Craig+	*Scobbie*	*Hunter*	*Paton*	*Watson*	*Mannus*
28/12/2016	L	H	Rangers	1	1		Clark	Anderson	Shaughnessy	Foster	Easton	Alston*	Wotherspoon&	Paton	Miller+	MacLean	Cummins	Scobbie*	Craig+	Swanson&	*Hunter*	*Kane*	*Watson*	*Mannus*
31/12/2016	L	A	Dundee	0	3		Clark	Anderson	Shaughnessy	Foster	Easton	Alston	Davidson	Paton+	Craig*	MacLean&	Swanson	Kane*	Wotherspoon+	Cummins&	*Scobbie*	*Miller*	*Watson*	*Mannus*
21/01/2017	SC4	H	Stenhousemuir	2	0		Clark	Anderson	Shaughnessy	Watson	Easton	Alston	Wotherspoon	Cummins+	Miller	MacLean	Swanson*	Craig*	Kane+	*C Thomson*	*Scobbie*	*Paton*	*Foster*	*Mannus*
25/01/2017	L	A	Celtic	0	1		Clark	Anderson	Shaughnessy	Watson	Scobbie	Paton	Wothesrpoon*	Craig	Miller	Kane&	Swanson+	Alston*	MacLean+	Cummins&	*Davidson*	*Easton*	*Craig Thomson*	*Mannus*
28/01/2017	L	H	Hamilton Accies	3	0		Clark	Anderson	Shaughnessy	Foster	Easton	Alston	Davidson	Paton	Cummins	MacLean+	Swanson*	Wotherspoon*	Craig+	Scobbie	*Miller*	*Watson*	*Kane*	*Mannus*
01/02/2017	L	A	Partick Thistle	1	0		Clark	Anderson	Shaughnessy	Foster	Easton	Miller	Davidson	Craig	Cummins	MacLean	Swanson*	Wotherspoon*	*Alston*	*Scobbie*	*Paton*	*Watson*	*Hunter*	*Mannus*
05/02/2017	L	H	Celtic	2	5		Clark	Scobbie	Shaughnessy	Foster+	Easton	Paton	Davidson	Wotherspoon*	Cummins	Watson	Swanson&	Alston*	MacLean+	Craig&	*Miller*	*Smith*	*Craig Thomson*	*Mannus*
11/02/2017	SC5	H	Partick Thistle	0	1		Clark	Anderson	Shaughnessy	Foster	Easton	Miller&	Davidson	Wotherspoon*	Cummins+	MacLean	Swanson	Alston*	Kane+	Craig&	*Scobbie*	*Paton*	*Watson*	*Mannus*
18/02/2017	L	A	Ross County	2	1		Clark	Anderson	Shaughnessy	Foster	Easton	Miller	Davidson*	Wotherspoon	Craig	MacLean+	Alston	Watson*	Kane+	*Jardine*	*Scobbie*	*Coulson*	*Craig Thomson*	*Mannus*
25/02/2017	L	H	Kilmarnock	0	2		Clark	Anderson	Shaughnessy	Foster	Easton	Miller*	Scobbie+	Wotherspoon	Kane	MacLean	Alston&	Paton*	Coulson+	Craig Thomson&	*Smith*	*Hunter*	*Jardine*	*Mannus*
01/03/2017	L	A	Rangers	2	3		Clark	Anderson	Shaughnessy	Foster	Easton	Watson&	Swanson+	Paton	Craig	MacLean	Alston*	Cummins*	Wotherspoon+	Coulson&	*Smith*	*Scobbie*	*Craig Thomson*	*Mannus*
11/03/2017	L	H	Dundee	2	0		Clark	Scobbie	Shaughnessy	Foster	Easton	Cummins	Swanson*	Paton	Craig	MacLean	Alston+	Davidson*	Craig Thomson+	*Hurst*	*Smith*	*Watson*	*Hunter*	*Mannus*
18/03/2017	L	A	Motherwell	2	1		Clark*	Scobbie	Shaughnessy	Foster	Easton	Cummins	Swanson	Paton	Craig	MacLean	Alston+	Mannus*	Davidson+	*Miller*	*Smith*	*Coulson*	*Craig Thomson*	*Hunter*
01/04/2017	L	A	Hamilton Accies	0	1		Mannus	Scobbie	Shaughnessy	Foster	Easton	Cummins	Swanson	Paton	Craig*	Davidson	Alston	Millar*	*Craig Thomson*	*Wotherspoon*	*Smith*	*Hurst*	*Clark*	
05/04/2017	L	H	Hearts	1	0		Mannus	Scobbie	Shaughnessy	Smith	Easton	Cummins	Wotherspoon*	Paton	Craig	MacLean	Alston	Miller*	*Craig Thomson*	*Cam Thomson*	*Coulson*	*Hunter*	*Clark*	
08/04/2017	L	A	Inverness CT	3	0		Mannus	Scobbie	Shaughnessy	Smith	Easton	Cummins	Coulson*	Paton	Craig	MacLean+	Alston&	Wotherspoon*	Miller+	Craig Thomson&	*Hurst*	*Hunter*	*Clark*	*Anderson*
15/04/2017	L	H	Aberdeen	1	2		Mannus	Scobbie	Shaughnessy	Foster	Easton	Coulson&	Wotherspoon	Paton	Craig+	Maclean	Alston*	Swanson*	Davidson+	Craig Thomson&	*Smith*	*Miller*	*Clark*	*Anderson*
29/04/2017	L	A	Aberdeen	2	0		Mannus	Anderson	Shaughnessy	Foster	Easton	Miller*	Wotherspoon+	Davidson	Craig	Swanson&	Cummins	Paton*	C Thomson+	Alston&	*Scobbie*	*Smith*	*Clark*	*Coulson*
06/05/2017	L	A	Celtic	1	4		Clark	Anderson	Shaughnessy	Foster	Easton	Alston+	Paton	MacLean	Craig	Swanson&	Cummins*	Craig Thomson*	Wotherspoon+	Kane&	*Scobbie*	*Smith*	*Hurst*	*Mannus*
13/05/2017	L	H	Partick Thistle	1	0		Mannus	Scobbie	Shaughnessy	Foster	Easton	Paton	Wotherspoon*	MacLean	Craig	Swanson+	Cummins	Alston*	Craig Thomson+	*Kane*	*Coulson*	*Smith*	*Gilchrist*	*Clark*
17/05/2017	L	H	Hearts	1	0		Mannus	Scobbie	Shaughnessy	Foster	Easton	Miller&	Wotherspoon	Craig Thomson*	Kane	Swanson+	Cummins	Alston*	Coulson+	Craig&	*Anderson*	*MacLean*	*Gilchrist*	*Clark*
21/05/2017	L	H	Rangers	1	2		Mannus	Scobbie	Shaughnessy	Foster	Easton	Miller	Alston	Craig Thomson+	Kane*	MacLean	Craig	Cummins*	Hurst+	Paton&	*Anderson*	*Jardine*	*Gilchrist*	*Clark*

ame	First Name	DOB	SQ	Nat	Pos	L A	L S	L G	SC A	SC S	SC G	LC A	LC S	LC G	UNS	Signed	Previous Club	Notes	Contract
on	Blair	23/03/1992	4	SCO	M	25	10	2	1	1	1	4	1		4	2016	Falkirk		End 2017/18
erson	Steven	19/12/1985	6	SCO	D	26		3	2			6		1	4	2004	Dundee United		End 2017/18
antyne	Cameron	22/04/2000		SCO	M											2016	St Johnstone Youths		
n	Ciaran	31/05/1999		SCO	D											2016	St Johnstone Youths		
k	Zander	26/06/1992	12	SCO	GK	26			2			3			15	2008	Hamilton Accies		End 2019/20
rie	Aaron	03/02/1997	39	SCO	D		1								11	2015	St Johnstone Youths	OL to Peterhead Jan-May 2017	End 2018/19
son	Michael	04/04/1988	17	ENG	M	7	7					1	3		12	2016	York City		End 2017/18
g	Liam	27/12/1986	26	SCO	M	27	9	5		2		5	1	1		2015	Hibernian		End 2018/19
mins	Graham	29/12/1987	29	ROI	F	17	13	5	2			3	1	1	6	2015	Exeter City		End 2017/18
dson	Murray	07/03/1988	8	SCO	M	18	4	3	1			2			2	2009	Livingston		End 2017/18
herty	Jamie	19/08/1999	41	SCO	F											2016	St Johnstone Youths		
ald	Gregor	27/04/2001		SCO	D											2016	St Johnstone Youths		
on	Brian	05/03/1988	24	SCO	D	38			2			6			1	2013	Dundee		End 2018/19
er	Richard	31/07/1985	19	SCO	D	33		1	1						1	2016	Ross County		End 2018/19
hrist	Ally	03/03/1995	28	SCO	D										3	2011	St johnstone Youths		End 2017/18
don	Liam	26/01/1996	23	SCO	D							1			13	2015	Hearts	OL to Peterhead Jan-May 2017	End 2018/19
nley	Joe	26/11/1989	20	NIR	F		1					1			3	2016	Peterborough United (OL)	Aug-Oct 2016	[redacted]
ter	George	03/08/1996	33	SCO	F										9	2015	Spartans	Freed May 2017	[redacted]
st	Mark	21/10/1995	30	SCO	F											2013	Livingston Youths	OL to East Fife Aug 16-May 2017	End 2017/18
st	Greg	08/04/1997		SCO	F		1								6	2015	Stirling Albion	OL to Berwick R Aug 16 -Jan 2017	End 2017/18
ine	Danny	17/01/1998		SCO	D										3	2015	Middlesbrough Youths		
nston	Joe	18/06/1999		SCO	F											2016	St Johnstone Youths		
e	Chris	05/09/1994	25	SCO	F	14	11	5		2		2	3	1	4	2010	St Johnstone Youths		End 2017/18
	Jason	06/02/1997	34	SCO	D											2014	Tynecastle Colts	OL to East Fife Jul 16-May 2017	End 2018/19
sden	Cameron	22/09/1999	35	SCO	D											2016	St Johnstone Youths		
Kenzie	Jamie	31/12/2000		SCO	M											2016	St Johnstone Youths		
Lean	Steven	23/08/1982	9	SCO	F	30	2	10	2		1	4	1	3	3	2012	Yeovil Town		End 2017/18
nus	Alan	19/05/1982	1	NIR	GK	12	2					3			29	2011	Shamrock Rovers		End 2017/18
ann	Alistair	04/12/1999	37	SCO	M											2016	St Johnstone Youths		
awl	Eoghan	31/07/1986	44	NIR	D											2015	Hull City	OL to Forfar A Oct 16-May 2017, Freed May 2017	[redacted]
ay	Brad	26/03/1993		SCO	D	2							1	1	5	2015	Hearts	Freed Aug 2016, joined Inverness CT	[redacted]
enzie	Ben	20/10/1997	45	SCO	GK											2016	St Johnstone Youths		End 2017/18
aren	Connor	20/02/1997	32	SCO	F				1						3	2014	Celtic Youths	OL to Stirling Alb Jan-May 2017, Freed May 2017	[redacted]
ar	Christopher	30/03/1983	7	SCO	M	14	3		1			3			12	2008	Morton		End 2017/18
eilly	Euan	02/05/2000		SCO	F											2016	St Johnstone Youths		
e	Greg	04/03/1998		SCO	D											2015	Hearts Youths	OL to Berwick R Mar-May	
on	Paul	18/04/1987	18	NIR	M	23	7	1				3	3		7	2016	Dundee United		End 2017/18
obie	Tom	31/03/1988	3	SCO	D	13	2					4			14	2012	Falkirk	OOC June 2017, joined Dundee United	[redacted]
ughnessy	Joe	06/07/1992	14	ROI	D	38		1	2			6				2015	Aberdeen		End 2018/19
pson	Paul	07/04/1997		SCO	M											2016	St Johnstone Youths		
lair	Ross	07/05/2001		SCO	GK											2016	St Johnstone Youths		
th	Clive	12/12/1997		WAL	D	2									10	2016	Preston NE (OL)	Jan-May 2017	[redacted]
thers	Shaun	10/01/2000		SCO	M											2016	St Johnstone Youths		
nson	Danny	28/12/1986	11	SCO	M	28	2	10	2			5	1	5		2016	Hearts	Joined Hibernian June 2017	
mson	Craig	10/03/1995		SCO	M	2	7	1				1	1		9	2013	St Johnstone Youths	OL to Stranraer Aug 16-Jan 2017	End 2017/18
mson	Cameron	28/11/1999		SCO	M										2	2016	St Johnstone Youths		
son	Keith	14/11/1989	22	SCO	M	3	1	1	1			1			9	2016	St Mirren		End 2017/18
therspoon	David	16/01/1990	10	SCO	M	20	13	1	2			2	1	1	2	2013	Hibernian		End 2018/19
n Goals								1											
V SIGNINGS																			
ean	Kyle			NIR	M											2017	Nottingham Forest		
ugall	Stefan															2017	Sheffield United		
ser	Scott															2017	Port Vale		

rce of Birthdates: St Johnstone FC website and transfermarkt.com

St Mirren FC 2016/17

Founded	1876
Ground	St Mirren Park, Greenhill Road
Postcode	PA3 1RU
Tel	0141 889 2558
Capacity	8023
Closest Railway Station	Paisley St James
Record Attendance	47438 v Celtic, LC, 20/8/49
Ground Record	7542 v Kilmarnock, 31/1/09
Record Win	15-0 v Glasgow University, SC, 30/1/1960
Record Defeat	0-9 v Rangersd, Lge, 4/12/1897
Most League Goals in a Season	45 Dunky Walker, 1921/2
Chairman	Stewart Gilmour
Chief Executive	Tony Fitzpatrick
Manager	Alex Rae (until Oct), Jack Ross
Assistant Manager	David Farrell (until Oct), James Fowler
Colours 2016/17 Top	White with Black Pin Stripe
Shorts	White
Sponsor	King of Trainers
Manufacturer	Carbrini
Change Colours 2016/17 Top	Black
Shorts	Black
Nicknames	Buddies
Web	www.saintmirren.net
Match Programme 2016/17	The Saint £3

During the first half of the season it looked like St Mirren w dead and buried. Under Alex Rae they struggled badly were well adrift.

The club brought Jack Ross in as Manager and slowly he be to turn things around. It was far from plain sailing and Sa Championship survival was not ensured until the very end, the transformation in fortunes was remarkable.

Saints also reached the Final of the Challenge Cup. Far fr being a distraction, wins in that competition seemed to s them on to greater things.

During the Summer Dundee coveted Jack Ross as their r manager but he elected to stay at St Mirren.

PREDICTION FOR 2017/18

Given the improvement brought about by Jack Ross St Mir could be dark horses this season. Rather than fight relegation, expect them to be in contention for promotion play off position at the least.

SOME SNIPPETS FROM HISTORY

The club's first game at Thistle Park was against John Elder FC on 6/9/1879 (0-2)
The club's first game at Westmarch was a 2-1 win over Queen's Park on 25/8/1883.

In 1888 the Westmarch ground boasted a running track and cricket square, as well as the football facilities. December 1889 saw the opening of a ne pavilion at Westmarch. Third Lanark visited for a special match and afterwards the teams adjourned to the Globe Hotel, Paisley.

In 1894 St Mirren were advised that their lease on Westmarch would not be extended. The ground was bought by a company who intended to promote trotting. The Paisley Daily Express reported the imminent move to Love Street thus:

"It is not improbable that the old brickfield at the foot of Love Street will be their ultimate choice. The nature of the ground forbids building extensions for some time, which fact will renderthe chance of securing a lengthy lease more probable. The removal will probably cost the club £500 but th central situation of the proposed new field will ensure the return of that sum in a few years".

The first game at Love Street was on 8/9/1894 against Celtic. Gates were opened at 2.30pm for a 4pm kick off and a crowd of 8000 turned up. Celtic won 3-0. Some contemporary reports refer to the ground as Fullerton Park. Paterson and McPherson (2005) clear this up by indicating that the ground belonged to a Mr John Fullerton and this name was used informally to describe the new location but was never properly adopted.

During 1895/6 the club generated additional revenue by allowing the adjacent slaughterhouse to use the field for grazing animals prior to their dispatch. For 1896/7 additional entrances were created through a passage from Caledonia Street – previous the only way in had been from Love Street. Barbed wire barricades were also erected.

During October 1899 the Scottish Rugby Union requested the use of Love Street for an Inter-District Match. This was granted.

St Mirren were peeved when the SFA chose Underwood Park (home of Abercorn) for an international match against Wales on 19/3/1890. However, St Mirren's consolation was to have two players in the Scotland team – Andy Brown and James Dunlop. Dunlop later died from an injury received in St Mirren match. On New Year's Day 1892 he cut himself on broken glass on the field at Abercorn's Underwood Park during a Friendly match. He contracted tetanus and died on January 11th 1892. Subscriptions were raised to erect a monument to Dunlop, and this still exists in Paisley's Woodside Cemetery.

Season 1904/5 brought ground problems. The club sought to extend theor lease on Love Street but found that the owners would prefer to sell the ground to them. They could not afford the asking price but found that the terms of any new lease would be much less favourable. The club began to look at alternative ground in the Shortroods area of the town. To finance the purchase of five acres of ground it was decided to convert the club into a Limited Liability Company. The first meeting of the re-constituted club took place on February 23rd 1905. At the same time the owners of the Love Street grounds accepted a reduced payment of £4000 for the site and the Directors went ahead with the purchase. Within a year there were plans fo ground improvements and 100 railway sleepers had been bought at 6d each to make a start!

Date	Comp	H/A	Opponents	F	A		HT		Referee	Crowd	Scorers
16/07/2016	LC	A	Livingston	3	2		1	0	G Duncan		Clarkson 2, Morgan
19/07/2016	LC	H	Ayr United	1	0		0	0	J Beaton	2098	Baird
23/07/2016	LC	A	Hamilton Accies	0	3		0	1	D Robertson	1379	
30/07/2016	LC	H	Edinburgh City	3	0		3	0	S Kirkland	1800	Shankland, Walsh, Baird
06/08/2016	L	H	Morton	1	1		0	1	S McLean	4997	Sutton
13/08/2016	L	A	Raith Rovers	1	3		0	1	K Graham	2140	Hardie
20/08/2016	L	H	Hibernian	0	2		0	2	D Robertson	4517	
27/08/2016	L	A	Ayr United	1	1		0	1	C Allan	2165	Walsh
03/09/2016	CC3	A	Albion Rovers	4	3	AET	3	3	M Roncone	711	Morgan, Mallan, Sutton, Shankland
10/09/2016	L	H	Queen of the South	1	3		1	2	B Cook	3102	Walsh
17/09/2016	L	A	Dumbarton	1	1		1	1	S Finnie	1101	Hardie
24/09/2016	L	A	Dunfermline Athletic	3	4		2	1	G Aitken	2732	Sutton 2, Hardie
01/10/2016	L	H	Falkirk	1	1		1	0	J Beaton	2334	Walsh
08/10/2016	CC4	A	Hibernian	2	1		1	1	W Collum	4393	Mallan, Clarkson
15/10/2016	L	H	Dundee United	0	2		0	1	N Walsh	3612	
29/10/2016	L	A	Hibernian	0	2		0	2	G Holt	14485	
01/11/2016	L	A	Morton	1	3		0	2	W Collum	3378	Gordon
05/11/2016	L	H	Dumbarton	0	1		0	0	J McKendrick	2758	
13/11/2016	CC4	H	Ayr United	2	1		0	0	C Allan	2199	Sutton 2
19/11/2016	L	H	Dunfermline Athletic	0	1		0	1	N Walsh	2126	
29/11/2016	SC3	H	Spartans	5	1		3	0	K Graham	1147	Shankland 2, Mallan, McAllister, Sutton
03/12/2016	L	A	Falkirk	1	3		1	0	C Thomson	4486	Morgan
06/12/2016	L	A	Queen of the South	3	2		1	2	C Allan	1147	Magennis, Gordon, Mallan
10/12/2016	L	H	Raith Rovers	1	0		0	0	B Cook	2630	Morgan
17/12/2016	L	H	Ayr United	1	1		0	0	G Aitken	3124	Sutton
24/12/2016	L	A	Dundee United	1	2		1	2	J McKendrick	7247	Sutton
31/12/2016	L	H	Morton	1	1		1	0	N Walsh	4902	McKenzie
07/01/2017	L	H	Queen of the South	0	3		0	1	M Northcroft	3105	
14/01/2017	L	A	Dunfermline Athletic	1	1		0	1	W Collum	4108	Mackenzie
21/01/2017	SC4	A	Dundee	2	0		1	0	B Madden	3622	Sutton, MacKenzie
28/01/2017	L	H	Falkirk	1	2		0	1	A Muir	3316	Loy
04/02/2017	L	A	Dumbarton	2	2		1	0	J Beaton	1377	Clarkson, Davis
11/02/2017	SC5	A	East Fife	3	2		1	1	D Robertson	1510	Smith, Morgan 2
19/02/2017	CCSF	H	TNS	4	1		0	1	K Kennedy (NI)	2044	McGinn, Mallan, Sutton, Loy
25/02/2017	L	A	Ayr United	2	0		0	0	C Thomson	2712	Morgan, Sutton
01/03/2017	L	H	Hibernian	2	0		1	0	E Anderson	3441	Demetriou 2
05/03/2017	SC6	A	Celtic	1	4		1	0	S McLean	27455	Davis
08/03/2017	L	A	Raith Rovers	0	2		0	0	C Allan	2124	
11/03/2017	L	H	Dunfermline Athletic	0	0		0	0	S Finnie	4582	
15/03/2017	L	H	Dundee United	3	2		2	1	G Aitken	3766	Davis, Mallan, Morgan
18/03/2017	L	A	Queen of the South	2	0		1	0	A Dallas	1728	Mallan, Loy
25/03/2017	CCF	N	Dundee United	1	2		1	1	N Walsh	8089	Loy
01/04/2017	L	H	Ayr United	6	2		4	0	G Duncan	4620	Mallan, McKenzie, McGinn, Magennis, Morgan, Smith
08/04/2017	L	H	Dumbarton	1	1		1	1	S Kirkland	3906	Magennis
11/04/2017	L	A	Morton	4	1		1	1	S Finnie	4609	Demettriou, Mallan, Sutton, McKenzie
15/04/2017	L	A	Falkirk	2	2		1	1	C Thomson	4734	Loy, McGinn
22/04/2017	L	A	Dundee United	2	3		1	1	C Charleston	6225	McKenzie, Todd
29/04/2017	L	H	Raith Rovers	5	0		2	0	K Clancy	4937	Mallan 2, McManus og, Loy, Morgan
06/05/2017	L	A	Hibernian	1	1		0	0	A Muir	19764	Loy

FRIENDLIES / OTHER GAMES

05/07/2016	H	Stirling Albion	4	3	at Ralston
09/07/2016	A	Stenhousemuir	3	1	
16/07/2016	A	Renfrew	4	3	U20
18/07/2016	A	Largs Thistle	4	1	U20
25/07/2016	A	Benburb	3	1	U20

Date	Comp	H/A	Opponents	F	A	1	2	3	4	5	6	7	8	9	10	11	12	13	14	15	16	17	18
16/07/2016	LC	A	Livingston	3	2	S Gallacher	Naismith	Irvine	Webster	Baird	Quinn+	Mallan	C Gallagher*	Morgan	Clarkson	Sutton	Hutton*	Stewart+	Gordon	Flanagan	O'Keefe	Langfield	
19/07/2016	LC	H	Ayr United	1	0	Langfield	Naismith	Irvine	Webster	Baird	Hutton	Mallan	C Gallagher*	Morgan	Clarkson	Sutton+	Walsh*	Shankland+	Gordon	McKenzie	McAllister	Stewart	S Gallacher
23/07/2016	LC	A	Hamilton Accies	0	3	Langfield	Naismith	Irvine	Webster	Baird	Hutton	Mallan	C Gallagher*	Morgan	Clarkson&	Sutton+	Walsh*	Shankland+	McCallister&	Gordon	O'Keefe	Stewart	S Gallacher
30/07/2016	LC	H	Edinburgh City	3	0	S Gallacher	Naismith	Stewart	Webster	Baird	Hutton	Mallan	Walsh&	Morgan	Clarkson*	Shankland+	Hardie*	Sutton+	C Gallacher&	Gordon	McAllister	McDonald	Langfield
06/08/2016	L	H	Morton	1	1	Langfield	Naismith	Irvine&	Webster	Baird	Hutton	Mallan	C Gallacher+	Morgan	Clarkson*	Shankland	Hardie*	Walsh+	Sutton&	Whyte	O'Keefe	McDonald	S Gallacher
13/08/2016	L	A	Raith Rovers	1	3	Langfield	Naismith+	Irvine	Webster	Baird	Hutton	Mallan&	C Gallacher*	Morgan	Hardie	Shankland	Walsh*	Sutton+	Clarkson&	Gordon	O'Keefe	McDonald	S Gallacher
20/08/2016	L	H	Hibernian	0	2	S Gallacher	Naismith	Irvine	Webster	Baird	Hutton	Mallan	Sutton+	Morgan*	Walsh	Shankland&	Hardie*	Clarkson+	Stewart&	Gordon	Whyte	McDonald	Langfield
27/08/2016	L	A	Ayr United	1	1	S Gallacher	Naismith	Irvine	Webster	Baird	Hutton+	Mallan	Sutton	Stewart*	Hardie	Clarkson	Walsh*	Shankland+	McLear	Gordon	Whyte	McDonald	Langfield
03/09/2016	CC3	A	Albion Rovers	4	3 AET	Langfield	McKenzie	Irvine	Webster	Walsh	Hutton&	Mallan	Sutton	Stewart*	Morgan	Clarkson+	McDonald*	Shankland+	Quinn&	Naismith	O'Keefe	Baird	S Gallacher
10/09/2016	L	H	Queen of the South	1	3	Langfield	Naismith*	Irvine	Webster&	McKenzie	Hutton	Mallan	Sutton+	Walsh	Morgan	Hardie	Shankland*	Clarkson+	Gordon&	Magennis	O'Keefe	Baird	S Gallacher
17/09/2016	L	A	Dumbarton	1	1	S Gallacher	Naismith	Irvine	Baird	McKenzie	Hutton&	Mallan	Sutton	Walsh	Morgan*	Hardie+	C Gallagher*	Shankland+	Whyte&	Webster	Clarkson	McAllister	Langfield
24/09/2016	L	A	Dunfermline Athletic	3	4	S Gallacher	Naismith	Irvine	Baird	McKenzie*	Hutton	Mallan	Sutton	Quinn	Morgan+	Hardie	Webster*	Walsh+	Whyte	Shankland	Clarkson	McDonald	Langfield
01/10/2016	L	H	Falkirk	1	1	Langfield	Naismith	Irvine	Baird	McKenzie	Hutton+	Mallan	Sutton	Quinn*	Morgan	Hardie	Walsh*	Clarkson+	Whyte	Shankland	McDonald	S Gallacher	
08/10/2016	CC4	A	Hibernian	2	1	Langfield	Naismith	Irvine	Baird	McKenzie	Hutton	Mallan	Sutton&	Quinn*	Morgan	Walsh+	Clarkson*	C Gallagher+	Shankland&	Willison	Whyte	O'Keefe	McDonald
15/10/2016	L	H	Dundee United	0	2	Langfield	Naismith	Irvine	Baird	McKenzie&	Hutton	Mallan*	Sutton	Quinn	Morgan	Hardie+	Shankland*	Walsh+	Clarkson&	McLear	Stewart	C Gallacher	S Gallacher
29/10/2016	L	A	Hibernian	0	2	Langfield	Naismith	Irvine	Baird	Gordon	Hutton&	Mallan	Clarkson+	Shankland	Morgan	Hardie*	Magennis*	Sutton+	C Gallagher&	Walsh	Mclear	Whyte	S Gallacher
01/11/2016	L	A	Morton	1	3	Langfield	Naismith	Irvine	Baird	Gordon	Hutton*	Mallan	Clarkson	Shankland&	Morgan	Walsh+	Sutton*	Magennis+	Hardie&	C Gallacher	McLear	Whyte	S Gallacher
05/11/2016	L	H	Dumbarton	0	1	Langfield	Naismith	Irvine	McKenzie	Gordon&	McAllister+	Mallan	Clarkson*	Magennis	Morgan	Sutton	Shankland*	Hardie+	C Gallacher&	Hutton	Mclear	Baird	S Gallacher
13/11/2016	CC4	H	Ayr United	2	1	S Gallacher	Naismith	Irvine	McKenzie	Baird+	McAllister&	Mallan	Clarkson*	Magennis	Morgan	Sutton	Shankland*	Walsh+	Stewart&	Hutton	McLear	C Gallacher	Langfield
19/11/2016	L	H	Dunfermline Athletic	0	1	S Gallacher	Naismith	Irvine	Gordon+	Baird	McAllister	Mallan	Clarkson*	Magennis&	Morgan	Sutton	Shankland*	Hardie+	McLear&	C Gallacher	Hutton	Stewart	Langfield
29/11/2016	SC3	H	Spartans	5	1	S Gallacher	Naismith	Irvine	Gordon*	McKenzie+	McAllister	Mallan	Shankland	Magennis	Morgan	Sutton&	Quinn*	Baird+	Orsi&	C Gallacher	McLear	Clarkson	Langfield
03/12/2016	L	A	Falkirk	1	3	S Gallacher	Naismith	Irvine	Quinn*	McKenzie	McAllister&	Mallan	Baird	Magennis	Morgan	Sutton+	Stewart*	Shankland+	C Gallacher&	Clarkson	McLear	Hardie	Langfield
06/12/2016	L	A	Queen of the South	3	2	S Gallacher	Naismith	Irvine	Quinn*	McKenzie	McAllister&	Mallan	Gordon	Magennis	Morgan	Sutton+	Shankland*	Hardie+	C Gallacher&	Clarkson	Mclear	Stewart	Langfield
10/12/2016	L	H	Raith Rovers	1	0	S Gallacher	Naismith	Irvine	Quinn+	McKenzie	McAllister	Shankland	Gordon*	Magennis	Morgan	Sutton&	Webster*	McLear+	Hardie&	Clarkson	Walsh	C Gallacher	Langfield
17/12/2016	L	H	Ayr United	1	1	S Gallacher	Naismith	Irvine	Quinn*	McKenzie	McAllister	Mallan	Webster&	Magennis	Morgan	Shankland+	Sutton*	Clarkson+	Hardie&	Baird	McLear	C Gallacher	Langfield
24/12/2016	L	A	Dundee United	1	2	S Gallacher	Naismith	Irvine	Quinn+	McKenzie*	McAllister&	Mallan	Webster	Magennis	Morgan	Sutton	Baird*	Clarkson+	Shankland&	C Gallacher	McLear	Hardie	Langfield
31/12/2016	L	H	Morton	1	1	S Gallacher	Naismith	Irvine	Quinn*	McKenzie	McAllister&	Mallan	Webster	Magennis+	Morgan	Sutton	McLear*	Clarkson+	C Gallacher&	Baird	Shankland	Hardie	Langfield
07/01/2017	L	H	Queen of the South	0	3	S Gallacher	Naismith	Irvine	Quinn	McKenzie	McAllister	Mallan	Webster+	Magennis*	Morgan	Sutton	Clarkson*	Shankland+	C Gallacher	Baird	McLear	Stewart	Langfield
14/01/2017	L	A	Dunfermline Athletic	1	1	Langfield	Naismith	Irvine	Quinn+	McKenzie	McAllister&	Mallan	Webster*	Storie	Loy	Sutton	Baird*	Morgan+	Magennis&	Clarkson	McLear	Fjelde	Willison
21/01/2017	SC4	A	Dundee	2	0	O'Brien	Fjelde	Irvine	Baird	McKenzie	McAllister&	Mallan	Morgan	Storie	Magennis*	Sutton+	Whyte*	Clarkson+	McPherson&	Webster	Mclear	O'Keefe	Langfield
28/01/2017	L	H	Falkirk	1	2	O'Brien	Fjelde	Irvine	Baird	McKenzie*	Smith	Mallan+	Morgan	Storie&	Loy	Sutton	Webster*	McGinn+	Todd&	Clarkson	Demetriou	Magennis	Langfield
04/02/2017	L	A	Dumbarton	2	2	O'Brien	Davis	Irvine	Eckersley+	McKenzie	Smith	Magennis	Morgan*	Storie	Clarkson&	McGinn	Sutton*	Demetriou+	Todd&	Baird	Fjelde	Webster	Langfield
11/02/2017	SC5	A	East Fife	3	2	O'Brien	Davis	Demetriou	Eckersley	McKenzie	Smith&	Mallan	Magennis	Storie+	Loy*	McGinn	Sutton*	Morgan+	Fjelde&	Baird	Irvine	Clarkson	Langfield
19/02/2017	CCSF	H	TNS	4	1	O'Brien	Davis	Demetriou	Eckersley&	Baird	Sutton	Mallan	Magennis	Storie*	Loy	McGinn+	Morgan*	Fjelde+	Irvine&	Webster	Whyte	O'Keefe	Langfield
25/02/2017	L	A	Ayr United	2	0	O'Brien	Davis	Demetriou	Eckersley	McKenzie	Sutton	Mallan+	Magennis	Smith*	Morgan	McGinn	Todd*	Fjelde+	Irvine	Baird	Loy	Storie	Langfield
01/03/2017	L	H	Hibernian	2	0	O'Brien	Davis	Demetriou	Irvine*	McKenzie	Sutton	Mallan	Magennis+	Smith&	Morgan	McGinn	Fjelde*	Todd+	Baird&	Webster	Loy	Storie	Langfield
05/03/2017	SC6	A	Celtic	1	4	O'Brien	Davis	Demetriou	Irvine	McKenzie+	Sutton*	Mallan	Magennis&	Smith	Morgan	McGinn	Loy*	Baird+	Storie&	Webster	O'Keefe	Fjelde	Langfield
08/03/2017	L	A	Raith Rovers	0	2	O'Brien	Davis	Demetriou+	Eckersley	McKenzie	Sutton	Mallan	Magennis*	Smith	Morgan	McGinn	Todd*	Loy+	Storie	Irvine	Baird	Fjelde	Langfield
11/03/2017	L	H	Dunfermline Athletic	0	0	O'Brien	Davis	Eckersley	Irvine	McKenzie	Sutton	Mallan	Todd*	Smith+	Morgan	McGinn	Loy*	Demetriou+	Storie	Magennis	Baird	Fjelde	Langfield
15/03/2017	L	H	Dundee United	3	2	O'Brien	Davis*	Eckersley	Irvine	McKenzie	Sutton	Mallan	Loy+	Smith&	Morgan	McGinn	Baird*	Magennis+	Storie&	Demetriou	Todd	Fjelde	Langfield
18/03/2017	L	A	Queen of the South	2	0	O'Brien	Magennis+	Eckersley	Irvine	McKenzie	Baird	Mallan	Loy*	Smith&	Morgan	McGinn	Sutton*	Storie+	Demetriou&	Webster	Todd	Fjelde	Langfield
25/03/2017	CCF	N	Dundee United	1	2	O'Brien	Magennis*	Eckersley	Irvine	McKenzie	Baird	Mallan	Loy	Sutton	Morgan	McGinn	O'Keefe*	Fjelde+	Demetriou	Webster	Whyte	Watters	Langfield
01/04/2017	L	H	Ayr United	6	2	O'Brien	Magennis	Demetriou	Eckersely	McKenzie&	Baird	Mallan+	Loy	Smith	Morgan*	McGinn	Sutton*	Todd+	Webster&	Gordon	Quinn	Fjelde	Langfield
08/04/2017	L	H	Dumbarton	1	1	O'Brien	Eckersley	Demetriou*	Irvine	McKenzie	Baird	Mallan	Loy&	Smith	Magennis+	McGinn	Sutton*	Todd+	Gordon&	Storie	Quinn	Fjelde	Langfield
11/04/2017	L	A	Morton	4	1	O'Brien	Magennis	Demetriou	Irvine	McKenzie	Baird	Mallan&	Loy*	Smith+	Sutton	McGinn	Storie*	Todd+	Quinn&	Gordon	Whyte	Fjelde	Langfield
15/04/2017	L	A	Falkirk	2	2	O'Brien	Magennis	Eckersley	Irvine	Mckenzie	Baird	Mallan	Loy&	Smith+	Sutton*	McGinn	Morgan*	Storie+	Todd&	Gordon	Quinn	Fjelde	Langfield
22/04/2017	L	A	Dundee United	2	3	O'Brien	Magennis	Eckersley	Irvine+	McKenzie	Baird	Mallan	Loy&	Smith*	Morgan	McGinn	Sutton*	Demetriou+	Todd&	Webster	Quinn	Storie	Langfield
29/04/2017	L	H	Raith Rovers	5	0	O'Brien	Magennis+	Eckersley	Irvine	McKenzie&	Baird	Mallan	Loy	Smith*	Morgan	McGinn	Demetriou*	Quinn+	Webster&	Sutton	Fjelde	Todd	Langfield
06/05/2017	L	A	Hibernian	1	1	O'Brien	Magennis	Eckersley	Irvine*	McKenzie	Baird	Mallan	Loy&	Smith+	Morgan	McGinn	Demetriou*	Quinn+	Sutton&	Webster	Fjelde	Todd	Langfield

Surname	First Name	DOB	SQ	Nat	Pos	L A	L S	L G	SC A	SC S	SC G	LC A	LC S	LC G	CC A	CC S	CC G	UNS	Signed	Previous Club	Notes	Contract
Baird	Jack	07/02/1997	15	SCO	D	21	4		1	2		4		2	4			11	2014	St Mirren Youth		End 2017/18
Barclay	Luke	01/01/1999	38	SCO	M														2016	St Mirren Youth		End 2017/18
Clarkson	David	10/09/1985	7	SCO	F	7	9	1		1		4		2	2	1	1	9	2016	Motherwell		OOC
Davis	Harry	24/09/1991		ENG	D	6		2	2		1				1				2017	Crewe Alexandra (OL)	Jan-May	[redacted]
Demetriou	Stelios	04/10/1990	2	CYP	D	6	6	3	2						1			3	2017	Doxa Katakopios		End 2017/18
Eckersley	Adam	07/09/1985	44	ENG	D	12			1						2				2017	FC Edmonton		End 2018/19
Fawkes	Lee	05/03/1999	41	SCO	M														2016	St Mirren Youth	OL to Johnstone Burgh Jan-May, Freed June 2017	[redacted]
Fjelde	Pat	26/07/1994	23	NOR	M	1	2		1	1						2		13	2017	Bryne FK	Freed June 2017	
Flanagan	Nathan	04/05/1997	31	SCO	F													1	2016	Hearts Youths	OL to Annan Athletic Dec-May	OOC
Gallacher	Scott	15/07/1989	12	SCO	GK	12			1			2			1			11	2016	Alloa Athletic	Freed Jan 2017, joined Hibernian	[redacted]
Gallagher	Calum	13/09/1994	11	SCO	F	2	6					3	1			1		9	2015	Rangers	Freed Jan 2017, joined Dumbarton	
Gordon	Ben	07/10/1985	5	SCO	D	6	2	2	1									10	2016	Livingston	OL to Alloa Sep-Oct, Freed June 2017	
Hardie	Ryan	17/03/1997	20	SCO	F	8	8	3					1					3	2016	Rangers (OL)	Jul-Sep	
Henry	Chris	22/02/1999	43	SCO	GK														2016	St Mirren Youth		End 2017/18
Hutton	Kyle	15/02/1991	14	SCO	M	11						3	1		2			3	2016	QOS	OL to Airdrie Nov-May, Freed June 2017	[redacted]
Irvine	Gary	17/03/1985	3	SCO	D	33			3			3			4	1		3	2016	Dundee		End 2017/18
Johnston	Craig	12/11/1999	33	SCO	F														2016	Hamilton Accies Youth	Freed June 2017	[redacted]
Langfield	Jamie	22/12/1979	1	SCO	GK	9						2			2			36	2015	Aberdeen		OOC
Loy	Rory	19/03/1988		SCO	F	11	2	5	1	1					2		2	2	2017	Dundee (OL)	Jan-May	[redacted]
Magennis	Kyle	26/08/1998	42	SCO	M	21	4	3	4						3			3	2016	St Mirren Youth		End 2019/20
Mallan	Stephen	25/03/1996	10	SCO	M	34		7	4		1	4			5		3		2014	St Mirren Youth	Transferred to Barnsley June 2017	[redacted]
McAllister	Kyle	21/01/1999		SCO	F	10			2		1		1		1			3	2016	St Mirren Youth	Transferred to Derby County Jan 2017	
MacPherson	Cameron	29/12/1998	40	SCO	M					1									2015	St Mirren Youth		
McDonald	Andrew	11/05/1998	39	SCO	D											1		8	2015	St Mirren Youth		End 2017/18
McGinn	Stephen	02/12/1988	8	SCO	M	14	1	2	2						2		1		2017	Wycombe Wanderers		End 2017/18
McKendry	Dylan	04/05/1999	32	SCO	D														2016	Celtic Youths		End 2017/18
McKenzie	Gary	15/10/1985	6	SCO	D	29		5	4		1				4			1	2016	Doncaster Rovers		End 2017/18
McLear	Lewis	26/05/1996	18	SCO	F		3											14	2015	St Mirren Youth		End 2017/18
McNaughton	Greig	22/03/1998	30	SCO	D														2016	Dundee United Youth	Freed June 2017	[redacted]
Morgan	Lewis	30/09/1996	17	SCO	M	31	2	6	3	1	2	4		1	4	1	1		2014	St Mirren Youth		End 2018/19
Morrison	Mark	31/12/1998	37	SCO	D														2015	St Mirren Youth		End 2017/18
Naismith	Jason	25/06/1994	2	SCO	D	21			1			4			2			1	2013	St Mirren Youth	Transferred to Ross County Jan 2017	[redacted]
O'Brien	Billy	21/11/1995		WAL / ENG	GK	15			3						2				2017	Manchester City (OL)	Jan-May	
O'Keefe	Conor	21/07/1998	36	SCO	M											1		10	2014	Celtic Youths		End 2017/18
Orsi	Kalvin	15/04/1997	34	SCO	F					1									2016	Aberdeen Youths	OL to Q Park Jan-May, Freed June 2017	[redacted]
Quinn	Rocco	07/09/1986	8	SCO	M	11	3			1		1			1	1		4	2016	Ross County		End 2017/18
Shankland	Lawrence	10/08/1995	25	SCO	F	7	10		1		2	1	2	1		3	1	3	2016	Aberdeen (OL)	Jul-Jan	[redacted]
Smith	Cammy	24/08/1995		SCO	F	15		1	2		1								2017	Aberdeen (OL)	Jan-May, Signed permanently June 2017	End 2018/19
Stewart	Jordan	05/03/1996	19	SCO	M	1	2					1	1		1	1		6	2016	St Mirren Youth	OL to Annan Jan-May, Freed June 2017 joined Clyde	[redacted]
Storie	Craig	13/01/1996		SCO	M	3	4		2	1					1			6	2017	Aberdeen (OL)	Jan-May	
Sutton	John	26/12/1983	9	ENG	F	24	11	7	3	1	2	3	1		5		4	1	2016	St Johnstone		End 2017/18
Todd	Josh	11/06/1994	25	ENG	M	1	10	1										4	2017	Dumbarton		End 2017/18
Walsh	Tom	11/06/1996	16	SCO	F	4	6	3				1	2	1	2	1		2	2016	Rangers (OL)	Jul-Jan	[redacted]
Watters	Ryan	12/05/1998	50	SCO	F													1	2017	Motherwell	Freed June 2017	
Webster	Andy	23/04/1982	4	SCO	D	10	5					4			1			10	2015	Coventry City	Freed June 2017	
Whyte	Darren	16/03/1997	35	SCO	M		1			1								11	2014	St Mirren Youth		
Willison	Reece	27/05/1999	28	SCO	GK													2	2015	Aberdeen Youths		OOC
Own Goals								1														
NEW SIGNINGS																						
Smith	Cammy	24/08/1995		SCO	F														2017	Aberdeen		End 2018/19
Stewart	Ross (A)	16/04/1995		SCO	GK														2017	Albion Rovers		End 2018/19
Stewart	Ross (B)	01/09/1996		SCO	F														2017	Albion Rovers		End 2018/19
Kirkpatrick	Jordan	06/03/1992		SCO	M														2017	Alloa Athletic		End 2018/19
Buchanan	Gregor	31/03/1990		SCO	D														2017	Dumbarton		End 2017/18
Samson	Craig	24/08/1984		SCO	GK														2017	Motherwell		End 2018/19
Reilly	Gavin	10/05/1993		SCO	F														2017	Hearts		End 2017/18
Hilson	Dale	23/12/1992		SCO	F														2017	Queen of the South		Dec 2017

Source of Birthdates - transfermarkt.com

Stenhousemuir FC 2016/17

Founded	1884
Ground	Ochilview Park
Postcode	FK5 4QL
Tel	01324 562 992
Capacity	3746
Closest Railway Station	Larbert
Record Attendance	12500 v East Fife, SC, 11/3/1950
Ground Record	01324 562992
Record Win	Ochilview
Record Defeat	2-11 v Dunfermline Athletic, 27/9/1930
Most League Goals in a Season	32 Robert Taylor, 1925/6
Chairman	Gordon Thompson
General Manager	Margaret Kilpatrick
Manager	Brown Ferguson
Assistant Manager	
Colours 2014/15 Top	Maroon with light blue trim
Shorts	Maroon
Sponsor	Gulnar Indian Restaurant
Manufacturer	Prostar
Change Colours 2016/17 Top	Blue and White Stripes
Shorts	Black
Nicknames	Warriors
Web	www.stenhousemuirfc.com
Match Programme 2016/17	£2

By all accounts the Warriors were operating on a tight budget for 2016/17 so relegation would have come as no great surprise. They were always around the foot of the table although a late revival almost saw them make it up to the play off position.

Like many lower league clubs Stenhousemuir make good use of loan players. Two lads from the Edinburgh clubs, Ally Roy from hearts and Oli Shaw from Hibs enhanced their reputations during season-long spells with Stenhousemuir. Both returned to extended contracts with their parent clubs.

It's a market that Brown Ferguson knows well and will no doubt utilise again in the future.

PREDICTION FOR 2017/18

There;s been a big clear out at Ochilview. The new players brought ni look to be of higher quality than those leaving which would suggest the club will be strong contenders for promotion this season.

Date	Comp	H/A	Opponents	F	A	HT		Referee	Crowd	Scorers
19/07/2016	LC	H	Queen's Park	0	2	0	1	C Napier	273	
23/07/2016	LC	A	Airdrieonians	0	2	0	1	G Duncan	532	
26/07/2016	LC	H	Partick Thistle	1	4	0	2	D Robertson	1433	McCroary
30/07/2016	LC	A	Queen of the South	0	1	0	0	K Graham	1013	
06/08/2016	L	A	Brechin City	1	2	0	1	D Munro	402	Kerr
13/08/2016	L	H	Queen's Park	1	2	1	0	J McKendrick	534	Stirling
17/08/2016	CC2	A	Rangers U20	3	1	2	0	G Irvine	324	McMenamin, Cook, McCrorie og
20/09/2016	L	A	Livingston	1	4	0	2	G Duncan	769	McMenamin
27/08/2016	L	H	Airdrieonians	2	2	1	0	G Ross	597	McMenamin, Kerr
03/09/2016	CC3	A	Queen of the South	1	7	0	4	G Aitken	1158	Cook
10/09/2016	L	A	Albion Rovers	0	4	0	0	S Millar	301	
17/09/2016	L	H	Peterhead	2	2	0	2	S Kirkland	331	McCormack, Kerr
24/09/2016	L	H	Alloa	2	2	0	1	C Napier	466	Furtado, Shaw
01/10/2016	L	A	East Fife	1	0	0	0	S Reid	563	McMenamin
15/10/2016	L	H	Stranraer	0	5	0	3	G Irvine	341	
22/10/2016	L	H	Brechin City	1	3	0	0	C Steven	352	Gilhaney
29/10/2016	L	A	Queen's Park	3	0	1	0	D Munro	538	Gilhaney, McMenamin, Roy
05/11/2016	L	A	Alloa	1	4	1	3	S Reid	458	Roy
19/11/2016	L	A	Stranraer	1	3	1	1	A Newlands	323	Roy
26/11/2016	SC3	A	Forres Mechanics	2	2	1	1	S Millar		Kerr, Furtado
03/12/2016	SC3R	H	Forres Mechanics	3	1	2	0	S Millar	289	McMenamin 3
10/12/2016	L	A	Airdrieonians	5	0	3	0	M Northcroft	791	Furtado, Marsh 2, Cook, Martinez
13/12/2016	L	H	Livingston	0	4	0	1	K Graham	334	
17/12/2016	L	H	Albion Rovers	1	0	0	0	G Beaton	371	Furtado
20/12/2016	L	H	East Fife	0	1	0	1	M Roncone	356	
26/12/2016	L	A	Peterhead	2	0	0	0	C Napier	427	McAllister og, McCormack
31/12/2016	L	H	Alloa	2	4	1	3	D Lowe	335	Cook, Shaw
07/01/2017	L	A	East Fife	0	1	0	1	K Graham	635	
14/01/2017	L	H	Stranraer	1	0	0	0	S Reid	392	Millar
21/01/2017	SC4	A	St Johnstone	0	2	0	2	E Anderson	2441	McLean, Alston
28/01/2017	L	H	Airdrieonians	4	2	1	1	C Napier	604	Cook 2, McMenamin, Mazana
04/02/2017	L	A	Brechin City	2	2	1	1	S Millar	403	Furtado, Shaw
11/02/2017	L	H	Queen's Park	0	2	0	1	G Irvine	423	
18/02/2017	L	A	Albion Rovers	1	1	0	1	B Cook	327	Robertson
04/03/2017	L	H	Peterhead	3	1	2	0	D Munro	362	Cook, Robertson, McMenamin
11/03/2017	L	A	Alloa	1	2	0	1	D Lowe	508	Grant
18/03/2017	L	A	Airdrieonians	0	1	0	0	S Kirkland	568	
21/03/2017	L	A	Livingston	0	1	0	1	B Cook	531	
25/03/2017	L	H	Albion Rovers	0	3	0	0	A Newlands	433	
01/04/2017	L	A	Stranraer	0	3	0	1	D Munro	440	
08/04/2017	L	H	East Fife	3	1	1	0	J McKendrick	455	Furtado 2, McMenamin
15/04/2017	L	H	Livingston	0	1	0	0	C Steven	472	
22/04/2017	L	A	Peterhead	1	0	1	0	S Finnie	587	Shaw
29/04/2017	L	A	Queen's Park	2	0	1	0	C Napier	764	Shaw 2
06/05/2017	L	H	Brechin City	1	1	0	1	G Aitken	557	Shaw

FRIENDLIES / OTHER GAMES

Date	H/A	Opponents	F	A	
28/06/2017	H	Hearts XI	2	1	
02/07/2016	H	Ayr United	0	2	
05/07/2016	H	Falkirk U20	2	3	
09/07/2016	H	St Mirren	1	3	
12/07/2016	H	Cowdenbeath	1	0	
20/07/2016	A	Steins Ams	2	2	U20

Date	Comp	H/A	Opponents	F	A	1	2	3	4	5	6	7	8	9	10	11	12	13	14	15	16	17	18
19/07/2016	LC	H	Queen's Park	0	2	McCabe	McCormack	Summers	Kerr	Meechan	Berry	Stirling	Millar*	Cook	McMenamin	Smith+	Gilhaney*	Docherty+	*Nash*	*Hamilton*	*Runciman*	*Howarth*	*McCroary*
23/07/2016	LC	A	Airdrieonians	0	2	McCabe	McCormack&	McMaster	Kerr	Meechan	Berry	Stirling	McCroary	Cook+	Gilhaney	Smith*	McMenamin*	Miller+	Docherty&	*Hamilton*	*Runciman*	*Howarth*	*Nash*
26/07/2016	LC	H	Partick Thistle	1	4	McCabe	McCormack	McMaster*	Kerr	Meechan	Berry	Miller	McCroary+	Cook	Gilhaney	McMenamin	Smith*	Nash+	*Docherty*	*Hamilton*	*Runciman*	*Howarth*	*Stirling*
30/07/2016	LC	A	Queen of the South	0	1	McCabe	McCormack&	Hamilton	Kerr	Meechan	Berry	Miller*	Stirling+	Cook	Gilhaney	McMenamin	J Smith*	McCroary+	Runciman&	*Docherty*	*McMaster*	*Howarth*	*Nash*
06/08/2016	L	A	Brechin City	1	2	McCabe	McCormack	Hamilton	Kerr	Meechan	Berry	Miller	Stirling*	Cook+	Gilhaney	McMenamin	Docherty*	Smith+	*Runciman*	*McCroary*	*McMaster*	*Howarth*	*Sinclair*
13/08/2016	L	H	Queen's Park	1	2	McCabe	McCormack	Hamilton	Kerr	Meechan	Berry	Shaw	Stirling+	Cook	Gilhaney	McMenamin*	McCroary*	Smith+	*Runciman*	*Docherty*	*Miller*	*Howarth*	*Sinclair*
17/08/2016	CC2	A	Rangers U20	3	1	McCabe	McCormack	Hamilton	Kerr	Meechan	Berry	Miller	Stirling*	Cook&	Gilhaney	McMenamin+	Sinclair*	Smith+	McCroary&	*Nash*	*Runciman*	*Howarth*	*McMaster*
20/09/2016	L	A	Livingston	1	4	McCabe	McCormack+	Hamilton	Kerr	Meechan	Berry*	Miller	Stirling&	Cook	Gilhaney	McMenamin	Roy*	Sinclair+	Shaw&	*McCroary*	*Smith*	*Howarth*	*McMaster*
27/08/2016	L	H	Airdrieonians	2	2	McCabe	McCormack	Summers	Kerr	Meechan	Shaw	Miller+	Stirling	Cook	Gilhaney&	McMenamin*	Roy*	Sinclair+	Smith&	*McCroary*	*Hamilton*	*S Robertson*	*McMaster*
03/09/2016	CC3	A	Queen of the South	1	7	McCabe	McCormack	Summers*	Kerr	Meechan&	Sinclair	Miller	Stirling+	Cook	Gilhaney	McMenamin	Docherty*	McCroary+	Hamilton&	*Smith*	*Runciman*	*S Robertson*	*McMaster*
10/09/2016	L	A	Albion Rovers	0	4	McCabe	McCormack	Hamilton	Paterson*	Meechan	McCroary	Furtado	Stirling	Allan	Shaw	Roy+	McMenamin*	Miller+	*Gilhaney*	*Smith*	*Runciman*	*Howarth*	*McMaster*
17/09/2016	L	H	Peterhead	2	2	McCabe	McCormack	Marsh	Kerr	Meechan+	McCroary	Furtado	Stirling	Cook	Shaw	Roy*	McMenamin*	Gilhaney+	*Millar*	*Summers*	*Runciman*	*Smith*	*Roman*
24/09/2016	L	H	Alloa	2	2	McCabe	McCormack	Marsh*	Kerr	Meechan	Berry	Furtado	Stirling+	Cook	Shaw	McMenamin	Gilhaney*	Roy+	*Millar*	*Summers*	*McCroary*	*Hamilton*	*Roman*
01/10/2016	L	A	East Fife	1	0	McCabe	McCormack	Marsh	Kerr	Meechan	Berry	Furtado&	Miller	Cook	Shaw+	McMenamin*	Gilhaney*	Roy+	McCroary&	*Summers*	*Hamilton*	*S Robertson*	*Smith*
15/10/2016	L	H	Stranraer	0	5	McCabe	McCormack	Marsh	Kerr	Meechan	Berry	Furtado	Miller*	Cook&	Shaw+	McMenamin	Stirling*	Roy+	Gilhaney&	*Summers*	*McCroary*	*S Robertson*	*Smith*
22/10/2016	L	H	Brechin City	1	3	McCabe	McCormack	Summers	Kerr	Meechan	Berry	Furtado	Gilhaney+	Miller&	Shaw*	McMenamin	Roy*	Smith+	McCroary&	*Stirling*	*Hamilton*	*S Robertson*	
29/10/2016	L	A	Queen's Park	3	0	Crawford	Marsh	Summers	Kerr	Meechan	Berry	Cook*	Gilhaney	Miller&	Roy	McMenamin+	Docherty*	McCroary+	Smith&	*Stirling*	*Hamilton*	*McCabe*	
05/11/2016	L	A	Alloa	1	4	Crawford+	Marsh	Summers	Kerr	Meechan	Berry	Cook*	Gilhaney	Miller&	Roy	McMenamin	McCormack*	McCabe+	Docherty&	*Hamilton*	*McCroary*		
19/11/2016	L	A	Stranraer	1	3	McCabe	Marsh	Summers	Kerr*	Meechan	Berry	Cook	Gilhaney&	Miller	Roy	McMenamin+	McCormack*	Furtado+	Manzana&	*Hamilton*	*McCroary*	*S Robertson*	*Shaw*
26/11/2016	SC3	A	Forres Mechanics	2	2	McCabe	Marsh	Summers	Kerr	McCormack	Berry*	Furtado	Gilhaney+	Miller	Roy	McMenamin	Mazana*	Nash+	*Robertson*	*Hamilton*	*McCroary*		
03/12/2016	SC3R	H	Forres Mechanics	3	1	McCabe	Marsh	Summers	Kerr	McCormack	Berry	Furtado&	Gilhaney*	Miller	Roy	McMenamin+	Cook*	McCroary+	Meechan&	*Hamilton*	*McMaster*	*Manzana*	*S Robertson*
10/12/2016	L	A	Airdrieonians	5	0	McCabe	Marsh	Summers	Kerr	McCormack&	Berry	Furtado	Cook*	Miller	Roy	McMenamin+	Mazana*	Shaw+	Meechan&	*Hamilton*	*McMaster*	*McCroary*	*S Robertson*
13/12/2016	L	H	Livingston	0	4	McCabe	Marsh+	Summers	Kerr	McCormack	Berry	Furtado	Cook	Miller	Roy*	McMenamin	Martinez*	Meechan+	*Gilhaney*	*Hamilton*	*McMaster*	*McCroary*	*S Robertson*
17/12/2016	L	H	Albion Rovers	1	0	McCabe	Meechan	Summers	Kerr	McCormack	Berry	Furtado	Cook	Miller	Roy*	McMenamin	Shaw*	*Walker*	*Gilhaney*	*Hamilton*	*Mazana-Martinez*	*McCroary*	*S Robertson*
20/12/2016	L	H	East Fife	0	1	McCabe	Meechan	Summers&	Kerr	McCormack	Berry	Furtado	Cook	Miller+	Roy*	McMenamin	Gilhaney*	Mazana-Martinez+	Walker&	*Hamilton*	*McMaster*	*McCroary*	*S Robertson*
26/12/2016	L	A	Peterhead	2	0	McCabe	Marsh	Summers	Hamilton	McCormack	Berry	Furtado*	Cook+	Miller	Gilhaney&	McMenamin	Roy*	McCroary+	Shaw&	*S Robertson*			
31/12/2016	L	H	Alloa	2	4	McCabe	Meechan	Summers	Hamilton	McCormack	Berry	Furtado&	Cook+	Miller	Gilhaney*	McMenamin	Shaw*	Mazana-Martinez+	Roy&	*Crawford*	*McMaster*	*McCroary*	
07/01/2017	L	A	East Fife	0	1	McCabe	Meechan	Summers	Marsh	McCormack*	Berry	Furtado	Cook	Miller	Shaw	McMenamin	Mazana*	*Hamilton*	*Runciman*	*McMaster*	*Crawford*		
14/01/2017	L	H	Stranraer	1	0	McCabe	Meechan	Summers	Marsh	Kerr	Berry	Furtado	Cook	Miller	Shaw*	McMenamin	McCormack*	*Hamilton*	*Smith*	*McCroary*	*Mazana-Martinez*	*Crawford*	
21/01/2017	SC4	A	St Johnstone	0	2	McCabe	Meechan	Summers	Kerr	McCormack	Berry	Furtado*	Cook	Miller&	Shaw	McMenamin+	Mazana*	Docherty+	McCroary&	*Hamilton*	*Runciman*	*McMaster*	*Crawford*
28/01/2017	L	H	Airdrieonians	4	2	McCabe	Meechan	Summers	Kerr	Marsh	Berry+	Furtado	Cook&	Miller	Shaw*	McMenamin	Mazana*	Roy+	Stirling&	*McCormack*	*Smith*	*McMaster*	*Crawford*
04/02/2017	L	A	Brechin City	2	2	Crawford	Meechan	Summers	Kerr	Marsh	Berry	Furtado&	Cook*	Miller	Shaw	McMenamin+	Roy*	McCormack+	Mazana&	*Duthie*	*Smith*	*Stirling*	*McCabe*
11/02/2017	L	H	Queen's Park	0	2	Crawford	Meechan&	Summers	Kerr	McCormack	Berry	Furtado	Cook	Stirling+	Shaw*	McMenamin	Roy*	Mazana+	Smith&	*Duthie*	*McCroary*	*Hamilton*	*Bowman*
18/02/2017	L	A	Albion Rovers	1	1	Crawford	Marsh	Summers	Kerr	McCormack	Berry	Furtado+	Cook	Miller	Roy*	McMenamin&	Robertson*	Mazana+	Smith&	*Duthie*	*Meechan*	*Stirling*	*Bowman*
04/03/2017	L	H	Peterhead	3	1	Crawford	Marsh	Summers	Kerr	Meechan	Berry+	Duthie&	Cook	Miller	Robertson	McMenamin*	Furtado*	Grant+	Stirling&	*Roy*	*Shaw*	*Manzana*	*Bowman*
11/03/2017	L	A	Alloa	1	2	Crawford	Marsh	Summers	Kerr	Meechan	Berry	Duthie&	Cook	Miller	Robertson+	Stirling*	Grant*	McMenamin+	Roy&	*Furtado*	*McCormack*	*Manzana*	*Bowman*
18/03/2017	L	A	Airdrieonians	0	1	Crawford	Marsh	Summers+	Kerr	Meechan	Berry	Furtado*	Cook	Miller	McMenamin	Robertson	Duthie*	Roy+	*Grant*	*Gilhaney*	*McCormack*	*Smith*	*Bowman*
21/03/2017	L	A	Livingston	0	1	Crawford	McCormack	Summers	Kerr	Meechan	Berry	Grant*	Duthie	Miller&	Roy	Robertson+	Furtado*	McMenamin+	Gilhaney&	*Hamilton*	*Smith*	*Bowman*	
25/03/2017	L	H	Albion Rovers	0	3	Crawford&	McCormack	Summers+	Kerr	Meechan	Berry	Cook	Duthie	Miller	McMenamin	Robertson*	Furtado*	Roy+	Bowman&	*Hamilton*	*Grant*	*Gilhaney*	
01/04/2017	L	A	Stranraer	0	3	Bowman	McCormack	Summers+	Kerr	Meechan	Roy*	Cook&	Duthie	Miller	McMenamin	Robertson	Shaw*	Furtado+	Gilhaney&	*Hamilton*	*Grant*	*McCabe*	
08/04/2017	L	H	East Fife	3	1	Bowman	Marsh	Gilhaney*	Kerr	Furtado&	Berry	Cook+	Duthie	Miller	McMenamin	Robertson	Meechan*	Shaw+	Mazana&	*Crawford*	*Grant*	*Roy*	*Summers*
15/04/2017	L	H	Livingston	0	1	Bowman	Marsh	Meechan+	Kerr	Furtado&	Gilhaney*	Cook	Duthie	Miller	McMenamin	Robertson	Shaw*	Mazana+	Roy&	*Crawford*	*Grant*	*Smith*	*McCormack*
22/04/2017	L	A	Peterhead	1	0	Bowman	Marsh	Berry	Kerr	Furtado+	Gilhaney*	Shaw	Duthie	Miller	McMenamin	Robertson	Meechan*	Summers+	*Roy*	*Mazana*	*Grant*	*McCabe*	
29/04/2017	L	A	Queen's Park	2	0	Bowman	Marsh+	Berry	Kerr	Furtado	Gilhaney*	Shaw	Duthie	Miller	McMenamin	Robertson	Grant*&	Meechan+	Summers&	*Mazana*	*McCormack*	*Roy*	*Crawford*
06/05/2017	L	H	Brechin City	1	1	Bowman	Marsh	Berry	Kerr	Furtado	Mazana*	Shaw	Duthie	Miller	McMenamin	Robertson	Roy*	Meechan	*Summers*	*Grant*	*McCormack*	*Smith*	*McCabe*

						L			SC			LC			CC							
Surname	First Name	DOB	SQ	Nat	Pos	A	S	G	A	S	G	A	S	G	A	S	G	UNS	Signed	Previous Club	Notes	Contract
Allan	Mark	14/05/1996		SCO	F	1														Trialist	Ex Stenhousemuir U20	
Berry	Vincent	19/08/1987		SCO	M	31			3			4			1				2016	Queen's Park	Freed June 2017, moved to USA	
Bowman	Graham	02/01/1993		SCO	GK	6	1											6	2017	Unattached	Ex Falkirk, OOC May 2017 joined Albion Rovers	
Cook	Alan	25/04/1992		SCO	F	30		5	1	1		4			2		2		2015	East Fife	OOC May 2017, joined East Fife	
Crawford	David	30/06/1985		SCO	GK	10												8	2016	Partick Thistle		
Docherty	Alan	25/10/1996		SCO	M		3			1			2			1		3	2016	Unattached		
Duthie	Connor	02/02/1997		SCO	M	10	1											3	2017	Dunfermline Athletic (OL)	Jan-May	
Furtado	Willis Alves	04/09/1997		FRA	M	24	5	6	3									1	2016	US Ivry	Freed May 2017	
Gilhaney	Mark	04/11/1984		SCO	F	14	7	2	2			3	1		2			5	2015	Dumbarton	May 2017 Retired	
Grant	Thomas	31/05/1995		SCO	M	1	3	1										7	2017	Fleetwood Town	OOC May 2017, joined Alloa Athletic	
Hamilton	Grant	06/05/1998		SCO	M	6						1			1	1		23	2015	Forth Valley Elite Acad	OL to Kilsyth R Jan-May, Freed May	
Howarth	James	28/07/1992		ENG	GK													9	2016	Ex Blyth Spartans	Freed Jan 2017	
Kerr	Fraser	17/01/1993		SCO	D	32		3	3		1	4			2				2016	Cowdenbeath	Freed May 2017	
Marsh	David	06/04/1990		SCO	D	23		2	2										2016	Clyde		
Mazana-Martinez	Carlos	03/11/1990		SPA	F	1	12	2		2								7	2015	Glasgow University		End 2017/1
McCabe	Colin	06/01/1997		ROI	GK	20	1		3			4			2			5	2016	Celtic (OL)	Jan-May	
McCormack	Jamie	01/02/1992		SCO	D	22	4	2	3			4			2			6	2015 Brechin City	Released May 2017	Freed May 2017	
McCroary	Liam	23/07/1996		SCO	M	2	5			2		2	1	1		2		16	2015	Raith Rovers	OL to Kilsyth Rangers Jan-Mar, Freed May	
McMaster	Liam	17/09/1999		SCO	D							2						15	2016	Forth Valley Elite Acad	OL to Dunipace Feb-May, Freed May	
McMenamin	Colin	12/02/1981		SCO	F	32	4	7	3		3	3	1		2		1		2014	Celtic Nation		
Meechan	Ross	10/11/1994		SCO	D	28	6		1	1		4			2			1	2014	Partick Thistle		End 2017/1
Miller	Kieran	14/10/1993		SCO	M	31	1	1	3			3	1		2			3	2014	Hamilton Accies	OOC May 2017 joined East Fife	End 2017/1
Nash	Paul	10/06/1998		SCO	M					1			1					4	2015	Forth Valley Elite Ascad	Ol to Dunipace Nov-Jan, Freed May	
Paterson	Jim	25/09/1979		SCO	D	1													2015	Dunfermline Athletic		
Robertson	Mason	23/07/1994		SCO	F	11	1	2											2016	Washington Huskies	OOC May 2017 joined Peterhead	
Robertson	Sean	24/08/1996		SCO	GK													13	2016	Stenhousemuir U20	OL to Camelon Sep-Jan, Dunipace Feb-May, Freed May	
Roman	Aldin			ROM	GK													2		Trialist, ex Cowdenbeath		
Roy	Alistair	26/07/1997		SCO	F	12	16	3	2									4	2016	Hearts (OL)	Aug-May	
Runciman	Calum	21/02/1999		SCO	M								1					11	2016	Forth Valley Elite Acad	OL to Dunipace Feb-May, Freed May	
Shaw	Ollie	12/09/1998		SCO	F	16	8	7	1		1							2	2016	Hibernian (OL)	Aug-May	
Sinclair	David	23/07/1990		SCO	M		2								1	1		2	2016	Bo'ness United	Freed Sep 2016	
Smith	Jack	27/12/1994		SCO	F		7					2	2			1		13	2016	East Kilbride	OL to East Kilbride Nov-Jan, Freed May 2017	
Stirling	Stephen	05/01/1990		SCO	M	9	3	1				3			2			5	2015	Stranraer		
Summers	Ciaran	16/04/1995		SCO	D	23	2		3			1			1			6	2013	Stenhousemuir U20		
Walker	Scott	05/03/1975		SCO	D		1											1		Trialist, ex Brechin City		
Own Goals								1									1					
NEW SIGNINGS																						
Longworth	Jamie																					
Scott	Martin			SCO	M														2017	Arbroath		
Halleran	Thomas																		2017	Forth Valley Elite Acad		
Sinclair	Robbie																		2017	Forth Valley Elite Acad		
Gracie	Joshua																		2017	Forth Valley Elite Acad		
Blockley	Nathan				M														2017	Peterhead		
Dunlop	Michael																		2017	Albion Rovers		
Dunlop	Ross																		2017	Albion Rovers		
McGuigan	Mark																		2017	Stranraer		
Smith	Chris																		2017	Stirling Albion		
Ferry	Mark																		2017	Albion Rovers		
Donaldson	Ruaridh																		2017	Bonnyrigg Rose		
Paton	Harry																		2017	Hearts (OL)		
McMinn	Lewis																		2017	Falkirk		
Ferns	Eddie																		2017	Arbroath		

Source of Birt

Stirling Albion FC 2016/17

Founded	1945
Ground	Forthbank Stadium
Postcode	FK7 7UJ
Tel	01786 450399
Capacity	3808
Closest Railway Station	Stirling
Record Attendance	26400 v Celtic, SC, 14/3/1959
Ground Record	3808 v Aberdeen, SC, 15/2/1996
Record Win	20-0 v Selkirk, SC, 8/12/1984
Record Defeat	0-9 v Dundee Utd, L, 30/12/1967;
	v Ross Co, SC, 6/2/2010
Most League Goals in a Season	27 Joe Hughes, 1969/70
Chairman	Stuart Brown
Secretary	Stuart Brown
Manager	Stuart McLaren (Until Oct), David Mackay
Assistant Manager	Martyn Corrigan (Until Oct), Ross Forsyth (until May)
	Frazer Wright (from May)
Colours 2016/17 Top	Red with white flashes
Shorts	Red
Sponsor	Prudential
Manufacturer	Macron
Change Colours 2014/15 Top	Yellow
Shorts	Blue
Nicknames	Binos
Web	www.stirlingalbionfc.co.uk
Match Programme 2016/17	None issued, monthly magazine produced
Theme Song	Twist and Shout

Many people were surprised that Stuart McLaren was given another season in charge at Stirling. He only lasted until thelate Autumn when results enforced a parting of the ways.

Stirling turned to former St Johnstone player Dave Mackay at a time when relegation to the Lowland League looked a distinct possibility. He shook up the team during the January transfer window and brought in enough quality to ensure they climbed the league to safety. One signing in particular, Frenchman Dylan Bikey, contributed a hatful of goals to help their cause.

PREDICTION 2017/18

There were signs of progress as the season went on and Stirling will be disappointed if they fail to make the play offs. Like other clubs the use of the loan market will be important—Mackay will have lots of contacts in the game and will surely use them to good effect.

Formation of the Club

On April 26th 1945 a meeting was held in the Golden Lion Hotel to discuss the future of senior football in Stirling. Only 17 members of the public turned up. The meeting had been called by Tom H Fergusson. Undaunted he set about the task of starting a new club. The club was formally established at a meeting in Fergusson's Coal Yard offices in Wallace Street, Stirling on May 10th 1945. 3000 £1 shares were issued and quickly bought by six local businessmen. It was resolved to try and buy the Annfield Estate which was on the market at the time. Failing that the club would look at leasing Strathallan Games Park in Bridge of Allan. Suggestions of sharing with Stirling County Cricket Club at William-field or Rugby Club at Bridgehaugh were dismissed.

Stirling Albion Supporters Club was established on May 15th 1945 at a meeting in the Old British Legion Hall, Thistle Street, Stirling.

The name of the club was the subject of debate. Stirling Villa was considered but Stirling Albion was chosen.

Tom Fergusson paid £5000 for the Annfield estate from his own pocket. His application to turn the Estate into a football ground was heard at a stormy Council Meeting on May 21st 1945. There was strong opposition from local residents. In the end the application was approved by 12-7 in a vote of the Council.

The first trial match was played on July 31st 1945 at Annfield. 3000 spectators attended.

The club's first real match was against Airdrie Reserves on August 11th 1945. Albion won 3-1 watched by 5000. The Airdrie team included Peter McKenzie who became Chairman of Stirling Albion from 1988-until 2010)

Date	Comp	H/A	Opponents	F	A	HT		Referee	Crowd	Scorers
16/07/2016	LC	H	Falkirk	1	0	1	0	C Steven	1315	DL Smith
19/07/2016	LC	A	Brechin City	1	2	1	1	G Beaton	362	Henderson
26/07/2016	LC	H	Elgin City	4	1	1	1	S Millar	522	Henderson 3, Ferns
30/07/2016	LC	A	St Johnstone	0	4	0	3	B Cook	2858	
02/08/2016	CC1	H	Hearts U21	2	3	2	0	S Reid	476	McKenzie 2
06/08/2016	L	A	Annan Athletic	2	3	1	3	G Irvine	421	Dickson, McKenzie
13/08/2016	L	H	Clyde	1	1	0	0	A Newlands	777	Forsyth
20/08/2016	L	H	Montrose	2	0	0	0	G Ross	497	D Smith, McKenzie
27/08/2016	L	A	Arbroath	3	5	1	1	G Beaton	601	Sukar og, Henderson, Ferns
10/09/2016	L	H	Edinburgh City	1	1	0	0	C Steven	465	McMillan
17/09/2016	L	A	Forfar Athletic	1	4	1	1	C Napier	625	Dickson
24/09/2016	L	H	Elgin City	0	4	0	3	J McKendrick	457	
01/10/2016	L	A	Cowdenbeath	2	0	1	0	G Irvine	342	Layne, D Smith
15/10/2016	L	H	Berwick Rangers	0	0	0	0	M Taylor	517	
22/10/2016	SC2	A	Linlithgow Rose	3	0	1	0	S Reid	942	Olanrewaju, McKenzie, Ferns
29/10/2016	L	A	Clyde	1	1	1	1	D Lowe	738	McKenzie
05/11/2016	L	H	Forfar Athletic	0	3	0	1	G Beaton	663	
12/11/2016	L	A	Elgin City	3	2	0	1	S Millar	585	McKenzie, Henderson, Mills
19/11/2016	L	H	Arbroath	2	2	0	1	D Munro	605	Dickson 2
03/12/2016	SC3	H	Wick Academy	2	0	1	0	S Finnie	572	Henderson, Nguene Bikey
06/12/2016	L	A	Berwick Rangers	2	3	2	2	G Ross	302	Nguene Bikey 2
10/12/2016	L	A	Edinburgh City	0	2	0	1	M Roncone	368	
17/12/2016	L	H	Annan Athletic	3	1	2	1	C Napier	694	D Smith, McMillan, Nguene Bikey
24/12/2016	L	A	Montrose	2	2	1	0	G Beaton	610	Steeves og, R Smith
31/12/2016	L	H	Cowdenbeath	1	2	0	0	A Muir	538	Nguene Bikey
07/01/2017	L	H	Clyde	3	0	1	0	S Reid	718	Kavanagh, Nguene Bikey 2
14/01/2017	L	A	Forfar Athletic	1	1	1	1	S Millar	632	D Smith
21/01/2017	SC4R	H	Clyde	2	2	1	1	M Northcroft	869	Nguene Bikey 2
28/01/2017	L	A	Annan Athletic	1	4	1	1	G Irvine	420	Henderson
31/01/2017	SC4R	A	Clyde	2	3	1	3	M Northcroft	625	Henderson 2
04/02/2017	L	H	Montrose	1	2	1	0	S Kirkland	494	Henderson
11/02/2017	L	H	Berwick Rangers	2	2	0	2	D Dickinson	515	Malone, Dickson
18/02/2017	L	A	Arbroath	1	1	0	0	R Milne	625	D Smith
25/02/2017	L	H	Edinburgh City	1	0	1	0	K Graham	501	Kavanagh
28/02/2017	L	H	Elgin City	1	0	0	0	C Napier	412	Dickson
04/03/2017	L	A	Cowdenbeath	2	0	1	0	G Beaton	381	R Smith, Dickson
11/03/2017	L	A	Montrose	3	1	1	0	S Kirkland	401	D Smith, Kavanagh, McLaren
18/03/2017	L	H	Annan Athletic	1	0	0	0	D Munro	531	D Smith
25/03/2017	L	A	Clyde	3	2	0	1	G Ross	606	Kavanagh, D Smith 2
01/04/2017	L	H	Forfar Athletic	0	3	0	2	M Northcroft	738	
08/04/2017	L	A	Berwick Rangers	1	0	1	0	C Napier	440	D Smith
15/04/2017	L	H	Cowdenbeath	0	3	0	2	S Millar	638	
22/04/2017	L	A	Elgin City	2	2	0	0	R Milne	785	D Smith, Nguene Bikey
29/04/2017	L	A	Edinburgh City	0	1	0	0	G Ross	388	
06/05/2017	L	H	Arbroath	1	1	0	1	K Graham	1748	Henderson

FRIENDLIES / OTHER GAMES					
05/07/2016	A	St Mirren	3	4	at Ralston
11/07/2016	A	Cumbernauld Colts	3	1	

Date	Comp	H/A	Opponents	F	A	1	2	3	4	5	6	7	8	9	10	11	12	13	14	15	16	17	18
16/07/2016	LC	H	Falkirk	1	0	C Smith	McMillan	Petrie	Verlaque	Scott Davidson	Hodge	McKenzie+	Dickson	McCue	D Smith*	Ferns&	Henderson*	Olanrewaju+	Mills&	Burns	Sam Davidson	Docherty	Binnie
19/07/2016	LC	A	Brechin City	1	2	Binnie	Mills	Forsyth	Verlaque	Scott Davidson+	Hodge	McKenzie	Dickson	Burns*	Henderson	Ferns&	McCue*	McMillan+	D Smith&	McAllister	Sam Davidson	Docherty	Fallens
26/07/2016	LC	H	Elgin City	4	1	C Smith	McMillan	Forsyth	Verlaque	R Smith+	Hodge	McKenzie	Dickson*	McCue	Henderson	Ferns&	D Smith*	Scott Davidson+	Docherty&	Mills	Sam Davidson	Olanrewaju	Binnie
30/07/2016	LC	A	St Johnstone	0	4	C Smith	McMillan+	Forsyth	Verlaque	R Smith	Hodge	D Smith	Dickson	McCue*	Henderson&	Ferns	McKenzie*	Scott Davidson+	Olanrewaju&	Mills	Kavanagh	Docherty	Binnie
02/08/2016	CC1	H	Hearts U21	2	3	Binnie	Mills	Burns	Scott Davidson	R Smith	Sam Davidson*	McKenzie&	Kavanagh	McCue	Olanrewaju+	Docherty	D Smith*	Ferns+	Henderson&	Verlaque	Mazel	McAllister	Fallens
06/08/2016	L	A	Annan Athletic	2	3	Binnie	Mills*	Forsyth	Verlaque+	Scott Davidson	Hodge	McKenzie	Dickson	D Smith	Henderson	Ferns	McCue*	Fowler+	McGeachie	Sam Davidson	Mazel	Docherty	Fallens
13/08/2016	L	H	Clyde	1	1	C Smith	McMillan	Forsyth	Verlaque	R Smith	Hodge	McKenzie+	Dickson	D Smith	Henderson*	Ferns	McCue*	Olanrewaju+	McGeachie	Scott Davidson	Mazel	Mills	Binnie
20/08/2016	L	H	Montrose	2	0	C Smith	McMillan	Forsyth	Verlaque	Scott Davidson	Hodge	McKenzie	Dickson	D Smith&	Henderson+	McCue*	Olanrewaju*	Ferns+	Morrison&	McGeachie	Mazel	Docherty	Binnie
27/08/2016	L	A	Arbroath	3	5	C Smith	McMillan	Forsyth	Verlaque	R Smith	Hodge	Layne*	Dickson	D Smith	Henderson	Ferns+	Olanrewaju*	Morrison+	Scott Davidson	McGeachie	Mazel	McCue	Binnie
10/09/2016	L	H	Edinburgh City	1	1	C Smith	McMillan	Forsyth&	McGeachie	Scott Davidson	McKenzie	Layne*	Dickson	D Smith+	Henderson	Ferns	Mazel*	Morrison+	Docherty&	Mills	R Smith	Verlaque	Binnie
17/09/2016	L	A	Forfar Athletic	1	4	C Smith	McMillan	Verlaque*	McGeachie	Scott Davidson	McKenzie	Petrie+	Dickson	D Smith	Olanrewaju	Ferns	Layne*	Henderson+	Mazel	Mills	R Smith	Morrison	Binnie
24/09/2016	L	H	Elgin City	0	4	C Smith	McMillan	Verlaque	McCue	Scott Davidson	McKenzie	Petrie	Dickson	D Smith	Henderson*	Layne+	Morrison*	Ferns+	Mills	R Smith	Docherty	Binnie	
01/10/2016	L	A	Cowdenbeath	2	0	C Smith	McMillan	Fowler	McGeachie	R Smith	McKenzie+	Petrie	Dickson	D Smith	Ferns	Layne*	Kavanagh*	Verlaque+	Scott Davidson	Morrison	Henderson	Docherty	Binnie
15/10/2016	L	H	Berwick Rangers	0	0	C Smith	McMillan	Hodge	McGeachie	Scott Davidson	McKenzie	Petrie	Dickson	D Smith*	Ferns&	Layne+	Olanrewaju*	Henderson+	Kavanagh&	Morrison	McCue	Verlaque	Binnie
22/10/2016	SC2	A	Linlithgow Rose	3	0	C Smith	McMillan	Hodge	McGeachie	Scott Davidson	McKenzie	Petrie	Dickson&	Henderson+	Ferns	Olanrewaju*	McCue*	Kavanagh+	Morrison&	Docherty	Cameron	Verlaque	Binnie
29/10/2016	L	A	Clyde	1	1	C Smith	McMillan	Hodge	Beith	Scott Davidson	McKenzie	Petrie	Dickson	McCue	Ferns+	Layne*	Kavanagh*	Olanrewaju+	Henderson	Verlaque	Morrison	Docherty	Binnie
05/11/2016	L	H	Forfar Athletic	0	3	C Smith	McMillan	Hodge	Beith	Scott Davidson	McKenzie	Petrie+	Dickson	McCue*	Ferns	Layne&	Verlaque*	Olanrewaju+	Kavanagh&	Henderson	Morrison	Docherty	Binnie
12/11/2016	L	A	Elgin City	3	2	C Smith	Robertson+	Hodge	Beith	Scott Davidson	McKenzie&	Petrie	Dickson	McMillan	Ferns	Henderson*	Kavanagh*	Verlaque+	Mills&	R Smith	Morrison	Docherty	Binnie
19/11/2016	L	H	Arbroath	2	2	C Smith	McMillan	Hodge*	Beith	Scott Davidson	McKenzie	Petrie	Dickson	Robertson	Ferns+	Henderson	Kavanagh*	McGeachie+	Mills	R Smith	Morrison	Docherty	Binnie
03/12/2016	SC3	H	Wick Academy	2	0	C Smith	McMillan*	McGeachie	Forsyth	Scott Davidson	McKenzie	Petrie&	Dickson	Colquhoun	Kavanagh+	Henderson	R Smith*	Nguene Bikey+	Ferns&	Verlaque	D Smith	Mills	Binnie
06/12/2016	L	A	Berwick Rangers	2	3	C Smith	McMillan	McGeachie	Robertson&	Scott Davidson	Beith	Petrie	Nguene Bikey	Colquhoun*	Kavanagh+	Henderson	Dickson*	Ferns+	Hodge&	R Smith	D Smith	Morrison	Binnie
10/12/2016	L	A	Edinburgh City	0	2	C Smith	McMillan	McGeachie	Forsyth	R Smith	Beith	McKenzie&	Dickson+	Colquhoun	Nguene Bikey	Henderson*	Kavanagh*	D Smith+	Ferns&	Verlaque	Hodge	Scott Davidson	Binnie
17/12/2016	L	H	Annan Athletic	3	1	C Smith	McMillan	McGeachie	Mills	R Smith+	Beith	Petrie	Morrison&	Colquhoun	D Smith*	Kavanagh	Nguene Bikey*	Scott Davidson+	McKenzie&	Henderson	Hodge	Ferns	Binnie
24/12/2016	L	A	Montrose	2	2	Binnie	McMillan	McGeachie*	Mills	R Smith	Beith	Petrie&	Morrison+	Colquhoun	D Smith	Nguene Bikey	Scott Davidson*	McKenzie+	Ferns&	Henderson	Dickson	Kavanagh	Fallens
31/12/2016	L	H	Cowdenbeath	1	2	Binnie	McMillan	McGeachie	Mills*	R Smith+	Dickson	Petrie	McKenzie	Colquhoun	D Smith&	Nguene Bikey	Morrison*	Scott Davidson+	Henderson&	Ferns	Verlaque	Kavanagh	Fallens
07/01/2017	L	H	Clyde	3	0	Binnie	McMillan	Quigley	Wright	Caddis	Beith	Robertson	McLaren+	Colquhoun	Kavanagh*	Nguene Bikey&	D Smith*	Henderson+	Dickson&	R Smith	Verlaque	Petrie	Fallens
14/01/2017	L	A	Forfar Athletic	1	1	Binnie	McMillan	Quigley	Wright	Caddis	Beith*	Robertson+	McLaren	Colquhoun	D Smith	Nguene Bikey	Henderson*	Dickson+	Cameron	R Smith	Verlaque	Petrie	Fallens
21/01/2017	SC4R	H	Clyde	2	2	Binnie	Davidson	Quigley	Wright	Caddis	Black*	Robertson	McLaren	Colquhoun+	D Smith	Nguene Bikey	Henderson*	Dickson+	Cameron	Forsyth	Verlaque	Petrie	C Smith
28/01/2017	L	A	Annan Athletic	1	4	C Smith	Davidson	Quigley	Wright	Caddis	Jeffries+	Robertson&	McLaren	Colquhoun*	D Smith	Henderson	Dickson*	Forsyth+	Black&	Mills	Cameron	Petrie	Binnie
31/01/2017	SC4R	A	Clyde	2	3	C Smith	Black*	Quigley	Wright&	Caddis	McMillan	Robertson	McLaren	Colquhoun+	D Smith	Henderson	Dickson*	Cameron+	R Smith&	Mills	Forsyth	Petrie	Binnie
04/02/2017	L	H	Montrose	1	2	C Smith	Caddis	Quigley	Wright	Dickson	McMillan	Robertson*	McLaren	Colquhoun	D Smith+	Henderson	Petrie*	Cameron+	R Smith	Mills	Forsyth	Black	Binnie
11/02/2017	L	H	Berwick Rangers	2	2	C Smith	McGeachie	Quigley	Forsyth	R Smith	McMillan*	Caddis+	McCue&	Dickson	D Smith	Henderson	Wright*	Malone+	McLaren&	Cameron	Petrie	Black	Binnie
18/02/2017	L	A	Arbroath	1	1	C Smith	McGeachie	Quigley	Wright	R Smith	Colquhoun	McLaren+	McCue*	Dickson	D Smith	Henderson&	Little*	Johnstone+	Kavanagh&	Caddis	Petrie	Black	Binnie
25/02/2017	L	H	Edinburgh City	1	0	C Smith	McGeachie	Quigley	Caddis	R Smith	Colquhoun	McLaren&	Kavanagh+	Dickson	D Smith*	Henderson	Johnstone*	Little+	Black&	McMullan	Mills	Docherty	Binnie
28/02/2017	L	H	Elgin City	1	0	C Smith	McGeachie	Forsyth	Caddis	R Smith	Black	McLaren*	Kavanagh	Dickson	McMullan	Henderson+	D Smith*	Johnstone+	Quigley	Wright	Colquhoun	Docherty	Binnie
04/03/2017	L	A	Cowdenbeath	2	0	C Smith	McGeachie	Quigley	Caddis	R Smith	Black	D Smith*	Kavanagh	Dickson	McMullan+	Henderson	McLaren*	Colquhoun+&	Forsyth&	Wright	Jeffries	Mills	Binnie
11/03/2017	L	A	Montrose	3	1	C Smith	McGeachie	Quigley	Caddis	R Smith	Black	D Smith	Kavanagh+	Dickson	McMullan*	Henderson&	McLaren*	Jeffries+	Petrie&	Wright	Forsyth	Mills	Binnie
18/03/2017	L	H	Annan Athletic	1	0	C Smith	McGeachie	Quigley	Jeffries+	R Smith&	Black	D Smith	Kavanagh	Dickson	McMullan	McLaren*	Morrison*	Henderson+	Wright&	Petrie	Forsyth	Mills	Binnie
25/03/2017	L	A	Clyde	3	2	C Smith	McGeachie	Quigley	Caddis	Wright	Black	D Smith	Kavanagh&	Dickson	McLaren+	Henderson*	Morrison*	Little+	Forsyth&	Petrie	McMullan	Mills	Binnie
01/04/2017	L	H	Forfar Athletic	0	3	C Smith	Forsyth	Quigley	Caddis	Wright	Black	D Smith	Kavanagh&	McMullen*	Morrison+	Nguene Bikey	Henderson*	Petrie+	Little&	McLaren	Jeffries	Mills	Binnie
08/04/2017	L	A	Berwick Rangers	1	0	C Smith	McGeachie	Quigley	Caddis	Forsyth	Black	D Smith&	Henderson*	Dickson	Morrison+	Nguene Bikey	Little*	Kavanagh+	McLaren&	McMillan	Jeffries	McMullan	Fallens
15/04/2017	L	H	Cowdenbeath	0	3	C Smith	McGeachie	Quigley	Caddis	Forsyth	Black&	D Smith	Henderson*	Dickson	Morrison*	Kavanagh+	McLaren*	Nguene Bikey+	Jeffries&	McMillan	Colquhoun	McMullan	Fallens
22/04/2017	L	A	Elgin City	2	2	C Smith	McGeachie	Quigley	Caddis	McMillan	Black	D Smith	Colquhoun	McLaren+	Morrison*	Nguene Bikey&	Jeffries*	Henderson+	Kavanagh&	Mills	Forsyth	McMullan	Binnie
29/04/2017	L	A	Edinburgh City	0	1	C Smith	McGeachie	Quigley	Caddis	McMillan	Black	D Smith+	Colquhoun	McLaren	Morrison*	Nguene Bikey&	Kavanagh*	Henderson+	McMullan&	McDonald	Mills	Forsyth	Binnie
06/05/2017	L	H	Arbroath	1	1	C Smith	McGeachie	Quigley	Caddis	Forsyth	Black	D Smith	Henderson+	McMullan*	Robertson&	Kavanagh	Nguene Bikey*	Morrison+	Vezza&	Colquhoun	McLaren	Mills	Binnie

			SQ	Nat	Pos	L			SC			LC			CC							
me	First Name	DOB				A	S	G	A	S	G	A	S	G	A	S	G	UNS	Signed	Previous Club	Notes	Contract
er	Kyle	13/07/1999		SCO	D														2016	Stirling Albion Youths		
	Angus	22/02/1996		SCO	M	10													2016	Hearts (OL)	Oct-Jan 2017	[redacted]
e	Cameron	08/11/1997		SCO	GK	5			1			1			1			35	2015	Stirling Albion Youths		End 2017/18
	Andy	20/09/1995		SCO	D	11	2		2									3	2017	Fauldhouse United		End 2017/18
	Scott	03/01/1997		SCO	D							1			1			1	2015	Stirling Albion Youths		
s	Liam	20/09/1993		SCO	M	16			2									1	2017	Ardrossan Winton Rovers		End 2017/18
ron	Ross	24/03/1998		SCO	F		1			1								5	2016	St Mirren Youths		
houn	Calvin	20/07/1996		SCO	M	13	1		3									3	2017	Dundee (OL)	Jan-May 2017	[redacted]
son	Scott	30/03/1996		SCO	D	12	3		3			2	2		1			4	2015	Stirling Albion Youths	OL to Cumbernauld Colts Jan-May 2017	End 2017/18
son	Sam	08/12/1997		SCO	D										1			4	2015	Stirling Albion Youths	OL to Linlithgow Rose Jan-May 2017	OOC
on	Sean	16/01/1992		SCO	M	26	4	7	2	2		4						1	2015	East Fife		End 2017/18
erty	Alex	01/01/1997		SCO	M		1						1		1			14	2016	Maryhill Black Star	OL to Maryhill Juniors Nov-May 2017, Freed May 2017	[redacted]
ns	Ronan	16/05/1999		SCO	GK													9	2015	Stirling Albion Youths		
	Eddie	18/04/1991		SCO	M	11	5	1	1	1	1	4		1		1		2	2016	Alloa	Freed Dec 2016, joined Arbroath	[redacted]
th	Ross	20/11/1982		SCO	D	12	3	1	1			3						7	2013	Dumbarton	Released May 2017	[redacted]
er	James	26/10/1980		SCO	M	1	1													Trialist	Ex QOS Manager	[redacted]
erson	Blair	10/08/1994		SCO	F	22	9	5	3	1	3	3	1	4		1		5	2016	Berwick Rangers		End 2017/18
e	Bryan	23/09/1987		SCO	M	9	1		1			4						2	2016	Forfar Athletic	Freed Dec 2016, joined Arbroath	[redacted]
es	Josh	13/01/1998		SCO	M	2	3											3	2017	Rangers (OL)	Jan-May 2017	[redacted]
tone	Andrew	30/09/1998		SCO	M		3													Trialist	ex Ayr United, Signed for Kirkintilloch Rob Roy Mar 2017	
nagh	Ross	26/04/1997		SCO	F	12	11	4	1	1					1			3	2014	Alloa Athletic Youths		End 2017/18
e	Isaac	16/05/1995		ENG	F	7	1	1											2016	Alloa (OL)	Aug-Nov 2016	[redacted]
	Andy	12/05/1989		NIR	F		5												2016	Preston North End		End 2017/18
ne	Aiden	19/02/1992		SCO	M		1	1												Trialist	Ex Queen's Park	[redacted]
	Aurelien	14/11/1982		FRA	D		1											6	2015	US Colomiers	Retired Sep 2016	[redacted]
ister	Tommy	03/01/1997		SCO	F													2	2015	Stirling Albion Youths	OL to Linlithgow Rose Aug-Dec, Freed Jan 2017	[redacted]
e	Jack	20/02/1995		SCO	M	6	2			1		3	1		1			2	2016	Airdrieonians	OL to Cumbernauld Colts Aug-Jan 2017	OOC
nald	Callum			SCO														1	2016	Stirling Albion Youths		
achie	Ross	04/05/1994		SCO	D	22	1		2									4	2012	Stirling Albion Youths		End 2017/18
nzie	Marc	11/07/1985		SCO	F	14	2	4	2		1	3	1		1		2		2016	Elgin City	Freed Dec 2016, joined Clyde	[redacted]
ren	Connor	20/02/1997		SCO	M	11	5	1	2									2	2017	St Johnstone (OL)	Jan-May 2017	[redacted]
ren	Regan			SCO															2016	Stirling Albion Youths	OL to Luncarty Jan-May 2017	
llan	Ross	20/10/1982		SCO	D	23		2	3			3	1					2	2015	Stenhousemuir	Released May 2017	[redacted]
ullan	Connor	19/11/1998		SCO	M	6	1											5	2016	Stirling Albion Youths	OL to Shotts BA, Dec 16-May 2017	End 2017/18
	Jamie	01/03/1996		SCO	D	4	1	1				1	1		1			20	2016	Rangers	Released May 2017	[redacted]
son	Callumn	05/07/1999		SCO	M	7	8			1								8	2016	Hearts (OL)	Sep 16-May 2017	
ne Bikey	Dylan	18/02/1995		FRA/CAM	F	10	3	7	1	1	3								2016	FC Dieppe	Transferred to Hearts Jan 2017, OL from Hearts Mar-May	[redacted]
ewaju	Moses	03/01/1996		ENG/NIG		1	6		1		1		2		1			1	2014	Rushden & Diamonds	Freed Jan 2017, joined Sauchie	[redacted]
e	Darren	26/07/1995		SCO	M	12	3		2			1						9	2016	Raith Rovers	Released May 2017	[redacted]
ey	Connor	04/12/1997		SCO	D	17			2									1	2017	Dundee (OL)	Jan-May 2017	[redacted]
rtson	William	14/04/1993		SCO	M	8			2										2017	Annan Athletic		End 2017/18
n	Chris	05/03/1986		SCO	GK	31			3			3						1	2015	Stenhousemuir	Released May 2017, joined Stenhousemuir	[redacted]
n	Ross	21/02/1992		SCO	D	14		2		2		2			1			9	2015	Peterhead		End 2017/18
n	Darren	27/03/1988		SCO	F	28	3	11	2			2	2	1		1		2	2011	Stenhousemuir		End 2017/18
	Alberto						1												2016	Stirling Albion Youths	OL to Carluke Rovers Nov-Jan	
que	David	11/08/1995			D	6	3					4						11	2015	Clydebank	Freed Jan 2017, joined Berwick Rangers	[redacted]
nt	Frazer	23/12/1979			D	7	2		2									3	2016	Dumbarton	Retired May 2017, appointed Assistant Manager	[redacted]
Goals								2														[redacted]
SIGNINGS																						
e	Steven				M														2017	Peterhead		
onald	Peter				F														2017	Clyde		

ce of Birthdates: SAFC Website, transfermarkt.com

Stranraer FC 2016/17

Founded	1870
Ground	Stair Park
Postcode	DG9 8BS
Tel	01776 703271
Capacity	2988
Closest Railway Station	Stranraer
Record Attendance	6500 v Rangers, 24/1/1948
Record Win	9-0 v St Cuthbert W, SC, 23/10/2010,
	v Wigtown & Bladnoch, SC, 22/10/2011
Record Defeat	1-11 v QOS, SC, 16/1/1932
Most League Goals in a Season	27 Derek Frye, 1977/8
Chairman	Iain Dougan
Match Secretary	Shaun Niven
Manager	Brian Reid
Assistant Manager	Lee Mair
Colours 2016/17 Top	Blue
Shorts	White
Sponsor	Stena Line
Manufacturer	Stanno
Change Colours 2016/17 Top	Black with luminous green trim
Shorts	Black with luminous green trim
Nicknames	Blues
Web	www.stranraerfc.org
Match Programme 2016/17	Beyond the Bandstand £2

Stranraer never really threatened to repeat their play position of 2015/16. However, they survived something to spare in what was a hugely compet league. Other than Livingston and Alloa there really nothing between the other eight clubs.

The lack of a regular scorer was probably what Stranraer a higher position. Their goals were sha around but if they had been able to get the best ou Christian Nade then their season might have borne fruit

PREDICTION FOR 2017/18

Stranraer will remain difficult to beat but they are unli to challenge seriously for the title. Expect to see ther mid table, possibly pushing towards the play off spots.

						L			SC			LC			CC							
			SQ	Nat	Pos	A	S	G	A	S	G	A	S	G	A	S	G	UNS				
Surname	**First Name**	**DOB**																	**Signed**	**Previous Club**	**Notes**	**Contra**
Agnew	Scott	11/07/1987		SCO	M	28	5	3	1	1		4			2			4	2016	St Mirren		End 20
Barbour	Ross	01/02/1993				1						3						4	2016	Kirkintilloch Rob Roy	Freed Sep 2016 joined Troon	
Barron	David	10/09/1987		SCO	D	24	1		2						1			1	2015	Greenock JFC		End 20
Belford	Cammy	16/10/1988		ENG	GK	36			2			2			3				2016	Wrexham		End 20
Bell	Steven	24/02/1985		SCO	M	32		3	2			2			3			1	2013	Dunfermline Athletic		End 20
Brown	Nathan	12/06/1997		SCO	GK													3	2012	St Cuthbert W		
Currie	Max	03/03/1997		SCO	GK							2						42	2015	Motherwell		End 20
Dempster	Mark	23/08/1998		SCO	D													1	2016	Kilmarnock Youth		
Dick	Liam	19/08/1995		SCO	D	34		1	2			4			2				2016	Falkirk		End 20
Donald	Michael	20/01/1989		SCO	M	9	3											2	2017	Ayr United	Freed May 2017	
Ewing	Mitchell			SCO	M													2	2016	Stranraer Youths		
Gibson	Willie	06/08/1984		SCO	M	32	1	8	2		1	4			3		1		2016	Dumbarton	OOC May 2017 joined Peterhead	
Johnstone	Andrew	30/09/1998		SCO	M		1											1		Trialist	ex Ayr United	
Kassarate	Amadou	14/01/1996		ENG / SEN			13	2										1	2017	Dumbarton (OL)	Feb-May	
Kemp	Calvin	01/08/1996		SCO	F	1	3					2	1			1		12	2016	Stranraer Youths	OL to Kilwining Rangers Aug-Jan	
Malcolm	Craig	31/12/1986		SCO	F	31	3	13	2			3	1	1	3		4	2	2014	Ayr United	OOC May 2017, joined Alloa Athletic	
Maley	Evan	09/06/1998		SCO	M											1		10	2015	Kilmarnock U20	OL to Troon Nov-May	
McCloskey	Sam	04/04/1995		SCO	M		1					1	1		1	1		8	2014	Bonnyton Thistle	OL to Kilwining Rangers Oct-Dec, Freed May	
McGowan	Christopher	01/01/2000		SCO	M													3	2016	Stranraer Youths		
McGuigan	Mark	07/11/1988		SCO	F	12	17	3	2			2	1		3		2	3	2015	Albion Rovers	OOC May 2017 joined Stenhousemuir	
McKeown	Frank	18/08/1986		SCO	D	6	5					4		2	2	1		7	2016	Morton	Freed Jan 2017 joined Alloa Athletic	
Morena	Guilermo	14/08/1992		ITA / GER	M	12	4			2			2		1	1		17	2016	Romagna Centro	Freed May 2017	
Nade	Christian	18/09/1984		FRA	F	4	2	1				2	2	1		2		2	2016	Dumbarton	Freed Dec 2017, rejoined Dumbarton	
Neill	Morgynn	10/03/1996		SCO	D	12	1		1										2017	Llivingston (OL)	Jan-May, signed permanently May	
Nuttall	Joe	27/01/1997		ENG	F	8	1	2	1										2016	Aberdeen (OL)	Nov-Jan	
Osadolor	Smart	26/03/1991		NIG	F								1					3	2016	Annan Athletic	Freed Aug 2016 joined East Kilbride FC	
Pettigrew	Craig	25/11/1986		SCO	D	10												2	2017	Dumbarton	Released May 2017, joined Auchinleck Talbot	
Richardson	David	01/01/1998		SCO	M													1	2016	Stranraer Youths		
Robertson	Scott	26/11/1987		SCO	D	33	1	1	2			4			3				2013	Arbroath		End 20
Sherry	Jack	01/01/1999		SCO	D													10	2015	St Mirren Youths		
Thomson	Ryan	13/04/1991		SCO	M	22	7	4	2			4			2	1		3	2015	Dunfermline Athletic		End 20
Thomson	Craig	10/03/1995		SCO	M	17	2	3							2				2016	St Johnstone (OL)	Aug-Jan	
Turner	Kyle	10/11/1997		SCO	M	20	8	2	1	1		1	3	1	2	1	1	6	2015	Stranraer Youths		End 20
Watt	Luke	20/06/1997		SCO	D	6	6											4	2016	Motherwell (OL)	Aug-Jan	
Whittaker	Jack	08/09/1997		SCO	M		1											1	2017	Kilmarnock (OL)	Jan-Feb	
Wilson	David	06/09/1994		SCO	M	6	7			1								4	2017	Partick Thistle (OL)	Jan-May	
Own Goals											1											
NEW SIGNINGS																						
Hamill	Jamie																		2017	Queen of the South		End 20
Wallace	Ryan																		2017	Albion Rovers		End 20
Neill	Morgynn																		2017	Livingston		End 20
Woods	Paul																		2017	East Kilbride		End 20
Lang	Tom																		2017	Dumbarton		End 20
Anderson	Grant																		2017	Peterhead		End 20

Source of Birthdates: transfermarkt.com

Date	Comp	H/A	Opponents	F	A	HT		Referee	Crowd	Scorers
16/07/2016	LC	A	Annan Athletic	2	1	0	0	S Reid	418	Nade, McKeown
19/07/2016	LC	H	East Stirlingshire	3	1	0	0	D Lowe	373	Malcolm, Turner, McKeown
25/07/2016	LC	A	Rangers	0	3	0	2	J Beaton	29575	
30/07/2016	LC	H	Motherwell	0	3	0	0	D Robertson	953	
06/08/2016	L	A	Livingston	1	5	0	2	C Steven	693	Malcolm
13/08/2016	L	H	Alloa	2	5	1	5	G Ross	448	Malcolm 2
16/08/2016	CC2	H	Spartans	7	1	3	0	C Napier	326	Malcolm 4, McGuigan, Gibson, Turner
20/08/2016	L	A	Airdrieonians	0	1	0	1	C Charleston	812	
27/08/2016	L	H	Peterhead	1	0	1	0	E Anderson	376	McGuigan
03/09/2016	CC3	H	Dumbarton	1	0	0	0	J McKendrick	401	McGuigan
10/09/2016	L	A	East Fife	0	2	0	1	M Roncone	555	
17/09/2016	L	H	Albion Rovers	3	2	2	0	K Graham	402	C Thomson 2, McGuigan
24/09/2016	L	A	Queen's Park	2	0	1	0	C Steven	534	Dick, Malcolm
01/10/2016	L	H	Brechin City	0	1	0	0	D Munro	402	
08/10/2016	CC4	H	Dundee United	0	1	0	0	G Aitken	629	
15/10/2016	L	A	Stenhousemuir	5	0	3	0	G Irvine	341	Gibson, Turner, Malcolm 2, Nade
22/10/2016	L	H	East Fife	1	1	0	1	J McKendrick	428	Bell
29/10/2016	L	A	Peterhead	0	2	0	0	C Steven	444	
05/11/2016	L	H	Queen's Park	0	2	0	1	G Ross	446	
12/11/2016	L	A	Albion Rovers	2	3	1	2	A Muir	321	Gibson, Nuttall
19/11/2016	L	H	Stenhousemuir	3	1	1	1	A Newlands	323	Bell, R Thomson, Nuttall
03/12/2016	SC3	H	East Kilbride	2	1	1	1	S Kirkland	331	Gibson, Strachan og
10/12/2016	L	H	Livingston	1	2	1	0	C Steven	333	Gibson
13/12/2016	L	A	Alloa	2	2	1	1	G Irvine	309	Agnew, Gibson
17/12/2016	L	A	Brechin City	0	2	0	2	K Graham	402	
24/12/2016	L	H	Airdrieonians	1	2	1	1	G Ross	317	Agnew
31/12/2016	L	A	Queen's Park	1	0	0	0	D Munro	556	Gibson
07/01/2017	L	H	Alloa	1	2	1	0	C Napier	383	C Thomson
14/01/2017	L	A	Stenhousemuir	0	1	0	0	S Reid	392	
21/01/2017	SC4	A	Aberdeen	0	4	0	2	D Robertson	8960	
28/01/2017	L	A	East Fife	0	0	0	0	S Millar	584	
04/02/2017	L	H	Albion Rovers	3	0	1	0	G Duncan	364	Malcolm 2, Bell
11/02/2017	L	A	Livingston	0	0	0	0	G Beaton	677	
18/02/2017	L	H	Peterhead	3	3	2	1	S Kirkland	459	R Thomson, Gibson 2
25/02/2017	L	H	Brechin City	2	0	1	0	S Reid	340	Gibson, Malcolm
04/03/2017	L	A	Airdrieonians	2	1	0	0	C Charleston	706	Malcolm, Thomson
11/03/2017	L	H	Queen's Park	1	1	0	1	G Ross	434	Malcolm
18/03/2017	L	H	Livingston	0	1	0	0	C Napier	523	
25/03/2017	L	A	Peterhead	2	2	2	1	G Beaton	449	Malcolm, Robertson
01/04/2017	L	H	Stenhousemuir	3	0	1	0	D Munro	440	Agnew, R Thomson, Kassarate
08/04/2017	L	A	Albion Rovers	0	3	0	1	G Irvine	377	
15/04/2017	L	H	Airdrieonians	2	1	1	0	S Finnie	489	McGuigan, Turner
22/04/2017	L	A	Brechin City	0	0	0	0	G Ross	403	
29/04/2017	L	A	Alloa	0	1	0	0	M Northcroft	507	
06/05/2017	L	H	East Fife	2	1	0	0	S Reid	462	Malcolm, Kassarate

FRIENDLIES / OTHER GAMES

02/07/2016	H	Partick Thistle XI	4	2	
05/07/2016	N	Dumbarton	2	1	at Benburb
08/07/2016	A	AFC Fylde	2	9	
14/07/2016	A	Newton Stewart	3	3	U17
16/07/2016	A	East Kilbride	3	5	U20
02/08/2016	N	Beith	2	7	U17, at Lochinch

Date	Comp	H/A	Opponents	F	A	1	2	3	4	5	6	7	8	9	10	11	12	13	14	15	16	17	18
16/07/2016	LC	A	Annan Athletic	2	1	Currie	Robertson	Dick	McKeown	Barbour	Agnew	McCloskey	Thomson	Gibson	Malcolm	Kemp	Nade*	Osadolor+	Turner&	*Brown*			
19/07/2016	LC	H	East Stirlingshire	3	1	Currie	Robertson	Dick	McKeown	Barbour	Agnew&	Nade+	Thomson	Gibson	Malcolm	Kemp*	McCloskey*	McGuigan+	Turner&	*Brown*	*Osadolor*	*Morena*	
25/07/2016	LC	A	Rangers	0	3	Belford	Robertson	Dick	McKeown	Barbour*	Agnew	Nade+	Thomson	Gibson	Bell	McGuigan&	Malcolm*	Turner+	Morena&	*McCloskey*	*Osadolor*	*Kemp*	*Currie*
30/07/2016	LC	H	Motherwell	0	3	Belford	Robertson	Dick	McKeown	Turner+	Agnew	Malcolm&	Thomson	Gibson	Bell	McGuigan*	Kemp*	Nade+	Morena&	*McCloskey*	*Osadolor*	*Barbour*	*Currie*
06/08/2016	L	A	Livingston	1	5	Belford	Robertson	Dick	McKeown	Turner	Agnew	Malcolm	Kemp*	Nade+	Bell	McGuigan	McCloskey*	Morena+	*Barbour*	*Currie*			
13/08/2016	L	H	Alloa	2	5	Belford	Robertson	Dick	Barbour*	Malcolm	Agnew	C Thomson+	R Thomson	Gibson	Bell	Nade&	Turner*	McGuigan+	Kemp&	*McCloskey*	*McKeown*	*Morena*	*Currie*
16/08/2016	CC2	H	Spartans	7	1	Belford	Robertson	McCloskey	McKeown	Malcolm&	Agnew*	C Thomson	R Thomson+	Gibson	Bell	McGuigan	Morena*	Turner+	Kemp&	*Barbour*	*Currie*		
20/08/2016	L	A	Airdrieonians	0	1	Belford	Robertson	Dick	McKeown	Malcolm	Agnew	C Thomson*	R Thomson	Gibson	Bell	McGuigan+	Turner*	Morena+	*Kemp*	*Barbour*	*Currie*	*McCloskey*	
27/08/2016	L	H	Peterhead	1	0	Belford	Barron	Dick	McKeown	Malcolm	Agnew	C Thomson	R Thomson	Gibson	Bell	McGuigan	Turner*	Morena+	Kemp&	*Nade*	*Currie*	*McCloskey*	*Sherry*
03/09/2016	CC3	H	Dumbarton	1	0	Belford	Robertson	Dick	McKeown	Malcolm*	Agnew+	Turner	R Thomson	Gibson	Bell	McGuigan&	Nade*	McCloskey+	Maley&	*Richardson*	*Currie*	*Dempster*	*Sherry*
10/09/2016	L	A	East Fife	0	2	Belford	Robertson	Dick	McKeown&	Malcolm*	Agnew	Turner+	R Thomson	Gibson	Bell	McGuigan	C Thomson*	Nade+	Barron&	*Watt*	*Currie*	*McCloskey*	*Morena*
17/09/2016	L	H	Albion Rovers	3	2	Belford	Robertson	Dick	Barron*	Malcolm	Morena+	Turner	C Thomson	Gibson	Bell	McGuigan	Watt*	Agnew+	*McKeown*	*McCloskey*	*Currie*		
24/09/2016	L	A	Queen's Park	2	0	Belford	Robertson	Dick	Barron&	Malcolm+	Morena	Turner	C Thomson	Gibson	Bell	McGuigan*	R Thomson*	Watt+	McKeown&	*McCloskey*	*Agnew*	*Brown*	
01/10/2016	L	H	Brechin City	0	1	Belford	Robertson	Dick*	Barron	Malcolm	Morena+	Turner	C Thomson&	Gibson	Bell	McGuigan	Watt*	R Thomson+	Agnew&	*McKeown*	*Maley*	*Sherry*	*Currie*
08/10/2016	CC4	H	Dundee United	0	1	Belford	Robertson	Dick	Barron	Malcolm	Morena+	Turner&	C Thomson*	Gibson	Bell	McGuigan	Nade*	R Thomson+	McKeown&	*Agnew*	*Currie*		
15/10/2016	L	A	Stenhousemuir	5	0	Belford	Robertson	Dick	Barron&	Malcolm	Morena	Turner	C Thomson*	Gibson	Bell	McGuigan+	Watt*	Nade+	McKeown&	*Agnew*	*Currie*	*R Thomson*	
22/10/2016	L	H	East Fife	1	1	Belford	Robertson	Dick	Watt	Malcolm	Morena+	Turner	C Thomson	Gibson	Bell	Nade*	R Thomson*	Agnew+	*McKeown*	*Currie*			
29/10/2016	L	A	Peterhead	0	2	Belford	Robertson	Dick	Watt	Malcolm	Morena+	Turner&	C Thomson	Gibson	Bell	Nade*	McKeown*	R Thomson+	Agnew&	*Currie*	*Ewing*	*Sherry*	
05/11/2016	L	H	Queen's Park	0	2	Belford	Robertson	Dick	Watt	Malcolm	McKeown*	Turner	C Thomson	Agnew	Bell	R Thomson+	Morena*	McGuigan+	*Nade*	*Currie*	*Ewing*	*Sherry*	
12/11/2016	L	A	Albion Rovers	2	3	Belford	Robertson	Dick	Watt	Malcolm	Morena*	Nuttall	C Thomson+	Gibson	Bell	R Thomson	Turner*	McGuigan+	*McKeown*	*Agnew*	*Currie*		
19/11/2016	L	H	Stenhousemuir	3	1	Belford	Robertson	Dick	Barron+	Malcolm*	McGuigan	Nuttall	Turner&	Gibson	Bell	R Thomson	C Thomson*	McKeown+	Agnew&	*Watt*	*Morena*	*Currie*	
03/12/2016	SC3	H	East Kilbride	2	1	Belford	Robertson	Dick	Barron	Malcolm+	McGuigan*	Nuttall	Turner	Gibson	Bell	R Thomson	Agnew*	Morena+	*Currie*	*Sherry*	*Watt*	*Maley*	
10/12/2016	L	H	Livingston	1	2	Belford	Robertson	Dick	Barron+	Morena	C Thomson	Nuttall	Turner	Gibson	Bell	Agnew*	McGuigan*	Watt+	*Sherry*	*McKeown*	*Malcolm*	*Currie*	*R Thomson*
13/12/2016	L	A	Alloa	2	2	Belford	Robertson	Watt	R Thomson	Morena	C Thomson	Nuttall*	Turner	Gibson	Bell	Agnew	McGuigan*	*McGowan*	*Sherry*	*Maley*	*Malcom*	*Currie*	
17/12/2016	L	A	Brechin City	0	2	Belford	Robertson	Dick	Watt	Morena&	C Thomson*	Nuttall+	Turner	Gibson	Bell	Agnew	Malcolm*	McGuigan+	McKeown&	*R Thomson*	*Currie*		
24/12/2016	L	H	Airdrieonians	1	2	Belford	Robertson	Dick	McKeown	Morena	C Thomson+	Nuttall	Turner*	Gibson	R Thomson	Agnew	Malcolm*	Johnstone+	Watt	*Sherry*	*Currie*	*Maley*	
31/12/2016	L	A	Queen's Park	1	0	Belford	Robertson	Dick	Barron	Morena	C Thomson+	Nuttall*	Turner	Gibson	Bell	Agnew	Malcolm*	Watt+	*Johnstone*	*Sherry*	*Currie*	*Maley*	
07/01/2017	L	H	Alloa	1	2	Belford	Robertson	Dick	Barron	Malcolm	C Thomson*	Wilson	Turner	Gibson+	Bell	Agnew	Nuttall*	R Thomson+	*Morena*	*McKeown*	*Currie*	*Maley*	
14/01/2017	L	A	Stenhousemuir	0	1	Belford	Robertson	Dick	Barron	Malcolm	Neill	Wilson	Turner*	Nuttall+	Pettigrew&	Agnew	McGuigan*	R Thomson+	Whittaker&	*Morena*	*Currie*	*Maley*	
21/01/2017	SC4	A	Aberdeen	0	4	Belford	Robertson	Dick	Barron*	Malcolm	Neill	R Thomson&	McGuigan+	Gibson	Bell	Agnew	Turner*	Wilson+	Morena&	*Whittaker*	*Currie*	*Maley*	
28/01/2017	L	A	East Fife	0	0	Belford	Robertson	Dick	Barron	Malcolm*	Neill	R Thomson+	Pettigrew	Gibson	Bell	Agnew	Donald*	McGuigan+	*Morena*	*Wilson*	*Currie*	*Turner*	*Maley*
04/02/2017	L	H	Albion Rovers	3	0	Belford	Robertson	Dick	Barron	Malcolm+	Neill	R Thomson	Donald*	Gibson	Bell	Agnew&	Turner*	McGuigan+	Wilson&	*Kemp*	*Currie*	*Kassarate*	*Morena*
11/02/2017	L	A	Livingston	0	0	Belford	Robertson	Dick	Barron	Malcolm+	Pettigrew	R Thomson	Donald*	Gibson	Bell	Agnew	Turner*	Kassarate+	Wilson	*Kemp*	*Currie*	*McGuigan*	*Morena*
18/02/2017	L	H	Peterhead	3	3	Belford	Robertson	Dick	Barron	Malcolm+	Pettigrew&	R Thomson	Donald*	Gibson	Bell	Agnew	Kassarate*	McGuigan+	Neill&	*Kemp*	*Currie*	*Turner*	*Wilson*
25/02/2017	L	H	Brechin City	2	0	Belford	Robertson	Dick	Barron	Malcolm+	Neill	R Thomson	Donald*	Gibson&	Bell	Agnew	Turner*	Kassarate+	McGuigan&	*Kemp*	*Currie*	*Wilson*	*Pettigrew*
04/03/2017	L	A	Airdrieonians	2	1	Belford	Robertson	Dick	Barron	Malcolm*	Neill	R Thomson	Donald+	Gibson	Bell	Agnew	Kassarate*	Wilson+	McGuigan	*Kemp*	*Currie*	*Turner*	*Pettigrew*
11/03/2017	L	H	Queen's Park	1	1	Belford	Robertson	Pettigrew	Barron	Malcolm	Turner+	R Thomson	Donald*	Gibson	Bell&	Agnew	Wilson*	Kassarate+	McGuigan&	*Kemp*	*Currie*	*Maley*	*Morena*
18/03/2017	L	H	Livingston	0	1	Belford	Robertson	Dick	Pettigrew	Malcolm&	Wilson*	R Thomson	McGuigan+	Gibson	Bell	Agnew	Turner*	Kassarate+	Kemp&	*Barron*	*Currie*	*McGowan*	*Morena*
25/03/2017	L	A	Peterhead	2	2	Belford	Robertson	Dick	Barron	Malcolm+	Wilson*	R Thomson	Neill	Gibson	Bell	Agnew&	Donald*	Kassarate+	McGuigan&	*Morena*	*Currie*	*Turner*	
01/04/2017	L	H	Stenhousemuir	3	0	Belford	Pettigrew	Dick	Barron	Malcolm*	Wilson&	R Thomson	Neill	Gibson+	Bell	Agnew	Kassarate*	McGuigan+	Donald&	*Morena*	*Currie*	*Turner*	*McGowan*
08/04/2017	L	A	Albion Rovers	0	3	Belford	Pettigrew	Dick	Barron	Malcolm	Wilson+	R Thomson	Neill	Donald&	Bell*	Agnew	Robertson*	Kassarate+	Gibson&	*Morena*	*Currie*	*Turner*	*McGuigan*
15/04/2017	L	H	Airdrieonians	2	1	Belford	Pettigrew	Dick	Barron	Malcolm	Robertson	Turner	Neill	Gibson*	McGuigan+	Agnew	Kassarate*	Wilson+	*Donald*	*Morena*	*Currie*	*Kemp*	
22/04/2017	L	A	Brechin City	0	0	Belford	Pettigrew&	Dick	Barron	Malcolm	Robertson	Turner*	Neill	Gibson	McGuigan+	Agnew	R Thomson*	Kassarate+	Wilson&	*Bell*	*Currie*	*Kemp*	*Donald*
29/04/2017	L	A	Alloa	0	1	Belford	Bell	Dick	Barron	Malcolm*	Robertson	R Thomson	Neill	Gibson+	Donald&	Agnew	Kassarate*	Wilson+	McGuigan&	*Morena*	*Currie*	*Kemp*	
06/05/2017	L	H	East Fife	2	1	Belford	Bell	Dick&	Barron	Malcolm+	Robertson	R Thomson	Neill	Gibson	Donald*	Agnew	Wilson*	Kassarate+	McGowan&	*McGuigan*	*Currie*	*Kemp*	*Morena*

Scottish Professional Football League Tables 2016/17

PREMIERSHIP	P	W	D	L	F	A	GD	PTS
Celtic	38	34	4	0	106	25	81	106
Aberdeen	38	24	4	10	74	35	39	76
Rangers (P)	38	19	10	9	56	44	12	67
St Johnstone	38	17	7	14	50	46	4	58
Hearts	38	12	10	16	55	52	3	46
Partick Thistle	38	10	12	16	38	54	-16	42
Ross County	38	11	13	14	48	58	-10	46
Kilmarnock	38	9	14	15	36	56	-20	41
Motherwell	38	10	8	20	46	69	-23	38
Dundee	38	10	7	21	38	62	-24	37
Hamilton Accies	*38*	*7*	*14*	*17*	*37*	*56*	*-19*	*35*
Inverness CT	38	7	13	18	44	71	-27	34

CHAMPIONSHIP	P	W	D	L	F	A	GD	PTS
Hibernian	36	19	14	3	59	25	34	71
Falkirk	36	16	12	8	58	40	18	60
Dundee United (R)	36	15	12	9	50	42	8	57
Morton	36	13	13	10	44	41	3	52
Dunfermline Ath (P)	36	12	12	12	46	43	3	48
QOSD	36	11	10	15	46	52	-6	43
St Mirren	36	9	12	15	52	56	-4	39
Dumbarton	36	9	12	15	46	56	-10	39
Raith Rovers	36	10	9	17	35	52	-17	39
Ayr United (P)	36	7	12	17	33	62	-29	33

LEAGUE ONE	P	W	D	L	F	A	GD	PTS
Livingston (R)	36	26	3	7	80	32	48	81
Alloa Athletic (R)	36	17	11	8	69	44	25	62
Airdrieonians	36	16	4	16	61	66	-5	52
Brechin City	36	15	5	16	43	49	-6	50
East Fife (P)	36	12	19	14	41	44	-3	46
Queen's Park (P)	36	12	10	14	37	51	-14	46
Stranraer	36	12	8	16	46	50	-4	44
Albion Rovers	36	11	9	16	41	48	-7	42
Peterhead	36	10	10	16	44	59	-15	40
Stenhousemuir	36	11	6	19	45	64	-19	39

LEAGUE TWO	P	W	D	L	F	A	GD	PTS
Arbroath	36	18	12	6	63	36	27	66
Forfar Athletic (R)	36	18	10	8	69	49	20	64
Annan Athletic	36	18	4	14	61	58	3	58
Montrose	36	14	10	12	44	53	-9	52
Elgin City	36	14	9	13	67	47	20	51
Stirling Albion	36	12	11	13	50	59	-9	47
Edinburgh City	36	11	10	15	38	45	-7	43
Berwick Rangers	36	10	10	16	50	65	-15	40
Clyde	36	10	8	18	49	64	-15	38
Cowdenbeath (R)	36	9	8	19	40	55	-15	35

Clubs in Bold Promoted or Relegated, Clubs in italics in Play Offs

PREMIERSHIP PLAY OFF

Rd 1	09/05/2017	Morton	Dundee United	1	2		3306
Rd 1	12/05/2017	Dundee United	Morton	3	0		6606
SF	16/05/2017	Dundee United	Falkirk	2	2		7043
SF	19/05/2017	Falkirk	Dundee United	1	2		7926
F	25/05/2017	Dundee United	Hamilton Accies	0	0		9368
F	28/05/2017	Hamilton Accies	Dundee United	1	0		5027

Hamilton Accies retain place in Premiership

CHAMPIONSHIP PLAY OFF

SF	10/05/2017	Airdrieonians	Alloa Athletic	1	0		1199
SF	10/05/2017	Brechin City	Raith Rovers	1	1		1022
SF	13/05/2017	Alloa Athletic	Airdrieonians	1	0	AET 4-3p	1181
SF	13/05/2017	Raith Rovers	Brechin City	3	3	AET, 3-4p	2932
F	17/05/2017	Brechin City	Alloa Athletic	1	0		7012
F	20/05/2017	Alloa Athletic	Brechin City	4	3	AET, 5-4p	1204

Brechin City promoted, Raith Rovers relegated

LEAGUE ONE PLAY OFF

SF	10/05/2017	Annan Athletic	Forfar Athletic	2	2		629
SF	10/05/2017	Montrose	Peterhead	1	1		1251
SF	13/05/2017	Forfar Athletic	Annan Athletic	4	2		665
SF	13/05/2017	Peterhead	Montrose	3	0		1096
F	17/05/2017	Forfar Athletic	Peterhead	2	1		958
F	20/05/2017	Peterhead	Forfar Athletic	1	5		1084

Forfar Athletic promoted, Peterhead relegated

PYRAMID / LEAGUE TWO PLAY OFF

Qua	29/04/2017	Buckie Thistle	East Kilbride	2	2		1000
Qual	06/05/2017	East Kilbride	Buckie Thistle	2	1		600
F	13/05/2017	East Kilbride	Cowdenbeath	0	0		600
F	20/05/2017	Cowdenbeath	East Kilbride	1	1	AET, 5-3p	1676

Cowdenbeath retain League Two position

SPFL MONTHLY AWARDS 2016/17

	Manager of the Month Premiership	Manager of the Month Championship	Manager of the Month League One	Manager of the Month League Two
August	Brendan Rodgers (Celtic)	Neil Lennon (Hibernian)	jack Ross (Alloa)	Gary Bollan (Forfar Athletic)
September	Richie Foran (ICT)	Peter Houston (Falkirk)	Gary Naysmith (East Fife)	Gary Bollan (Forfar Athletic)
October	Brendan Rodgers (Celtic)	Jim Duffy (Morton)	David Hopkin (Livingston)	Jim Weir (Elgin City)
November	Robbie Neilson (hearts)	Ray McKinnon (Dundee United)	Mark Wilson (Airdrieonians)	Gary Jardine (Edinburgh City)
December	Brendan Rodgers (Celtic)	Stephen Aitken (Dumbarton)	Barry Smith (East Fife)	Gary Jardine (Edinburgh City)
January	No award	Neil Lennon (Hibernian)	Jim McInally (Peterhead)	Gary Bollan (Forfar Athletic)
February	Paul Hartley (Dundee)	Peter Houston (Falkirk)	Jim Goodwin (Alloa)	Jim Chapman (Annan Athletic)
March	Derek McInnes (Aberdeen)	Jack Ross (St Mirren)	David Hopkin (Livingston)	Dave Mackay (Stirling Albion)
April	Brendan Rodgers (Celtic)	Jack Ross (St Mirren)	David Hopkin (Livingston)	Dick Campbell (Arbroath)
	Premier Player of the Month	Championship Player of the Month	League 1 Player of the Month	League 2 Player of the Month
August	Liam Boyce (Ross County)	Jason Cummings (Hibernian)	Jordan Kirkpatrick (Alloa)	Josh Peters (Forfar Athletic)
September	Moussa Dembele (Celtic)	Cammy Bell (Dundee United)	Jamie Insall (East Fife)	Thomas O'Brien (Forfar Athletic)
October	Adam Barton (Partick Thistle)	Thomas O'Ware (Morton)	Liam Buchanan (Livingston)	Shane Sutherland (Elgin City)
November	Bjorn Johnsen (Hearts)	John McGinn (Hibernian)	Rohan Ferguson (Airdrieonians)	Marc Laird (Edinburgh City)
December	Stuart Armstrong (Celtic)	Mark Docherty (Dumbarton)	Jonathan Page (East Fife)	Andrew Stobie (Edinburgh City)
January	No award	Ross Forbes (Morton)	Michael Dunlop (Albion Rovers)	Shane Sutherland (Elgin City)
February	Moussa Dembele (Celtic)	Jason Cummings (Hibernian)	Willie Gibson (Stranraer)	Gavin Skelton (Annan Athletic)
March	Stuart Armstrong (Celtic)	Efe Ambrose (Hibernian)	Andy jackson (Brechin City)	Gary Rutherford (Berwick Rangers)
April	Liam Boyce (Ross County)	Stevie Mallan (St Mirren)	Liam Buchanan (Livingston)	Ryan McCord (Arbroath)

SCOTTISH FOOTBALL WRITERS AWARDS 2016/17

Player of the Year: Scott Sinclair (Celtic)
Manager of the Year: Brendan Rodgers (Celtic)
Young Player of the Year: Kieran Tierney (Celtic)

SCOTTISH FOOTBALL WRITERS ASSOCIATION - RECENT AWARDS

	Player of the Year		Young Player of the Year		Manager of the Year	
1986/7	Brian McClair	Celtic			Jim McLean	Dundee United
1987/8	Paul McStay	Celtic			Billy McNeill	Celtic
1988/9	Richard Gough	Rangers			Graeme Souness	Rangers
1989/90	Alex McLeish	Aberdeen			Andy Roxburgh	Scotland
1990/1	Maurice Malpas	Dundee United			Alex Totten	St Johnstone
1991/2	Ally McCoist	Rangers			Walter Smith	Rangers
1992/3	Andy Goram	Rangers			Walter Smith	Rangers
1993/4	Mark Hateley	Rangers			Walter Smith	Rangers
1994/5	Brian Laudrup	Rangers			Jimmy Nicholl	Raith Rovers
1995/6	Paul Gascoigne	Rangers			Walter Smith	Rangers
1996/7	Brian Laudrup	Rangers			Walter Smith	Rangers
1997/8	Craig Burley	Celtic			Wim Jansen	Celtic
1998/9	Henrik Larsson	Celtic			Dick Advocaat	Rangers
1999/00	Barry Ferguson	Rangers			Dick Advocaat	Rangers
2000/1	Henrik Larsson	Celtic			Martin O'Neill	Celtic
2001/2	Paul Lambert	Celtic	James McFadden	Motherwell	Martin O'Neill	Celtic
2002/3	Barry Ferguson	Rangers	Zurab Khizanishvili	Dundee	Alex McLeish	Rangers
2003/4	Jackie McNamara	Celtic	Craig Gordon	Hearts	Martin O'Neill	Celtic
2004/5	John Hartson	Celtic	Derek Riordan	Hibernian	Tony Mowbray	Hibernian
2005/6	Craig Gordon	Hearts	Steven Naismith	Kilmarnock	Gordon Strachan	Celtic
2006/7	Shunsuke Nakamura	Celtic	Scott Brown	Hibernian	Gordon Strachan	Celtic
2007/8	Carlos Cuellar	Rangers	Steven Fletcher	Hibernian	Walter Smith	Rangers
2008/9	Gary Caldwell	Celtic	Steven Fletcher	Hibernian	Csaba Laszlo	Hearts
2009/10	David Weir	Rangers	Danny Wilson	Rangers	Walter Smith	Rangers
2010/1	Emilio Izaguirre	Celtic	David Goodwillie	Dundee United	Mixu Paatelainen	Kilmarnock
2011/2	Charlie Mulgrew	Celtic	James Forrest	Celtic	Neil Lennon	Celtic
2012/3	Leigh Griffiths	Hibernian	Stuart Armstrong	Dundee United	Neil Lennon	Celtic
2013/4	Kris Commons	Celtic	Stevie May	St Johnstone	Derek McInnes	Aberdeen
2014/5	Craig Gordon	Celtic	Ryan Christie	ICT	John Hughes	ICT
2015/6	Leigh Griffiths	Celtic	Kieran Tierney	Celtic	Jim McIntyre	Ross County
2016/7	Scott Sinclair	Celtic	Kieran Tierney	Celtic	Brendan Rodgers	Celtic

PFA SCOTLAND AWARDS 2016/17

Player of the Year	Scott Sinclair (Celtic)
Young Player of the Year	Kieran Tierney (Celtic)
Manager of the Year	Brendan Rodgers (Celtic)
Championship Player of the Year	John McGinn (Hibernian)
League One Player of the Year	Liam Buchanan (Livingston)
League Two Player of the Year	Shane Sutherland (Elgin City)
Goal of the Season	Moussa Dembele (Celtic)
Merit Award	Scottish Women's National team

Premiership Team of the Year	**Championship Team of the Year**	**League One Team of the Year**	**League Two Team of the Year**
Joe Lewis (Aberdeen)	Cammy Bell (Dundee United)	Neil Parry (Alloa)	Chris Smith (Stirling Albion)
Shay Logan (Aberdeen)	Nicky Devlin (Ayr United)	Ryan McGeever (Queen's Park)	Ricky Little (Arbroath)
Mikael Lustig (Celtic)	Darren McGregor (Hibernian)	Andy Graham (Alloa)	Thomas O'brien (Forfar Athletic)
Liam Lindsay (Partick Thistle)	Thomas O'Ware (Morton)	Jonathan Page (East Fife)	Colin Hamilton (Arbroath)
Kerian Tierney (Celtic)	Lewis Stevenson (Hibernian)	Calum Waters (Alloa)	Archie MacPhee (Elgin City)
Stuart Armstrong (Celtic)	Stephen Mallan (St Mirren)	Scott Pittman (Livingston)	Brian Cameron (Elgin City)
Scott Brown (Celtic)	John McGinn (Hibernian)	Shaun Byrne (Livingston)	Thomas Reilly (Elgin City)
Kenny McLean (Aberdeen)	Ross Forbes (Morton)	Jordan Kirkpatrick (Alloa)	Bobby Linn (Arbroath)
Jonny Hayes (Aberdeen)	Tony Andreu (Dundee United)	Andy Ryan (Airdrieonians)	Steven Doris (Arbroath)
Moussa Dembele (Celtic)	Stephen Dobbie (QOS)	Liam Buchanan (Livingston)	Shane Sutherland (Elgin City)
Scott Sinclair (Celtic)	Jason Cummings (Hibernian)	Cdanny Mullen (Livingston_	Peter MacDonald (Clyde)

PREMIERSHIP GOAL STATS 2016/17

TOP SCORERS

31	Leigh Griffiths	Celtic
21	Kane Hemmings	Dundee
20	Adam Rooney	Aberdeen
15	Louis Moult	Motherwell
14	Steven McLean	St Johnstone
14	Kris Doolan	Partick Thistle
14	Liam Boyce	Ross County
12	Juanma Delgado	Hearts
12	Billy McKay	Dundee United
11	Miles Storey	ICT
10	Niall McGinn	Aberdeen
10	Scott McDonald	Motherwell
10	Josh Magennis	Kilmarnock
9	Greg Stewart	Dundee
9	David Wotherspoon	St Johnstone
9	Rory Loy	Dundee
9	Osman Sow	Hearts

SHUT OUTS

16	Neil Alexander	Hearts
14	Craig Gordon	Celtic
10	Danny Ward	Aberdeen
10	Tomas Cerny	Partick Thistle
10	Michael McGivern	Hamilton
9	Owain Fon Williams	ICT
7	Jamie McDonald	Kilmarnock
7	Scott Bain	Dundee
6	Connor Reipley	Motherwell
5	Scott Fox	Ross County
5	Alan Mannus	St Johnstone

TOP ASSISTS

11	Jonny Hayes	Aberdeen
10	Niall McGinn	Aberdeen
9	Greg Stewart	Dundee
7	Tom Rogic	Celtic
7	Graham Cummins	St Johnstone
7	Ali Crawford	Hamilton Accies
6	Kallum Higginbotham	Kilmarnock
6	Mikael Lustig	Celtic
6	Callum McGregor	Celtic

PENALTY KICKS

Team	For	Home	Away	Scored	Missed	Saved
Hearts	12	8	4	10		2
Aberdeen	9	7	2	9		
Celtic	8	4	4	5	2	1
Dundee United	7	4	3	7		
ICT	7	5	2	7		
Hamilton	6	3	3	4		2
St johnstone	6	3	3	4	1	1
Ross County	5	3	2	5		
Motherwell	5	2	3	3		2
Kilmarnock	4	2	2	4		
Dundee	4	3	1	3		1
Partick Thistle	1	1		1		

SPFA PLAYER OF THE YEAR AWARDS

Season	Premier			Division One			Division Two			Division Three			Young Player		
1977/8	Johnstone	Derek	Rangers	Pirie	Billy	Dundee	Smith	David	Berwick Rangers				Payne	Graeme	Dundee United
1978/9	Hegarty	Paul	Dundee United	McLaughlin	Brian	Ayr United	Leonard	Mike	Dunfermline Athletic				Stewart	Raymond	Dundee United
1979/80	Provan	Davie	Celtic	Clark	Sandy	Airdrieonians	Leetion	Paul	Falkirk				MacDonald	John	Rangers
1980/1	McGhee	Mark	Aberdeen	Sinclair	Eric	Dundee	Robertson	Jimmy	Queen of the South				Nicholas	Charlie	Celtic
1981/2	Clark	Sandy	Airdrieonians	McLaughlin	Brian	Motherwell	Nevin	Pat	Clyde				McAvennie	Frank	St Mirren
1982/3	Nicholas	Charlie	Celtic	McCabe	Gerry	Clydebank	Colquhoun	John	Stirling Albion				McStay	Paul	Celtic
1983/4	Miller	Willie	Aberdeen	McCabe	Gerry	Clydebank	Liddle	Jim	Forfar Athletic				Robertson	John	Hearts
1984/5	Duffy	Jim	Morton	McCabe	Gerry	Clydebank	Slaven	Bernie	Albion Rovers				Levein	Craig	Hearts
1985/6	Gough	Richard	Dundee United	Brogan	John	Hamilton Accies	Smith	Mark	Queen's Park				Levein	Craig	Hearts
1986/7	McClair	Brian	Celtic	Holmes	Jim	Morton	Sludden	John	Ayr United				Fleck	Robert	Rangers
1987/8	McStay	Paul	Celtic	Taylor	Alex	Hamilton Accies	Templeton	Henry	Ayr United				Collins	John	Hibernian
1988/9	Snelders	Theo	Aberdeen	Jack	Ross	Dunfermline Athletic	Hunter	Paul	East Fife				McKinlay	Billy	Dundee United
1989/90	Bett	Jim	Aberdeen	Eadie	Ken	Clydebank	Watters	Willie	Kilmarnock				Crabbe	Scott	Hearts
1990/1	Elliot	Paul	Celtic	Stainrod	Simon	Falkirk	Todd	Kevin	Berwick Rangers				Jess	Eoin	Aberdeen
1991/2	McCoist	Ally	Rangers	Dalziel	Gordon	Raith Rovers	Thomson	Andy	Queen of the South				O'Donnell	Phil	Motherwell
1992/3	Goram	Andy	Rangers	Dalziel	Gordon	Raith Rovers	Ross	Sandy	Brechin City				Jess	Eoin	Aberdeen
1993/4	Hateley	Mark	Rangers	Cadette	Richard	Falkirk	Thomson	Andy	Queen of the South				O'Donnell	Phil	Motherwell
1994/5	Laudrup	Brian	Rangers	Crawford	Steven	Raith Rovers	McInnes	Derek	Morton	Bingham	David	Forfar Athletic	Miller	Charlie	Rangers
1995/6	Gascoigne	Paul	Rangers	O'Boyle	George	St Johnstone	McCormick	Steve	Stirling Albion	Young	Jason	Livingston	McNamara	Jackie	Celtic
1996/7	Di Canio	Paulo	Celtic	Grant	Roddy	St Johnstone	Ritchie	Paul	Hamilton Accies	Stewart	Iain	Inverness CT	Winters	Robbie	Dundee United
1997/8	McNamara	Jackie	Celtic	Grady	James	Dundee	Lovering	Paul	Clydebank	Irvine	Willie	Alloa	Naysmith	Gary	Hearts
1998/9	Larsson	Henrik	Celtic	Latapy	Russell	Hibernian	Bingham	David	Livingston	Tarrant	Neil	Ross County	Ferguson	Barry	Rangers
1999/00	Viduka	Mark	Celtic	Crawford	Steven	Dunfermline Athletic	Carrigan	Brian	Clyde	Milne	Steven	Forfar Athletic	Miller	Kenny	Hibernian
2000/1	Larsson	Henrik	Celtic	Bingham	David	Livingston	McLean	Scott	Partick Thistle	Hislop	Steven	East Stirlingshire	Petrov	Stilian	Celtic
2001/2	Amoruso	Lorenzo	Rangers	Coyle	Owen	Airdrieonians	O'Neil	John	Queen of the South	McManus	Paul	East Fife	McNaughton	Kevin	Aberdeen
2002/3	Ferguson	Barry	Rangers	Wyness	Dennis	Inverness CT	Templeman	Chris	Brechin City	Williams	Alex	Morton	McFadden	James	Motherwell
2003/4	Sutton	Chris	Celtic	Harty	Ian	Clyde	Tosh	Paul	Forfar Athletic	Moore	Michael	Stranraer	Pearson	Steven	Celtic
2004/5	*Ricksen	Fernand	Rangers	Latapy	Russell	Falkirk	Hampshire	Steven	Brechin City	Bingham	David	Gretna	Riordan	Derek	Hibernian
	*Hartson	John	Celtic												
2005/6	Maloney	Shaun	Celtic	Rankin	John	Ross County	Gray	James	Gretna	Paatelainen	Markus	Cowdenbeath	Maloney	Shaun	Celtic
2006/7	Nakamura	Shunsuk	Celtic	McMenamin	Colin	Gretna	Russell	Iain	Brechin City	Chaplain	Scott	Albion Rovers	Naismith	Steven	Kilmarnock
2007/8	McGeady	Aiden	Celtic	Dorrans	Graham	Livingston	Russell	Allan	Airdrie United	Smart	Jonathan	East Fife	McGeady	Aiden	Celtic
2008/9	Brown	Scott	Celtic	Griffiths	Leigh	Livingston	Prunty	Bryan	Ayr United	Barr	Bobby	Albion Rovers	McCarthy	James	Hamilton Accies
2009/10	Davis	Steven	Rangers	Rooney	Adam	Inverness CT	McAllister	Rory	Brechin City	Winters	Robbie	Livingston	Wilson	Danny	Rangers
2010/1	Izaguirre	Emilio	Celtic	Baird	John	Raith Rovers	McAllister	Rory	Brechin City	Swankie	Gavin	Arbroath	Goodwillie	David	Dundee United
2011/2	Mulgrew	Charlie	Celtic	El Alagui	Farid	Falkirk	Robertson	Jon	Cowdenbeath	May	Stevie	Alloa	Forrest	James	Celtic
2012/3	Higdon	Michael	Motherwell	Taylor	Lyle	Partick Thistle	Clark	Nicky	Queen of the South	Wallace	Lee	Rangers	Griffiths	Leigh	Hibernian
2013/4	Commons	Kris	Celtic	Hemmings	Kane	Cowdenbeath	Wallace	Lee	Rangers	McAllister	Rory	Peterhead	Robertson	Andrew	Dundee United
2014/5	Johansen	Stefan	Celtic	Allan	Scott	Hibernian	McManus	Declan	Morton	Linn	Bobby	Arbroath	Denayer	Jason	Celtic
2015/6	Griffiths	Leigh	Celtic	Wallace	Lee	Rangers	El Bakhtoui	Faisal	Dunfermline Athletic	Austin	Nathan	East Fife	Tierney	Kieran	Celtic
2016/7	Sinclair	Scott	Celtic	McGinn	John	Hibernian	Buchanan	Liam	Livingston	Sutherland	Shane	Elgin City	Tierney	Kieran	Celtic

* Joint Winners

PFA SCOTLAND DIVISION TEAM OF THE YEAR

PREMIERSHIP TEAM OF THE YEAR

2006/7

GK	Artur Boruc	Celtic
DF	Steven Whittaker	Hibernian
DF	Russell Anderson	Aberdeen
DF	Stephen McManus	Celtic
DF	Lee Naylor	Celtic
MF	Scott Brown	Hibernian
MF	Barry Ferguson	Rangers
MF	Shunsuke Nakamura	Celtic
FW	Steven Naismith	Kilmarnock
FW	Kris Boyd	Rangers
FW	Scott McDonald	Motherwell

2007/8

GK	Artur Boruc	Celtic
DF	Steven Whittaker	Rangers
DF	Carlos Cuéllar	Rangers
DF	Gary Caldwell	Celtic
DF	Saša Papac	Rangers
MF	Shunsuke Nakamura	Celtic
MF	Barry Ferguson	Rangers
MF	Barry Robson	Dundee United / Celtic
MF	Aiden McGeady	Celtic
FW	Jan Vennegoor of Hesselink	Celtic
FW	Scott McDonald	Celtic

2008/9

GK	Allan McGregor	Rangers
DF	Andreas Hinkel	Celtic
DF	Madjid Bougherra	Rangers
DF	Gary Caldwell	Celtic
DF	Saša Papac	Rangers
MF	Scott Brown	Celtic
MF	Steven Davis	Rangers
MF	Pedro Mendes	Rangers
MF	Aiden McGeady	Celtic
FW	Kenny Miller	Rangers
FW	Scott McDonald	Celtic

2009/10

GK	Allan McGregor	Rangers
DF	Steven Whittaker	Rangers
DF	David Weir	Rangers
DF	Andy Webster	Dundee United
DF	Saša Papac	Rangers
MF	Jim O'Brien	Motherwell
MF	Steven Davis	Rangers
MF	Liam Miller	Hibernian
MF	Lee McCulloch	Rangers
FW	Kenny Miller	Rangers
FW	Kris Boyd	Rangers

2010/11

GK	Allan McGregor	Rangers
DF	Mark Wilson	Celtic
DF	Marius Žaliukas	Heart of Midlothian
DF	Madjid Bougherra	Rangers
DF	Emilio Izaguirre	Celtic
MF	Steven Naismith	Rangers
MF	Beram Kayal	Celtic
MF	Alexei Eremenko	Kilmarnock
FW	David Goodwillie	Dundee United
FW	Conor Sammon	Kilmarnock
FW	Gary Hooper	Celtic

2011/12

GK	Darren Randolph	Motherwell
DF	Adam Matthews	Celtic
DF	Gavin Gunning	Dundee United
DF	Charlie Mulgrew	Celtic
DF	Paul Dixon	Dundee United
MF	James Forrest	Celtic
MF	Steven Davis	Rangers
MF	Gary Mackay-Steven	Dundee United
FW	Johnny Russell	Dundee United
FW	Jon Daly	Dundee United
FW	Gary Hooper	Celtic

2012/3

GK	Darren Randolph	Motherwell
DF	Adam Matthews	Celtic
DF	Shaun Hutchinson	Motherwell
DF	Kelvin Wilson	Celtic
DF	Charlie Mulgrew	Celtic
MF	Andrew Shinnie	Inverness Caledonian Thistle
MF	Victor Wanyama	Celtic
MF	Nicky Law	Motherwell
FW	Niall McGinn	Aberdeen
FW	Michael Higdon	Motherwell
FW	Leigh Griffiths	Hibernian

2013/4

GK	Fraser Forster	Celtic
DF	Graeme Shinnie	Inverness Caledonian Thistle
DF	Virgil van Dijk	Celtic
DF	Mark Reynolds	Aberdeen
DF	Andrew Robertson	Dundee United
MF	Stuart Armstrong	Dundee United
MF	Peter Pawlett	Aberdeen
MF	Kris Commons	Celtic
FW	Stevie May	St Johnstone
FW	Kris Boyd	Kilmarnock
FW	Nadir Ciftci	Dundee United

2014/5

GK	Craig Gordon	Celtic
DF	Shay Logan	Aberdeen
DF	Jason Denayer	Celtic
DF	Virgil van Dijk	Celtic
DF	Graeme Shinnie	Inverness Caledonian Thistle
MF	Stuart Armstrong	Dundee United / Celtic
MF	Scott Brown	Celtic
MF	Stefan Johansen	Celtic
FW	Nadir Çiftçi	Dundee United
FW	Adam Rooney	Aberdeen
FW	Greg Stewart	Dundee

2015/6

GK	Scott Bain	Dundee
DF	Shay Logan	Aberdeen
DF	Alim Öztürk	Heart of Midlothian
DF	Andrew Davies	Ross County
DF	Kieran Tierney	Celtic
MF	Jonny Hayes	Aberdeen
MF	Kenny McLean	Aberdeen
MF	Graeme Shinnie	Aberdeen
FW	Kane Hemmings	Dundee
FW	Leigh Griffiths	Celtic
FW	Greg Stewart	Dundee

2016/7

GK	Joe Lewis	Aberdeen
DF	Shay Logan	Aberdeen
DF	Mikael Lustig	Celtic
DF	Liam Lindsay	Partick Thistle
DF	Kieran Tierney	Celtic
MF	Stuart Armstrong	Celtic
MF	Scott Brown	Celtic
MF	Kenny McLean	Aberdeen
FW	Jonny Hayes	Aberdeen
FW	Moussa Dembélé	Celtic
FW	Scott Sinclair	Celtic

FIRST DIVISION / CHAMPIONSHIP

2011/2

GK	Michael McGovern	Falkirk
DF	Kieran Duffie	Falkirk
DF	Scott Boyd	Ross County
DF	Grant Munro	Ross County
DF	Aaron Taylor-Sinclair	Partick Thistle
MF	Nicky Riley	Dundee
MF	Mark Millar	Falkirk
MF	Ryan Conroy	Dundee
FW	Michael Gardyne	Ross County
FW	Farid El Alagui	Falkirk
FW	Colin McMenamin	Ross County

2012/3

GK	Scott Fox	Partick Thistle
DF	Stephen O'Donnell	Partick Thistle
DF	Jordan McMillan	Partick Thistle
DF	Callum Morris	Dunfermline Athletic
DF	Aaron Taylor-Sinclair	Partick Thistle
MF	Stefan Scougall	Livingston
MF	Michael Tidser	Greenock Morton
MF	Stuart Bannigan	Partick Thistle
FW	Brian Graham	Raith Rovers
FW	Lyle Taylor	Falkirk
FW	Chris Erskine	Partick Thistle

2013/4

GK	Michael McGovern	Falkirk
DF	Paul McGinn	Dumbarton
DF	Will Vaulks	Falkirk
DF	Stephen Kingsley	Falkirk
DF	Ziggy Gordon	Hamilton Academical
MF	Tony Andreu	Hamilton Academical
MF	Mark Millar	Falkirk
MF	Ali Crawford	Hamilton Academical
FW	Rory Loy	Falkirk
FW	Kane Hemmings	Cowdenbeath
FW	Peter MacDonald	Dundee

2014/5

GK	Neil Alexander	Heart of Midlothian
DF	David Gray	Hibernian
DF	Alim Öztürk	Heart of Midlothian
DF	Danny Wilson	Heart of Midlothian
DF	Lewis Stevenson	Hibernian
MF	Scott Allan	Hibernian
MF	Morgaro Gomis	Heart of Midlothian
MF	Jamie Walker	Heart of Midlothian
FW	Gavin Reilly	Queen of the South
FW	Rory Loy	Falkirk
FW	Osman Sow	Heart of Midlothian

2015/6

GK	Danny Rogers	Falkirk
DF	James Tavernier	Rangers
DF	Darren McGregor	Hibernian
DF	Peter Grant	Falkirk
DF	Lee Wallace	Rangers
MF	Jason Holt	Rangers
MF	John McGinn	Hibernian
MF	Barrie McKay	Rangers
FW	John Baird	Falkirk
FW	Martyn Waghorn	Rangers
FW	Jason Cummings	Hibernian

2016/7

GK	Cammy Bell	Dundee United
DF	Nicky Devlin	Ayr United
DF	Darren McGregor	Hibernian
DF	Thomas O'Ware	Greenock Morton
DF	Lewis Stevenson	Hibernian
MF	Stevie Mallan	St Mirren
MF	John McGinn	Hibernian
MF	Ross Forbes	Greenock Morton
FW	Tony Andreu	Dundee United
FW	Stephen Dobbie	Queen of the South
FW	Jason Cummings	Hibernian

SECOND DIVISION / LEAGUE ONE

2011/2

GK	Stephen Grindlay	Dumbarton
DF	Mark Baxter	Arbroath
DF	Joe Mbu	Cowdenbeath
DF	John Armstrong	Cowdenbeath
DF	Kenny Adamson	Cowdenbeath
MF	Josh Falkingham	Arbroath
MF	Jon Robertson	Cowdenbeath
MF	Scott Agnew	Dumbarton
FW	Ryan Donnelly	Airdrie United
FW	Steven Doris	Arbroath
FW	Ryan Wallace	East Fife

2012/3

GK	Lee Robinson	Queen of the South
DF	Chris Mitchell	Queen of the South
DF	Mark Durnan	Queen of the South
DF	Ben Gordon	Alloa Athletic
DF	Chris Higgins	Queen of the South
MF	Alan Trouten	Brechin City
MF	Ryan McCord	Alloa Athletic
MF	Daniel Carmichael	Queen of the South
FW	Andy Jackson	Brechin City
FW	Nicky Clark	Queen of the South
FW	Steven Doris	Arbroath

2013/4

GK	Cammy Bell	Rangers
DF	Ryan Williamson	Dunfermline Athletic
DF	Callum Morris	Dunfermline Athletic
DF	Lee McCulloch	Rangers
DF	Lee Wallace	Rangers
MF	Andy Stirling	Stranraer
MF	Andy Geggan	Dunfermline Athletic
MF	Nicky Law	Rangers
FW	Michael Moffat	Ayr United
FW	Jon Daly	Rangers
FW	Gavin Swankie	Forfar Athletic

2014/5

GK	Rab Douglas	Forfar Athletic
DF	Mark Russell	Greenock Morton
DF	Stuart Malcolm	Forfar Athletic
DF	Frank McKeown	Stranraer
DF	Paddy Boyle	Airdrieonians
MF	Alan Trouten	Brechin City
MF	Jamie Stevenson	Peterhead
MF	Willie Gibson	Stranraer
FW	Gavin Swankie	Forfar Athletic
FW	Declan McManus	Greenock Morton
FW	Bobby Barr	Brechin City

2015/6

GK	Graeme Smith	Peterhead
DF	Nicky Devlin	Ayr United
DF	Michael Dunlop	Albion Rovers
DF	Ben Richards-Everton	Dunfermline Athletic
DF	Paddy Boyle	Ayr United
MF	Liam Watt	Airdrieonians
MF	Andy Geggan	Dunfermline Athletic
MF	Joe Cardle	Dunfermline Athletic
FW	Greig Spence	Cowdenbeath
FW	Rory McAllister	Peterhead
FW	Faissal El Bakhtaoui	Dunfermline Athletic

2016/7

GK	Neil Parry	Alloa Athletic
DF	Ryan McGeever	Queen's Park
DF	Andy Graham	Alloa Athletic
DF	Jonathan Page	East Fife
DF	Calum Waters	Alloa Athletic
MF	Scott Pittman	Livingston
MF	Shaun Byrne	Livingston
MF	Jordan Kirkpatrick	Alloa Athletic
FW	Andy Ryan	Airdrieonians
FW	Liam Buchanan	Livingston
FW	Danny Mullen	Livingston

THIRD DIVISION / LEAGUE TWO

2011/2		
GK	Scott Bain	Alloa Athletic
DF	Michael Doyle	Alloa Athletic
DF	Ricky Little	Queen's Park
DF	Ryan Harding	Alloa Athletic
DF	Daryll Meggatt	Queen's Park
MF	Ryan McCord	Alloa Athletic
MF	Stephen Stirling	Stranraer
MF	Daniel Moore	Elgin City
FW	Jamie Longworth	Queen's Park
FW	Stevie May	Alloa Athletic
FW	Kevin Cawley	Alloa Athletic

2012/3		
GK	Jamie Barclay	Clyde
DF	Stephen McNally	Montrose
DF	Ricky Little	Queen's Park
DF	Lee McCulloch	Rangers
DF	Lee Wallace	Rangers
MF	Lee Currie	Berwick Rangers
MF	David Anderson	Queen's Park
MF	Daniel Moore	Elgin City
FW	Andrew Little	Rangers
FW	Rory McAllister	Peterhead
FW	David Templeton	Rangers

2013/4		
GK	Graeme Smith	Peterhead
DF	Devon Jacobs	Berwick Rangers
DF	Steven Noble	Peterhead
DF	Michael Dunlop	Albion Rovers
DF	Kieran MacDonald	Clyde
MF	Blair Spittal	Queen's Park
MF	David Anderson	Queen's Park
MF	Lee Currie	Berwick Rangers
FW	Kenny MacKay	Annan Athletic
FW	Rory McAllister	Peterhead
FW	Andy Rodgers	Peterhead

2014/5		
GK	Neil Parry	Albion Rovers
DF	Shaun Rooney	Queen's Park
DF	Michael Dunlop	Albion Rovers
DF	Marvin Andrews	Montrose
DF	Ross Dunlop	Albion Rovers
MF	Bobby Linn	Arbroath
MF	Darren Miller	Queen's Park
MF	Paul Woods	Queen's Park
FW	Shane Sutherland	Elgin City
FW	Peter Weatherson	Annan Athletic
FW	Simon Murray	Arbroath

2015/6		
GK	Chris Smith	Stirling Albion
DF	Ricky Little	Arbroath
DF	Jonathan Page	East Fife
DF	Gary Naysmith	East Fife
DF	Scott Linton	Clyde
MF	Matty Flynn	Annan Athletic
MF	Kyle Wilkie	East Fife
MF	Bobby Linn	Arbroath
FW	Peter Weatherson	Annan Athletic
FW	Nathan Austin	East Fife
FW	Craig Gunn	Elgin City

2016/7		
GK	Chris Smith	Stirling Albion
DF	Ricky Little	Arbroath
DF	Thomas O'Brien	Forfar Athletic
DF	Colin Hamilton	Arbroath
DF	Archie MacPhee	Elgin City
MF	Brian Cameron	Elgin City
MF	Thomas Reilly	Elgin City
MF	Bobby Linn	Arbroath
FW	Steven Doris	Arbroath
FW	Shane Sutherland	Elgin City
FW	Peter MacDonald	Clyde

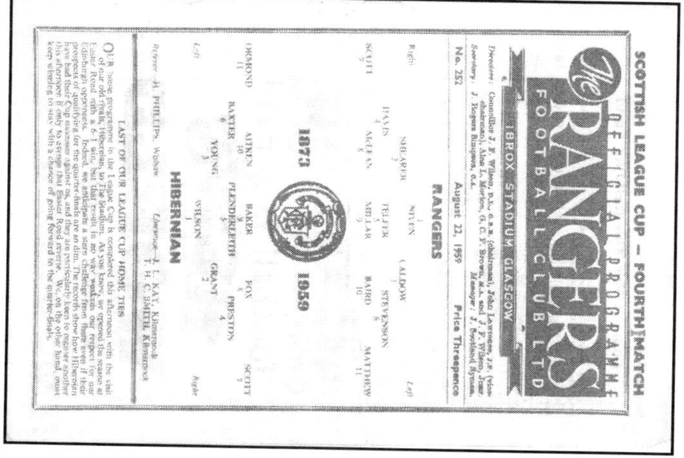

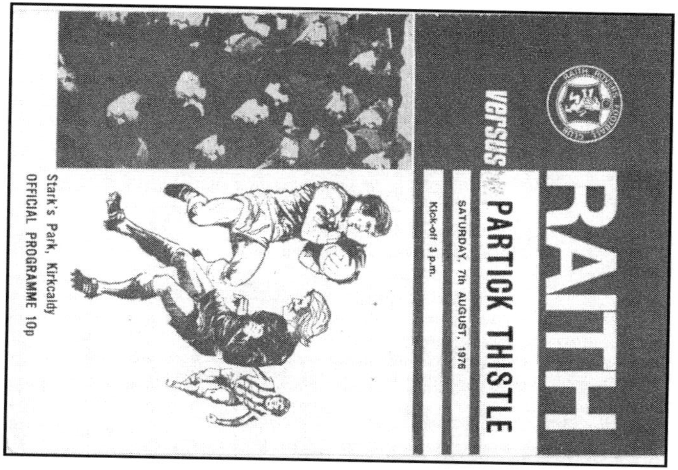
RAITH
versus
PARTICK THISTLE
SATURDAY, 7th AUGUST, 1976
Kick-off 3 p.m.
Stark's Park, Kirkcaldy
OFFICIAL PROGRAMME 10p

SPFL CLUB TOP LEAGUE SCORERS 1975/6-Date

ABERDEEN

Season	Player	Goals
1975/6	Jocky Scott	14
1976/7	Joe Harper	18
1977/8	Joe Harper	17
1978/9	Joe Harper	19
1979/80	Steve Archibald / Drew Jarvie	12
1980/1	Mark McGhee	18
1981/2	John Hewitt	11
1982/3	Mark McGhee	17
1983/4	Mark McGhee / Gordon Strachan	13
1984/5	Frank McDougall	22
1985/6	Frank McDougall	14
1986/7	Billy Stark	12
1987/8	Jim Bett	10
1988/9	Charlie Nicholas	16
1989/90	Charlie Nicholas	11
1990/1	Hans Gillhaus	14
1991/2	Eoin Jess	12
1992/3	Duncan Shearer	22
1993/4	Duncan Shearer	17
1994/5	Billy Dodds	15
1995/6	Scott Booth / Joe Miller	9
1996/7	Billy Dodds	15
1997/8	Billy Dodds	10
1998/9	Eoin Jess	14
1999/00	Arild Stavrum	9
2000/1	Arild Stavrum	17
2001/2	Robbie Winters	13
2002/3	Paul Sheerin	8
2003/4	Scott Booth	8
2004/5	Darren Mackie	12
2005/6	Stephen Lovell / Jamie Smith	8
2006/7	Darren Mackie	13
2007/8	Lee Miller	12
2008/9	Lee Miller	10
2009/10	Steven McLean	5
2010/1	Scott Vernon	10
2011/2	Scott Vernon	11
2012/3	Niall McGinn	20
2013/4	Niall McGinn	13
2014/5	Adam Rooney	18
2015/6	Adam Rooney	20

AIRDRIE

Season	Player	Goals
1975/6	Derek Whiteford	8
1976/7	Derek Whiteford	15
1977/8	Joe Cairney	22
1978/9	Sandy Clark	23
1979/80	Sandy Clark	22
1980/1	Sandy Clark	10
1981/2	Sandy Clark	15
1982/3	Blair Millar	12
1983/4	John Flood	11
1984/5	David McCabe	21
1985/6	John Flood	11
1986/7	David McCabe	13
1987/8	David McCabe	20
1988/9	Kenny MacDonald	22
1989/90	Owen Coyle	10
1990/1	Owen Coyle	20
1991/2	Owen Coyle	11
1992/3	Owen Coyle	9
1993/4	David Kirkwood	10
1994/5	Andy Smith	12
1995/6	Jim McIntyre	9
1996/7	Paddy Connolly / Steve Cooper / Brian McPhee	8
1997/8	Brian McPhee	12
1998/9	Steve Cooper	8
1999/00	Alex Neil / Neil Thompson	5
2000/1	Davide Fernandez	7
2001/2	Owen Coyle	23
2002/3		
2003/4		
2004/5		
2005/6		
2006/7		
2007/8		
2008/9		
2009/10		
2010/1		
2011/2		
2012/3		
2013/4		
2014/5		
2015/6		

ALBION ROVERS

Season	Player	Goals
1975/6	John Brogan	7
1976/7	Donnie McLean	20
1977/8	Donnie McLean	23
1978/9	Bruce Cleland	24
1979/80	Peter Houston	18
1980/1	Ian Campbell	12
1981/2	Steve Evans	16
1982/3	Steve Evans	12
1983/4	Tommy McGorm	11
1984/5	Bernie Slaven	27
1985/6	Sammy Conn / Vic Kasule / Alan Rodgers	6
1986/7	Chris Wilson	11
1987/8	Ally Graham	10
1988/9	Jim Chapman	15
1989/90	Mike McAnenay	10
1990/1	Mike McAnenay	12
1991/2	Gerry McCoy	11
1992/3	Martin Scott	16
1993/4	Martin Scott	17
1994/5	Martin Scott	7
1995/6	Gordon Young	12
1996/7	Willie Watters	11
1997/8	Willie Watters	13
1998/9	David Lorimer	10
1999/00	Ian Diack	7
2000/1	Mark Booth	6
2001/2	Colin McLean	11
2002/3	Jim Mercer	10
2003/4	Paul McManus	18
2004/5	John Bradford	7
2005/6	Scott Chaplain	8
2006/7	Scott Chaplain	18
2007/8	John Gemmell	11
2008/9	Bobby Barr	11
2009/10	Marc McCusker	6
2010/1	Robert Love	10
2011/2	John Gemmell	9
2012/3	David Crawford	10
2013/4	Scott Chaplain	9
2014/5	Mark McGuigan	11
2015/6	Ally Love	13

ALLOA

Season	Player	Goals
1975/6	Billy Morrison	
1976/7	Gordon Forrest	
1977/8	Donnie Wilson	
1978/9	Willie Irvine	
1979/80	Colin McIntosh	
1980/1	Alan Holt	
1981/2	Scott Murray	
1982/3	Lennie McComb	
1983/4	David Lloyd	
1984/5	David Lloyd	
1985/6	Mike Jamieson / Stuart Sorbie	
1986/7	Stuart Sorbie	
1987/8	Paul Rutherford	
1988/9	Charlie Lytwyn	
1989/90	Peter Lamont	
1990/1	John Irvine	
1991/2	Mike Hendry	
1992/3	Barrie Moffat	
1993/4	Willie Newbigging	
1994/5	Barrie Moffat	
1995/6	Barrie Moffat / Steve Rixon	
1996/7	Willie Irvine	
1997/8	Willie Irvine	
1998/9	Martin Cameron / Willie Irvi	
1999/00	Martin Cameron	
2000/1	Ross Hamilton	
2001/2	Gareth Hutchison	
2002/3	Robert Sloan	
2003/4	Ross Hamilton	
2004/5	Andy Brown	
2005/6	Jamie Stevenson	
2006/7	Graeme Brown	
2007/8	Graeme Brown	
2008/9	Andy Scott	
2009/10	Steven Noble	
2010/1	Brian Prunty	
2011/2	Stevie May	
2012/3	Kevin Cawley	
2013/4	Kevin Cawley	
2014/5	Liam Buchanan	
2015/6	Michael Duffy / Ian Flanniga	

ANNAN ATHLETIC

Season	Player	Goals
1975/6		
1976/7		
1977/8		
1978/9		
1979/80		
1980/1		
1981/2		
1982/3		
1983/4		
1984/5		
1985/6		
1986/7		
1987/8		
1988/9		
1989/90		
1990/1		
1991/2		
1992/3		
1993/4		
1994/5		
1995/6		
1996/7		
1997/8		
1998/9		
1999/00		
2000/1		
2001/2		
2002/3		
2003/4		
2004/5		
2005/6		
2006/7		
2007/8		
2008/9	Michael Jack	15
2009/10	Graham Bell	9
2010/1	Ian Harty	14
2011/2	Scott Gibson / Aaron Juirhead / Sean O'Connor	7
2012/3	Alistair Love	12
2013/4	Kenny Mackay	13
2014/5	Peter Weatherson	22
2015/6	Peter Weatherson	16

ARBROATH

Season	Player	Goals
1975/6	Jimmy Bone	13
1976/7	Jimmy Bone	15
1977/8	John Fletcher	9
1978/9	Steve Mylles / Tommy Yule	9
1979/80	Tommy Yule	10
1980/1	Ian Harley	15
1981/2	Dougie Robb	21
1982/3	Billy Steele	15
1983/4	Ian Harley	18
1984/5	Rod Brown	6
1985/6	Mark McWalter	14
1986/7	Jim Fotheringham	14
1987/8	Alan McKenna	13
1988/9	Jim Fotheringham	11
1989/90	Jim Marshall	12
1990/1	Martin Bennett / Stuart Sorbie	10
1991/2	Stuart Sorbie	12
1992/3	Stuart Sorbie	19
1993/4	Danny Diver	10
1994/5	Steven Tosh	11
1995/6	Stephen McCormick / David Pew	8
1996/7	Brian Grant	5
1997/8	Billy Spence	16
1998/9	Colin McGlashan	12
1999/00	Colin McGlashan	16
2000/1	Steven Mallan	10
2001/2	Graeme Bayne / Colin McGlashan	6
2002/3	Murray McDowell / John Cusick	4
2003/4	John McGlashan	10
2004/5	Greg Henslee	11
2005/6	Jay Stein	9
2006/7	Willie Martin	9
2007/8	Barry Scott	11
2008/9	Barry Scott / Barry Sellars	6
2009/10	Stephen Hislop	8
2010/1	Gavin Swankie	22
2011/2	Steven Doris	21
2012/3	Steven Doris	11
2013/4	Alan Cook	12
2014/5	Simon Murray	19
2015/6	Bobby Linn	11

AYR UNITED

Season	Player	Goals
1975/6	Johnny Graham	16
1976/7	Walker McCall	16
1977/8	Walker McCall	12
1978/9	Brian McLaughlin	19
1979/80	Derek Frye	16
1980/1	Derek Frye / Eric Morris	10
1981/2	Derek Frye	13
1982/3	Mike Larnach / Derek Frye / Alan McInally	7
1983/4	Alan McInally	15
1984/5	Gerry Collins	8
1985/6	David Irons	6
1986/7	John Sludden	26
1987/8	John Sludden	31
1988/9	Henry Templeton	17
1989/90	Tommy Bryce	10
1990/1	Tommy Bryce	11
1991/2	Ally Graham	14
1992/3	Ally Graham	9
1993/4	Sammy McGivern	12
1994/5	Justin Jackson	4
1995/6	Brian Bilsland / Isaac English	5
1996/7	Stevn J Kerrigan	14
1997/8	Laurent D'Jaffo	10
1998/9	Greg Hurst	18
1999/00	Greg Hurst	14
2000/1	Eddie Annand	18
2001/2	Eddie Annand	14
2002/3	Stuart Kean	7
2003/4	Stuart Kean	9
2004/5	Stuart Kean	10
2005/6	Jerome Vareille	13
2006/7	Gareth Wardlaw	7
2007/8	Alex Williams	16
2008/9	Brian Prunty	15
2009/10	Mark Roberts	8
2010/1	Mark Roberts	21
2011/2	Michael Moffat / Mark Roberts	8
2012/3	Michael Moffat	16
2013/4	Michael Moffat	26
2014/5	Alan Forrest	9
2015/6	Craig Moore	14

BERWICK RANGERS

Season	Player	Goals
1975/6	Ian Smith	
1976/7	Billy Laing	
1977/8	Eric Tait / Billy Laing	
1978/9	Jim Morton	
1979/80	Eric Tait	
1980/1	Eric Tait	
1981/2	Mickey Lawson	
1982/3	Stuart Romaines / Ian Cashmore	
1983/4	Peter Davidson	
1984/5	Peter Davidson	
1985/6	John Sokuluk	
1986/7	Eric Tait	
1987/8	Mark Cameron / Hugh Douglas / Tom Gra	
1988/9	John Hughes	
1989/90	Scott Sloan	
1990/1	Kevin Todd	
1991/2	Steve Bickmore	
1992/3	David Scott	
1993/4	Willie Irvine	
1994/5	Warren Hawke	
1995/6	Willie Irvine	
1996/7	Paul Forrester	
1997/8	Paul Forrester	
1998/9	Moray Ieask	
1999/00	Marc Anthony	
2000/1	Gary Wood	
2001/2	Gary Wood	
2002/3	Alex Burke / Gary Wood	
2003/4	Gareth Hutchison	
2004/5	Gareth Hutchison /Darren Smith	
2005/6	Kevin Haynes	
2006/7	Gary Wood	
2007/8	Ian Diack	
2008/9	Darren Gribben	
2009/10	Damon Gray	
2010/1	Darren Gribben	
2011/2	Darren Gribben	
2012/3	Darren Lavery	
2013/4	Lee Currie	
2014/5	Darren Lavery	
2015/6	Blair henderson	

BRECHIN CITY			CELTIC			CLYDE			CLYDEBANK		
1975/6	Albert Rice	7	1975/6	Kenny Dalglish	24	1975/6	Neil Hood	14	1975/6	Davie Cooper	13
1976/7	Ronnie Robb	16	1976/7	Ronnie Glavin	19	1976/7	Neil Hood	16	1976/7	Joe McCallan	27
1977/8	Jim Morton	10	1977/8	Johannes Edvaldsson	10	1977/8	Neil Hood	21	1977/8	John McCormack	5
1978/9	Ian Campbell	16	1978/9	Andy Lynch / Tom McAdam	7	1978/9	Joe Ward	10	1978/9	Blair Miller	28
1979/80	Ian Campbell	25	1979/80	George McCluskey	10	1979/80	Neil Hood	11	1979/80	Blair Miller	17
1980/1	Ian Campbell	11	1980/1	Frank McGarvey	23	1980/1	Danny Masterton	19	1980/1	Blair Miller	18
1981/2	Ian Campbell	16	1981/2	George McCluskey	21	1981/2	Danny Masterton	23	1981/2	Blair Miller	20
1982/3	Ian Campbell	24	1982/3	Charlie Nicholas	29	1982/3	Danny Masterton	14	1982/3	Bobby Williamson	21
1983/4	Ian Campbell	19	1983/4	Brian McClair	23	1983/4	Derek Frye	17	1983/4	Tommy Coyne	10
1984/5	Ken Eadie	17	1984/5	Brian McClair	19	1984/5	Derek Frye	19	1984/5	Michael Conroy	11
1985/6	Ken Eadie	22	1985/6	Brian McClair	22	1985/6	Derek Frye	12	1985/6	Michael Conroy / David Lloyd	7
1986/7	Charlie Adam	12	1986/7	Brian McClair	35	1986/7	Jim Murphy	12	1986/7	Michael Conroy / Stuart Gordon	9
1987/8	Graham Buckley	15	1987/8	Andy Walker	26	1987/8	Colin McGlashan	16	1987/8	Michael Conroy	11
1988/9	Charlie Adam	15	1988/9	Mark McGhee	16	1988/9	Colin McGlashan	16	1988/9	Ken Eadie	21
1989/90	Gordon Lees	12	1989/90	Dariusz Dziekanowski	8	1989/90	Colin McGlashan	11	1989/90	Ken Eadie	21
1990/1	Paul Ritchie	14	1990/1	Tommy Coyne	18	1990/1	Steve Mallan	8	1990/1	Ken Eadie	29
1991/2	Paul Ritchie	12	1991/2	Charlie Nicholas	21	1991/2	David Thompson	16	1991/2	Ken Eadie	22
1992/3	Sandy Ross	23	1992/3	Andy Payton	13	1992/3	Frank McGarvey	16	1992/3	Craig Flannigan	21
1993/4	Marc Miller	10	1993/4	Pat McGinlay	10	1993/4	Ian McConnell / Gordon Parks	5	1993/4	Ken Eadie / Craig Flannigan	11
1994/5	Gavin Price / Ray Smith	6	1994/5	John Collins	8	1994/5	John Dickson	10	1994/5	Ken Eadie	9
1995/6	Sandy Ross	8	1995/6	Pierre Van Hooijdonk	26	1995/6	Eddie Annand	21	1995/6	James Grady	11
1996/7	Stephen P Kerrigan	7	1996/7	Jorge Cadete	25	1996/7	Eddie Annand	21	1996/7	James Grady	8
1997/8	Craig Feroz	7	1997/8	Henrik Larsson	16	1997/8	Paul Brownlie	8	1997/8	Colin McDonald	13
1998/9	John Dickson	15	1998/9	Henrik Larsson	29	1998/9	Steve Convery	12	1998/9	Colin McDonald	9
1999/00	Ben Honeyman	11	1999/00	Mark Viduka	25	1999/00	Brian Carrigan	18	1999/00	Ian Cameron	5
2000/1	Roddy Grant	22	2000/1	Henrik Larsson	35	2000/1	Andrew Kane	7	2000/1	Alex Burke	8
2001/2	Chris Templeman	15	2001/2	Henrik Larsson	29	2001/2	Leigh Hinds	11	2001/2	Alex Burke	9
2002/3	Chris Templeman	21	2002/3	Henrik Larsson	28	2002/3	Pat Keogh	12	2002/3	Jerome Vareille	17
2003/4	Chris Templeman	5	2003/4	Henrik Larsson	30	2003/4	Ian Harty	25	2003/4	Owen Coyle / Alan Gow	12
2004/5	Steve Hampshire	17	2004/5	John Hartson	23	2004/5	Ian Harty	15	2004/5	Owen Coyle	14
2005/6	Kevin Byers	6	2005/6	John Hartson	18	2005/6	Alex Williams	13	2005/6	Brian Prunty	15
2006/7	Ian Russell	21	2006/7	Jan Vennegoor of Hesselink	13	2006/7	Gary Arbuckle	11	2006/7	Gary Twigg	10
2007/8	Charlie King	10	2007/8	Scott McDonald	25	2007/8	Pat Clarke	6	2007/8	Allan Russell	19
2008/9	Gary Twigg	12	2008/9	Scott McDonald	16	2008/9	Pat Clarke	11	2008/9	Simon Lynch	10
2009/10	Rory McAllister	21	2009/10	Robbie Keane	12	2009/10	Willie Sawyers	10	2009/10	John Baird	11
2010/1	Rory McAllister	19	2010/1	Gary Hooper	20	2010/1	Marc McCusker	11	2010/1	Scott Gemmill	9
2011/2	Paul McManus	15	2011/2	Gary Hooper	24	2011/2	John Neill	7	2011/2	Ryan Donnelly	21
2012/3	Alan Trouten	17	2012/3	Gary Hooper	19	2012/3	John Sweeney / Kevin Watt	9	2012/3	John Boyle	10
2013/4	Andy Jackson	12	2013/4	Kris Commons	27	2013/4	Stefan McCluskey	11	2013/4	Jim Lister	9
2014/5	Alan Trouten	15	2014/5	Leigh Griffiths	14	2014/5	Scott McManus	7	2014/5	Brian Prunty	14
2015/6	Robbie Thomson	15	2015/6	Leigh Griffiths	31	2015/6	Sean Higgins / Scott Linton	9	2015/6	Jim Lister	8

COWDENBEATH			DUMBARTON			DUNDEE			DUNDEE UNITED		
1975/6	John Murphy	10	1975/6	John Bourke	17	1975/6	Gordon Wallace	12	1975/6	Tom McAdam	12
1976/7	George Hunter	17	1976/7	John Bourke	19	1976/7	Billy Pirie	36	1976/7	Paul Sturrock	15
1977/8	Billy Steele	20	1977/8	Derek Whiteford / John Whiteford	15	1977/8	Billy Pirie	35	1977/8	George Fleming	9
1978/9	Billy Steele	20	1978/9	Raymond Blair	9	1978/9	Billy Pirie	16	1978/9	David Dodds	10
1979/80	Billy Steele	13	1979/80	Graeme Sharp	16	1979/80	Ian Redford	9	1979/80	Willie Pettigrew	14
1980/1	Jim Liddle	18	1980/1	Brian Gallagher	14	1980/1	Eric Sinclair	19	1980/1	David Dodds	14
1981/2	Gordon Forrest	16	1981/2	Raymond Blair	9	1981/2	Ian Ferguson	12	1981/2	Paul Sturrock	15
1982/3	Willie Gibson	13	1982/3	Raymond Blair	10	1982/3	Ian Ferguson	9	1982/3	David Dodds	22
1983/4	Ian Paterson	7	1983/4	Joe Coyle	15	1983/4	Walker McCall	13	1983/4	David Dodds	15
1984/5	Kenny Ward	16	1984/5	Joe Coyle	7	1984/5	Ray Stephen	8	1984/5	Paul Sturrock	14
1985/6	Colin McGlashan	15	1985/6	Gerry McCoy	13	1985/6	Ray Stephen	14	1985/6	David Dodds	12
1986/7	Billy Blackie / Roddy Grant	14	1986/7	Gerry McCoy	21	1986/7	Graham Harvey	12	1986/7	Ian Ferguson	16
1987/8	Roddy Grant	11	1987/8	Owen Coyle	14	1987/8	Tommy Coyne	33	1987/8	Ian Ferguson	11
1988/9	Alan McGonnigal	8	1988/9	Stuart MacIver	13	1988/9	Tommy Coyne	9	1988/9	Mixu Paatelainen	10
1989/90	Sandy Ross	16	1989/90	Charlie Gibson	20	1989/90	Billy Dodds	13	1989/90	Darren Jackson / Mixu Paatelainen	7
1990/1	Alan McKenzie	15	1990/1	John McQuade	14	1990/1	Keith Wright	15	1990/1	Darren Jackson	12
1991/2	Graham Buckley	21	1991/2	Jimmy Gilmour	19	1991/2	Billy Dodds	19	1991/2	Duncan Ferguson	15
1992/3	Willie Callaghan	9	1992/3	John McQuade	15	1992/3	Billy Dodds	16	1992/3	Paddy Connolly	16
1993/4	Willie Callaghan	11	1993/4	Charlie Gibson	13	1993/4	Dragutin Ristic / George Haw	6	1993/4	Craig Brewster	16
1994/5	Mark Yardley	23	1994/5	Martin Mooney	17	1994/5	George Shaw / Gerry Britton / Jim Hamilton	12	1994/5	Craig Brewster	7
1995/6	David Scott	11	1995/6	Martin Mooney	5	1995/6	Jim Hamilton	14	1995/6	Craig Brewster / Gary McSwegan	17
1996/7	Gary Wood	6	1996/7	Hugh Ward	7	1996/7	Jerry O'Driscoll	10	1996/7	Kjell Olofsson	12
1997/8	Willie Stewart	6	1997/8	Colin McKinnon	10	1997/8	James Grady	15	1997/8	Kjell Olofsson	18
1998/9	Willie Stewart	7	1998/9	Paddy Flannery	17	1998/9	Eddie Annand	9	1998/9	Billy Dodds	17
1999/00	Murray McDowell	13	1999/00	Paddy Flannery	14	1999/00	Willie Falconer	13	1999/00	Billy Dodds	9
2000/1	Murray McDowell	10	2000/1	Paddy Flannery	17	2000/1	Juan Sara	14	2000/1	Derek Lilley	6
2001/2	Graeme Brown	17	2001/2	Paddy Flannery	18	2001/2	Juan Sara	11	2001/2	Derek Lilley / Jim McIntyre / Stephen Thomsnon	6
2002/3	Graeme Brown / Kevin Gordon	10	2002/3	Paddy Flannery / Gary McCutcheon	8	2002/3	Stephen Lovell	13	2002/3	Jim McIntyre	9
2003/4	Dene Shields	12	2003/4	Ian Russell	10	2003/4	Nacho Novo	20	2003/4	Billy Dodds / Jim McIntyre	10
2004/5	Darren Gribben	12	2004/5	Ian Russell	11	2004/5	Stephen Lovell	12	2004/5	Jim McIntyre	11
2005/6	Liam Buchanan	17	2005/6	Andy Rodgers	12	2005/6	Simon Lynch	12	2005/6	Lee Miller	8
2006/7	Liam Buchanan	20	2006/7	Stephen Dobbie	10	2006/7	Derek Lyle	12	2006/7	Barry Robson	11
2007/8	Pat Clarke	6	2007/8	Fergus Tiernan	6	2007/8	Kevin McDonald	9	2007/8	Noel Hunt	13
2008/9	John Gemmell	12	2008/9	Ross Clark	14	2008/9	Mickael Antoine-Curier	14	2008/9	Fran Sandaza	10
2009/10	Gareth Wardlaw	16	2009/10	Scott Chaplain	10	2009/10	Gary Harkins	14	2009/10	John Daly	13
2010/1	Greg Stewart	9	2010/1	Jon McShane	13	2010/1	Stephen Higgins	9	2010/1	David Goodwillie	17
2011/2	Marc McKenzie	18	2011/2	Bryan Prunty	14	2011/2	Ryan Conroy / Steven Milne	11	2011/2	John Daly	19
2012/3	Jamie Stevenson	8	2012/3	Jim Lister	12	2012/3	Ryan Conroy	6	2012/3	Jonny Russell	13
2013/4	Kane Hemmings	18	2013/4	Chris Kane / Mitch Megginson	1o	2013/4	Peter MacDonald	17	2013/4	Nadir Ciftci	11
2014/5	Kudus Oyenuga	6	2014/5	Gary Fleming	6	2014/5	Greg Stewart	13	2014/5	Nadir Ciftci	14
2015/6	Greg Spence	17	2015/6	Gary Fleming / Christian Nade	7	2015/6	Kane Hemmings	21	2015/6	Billy McKay	12

DUNFERMLINE ATH

Season	Top scorer	Goals
1975/6	Ken Mackie	10
1976/7	Alan Evans	13
1977/8	Bobby Morrison	11
1978/9	Mike Leonard	20
1979/80	Sandy McNaughton	17
1980/1	Sandy McNaughton	20
1981/2	Sandy McNaughton	13
1982/3	Steve Morrison	8
1983/4	Steve Morrison	9
1984/5	John Watson	15
1985/6	John Watson	24
1986/7	John Watson	13
1987/8	Craig Robertson	13
1988/9	Ross Jack	18
1989/90	Ross Jack	16
1990/1	Ross Jack	8
1991/2	David Moyes	5
1992/3	Hamish French	12
1993/4	George O'Boyle	17
1994/5	Stewart Petrie	14
1995/6	Stewart Petrie	13
1996/7	Gerry Britton	13
1997/8	Andy Smith	16
1998/9	Andy Smith	8
1999/00	Steven Crawford	16
2000/1	Steven Crawford	9
2001/2	Barry Nicholson	7
2002/3	Steven Crawford	19
2003/4	Steven Crawford	13
2004/5	Andy Tod	6
2005/6	Mark Burchill	12
2006/7	Steven Crawford	5
2007/8	Mark Burchill	11
2008/9	Andy Kirk	12
2009/10	Willie Gibson	9
2010/1	Andy Kirk	12
2011/2	Andy Kirk	11
2012/3	Andy Barrowman	10
2013/4	Ryan Wallace	10
2014/5	Faisal El Bakhtoui / Gozie Ugwu	7
2015/6	Faisal El Bakhtoui	22

EAST FIFE

Season	Top scorer	Goals
1975/6	Drew Rutherford / Kevin Hegarty	8
1976/7	Willie Gillies / Kevin Hegarty	7
1977/8	Ken Mackie	11
1978/9	Ken Mackie	17
1979/80	John Lumsden / Ken Mackie	7
1980/1	Robin Thomson	10
1981/2	Gordon Scott	16
1982/3	Robin Thomson	13
1983/4	Gordon Durie	16
1984/5	Gavin Murray	12
1985/6	Steve Kirk	14
1986/7	Brian McNaughton	15
1987/8	Paul Hunter	17
1988/9	Paul Hunter	9
1989/90	Paul Hunter	14
1990/1	Willie Brown / Ronnie Scott	10
1991/2	John Sludden	21
1992/3	Robert Scott	16
1993/4	Robert Scott	10
1994/5	Robert Scott	14
1995/6	Robert Scott	11
1996/7	Matt Dyer / Paul Ronald	4
1997/8	Matt Dyer	11
1998/9	Barrie Moffat	13
1999/00	Barrie Moffat	11
2000/1	Steven P Kerrigan	8
2001/2	Paul McManus	11
2002/3	Kenny Deuchar	20
2003/4	Kenny Deuchar	11
2004/5	Steven Nicholas	9
2005/6	John Bradford / Greg McDonald	7
2006/7	Craig O'Reilly	13
2007/8	Paul McManus	17
2008/9	Paul McManus	12
2009/10	Paul McManus	15
2010/1	Bobby Linn	13
2011/2	Ryan Wallace	20
2012/3	Scott McBride	11
2013/4	Liam Buchanan	11
2014/5	Kevin Smith	12
2015/6	Nathan Austin	22

EAST STIRLINGSHIRE

Season	Top scorer	Goals
1975/6	Jim Mullin	8
1976/7	Ian Cochrane	11
1977/8	Jim Docherty	14
1978/9	Jim Docherty	14
1979/80	Ally Grant	14
1980/1	Paul Lamont	7
1981/2	Jim Blair / Paul Lamont / Raymond Edgar	4
1982/3	Charlie Gibson	6
1983/4	Charlie Gibson	13
1984/5	Steve Maskrey	12
1985/6	Steve Maskrey	12
1986/7	Alan McGonnigal / John Paisley / David Strange	5
1987/8	Gary Murray	9
1988/9	Billy McNeill	16
1989/90	Billy McNeill / Colin Wilson / David Wilcox	4
1990/1	Charlie Lytwyn / Derek Walker	10
1991/2	Danny Diver	18
1992/3	Paul Roberts	9
1993/4	Mungo McCallum	12
1994/5	Michael Geraghty	16
1995/6	Peter Dwyer	21
1996/7	Grant Inglis	9
1997/8	David Watt	13
1998/9	Billy McNeill	8
1999/00	Gary Higgins / Steven Laidlaw	9
2000/1	Steven Hislop	16
2001/2	Kevin Gordon	11
2002/3	Jordan Leishman / Derek Ure	5
2003/4	Derek Ure	9
2004/5	Joe Robertson	7
2005/6	Ian Diack	8
2006/7	Marc McKenzie	5
2007/8	Andy Brand	11
2008/9	Brian Graham	15
2009/10	Simon Lynch	13
2010/1	Kevin Cawley	8
2011/2	Kevin Turner	6
2012/3	Paul Quinn	11
2013/4	Paul Quinn	7
2014/5	David McKenna	12
2015/6	David McKenna	8

ELGIN CITY

Season	Top scorer	Goals
1975/6		
1976/7		
1977/8		
1978/9		
1979/80		
1980/1		
1981/2		
1982/3		
1983/4		
1984/5		
1985/6		
1986/7		
1987/8		
1988/9		
1989/90		
1990/1		
1991/2		
1992/3		
1993/4		
1994/5		
1995/6		
1996/7		
1997/8		
1998/9		
1999/00		
2000/1	Colin Milne / David Ro	
2001/2	Ian Gilzean	
2002/3	Kevin Steele	
2003/4	Alex Bone	
2004/5	Willie Martin	
2005/6	Martin Johnston	
2006/7	Martin Johnston	
2007/8	Darren Shallicker	
2008/9	Darren Shallicker	
2009/10	Craig Gunn	
2010/1	Jason Crooks	
2011/2	Craig Gunn	
2012/3	Stuart Leslie	
2013/4	Craig Gunn	
2014/5	Craig Gunn	
2015/6	Craig Gunn	

FALKIRK

Season	Top scorer	Goals
1975/6	John Whiteford	17
1976/7	Bobby Ford	5
1977/8	Ally McRoberts	13
1978/9	Ally McRoberts	11
1979/80	Paul Leetion	13
1980/1	Colin Spence	5
1981/2	Willie Herd	10
1982/3	Peter Houston	8
1983/4	Kevin McAllister	11
1984/5	Gerry McCoy	22
1985/6	Jimmy Gilmour	15
1986/7	Ken Eadie	6
1987/8	Crawford Baptie	9
1988/9	Alex Rae	12
1989/90	Derek McWilliams	17
1990/1	Simon Stainrod	16
1991/2	Kevin McAllister / Eddie May	9
1992/3	Richard Cadette	8
1993/4	Richard Cadette	18
1994/5	Colin McDonald	9
1995/6	Paul McGrillen	6
1996/7	Mark McGraw	8
1997/8	David Moss	12
1998/9	Marino Keith	17
1999/00	Scott Crabbe	14
2000/1	Gareth Hutchison	11
2001/2	Lee Miller	11
2002/3	Owen Coyle	20
2003/4	Jason Lee	8
2004/5	Darrell Duffy	17
2005/6	Darrell Duffy	9
2006/7	Anthony Stokes	14
2007/8	Michael Higdon / Pedro Moutinho	8
2008/9	Stephen Lovell	8
2009/10	Pedro Moutinho / Ryan Flynn / Carl Finnegan	
2010/1	Mark Stewart	15
2011/2	Faroud El Alagui	18
2012/3	Lyle Taylor	24
2013/4	Rory Loy	20
2014/5	Rory Loy	9
2015/6	John Baird	17

FORFAR ATHLETIC

Season	Top scorer	Goals
1975/6	Sandy White	10
1976/7	Sandy White	10
1977/8	Alex Rae	11
1978/9	Alex Rae	11
1979/80	John Clark	20
1980/1	Neil Watt	13
1981/2	John Clark / Steve Hancock	9
1982/3	Kenny MacDonald	16
1983/4	Jim Liddle	22
1984/5	Kenny MacDonald	14
1985/6	John Clark	10
1986/7	Kenny MacDonald	17
1987/8	Kenny MacDonald	20
1988/9	Kenny Ward	12
1989/90	Craig Brewster	8
1990/1	Gary Whyte	12
1991/2	Gordon Winter	8
1992/3	Stewart Petrie	21
1993/4	David Bingham	13
1994/5	David Bingham	22
1995/6	Gary Higgins	12
1996/7	Ben Honeyman	17
1997/8	Martin McLauchlan	14
1998/9	Ralph Brand	10
1999/00	Steven Milne	16
2000/1	Willie Stewart	9
2001/2	Paul Tosh	19
2002/3	Martin Bavidge	15
2003/4	Paul Tosh	18
2004/5	Paul Shields	20
2005/6	Darren Gribben	10
2006/7	Darren Gribben	11
2007/8	John Ovenstone / Michael Stuart	4
2008/9	Ross Campbell	13
2009/10	Ross Campbell	16
2010/1	Ross Campbell	11
2011/2	Chris Templeman	16
2012/3	Gavin Swankie / Chris Templeman	10
2013/4	Dale Hilson	12
2014/5	Gavin Swankie	11
2015/6	Andy Ryan	9

GRETNA

Season	Top scorer	Goals
1975/6		
1976/7		
1977/8		
1978/9		
1979/80		
1980/1		
1981/2		
1982/3		
1983/4		
1984/5		
1985/6		
1986/7		
1987/8		
1988/9		
1989/90		
1990/1		
1991/2		
1992/3		
1993/4		
1994/5		
1995/6		
1996/7		
1997/8		
1998/9		
1999/00		
2000/1		
2001/2		
2002/3	Mark Dobie	10
2003/4	Martin Cameron	17
2004/5	Kenny Deuchar	38
2005/6	Kenny Deuchar	18
2006/7	Colin McMenamin	24
2007/8	Kenny Deuchar	6
2008/9		
2009/10		
2010/1		
2011/2		
2012/3		
2013/4		
2014/5		
2015/6		

HAMILTON ACCIES

Season	Top scorer
1975/6	Billy Thomas
1976/7	Joe McGrogan
1977/8	Joe McGrogan
1978/9	Bobby Graham
1979/80	Jaimie Fairlie / Bobby Graham
1980/1	Jamie Fairlie
1981/2	Jamie Fairlie
1982/3	Jamie Fairlie
1983/4	Doug Somner
1984/5	John McGachie
1985/6	John Brogan
1986/7	John Brogan
1987/8	Mark Caughey
1988/9	Stuart Gordon / Colin Harris
1989/90	Colin Harris
1990/1	George McCluskey
1991/2	Gary Clark
1992/3	Paul McDonald
1993/4	Peter Duffield
1994/5	Peter Duffield
1995/6	Paul Hartley
1996/7	Paul Ritchie
1997/8	Paul Ritchie
1998/9	Gary Wales
1999/00	Darren Henderson / Nicky Henderson
2000/1	David McFarlane
2001/2	Michael Moore
2002/3	Brian McPhee
2003/4	Brian McPhee
2004/5	Scott Tunbridge
2005/6	Brown Ferguson
2006/7	Richard Offiong
2007/8	Richard Offiong
2008/9	James McCarthy / Simon Mensing/ Richard Offi
2009/10	Simon Mensing
2010/1	Dougie Imrie / Mickael Antoine-Curier
2011/2	Jon McShane
2012/3	Stevie May
2013/4	Tony Andreu / James Keatings
2014/5	Tony Andreu
2015/6	Carlton Morris

HEARTS			HIBERNIAN			INVERNESS CT			KILMARNOCK		
1975/6	Drew Busby / Willie Gibson	8	1975/6	Arthur Duncan	13	1975/6			1975/6	Ian Fallis	10
1976/7	Willie Gibson	15	1976/7	Bobby Smith	8	1976/7			1976/7	Ian Fallis	10
1977/8	Willie Gibson	20	1977/8	Ally MacLeod	16	1977/8			1977/8	Donny McDowell	13
1978/9	Derek O'Connor	8	1978/9	Ralph Callachan	9	1978/9			1978/9	John Bourke	21
1979/80	Willie Gibson	17	1979/80	Ally MacLeod	8	1979/80			1979/80	Bobby Street	9
1980/1	Willie Gibson / Derek O'Connor	4	1980/1	Ally MacLeod	15	1980/1			1980/1	John Bourke	5
1981/2	Willie Pettigrew	16	1981/2	Gordon Rae	11	1981/2			1981/2	John Bourke	14
1982/3	John Robertson	21	1982/3	Gordon Rae / Gary Murray	6	1982/3			1982/3	Brian Gallagher	9
1983/4	John Robertson	13	1983/4	Willie Irvine	18	1983/4			1983/4	Robert Clark	11
1984/5	Sandy Clark / John Robertson	8	1984/5	Gordon Durie / Paul Kane	8	1984/5			1984/5	Blair Millar	12
1985/6	John Robertson	20	1985/6	Steve Cowan	19	1985/6			1985/6	Ian Bryson	14
1986/7	John Robertson	16	1986/7	George McCluskey	9	1986/7			1986/7	Ian Bryson	10
1987/8	John Robertson	26	1987/8	Paul Kane	10	1987/8			1987/8	Colin Harkness	16
1988/9	John Colquhoun / Ian Ferguson	5	1988/9	Steve Archibald	13	1988/9			1988/9	Willie Watters	12
1989/90	John Robertson	17	1989/90	Keith Houchen	8	1989/90			1989/90	Willie Watters	23
1990/1	John Robertson	12	1990/1	Paul Wright	6	1990/1			1990/1	Bobby Williamson	14
1991/2	Scott Crabbe	15	1991/2	Mickey Weir	11	1991/2			1991/2	Callum Campbell / Ally Mitchell	10
1992/3	John Robertson	11	1992/3	Darren Jackson	13	1992/3			1992/3	George McCluskey	11
1993/4	John Robertson	10	1993/4	Keith Wright	16	1993/4			1993/4	Bobby Williamson	7
1994/5	John Robertson	10	1994/5	Darren Jackson / Michael O'Neill	10	1994/5	Charlie Christie / Alan Hercher	6	1994/5	Colin McKee	6
1995/6	John Robertson	11	1995/6	Darren Jackson / Keith Wright	9	1995/6	Ian Stewart	23	1995/6	Paul Wright	13
1996/7	John Robertson	14	1996/7	Darren Jackson	11	1996/7	Ian Stewart	27	1996/7	Paul Wright	15
1997/8	Jim Hamilton	14	1997/8	Steve Crawford	9	1997/8	Ian Stewart	16	1997/8	Paul Wright	10
1998/9	Stephane Adam	10	1998/9	Steve Crawford	14	1998/9	Scott McLean	19	1998/9	Ally McCoist	7
1999/00	Gary McSwegan	13	1999/00	Kenny Miller	11	1999/00	Barry Wilson	13	1999/00	Christophe Cocard	8
2000/1	Colin Cameron / Andy Kirk	12	2000/1	Mixu Paatelainen	11	2000/1	Dennis Wyness	24	2000/1	Paul Wright	8
2001/2	Kevin McKenna	9	2001/2	Gary O'Connor	10	2001/2	Dennis Wyness	18	2001/2	Alan Johnson	7
2002/3	Mark De Vries	15	2002/3	Tom McManus	12	2002/3	Dennis Wyness	19	2002/3	Kris Boyd	12
2003/4	Mark De Vries	12	2003/4	Derek Riordan	15	2003/4	Paul Ritchie	14	2003/4	Kris Boyd	15
2004/5	Paul Hartley	11	2004/5	Derek Riordan	20	2004/5	Barry Wilson	11	2004/5	Kris Boyd	17
2005/6	Rudi Skacel	16	2005/6	Derek Riordan	17	2005/6	Craig Dargo	17	2005/6	Kris Boyd	15
2006/7	Andrius Velicka	10	2006/7	Chris Killen	13	2006/7	Craig Dargo	10	2006/7	Steven Naismith	16
2007/8	Andrius Velicka	11	2007/8	Steven Fletcher	13	2007/8	Don Cowie	9	2007/8	Colin Nish	7
2008/9	Bruno Aguiar	7	2008/9	Steven Fletcher / Derek Riordan	12	2008/9	Adam Rooney	5	2008/9	Kevin Kyle	8
2009/10	Suso Santana	6	2009/10	Anthony Stokes	22	2009/10	Adam Rooney	24	2009/10	Kevin Kyle	8
2010/1	Rudi Skacel	13	2010/1	Derek Riordan	11	2010/1	Adam Rooney	15	2010/1	Connor Sammon	15
2011/2	Rudi Skacel	11	2011/2	Gary O'Connor	12	2011/2	Gregory Tade	9	2011/2	Dene Shiels	13
2012/3	John Sutton	8	2012/3	Leigh Griffiths	23	2012/3	Billy McKay	23	2012/3	Paul Heffernan / Cillian Sheridan	9
2013/4	Callum Paterson	11	2013/4	James Collins / Liam Craig	6	2013/4	Billy McKay	18	2013/4	Kris Boyd	22
2014/5	Genero Zeefuik	12	2014/5	Jason Cummings	18	2014/5	Billy McKay	10	2014/5	Topi Obadeyi	9
2015/6	Juanma Delgado	12	2015/6	Jason Cummings	18	2015/6	Miles Storey	11	2015/6	Josh Magennis	10

LIVINGSTON / MEADOWBANK			MONTROSE			MORTON			MOTHERWELL		
1975/6	Kenny Davidson	7	1975/6	Bobby Livingstone	12	1975/6	Rikki Sharp / John Goldthorp / Ian Harley	5	1975/6	Willie Pettigrew	22
1976/7	Kenny Davidson / Jimmy Hancock	8	1976/7	Dougie Robb	13	1976/7	Andy Ritchie	22	1976/7	Willie Pettigrew	21
1977/8	Kenny Davidson / Jimmy Hancock / Tom Downie	6	1977/8	Bobby Livingstone	10	1977/8	John Goldthorp / Andy Ritchie	20	1977/8	Vic Davidson	8
1978/9	Gerry Adair	7	1978/9	Gary Murray	12	1978/9	Andy Ritchie	22	1978/9	Willie Pettigrew	6
1979/80	John Jobson	17	1979/80	Gary Murray	15	1979/80	Andy Ritchie	19	1979/80	Willie Irvine	13
1980/1	John Jobson	12	1980/1	Gary Murray / Dougie Robb	12	1980/1	Andy Ritchie	8	1980/1	Albert Kidd	13
1981/2	John Jobson	15	1981/2	Ian Campbell	9	1981/2	Andy Ritchie	6	1981/2	Willie Irvine	20
1982/3	Tom Hendrie	13	1982/3	Eddie Copeland	12	1982/3	Jim Rooney	6	1982/3	Brian McClair	11
1983/4	Chris Robertson	10	1983/4	Neil Burke	7	1983/4	John McNeil	17	1983/4	John Gahagan	7
1984/5	Adrian Sprott	14	1984/5	Doug Somner	12	1984/5	Jim Gillespie	5	1984/5	Andy Harrow	9
1985/6	Darren Jackson	17	1985/6	Martin Allan	6	1985/6	John McNeil	14	1985/6	John Reilly	9
1986/7	John McGachie	21	1986/7	Ian Paterson	10	1986/7	Rowan Alexander	23	1986/7	Steve Kirk / Andy Walker	10
1987/8	John McGachie	14	1987/8	Hamish Mackay	11	1987/8	Jim Boag	8	1987/8	Steve Cowan	9
1988/9	David Roseburgh	6	1988/9	Gary Murray	21	1988/9	Rowan Alexander	11	1988/9	Steve Kirk	14
1989/90	Brian McNaughton	8	1989/90	Danny Powell	11	1989/90	Rowan Alexander	11	1989/90	Nick Cusack	11
1990/1	David Roseburgh	15	1990/1	Gary Murray	11	1990/1	David McCabe	21	1990/1	Dougie Arnott	14
1991/2	David Roseburgh	8	1991/2	John McGachie	9	1991/2	Alex Mathie	18	1991/2	Dougie Arnott	8
1992/3	Paul Rutherford	9	1992/3	Derek Grant	10	1992/3	Alex Mathie	13	1992/3	Steve Kirk	10
1993/4	Ian Little	12	1993/4	Derek Grant	12	1993/4	Rowan Alexander	11	1993/4	Tommy Coyne	12
1994/5	Lee Bailey	6	1994/5	Colin McGlashan	19	1994/5	Derek Lilley	16	1994/5	Tommy Coyne	16
1995/6	Jason Young	18	1995/6	Colin McGlashan	16	1995/6	Derek Lilley	14	1995/6	Willie Falconer	5
1996/7	Graham Harvey	15	1996/7	Colin McGlashan	11	1996/7	Derek Lilley	15	1996/7	Tommy Coyne	11
1997/8	Graham Harvey	15	1997/8	Colin McGlashan	20	1997/8	Warren Hawke	10	1997/8	Tommy Coyne	15
1998/9	John Robertson	12	1998/9	Scott Taylor	7	1998/9	Kevin Thomas	9	1998/9	Owen Coyle /John Spencer	7
1999/00	David Bingham	15	1999/00	Scott Taylor	12	1999/00	Harry Curran	9	1999/00	John Spencer	11
2000/1	David Bingham	14	2000/1	John Mitchell	7	2000/1	Ross Matheson	9	2000/1	Stuart Elliott	10
2001/2	Barry Wilson	9	2001/2	Steven Laidlaw	13	2001/2	Scott Bannerman / Sean O'Connor	8	2001/2	Stuart Elliott / James McFadden	10
2002/3	Rolando Zarate	9	2002/3	Steven P Kerrigan	8	2002/3	Alex Williams	23	2002/3	James McFadden	13
2003/4	Derek Lilley	12	2003/4	Scott Michie	14	2003/4	Alex Williams	15	2003/4	David Clarkson	11
2004/5	Burton O'Brien	8	2004/5	Craig Smart	14	2004/5	Chris Millar / Peter Weatherson`	11	2004/5	Scott McDonald	15
2005/6	Richard Brittain / Robert Snodgrass	4	2005/6	Greg Henslee	10	2005/6	Derek Lilley	12	2005/6	Richie Foran	11
2006/7	Stephen Craig	7	2006/7	Andy Rodgers	10	2006/7	Peter Weatherson	15	2006/7	Scott McDonald	15
2007/8	Graham Dorrans	11	2007/8	John Baird	18	2007/8	Peter Weatherson	9	2007/8	Chris Porter	14
2008/9	Leigh Griffiths	17	2008/9	Roddy Hunter	9	2008/9	Brian Wake	9	2008/9	David Clarkson	14
2009/10	Andy Halliday	14	2009/10	Paul Tosh	9	2009/10	Peter Weatherson	10	2009/10	Lucas Jutkiewicz / John Sutton	12
2010/1	Ian Russell	22	2010/1	Paul Tosh	12	2010/1	Allan Jenkins	8	2010/1	Nick Blackman / John Sutton	10
2011/2	Rory Boulding / Mark McNulty	11	2011/2	Martin Boyle	22	2011/2	Peter MacDonald	10	2011/2	Michael Higdon	14
2012/3	Ian Russell	15	2012/3	Martin Boyle	9	2012/3	Peter MacDonald	14	2012/3	Michael Higdon	26
2013/4	Marc McNulty	17	2013/4	Bryan Deasley	10	2013/4	Dougie Imrie	9	2013/4	John Sutton	22
2014/5	Jordan White	11	2014/5	Gary Wood	10	2014/5	Declan McManus	20	2014/5	John Sutton	12
2015/6	Liam Buchanan	11	2015/6	Gary Fraser	19	2015/6	Denny Johnstone	14	2015/6	Louis Moult	15

PARTICK THISTLE

Season	Player	Goals
1975/6	Doug Somner	16
1976/7	Doug Somner	11
1977/8	Doug Somner	15
1978/9	Doug Somner	11
1979/80	Colin McAdam	17
1980/1	Tony Higgins / Alex O'Hara	7
1981/2	Maurice Johnston	9
1982/3	Maurice Johnston	21
1983/4	Kenny McDowall	13
1984/5	Alan Logan	12
1985/6	Gordon Smith	11
1986/7	Colin West	10
1987/8	Eddie Gallagher	13
1988/9	Gerry McCoy	19
1989/90	Calum Campbell	18
1990/1	David Elliot	13
1991/2	Colin McGlashan	18
1992/3	Gerry Britton	12
1993/4	Albert Craig	14
1994/5	Wayne Foster	7
1995/6	Andy Lyons / Rod McDonald	5
1996/7	David Moss	11
1997/8	Jered Stirling	6
1998/9	Robert Dunn	10
1999/00	Robert Dunn	5
2000/1	Scott McLean	16
2001/2	Gerry Britton	12
2002/3	Alex Burns	16
2003/4	James Grady	15
2004/5	Juan Escalas	10
2005/6	Mark Roberts	10
2006/7	Mark Roberts	16
2007/8	Liam Buchanan	11
2008/9	Gary Harkins	9
2009/10	Liam Buchanan	10
2010/1	Kris Doolan	15
2011/2	Kris Doolan	13
2012/3	Steven Lawless	13
2013/4	Kris Doolan	11
2014/5	Kris Doolan	9
2015/6	Kris Doolan	14

PETERHEAD

Season	Player	Goals
1975/6		
1976/7		
1977/8		
1978/9		
1979/80		
1980/1		
1981/2		
1982/3		
1983/4		
1984/5		
1985/6		
1986/7		
1987/8		
1988/9		
1989/90		
1990/1		
1991/2		
1992/3		
1993/4		
1994/5		
1995/6		
1996/7		
1997/8		
1998/9		
1999/00		
2000/1	Craig Yeats	11
2001/2	Ian Stewart	19
2002/3	Ian Stewart	21
2003/4	Martin Johnston	18
2004/5	Scott Michie	21
2005/6	Bobby Linn	11
2006/7	Martin Bavidge	11
2007/8	Martin Bavidge	15
2008/9	Martin Bavidge	9
2009/10	Martin Bavidge	11
2010/1	Dennis Wyness	8
2011/2	Rory McAllister	20
2012/3	Rory McAllister	21
2013/4	Rory McAllister	32
2014/5	Rory McAllister	8
2015/6	Rory McAllister	22

QOS

Season	Player	Goals
1975/6	Peter Dickson / Ian Reid	11
1976/7	Peter Dickson	15
1977/8	Tommy Bryce	8
1978/9	Tommy Bryce	12
1979/80	Rowan Alexander	21
1980/1	Jim Robertson	19
1981/2	Gerry Phillips	12
1982/3	Rowan Alexander	23
1983/4	John Robertson	9
1984/5	George Cloy	9
1985/6	Tommy Bryce / Stewart Cochrane	15
1986/7	Tommy Bryce	20
1987/8	Jim Hughes	17
1988/9	Gary Fraser	7
1989/90	Stuart Gordon	8
1990/1	Andy Thomson	11
1991/2	Andy Thomson	26
1992/3	Andy Thomson	21
1993/4	Andy Thomson	29
1994/5	Duncan Campbell / Steve Mallan	9
1995/6	Steve Mallan	12
1996/7	Steve Mallan	13
1997/8	Steve Mallan	10
1998/9	Steve Mallan	15
1999/00	Steve Mallan	13
2000/1	Peter Weatherson	16
2001/2	John O'Neil	19
2002/3	John O'Neil	9
2003/4	Alex Burke	13
2004/5	David McNiven	12
2005/6	John O'Neil	10
2006/7	John O'Neil	8
2007/8	Stephen Dobbie	16
2008/9	Stephen Dobbie	23
2009/10	Derek Holmes	12
2010/1	Colin McMenamin	11
2011/2	Sam Parkin	6
2012/3	Nicky Clark	23
2013/4	Ian Russell	13
2014/5	Derek Lyle	15
2015/6	Derek Lyle	13

QUEEN'S PARK

Season	Player	Goals
1975/6	Sandy McNaughton / Hugh McGill	8
1976/7	Bernie Donnelly	15
1977/8	Bernie Donnelly	8
1978/9	Ian Ballantyne	13
1979/80	Jim Gillespie	21
1980/1	Gerry McCoy	17
1981/2	Gerry Crawley	10
1982/3	Jimmy Gilmour	10
1983/4	Lex Grant	17
1984/5	Jim Nicholson	18
1985/6	Gary Fraser	11
1986/7	Ross Caven	13
1987/8	Paul O'Brien	17
1988/9	Mike Hendry	9
1989/90	Mike Hendry	10
1990/1	Mike Hendry	17
1991/2	Steve McCormick	17
1992/3	Ross Caven	11
1993/4	John O'Neil	18
1994/5	Steve McCormick	8
1995/6	Scott Edgar / Kevin McGoldrick	6
1996/7	Danny Ferry	7
1997/8	Scott Edgar	8
1998/9	Scott Edgar	7
1999/00	Mark Gallagher	13
2000/1	Mark Gallagher	7
2001/2	Steven Canning / Ross Jackson	5
2002/3	John Gemmell	8
2003/4	Stephen Reilly	7
2004/5	Frank Carroll	14
2005/6	Mark Ferry	8
2006/7	David Weatherston	16
2007/8	Alan Trouten	12
2008/9	Paul Cairney	8
2009/10	Barry Douglas	8
2010/1	Jamie Longworth	12
2011/2	Jamie Longworth	20
2012/3	Lawrence Shankland	11
2013/4	Blair Spittal	8
2014/5	Paul Woods	9
2015/6	Paul Woods	11

RAITH ROVERS

Season	Player	Goals
1975/6	Malcolm Robertson / Gordon Wallace	9
1976/7	Gordon Wallace	8
1977/8	Ronnie Duncan	11
1978/9	Gordon Wallace	14
1979/80	Ian Ballantyne	13
1980/1	Ian Ballantyne	12
1981/2	Ian Ballantyne	12
1982/3	Colin Harris	18
1983/4	Jim Kerr	16
1984/5	Keith Wright	22
1985/6	Paul Smith / Keith Wright	21
1986/7	Colin Harris	22
1987/8	Gordon Dalziel	25
1988/9	Gordon Dalziel	11
1989/90	Gordon Dalziel	20
1990/1	Gordon Dalziel	25
1991/2	Gordon Dalziel	26
1992/3	Gordon Dalziel	32
1993/4	Gordon Dalziel	8
1994/5	Gordon Dalziel	15
1995/6	Colin Cameron	9
1996/7	Peter Duffield / Danny Lennon	5
1997/8	Paul Hartley / Keith Wright	10
1998/9	Craig Dargo	8
1999/00	Craig Dargo	12
2000/1	Paul Tosh	9
2001/2	Nacho Novo	19
2002/3	Karl Hawley	7
2003/4	John Sutton	13
2004/5	Pat Clarke / John Martin	4
2005/6	Paul McManus	15
2006/7	Paul McManus	7
2007/8	Graham Weir	10
2008/9	Kevin Smith	18
2009/10	Gregory Tade	5
2010/1	John Baird	13
2011/2	Brian Graham	11
2012/3	Brian Graham	18
2013/4	Greg Spence	9
2014/5	Mark Stewart	10
2015/6	Mark Stewart	10

RANGERS

Season	Player	Goals
1975/6	Derek Johnstone	15
1976/7	Derek Parlane	16
1977/8	Derek Johnstone	25
1978/9	Gordon Smith	11
1979/80	Derek Johnstone	14
1980/1	Colin McAdam	12
1981/2	John MacDonald	14
1982/3	John MacDonald	10
1983/4	Sandy Clark / Ally McCoist	9
1984/5	Ally McCoist	12
1985/6	Ally McCoist	24
1986/7	Ally McCoist	33
1987/8	Ally McCoist	31
1988/9	Kevin Drinkell	12
1989/90	Maurice Johnston	15
1990/1	Mark Walters	11
1991/2	Ally McCoist	34
1992/3	Ally McCoist	34
1993/4	Mark Hateley	22
1994/5	Mark Hateley	13
1995/6	Gordon Durie	17
1996/7	Brian Laudrup	16
1997/8	Marco Negri	32
1998/9	Rod Wallace	18
1999/00	Jorg Albertz	17
2000/1	Tore Andree Flo	11
2001/2	Tore Andree Flo	17
2002/3	Ronald de Boer / Barry Ferguson	16
2003/4	Shota Arveladze	12
2004/5	Nacho Novo	19
2005/6	Kris Boyd	17
2006/7	Kris Boyd	20
2007/8	Kris Boyd	14
2008/9	Kris Boyd	27
2009/10	Kris Boyd	23
2010/1	Kenny Miller	21
2011/2	Nikica Jelavic	15
2012/3	Andy Little	22
2013/4	John Daly	20
2014/5	Nicky Law	10
2015/6	Martin Waghorn	20

ROSS COUNTY

Season	Player	Goals
1975/6		
1976/7		
1977/8		
1978/9		
1979/80		
1980/1		
1981/2		
1982/3		
1983/4		
1984/5		
1985/6		
1986/7		
1987/8		
1988/9		
1989/90		
1990/1		
1991/2		
1992/3		
1993/4		
1994/5	Brian Grant	12
1995/6	Colin Milne	5
1996/7	Derek Adams	22
1997/8	Derek Adams	16
1998/9	Steven Ferguson / Neil Tarrant	17
1999/00	George Shaw	13
2000/1	Alex Bone	14
2001/2	Steven Hislop	14
2002/3	Graham Bayne	6
2003/4	David Winters	10
2004/5	Alex Burke / David Winters	6
2005/6	John Rankin	12
2006/7	Don Cowie	7
2007/8	Andy Barrowman	24
2008/9	Stephen Craig / Sean Higgins	10
2009/10	Richard Brittain	9
2010/1	Andy Barrowman	5
2011/2	Colin McMenamin	19
2012/3	Richard Brittain	9
2013/4	Melvin De Leeuw	9
2014/5	Liam Boyce	10
2015/6	Liam Boyce	15

ST JOHNSTONE

1975/6	Jim O'Rourke
1976/7	Ian Anderson
1977/8	Derek O'Connor
1978/9	John Brogan
1979/80	John Brogan
1980/1	Ally McCoist
1981/2	Jim Morton
1982/3	John Brogan
1983/4	John Brogan
1984/5	Joe Reid
1985/6	Willie Brown
1986/7	Willie Brown
1987/8	Willie Watters
1988/9	Steve Maskrey
1989/90	Roddy Grant
1990/1	Harry Curran
1991/2	Paul Wright
1992/3	Paul Wright
1993/4	Paul Wright
1994/5	George O'Boyle
1995/6	George O'Boyle
1996/7	Roddy Grant
1997/8	George O'Boyle
1998/9	Gary Bollan / Roddy Grant / Miguel Simac
1999/00	Nathan Lowndes
2000/1	Keigan Parker
2001/2	Paul Hartley
2002/3	Chris Hay
2003/4	Mixu Paatelainen
2004/5	Peter MacDonald
2005/6	Jason Scotland
2006/7	Jason Scotland
2007/8	Andy Jackson
2008/9	Steven Milne
2009/10	Liam Craig
2010/1	Liam Craig
2011/2	Fran Sandaza
2012/3	Liam Craig / Mrray davidson
2013/4	Stevie May
2014/5	Brian Graham
2015/6	Steven MacLean

T MIRREN

975/6	Donnie McDowell	12
976/7	Derek Hyslop / Frank McGarvey	17
977/8	Frank McGarvey	17
978/9	Frank McGarvey	13
979/80	Doug Somner	25
980/1	Doug Somner	13
981/2	Frank McAvennie	13
982/3	Frank McDougall	9
983/4	Frank McDougall	13
984/5	Frank McAvennie	16
985/6	Gardner Speirs	7
986/7	Frank McGarvey	10
987/8	Paul Chalmers	10
988/9	Paul Chalmers	11
989/90	Gudmundur Torfason	12
990/1	Paul Kinnaird / Kenny McDowall / Gudmundur Torfason	4
991/2	Gudmundur Torfason	8
992/3	Barry Lavety	18
993/4	Barry Lavety	10
994/5	Barry Lavety	7
995/6	Barry Lavety	11
996/7	Mark Yardley	15
997/8	Junior Mendes	9
998/9	Mark Yardley	11
999/00	Mark Yardley	19
2000/1	Ricky Gillies	10
2001/2	Ricky Gillies / Brian McGinty	6
2002/3	Martin Cameron	12
2003/4	Ricky Gillies	8
2004/5	John O'Neil	7
2005/6	John Sutton	14
2006/7	John Sutton	12
2007/8	Billy Mehmet	6
2008/9	Andy Dorman	10
2009/10	Andy Dorman	6
2010/1	Michael Higdon	14
2011/2	Steven Thompson	13
2012/3	Steven Thompson	13
2013/4	Steven Thompson	13
2014/5	Kenny McLean	7
2015/6	Steven Mallan	11

STENHOUSEMUIR

1975/6	Jim Wight	14
1976/7	Frank Coulston	7
1977/8	Frank Wilson	14
1978/9	Sandy McNaughton	16
1979/80	David Jack	12
1980/1	Stevie Hancock	20
1981/2	Brian Jenkins	8
1982/3	Gavin Murray	15
1983/4	Gordon Forrest	14
1984/5	Harry Erwin / Sandy McNaughton	6
1985/6	Jim Sinnet	11
1986/7	Alan Bateman / Peter Russell /John Waddell	5
1987/8	Tom Condie	10
1988/9	Colin Walker	9
1989/90	Stephen McCormick	15
1990/1	Tony Speirs	17
1991/2	Miller Mathieson	9
1992/3	Miller Mathieson	26
1993/4	Miller Mathieson	14
1994/5	Gareth Hutchison	10
1995/6	Miller Mathieson	10
1996/7	Ian Little	14
1997/8	Ian Little	15
1998/9	Ross Hamilton	11
1999/00	Martin Mooney	8
2000/1	Isaac English	18
2001/2	Willie Irvine	7
2002/3	Mark Booth	9
2003/4	Andy Brown	5
2004/5	Paul McGrillen	18
2005/6	Colin Cramb	16
2006/7	John Demspter	10
2007/8	Scott Dalziel	9
2008/9	Scott Dalziel	14
2009/10	Kevin Motion	7
2010/1	Grant Anderson	7
2011/2	Andy Rodgers	14
2012/3	John Gemmell	18
2013/4	John Gemmell	11
2014/5	Colin McMenamin	15
2015/6	Alan Cook	8

STIRLING ALBION

1975/6	Mickey Lawson	18
1976/7	Bobby Gray	13
1977/8	Billy Steele	13
1978/9	Billy Steele	7
1979/80	Andy Kennedy	11
1980/1	Graeme Armstrong / Billy Steele	4
1981/2	John Colquhoun	13
1982/3	John Colquhoun	21
1983/4	Willie Irvine	12
1984/5	Willie Irvine	21
1985/6	Willie Irvine	17
1986/7	Steve Gavin / Charlie Gibson	7
1987/8	John Brogan	23
1988/9	Charlie Gibson	18
1989/90	Joe Reid	16
1990/1	David Lloyd	14
1991/2	Willie Watters	17
1992/3	Willie Watters	11
1993/4	Willie Watters	13
1994/5	Willie Watters	15
1995/6	Steve McCormick	25
1996/7	Alex Bone	9
1997/8	Alex Bone	13
1998/9	Alex Bone	21
1999/00	Ally Graham	17
2000/1	Craig Feroz / Ally Graham	5
2001/2	Alex Williams	17
2002/3	Steven Nicholas	11
2003/4	Scott McLean	21
2004/5	Scott McLean	9
2005/6	Paddy Connolly	14
2006/7	Colin Cramb	14
2007/8	Chris Aitken	8
2008/9	Martin Grehan / David McKenna	12
2009/10	Martin Grehan	8
2010/1	Gordon Smith	11
2011/2	Alan Cook	8
2012/3	Jordan White	13
2013/4	Jordan White	15
2014/5	Gordon Smith	8
2015/6	Steven Doris / Darren Smith	9

STRANRAER

1975/6	J Traynor	12
1976/7	Derek Frye	24
1977/8	Derek Frye	27
1978/9	Drew Harvey	11
1979/80	Ian Gibb	15
1980/1	Hugh Hay	7
1981/2	Sean Sweeney	11
1982/3	Sean Sweeney	11
1983/4	Jim McGuire	11
1984/5	Sean Sweeney	10
1985/6	Jim McGuire / Stuart Mauchlen	8
1986/7	Bruce Cleland	13
1987/8	Bruce Cleland	8
1988/9	David Lloyd	11
1989/90	Colin Harkness	13
1990/1	Colin Harkness	14
1991/2	Tommy Sloan	14
1992/3	Tommy Sloan	19
1993/4	Tommy Sloan	16
1994/5	Darren Henderson / Tommy Sloan	4
1995/6	Lex Grant	6
1996/7	Paul McIntyre	7
1997/8	Graham Young	11
1998/9	Paul Ronald / Graham Young	5
1999/00	Paul Ronald	12
2000/1	Ian Harty	13
2001/2	Ian Harty	16
2002/3	Ian Harty	12
2003/4	Michael Moore	24
2004/5	David Graham	14
2005/6	David Hamilton	9
2006/7	Michael Moore	12
2007/8	Michael Mullen	13
2008/9	Gregory Tade	7
2009/10	Michael Moore / Armand One	8
2010/1	Armand One	17
2011/2	Craig Malcolm	15
2012/3	Craig Malcolm	18
2013/4	Jamie Longworth	14
2014/5	Jamie Longworth	11
2015/6	Craig Malcolm	12

PLAYER STATS - PREMIERSHIP GOALS		GP	GS	Mins	G	P
1 Boyce, Liam	Ross County	34	34	2970	23	5
2 Sinclair, Scott	Celtic	35	30	2775	21	5
3 Dembélé, Moussa	Celtic	29	20	1917	17	4
4 Armstrong, Stuart	Celtic	31	25	2281	15	0
4 Moult, Louis	Motherwell	31	30	2637	15	2
6 Doolan, Kris	Partick Thistle	37	29	2645	14	0
7 Griffiths, Leigh	Celtic	23	15	1299	12	1
7 Rooney, Adam	Aberdeen	38	32	2852	12	3
7 Walker, Jamie	Hearts	34	28	2484	12	4
10 Miller, Kenny	Rangers	37	32	2768	11	0
11 McGinn, Niall	Aberdeen	36	30	2630	10	0
11 MacLean, Steven	St Johnstone	32	30	2666	10	0
11 Swanson, Danny	St Johnstone	30	28	2347	10	6
14 Roberts, Patrick	Celtic	32	20	1901	9	0
14 Hayes, Jonny	Aberdeen	32	32	2794	9	0
14 McDonald, Scott	Motherwell	35	34	2961	9	0
17 Crawford, Ali HA	Hamilton Accies	33	31	2720	8	0
17 Boyd, Kris	Kilmarnock	27	22	2037	8	1
17 Paterson, Callum	Hearts	20	20	1662	8	0
17 Fisher, Alex	Inverness CT	21	9	1029	8	0
17 Coulibaly, Souleymane	Kilmarnock	21	18	1637	8	1
17 Waghorn, Martyn	Rangers	32	20	1886	8	2
17 Haber, Marcus	Dundee	27	27	2346	8	0
24 D'Acol, Alexandre	Hamilton Accies	29	24	1849	7	2
24 Christie, Ryan	Aberdeen	18	10	906	7	0
24 Rogic, Tom	Celtic	22	15	1272	7	0
24 Tansey, Greg	Inverness CT	37	37	3265	7	2
24 Garner, Joe	Rangers	31	21	1891	7	0
24 Gonçalves, Esmael	Hearts	15	15	1266	7	1
30 Lindsay, Liam	Partick Thistle	36	36	3170	6	0
30 Forrest, James	Celtic	28	23	1750	6	0
30 McGregor, Callum	Celtic	31	20	1935	6	0
30 Considine, Andrew	Aberdeen	36	36	3193	6	0
30 O'Hara, Mark DUN	Dundee	28	26	2282	6	0
30 Sammon, Conor	Kilmarnock	34	23	2084	6	1
30 Johnsen, Bjorn	Hearts	34	22	1908	6	0

PREMIERSHIP RED CARDS		GP	GS	Mins	YC	RC
1 MacKinnon, Darian	Hamilton Accies	33	32	2846	8	2
1 Stockley, Jayden	Aberdeen	27	8	854	2	2
3 Elliot, Christie	Partick Thistle	31	26	2403	5	1
3 Osman, Abdul	Partick Thistle	31	30	2577	7	1
3 Welsh, Sean	Partick Thistle	21	18	1588	5	1
3 McMann, Scott	Hamilton Accies	23	21	1908	4	1
3 Foster, Richard	St Johnstone	34	34	2917	6	1
3 McShane, Ian	Ross County	8	5	505	0	1
3 Brown, Scott	Celtic	33	33	2913	11	1
3 McGregor, Callum	Celtic	31	20	1935	2	1
3 Jack, Ryan	Aberdeen	26	25	2253	3	1
3 Reynolds, Mark	Aberdeen	26	22	1878	6	1
3 O'Hara, Mark DUN	Dundee	28	26	2282	4	1
3 Taylor, Greg	Kilmarnock	34	34	3033	8	1
3 Buaben, Prince	Hearts	20	11	828	4	1
3 Nicholson, Sam	Hearts	19	13	1173	1	1
3 Walker, Jamie	Hearts	34	28	2484	6	1
3 McDonald, Scott	Motherwell	35	34	2961	6	1
3 Swanson, Danny	St Johnstone	30	28	2347	7	1
3 Devine, Daniel	Partick Thistle	30	28	2500	6	1
3 Horner, Lewis	Inverness CT	10	5	519	2	1
3 Polworth, Liam	Inverness CT	32	26	2382	3	1
3 Tansey, Greg	Inverness CT	37	37	3265	4	1
3 Warren, Gary	Inverness CT	33	33	2941	5	1
3 Williams, Danny	Dundee	23	11	1141	4	1
3 Hill, Clint	Rangers	23	22	1888	5	1
3 McEveley, James	Ross County	21	18	1617	9	1
3 Van der Weg, Kenny	Ross County	33	29	2659	4	1
3 McHugh, Carl	Motherwell	19	19	1639	5	1
3 Kiernan, Rob	Rangers	24	24	2130	4	1
3 O'Halloran, Michael	Rangers	16	6	627	2	1
3 Lucas, Lee	Motherwell	10	6	578	2	1
3 Hendrie, Luke	Kilmarnock	32	32	2822	6	1
3 Gomis, Kevin	Dundee	22	22	1755	4	1
3 Chow, Tim	Ross County	30	26	2231	8	1
3 Senderos, Philippe	Rangers	3	3	255	1	1
3 Cole, Larnell	Inverness CT	21	13	1137	4	1
3 O'Brien, Jim	Ross County	16	8	781	7	1
3 Gonçalves, Esmael	Hearts	15	15	1266	3	1
3 Skondras, Giannis	Hamilton Accies	13	11	997	6	1

PREMIERSHIP YELLOW CARDS		GP	GS	Mins	YC	RC
1 Devlin, Mikey	Hamilton Accies	28	28	2467	12	0
2 Brown, Scott	Celtic	33	33	2913	11	1
2 Shinnie, Graeme	Aberdeen	36	35	3121	11	0
2 McGowan, Paul	Dundee	36	35	3169	11	0
5 Imrie, Douglas	Hamilton Accies	37	36	3188	10	0
5 Dicker, Gary	Kilmarnock	36	36	3239	10	0
5 O'Dea, Darren	Dundee	35	35	3096	10	0
5 Craig, Liam	St Johnstone	36	27	2493	10	0
5 Vigurs, Iain	Inverness CT	32	28	2373	10	0
5 Paton, Paul	St Johnstone	27	22	2053	10	0
11 McEveley, James	Ross County	21	18	1617	9	1
11 Garner, Joe	Rangers	31	21	1891	9	0
13 Gillespie, Grant	Hamilton Accies	31	28	2502	8	0
13 MacKinnon, Darian	Hamilton Accies	33	32	2846	8	2
13 Taylor, Greg	Kilmarnock	34	34	3033	8	1
13 Lasley, Keith	Motherwell	28	25	2104	8	0
13 Davidson, Murray	St Johnstone	23	19	1741	8	0
13 MacLean, Steven	St Johnstone	32	30	2666	8	0
13 McKay, Brad	Inverness CT	28	27	2380	8	0
13 Draper, Ross	Inverness CT	37	35	3033	8	0
13 Tremarco, Carl	Inverness CT	29	29	2375	8	0
13 Donati, Massimo	Hamilton Accies	31	26	2306	8	0
13 Chow, Tim ROS	Ross County	30	26	2231	8	1
24 Osman, Abdul	Partick Thistle	31	30	2577	7	1
24 Crawford, Ali	Hamilton Accies	33	31	2720	7	0
24 Boyce, Liam	Ross County	34	34	2970	7	0
24 Davies, Andrew	Ross County	32	32	2813	7	0
24 Considine, Andrew	Aberdeen	36	36	3193	7	0
24 Igor Rossi	Hearts	20	20	1779	7	0
24 Moult, Louis	Motherwell	31	30	2637	7	0
24 Swanson, Danny	St Johnstone	30	28	2347	7	1
24 Heneghan, Ben	Motherwell	37	37	3330	7	0
24 Sarris, Giorgos	Hamilton Accies	30	30	2655	7	0
24 Tavernier, James	Rangers	36	35	3145	7	0
24 O'Brien, Jim	Ross County	16	8	781	7	1
36 Booth, Callum	Partick Thistle	31	31	2790	6	0
36 Edwards, Ryan	Partick Thistle	38	33	3003	6	0
36 Curran, Craig	Ross County	34	26	2195	6	0
36 Foster, Richard	St Johnstone	34	34	2917	6	1
36 Woods, Martin	Ross County	29	27	2197	6	0
36 Hayes, Jonny	Aberdeen	32	32	2794	6	0
36 Reynolds, Mark	Aberdeen	26	22	1878	6	1
36 Smith, Liam	Hearts	20	12	1345	6	0
36 Walker, Jamie	Hearts	34	28	2484	6	1
36 Etxabeguren, Julen	Dundee	17	14	1306	6	0
36 Kerr, Cameron	Dundee	36	35	3143	6	0
36 McDonald, Scott	Motherwell	35	34	2961	6	1
36 Wotherspoon, David	St Johnstone	33	20	1922	6	0
36 Devine, Daniel	Partick Thistle	30	28	2500	6	1
36 Tait, Richard	Motherwell	25	25	2150	6	0

PREMIERSHIP[SHUT OUTS		GP	GS	Mins	GA	CS
1 Gordon, Craig	Celtic	35	34	3105	20	19
2 Lewis, Joe	Aberdeen	38	38	3420	35	14
3 Foderingham, Wesley	Rangers	37	37	3330	43	12
4 Hamilton, Jack	Hearts	35	35	3150	47	10
5 Clark, Zander	St Johnstone	26	26	2256	32	9
6 Cerny, Tomas	Partick Thistle	27	27	2334	30	8
7 Fox, Scott	Ross County	36	36	3195	54	7
8 MacDonald, Jamie	Kilmarnock	24	24	2160	41	6
8 Mannus, Alan	St Johnstone	14	12	1164	14	6
10 Matthews, Remi	Hamilton	17	17	1522	21	5
11 Woods, Gary	Hamilton	21	21	1890	34	4
11 Bain, Scott	Dundee	36	36	3240	62	4
11 Samson, Craig	Motherwell	34	34	3060	64	4
11 Woodman, Freddie	Kilmarnock	14	14	1260	15	4
15 Mitchell, David	Dundee	2	2	180	0	2
15 Williams, Owain Fon	Inverness CT	32	32	2880	60	2
17 Esson, Ryan	Inverness CT	6	6	540	11	1
17 Griffiths, Russell	Motherwell	4	4	360	5	1
19 Scully, Ryan	Partick Thistle	7	6	589	9	0
19 McCarey, Aaron	Ross County	3	2	225	4	0
19 Noring, Viktor	Hearts	3	3	270	5	0
19 De Vries, Dorus	Celtic	4	4	315	5	0
19 Thomson, Robbie	Hamilton	1	0	8	1	0
19 Stuckmann, Thorsten	Partick Thistle	5	4	362	7	0
19 Ridgers, Mark	Partick Thistle	2	1	135	8	0
19 Alnwick, Jak	Rangers	1	1	90	1	0

LEAGUE POSITIONS SINCE 1994 (creation of the 4 Division structure)

	94/5	95/6	96/7	97/8	98/9	99/0	00/1	01/2	02/3	03/4	04/5	05/6	06/7	07/8	08/9	09/10	10/1	11/2	12/3	13/4	14/5	15/6	16/7
Aberdeen	A9	A3	A6	A6	A8	A10	A7	A4	A8	A11	A4	A6	A3	A4	A4	A9	A9	A9	A8	A3	A2	A2	A2
Airdrieonians (1)	B4	B8	B2	B4	B4	B9	B8	B2														C5	C3
Albion Rovers	D10	D10	D5	D5	D7	D10	D7	D3	D3	D8	D9	D8	D6	D7	D8	D5	D2+	C9	C10-	D7	D1+	C6	C8
Alloa	D5	D9	D4	D1+	C5	C2+	B10-	C2+	B9-	C7	C6	C9	C7	C4	C8	C2	C9-	D1+	C2+	B8	B9	B10-	C2
Annan Athleic															D7	D8	D4	D6	D8	D2	D5	D5	D3
Arbroath	D7	D5	D10	D2+	C7	C4	C2+	B7	B10-	C8	C9-	D4	D2	D4+	C7	C9-	D1+	C2	C5	C10-	D3	D9	D1+
Ayr United	B9-	C6	C1+	B7	B3	B7	B2	B3	B6	B9-	C8	C6	C5	C7	C2+	B10-	C2+	B9-	C7	C4	C8	C2+	B10-
Berwick Rangers	C5	C3	C10-	D6	D5	D2+	C3	C6	C5	C5	C10-	D2	D1+	C10-	D9	D6	D6	D7	D4	D5	D8	D6	D8
Brechin City	C10-	D2+	C7	C10-	D3	D8	D3	D1+	C2+	B10-	C1+	B10-	C4	C6	C3	C4	C4	C8	C3	C8	C4	C7	C4+
Celtic	A4	A2	A2	A1	A2	A2	A1	A1	A2	A1	A2	A1	A1	A1	A2	A2	A2	A1	A1	A1	A1	A1	A1
Clyde	C6	C5	C4	C8	C3	C1+	B5	B5	B2	B2	B3	B5	B5	B9	B10-	C10-	D10	D9	D9	D4		D3	D9
Clydebank / Airdrie*	B8	B7	B9-	C2+	B7	B10-	C5	C4	C3	C1+	B5	B6	B9-	C2+	B9	B9-	C6	C4+	B10-	C6	D6		
Cowdenbeath	D9	D8	D7	D8	D9	D5	D2+	C8	C10-	D5	D3	D1+	C6	C9-	D2+	C3+	B9-	C1+	B8	B9	B10-	C9-	D10
Dumbarton	C2+	B10-	C9-	D10	D4	D6	D6	D2+	C6	C3	C7	C10-	D5	D8	D1+	C6	C7	C3+	B7	B5	B7	B8	B8
Dundee	B3	B5	B3	B1+	A5	A7	A6	A9	A6	A7	A12-	B7	B3	B2	B4	B2	B6	B2+	A12-	B1+	A6	A8	A10
Dundee United	A10-	B2+	A3	A7	A9	A8	A11	A8	A11	A5	A9	A9	A9	A5	A5	A3	A4	A4	A6	A4	A5	A12-	B3
Dunfermline Ath	B2	B1+	A5	A8	A10-	B2+	A9	A6	A5	A4	A11	A11	A12-	B5	B3	B3	B1+	A12-	B9-	C2	C7	C1+	B5
East Fife	C8	C2+	B10-	C6	C9-	D4	D4	D8	D2+	C9-	D8	D7	D4	D1+	C6	C7	C5	C6	C9	C9-	D4	D1+	C5
East Stirlingshire	D4	D7	D9	D4	D8	D7	D8	D7	D10	D10	D10	D10	D10	D9	D3	D3	D9	D10	D10	D8	D9	D10-	
Edinburgh City																							D7
Elgin City							D10	D6	D9	D9	D6	D5	D9	D6	D10	D9	D7	D4	D5	D9	D7	D2	D5
Falkirk	A5	A10-	B5	B2	B2	B3	B3	B9	B1	B4	B1+	A10	A7	A7	A10	A12-	B3	B3	B3	B3	B5	B2	B2
Forfar Athletic	D1+	C9-	D2+	C7	C10-	D3+	C8	C3	C4	C6	C5	C8	C10-	D10	D6	D2+	C3	C7	C4	C7	C3	C10	D2+
Gretna									D6	D3	D1+	C1+	B1+	A12-									
Hamilton Accies	B6	B9-	C2+	B8	B9-	C10-	D1+	C5	C8	C2+	B7	B3	B4	B1+	A9	A7	A12-	B4	B5	B2+	A7	A10	A11
Hearts	A6	A4	A4	A3	A6	A3	A5	A5	A3	A3	A5	A2	A4	A8	A3	A6	A3	A5	A10	A12-	B1+	A3	A5
Hibernian	A3	A5	A9	A10-	B1+	A6	A3	A10	A7	A8	A3	A4	A6	A6	A6	A4	A10	A11	A7	A11-	B2	B3	B1+
Inverness CT	D6	D3	D1+	C5	C2+	B6	B4	B6	B4	B1+	A8	A7	A8	A9	A12-	B1+	A7	A10	A4	A5	A3	A7	A12-
Kilmarnock	A7	A7	A7	A4	A4	A9	A4	A7	A4	A10	A7	A5	A5	A1	A8	A11	A5	A7	A9	A9	A10	A11	A8
Livingston	C9-	D1+	C3	C3	C1+	B4	B1+	A3	A9	A9	A10	A12-	B6	B7	B7-	D1+	C1+	B5	B4	B6	B8	B9-	C1
Montrose	D2+	C10-	D6	D9	D10	D9	D9	D5	D7	D6	D5	D9	D8	D3	D5	D10	D8	D8	D6	D6	D10	D8	D4
Morton	C1+	B3	B8	B5	B6	B8	B9-	C10-	D1+	C4	C3	C2	C1+	B8	B6	B8	B7	B8	B2	B10-	C1+	B5	B4
Motherwell	A2	A8	A8	A9	A7	A4	A8	A11	A12	A6	A6	A8	A10	A3	A7	A5	A6	A3	A2	A2	A11	A5	A9
Partick Thistle	A8	A9-	B6	B9-	C8	C5	C1+	B1+	A10	A12-	B9-	C4+	B7	B6	B2	B6	B5	B6	B1+	A10	A8	A9	A6
Peterhead							D5	D4	D4	D4	D2+	C3	C8	C5	C4	C5	C10-	D5	D2	D1+	C6	C3	C9-
Queen of the S	C7	C7	C5	C4	C4	C9	C6	C1+	B5	B5	B4	B8	B8	B4	B5	B4	B4	B10-	C1+	B4	B4	B7	B6
Queen's Park	D8	D6	D8	D7	D6	D1+	C9-	D10	D8	D7	D4	D6	D3+	C8	C9-	D4	D3	D2	D3	D10	D2	D4+	C6
Raith Rovers	B1+	A6	A10-	B3	B8	B5	B7	B10-	C1+	B8	B10-	C7	C3	C3	C1+	B7	B2	B7	B6	B7	B6	B4	B9-
Rangers	A1	A1	A1	A2	A1	A1	A2	A2	A1	A2	A1	A3	A2	A2	A1	A1	A1	A2-	D1+	C1+	B3	B1+	A3
Ross County	D3	D4	D3	D3	D1+	C3+	B6	B4	B8	B6	B6	B4	B10-	C1+	B8	B5	B8	B1+	A5	A7	A9	A6	A7
St Johnstone	B5	B4	B1+	A5	A3	A5	A10	A12-	B3	B3	B8	B2	B2	B3	B1+	A8	A8	A6	A3	A6	A4	A4	A4
St Mirren	B7	B6	B4	B6	B5	B1+	A12-	B8	B7	B7	B2	B1+	A11	A10	A11	A10	A11	A8	A11	A8	A12-	B6	B7
Stenhousemuir	C4	C4	C6	C9-	D2+	C8	C7	C9	C7	C10-	D7	D3	D7	D5	D4+	C8	C8	C5	C6	C5	C9	C8	C10-
Stirling Albion	C3	C1+	B7	B10-	C6	C7	C10-	D9	D5	D2+	C4	C5	C2+	B10-	C5	C1+	B10-	C10-	D7	D3+	C10-	D7	D6
Stranraer	B10-	C8	C8	C1+	B10-	C6	C4	C7	C9-	D1+	C2+	B9-	C9-	D2+	C10-	D7	D5	D3+	C8	C3	C2	C4	C7

A Premier Division / Premiership

B Division One / Championship

C Division Two / League One

D Division Three / League Two

* Clydebank changed their name to Airdrie United in 2002, then to Airdrieonians in 2013

SPFL ATTENDANCE FIGURES 2016/17

Premiership	AB	CEL	DUN	HAM	HEA	ICT	KIL	MOT	PAR	RAN	ROS	SJ	Total	Home	Mean
Aberdeen		17105	10512	13131	13559	11356	*8195*	10384	11049	19263	10091	11501			
		16015			12178	11507		12524	10094	**19332**	11774	10606	240176	19	12640
Celtic	53985		53589	55076	58247	54152	57679	54159	55733	58348	55355	*51057*			
	57758			54685	**58967**		53532	56366	54047	58545		52796	1054076	19	55477
Dundee	6321	8827		5287	6160	5094	5111	5471	4783	**9702**	4742	6492			
	7314	8968		6489		5574	*4708*		5328	9017	6812		122200	19	6431
Hamilton	2315	5003	1853		2339	*1611*	2228	3526	2210	**5292**	1609	1705			
	2006		2616			1745	2159	4173			1548	1662	48082	19	2530
							2482								
Hearts	16630	16777	16512	15497		15880	16696	16129	16418	**16803**	16231	16421			
	16552	16539	16304	15881		16372			15930	16570	*15470*		309612	19	16295
Inverness	4867	6061	2884	*2473*	3565		2592	3097	2823	**7012**	4204	2729			
		5948	2606	2478			2780	5351		6415	4123	2961	74969	19	3945
Kilmarnoc	4592	10962	3615	3387	3917	3294		4308	4169	**11800**	3207	*3056*			
	3972		4040		4110	3137		4726	4519	9548	3951		94310	19	4963
Motherwe	3428	**8535**	4078	4514	4666	*3131*	3684		3759	7902	3177	3739			
			4002	4644	4651	3696	5246				3870	3588	85229	19	4485
			4919												
Partick Th	3974	7609	3758	2843	4919	2943	3584	3227		**7951**	3777	2885			
	3924	7847		3057	4143	3082		3920		6799	3149	*2257*	85648	20	4282
Rangers	50003	**50126**	48773	49125	50039	48528	49302	48716	49680		47935	46563			
	48289	49822		49090	47809			49198	49748		49428	*46800*	928974	19	48893
Ross Coun	4467	6290	3669	3275	4042	5111	3263	3019	2935	**6590**		3299			
		6205	2819	4871		4928	3380	*2511*				3187	73861	18	4103
St Johnsto	5728	6823	3646	3279	5456	*2549*	2930	2836	3096	**7979**	2554				
	5132	6548	4195		4197		2933		3630	6799					
					3141								83451	19	4392
Total	301257	228890	183878	285951	270368	180827	224289	270733	278808	253072	231142	251197			
Away	19	19	19	19	19	19	19	19	18	19	20	19			
Mean	15855	12046	9677	15050	14229	9517	11804	14249	15489	13319	11557	13220			

Championship	AYR	DUM	UTD	PARS	FAL	HIB	MOR	QUE	RAI	STM	Total	Home	Mean
Ayr United		1441	2049	2883	1414	**3100**	1441	1842	1550	2165			
		1608	*1205*	2261	1614	2152	1576	1476	1103	2712	33592	18	1866
Dumbarton	1005		1475	1018	832	1339	1147	840	*600*	1101			
	1198		1221	1142	**1660**	1523	1323	825	719	1377	20345	18	1130
Dundee United	6427	5979		5996	7046	**10925**	5829	7058	7434	7247			
	4661	5107		5304	6313	9532	6065	6136	5232	6225	118516	18	6584
Dunfermline Athletic	3250	3496	5563		6134	**7622**	3101	3973	5649	2732			
	3276	3320	4670		5076	7058	3339	*2653*	4865	4108	79885	18	4438
Falkirk	4345	4311	5488	6377		6458	4432	4170	4773	4486			
	5038	*4160*	5028	5953		**6747**	4584	4673	4823	4737	90583	18	5032
Hibernian	15056	13881	15492	16477	14551		14508	*13861*	15409	14485			
	14349	14093	18786	14437	16140		15149	17054	13604	**19764**	277096	18	15394
Morton	1859	1586	2578	1756	2079	2156		1628	1528	3378			
	2390	2094	2159	2670	2397	4229		*1451*	1957	**4609**	42504	18	2361
Queen of the South	1982	1261	2316	1561	1841	**3703**	1695		1864	*1147*			
	1594	1289	1514	1849	1995	3007	1588		1484	1728	33418	18	1856
Raith Rovers	1241	1636	4361	5114	2320	3753	*1161*	1244		2140			
	3054	1413	2192	**5899**	2202	4172	1720	1609		2124	47355	18	2630
St Mirren	3124	2758	3612	*2126*	2334	4517	**4997**	3102	2630				
	4620	3906	3766	4582	3316	3441	4902	3105	4937		65775	18	3654
Total Away	78469	73339	83475	87405	79264	85434	78557	76700	80161	86265			
Away	18	18	18	18	18	18	18	18	18	18			
Mean	4359	4074	4637	4855	4403	4746	4364	4261	4453	4792			

Bold = Biggest Home

Italic = Smallest Home

League One	AIR	ALB	ALL	BRE	EF	LIV	PET	QP	STE	STR	Total	Home	Mean
Airdrieonians		972	790	739	814	1048	*482*	702	791	812			
		1633	757	676	833	1012	599	1011	568	706	14945	18	830
Albion Rovers	**1199**		411	*228*	419	413	360	444	301	321			
	873		348	332	488	454	285	512	327	377	8092	18	449
Alloa	644	453		*386*	652	**712**	504	442	458	309			
	540	606		662	436	565	504	675	508	507	9563	18	531
Brechin City	466	*283*	413		414	517	431	447	402	402			
	346	422	372		525	523	**553**	393	403	403	7715	18	428
East Fife	706	682	*412*	609		784	486	557	563	555			
	908	539	612	642		661	636	692	635	584	11263	18	625
Livingston	989	702	977	858	907		712	819	769	693			
	832	*548*	**1099**	746	773		891	821	531	677	14344	18	796
Peterhead	475	503	365	621	492	569		519	427	444			
	524	*423*	**681**	483	495	582		442	587	449	9081	18	504
Queen's Park	**957**	662	664	632	571	698	524		538	534			
	922	677	657	*481*	566	701	501		764	556	11605	18	644
Stenhousemuir	597	371	466	352	356	334	*331*	534		341			
	604	433	335	557	455	472	362	423		392	7715	18	428
Stranraer	*317*	402	448	402	428	333	376	446	323				
	489	364	383	340	462	**523**	459	434	440		7369	18	409
Total	12388	10675	10190	9746	10086	10901	8996	10313	9335	9062			
Away	18	18	18	18	18	18	18	18	18	18			
Average	688	593	566	541	560	605	499	572	518	503			

League Two	ANN	ARB	BER	CYD	COW	EDC	ELG	FOR	MON	SA	Total	Home	Mean
Annan Athletic		326	430	421	241	351	353	403	*289*	421			
		456	460	398	386	379	328	432	**461**	420	6955	18	386
Arbroath	*482*		502	615	588	582	584	862	**1731**	601			
	566		539	566	519	775	807	1008	1156	625	13108	18	728
Berwick Rangers	366	390		469	454	515	407	421	361	*302*			
	355	425		336	408	**695**	403	480	452	440	7679	18	426
Clyde	467	559	546		538	461	616	660	445	**738**			
	462	465	710		395	484	465	490	*365*	606	9472	18	526
Cowdenbeath	331	317	327	309		325	315	277	270	342			
	258	501	343	460		309	278	**571**	302	381	6216	18	345
Edinburgh City	*246*	**590**	419	432	382		352	547	309	368			
	378	481	423	302	577		396	352	341	388	7283	18	404
Elgin City	583	*519*	535	713	650	610		**1091**	586	585			
	638	640	588	881	909	563		709	781	785	12366	18	687
Forfar Athletic	*337*	786	477	659	516	491	537		740	635			
	917	**1564**	477	741	547	446	551		725	632	11778	18	654
Montrose	340	794	*283*	396	393	388	302	630		610			
	384	1002	1222	**1324**	432	454	562	984		401	10901	18	605
Stirling Albion	694	605	517	777	538	465	457	663	497				
	531	**1748**	515	718	638	501	*412*	738	494		11508	18	639
Total Away	8335	12168	9313	10517	9111	8794	8125	11318	10305	9280			
	18	18	18	18	18	18	18	18	18	18			
Average Away	463	676	517	584	506	488	451	628	572	515			

Club Largest Home in Bold
Smallest Home in Italics

The question of the accuracy of attendance figures is a vexed one. Different clubs use different methods in "calculating" match attendances. Dunfermline Athletic issued the following statement at the end of the season:

"It now appears that the majority of clubs in the SPFL count all of their season ticket holders (even if they do not attend a specific match), into their published match day attendance figure, something that we as a club have never done. Therefore, our Board has decided to change its policy on this as from next season, so that we are on an equal terms, and published figures do not appear to disadvantage our club, which is the case at present."

This confirms what was already well-known – that attendance figures now relate to "tickets sold" rather than "people attending". The big Glasgow clubs, for example, start calculating the attendance with their stadium capacity, and simply deduct any unsold places to arrive at the attendance figure.

At Celtic this caused a huge disparity in 2015/16. Published attendances were frequently in the 45-50,000 bracket when actual attendances were around the 25-30,000 mark. This differential was much less marked in 2016/17 when actual attendances were much closer to the published figures, other than for a few midweek games. However, the actual increase in people going to games would not be reflected in official attendance figures and summaries.

CLUB TWITTER FOLLOWERS 2016/17

	Pos 2017	Pos 2016	Up / Down	Jul-17	Jul-16	Jul-15
Celtic	1	1		473000	337000	287000
Rangers	2	2		338000	241000	188000
Aberdeen	3	3		78200	55600	43800
Hearts	4	4		64100	49600	40100
Hibernian	5	5		59500	45900	33500
Dundee United	6	6		43300	34200	27200
Dundee	7	7		34800	25400	19300
Motherwell	8	8		28200	22600	19000
St Johnstone	9	9		27200	20600	16000
Inverness CT	10	10		24100	19400	16200
Kilmarnock	11	11		23200	17000	12900
St Mirren	12	12		20100	16000	13400
Partick Thistle	13	13		19700	15400	12200
Falkirk	14	14		17700	14200	10300
Hamilton Accies	15	15		17400	13000	10100
Dunfermline Athletic	16	16		15200	12300	9732
Raith Rovers	17	18	1	13600	10600	8058
Cowdenbeath	18	17	-1	13300	11500	9723
Morton	19	19		13200	10200	8089
Livingston	20	21	1	11400	9015	7265
Stenhousemuir	21	20	-1	10800	9241	8068
Clyde	22	26	4	10700	7142	5598
Queen of the South	23	23		10400	7820	6534
Albion Rovers	24	24		10100	7666	6177
Edinburgh City	25	37	12	9943	4869	2898
East Fife	26	22	4	9772	7924	6524
Stirling Albion	27	25	-2	9497	7605	6146
Ross County	28	35	7	9016	5488	2204
Airdrieonians	29	29		8860	6688	5022
Berwick Rangers	30	28	-2	8504	6743	5531
Ayr United	31	31		8441	6435	4808
Stranraer	32	30	2	8429	6516	4809
Elgin City	33	32	1	8237	6360	4988
Queen's Park	34	33	-1	7905	5971	4560
Dumbarton	35	27	-8	7684	6978	5827
Forfar Athletic	36	34	-2	7589	5678	4336
Montrose	37	36	-1	6816	5118	3922
Annan Athletic	38	38		5342	4003	2823
Brechin City	39	41	2	5268	2868	2709
Peterhead	40	39	-1	4918	3549	2246
Arbroath	41	40	-1	4509	3064	2210
Alloa Athletic	42	42		2758	1929	1371

LOWLAND LEAGUE		
Spartans	7614	6833
East Stirlingshire	6771	5419
East Kilbride	5369	3323
Selkirk	3495	3047
Gala Fairydean Rovers	3285	2595
Whitehill Welfare	2898	2383
Cumbernauld Colts	2972	2336
Gretna 2008	2655	2219
Preston Athletic		2010
Stirling University	2436	1916
Dalbeattie Star	1929	1508
Edinburgh University	1727	1430
Vale of Leithen	1629	1405
BSC Glasgow	2009	1403
Threave Rovers		1282
Hawick Royal Albert	1208	672
Civil Service Strollers	749	359
Edusport Academy	1575	
HIGHLAND LEAGUE		
Formartine United	11900	12900
Brora Rangers	4193	3718
Inverurie Locos	3941	3400
Wick Academy	3333	3045
Fort William	3042	2600
Fraserburgh	3064	2544
Huntly	2754	2214
Cove Rangers	2776	2097
Forres Mechanics	2542	2008
Deveronvale	2337	1906
Clachnacuddin	1885	1883
Lossiemouth	2247	1724
Strathspey Thistle	1752	1579
Buckie Thistle	2596	1381
Turriff United	1722	1166
Rothes	1622	1088
Keith	1643	1038
Nairn County	1118	366

VIEWING FIGURES FOR TELEVISED MATCHES

This information refers to Satellite tv only—figures were not available for terrestrial or BBC Alba matches.

Champions League	Lincoln Red Imps vs Celtic	12/07/2016	19:00	BT Sport 2	156000
League Cup	Arbroath vs Dundee United	15/07/2016	19:30	BT Sport 1	42000
League Cup	Motherwell vs Rangers	16/07/2016	15:00	BT Sport 1	80000
League Cup	East Stirlingshire vs Rangers	22/07/2016	19:30	BT Sport 1	109000
League Cup	St Johnstone vs Falkirk	23/07/2016	15:00	BT Sport 1	28000
Friendly	Celtic vs Leicester	23/07/2016	17:30	Sky Sports 1	273000
League Cup	Rangers vs Stranraer	25/07/2016	19:30	BT Sport 1	105000
League Cup	Dundee Utd vs Dunfermline	31/07/2016	15:00	BT Sport 1	44000
Friendly	Celtic vs Barcelona	30/07/2016	17:30	Sky Sports 1	226000
SPFL Premiership	Rangers vs Hamilton	06/08/2016	12:30	Sky Sports 1/5	251000
SPFL Premiership	St Johnstone vs Aberdeen	07/08/2016	12:00	Bt Sport 1	77000
SPFL Premiership	Hearts vs Celtic	07/08/2016	14:00	Sky Sports 1/5	332000
SPFL Premiership	Dundee vs Rangers	13/08/2016	12:00	BT Sport 1	111000
League Cup	Celtic vs Motherwell	10/08/2016	19:30	BT Sport 1	92000
Champions League	Celtic vs Hapoel Beer Sheva	17/08/2016	19:45	BT Sport 2	152000
SPFL Premiership	St Johnstone vs Celtic	20/08/2016	12:00	BT Sport 1	74000
SPFL Premiership	Kilmarnock vs Rangers	26/08/2016	19:45	BT Sport 1	150000
Champions League	Hapoel Beer Sheva vs Celtic	23/08/2016	19:45	BT Sport	200000
International	Malta vs Scotland	04/09/2016	19:00	Sky Sports	359000
SPFL Premiership	Celtic vs Rangers	10/09/2016	12:00	Sky Sports 1	321000
SPFL Premiership	Inverness vs Celtic	18/09/2016	15:00	BT Sport 1	186000
Champions League	Barcelona vs Celtic	14/09/2016	19:45	BT Sport 3	246000
SPFL Premiership	Dundee vs Aberdeen	18/09/2016	12:15	Sky Sports 2	70000
League Cup	Rangers vs Queen of the South	20/09/2016	19:30	BT Sport 1	85000
League Cup	Celtic vs Alloa	21/09/2016	19:30	BT Sport 1	142000
League Cup	Aberdeen vs St Johnstone	22/09/2016	19:30	BT Sport 1	105000
SPFL Premiership	Aberdeen vs Rangers	25/09/2016	13:00	Sky Sports 1/5	303000
SPFL Premiership	Dundee vs Celtic	01/10/2016	12:45	BT Sport 1	123000
Champions League	Celtic vs Man City	28/09/2016	19:45	BT Sport 2	592000
SPFL Premiership	Motherwell vs Hearts	30/09/2016	19:45	BT Sport 2	58000
SPFL Championship	Hibs vs Dundee United	02/10/2016	12:00	Sky Sports 2	48000
International	Scotland vs Lithuania	08/10/2016	19:45	Sky Sports 2	298000
SPFL Premiership	Inverness vs Rangers	14/10/2016	19:45	BT Sport 1	107000
League Cup	Morton vs Aberdeen	22/10/2016	12:00	BT SPort 1	100000
League Cup	Celtic vs Rangers	23/10/2016	15:00	BT Sport 1	382000
Champions League	Celtic vs Borussia Moenchengladbach	19/10/2016	19:45	BT Sport ESPN	117000
SPFL Premiership	St Johnstone vs Dundee	23/10/2016	13:00	Sky Sports 5	37000
SPFL Premiership	Ross County vs Celtic	26/10/2016	19:45	BT Sport 1	97000
SPFL Premiership	Aberdeen vs Celtic	29/10/2016	12:00	Sky Sports 5	70000
Champions League	Borussia Moenchengladbach vs Celtic	01/11/2016	19:45	BT ESPN	189000
SPFL Premiership	Partick Thistle vs Aberdeen	04/11/2016	19:45	BT Sport 1	N/A
SPFL Premiership	Ross County vs Rangers	06/11/2016	12:15	Sky Sports 2	83000
International	England vs Scotland	11/11/2016	20:00	ITV	6380000
SPFL Premiership	Kilmarnock vs Celtic	18/11/2016	19:45	BT Sport 1	89000
League Cup	Celtic vs Aberdeen	27/11/2016	15:00	BT Sport 1	165000
Champions League	Celtic vs Barcelona	23/11/2016	19:45	BT ESPN	216000
SPFL Premiership	Partick Thistle vs Rangers	26/11/2016	12:15	Sky Sports 1/5	151000
SPFL Championship	Dundee Utd vs Hibs	02/12/2016	19:45	BT Sport 2	52000
SPFL Premiership	Motherwell vs Celtic	03/12/2016	12:15	Sky Sports 5	90000

Champions League	Manchester City vs Celtic	06/12/2016	19:45	BT Sport 3	N/A
SPFL Premiership	Partick Thistle vs Celtic	09/12/2016	19:45		N/A
SPFL Premiership	Hamilton vs Rangers	16/12/2016	19:45	BT Sport 1	147000
SPFL Premiership	Motherwell vs Aberdeen	23/12/2016	19:45	BT Sport 1	103000
SPFL Premiership	Hamilton vs Celtic	24/12/2016	12:30	Sky Sports 1/5	156000
SPFL Premiership	St Johnstone vs Rangers	28/12/2016	19:45	BT Sport 1	156000
SPFL Premiership	Hearts vs Aberdeen	30/12/2016	19:45	BT Sport 2	74000
SPFL Premiership	Rangers vs Celtic	31/12/2016	12:30	Sky Sports 1/5	734000
Scottish Cup	Rangers vs Motherwell	21/01/2017	12:30	Sky Sports 2/5	124000
Scottish Cup	Albion Rovers vs Celtic	22/01/2017	15:00	Sky Sports 5	8900
SPFL Premiership	Aberdeen vs Dundee	27/01/2017	19:45	BT Sport 1	3700
SPFL Premiership	Motherwell vs Rangers	28/01/2017	12:15	Sky Sports 1	157000
SPFL Premiership	Celtic vs Hearts	29/01/2017	12:15	Sky Sports 1/5	21100
SPFL Premiership	Motherwell vs Hearts	04/02/2017	12:15	BT Sport 1	6700
SPFL Premiership	Hearts vs Rangers	01/02/2017	19:45	BT Sport 2	15500
SPFL Premiership	St Johnstone vs Celtic	05/02/2017	12:15	Sky Sports 5	7800
Scottish Cup	Hearts vs Hibs	12/02/2017	12:30	Sky Sports 2/Mix	19200
scottish Cup	Rangers vs Morton	12/02/2017	15:00	Sky Sports 2	17000
SPFL Premiership	Kilmarnock vs Aberdeen	19/02/2017	12:30	Sky SPorts 1	17400
SPFL Premiership	Dundee vs Rangers	19/02/2017	15:00	Sky SPorts 1/5	20800
SPFL Premiership	Inverness vs Rangers	24/02/2017	19:45	BT Sport 1	11900
SPFL Premiership	Hamilton vs Aberdeen	28/02/2017	19:45	BT Sport 1	5600
SPFL Premiership	Inverness vs Celtic	01/03/2017	19:45	Sky Sports 1	N/
Scottish Cup	Rangers vs Hamilton	04/03/2017	12:45	Sky Sports 2	11100
Scottish Cup	Celtic vs St Mirren	05/03/2017	12:45	Sky Sports 5	15200
SPFL Championship	Dundee Utd vs Hibs	10/03/2017	19:45	BT Sport 1	6500
SPFL Premiership	Celtic vs Rangers	12/03/2017	12:00	Sky Sports 1/5	46500
SPFL Premiership	Aberdeen vs Hearts	18/03/2017	12:30	BT Sport 1	5200
SPFL Premiership	Dundee vs Celtic	19/03/2017	12:30	Sky Sports 2	14900
International	Scotland vs Canada	22/03/2017	19:45	Sky Sports	9300
International	Scotland vs Slovenia	26/03/2017	19:45	Sky Sports 1	29900
SPFL Premiership	Dundee vs Aberdeen	31/03/2017	19:45	BT Sport 1	
SPFL Premiership	Hearts vs Celtic	02/04/2017	12:30	Sky Sports 2/Mix	16200
SPFL Premiership	Kilmarnock vs Rangers	05/04/2017	19:45	Sky Sports 2	490
SPFL Premiership	Aberdeen vs Rangers	09/04/2017	12:30	Sky Sports 2	680
SPFL Premiership	Ross County vs Celtic	16/04/2017	12:30	Sky Sports 2	750
Scottish Cup	Celtic vs Rangers	23/04/2017	12:00	Sky Sports 2	3860
SPFL Premiership	Rangers vs Celtic	29/04/2017	12:00	Sky Sports	3090
SPFL Premiership	Ross County vs Inverness	28/04/2017	19:45	BT Sport 1	
SPFL Premiership	Inverness vs Hamilton	06/05/2017	12:30	Sky Sports	490
SPFL Premiership	Aberdeen vs Celtic	12/05/2017	19:45	BT Sport 1	
SPFL Premiership	Rangers vs Hearts	13/05/2017	12:30	Sky Sports	880
SPFL Championship	Dundee United vs Falkirk	16/05/2017	19:45	BT Sport 1	630
SPFL Championship	Falkirk vs Dundee United	19/05/2017	19:45	BT Sport 1	1220
SPFL Premiership	Partick Thistle vs Celtic	18/05/2017	19:45	Sky Sports 5	520
SPFL Premiership	Celtic vs Hearts	21/05/2017	12:30	Sky Sports 2	2000
SPFL Championship	Dundee United vs Hamilton Accies	25/05/2017	19:45	BT Sport 1	
SPFL Championship	Hamilton Accies vs Dundee United	28/05/2017	15:00	BT Sport 1	
Scottish Cup	Celtic vs Aberdeen	27/05/2017	15:00	Sky Sports 1	2270

PRICE OF FOOTBALL SURVEY 2016/17

	Cheapest season ticket	Dearest season ticket	Lowest matchday ticket	Highest matchday ticket	Programme	Pie	Tea	Cheapest adult away	Dearest adult away	Adult shirt	Junior shirt
Aberdeen	£319	£406	£22	£28	£3	£1.95	£2.20	£25	£25	£50	£40
Celtic	£337	£559	£23	£49	£3	£2.30	£2.20	£23	£49	£53	£40
Dundee	£340	£385	£22	£25	£3	£1.95	£2.10	£22	£25	£45	£35
Hamilton	£150	£150	£22	£22	£2.50	£2.10	£1	£22	£22	£49	£39
Hearts	£280	£480	£18	£32	£3.50	£2.20	£2	£18	£28	£45	£35
Inverness	£297	£380	£22	£30	£3	£2.20	£2.20	n/a	£25	£35	£25
Kilmarnock	£280	£330	£20	£26	£3	£2.20	£2	£20	£26	£45	£36
Motherwell	£310	£420	£19	£27	£3	£2.20	£1.90	£23	£27	£45	£35
Partick Thistle	£308	£340	£22	£25	£3	£2.20	£2	£22	£25	£40	£30
Rangers	£295	£625	£22	£49	£3.50	£2.50	£2.50	£24	£49	£47.99	£36.99
Ross County	£300	£360	£20	£26	£2	£2.20	£1.20	£20	£26	£40	£30
St Johnstone	£310	£375	£23	£24	£2.50	£2.10	£2	£23	£27	£40	£35
Ayr United	£220	£220	£17	£17	£2	£1.50	£1	£17	£17	£55	£45
Dumbarton	£215	£250	£18	£20	£2.50	£1.90	£1.90	£18	£20	£40	£35
Dundee United	£279	£440	£20	£25	£2.50	£1.90	£2.10	£20	£22	£45	£36
Dumfermline	£225	£285	£17	£19	£3	£2	£1.70	£17	£17	£40	£35
Falkirk	£225	£325	£18	£20	£2.50	£1.90	£1.60	£18	£18	£45	£35
Greenock Morton	£250	£270	£18	£18	£2	£1.50	£1	£18	£18	£45	£38
Hibernian	£335	£380	£22	£22	£3	£2.40	£2.20	£22	£22	£45	£36
Queen of the South	£256	£256	£16	£16	£2.50	£1.60	£1.20	£16	£16	£40	£35
Raith Rovers	£250	£300	£15	£20	£2	£1.80	£0.80	£15	£20	£40	£30
St Mirren	£275	£350	£20	£22	£3	£2.15	£2.05	£20	£20	n/a	n/a
Airdrieonians	£235	£250	£16	£16	£2	n/a	n/a	£16	£16	£45	£35
Albion Rovers	£180	£180	£14	£14	£2	£2	£1	£14	£14	£40	£30
Alloa	£190	£220	£16	£16	£2	£1.50	£1	£16	£16	£35	£30
Brechin City	£185	£200	£13	£13	£2	£2	£1	£13	£13	£35	£26
East Fife	£162	£180	£13	£13	£2	£1.70	£1.30	£13	£13	£40	£35
Livingston	£180	£180	£12	£12	£2.50	£1.50	£1.70	£12	£12	£39.99	£29.99
Peterhead	£165	£215	£12	£12	£2.50	£2	£1.40	£12	£12	£45	£35
Queen's Park	£160	£160	£12	£12	n/a	£2.30	£2.30	£12	£12	£40	£35
Stenhousemuir	£180	£180	£12	£13	n/a	£2	£1.50	£12	£13	£36.99	£26.99
Stranraer	£185	£215	£15	£15	£2	£1.50	£1	£15	£15	£40	£32
Annan Athletic	£120	£145	£12	£12	£2	£1.50	£1	£12	£12	£35	£25
Arbroath	£180	£180	£13	£13	£2	£1.50	£1	£13	£13	£38	£32
Berwick Rangers	£144	£150	£12	£12	£2.50	£2	£1.50	£12	£12	£35	£25
Clyde	£166.25	£175	£13	£13	£2.50	£2	£1.50	£13	£13	£40	£32.50
Cowdenbeath	£160	£170	£12	£12	£2.50	£2	£1	£12	£12	£40	£30
Edinburgh City	£120	£120	£12	£12	£2	£1.50	£1	£12	£12	£29.99	£19.99
Elgin City	£145	£175	£12	£14	£2	£1.80	£1	£12	£14	£35	£25
Forfar Athletic	£180	£190	£12	£13	£2	£1.20	£0.80	£12	£13	£36	£26
Montrose	£175	£295	£12	£12	£2	£2	£1	£12	£12	£45	£36
Stirling Albion	£170	£170	£13	£13	£3	£2	£1.50	£13	£13	£40	£35

Source: BBC Price of Football Survey

CHAMPIONS LEAGUE DIVVY-UP 2016/17

UEFA CHAMPIONS LEAGUE MONEY 2016/17 (Million Euros)

	Celtic	Leicester	Arsenal	Spurs	Man City
Participation	***12.7***	***12.7***	***12.7***	***12.7***	***12.7***
PO Eliminated					
PO Winners	2				2
GS Results	1.5	7.2	8.4	4.2	24.8
last 16		6	6		18
QF		6.5			6.5
SF					
RU					
Winners					
Prize Money	3.5	19.7	14-Apr	4.2	13
TV Pool	14.3	45.7	35.3	24.9	22.5
Total Revenue	***30.5***	***78.1***	***62.4***	***41.8***	***48.2***

The Managers League Club Managers Since 1970

ABERDEEN
1965-71 Eddie Turnbull
1971-75 Jimmy Bonthrone
1975-77 Ally McLeod
1977-78 Billy McNeill
1978-86 Alex Ferguson
1986-88 Ian Porterfield
1988-91 Alex Smith / Jocky Scott
1991-92 Alex Smith
1992-95 Willie Miller
1995-97 Roy Aitken
1997-98 Alex Miller
1998-99 Paul Hegarty
1999-2002 Ebbe Skovdahl
2002-04 Steve Paterson
2004-09 Jimmy Calderwood
2009-10 Mark McGhee
2010-13 Craig Brown
2013- Derek McInnes

AIRDRIEONIANS /AIRDRIE UNITED
1967-70 Ralph Collins
1970-76 Ian McMillan
1976-78 Jackie Stewart
1978-82 Bobby Watson
1982-83 Bill Munro
1983-85 Ally McLeod
1985-86 Ian McMillan
1987-87 Derek Whiteford
1987-89 Gordon McQueen
1989-91 Jimmy Bone
1991-99 Alex McDonald
1999-2000 Gary Mackay
2000-01 Steve Archibald
2001-02 Ian McCall
2006-06 Sandy Stewart
2006-10 Kenny Black
2010-13 Jimmy Boyle
2013-2015 Gary Bollan
2015-2016 Eddie Wolecki-Black
2016 Danny Lennon (Interim)
2016 Kevin McLeish (Interim)
2016-17 Mark Wilson
2017-

ALBION ROVERS
1969-72 Bobby Flavell
1972-73 Frank Beattie
1973-74 Ralph Brand
1974-76 George Caldwell
1976-81 Sam Goodwin
1981 Harry Hood
1981 Joe Baker
1981-82 Derek Whiteford
1982-83 Martin Ferguson
1983-84 Billy Wilson
1984 Benny Rooney
1984 Andy Ritchie
1984-85 Joe Baker
1986-87 Tommy Gemmell
1987-91 Dave Provan
1991-92 Mick Oliver
1992-93 Billy McLaren
1993-94 Tommy Gemmell
1994-95 Tom Spence
1995 Jimmy Crease
1996-98 Vinnie Moore
1998-99 Billy McLaren
1999-00 Mark Shanks
2000-02 John McVeigh
2002-03 Peter Hetherston
2003-05 Kevin McAllister
2005 Jimmy Lindsay
2005-07 Jim Chapman
2007-08 John McCormack
2008-12 Paul Martin
2012-13 Todd Lumsden
2013-14 James Ward
2014-17 Darren Young
2017- Brian Kerr

ALLOA ATHLETIC
1969-71 Duncan McCallum
1971-72 Ian Crawford
1972-74 Dan McLindon
1974-80 Hugh Wilson
1980-82 Alex Totten
1982-84 Willie Garner
1984-86 Jimmy Thomson
1986-87 Dom Sullivan
1987-90 Gregor Abel
1990 Billy Little
1990-93 Hugh McCann
1993-95 Billy Lamont
1995-96 Pat McAulay
1996-98 Tom Hendrie
1999-2003 Terry Christie
2003-06 Tom Hendrie
2006-11 Alan Maitland
2011-14 Paul Hartley
2014-15 Barry Smith
2015 Danny Lennon
2015- 16 Jack Ross
2016- Jim Goodwin

ANNAN ATHLETIC
2006-12 Harry Cairney
2013-17 Jim Chapman
2017- Peter Murphy

ARBROATH
1962-80 Albert Henderson
1980-83 Ian Stewart
1983-85 George Fleming
1985-86 Jimmy Bone
1987-90 John Young
1990-91 Ian Gibson
1991 Walter Borthwick
1991-92 Michael Lawson
1992-94 Danny McGrain
1994 Jocky Scott
1994 Donald Park / George Mackie
1995-96 John Brogan
1996-97 Tommy Campbell
1997-2000 Dave Baikie
2000-03 John Brownlie
2003-04 Stevie Kirk
2004-05 Harry Cairney
2005-09 John McGlashan
2009-10 Jim Weir
2010-14 Paul Sheerin
2014-15 Allan Moore
2015-16 Todd Lumsden
2016- Dick Campbell

AYR UNITED
1966-75 Ally McLeod
1975-78 Alex Stuart
1978 Ally McLeod
1979-83 Willie McLean
1983-85 George Caldwell
1985-90 Ally McLeod
1991-93 George Burley
1993-95 Simon Stainrod
1995-2002 Gordon Dalziel
2002-04 Campbell Money
2004-05 Mark Shanks
2005-07 Robert Connor
2007 Neil Watt
2007-12 Brian Reid
2012-14 Mark Roberts
2015- Ian McCall

BERWICK RANGERS
1969-75 Harry Melrose
1975 Walter Galbraith
1976 Gordon Haig
1976-80 Dave Smith
1980-82 Frank Connor
1982-83 Jim McSherry
1983-87 Eric Tait
1987-88 Jimmy Thomson
1988-90 Jim Jefferies
1990-92 Ralph Callachan
1992 John Anderson
1992-94 Jimmy Crease
1994-96 Tom Hendrie
1996 Ian Ross
1996-97 Jimmy Thomson
1997-2004 Paul Smith
2004-05 Sandy Clark
2005-07 John Coughlin
2007-08 Michael Renwick
2008 Alan McGonnigal
2008-11 Jimmy Crease
2011-14 Ian Little
2014-15 Colin Cameron
2015- John Coughlin

BRECHIN CITY
1962-70 John Gilmartin
1970-71 Frank Sandeman
1971-72 Bobby Methven
1972-73 Kenny Dick
1973-77 Charlie Dunn
1977-80 Ian Stewart
1980-82 Doug Houston
1982-86 Ian Fleming
1987-93 John Ritchie
1993-94 Ian Redford
1994-2000 John Young
2000-05 Dick Campbell
2005-06 Ian Campbell
2006-08 Michael O'Neill
2009-10 Jim Duffy
2010-12 Jim Weir
2012-15 Ray McKinnon
2015- Darren Dods

CELTIC
1965-78 Jock Stein
1978-83 Billy McNeill
1983-87 Davie Hay
1987-91 Billy McNeill
1991-93 Liam Brady
1993-94 Lou Macari
1994-97 Tommy Burns
1997-98 Wim Jansen
1998-99 Jozef Venglos
1999-00 John Barnes
2000-05 Martin O'Neill
2005-09 Gordon Strachan
2009-10 Tony Mowbray
2010-14 Neil Lennon
2014-16 Ronnie Deila
2016- Brendan Rogers

CLYDE
1968-73 Archie Robertson
1973-77 Stan Anderson
1977 Billy McNeill
1977-86 Craig Brown
1986-92 John Clark
1992-96 Alex Smith
1996-98 Gardner Speirs
1998-02 Alan Maitland
2002-04 Alan Kernaghan
2004-05 Billy Reid
2005-06 Graham Roberts
2006-07 Joe Miller
2007-08 Colin Hendry
2008-09 John Brown
2009-10 John McCormack
2010-11 Stuart Miller
2011-14 Jim Duffy
2014-17 Barry Ferguson
2017 JP McGovern / Peter MacDonal
2017- Jim Chapman

COWDENBEATH
1968-74 Andy Matthew

1974 Bert Paton
1974-75 Dan McLindon
1975-77 Frank Connor
1977-80 Paddy Wilson
1980 Pat Stanton
1980-82 Andy Rolland
1982-83 Hugh Wilson
1983-84 Willie McCulloch
1984-85 John Clark
1985-87 Joe Craig
1987 Dick Campbell
1987-88 John Blackley
1988-92 John Brownlie
1992-93 Andy Harrow
1993-94 John Reilly
1994-95 Paddy Dolan
1995-97 Tom Steven
1997 Sammy Conn
1997-2000 Craig Levein
2000 Peter Cormack
2000-02 Gary Kirk
2002-04 Keith Wright
2004-05 Dave Baikie
2005-06 Mixu Paatelainen
2006-08 Brian Welsh
2008-10 Danny Lennon
2010-11 Jimmy Nicholl
2011-13 Colin Cameron
2013-15 Jimmy Nicholl
2015-16 Colin Nish
2016-17 Liam Fox
2017 Gary Locke
2017- Billy Brown

DUMBARTON
1968-73 Jackie Stewart
1973-77 Alex Wright
1977-80 Davie Wilson
1980-81 Sean Fallon
1981-84 Billy Lamont
1984-86 Davie Wilson
1986 Derek Whiteford
1986-87 Alex Totten
1987-88 Mark Clougherty
1988 Bertie Auld
1988-90 Jim George
1990-93 Billy Lamont
1993-95 Murdo McLeod
1995-96 Jim Fallon
1996-99 Ian Wallace
1999-2000 Jimmy Brown
2000-02 Tom Carson
2002-03 David Winnie
2003-04 Brian Fairley
2004-06 Paul Martin
2006-07 Gerry McCabe
2007 John Brown
2007-2010 Jim Chapman
2010-12 Alan Adamson
2012-15 Ian Murray
2015- Steven Aitken

DUNDEE
1968-71 John Prentice
1972-77 Davie White
1977-80 Tommy Gemmell
1980-83 Donald Mackay
1983-86 Archie Knox
1986-88 Jocky Scott
1988-89 Dave Smith
1989-91 Gordon Wallace
1991-92 Ian Munro
1992-93 Simon Stainrod
1993-96 Jim Duffy
1996-98 John McCormack
1998-2000 Jocky Scott
2000-02 Ivano Bonetti
2002-05 Jim Duffy
2005-06 Alan Kernaghan
2006-08 Alex Rae
2008-10 Jocky Scott
2010 Gordon Chisholm
2010-13 Barry Smith
2013-14 John Brown
2014-17 Paul Hartley
2017- Neil McCann

DUNDEE UNITED
1959-71 Jerry Kerr
1971-93 Jim McLean
1993-95 Ivan Golac
1995-96 Billy Kirkwood
1996-98 Tommy McLean
1998-2000 Paul Sturrock
2000-02 Alex Smith
2002-03 Paul Hegarty
2003-05 Ian McCall
2005-06 Gordon Chisholm
2006 Craig Brewster
2006-09 Craig Levein
2009-13 Peter Houston
2013-15 Jackie McNamara
2015-16 Mixu Paatelainen
2016- Ray McKinnon

DUNFERMLINE ATHLETIC
1967-70 George Farm
1970-72 Alex Wright
1972-75 George Miller
1975-80 Harry Melrose
1980-82 Pat Stanton
1982-83 Tom Forsyth
1983-90 Jim Leishman
1990-91 Ian Munro
1991-93 Jocky Scott
1993-99 Bert Paton
1999 Dick Campbell
1999-2004 Jimmy Caldwerwood
2004-05 Davie Hay
2005-06 Jim Leishman
2006-07 Steven Kenny
2007-12 Jim McIntyre
2012-14 Jim Jefferies
2014-15 John Potter
2015- Alan Johnston

EAST FIFE
1969-70 Bill Baxter
1970-73 Pat Quinn
1973-76 Frank Christie
1976-78 Roy Barry
1978-87 Dave Clarke
1987-93 Gavin Murray
1993-94 Alex Totten
1994-96 Steve Archibald
1996-97 Jimmy Bone
1997-99 Stevie Kirk
1999-2001 Rab Shannon
2001-02 Dave Clarke
2002-06 Jim Moffat
2006-09 David Baikie
2009-10 Stevie Crawford
2010-12 John Robertson
2012 Gordon Durie
2012-13 Billy Brown
2013 Willie Aitchison
2013-16 Gary Naysmith
2016-17 Barry Smith
2017- Darren Young

EDINBURGH CITY
2010- Gary Jardine

ELGIN CITY
2000-02 Alex Caldwell
2002-03 Harry McFadden
2003-05 David Robertson
2006 Brian Irvine
2007-08 Robbie Williamson
2009-14 Ross Jack
2014 Barry Wilson
2014- Jim Weir

FALKIRK
1968-73 Willie Cunningham
1973-75 John Prentice
1975-77 George Miller
1977-79 Billy Little
1979-82 John Hagart
1982-83 Alex Totten
1983-84 Gregor Abel
1984-87 Billy Lamont
1987-88 Dave Clarke
1988-89 Jim Duffy
1989-90 Billy Lamont
1990-95 Jim Jefferies
1995-96 John Lambie
1996 Eamonn Bannon
1996-2002 Alex Totten
2002-03 Ian McCall
2003 John Hughes / Owen Coyle
2003-09 John Hughes
2009-10 Eddie May
2010-13 Steven Pressley
2013-14 Gary Holt
2014- Peter Houston

FORFAR ATHLETIC
1969-71 Ian Campbell
1971-73 Alan Kennedy
1973-74 Dave Easson
1974-76 Jerry Kerr
1976-80 Archie Knox
1980 Steve Murray
1980-82 Alex Rae
1982-86 Doug Houston
1986-89 Henry Hall
1989-90 Bobby Glennie
1990-92 Paul Hegarty
1992-96 Tommy Campbell
1996-2000 Ian McPhee
2000-2003 Neil Cooper
2003-04 Raymond Stewart
2004-05 Brian Fairley
2005-06 Ray Farningham
2006-07 George Shaw
2007-08 Jim Moffat
2008-15 Dick Campbell
2015- Gary Bollan

HAMILTON ACCIES
1969-70 Tommy Ewing
1970-71 Bobby Shearer
1971-72 Ronnie Simpson
1972-78 Eric Smith
1978-82 Davie McParland
1982-83 John Blackley
1983-84 Bertie Auld
1984-88 John Lambie
1988-89 Jim Dempsey
1989-90 John Lambie
1990-92 Billy McLaren
1992-96 Ian Munro
1996-98 Sandy Clark
1998-99 Colin Miller
1999-2002 Ally Dawson
2002-03 Chris Hillcoat
2003-05 Allan Maitland
2005-13 Billy Reid
2013-15 Alex Neil
2015- Martin Canning

HEARTS
1966-70 John Harvey
1970-74 Bobby Seith
1974-77 John Hagart
1977-80 Willie Ormond
1980-81 Bobby Moncur
1981 Tony Ford
1981-86 Alex MacDonald
1986-88 Alex MacDonald / Sandy Jardine
1988-90 Alex MacDonald
1990-93 Joe Jordan
1993-94 Sandy Clark
1994-95 Tommy McLean
1995-2000 Jim Jefferies
2000-04 Craig Levein
2004-05 John Robertson
2005 George Burley
2005-06 Graham Rix
2006-07 Valdas Ivanauskis
2007-08 Anatoly Korobochka
2008 Stephen Frail
2008-10 Csabo Laszlo
2010-11 Jim Jefferies
2011-12 Paulo Sergio
2012-13 John McGlynn
2013-14 Gary Locke

2014-16 Robbie Neilson
2016- Ian Cathro

HIBERNIAN
1969-70 Willie McFarlane
1970-71 Dave Ewing
1971-80 Eddie Turnbull
1980 Willie Ormond
1980-82 Bertie Auld
1982-84 Pat Stanton
1984-86 John Blackley
1986-96 Alex Miller
1996 Jocky Scott
1996-98 Jim Duffy
1998-2001 Alex McLeish
2001-02 Franck Sauzee
2002-04 Bobby Williamson
2004-06 Tony Mowbray
2006-07 John Collins
2008-09 Mixu Paatelainen
2009-10 John Hughes
2010-11 Colin Calderwood
2011-13 Pat Fenlon
2013-14 Terry Butcher
2014-16 Alan Stubbs
2016- Neil Lennon

INVERNESS CALEDONIAN THISTLE
1994-95 Sergei Baltacha
1995-2002 Steve Paterson
2002-04 John Robertson
2004-06 Craig Brewster
2006-07 Charlie Christie
2007-09 Craig Brewster
2009-13 Terry Butcher
2013-16 John Hughes
2016-17 Richie Foran
2017- John Robertson

KILMARNOCK
1968-73 Walter McCrae
1973-77 Willie Fernie
1977-81 Davie Sneddon
1981-84 Jim Clunie
1984-88 Eddie Morrison
1988-92 Jim Fleeting
1992-94 Tommy Burns
1994-96 Alex Totten
1996-2002 Bobby Williamson
2002-10 Jim Jefferies
2010 Jimmy Caldwerwood
2010-11 Mixu Paatelainen
2011-13 Kenny Shiels
2013-15 Alan Johnston
2015-16 Gary Locke
2016-17 Lee Clark
2017- Lee McCulloch

LIVINGSTON / MEADOWBANK THISTLE
1974-75 John Bain
1976-77 Alec Ness
1977-80 Willie McFarlane
1980-92 Terry Christie
1992-93 Donald Park
1993-94 John Brownlie
1994-95 Michael Lawson
1995-98 Jim Leishman
1998-2000 Raymond Stewart
2000-03 David Hay / Jim Leishman
2003 Marcio Maximo Barcellos
2003-04 David Hay
2004 Allan Preston
2004-05 Richard Gough
2005-06 Paul Lambert
2006-07 John Robertson
2007-08 Mark Proctor
2008 Roberto Landi
2008-09 Paul Hegarty
2009 John Murphy
2009-12 Gary Bollan
2012 John Hughes
2012-13 Gareth Evans
2013 Richie Burke
2013-14 John McGlynn
2014-15 Mark Burchill
2015- David Hopkin

MONTROSE
1969/75 Alex Stuart
1975-79 Kenny Cameron
1979-82 Bobby Livingstone
1982-83 Steve Murray
1983 Denis D'Arcy
1983-90 Ian Stewart
1990-91 Doug Rougvie / Chic McClelland
1992-93 Jim Leishman
1993-95 John Holt
1995-96 Andy Dornan
1996-97 David Smith
1997-98 Tommy Campbell
1998-2000 Kevin Drinkell
2000-03 John Sheran
2003-05 Henry Hall
2005-06 Eddie Wolecki
2006 Eddie Wolecki / David Robertson
2006-07 David Robertson
2007-08 Jim Weir
2009-11 Steven Tweed
2011-12 Ray Farningham
2012-14 Stuart Garden
2014-15 George Shields
2015-16 Paul Hegarty
2016- Stuart Petrie

MORTON
1961-72 Hal Stewart
1972 Eric Smith
1972-74 Hal Stewart
1974-75 Erik Sorensen
1975-76 Joe Gilroy
1976-83 Benny Rooney
1983 Alex Miller
1983-84 Tommy McLean
1984-85 Willie McLean
1985-97 Allan McGraw
1997-2000 Billy Stark
2000 Ian McCall
2000-01 Allan Evans
2001 Ally Maxwell
2001-02 Peter Cormack
2002 Dave McPherson
2002-04 John McCormack
2004-08 Jim McInally
2008-09 David Irons
2009-10 James Grady
2010-13 Allan Moore
2013-14 Kenny Shiels
2014- Jim Duffy

MOTHERWELL
1965-73 Bobby Howitt
1973-74 Ian St John
1974-77 Willie McLean
1977-78 Roger Hynd
1978-81 Ally McLeod
1981-82 David Hay
1982-83 Jock Wallace
1983-84 Bobby Watson
1984-94 Tommy McLean
1994-98 Alex McLeish
1998 Harry Kampman
1998-2001 Billy Davies
2001-02 Eric Black
2002-06 Terry Butcher
2006-07 Maurice Malpas
2007-09 Mark McGhee
2009 Jim Gannon
2009-10 Craig Brown
2010-14 Stuart McCall
2014-15 Ian Barraclough
2015-17 Mark McGhee
2017- Stephen Robinson

PARTICK THISTLE
1968-70 Scot Symon
1970-74 Davie McParland
1974-80 Bertie Auld
1980-84 Peter Cormack
1984-86 Benny Rooney
1986 Bertie Auld
1986-87 Derek Johnstone
1987-88 Billy Lamont
1988-89 John Lambie
1989-90 Sandy Clark
1990-95 John Lambie
1995-97 Murdo McLeod
1997-98 John McVeigh
1998-99 Tommy Bryce
1999-2003 John Lambie
2003-04 Derek Whyte / Gerry Britton
2005-07 Dick Campbell
2007-11 Ian McCall
2011-13 Jackie McNamara
2013- Alan Archibald

PETERHEAD
2000-03 Ian Wilson
2004-06 Iain Stewart / Paul Mathers
2006-08 Steve Paterson
2008-11 Neale Cooper
2011 John Sheran
2011- Jim McInally

QUEEN OF THE SOUTH
1970 Harold Davis
1971-73 Jim Easton
1973-74 Willie McLean
1975-78 Mike Jackson
1978 Willie Hunter
1979-80 Billy Little
1980 George Herd
1982 Harry Hood
1982-84 Drew Busby
1984-86 Nobby Clark
1986-87 Mike Jackson
1987-88 Davie Wilson
1988-89 Tom McGinn
1989-90 Billy McLaren
1990-91 Frank McGarvey
1991-92 Ally McLeod
1992-93 Derek Frye
1993-96 Billy McLaren
1996-98 Mark Shanks / Rowan Alexander
1998-99 Rowan Alexander
1999-00 George Rowe / Ken Eadie
2000-04 John Connolly
2004-05 Iain Scott
2005-07 Ian McCall
2007-10 Gordon Chisholm
2010-11 Kenny Brannigan
2011-12 Gus McPherson
2012-13 Allan Johnston
2013-14 Jim McIntyre
2014-16 James Fowler
2016 Gavin Skelton
2016- Gary Naysmith

QUEEN'S PARK
1969-74 Tommy Duncan
1974-76 Davie McParland
1976-79 Joe Gilroy
1979-94 Eddie Hunter
1995-97 Hugh McCann
1997-98 Graeme Elder
1998-2002 John McCormack
2003-04 Kenny Brannigan
2004-08 Billy Stark
2008-13 Garner Speirs
2014- Gus McPherson

RAITH ROVERS
1069-70 Jimmy Millar
1970-71 Bill Baxter
1971-74 George Farm
1974-75 Bert Paton
1975-78 Andy Matthew
1978-79 Willie McLean
1979-83 Gordon Wallace
1983-86 Bobby Wilson
1986-90 Frank Connor
1990-96 Jimmy Nicholl
1996 Jimmy Thomson
1996 Tommy McLean

1996-97 Iain Munro
1997-99 Jimmy Nicholl
1999 John McVeigh
1999-2001 Peter Hetherston
2001-02 Jocky Scott
2002-04 Antonio Calderon
2004 Claude Anelka
2004-06 Gordon Dalziel
2006 Craig Levein
2006-12 John McGlynn
2012-15 Grant Murray
2015-16 Ray McKinnon
2016-17 Gary Locke
2017 John Hughes
2017- Barry Smith

RANGERS
1969-72 Willie Waddell
1972-78 Jock Wallace
1978-83 John Greig
1983-86 Jock Wallace
1986-91 Graeme Souness
1991-98 Walter Smith
1998-2001 Dick Advocaat
2001-06 Alex McLeish
2006-07 Paul Le Guen
2007-11 Walter Smith
2011-14 Ally McCoist
2014-15 Kenny McDowall
2015 Stuart McCall
2015-17 Mark Warburton
2017- Pedro Caixinha

ROSS COUNTY
1994-96 Bobby Wilson
1996-2002 Neale Cooper
2002-2005 Alex Smith
2005 John Robertson
2005-06 Gardner Speirs
2006-07 Scott Leitch
2007 Dick Campbell
2007-10 Derek Adams
2010-11 Willie McStay
2011 Jimmy Calderwood
2011-14 Derek Adams
2014- Jim McIntyre

ST JOHNSTONE
1967-73 Willie Ormond
1973-76 Jackie Stewart
1976-78 Jim Storrie
1978-80 Alex Stuart
1980-85 Alex Rennie
1985-87 Ian Gibson
1987-92 Alex Totten
1992-93 John McClelland
1993-98 Paul Sturrock
1998-2001 Sandy Clark
2001-04 Billy Stark
2004-05 John Connolly
2005-07 Owen Coyle
2007-11 Derek McInnes
2011-13 Steve Lomas
2013- Tommy Wright

ST MIRREN
1966-70 Alex Wright
1970-72 Wilson Humphries
1972-73 Tommy Bryceland
1973-74 Willie Cunningham
1974-78 Alex Ferguson
1978-80 Jim Clunie
1980-83 Ricky McFarlane
1983-86 Alex Miller
1986-88 Alex Smith
1988-91 Tony Fitzpatrick
1991-92 David Hay
1992-96 Jimmy Bone
1996 Iain Munro
1996-98 Tony Fitzpatrick
1998-2002 Tom Hendrie
2002-03 John Coughlin
2003-10 Gus McPherson
2010-14 Danny Lennon
2014 Tommy Craig
2014-15 Gary Teale
2015 Ian Murray
2015-16 Alex Rae
2016- Jack Ross

STENHOUSEMUIR
1969-74 Alex Smith
1974-81 Harry Glasgow
1981-84 Jim Black
1984-86 Archie Rose
1987 Billy Henderson
1987-89 Alex Rennie
1989-91 Jim Meakin
1991-92 Dennis Lawson
1992-99 Terry Christie
1999-00 Graeme Armstrong
2000-1 Brian Fairley
2001-02 Jimmy Bone
2002-04 John McVeigh
2004-05 Tony Smith / Des McKeown
2005-06 Des McKeown
2006-07 Campbell Money
2007-10 John Coughlin
2010-12 Davie Irons
2012-14 Martyn Corrigan
2014-15 Scott Booth
2015- Brown Ferguson

STIRLING ALBION
1969-70 Frank Joyner
1971-73 Bob Shankly
1973-74 Frank Beattie
1974-86 Alex Smith
1986-88 George Peebles
1988 Jim Fleeting
1988-94 John Brogan
1994-98 Kevin Drinkell
1998-2000 John Philliben
2000-02 Raymond Stewart
2002-2010 Allan Moore
2010-11 John O'Neill
2011 Jocky Scott
2011-14 Greig McDonald
2014-16 Stuart McLaren
2016- Dave MacKay

STRANRAER
1970-71 Dan McLindon
1973-75 Eric Caldow
1975-76 John Hughes
1980-81 Neil Hood
1981 Gordon Hamilton
1982-85 Davie Sneddon
1986 John Clark
1986-87 Robert Clark
1897-96 Alex McAnespie
1996-99 Campbell Money
1999-03 Billy McLaren
2003-06 Neil Watt
2006-08 Gerry Britton
2008-09 Derek Ferguson
2009-12 Keith Knox
2012-15 Stephen Aitken
2015-17 Brian Reid
2017- Stephen Farrell

The Managers—as at 23/6/16, by date of appointment

1	30/01/2010	Gary Jardine	Edinburgh City
2	07/10/2011	Jim McInally	Peterhead
3	30/01/2013	Alan Archibald	Partick Thistle
4	08/04/2013	Derek McInnes	Aberdeen
5	10/06/2013	Tommy Wright	St Johnstone
6	22/01/2014	Gus McPherson	Queen's Park
7	19/05/2014	Jim Duffy	Morton
8	12/06/2014	Peter Houston	Falkirk
9	09/09/2014	Jim McIntyre	Ross County
10	27/11/2014	Jim Weir	Elgin City
11	06/01/2015	Ian McCall	Ayr United
12	23/01/2015	Martin Canning	Hamilton Accies
13	03/04/2015	Brown Ferguson	Stenhousemuir
14	08/05/2015	Alan Johnston	Dunfermline Athletic
15	26/05/2015	Steven Aitken	Dumbarton
16	10/06/2015	Darren Dods	Brechin City
17	06/11/2015	John Coughlin	Berwick Rangers
18	21/12/2015	Gary Bollan	Forfar Athletic
19	06/01/2016	David Hopkin	Livingston
20	08/03/2016	Dick Campbell	Arbroath
21	12/05/2016	Ray McKinnon	Dundee United
22	20/05/2016	Brendan Rodgers	Celtic
23	08/06/2016	Neil Lennon	Hibernian
24	10/10/2016	Jim Goodwin	Alloa Athletic
25	10/10/2016	Jack Ross	St Mirren
26	10/11/2016	Dave Mackay	Stirling Albion
27	04/12/2016	Stewart Petrie	Montrose
28	05/12/2016	Ian Cathro	Hearts
29	08/12/2016	Gary Naysmith	Queen of the South
30	20/01/2017	Stephen Farrell	Stranraer
31	10/03/2017	Gary Locke	Cowdenbeath
32	11/03/2017	Pedro Caixinha	Rangers
33	15/03/2017	Stephen Robinson	Motherwell
34	08/05/2017	Brian Kerr	Albion Rovers
35	20/05/2017	Jim Chapman	Clyde
36	29/05/2017	Barry Smith	Raith Rovers
37	02/06/2017	Neil McCann	Dundee
38	02/06/2017	Peter Murphy	Annan Athletic
39	02/06/2017	Darren Young	East Fife
40	05/06/2017	Lee McCulloch	Kilmarnock
41	11/06/2017	John Robertson	Inverness CT
42			Airdrieonians

Scottish Cup 2016/17

1st Preliminary Round	Res	Att	
Edusport Academy v Colville Park	2-2	27	
Newton Stewart v Beith	0-4	191	
Wigtown & Bladnoch v Auchinleck Talbot	0-4	167	
Glasgow Uni v Bonnyrigg Rose	2-8	70	at Airdrie
St Cuthberts Wanderers v Leith Athletic	0-3	57	
1st Preliminary Round Replays			
Colville Park v Edusport Academy	1-0	41	at Benburb
2nd Preliminary Round			
Leith Athletic v Coldstream	1-0	73	at Spartans
Bonnyrigg Rose v Burntisland Shipyard	14-0	387	
Colville Park v Girvan	0-1	77	at Benburb
Beith v Auchinleck Talbot	2-2	692	
Threave Rovers v Linlithgow Rose	1-2	278	
Banks O'Dee v Golspie Sutherland	4-0	68	
2nd Preliminary Round Replays			
Auchinleck Talbot v Beith	0-3	563	
1st Round			
Turriff United v Bonnyrigg Rose	1-1	304	
Leith Athletic v Cumbernauld Colts	0-0	174	at Spartans
Forres Mechanics v Lossiemouth	2-2	244	
Ft William v Brora Rangers	1-4	45	
East Kilbride v Vale of Leithen	9-1	154	
BSC Glasgow v Rothes	3-1	70	at Alloa
Edinburgh University v Whitehill Welfare	0-1	108	
Deveronvale v Gretna 2008	0-3	198	
Gala Fairydean Rovers v Fraserburgh	3-1	160	
Keith v Banks o'Dee	0-1	107	
Civil Service Strollers v Hawick Royal Albert	1-1	43	
Nairn County v Preston Athletic	2-3	121	
Inverurie Loco Works v Buckie Thistle	0-6	553	
Dalbeattie Star v Wick Academy	1-3	105	
Beith v Strathspey Thistle	6-0	373	
Clachnacuddin v Stirling University	1-2	129	
Selkirk v Linlithgow Rose	0-3	177	
Girvan v Huntly	1-2	68	
1st Round Replays			
Bonnyirgg Rose v Turriff United	4-1	676	
Cumbernauld Colts v Leith Athletic	1-0	167	
Lossiemouth v Forres Mechanics	0-4	245	
Hawick Royal Albert v Civil Service Strollers	6-2	75	
2nd Round			
Annan Athletic v East Stirlingshire	0-0	302	
Banks o'Dee v Formartine United	2-2	199	
Brora Rangers v Clyde	0-2	291	
BSC Glasgow v Beith	0-1	270	at Alloa
Bonnyrigg Rose v Cove Rangers	2-1	657	
Berwick Rangers v Hawick Royal Albert	2-3	477	
Linlithgow Rose v Stirling Albion	0-3	1063	
Wick Academy v Whitehill Welfare	4-1	403	
Preston Athletic v Montrose	0-3	257	
Huntly v Spartans	0-2	181	
Edinburgh City v Forfar Athletic	0-0	328	
Cowdenbeath v East Kilbride	0-1	286	
Cumbernauld Colts v Forres Mechanics	2-2	187	
Arbroath v Stirling University	3-1	412	
Gala Fairydean Rovers v Elgin City	0-4	275	
Buckie Thistle v Gretna 2008	1-1	586	
2nd Round Replays			
East Stirlingshire v Annan Athletic	1-2	114	
Formartine United v Banks O'Dee	7-2	136	
Forfar Athletic v Edinburgh City	0-1	388	
Forres Mechanics v Cumbernauld Colts	4-0	268	
Gretna 2008 v Buckie Thistle	2-6	174	

3rd Round			
Elgin City vs. Hawick Royal Albert	8-1	549	
Airdrieonians vs. Livingston	1-2	780	
Buckie Thistle vs. Dunfermline Athletic	3-5	1441	
Stirling Albion vs. Wick Academy	2-0	572	
St Mirren vs. Spartans	5-1	1147	
Stranraer vs. East Kilbride	2-1	331	
Forres Mechanics vs. Stenhousemuir	2-2	369	
East Fife vs. Edinburgh City	1-1	339	
Albion Rovers vs. Queen of the South	2-1	387	
Clyde vs. Arbroath	5-0	368	
Formartine United vs. Annan Athletic	4-0	124	
Beith Juniors vs. Greenock Morton	0-6	1693	
Brechin City vs. Ayr United	0-1	308	
Bonnyrigg Rose vs. Dumbarton	0-0	1552	
Peterhead vs. Alloa Athletic	0-1	563	
Queen's Park vs. Montrose	2-0	348	
3rd Round Replays			
Stenhousemuir v Forres Mechanics	3-1	291	
Dumbarton v Bonnyrigg Rose	0-1	632	
Edinburgh City v East Fife	0-1	397	
4th Round			
Ross County v Dundee United	6-2	2440	
St Johnstone v Stenhousemuir	2-0	2441	
Albion Rovers v Celtic	0-3	8319	
Livingston v East Fife	0-1	726	
Rangers v Motherwell	2-1	31921	
Aberdeen v Stranraer	4-0	8960	
Elgin City v Inverness Caledonian Thistle	1-2	3624	
Raith Rovers v Heart of Midlothian	1-1	5036	
Kilmarnock v Hamilton Academical	0-1	2944	
Bonnyrigg Rose v Hibernian	1-8	13000	at Heart
Ayr United v Queens Park	0-0	1326	
Partick Thistle v Formartine United	4-0	2782	
Stirling Albion v Clyde	2-2	869	
Alloa Athletic v Dunfermline Athletic	2-3	1871	
Dundee v St Mirren	0-2	3622	
Greenock Morton v Falkirk	2-0	2349	
4th Round Replays			
Queens Park v Ayr United	(Ayr	1026	
Clyde v Stirling Albion	3-2	625	
Heart of Midlothian v Raith Rovers	4-2	10740	
5th Round			
Dunfermline Athletic v Hamilton Academical	1-1	2945	
Heart of Midlothian v Hibernian	0-0	16971	
St Johnstone v Partick Thistle	0-1	2884	
Ayr United v Clyde	1-1	1554	
East Fife v St Mirren	2-3	1483	
Ross County v Aberdeen	0-1	4671	
Celtic v Inverness Caledonian Thistle	6-0	25881	
Rangers v Greenock Morton	2-1	30295	
5th Round Replays			
Hamilton Academical v Dunfermline Athletic	(Hamil	1222	
Clyde v Ayr United	1-2 aet	965	
Hibernian v Heart of Midlothian	3-1	20205	
Quarter-Finals			
Aberdeen v Partick Thistle	1-0	11333	
Celtic v St Mirren	4-1	27455	
Hibernian v Ayr United	3-1	13602	
Rangers v Hamilton Academical	6-0	27287	
Semi-finals			
Aberdeen v Hibernian	3-2	31969	at Ham
Celtic v Rangers	2-0	49645	at Ham
final			
Aberdeen v Celtic	1-2	48713	at Ham

Appearances etc. for Non SPFL teams in Scottish Cup 2016/17

NB team line-ups etc. for SPFL sides are included in the club grids earlier in this book. It has not been possible to trace all line ups for round one. The Press Association, who provide information for the media, only cover the Cup from Round Two. Thanks to those clubs who responded to requests for information.

Many thanks to Jock Gardiner for obtaining attendances for the early round matches from the SFA.

First Preliminary Round

Saturday August 13th 2016

Wigtown and Bladnoch 0 Auchinleck Talbot 4 (Shankland 2, Wilson 2) (HT 0-0)
Referee – Mike Taylor
W&B: Roddie, McIntyre, Rennie, Agnew, Richardson, Cluckie, Jones, Dunn, Jamieson, Dougan, Miller
Subs – Robertson, Lowe, Chilton, Rose, Gerrit, Whyte (gk)
AT: Leishman, Lyle, Pope, McGoldrick, Boyle, Latta, Young (Sub Hyslop), S Wilson, Milliken, Shankland (Sub Drummond), Pooler (Sub White)
Subs – McPherson, G Wilson, Hewitt (gk)

Newton Stewart 0 Beith 4 (Frize 2, Christie, McPherson) (HT 0-2)
Referee- Duncan Smith
NS:
B: McBain, Fisher, Sheridan, McDonald, McArthur, McGlinchey, Frize, Wilson, Collins (Sub Christie), Burke (sub McGowan), McLean (Sub McPherson). Subs Martin, Docherty, McLaughlin, MacPherson

Edusport Academy 2 (Bouchentouf, Hoareau) Colville Park 2 (Mulvay, McLaughlin) (HT 1-2)
Referee – Chris Graham
EA: Gregoire, Ngongo, Reid, Kyenge, Brunet, McCann, Parendel, Moutou (Sub McLaren), Toure, Bouchentouf, Hoareau. Subs Prevot, Tshibangu, Hussenet, Boulalem
CP: Cowie, Peebles (Sub McAuley), Murray, McKay, Mulvey, McDevitt, Bradley, Burden (sub Clearie), McLaughlin, Craig (Sub McIntosh), Cusack. Subs Ward, Greenlees, Pearce, Bradshaw

St Cuthbert Wanderers 0 Leith Athletic 3 (Fee 2, Own Goal) (HT
Referee - Steven Reid
SCW: Wilson, Jackel (Henderson 86), O'Sullivan, Cameron, Loudon, Dingwall (Rudd 74), Middlemiss, McMurdo, Donley, Milligan, Carnochan (Hunter 65). Subs: Cunningham, Gordon, Ourham, Wilson.
LA: Gordon, Black, Fee, Lowson, Glynn, Beaton, Tracey (McKinlay 82), Wilkie, Hainey (Mason 73), Kneeshaw (Combe 73), Wilson. Subs: Fairnie, Allan, Laverty, Simpson.

Sunday August 14th 2016

Glasgow University 2 (D Thomson 2) Bonnyrigg Rose 8 (Jamieson 4, Tobin, McLaren 2, Moyes (HT 1-3)
Referee- Scott Millar
GU: Middlemass, M Thomson (J Mitchell 73), O Mitchell, Woodley, Warrillow, M Baxter, J Baxter (Lee 76), Davidson (Paterson 55), D Thomson, Cameron, Kerins. Subs Unused: McLay, McCaffrey, Hendry, Oladunjoye
BR: Andrews (Sub Rooney), Horne, Donaldson, Young, Stewart (sub Nelson), Moyes, McLaren (sub McGachie), Kidd, Jamieson, King, Tobin. Subs: Hoskins, McIntosh

First Preliminary Round Replay

Saturday August 20th

Colville Park 1 (McKay) Edusport Academy 0 (HT 1-0)
Referee: Chris Graham
CP: Cowie, Murray, Campbell, Mulvay, McDevitt, Bradley, Cusack, Clearie, McLaughlin, McKay, Craig. Subs Murden, McAuley, Pearce. Unused Subs Monteith, Bradshaw, Greenlees, McIntosh
ES: Gregoire, Ngongo, Reid, Kyenge, Brunet, McCann, McLaren, Moutou, Toure, Bouchentouf, Hoareau. Subs Prevot, Tshibangu, Hussenet, Boulalem, Parandel.

Second Preliminary Round

Saturday September 3rd

Bonnyrigg Rose 14 (McIntosh 7, Kidd, McGachie, Tobin, Jamieson 2, Moyes, Donaldson) Burntisland Shipyard 0 (HT 5-0)
Referee Lloyd Wilson
BR: Andrews, Brown, Donaldson, Moyes, Hoskins (Sub Young), Stewart (Sub Nelson), Jamieson (Sub Turner), Tobin, McGachie, Kidd, McIntosh. Subs not used - McLeish, Rooney:
BSY: Taylor, Saunders, Fleming, Ford, McIntosh, Paterson, Watt (Sub Bowman), McDonald, Aitken, Roberts (Sub Black), Kellachan (Sub Hall). Subs not used Butt, McKay, Prendergast.

Beith 2 (Wilson, Docherty) Auchinleck Talbot 2(Pope, Young) (HT 1-1)
Referee: Peter Stuart
B: Grindlay, MacDonald, Docherty, McLaughlin, Sheridan, Wilson, McGlinchey, Frize, Mclean, Christie, McGowan. Subs Collins, Watt, Burke, McPherson, Fisher, Martin, McBain
AT: lesihman, Lyle, Pope, McGoldrick, Boyle, Latta, Whyte, Hyslop, Wilson, Milliken, Young. Subs Stevenson, Pooler, Harvey, Wilson, McCracken, Hewitt

Threave Rovers 1 (Irving) Linlithgow Rose 2 (Weir, Batchelor) (HT 1-2)
Referee: Stephen Brown
TR: Gemmell, Gray, Jamieson, Paterson, Wilby, Blain, Cooper, Goodwin, Irving, A Barnes, Liddell. Subs C Barnes, Tait, D Milligan, McHurtrie, Graham, S Milligan
LR: Barnard, R Donaldson, Hamill, B Donaldson, Thom, Beaumont, Batchelor, Shirra, Kelbie, Coyne, Weir. Subs Kelly, McAllister, Myles, McNab, Hill

Leith Athletic 1 (Hainey) Coldstream 0, HT 1-0
Referee: David Dickinson
LA: Gordon, Black, Simpson (Sub Kneeshaw), Lowson, Glynn, Beaton (Sub Mason), McKinlay, Allan, Hainey (Sub Melvin), Ferguson, Fee. Subs Fairnie, Burns, Tracey, McPherson.
C: Walters, Wales, Logan, Inglis, Hossack, Hebdon, Robinson, Beasley, Sutherland, Steele ISub Gray), Brown (Sub Johnston). Subs not used Nisbet, Bowline.

Banks o' Dee 4 (K Winton, Henderson, Heads, Lennox) Golspie Sutherland 0, HT
Referee: Lorraine Clark
BOD: Shearer, Duguid, Whyte, Heads, McCall, K Winton, Henderson, Forbes, Watt, Lennox, Phillipson. Subs used: J Winton, Hamilton, Buchanan

Colville Park 0 Girvan 1 (Jardine), HT 0-0
Referee: Duncan Williams
CP
G: Johnston, McDowall, Doolan, Mossie, Frame, Dinwoodie, Murphy, Reilly, Cunningham, Paterson, Jardine.Subs used Reid, Cameron, Stevenson

Replay

Saturday September 10th

Auchinleck Talbot 0 Beith 3 (McGowan, Christie, McLaughlan)
Referee: Peter Stuart
Auchinleck: Leishman, Lyle, Pope, McGoldrick, McCracken, Wilson, Young, White, Wilson, Milliken, Hyslop. Subs: Pooler, Stevenson, Harvey, Boyle, Thomson, Shankland, Hewitt
Beith: Grindlay, MacDonald, Docherty, McLaughlan, Sheridan, Wilson, McGlinchey, Frize, McLean, Christie, McGowan. Subs: Collins, Watt, Burke, McPherson, Fisher, Martin, McBain.

First Round

Saturday September 24th

Beith 6 (Christie, McGowan, McLean 2, McPherson, Docherty) Strathspey Thistle 0, H.T. 4-0
Referee: Stephen Graham
B: Grindlay, McGlinchey, Docherty, Sheridan, MacDonald, Watt, Frize, McGowan (Sub Martin), Burke (Sub Collins), Christie, McLean (Sub McPherson)
ST:

BSC Glasgow 3 (Bowers, Ferris, Rothes 1 (Stuart) , H.T 2-1
Referee: Graham Grainger
BSC: Wilton, Bowers, Keys (Sub Beckett), Kasongo, Bell, Redpath (Sub Duncan), Ferris, Dryden (Sub Cunningham), Jones, Woods, Traynor. Unused Subs Barr, Toner, Niven
R: McIntosh, Henderson, Sharp, Watt, Jennings, Smith, Davidson, McMillan (Sub McNamara), Stuart, Gauld, Stables Sub Johnson used, Unused – S McIntosh, C McIntosh, Riddell, Ezekiel

Civil Service Strollers 1 Hawick Royal Albert 1
Referee: Calum Haswell
CSS: Burnside, Laird, Dingwall (Sub Finnie), Turnbull, Milven, Cunningham, Milligan (Sub Anderson), Downie, Froude, Martin (Sub Rixon), Boyle. Unused subs: Brown, Watson, Greenhill
HRA: Rankin, Saunderson, Spence, Johnson, Smeaton, Conaghan, Stevenson, McPartlin, Morris, Mitchell, Pettigrew. Subs Atkin, McInally, Hunter, Boyd, Meikle, Begbie

Clachnacuddin 1 (Finnis) Stirling University 2 (Fitzpatrick 2), H.T. 1-2
Referee: Liam Duncan
C: Campbell, McIntosh, Finnis, MacKillop, Grant, Robertson, Smith, Callum, Penright, Leslie, MacLenn. Subs MacDonald, Lawrie, Jones, Beatson, Kennedy, MacLeod, Shewan
SU: Marshall, Jones, Kellock, Cuff, Nixon, Moyes, Gillen, Hunter, Geddes, McCafferty, Fitzpatrick. Subs Hughes, Tuohy, McAnespie, Kane, Cowley, Byrne, Emmott

Dalbeattie Star 1 (Muir) Wick Academy 3 (Pickles, McAdie, Anderson), H.T. 1-2
Referee: Duncan Williams
DS: Parker, Maxwell, Thorburn (Sub Degnam), Dunlingson (Sub Todd), Wells (Sub Wilson), Baty, Muir, Graham, Anderson, Sloan, McHarrie. Subs not used Neil, Mason, Proudlock, Morton
WA: S McCarthy, Steven, Manson, Farquhar, Mackay, Steven, S Mackay, Anderson (Sub McGregor), Weir (Sub Hardwick), MacAdie, Pickles. Subs not used D McCarthy, Petrie, A Mackay, Mclean

Deveronvale 0 Gretna 2008 3 (Telfer, McCartney, Reynard) H.T. 0-2
Referee: Gavin Duncan
Dev: Blanchard, Rae, Dunbar, Begg, Forbes, Blackhall, Sutherland, Cowie, Davidson, Noble, Watt. Subs Souter, Keith, Manson, Duguid, Ross, Aitken, Thomson
G: Armstrong, Branna, Wadge, Rudd, Inglis, Dickinson, Reynard, Hope, McCartney, Murray, Telfer. Subs Ballantyne, Wood, Neil, Studaholme

East Kilbride 9 (Vitoria 3, Winters 2, Strachan 2, Capuano, Hughes) Vale of Leithen 1(Lynch) H.T.
Referee: Lorraine Clark
EK: McGinley, Capuano, Howie, Proctor, Russell, Gibson, Coll, Strachan, McBride, Vitoria (Sub Hughes), Winters Subs not used: Stevenson, McNeil, Winter, Millar, McLaren, Kean
VOL: McQueen, Scott-Mercer, Patterson, Lynch, O'Donnell, Hunter, McIntosh, Manson, Atkinson, McLeod, Motion. Subs Shiel, Brady, Stevens, Stewart, Edwards, Lamb

Edinburgh University 0 Whitehill Welfare 1 (Hall), H.T. 0-1
Referee: Lloyd Wilson
EU: Davidson, McMillan, Murray, Irvine, Swan, Daniels-Yeoman, Collins, Ritchie, Guthrie, McCrory-Irvine, Evans. Subs Smith, Mair, Verkalk, Hely, Matthew
WW: Young, Hall, O'Hara, Murray, Williams, McGregor, Dodds (Sub Martin), McCulloch, Osborne, Swan, Denton (Sub Manson). Subs not used: Keane, Kerr, Gormley, Jardine

Forres Mechanics 2 (Fraser, Knight) Lossiemouth 2 (Miller, Scott) H.T. 1-0
Referee: Duncan Smith
FM: Knight, Allan, Grant, G Fraser, Groat, Moore, L Fraser, Graham, Scott, Finlayson, Soane. Subs Forbes, Baxter, Brown, McIver, Paterson, Mclean, Storrier
Lossie: McConnachie, Gordon, Ross, Rodrigues, Flett, McMullan, Farquhar, Miller, Scptt, Bellingham, Archibald. Subs Ross, Bell, Hall, Smith, Mathers, Wardrop, Farquhar

Fort William 1 (Highet) Brora Rangers 4 (Sutherland, Campbell 2 Ross) H.T. 1-0
Referee: Gary Docherty
FW:
BR: Malin. Pickles. Ross. Williamson. Macdonald. Pollock. Gillespie. Maclean. Sutherland. Mackay. Greig.

Gala Fairydean 2 (Stuart Noble, Hay) Fraserburgh 1 (Harris), HT 1-1
Referee: David Dickinson
Gala: Wright, Steven, Main, Waugh, Herdman, McColm, Miller, Hope, Scott Noble, Palicza, Bonnar. Subs Simpson, Windram, Bonnington, Collins, Nicol, Steven Noble
Fr: Leask, Dickson, McBride, Buchan, Hay, Cowie, Rae, West, Harris, Johnston, Combe. Subs Flinn, Taylor, Campbell, Buchan, Christie, Cowie, Lawrence

Girvan 1 (Reilly) Huntly 2 (Duncanson 2) H.T. 1-1
Referee: Matthew McDermid
G: Johnson, Reid, Frame, Mossie, Doolan, McDowell, Dinwoodie (Sub McCreadie), Murphy, Jardine (Sub Stevenson), Paterson (Sub Cunningham), Reilly. Subs
H: Grant, Naismith, Allan, Robertson (Sub Ingram), Johnston (Sub Ritchie), Burr, Duncan, Murison, Napier, Duncanson, Wyness (Sub Hodge). Subs

Inverurie Loco Works 0 Buckie Thistle 6 (Fraser 2, Dorrat, Urquhart 2, Murray) H.T. 0-1
Referee: David Watt
IL: Mathieson, Rennie, Mitchell, Crisp (McCabe 50), Jeffrey (Leyden 60), Adams, Souter, McLean, Hunter, Bavidge, Laing (Charlesworth 55). Unused subs – Selfridge, Wilson, Morrison, Cook.
BT: Salmon, Cheyne (Macrae 77), MacKinnon, Munro, Dorrat (Carroll 75), Copeland (Murray 62), McLean, Fraser, Urquhart, Low, McLeod. Unused subs – Strong, J. Fraser, Scott, Taylor.

Keith 0 Banks o' Dee 1 (Henderson) H.T. 0-1
Referee: Billy Baxter
K: Dey, Cooper, Spink, Milne, Ralton, Whelan, Brownie, Fraser, Barbour, Ewen, MacAskill. Subs Clark, Hall, Raffell, Duncan, Cormack, Smith, Bell
BOD: Shearer, Buchanan, Whyte, McCall, Robertson, J Winton, Lennox, K Winton, Henderson, Phillipson, Forbes. Subs used Heads

Nairn County 2 (Naismith 2) Preston Athletic 3 (Park, O'Rourke, Barclay), H.T. 0-3
Referee: Steven Traynor
Nairn: S McKenzie, McLeod, Riddell, McIntosh, C McLean, Kerr, Mackay, Mclean, Main, D McLean, K McKenzie. Subs D McKenzie, Naismith. Unused – Main, Morganti, McLeod, Moir, MacRae
PA: Pennycuik, Law, Cochrane, Cowan, Colquhoun, Todd (Sub MacLeod), Stevenson, Barclay, Henderson (Sub Shave), Park, O'Rourke (Sub Lawson)

Selkirk 0 Linlithgow Rose 3 (Weir, Coyne, Kelbie) H.T.
Referee: Calum Scott
S: Wilson, Samson, Christie, Harley, Fleming, Miller, King, McCormack, Baxter, Addison, Doyle. Subs O'Connor, Fairm Neil, Scott, Collin, Beagley, Robertson
LR: Hill, B Donaldson, R Donaldson, McKenzie, Thom, Hamill, Batchelor (Sub Kelbie), Shirra, McNab, Coyne, Weir. Subs BeaumontGray, McAllister, Barnard

Turriff United 1 (Herd) Bonnyrigg Rose 1 (McLaren)
Referee: Stephen Brown
TU: Main, Davidson, Herd, Wood, Bowden, Chalmers, C Booth, Young, Kleczkowski, D Booth, Allan. Subs: Nowossielski, Mair, Smith, Moir, Vastano, Sherman.
BR: Andrews, Horne, Donaldson, Young, Hoskins, Stewart, Jamieson, Turner, McGachey, Nelson, Kidd. Subs: Moyes, Gray,

Brown, McLaren, Rooney.

Sunday September 25th

Leith Athletic 0 Cumbernauld Colts 0
Referee: C Fordyce
LA: Gordon, Black, Fee, Lowson, Melvin, Mason (Beaton 21), McKinlay, Wilkie (Allan 65), Hainey, Kneeshaw (Ferguson 79), Wilson.
CC: Fahey, Batchelor, Kirwin, McFarlane, Ward, Pirrie (Broadfoot 68), Ronald (Tennant 72), Murray, Selkirk, Black (Ballantyne), O'Neill.

First Round Replays

Saturday October 1st

Bonnyrigg Rose 4 (Hoskins, McGachie, McLaren, McIntosh) Turriff United 1(Smith) H.T. 1-0
Referee:
Bonnyrigg Rose: Andrews, Horne, Donaldson, Young, Hoskins, Stewart, Jamieson (Moyes), Turner, McGachie (McIntosh), Nelson (McLaren), Kidd
Turriff United: Main, Davidson, Herd, Wood, Bowden, Chalmers, Gray, Young, Kleczkowski (D Booth), C Booth, Allan (Smith)

Lossiemouth 0 Forres Mechanics 4 (G Fraser, L Fraser 2, Graham), H.T. 0-2

Hawick Royal Albert 6 (Morris 4, Mitchell 2) Civil Service Strollers 2 (Cunningham, Froude) H.T. 4-0
Hawick Royal Albert: Rankin, Stevenson (Begbie 86), Spence, Johnson, Smeaton (Boyd 83), Meikle, Hunter, McPartlin, Morris (Pettigrew 80), Mitchell, McInally. Sub: Aitkin. Civil Service Strollers: Burnside, Laird, Dingwall, Turnbull, Milven, Cunningham, Milligan, Downie (Pacheco 60), Froude, Finnie (Anderson 60), Boyle. Subs: Ballantyne, Watson, Clapperton.

Wednesday October 5th

Cumbernauld Colts 1 (Ronald) Leith Athletic 0 H.T. 1-0
CC: Fahey, Tennent, Kirwan, McFarlane, Ward, Ballantyne (Sub Black), Ronald, Barclay (Sub Pirrie), Selkirk, Murray (Sub Broadfoot), O'Neill Subs not used: Giles, Morris, Hunter, Foggin
LA:

Second Round

Saturday October 22nd

Buckie Thistle 1 (McLeod) Gretna 1 (Murray) H.T.
Referee: D Williams
BT: Salmon, Munro, Dorrat, Taylor (Sub Angus), McLean, Carroll (Sub Wood), Low, Cheyne (Sub MacKinnon), Fraser, Urquhart, McLeod. Subs not used: Fraser, Murray, Strong, Copeland
Gretna: Wood, Murray, Armstrong, Brannan, Renyard, Hope, Hunter, Murray, Neill (Sub Inglis), McCartney, Simpson. Subs not used: Studholme, Ballantyne

Gala Fairydean Rovers 0 Elgin City 4, H.T. 0-3
Ref: G Irvine
GFR: Wright, Stephen , Main, Millar, Hope (Sub Windram), Smith, McColm (Sub Bonnington), Bonnar, Watson, Noble, Paliczka (Sub Collins). Subs not used: Senton, Waugh, Clapperton, Simpson

Linlithgow Rose 0 Stirling Albion 3, H.T. 0-1
Ref: S Reid
LR: Hill, Mckenzie, Thom, Donaldson, Leiper (Sub Small), Beaumont, McNab (Sub Kelly), Batchelor, Coyne, Kelbie (Sub Weir), Gray. Unused subs: Shirra, Barnard

Brora Rangers 0 Clyde 2, H.T. 0-0
Ref: S Lambie
BR: Malin, Tokeley, Williamson, Morrison (Sub Mclean), Pollok (Sub Mackay), Brindle, Pickles, Lisle, Sutherland (Sub Greig), MacDonald, Ross. Unused subs: Campbell, Gillespie, Ross, Cormack

Wick Academy 4 Whitehill Welfare 1 H.T. 0-1
Referee: S Brown
WA: McCallum, G Steven (Sub Hardwick), M Steven, D Mackay, S Mackay (Sub MacAdie), Farquhar, Manson, Pickles, Allan, Weir (Sub MacGregor), Anderson. Unused subs: A Mackay, McCarthy, McLean
WW: Young, O'Hara, Keane, Williams, Hall (Sub Kerr), Osbourne, Swan, McCulloch, McGregor, Manson (Sub Denton), Gormley (Sub Martin). Subs unused: Gilbertson, Hislop

Cumbernauld Colts 2 (Selkirk, Barclay) Forres Mechanics 2 (Graham, Soane), H.T. 1-1
Ref: L Wilson
CC: Fahey, Kirwan, Ward, McFarlane, Barclay, Murray (Sub Pirrie), O'Neill, Broafdoot, Batchelor, Ronald, Selkirk. Subs not used: Black, Hunter, brown, Foggin, Giles, Tennant
FM: Knight, Allan, Grant, Fraser, Finlayson (Sub Moore), Fraser, Soane, Scott, Khutishvili (Sub McLellan), Cameron (Sub McGivern), Graham. Unused subs: Groat, Storrier, Forbes, Baxter

Arbroath 3 (Hamilton, Linn, Doris) Stirling University 1 (Geddes) H.T. 3-1
Referee: G Beaton
SU: Marshall, Ashe, Nixon, Kellock, Mailer, Faulds, Jones, Leigh, Gillen, Geddes, McCafferty (Sub Hunter) Unused subs: Cowley, McAnespie, Hughes, Dorcz, Moyes, Byrne

Huntly 0 Spartans 2 (Thompson, Townsley) H.T. 0-2
Referee: P Stuart
H: Grant, Webb, Still (Sub Murison), Allan, Johnston, Croll, Napier, Naismith (Sub Ingram), Thoirs, Duff (Burr), Duncanson. Subs not used: Pennycook, Hodge, Morrice, Ritchie
Sp: Carswell, Townsley, Stevenson, Thompson, Greenhill, Comrie (Sub Watson), Maxwell, Herd, Ward, Dishington, Johnston (Sub Haye). Subs not used: beesley, Gilpin, Mair, Tolmie, Horribine

Banks o' Dee 2 (Dawson og, Lennox) Formartine United 2 (Young, Barbour), H.T. 0-1
Ref: C Graham
BOD: Shearer, Robertson, Duguid (Sub Heads), Whyte, J Winton, McCall, K Winton, Hamilton (Sub Sopel), Lennox, Hall, Henderson (Sub Phillipson) Subs not used: Stephen, Forbes, Buchanan
FU: Reid, Lawson, Anderson, Rodger, Masson (Sub Berton), Michie, Ferries (Sub Gauld), Jamieson, Wood (Sub Young), Barbour, Dingwall. Subs not used: MacDonald, Stuart Smith

Bonnyrigg Rose 2 (Hoskins, Kidd) Cove Rangers 1 (Smith), H.T. 0-0
Ref: W Wilson
BR: Andrews, Brown (Sub Horne), Hoskins, Young, Donaldson, Stewart, Nelson (Sub McLaren), Kidd, Jamieson (Sub McGachie), Turner, McIntosh. Subs not used: Moyes, Gray, King, Rooney
CR: McKenzie, Smith, Kelly, Walker, Watson (Sub Park), Redford,, Yule, Milne, Duff, Scully (Sub Stott), Megginson. Unused subs: McBain, McCafferty, Lawrie, McDonald

Preston Athletic 0 Montrose 3 H.T. 0-0
Ref: C Napier
PA: Pennycuick, Cowan, Cochrane (Sub Jardine), Siegel, Colquhoun, Innes (Sub henderson), Stevenson, Mcleod, O'Rourke, Neto, Ritchie (Sub Park). Unused subs: Lawson, Baines, Graham, Erskine

Cowdenbeath 0 East Kilbride 1 (Victoria) H.T. 0-1
Referee: G Ross
EK: Kean, Russell, Capuano, Howie, McLaren, Strachan, McBride, Winters, Gibbons, Hardie (Sub Hughes), Victoria (Sub Millar). Subs not used Winters, McNeil, Marenghi, McGinley, Stevenson

Berwick Rangers 2 Hawick Royal Albert 3 (Morris 3)
Ref: M Roncone
HRA: Ranking, McInally, Saunderson, Spence, Meikle (Sub Crease), Stevenson, Conaghan, Johnstone, Partlin, Morris, Hunter. Subs not used: Boyd, Pettigrew, Brown, Darling

Annan Athletic 0 East Stirlingshire 0
Ref: A Newlands
ES: Barclay, MacGregor, Greene, Grant, Allison, ure, Sludden, Faulds, D Grant (Sub Glasgow), White (Sub Shaw), Rodgers. Unused subs: Ramsay, Murray, McGuigan, Peddie, Hogg

BSC Glasgow 0 Beith 1 (McLaughlin), HT 0-0
Ref: Lorraine Clark
BSC: Wilton, Duncan, Traynor, Keys (Sub Jones), Redpath, Cunningham, Bell, Toner, Dryden (Sub Corrieri), Woods, Ferris (Sub Holms) Unused subs: S Barr, C Kasango, M Beckett, A Bembo
Beith: Grindlay, McLaughlin, Sheridan, Wilson, Docherty (Sub Watt), McGowan, McGlinchey, MacDonald, Frize, McLean (Sub Collins), Christie (Sub McPherson) Unused subs: Burke, Martin, Fisher, McBain

Second Round Replays

Saturday October 29th

East Stirlingshire 1 (Sludden) Annan Athletic 2 (Mckenna, Ashgar) H.T. 1-1
Referee: A Newlands
ES: Barclay, McGregor (Sub Murray), Greene, A Grant, Allison, Ure, Sludden, Faulds, D Grant, White (Sub Glasgow), Rodgers. Subs not used: Ramsay, McGuigan, Shaw, Hogg, Peddie

Formartine United 7 (Anderson, Masson 3, Gauld, Rodger, Barbour) Banks o' Dee 2 (Henderson, Buchanan)
Referee: D Smith
FU: MacDonald, Crawford (Sub Henry), Anderson, Rodger (Sub Lawrence), Masson, Michie, Ferries, Jamieson, Gauld (Sub Burnett), Barbour, Dingwall. Subs not used Berton, Reid, Stuart Smith
BOD: Shearer, Robertson, Heads, Whyte, Winton, McCall, Phillipson (Sub Forbes), Lennox, Watt (Sub McLeod), Hall (Sub Buchanan), Henderson. Subs not used Sopel, Stephen

Forres Mechanics 4 (McGovern, Soane, Fraser, Scott) Cumbernauld Colts 0, H.T. 1-0,
Referee: M Roncone
FM: Knight, Allan (Sub Cameron), Grant, G Fraser, Finlayson, L Fraser, Soane (Sub Moore), Scott, Khutishvili (Sub Groat), McGovern, Graham. Subs not used: Forbes, Baxter, Storrier, McLean
CC: Fahey, Kirwan, Ward, McFarlane, Barclay, Murray (Sub Black), O'Neill (Sub Brown), Broadfoot, Batchelor, Ronald, Selkirk. Subs not used Foggin, Giles, McKenzie, Pirrie, Sheridan

Gretna 2008 2 (Neill, Murray) Buckie Thistle 6 (McLeod 5, Dorrat)
Referee:
G: Ballantyne, Wood (Sub Dickinson), Brannan, R Murray, Hope, Hunter, Rudd (Sub Studholme), Telfer, Connor Murray, Neill, McCartney (Sub J Murray). Sub not used Inglis
BT: Salmon, Munro, MacKinnon (Sub MacRae), Dorrat, Wood, Taylor, McLean, Low (Sub Copeland), Fraser, Urquhart, McLeod (Sub Fraser). Subs not used Angus, Scott, Carroll, Strong

Third Round

Saturday November 26th

Bonnyrigg Rose 0 Dumbarton 0
Ref: S Finnie
BR: Andrews, Hoskins, Young, Donaldson, Horne, Stewart, Nelson (Sub Gray), Kidd, Turner, McIntosh (Sub McLaren), McGachie. Unused subs: Moyes, Rooney, Archibald

Elgin City 8 (Sutherland 4, Cameron 2, McLeish, Gunn) Hawick Royal Albert 1 (Mitchell), HT 3-1
Ref: M Northcroft
HRA: Raking, Saunderson (Sub Spence), Meikle, Stevenson, Conaghan, Johnstone (Sub Darling), Mitchell, Hughes, Morris, Hunter, McPartlin (Sub McInally). Subs Aitken, Pettigrew, Sonkur

Buckie Thistle 3 (McLeod, Angus 2) Dunfermline Athletic 5 (Paton, Munro og, Higginbotham, McMullan 2), H.T. 2-2
Ref: C Charleston
BT: Salmon, Munro, Mckinnon, Dorratt, McLean (Sub Wood), Angus, Cheyne, Copeland (Sub Milne), Fraser, Urquhart, McLeod. Subs not used: Carroll, Strong, Scott, MacRae, Low

Forres Mechanics 2 (Allan, Fraser) Stenhousemuir 2 (Furtado, Kerr) H.T. 1-1
Ref: S Millar
FM: Knight, Allan, Grant, G Fraser, Finlayson, L Fraser, Soane, Khutashvili, MacPherson (Sub Cameron), McGovern (Sub Groat), Graham (Sub Baxter). Subs not used: Moore, McLean, Scott, Storrier
Tuesday November 29th

St Mirren 5 (Shankland 2, McAllister, Mallin, Sutton) Spartans 1 (Beesley)
Ref: K Graham
S: Carswell, Malone, Townsley, Stevenson, Thomson, Tolmie (Sub Salutregi), Herd, Brown, Dishington, Mair (Sub Maxwell), Haye (Sub Beesley). Subs not used: Gilpin, Ward, Watson, Comrie

Saturday December 3rd

Stranraer 2 (Gibson, Strachan) v East Kilbride 1 (Winter)
Ref: S Kirkland
EK: Kean, Proctor, Russell, Coll (Sub Smith), Capuano (Sub McLaren), Howie, Strachan, Winter, Marenghi (Sub McBride), Hughes, Victoria. Subs not used: Stevenson, McNeil, Hardie, McGinley

Replays

Saturday December 3rd

Stenhousemuir 3 (McMenamin 3) Forres Mechanics 1 (Baxter), H.T. 2-0
Referee: S Millar
FM: Knight, Allan, Grant, Fraser, Finlayson (Sub Groat), L Fraser, Soane (Sub Baxter), Khutishvili (Sub Cameron), MacPherson, McGovern, Graham. Subs not used Hutcheson, McLean, Storrier, Paterson

Tuesday December 6th

Dumbarton 0 Bonnyrigg Rose 1 (Nelson) H.T. 0-0
Referee: G Aitken
BR: Andrews, Hoskins, Young, Donaldson, Horne, Stewart, Nelson, Kidd (Sub Gray), Turner, McIntosh (Sub McLaren), McGachie (Sub Moyes). Subs not used Rooney, Archibald

Round Four

Saturday January 21st

Bonnyrigg Rose 1 (Hoskins) Hibernian 8 (Shinnie, Keatings 2, Humphrey, Cummings 2, Stevenson, Forster)
Referee: A Muir Att 12451
BR: Andrews, Hoskins, Young, Donaldson, Horne, Stewart (Sub Brown), Nelson, Kidd, Turner (Sub Gray), McIntosh (Sub McLaren), McGachie. Subs not used: Jamieson, Rooney, Moyes, Archibald

Scottish Cup Finals 1873-2017

Season	Winner	Score	Runner-up	Venue	Attendance
1873–74	Queen's Park (1)	2–0	Clydesdale	Hampden Park (original)	2,500
1874–75	Queen's Park (2)	3–0	Renton	Hampden Park (original)	7,000
1875–76	Queen's Park	1–1	3rd Lanark RV	Hamilton Crescent	6,000
(R)	Queen's Park (3)	2–0	3rd Lanark RV	Hampden Park (original)	10,000
1876–77	Vale of Leven	1–1	Rangers	Hamilton Crescent	8,000
(R)	Vale of Leven	1–1	Rangers	Hamilton Crescent	15,000
(SR)	Vale of Leven (1)	3–2	Rangers	Hampden Park (original)	12,000
1877–78	Vale of Leven (2)	1–0	3rd Lanark RV	Hampden Park (original)	5,000
1878–79	Vale of Leven	1–1	Rangers	Hampden Park (original)	9,000
(R)	Vale of Leven (3)	wo	Rangers	Hampden Park (original)	
1879–80	Queen's Park (4)	3–0	Thornliebank	Hampden Park (original)	4,000
1880–81	Queen's Park	2–1 *	Dumbarton	Kinning Park	15,000
(R)	Queen's Park (5)	3–1	Dumbarton	Kinning Park	10,000
1881–82	Queen's Park	2–2	Dumbarton	Cathkin Park (first)	12,500
(R)	Queen's Park (6)	4–1	Dumbarton	Cathkin Park (first)	14,000
1882–83	Dumbarton	2–2	Vale of Leven	Hampden Park (original)	15,000
(R)	Dumbarton (1)	2–1	Vale of Leven	Hampden Park (original)	12,000
1883–84	Queen's Park (7)	wo	Vale of Leven	Cathkin Park (first)	
1884–85	Renton	0–0	Vale of Leven	Hampden Park (second)	3,000
(R)	Renton (1)	3–1	Vale of Leven	Hampden Park (second)	5,500
1885–86	Queen's Park (8)	3–1	Renton	Cathkin Park (first)	7,000
1886–87	Hibernian (1)	2–1	Dumbarton	Hampden Park (second)	15,000
1887–88	Renton (2)	6–1	Cambuslang	Hampden Park (second)	10,000
1888–89	3rd Lanark RV	3–0 *	Celtic	Hampden Park (second)	17,000
(R)	3rd Lanark RV (1)	2–1	Celtic	Hampden Park (second)	13,000
1889–90	Queen's Park	1–1	Vale of Leven	Ibrox Park (first)	11,000
(R)	Queen's Park (9)	2–1	Vale of Leven	Ibrox Park (first)	13,000
1890–91	Heart of Midlothian (1)	1–0	Dumbarton	Hampden Park (second)	10,836
1891–92	Celtic	1–0 *	Queen's Park	Ibrox Park (first)	40,000
(R)	Celtic (1)	5–1	Queen's Park	Ibrox Park (first)	26,000
1892–93	Queen's Park	0–1 *	Celtic	Ibrox Park (first)	18,771
(R)	Queen's Park (10)	2–1	Celtic	Ibrox Park (first)	13,239
1893–94	Rangers (1)	3–1	Celtic	Hampden Park (second)	17,000
1894–95	St Bernard's (1)	2–1	Renton	Ibrox Park (first)	10,000
1895–96	Heart of Midlothian (2)	3–1	Hibernian	Logie Green	17,034
1896–97	Rangers (2)	5–1	Dumbarton	Hampden Park (second)	14,000
1897–98	Rangers (3)	2–0	Kilmarnock	Hampden Park (second)	13,000
1898–99	Celtic (2)	2–0	Rangers	Hampden Park (second)	25,000
1899–1900	Celtic (3)	4–3	Queen's Park	Ibrox Park	15,000
1900–01	Heart of Midlothian (3)	4–3	Celtic	Ibrox Park	15,000
1901–02	Hibernian (2)	1–0	Celtic	Celtic Park	16,000
1902–03	Rangers	1–1	Heart of Midlothian	Celtic Park	13,000
(R)	Rangers	0–0	Heart of Midlothian	Celtic Park	35,000
(SR)	Rangers (5)	2–0	Heart of Midlothian	Celtic Park	30,000
1903–04	Celtic (4)	3–2	Rangers	Hampden Park	64,472
1904–05	Third Lanark	0–0	Rangers	Hampden Park	54,000
(R)	Third Lanark (2)	3–1	Rangers	Hampden Park	55,000
1905–06	Heart of Midlothian (4)	1–0	Third Lanark	Ibrox Park	30,000
1906–07	Celtic (5)	3–0	Heart of Midlothian	Hampden Park	50,000
1907–08	Celtic (6)	5–1	St. Mirren	Hampden Park	58,000
1909–10	Dundee	2–2	Clyde	Ibrox Park	60,000
(R)	Dundee	0–0 AET	Clyde	Ibrox Park	25,000
(SR)	Dundee (1)	2–1	Clyde	Ibrox Park	25,000
1910–11	Celtic	0–0	Hamilton Academical	Ibrox Park	45,000

Season	Winner	Score	Runner-up	Venue	Attendance
(R)	Celtic (7)	2–0	Hamilton Academical	Ibrox Park	25,000
1911–12	Celtic (8)	2–0	Clyde	Ibrox Park	45,000
1912–13	Falkirk (1)	2–0	Raith Rovers	Celtic Park	45,000
1913–14	Celtic	0–0	Hibernian	Ibrox Park	56,000
(R)	Celtic (9)	4–1	Hibernian	Ibrox Park	40,000
1919–20	Kilmarnock (1)	3–2	Albion Rovers	Celtic Park	95,000
1920–21	Partick Thistle (1)	1–0	Rangers	Celtic Park	28,294
1921–22	Morton (1)	1–0	Rangers	Hampden Park	70,000
1922–23	Celtic (10)	1–0	Hibernian	Hampden Park	82,000
1923–24	Airdrieonians (1)	2–0	Hibernian	Ibrox Park	65,000
1924–25	Celtic (11)	2–1	Dundee	Hampden Park	75,31
1925–26	St. Mirren (1)	2–0	Celtic	Hampden Park	98,00
1926–27	Celtic (12)	3–1	East Fife	Hampden Park	80,07
1927–28	Rangers (6)	4–0	Celtic	Hampden Park	118,11
1928–29	Kilmarnock (2)	1–0	Rangers	Hampden Park	114,78
1929–30	Rangers	0–0	Partick Thistle	Hampden Park	107,47
(R)	Rangers (7)	2–1	Partick Thistle	Hampden Park	103,68
1930–31	Celtic	2–2	Motherwell	Hampden Park	104,86
(R)	Celtic (13)	4–2	Motherwell	Hampden Park	98,50
1931–32	Rangers	1–1	Kilmarnock	Hampden Park	112,00
(R)	Rangers (8)	3–0	Kilmarnock	Hampden Park	104,60
1932–33	Celtic (14)	1–0	Motherwell	Hampden Park	102,33
1933–34	Rangers (9)	5–0	St. Mirren	Hampden Park	113,43
1934–35	Rangers (10)	2–1	Hamilton Academical	Hampden Park	87,74
1935–36	Rangers (11)	1–0	Third Lanark	Hampden Park	88,85
1936–37	Celtic (15)	2–1	Aberdeen	Hampden Park	147,36
1937–38	East Fife	1–1	Kilmarnock	Hampden Park	80,09
(R)	East Fife (1)	4–2 AET	Kilmarnock	Hampden Park	92,71
1938–39	Clyde (1)	4–0	Motherwell	Hampden Park	94,00
1946–47	Aberdeen (1)	2–1	Hibernian	Hampden Park	82,14
1947–48	Rangers	1–1 AET	Morton	Hampden Park	129,17
(R)	Rangers (11)	1–0 AET	Morton	Hampden Park	133,75
1948–49	Rangers (12)	4–1	Clyde	Hampden Park	108,43
1949–50	Rangers (13)	3–0	East Fife	Hampden Park	118,26
1950–51	Celtic (16)	1–0	Motherwell	Hampden Park	131,9
1951–52	Motherwell (1)	4–0	Dundee	Hampden Park	136,2
1952–53	Rangers	1–1	Aberdeen	Hampden Park	129,7
(R)	Rangers (14)	1–0	Aberdeen	Hampden Park	113,7
1953–54	Celtic (17)	2–1	Aberdeen	Hampden Park	130,0
1954–55	Clyde	1–1	Celtic	Hampden Park	106,2
(R)	Clyde (2)	1–0	Celtic	Hampden Park	68,8
1955–56	Heart of Midlothian (5)	3–1	Celtic	Hampden Park	132,8
1956–57	Falkirk	1–1	Kilmarnock	Hampden Park	83,0
(R)	Falkirk (2)	2–1 AET	Kilmarnock	Hampden Park	79,7
1957–58	Clyde (3)	1–0	Hibernian	Hampden Park	95,1
1958–59	St. Mirren (2)	3–1	Aberdeen	Hampden Park	108,5
1959–60	Rangers (15)	2–0	Kilmarnock	Hampden Park	108,0
1960–61	Dunfermline Athletic	0–0	Celtic	Hampden Park	113,6
(R)	Dunfermline Athletic (1)	2–0	Celtic	Hampden Park	87,8
1961–62	Rangers (16)	2–0	St. Mirren	Hampden Park	127,9
1962–63	Rangers	1–1	Celtic	Hampden Park	129,6
(R)	Rangers (17)	3–0	Celtic	Hampden Park	120,2
1963–64	Rangers (18)	3–1	Dundee	Hampden Park	120,9
1964–65	Celtic (18)	3–2	Dunfermline Athletic	Hampden Park	108,8

1965–66	Rangers	0–0	Celtic	Hampden Park	126,552
(R)	Rangers (19)	1–0	Celtic	Hampden Park	98,202
1966–67	Celtic (19)	2–0	Aberdeen	Hampden Park	126,102
1967–68	Dunfermline Athletic (3)	3–1	Heart of Midlothian	Hampden Park	56,365
1968–69	Celtic (20)	4–0	Rangers	Hampden Park	132,000
1969–70	Aberdeen (2)	3–1	Celtic	Hampden Park	108,434
1970–71	Celtic	1–1	Rangers	Hampden Park	120,092
(R)	Celtic (21)	2–1	Rangers	Hampden Park	103,332
1971–72	Celtic (22)	6–1	Hibernian	Hampden Park	106,102
1972–73	Rangers (20)	3–2	Celtic	Hampden Park	122,714
1973–74	Celtic (23)	3–0	Dundee United	Hampden Park	75,959
1974–75	Celtic (24)	3–1	Airdrieonians	Hampden Park	75,457
1975–76	Rangers (21)	3–1	Heart of Midlothian	Hampden Park	85,354
1976–77	Celtic (25)	1–0	Rangers	Hampden Park	54,252
1977–78	Rangers (22)	2–1	Aberdeen	Hampden Park	61,563
1978–79	Rangers	0–0	Hibernian	Hampden Park	50,610
(R)	Rangers	0–0 AET	Hibernian	Hampden Park	33,504
(SR)	Rangers (23)	3–2 AET	Hibernian	Hampden Park	30,602
1979–80	Celtic (26)	1–0	Rangers	Hampden Park	70,303
1980–81	Rangers	0–0AET	Dundee United	Hampden Park	53,000
(R)	Rangers (24)	4–1	Dundee United	Hampden Park	43,099
1981–82	Aberdeen (3)	4–1 AET	Rangers	Hampden Park	53,788
1982–83	Aberdeen (4)	1–0 AET	Rangers	Hampden Park	62,979
1983–84	Aberdeen (5)	2–1 AET	Celtic	Hampden Park	58,900
1984–85	Celtic (27)	2–1	Dundee United	Hampden Park	60,346
1985–86	Aberdeen (6)	3–0	Heart of Midlothian	Hampden Park	62,841
1986–87	St. Mirren (3)	1–0 AET	Dundee United	Hampden Park	51,782
1987–88	Celtic (28)	2–1	Dundee United	Hampden Park	74,000
1988–89	Celtic (29)	1–0	Rangers	Hampden Park	72,069
1989–90	Aberdeen (7)	0–0 †	Celtic	Hampden Park	60,493
1990–91	Motherwell (2)	4–3 AET	Dundee United	Hampden Park	57,319
1991–92	Rangers (25)	2–1	Airdrieonians	Hampden Park	44,045
1992–93	Rangers (26)	2–1	Aberdeen	Celtic Park	50,715
1993–94	Dundee United (1)	1–0	Rangers	Hampden Park	37,450
1994–95	Celtic (30)	1–0	Airdrieonians	Hampden Park	36,915
1995–96	Rangers (27)	5–1	Heart of Midlothian	Hampden Park	37,730
1996–97	Kilmarnock (3)	1–0	Falkirk	Ibrox Stadium	48,953
1997–98	Heart of Midlothian (6)	2–1	Rangers	Celtic Park	48,946
1998–99	Rangers (28)	1–0	Celtic	Hampden Park	52,670
1999–00	Rangers (29)	4–0	Aberdeen	Hampden Park	50,865
2000–01	Celtic (31)	3–0	Hibernian	Hampden Park	51,824
2001–02	Rangers (30)	3–2	Celtic	Hampden Park	51,138
2002–03	Rangers (31)	1–0	Dundee	Hampden Park	47,136
2003–04	Celtic (32)	3–1	Dunfermline Athletic	Hampden Park	50,846
2004–05	Celtic (33)	1–0	Dundee United	Hampden Park	50,635
2005–06	Heart of Midlothian (7)	1–1 AET + pk	Gretna	Hampden Park	51,232
2006–07	Celtic (34)	1–0	Dunfermline Athletic	Hampden Park	49,600
2007–08	Rangers (32)	3–2	Queen of the South	Hampden Park	48,821
2008–09	Rangers (33)	1–0	Falkirk	Hampden Park	50,956
2009–10	Dundee United (2)	3–0	Ross County	Hampden Park	47,122
2010–11	Celtic (35)	3–0	Motherwell	Hampden Park	49,618
2011–12	Heart of Midlothian (8)	5–1	Hibernian	Hampden Park	51,041
2012–13	Celtic (36)	3–0	Hibernian	Hampden Park	51,254
2013-14	St Johnstone (1)	2-0	Dundee United	Celtic Park	47,545
2014-15	Inverness CT (1)	2-1	Falkirk	Hampden Park	37,149
2015-16	Hibernian (3)	3-2	Rangers	Hampden Park	50,701
2016-17	Celtic (37)	2-1	Aberdeen	Hampden Park	48,713

* Match Void

Scottish Cup Format 2017/18

1st Preliminary Round (3 ties)
4 Qualifiers (Kelty Hearts, Colville Park, Glenafton Ath, Lothian Thistle HV)
1 unlicensed SFA member (Newton Stewart)
+ 3 drawn randomly from Linlithgow, Banks o' Dee, Girvan, St Cuthbert, Burntisland, Coldstream, Preston Ath, Threave, Golspie S, Glasgow Uni

2nd Prelim Round (6 ties)
4 Winners from 1st Preliminary Round
8 drawn randomly from Linlithgow, Banks o' Dee, Girvan, St Cuthbert, Burntisland, Coldstream, Preston Ath, Threave, Golspie S, Glasgow Uni

Round 1 (18 ties)
14 Lowland League teams (placed 3-15 in 2016/17 + Edusport), 16 Highland League Clubs (placed 2-18 last season), plus 6 winners from 2nd Prelim Round

Round 2 (16 ties)
10 League Two teams. 2 Lowland League teams (East Kilbride and Shire), 2 Highland League teams (Buckie and Cove), plus 18 Round 1 winners

Round 3 (16 ties)
6 Championship teams from 2016/17 (places 5-10) , 10 League 1 teams (placed 1-9 from 2016/17 but 2016/17 League 2 Champions), plus 16 Round 2 winners

Round 4 (16 ties)
12 Premier Teams from 2016/17, 4 Championship teams plus 16 Round 3 winners

Competition Dates:

Preliminary Round One – Saturday, 12 August 2017
Preliminary Round Two – Saturday, 2 September 2017
Round One – Saturday, 23 September 2017
Round Two – Saturday, 14 October 2017
Round Three – Saturday, 18 November 2017
Round Four – Saturday, 20 January 2018
Round Five – Saturday, 10 February 2018
Round Six – Saturday, 3 March 2018
Semi-finals – Saturday, 14 and Sunday, 15 April 2018
Final – Saturday, 19 May 2018

Preliminary Round Draws (made July 10th 2017)

First Preliminary Round (August 12)
Kelty Hearts v Lothian Thistle Hutchison Vale
Glenafton Athletic v Newton Stewart
Burntisland Shipyard v Colville Park

Second Preliminary Round (September 2)
Banks o' Dee v Linlithgow Rose
Glasgow University v Threave Rovers
Burntisland SY or Colville Park v Preston Athletic
Kelty Hearts or Lothian Thistle HV v Coldstream
Glenafton Ath or Newton Stewart v Golspie Sutherland
St Cuthbert Wanderers v Girvan

Scottish League (Betfred) Cup 2016/17

The format of the competition was changed for 2016/17. The four clubs competing in Europe were exempted from the group stages. The remaining 38 clubs, plus East Stirlingshire and Cove Rangers, were drawn into 8 groups of 5. The draw was regionalised and seeded. Teams met each other once. Drawn matches went to a penalty kicks, with 2 points to the winners and 1 to the losers of the shoot-out. The 8 Group winners and the 4 best runners-up qualified for the First Round, with the 4 European entrants joining at that stage.

Details of team-line ups, dates, attendances etc are within the relevant club grids earlier in this book.

GROUP A															
Pos	Team	Pld	W	PW	PL	L	GF	GA	GD	Pts	PET	EF	DND	FOR	DUM
1	Peterhead (Q)	4	2	1	0	1	8	6	2	8			2–1	2–0	
2	East Fife (X)	4	2	1	0	1	5	4	1	8	2–1		1–1, 4-2p		
3	Dundee	4	2	0	1	1	15	5	10	7				7–0	6–2
4	Forfar Athletic	4	1	1	0	2	4	11	-7	5		2–0			2–2, 5-3p
5	Dumbarton	4	0	0	2	2	7	13	-6	2	3–3, 5-6p	0-2			

GROUP B															
Pos	Team	Pld	W	PW	PL	L	GF	GA	GD	Pts	STJ	FAL	STI	BRE	ELG
1	St Johnstone (Q)	4	3	0	1	0	11	2	9	10		3–0	4–0		
2	Falkirk (X)	4	2	0	0	2	5	4	1	6				2–0	3–0
3	Stirling Albion	4	2	0	0	2	6	7	-1	6		1–0			4–1
4	Brechin City	4	1	1	0	2	5	8	-3	5	1-1, 4-2p		2-1		
5	Elgin City	4	1	0	0	3	6	12	-6	3	1–3			4–2	

GROUP C															
Pos	Team	Pld	W	PW	PL	L	GF	GA	GD	Pts	INV	DUFC	PARS	COW	ARB
1	Inverness CT (Q)	4	3	0	1	0	15	3	12	10		1–1, 1-4p			7-0
2	Dundee United (X)	4	2	2	0	0	10	3	7	10			2–0	6–1	
3	Dunfermline Athletic	4	2	0	0	2	7	7	0	6	1–5				3–0
4	Cowdenbeath	4	1	0	0	3	4	11	-7	3	1–2		0–3		
5	Arbroath	4	0	0	1	3	1	13	-12	1		1–1, 3-5p		0–2	

GROUP D															
Pos	Team	Pld	W	PW	PL	L	GF	GA	GD	Pts	ALO	RAI	ROS	COVE	MON
1	Alloa Athletic (Q)	4	4	0	0	0	10	2	8	12			3–2	4–0	
2	Raith Rovers (X)	4	2	1	0	1	5	4	1	8	0–1				2–1
3	Ross County	4	2	0	1	1	11	4	7	7		1–1, 3-4p		7–0	—
4	Cove Rangers	4	1	0	0	3	4	13	-9	3		1–2			3–0
5	Montrose	4	0	0	0	4	1	8	-7	0	0–2		0–1		

Group E															
Pos	Team	Pld	W	PW	PL	L	GF	GA	GD	Pts	PAR	QOS	AIR	QPA	STE
1	Partick Thistle (Q)	4	4	0	0	0	9	2	7	12		2–1		2–0	
2	Queen of the South (X)	4	3	0	0	1	6	2	4	9			2–0		1–0
3	Airdrieonians	4	1	1	0	2	5	7	-2	5	0–1				2–1
4	Queen's Park	4	1	0	1	2	5	7	-2	4		0–2	3–3, 7-8p		
5	Stenhousemuir	4	0	0	0	4	2	9	-7	0	1–4			0–2	

GROUP F															
Pos	Team	Pld	W	PW	PL	L	GF	GA	GD	Pts	RAN	MOT	STR	ANN	SHI
1	Rangers (Q)	4	4	0	0	0	10	0	10	12			3–0	2–0	
2	Motherwell (X)	4	3	0	0	1	9	3	6	9	0–2				3–0
3	Stranraer	4	2	0	0	2	5	8	-3	6		0–3			3–1
4	Annan Athletic	4	1	0	0	3	4	7	-3	3		1–3	1–2		
5	East Stirlingshire	4	0	0	0	4	1	11	-10	0	0–3			0–2	

Date	Comp	H/A	Opponents	F	A	HT		Referee	Crowd	Scorers	1	2	3	4	5	6	7	8	9	10	11	12	13	14	15	16	17	18
EAST STIRLINGSHIRE																												
19/07/2016	LC	A	Stranraer	1	3	0	0	D Lowe	373	Glasgow	Dolan	Greene	Murray	A Grant	Fisher	MacGregor	McGuigan	Ure*	Glasgow+	McMillan	D Grant&	Comrie*	Hogg+	White&	Buist	*Peddie*	*Shaw*	
23/07/2016	LC	H	Rangers	0	3	0	2	C Allan	2246		Dolan	Greene	Murray	A Grant	Fisher	MacGregor*	McGuigan	Ure	Faulds	Hogg&	D Grant+	Comrie*	McMillan+	White&	Buist	*Peddie*	*Shaw*	
26/07/2016	LC	A	Motherwell	0	3	0	0	C Charleston	2503		Dolan	Greene	Murray*	A Grant	Fisher	MacGregor	McGuigan&	Ure	Faulds	Hogg+	D Grant	Sludden*	Comrie+	Peddie&	Buist	*White*	*Shaw*	*McMillan*
30/07/2016	LC	H	Annan Athletic	0	2	0	0	M Roncone	134		Dolan	Greene	Buist+	A Grant	Fisher	MacGregor	McGuigan&	Ure	Sludden	Hogg*	D Grant	Murray*	McMillan+	Rodgers&	Peddie	*White*	*Shaw*	*Comrie*
COVE RANGERS																												
15/07/2016	LC	H	Raith Rovers	1	2	1	1	G Beaton	362	Stott	McKenzie	Redford	Lawrie&	Walker	Kelly	Yule	Scully*	Burnett	Stott+	Megginson	J Smith	Park*	Milne+	Donaldson&	Watson	*Duff*	*McCulloch*	*McCafferty*
19/07/2016	LC	A	Alloa	0	4	0	1	S Reid	213		McKenzie	Milne	Watson*	Walker	Kelly	Duffy	Scully+	Burnett	Park*	Megginson	J Smith	Stott*	Buchan+	McCulloch&	*S Smith*	*Dunbar*	*McCafferty*	
27/07/2016	LC	H	Montrose	3	0	1	0	M Taylor	189	Walker, MegginsoN, Park	McKenzie	Redford	Watson	Walker	Kelly*	Yule	Scully	Duff	Buchan+	Megginson	J Smith&	Milne*	Park+	Donaldson&	*McBain*	*Burnett*	*McCulloch*	*McCafferty*
30/07/2016	LC	A	Ross County	0	7	0	1	M Northcroft	722		McKenzie	Redford	Milne	Walker	Kelly	Yule	Scully&	Burnett	Buchan*	Megginson	J Smith+	McBain*	Park+	McCulloch&	*Donaldson*	*Watson*	*S Smith*	*McCafferty*

GROUP G														
Pos	Team	Pld	W	PW	PL	L	GF	GA	GD	Pts	HAM	AYR	STM	LIV	EDC
1	Hamilton Academical (Q)	4	3	0	0	1	10	5	5	9			3–0	2–1	
2	Ayr United (X)	4	3	0	0	1	5	2	3	9	2–1				1–0
3	St Mirren	4	3	0	0	1	7	5	2	9		1–0			3–0
4	Livingston	4	1	0	0	3	6	7	-1	3		0–2	2–3		
5	Edinburgh City	4	0	0	0	4	2	11	-9	0	2–4			0–3	

GROUP H															
Pos	Team	Pld	W	PW	PL	L	GF	GA	GD	Pts	MOR	KIL	CLY	ALB	BER
1	Morton (Q)	4	3	1	0	0	5	0	5	11			1–0		2–0
2	Kilmarnock (X)	4	2	0	1	1	5	5	0	7	0–2			0–0, 3-5p	
3	Clyde	4	1	1	0	2	4	5	-1	5		1–2			1–1
4	Albion Rovers	4	0	2	1	1	1	2	-1	5	0–0, 3-4p		1–2		
5	Berwick Rangers	4	0	0	2	2	3	6	-3	2	2–3		0–0, 4-5p		

KO STAGES						
Rd 1	9/8/16	Alloa Athletic	Inverness CT	1	0	613
	9/8/16	Rangers	Peterhead	5	0	27076
	9/8/16	Dundee United	Partick Thistle	3	1	5036
	9/8/16	Hamilton Accies	Morton	1	2	1112
	9/8/16	Hibernian	Queen of the South	1	3	7647
	10/8/16	Celtic	Motherwell	5	0	20165
	10/8/16	St Johnstone	Hearts	3	2	4314
	10/8/16	Ayr United	Aberdeen	1	2	2653
QF	20/9/16	Morton	Dundee United	2	1	2149
	20/9/16	Rangers	Queen of the South	5	0	26079
	21/9/16	Celtic	Alloa Athletic	2	0	15900
	22/9/16	Aberdeen	St Johnstone	1	0	8829
SF	22/10/16	Morton	Aberdeen	0	2	16183
	23/10/16	Rangers	Celtic	0	1	50697
F	27/11/16	Aberdeen	Celtic	0	3	49626

Betfred Scottish League Cup Format 2017/18

Group A - Inverness CT, Falkirk, Stirling Albion, Brechin City, Forfar Athletic

Group B - Hearts, Dunfermline, Peterhead, East Fife, Elgin City

Group C - Dundee, Dundee United, Cowdenbeath, Buckie Thistle, Raith Rovers

Group D - Ross County, Hibernian, Montrose, Alloa, Arbroath

Group E - Kilmarnock, Dumbarton, Ayr United, Clyde, Annan Athletic

Group F - Motherwell, Morton, Edinburgh City, Queen's Park, Berwick Rangers

Group G - Hamilton Accies, Queen of the South, Albion Rovers, Stenhousemuir, East Kilbride

Group H - Partick Thistle, St Mirren, Airdrie, Stranraer, Livingston

Same rules apply as in 2016/17 - drawn matches to be decided on a penalty shoot-pout with a bonus po for the winner. Eight group winners plus 4 best runners-up will qualify for the KO stages where they w be joined by Celtic, Rangers, St Johnston e and Aberdeen.

Scottish League Cup Finals 1947-2017

Season	Winner	Score	Runner-up	Venue	Attendance	Losing SF	
1946–47	Rangers	4 – 0	Aberdeen	Hampden Park	82,700	Hearts	Hibernian
1947–48	East Fife	0 – 0 AET	Falkirk	Hampden Park	53,785	Aberdeen	Rangers
1947–48 (R)	East Fife	4 – 1	Falkirk	Hampden Park	31,000		
1948–49	Rangers	2 – 0	Raith Rovers	Hampden Park	57,450	Hamilton Accies	Dundee
1949–50	East Fife	3 – 0	Dunfermline Athletic	Hampden Park	39,744	Rangers	Hibernian
1950–51	Motherwell	3 – 0	Hibernian	Hampden Park	64,074	Ayr United	QOS
1951–52	Dundee	3 – 2	Rangers	Hampden Park	92,325	Celtic	Motherwell
1952–53	Dundee	2 – 0	Kilmarnock	Hampden Park	51,830	Rangers	Hibernian
1953–54	East Fife	3 – 2	Partick Thistle	Hampden Park	38,529	Rangers	Hibernian
1954–55	Heart of Midlothian	4 – 2	Motherwell	Hampden Park	55,640	East Fife	Airdrie
1955–56	Aberdeen	2 – 1	St. Mirren	Hampden Park	44,106	Rangers	Motherwell
1956–57	Celtic	0 – 0 AET	Partick Thistle	Hampden Park	58,794	Dundee	Clyde
1956–57 (R)	Celtic	3 – 0	Partick Thistle	Hampden Park	31,156		
1957–58	Celtic	7 – 1	Rangers	Hampden Park	82,293	Brechin City	Clyde
1958–59	Heart of Midlothian	5 – 1	Partick Thistle	Hampden Park	59,690	Kilmarnock	Celtic
1959–60	Heart of Midlothian	2 – 1	Third Lanark	Hampden Park	57,994	Cowdenbeath	Arbroath
1960–61	Rangers	2 – 0	Kilmarnock	Hampden Park	82,063	Hamilton Accies	QOS
1961–62	Rangers	1 – 1 AET	Heart of Midlothian	Hampden Park	88,000	Stirling Albion	St Johnstone
1961–62 (R)	Rangers	3 – 1	Heart of Midlothian	Hampden Park	47,500		
1962–63	Heart of Midlothian	1 – 0	Kilmarnock	Hampden Park	51,000	Rangers	St Johnstone
1963–64	Rangers	5 – 0	Morton	Hampden Park	105,907	Berwick Rangers	Hibernian
1964–65	Rangers	2 – 1	Celtic	Hampden Park	91,423	Dundee United	Morton
1965–66	Celtic	2 – 1	Rangers	Hampden Park	107,609	Kilmarnock	Hibernian
1966–67	Celtic	1 – 0	Rangers	Hampden Park	94,532	Aberdeen	Airdrie
1967–68	Celtic	5 – 3	Dundee	Hampden Park	66,660	St Johnstone	Morton
1968–69	Celtic	6 – 2	Hibernian	Hampden Park	74,240	Dundee	Clyde
1969–70	Celtic	1 – 0	St. Johnstone	Hampden Park	73,067	Ayr United	Motherwell
1970–71	Rangers	1 – 0	Celtic	Hampden Park	106,263	Cowdenbeath	Dumbarton
1971–72	Partick Thistle	4 – 1	Celtic	Hampden Park	62,740	St Mirren	Falkirk
1972–73	Hibernian	2 – 1	Celtic	Hampden Park	71,696	Aberdeen	Rangers
1973–74	Dundee	1 – 0	Celtic	Hampden Park	27,924	Kilmarnock	Rangers
1974–75	Celtic	6 – 3	Hibernian	Hampden Park	53,848	Falkirk	Airdrie
1975–76	Rangers	1 – 0	Celtic	Hampden Park	58,806	Partick Thistle	Montrose
1976–77	Aberdeen	2 – 1 AET	Celtic	Hampden Park	69,707	Rangers	Hearts
1977–78	Rangers	2 – 1 AET	Celtic	Hampden Park	60,168	Forfar Athletic	Hearts
1978–79	Rangers	2 – 1	Aberdeen	Hampden Park	54,000	Hibernian	Celtic
1979–80	Dundee United	0 – 0 AET	Aberdeen	Hampden Park	27,173	Hamilton Accies	Morton
1979–80 (R)	Dundee United	3 – 0	Aberdeen	Dens Park	28,933		
1980–81	Dundee United	3 – 0	Dundee	Dens Park	24,466	Ayr United	Celtic
1981–82	Rangers	2 – 1	Dundee United	Hampden Park	53,777	Aberdeen	St Mirren
1982–83	Celtic	2 – 1	Rangers	Hampden Park	55,572	Dundee United	Hearts
1983–84	Rangers	3 – 2 AET	Celtic	Hampden Park	66,369	Dundee United	Aberdeen
1984–85	Rangers	1 – 0	Dundee United	Hampden Park	44,698	Meadowbank Th	Hearts
1985–86	Aberdeen	3 – 0	Hibernian	Hampden Park	40,061	Dundee United	Rangers
1986–87	Rangers	2 – 1	Celtic	Hampden Park	74,219	Dundee United	Motherwell
1987–88	Rangers	3 – 3 AET + pk	Aberdeen	Hampden Park	71,961	Dundee	Motherwell
1988–89	Rangers	3 – 2	Aberdeen	Hampden Park	72,122	Dundee United	Hearts
1989–90	Aberdeen	2 – 1 AET	Rangers	Hampden Park	61,190	Dunfermline Ath	Celtic
1990–91	Rangers	2 – 1 AET	Celtic	Hampden Park	62,817	Dundee United	Aberdeen
1991–92	Hibernian	2 – 0	Dunfermline Athletic	Hampden Park	40,377	Airdrie	Rangers
1992–93	Rangers	2 – 1 AET	Aberdeen	Hampden Park	54,298	St Johnstone	Celtic
1993–94	Rangers	2 – 1	Hibernian	Celtic Park	47,632	Dundee United	Celtic
1994–95	Raith Rovers	2 – 2 AET + pk	Celtic	Ibrox Stadium	45,384	Aberdeen	Airdrie
1995–96	Aberdeen	2 – 0	Dundee	Hampden Park	33,096	Rangers	Airdrie
1996–97	Rangers	4 – 3	Heart of Midlothian	Celtic Park	48,559	Dunfermline Ath	Dundee
1997–98	Celtic	3 – 0	Dundee United	Ibrox Stadium	49,305	Dunfermline Ath	Aberdeen
1998–99	Rangers	2 – 1	St. Johnstone	Celtic Park	45,533	Hearts	Airdrie
1999–00	Celtic	2 – 0	Aberdeen	Hampden Park	50,073	Dundee United	Kilmarnock

2000–01	Celtic	3 – 0	Kilmarnock	Hampden Park	48,830	St Mirren	Rangers
2001–02	Rangers	4 – 0	Ayr United	Hampden Park	50,076	Hibernian	Celtic
2002–03	Rangers	2 – 1	Celtic	Hampden Park	52,000	Dundee United	Hearts
2003–04	Livingston	2 – 0	Hibernian	Hampden Park	45,500	Dundee	Rangers
2004–05	Rangers	5 – 1	Motherwell	Hampden Park	50,182	Dundee United	Hearts
2005–06	Celtic	3 – 0	Dunfermline Athletic	Hampden Park	50,090	Motherwell	Livingsto
2006–07	Hibernian	5 – 1	Kilmarnock	Hampden Park	52,000	St Johnstone	Falkirk
2007–08	Rangers	2 – 2 AET + pk	Dundee United	Hampden Park	50,019	Aberdeen	Hearts
2008–09	Celtic	2 – 0 AET	Rangers	Hampden Park	51,193	Dundee United	Falkirk
2009–10	Rangers	1 – 0	St. Mirren	Hampden Park	44,538	St Johnstone	Hearts
2010–11	Rangers	2 – 1 AET	Celtic	Hampden Park	51,181	Motherwell	Aberdee
2011–12	Kilmarnock	1 – 0	Celtic	Hampden Park	49,572	Ayr United	Falkirk
2012–13	St. Mirren	3 – 2	Heart of Midlothian	Hampden Park	44,036	Inverness CT	Celtic
2013–14	Aberdeen	0 – 0 AET + pk	Inverness CT	Celtic Park	51,143	St Johnstone	Hearts
2014-15	Celtic	2-0	Dundee United	Hampden Park	49,259	Aberdeen	Rangers
2015-16	Ross County	2-1	Hibernian	Hampden Park	38,796	St Johnstone	Celtic
2016-17	Celtic	3-0	Aberdeen	Hampden Park	49,629	Rangers	Morton

Alternative names / sponsors for the League Cup have been:

1979-81	Bell's Scottish League Cup
1983-84	Final only, sponsored by Telejector
1984-92	Skol Cup
1994-97	Coca Cola Cu
1999-2008	CIS Insurance Cup
2008-11	Co-operative Insurance Cup
2011-13	Scottish Communities League Cup
2014-15	Semi Finals and Final only, The Scottish League Cup presented by QTS
2015-16	The Scottish League Cup, presented by Utilita
2016-17	Betfred Cup

Winners (Not including war-time seasons)			
Rangers	27	Motherwell	1
Celtic	16	Partick Thistle	1
Aberdeen	6	Raith Rovers	1
Hearts	4	Livingston	1
Hibernian	3	Kilmarnock	1
Dundee	3	St Mirren	1
East Fife	3	Ross County	1
Dundee United	2		

Scottish League Cup Finals 1940-1947

Some sources include the War Time versions of the League Cup in the records. It is certainly true that the format of the competition (Groups, followed by knock out) was established during the War. However, War Time games are not normally included in football records and are regarded as "unofficial".

Season	Winner	Score	Runner-up	Venue	Attendance	Losing SF	
1940-41	Rangers	1-1	Hearts	Hampden Park	75,000	St Mirren	Celtic
1940-41 (R)	Rangers	4-2	Hearts	Hampden Park	70,000		
1941-42	Rangers	1-0	Morton	Hampden Park	43,000	Partick Thistle	Celtic
1942-43	Rangers	1-1 + corners	Falkirk	Hampden Park	20,000	Hamilton Accies	Third Lanark
1943-44	Hibernian	0-0 + corners	Rangers	Hampden Park	63,000	Celtic	Clyde
1944-45	Rangers	2-1	Motherwell	Hampden Park	80,000	Queen's Park	Motherwell
1945-46	Aberdeen	3-2	Rangers	Hampden Park	135,000	Airdrie	Hearts

Irn Bru Challenge Cup 2016/17

Rd	DATE	H	A	F	A		ATT	NOTES
1	02/08/2016	Berwick Rangers	Spartans	0	3		302	
1	02/08/2016	Celtic U20	Annan Athletic	5	1		216	at Cappielow
1	02/08/2016	Clyde	Partick Thistle U20	0	5		351	
1	02/08/2016	Cove Rangers	Dundee U20	2	1		190	at Forfar Ath
1	02/08/2016	East Stirlingshire	Montrose	0	3		149	
1	02/08/2016	Formartine United	Aberdeen U20	2	5		305	
1	02/08/2016	Inverness CT U20	Arbroath	0	3		296	
1	02/08/2016	Motherwell U20	Edinburgh City	2	1		402	
1	02/08/2016	Queen's Park	Kilmarnock U20	5	2		299	
1	02/08/2016	Ross County U20	Brora Rangers	2	3		350	
1	02/08/2016	St Johnstone U20	Turriff United	1	2		320	
1	02/08/2016	Stirling Albion	Hearts U20	2	3		476	
1	03/08/2016	Cumbernauld Colts	Hamilton Accies U20	0	3		119	
1	10/08/2016	Rangers U20	Stirling University	4	0		493	at Stirling Albion
2	16/08/2016	Aberdeen U20	Forfar Athletic	1	3		221	at Formartine
2	16/08/2016	Albion Rovers	Hamilton Accies U20	2	0		114	
2	16/08/2016	Brechin City	Cove Rangers	4	1		242	
2	16/08/2016	Cowdenbeath	Celtic U20	1	2		449	
2	16/08/2016	Elgin City	Hearts U20	2	0		350	
2	16/08/2016	Motherwell U20	Airdrieronians	1	2		1007	
2	16/08/2016	Partick Thistle U20	Queen's Park	1	1	5-6p	436	
2	16/08/2016	Peterhead	Brora Rangers	3	2		399	
2	16/08/2016	Stranraer	Spartans	7	1		326	
2	17/08/2016	Arbroath	East Fife	2	3		335	
2	17/08/2016	Rangers U20	Stenhousemuir	1	3		324	at Stirling Albion
2	17/08/2016	Turriff United	Montrose	1	0		180	
3	03/09/2016	Albion Rovers	St Mirren	3	4		711	
3	03/09/2016	Alloa Athletic	East Fife	3	0		444	
3	03/09/2016	Brechin City	Dunfermline Athletic	1	5		577	
3	03/09/2016	Dundee United	Peterhead	3	2		3520	
3	03/09/2016	Falkirk	Elgin City	6	1		1591	
3	03/09/2016	Forfar Athletic	Raith Rovers	3	2		690	
3	03/09/2016	Livingston	Celtic U20	5	1		1214	
3	03/09/2016	Queen of the South	Stenhousemuir	7	1		1158	
3	03/09/2016	Queen's Park	Morton	2	0		1085	
3	03/09/2016	Stranraer	Dumbarton	1	0		401	
3	04/09/2016	Ayr United	Airdrieronians	3	2		1135	
3	04/09/2016	Turriff United	Hibernian	0	3		1791	
4	07/10/2016	Ayr United	Falkirk	1	0		1247	
4	07/10/2016	Crusaders	Livingston	1	2			
4	08/10/2016	Bala Town	Alloa Athletic	2	4		591	
4	08/10/2016	Dunfermline Athletic	Queen's Park	2	1		1930	
4	08/10/2016	Forfar Athletic	TNS	1	3		691	
4	08/10/2016	Hibernian	St Mirren	1	2		4393	
4	08/10/2016	Stranraer	Dundee United	0	1		629	
4	09/10/2016	Queen of the South	Linfield	2	0		2358	
4R	01/11/2016	Crusaders	Livingston	0	3			
5	12/11/2016	Dunfermline Athletic	Dundee United	0	1		2576	
5	12/11/2016	Queen of the South	Alloa Athletic	2	0		1180	
5	13/11/2016	Livingston	TNS	0	3		733	
5	13/11/2016	St Mirren	Ayr United	2	1		2199	
SF	18/02/2017	Queen of the South	Dundee United	2	3		1526	
SF	19/02/2017	St Mirren	TNS	4	1		2044	
F	25/03/2017	St Mirren	Dundee United	1	2		8089	at Motherwell

In an attempt to invigorate the competition the format was altered to include the Premiership Under 20 sides, plus entrants from Northern Ireland and Wales and the Highland and Lowland Leagues.

The jury remains out on the success of bringing in the U20 sides. Some clubs embraced the concept whilst others seemed to regard it as an inconvenience. There were four wins for U20- sides against SPFL opponents with Celtic taking two scalps, Annan Athletic and Cowdenbeath.

Some lower league sides, faced with U20 opponents, opted to field under-strength sides. Clyde fielded an entirely U20 side against Partick and Stirling played mainly fringe players against Hearts. Both were beaten.

Linfield brought a substantial support for their match at Dumfries but fell at the first hurdle. Crusaders were given a second chance after defeat by Livingston - the Scottish side fielded Alan Lithgow whilst under suspension. Strangely he had served the suspension before the replayed game and was eligible to play in it.

TNS were the most successful of the non-Scots sides. They were comfortable winners against Forfar and Livingston but collapsed in the second half against St Mirren. Many observers reckoned this was because they seldom came up against full-time sides and most of their Welsh opponents were on their uppers by the last half hour.

The Highland and Lowland League sides made little impact on the competition. Spartans had a notable win over Berwick Rangers but crashed out heavily to Stranraer.

Attendances were disappointing with several clubs recording season-low figures.

The admission of Colts teams to the Irn Bru Cup presents a conundrum for statisticians. Are these first-team appearances or not? For the purposes of the Almanac we will regard the Colts teams as separate clubs from their parent teams - and appearances / goals will count as first team statistics. For example, during 2016/17 Shug McGlumpher may have played 2 first team games for Stoneybridge Thistle Colts in the Irn Bru Cup, and six first team games for Stoneybridge Thistle in the SPFL. We regard them as two separate clubs.

Details overleaf.

Irn Bru Challenge Cup 2016/17 - Colt Team Line Ups, Scorers etc

		V	Opponents	F	A		H	T	Ref	Att	Scorers	1	2	3	4	5
ABERDEEN																
02/08/2016	CC	A	Formartine United	5	2		1	0	G Beaton	305	Wright 3, Norris, Nuttall	Craddock	Henry	Harvie	Roscoe	Omolokun*
16/08/2016	CC	H	Forfar Athletic	1	3	At Formar	0	1	M Roncone	221	Omolokun	Craddock	Robertson	Wells	Roscoe	Omolokun
CELTIC																
02/08/2016	CC	H	Annan Athletic	5	1	At Mortor	3	1	D Dickinson	216	Nesbitt 2, Hendry, Aitchison, Crossan	Doohan	Ralston	McIlduff	McCart	Ajer
16/08/2016	CC	A	Cowdenbeath	2	1		0	1	S Kirkland	449	Aitchison, Crossan	Doohan	Ralston	McIlduff	McCart	Ajer
03/09/2016	CC3	A	Livingston	1	5		1	5	S Kirkland	1214	Hendry	Doohan	Ralston	McIlduff	McCart	Nesbitt
DUNDEE																
02/08/2016	CC	A	Cove Rangers	1	2	at Forfar	1	0	M Roncone	190	Warwick	Gourlay	Gallacher	Quigley	Smyth	Waddell
HAMILTON ACCIES																
02/08/2016	CC	A	Cumbernauld Colts	3	0		0	1	C Graham	219	Cunningham, Boyd, Tierney	Marshall	Reilly	Quitongo&	Want	Breslin
16/08/2016	CC	A	Albion Rovers	0	2		0	1	S Millar	114		Marshall	Reilly	Quitongo	Want	Breslin
HEARTS																
02/08/2016	CC	A	Stirling Albion	3	2		0	2	S Reid	476	Jones, Roy, McLean	Mason	Godinho+	Reid	Baur	Jones
16/08/2016	CC	A	Elgin City	0	2		0	1	G Beaton	350		Mason	Godinho	Reid	Baur	Jones
INVERNESS CT																
02/08/2016	CC	H	Arbroath	0	3		0	2	A Shepherd	296		Foster	Stark+	Rennie	Gilchrist	McRitchie
KILMARNOCK																
02/08/2016	CC	A	Queen's Park	2	5		2	3	G Aitken	299	Hawkshaw, Queen	Miller	Queen*	Liddington	A Wilson	Clark+
MOTHERWELL																
02/08/2016	CC	H	Edinburgh City	2	1		1	0	L Wilson	402	Mackin, Fry	Morrison	McMillan	Armstrong	Maguire	Watt
16/08/2016	CC	H	Airdrieonians	1	2		0	1	M Taylor	1007	Mackin	Morrison	McMillan	Armstrong	Maguire	Watt
PARTICK THISTLE																
02/08/2016	CC	A	Clyde	5	0		0	0	D Lowe	351	Nisbet 3, Penrice, McLaughlin	Cullen	McInally	Penrice*	Syme	McMullin
16/08/2016	CC	H	Queen's Park	1	1	AET, 5-6p	0	0	D Munro	436	McMullin	Cullen	McInally	Penrice	Syme	McMullin
RANGERS																
10/08/2016	CC	H	Stirling University	4	0	at Stirling	4	0	S Luke	493	Jeffries 2, Hardie, Burt	Robbie McCrorie	Lyon	Gray	Ross McCrorie	Bradley
17/08/2016	CC	H	Stenhousemuir	1	3	at Stirling	0	2	G Irvine	324	Hardie	Robbie McCrorie	Lyon	Gray+	Ross McCrorie	Bradley
ROSS COUNTY																
02/08/2016	CC	H	Brora Rangers	2	3	AET	0	1	B Dempster	350	Morrison, Wallace	Munro	Tumilty&	Malcolm	Brownlie	S Morrisc
ST JOHNSTONE																
02/08/2016	CC	H	Turriff United	1	2		1	0	C Fordyce	320	Hurst	MacKenzie	Lumsden	Thompson	Comrie	Brian

Irn Bru Challenge Cup 2016/17 - Highland / Lowland League Team Line Ups, Scorers etc

Date		V	Opponents	F	A		H	T	Ref	Att	Scorers	1	2	3	4
BRORA RANGERS															
02/08/2016	CC	A	Ross County U20	3	2	AET	1	0	B Dempster	350	Pollock, Murray, Campbell	Malin	Ross	A MacDonald&	Williamsc
16/08/2016	CC	A	Peterhead	2	3		1	0	M Northcroft	399	Sutherland, Brindle	Malin	Ross	A MacDonald	Williamsc
COVE RANGERS															
02/08/2016	CC	H	Dundee U20	2	1		0	1	M Roncone	190	Buchan, Scully	McCafferty	Watson	Milne	Duff
16/08/2016	CC	A	Brechin City	1	4		1	2	G Ross	242	Milne	McKenzie	McCulloch	Milne	Duff
CUMBERNAULD COLTS															
03/08/2016	CC	H	Hamilton Accies U20	0	3		0	1	C Graham	219		Fahey	Batchelor	Ramsay	Kirwan
EAST STIRLINGSHIRE															
02/08/2016	CC	H	Montrose	0	3		0	1	C Napier	149		Dolan	Greene	Buist	A Grant
FORMARTINE UNITED															
02/08/2016	CC	H	Aberdeen U20	2	5		0	1	G Beaton	305	Gauld, Rodger	MacDonald	Michie+	Smith	Crawforc
SPARTANS															
02/08/2016	CC	A	Berwick Rangers	3	0					302	Maxwell, Dishington, Stevenson	Carswell	Thomson	Brown	Townsley
16/08/2016	CC	A	Stranraer	1	7		0	3	C Napier	326	Malone	Carswell	Thomson	Brown+	Townsley
STIRLING UNIVERSITY															
10/08/2016	CC	A	Rangers U20	0	4	at Stirling	0	4	S Luke	320		Hughes	Cuff	Kellock	Ashe
TURRIFF UNITED															
02/08/2016	CC	A	St Johnstone U20	2	1					320	McKenzie og, Booth	Main	Davidson	Herd	Wood
17/08/2016	CC	H	Montrose	1	0		0	0	G Duncan	180	Kiecvkowski	Main	Davidson	Herd	Wood
04/09/2016	CC	H	Hibernian	0	3		0	2	E Anderson	1791		Main	Davidson	Herd	Wood

6	7	8	9	10	11	12	13	14	15	16	17	18
Thomas	Wright+	McLennan	F Ross	Nuttall&	Norris	Wells*	Anderson+	Dangana&	Robertson	Ellis		
Thomas	Wright	McLennan+	F Ross*	Nuttall&	Henry	Norris*	Anderson+	Hutchison&	Dangana	S Ross	McPherson	Mair
Wardrop	Nesbitt	J Thomson&	Hendry+	Miller	Aitchison*	Crossan*	T Thomson+	Hill&	Higgins	Hazard	Johnston	Murray
Wardrop	Nesbitt*	J Thomson	Hendry+	Miller	Aitchison	Crossan*	Johnston+	Hill	Higgins	Hazard	Archibald	Murray
Wardrop	Hill	J Thomson	Hendry	Miller	Crossan*	Aitchison*	Higgins	Archibald	Payne	Kerr	Johnston	Hazard
Warwick	Coupe+	Berry	Clark	M Smith*	Skelly	Henvey*	Rice+	C Ferry	Gibb	Anderson		
Hughes	Cunningham	Ferguson*	Boyd	Tierney	Kelly+	Smith*	Connelly+	O'Halloran&	Wilson	Boyd	Slaven	Connolly
Hughes	McKirdy	Smith*	Boyd	Tierney	Kelly	Henry*	Ferguson	O'Halloran	Wilson	Boyd	Sheridan	Connolly
Petkov*	Morrison	Paton	Irving	Zanatta	MacLean&	Roy*	Vladislav+	Currie&	I Smith	K Smith	Baxter	
Currie	Morrison	Paton	Irving*	Zanatta+	MacLean&	Roy*	Vladislav+	I Smith&	Petkov	K Smith	Baxter	
McArthur*	Brown	MacLennan	Wilson	MacRae	Robertson&	MacDonald*	Chalmers+	Wilson&	MacKinnon			
I Wilson	Frizzell	Hawkshaw	Dempsie	Morrison	McLean&	Whittaker*	Wylie+	McLevy&	Lyle	Cameron	McDonald	Barr
Campbell	Turnbull*	Hastie&	Fry	MacLean	Mackin+	Falconer*	Scott+	Livingstone&	Stevenson	Moore	Semple	
Campbell	Turnbull+	Hastie*	Fry	MacLean&	Mackin	Falconer*	Scott+	Moore&	Stevenson	Livingstone		
Wilson	Lamont&	Nisbet+	McCarthy	Docherty	McLaughlin	Fleming*	J Stokes+	Hall&	Higgins	Livesey		
Wilson	Lamont	Nisbet*	McCarthy	Docherty	McLaughlin+	J Stokes*	Higgins+	Fleming	I Stokes	Livesey	Hall	
Barjonas	Jeffries	Thompson*	Burt&	Hardie+	Rudden	S Kelly*	Dallas+	Ashmore&	Wilson	White	Gibson	Wright
Barjonas*	Jeffries	Thompson	Burt&	Hardie	Rudden	Dallas*	Wilson+	Gibson&	Jamieson	S Kelly	Ashmore	Wright
MacLennan	McIver	Wallace+	Keillor-Dunn*	R Dingwall	G Morrison	Grant*	Gallagher+	Kelly&	Ramsey	Herbert		
McCann	McLaren	Jardine*	Simpson	G Hurst	Docherty+	Johnson*	O'Reilly+	Sinclair	Donald	Ballantyne	Struthers	McKenzie

7	8	9	10	11	12	13	14	15	16	17	18
Pollock*	Greig+	MacLean	Mackay	Campbell	Sutherland*	Gillespie+	C McDonald&	Brindle	Grant	Cormack	
Pollock+	Greig	Brindle*	Sutherland&	Gillespie	Mackay*	Campbell+	Grant&	Houston	C McDOnald	Cormack	
Buchan	Burnett	McCulloch	McBain+	J Smith	Scully*	Yule+	Redford	Walker	McKenzie	S Smith	
Buchan+	Stott&	Megginson	McBain*	J Smith	Yule*	Scully+	Burnett&	Lawrie	Dunbar	Redford	McCafferty
McKenzie*	Pirrie	O'Neill	Hunter+	Murray	Ronald*	Brown+	Barclay&	Giles	Black	Milne	Bateman
McGuigan&	Ure	Sludden*	McMillan	D Grant+	Rodgers*	McGregor+	Comrie&	Hogg	White	Shaw	Murray
Dingwall	Anderson	Rodger	Gethins*	Barbour	Gauld*	McVitie+	Berton&	Henry	Young	Reid	
Maxwell*	Dishington	Stevenson	Greenhill	Horribine+	Beesley*	Raiker+	Girdwood	Malone	Gilpin		
Beesley*	Dishington	Stevenson	Greenhill	Tolmie	Horribine*	Maxwell+	Malone&	Gilpin			
Faulds+	Gillen&	McCafferty	Geddes*	Bonar	MacEwan*	Fitzpatrick+	Hunter&	McAnespie	Moyes	Quinn	Touhy
Nowosielski&	Young	McKenzie*	Kieczkowski+	D Booth	C Booth*	Walker+	Chalmers&	Moir	Mair	Smith	Sherman
Nowosielski*	Young	McKenzie	Kieczkowski+	D Booth	Mair*	Gray+	Chalmers&	Moir	Walker	Allan	Sherman
Nowosielski*	Young	McKenzie	Kieczkowski+	D Booth&	Gray*	Clark+	Allan&	Chalmers	Mair	Smith	Sherman

ABERDEEN		A	S	G
Craddock	David	2		0
Henry	Jamie	2		
Robertson	Sam	1		
Harvie	Daniel	1		
Wells	Toby	1	1	
Roscoe	Sam	2		
Omolukun	Kesi	2		1
Thomas	Dylan	2		
Wright	Scott	2		3
McLennan	Connor	2		
Ross	Francis	2		
Nuttall	Joe	2		1
Norris	Aaron	1	1	1
Anderson	Bruce		2	
Dangana	David		1	
Hutchison	Lewis		1	

CELTIC		A	S	G
Doohan	Ross	3		
Ralston	Anthony	3		
McCart	Jamie	3		
McIlduff	Aidan	3		
Ajer	Kristoffer	2		
Nesbitt	Aidan	3		2
Wardrop	Sam	3		
Hill	Mark	1		
Thomson	Joe	3		
Hendry	Regan	3		2
Miller	Calvin	3		
Aitchison	Jack	2	1	2
Crossan	Paul John	1	2	2
Archibald	Theo		1	
Johnston	Michael		1	

DUNDEE		A	S	G
Gourlay	Kyle		1	
Gallacher	Sean		1	
Quigley	Conor		1	
Smyth	Matthew		1	
Waddell	Kerr		1	
Warwick	Greg		1	
Coupe	Connor		1	
Berry	Taylor		1	
Clark	Kyle		1	
Smith	Mark		1	
Skelly	Josh		1	
Henvey	Matthew			1
Rice	Brian			1

HAMILTON ACCIES		A	S	G	
Marshall	Alexander		2		
Reilly	Ben		2		
Quitongo	Rico		2		
Want	Shaun		2		
Breslin	Jack		2		
Hughes	Ronan		2		
McKirdy	Sean		1		
Cunningham	Ross		1		1
Ferguson	Lewis		1		
Smith	Lewis		1	1	
Boyd	Steven		2		1
Tierney	Ryan		2		1
Kelly	Marc		2		
Henry	Dylan			1	
Connolly	Steffen			1	
O'Halloran	Daniel			1	

HEARTS		A	S	G
Mason	Kelby	2		
Godinho	Marcus	2		
Reid	Aaron	2		
Baur	Daniel	2		
Jones	Leon	2		1
Petkov	Alex	1		
Currie	Rory	1	1	
Morrison	Callumn	2		
Paton	Harrison	2		
Irving	Andrew	2		
Zanatta	Dario	2		
MacLean	Russell	2		1
Roy	Alistair		2	1
Vladislav	Yves		2	
Smith	Ian		1	

INVERNESS CT		A	S	G
Foster	Stephen	1		
Stark	Ali	1		
Rennie	Stephen	1		
Gilchrist	Cameron	1		
McRitchie	Ryan	1		
McArthur	Stuart	1		
Brown	Christopher	1		
MacLennan	Blair	1		
Wilson	Jamie	1		
MacRae	Andrew	1		
Robertson	Sam	1		
MacDonald	Liam		1	
Chalmers	Kieran		1	
Wilson	Aidan		1	

KILMARNOCK		A	S	G
Miller	Ross		1	
Queen	Taylor		1	
Liddington	Sam		1	
Wilson	Aidan		1	
Clark	Lewis		1	
Wilson	Iain		1	
Frizzell	Adam		1	
Hawkshaw	Dean		1	
Dempsie	Thomas		1	
Morrison	Lewis		1	
McLean	Scott		1	
Whittaker	Jack			1
Wylie	Ross			1
McLevy	Ewan			1

MOTHERWELL		A	S	G
Morrison	Peter	2		
McMillan	Jack	2		
Armstrong	Jordan	2		
Maguire	Barry	2		
Watt	Luke	2		
Campbell	Allan	2		
Turnbull	David	2		
Hastie	Jake	2		
Fry	Tom	2		1
MacLean	Ross	2		
Mackin	Dylan	2		2
Falconer	Dylan		2	
Scott	James		2	
Livingstone	Adam		1	
Moore	Josh		1	

PARTICK THISTLE		A	S	G
Cullen	Conor	2		
McInally	Matthew	2		
Penrice	James	2		1
Syme	David	2		
McMullin	Michael	2		
Wilson	Callum	2		
Lamont	Mark	2		
Nisbet	Kevin	2		3
McCarthy	Andrew	2		
Docherty	Dominic	2		
McLaughlin	Neil	2		1
Fleming	Ross		1	
Stokes	James		2	
Higgins	Connor		1	
Hall	Jamie		1	

RANGERS		A	S	G
McCrorie	Robbie	2		
Lyon	Ross	2		
Gray	Scott	2		
McCrorie	Ross	2		
Bradley	Kyle	2		
Barjonas	Jamie	2		
Jeffries	Josh	2		2
Thompson	Jordan	2		
Burt	Liam	2		1
Hardie	Ryan	2		2
Rudden	Zac	2		
Kelly	Stephen		1	
Dallas	Andrew		2	
Wilson	Aiden		1	
Ashmore	Max		1	
Gibson	Jordan		1	

ROSS COUNTY		A	S	G
Munro	Ross	1		
Tumilty	Reghan	1		
Brownlie	David	1		
Morrison	Sam	1		
MacLennan	Tom	1		
McIver	Ross	1		
Wallace	James	1		[illegible]
Keiller-Dunn	Davis	1		
Malcolm	Blair	1		
Dingwall	Russell	1		
Morrison	Greg	1		
Grant	Ethan		1	
Gallagher	Mark		1	
Kelly	Tom		1	

ST JOHNSTONE		A	S	G
Mackenzie	Ben	1		
Lumsden	Cameron	1		
Thompson	Cameron	1		
Comrie	Aaron	1		
Brian	Ciaran	1		
McCann	Alistair	1		
McLaren	Connor	1		
Jardine	Daniel	1		
Simpson	Paul	1		
Hurst	Greg	1		
Docherty	Jamie	1		
Johnston	Joseph		1	
O'Reilly	Ewan		1	

Scottish League Challenge Cup Finals 1991-2017

Season	Winner	Score	Runner-up	Venue	Att
1990–91	Dundee (1)	3–2 AET	Ayr United	Fir Park	11,506
1991–92	Hamilton Academical (1)	1–0	Ayr United	Fir Park	9,663
1992–93	Hamilton Academical (2)	3–2	Morton	Love Street	7,391
1993–94	Falkirk (1)	3–0	St. Mirren	Fir Park	13,763
1994–95	Airdrieonians (1)	3–2 AET	Dundee	McDiarmid Park	8,844
1995–96	Stenhousemuir (1)	0–0 aet + pens	Dundee United	McDiarmid Park	7,856
1996–97	Stranraer (1)	1–0	St. Johnstone	Broadwood	5,222
1997–98	Falkirk (2)	1–0	Queen of the South	Fir Park	9,735
1998–99	No competition				
1999–2000	Alloa Athletic (1)	4–4 aet + pens	Inverness Caledonian Thistle	Excelsior Stadium	4,043
2000–01	Airdrieonians (2)	2–2 aet + pens	Livingston	Broadwood	5,623
2001–02	Airdrieonians (3)	2–1	Alloa Athletic	Broadwood	4,548
2002–03	Queen of the South (1)	2–0	Brechin City	Broadwood	6,428
2003–04	Inverness Caledonian Thistle (1)	2–0	Airdrie United	McDiarmid Park	5,428
2004–05	Falkirk (3)	2–1	Ross County	McDiarmid Park	7,471
2005–06	St. Mirren (1)	2–1	Hamilton Academical	Excelsior Stadium	9,613
2006–07	Ross County (1)	1–1 aet + pens	Clyde	McDiarmid Park	4,062
2007–08	St. Johnstone (1)	3–2	Dunfermline Athletic	Dens Park	6,446
2008–09	Airdrie United (1)	2–2 aet + pens	Ross County	McDiarmid Park	4,091
2009–10	Dundee (2)	3–2	Inverness Caledonian Thistle	McDiarmid Park	8,031
2010–11	Ross County (2)	2–0	Queen of the South	McDiarmid Park	5,124
2011–12	Falkirk (4)	1–0	Hamilton Academical	Almondvale	5,210
2012–13	Queen of the South (2)	1–1 aet + pens	Partick Thistle	Almondvale	9,452
2013-14	Raith Rovers (1)	1-0 aet	Rangers	Easter Road	19,983
2014-15	Livingston (1)	4-0	Alloa Athletic	McDiarmid Park	2,869
2015-16	Rangers (1)	4-0	Peterhead	Hampden Park	48,133
2016-17	Dundee United (1)	2-1	St Mirren	Fir Park	8,089
WINNERS (25)					
4	Falkirk				
3	Airdrieonians				
2	Hamilton Accies, Queen of the South, Ross County, Dundee				
1	Livingston, Raith Rovers, Airdrie United, St Johnstone, St Mirren, Inverness CT, Alloa Athletic, Stranraer, Stenhousemuir, Rangers, Dundee United				

Alternative Names / Sponsors for the Challenge Cup have been:

1990/1	B and Q Centenary Cup
1991/2-1994/5	B and Q Cup
1995/6-1997/8	Scottish League Challenge Cup
1998/9	No competition
1999/00-2001/2	Bells Challenge Cup
2002/3-2005/6	Bells Cup
2006/7-2007/8	Scottish League Challenge Cup
2008/9-2010/11	ALBA Challenge Cup
2011/12-2013/4	Ramsdens Cup
2014/15-2015/16	Petrofac Training Cup
2016-17	Irn Bru Cup

IRN BRU CHALLENGE CUP 2017/18

Some changes have been made to the format for 2017/18, with one round removed from the competition.

Round One has 48 clubs - 8 from the SPFL Championship, 10 from SPFL 1, 10 from SPFL 2, 4 from Highland League (Cove, Buckie, Brora and Formartine), 4 from Lowland Le8gue (East Kilbride, East Stirlingshire, Spartans and Stirling University, plus the Colt sides of the 12 Premiership clubs. The draw is split into North and South Sections with 6 Colt teams in each. Othjerwise it is unseeded.

Round Two has 32 clubs - the 24 winners from Round One, two each from Wales (TNS and Connah's Quay), Northern Ireland (Linfield and Crusaders), 2 from the Irish Republic (Bray Wanderers and Sligo Rovers) plus Falkirk and ICT.

SPFL Development League 2016/17

	ABE	CEL	D	DU	DA	F	HAM	HEA	HIB	ICT	KIL	MOT	PAR	RAN	ROS	SJ	SM
Aberdeen		Jan 24 1-0*	Aug 23 2-2*	Feb 27 0-3#	Mar 28 4-0£	Apr 6 2-0#	Oct 26 4-1*	Apr 25 1-3£	Oct 13 2-1#	Feb 7 3-0^	Mar 14 4-2#	Dec 20 1-9&	Dec 7 1-2&	Sep 20 1-1#	Apr 10 0-1#	Apr 14 2-0*	Sep 6 1-2*
Celtic	Apr 20 4-0*		Feb 21 1-0#	Apr 17 1-0*	Dec 27 0-3#	Mar 13 0-0*	Dec 12 2-2*	Oct 3 3-1*	Apr 6 3-0#	Mar 30 4-1#	May 1 2-2*	Feb 10 3-2&	Feb 6 5-2*	Apr 14 4-0*	Sep 19 0-1*	Aug 29 1-1*	Mar 7 2-0#
Dundee	May 2 0-2*	Oct 10 0-1*		Dec 16 3-3*	Feb 13 2-0*	Nov 29 0-0*	Sep 13 0-2*	Mar 14 1-2*	Aug 30 2-2*	Dec 13 0-1*	Apr 27 1-1#	Nov 15 0-0*	Oct 24 1-2*	Apr 18 0-5*	Feb 27 0-1*	Sep 27 1-0*	Apr 3 0-3*
Dundee United	Oct 18 3-2&	Mar 17 0-6£	Sep 6 0-3#		Apr 14 2-2^	Feb 7 1-1^	Nov 9 2-2&	Dec 21 2-2^	Mar 7 1-2^	Feb 21 3-1£	Mar 30 2-0#	Jan 25 0-3^	Aug 23 1-2*	Oct 4 4-0#	Apr 25 2-2^	Apr 28 1-1£	Sep 19 4-1#
Dunfermline Athletic	Nov 15 1-0#	Sep 6 0-1*	Oct 3 1-0*	Nov 29 1-0#		Mar 6 0-2#	Apr 18 1-4#	Sep 28 2-3#	Apr 3 0-3#	Apr 6 1-1#	Dec 13 1-1#	Feb 21 3-2#	Sep 19 0-1*	Nov 1 1-0#	Jan 24 4-0#	May 2 2-1#	Oct 18 5-1#
Falkirk	Sep 13 1-4*	Feb 2 0-4*	Apr 11 3-0*	Sep 27 5-1*	Oct 24 2-1*		Mar 16 1-2*	Nov 22 1-1*	Jan 30 1-4*	Dec 27 2-3*	Oct 11 4-1*	Dec 6 3-1*	Mar 28 3-1*	Aug 30 1-3*	Nov 8 3-2*	Feb 28 2-2*	Apr 25 3-2*
Hamilton Accies	Mar 7 3-2*	May 4 0-0*	Jan 24 4-0*	Mar 23 3-1*	Dec 7 3-0*	Oct 4 2-2*		Sep 6 1-0*	Nov 1 0-2*	Oct 18 5-0*	Nov 22 3-0*	Sep 19 1-2*	Dec 21 2-1*	Feb 21 1-0*	Aug 23 1-2*	Apr 11 2-2*	Feb 7 3-1*
Hearts	Dec 14 0-2#	Feb 13 1-0*	Oct 31 2-1*	Aug 29 1-1*	Feb 6 1-1*	Apr 3 3-1*	Jan 16 3-0*		May 1 3-1^	Apr 17 3-1#	Sep 12 0-1*	Mar 20 0-3*	Feb 28 5-1&	Nov 28 1-2*	Oct 10 0-2*	Jan 30 3-0*	Nov 14 1-2
Hibernian	Feb 21 4-1*	Apr 11 2-1*	Dec 20 4-1*	Oct 25 1-0*	Nov 22 3-0*	Sep 20 3-3*	Mar 14 0-3*	Aug 23 2-2*		Oct 4 1-0#	Nov 8 1-4*	Sep 6 3-1*	Apr 25 4-0*	Feb 7 1-2&	Dec 6 0-2*	Mar 28 5-0*	Jan 25 3-2&
Inverness CT	Sep 26 0-2#	Dec 16 0-1&	Apr 25 1-2#	Oct 10 1-1&	Nov 9 1-0	Sep 6 0-3#	Feb 27 0-3^	Dec 7 2-2&	Feb 14 2-2#		Oct 25 3-1&	Aug 23 1-3*	Apr 11 1-3#	Jan 25 2-1#	Nov 22 2-2^	Mar 14 2-1#	Dec 20 1-0&
Kilmarnock	Nov 1 4-1*	Aug 23 3-4*	Sep 20 2-4*	Nov 15 3-4*	Apr 25 1-2*	Feb 21 1-2*	Apr 3 0-4*	Jan 24 1-0*	Mar 21 1-2*	Mar 7 2-0*		Feb 7 1-0*	Sep 6 1-3*	Oct 18 4-2*	Dec 20 4-1*	Dec 7 1-1*	Oct 4 1-1*
Motherwell	Aug 30 2-2*	Feb 27 1-0*	Mar 28 0-0*	Sep 13 3-0*	Oct 10 4-0*	Apr 18 3-2*	Jan 30 4-3*	Nov 9 0-1*	Oct 18 0-3*	May 1 3-0#	Sep 27 1-0*		Mar 14 3-6*	Dec 14 2-1*	Oct 25 1-1*	Feb 14 3-1*	Apr 10 4-0*
Partick Thistle	Apr 17 2-1#	Oct 7 1-0*	Mar 7 3-0#	May 1 4-2#	Jan 30 1-3#	Nov 15 2-1*	Aug 30 3-3*	Oct 18 3-1*	Dec 13 0-3#	Nov 29 2-2#	Jan 17 5-0#	Nov 1 1-2*		Apr 3 2-3#	Feb 14 2-6#	Sep 13 2-3*	Apr 28 1-0*
Rangers	Jan 30 2-2*	Jan 17 0-1#	Dec 7 3-0*	Feb 14 2-1*	Mar 15 3-3#	Jan 10 1-2*	Oct 10 2-2*	Apr 10 2-1*	Sep 27 2-1*	Sep 13 2-1*	Feb 28 1-0#	May 4 2-1&	Nov 22 0-0*		Mar 28 1-1*	Oct 25 1-2*	Aug 23 0-1*
Ross County	Jan 19 2-1*	Mar 3 1-1*	Oct 18 4-1*	Dec 14 3-1*	Sep 13 2-4#	Mar 21 2-0*	May 1 1-2#	Feb 20 4-1*	Apr 18 2-0#	Apr 3 1-0*	Aug 30 2-1*	Mar 7 1-0*	Oct 4 4-2#	Nov 15 2-3#		Feb 10 2-2*	Apr 6 1-0*
St Johnstone	Mar 21 1-2*	Dec 20 0-2#	Feb 7 1-3&	Apr 3 3-2*	Aug 23 1-2*	Oct 17 0-1#	Nov 28 0-2#	Sep 19 0-0*	Nov 15 1-2#	Oct 31 2-0*	Apr 18 3-4*	Oct 3 1-1*	Jan 24 1-0#	Mar 7 0-3#	Sep 6 0-2*		Feb 21 2-2#
St Mirren	Jan 16 2-3*	Oct 24 1-4*	Nov 22 1-4#	Jan 30 2-1*	Feb 27 2-4#	Dec 13 0-2#	Sep 27 1-3*	Mar 28 2-1#	Sep 13 1-2*	Aug 30 5-2*	Feb 14 4-3*	Nov 30 1-1#	Nov 8 2-1#	May 1 2-3*	Mar 14 1-3#	Oct 10 1-1*	

ABD
27/9/16 Rangers v Hibernian, Abandoned half time due to linesman falling ill, result stood

KEY TO VENUES 2016/17	*	#	&	^	£
Aberdeen	Brechin City FC	Peterhead FC	Montrose FC	Banks o Dee JFC	Formartine Utd FC
Celtic	Morton FC	Lennoxtown	Dumbarton FC		
Dundee	Montrose FC	Dens Park			
Dundee United	Arbroath FC	Tannadice	Brechin City FC	Forfar Ath FC	St Andrews Univ
Dunfermline Athletic	East End Park	Kelty Hearts JFC			
Falkirk	Falkirk Stadium				
Hamilton Accies	New Douglas Park				
Hearts	Stenhousemuir FC	Riccarton Astro	Riccarton Grass	ORIAM Indoors	
Hibernian	ORIAM Indoors	Riccarton Astro	Hibernian TC		
Inverness CT	Bairn County FC	Caledonian Stadium	Clachnacuddin FC	Highland Football Acad	
Kilmarnock	Rugby Park				
Motherwell	Airdrie FC	Stirling Albion FC			
Partick Thistle	Firhill	Airdrie FC			
Rangers	Stirling Albion FC	Auchenhowie	Ibrox		
Ross County	Highland Football Acad	Victoria Park			
St Johnstone	McDiarmind Park	Airdrie FC	Forfar Ath FC		
St Mirren	St Mirren Park	Renfrew JFC			

FORMAT 2017/18

Rangers have withdrawn from the League to pursue a programme of Friendly matches against what they describe as "more challenging" opposition.

At the time of gling to press the composition of the league for 2017/18 had not been decided. However, it was believed that Dunfermline Athletic and Inverness Cy had also withdrawn.

	Team	P	W	D	L	F	A	W	D	L	F	A	GD	Pts
1	Ross County	32	11	2	3	34	19	9	4	3	29	21	23	66
2	Hamilton Accies	32	10	3	3	34	15	9	4	3	38	24	33	64
3	Celtic	32	10	4	2	35	15	9	2	5	26	11	35	63
4	Hibernian	32	10	2	4	37	22	9	2	5	30	21	24	61
5	Motherwell	32	10	3	3	34	20	7	3	6	32	19	27	57
6	Rangers	32	7	5	4	24	19	8	1	7	29	28	6	51
7	Falkirk	32	8	2	6	35	32	6	5	5	22	20	5	49
8	Partick Thistle	32	8	2	6	34	30	7	1	8	27	34	-3	48
9	Aberdeen	32	8	2	6	29	27	6	2	8	27	31	-2	46
10	Dunfermline	32	7	2	7	20	21	6	3	7	25	32	-8	44
11	Hearts	32	8	2	6	27	19	4	5	7	21	27	2	43
12	Kilmarnock	32	6	2	8	30	31	3	3	10	21	37	-17	32
13	St. Mirren	32	5	2	9	28	38	4	2	10	18	32	-24	31
14	Dundee United	32	5	6	5	28	30	2	3	11	21	36	-17	30
15	Dundee	32	2	5	9	11	25	5	2	9	21	32	-25	28
16	Inverness CT	32	5	4	7	19	27	2	2	12	13	39	-34	27
17	St. Johnstone	32	3	3	10	16	28	2	7	7	18	31	-25	25

It was quite an achievement for Ross County to win the Development League title. The Dingwall club had a settled team of talented youngsters, only occasionally augmented with over-age players.

Celtic, who had dominated this league for several years, had a gruelling programme including European matches and this eventually caught up with them.

Venues for matches are many and varied. Clubs get incentive payments for playing matches at their home stadium. This is supposed to benefit players by performing in a "stadium atmosphere". Matches are usually played on Tuesdays, some in the afternoon, but many with a 6pm Kick Off.

SPFL Development League East and West 2016/17

	ALL	BER	COW	FOR	LIV	RAI	STI	
Alloa		Oct 17	Nov 28	Feb 6	Nov 14	Sep 26	Oct 3	
		2-1	3-0	0-3	2-4	0-4	3-2	
		Dec 5				Feb 20	Mar 6	
		1-4				0-1	4-4	
Berwick Rangers	Apr 12		Nov 16	Oct 12	Jan 23	Mar 27	Sep 14	* Newtongrange Star
	3-0		6-0	2-1	1-1	1-3	4-3	
				Apr 26		Apr 3	Feb 22	
				2-2		0-2	3-1*	
Cowdenbeath	Oct 10	Sep 19		Nov 21	Oct 24	Feb 1	Oct 31	* Kelty Hearts
	0-3*	2-2*		3-4	2-1*	1-2*	2-2*	
	Mar 13	Feb 27			Mar 27			
	1-2*	2-7*			4-2*			
Forfar Athletic	Oct 25	Nov 29	Oct 4		Sep 13	Jan 17	Nov 15	
	0-2	3-1	6-0		2-4	2-1	2-1	
	Mar 28		Mar 7		Apr 11			
	5-1		6-1		6-0			
Livingston	Sep 19	Sep 5	Feb 6	Nov 7		Nov 21	Oct 17	* Almondvale Astro
	4-3*	0-2	3-1*	5-1		3-3	2-6*	
	Feb 27	Feb 13					Mar 20	
	1-1	1-2*					2-0*	
Raith Rovers	Nov 8	Oct 26	Oct 18	Sep 6	Oct 4		Nov 29	* Kelty Hearts
	6-1	3-6*	7-0	2-6	2-2		2-0	
			Mar 22	Feb 14	Apr 25			
			5-0*	1-0	2-1			
Stirling Albion	Nov 22	Dec 13	Sep 6	Sep 20	Apr 4	Oct 11		* Forthbank Astro
	2-0	5-0*	5-1*	5-1*	3-4*	2-2*		
			Feb 14	May 2		Mar 14		
			4-1*	1-0*		0-2*		

Matches played at normal home ground unless otherwise indicated

	AIR	ALB	AYR	CLY	MOR	QOS	QP	STRA	
Airdrieonians		Jan 11	Feb 15	Nov 9	Sep 22	Oct 26	Dec 7	Oct 12	* Ravenscraig
		2-1*	1-3*	0-0*	1-2*	1-3*	3-1*	0-4*	
			Nov 2		Feb 28	Mar 29		Mar 15	
			0-4*		3-5*	3-3*		1-2*	
Albion Rovers	Oct 3		Feb 2	Oct 17	Feb 8	Oct 31	Nov 14	Sep 12	
	4-0		4-2	6-2	4-0	0-2	2-0	1-2	
	Apr 11			Mar 23				Feb 20	
	2-4			5-2				1-1	
Ayr United	Sep 5	Oct 10		Sep 20	Nov 21	Sep 13	Oct 24	Dec 6	* Cumnock JFC
	5-0*	5-4		5-0	0-0	6-0*	2-2*	3-0#	# Belmont Acad
		Mar 13		Feb 27			Mar 27		
		1-2*		0-2*			2-2		
Clyde	Sep 11	Dec 18	Nov 13		Dec 6	Oct 2	Oct 30	Oct 23	* Broadwood Astro
	3-1*	1-2	3-2		1-8#	3-5*	1-4	3-3*	# Lennoxtown
	Feb 19				Mar 14	Mar 5		Apr-23	
	3-1*				2-1*	0-1*		2-3*	
Morton	Nov 15	Oct 24	Mar 7	Oct 10		Apr 5	Sep 13	Feb 14	* Lennoxtown
	3-0	5-2	2-2	3-0		2-0	2-1	2-1	
		Apr 3					Mar 30		
		3-0*					1-1		
Queen of the South	Feb 7	Sep 6	Nov 8	Nov 22	Oct 18		Oct 11	Sep 19	
	3-1	2-1	2-1	2-1	2-3		2-1	2-1	
		Feb 14			Mar 21		Mar 14	Feb 28	
		2-0			4-0		2-1	5-0	
Queen's Park	Oct 17	Sep 19	Feb 6	Sep 5	Dec 14	Nov 28		Oct 3	* New Lesser Hampden
	1-2*	0-0*	0-2*	1-1*	0-3*	1-2		2-1*	
	Mar 20	Feb 27		Feb 13					
	1-0*	1-3*		4-1*					
Stranraer	Nov 28	Nov 7	Oct 17	Apr 18	Sep 6	Nov 14	Apr 3		* New Lesser Hampden
	1-3	1-1	1-3	2-0#	2-2	0-1	4-1*		# Beith JFC
			Mar 20		Oct 31		Mar 6		
			3-3		1-4		1-2		

Games played at normal club home ground unless otherwise indicated

			Home					Away						
	Team	P	W	D	L	F	A	W	D	L	F	A	GD	Pts
1	Raith Rovers	18	6	1	2	30	16	6	2	1	20	9	25	39
2	Berwick Rangers	18	5	2	2	22	13	5	1	3	25	19	15	33
3	Forfar Athletic	18	7	0	2	32	11	3	1	5	18	21	18	31
4	Livingston	18	4	2	3	21	17	3	2	4	19	24	-1	25
5	Stirling Albion	18	6	1	2	27	11	1	2	6	19	24	11	24
6	Alloa Athletic	18	3	1	5	15	23	3	1	5	11	22	-19	20
7	Cowdenbeath	18	2	2	5	17	25	0	0	9	4	45	-49	8

			Home					Away						
	Team	P	W	D	L	F	A	W	D	L	F	A	GD	Pts
1	Queen of South	21	10	0	1	28	10	7	1	2	18	16	20	52
2	Morton	21	8	2	0	26	7	6	2	3	28	20	27	46
3	Ayr United	21	5	3	3	29	13	4	2	4	22	19	19	32
4	Albion Rovers	21	6	1	3	29	15	3	2	6	16	23	7	30
5	Stranraer	21	2	3	5	16	20	4	2	5	18	22	-8	23
6	Queen's Park	21	3	2	5	11	15	2	3	6	16	22	-10	20
7	Clyde	21	4	1	6	22	31	1	2	7	9	28	-28	18
8	Airdrieonians	21	2	2	7	15	28	3	0	7	12	26	-27	17

Club Academy Scotland U17 League 2016/17

		P	W	D	A	F	A	GD	PTS
1	Celtic	26	23	0	3	121	13	108	69
2	Aberdeen	26	20	3	3	79	33	46	63
3	Rangers	26	19	3	4	84	35	49	60
4	Hamilton Accies	26	19	2	5	83	32	51	59
5	St Mirren	26	12	6	8	56	61	-5	42
6	Partick Thistle	26	11	8	7	53	54	-1	41
7	Hearts	26	8	5	13	50	72	-22	29
8	Dundee United	26	8	5	13	40	67	-27	29
9	Motherwell	26	7	4	15	57	72	-15	25
10	Forth Valley E;itce Academy	26	6	6	14	43	63	-20	24
11	Kilmarnock	26	6	6	14	33	61	-28	24
12	Hibernian	26	6	5	15	27	48	-21	23
13	Fife Elite Academy	26	5	1	20	39	97	-58	16
14	Ayr United	26	3	4	19	25	82	-57	13

This League is very significant because the Champions, as it stands, are guaranteed entry to the following season's UEFA Youth League. Despite this matches are seldom publicised and the League table is seldom seen.

Club Academy Scotland operates Leagues at Under 11, 12, 13, 14, 15 and 17. The younger age groups are "non competitive" and fixtures / results are not published under an SFA directive.

However, that directive does not cover the Under 17 Category and there is much good football to be seen there. Membership of the different Club Academy Scotland leagues for 2016/17 is shown below.

Under 11 Elite
Aberdeen
Ayr United
Celtic
Dundee
Dundee United
Fife Elite Academy
Forth Valley Elite Academy
Hamilton Accies
Hearts
Hibernian
Inverness CT
Kilmarnock
Morton
Motherwell
Partick Thistle
Queen's Park
Rangers
St Mirren

Under 12 Elite
Aberdeen
Ayr United
Celtic
Dundee
Dundee United
Fife Elite Academy
Forth Valley Elite Academy
Hamilton Accies
Hearts
Hibernian
Inverness CT
Kilmarnock
Morton
Motherwell
Partick Thistle
Queen's Park
Rangers
St Mirren

Under 13 Elite
Aberdeen
Ayr United
Celtic
Dundee United
Fife Elite Academy
Forth Valley Elite Academy
Hamilton Accies
Hearts
Hibernian
Kilmarnock
Motherwell
Partick Thistle
Rangers
St Mirren

Under 13
Airdrieonians
Alloa
Dumbarton
Dundee
Elgin City
Inverness CT
Livingston
Morton
Queen of the South
Queen's Park
Ross County
St Johnstone
Stirling Albion

Under 14 Elite
Aberdeen
Ayr United
Celtic
Dundee United
Fife Elite Academy
Forth Valley Elite Academy
Hamilton Accies
Hearts
Hibernian
Kilmarnock
Motherwell
Partick Thistle
Rangers
St Mirren

Under 14
Airdrieonians
Alloa
Dumbarton
Dundee
Elgin City
Inverness CT
Livingston
Morton
Queen's Park
Ross County
St Johnstone
Stirling Albion

Under 15 Elite
Aberdeen
Ayr United
Celtic
Dundee United
Fife Elite Academy
Forth Valley Elite Academy
Hamilton Accies
Hearts
Hibernian
Kilmarnock
Motherwell
Partick Thistle
Rangers
St Mirren

Under 15
Airdrieonians
Alloa
Dumbarton
Dundee
Elgin City
Inverness CT
Livingston
Montrose
Morton
Queen's Park
Queen of the South
Ross County
St Johnstone
Stirling Albion
Stranraer

Under 17 Elite
Aberdeen
Ayr United
Celtic
Dundee United
Fife Elite Academy
Forth Valley Elite Academy
Hamilton Accies
Hearts
Hibernian
Kilmarnock
Motherwell
Partick Thistle
Rangers
St Mirren

Under 17
Airdrieonians
Alloa
Celtic
Dumbarton
Dundee
Elgin City
Inverness CT
Livingston
Montrose
Morton
Queen's Park
Queen of the South
Ross County
St Johnstone
Stirling Albion
Stranraer

Project Brave

Until 2016/17 both Elite Academies and "Ordinary" Academies attracted funding from the SFA, provided clubs met certain criteria. The formation of the Academies was designed to ensure that young players received the best possible coaching in a safe and regulated environment.

Currently around 2500 young players are involved in Club Academy Scotland, across around 100 teams in 29 Club Academies. As part of the SFA's Project Brave, the number of players participating is to be reduced by around 50%, with resources directed at fewer teams. It is anticipated that there will be a maximum of 16 Academy Clubs, chosen against independently-audited selection criteria.
From 2018 any clubs involved in Club Academy Scotland will require to have 6 full-time coaches.

The smaller clubs have been loudest in their criticism of the changes. However, the SFA has pointed to Germany as a comparison where a total of just 5000 players participate in centrally-funded academies.

Ultimately the aim is for Club Academy Scotland to run up to the Under 18 age group level. Above that age Reserve Team football may be introduced along with the possibility of "Colt" teams from the Academy Clubs participating in the SPFL structure.

The aim of the proposed changes is to achieve better player progression and development in the 16-20 age group.

SPFL DEVELOPMENT LEAGUE - MANAGERS / COACHES 2016/17

Aberdeen	Head Coach	Paul Sheerin
Airdrieonians	Coach	Kevin McBride
Albion Rovers	Coach	Brian Kerr
Alloa Athletic	Head of Youth Devt	Graeme Liveston
Annan Athletic	No Under 20 side	
Arbroath	No Under 20 side	
Ayr United	Head of Youth	David White
Berwick Rangers	Head of Youth Devt	Derek McKenzie
	Coach	Neil Oliver
Brechin City	No Under 20 side	
Celtic	Head of Youth Devt	Chris McCart
	Head Coach	Tommy McIntyre
Clyde	Head Coach	Richard Fox
Cowdenbeath	Development Coaches	Brian Nelson / Dean Ewing
Dumbarton	Head of Youth	Tony McNally (Until May)
Dundee	Head of Youth	Jimmy Boyle
Dundee United	Head of Youth	Brian Grant
	Head Coach	Dave Bowman
Dunfermline Athletic	Head Coach	John Potter
East Fife	No Under 20 side	
Edinburgh City	Manager	Rob Hart
Elgin City	No Under 20 side	
Falkirk	Head Coach	Alan Maybury
Forfar Athletic	Coach	Barry Sellars
Hamilton Accies	Head of Youth	George Cairns
	Coach	Guillaume Beuzelin
Hearts	Head Coach	Jon Daly
Hibernian	Head of Academy Coaching	Eddie May
Inverness CT	Head Coach	Duncan Shearer
Kilmarnock	Head Coach	Paul Stephenson
Livingston	Coach	David Martindale
Montrose	No Under 20 side	
Morton	Head Coach	Andy Millen
Motherwell	Manager	Stephen Craigan
Partick Thistle	Coach	Scott MacKenzie / Ryan Wilkie
Peterhead	No Under 20 side	
Queen's Park	Coach	Alan Mahood
Queen of the South	Coach	Eddie Warwick
Raith Rovers	Head of Player Development	Craig Easton
Rangers	Head of Youth	Craig Mulholland
	Head Coach	Graeme Murty
Ross County	Manager	Stuart Kettlewell
St Johnstone	Head Coach	Alex Cleland
St Mirren	Head of Youth Devt	Allan McManus
Stenhousemuir	No Under 20 side	
Stirling Albion	Coach	Ross Forsyth / Andy Todd
Stranraer	Manager	Stuart Wild

Scottish FA Youth Cup 2016/17

Round	Date	Home	Away	F	A		Notes
1	28/08/2016	Deveronvale	Inverurie Locos	0	2		
1	28/08/2016	Turriff United	Keith	0	7		Keith expelled for fielding overage player
1	26/08/2016	Aberdeen	Fraserburgh	4	1		
1	28/08/2016	Clyde	Queen's Park	1	5		at Broadwood Outside Pitch
1	28/08/2016	Dunfermline Athletic	Berwick Rangers	3	1	AET	
1	02/09/2016	Heriot Watt University	Partick Thistle	0	6		
1	04/09/2016	Edusport Academy	Alloa Athletic	2	1		at Spartans
2	25/09/2016	Buckie Thistle	Clachnacuddin	2	8		
2	25/09/2016	Banks o' Dee	Montrose	2	1		
2	25/09/2016	Formartine United	Lossiemouth	3	3	AET, 3-5p	
2	25/09/2016	Inverurie Locos	Forfar Athletic	1	3		
2	29/09/2016	Turriff United	Aberdeen	0	13		
2	25/09/2016	Stranraer	Annan Athletic	2	3		
2	25/09/2016	Edusport Academy	Lothian Thistle HV	3	0		
2	25/09/2016	Edinburgh City	Preston Athletic	3	1		
2	23/09/2016	Spartans	Whitehill Welfare	3	1		
2	25/09/2016	Livingston	Dunfermline Athletic	0	4		
2	25/09/2016	Stirling Albion	Queen's Park	2	1	AET	
2	25/09/2016	Falkirk	Albion Rovers	3	1		
2	25/09/2016	East Kilbride	BSC Glasgow	5	1		
2	23/09/2016	Hamilton Accies	Raith Rovers	2	1		
2	25/09/2016	Cowdenbeath	Partick Thistle	2	3	AET	
2	09/10/2016	Tynecastle	Hibernian	2	4		
3	06/11/2016	St Mirren	Dunfermline Athletic	0	2		
3	06/11/2016	Ayr United	Inverness CT	0	0	AET, 6-5p	
3	23/10/2016	Hearts	Annan Athletic	10	0		
3	06/11/2016	Queen of the South	Airdrieonians	2	1		
3	05/11/2016	Celtic	Edinburgh City	21	0		at Lennoxtown
3	06/11/2016	Partick Thistle	East Kilbride	4	1		
3	06/11/2016	Spartans	Clachnacuddin	3	1		
3	03/11/2016	Forfar Athletic	St Johnstone	0	0	AET, 3-4p	
3	07/11/2016	Rangers	Edusport Academy	3	0		at Stirling Albion
3	06/11/2016	Lossiemouth	Dundee United	0	9		
3	06/11/2016	Kilmarnock	Stirling Albion	6	1		
3	14/11/2016	Falkirk	Ross County	3	2		
3	06/11/2016	Motherwell	Cumbernauld Colts	1	0		
3	06/11/2016	Dundee	Hibernian	0	2		
3	06/11/2016	Aberdeen	Hamilton Accies	1	1	AET, 4-3p	
3	06/11/2016	Morton	Banks o' Dee	10	1		
4	04/12/2016	Spartans	Falkirk	1	4		
4	04/12/2016	Hearts	Rangers	2	5		at ORIAM
4	01/12/2016	Aberdeen	Hibernian	1	2		at Brechin
4	03/12/2016	Celtic	Dundee United	5	0		at Lennoxtown
4	04/12/2016	Motherwell	Morton	3	1		
4	04/12/2016	Ayr United	Dunfermline Athletic	1	0		
4	04/12/2016	St Johnstone	Partick Thistle	1	2		
4	30/11/2016	Kilmarnock	Queen of the South	3	2	aet	
5	22/01/2017	Ayr United	Kilmarnock	3	4	aet	
5	22/01/2017	Rangers	Falkirk	5	1		
5	22/01/2017	Partick Thistle	Motherwell	3	4		
5	17/02/2017	Hibernian	Celtic	0	1		at ORIAM
SF	12/03/2017	Kilmarnock	Rangers	1	4	aet	
SF	03/04/2017	Celtic	Motherwell	1	0		at Lennoxtown
F	26/04/2017	Celtic	Rangers	3	0		at Hampden

The final, at Hampden, was not open to the public. Tickets were issued by both clubs to the families of players, and through their youth and community programmes.

Celtic's 21-0 win over Edinburgh City was the biggest victory margin of the tournament. However, it is not a record—Ayr United defeated Selkirk by 25-0 in 2015/16.

FINAL

Celtic 3 Rangers 0
Wednesday 26th April 2016, Hampden Park, Glasgow

(Wardrop 39, Miller 45, McIlduff 53)

Celtic: Hazard, Ralston, Wardrop, Kerr, McIlduff, Hill (Hendry), Thomson (McInroy), Johnson, Nesbitt, Miller, Aitchison
Unused subs: Doohan (GK), Archibald, Crossan, Duffy, Watson
Rangers: Robby McCrorie, Houston, Ross McCrorie, Wilson, Lyon; Ashmore, Barjonas, Gilmour (Jeffries), Rudden (Gibson), Dallas (Burt), Atakayi
Unused subs: Wright (GK), Bradley, Abaradan, Krones

ALL TIME SFA YOUTH CUP FINALS					
YEAR	WINNERS	RUNNERS-UP	RES		VENUE
1983–84	Celtic	Rangers	2 – 0	AET	Celtic Park
1984–85	Aberdeen	Celtic	5 – 3		Pittodrie Stadium
1985–86	Aberdeen	Queen of the South	2 – 0		Palmerston Park
1986–87	Celtic	Motherwell	2 – 1		Fir Park
1987–88	Dunfermline Athletic	Dundee	2 – 1		East End Park
1988–89	Celtic	Dundee United	1 – 0		Tannadice Park
1989–90	Dundee United	Hibernian	0 – 0	AET, pens	Easter Road
1990–91	Dundee United	Hibernian	2 – 0		Tannadice Park
1991–92	Hibernian	Ayr United	2 – 0		Easter Road
1992–93	Heart of Midlothian	Rangers	3 – 1		Ibrox Stadium
1993–94	Rangers	Airdrieonians	5 – 3		Broomfield Park
1994–95	Rangers	St Johnstone	2 – 0		Hampden Park
1995–96	Celtic	Dundee	4 – 1		Hampden Park
1996–97	Celtic	Rangers	3 – 2		Broadwood Stadium
1997–98	Heart of Midlothian	Dundee United	2 – 0		Tynecastle Stadium
1998–99	Celtic	Dundee	4 – 0		Celtic Park
1999–00	Heart of Midlothian	Rangers	5 – 3		Hampden Park
2000–01	Aberdeen	Celtic	2 – 0		Hampden Park
2001–02	Rangers	Ayr United	4 – 2		New Douglas Park
2002–03	Celtic	Aberdeen	3 – 1	AET	McDiarmid Park
2003–04	Kilmarnock	Rangers	1 – 0		Rugby Park
2004–05	Celtic	St Mirren	2 – 0		Hampden Park
2005–06	Celtic	Heart of Midlothian	3 – 1		Celtic Park
2006–07	Rangers	Celtic	5 – 0		Hampden Park
2007–08	Rangers	Celtic	3 – 1	AET	Hampden Park
2008–09	Hibernian	Rangers	2 – 1	AET	Hampden Park
2009–10	Celtic	Rangers	2 – 0		Hampden Park
2010–11	Celtic	Rangers	2 – 1	AET	Hampden Park
2011–12	Celtic	Queen of the South	8 – 0		Hampden Park
2012–13	Celtic	Dunfermline Athletic	3 – 1		Hampden Park
2013–14	Rangers	Heart of Midlothian	2 – 2	AET, pens	St Mirren Park
2014–15	Celtic	Rangers	5 – 2		Hampden Park
2015–16	Motherwell	Heart of Midlothian	5 – 2		Hampden Park
2016-17	Celtic	Rangers	3-0		Hampden Park

WINNERS

15	Celtic
6	Rangers
3	Hearts, Aberdeen
2	Hibernian, Dundee United
1	Dunfermline Athletic, Kilmarnock, Motherwell

RUNNERS UP

10	Rangers
4	Celtic
3	Hearts, Dundee
2	Hibernian, Dundee United, Queen of the South, Ayr United
1	Aberdeen, Dunfermline Athletic, Motherwell, St Mirren, St Johnstone, Airdrieonians

UEFA Youth Champions League 2016/17

CELTIC FC RESULTS GROUP STAGE					Att	Scorers	1	2	3	4	5	6	7	8	9	10	11	12	14	15	16	17	18	19
13/09/2016	A$	CF Barcelona	1	2	480	Aitchison	Doohan	Ralston	Archibald	McCart*	Ajer	Wardrop	Hill	Aitchison	Hendry	Miller	Crossan+	Kerr*	Johnston+	*Church*	*Higgins*	*Payne*	*McAdam*	*Hazard*
28/09/2016	H"	Manchester City	0	4	246		Hazard	Ralston	McCart	Wardrope	Ajer	Archibald+	Hill&	Aitchison	Hendry	Miller	Crossan*	Johnston*	Church+	Payne&	*Kerr*	*Duffy*	*McInroy*	*Doohan*
19/10/2016	H"	Borussia Moenchengladbach	1	1	341	Johnston	Doohan	Ralston	McCart	Johnson	Kerr	Wardrop	Hill	Higgins*	Hendry&	Miller	Aitchison+	Payne*	Crossan+	Archibald&	*Duffy*	*Church*	*McAdams*	*Hazard*
01/11/2016	A>	Borussia Moenchengladbach	1	4	777	Hendry	Doohan	Ralston	McCart	Hendry*	Kerr	Wardrop	Ajer	Hill	Miller	Archibald	Aitchison+	Crossan*	Higgins+	*Church*	*Payne*	*Duffy*	*McAdams*	*Hazard*
23/11/2016	H"	CF Barcelona	1	4	296	Aitchison	Doohan	Ralston	McCart	Hendry+	Kerr	Wardrop	Crossan*	Hill	Ajer	Miller	Aitchison	Johnston*	Archibald+	*Church*	*Higgins*	*Duffy*	*McAdams*	*McInroy*
06/12/2016	A*	Manchester City	2	3	613	Johnston, Archibald	Doohan	Ralston	Higgins*	Hendry	Kerr	Archibald+	Johnston	Hill&	Ajer	Miller	Aitchison	McInroy*	Crossan+	Henderson&	*Duffy*	*McAdams*	*Walsh*	*Deas*

$ at Mini Estadi, Nou Camp

" at Cappielow

* at Man City Mini Stadium

> at Fohlenplatz

Celtic qualified automatically for the Group Stages in 2016/17.

FA Premier League International Cup 2016/17

Celtic were invited to take part in this competition for the third year in succession.

The FA Premier League International Cup involved 24 sides.

Celtic Results

(Group E)

9/11/16 A	v Aston Villa	3-0
16/11/16	A v Norwich City	0-3
30/11/16	N v Valencia*	3-0

* at Southampton FC Training Ground

Knock Out Stage Results

Quarter Finals

Swansea City v Hertha Berlin	5-1
Norwich City v Dinamo Zagreb	6-0
Sundeland v Athletic Bilbao	2-0
Manchester Utd v Porto	0-2

Semi Finals

Norwich City v Sunderland	0-1
Swansea City v Porto	0-1

Final (May 17 2017)
Porto v Sunderland

ESMGO Youth Tournament, Gonfreville, France

Hamilton Accies retained this prestigious trophy with an impressive set of results against quality opposition.

27th ESMGO Youth Tournament, at Gonfreville				
Group Games				
G June 3	Charlton Athletic	6	0	
G June 4	ESMGO	1	0	
G June 4	Dumnkerque	4	2	
SF June 5	Le Havre	2	0	
F June 5	Moscow Dynamo	2	1	Att 650

Accies squad:

Ross Connelly, Kieran McDougall, Ciaran McAndrew, Leon McCann, Taylor Wilson, Adam Douglas, Daryl Meikle, Lewis Smith (c), Steffen Connelly, Sean Slaven, Charlie Reilly, Liam Scullion, Marley Redfern, Andy Winter, Jamie Hamilton and Deaglan Moynes.

UEFA YOUTH LEAGUE 2017/18

The Tournament will be made up of 64 teams as follows:

32 Clubs whose first teams have qualified for the 2017/18 Champions League group stages.

Plus

The domestic youth champions of the 32 countries highest in the UEFA rankings

If a team "double qualifies" then the youth champions from the next highest-ranked UEFA nation will qualify.

NB Youth Champions entry is based on the Under 17 domestic league—i.e. the players who won their league should play in the following season's UEFA Youth League.

Currently Scotland sits 25th in the UEFA rankings and the champions (Celtic) are guaranteed a place in the "Domestic Champions" path. This involves home and away knock out ties against other domestic champions.

Should Celtic's first team reach the group stage of the Champions League then their youths will enter the "Champions League" path with 6 games guaranteed in a group with opponents identical to the first team.

SCOTS IN ENGLISH PREMIERSHIP CLUB ACADEMIES				
Crean	Alex	Arsenal	GK	Ex Celtic
Kerr	Josh	Brighton	D	Ex Celtic
Leitch	Robbie	Burnley	M	Ex Motherwell
Sammut	Ruben	Chelsea	M	
St Clair	Harvey	Chelsea	M	
Gilmour	Billy	Chelsea	M	Ex Rangers
Bramall	Danny	Everton	M	
Hornby	Fraser	Everton	M	
Taylor	Cameron	Huddersfield Town	D	
Fulton	Ryan	Liverpool	GK	
Johnston	George	Liverpool	D	
McTominay	Scott	Manchester United	M	
Hamilton	Ethan	Manchester United	M	
Gallacher	Owen	Newcastle United	M	
Freeman	Kieran	Southampton	D	
Souttar	Harry	Stoke City	D	Ex Dundee United
Biabi	Botti	Swansea City	F	Ex Falkirk
Byers	George	Swansea City	M	
McBurnie	Oliver	Swansea City	F	
Blair	Ryan	Swansea City	F	Ex Falkirk
Elliot	Jordan	Swansea City	M	
Jakubiak	Alex	Watford	M	
Meredith	Dan	West Bromwich Albion	D	

Referees 2015/16

Category 1
REFEREES
Greg Aitken
Crawford Allan
Euan Anderson
Graham Beaton
John Beaton
Craig Charleston
Kevin Clancy
William Collum
Barry Cook
Andrew Dallas
Gavin Duncan
Stephen Finnie
Kevin Graham
Grant Irvine
Steven Kirkland
David Lowe
Bobby Madden
John McKendrick
Steven McLean
Scott Millar
Ryan Milne (Aberdeen)
Alan Muir
David Munro
Craig Napier
Alan Newlands
Mat Northcroft
Steven Reid
Don Robertson
Mike Roncone
Gavin Ross
Colin Steven
Craig Thomson
Nick Walsh

Category 1
DEVELOPMENT REFEREES
Mike Taylor

Category 2
REFEREES
Stephen Brown
Lorraine Clark
David Dickinson
Chris Graham
Scott Lambie
Duncan Smith
Peter Stuart
Duncan Williams
Lloyd Wilson

Category 2
DEVELOPMENT REFEREES
Evan Cairns
Jordan Curran
Garry Doherty
Liam Duncan
Chris Fordyce
Chris Gentles
Stephen Graham
Graham Grainger
Kyle Hall
Calum Haswell
Craig King
Stewart Luke
Matthew MacDermid
Chris McNab
Calum Scott
Ronnie Strain
Gavin Thomson
Steven Traynor
William Wilson

Category 3
SPECIALIST ASSISTANT REFEREES
Michael Banks
Sean Carr
Graham Chambers
Frank Connor
Willie Conquer
Anthony Cooper
Gordon Crawford
Ralph Gordon
Gavin Harris
Ross Haswell
Gary Hilland
Stuart Hodge
Joseph Lawson
Graeme Leslie
Alastair Mather
John McCrossan
David McGeachie
Mark McLean
Kylie McMullan
Graham McNeillie
Andrew McWilliam
Andy Milne
Stephen Mitchell
Alan Mulvanny
Dougie Potter
David Roome
Alasdair Ross
Douglas Ross
Ivan Stankovic
Stuart Stevenson
Graeme Stewart
Jordan Stokoe
Brian Templeton
Raymond Whyte

Category 3
SPECIALIST ASSISTANT
REFEREE DEVELOPMENT
David Doig
David Dunne
Willie Ferguson
Kevin McElhinney
David McKniff
Paul O'Neill
Chris Phillips
Calum Spence

Category 3
REFEREES
Mark Ainslie
Ross Anderson
Connor Ashwood
Billy Baxter
Jonathan Bell
Euan Birch
Ross Birrell
David Burns
Jim Burns
Liam Butler
George Calder
Thomas Clark
Derek Crothers
Finlay Currie
Ben Dempster
Garry Farmer
Craig Ferguson
Graham Fraser
Tony Fullerton
Alan Grainger
Daniel Graves
Alastair Grieve
Ross Hardie
Xander Harrison
Alan Hogg
David Ingram
Tony Kelly
George King
Drew Kirkland
Ryan Lee
Scott Leslie
Scott Love
Alan Macfadyen
Simon MacLean
Colin McAlpine
Martin McCarthy
Colin McDonald
Dan McFarlane (Aberdeen)
Daniel McFarlane (Lanarkshire)
Mark McHendry
Chris McTiernan
Ross Menzies
Richard Murray
Ryan Oliver
Jordan Paterson
Colin Pensom
Alan Proctor
Barry Reid
George Robertson
Thomas Shaw
Alex Shepherd
Will Smith
Iain Snedden
Greg Soutar
Steven Strang
Andy Taylor
Craig Walker
David Watt
Colin Whyte
Craig Wilson

Category 3
DEVELOPMENT REFEREES
Michael Addy
Boise Allan
Scott Anderson
Nicolle Andrews
Scott Annandale
Adam Barclay
Harry Bruce
Corey Craig
Andrew Craven
Paul Cummings
David Currie
Billy Dewar-Riddick
Barry Dickson
Lee Dixon
Calum Doyle
Colin Drummond
Fabrice Dubois
Eddie Ferguson
Blair Fraser
Jonathan Gall
Gary Hanvidge
Greig Haynes
Martin Hristov
Elliott Husband Powton
Mark Kane
Ryan Kennedy
Alastair Leghorn
Kevin Lindsay
Gary Logan
Lee Macaulay
Michael MacDermid
Laurie Mackinnon
Gary MacLean
David MacLennan
Ross MacLeod
Craig Macrae
Nicky Marshall
Neil Matheson
Filippo Mazzoni
Paul McAvinue
Gordon McCabe
Michael McCart
Gary McGregor
Steven McKay
Philip McLean
Ryan Milne (Angus & Perthshire)
David Milton
Alasdair Morrison
Darren Munro
Graeme Murphy
Chris Newman
Stephen Nicol
Lee Pirie
Chris Rae
Mark Rennie
Steven Rintoul

Nikki Smith
John Stewart
Andrew Strang
Danny Taylor
Cameron Telfer
Robert Thomson (Lanarkshire)
Paul Timmons
Keiran Trayner
Steven Wilson

Category 4
REFEREES
George Anderson
Ian Bailey
Ally Bruce
Glen Carruthers
Billy Cooper
Derek Davidson
Gavin Dearie
Graham Elder
Derek Folganan
Liam Gallagher
Michael Gill
Paul Hanlon
Graeme Jack
Scott Jamieson
Graham John
George MacDonald
Rodney Marshall
Keith Maskell
Jim McCunnie
Stephen McDade
Mike McIlvenny
David McKenzie
Dave McLaren
Arthur Murphy
John Nicolson
Morag Pirie
Caryl Potten
Stewart Riddoch
Jamie Shepherd
Graeme Smith
Catalin Stan
Sean Sutherland
Rab Thomson (Edinburgh

Referees' Associations' Managers
Aberdeen & District RA
Sandy Roy
(Incorporating Orkney and Shetland)
Mike Pocock (Assistant Manager)

Angus & Perthshire RA
Neil Watters
Steve Pullar (Assistant Manager)

Ayrshire RA
Dougie Smith
Jim Laird (Assistant Manager)

Edinburgh & District RA
Martin Clark
Mark Doyle (Assistant Manager)

Fife RA
Stuart Macaulay
Derek Lowe (Assistant Manager)

Glasgow RA
Alan Cunningham
Bryan Robertson (Assistant Manager)

Lanarkshire RA
Brian Winter
George Drummond (Assistant Manager)

Moray & Banff RA
Bill Machray

North of Scotland RA
Bill Machray
Billy Murray (Assistant Manager)

Renfrewshire RA
Joe McDowall
John Brown (Assistant Manager)

South of Scotland RA
Graeme Alison

Stirlingshire RA
Ricky Mooney
Brian McGarry (Assistant Manager)

Referee Observers
Graeme Alison
Les Norris
Iain Brines
Mike Pocock
Jim Bruce
Bryan Robertson
Brian Cassidy
Sandy Roy
Martin Clark
Dougie Smith
George Clyde
Eddie Smith
Gerry Evans
George Smith
Alan Freeland
Louis Thow
Ian Fyfe
Kevin Toner
Douglas Hope
Paul Watson
Bill Machray
Neil Watters
Craig Mackay
Brian Winter
Douglas Yeats
John Young
Calum Murray
Willie Young
Euan Norris

Assistant Referee Observers
Martin Cryans
John McElhinney
Alan Cunningham
Brian McGarry
George Drummond
Derek Rose
Stuart Macaulay
Stewart Shearer
Joe McDowall
Keith Sorbie

Scottish Referees on FIFA / UEFA List 2017

REFEREES (Year of Birth, Year of first FIFA appointment)

Elite
Willie Collum (1979 / 2006)
Craig Thomson (1972 / 2002)

Category One
John Beaton (1983 / 2012)
Bobby Madden (1978 / 2010)

Category Two
Kevin Clancy (1983 / 2012)
Andrew Dallas (1983 / 2015)

Category Three
Don Robertson

Women Elite
Morag Pirie (1975 / 2005)

Women Category One
Lorraine Clark (1985 / 2010)

Women Category Two
None

Women Category Three
None

FIFA / UEFA Assistant Referees (Men)
Alan Mulvanny (1985 / 2016)
Alistair Mather (xxx/2017)
Stuart Stevenson (1981 / 2012)
David McGeachie (1986 / 2013)
Francis Connor (1981 / 2015)
Douglas Ross (1983 / 2015)
Graeme Stewart (1985 / 2015)
Douglas Potter (1985 / 2016)
Sean Carr (1983 / 2016)
Jordan Stokoe (xxxx / 2017)

Assistant Referees (Women)
Vikki Allan
Molly Alexander
Kylie McMullan (1988 / 2013)
Vikki Robertson (1984 / 2015)

Referees - Severity Index 2016/17

The table below is provided for a little bit of fun - not for any ulterior purpose. It shows the total number of SPFL games handled (G), total Yellow (Y) and Red (R) cards issued during 2016/17. Yellow Cards are given 1 point each, red cards are given three points each to reach a total, and the total is then divided by the number of games to give the (PPG) - the severity index.

Of course the fewer games a referee handles the less likely they are to be representative of all games therefore figures for those with a low games total must be treated with particular caution.

A further note of caution—a referee in the middle of the list may be very good or they could be erratic with some lenient games and some severe games..

	2016/17				2015/16				2014/15			
SEVERE	G	Y	R	PPG	G	Y	R	PPG	G	Y	R	PPG
Gavin Ross	25	148	13	7.48	25	106	9	5.32	26	102	6	4.61
Steven Kirkland	26	103	13	5.46	23	69	5	3.65	17	43	4	3.23
Craig Charleston	28	118	8	5.07	30	119	5	4.47	34	7	15	4.47
Colin Steven	20	80	7	5.05	24	102	7	5.12	26	89	5	4
Barry Cook	25	114	4	5.04	30	119	7	4.67	27	97	3	3.93
Steven McLean	32	134	9	5.03	40	143	5	3.95	38	126	7	3.87
Nick Walsh	35	142	9	4.83	31	122	12	5.1	28	83	4	3.39
David Munro	21	77	8	4.81	26	69	4	3.11	19	55	2	3
Stephen Finnie	32	135	5	4.69	37	155	8	4.84	33	133	3	4.3
Craig Napier	25	81	12	4.68	12	33	1	3				
Andrew Dallas	30	117	6	4.50	26	106	3	4.42	32	119	7	4.37
Gavin Duncan	28	117	3	4.50	24	103	5	4.92	21	76	6	4.48
Alan Newlands	26	97	6	4.42	27	93	4	3.89	40	3	3	4.67
Graeme Beaton	22	79	6	4.41								
Kevin Clancy	32	139	3	4.34	38	145	7	4.37	35	124	4	3.89
Mike Roncone	27	96	7	4.33	26	102	10	5.08	6	27	2	5.5
Scott Millar	23	79	6	4.22	9	30	4	4.67				
Ryan Milne	8	30	1	4.13	4	12	2	4.5	7	15	2	3
John Beaton	39	142	6	4.10	40	144	9	4.27	33	14	4	3.82
Craig Thomson	38	133	7	4.05	43	183	7	4.74	45	1269	7	4.22
Kevin Graham	24	85	4	4.04	28	109	8	4.75	29	103	7	4.28
Alan Muir	32	120	3	4.03	35	108	5	3.51	31	113	7	4.32
Don Robertson	33	111	7	4.00	39	105	8	3.31	25	101	6	3.4
David Dickinson	3	12	0	4.00								
William Collum	43	134	8	3.67	46	142	7	3.54	48	142	17	4.02
Grant Irvine	24	76	3	3.54	11	35	3	4	15	38	1	2.73
Greg Aitken	30	97	3	3.53	27	95	12	4.85	34	88	13	3.73
Euan Anderson	29	95	2	3.48	32	89	5	3.25	33	129	4	4.27
Mat Northcroft	24	74	3	3.46	21	75	3	4	25	75	5	3.6
Crawford Allan	31	96	3	3.39	31	97	5	3.61	34	83	4	2.79
David Lowe	27	74	4	3.19	26	71	2	2.96	6	18	0	3
Mike Taylor	3	6	1	3.00	7	18	1	3	3	7	2	4.33
Bobby Madden	39	82	2	2.93	37	130	11	4.41	41	135	11	4.1
Steven Reid	25	59	2	2.60	12	42	1	3.75				
John McKendrick	24	51	2	2.38	32	71	0	2.21	35	84	2	2.57
LENIENT												
Brian Colvin					15	49	3	3.87	29	100	7	4.17
George Salmond					27	91	6	4.04	30	77	4	2.97
Peter Newlands									10	40	3	4.9
Calum Murray									36	21	8	4.03
Graham Beaton									4	14	0	3.5
Des Roache									13	48	0	3.69

IFAB and Proposed Rule Changes

WHAT IS IFAB?

The International Football Association Board meets for it's AGM every March. It meets on rotation in England, Scotland, Wales, Northern Ireland and at FIFA HQ. The IFAB Board has 8 members—four from FIFA and one each from the four British Associations. For decisions to be passed they must be approved by 6 out of the 8 members.

The 132nd Annual General Meeting will be hosted by FIFA in February or March 2018

In June 2017 IFAB issued a discussion document proposing various law changes:

Scrap 45 minute halves and replace with 2 x 30 minute halves. However, referee's watch to be stopped when ball out of play.

Players not allowed to score on rebound from a penalty – if the penalty is saved and the ball remains in play then a goal kick is awarded.

Link the referee's watch to a stadium clock

Players can pass to themselves at a free kick

Only team captain's may speak to the referee

Goal kicks could be taken when ball is moving

Goal kicks to be taken on the same side as the ball went out

A clearer definition of handball

A player who scores or stops a goal with his hand to be red carded

Goalkeeper handling a back-pass or throw in from a team mate to concede a penalty

Referee could award a goal if ball is stopped by handling on or close to goal line

Referees only to blow for half or full time when ball is out of play

Red and Yellow Cards 2016/17

PREMIERSHIP RED CARDS		GP	GS	Mins	YC	RC
MacKinnon, Darian	Hamilton Accies	33	32	2846	8	2
Stockley, Jayden	Aberdeen	27	8	854	2	2
Elliot, Christie	Partick Thistle	31	26	2403	5	1
Osman, Abdul	Partick Thistle	31	30	2577	7	1
Welsh, Sean	Partick Thistle	21	18	1588	5	1
McMann, Scott	Hamilton Accies	23	21	1908	4	1
Foster, Richard	St Johnstone	34	34	2917	6	1
McShane, Ian	Ross County	8	5	505	0	1
Brown, Scott	Celtic	33	33	2913	11	1
McGregor, Callum	Celtic	31	20	1935	2	1
Jack, Ryan	Aberdeen	26	25	2253	3	1
Reynolds, Mark	Aberdeen	26	22	1878	6	1
O'Hara, Mark DUN	Dundee	28	26	2282	4	1
Taylor, Greg	Kilmarnock	34	34	3033	8	1
Buaben, Prince	Hearts	20	11	828	4	1
Nicholson, Sam	Hearts	19	13	1173	1	1
Walker, Jamie	Hearts	34	28	2484	6	1
McDonald, Scott	Motherwell	35	34	2961	6	1
Swanson, Danny	St Johnstone	30	28	2347	7	1
Devine, Daniel	Partick Thistle	30	28	2500	6	1
Horner, Lewis	Inverness CT	10	5	519	2	1
Polworth, Liam	Inverness CT	32	26	2382	3	1
Tansey, Greg	Inverness CT	37	37	3265	4	1
Warren, Gary	Inverness CT	33	33	2941	5	1
Williams, Danny	Dundee	23	11	1141	4	1
Hill, Clint	Rangers	23	22	1888	5	1
McEveley, James	Ross County	21	18	1617	9	1
Van der Weg, Kenny	Ross County	33	29	2659	4	1
McHugh, Carl	Motherwell	19	19	1639	5	1
Kiernan, Rob	Rangers	24	24	2130	4	1
O'Halloran, Michael	Rangers	16	6	627	2	1
Lucas, Lee	Motherwell	10	6	578	2	1
Hendrie, Luke	Kilmarnock	32	32	2822	6	1
Gomis, Kevin	Dundee	22	22	1755	4	1
Chow, Tim	Ross County	30	26	2231	8	1
Senderos, Philippe	Rangers	3	3	255	1	1
Cole, Larnell	Inverness CT	21	13	1137	4	1
O'Brien, Jim	Ross County	16	8	781	7	1
Gonçalves, Esmael	Hearts	15	15	1266	3	1
Skondras, Giannis	Hamilton Accies	13	11	997	6	1

PREMIERSHIP YELLOW CARDS		GP	GS	Mins	YC	RC
1 Devlin, Mikey	Hamilton Accies	28	28	2467	12	0
2 Brown, Scott	Celtic	33	33	2913	11	1
2 Shinnie, Graeme	Aberdeen	36	35	3121	11	0
2 McGowan, Paul	Dundee	36	35	3169	11	0
5 Imrie, Douglas	Hamilton Accies	37	36	3188	10	0
5 Dicker, Gary	Kilmarnock	36	36	3239	10	0
5 O'Dea, Darren	Dundee	35	35	3096	10	0
5 Craig, Liam	St Johnstone	36	27	2493	10	0
5 Vigurs, Iain	Inverness CT	32	28	2373	10	0
5 Paton, Paul	St Johnstone	27	22	2053	10	0
11 McEveley, James	Ross County	21	18	1617	9	1
11 Garner, Joe	Rangers	31	21	1891	9	0
13 Gillespie, Grant	Hamilton Accies	31	28	2502	8	0
13 MacKinnon, Darian	Hamilton Accies	33	32	2846	8	2
13 Taylor, Greg	Kilmarnock	34	34	3033	8	1
13 Lasley, Keith	Motherwell	28	25	2104	8	0
13 Davidson, Murray	St Johnstone	23	19	1741	8	0
13 MacLean, Steven	St Johnstone	32	30	2666	8	0
13 McKay, Brad	Inverness CT	28	27	2380	8	0
13 Draper, Ross	Inverness CT	37	35	3033	8	0
13 Tremarco, Carl	Inverness CT	29	29	2375	8	0
13 Donati, Massimo	Hamilton Accies	31	26	2306	8	0
13 Chow, Tim ROS	Ross County	30	26	2231	8	1
24 Osman, Abdul	Partick Thistle	31	30	2577	7	1
24 Crawford, Ali	Hamilton Accies	33	31	2720	7	0
24 Boyce, Liam	Ross County	34	34	2970	7	0
24 Davies, Andrew	Ross County	32	32	2813	7	0
24 Considine, Andrew	Aberdeen	36	36	3193	7	0
24 Igor Rossi	Hearts	20	20	1779	7	0
24 Moult, Louis	Motherwell	31	30	2637	7	0
24 Swanson, Danny	St Johnstone	30	28	2347	7	1
24 Heneghan, Ben	Motherwell	37	37	3330	7	0
24 Sarris, Giorgos	Hamilton Accies	30	30	2655	7	0
24 Tavernier, James	Rangers	36	35	3145	7	0
24 O'Brien, Jim	Ross County	16	8	781	7	1
36 Booth, Callum	Partick Thistle	31	31	2790	6	0
36 Edwards, Ryan	Partick Thistle	38	33	3003	6	0
36 Curran, Craig	Ross County	34	26	2195	6	0
36 Foster, Richard	St Johnstone	34	34	2917	6	1
36 Woods, Martin	Ross County	29	27	2197	6	0
36 Hayes, Jonny	Aberdeen	32	32	2794	6	0
36 Reynolds, Mark	Aberdeen	26	22	1878	6	1
36 Smith, Liam	Hearts	20	12	1345	6	0
36 Walker, Jamie	Hearts	34	28	2484	6	1
36 Etxabeguren, Julen	Dundee	17	14	1306	6	0
36 Kerr, Cameron	Dundee	36	35	3143	6	0
36 McDonald, Scott	Motherwell	35	34	2961	6	1
36 Wotherspoon, David	St Johnstone	33	20	1922	6	0
36 Devine, Daniel	Partick Thistle	30	28	2500	6	1
36 Tait, Richard	Motherwell	25	25	2150	6	0

Ango-Scots 2016/17

Listed below are League appearances made by scots and known scots-eligible players in the top four levels of English

ANGLO-SCOTS 2016/17				League			Cup
Name		Club	Div	Apps	Subs	Gls	Only
Adam	Charlie	Stoke City	Prem	17	7	1	
Aldred	Tom	Blackpool	Lge 2	47	0	2	
Allan	Scott	Rotherham United	Cham	4	6	0	
Andreu	Tony	Norwich City	Cham	0	0	0	x
Anya	Ikechi	Watford	Prem	0	1	0	
Anya	Ikechi	Derby County	Cham	14	12	1	
Archer	Jordan	Millwall	Lge 1	39	0	0	
Bannan	Barry	Sheffield Wednesday	Cham	43	1	1	
Bardsley	Phil	Stoke City	Prem	14	1	0	
Berra	Christophe	Ipswich Town	Cham	44	0	2	
Black	Ian	Shrewsbury Town	Lge 1	14	4	3	
Black	Ian	Blackpool	Lge 2	1	12	0	
Boyd	George	Burnley	Prem	33	3	2	
Boyle	Will	Cheltenham Town	Lge 2	21	2	0	
Bridcutt	Liam	Leeds United	Cham	22	3	0	
Broadfoot	Kirk	Rotherham United	Cham	3	0	0	
Bryson	Craig	Derby County	Cham	23	11	2	
Burke	Oliver	Nottingham Forest	Cham	4	1	4	
Caddis	Paul	Birmingham City	Cham	0	0	0	x
Caddis	Paul	Bury	Lge 1	13	0	0	
Cairney	Tom	Fulham	Cham	45		12	
Cameron	Kyle	Newport County	Lge 2	6	0	0	
OL from Newcastle United							
Clark	Nicky	Bury	Lge 1	2	1	0	
Conway	Craig	Blackburn Rovers	Cham	34	8	6	
Cooper	Liam	Leeds United	Cham	8	3	0	
Cooper	Alex	Cheltenham Town	Lge 2	0	1	0	
Coutts	Paul	Sheffield United	Lge 1	40	3	2	
Cuthbert	Scott	Luton Town	Lge 2	37	1	1	
Davey	Alex	Crawley Town	Lge 2	8	6	0	
Diamond	Zander	Northampton Town	Lge 1	37	2	0	
Dorrans	Graeme	Norwich City	Cham	22	1	6	
Erwin	Lee	Oldham Athletic	Lge 1	25	9	8	
OL from Leeds Utd							
Feruz	Islam	Swindon Town	Lge 1	4	0	0	
Findlay	Stuart	Newcastle United	Cham	0	0	0	x
Fleck	John	Sheffield United	Lge 1	41	3	4	
Fletcher	Darren	West Bromwich Albion	Prem	34	1	2	
Fletcher	Steven	Sheffield Wednesday	Cham	23	12	10	
Flynn	Ryan	Oldham Athletic	Lge 1	31	6	1	
Forsyth	Craig	Derby County	Cham	3	0	1	
Fox	Danny	Nottingham Forest	Cham	22	1	0	
Fraser	Ryan	AFC Bournemouth	Prem	19	9	3	
Fulton	Jay	Swansea City	Prem	9	2	0	
Fulton	Ryan	Chesterfield	Lge 1	26	0	0	
Furlong	Conor	Milton Keynes Dons	Lge 1	0	0	0	x
Gallagher	Paul	Preston North End	Cham	28	3	1	
Gilks	Matt	Wigan Athletic	Cham	0	0	0	
Goodwillie	David	Plymouth Argyle	Lge 2	5	11	1	
Greer	Gordon	Blackburn Rovers	Cham	19	2	0	
Grimmer	Jack	Fulham	Cham	0	0	0	x
Grimmer	Jack	Shrewsbury Town	Lge 1	22	2	0	
Gunner	Callum	Swindon Town	Lge 1	0	0	0	
Hanley	Grant	Newcastle United	Cham	5	5	1	
Hendrie	Stephen	Blackburn Rovers	Cham	2	2	0	
OL from West Ham							
Hendry	Jack	Wigan Athletic	Cham	0	0	0	
Hendry	Jack	Milton Keynes Dons	Lge 1	6	1	0	
OL from Wigan Ath							
Hutton	Akan	Aston Villa	Cham	18	1	0	
Iacovitti	Alex	Nottingham Forest	Cham	2	0	0	
Iacovitti	Alex	Mansfield Town	Lge 2	4	4	0	
OL from Nottingham Forest							
Jakubiak	Alex	Wycombe Wanderers	Lge 2	9		1	
Johnstone	Denny	Colchester United	Lge 2	15	13	2	
Jones	James	Crewe Alexandra	Lge 2	42	3	10	
Kelly	Sean	AFC Wimbledon	Lge 1	22	4	2	
Kelly	Liam	Leyton Orient	Lge 2	19	2	4	

Kennedy	Matthew	Cardiff City	Cham	0	2	0	
Kennedy	Matty	Plymouth Argyle	Lge2	15		5	
Kettings	Chris	Oldham Athletic	Lge 1	0	0	0	
King	Adam	Southend United	Lge 1	5	2	0	
Kingsley	Stephen	Swansea City	Prem	12	1	0	
Love	Donald	Sunderland	Prem	5	6	0	
MacDonald	Alex	Oxford United	Lge 1	18	5	1	
MacDonald	Alex	Mansfield Town	Lge 2	13	5	1	
Mackail-Smith	Craig	Peterborough United	Lge 1	13	5	5	
Mackail-Smith	Craig	Luton Town	Lge 2	0	2	0	
Mackie	Jamie	QPR	Cham	11	7	1	
MacLeod	Lewis	Brentford	Cham	10	3	0	
Maguire	Chris	Oxford United	Lge 1	40	2	13	
Maloney	Shaun	Hull City	Prem	2	7	1	
Marshall	David	Hull City	Prem	16	0	0	
Marshall	David	Cardiff City	Cham	4	0	0	
Martin	Chris	Fulham	Cham	27	4	10	
Martin	Russell	Norwich City	Cham	36	1	1	
May	Stevie	Preston North End	Cham	2	2	1	
McAlister	Jim	Blackpool	Lge 2	18	4	0	
McArthur	James	Crystal Palace	Prem	24	5	5	
McBurnie	Oliver	Swansea City	Prem	0	5	0	
McCallum	Marc	Plymouth Argyle	Lge 2	2	2	0	
McCormack	Ross	Aston Villa	Cham	13	7	3	
McCormack	Ross	Nottingham Forest	Cham	3	4	1	
McDonald	Kevin	Fulham	Cham	43	0	3	
McGinn	Paul	Chesterfield	Lge 1	17	1	1	
McGinn	Stephen	Wycombe Wanderers	Lge 2	5	0	0	
McGregor	Allan	Cardiff City	Cham	19	0	0	
McKay	Paul	Leeds United	Cham	0	0	0	x
McKee	Joe	Carlisle United	Lge 2	4	0	0	
McLaughlin	Jon	Burton Albion	Cham	43	0	0	
McNulty	Marc	Bradford City	Lge 1	5	10	1	
McNulty	James	Rochdale	Lge 1	23	2		
McNulty	Mark	Sheffield United	Lge 1	1	3	0	
Miller	Gary	Plymouth Argyle	Lge 2	37	4	0	
Morrison	James	West Bromwich Albion	Prem	16	13	5	
Muirhead	Robbie	Milton Keynes Dons	Lge 1	12	7	2	
Mulgrew	Charlie	Blackburn Rovers	Cham	26	2	3	
Murphy	Jamie	Brighton	Cham	18	12	2	
Naismith	Steven	Norwich City	Cham	21	9	5	
Naismith	Kai	Portsmouth	Lge 2	22	15	13	
Ness	Jamie	Scunthorpe United	Lge 1	8	3	0	
O'Brien	Jim	Shrewsbury Town	Lge 1	14	4	0	
O'Donnell	Stephen	Luton Town	Lge 2	27	3	1	
Palmer	Liam	Sheffield Wednesday	Cham	15	6	0	
Phillips	Matt	West Bromwich Albion	Prem	26	1	4	
Rhodes	Jordan	Middlesbrough	Prem	2	4	0	
Rhodes	Jordan	Sheffield Wednesday	Cham	13	4	3	
Ritchie	Matt	Newcastle United	Cham	40	2	12	
Robertson	Andrew	Hull City	Prem	31	2	1	
Robertson	Chris	AFC Wimbledon	Lge 1	13		1	
Robertson	Clark	Blackpool	Lge 2	47	0	1	
Ruddy	Jack	Bury	Lge 1				
Russell	Jonny	Derby County	Cham	29	7	2	
Scougall	Stefan	Sheffield United	Lge 1	6	19	4	
Shearer	Scott	Mansfield Town	Lge 2	25	0	0	
Slater	Craig	Colchester United	Lge 2	23	5	3	
Snodgrass	Robert	West Ham United	Prem	8	7	0	
Snodgrass	Robert	Hull City	Prem	19	1	7	
Spence	Kyle	Coventry City	Lge 1	0	1	0	
Stewart	Greg	Birmingham City	Cham	6	15	0	
Taylor-Sinclair	Aaron	Doncaster Rovers	Lge 2	4	0	0	
Wallace	Ross	Sheffield Wednesday	Cham	35	7	5	
Wallace	Murray	Scunthorpe United	Lge 1	44	0	0	
Watt	Tony	Charlton Athletic	Lge 1	9	7	2	
Whittaker	Steven	Norwich City	Cham	7	5	0	
Wylde	Gregg	Millwall	Lge 1	2	3	0	
Wylde	Gregg	Northampton Town	Lge 1	6	6	1	
Young	Jordan	Swindon Town	Lge 1	1	1	0	

The "Pyramid"

The divide between Scottish League Football and "Non League" football used to be clear and distinct. The Scottish League (and later the Scottish Premier League) were a closed shop. The only opportunities for clubs to gain entry were through expanding the size of the leagues or if one of the member clubs folded. Access was gained through an application and election process.

After Ferranti Thistle were elected in 1974 (changing their name to Meadowbank in the process), there were no further vacancies until 1994. Re-organisation of the League structure left two vacancies and the newly merged Caledonian Thistle and Ross County were elected. Six years later a further re-organisation created two more places. Perhaps enthused by the success of Inverness and Ross County, the SFL clubs chose two more Highland League clubs to join the fold – Elgin City and Peterhead.

In 2002 Airdrieonians FC closed down. In the election that followed it was Gretna who were successful, ahead of a reformed paper-based Airdrie United club. Undeterred, the men behind Airdrie United bought out struggling Clydebank, changed their name to Airdrie United, and transplanted them from West Dunbartonshire to North Lanarkshire. Indeed, by being unsuccessful in the first ballot, they actually moved straight into a higher division than they would have it they had been successful!

Gretna's meteoric rise was followed by an equally meteoric fall. By 2008 they had folded. During the early 2000s Edinburgh-based Spartans had emerged as a force in non-league football. The power of the Highland League had been weakened by the loss of five of their top clubs to the Scottish League, and it was Spartans who took over the mantle of Cup giant killers. They also had plans for a magnificent new stadium in north Edinburgh.

Unfortunately for Spartans the 2008 vacancy came at a bad time. Their ground was one year away from completion and the club had upset some parties in Scottish Football with a rather over-bearing campaign. Annan Athletic were elected to fill the vacancy in the Scottish League.

This led to a clamour for a more merit-based system of choosing League members and also for an end to the "closed shop" of League football.

However, one major problem was the fragmented system of football that existed below the Scottish League. In the Highlands and Aberdeen area the Highland League was dominant. In the far South West the largely Amateur South of Scotland League was the top level of local football. Both these were "Senior" Leagues. In the East, there was a Senior East of Scotland League in Edinburgh and the Borders. However, over the most populous parts of Scotland there was effectively no Senior non-league football – the Junior game was predominant.

Junior football was a misnomer. There were no age restrictions and it had a mixture of semi-professional and amateur clubs. Across Ayrshire, Renfrewshire, Glasgow, Dunbartonshire, Lanarkshire, Stirlingshire, Fife, the Lothians, Perthshire and Angus it was the strongest level of football outside the Scottish League. In the North Junior football was very much the lesser partner to the Highland League. In its heyday Junior football attracted enormous crowds. Even in the early 21st Century the top clubs could attract decent attendances and often paid wages that were way in excess of lower Scottish League clubs.

In the early 2000s the Juniors re-organised into three regions, North, West and East. Each had its own pyramid system with promotion to the Regional Super League. There was no advancement from there and no apparent wish for it.

Junior and Senior Non League football were two separate worlds. Senior Non League clubs, some through historical accident, participated in the qualifying rounds of the Scottish Cup. Some played on roped off public parks - grounds that would have been rejected by the Juniors. From 2007 the SFA invited four Junior clubs per season to enter the Scottish Cup – the three Regional Super League champions and the winners of the Scottish Junior Cup. The Junior entrants showed that they were the better of most Senior non league clubs and a match for the best. Both Auchinleck Talbot and Irvine Meadow had great Cup runs, and some Senior clubs suffered crushing defeats at the hands of Junior opposition.

Changes in the leadership at the SFA helped lead to a move towards creating a pyramid system. It was proposed that a Lowland League be formed, to run in tandem with the Highland League. Rather than taking a lead role in creating the Lowland League, the SFA allowed it to evolve. The big break for the Lowland League came in 2013 with the amalgamation of the Scottish Premier League and the Scottish Football League. The newly formed SPFL agreed that from 2014/15 the bottom club would play off against the winners of a match between the Highland and Lowland League Champions with a place in the SPFL at stake.

The Lowland League was set up at very short notice. The Scottish Junior FA did nothing to encourage clubs to take an interest. The vast majority were entirely happy to continue in their own set-up which served them well. They had no ambitions to join the SPFL.

The Lowland League started in 2013 with its membership coming from the East and South of Scotland Leagues and just one club from the West of Scotland, former Amateur team East Kilbride FC. In 2014 two more teams were added including BSC Glasgow, a youth club starting their first ever adult side. The major Junior clubs still showed no interest whatsoever. A few smaller Junior clubs did indicate a degree of interest but it never translated into any concrete applications.

The "Pyramid" that had been created was fraught with problems. The Highland League refused to reduce in size from eighteen to sixteen and refused to countenance automatic promotion / relegation from below. Many of the Lowland League clubs faced large bills for ground improvements – membership from 2015 onwards was tied into the SFA's club licensing scheme.

To be members of the Lowland or Highland Leagues clubs had to be in possession of a licence. The process of applying for a licence was not restricted to members of these Leagues. Two Junior clubs, Linlithgow Rose and Banks o' Dee did so, were successful, and thereby became full SFA members and eligible to play in the Scottish Cup every year. However, as their applications were being processed the rules were changed so that achieving a licence meant committing to the SFA's Pyramid (i.e. the Highland or Lowland Leagues). The current situation is that any club, Senior or Junior, seeking a licence must join the Highland, Lowland, East of Scotland or South of Scotland League.

The Lowland League has embraced the concept of a Pyramid by opening up relegation / promotion. The winners of the East of Scotland and South of Scotland Leagues, subject to them having licences, play off and the winners will then meet the bottom team in the Lowland League. In 2015 and 2016 neither of the East or South League winners were licensed. The Lowland League expanded further by adding Cumbernauld Colts, Civil Service Strollers and Hawick Royal Albert.

BSC Glasgow, East Kilbride and Cumbernauld Colts operate within the geographical area that is dominated by Junior football. However, this effectively leaves them with two-thirds of Scotland's population as a catchment area for players. Financially they are competing with the top Junior sides in recruiting quality players. The irony of this is that some of the original "mover and shakers" for a Lowland League – Spartans and Whitehill Welfare for example, are in danger of being outmuscled by the new kids on the block. Preston Athletic were relegated out of the Lowland League in 2017.

Edinburgh City won the Lowland League in 2015 but lost the play off against Highland League Champions Brora Rangers. Brora then lost to Montrose and the status quo was maintained. Just months earlier Brora had stated that they did not want promotion to the SPFL but that they would "reluctantly" accept it in the event of them being successful in the play offs.

City won the Lowland League again in 2015/16 and then defeated Cove Rangers the Highland League Champions. The Play Off against East Stirlingshire saw the Lowland League Champions prevail - they were promoted and the Shire lost their SPFL status. At the top end, at least, the pyramid could said to be working.

However, at the bottom end of the Lowland League things were not so healthy. Leith Athletic won the East of Scotland League but were not licensed. St Cuthbert Wanderers were winners of the South of Scotland League - by all accounts they could have been licensed but work was delayed and they did not qualify for promotion. The feeling amongst many was that the club did not want to go up to the Lowland League. This meant that Threave Rovers, bottom of the Lowland League, could have been reprieved but they resigned in order to return to the South of Scotland League.

In 2016/17 East Kilbride won the Lowland League by some distance from East Stirlingshire. They defeated Buckie Thistle in the first play-off but lost out to Cowdenbeath on penalty kicks.

The leading clubs in the East of Scotland League, Leith Athletic and Lothian Thistle Hutchison Vale, were not licensed. It was clear early on in the season that one of them would win the League—Lothian Thistle proving successful. Things were different in the South of Scotland League—licensed club Wigtown & Bladnoch looked odds-on to win the league until they suffered an amazing late collapse. Edusport Academy, a licensed club but quite unlike any other, won the title and were promoted.

The biggest question as 2016/17 came to an end was if any Junior clubs might be tempted to jump ship to the Seniors. The attraction of gaining a licence and an annual place in the Scottish Cup was enough to convince East Super League Champions Kelty Hearts to take the plunge. With generous sponsors, superb facilities and a strong infrastructure they applied to join the East of Scotland League. Clearly they hope to win that at the first attempt and have stated that their aim is to progress upwards to the

SPFL.

Rumours persisted that there might be major changes at the end of 2017/18 to accommodate "Colts" clubs, amongst other priorities. Kelty may feel that they have given themselves a head start over other Junior clubs who might be tempted to make the same move. Bo'ness United, Linlithgow Rose and Bonnyrigg Rose have all been mentioned in this context.

Meanwhile, two of the smaller Senior clubs with no ambitions for SPFL football, Easthouses and Craigroyston, moved to the Juniors.

So, is there any possibility of a real pyramid happening, involving Senior and Junior clubs. The first point to make is that the vast majority of clubs have nothing to gain from this as they are happy playing at the level in which they operate. They have no ambitions to join the SPFL. It seems South of Scotland League clubs have no ambition to join the Lowland League. In the North the Highland League continues as a closed shop—if any club north of the Tay wanted to replicate Kelty's move they would be unable to do so.

The Junior FA has adopted the ostrich position over the last decade or so. At their AGM they seemed unconcerned that one of their Champion clubs was leaving. Mind you, if others follow they will probably be from the East—could we eventually see a split with East clubs belonging to the Lowland / East of Scotland Leagues and the Juniors being concentrated in the West?

Edinburgh City have shown that it is possible to bridge the gap between the Lowland League and the SPFL. East Stirlingshire, aided by a parachute payment, were relatively successful in the Lowland League. Realistically only East Kilbride, East Stirlingshire, Spartans, BSC Glasgow, Cumbernauld Colts, Gala Fairydean Rovers and Kelty Hearts of the current Pyramid clubs could aspire to SPFL membership. In the North there are doubts as to whether any clubs, apart from Cove Rangers, are keen on moving upwards.

The complicated and dysfunctional system that we have evolved to seems to be massively unsettling and disruptive to suit the ambitions of a small number of clubs.

Club Licensing

Club Licensing Status as at June 2017 is shown below. (source SFA website)

CLUB	Current Status	Last Review	Next Review	Ground	1st Team	Legal / Admin Finance	UEFA Licence	Youth
Premiership								
Aberdeen	Silver	Apr-17	2018	Silver	Gold	Gold	Granted	Silver
Celtic	Platinum	Apr-17	2018	Gold	Gold	Gold	Granted	Platinum
Dundee	Bronze	Apr-17	2018	Bronze	Silver	Bronze	Granted	Bronze 2
Hamilton Accies	Silver	Apr-17	2018	Silver	Silver	Silver	Granted	Silver
Hearts	Bronze	Apr-17	2018	Bronze	Gold	Bronze	Granted	Silver
Hibernian	Silver	May-17	2018	Gold	Silver	Gold	N/A	Silver
Kilmarnock	Silver	Apr-17	2018	Silver	Silver	Gold	Granted	Silver
Motherwell	Silver	Apr-17	2018	Silver	Silver	Gold	Granted	Silver
Partick Thistle	Silver	Apr-17	2018	Silver	Silver	Gold	Granted	Silver
Rangers	Silver	Apr-17	2018	Gold	Silver	Silver	Granted	Platinum
Ross County	Bronze	Apr-17	2018	Silver	Gold	Gold	Granted	Bronze 2
St Johnstone	Bronze	Apr-17	2018	Bronze	Gold	Gold	Granted	Bronze 2
Championship								
Brechin City	Bronze	Feb-17	2018	Bronze	Bronze	Bronze	N/A	N/A
Dumbarton	Bronze	May-17	2018	Bronze	Silver	Bronze	N/A	Bronze 2
Dundee United	Bronze	May-17	2018	Silver	Silver	Bronze	N/A	Silver
Dunfermline Athletic	Entry	Aug-16	2017	Silver	Silver	Entry	N/A	Fife Elite Acad
Falkirk	Silver	Feb-17	2018	Silver	Silver	Gold	N/A	Forth Valley El Acad
Greenock Morton	Bronze	Oct-16	2017	Bronze	Silver	Bronze	N/A	Bronze 2
Inverness CT	Bronze	Apr-17	2018	Bronze	Silver	Silver	Refused	Bronze 2
Livingston	Bronze	Aug-16	2017	Bronze	Bronze	Bronze	N/A	Bronze 2
QOS	Bronze	Feb-17	2018	Bronze	Bronze	Gold	N/A	Bronze 1
St Mirren	Gold	May-17	2018	Gold	Gold	Gold	N/A	Gold
League One								
Airdrieonians	Bronze	Aug-16	2017	Silver	Bronze	Bronze	N/A	Bronze 2
Albion Rovers	Entry	May-17	2018	Entry	Entry	Bronze	N/A	N/A
Alloa Athletic	Bronze	May-17	2018	Bronze	Bronze	Bronze	N/A	Bronze 2
Arbroath	Bronze	Feb-17	2018	Bronze	Silver	Bronze	N/A	N/A
Ayr United	Bronze	Aug-16	2017	Bronze	Bronze	Bronze	N/A	Silver
east Fife	Bronze	May-17	2018	Bronze	Silver	Bronze	N/A	Fife Elite Acad
Forfar Athletic	Bronze	Feb-17	2018	Bronze	Bronze	Bronze	N/A	N/A
Queen's Park	Bronze	Aug-16	2017	Gold	Silver	Silver	N/A	Bronze 2
Raith Rovers	Bronze	May-16	2017	Bronze	Bronze	Bronze	N/A	Fife Elite Acad
Stranraer	Bronze	May-17	2018	Bronze	Bronze	Bronze	N/A	Bronze 1
League Two								
Annan Athletic	Bronze	Feb-17	2018	Bronze	Bronze	Bronze	N/A	N/A
Berwick Rangers	Bronze	May-17	2018	Bronze	Bronze	Bronze	N/A	N/A
Clyde	Bronze	Aug-16	2017	Bronze	Bronze	Bronze	N/A	N/A
Cowdenbeath	Bronze	May-17	2018	Bronze	Bronze	Bronze	N/A	Fife Elite Acad
Edinburgh City	Entry	Aug-16	2017	Entry	Entry	Entry	N/A	N/A
Elgin City	Bronze	Aug-16	2017	Bronze	Bronze	Gold	N/A	Bronze 2
Montrose	Entry	Aug-16	2017	Bronze	Entry	Entry	N/A	Bronze 1
Peterhead	Bronze	May-17	2018	Bronze	Bronze	Silver	N/A	N/A
Stenhousemuir	Bronze	May-17	2018	Bronze	Bronze	Bronze	N/A	Forth Val El Acad
Stirling Albion	Bronze	Aug-16	2017	Bronze	Bronze	Silver	N/A	Bronze 2

Highland League								
Brora Rangers	Entry	Feb-17	2017	Entry	Entry	Entry	N/A	Entry
Buckie Thistle	Entry	Aug-16	2017	Entry	Entry	Entry	N/A	Entry
Clachnacuddin	Entry	Oct-16	2017	Entry	Entry	Entry	N/A	Entry
Cove Rangers	Entry	Aug-16	2017	Entry	Entry	Entry	N/A	Entry
Deveronvale	Entry	Aug-16	2017	Entry	Entry	Entry	N/A	N/A
Formartine United	Entry	Oct-16	2017	Entry	Entry	Entry	N/A	Entry
Forres Mechanics	Entry	May-16	2017	Entry	Entry	Entry	N/A	Entry
Fort William	Entry	Oct-16	2017	Entry	Entry	Entry	N/A	Entry
Fraserburgh	Entry	May-17	2018	Entry	Entry	Entry	N/A	Entry
Huntly	Entry	Aug-16	2017	Entry	Entry	Entry	N/A	Entry
Inverurie Loco Works	Entry	Feb-17	2018	Entry	Entry	Entry	N/A	Entry
Keith	Entry	May-17	2018	Entry	Entry	Entry	N/A	Entry
Lossiemouth	Entry	Aug-16	2017	Entry	Entry	Entry	N/A	Entry
Nairn County	Entry	May-16	2017	Bronze	Entry	Entry	N/A	Entry
Rothes	Entry	Aug-16	2017	Entry	Entry	Entry	N/A	Entry
Strathspey Thistle	Entry	Aug-16	2017	Entry	Entry	Entry	N/A	Entry
Turriff United	Entry	Apr-17	2018	Entry	Entry	Entry	N/A	Entry
Wick Academy	Entry	Oct-16	2017	Entry	Entry	Entry	N/A	Entry
Lowland League								
BSC Glasgow	Entry	Oct-16	2017	Bronze	Entry	Entry	N/A	N/A
Civil Service Strollers	Entry	Oct-16	2017	Entry	Entry	Entry	N/A	N/A
Cumbernauld Colts	Entry	May-17	2018	Bronze	Entry	Entry	N/A	N/A
Dalbeattie Star	Entry	Oct-16	2017	Entry	Entry	Entry	N/A	N/A
East Kilbride	Entry	Oct-16	2017	Entry	Entry	Entry	N/A	Entry
East Stirlingshire	Entry	May-17	2018	Entry	Entry	Entry	N/A	Forth Vall El Acad
Edinburgh University	Entry	May-17	2018	Entry	Entry	Entry	N/A	N/A
Edusport Academy	Entry	Aug-16	2017	Entry	Entry	Entry	N/A	N/A
Gala Fairydean Rovers	Entry	Aug-16	2017	Entry	Entry	Entry	N/A	N/A
Gretna 2008	Entry	May-17	2018	Entry	Entry	Entry	N/A	N/A
Hawick Royal Albert	Entry	Aug-16	2017	Entry	Entry	Entry	N/A	N/A
Selkirk	Entry	Aug-16	2017	Entry	Entry	Entry	N/A	N/A
Spartans	Bronze	Aug-16	2017	Bronze	Bronze	Bronze	N/A	N/A
University of Stirling	Entry	Oct-16	2017	Entry	Entry	Entry	N/A	N/A
Vale of Leithen	Entry	Oct-16	2017	Entry	Entry	Entry	N/A	N/A
Whitehill Welfare	Entry	Aug-16	2017	Entry	Entry	Entry	N/A	N/A
East of Scotland league								
Burntisland Shipyard	Entry	Oct-16	2017	Entry	Entry	Entry	N/A	N/A
Coldstream	Entry	May-17	Aug-17	Entry	Entry	Entry	N/A	N/A
Preston Athletic	Entry	Aug-16	2017	Entry	Entry	Entry	N/A	N/A
South of Scotland League								
Newton Stewart	Refused	May-17	Aug-17	Refused	Entry	Entry	N/A	N/A
St Cuthbert Wanderers	Entry	May-17	2018	Entry	Entry	Entry	N/A	N/A
Threave Rovers	Entry	Aug-16	2017	Entry	Entry	Entry	N/A	N/A
Wigtown & Bladnoch	Entry	Aug-16	2017	Entry	Entry	Entry	N/A	N/A
North Caledonian League								
Golspie Sutherland	Entry	Oct-16	2017	Entry	Entry	Entry	N/A	N/A
Junior Leagues								
Banks o' Dee	Entry	Feb-16	2017	Entry	Entry	Entry	N/A	N/A
Girvan	Entry	May-17	2018	Entry	Entry	Entry	N/A	N/A
Linlithgow Rose	Entry	Aug-16	2017	Entry	Entry	Entry	N/A	N/A
Amateur Leagues								
Glasgow University	Entry	May-17	2018	Entry	Entry	Entry	N/A	N/A

Junior Football

The structure and organisation of Junior football is quite complex and those not familiar with the Junior game can easily be confused by it. The Scottish Junior Football Association is the parent body for Junior football in Scotland. The name Junior does not imply any age-restriction - the use of the term Junior simply relates to the fact that in late Victorian times this grade of football was played on amore local basis than Senior football.

The Scottish Junior Cup is the only competition that is run by the SJFA. It was first contested in 1886/7 and is regarded as the "holy grail" of the Junior game. The SJFA acts as a parent body for the 3 Junior Regions, East, West and North.

This tri-partite system dates from the early 2000s. Prior to that, from 1968, there were six Junior regions - North, Tayside, Fife, Lothians, Central and Ayrshire. Prior to 1968 there were various County and District Junior Leagues and Cups, each of which was run independently.

The three Regions are responsible for League and Cup fixtures. The SJFA acts as a point of appeal if clubs dispute any decisions made by their Regional JFA. The number of Cups organised by the Regions has been greatly reduced in recent years. It is not so long since a club could participate in seven or eight different Cup competitions, in addition to their League games and the Scottish Junior Cup.

Junior football has been careful to guard its independence. In 2007 the Scottish Football Association decided to allow four Junior clubs to participate in the Scottish Cup each year - the three Regional Champions and the Scottish Junior Cup holders. They joined the Scottish Premier League, Scottish League and Senior Non League clubs in the draw. The results show that the top Junior clubs are amongst the most powerful "Non League" clubs in Scotland.

Attempts have been made to merge the Senior and Junior "Non League" games in Scotland. The Senior Highland League has existed for over one hundred years and more recently the SFA created a Lowland League. Junior clubs were invited to apply but none did so. However, in 2017 Kelty Hearts, the East Region Champions, resigned from Junior football to join the East of Scotland League, hoping to rise up and achieve SPFL status.

Why have more Junior clubs not become involved? Most have no ambitions at all to be part of a national pyramid system. They idea of the Lowland League is to create a pathway to promotion to the Scottish Professional Football League. So far only Kelty has seen this as a journey they wish to embark on although it is rumoured that more from the East may be interested in following.

Junior football thrives on local competition and rivalries. Crowds at the top level of Junior football reach a decent level, attracted by the cheap admission prices an the lack of regulation. The prospect of promotion to the lower reaches of the SPFL is not an attractive one for Junior clubs.

This does not mean that some clubs do not want to improve facilities and infrastructure. Linlithgow Rose and Banks o' Dee are excellent examples. They completed all the work necessary to become SFA licensed clubs which means they are now admitted to the Scottish Cup on an annual basis. However, during the process of their application the goalposts were moved to include a commitment to the principle of a pyramid system. This has discouraged other Junior clubs from taking the same path—in order to apply for a licence kelty had to move to the East of Scotland (Senior) league.

Junior football is the main grade of "Non League" football played in Scotland. It dominates the most populous areas and generates considerable local pride and interest.

The Annual General Meeting of the Scottish Junior FA takes place on the third Saturday in June. All fixtures require to be completed by then. The AGM is held in each of the three regions on a rotational basis. All decisions are made on the basis of one club one vote and all motions are submitted by the clubs themselves. The AGM also votes on the admission of any new clubs to the SJFA. All new clubs making application for membership of the Scottish Junior Football Association must have a ground complying with the following requirements:
(a) Must be enclosed with a suitable fence to keep spectators from gaining entry to the ground without payment;
(b) Must have a pavilion situated inside the ground and closely adjacent to playing field with separate stripping accommodation for home and visiting teams and for match official, all with adequate toilet and washing facilities;
(c) The playing field must be properly fenced to keep spectators from encroaching on the field;
(d) Grounds and facilities must satisfy the inspection of the Scottish Junior Football Association. Ground inspection fee of £40 must accompany application for membership and clubs will be responsible for expenses incurred for any further inspections required.

No new clubs applied for membership in 2017. Harthill Royal returned from a spell in abeyance and will compete in 2017/18. Fochabers Juniors resigned. The concept of "abeyance" is not uncommon in Junior football. If a club faces difficulties of some sort they may opt to become non-playing members. Some will return and some will fold.

One feature that differentiates Junior football from the other grades is the Reinstatement rule. Any player who has been senior (i.e. with an SPFL, Highland, Lowland, East or South of Scotland club) must be reinstated to play Junior football. This involves paying a fee but is otherwise now a formality. At one time players could only go from Senior to Junior if they had previously been Junior. A young lad who joined a Senior side without having played Junior football would be debarred from playing at Junior level. To get round this professional clubs used to register a player with a Junior side for one day, then sign him from them, so that he could go back Junior if he failed to make the grade. The best example of this would be former Rangers and Scotland player John Greig, apparently signed from Whitburn Juniors, although he never played for them.

SCOTTISH JUNIOR FOOTBALL ASSOCIATION

HON. PRESIDENT
Peter Gardiner, Ex President SFA

HON. VICE-PRESIDENTS
David Roy, Past President
Matt Spiers, Ayrshire Region
Ron Ross, Fife Region
J. Gordon Law,Past President
Jack Whitehead, North Region
John Reilly, Past President
Joseph P. Black, Assistant Secretary
John Brodie, Former Treasurer
Robert Smith, Past President
J.Scott Robertson, Secretary, West Region
George Rose, Past President
Tom Anderson, Past President
George Morton, Past President

PRESIDENT
Harry Lawrie (Fauldhouse United)

VICE PRESIDENT
Felix McKenna (St Anthonys)

SECRETARY
Tom Johnston

ASST. SECRETARY / TREASURER
Iain McQueen

S.J.F.A. OFFICES
HAMPDEN PARK, GLASGOW G42 9DD
TELEPHONE: 0141 620 4560
FAX: 0141 620 4561
email: scottishjuniorfa@scottish-football.com

AUDITORS
Peter Deans Chartered Accountants, Denny

MANAGEMENT COMMITTEE

WEST REGION
Colin Chisholm, (Auchinleck Talbot)
Jim Wilson, (Vale of Clyde)
Matt Bamford, (Clydebank)
Scott Wilson (Cambuslang Rangers)

EAST REGION
William L. Donaldson M.B.E., J.P., (Linlithgow Rose)
Douglas Hynd (Oakley United)
Ian Sherlock, (Whitburn)
James Provan, (Broxburn Athletic)

NORTH REGION
Norman Mackay, (Dyce Juniors)
George Rose, (New Elgin)

REGIONAL SECRETARIES

WEST REGION
SECRETARY
J. Scott Robertson
email: jayessar@sky.com

ASSISTANT SECRETARY
John Fyfe
email: Assistant-Secretary@West-Region-SJFA.co.uk

EAST REGION
SECRETARY
John Reilly,
email: rjohnreilly18@yahoo.co.uk

ASSISTANT SECRETARY
Syd McAlpine
email: sydmcalpine@hotmail.co.uk

NORTH REGION
SECRETARY
Richard Easton
email: richardeaston5@aol.com

ASSISTANT SECRETARY
Angela Cumming
email: angelacumming@hotmail.co.uk

FIFE AND LOTHIANS ASSOCIATION
SECRETARY
Mark Stevens
email: fifeandlothiansecretary@outlook.com

At the 2017 AGM, held in Perth on June 17, Felix McKenna became the new President of the SJFA.

Some Interesting Points from the SJFA Rules

ALTERATIONS TO SJFA RULES

Any proposed amendments must be sent to the SJFA by the end of April each year, prior to the AGM.

If any new rule is passed it cannot be rescinded for at least two years. If a proposed change is defeated, no similar motion can be proposed for at least two years.

PUBLIC LIABILITY INSURANCE

All clubs must have adequate Public Liability Insurance, intimated to the SJFA by July 1st each year.

MEMBERSHIP FEE
SJFA membership costs clubs £35 per year.

MANAGEMENT COMMITTEE
Each Region is entitled to one member for each 20 clubs or part thereof.

SCOTTISH JUNIOR CUP COMPETITION RULES
If a club is unable to fulfil a home tie at its own ground it must use a suitable venue within the same Region and within ten miles of their home ground. Suitable venue means a ground that efficiently prevents unpaid public access and has adequate changing / toilet facilities. If a club cannot meet these requirements then the fixture will be reversed. In neither team's ground meets the requirements the SJFA will determine the venue.

Any club who scratches or withdraws from the Cup will be banned from the next season's competition.

The winners and runners up both receive 20 medals from the SJFA.

The home club must pay a guarantee to visiting clubs in Scottish Junior Cup ties, as follows:

Distance travelled (one way)	
0-25 miles	£55
26-50 miles	£95
51-75 miles	£120
76-100 miles	£170
101-150 miles	£220
151-200 miles	£270
201-250 miles	£310
251-300 miles	£340

Clubs travelling 201 miles or more, will get an additional sum, worth 50% of the above, from the SJFA.

COMPETITIONS
Every competition organised by one of the Regions or any other combination of clubs (e.g. the Fife & Lothians JFA) must have a permit. These are obtained from the SJFA at a cost of £3 per competition, or £1 if the competition has fewer than seven entrants.

All Friendly matches require a permit, costing £3. The SFA appoint referees for all such matches.

MATCHES / PLAYERS
No club is required to play on a Sunday, other than in the Semi Final and Finals of the Scottish Junior Cup. If both clubs agree to a Sunday date for other games than that is allowed but no player can be penalised for refusing to take part.

Any player previously signed for a Senior club on a Professional, Non – Contract or Amateur form must be reinstated before they can play in a Junior game – even as a trialist. If a player does get reinstated to play for a Junior club then that reinstatement lapses after 14 days if they have not been signed by that Junior club.

No club can have more than 25 signed players at any one time, plus 20 youth players.

TEMPORARY TRANSFERS
Not allowed between clubs in the same League division. Clubs limited to signing four players on loan during one season.

PROTESTS
For a Cup tie to be replayed, one of the following must have occurred:
Playing a Senior player (i.e. not reinstated)
Playing a suspended player
Playing a player registered with another Junior club
Playing an un-registered player
Playing a player who has appeared already in the Cup for another club (cup-tied)

Protests must be made by recorded delivery letter, postmarked no more than 3 days after the match and sent to the opposing club Sevretary and the SJFA Secretary. Fee of £50 not returnable in event of protest being dismissed. Meeting to be held within 7 days of receipt of protest to determine outcome.

Scottish Junior Football Club Directory

NIOR CLUB SECRETARIES AND OTHER CLUB DETAILS
revised on SJFA website, June 2017)

erdeen East End
Brian Malcolm, 70 Cove Gardens, Cove Bay, Aberdeen,
12 3QR Tel: (H) 01224 896784 (M) 07717227951
ail: b.malcolm@sky.com
contact: Jim Kirkwood Tel: (M) 07423062639
ail: kirkyfootball18@hotmail.co.uk
ound: New Advocates Park, Aberdeen, AB24 1RG Tel: 01224
3977

erdeen University
Paul Spence, 81 Sunnyside Road, Aberdeen, AB24 3LT Tel:
07922319513
ail: paul.stephen.spence.13@aberdeen.ac.uk
contact: James Macarthur Tel: (M) 07780463679
ail: avs033@abdn.ac.uk
ound: Hillhead Centre, Don Street, Old Aberdeen, Aberdeen,
245 1UH Tel:
ound formerly known as Keith Park

nbank United
Scott Taylor, 35 Castlehill Road, Ayr, KA7 2HY
: (H) 01292 262339 (W) 01292 261384 (M) 07870649413
ail: scott@lcshopfitters.co.uk
contact: John Cree Tel: (H) 01292 521319 (B) 01292 264115
07947194411
ail: grace@lcshopfitters.co.uk
ound: New Pebble Park, Weston Avenue, Annbank, KA6 5EE
:

broath Victoria
Neil Hardie, 73 Keptie Street, Arbroath, DD11 3AN
: (H) 01241 876326 (W) 01307 473267 (M) 07774030028
ail: neilhardievics@btinternet.com
. contact: Russell Ruxton Tel: (H) 01241 872855 (M)
746024889
ail:
ound: Ogilvy Park, Cairnie Loan, Arbroath, DD11 4DS Tel:

deer Thistle
Peter McBlain, 4 Darg Road, Stevenston, KA20 3AY Tel: (M)
767898818
ail: petermcblain@hotmail.com
. contact: Boyd Miller Tel: (H) 01294 603793 (M)
920277994
ail: boydmiller@atfc1900.plus.com
ound: Ardeer Stadium, Stevenston, KA20 3JD Tel:

drossan Winton Rovers
Bobby Macnamara, 3 Verona Place, Ardrossan, Ayrshire,
22 8EJ Tel: (H) 01294 604697 (M) 07969241895
ail: wintonrovers@hotmail.com
. contact: Pat Breen Tel: (B) 01294 464733 (M) 07866445538
ail: breenroofing@aol.com
ound: Winton Park, Winton Street, Ardrossan, KA22 8JG Tel:

madale Thistle
Scott Watson, 52 Hailstones Crescent, Armadale, West
thian, EH48 3PH Tel: (H) 01501 734607 (M) 07790343794
ail: armadalethistle@gmail.com
. contact: John Lee Tel: (H) 01501 731366 (M) 07951936152
ail: johnlee1940@aol.com
ound: Volunteer Park, North Street, Armadale, EH48 3QD
l:
ckname: The Dale

niston Rangers
Allan Hares, 14 Carrick Crescent, Easthouses, Dalkeith,
dlothian, EH22 4HE Tel: (M) 07734924577
ail: allan.hares@aol.com
. contact: Denise Scott Tel: (M) 07788692883
ail: dsctt665@aol.com
ound: Newbyres Park, 15 Hunterfield Road, Gorebridge, EH23
P Tel:
ckname: Arnie

Arthurlie
Mr Stephen Connelly, 1 Northpark Avenue, Barrhead, G78 1QL
Tel: (H) 01698 743063 (M) 07947539341
Email: stevoevo@yahoo.co.uk
Alt. contact: David Blakey Tel: (M) 07763192814
Email:
Ground: Dunterlie Park, 42 Carlibar Road, Barrhead, G78 1AA
Tel: 0141 580 1029
Nickname: the Lie (pronounced Lee)

Ashfield
Mr Thomas Robertson, 861 Crow Road, Flat 2 / 5, Anniesland,
Glasgow, G13 1LE Tel: (H) 0141 950 6991 (W) 0141 287 2279
(M) 07703520219
Email: tam-robertson@hotmail.co.uk
Alt. contact: Jim Ross Tel: (H) 0141 762 1757 (M) 07979203543
Email: jamesb.ross@btinternet.com
Ground: Saracen Park, 404 Hawthorn Street, Glasgow, G22 6RU
Tel:

Auchinleck Talbot
Mr Henry Dumigan, 16 Main Street, Auchinleck, KA18 2AA Tel:
(H) 01290 421785 (M) 07929525494
Email: henry.dumigan@sky.com
Alt. contact: Morton Wright Tel: (M) 07972719553
Email: morton.wright.mw@gmail.com
Ground: Beechwood Park, Beechwood Avenue, Auchinleck,
KA18 2AR Tel: 07786637584
Nickname: Bot

Banchory St Ternan
Ms Wendy Sadler, 12 Sycamore Road, Banchory, AB31 5JP Tel:
(H) 01330 823115 (M) 07817653741
Email: wendysadler@hotmail.co.uk
Alt. contact: John Watson Tel: (M) 07831862070
Email:
Ground: Milton Park, Crathes by Banchory, AB31 5QH Tel:
Nickname: Saints

Banks o' Dee
Mr Tom Ewan, 231 North Anderson Drive, Stockethill, Aberdeen,
AB16 5NH Tel: (H) 01224 699983 (W) (M) 07712473408
Email: tom.ewan@mac.com
Alt. contact: Brian Winton Tel: (H) 01224 575319 (M)
07595336302
Email: brian.winton@btopenworld.com
Ground: Spain Park, Abbotswell Road, Aberdeen, AB12 3AB Tel:
Nickname: Rechabites

Bathgate Thistle
Mr Robert Napier, 5 Young Crescent, Bathgate, West Lothian,
EH48 2SN Tel: (H) 01506 635594 (W) 03000527207 (M)
07864071506
Email: robertnapier21@btinternet.com
Alt. contact: Jim Walker Tel: (H) 01506 652483 (M) 07909891663
Email: bathgatenewland@aol.com
Ground: Creamery Park, Hardhill Road, Bathgate, EH48 2BW

Beith
Mr Chris Irving, 22 Netherlee Crescent, Dalry, KA24 5HF Tel: (M)
07787297348 (B) 07717651721
Email: chris@mctaggartconstruction.co.uk
Alt. contact: tbc
Email: tbc
Ground: Bellsdale Park, Meadowside Terrace, Beith, KA15 2AF
Tel:
Nicknames: The Cabes, The Mighty

Bellshill Athletic
Mr Scott Lennox, 15 Burnside Avenue, Mossend, Bellshill, ML4
2PD Tel: (H) 01698 299610 (M) 07722439337
Email: sc.ott@blueyonder.co.uk
Alt. contact: Edward Lynas Tel: (M) 07749826357
Email: eddiel56@hotmail.com
Ground: Rockburn Park, Carnoustie Place, Bellshill, ML4 3EU
Tel:

Benburb FC
Mr John Smith, Flat 1 / 2, 66B Dormanside Road, Pollok, Glasgow, G53 5XY Tel: (M) 07934846151
Email: benburbfootballclub@gmail.com
Alt. contact: Archie Wiseman Tel: (M) 07969954415
Email:
Ground: New Tinto Park, 282 Craigton Road, Glasgow, G51 4XE Tel:
Nickname: Bens

Blackburn United
Mr Paul Meechan, 56 Jardine Place, Bathgate, West Lothian, EH48 4GU Tel: (M) 07540434899
Email: pgmeechan@yahoo.co.uk
Alt. contact: Ian McGinty Tel: (M) 07764681679
Email: blackburnunited@googlemail.com
Ground: Blackburn United Community FC, ash Grove, Blackburn, EH4 7LL Tel:
Nickname: Burnie

Blairgowrie Juniors
Mr Martin Mackay, Rose Cottage, 24 Hay Street, Alyth, PH11 8DQ Tel: (H) 01828 633273 (M) 07858089312
Email: martin.mackay2@googlemail.com
Alt. contact: Mike Coyle Tel: (H) 01250 872682 (M) 07504650475
Email: mike.coyle@email.com
Ground: Davie Park, Rattray, Blairgowrie, PH10 7BJ Tel:
Nicknames: Berrypickers

Blantyre Victoria
Mr Duncan Sinclair, 7 Angle Street, Stonehouse, ML9 3LB Tel: (M) 07831327483
Email: blantyrevics21@hotmail.co.uk
Alt. contact: Alison Paterson Tel: (H) 01698 825450 (M) 07413621171
Email: patersonbvfc@live.co.uk
Ground: Castle Park, Forrest Street, Blantyre, G72 0JL Tel:

Bo'ness United
Mr Douglas Argent, 9 Forthview Crescent, Bo'ness, EH51 0LR Tel: (H) 01506 200934 (W) (M) 07762947836
Email: douglasargentbufc@virginmedia.com
Alt. contact: John Aitchison Tel: (H) 01506 511115 (M) 07899876296
Email: johnaitchison@blueyonder.co.uk
Ground: Newtown Park, Jamieson Avenue, Boness, EH51 0DP Tel: 01506 822313
Nickname: BU (Bee You)

Bonnyrigg Rose
Mr Robert Dickson, 21 Quarryfoot Gardens, Bonnyrigg, Midlothian, EH19 2DH Tel: (H) 0131 663 7498 (M) 07762368986
Email: rob.dickson226@btinternet.com
Alt. contact: Charlie Kirkwood Tel: (M) 07718933693
Email: juileskirk50@aol.com
Ground: New Dundas Park, Town Centre, Bonnyrigg, EH19 3AE Tel:

Brechin Victoria
Mr Clark Crighton, 75 Drumachlie Park, Brechin, DD9 7BT Tel: (H) 01356 622239 (M) 07526469706
Email: c.crighton2@hotmail.com
Alt. contact: Brian Eaton Tel: (H) 01356 623534 (M) 07740861898
Email: brian.eaton@brechinvics.co.uk
Ground: Victoria Park, Behind Nursery Park Off River Street, Brechin, DD9 7EY Tel:

Broughty Athletic
Mr Gordon Deuchars, 5A Victoria Street, Monifieth, Angus, DD5 4HP Tel: (W) 01382 770820 (M) 07788750760
Email: gordon@gaengineering.net
Alt. contact: Ronnie McKenzie Tel: (H) 01382 738367 (M) 07746553090
Email: ronniemckenzie35@gmail.com
Ground: Whitton Park, Arbroath Road, Broughty Ferry Tel:
Nockname: The Fed

Broxburn Athletic
Mr Jim Provan, 24 Hillview Avenue, Broxburn, EH52 5SB Tel: (H) 01506 854389 (M) 07753708841
Email: jamesprovan@hotmail.com
Alt. contact: Alan Cunningham Tel: (H) 01506 855458 (M 07831391850
Ground: Albyn Park, Greendykes Road, Broxburn, EH52 01506 858057

Buchanhaven Hearts
Mr Graeme Mackie, 51 Richmondhill Road, Peterhead, A Tel: (H) 01779 481966 (W) 01779 480290 (M) 07950974
Email: graeme@billmackieengltd.co.uk
Alt. contact: David Buchan Tel: (H) 01779 470722 (B) 017 480290 (M) 07518244499
Email: graeme@billmackieengltd.co.uk
Ground: Raemoss Park, Victoria Road, Peterhead, AB42 Tel:
Nickname: Hearties

Buckie Rovers
Mr David Roberts, 23 Ogilvie Park, Cullen, Buckie, AB56 (H) 01542 840861 (M) 07929444254
Email: david1955roberts@gmail.com
Alt. contact: David Findlay Tel: (H) 01542 649335 (M) 07887524689
Email: parro55@hotmail.com
Ground: Merson Park, Barrhill Road, Buckie, AB56 1DS

Burghead Thistle
Mr Billy Stewart, Ar-Nead, Grant Street, Burghead, IV30 5 (M) 07971765227
Email: arnead@btinternet.com
Alt. contact: Eddie Leggat Tel: (H) 01343 831138 (M) 07917775202
Email: leggat@uwclub.net
Ground: Forrest Park, Burghead, IV30 5YJ Tel:
Nickname: The Broch

Cambuslang Rangers
Mr Scott Wilson, 3A Tontine Place, Rutherglen, Glasgow, 5HE Tel: (M) 07951595710
Email: cambuslangrangers@gmail.com
Alt. contact: William Miller Tel: (H) 0141 641 0255 (M) 07891199896
Email: borgie.lang@talktalk.net
Ground: Somervell Park, Somervell Street, Cambuslang, Tel:
Nickname: The Lang

Camelon Juniors
Mr Tony Davidson, 65 Skaithmuir Crescent, Carronshore, FK2 8BU Tel: (H) (W) (M) 07426137866
Email: tony_d1967@icloud.com
Alt. contact: Alex Graham Tel: (H) 01324 557254 (M) 07858964678
Email: bigzam@blueyonder.co.uk
Ground: Carmuirs Park, Fairlie Drive, Camelon Tel: 0132 638060
Nickname: The Mariners

Carluke Rovers
Ms Tracey Cranston, 22 Greenfield Road, Carluke, ML8 5 (H) 01555 752344 (M) 07909548465
Email: cranstt@sky.com
Alt. contact: Ian McKnight Tel: (M) 07464598150
Email: ian@imsportsmemorabilia.co.uk
Ground: John Cummings Stadium, Carluke, ML8 4EA Te
Nickname: The Jam Makers

Carnoustie Panmure
Mr Andrew Finlay, 156 Kinloch Street, Carnoustie, Angus, 7JQ Tel: (M) 07516000984
Email: andrew.finlay@hotmail.co.uk
Alt. contact: Mrak Johnson Tel: (M) 07825883608 Email: mark.johnson1970@hotmail.co.uk
Ground: Laing Park, Pitskelly Road, Carnoustie, DD7 7Q
Nickname: The Gowfers

Clydebank
Mr Matt Bamford, 191 Broomhill Crescent, Bonhill, Alexan G83 9QZ Tel: (H) 01389 710990 (W) 0141 771 9567 (M)

04628113.
ail: mbamford@blueyonder.co.uk
contact: Gordon Robertson Tel: (H) 0141 586 7193 (M)
'19431894
ail: gordonrobertson1965@hotmail.co.uk
und: Holm Park, Clydebank, G81 1LX Tel:
kname: The Bankies

ony Park Juniors
Douglas Benzie, 39 Selbie Drive, Iverurie, Aberdeenshire,
51 3YB Tel: (H) 01467 629253 (M) 07712240583
ail: dbenzie14150@gmail.com
contact: Roger Langtree Tel: (H) 01467 621357 (M)
13002781
ail: roger.langtree@btinternet.com
und: Colony Park, Harlaw Road, Inverurie, AB51 4SG Tel:

upar Angus
Gillian McColl, 31 Strathmore Avenue, Coupar Angus, PH13
) Tel: (H) 01828 628743 (M) 07874364722
ail: gmccoll06@tiscali.co.uk
contact: Bill McGregor Tel: (H) 01250 874461 (M)
'90770692
ail: bill.mcgregor@briggsequipment.co.uk
und: Foxhall Park, Forfar Road, Coupar Angus, PH13 9AN
:

aigmark Burntonians
David Conway, 11 High Street, Dalmellington, Ayrshire, KA6
U Tel: (H) 01292 551978 (M) 07503066955
ail: dconway430@btinternet.com
contact: Jamie Conway Tel: (H) 01292 551978 (M)
'47161580
ail: jamieconway1@hotmail.com
und: Station Park, Ayr Road, Dalmellington, KA6 7SJ Tel:

aigroyston FC
Jim Sivewright, 16 / 9 Marchmont Crescent, Edinburgh, EH9
. Tel: (H) 0131 228 1803 (M) 07817530152
ail: jimsivewright@hotmail.co.uk
contact: Keith Richardson Tel: (H) 0131 443 0428 (M)
969423769
ail: keithmrichardson@hotmail.co.uk
und: Tel:
kname: Craigie

ossgates Primrose
Kevan McArthur, 83 Droverhall Avenue, Crossgates,
wdenbeath, KY4 8BP Tel: (H) 01383 512963 (M)
341309932
ail: kevanmac1965@sky.com
contact: Gavin Wilson Tel: (H) 01383 623296 (M)
575334567
ail: gavingwilson9602@gmail.com
und: Humbug Park, Inverkeithing Road, Crossgates, Fife,
4 8AT Tel:

uden Bay
Terry Dando, 16 Slains Crescent, Cruden Bay, Peterhead,
42 0PZ Tel: (H) 01779 812796 (W) 01224 711100 (M)
931154524
ail: terrydando@outlook.com
contact: Graham Heddle Tel: (H) 01779 813282 (M)
876340139
ail: graham.heddle@yahoo.com
und: Watson Park, Cruden Bay, AB42 0PJ Tel:

lter JFC
Angus Johnstone, 153 Hardgate, Aberdeen, AB11 6XQ Tel:
) 01224 876733 (M) 07765256627
ail: gus.culter@gmail.com
contact: Doug Jamieson Tel: (H) 01224 321663 (M)
979346043
ail: doug.jamieson46@gmail.com
und: Crombie Park, Malcolm Road, Peterculter, AB14 0XB
: 01224 735727
onouned Coo-ter

mbernauld United
Alan Robertson, 5 Southerness Drive, Westerwood,
mbernauld, G67 0HU Tel: (H) 01236 451850 (M)
07932956855
Email: arobertson1808@gmail.com
Alt. contact: George Watson Tel: (H) 01236 720703 (M)
07977497605
Email: george.watson@paper.co.uk
Ground: Guys Meadow Stadium, Old Glasgow Road, Cumbernauld
Village, G67 2SA Tel:
01236 722883

Cumnock
Mr George Morton, 27 Gray Street, Cumnock, KA18 1EZ Tel: (H)
01290 423992 (W) (M) 07966 767405
Email: cumnockjuniors@gmail.com
Alt. contact: Neil Robertson Tel: (H) 01563 405104 (M)
07926501845
Email: nero@sky.com
Ground: Townhead Park, Townhead Street, Cumnock, KA18 1LZ
Tel: 01290 423027
Nickname: The Nock

Dalkeith Thistle
Mr Duncan Purdie, 49 Echline Grove, South Queensferry, EH30
9RU Tel: (H) 0131 331 5642 (M) 07762550391
Email: dunx@tesco.net
Alt. contact: Barclay Ewing Tel: (H) 0131 660 9841 (M)
07795441113
Email: ewingbarclay73@yahoo.com
Ground: Kings Park, Croft Street, Dalkeith, EH22 3BA Tel:

Dalry Thistle
Mr Hugh Aitken, 45 Stockbridge Crescent, Kilbirnie, Ayrshire, KA25
7HG Tel: (H) 01505 683558 (W) 07968862364 (M) 07724178388
Email: dalrythistlefc@live.co.uk
Alt. contact: Steven Aitken Tel: (H) 01505 685339 (B) 01294
834660 (M) 07547175264
Email: aitkesh@live.co.uk
Ground: Merksworth Park, Dalry, KA24 4BA Tel:

Darvel
Mr Alec Smith, 20 Loch View, Kilmarnock, KA3 7NP Tel: (H) 01563
523434 (M) 07539232304
Email: aalexlyn@aol.com
Alt. contact: John Gall Tel: (B) 01563 522685 (M) 07977064245
Email: john@browningsbakers.com
Ground: Recreation Park, Irvinebank Road, KA17 0HA Tel:

Deveronside
Ms Linda Legge, 14 Gellyhill Street, Macduff, AB44 1TN
Tel: (H) 01261 833273 (W) 01261 818303 (M) 07840073441
Email: admin@prsct.org
Alt. contact: Alastair Clark Tel: (H) 01261 818574 (M) 07769214422
Email: aclark.1964@talktalk.net
Ground: Myrus Centre, Macduff, AB44 1AA

Downfield
Mr Jim Kelly, 10 Buttars Place, Dundee, DD2 4PN
Tel: (H) 01382 203400 (W) 01382 624525 (M) 07775647726
Email: jim@rvbc.co.uk
Alt. contact: Alex Duncan Tel: (H) 01382 508241 (B) 01382 203400
(M) 07505736928
Email: spiders1906@gmail.com
Ground: Downfield Park, Balgowan Avenue, Dundee, DD3 0JB Tel:
01382 810594
Nickname: The Spiders

Dufftown
Mr Harry Officer, 16 Macduff Place, Dufftown, Keith, Banffshire,
AB55 5AH Tel: (H) 01340 821279 (M) 07875458405
Email: hofficer2@gmail.com
Alt. contact: Alan Murray Tel: (H) 01343 556320 (M) 07876547467
Email: alan.murray@deveronhomes.co.uk
Ground: Westburn Park, Hill Street, AB55 4AW Tel: 01340 821368

Dunbar United
Mr Malcolm Jones, Elderside, Spott, Dunbar, EH42 1RE Tel: (H)
01368 864130 (M) 07968443889
Email: p.m.jones@live.co.uk
Alt. contact: Ian Livie Tel: (H) 01368 862724 (M) 07570993282
Email: ianlivie461@btinternet.com

Ground: New Countess Park, Countess Road, Dunbar, EH42 1RF Tel:
Nickname: The Seasiders

Dundee East Craigie
Mr Jack Stephenson, 92 Finella Terrace, Dundee, DD4 9NE Tel: (H) 01382 502712 (M) 07773582908
Email: jakestephenson583@yahoo.co.uk
Alt. contact: Adrian Shearer Tel: (M) 07757550401
Email: shades43@hotmail.co.uk
Ground: Craigie Park, Dundee, DD4 7HX Tel:
Nickname: The Shipbuilders

Dundee North End
Mr Phil Hart, 295A Strathmore Avenue, Dundee, DD3 6SG Tel: (H) 01382 505114 (M) 07806664545
Email: dundeenorthend@virginmedia.com
Alt. contact: Kenneth Grubb Tel: (M) 07402222343
Email: the.dokens@gmail.com
Ground: North End Park, Fairmuir Street, Dundee, DD3 8HU Tel: 01382 810166
Nickname: The Dokens

Dundee Violet JFC
Mr Brian Coutts, 4 Bright Street, Lochee, Dundee, DD2 3DE Tel: (M) 07720443374
Email: briancouttsdvjfc@gmail.com
Alt. contact: Dave Don Tel: (M) 07780700349
Ground: Glenesk Park, Balfield Road, Dundee, DD3 6AG Tel:
Nickname: The Pansies

Dundonald Bluebell
Mr Allan Halliday, 62 Balmanno Green, Glenrothes, KY7 4TD Tel: (M) 07725199773
Email: allan.halliday@fife.gov.uk
Alt. contact: Douglas Rogerson Tel: (M) 07977403855
Email: rogersonplumbing@btconnect.com
Ground: Moorside Park, Dundonald Park, Cardenden, KY5 0DG Tel:
Nickname: Bell

Dunipace
Mr Ian Duncan, 7 Spence Street, Bonnybridge, FK4 1NH Tel: (H) 01324 813463
Email: derekabrown@hotmail.co.uk
Alt. contact: Stephen Tait Tel: (H) 01324 820887 (B) 0141 578 0200 (M) 07403228220
Email: stephentait31@aol.com
Ground: Westfield Park, Townhouse Street, Denny, FK6 5DW Tel:

Dyce
Mr Keith McIntosh, 15 Wellside Avenue, Kingswells, Aberdeen, AB15 8EF Tel: (H) (W) 01224 332400 (M) 07787127574
Email: keith.mcintosh@raeburns.co.uk
Alt. contact: Norman Mackay Tel: (H) 01224 311795 (M) 07768273630
Email: normanmackay65@yohoo.co.uk
Ground: Ian Mair Park, Dyce Drive, Dyce Tel:

East Kilbride Thistle
Mr Martin Sutherland, 15 Galloway Road, Brancumhall, East Kilbride, G74 3NR Tel: (M) 07941876698
Email: fudgesutherland@hotmail.co.uk
Alt. contact: Jimmy Stewart Tel: (M) 07572222876
Email: jimmy1968@hotmail.co.uk
Ground: Showpark, 17 Maxwell Drive, East Kilbride, G74 4HG Tel: 01355 243066
Nickname: The Jags

Easthouses Lily MWFC
Mr James Forrest, 5 Oak Crescent, Mayfield, Dalkeith, EH22 5JX Tel: (H) 0131 663 5082 (M) 07762596477
Email: jamesdot@hotmail.co.uk
Alt. contact: James Florence Tel: (H) 0131 663 9609 (M) 07902908766
Email: jamesflorence4511@yahoo.co.uk
Ground: Easthouses Lily MWFC, Newbattle Complex, off Broadhurst Road, Easthouses, Dalkeith, EH22 4EW Tel:
Nickname: Hooses

Edinburgh United
Mr Kevin Hanratty, 23 Easter Currie Terrace, Edinburgh, EH14 5LF Tel: (M) 07525349008
Email: juniors@edinburghunitedfc.co.uk
Alt. contact: Brian Smith Tel: (M) 07974173175
Email: BS011J8849@blueyonder.co.uk
Ground: Paties Road, Stadium, Katesmill Road, Edir
EH14 1JF Tel:

Ellon United
Mr Irvine Morris, 14 Hillhead Road, Ellon, Aberdeens
AB41 9LF Tel: (H) 01358 721321 (M) 07791026406
Email: r.morris645@btinternet.com
Alt. contact: William Gordon Tel: (H) 01358 721404 07922662250
Email: billy.gogsi@btinternet.com
Ground: The Meadows, Meadows Way, Ellon, AB41
Tel: 01358 725162

Fauldhouse United
Mr Dave Huddlestone, 76E Sheephousehill, Fauldho
West Lothian, EH47 9EG Tel: (H) 01501 771017 (M) 07881938534
Email: dave.huddlestone@live.co.uk
Alt. contact: Colin Cunningham Tel: (H) 01501 77071
07887902667
Email: colin@gmfinancialservices.co.uk
Ground: Parkview, Fauldhouse, EH47 9JS Tel:
Nickname: The Hoose

Forfar Albion
Mr Jack Florence, Balquharn Cottage, Fern, By Brec
DD9 7RS Tel: (H) 01356 650305 (M) 07899937340
Email: jackflorence1969@gmail.com
Alt. contact: Andy Ferrar Tel: (M) 07599235529 Emai
Ground: Guthrie Park, Lochside Road, Forfar, DD8 3
Forfar West End
Mr Ian Gowans, 13 Sheriff Park Gardens, Forfar, DD
Tel: (H) 01307 465271 (W) 01307 463173 (M) 07517
Email: ian@rammsayladders.co.uk
Alt. contact: Alan Morrison Tel: (M) 07979192149
Email: cammymo@aol.com
Ground: Strathmore Park,Raig o' Loch Road, Forfar,
1BT Tel: 01307 462935
Nickname: The Westies

Forres Thistle
Mr Dutch Holland, 15 Highfield, Forbeshill, Forres, IV
Tel: (H) 01309 676666 (W) 01309 675000 (M) 07769
Email: dutchinforres@btinternet.com
Alt. contact: James Sutherland Tel: (H) 01309 67656
01309 676585 (M)
07801354129
Email: mscs.ltd@hotmail.co.uk
Ground: Logie Park, West Pilmuir, Forres, IV36 1PH

Forth Wanderers
Mr Stewart Barrett, 24 Cloglands, Forth, ML11 8ED T
01555 811500 (M) 07990578773
Email: stewsy15@aol.com
Alt. contact: Stuart Smith Tel: (H) 01555 811573 (M) 07807339725
Email: matthewpepsi12@aol.com
Ground: Kingshill Park, Main Street, Forth Tel:

Fraserburgh United
Mr Gordon Laird, 23 Ailsa Court, Fraserburgh, Aberdeenshire, AB43 9SH Tel: (H) 01346 516828
Email: gordonlaird23@aol.com
Alt. contact: Colin Smith Tel: (M) 07710662555
Ground: College Park, Henderson Road, Fraserburgh
9GA Tel:

Gartcairn JFC
Mr Robert McCallum, 76 Inverlochy Road, Airdrie, ML
Tel: (H) 01236 749344 (M) 07818002241
Email: Robert@gartcairn.com
Alt. contact: Craig Armstrong Tel: (M) 07949054206
Email: craig@exselgroup.com
Ground: MTC Park, Waverley Drive, Airdrie, ML6 6HE

Girvan FC
Mr Andrew Sinclair, 2 Todd Street, Girvan, KA26 0DX Tel: (M) 07759753425
Email: andrewsinclair35@hotmail.com
Alt. contact: Tom McCreadie Tel: (H) 01465 714681 (M) 07736397531
Email: t_mccreadie@hotmail.com
Ground: Hamilton Park, Vicerton Street, Girvan, KA26 9HF Tel:

Glasgow Perthshire
Ms Carol Cunningham, 64 Mosspark Avenue, Glasgow, G52 1LQ Tel: (H) 0141 419 9308 (M) 07860848699
Email: carolglasgowperthshire@hotmail.com
Alt. contact: Andy Halliday Tel: (M) 07802697538
Ground: Keppoch Park, Ashfield Street, Possilpark, Glasgow, G22 5HE Tel:
Nickname: Shire

Glenafton Athletic & Sporting Club
Mr John Stewart, 1 Woodend Cottages, Drongan, Ayrshire, KA6 7BT Tel: (H) 01292 591734 (M) 07831232638
Email: glenaftonathletic@live.co.uk
Alt. contact: Ian Young Tel: (B) 01290 338306 (M) 07761600041
Email: ianyounglowes@live.co.uk
Ground: Loch Park, 115 Main Street, New Cumnock, KA18 4AE Tel: 01290 338022
Nickname: Glens

Glenrothes
Mr Willie Drew, 88 Falcon Drive, Glenrothes, KY7 5HR Tel: (H) 01592 759189 (M) 07927385918
Email: williedrew@hotmail.co.uk
Alt. contact: Douglas Cooper Tel: (H) 01592 759189 (M) 07813307375
Email: dsddecorators@blueyonder.co.uk
Ground: Warout Stadium, Warout Road, Glenrothes, KY7 4JY Tel:
Nickname: Glens

Glentanar
Mr Bill Hay, 139 Lang Stracht, Aberdeen, AB15 6LB Tel: (H) 01224 319148 (M) 07946464015
Email: billhay7@btinternet.com
Alt. contact: Derek Thomson Tel: (H) 01224 313522 (B) 01224 752697 (M) 07435663695
Email: derek.4.thomson@bt.com
Ground: Woodside Sports Complex, Station Road, Woodside, Aberdeen, AB24 2UL Tel: 01224 276141

Greenock
Mr Alex Wilson, 81 Waverley Street, Greenock, PA16 9DG Tel: (H) 01475 716561 (M) 07958652104
Email: alec.wilson3@outlook.com
Alt. contact: Neil Docherty Tel: (H) 01475 724752 (M) 07831143169
Email: neil2doc@gmail.com
Ground: Ravenscraig Stadium, Greenock Tel:

Haddington Athletic
Mr Tom Thornton, 14 / 3 Redhall Place, Edinburgh, EH14 2DL Tel: (H) 0131 443 7188 (M) 07878333586
Email: T_Thornton_2006@yahoo.co.uk
Alt. contact: Drew Donaldson Tel: (H) 01620 824704 (M) 07753513789
Email: drew_donaldson@btopenworld.com
Ground: Millfield, Mill Wynd, Haddington, EH41 4DB Tel: 01620 826547
Nickname: Hi Hi

Hall Russell United
Mr John V. Carroll, 140 Osborne Place, Aberdeen, AB25 2DU Tel: (H) 01224 641694 (W) 01224 643106 (M) 07749673786
Email: jvcarroll@btconnect.com
Alt. contact: Iain Hay Tel: (B) 01224 622868 (H) 01224 325400 (M) 07899901262
Email: iain-hay@ajg.com
Ground: Denmore Park, Bridge of Don, Aberdeen, AB23 8JW Tel:

Harthill Royal
Mr Archie Brown, 49 Cunningham Drive, Harthill, Shotts, ML7 5NY Tel: (H) 01501 750391 (M) 0774 3853415
Email: archiebrown2212@outlook.com
Alt. contact: Keith Cooper Tel: (H) 01501 751325 (M) 07774870953
Email: keith.cooper@aggregate.com
Ground: Gibbshill Park, East Main Street, Harthill, ML7 5QQ Tel:
Ground formerly known as Beechbank Park

Hermes
Mr Alex M. Fiddes, 345 Clifton Road, Aberdeen, AB24 4DT Tel: (H) 01224 487466 (M) 07958080854
Email: afid@btopenworld.com
Alt. contact: Leslie Hutton Tel: (H) 01224 317501 (M) 07816753128
Email: leslie.hutton@btinternet.com
Ground: Uniconn Park, Bridge of Don, Aberdeen, AB23 8JW Tel:
Ground formerly known as Lochside Park

Hill of Beath Hawthorn
Mr Neil MacLagan, 61 Bowton Road, Kinross, KY13 8EH Tel: (M) 07790406597
Email: neilmaclagan@hotmail.co.uk
Alt. contact: Lenny Munro Tel: (M) 078097269752
Email: leonardmunro59@hotmail.co.uk
Ground: Keirs Park, Hawthorn Crescent, Hill of Beath, KY4 8EF Tel:
Nickname: Haws

Hurlford United
Mr George Jaconelli, 8 Mansewell Road, Prestwick, KA9 1BB Tel: (H) 01292 479722 (M) 07858667131
Email: gjaconelli@hotmail.com
Alt. contact: John Sibbald Tel: (H) 01563 520884 (M) 07788594860
Email: johnsibbald@yahoo.co.uk
Ground: Blair Park, Blair Road, Hurlford Tel:
Nickname The Ford

Inverness City
Ms Violet Wardhaugh, Station House, Dalcross, Inverness, IV2 7JJ Tel: (H) 01667 493278 (M) 07711446658
Email: violet@wardhaugh.fsworld.co.uk
Alt. contact: Alastair Wardhaugh Tel: (H) 01667 493278 (M) 07802461504
Email: alastairwardhaugh@gmail.com
Ground: Bught Park, Inverness Tel:

Irvine Meadow XI
Mrs Lyn McFarlane, 5 Norman Crescent, Irvine, Ayrshire, KA12 8SB Tel: (H) 01294 272424 (M) 07854767062
Email: lynmcfarlane9@gmail.com
Alt. contact: Stewart Griffiths Tel: (M) 07534772397
Email: stewart.griffiths55@virgin.net
Ground: Meadow Park, Wilson Avenue, Irvine, KA12 0TW Tel: 01294 274459
Nickname: Medda

Irvine Victoria
Mr David Loach, 6 Pladda Crescent, Broomlands, Irvine, KA11 1DP Tel: (H) 01294 222115 (M) 07969486913
Email: davidloach14@googlemail.com
Alt. contact: Robert Hanvey Tel: (H) 01294 271346 (M) 07784317698
Email: bobharvey@yahoo.co.uk
Ground: Victoria Park, Boyle Street, Irvine, KA12 8PG Tel:

Islavale
Mr Brian Rae, Beechlea, 4 Muldearie View, Keith, AB55 5TF Tel: (H) 01542 886336 (M) 07816346605

Email: raeflor@aol.com
Alt. contact: Sandy McCombie Tel: (M) 07740173436
Email: kilvrecht21@aol.com
Ground: Simpson Park, Westerton Road, Keith, AB55 5EP Tel:

Jeanfield Swifts
Mr Bob Bissett, 7 Farm Road, Perth, PH2 7JJ Tel: (H) 01738 561298 (M) 07862725223
Email: bobbissett1@hotmail.com
Alt. contact: John Soutar Tel: (H) 01738 636887 (M) 07583684516
Email: jean_soutar@hotmail.com
Ground: Riverside Stadium, Bute Drive, Perth, PH1 3BG Tel:

Johnstone Burgh
Mr Ricky Cantwell, 11 Cruachan Avenue, Renfrew, PA4 0PH Tel: (H) 0141 561 6010 (M) 07719323744
Email: richard.cantwell@ntlworld.com
Alt. contact: David Brolly Tel: (M) 07754204932
Ground: Keanie Park, Auchenlodment Road, Johnstone, PA5 9PE Tel: 01505 322200

Kello Rovers
Ms Gillian Keggans, 32 Sandyknowe Crescent, Kelloholm, Dumfriesshire, DG4 6SX Tel: (H) 01659 66632 (M) 07800864158
Email: gillian.keggans@btinternet.com
Alt. contact: Mark Keggans Tel: (H) 01659 66632 (M) 07846101474
Ground: Nithside Park, Kirkconnel, DG4 6NB Tel:

Kennoway Star Hearts
Ms Jane Anderson, 3 Pentland Drive, KEnnoway, Fife, KY8 5TX Tel: (H) 01333 353375 (M) 07375470137
Email: janeandersonksh@gmail.com
Alt. contact: Brian Davidson Tel: (H) 01333 352392 (M) 07802772313
Email: brian651davidson@btinternet.com
Ground: Treaton Park, Star, Fife, KY7 6LJ Tel:
Nickname: The Budgies

Kilbirnie Ladeside
Mr Gordon Ronney, Habost, Duchal Road, Kilmacolm, PA13 4AS Tel: (H) 01505 874406 (W) 07881788854 (M) 07889403298
Email: gronney@rjmcleod.co.uk
Alt. contact: Ian McDonald Tel: (H) 01505 504201 (M) 07748416316
Email: ianandliz.mcdonald@btinternet.com
Ground: Valefield, Kirkland Road, Kilbirnie Tel:
Nickname: The Blasties

Kilsyth Rangers
Mr William Dunbar, 19 Cavalry Park, Kilsyth, G65 0AU Tel: (M) 07776066696
Email: wiliamdunbar1967@gmail.com
Alt. contact: John Ferguson Tel: (H) 01236 824306 (M) 07443890755
Email: jrfwx@tiscali.co.uk
Ground: Duncansfield, Haugh Road, Kilsyth, G65 9JX Tel:

Kilwinning Rangers
Mr William Allan, 84 Ladyford Avenue, Kilwinning, Ayrshire, KA13 6DS Tel: (H) 01294 551063 (M) 07881883260
Email: willie.allan@btinternet.com
Alt. contact: John Bennett Tel: (H) 01294 552213 (M) 07810435483
Ground: Abbey Park, Dovecot Lane, Kilwinning, KA13 6DU Tel:
Nickname: The Buffs

Kinnoull
Mr Charlie Grieve, 46 South Inch Park, Perth, PH2 8BU Tel: (H) 01738 446747 (M) 07557792832
Email: kinnoull@grieve.myzen.co.uk
Alt. contact: Chris Jones Tel: (M) 07940814370
Ground: Tulloch Park, Tulloch Road, Perth, PH1 2RW Tel:
Nickname: Noull

Kirkcaldy YMCA
Mr James Douglas, 3 McIntosh Court, Kirkcaldy, KY2 6RQ Tel: (H) 01592 649759 (M) 07976838352
Email: jim.douglas444@gmail.com
Alt. contact: Ramsay Budd Tel: (H) 01592 202066 (M) 07504004067
Email: ramsaybudd@hotmail.com
Ground: Denfield Park, Den Road, Kirkcaldy, KY11 2ER Tel:
Nickname: YM

Kirkintilloch Rob Roy
Mr Charles O'Brien, 33 Eastermains, Kirkintilloch, G66 2UT Tel: (H) 0141 237 1927 (M) 07955095707
Email: charlesobrien33@hotmail.com
Alt. contact: James Black Tel: (H) 0141 776 0316 (M) 07707048309
Email: jimblack0316@hotmail.com
Ground: Currnetly ground sharing with Cumbernauld United
Nickname: the Rabs, The Roy

Kirriemuir Thistle
Ms Linda Coupar, 5 Kirkwynd, Kirriemuir, DD8 4BH Tel: (H) 01575 574450 (M) 07840023010
Email: lcouparkirrie@hotmail.com
Alt. contact: Andy Stewart Tel: (H) 01575 572274 (M) 07756769130
Email: andy.spark@btinternet.com
Ground: Westview Park, Southmuir, Kirriemuir, DD8 5LG Tel: 01575 572722
Nickname: Kirrie

Lanark United
Mr Tom Anderson, 45 Wellwood Avenue, Lanark, ML11 7HS Tel: (H) 01555 663796 (M) 07721047708
Email: thomasanderson179@btinternet.com
Alt. contact: George Reid Tel: (H) 01555 661788 (M) 07748540871
Ground: Moor Park, Hyndford Road, Lanark, ML11 9BG Tel: 07721047708 (on match days)
Nickname: The Yowes

Largs Thistle
Mr Kenneth Smailes, 1 Douglas Place, Largs, KA30 8PU Tel: (M) 07787575615
Email: kennysmailes@gmail.com
Alt. contact: Stuart McAulay Tel: (M) 07854979706
Email: aqto51@dsl.pipex.com
Ground: Barrfields Stadium, Brisbane Road, Largs, KA30 8NN Tel:

Larkhall Thistle
Mrs Fiona Tierney, 63 Earls Park Avenue, Glasgow, G43 2HE Tel: (H) 0141 577 7055 (M) 07706681274
Email: fetierney@yahoo.co.uk
Alt. contact: Hugh Kerr Tel: (H) 01698 309391 (M) 07746875347
Email: mrkerr@blueyonder.co.uk
Ground: Gasworks Park, Raploch Street, Larkhall, ML9 1AJ Tel:

Lesmahagow
Mr Andrew Irving, 60 Auldton Drive, Lesmahagow, ML11 0BY Tel: (H) 01555 895828 (W) 01555 662244 (M) 07703772123
Email: irvandr4@aol.com
Alt. contact: George Brownlie Tel: (H) 01555 892771 (M) 07989688219
Ground: Craighead Park, Pathfoot Smithy, Lesmahagow, ML11 0AG Tel:
Nickname: Gow

Lewis United
Mr George Copland, 64 Summerhill Crescent, Aberdeen, AB15 6ED Tel: (H) 01224 321683 (M) 07847059778
Email: ekcgmc64@sky.com
Alt. contact: Barry Watson Tel: (M) 07887520923
Email: barrywatson@aol.com
Ground: Aberdeen Sports Village, Linksfield Road, Aberdeen, AB24 5RU Tel:

Linlithgow Rose
Mr William Calder, 56 Braehead Road, Linlithgow, West Lothian, EH49 6DY Tel: (M) 07784640512
Email: calder.william@hotmail.co.uk
Alt. contact: David Roy Tel: (H) 01506 842197 (M) 07811220307
Ground: Prestonfield, Braehead Road, Linlithgow, EH49 6HF Tel: 01506 843736
Nickname: The Gallant, The Rosey-Posey

Livingston United
Mr Scott Burgess, 32 Alderstone Place, Alderstone, Livingston, EH54 7FE Tel: (H) 01506 798186 (W) 07747195312 (M) 07917732030
Email: scottburguss@live.co.uk
Alt. contact: Robert Ramsay Tel: (H) 01236 763383 (M) 07799612789
Email: r.ramsay5@btinternet.com
Ground: Station Park, 68-74 Deans South, Deans, Livingston, EH54 8QU Tel:

Lochee Harp
Mr James Kelly, 20 Leven Street, Broughty Ferry, Dundee, DD5 3JE Tel: (H) 01382 778006 (M) 07581513332
Email: kelly.jim1@sky.com
Alt. contact: Jack Kelly Tel: (H) 01382 827457
Ground: Beechwood Park, Kings Cross Road, Dundee, DD3 2PU Tel: Lochee have vacated Beechwood Park and will ground-share until their own new ground is ready

Lochee United
Mr Larry Duncan, 38 Lintrathen Gardens, Dundee, DD3 8EJ Tel: (H) 01382 884188 (M) 07808587741
Email: larry@larryduncan.co.uk
Alt. contact: Tom McMillan Tel: (H) 01382 419462 (M) 07584102202
Email: tommcmillan1954@hotmail.com
Ground: Thomson Park, Napier Drive, Lochee, Dundee, DD2 2SJ Tel:
Nickname: The Bluebells, Chee

Lochgelly Albert
Mr Ian Patrick, 88 South Street, Lochgelly, Fife, KY5 9LB Tel: (H) 01592 780155 (M) 07740982985
Email: ipatrick1926@gmail.com
Alt. contact: Jock Kinnell Tel: (H) 01592 781769 (M) 07568505304
Ground: Gardiners Park, South Street, Lochgelly, KY5 9LJ Tel:
Nickname: The Berts

Lochore Welfare
Mr John Kirkland, 9 Denholm Way, Crosshill, Fife, KY5 8BW Tel: (H) 01592 305064 (M) 07813977113
Email: johnkirkland14@hotmail.com
Alt. contact: Michelle Kirkland Tel: (H) 01592 305064 (M) 07772710645
Email: michelleconnelly@live.co.uk
Ground: Central Park, Lochore Tel:

Longside
Mr Gavin Davidson, 15 Bruce Brae, Longside, Peterhead, AB42 4SY Tel: (H) 01779 821347 (W) 01779 471500 (M) 07748558461
Email: gavin.davidson@travisperkins.co.uk
Alt. contact: Stephen Wallace Tel: (M) 07813724908
Email: stephenjwallace@aol.com
Ground: Davidson Park, Off Station Road, Longside, AB42 4GR Tel: 01779 821789

Lugar Boswell Thistle
Mr Lauchlan Millar, 10 Castlehill, New Cumnock, KA18 4AF Tel: (M) 07502456899
Email: lauchlan1974@googlemail.com
Alt. contact: Derek McMurdo Tel: (M) 07791923614
Email: dmcmurdo@rjtexcavations.co.uk
Ground: Rosebank Park, Lugar, KA18 3LT Tel:
Nickname: The Jaggy Bunnets

Luncarty
Mr Michael Dalton, 56 Crammond Place, Perth, PH1 3BN Tel: (H) 01738 315177 (M) 07805364097
Email: mdalton906@hotmail.com
Alt. contact: Jim Meiklejohn Tel: (H) 01738 828071 (M) 07535711182
Ground: Brownlands Park, Main Road, Luncarty, PH1 3EP Tel: 01738 828836

Maryhill
Mr Gordon Anderson, 14 Lomond Drive, Bishopbriggs, Glasgow, G64 3BZ Tel: (H) 0141 563 0969 (W) 0141 287 2949 (M) 07693804869
Email: gordon.a@ntlworld.com
Alt. contact: Gordon Boyd Tel: (H) 0141 563 0483 (B) 0141 224 0609 (M) 07984731365
Email: gordon.boyd@rbs.co.uk
Ground: Lochburn Park, 18 Lochburn Road, Glasgow, G20 9AQ Tel: 0141 946 8850

Maud
Mr Graham Lawson, 24 Burnside Road, Mintlaw, Peterhead, AB42 5GE Tel: (H) 01771 623575 (W) 01779 472486 (M) 07825585524
Email: maudjfc@aol.com
Alt. contact: Bruce Lawson Tel: (H) 01779 472486 (M) 07709065555
Email: brucetown@yahoo.com
Ground: Pleasure Park, In Village of Maud, AB42 4NP Tel: 01771 613259

Maybole
Mr Alex Meek, 2 Gardenrose Path, Maybole, KA19 8AG Tel: (H) 01655 883419
Email: elizabeth.meek@live.co.uk
Alt. contact: William Galloway Tel: (H) 01655 882595 (M) 07951650067
Email: leadywellcleaning@btinternet.com
Ground: Ladywell Stadium, Dailly Road, Maybole, KA19 7AZ Tel:

Montrose Roselea
Mr Alan Simpson, 20B Ramsay Street, Montrose, Angus, DD10 8BS Tel: (H) 01674 677565 (M) 07593015043
Email: simmobc1@talktalk.net
Alt. contact: Roy Gill Tel: (H) 01674 672920 (B) 01674 673651 (M) 07908763219
Email: gill.fin@btinternet.com
Ground: Broomfield Park, Broomfield Road, Montrose, DD10 8TZ Tel:

Muirkirk
Mr Billy Tait, 17 Kings Way, Cumnock, KA18 1TN Tel: (H) 01290 425377 (M) 07596089828
Email: billy@taitb.fsnet.co.uk
Alt. contact: Isabel Davidson Tel: (H) 01290 661069 (M) 07814510259
Email: delandbell@aol.com
Ground: Burnside Park, Furnace Road, Muirkirk, KA18 3RE Tel:

Musselburgh Athletic
Ms May McGlynn, 47 Inchview Crescent, Wallyford, East Lothian, EH21 8LS Tel: (H) 0131 665 5854 (M) 07951745018
Email: mcglynncharlie47@aol.com
Alt. contact: Charlie McGlynn Tel: (H) 0131 665 5854 (M) 07951745018
Email: mcglynncharlie47@aol.com
Ground: Olivebank, Market Street, Musselburgh, EH21 6QA Tel: 0131 653 3319
Nickname: Burgh

Nairn St Ninian
Mr Derek Davidson, 8 Mill Road Terrace, Nairn, IV12 5EG Tel: (H) 01667 459332 (M) 07743165525
Email: derekdavidson789@btinternet.com
Alt. contact: Alan Simpson Tel: (H) 01667 453860 (M) 07730368676
Email: o.simpson276@btinternet.com
Ground: Showfield, Lodgehill Road, Nairn, IV12 4QL Tel:

Neilston

Mr Mark Kirkland, 51 Whitesbridge Avenue, Paisley, PA3 3BL
Tel: (H) 0141 889 6614 (M) 07557391616
Email: kirky313@hotmail.co.uk
Alt. contact: Kevin Robertson Tel: (M) 07324064230
Email: admin@neilstonjuniors.com
Ground: Brig-o-Lea Stadium, Uplawmoor Road, Neilston, G78 3LB Tel:
Nickname: The Farmers Boys

New Elgin
Mr George Rose, 10 Rowan Court, Elgin, Moray, IV30 4BB Tel: (H) 01343 550734 (W) 07779999219 (M) 07580508190
Email: gernejfc@yahoo.co.uk
Alt. contact: Joyce Rose Tel: (H) 01343 550734 (M) 07967186467
Email: gernejfc@yahoo.co.uk
Ground: Nicol-Togneri Park, Pinefield, Elgin, IV30 3AF Tel:

Newburgh
Mr Kevin Bartlett, 10 Lyall Place, Newburgh, Fife, KY14 6AN Tel: (M) 07743180205
Email: kevin.101@btinternet.com
Alt. contact: Graham Strachan Tel: (M) 07516625033
Email: grstrachan@btinternet.com
Ground: East Shore Park, Coach Road, Newburgh, Fife, KY14 6BY Tel:

Newburgh Thistle
Mr Robert Jarvie, 123 Fairview Drive, Danestone, Aberdeen, AB22 8ZZ Tel: (H) 01224 824807 (W) 01224 797078 (M) 07759144836
Email: bjarvie@talktalk.net
Alt. contact: Susan Raeburn Tel: (H) 01224 703572 (B) 01224 797044 (M) 07833794614
Email: sraeburn@rwgroup.com
Ground: Gallowhills Park, Beach Road, Newburgh, AB41 6BY Tel:

Newmachar
Ms Angela Cumming, 4 Station Road, Newmachar, Aberdeen, AB21 0PW Tel: (H) 01651 862396 (M) 07731613405
Email: angelacumming@hotmail.co.uk
Alt. contact: Ian Cooper Tel: (H) 01466 410129 (M) 07563157069
Email: ian.cooper1963@gmail.com
Ground: Charlie Gordon Park, Newmachar, AB21 0QD Tel:

Newmains United Community Football Club
Mr Bill Carrigan, 17 Swisscot Walk, Hamilton, ML3 8DX Tel: (M) 07982687545
Email: bill.carrigan2@gmail.com
Alt. contact: TBC Tel: Email:
Ground: Victoria Park, Overtown Road, Newmains, ML2 8HF Tel:
Nickname: The Dahlies

Newtongrange Star
Mr Joe Wilson, 10 South Belton Farm Cottages, Dunbar, East Lothian, EH42 1RG Tel: (H) 01368 862729 (W) 01368 862266 (M) 07766760857
Email: joe.starblue@gmail.com
Alt. contact: Stan Adams Tel: (M) 07588326160
Ground: New Victoria Park, Dalhousie Road, Newtongrange, EH22 4NG Tel: 0131 663 3362
Nickname: Star

Oakley United
Mr Douglas Hynd, 4 Woodburn Crescent, Oakley, KY12 9RS Tel: (H) 01383 851779 (M) 07775518846
Email: douglas.hynd93@gmail.com
Alt. contact: Alec Wright Tel: (H) 01383 850593 (M) 07588410992
Email: alec.wright@live.co.uk
Ground: Blairwood Park, Blairwood Walk, KY12 9RA Tel:

Penicuik Athletic
Mr Neil Gordon, 103 Rullion Road, Penicuik, EH26 9JA
Tel: (H) 01968 677395 (W) 0131 653 2481 (M) 07936156451
Email: neil@johnmckayinsurance.co.uk
Alt. contact: John Fraser Tel: (H) 01968 676515 (M) 07713247144
Ground: Penicuik Park, Carlops Road, Penicuik, EH26 9HU Tel:
Nickname: Cuiky

Petershill
Mr Derek Crozier, 6 Holly Drive, Glasgow, G21 4EQ Tel: (H) 0141 558 7325 (M) 07711867748
Email: derekcroz_99@yahoo.co.uk
Alt. contact: Albert Moffat Tel: (H) 0141 558 8344 (M) 07969139880
Ground: Petershill Park, 28/30 Adamswell Street, Springburn, Glasgow, G21 4DD Tel: 0141 276 8446
Nickname: Peasy

Pollok
Mr Stuart McCulloch, 67 Alexander Avenue, Eaglesham, G76 0DS Tel: (H) 01355 303204 (M) 07985741541
Email: secretary@pollokfc.com
Alt. contact: Francis McNeil Tel: (H) 0141 881 0026 (M) 07847542590
Ground: Newlandsfield Park, Glasgow, G43 2XR Tel: 0141 632 4929
Nickname: Lok

Port Glasgow
Mr Robert Spence, 69 Montrose Avenue, Port Glasgow, PA14 5YJ Tel: (H) 01475 790364 (M) 07593421998
Email: spencemontrose@yahoo.co.uk
Alt. contact: Peter Loughlin Tel: (H) 01475 719160 (M) 07946814951
Email: pete.loughlin@gmail.com
Ground: Port Glasgow Community Stadium, Parklea Playing Fields, Port Glasgow, PA14 6TR Tel:
Nickname: The Undertakers

Pumpherston
Mr William Rogers, 5 Ormiston Drive, , East Calder, West Lothian, EH53 0NR Tel: (H) 01506 490981 (M) 07786021303
Email: billy.rogers@hotmail.co.uk
Alt. contact: Robert Rogers Tel: (H) 01506 431218 (M) 07999967056
Email: rogersfaepumphy@hotmail.co.uk
Ground: Recreation Park, Pumpherston Tel:
Nickname: Pumpny

Renfrew
Mr Allan McCafferty, 19 Tirry Way, Renfrew, PA4 0YE Tel: (H) 0141 561 1784 (M) 07958018561
Email: j.mccafferty@ntlworld.com
Alt. contact: John Gilmour Tel: (H) 0141 886 4094 (B) 07768568160 (M) 07731863279
Email: john.gilmour7@sky.com
Ground: New Western Park, 1 Argyle Avenue, Renfrew, PA4 9EF Tel: 07799952106
Nickname: Frew

Rossvale FC
Mr Andy Sandilands, 49 Iona Ridge, Hamilton, ML3 8PZ Tel: (M) 07908713302
Email: andysandilands49@gmail.com
Alt. contact: Dom McInally Tel: (H) 0141 569 7580 (M) 07900928481
Email: dommci@ntlworold.com
Ground: Petershill Park, 28/30 Adamswell Street, Springburn, Glasgow, G21 4DD Tel: 0141 276 8446

Rosyth
Mr Alfie Blair, 35 Hudson Road, Rosyth, Fife, KY11 2EW Tel: (M) 07727188293
Email: alfie.blair@yahoo.co.uk
Alt. contact: Raymond Fairbairn Tel: (M) 07817160420
Ground: Recreation Park, Admiralty Road, Rosyth, KY11 2BN Tel:
Likely to vacate ground before end 2017

Royal Albert Athletic
Mr Peter Higgins, 81 Margaretvale Drive, Larkhall, ML9 1EH Tel: (H) 01698 888498 (W) 01355 585954 (M) 07719384581
Email: peter.higgins@uk.issworld.com
Alt. contact: Donald Campbell Tel: (M) 07720760149
Email: dc009d2067@blueyonder.co.uk
Ground: Tilework Park, Stonehouse Tel:

Rutherglen Glencairn
Mr Alex J. Forbes, 83 Dryburgh Avenue, Rutherglen, G73 3ES Tel: (H) 0141 643 1406 (M) 07787737654
Email: alexforbes83@hotmail.co.uk
Alt. contact: Alex McArthur Tel: (M) 07967535513
Email: mcarthuramas@aol.com
Ground: Clyde Gateway Stadium, Toryglen Road, Rutherglen, G73 1JH Tel:
Nickname: Glens

St. Andrews United
Mr Johnny Strachan, 115 Elgin Drive, Glenrothes, KY6 2JS Tel: (H) 01592 755239 (M) 07511459354
Email: johnny6513@hotmail.co.uk
Alt. contact: Ian Barrett Tel: (M) 078869588843
Email: oorboom11@hotmail.co.uk
Ground: Recreation Park, Langlands Road, St Andrews, KY16 8BN Tel: 01334 477365
Nickname: Saints

St. Anthony's
Mr Felix McKenna, 20 Overton Road, Glasgow, G72 7QP Tel: (H) 0141 641 9659 (W) 0141 778 8300 (M) 07790169666
Email: felix.mckenna@theants.co.uk
Alt. contact: James McKenna Tel: (M) 07506957547
Ground: McKenna Park, Fulbar Road/Shieldhall Road, Glasgow, G51 4HU Tel:
Nickname: The Ants

St. Rochs
Mr Andy Cameron, James McGrory Park, 713 Royston Road, Glasgow, G21 2AA Tel: (H) 0141 548 8689 (M) 07513231176
Email: andy.cameron@drs.glasgow.uk
Alt. contact: Paul Reddie Tel: (M) 07986561745
Ground: James McGrory Park, 713 Royston Road, Glasgow , G21 2AA Tel:
Nickname: The Candy

Saltcoats Victoria
Mr Gordon Hunter, 11 Wilson Street, Airdrie, ML6 0EE Tel: (M) 07505488430
Email: gordonianhunter@postmaster.co.uk
Alt. contact: Robert Latta Tel: (M) 07788562402
Email: rlat1312@hotmail.co.uk
Ground: Campbell Park, Blakery Road, Saltcoats, KA21 6AP Tel:

Sauchie
Mr Robbie McKenzie, 39 St Serfs Grove, Clackmannan, FK10 4SR Tel: (H) 01259 215268 (W) 07554807338 (M) 07759162431
Email: robbie.49er@hotmail.co.uk
Alt. contact: Lorna Duncan Tel: (H) 01259 216242 (M) 07762130534
Email: lorna.duncan211@btinternet.com
Ground: Beechwood Park, Sauchie, FK10 3AX Tel: 01259 722933

Scone Thistle
Mr Jon Baker, 28 Cross Street, Scone, Perth, PH2 6LR Tel: (M) 07984408366
Email: jb@sconethistlefc.org
Alt. contact: Derek Adam Tel: (M) 07736037243
Email: derek.adam@sconethistlefc.org
Ground: Farquharson Park, Stormont Road, Scone, PH2 6NT Tel:
Nickname: The Jags

Shettleston JFC
Mr Les Turnbull, 9 Oban Court, Fergus Drive, Glasgow, G20 6AS Tel: (W) 0141 778 6415 (M) 07469706499
Email: info@shettlestonjuniors.co.uk
Alt. contact: Bernard Beacon Tel: (B) 0141 778 6415 (M) 07958777104
Email: berniebeacon@msn.com
Ground: Greenfield Park, 401 Old Shettleston Road, Glasgow, G32 7JN Tel: 0141 778 6415
Nickname: The Town

Shotts Bon Accord
Mr Alex Hendry, 42 Main Street, Fauldhouse, West Lothian, EH47 9HP Tel: (H) 01501 771101 (M) 07760571381
Email: hendrya1@sky.com
Alt. contact: Stewart McLuckie Tel: (H) 01501 823420 (M) 07962086610
Email: stewart.mcluckie@outlook.com
Ground: Hannah Park, Dykehead, Shotts, ML7 5EY Tel: 01501 821542
Nickname: The Bonny

Spey Valley United JFC
Mr Graeme Mackie, 12 Dorback Place, Nethybridge, PH25 3AB Tel: (M) 07719777125
Email: graememackie1@btinternet.com
Alt. contact: Liam Simpson Tel: (M) 07873112855
Email: liam.simpson@mcgowanltd.co.uk
Ground: Cromdale Park, Cromdale, PH26 3LW Tel:

Stonehaven
Mr Neale Scott, 149 Kincorth Circle, Aberdeen, AB12 5NS Tel: (H) 01224 943069 (M) 07738293966
Email: stonehavenjfc@hotmail.co.uk
Alt. contact: Chuck Thorn Tel: (H) 01224 745080 (M) 07763458841
Email: chuckthorne@aol.com
Ground: Glenury Park, Stonehaven, AB39 3LA Tel:

Stoneyburn
Mr Steven MacMillan, 1 Meadow Drive, Stoneyburn, EH47 8DZ Tel: (H) 01501 762032 (M) 07824662273
Email: stevielyn22uk@yahoo.com
Alt. contact: Derek Sutherland Tel: (M) 07969346582
Ground: Beechwood Park, Strathyre Drive, EH47 8AZ Tel:
Nickname: Fulshie

Stoneywood Parkvale
Mr Brian Hay, 21 Overton Park, Dyce, Aberdeen, AB21 7FT Tel: (H) 01224 725152 (M) 07876258116
Email: hayubrian@aol.com
Alt. contact: alan Stables Tel: (H) 01224 826146 (M) 07979854110
Email: alan@danestonemortgage.com
Ground: Clark Commercial Park, Market Street, Dyce, Aberdeen, AB21 9JH Tel:

Sunnybank
Ms Yvonne Mearns, 3 Chapman Walk, Aberdeen, AB16 7DG Tel: (H) 01224 691498 (M) 07973262025
Email: ymearns@yahoo.co.uk
Alt. contact: Lesley Christie Tel: (H) 01224 680242 (M) 07709192286
Email: lesley.christie@john-clark.co.uk
Ground: Heathryfold Park, Heathryfold, Aberdeen, AB16 7DS Tel: 01224 696309
Nickname: The Bankers

Tayport
Mr John Morris, 37 Elizabeth Street, Tayport, DD6 9ND Tel: (H) 01382 553320 (M) 07889170364
Email: johnmorris37@btinternet.com
Alt. contact: John Aitken Tel: (H) 01382 552789 (M) 07790225110
Email: tinkboy@hotmail.co.uk
Ground: The Canniepairt, Shanwell Road, Tayport, DD6 9DX Tel:

Thorniewood United
Mr Ian McLaughlin, 75 Greenrig, Uddingston, G71 7TD Tel: (H) 01698 810071 (W) 01698 201617 (M) 07758249811
Email: ianmclaughlan@blueyonder.co.uk
Alt. contact: John Miller Tel: (H) 01236 421456 (M)

07894709243
Ground: Robertson Park, Old Edinburgh Road, Uddingston, G71 6HQ Tel: 01698 816471

Thornton Hibs
Mr Craig Gilbert, Haslemere, 64 Emsdorf Street, Lundin Links, Fife, KY8 6HL Tel: (M) 07769217025
Email: proplumbservices@btinternet.com
Alt. contact: Audrey McDonald Tel: (M) 07834095069
Email: audrey.mcdonald@lloydbanking.com
Ground: Memorial Park, Old Main Street, Thornton, Fife, KY1 4AL Tel:

Tranent
Mr Robert McNeill, 11 Meadowmill Loan, Tranent, East Lothian, EH33 1FE Tel: (H) 01875 611830 (M) 07724727813
Email: robert.mcneill49@btinternet.com
Alt. contact: Colin Martin Tel: (M) 07746981719
Email: colinmartin06@gmail.com
Ground: Forresters Park, Lindores Drive, Tranent, EH33 1HY Tel:
Nickname: The Belters

Troon
Ms Sharon McSkimming, 15B Gillies Street, Troon, KA10 6QH Tel: (H) 01292 318076 (M) 07932214639
Email: shazhamltn@aol.com
Alt. contact: Richard Henderson Tel: (M) 07989475597
Email: 13hender@gmail.com
Ground: Portland Park, Portland Street, Troon, KA10 6QN Tel:

Vale of Clyde
Mr Jim Wilson, 183 Easterhill Street, Tollcross, Glasgow, G32 8LD Tel: (H) 0141 778 3340 (W) 0141 777 9050 (M) 07772973091
Email: sales@saltirecarpetsandbeds.co.uk
Alt. contact: John Morrison Tel: (H) 0141 573 8756 (B) 01236 734061 (M) 07852230990
Email: johnmorrison@9me.com
Ground: Fullarton Park, Easterhill Street, Tollcross , Glasgow, G32 8LD Tel: 0141 778 3340 (Jim Wilson - Secretary)
Nickname: Tin Pail

Vale of Leven F&AC
Mr Angus Wallace, 30 Whitehaugh Drive, Paisley, PA1 3PG Tel: (H) 0141 840 1556 (M) 07950075210
Email: anguswallace@btinternet.com
Alt. contact: Hugh Hamill Tel: (H) 01389 841050 (B) 0141 341 3922 (M) 07768670569
Email: h.hamill@hillebrandgroup.com
Ground: Millburn Park, Leven Street, Alexandria, G83 0SR Tel: 01389 752164

West Calder United
Ms Christine Lowther, 64 Parkhead Crescent, West Calder, West Lothian, EH55 8AX Tel: (H) 01506 794758 (M) 07557143517
Email: westcalderjuniors@hotmail.co.uk
Alt. contact: Lyndsay Lammie Tel: (H) 01506 871903 (M) 07850567728
Email: westcalderjuniors@hotmail.co.uk
Ground: Hermand Park, Harburn Road, West Calder, EH55 8WW Tel:
Nickname: Cauther

Whitburn
Ms Ann Haddow, 2 Loch Maree Way, Whitburn, West Lothian, EH47 0RW Tel: (H) 01501 743316 (M) 07917753017
Email: annhaddie@yahoo.com
Alt. contact: Ian Sherlock Tel: (H) 01501 743771
Ground: Central Park, East Main Street, Whitburn, EH47 0RE Tel: 01501 740557
Nickname: Burn

Whitehills
Mr Martyn Tevendale, 8 Seafield Place, Whitehills, Banff, AB45 2NG Tel: (H) 01261 861696
Email: martyntevendale@gmail.com
Alt. contact: Michael Watson Tel: (H) 01261 861040 (M) 07946830509
Email: michaelgwatson@tiscali.co.uk
Ground: School Park, Loch Street, Whitehills Tel:

Whitletts Victoria
Mr John Dalton, Barsalloch, 23 Sorn Road, Mauchline, Ayrshire, KA5 6AW Tel: (H) 01290 721971 (M) 07759637350
Email: jbd@sky.com
Alt. contact: Andrew McKissock Tel: (H) 01292 266361 (M) 07519344387
Email: andrew.mckissock@sky.com
Ground: Dam Park Stadium, Content Avenue, Ayr, KA8 0ET Tel: 01292 619595

Wishaw
Mr Robert Watson, 16 Binniehill Road, Cumbernauld, G68 9JJ Tel: (H) 01236 725042 (M) 07764223057
Email: wishawjuniors@hotmail.com
Alt. contact: William Kilgour Tel: (M) 07824594754
Email: william.kilgour@sky.com
Ground: The Beltane, Wishaw, ML2 0HL Tel:

Yoker Athletic
Mr John Cuthbertson, Flat 2, 21 Second Avenue, Clydebank, G81 3BD Tel: (H) 0141 952 7548 (M) 07769586845
Email: john.cuthbertson@yokerathletic.com
Alt. contact: Campbell Bissland Tel: (B) 0141 343 5434 (M) 07850150681
Email: campbell.bissland@yokerathletic.com
Ground: Holm Park, Yoker, G81 1LU Tel:
Nickname: Whey Ho

SCOTTISH JUNIOR CUP 2016/17

und	Date	Home	Away	F	A	
	24/09/2016	Armadale Thistle	Kennoway Star Hearts	1	3	
	24/09/2016	Wishaw	Cumnock	2	0	
	24/09/2016	Kirriemuir Thistle	Easthouses MW	4	0	
	24/09/2016	Whitletts Victoria	Buckie Rovers	5	2	
	24/09/2016	Ellon United	Glasgow Perthshire	0	1	
	24/09/2016	Newburgh Thistle	Sauchie	0	5	
	24/09/2016	Ardeer Thistle	East Kilbride Thistle	0	1	
	24/09/2016	Buchanhaven Hearts	Culter	0	2	
	24/09/2016	Thornton Hibs	Dunbar United	2	2	
	24/09/2016	New Elgin	Dundee North End	1	8	
	24/09/2016	Jeanfield Swifts	Lugar Boswell Thistle	3	0	
	24/09/2016	Livingston United	Cruden Bay	7	0	
	24/09/2016	Pumpherston	Kirkcaldy YM	3	0	
	01/10/2016	Saltcoats Vics	Renfrew	0	2	
	24/09/2016	West Calder United	Stoneywood Parkvale	3	0	
	24/09/2016	Vale of Clyde	Sunnybank	8	0	
	24/09/2016	Irvine Victoria	Newtongrange Star	2	1	
	24/09/2016	Newburgh	Hermes	0	5	
	24/09/2016	Largs Thistle	Blantyre Vics	0	1	
	24/09/2016	Port Glasgow	Whitehills	5	0	
	24/09/2016	Lochee United	Hurlford United	2	1	
	24/09/2016	Bo'ness United	Bellshill Athletic	3	3	
	24/09/2016	Lesmahagow	Irvine Meadow	0	2	
	24/09/2016	Haddington Athletic	Troon	1	0	
	24/09/2016	East Craigie	Bathgate Thistle	1	3	
	24/09/2016	Broxburn Athletic	Glenafton Athletic	3	3	
	24/09/2016	Ardrossan Winton Rovers	Dundonald Bluebell	2	1	
	24/09/2016	Camelon	Whitburn	3	4	
	24/09/2016	St Rochs	Kilwinning Rangers	0	1	
	24/09/2016	Kilbirnie Ladeside	Banchory St Ternan	6	0	
	24/09/2016	Arbroath Vics	Crossgates Primrose	4	4	
	01/10/2016	Crossgates Primrose	Arbroath Vics	1	3	
	01/10/2016	Bellshill Athletic	Bo'ness United	1	6	
	01/10/2016	Dunbar United	Thornton Hibs	3	3	4-3p
	01/10/2016	Glenafton Athletic	Broxburn Athletic	3	1	
	22/10/2016	Brechin Vics	Sauchie	1	4	
	22/10/2016	Craigmark Burntonians	Penicuik Athletic	0	4	
	22/10/2016	Kelty Hearts	Aberdeen University	6	1	
	22/10/2016	Shotts Bon Accord	Haddington Athletic	3	3	
	22/10/2016	Dunbar United	Kennoway Star Hearts	5	0	
	22/10/2016	Musselburgh Athletic	Craigroyston	8	4	
	22/10/2016	Forfar Albion	Blackburn United	0	11	
	22/10/2016	Glenafton Athletic	Livingston United	8	1	
	22/10/2016	Kinnoull	Glasgow Perthshire	1	2	
	22/10/2016	Luncarty	Fraserburgh United	4	1	
	22/10/2016	Coupar Angus	Forth Wanderers	3	5	
	22/10/2016	Dundee North End	Wishaw	5	0	
	22/10/2016	Inverness City	Scone Thistle	2	5	
		at Clachnacudin FC				
	22/10/2016	Royal Albert	Larkhall Thistle	1	3	
		at Larkhall Thistle FC				
	22/10/2016	Pollok	Glentanar	4	0	
	22/10/2016	Annbank United	Auchinleck Talbot	1	2	
	22/10/2016	Arbroath Vics	Whitburn	3	4	
	22/10/2016	Ashfield	Stoneyburn	1	1	
	22/10/2016	Benburb	Dyce	5	3	
	22/10/2016	Blantyre Vics	Tayport	2	0	
	22/10/2016	Burghead Thistle	Stonehaven	0	3	

2	22/10/2016	Cambuslang Rangers	Lochgelly Albert	1	2	
2	22/10/2016	Carluke Rovers	Deveronside	1	0	
2	22/10/2016	Colony Park	Kirkintilloch Rob Roy	0	4	
2	22/10/2016	Cumbernauld United	Rutherglen Glencairn	2	1	
2	22/10/2016	Darvel	Ardrossan Winton Rove	1	1	
2	22/10/2016	Downfield	Nairn St Ninian	1	0	
2	22/10/2016	Dufftown	Pumpherston	3	2	
2	22/10/2016	Dundee Violet	Blairgowrie	4	1	
2	22/10/2016	Aberdeen East End	Lochee United	0	6	
2	22/10/2016	East Kilbride Thistle	Forres Thistle	3	1	
2	22/10/2016	Edinburgh United	Dunipace	3	1	
2	22/10/2016	Fauldhouse United	St Anthonys	5	0	
2	22/10/2016	Forfar West End	Culter	0	2	
2	22/10/2016	Gartcairn	Newmachar United	5	0	
2	22/10/2016	Girvan	Muirkirk	5	2	
2	22/10/2016	Glenrothes	Hill of beath Hawthorn	1	6	
2	22/10/2016	Greenock	Vale of Leven	2	1	
2	22/10/2016	Hall Russell United	Maybole	0	2	
2	22/10/2016	Irvine Meadow	Oakley United	4	0	
2	22/10/2016	Jeanfield Swifts	St Andrews United	1	0	
2	22/10/2016	Johnstone Burgh	Broughty Athletic	1	2	
2	22/10/2016	Kello Rovers	Carnoustie Panmure	1	2	
2	22/10/2016	Kilwinning Rangers	Arthurlie	0	0	
2	22/10/2016	Kirriemuir Thistle	Whitletts Vicsd	3	0	
2	22/10/2016	Lanark United	Neilston	0	0	
2	22/10/2016	Lewis United	Rosyth	1	3	
2	22/10/2016	Lochee Harp	Maryhill	3	5	
2	22/10/2016	Lochore Welfare	Kilsyth Rangers	0	4	
2	22/10/2016	Maud	Spey Valley United	5	1	
2	22/10/2016	Newmains United	Hermes	1	1	
2	22/10/2016	Petershill	Dalkeith Thistle	2	1	
2	22/10/2016	Renfrew	Bathgate Thistle	6	4	
2	22/10/2016	Shettleston	Montrose Roselea	2	0	
2	22/10/2016	Tranent	Longside	4	3	
2	22/10/2016	West Calder United	Arniston Rangers	0	2	
2	22/10/2016	Yoker Athletic	Irvine Vics	2	3	
2	22/10/2016	Port Glasgow	Thorniewood	1	1	
2	22/10/2016	Islavale	Fochabers	9	0	
2	29/10/2016	Linlithgow Rose	Clydebank	3	0	
2	29/10/2016	Vale of Clyde	Beith	0	3	
2	29/10/2016	Bonnyrigg Rose`	Rossvale	3	1	
2	29/10/2016	Dalry Thistle	Bo'ness United	0	4	
2	05/11/2016	Banks o' Dee	Kilbirnie Ladeside	1	0	
2R	29/10/2016	Hermes	Newmains United	6	0	
2R	29/10/2016	Haddington Athletic	Shotts Bon Accord	3	3	4-3p
2R	29/10/2016	Stoneyburn	Ashfield	1	2	
2R	29/10/2016	Ardrossan Winton Rovers	Darvel	1	2	
2R	29/10/2016	Arthurlie	Kilwinning Rangers	1	3	
2R	29/10/2016	Neilston	Lanark United	2	1	
2R	29/10/2016	Thorniewoood United	Port Glasgow	3	1	
3	19/11/2016	Kilsyth Rangers	Lochgelly Albert	3	0	
3	19/11/2016	Penicuik Athletic	Scone Thistle	2	0	
3	19/11/2016	Haddington Athletic	Neilston	2	1	
3	19/11/2016	Blackburn United	Girvan	2	5	
3	19/11/2016	Glasgow Perthshire	Kirkintilloch Rob Roy	3	4	
3	19/11/2016	Petershill	Carnoustie Panmure	1	0	
		at St Anthony's FC				
3	19/11/2016	Banks o' Dee	Sauchie	0	5	
3	19/11/2016	Renfrew	Arniston Rangers	1	0	

3	19/11/2016	Dufftown	Dunbar United	1	2	
3	19/11/2016	Gartcairn	Whitburn	3	0	
3	19/11/2016	Maybole	Benburb	2	3	
3	19/11/2016	Maryhill	Forth Wanderers	2	0	
3	19/11/2016	Darvel	Irvine Meadow	1	1	
3	19/11/2016	Irvine Victoria	Carluke Rovers	1	2	
3	19/11/2016	Larkhall Thistle	Fauldhouse United	1	2	
3	19/11/2016	Kilwinning Rangers	Shettleston	5	2	
3	19/11/2016	Beith	Islavale	9	0	
3	19/11/2016	Kelty Hearts	Ashfield	7	1	
3	19/11/2016	Pollok	Auchinleck Talbot	1	1	
3	19/11/2016	Edinburgh United	Maud	2	1	
3	19/11/2016	Cumbernauld United	Tranent	2	1	
3	26/11/2016	Blantyre Vics	Bo'ness United	2	2	
		at Hamilton Accies FC, Att 574				
3	03/12/2016	Jeanfield Swifts	Hermes	2	3	
3	03/12/2016	Kirriemuir Thistle	Hill of Beath Hawthorn	1	4	
3	03/12/2016	Lochee United	Musselburgh Athletic	2	3	
3	03/12/2016	Dundee North End	Linlithgow Rose	0	5	
3	03/12/2016	Violet	Glenafton Athletic	0	2	
3	03/12/2016	Stonehaven	Greenock	1	1	
3	03/12/2016	Luncarty	Rosyth	3	2	
3	03/12/2016	East Kilbride Thistle	Culter	1	1	
3	03/12/2016	Downfield	Broughty Athletic	1	5	
3	03/12/2016	Thorniewoood United	Bonnyrigg Rose	1	1	
3R	03/12/2016	Bo'ness United	Blantyre Vics	2	2	3-4p
		15 minutes extra time played in error				
3R	03/12/2016	Irvine Meadow	Darvel	5	3	
3R	03/12/2016	Auchinleck Talbot	Pollok	4	0	
3R	10/12/2016	Culter	East Kilbride Thistle	1	2	
3R	10/12/2016	Greenock	Stonehaven	3	2	
3R	10/12/2016	Bonnyrigg Rose`	Thorniewood United	4	0	
4	21/01/2017	Broughty Athletic	Sauchie	0	4	
4	21/01/2017	Cumbernauld United	Luncarty	1	3	
4	21/01/2017	Beith	Auchinleck Talbot	0	1	
4	21/01/2017	Linlithgow Rose	Blantyre Vics	4	0	
4	21/01/2017	Renfrew	Greenock	2	0	
4	21/01/2017	Carluke Rovers	Irvine Meadow	1	0	
4	21/01/2017	Dunbar United	Benburb	3	1	
4	21/01/2017	Edinburgh United	Kilwinning Rangers	0	2	
4	21/01/2017	Fauldhouse United	Maryhill	0	0	
4	21/01/2017	Gartcairn	Hermes	1	1	
4	21/01/2017	Girvan	Penicuik Athletic	2	3	
4	21/01/2017	Kelty Hearts	Hill of Beath Hawthorn	5	0	
4	21/01/2017	Petershill	Haddington Athletic	7	1	
4	28/01/2017	East Kilbride Thistle	Glenafton Athletic	0	4	
4	28/01/2017	Kilsyth Rangers	Bonnyrigg Rose	2	2	
4	11/02/2017	Kirkintilloch Rob Roy	Musselburgh Athletic	2	1	
		at Benburb FC				
4R	04/02/2017	Bonnyrigg Rose`	Kilsyth Rangers	3	0	
5	11/03/2017	Maryhill	Linlithgow Rose	2	4	
		at St Anthony's FC				
5	18/02/2017	Dunbar United	Glenafton Athletic	0	3	
5	18/02/2017	Penicuik Athletic	Kirkintilloch Rob Roy	2	4	
5	18/02/2017	Auchinleck Talbot	Luncarty	4	0	
5	18/02/2017	Kelty Hearts	Kilwinning Rangers	1	2	
5	18/02/2017	Gartcairn	Carluke Rovers	2	2	
5	18/02/2017	Renfrew	Sauchie	2	4	
5	18/02/2017	Petershill	Bonnyrigg Rose	0	2	

5R	25/02/2017	Carluke Rovers	Gartcairn	2	3
6	18/03/2017	Auchinleck Talbot	Kilwinning Rangers	2	0
6	18/03/2017	Bonnyrigg Rose`	Kirkintilloch Rob Roy	2	0
6	18/03/2017	Glenafton Athletic	Sauchie	1	0
6	18/03/2017	Linlithgow Rose	Gartcairn	7	0
SF	15/04/2017	Glenafton Athletic	Bonnyrigg Rose	1	0
SF	15/04/2017	Linlithgow Rose	Auchinleck Talbot	0	0
SF	22/04/2017	Bonnyrigg Rose`	Glenafton Athletic	0	0
SF	22/04/2017	Auchinleck Talbot	Linlithgow Rose	1	0
F	04/06/2017	Glenafton Athletic	Auchinleck Talbot	2	1
		at Rugby Park, Kilmarnock, Att 6144			

FINAL DETAILS

Glenafton Athletic 2 Auchinleck Talbot 1, Att 6144

0-1	17m	Keir Milliken
1-1	28m	Cammy Marlow
2-1	75,	Alan Cairns

MoM	Dan Orsi
Referee:	David Dickinson

Glenafton Athletic: 1. Brian McGarrity 2. Kyle McAusland 3. Alan Cairns 4. Craig Menzies 5. Ryan MChesney 6. Ally Park 7. Dan Orsi 8. Cameron Marlow 9. Chris Dallas (15. John Carter) 10. Mick McCann (14. Joe Andrew) 11. Darren McGill (16. Conor Lynass). Subs not used 12. David Gray GK. Blair Lochhead

Auchinleck Talbot: 1. Andy Leishman 2. Ross Harvey 3. Willie 4. Martin McGoldrick 5. Steven White, 6.Stephen Wilson 7. Bryan Young 8. Craig McCracken (12 Mark Shankland) 9. Keir Milliken 10. Graham Wilson 11. Dwayne Hyslop. **Subs Unused:** Dylan Pooler, Klark Thomson, Neil McPherson, Dylan Stevenson.

TEAMS IN LAST 16 OF THE SCOTTISH JUNIOR CUP (Round 5)

	2006/7	2007/8	2008/9	2009/10	2010/11	201/12	2012/13	2013/14	2014/15	2015/16	2016/17
Ardrossan Winton Rovers					5						
Arthurlie	SF		QF			5			5	QF	
Ashfield			5			5					
Auchinleck Talbot		QF	W	5	W	F	W		W	QF	F
Ballingry Rovers		5									
Bathgate Thistle		W		QF							
Beith			5		5					W	
Bo'ness United				5	SF	QF	QF	QF			
Bonnyrigg Rose					QF	SF			5	5	SF
Camelon	5	5	5				QF	SF	5	QF	
Carluke Rovers											5
Carnoustie Panmure			5							5	
Clydebank		QF	F	SF							
Cumnock		F					QF	QF			
Dalry Thistle					SF			5			
Darvel										5	
Dunbar United											5
Dundonald Bluebell							5	QF			
East Kilbride Thist	5										
Fauldhouse United									5		
Gartcairn											QF
Glenafton Athletic		QF						F			W
Glenrothes			5		5						
Haddington Athletic					5						
Hermes										5	
Hill of Beath Hawthorn				QF							
Hurlford United								W	SF	SF	
Irvine Meadow	5		QF	QF	QF	QF	5	SF			
Jeanfield Swifts							5				
Kelty Hearts	F					5	QF			5	5
Kilbirnie Ladeside					QF	5			5	QF	
Kilsyth Rangers	5						5	5			
Kilwinning Rangers	SF					QF				SF	QF
Kinnoull						5					
Kirkintilloch Rob Roy			SF	5	QF		5				QF
Lanark United	QF	QF	5								
Largs Thistle				F		SF					
Larkhall Thistle						5					
Lesmahagow									5		
Linlithgow Rose	W			W			F		SF	5	SF
Lochee United	5	5		SF		5	5				
Luncarty											5
Maryhill				5							5
Maybole		5									
Montrose Roselea			5								
Musselburgh Athletic	5	5			F				F		
Neilston	QF	5									
Newtongrange Star		5	QF	5					5		
Penicuik Athletic								5	QF		5
Petershill	5		QF		5					5	5
Pollok	QF	SF	SF				5		QF	F	
Pumpherston							5				
Renfrew					5						5
Rossvale										5	
Rutherglen Glencairn				5			SF	5			
Sauchie					5			5			QF
Shettleston					5				QF		
Shotts Bon Accord		5		5		W	SF	5			
St Andrews United						QF			5		
St Rochs						5					
Tayport				QF				5			
Thorniewood United			5								
Thornton Hibs		SF									
Tranent	5										
Whitletts Vics				5				QF			
Yoker Athletic	QF							5	QF		

SCOTTISH JUNIOR CUP FORMAT

The Scottish Junior Cup uses one of the most "open" draw systems possible.

The First Round is held at the end of September and is used to reduce the number of competing teams to 128. This usually means around 40 ties are drawn. Clubs who are participating in the Scottish Cup (Senior) are given byes in Round One of the Scottish Junior Cup.

Other than that the draw is unseeded and not structured in any way.

In bygone days the early rounds were organised in Regions. As recently as the 1970s there were North and South sections. Before that smaller geographical groups ensured that all parts of Scotland were represented in the last 32.

In the 1950s this included the Argyllshire Juniors which was comprised of around half a dozen teams, all from the Kintyre peninsula.

The Semi Finals are now played on a two-leg basis. They used to be played as one-off matches on neutral (usually senior) grounds. However, increasing costs and falling crowds led to the change. The money from the Semi Finals now remains within the Junior game rather than being paid to senior clubs.

The venue for the Final is usually decided around April.

JUNIOR CLUBS IN THE SCOTTISH CUP

Since 2007/8 the 3 Regional Champions and the Scottish Junior Cup winners have been eligible to play in the Scottish Cup. They join Girvan who are "legacy members" of the SFA from their days as a Senior clubs, and Linlithgow Rose and Banks o' Dee who achieved club licenses in recent seasons.

The Junior clubs participating have been:

Auchinleck Talbot	2009/10, 2011/12, 2013/14, 2014/15 2015/16, 2016/17
Banks o' Dee	2008/9, 2009/10, 2014/15-2017/18 inclusive
Bathgate Thistle	2008/9
Beith	2010/11, 2016/17
Bo'ness United	2010/11, 2011/12, 2014/15
Bonnyrigg Rose	2009/10, 2012/13. 2016/17
Culter	2007/8, 2011/12, 2013/14, 2014/15
Girvan	2007/8-2016/17 inclusive
Glenafton Ath	2017/18
Hermes	2012/13, 2015/16
Hurlford United	2014/15
Irvine Meadow	2009/10, 2011/12, 2012/13
Kelty Hearts	2015/16, 2017/18
Lochee United	2008/9
Linlithgow Rose	2007/8, 2010/11, 2013/14, 2014/15-2017/18 inclusive
Pollok	2007/8, 2008/9
Shotts Bon Accord	2012/13
Sunnybank	2010/11

Dates for 2017/18 Scottish Junior Cup are :

Round 1	23 Sep 2017	(Byes given to Junior clubs involved in the senior Scottish Cup)
Round 2	28 Oct 2017	
Round 3	25 Nov 2017	
Round 4	20 Jan 2018	
Round 5	17 Feb 2018	
Round 6	17 Mar 2018	
Semis	14/15 Apr 2018	21/22 Apr 2018
Final	27 May 2018	

SCOTTISH JUNIOR CUP FINALS and SEMI FINALISTS

ason	Winners	Runners Up				LOSING SEMI FINALISTS	
86/87	Fairfield Govan	Edinburgh Woodburn	3	1	after protest	Westburn	Burnbank Swifts
87/88	Wishaw Thistle	Maryhill	3	1	after 2 protests	Hamilton West End	Carluke Milton Rovers
88/89	Burnbank Swifts	West Benhar Violet	4	1		Hamilton West End	Edinburgh Woodburn
89/90	Burnbank Swifts	Benburb	3	1	after protest	Kilmarnock Shawbank	Carluke Milton Rovers
90/91	Vale of Clyde	Chrytson Athletic	2	0	after 1-1 draw	Leith Rangers	Newton Thistle
91/92	Minerva	West Benhar Violet	5	2		Vale of Clyde	Darvel
92/93	Vale of Clyde	Dumbarton Fern	3	2	after 1-1 draw	Crown Athletic	Haywood Wanderers
93/94	Ashfield	Renfrew Victoria	3	0	after 1-1 draw	Broxburn Athletic	Blantyre Vics
94/95	Ashfield	West Calder Wanderers	2	1	after 1-1 draw	Lenzie	Glasgow Perthshire
95/96	Cambuslang Hibs	Parkhead	2	1		Broxburn Athletic	Strathclyde
96/97	Strathclyde	Dunfermline Juniors	2	0		Captain Colt's Rovers	Ashfield
97/98	Dalziel Rovers	Parkhead	2	1		Captain Colt's Rovers	Glenbuck Cherrypickers
98/99	Parkhead	Westmarch XI	4	1		Dalziel Rovers	Duntocher Hibs
99/00	Maryhill	Rugby XI	3	2		Holytown Thistle	Cambuslang Hibs
00/01	Burnbank Athletic	Maryhill	2	0		Parkhead Athletic	Renfrew Vics
01/02	Glencairn	Maryhill	1	0		Dunipace	Strathclyde
02/03	Parkhead	Larkhall Thistle	3	0		Ardeer Thistle	Burnbank Athletic
03/04	Vale of Clyde	Parkhead	3	0		Maryhill	Darvel
04/05	Ashfield	Renfrew Victoria	2	1		Maryhill	Arniston Rangers
05/06	Dunipace	Rob Roy	1	0	after 2-2 draw	Maryhill	Kirkintilloch Rob Roy
06/07	Strathclyde	Maryhill	1	0	after two 1-1 draws	St Ninian's Thistle	Clydebank
07/08	Larkhall Thistle	Queen's Park Hampden XI	1	0		St Ninian's Thistle	Cowie Wanderers
08/09	Kilwinning Rangers	Strathclyde	1	0	ater 0-0 draw	Penicuik	Yoker Athletic
09/10	Ashfield	Kilwinning Rangers	3	0	after protest	Port Glasgow	Arniston Rangers#
10/11	Burnbank Athletic	Petershill	1	0	after 2-2 draw	Cambuslang Rangers	Ardrossan Winton Rovers
11/12	Petershill	Denny Hibs	5	0		Cambuslang Rangers	Kilbirnie Ladeside
12/13	Inverkeithing United	Dunipace	1	0		Kilbirnie Ladeside	Larkhall Thistle
13/14	Larkhall Thistle	Ashfield	1	0	after draws 0-0, 1-1	Renfrew	Yoker Athletic
14/15	Parkhead	Port Glasgow	2	0		Ashfield	Petershill
15/16	Petershill	Parkhead	2	0		Cambuslang Rangers	Larkhall Thistle
16/17	St Mirren Juniors	Renfrew	1	0	after 0-0 draw	Cambuslang Rangers	Bellshill Athletic
17/18	Petershill awarded cup					St Mirren Juniors	Parkhead / Renfrew
18/19	Glencairn	St Anthonys	1	0	after 1-1 draw	Kilsyth Emmet	Parkhead
19/20	Parkhead	Cambuslang Rangers	2	0		Cumnock	Burnbank
20/21	Rob Roy	Ashfield	1	0		Cambuslang Rangers	Parkhead
21/22	St Rochs	Kilwinning Rangers	2	1	after protest	Cambuslang Rangers	Rutherglen Glencairn
22/23	Musselburgh Bruntonians	Arniston Rangers	2	0		Carluke Rovers	Port Glasgow Ath Juniors
23/24	Parkhead	Baillieston	3	1	after 1-1 draw	Auchinleck Talbot	Blantyre Celtic
24/25	Saltcoats Victoria	St Anthonys	2	1	after draws 1-1, 3-3	Shettleston	Shieldmuir Celtic
25/26	Strathclyde	Bridgeton Waverley	2	0	after 1-1 draw	Parkhead Athletic	St Rochs
26/27	Glencairn	Cambuslang Rangers	2	1		Tranent	Darvel
27/28	Maryhill Hibs	Burnbank Athletic	6	2		Coalburn	Saltcoats Vics
28/29	Dundee Violet	Denny Hibs	4	0	after protest and 2-2 draw	Coalburn	Burnbank Athletic
29/30	Newtongrange Star	Hall Russell	3	0		Croy Celtic	Larkhall Royal Albert
30/31	Denny Hibs	Burnbank Athletic	1	0		Rothesay Royal Vivs	Lochee Harp
31/32	Glasgow Perthshire	Rob Roy	2	1		Larkhall Thistle	Rosslyn Juniors
32/33	Yoker Athletic	Tranent	4	2	after 0-0 draw	Renfrew	Bonnyrigg Rose
33/34	Benburb	Bridgeton Waverley	3	1		Lochee Harp	Ardrossan Winton Rovers
34/35	Tranent	Petershill	6	1		Shawfield	Wishaw
35/36	Benburb	Yoker Athletic	1	0	after 1-1 draw	Renfrew	St Anthonys
36/37	Arthurlie	Rob Roy	5	1		Morton Juniors	Glasgow Perthshire
37/38	Cambuslang Rangers`	Benburb	3	2		Dunipace	Blantyre Celtic
38/39	Glencairn	Shawfield	2	1		Benburb	Cambuslang Rangers
39/40	Maryhill	Morton Juniors	1	0		Larkhall Royal Albert	Arthurlie
40/41	Glasgow Perthshire	Armadale Thistle	3	1	after draws 2-2, 0-0	Petershill	Winchburgh Albion
41/42	Clydebank	Vale of Clyde	4	2		Polkemmet	St Anthonys
42/43	Rob Roy	Benburb	3	1	after draws 1-1, 0-0	Bedlay	Petershill
43/44	Glasgow Perthshire	Blantyre Vics	1	0		Ardeer Recreation	Maryhill
44/45	Burnbank Athletic	Cambuslang Rangers	3	1	after protest	St Rochs	Pollok
45/46	Fauldhouse United	Arthurlie	2	0		Polkemmet	Blantyre Celtic

1946/47	Shawfield	Bo'ness United	2	1	after 1-1 draw	Irvine Meadow	Renfrew
1947/48	Bo'ness United	Irvine Meadow	2	1		Bathgate Thistle	Shawfield
1948/49	Auchinleck Talbot	Petershill	3	2		Benburb	Newtongrange Star
1949/50	Blantyre Vics	Cumnock	3	0		Ardeer Recreation	Stoneyburn
1950/51	Petershill	Irvine Meadow	1	0		Broxburn Athletic	Armadale Thistle
1951/52	Kilbirnie Ladeside	Camelon	1	0		Lugat Boswell Thistle	Carnoustie Panmure
1952/53	Vale of Leven	Annbank United	1	0		Arniston Rangers	Ashfield
1953/54	Sunnybank	Lochee Harp	2	1		Clydebank	Baillieston
1954/55	Kilsyth Rangers	Duntocher Hibs	4	1	after 1-1 draw	Ashfield	Armadale Thistle
1955/56	Petershill	Lugar Boswell Thitle	4	1		Whitletts Vics	Broxburn Athletic
1956/57	Banks o' Dee	Kilsyth Rangers	1	0		Loanhead Mayflower	Duntocher Hibs
1957/58	Shotts Bon Accord	Pumpherston	2	0		Baillieston	Irvine Meadow
1958/59	Irvine Meadow	Shettleston	2	1		Carluke Rovers	Johnstone Burgh
1959/60	St Andrews United	Greenock	3	1		Thornton Hibs	Ardeer Thistle
1960/61	Dunbar United	Cambuslang Rangers	2	0	after 2-2 draw	Ashfield	Dundee St Josephs
1961/62	Rob Roy	Renfrew	1	0	after 1-1 draw	Glenafton Athletic	Newburgh
1962/63	Irvine Meadow	Glenafton Athletic	2	1		Bonnyrigg Rose	Craigmark Burntonians
1963/64	Johnstone Burgh	Cambuslang Rangers	3	0	after 1-1 draw	Irvine Meadow	Kirkintilloch Rob Roy
1964/65	Linlithgow Rose	Baillieston	4	1		Aberdeen Rosemount	Kilsyth Rangers
1965/66	Bonnyrigg Rose	Whitburn	6	1	after 1-1 draw	Penicuik Athletic	Shettleston
1966/67	Kilsyth Rangers	Glencairn	3	1	after 1-1 draw	Carluke Rovers	Johnstone Burgh
1967/68	Johnstone Burgh	Glenrothes	4	3	after 2-2 draw	Larkhall Thistle	Lochee Harp
1968/69	Cambuslang Rangers`	Rob Roy	1	0		Irvine Meadow	Linlithgow Rose
1969/70	Blantyre Vics	Penicuik Athletic	1	0	after 2-2 draw	Ardrossan Winton Rovers	Ashfield
1970/71	Cambuslang Rangers`	Newtongrange Star	2	1		Dalkeith Thistle	Broxburn Athletic
1971/72	Cambuslang Rangers`	Bonnyrigg Rose	3	2	after 1-1 draw	Newtongrange Star	Johnstone Burgh
1972/73	Irvine Meadow	Cambuslang Rangers	1	0	after draws 3-3, 2-2	East Kilbride Thistle	Newburgh
1973/74	Cambuslang Rangers`	Linlithgow Rose	3	1		Glasgow Perthshire	Blantyre Vics
1974/75	Glenrothes	Glencairn	1	0		Kilbirnie Ladeside	Ashfield
1975/76	Bo'ness United	Darvel	3	0		Lanark United	Kilbirnie Ladeside
1976/77	Kilbirnie Ladeside	Rob Roy	3	1		Shettleston	Lesmahagow
1977/78	Bonnyrigg Rose	Stonehouse Violet	1	0		Carnoustie Panmure	Renfrew
1978/79	Cumnock	Bo'ness United	1	0		Pollok	Glenafton Athletic
1979/80	Baillieston	Benburb	2	0	AET and 2-2 draw	Dunipace	Lochee United
1980/81	Pollok	Arthurlie	1	0		Bo'ness United	Forth Wanderers
1981/82	Blantyre Vics	Baillieston	1	0		Bonnyrigg Rose	Kirkintilloch Rob Roy
1982/83	East Kilbride Thistle	Bo'ness United	2	0		Auchinleck Talbot	Pollok
1983/84	Bo'ness United	Baillieston	2	0		Auchinleck Talbot	Darvel
1984/85	Pollok	Petershill	3	1	after 1-1 draw	Darvel	Downfield
1985/86	Auchinleck Talbot	Pollok	3	2		Cumnock	Kilbirnie Ladeside
1986/87	Auchinleck Talbot	Kilbirnie Ladeside	1	0	after 1-1 draw	Irvine Meadow	Arthurlie
1987/88	Auchinleck Talbot	Petershill	1	0		Newtongrange Star	Whitburn
1988/89	Cumnock	Ormiston Primrose	1	0		Shotts Bon Accord	Lesmahagow
1989/90	Hill of Beath Hawthorn	Lesmahagow	1	0		Linlithgow Rose	Whitburn
1990/91	Auchinleck Talbot	Newtongrange Star	1	0		Arthurlie	Glenafton Athletic
1991/92	Auchinleck Talbot	Glenafton Athletic	4	0		Beith	Whitburn
1992/93	Glenafton Athletic	Tayport	1	0		Auchinleck Talbot	Lesmahagow
1993/94	Largs Thistle	Glenafton Athletic	1	0		Arthurlie	Kilwinning Rangers
1994/95	Camelon	Whitburn	2	0	AET	Lochee United	Glenafton Athletic
1995/96	Tayport	Camelon	2	1		Auchinleck Talbot	Pollok
1996/97	Pollok	Tayport	3	1		Blantyre Vics	Arthurlie
1997/98	Arthurlie	Pollok	4	0		Maryhill	Kilwinning Rangers
1998/99	Kilwinning Rangers	Kelty Hearts	1	0		Petershill	Arthurlie
1999/00	Whitburn	Johnstone Burgh	2	2	AET, 4-3 pens	Benburb	Shotts Bon Accord
2000/1	Renfrew	Carnoustie Panmure	0	0	AET, 6-5 pens	Auchinleck Talbot	Shettleston
2001/2	Linlithgow Rose	Auchinleck Talbot	1	0		Kilwinning Rangers	Tayport
2002/3	Tayport	Linlithgow Rose	1	0		Bo'ness United	Maryhill
2003/4	Carnoustie Panmure	Tayport	0	0	AET, 6-5 pens	Glenrothes	Hill of Beath Hawthorn
2004/5	Tayport	Lochee United	2	0		Maryhill	Renfrew
2005/6	Auchinleck Talbot	Bathgate Thistle	2	1		Irvine Meadow	Tayport
2006/7	Linlithgow Rose	Kelty Hearts	2	1	AET	Kilwinning Rangers	Arthurlie
2007/8	Bathgate Thistle	Cumnock	2	1		Pollok	Thornton Hibs
2008/9	Auchinleck Talbot	Clydebank	2	1		Pollok	Kirkintilloch Rob Roy
2009/10	Linlithgow Rose	Largs Thistle	1	0		Lochee United	Clydebank
2010/11	Auchinleck Talbot	Musselburgh Athletic	2	1	AET	Bo'ness United	Dalry Thistle
2011/12	Shotts Bon Accord	Auchinleck Talbot	2	1		Largs Thistle	Bonnyrigg Rose
2012/13	Auchinleck Talbot	Linlithgow Rose	1	0		Rutherglen Glencairn	Shotts Bon Accord
2013/14	Hurlford United	Glenafton Athletic	3	0		Irvine Meadow	Camelon
2014/15	Auchinleck Talbot	Musselburgh Athletic	2	1		Linlithgow Rose	Hurlford United
2015/16	Beith	Pollok	1	1	4-3p	Hurlford United	Kilwinning Rangers
2016/17	Glenafton Athletic	Auchinleck Talbot	2	1		Bonnyrigg Rose	Linlithgow Rose

EAST REGION JUNIORS

The East Region of Scottish Junior football extends from Brechin in the north to Dunbar in the south-east and Fauldhouse in the south west. It includes the counties of Angus, Perthshire, Fife, East, Mid and West Lothian, Clackmannanshire, parts of Stirlingshire as well as the cities of Dundee and Edinburgh.

The East Region was formed in 2002 by the amalgamation of the Lowlands, Fife and Tayside Regions. Initially there was a Region-wide Super League fed by three District Leagues. A Premier Division (tier 2) was introduced in 2006. From 2013 the top two divisions were expanded to sixteen clubs and the three lower leagues amalgamated into two. This meant that the Fife clubs were split between the North and South Divisions.

Two teams are relegated and promoted between the Super and Premier Divisions with the 3rd bottom and 3rd top playing off. Two teams are promoted from each of the lower leagues with four relegated from the Premier Division. There is no official policy on the composition of the lower leagues but some teams have been switched to try and maintain parity of size.

All clubs compete in the Scottish Junior Cup and the East of Scotland Junior Cup. Below that the Cup competitions are based on the old districts which existed until 2002—Tayside, Fife and Lothians.

The entrants to the long-established Fife and Lothians Cup are self explanatory. The Tayside clubs compete in a similar competition with the North (Aberdeen etc.) Juniors. There is also provision for a Fife-Tayside competition should there be room in the fixture list. These competitions are known as Inter-District Cups.

Tayport represent a slight anomaly. Although located in Fife, the club chose to join the old Tayside Region when they joined the Juniors in 1990. They have regularly applied for membership of the Fife and Lothians FA but have always been rejected.

In recent years the 'domestic' knock-out cups have been pruned due to fixture congestion. Until a few years ago there were three knock out cups in each district; in 2009/10 just one was played in each District and from 2010/11 none at all.

LEAGUE STRUCTURE

SUPER LEAGUE (16)
Two teams relegated
One team in relegation Play Off

PREMIER LEAGUE (16)
Two teams promoted
One team in promotion Play Off
Four teams relegated

NORTH LEAGUE
Two teams promoted

SOUTH LEAGUE
Two teams promoted

League Composition 2017/18

SUPER	PREMIER	NORTH	SOUTH
Bo'ness United	Arniston Rangers	Arbroath Vics	Armadale Th (R)
Bonnyrigg Rose	Bathgate Thistle	Blairgowrie	Craigroyston
Broughty Athletic	Blackburn United (P)	Brechin Vics	Crossgates Primrose
Broxburn Athletic	Dalkeith Th	Coupar Angus	Easthouses Lily
Camelon	Downfield	Dundee NE	Edinburgh United
Carnoustie Panmure	Dunbar Utd (P)	East Craigie	Harthill Royal
Dundonald Bluebell	Fauldhouse United (R)	Forfar Albion	Kirkcaldy YM
Forfar West End (P)	Glenrothes	Kinnoull	Livingston Utd
Hill of Beath Hawthorn	Haddington Ath	Lochee Harp	Lochgelly Albert
Jeanfield Swifts	Kirrie Thistle (P)	Lochore Welfare	Oakley United
Kennoway Star Hearts (P)	Musselburgh Athletic (R)	Luncarty	Pumpherston
Linlithgow Rose	St Andrew's Utd	Newburgh	Rosyth
Lochee United	Tayport	Scone Thistle	Stoneyburn
Newtongrange Star	Thornton Hibs (P)	Violet (R)	West Calder Utd
Penicuik Athletic	Tranent		
Sauchie (P)	Whitburn		

Mcbookie.com East Super League 2016/17

	BU	BONY	BRTY	BROX	CAM	CAR	DDB	FAU	HOB	JEA	KEL	LIN	LOC	MUS	NEW	PEN
Bo'ness United		Sep 17 2-3	Nov 5 3-0	Mar 4 0-1	Oct 8 0-0	Aug 13 4-1	Aug 27 2-1	Feb 18 7-0	Aug 10 1-2	Feb 11 5-1	Jan 7 1-2	May 13 2-0	Mar 25 3-4	Apr 22 5-1	Dec 17 4-1	May 6 5-0
Bonnyrigg Rose	Apr 8 2-0		Aug 20 4-0	Sep 10 3-1	Aug 24 1-0	May 27 5-0	Apr 29 4-0	Feb 25 2-0	Nov 5 1-0	May 24 5-0	Aug 6 2-4	May 31 0-2	Mar 11 3-0	May 8 1-2	Jan 14 3-0	Aug 17 3-0
Broughty Athletic	Feb 25 0-1	May 20 0-6		Apr 29 1-6	Oct 29 0-1	Oct 8 3-4	Mar 18 3-1	Aug 13 3-2	Sep 17 1-0	Aug 10 3-3	Apr 15 0-0	Dec 10 2-2	Jun 3 2-3	Aug 27 2-0	Apr 8 2-2	Oct 1 1-0
Broxburn Athletic	Nov 12 1-3	May 3 1-0	May 10 0-2		Mar 18 5-0	Dec 17 3-0	Aug 13 1-2	Aug 10 4-0	May 6 0-3	Aug 27 7-3	Nov 26 1-2	Apr 8 0-1	Dec 10 3-1	Sep 17 1-5	Oct 22 1-1	Jan 28 3-3
Camelon	May 3 1-5	Apr 24 1-2	Jan 28 5-2	Jan 7 1-1		Sep 17 2-3	Oct 22 3-3	Aug 27 2-1	Apr 22 2-2	Apr 1 1-2	Feb 11 0-3	Aug 10 2-1	Oct 1 2-1	Dec 17 1-1	Mar 25 1-1	Dec 3 0-1
Carnoustie Panmure	May 20 1-3	Oct 15 2-1	Aug 17 0-4	Aug 20 1-6	Dec 10 1-1		Feb 25 2-2	Mar 18 4-0	Jan 28 2-0	Apr 29 0-1	Apr 1 1-5	Nov 12 1-0	Apr 15 0-2	Sep 24 1-2	Aug 6 2-4	Sep 10 1-5
Dundonald Bluebell	Apr 15 5-0	Jan 7 3-1	Sep 10 1-2	Oct 15 5-6	Aug 6 1-0	Dec 3 2-3		Oct 29 1-2	Apr 1 1-0	Oct 1 4-2	Mar 25 2-1	Jan 28 1-1	Aug 17 2-3	Apr 8 3-1	Nov 19 0-0	Aug 20 2-6
Fauldhouse United	Aug 17 1-3	May 1 0-2	Mar 25 0-2	Apr 15 1-3	Apr 8 1-3	Oct 1 2-2	Mar 11 0-5		Dec 17 1-2	May 6 0-2	Aug 20 1-3	Nov 5 1-4	Aug 6 0-5	Oct 15 1-4	Sep 10 4-2	May 3 0-0
Hill of Beath Hawthorn	Dec 10 0-2	Mar 25 2-3	Apr 19 1-3	Aug 6 3-3	Aug 17 0-1	Oct 29 1-1	Nov 12 4-4	Sep 24 3-1		Mar 11 3-1	Sep 10 2-5	May 3 1-0	May 20 0-2	Apr 15 1-1	Aug 20 3-0	Apr 29 0-2
Jeanfield Swifts	Aug 20 0-5	May 13 1-3	Dec 17 1-1	Feb 18 3-3	Sep 10 4-0	Mar 25 2-2	Feb 4 2-3	Nov 12 1-3	Oct 15 3-1		Aug 17 2-3	Jun 3 0-1	Apr 8 0-0	May 20 2-1	Apr 15 4-4	Aug 6 2-3
Kelty Hearts	Apr 29 2-1	Jun 3 3-0	Nov 12 3-1	Mar 11 2-0	Oct 15 1-1	Aug 27 5-0	Aug 10 1-0	Dec 3 3-0	May 13 4-1	Feb 25 1-2		Sep 17 2-0	Jan 28 4-1	Aug 13 3-1	Oct 1 5-3	Dec 17 3-3
Linlithgow Rose	Sep 10 0-3	Dec 17 0-1	Aug 6 1-2	Aug 17 2-1	Apr 29 1-1	Feb 11 1-2	Apr 24 2-2	May 8 3-1	Oct 1 0-0	Jan 7 1-1	May 20 0-2		Aug 20 4-1	May 17 2-0	May 1 0-1	Mar 25 0-2
Lochee United	Jan 21 2-2	Aug 27 0-3	May 6 2-0	Apr 22 1-0	Feb 18 4-0	Aug 10 3-0	Dec 17 0-2	Apr 1 2-0	Aug 13 1-3	Sep 17 5-2	Nov 5 0-5	May 27 103		Mar 18 0-0	Apr 29 1-2	Nov 12 2-0
Musselburgh Athletic	Aug 6 1-0	Nov 12 0-1	May 13 1-2	Mar 25 1-2	Aug 20 1-1	Jan 21 3-3	Oct 8 1-2	Apr 29 4-0	Jan 7 1-1	Oct 29 2-2	Dec 10 1-2	May 6 2-2	Sep 10 1-1		Aug 17 1-1	Feb 25 2-3
NewtongrangeStar	Mar 18 0-0	Aug 10 0-1	Jan 7 1-1	Dec 3 2-2	Nov 12 2-0	Apr 22 4-1	Sep 17 1-4	Dec 10 2-1	Feb 18 2-3	Aug 13 0-2	Feb 4 2-4	Aug 27 2-3	Oct 29 0-2	Apr 26 1-0		Oct 15 2-4
Penicuik Athletic	Feb 4 1-1	May 10 1-4	Mar 4 1-1	Oct 29 5-3	Apr 15 1-1	Apr 8 0-2	Dec 10 5-1	Sep 17 6-1	Aug 27 4-0	Mar 18 4-0	Sep 24 0-1	Aug 13 0-2	May 13 2-3	Aug 10 1-1	Mar 11 3-0	

			Home					Away						
		P	W	D	L	F	A	W	D	L	F	A	GD	Pts
1	**Kelty Hearts**	30	12	2	1	42	14	13	1	1	42	15	55	78
2	Bonnyrigg Rose	30	12	0	3	39	9	11	0	4	31	16	45	69
3	Boness United	30	9	1	5	44	17	8	3	4	29	17	39	55
4	Penicuik Athletic	30	6	4	5	34	21	8	3	4	31	26	18	49
5	Lochee United (P)	30	7	2	6	24	22	8	2	5	29	26	5	49
6	Dundonald Bluebell (P)	30	7	2	6	33	27	6	4	5	32	31	7	45
7	Broughty Athletic	30	5	4	6	23	31	7	3	5	23	24	-9	43
8	Broxburn Athletic	30	6	2	7	31	26	6	4	5	38	31	12	42
9	Linlithgow Rose	30	4	4	7	17	20	7	3	5	22	17	2	40
10	Hill of Beath Hawthorn	30	4	4	7	24	29	5	3	7	18	24	-11	34
11	Carnoustie Panmure	30	4	2	9	19	36	5	4	6	24	40	-33	33
12	Camelon Juniors	30	4	5	6	24	29	3	6	6	10	23	-18	32
13	Jeanfield Swifts (P)	30	3	5	7	27	33	5	3	7	24	41	-23	32
14	*Newtongrange Star*	30	4	3	8	21	28	3	6	6	22	34	-19	30
15	**Musselburgh Athletic**	30	2	7	6	22	23	4	4	7	20	25	-6	29
16	**Fauldhouse United**	30	1	2	12	13	42	2	0	13	12	47	-64	11

Play Off Matches

27/5/17
Forfar West End v Newtongrange Star
3-1, Att 250

3/6/17
Newtongrange Star v Forfar West End
1-0, Att 750

Aggregate
Forfar West End v Newtongrange Star
3-2

Newtongrange were reprieved due to resignation of Kelty Hearts.

Kelty Hearts set the pace, aided by being able to fulfil most of their fixtures due to their artificial pitch. Bonnyrigg Rose, with a huge backlog of games, knew exactly what they had to and mounted a strong chase. Ultimately the number of games proved too much for them—had they won their final two, at home to Linlithgow and away to Kelty, they would have caught the Fife side. In the event, they lost both.

Bonnyrigg did bring great credit to the East region by beating SPFL Championship side Dumbarton in the Scottish Cup, earning a money -spinning tie against Hibernian, played at Tynecastle.

Fauldhouse United were adrift from the rest of the division. A late run by Newtongrange Star lifted them into the play-off spot, consigning Musselburgh to an unexpected relegation.

The three promoted clubs all did well. Jeanfield will be delighted to have survived whilst Lochee United and Dundonald Bluebell performed far above expectations.

The biggest disappointments were certainly Linlithgow Rose who flirted with relegation at one stage before a late recovery. Bo'ness United also had a disappointing season by their own exacting standards.

Kelty Hearts will not be defending their title having taken the decision to move to Senior football and chase the dream of a place in the SPFL. Bonnyrigg, with cash banked from last season's Cup exploits, will surely be the team to catch in 2017/18.

EAST JUNIOR SUPER LEAGUE - ALL TIME POSITIONS

	2002-3	2003-4	2004-5	2005-6	2006-7	2007-8	2008-9	2009-10	2010-11	2011-12	2012-13	2013-14	2014-15	2015-16	2016-17
Armadale Thistle												11	14		
Arniston Rangers	4	5	9	11											
Ballingry Rovers												13	Res		
Bathgate Thistle	3	7	7	2	7	8	8	3	8	11					
Bo'ness United		6	5	7	11		10	1	1	4	4	1	2	4	3
Bonnyrigg Rose	6	3	4	6	2	4	1	10	4	1	2	3	7	1	2
Broughty Athletic														10	7
Broxburn Athletic											6	7	8	6	8
Camelon			11		10	3	2	6	10	6	3	5	12	11	12
Carnoustie Panmure	10		8	8	4	11				10	9	12	13	12	11
Dundee North End	9	12		12											
Dundee Violet	12														
Dundonald Bluebell															6
Edinburgh United	11														
Fauldhouse United													10	13	16
Forfar West End							11		6	Res					
Glenrothes	8	8	6	10		9	7	12							
Hill of Beath Haws	2	11		3	6	10	6	8	2	2	8	6	9	8	10
Jeanfield Swifts															13
Kelty Hearts		10				7	5	9	9	5	5	14	1	2	1
Kinnoull					12										
Linlithgow Rose	5	1	3	5	1	5	3	2	3	3	1	2	3	3	9
Lochee United		4	1	9	5	1	9	5	5	7	10	10	15		5
Musselburgh Athletic								7	7	8	7	8	11	7	15
Newtongrange Star								4	12			4	4	5	14
Oakley United	7	9	10		9	12									
Penicuik Athletic													6	9	4
Sauchie											11	9	5	14	
St Andrews United										9	12	16		15	
Tayport	1	2	2	1	8	6	12		11			15		16	
Thornton Hibs			12												
Whitburn				4	3	2	4	11							

East Juniors Super League Playing Squads 2016/17

B These are not comprehensive lists of players used - there will be some omissions. However, all players listed were associated with e club concerned during 2016/17.

'ness United
anager: Allan McGonnigal
sistant: Steve Pittman Coach: ssell Lee
ss Campbell (2014 Clydebank)
ott Christie (2015 Linlithgow Rose, Hamilton Accies, Stirling Albion, 'ness Utd)
arlie Clark
n Collumbine (On Loan to madale Th Feb-May 2017)
ewart Devine (2011 Stranraer, tired 2017, ex Stirling Albion)
ris Donnelly (2011 Heriot Watt iiv)
ser Eddington (2016 nhousemuir, Ex North rchiston BC)
in El-Zubaidi (2017 Ex wdenbeath, Hamilton Accies)
chael Gemmell (2015 Hill of Beath ws, Ex Gairdoch Utd, Airdrie Utd, nadale Th, Bonnyrigg Rose)
tt Gibb (2011 Stenhousemuir, Ex kirk, Stirling Alb, Drogheda ted, N Ireland U21 Cap)
art Hunter (2011 Bathgate Thistle)
Darren Jamieson (2016 Livingston, then transferred to Hamilton Accies)
Fraser Keast (2016 Broxburn Ath, Ex Airdrie Utd)
Roddy McLennan (2016 Linlithgow Rose, Ex Clyde)
Ruari McLennan (2016 Linlithgow Rose, Ex Clyde)
John Miller (2016 Broxburn Ath, ex Dalkeith Th)
Andrew Murphy (2017 Queen's Park)
Paul Murphy (2016 Cumnock, then transferred to Petershill, ex Glenafton Ath, Bo'ness United)
Ross Philp (2014 Kelty Hearts, Ex Alloa)
Scott Ritchie (2016 Whitburn, Ex Bo'ness Utd, Alloa U20)
Connor Scullion (2017 Hamilton Accies On Loan, Jan-May)
Jack Simpson (2016 Hamilton Accies)
Robert Sloan (2013 East Fife, Ex Hearts, St Johnstone, Alloa)
Calum Smith (2016 Kelty HeaRTS, EX Linlithgow R)
Will Snowdon (2007 Stranraer, Ex Ipswich T, Livingston, Partick Th)
Colin Strickland (2016 Linlithgow Rose, Ex Whitburn)
Ross Tierney (On Loan to Armadale Th Feb-May 2017)
Nicky Walker (ex Spartans, Stirling Albion, Brechin C etc, Retired Sep 2016)
Marty Wright (2015 Camelon, ex Dunipace)

Bonnyrigg Rose
Manager: Robbie Horn Assistant: David Burrell Coaches: Jim McQueen, Kevin McLeish
Michael Andrews (2015 Cowdenbeath, ex Berwick R, Brechin C, E Fife, Montrose, Falkirk, E Stirling), Dylan Rooney (2015 East Fife),
Alan Horne (2013 Tranent),
Ewan Moyes (2015 Montrose, ex E Fife, Gateshead, Hibernian, Brechin C, Arbroath, Livingston), Jonathan Brown (2014 Brechin C, ex Livingston, Hearts, Stirling Albion),
Dean Hoskins (2015 Berwick R, ex Spartans),
Ruaridh Donaldson (2015 Tayport),
Kerr Young (2016 Berwick R, ex Dunfermline Ath),
Scott Gray (2015 Airdrie, ex St Johnstone Youths),
Jonathan Stewart (2014 East Fife, ex Dundee, Hearts, Brechin C),
Andrew Kidd (2015 Whitehill W),
Adam Nelson (2015 Linlithgow R, ex Musselburgh Ath, Brechin C, Elgin City, Blackburn Rovers), Lewis Turner (2015 Musselburgh Ath, Ex Berwick R, Newtongrange Star, Livingston, Dunfermline Ath Youths),
Alex King (ex Linlithgow R, Bonnyrigg R),
Sean Jamieson (2016 Musselburgh Ath, Ex Newtongrange S, E Fife, Haddington Ath),
Keiran McGachie (2015 Civil Service S, Ex Clyde, Annan Ath, Motherwell, Stenhousemuir),

Fraser McLaren (2015 Peterhead, Ex Berwick R, Gretna, Montrose, Ayr Utd),
Wayne McIntosh (2015 Whitehill Welfare, Ex Tynecastle, Lothian Th, Arniston R)
Sean Brennan (2017 Berwick Rangers OL Feb-May, ex Hibernian)
Ross Archibald (2011 Spartans, ex Brechin C, Blyth Spartans)
Chris Tobin (2015 Civil Service St, Ex Hearts U20, St Johnstone U20, CSS, Brechin C)
David Burrell (2015 Penicuik Ath, Ex Craigroyston)

Broughty Athletic
Manager: Keith Gibson
Assistant: Stewart Petrie (until Nov 2016), Charlie King (from Dec 2016) Coaches: Tony McAuley, Mark Murray
Iain Ross (2013 Tayport, Ex Lochee Utd)
John Sinclair (ex Dryburgh U19)
Josh Allardyce (2016 Carnoustie Panmure)
Jamie McCunnie (2013 Stirling Albion, ex Dundee Utd, Ross Co, Dunfermline Ath, Hartlepool Utd, E Fife, Haukar, Grindavik, IR, Scotland U21 Cap)
Ryan Blair (2016 NCR Amateurs)
Drew Fleming (2017 Tayport)
Barry Myles (2015 Carnoustie Panmure, ex Arbroath)
Frank Lannen (2015 Forfar Ath U20)
Jonathan Smart (2015 Dundee NE, Ex Raith Rovers, Rowantree, E Fife, Montrose, Ballingry R)
Ryan Suttie (2015 Tayport, Ex Arbroath St Andrews Utd)
Paul McLellan (2015 Forfar Ath, Ex Celtic U17, Dundee NE)
Jamie Winter (2013 Montrose, Ex Leeds Utd, Aberdeen, St johnstone, Chesterfield, Formartine Utd)
Brian Clark (ex Dundee FC, Arbroath FC, Carnoustie Panmure, Lochee United, Downfield JFC)
Grant Lawson (2015 Tayport, Ex Lochee Utd, Violet)
Jake Mair (ex Arbroath, Tayport, Violet)
Danny Cavanagh (2016 Tayport, ex Montrose, Downfield, Lochee Utd, Dundee U20. Retired Nov 2016)
Ross McCord (2016 Montrose, Ex Dundee Utd, Stirling Albion, Montrose, Alloa)
Derryn Kesson (2015 Broughty U19)
Stewart McConnachie (2015 Violet)
Richard "Shaka" Roy (2017 Hamilton Accies, Ex Trindard & Tobago Defence Force, 8 Full caps for T and T)
Kevin Buchan (2016 Cove Rangers, Ex Dundee, ICT, Peterhead, Lochee Utd, Arbroath, Brechin C, Broughty Ath)
James Collier (2016 Montrose Roselea)

Broxburn Athletic
Manager: Max Christie Coach: Ian McLaren
Connor Wallace (2015 Bo'ness Utd, Ex Livingston Utd)
Shaun Donoghue (ex Broxburn Ath Colts)
Craig Purves (2014 Livingston Utd)
Craig Young (ex Armadale Th, Blackburn Utd, Cowdenbeath, Harthill, Ross County)
Darren Cole (2016 Livingston, Ex Rangers, Partick Thistle, Morton, 2 U21 caps for Scotland)
Frazer Paterson (2017 Edinburgh City, Ex Heriot Watt Uni, Haddington AFC)
Grant Gavin (ex Dalkeith Th, Raith R)
Marcus Miller (ex Broxburn Ath Colts, Livingston)
Moussa Mambuya (2014 Livingston, Ex Anderlecht, Genk, Heusden-Zolder, KFCVW Hamme, Leirse SK, Tongeren, VVV Venlo, Helmond Sport, Doxa Katokopias, En. Parlimni, 1 Full Cap for Congo DR)
Alan Lawson (2016 Fauldhouse United, Ex Stenhousemuir, Bo'ness Utd)
Craig Scott (2015 Bo'ness Utd, Ex E Stirling, Whitburn)
Darren Gribben (2016 Arthurlie, Ex Hamilton Accies, Cowdenbeath, Forfar Ath, Stirling Alb, Stranraer, Berwick R, Dumbarton, Bo'ness Utd, Arbroath, Stranraer)
Michael Linton (ex Dalkeith Th, Easthouses)
Nicholas Locke (2013 Alloa, Ex Edinburgh City, Sauchie)
Ross Nimmo (ex Broxburn Ath Colts, Falkirk)
Scott Richards (ex Broxburn Colts, Rangers Youths)
Scott McNaughton (ex Arniston R, Bonnyrigg Rose Ams, Dalkeith Th, Hutchison Vale, Lochend YC, North Merchiston, Tynecastle)
Alexander "Zander" Miller (2015 Bo'ness Utd)
Darren Downie (ex Armadale Th)
Keiran Anderson (2015 Bo'ness Utd, Ex Stenhousemuir, Whitburn)
Michael Browne (Ex Blackridge Th, Fauldhouse Utd, Livingston, Whitburn)
Ross Donnelly (ex Fauldhouse Utd, Stoneyburn)

Camelon Juniors
Manager: Murray McDowell (June-Sep), Karl Lejman (Iep-Oct), Gordon Herd (Oct-)
Assistants Stevie Kay / Ryan Blackadder (June-Sep), Colin Allison / Eamonn Fullerton (Oct)
Colin "Scifo" Allison (2009 Ex Bo'ness Utd, Linlithgow Rose, Shotts Bon Accord, Fauldhouse Utd
Craig Donaldson (2014 Bo'ness Utd, Ex E Stirlingshire)
David Kane (2015 Steins Thistle)
Eamon Fullerton (2009 Bo'ness Utd, Ex Livingston, Raith R, Kelty H)
Alan Benton (2016 Cumbernauld Colts, Ex Maryhill, Albion R, Linlithgow R, Steins Th, Camelon))
Alan Docherty (OL from Stenhousemuir)
Andy Kay (2016 E Stirlingshire, Ex Motherwell, Dunipace)
Calum Scott
David Mitchell (2016 Falkirk Juniors)
David O'Brien (2016 Ex Morton, Ayr Utd, Dundee, Stirling Albion)
Don Morrison (2016 Bo'Ness Utd, ex Armadale Th, Stirling Albion, Scotland Schools Cap)
Gordon Herd (2016 Steins Th, ex Linlithgow Rose)
Jason Deans (2016 Fauldhouse United)
Jason Bolam (2016 Falkirk Juniors)
Jason Walton
Jordan Devlin
Jordan Herron (2016 Stirling Albion)
Morgan Reid (2016 Stirling Albion OL)
Scott Taylor
Stuart Bell
Divine Shanganya (2017 Clyde OL, Ex St Catharine College)
James Donaldson (2017 Bannockburn Ams)
Ryan Kane (2017 Pennies AFC)
Wayne Meikle (2017 Linlithgow Thistle)
Mark Flynn

Carnoustie Panmure
Mannager: Alan McSkimming, Assistants: Grant Miller, Bobby Brown
Alan Cormack (2015 Broughty Ath, Ex Lochee Harp)
Jamie Robbie (2016 Brechin Vics)
Danny Millar (2011 Forfar WE)
Bailey Steel
Adam Harwood (2016 Montrose OL, Ex Portadown, Dundee United)
Darren Cooper
Ewan Buggins (2013 Brechin Vics)
Ryan Roche
Liam Gibb (2016 Dundee FC Youths)
Gordon McDonald (2015 Broughty Ath, Ex Arbroath FC Youths)
Steven Cook
John Black
Jamie McCabe (2015 Dundee NE, ex Dundee FC Youths)
John Roberts (2010 Forfar WE)
Liam Scott (ex Dundee United Youth, Brechin City Youths)
Roddy Black (2013 Cove Rangers, Ex Arbroath, Brechin City)
Michael McIlravey (ex Arbroath)
Luke McGeehan (2014 Derry City)
Sam Simpson (2014 Dundee NE)
Pat Smith (ex Arbroath, Monifieth Athletic)
Robert Urquhart (2016 Violet, Ex Arbroath, Montrose)
Scott Gray
Murray Mackintosh (2017 Forfar Athletic OL)

Dundonald Bluebell
Manager: Stevie Kay Assistant: Lee Dair (from Oct), Lee Richardson (Until Oct) Coach: Roy Ness
James Lennox (2011 Lochgelly Albert, ex Bowhill Rovers)
Rhory Mooney (2016 Ex Dunfermline Athletic, Cowdenbeath, Hill of Beath Haws, to St Andrews Utd Oct 2016)
Mark Forbes (2014 Ex Dunfermline Ath, Cowdenbeath, Kelty H)
Scott Mayne (2012 Ex Kennoway, to St Andrews Utd Oct 2016)
Ross Drummond (2016 Ex Berwick R, Dunfermline Ath)
Stuart McDonald (2015 ex Kelty H, Cowdenbeath, Hearts Youth) to Glenrothes Jan 2017
Callum Rarity (2016 Ex Broxburn Ath, Whitburn, Armadale Th, Harthill)
Jason Quinn (2013 ex Burntisland SY, Kirkcaldy YM)
Ryan MacDonald (2016 Ex Cowdenbeath, Raith R)
Derek Wallace (2008 Ex Cowdenbeath) To St Andrews Utd Jan 2017
Scott Orrock (2013 Ex East Fife, Kirkcaldy YM, to St Andrews Utd Oct 2016)
Ricky Patrick (2016 Ex St Andrews Utd, East Fife)
Lewis McKenzie (2016 Ex HOB Haws)
Callum Young (2012 Ex Cowdenbeath, Kelty H)

Brodie Gray (2016 E Fife, Ex Kennoway SH)
Scott Lawrie (2014 Ex Ballingry R, kelty H, Cowdenbeath),
Gregg Meikle (2015 Ex Glenrothes, Ballingry R, Kirkcaldy YM)
Paul Quinn (2016 Ex Albion R, E Stirlingt, Cumnock)
Ben Anthony (2014 Ex Alloa, Cowdenbeath HOB Haws, to St Andrews Utd Oct 2016)
Josh Thomson (2017 Arbroath)
Darren Wright (Ex HOB Haws)
Jordan Laird (2017 Ex Dundonald BB)
Sam Buchan (2017 St Andrews Utd)
Craig Wedderburn (2016 St Andrews Utd, ex Raith R, Stirling Albion)
Barry Sibanda (2016 St Andrews United)
Ross Lennie (2017 Montrose)
John Duffy (2016 Rosyth)
James Ward (2016 Ex Oakley Utd, Sauchie)

Fauldhouse United
Manager: David Cowan (until Jan), Jon Connolly (from Jan)
Jon Connolly (2016 St Ants, Ex Ipswich Town, Albion Rovers, Thorniewood United, Motherwell, Dumbarton, Cumnock, East Stirlingshire, Dunipace, Linlithgow Rose, Larkhall Thistle, Bo'ness United, Fauldhouse Utd, Cambuslang R, St Anthonts, Kirkintilloch RR, Thorniewood Utd, Kilwinning R, Kirkintilloch RR, Vale of Clyde, Rossvale)
Jonathan Grier (2016 Carluke R, Ex Albion R, Airderie, Cambuslang R)
Sam Watson
McCauley Wilson (2016 Airdrie, Ex Beith, Benburb)
Jamie McKay (2016 Armadale Th, Ex E Stirling, Whitburn)
Gary Fallon (2013 Bellshill Th, ex Motherwell, Bathgate Th)
Aiden Ward (2016 Carluke R, ex Hibernian, Airdrie)
Declan Byrne (2016 Cowdenbeath, Ex Airdrie)
James Martin (2016 Preston Ath, Ex Hamilton Accies, Partick Th, KV Turnhout, E Kilbride)
Kyle Richford (2016 Airdrie, Ex BSC Glasgow, Campsie BW)
John Boyle (2016 Ex Airdrie, Raith R, E Fife, Bellshill Ath, Auchinleck T)
Gary Bonnes (ex Sauchie)
Andrew Gilchrist (2016 Preston Ath, Ex Hibernian, Airdrie, Forth W, Wishaw)
Kyle Miller – transferred to Pumpherston Nov 2016
Ryan Stewart (2015 Ex Hearts, Brechin C, East Fife)
Mark Wilkins
Scott Sally (2016 Bellshill Ath, Ex Airdrie, Albion R, Irvine M, Petershill)
Ryan McSherry (2016 Preston Ath, Ex Airdrie, Rossvale, Edusport Acad)
Rhys Devlin (2016 Arthurlie, Ex St Mirren, Airdrie, E Stirling)
Gavin McQuillan
Andy Black (2016 Dundee, joined Stirling Albion Jan 2017)

Hill of Beath Hawthorn
Manager: Bobby Wilson
Shaun Leishman (2014 Kirkcaldy YM, ex Lochgelly Albert, Burntisland SY)
Rikki Dair
Calum Adamson (ex Lochgelly Albert, Cowdenbeath Central BC)
Stuart Hall (2009 Montrose, Ex Raith Rovers, Thornton Hibs)
Kevin Conners (2014 Ballingry Rovers, ex Oakley United)
Adam Moffat (2013 Ballingry Rovers, ex Kelty H)
Aaron Hay
John McCulloch (2008 Dunfermline Athletic)
Lee Bryce (2014 Ballingry R, Ex Raith R, E Fife, Tayport, Arbroath, Dundonald BB)
Colin Wilson (2015 Bonnyrigg Rose, Ex Raith Rovers, Musselburgh Ath,, Montrose)
Russell Grierson
Greig Smith (2013 Berwick Rangers, ex Alloa)
Lee Reid
Craig McGuire (2016 Lochore W, ex Lochgelly Albert)
Scott Renton (2016 Lochore Welfare, Ex HOB Haws)
Tam Hampson (2016 Rosyth, trials with Berwick Rangers July 2016)
Dale Allan (2013 Ex Crossgates P, East Fife, Dundonald BB)
Stephen Forbes
Scott McCrindle (Transferred to Oakley Utd Oct 2016)

Jeanfield Swifts
Manager: Ross Gunnion
Assistant: John AndersonCoaches: Eric Fleming, Scott Cummings, Michael Dott
Stephen Blair (ex Kinnoull)
Jordan Kinnon (ex Jeanfield Swifts U19)
Mark Mitchell (ex Luncarty, Kinnoull, Newburgh, Bankfoot, Scone Thistle, St Johns AFC, Kinrossie Caledonian)
Mark Duigan (ex Hill of Beath Hawthorn, Kinnoull, East Stirlingshire, Blairgowrie, Coupar Angus)
James Yates (ex Forfar Athletic, Broughty Athletic, Coupar Angus)
Chris Anton (ex Kinnoull, Tayport, Forfar Athletic, Cowdenbeath, Ross County)
Lee Deans (ex Auchterarder AFC, Kinnoull)
Sean Fleming (ex Kinnoull, Bankfoot, Montrose, Peterhead, Albion Rovers, Dundee United)
Ross Gunnion (ex Bankfoot JFC, Tayport JFC, Kinnoull JFC)
Stuart McDermid (ex Jeanfield Swifts U19)
Scott Mollison (ex Fair City AFC, Dundee, Forfar Athletic)
Jack Parr (Ex Cowdenbeath, Kinnoull, St Johnstone)
Chris "Kiffy" Scott (ex Lochee United, Arbroath)
Keith Dewar (ex Scone Thistle, Kinnoull, Blairgowrie, Bankfoot)
Kevin Fowler (Ex Luncarty, St Johns AFC, Kinnoull, Bankfoot)
Anthony Holt (signed 2005)
Daniel Kelly (ex Luncarty, Letham AFC)
Stevie McManus (ex St Andrews United, Tayport, Kinnoull, Brechin, Montrose, St Johnstone)
Fraser Smith (ex Lochee United, Kirrie Thistle, Coupar Angus, Dundee United)
John Anderson (ex Luncarty, Scone Thistle)
Lewis Baker (2016 AM Soccer)
Richard Donovan (2016 Jeanfield Swifts U19)
Michael Fotheringham (2017 Letham Whites)
Robbie Holden (ex St Andrews United, Forfar West End, Kinnoull, Tayport, Dundee North End)
Scott Sutherland (ex Cowdenbeath, Dunfermline)

Kelty Hearts
Manager: Tom Courts Assistant: Sean Grady
Coaches: Greg McEwan, Paul Shields
Kyle Allison (2014 Ballingry Rovers, Ex Linlithgow R, Dunfermline Ath, ICT Youths, Cowdenbeath Youths),
Kyle Marley (2016 Thornton Hibs),
Tom Courts (2008 Hill of Beath H, Ex E Fife, Kelty Hearts, Livingston, Cowdenbeath, Milton Ams),
Murray Carstairs (2015 Dundonald BB, ex Ballingry R, Glenrothes, Thornton Hibs),
Sean O'Neil (2014 Kirkcaldy YM, Ex Bamber Bridge, Leigh RMI, Dundonald BB),
Garry Leighton (2014 Glenrothes, Ex Dunfermline Ath Youths, Kelty H, Rosyth, Ballingry R, Oakley Utd),
Devon Jacobs (2015 Berwick Rangers, Ex Stirling Albion, Livingston),
Shaun Greig (2014 Kirkcaldy YM, ex Dundonald BB, Star Hearts),
Brian Ritchie (2012 Oakley Utd),
Neil "Nelly" McCabe (2010 Raith Rovers),
Neil "Cabey" McCabe (2016 E Stirling, Ex Forfar Ath, Cowdenbeath, Kelty H, Livingston, Falkirk Youths),
Stephen Husband (Ex Cowdenbeath, Hearts, Livingston, Blackpool, Stockport Co, Dunfermline Ath, Forfar Ath),
Conrad Courts (2014 Ballingry R, Ex E Fife Youths, Lochore W, Hill of Beath Haws, Linlithgow Rose),
Craig Thomson (2016 Newtongrange Star, Ex Hearts, FBK Kaunas, Suduva, Arniston R),
Jason Penman (ex Lochgelly Albert OL),
Archie Campbell (ex Cowdenbeath Youth, Rangers, Morton, Dumbarton, Clyde),
Scott Dalziel (2015 Berwick R, ex Armadale Th, Cowdenbeath, East Fife, Stenhousemuir, Brechin C), Stuart Cargill (2012 Dundonald BB, ex E Fife),
Jordan Moore (2016 Limerick, Ex Dundee United, Airdrie, Dunfermline Ath, Queen's Park)
Jordyn Sheerin (2017 Berwick R, ex Musselburgh Ath, E Stirling, Livingston)
Jack Wilson (OL to Lochgelly Albert)
Josh McPhie (OL to Glenrothes)

Linlithgow Rose
Manager: David McGlynn (until Oct), Todd Lumsden (from Oc-Apr), then Jimmy Crease / Alan Millar
Assistant: Steven Hislop (Oct-Apr)
Coach: Steve Ellison
Darren Hill (2016 Forfar Ath, Ex Falkirk, E Stirling, Arbroath, Hamilton Accies)
Richie Barnard (2016 E Stirling, Ex Aldershot, Millwall, Maidenhead Utd, Aldershot T, QOS, Slough Town, Carshalton Ath, Wealdstone, Weymouth, Farnborough Town, Basingstokle Town, Camelon)
Joe Hamill (2015 Bonnyrigg R, ex Hearts, Leicester C, Livingston, QOS, Ostersunds, Raith R, Formartine Utd, Airdrie, transferred to Haddington Ath Feb 2017)
Gary Thom (2014 East Fife, Ex Stenhousemuir, Bonnyrigg Rose, Stirling Albion)

Bradley Donaldson (2016 Cowdenbeath, Ex Hibernian, Arbroath, Livingston, Transferred to Musselburgh Ath Feb 2017)
Colin Leiper (2015 Bo'ness United, Ex Raith R, Whitburn, Bathgate Th, Camelon)
Jamie McKenzie (2011 Chalkanoros, Ex Hibernian, Montrose, Sligo Rovers, Aris Limassol, Galway United)
Robbie McNab (2016 Stirling Albion, Ex Falkirk, Spartans)
Reece Donaldson (2016 E Stirling, Ex Raith R, Peterhead)
Jack Beaumont (2016 Cowdenbeath, ex Hutchie Vale, Livingston)
Graham Weir (2015 Stirling Albion, Ex Hearts, QOS, Raith R, Brechin C)
Mark Williams (2016 Cumnock, Ex St Mirren, Alloa, Arbroath, Q Park)
Andy Shirra (2011 Bo'ness Utd, ex Camelon, Stenhousemuir. Transferred to Sauchie Jan 2017)
Ross Gray (2016 Spartans, Ex Cowdenbeath, Livingston, Berwick R, Selkirk)
Jackie Myles (2016 Musselburgh Ath, Ex Haddington Ath)
Tommy Coyne (2009 Albion R, Ex Kilmarnock, Dumbarton, Stirling Albion)
Kevin Kelbie (2014 Camelon, Ex Rangers, Alloa, Northern Oklahoma Coll, Glentoran, Ballymena Utd, Morton, Glenavon, Stirling Albion)
Blair Batchelor (2014 Camelon, Ex St Johnstone, Raith R)
Lewis Small (2016 Falkirk, Ex Stirling Albion, Stenhousemuir)
Conner Kelly (2015 Sauchie, Ex Falkirk, Alloa, E Stirling)
Tommy McAllister (2016 Stirling Albion)
Harvey Swann (2017 Cowdenbeath, Ex Whitehill W)
Sean Muhsin (2017 Edinburgh City, Ex Hibernian, St Andrews Utd, Dunfermline Ath, Heriot Watt Uni, Spartans)

Lochee United
Manager: George ShieldsAssistant: Ray Farningham
Paul Blackwood
Charlie Cargill
Bryan Deasley (2015 Montrose, Ex Dundee, Cowdenbeath, Arbroath, Forfar Ath, Peterhead, Carnoustie P, Montrose)
Ross Gallacher
Philip Hagan (2011 Linlithgow Rose, Ex Violet, Raith R, Lochee Harp)
Graham Hay (2015 Arbroath, Ex Dundee, Montrose, Lochee Utd, Brechin C, Formartine Utd)
Greg Kirk
Scott McComiskie
Reece Ritchie
Scott Webster (2015 Cove Rangers, Ex Brechin C, Forfar Ath)
Ryan Winter (2014 Montrose)
Mark Fotheringham
Stephen McNally
Paul Lunan (2016 Broughty Ath, Ex Dundee, Forfar Ath, Arbroath, Violet, Montrose)
Kris Rollo
Jamie Montgomery
Cameron McMahon
Dougie Cameron (2016 Broughty Ath, Ex Dundee, Peterhead, Forfar Ath, E Fife, Montrose, Ballingry R)
Aaron Whitehead
Connor Birse (2015 Arbroath, ex Arbroath Vics)

Musselburgh Athletic
Manager: Calvin Shand
Kieron Renton (2016 ex Blackburn rovers, Elgin City, Raith Rovers, Stenhousemuir, Musselburgh Athletic, Newtongrange Star)
John McManus (2016 Newtongrange Star)
Matty Lynch (2016, Ex Hibs, Cowdenbeath, Penicuik, Arniston, Haddington)
David Dunn (2016, ex Hearts, Forfar, Bonnyrigg, Newtongrange)
Barry Hogg (2017, Berwick Rangers)
Declan O'Kane (2016, Ex Hearts, Dunfermline, Montrose, East Fife)
Sean Murphy (2016, ex Livingston, Leith Ath)
Gary Cherrie (2016, ex Tynecastle, Newtongrange Star)
Connor Spowart (2016 Dalkeith Th)
Mathu King (2016, Ex Celtic U17, Hearts, Forfar, Arbroath, Musselburgh Athletic, Newtongrange Star)
Jed Davie (2014, ex Livingsgton, Musselburgh Ath U19)
Bradley Donaldson (2017, Ex Hibernian, Livingston, Cowdenbeath, Linlithgow Rose)
Michael Moffat (2016, ex Spartans, Haddington Ath)
Conor Thomson (2016, ex Livingston, Dundee, Montrose, Penicuik, Musselburgh Athletic, Bonnyrigg, Penicuik)
David Porcher (2016, Ex H ibs U17, Stenhousemuir U20, Preston Athletic)
Ewan Ralton (2016,
David McKenzie (2016, Edinburgh City)
Chris Gray
Dachi Khutashvili (ex Elgin C, Forres Mechanics, ICT)
Luke Mancini (ex Edinburgh City)

Newtongrange Star
Manager: Steven McLeish
Coach: Murray Hunter, Walter Martyniuk, John O'Hara (until Dec)
John Dodds (2016 Musselburgh Ath, ex Maybole, Ayr Utd, QOS, E Fife, Selkirk, Gala Fairydean R))
Murray Jackson (2016 Musselburgh Ath, Ex Cowdenbeath, Stirling Albion, Spartans)
Mike Noble (2016 Haddington Ath, Craigroyston, Dundee Utd, Rangers)
Brian Murray (2015 Civil Service S, Ex Musselburgh Ath, Bonnyrigg R)
David Bonnar (2016 Gala Fairydean R)
Craig Meikle (2016 Penicuik Ath, ex Bonnyrigg R, Musselburgh Ath))
Dale Richardson (2016 Peebles Rovers)
Gary Hamilton (2016 Musselburgh Ath, ex Coldstream, Spartans)
David Morris (2016 Berwick R, ex East Fife, Arniston R, Dalkeith Th)
Jack Wilson (ex Haddington Ath, ex Hibernian, Doncaster R, Musselburgh Ath)
Kenny O'Brien (2016 Vale of Leithen, Ex Edinburgh City, Alloa, Berwick R)
Jordan Cropley (ex Haddington Ath, ex Hibernian, Berwick R, Arniston R)
Jack Wright (2016 Musselburgh Ath, ex Cowdenbeath, Edina Hibs)
Kevin Bracks (2016 Musselburgh Ath, ex Berwick R, Bonnyrigg R, Tranent, Vale of Leithen, Haddington Ath)
Lee Currie (2015 Berwick R, ex Hibernian, Stenhousemuir)
Sean Lally (2016 Dalkeith Th)
Stuart Roseburgh (Retired due to injury Jan 2017)
Andrew Sinclair (2016 Haddington Athletic On Loan)
Errol Douglas (2016 Ex Spartans, Bonnyrigg R, Craigroyston, Stenhousemuir)
James Flynn (2016 Whitehill W U20)
Sean Paliczka (2016 Ex Bonnyrigg R, penicuik Ath, Gala F, Musselburgh Ath)
Jack Cook (2017 Berwick Rangers On Loan, Ex Huthison Vale, Livingston, St Francis Brooklyn))
Kyle Lander (2016 St Johnstone, ex Stirling Albion, Livingston, Edina Hibs)
Liam Amos (2016 Haddington Ath – 3rd spell with Nitten, ex Raith R, St Andrews Utd, Bonnyrigg R)
Neil Martyniuk (2016 Edinburgh City on loan, ex Hibernian, St Johnstone, Berwick R)
Jim Young (2016 Amateur football, ex Peebles, Civil Service St, Whitehill W, Lothian Th, Alloa)
Lewis Swaney (2016 Berwick Rangers On Loan, Sep-Dec)
Scott Swaney (2016 Musselbur Ath, Ex Newtongrange Star)

Penicuik Athletic
Manager: Johnny HarveyAssist Ryan GayCoaches: Dave Lees, K Wright, John Menzies
Aaron Somerville (2016 Whitel Welfare, ex Vale of Leithen, Newtongrange Star)
Andy Forbes (Ex Inverurie Locc Heriot Watt Uni, Haddington A
Andy Jack (ex Dalkeith Th, Whi W, Craigroyston, Tranernt, Hav RA, Coldstream, Tynecastle, Ormiston, Newtongrange Star)
Billy Bald (ex Berwick R, Hiber St Mirren, Linlithgow R, Bonny R)
Callum Connolly
Conar Easton
Craig Hume (ex Tranent, Lothi Lochend Ams, E Stirlingshire, Ath, Edinburgh Utd)
Darrell Young (ex Bonnyrigg R "A")
John MacDonald (ex Dunferm Ath, Lothian Th, Edinburgh Ci Newtongrange Star)
Jordan Lister (2013 Bonnyrigg "A")
Keith Lough (ex Detroit City, Berwick R, Vale of Leithen, Ga Fairydean)
Kyle Scott (2016 OL from Ber
Lewis Barr (ex East Fife)
Neil Janczyk (ex hearts, Raith Stranraer, St Johnstone, Brec Berwick R, Clyde)
Ross Montgomery (ex Bonny
Ryan Gay (ex Newtongrange
Ryan McCallum (ex Cowdenb Arniston R, Musselburgh Ath Bonnyrigg R)
Sam Jones (2016 OL from Be Rangers, ex Loanhead MW, Hibernian, Hutchison Vale)
Stephen Scott (2016, OL from Berwick Rangers)
Steven Noble (ex Newtongra Star)
Wayne Sproule (ex Cowdent Falkirk, Tynecastle, Whitehil Vale of Leithen, Haddington
Youssef Bajaoui
Craig Noble
Craig Hume (ex Tranent, Loc Ams, E Stirling, Edinburgh U Ath, Haddinton Ath)
Chris Inglis (ex Cowdenbeat Bonnyrigg R, St bernards U2 Haddington Ath, Tynecastle Tranent, Vale of Leithen, Ed Utd)
Sebastian Pyda (ex Spartans Fairydean, Motor Lublin, St Poniatowa)
Jordan Lister

East Juniors Early Season Fixtures 2017/18

Saturday 5 August 2017 (2.30pm)
McBookie.com East Super League
Bo'ness Utd v Carnoustie Panmure
Broughty Athv Sauchie
Broxburn Ath v Jeanfield Swifts
Camelon v Kennoway Star Hearts
Forfar West End v Bonnyrigg Rose
Lochee Utdv Hill of Beath Hawthorn
Newtongrange Star v Dundonald BB
Penicuik Ath v Linlithgow Rose

McBookie.com East Premier League
Blackburn Utd v Downfield
Dunbar Utd v Glenrothes
Fauldhouse Utd v Dalkeith Thistle
Haddington Ath v Bathgate Thistle
Kirriemuir Thistle v Whitburn
Musselburgh Ath v Tayport
Thornton Hibs v Arniston Rangers
Tranent v St Andrews Utd

McBookie.com East North League
Brechin Vics v Blairgowrie
Dundee East Craigie v Scone Thistle
Forfar Albion v Dundee Violet
Lochee Harp v Coupar Angus
Lochore Welfare v Dundee North End
Luncarty v Kinnoull
Newburgh v Arbroath Vics

McBookie.com East South League
Craigroyston v Lochgelly Albert
Harthill Royal v Kirkcaldy YM
Livingston Utd v Crossgates Primrose
Oakley Utd v Edinburgh Utd
Pumpherston v West Calder Utd
Rosyth v Armadale Thistle
Stoneyburn v Easthouses Lily MW

Wednesday 9 August 2017 (6.45pm)

McBookie.com East Super League
Bonnyrigg Rose v Broxburn Ath
Broughty Ath v Forfar West End
Carnoustie Panmure v Lochee Utd
Hill of Beath Hawthorn v Kennoway Star Hearts
Jeanfield Swifts v Dundonald Bluebell
Linlithgow Rose v Camelon
Penicuik Ath v Newtongrange Star
Sauchie v Bo'ness Utd

McBookie.com East Premier League

Arniston Rangers v Tranent
Bathgate Thistle v Blackburn Utd
Dalkeith Thistle v Haddington Ath
Downfield v Kirriemuir Thistle
Dunbar Utd v Musselburgh Ath
St Andrews Utd v Thornton Hibs
Tayport v Glenrothes
Whitburn v Fauldhouse Utd

Saturday 12 August 2017 (2.30pm)
McBookie.com East Super League
Bonnyrigg Rose v Camelon
Carnoustie Panmure v Broxburn Ath
Dundonald Bluebell v Penicuik Ath
Hill of Beath Hawthorn v Forfar WE
Jeanfield Swifts v Bo'ness Utd
Kennoway Star Heart v Broughty Ath
Linlithgow Rose v Newtongrange Star
Sauchie v Lochee Utd

McBookie.com East Premier League
Arniston Rangers v Blackburn Utd
Bathgate Thistle v Thornton Hibs
Dalkeith Thistle v Musselburgh Ath
Downfield v Tranent
Kirriemuir Thistle v Fauldhouse Utd
St Andrews Utd v Haddington Ath
Tayport v Dunbar Utd
Whitburn v Glenrothes

McBookie.com East North League
Arbroath Vics v Forfar Albion
Blairgowrie v Kinnoull
Coupar Angus v Dundee East Craigie
Dundee North End v Luncarty
Dundee Violet v Lochore Welfare
Newburgh v Lochee Harp
Scone Thistle v Brechin Vics

McBookie.com East South League
Armadale Thistle v Oakley Utd
Crossgates Primrose v Craigroyston
Easthouses Lily MW v Edinburgh Utd
Kirkcaldy YM v Stoneyburn
Lochgelly Albert v Rosyth
Pumpherston v Livingston Utd
West Calder Utd v Harthill Royal

Wednesday 16 August 2017 (6.45pm)

McBookie.com East Super League
Bo'ness Utd v Penicuik Ath
Broxburn Ath v Linlithgow Rose
Camelon v Sauchie
Dundonald Bluebell v Hill of Beath Hawthorn
Forfar West End v Carnoustie Panmure
Kennoway Star Heart v Jeanfield Swifts
Lochee Utd v Broughty Ath
Newtongrange Star v Bonnyrigg Rose

McBookie.com East Premier League
Blackburn Utd v Whitburn
Fauldhouse Utd v Bathgate Thistle
Glenrothes v St Andrews Utd
Haddington Ath v Dunbar Utd
Kirriemuir Thistle v Tayport
Musselburgh Ath v Arniston Rangers
Tranent v Dalkeith Thistle
Thornton Hibs v Downfield

Saturday 19 August 2017 (2.30pm)

McBookie.com East Super League

Bo'ness Utd v Bonnyrigg Rose
Broughty Ath v Jeanfield Swifts
Broxburn Ath v Kennoway Star Hearts
Camelon v Hill of Beath Hawthorn
Forfar West End v Dundonald Bluebell
Lochee Utd v Linlithgow Rose
Newtongrange Star v Carnoustie Pa
Penicuik Ath v Sauchie

McBookie.com East Premier League
Blackburn Utd v St Andrews Utd
Dunbar Utd v Dalkeith Thistle
Fauldhouse Utd v Downfield
Glenrothes v Arniston Rangers
Haddington Ath v Kirriemuir Thistle
Musselburgh Ath v Bathgate Thistle
Thornton Hibs v Whitburn
Tranent v Tayport

McBookie.com East North League
Brechin Vicsv Coupar Angus
Dundee East Craigie v Newburgh
Dundee North End v Dundee Violet
Kinnoull v Scone Thistle
Lochee Harp v Forfar Albion
Lochore Welfare v Arbroath Vics
Luncarty v Blairgowrie

McBookie.com East South League
Easthouses Lily MW v Armadale Thistle
Edinburgh Utd v Kirkcaldy YM
Harthill Royal v Pumpherston
Livingston Utd v Craigroyston
Oakley Utd v Lochgelly Albert
Rosyth v Crossgates Primrose
Stoneyburn v West Calder Utd

Saturday 26 August 2017 (2.30pm)

McBookie.com East Super League

Bonnyrigg Rose v Lochee Utd
Carnoustie Panmure v Camelon
Dundonald Bluebell v Broughty Ath
Hill of Beath Hawthorn v Penicuik Ath
Jeanfield Swifts v Newtongrange Star
Kennoway Star Hearts v Bo'ness Utd
Linlithgow Rose v Forfar West End
Sauchie v Broxburn Ath

McBookie.com East Premier League

Arniston Rangers v Haddington Ath
Bathgate Thistle v Tranent
Dalkeith Thistle v Blackburn Utd
Downfield v Glenrothes
Kirriemuir Thistle v Thornton Hibs
St Andrews Utd v Musselburgh Ath
Tayport v Fauldhouse Utd
Whitburn v Dunbar Utd

McBookie.com East North League

Arbroath Vics v Brechin Vics
Blairgowrie v Dundee East Craigie
Coupar Angus v Dundee North End
Dundee Violet v Luncarty
Forfar Albion v Lochore Welfare
Kinnoull v Lochee Harp
Scone Thistle v Newburgh

McBookie.com East South League

Armadale Thistle v Rosyth
Craigroyston v Oakley Utd
Crossgates Primrose v Easthouses Lily MW
Edinburgh Utd v Stoneyburn
Kirkcaldy YM v Pumpherston
Lochgelly Albert v Harthill Royal
West Calder Utd v Livingston Utd

Saturday 2 September 2017 (2.30pm)

East of Scotland Cup 1st Round
Lochgelly Albert v Lochee Utd
Camelon v Glenrothes
Broxburn Ath v Oakley Utd
Broughty Ath v Dundee East Craigie
Lochore Welfare v Kirkcaldy YM
Dundonald Bluebell v Newburgh
Haddington Ath v Kinnoull
Tayport v Linlithgow Rose
Rosyth v Coupar Angus
St Andrews Utd v Musselburgh Ath
Arniston Rangers v Dunbar Utd
Livingston Utd v Craigroyston
Whitburn v Thornton Hibs
Dundee Violet v Bo'ness Utd
Dundee North End v Bonnyrigg Rose
Fauldhouse Utd v Easthouses Lily MW
Penicuik Ath v Bathgate Thistle
Blairgowrie v Harthill Royal
Tranent v Sauchie
West Calder Utd v Carnoustie Panmure
Pumpherston v Edinburgh Utd
Forfar Albion v Crossgates Primrose
Luncarty v Stoneyburn
Scone Thistle v Blackburn Utd
Kirriemuir Thistle v Lochee Harp
Jeanfield Swifts v Kennoway Star Hearts
Armadale Thistle v Forfar West End
Hill of Beath Hawthorn v Arbroath Vics

McBookie.com East Premier League

Downfield v Dalkeith Thistle

Saturday 9 September 2017 (2.30pm)

McBookie.com East Super League
Bo'ness Utd v Linlithgow Rose
Broughty Ath v Camelon
Broxburn Ath v Hill of Beath Hawthorn
Forfar West End v Jeanfield Swifts
Kennoway Star Hearts v Carnoustie Panmure
Lochee Utd v Dundonald Bluebell
Newtongrange Star v Sauchie
Penicuik Ath v Bonnyrigg Rose

McBookie.com East Premier League
Blackburn Utd v Tayport
Dunbar Utd v Arniston Rangers
Fauldhouse Utd v St Andrews Utd
Glenrothes v Bathgate Thistle
Haddington Ath v Downfield
Musselburgh Ath v Thornton Hibs
Tranent v Kirriemuir Thistle
Whitburn v Dalkeith Thistle

McBookie.com East North League
Brechin Vics v Kinnoull
Dundee East Craigie v Arbroath Vics
Dundee North End v Forfar Albion
Lochee Harp v Dundee Violet
Luncarty v Scone Thistle
Newburgh v Coupar Angus

McBookie.com East South League
Easthouses Lily MW v West Calder Utd
Harthill Royal v Edinburgh Utd
Livingston Utd v Kirkcaldy YM
Oakley Utd v Crossgates Primrose
Pumpherston v Armadale Thistle
Rosyth v Craigroyston
Stoneyburn v Lochgelly Albert

Saturday 16 September 2017 (2.30pm)

McBookie.com East Super League
Broxburn Ath v Newtongrange Star
Camelon v Lochee Utd
Carnoustie Panmure v Penicuik Ath
Dundonald Bluebell v Kennoway Star Hearts
Hill of Beath Hawthorn v Bo'ness Utd
Jeanfield Swifts v Bonnyrigg Rose
Linlithgow Rose v Broughty Ath
Sauchie v Forfar West End

McBookie.com East Premier League
Arniston Rangers v Fauldhouse Utd
Bathgate Thistle v Dunbar Utd
Dalkeith Thistle v Glenrothes
Downfield v Musselburgh Ath
Kirriemuir Thistle v Blackburn Utd
St Andrews Utd v Whitburn
Tayport v Haddington Ath
Thornton Hibs v Tranent

McBookie.com East North League
Arbroath Vics v Dundee North End
Blairgowrie v Lochee Harp
Coupar Angus v Luncarty
Dundee Violet v Brechin Vics
Forfar Albion v Newburgh
Kinnoull v Dundee East Craigie
Scone Thistle v Lochore Welfare

Mcbookie.com East Premier League 2016/17

	ARM	ARN	BAT	DAL	DOW	FAL	FOR	GLE	HAD	KSH	SAU	STA	TAY	TRA	VIO	WHI
Armadale Thistle		Feb 18 1-1	Apr 29 2-6	Oct 29 0-5	Apr 22 1-2		Oct 1 1-1	Jan 21 2-4	Mar 11 0-6	Dec 17 0-9	Dec 10 0-2	Sep 10 1-1	Aug 13 1-1	Mar 25 2-3	Nov 5 1-2	Aug 10 3-2
Arniston Rangers	Oct 15 1-0		Mar 18 0-1	Apr 8 2-5	Aug 13 2-3		Apr 1 0-0	Dec 10 2-1	Aug 10 2-2	Sep 10 0-3	May 13 0-6	Apr 15 1-1	Sep 24 1-1	Dec 17 2-2	Nov 12 3-1	May 9 1-0
Bathgate Thistle	Dec 3 1-2	Oct 29 4-1		Dec 17 3-1	Nov 12 2-2		Apr 22 2-1	Aug 13 3-0	Sep 10 6-1	Feb 18 3-1	Aug 6 0-4	Aug 20 1-2	Apr 15 1-3	Oct 15 1-2	Jan 21 5-1	Apr 1 1-4
Dalkeith Thistle	Apr 15 3-0	Aug 17 0-1	Sep 17 1-1		Oct 1 1-0		Aug 27 1-4	Feb 4 4-0	Nov 5 1-2	Aug 20 0-2	Dec 3 1-2	Jan 28 2-1	Mar 18 1-0	Mar 11 0-1	Feb 18 3-1	Jan 7 3-1
Downfield	Aug 6 3-0	May 6 1-4	Mar 11 1-1	Jan 21 2-4			Aug 17 0-2	Sep 10 2-0	Apr 15 0-1	Apr 8 0-3	May 26 0-1	Oct 29 4-2	Feb 18 1-5	Sep 24 1-1	Dec 17 2-1	May 13 3-3
Falkirk JFC																
Forfar West End	Feb 25 5-1	Aug 20 0-1	Feb 11 2-1	Dec 10 6-1	Mar 18 0-0			Dec 17 3-2	Mar 25 4-1	Oct 29 2-1	Apr 29 3-0	Sep 24 1-0	Aug 10 3-2	Sep 10 2-1	Apr 15 4-0	Aug 13 2-1
Glenrothes	Aug 27 1-0	Apr 22 3-3	Nov 5 3-1	Sep 24 0-1	Mar 25 4-2		Sep 17 3-0		Aug 20 2-1	Jan 28 1-2	Apr 15 1-3	Aug 17 0-2	Oct 15 2-0	Apr 8 0-3	Apr 1 2-1	Dec 3 2-1
Haddington Athletic	Sep 17 3-0	Dec 3 1-2	Apr 8 2-2	Mar 4 1-0	Jan 28 1-3		Aug 6 1-1	Mar 18 5-1		Nov 12 0-2	Apr 1 0-0	Dec 17 3-0	Aug 27 1-3	Aug 17 3-1	Oct 15 7-0	Apr 29 2-4
Kennoway Star Hearts	Aug 17 2-1	Mar 11 1-1	Aug 27 3-1	Nov 19 0-2	Jan 7 6-2		Jan 21 3-0	Aug 6 6-3	Feb 25 3-3		Mar 25 4-2	Apr 1 1-1	Nov 5 3-2	Dec 3 0-3	Sep 17 3-1	Oct 1 2-1
Sauchie	Apr 8 1-0	Jan 7 2-1	Apr 26 1-1	Apr 19 3-1	Aug 20 3-1		Nov 12 0-1	Aug 10 3-1	Oct 1 4-2	Aug 13 5-0		Mar 11 6-0	May 6 2-1	May 3 1-2	May 10 3-1	Sep 10 4-2
St Andrews United	Feb 4 4-1	Oct 1 0-4	Dec 10 0-1	Aug 6 2-3	Apr 29 1-3		Dec 3 0-1	Feb 18 0-2	Aug 13 4-0	Aug 10 3-1	Sep 17 0-4		Apr 8 0-1	Nov 5 0-1	Aug 27 3-3	Mar 18 3-3
Tayport	Feb 11 3-1	Mar 25 1-2	Jan 7 1-1	Sep 10 2-1	May 20 6-0		Oct 8 1-0	Apr 29 0-0	Dec 10 4-3	Mar 4 3-4	Oct 29 2-2	Nov 12 2-2		Aug 6 1-1	Aug 17 2-1	Aug 20 3-1
Tranent	Nov 12 0-1	Sep 17 0-1	Jan 28 2-2	Aug 10 1-1	Dec 10 4-2		Feb 18 2-1	Oct 1 4-1	Jan 7 1-1	Mar 18 1-3	Aug 27 2-6	Feb 11 2-1	Apr 1 0-1		Apr 29 5-1	Oct 29 1-3
Violet	May 13 5-3	Jan 28 0-2	Oct 1 1-3	Aug 13 1-1	Aug 10 1-4		Jan 7 3-4	Oct 29 6-1	May 6 2-1	Dec 10 0-3	May 20 0-6	Mar 25 2-2	Apr 26 1-2	Aug 20 2-3		May 27 2-2
Whitburn	Apr 26 2-1	Aug 27 1-2	Aug 17 1-1	Mar 25 2-2	Sep 17 3-3		Apr 8 0-1	May 20 2-2	Feb 18 0-4	Apr 15 1-4	Jan 28 0-1	Oct 15 2-2	Dec 17 2-2	Apr 22 1-2	Aug 6 5-1	

			Home					Away							
		P	W	D	L	F	A	W	D	L	F	A	GD	Pts	
1	**Sauchie Juniors**	28	11	1	2	38	14	10	2	2	39	13	50	66	66
2	**Kennoway Star Hearts**	28	9	3	2	37	23	10	0	4	38	19	33	60	60
3	*Forfar West End*	28	12	1	1	37	12	6	3	5	17	17	25	58	58
4	Tranent Juniors (P)	28	5	3	6	25	25	9	3	2	26	16	10	48	48
5	Tayport	28	7	5	2	31	19	6	3	5	24	19	17	47	47
6	Arniston Rangers	28	4	5	5	17	26	9	3	2	26	15	2	47	47
7	Dalkeith Thistle	28	7	1	6	21	16	6	3	5	28	25	8	43	43
8	Bathgate Thistle	28	7	1	6	33	25	4	7	3	23	20	11	41	41
9	Haddington Athletic	28	6	3	5	30	19	4	3	7	28	33	6	36	36
10	Downfield (P)	28	4	3	7	20	28	5	3	6	27	35	-16	33	33
11	Glenrothes (P)	28	8	1	5	24	20	2	2	10	18	42	-20	33	33
12	Whitburn Juniors (P)	28	2	6	6	22	28	3	3	8	28	32	-10	24	24
13	**St Andrews United**	28	3	2	9	20	28	2	6	6	17	28	-19	23	23
14	**Dundee Violet**	28	3	3	8	26	37	1	1	12	15	48	-44	16	16
15	**Armadale Thistle**	28	1	4	9	15	45	2	0	12	11	34	-53	13	13

Sauchie were unlucky to have been relegated in 2016 and they bounced back at the first attempt. Joining them in promotion were surprise packets Kennoway Star Hearts in only their fourth season s a Junior club. Forfar West End made the Play off and defeated Newtongarnge Sar on aggregate.

Armadale Thistle and Dundee Violet struggled throughout the season and were relegated by some distance. St Andrews United would have joined them but they were reprieved as knock-on effect of Kelty Hearts resigning from Junior football.

Tranent could lay claim to being team of the year with wins in both of the regional cups. Perhaps their Cup exploits distracted them in the League as they finished ten points off the promotion spots.

EAST PREMIER LEAGUE ALL-TIME POSITIONS

	2006-7	2007-8	2008-9	2009-10	2010-11	2011-12	2012-13	2013-14	2014-15	2015-16	2016-17
Armadale Thistle	5	11		9	7	10	4			13	15
Arniston Rangers	8	8	6	4	9	12		9	6	4	6
Ballingry Rovers			7	6	6	7	2				
Bathgate Thistle							6	8	13	6	8
Blairgowrie			8	11							
Bo'ness United		1									
Broughty Athletic					8	9	12	7	3		
Broxburn Athletic					3	2					
Carnoustie Panmure			3	5	2						
Dalkeith Thistle							7	3	4	7	7
Downfield						11					10
Dundee North End	6	5	12						15	12	
Dundee Violet							10	11	8		14
Dundonald Bluebell		9	11						5	2	
Edinburgh United									9	15	
Falkirk										10	
Fauldhouse United			9	10				2			
Forfar West End		2		2					10	8	3
Glenrothes	1				4	8	11	5	14		11
Haddington Athletic										5	9
Jeanfield Swifts							8	4	7	1	
Kelty Hearts	2										
Kennoway Star Hearts										9	2
Kinnoull		7	5	3	10			10	16		
Kirkcaldy YM								13			
Kirrie Thistle								15			
Livingston United								14			
Lochee Harp	11										
Lochee United										3	
Montrose Roselea	7	10		12				12	11	11	
Musselburgh Athletic	4	4	1								
Newtongrange Star		3	2			6	1				
Oakley United			10			5	9	6	12	16	
Penicuik Athletic	9	6	4	7	5	4	5	1			
Pumpherston								16			
Rosyth	3	12									
Sauchie						1					1
Scone Thistle	12										
St Andrews United	10			8	1	3	3		2		13
Tayport				1					1		5
Thornton Hibs					12					14	
Tranent											4
Whitburn					11						12

East Juniors Premier League Playing Squads 2016/17

NB These are not comprehensive lists of players used - there will be some omissions. However, all players listed were associated with the club concerned during 2016/17.

Armadale Thistle
Manager: Jamie Mackay (from Dec), James McAllister
Bruno Maltoni (ex VF Collgiana, Sestese, Vallee 'Aoste, Imolese, Alghero, Tavolara Calcio, Carluke Rovers, Glenafton Ath, Edusport Acad, Petershill, BSC Glasgow)
Darren Downie (ex Bo'ness Utd)
Kieran Brennan (to Arthurlie Feb 2017)
Aiden McKee
Dylan Rooney (ex E Fife, Bonnyrigg R)
Alan Keir
Scott Brown (ex Stenhousemuir)
Scott Hislop
Duffy
Bryan King
Gary Brown (ex Annan Ath, Bo'ness Utd, Crossgates P)
McAllister
Ross Tierney (2017 Bo'ness Utd OL)
Roger
Simon Marriot
Liam Gray
Liam Kane
Sam Collumbine (2017 Bo'ness Utd OL)
Lee Brown
Callum Robertson
Gardner
Lewis Milton (ex Hamilton Accies)

Arniston Rangers
Manager: Jock Landells
Dale Cornet
Danny McFadden
John Faulkner
David Jeffrey (ex Preston Ath, Berwick Rangers, Craigroyston, Easthouses Lily, Civil Service Strollers)
Greg Callaghan (ex Bonnyrigg Rose U21)
Declan Brady (ex Bathgate Th)
Michael Deland (ex hearts, Berwick R, Newtongrange Star)
Ryan Porteous (2016 OL from Berwick R)
Scott Lucas (ex Berwick R)
Darren McTernan
Kevin Moffat (ex Bonnyrigg R, Hearts, Hibernian, Tynecastle Hearts, Craigroyston, Falkirk, Arbroath, Whitehill W)
Mikey Langdale
Lumbert Kataleza (ex Edinburgh Utd)
Danny "Gus" McFadden
Darren Leslie
Kirean Somerville (2016 Livingston)
Kevin Airlie
Chris Tobin (ex Bonnyrigg Rose)
Kyle Houldcroft- Doig
Kieran Watson
Nicky Faulds (ex Gretna, Lugar BYT, Girvan, Hurlford Utd, Ardrossan WR)
Jordan Lister (Oct 2016 from Penicuik Ath)
Danny Thomson (ex hearts, Inlgewood Utd, Raith Rovers)
Kyle Meaney
Ross Pullen (ex Bonnyrigg Rose U21)

Bathgate Thistle
Manager: Andrew ColleyAssistant: David Strathie
Coaches: Andy Malone, Gavin Kirkwood
Michael Watson (ex Armadale Th, Freed Mar 2017))
James Penman (2016 Falkirk Athletic)
Darren McIntosh (freed Mar 2017)
Darren McIsaac
Hassan Nyang (ex Thurrock, Horsham, Three Bridges, Stenhousemuir, Gambian internationalist)
Jamie Clark (2016 Armadale Th, Ex Alloa, Stirling Albion, Bo'ness United)
George Bonnar
Grant McDonald (ex Polbeth United, Livingston, Hutchison Vale)
Reece Boyle (2016 Sauchie, Ex Stirling Albion, E Stirlingshire, Oakley Utd)
Ritchie Hutton (freed Mar 2017)
David Taylor (2016 Armadale Th, Ex Airdrie Utd, Shotts BA, Loche Harp, Forfar WE)
Sid Easton
Gordon Harris
Rhys Minnock (freed Mar 2017)
Stuart McLeod
Darren Dalrymple (2016 Broxburn Ath, Ex Kilsyth R, Albion R, Stirling Uni, Armadale Th)
Robbie Feeney (2016 Bo'ness Utd, ex Armadale Th)
Jordan Thomson
Iain Griffin (2016 Glenrothes)
Liam Healy
Jack Kelly
Adam Kennedy
John-James Henderson
Jack Henderson
Steven MacMillan
Martin Lawrie (2017 Blackburn United)
Michael Fairbanks (2017 Whitburn)
James Penman
Michael Fairbanks

Dalkeith Thistle
Manager: Kevin Haynes
Assistant: Andy DonlevyCoaches: Willie Jamieson, Willie Auld, Michael Burgess, Ross Combe
James McQueen (ex Nitten Star)
Shaun Murray
Callum McNeill (ex Bonnyrigg Rose, Raith R, Cowdenbeath)
Ryan McQueenie
John Robertson

Tyron McLean
Dean Whitson
Michael Hunter (ex Musselburgh Ath, Stenhousemuir, E Stirling)
James Redpath (ex North Merchiston, Stenhousemuir, Leith Ath)
Darryl Devlin
Stewart Adams
Dan Greig
Scott Waugh
Paul Tansey (ex Edina H, Mussleburgh Ath, E Fife, Nitten Star, Selkirk)
Darren McGlashan (ex Whitehill W, Preston Ath)
Blake Wales
David Paterek
Alan Murray
Shaun Murray
Lewis Turkington (ex Bonnyrigg U21, Livingston, joined Preston Ath Feb 2017)
Duncan Muir
Daniel Greig
Michael Hunter

Downfield
Manager:
Matty Smith (2017 Menzieshill Ams)
Craig Smith
Mark Bannon
Jordan Timmons
Jack Neave
Robert Smith
Mark Stewart
Kieran Small
Ballantyne
Gary Archibald
J Thomson
Ryan Rigden
Birmingham
Marc O'Leary
Kenneth
Blair

Dundee Violet
Manager: Ralph Henderson
Gary Robertson
Gary Thane
Davie O'Neill
Ben Middleton
Kit Bremner
Scott Tovey
Lee Milton
Ryan Dignan
Gavin Hood
Ben Finnie
Kevin Scott
Connor McLeod
Connor Hart
George Duncan
Craig Bachelor
Sean McVicar
Barry Wilson

Ciaran Conway
Aaron Kane
Mitchell Hay

Forfar West End
Manager:
Darryl Burns (ex Dundee Utd, Arbroath, Newburgh, Forfar WE, Broughty Ath, Lochee Utd)
Craig Bell (ex Dundee Utd, Carnoustie P, Montrose)
Ross McDonald (ex Dundee Utd)
Craig Stephen
Liam Godfrey
David Rae (ex Montrose, Broughty Ath)
Mark Godfrey
Callum Petrie
Danny Ross
Ryan Stirton
Scott Fullerton (ex Arbroath)
Andy Walls
Matthew Ramsay
Connor Ireland
Kieran CRichton
Reynolds
Daryl McKenzie
Callum Walls
Adam Braid
Graeme Hart
Robbie Norrie
Blair Fleming
Matty Reynolds

Glenrothes
Manager: Willie Campbell
Aidan Anderson (ex Oakley Utd)
Blair Smart (ex Burtnisland SY, Thornton Hibs, Newburgh)
Callum Kinnes (ex Oakley Utd)
Conor Schiavone (ex Dunfermline Ath, Balligry R, Dundonald BB, Kirkcaldy YM, Lochgelly Alb, St Andrews Utd)
Craig Wallace (ex Dundee, Bo'ness Utd, Kelty H, Dundonald BB)
Dion Gear
Gary Pearson
Gavin Moffat
Jack Small
James Russell (ex Tayport, Kirrie Th)
Josh McPhie
Lewis Hamill
M Miller
Rhys Sneddon
Ricki Cooper
Ross Mutch
Ryan MacDonald (ex Raith R, Cowdenbeath, Dundonald BB)
Scott Costello
Scott Napier
Stephen Forbes (ex Rangers, Dundonald BB)
Stewart MacDonald

Haddington Athletic
Manager: Brian Johnston
Sinclair Inglis (ex Tranent, Vale of Leithen, Edinburgh Utd)
Grant Goodfellow
Kevin Keane (ex Lothian Th, Whitehill W, Preston Ath)
Robert Berry
Chris Cairney
Arran Ponton
Euan Bald
Keiran Ingram
George Cunningham
Michael Fairnie (ex Tranent, Haddington Ath, Edinburgh Utd)
Scott Moffat (Sep 2016 Whitehill Welfare)
Paul Devlin (ex Leith Ath, Whitehill W, Peebles R, Tynecastle, Edinburgh City, Preston Ath)
Chris Inglis (ex Cowdenbeath, Bonnyrigg R, St Bernards U21, Tranent, Vale of Leithen, Edinburgh Utd, Penicuik Ath)
Stewart Johnston
Jamie Chapman
Andrew Jones
William Kidd
Scott Wright (ex Ormiston)
Dean Woods
Joe Hamill (ex E Stirlingshire, Hearts, Leicester C, Livingston, QOS, Ostersunds FK, Raith R, Formartine Utd, Airdrie, Bonnyrigg R, Linlithgow R)

Kennoway Star Hearts
Manager:
Robbie Paterson
Scott Young
Ross Brewster (ex E Fife, HOB Haws)
Mark Partridge
Nathan Doig (ex E Fife)
Michael Lee (ex Dundee Utd, Glenrothes, HOB Haws)
Liam Craig
Stephen Davidson
Kyle Wilson
Kevin Byers
Liam Rolland
Sean Simpson
Kieran Band
Matthew Gay
Liam Mann
Calum Sutherland

St Andrew's United
Manager: Craig Morrison
Shaun Hunter (ex Kelty H, Cowdenbeath)
Dylan Honeyman (ex Eastvale, E Fife, Newburgh, Glenrothes)
Michael Perrie
Ryan McInnes

Lee Schiavone (ex Dunfermline Ath, Alloa, Cowdenbeath, Ballingry R, Thornton H)
Daryl Falconer (ex E Fife, Dundonald BB, Newburgh, Glenrothes)
Graeme Nutt (ex Steelend Vics, Lochore W , Oakley Utd)
Aiden Hendry
Ben Antony (ex Alloa, Cowdenbeath, HOB Haws, Dundonald BB)
Scott Orrock (ex Kirkcaldy YM, Dundonald BB)
Lee Duffy
Scott Mayne (ex Kennoway Ams, Dundonald BB)
Rhory Mooney
Michael Fleming (ex Cowdenbeath, Ballingry R, HOB Haws, Oakley United)
Jason Quinn
Ross Graham (ex Kelty H, Ballingry R, Dundonald BB, Montrose, Berwick R)

Sauchie
Manager: Fraser Duncan
Jordan Allan (ex Clyde, Bo'ness Utd, Hamilton Accies, Whitburn)
Darren Dolan (ex E Stirling)
Greg Maitland
Steve Dolan
Jon Tully (ex Peterhead, E Stirling)
Stuart McFarlane
Jordan Tapping (ex E Stirling, Oakley Utd)
Iain Syme
Gary McCulloch
Anthony McTaggart
Martyn Shields
Colin Samuel (ex Khelwalas, Jabloteh, Falkirk, Dundee Utd, Toronto FC, St johnstone, Luton Town, Arbroath, E Fife, Trinidand & Tobago International)
Moses Olenrewaju (ex Stevenage, Rushden & Diamonds, Stirling Albion)
Ryan Miller
Brian Morgan
Darren Cummings (ex Stirling Albion, Bo'ness United)
Ian Diack (ex Celtic, Albion R, Arbroath, Morton, E Stirling, Stenhousemuir, Berwick R, Brechin C, Pollok, Kirkintilloch RR, Linlithgow R, Kilbirnie L)
Josh Flood (ex Stirling Albion, Albion R, Irvine M, Shotts BA)
James McAteer (ex Falkirk JFC, Bo'ness Utd)
Ben Hutchison
Mark Sharp

Sean Heaver

Tayport
Manager: John Ovenstone
Assistant: Steve Kerrigan
Coach: Allan Ramsay, Jim Moffat
Gavin Sorley (ex Coupar Angus, Scone Th, Harthill Royal, Kinnoull, E Stirling, Berwick R, St Andrews Utd)
Kieran Conway
Craig Sturrock
Daniel Sanchez
Pavel Ostrovskis
Stuart Walton (ex Alloa, Dundonald BB)
Alan Tulleth (ex Dundee, St Andrews Utd, Newburgh)
Grant Mowatt
David Geekie
Liam Ross
Struan Christie
Marc Ogg
Sergio Alvarez (ex Atl Victoria, Arbroath)
Connaire Connelly
Grant Paterson
Dale Reid (ex Montrose)
Duncan Bruce
Fraser Anderson
Taylor Carroll
Gary Sutherland (ex Dunfermline Ath, Craigroyston, St Andrews Utd, Dundee NE)

Tranent
Managers: Darren Smith / Kenny Rafferty
Murray Jackson (ex Cowdenbeath, Stirling Albion, Spartans, Musselburgh Ath, Nitten Star)
Liam Robertson (son of John Robertson, ex Hearts)
Alexander Christie (ex Musselburgh Ath)
Neil Smeaton
Jamie Patterson
Craig Wojtowycz
Jamie Todd
Guy Kerr (ex Dunfermline Ath, ICT, Elgin C, Berwick R, E Fife, Musselburgh Ath, Penicuik Ath, Newtongrange Star, Arniston R)
Lewis Hawkins
Darren Smith (ex Hutchison Vale, Berwick R, Brechin C, Raith R, Alloa, E Fife, Arbroath, Stirling Albion, Musselburgh Ath)
Jack Wright
Ben Miller (ex Berwick R, Arniston R)
Lloyd Fiddler
Stephen Manson
Thomas Watters
Joe Murray
Kenny Fisher (ex Dalkeith Th, Edinburgh Utd)
Kane Patterson
Kyle Mitchell

Whitburn
Manager: Tom Hendrie (until October), Andy Cunningham (from November)
A Gilmour
Aaron Gunn
Adam Porteous
Allan
C Robertson
Connor McQueenie
Dean Wilson
Dewi Taylor (ex Dunipace U19)
Gary Brass (ex Stirling Albion, Camelon)
Graham
Greg Skinner
Jack Hamilton (ex Stenhousemuir, E Stirling)
James Martin
Jake Moyes
James McGrane
JJ Henderson
Johnstone
Jordan Bain (ex Broxburn Ath)
Kieran Baksh
Jason Walton
Kris Russell
Lee Brown
Martin Hubbocks
Martin Russell
McAteer
Michael Adams (ex West Calder)_
Patrick
Peter Douglas Horne
Russell Hogarth
Steven McMeechan
Thomson
W Gardner

McBookie.com East League North Division 2016/17

	ARB	BLA	BRE	COU	DNE	EAS	FOR	KIN	KIR	LHA	LWE	LUN	NEW	SCO	THO
Arbroath Vics		Apr 22 3-2	Apr 29 1-3	Dec 10 2-4	May 13 2-3	Sep 10 3-6	Mar 11 3-1	Aug 6 2-3	Oct 15 4-5	Feb 25 0-0	Nov 5 0-5	Aug 20 1-1	Feb 4 3-2	Jan 28 1-2	Apr 15 0-3
Blairgowrie	Jan 21 1-3		Oct 8 4-0	Sep 24 4-2	Apr 15 2-3	Feb 18 1-1	Sep 10 3-1	May 13 1-3	Aug 20 2-2	Mar 18 1-2	Dec 17 6-3	Apr 1 1-2	Apr 29 4-3	Nov 12 2-1	Feb 11 0-6
Brechin Vics	Sep 17 3-4	May 6 0-2		May 10 3-6	Apr 1 0-3	Dec 10 0-6	Apr 15 5-4	Feb 4 1-3	Nov 12 1-3	Aug 27 3-1	Mar 25 2-3	Oct 1 0-6	Oct 29 1-6	Aug 13 2-3	Jan 21 1-5
Coupar Angus	Mar 25 4-0	Dec 3 3-3	Aug 20 1-1		Oct 29 1-3	Apr 1 0-3	Oct 8 1-1	Nov 5 0-3	Feb 25 0-5	Sep 17 4-7	Apr 22 3-1	Apr 26 1-2	May 13 5-0	Mar 11 1-4	Aug 6 0-3
Dundee North End	Feb 18 7-0	Dec 10 1-1	Sep 10 5-1	Apr 29 3-0		Apr 26 0-2	Aug 6 5-1	Jan 21 1-1	Dec 17 0-2	Nov 12 1-1	Apr 8 3-0	Feb 4 1-2	Oct 1 5-3	May 24 2-2	Aug 20 0-2
East Craigie	Dec 17 2-2	Oct 29 3-1	Mar 18 3-0	Aug 13 3-0	Aug 27 5-2		Jan 21 10-0	Apr 29 0-1	Nov 5 1-5	Apr 8 2-1	Oct 1 3-1	Apr 15 3-3	Sep 17 4-3	Feb 25 1-0	May 13 0-2
Forfar Albion	Aug 13 2-1	Apr 8 0-5	Nov 5 1-5	Mar 18 2-2	Feb 11 0-5	Apr 22 1-6		Mar 25 0-5	Sep 17 0-7	Oct 29 0-2	Aug 27 2-2	Apr 29 0-13	Dec 17 1-5	May 6 1-4	Feb 25 0-8
Kinnoull	May 6 2-1	Aug 27 1-2	Dec 3 3-1	Apr 15 4-1	May 27 0-3	Jan 7 2-2	Oct 1 8-0		Mar 18 2-2	Sep 24 3-0	Feb 11 5-1	Oct 29 3-3	Aug 13 3-0	Apr 1 2-2	Dec 17 1-4
Kirrie Thistle	Apr 26 6-0	Mar 25 3-1	Apr 8 7-0	May 6 9-0	May 31 2-3	May 10 1-1	May 3 6-0	Sep 10 2-4		Dec 10 4-2	Aug 13 10-1	Jan 7 6-3	Jan 28 5-0	Oct 1 5-3	Oct 29 6-1
Lochee Harp	Dec 3 4-3	Oct 1 4-4	May 20 8-1	Jan 7 3-4	Apr 22 1-5	Aug 20 3-2	Apr 1 6-0	Feb 18 1-1	Apr 15 0-4		Apr 29 3-1	Aug 6 2-3	Nov 5 1-4	Dec 17 1-2	Mar 25 0-4
Lochore Welfare	May 20 0-3	Aug 6 0-7	May 13 5-1	Nov 12 0-4	Jan 7 0-3	May 6 2-6	Feb 4 2-2	Aug 20 0-5	Apr 1 0-10	Jan 21 1-2		Sep 10 1-4	Apr 15 5-1	Oct 29 0-4	Sep 17 2-5
Luncarty	Mar 18 2-1	Sep 17 2-3	Apr 22 4-0	Dec 17 2-4	Aug 13 1-1	Feb 11 0-0	Nov 12 7-3	Apr 8 2-2	May 15 2-3	May 13 2-1	Mar 11 6-0		Aug 27 3-0	Sep 24 0-1	May 6 1-2
Newburgh	Nov 12 2-3	Jan 7 1-4	Feb 18 1-1	Jan 21 1-4	Mar 11 2-5	Mar 25 1-2	Aug 20 3-3	Dec 10 3-0	Aug 6 1-5	May 6 2-2	Oct 15 5-0	May 20 2-3		Dec 3 0-6	Sep 10 1-6
Scone Thistle	Apr 8 2-3	Feb 4 3-1	Jan 7 3-0	Aug 27 4-1	Sep 17 2-7	Aug 6 1-0	Dec 10 6-2	Oct 15 2-3	May 13 1-1	Sep 10 2-1	Feb 18 5-2	Mar 25 1-1	Apr 22 3-0		Nov 5 0-2
Thornton Hibs	Aug 27 5-1	Sep 3 4-5	May 27 6-0	Apr 8 5-0	May 15 2-2	Oct 22 2-0	May 20 4-0	Apr 22 2-2	Apr 29 0-0	Aug 13 6-0	Dec 3 4-1	Dec 10 1-1	Apr 1 5-0	Mar 18 1-1	

ABD
11/3/17, Blairgowrie v Kinnoull, 0-1, 38 mins, Player injury

			Home					Away						
		P	W	D	L	F	A	W	D	L	F	A	GD	Pts
1	**Kirriemuir Thistle**	28	11	1	2	72	18	10	4	0	54	14	94	68
2	**Thornton Hibs (R)**	28	8	5	1	47	13	13	0	1	53	12	75	68
3	Dundee North End	28	6	4	4	34	18	11	2	1	48	20	44	57
4	Kinnoull	28	7	4	3	39	22	9	4	1	36	17	36	56
5	East Craigie	28	9	2	3	40	21	7	4	3	37	17	39	54
6	Scone Thistle	28	8	2	4	35	24	8	3	3	35	19	27	53
7	Luncarty	28	6	3	5	34	21	8	5	1	47	23	37	50
8	Blairgowrie	28	6	2	6	32	32	7	3	4	40	28	12	44
9	Lochee Harp	28	5	2	7	37	38	4	3	7	22	31	-10	32
10	Coupar Angus	28	3	3	8	24	36	6	1	7	32	45	-25	31
11	Arbroath Vics	28	3	2	9	25	40	5	1	8	25	42	-32	27
12	Newburgh	28	2	3	9	25	44	3	0	11	27	48	-40	18
13	Brechin Vics	28	2	0	12	22	55	2	2	10	14	52	-71	14
14	Lochore Welfare	28	2	1	11	18	57	2	1	11	21	57	-75	14
15	Forfar Albion	28	1	2	11	10	70	0	3	11	18	69	-111	8

The League quickly developed into a two-horse race between Kirrie Thistle and Thornton Hibs. The monly question was who would be Champions and who would be Runners-Up - in the end it was Kirrie who triumphed by the smallest of margins.

Great credit is due to both clubs for earning promotion considering how limited are the resources available to them. Both have been in the Premier League recently and have struggled - perhaps they will fare better next season.

Lochee Harp bid farewell to Beechwood Park at the end of the season. They will groundshare until their own new ground is ready.

Lochore Welfare deserve credit for completing the season. They looked likely to drop out last Summer but survived and managed to fulfil their commitments.

Forfar Albion again finished bottom,

East Juniors North Division 2006-2017	2006/7	2007/8	2008/9	2009/10	2010/11	2011/12	2012/13	2013/14	2014/15	2015/16	2016/17
Arbroath SC	2	0	6	10	7						
Arbroath Victoria	10	5	5	3	5	4	6	11	6	12	11
Blairgowrie	4	1			8	9	8	6	4	4	8
Brechin Vics	12	11	11	9	9	7	10	13	9	13	13
Broughty Athletic	6	2	2	1							
Coupar Angus	11	10	9	12	3	11	12	16	Ab	9	10
Downfield	3	8	8	5	1		7	3	3	1	
Dundee North End				8	2	2	5	1		5	3
East Craigie	7	7	7	7	1	5	3	10	5	8	5
Forfar Albion	9	12	2	11	12	10	11	15	15	15	15
Forfar West End	1						4	2			
Glenrothes										2	
Kennoway Star Hearts								5	2		
Kinnoull										7	4
Kirkcaldy YM									13		
Kirrie Thistle	8	6	10	4	7	6	1		14	3	1
Lochee Harp		4	4	6	10	8	9	14	10	11	9
Lochore Welfare								9	12	6	14
Luncarty								8	8		7
Montrose Roselea			1		4	3	2				
Newburgh								4	7	14	12
Scone Thistle								12	11	10	6
Thornton Hibs								7	1		2
Violet	5	3	3	2	3	1					

East Juniors South Division 2006-2017	2006/7	2007/8	2008/9	2009/10	2010/11	2011/12	2012/13	2013/14	2014/15	2015/16	2016/17
Armadale Thistle			1								
Arniston Rangers							4				
Blackburn United	10	6	9	5	7	6	10	3	5	3	2
Broxburn Athletic	3	4	4	1							
Craigroyston											10
Crossgates Primrose								13	14	Res	12
Dalkeith Thistle	14	7	8	9	12	1					
Dunbar United	9	10	12	8	10	9	6	6	6	4	1
Dundonald Bluebell								2			
Easthouses Lily MY										6	5
Edinburgh United	8	8	5	7	8	14	15	1			7
Falkirk JFC						3	13	7	2		
Fauldhouse United	6	1			2	4	1				
Haddington Athletic	5	2	11	10	4	2	5	4	1		
Harthill Royal	7	3	7	12	14	15	14	14	13		
Kirkcaldy YM										9	14
Livingston United	15	12	14	13	3	7	3		10	11	11
Lochgelly Albert								9	7	5	4
Newtongrange Star	1										
Oakley United											9
Pumpherston	4	11	13	14	13	12	2		11	10	3
Rosyth								12	3	7	8
Sauchie	2	5	3	4	1						
Spartans				2	9	10	9				
Stoneyburn	13	13	10	11	6	11	12	11	9	12	13
Tranent	11	12	2	3	5	5	7	8	12	1	
West Calder United	12	9	6	6	11	13	11	10	8	8	6
Whitburn						8	8	5	4	2	

East Juniors Central Division - All Time Positions	2006-7	2007-8	2008-9	2009-10	2010-11	2011-12	2012-13
Ballingry Rovers	3	1					
Bankfoot Athletic	12	10	7	7	6	5	12
Crossgates Primrose	10	6	8	10	9	9	10
Dundonald Bluebell	1			5	2	2	3
Jeanfield Swifts	7	5	4	4	4	1	
Kinnoull						3	1
Kirkcaldy YM	2	Ab	3	3	3	7	2
Lochgelly Albert	4	3	9	11	5	4	8
Lochore Welfare	5	7	6	6	7	11	5
Luncarty	6	11	13	14	13	13	13
Newburgh	11	9	12	12	11	6	4
Oakley United				2	1		
Rosyth			2	8	12	10	6
Scone Thistle		8	11	13	10	Ab	11
St Andrews United		2	1				
Steelend Vics	8	12	10	9	8	12	9
Thornton Hibs	9	4	5	1		8	7

From 2006 until 2013 the third tier of the East Region operated with three Divisions. The Perth area clubs were transferred from Tayside and grouped with the Fife clubs to form a Central Division. In 2013 a two-division set-up was established with the Central Division clubs split between the North and South Leagues. Fife clubs are vulnerable to being switched between divisions without consultation.

East Juniors North Division Playing Squads 2016/17

NB These are not comprehensive lists of players used - there will be some omissions. However, all players listed were associated with the club concerned during 2016/17

Arbroath Victoria
Co-Managers: David McLeish, Mark Fotheringham, David Sturrock
Mark Anderson
Josh Allardyce
Joantahan Bastow
Josh Chalmers
Scott Donald
Kevin Durno
Kyle Findlater
Steve Florence (ex Arbroath, Forfar Ath)
Rikki Gillespie
Lee Jones
Craig Kear
Ryan Lewis
Kellon Lyons
Corey McCulloch
Ross Paterson
David Sturrock
Marc Walker
Calum Walls
Gary Warren
Charlie Wilson

Blairgowrie
Manager:
Allan Cruikshank
Danny Miller
Darren Neave
Gary Axworthy
Gordon Norrie
Gordon O'Brien (ex St Johnstone, Berwick R)
Gordon Pirie
Greg McDonald
Ian Plenderleith (ex Broughty Ath)
James Simpson
Jamie Duncan
John Black
Keir Reilly
Mark Brash (ex Broughty Ath)
Paul Maloney
Paul Scott
Robbie Hood
Ross Mitchell
Rudi Brown
Ryan Menzies
Sean Kelly (Ex Dundee NE, Montrose, Broughty Ath, Downfield)
Stefan Brown
Steven Findlay
Stewart Nicoll

Brechin Vics
Manager: Charlie King (until December), Paul Tosh / Wayne Harrison (from December)
Leighton Davidson
Gregor O'Neill
Barrie Gourlay
Blair Stephen
Ryan Milne
Kerr Hendry
Matty Johnston
Steven Eaton
Sean Ferrar
Connor Mitchell
David Steel
Colin Lawson
Douglas Crowe
Adam Renilson
Sam Wood
Jordan Rausch
Scott Black
Scott Ferries
Paul Tosh

Coupar Angus
Manager: Logan McConachie
Murray Irvine
Alex Gibb (2016 Dundee NE)
Chris Liversedge (ex Banks o Dee, Carnoustie Panmure)
Tom Casey
Dylan Cook (2016 Forfar Albion)
Daniel Neath (2016 Carnoustie Panmure)
Murray Irvine
Blair Fleming
Alex Gibb
Joe Grimes
Martyn McCabe (2016 Lochee Harp)
Scott Bennett (ex Stirling Albion, Stenhousemuir, Montrose)
Dougie Inglis
Alan Leith
Struan Docherty (2016 Forfar WE OL)
Jack Shaw
Jonathan White
Joe Sturrock
Nathan Ireland
Ross Nicholson
John Miller
Aaron Ogilvie
Callum Hill
Adam Mitchell
Ryan Duncan
Michael Cook
Blair Fleming (2016 Forfar WE OL)

Dundee North End
Manager: Ross Lunan
Marc Mackie
Martin Strachan
Ryan Smith
Neal Ferrie
G Robertson
Bradie Heggie
Michael Stewart
Winter
Ross Sievwright
Ryan Shaw
Paul Lunan
Gary Sutherland (to Tayport Jan 2017)
Dayle Robertson
Lee Cameron (ex Dundee)
McBride
Ryan Hunter
William Johnston
Gavin Burns
Patrick Martin
Zak Wilson
Craig Scrimgeour

East Craigie
Manager: Sean Wilkie
Adam Braid
Andy McDonald
Conan Howett
Darren Gray
David Black
Euan Faulkner
Finlay Baird
Gary Welsh
Graeme McLeish
Greg Warwick
James Malone
Jon Ross-Craig
Kris Ward
Lee Maloney
Liam Dunn
Liam McCartney
Lloyd Spowatt
Logan Irvine
Mark Ferrie
Mark Middleton
Nicky Mann
Ranald Bowie
Ross McFarlane
Ryan Welsh
Ryan White
Sean Reekie

Forfar Albion
Manager: David Thomson
Alistair Nicholson
Alistair Wilson
Ben English
Ben Lees
Caelan Flynn
Callum Martin
Calvin Brady
Chris Campbell
Connor Airlie
Connor Yeats
Dan Duggan
Dan Thomson
Darren Mackie
David Cargill
David Scott
Derek Johnston
Dylan Phillips
Gatreth Mowatt
Gary Grant
Gavin Anderson
Jake Porter
Jason King
Jayden Murphy
Josh Alexander
Josh Moncreiff
Justin McCabe
Kieran Crighton
Kyle MacLeod
Lawrie Mitchell
Lee Anderson
Lewis Starkey
Liam Harper
Marlk Caldwell
Martyn Gellatly
Matthew Dorward
Matthew Muir
Michael Malone
Owen McCabe
Ross McCleary
Ryan Anderson
Ryan Burry
Ryan Carr
Ryan Murphy
Ryan Sievwright
Sameer Al Nadaf
Sean Colvin
Steve Clark
Vince Kenny
William Milligan

Kinnoull
Manager: Alan Cameron
Sean Burton
Rhys Davies
Mark Smith
Gordon Chalmers
Kieran Donald
Allan Ferguson
Rab Kinnaird
Lewis Mackie
David Gray
Liam Woolley
Tom Whyte
Chris McCaffrey
Robbie Morrie
Greg Whyte
Mark McDonald
Greg Fleming
Dominic Blair

Jordan Davidson
Youssef Elseedawy
Richard Cargill
Ryan Gray
Jay Kinnear

Kirrie Thistle
Manager: Jim Finlayson
Adam O'Connor
Blair Mudie
Bryan Duell
Chris Hutchison
Darren Cox
Darren Scott
Davie Millar
Dean Thomson
Derek Patterson
Gary Archibald
John Farquharson
Jonny Snowdon
Kamil Kadela
Lewis Fyfe
Nathan Tosh
Paul Constable
Ryan Sloan
Ryan Strachan
Scott Drum
Sean Diamond
Stephen Duffy
Stewart Russell
Stewart McKenna

Lochee Harp
Manager: David Martin
Graham Allan
Darren Brown
David Buchan
James Cochrane
Joe Colquhoun
Darryl Gowans
Mark Kelly
Connor MacLeod
Martyn McCabe
Sam McDonald
Paul Moran
Frankie Mullen
Aarn Opeku
Gordon Ramsey
Liam Roddy

Lochore Welfare
Manager: Andy Healy
Scott Warrender
Gary Inglis
Callum Watt
Dean Ewing
James Davies
Kevin Brown
Ben Rolland
Kytle Fraser
Callum Esson
James Adam
Logan Greig Donaldson
Scott Morrison
Kearyn Hicks
Calum Reid
Kieran Annandale
Cassells
Lewis Thompson
Laird
Adam Haddow
Gray
Renton
Scott Rowland
Ewan Robertson
Joe Kirby
Ryan Brocklebank
Colin Sutherland

Luncarty
Manager: Jon Kelly
Alexander Whytock
Andy Kirkcaldy
Dan Walker
Danny Dobie
Darren Gray
Darren Kelly
Duncan Bruce
Gerry Kelly
Jake DOlzanski
Jamie McKenzie
Jamie Reid
Jon Kelly
Jordan Kinnon
Kyle Sandilands
Ledwis Allan
Martin Maher
Neil Ritchie
Regan McLaren (OL from Stirling Albion)
Richard Doig
Richie Montgomery
Robbie Miller
Ross Mitchell
Steve McCallister
Stuart Nicol

Newburgh
Manager: Paul Martin (Until April), Kurt Herd (until May), Alan Fortune (from May 2017)
Liam Keiller
Gavin Thomson
Fairweather
Cammy Black
Graham Scrimgeour
Fraser Wilson
Stuart Hill
Steven Harris
Hatch
Scott Findlay
Cunningham
Duddy
Andrew Reade
Gary Spence
Tom Gooding
James Robson
Neal Craig
Martin Forbes
Cumberland Bowers
Chris Chimiak
Brad Ronan
Fraser Wilson
Kyle Baker
Cameron Williamson

Scone Thistle
Manager: Derek Lawson
Abdourahman Njie
Andrew McKenzie
Arran McKay
Ben Ayton
Ben Boucher-Myers
Ben Moffat
Craig Mitchell
David Winton
Derek Angus
Fraser MacDonald
Fraser Mills
Gary Fergus
Gary Mackie
Graham Michie
Josh Gorton
Kenny Hynd
Kevin Sinclair
Lewis Avolio
Martin Strachan
Max Avolio
Scott Lafferty
Sean Fergus
Sean Whitworth
Stephen Moon
Willie Laing

Thornton Hibs
Manager: Craig Gilbert
Assistant: Graeme Turnbull
Player / Coach: John Paul Burns
Bryan Strachan
Chris Ireland
Coco Mullen
Dale Robertson
Dean Gear
Dean McMillan
Ewan Henderson
Garry Thomson Jnr
Garry Thomson Snr
Ian Hepburn
Ian Shanks
Jimmy Shields
John Paul Burns
Matthew Clark
Matthew Robertson
Max Coleman
Nicholas McGowan
Raymond Crichton
Shaun Keatings (2016 St Andrews Utd, ex Dundonald BB, Kirkcaldy YMCA)
Stuart Drummond
Ian Hepburn

EAST OF SCOTLAND CUP DRAW 2017/18

ROUND 1 (to be played 3/9/16)
Lochgelly Albert v Lochee Utd
Camelon v Glenrothes
Broxburn Ath v Oakley Utd
Broughty Ath v Dundee East Craigie
Lochore Welfare v Kirkcaldy YM
Dundonald Bluebell v Newburgh
Haddington Ath v Kinnoull
Tayport v Linlithgow Rose
Rosyth v Coupar Angus
St Andrews Utd v Musselburgh Ath
Arniston Rangers v Dunbar Utd
Livingston Utd v Craigroyston
Whitburn v Thornton Hibs
Dundee Violet v Bo'ness Utd
Dundee North End v Bonnyrigg Rose
Fauldhouse Utd v Easthouses Lily MW
Penicuik Ath v Bathgate Thistle
Blairgowrie v Harthill Royal
Tranent v Sauchie
West Calder Utd v Carnoustie Panmure
Pumpherston v Edinburgh Utd
Forfar Albion v Crossgates Primrose
Luncarty v Stoneyburn
Scone Thistle v Blackburn Utd
Kirriemuir Thistle v Lochee Harp
Jeanfield Swifts v Kennoway Star Hearts
Armadale Thistle v Forfar West End
Hill of Beath Hawthorn v Arbroath Vics

McBookie.com East League South Division 2016/17

	BLA	CRA	PRIM	DUN	EAS	EDI	KIR	LIV	ALB	OAK	PUM	ROS	STO	WCU
Blackburn United		Dec 10 3-0	Apr 15 6-0	Oct 29 1-0	Jan 7 4-0	Aug 27 2-0	Nov 12 2-1	Oct 1 4-2	Sep 17 2-2	Aug 13 8-1	Jan 21 3-2	Feb 18 3-1	Mar 25 2-1	Nov 26 3-0
Craigroyston	Aug 20 1-2		Jan 28 3-1	Dec 3 0-5	Mar 4 1-4	Mar 25 5-5	Oct 15 4-4	Nov 5 2-2	Dec 17 0-2	Sep 10 4-2	Nov 12 3-6	Feb 11 0-1	Mar 18 1-2	Aug 6 1-1
Crossgates Primrose	Aug 6 1-3	Aug 27 1-3		Apr 8 1-5	Oct 29 1-2	Feb 4 1-3	Oct 22 2-2	Dec 3 6-0	May 13 1-3	Dec 17 2-3	Sep 17 0-4	Jan 21 1-1	Apr 29 1-2	Feb 18 2-5
Dunbar United	Apr 29 1-0	Apr 1 2-0	Dec 10 3-2		Feb 25 3-0	Apr 22 7-1	Aug 27 3-0	Aug 13 4-1	Nov 12 4-2	Nov 5 2-0	Mar 11 3-1	Sep 17 3-0	Aug 6 3-0	Jan 28 8-1
Easthouses Lily	Oct 15 1-2	Nov 19 4-2	Mar 11 3-1	Aug 20 2-4		Feb 18 3-3	Sep 17 3-2	Apr 15 0-0	Mar 25 1-2	Jan 28 3-1	Aug 6 0-5	Dec 17 2-1	Sep 10 2-1	Dec 3 0-2
Edinburgh United	Jan 28 0-0	Oct 1 1-0	Sep 10 3-3	Oct 15 1-4	Apr 8 1-0		Aug 6 4-1	Mar 11 0-0	Dec 3 1-1	Apr 15 4-2	Dec 17 2-3	Aug 20 3-2	May 6 4-0**	Jan 7 3-6
Kirkcaldy YM	Mar 18 1-4	Feb 4 0-5	Mar 25 1-3	Apr 15 1-7	Jan 21 0-2	Oct 8 1-7		Sep 10 1-1	Aug 20 1-1	Feb 18 0-3	Dec 3 2-7	Oct 1 1-1	Jan 7 3-2	Dec 17 0-3
Livingston United	Dec 17 0-3	Apr 8 5-0	Oct 15 4-5	May 6 0-5	Aug 27 3-5	Nov 12 2-6	Jan 28 5-3		Aug 6 1-10	Apr 22 1-1	Mar 25 0-2	Jan 7 0-2	Aug 20 5-0	Sep 17 1-6
Lochgelly Albert	Apr 8 1-0	Oct 29 3-2	Jan 7 1-1	May 20 2-0	Aug 13 4-2	Apr 29 3-3	Dec 10 2-0	Apr 1 2-1		Sep 24 0-2	Oct 15 4-2	May 3 3-1	Apr 22 4-0	Aug 27 2-0
Oakley United	Mar 11 1-6	Jan 7 5-0	Aug 20 3-3	Mar 25 0-4	Nov 12 1-4	Sep 17 3-2	Apr 8 3-2	Oct 29 3-2	Jan 21 4-2		Feb 4 3-3	Aug 6 1-4	Dec 10 4-4	Oct 15 2-1
Pumpherston	Sep 10 3-6	Feb 18 3-0	Apr 1 4-3	Jan 7 4-0	Dec 10 8-2	Oct 29 5-2	Aug 13 4-1	Nov 19 5-0	May 6 1-1	Oct 1 3-2		Apr 8 3-0	Nov 5 4-1	Mar 18 4-0
Rosyth	Sep 24 2-0	Aug 13 3-3	Apr 22 6-2	Feb 4 1-4*	Apr 29 1-0	Dec 10 2-1	Apr 1 0-0	May 20 3-1	Sep 10 0-2	Mar 4 4-0*	Aug 27 0-6		May 13 6-2	Nov 5 1-2
Stoneyburn	Dec 3 0-2	Sep 17 1-3	Aug 13 1-3	Dec 17 0-5	Apr 1 0-2	Sep 24 1-6	Mar 11 2-1	Feb 18 1-2	Oct 1 0-1	Aug 27 1-0	Apr 15 0-1	Jan 28 1-2		Apr 8 1-1
West Calder United	Apr 22 0-1	Mar 11 1-4	Nov 12 6-0	Sep 10 1-1	Oct 1 3-3	Aug 13 2-1	Oct 29 5-2	Dec 10 4-0	Apr 15 1-2	Apr 1 2-0	Aug 20 2-4	Mar 25 3-2	Nov 19 1-1	

* at Kelty (Rosyth ground unavailable due to generator issues)
** at Newtongrange (Double booking at Paties Road)

			Home					Away						
		P	W	D	L	F	A	W	D	L	F	A	GD	Pts
1	**Dunbar United**	26	13	0	0	46	8	9	1	3	44	13	69	67
2	**Blackburn United**	26	12	1	0	43	10	9	1	3	29	12	50	65
3	Pumpherston Juniors	26	11	1	1	50	18	9	1	3	46	22	56	62
4	Lochgelly Albert	26	10	2	1	31	14	7	4	2	34	17	34	57
5	Easthouses Lily MW	26	6	2	5	24	29	6	1	6	26	30	-9	39
6	West Calder United	26	6	3	4	31	21	5	2	6	22	28	4	38
7	Edinburgh United (R)	26	6	4	3	27	22	4	3	6	40	37	8	37
8	Rosyth	26	7	2	4	29	23	4	2	7	18	24	0	37
9	Oakley United (R)	26	6	3	4	33	37	3	1	9	17	34	-21	31
10	Craigroyston	26	2	4	7	25	37	4	1	8	22	32	-22	23
11	Livingston United	26	4	1	8	27	42	1	4	8	12	35	-38	20
12	Crossgates Primrose	26	1	2	10	20	36	3	3	7	27	44	-33	17
13	Stoneyburn Juniors	26	2	1	10	9	29	2	2	9	16	40	-44	15
14	Kirkcaldy YM	26	1	3	9	12	46	0	3	10	19	39	-54	9

For much of the season there was a three-way fight between Dunbar, Blackburn and Pumpherston for the two promotion places. In the end Dunbar were worthy champions, finally fulfilling their potential and achieving promotion. Blackburn have enjoyed a "bounce" from their new facilities and deservedly joined them in the step up.

Both relegated clubs, Edinburgh and Oakley, struggled for any sort of consistency. Newcomers Craigroyston were in a similar position. Crossgates Primrose returned from a spell in abeyance and seem to be thriving.

Rosyth had ongoing issues with their ground. Recreation Park has been sold by the council and they are on notice to leave. Problems with the electricity supply meant they had to move a number of games to Kelty.

Kirkcaldy YM suffered at the hands of vandals with their facilities at Denfield Park being torched. They suffered on the field as well, finishing some way adrift at the bottom.

Harthill Royal will be returning for 2017/18 following a couple of seasons in abeyance.

East Juniors South Division Playing Squads 2016/17

NB These are not comprehensive lists of players used - there will be some omissions. However, all players listed were associated with the club concerned during 2016/17.

Blackburn United
Manager: Mark Campbell
James Mildren
Martin Lawrie
Andy McQuillan
Aaron Gowans
Fraser Spence
Ross Williamson
Craig Young
Gavin King
John Drummond
Ewan Herriot
Chris Marshall
Gordon Wilson
Danny Campbell
David Swan
Scott Mackie
Ross Donnelly
Scott Woodhouse
Darren Mitchell
Fraser Cormack
Gavin McQuillan
Gary Calvey
Lee Meekison
Dean McCarthur
Darren Fleming
Craig Easton
Ryan Conroy
Jack McLaren
Kenny Govan
Ross Mitchell
Bailey Warren-Black
Ross Gowrie

Craigroyston
Manager: Graham Buckley (until May)
Assistant: Neil Nisbet
Coaches: Kenny Jack, Dave Ewing
Adam Robertson
Andrew Fleming
Andrzej Reske
Cameron Dickson
Chris Rooney
Chris Taylor
Chris Inglis
Craig Sutherland
Dale Pennycuick
David Aitken
Euan Rodgers
Gary Calvey
Gary Dolan
Jack Verth
Jamie Hawkins
Jason Young
Keith Buckley
Kieron Beveridge
Kyle Boggie
Lewis Swaney
Ollie Fleming
Paul Tansey
Ross Nisbet
Sam Kingb
Stephane Murray
Stewart Fisher
Zak Williams

Crossgates Primrose
Manager: Andy Brown
Connor Kirton
Alistair Campbell
Brian Foster
Ben Brown
Conor Gray
Dale Prattis
Dale Mason
Dave Graham
David Mason
Ethan Anderson
Gordon Brown
Greg Pearson
Jamie McNeish
Jamie McNeill
Liam Forbes
Liam McComish
Mark Higgins
Matthew Christie
Rhys Parker
Ryan Graham
Robert Wilson
Ross Day
Scott Devaney
Scott Donaldson
Scott Hope
Stuart Allan
Stuart Donaldson
Stephen Stark
Wayne Beveridge
William Campbell

Dunbar United
Manager: Geoff Jones Assistant Manager: Derek Aitken
Coaches: Ryan Grant, Sandy Inglis, Graeme Lennie
Ano Subasic
Chris Grant
Chris Gordon (2017 Tranent)
Chris Hogg
Chris King
Chris Moffat
Connor Pant
Darren Gillon
Darren Handling
Dean Ballantyne
John Johnstone
Keith Tait
Kevin Smith
Liam McCathie
Sam Young
Scott Gibson
Scott Devlin
Steven Kean
Steven Tait
Taylor Aitchison
Wes Mitchell
Chris Grant
Kieran Ingram (2017 Berwick Rangers OL)

Easthouses Lily
Manager: David McQueenie
Billy Taylor
Shaun Moffat
Ross Hamilton
Gavin Tainsh
David Arthur
Lewis Russell
Stephen Barrie
Kenny McMillan
Gary Shearer
Paul McDermott
Stephen Ferguson
Ryan Kecheran
Danny Watson
David McQueenie
Liam Hall
Mark McEwan
Steven Campbell
Ross McManus
Graeme Young
James Glodek
Patrick Barnett
Paul Neilson
Stephen Hay

Edinburgh United
Manager: Callum Elliot (until December), John O'Hara
Asher Tuffail
Connor Easton
John Armstrong
Ronald Fleming
Liam McDade
Jason Darling
Elliot Grieve
Mark Hendrie
Josh Lawrie
Gabriele Auriemma
Euan Lee
Shaun Conlon
Sean Guiney
Craig Sutherland
Scott Sutherland
Chris Hendrie
Ewan Watson
Nicky Motion
Taylor Hendry
Sebastian Pyda
Sean Martin
Ross Elliot
Jordan Hpkinson
Haydn Crane
Ben Maxwell
Ryan Sclater

Kirkcaldy YM
Manager: Kenny Crawford
Jordan Mushet
Kieran Matthew
Blair Grubb
David Hutchison
Todd Arthur
Stephen King
Scott Small
Gordon Preston
David Byrne
Joe Kinninmonth
Matthew Miller
Connor McManus
Calum Geddes
Lee Henderson
Liam MacDuff
Neil Linton
Glen Barr
Adam Doig
Kyle Fenton
Michael Lawson
Gregor Brown
Daniel MacLeod

Livingston United
Manager: Robert Thomson
Aaron Kane
Alastair Griffin
Bobby Thomson
Callum Wilkinson
Callum Mitchell
Craig Russell
Daniel Forbes
Daniel Robertson
Darren Mclean
Euan Clark
Gareth Roberts
Gary O'Hara
Greig Fowler
Jack Henderson
Jack McWilliams
Jack Townsley
Jake Hughes
John Drummond
John Duncan
Jordan Conlon
Kenneth Govan
Kieran McKee
Kieran McGurk
Kyle Miller
Marc Fleming
Mark McArthur
Mitchell
Paul Clarkson
Richard Kay
Ross Crawford
Ross Gowrie
Sam Rodger
Sebastian Tinning
Sean McLaughlin
Sean McIntosh
Wade

Lochgelly Albert
Manager: Craig Ness
Andy Watt
Colin Rushford
Craig Bateson
Craig Paterson
Douglas Swan
Dylan Hunter
Fraser Sutherland
Gary Pearson
Gregor Colquhoun
Iain Millar
Jack Wilson
John Ferguson
Lee Wilson
Lewis Elder
Lewis Grierson
Martin Rennie
Ryan McEwan
Ryan Robertson
Scott Gibson
Scott Murray
Steven Brown
Steven Page

Oakley United
Manager: Lee Richardson (from Sep) Assistant: John Steel
Andrew McDonald
Alistair MacDonald
Andrew Watt
Brian Breen
Cameron Smith
Conor Drury
Derek Murray
Ewan Watson
Gary Inglis
Graeme Moore
Gregor MacDOnald
Greig Renton
Jamie McGuire
Jason Ward
John Rushford
Josh Wilson
Kevin Brown
Kevin Goodwin
Kevin Gollan
Lee Celentano
Lovemore Demba
Lyall Kellichan
Peter Goldie
Reece Fraser
Reece Strachan
Rory McCann
Rory George
Ross Colquhoun
Ross Harkness
Ross Rennie
Ryan Adamson
Ryan Ewing
Scott Powrie
Scott Morrison
Stanley Chitmere
Tony Doubleday
William Campbell
Yannis Illiopolous

Pumpherston
Manager: Craig Martin
Connor Shaw
Allan McRitchie
Alexander Murray
Barry Nicholson
Bismark Ansong
Bobby Nwanze
Chris Norris
Craig Hepburn
Darryl Butler
Derek Shaw
Gerry McLauchlan
Haydn Crane
Ian Douglas
Jack McLaren
Kyle Miller
Lee Fairley
Marcus Miller
Mark Wilkins
Nicky Rendall
Norrie Dunnett
Ross Elliot
Ryan Slessor
Scott Oliver

Rosyth
Manager: Kevin Smith
Quinn Franklin
Mark Rowbotham
Sean Johnstone
Gregg Robertson
Mark McCulloch
Mark Morrison
Gavin McCann
Steven Slimmings
Scott Gilfillan
Greg Page
Michael McMillan
Ryan O'Connor
Blair Duff
Egidijus Savickas
Dean Ogg
Andy Lawson
Tom Hampson
John Duffy
Scott Russell
Darryl Healey
Ciaran Chalmers
Ross Wortley

Stoneyburn
Manager: Allan Brown
Coach: Brian Fleming
Lee Holliday
Lee Dawson
Steven Dick
Aaron Menzies
Darryl Drew
Craig Gilhooley
John Milroy
Richie Barr
Evan Drew
Lee Henry
James McGrane
David Watson
Graeme Millar
Joe Brady
Dean Clark
Ben Mackay
Dean Clements
Lee Knox
Callum Wilson
Stephen King
Daniel Waddell
Ewan Clark
Steven Sutherland
Mark Donoghue
Graeme Millar
Craig Watt

West Calder United
Manager: Gareth Alexander
Alistair McInnes
Andrew Mochan
Anthony McLaughlin
Darren Fleming
David Cane
David Love
Dean McLean
Declan Winters
Grant Sneddon
Greg Nicol
Jack McGurk
Jamie McDowell
Jordan Hamilton
Jordan Thomson
Jordan Harvey Devine
Keith Paton
Lewis McCarthur
Michael Adams
Nicholas Miller
Paul McLaughlin
Ross Morrison
Sean McLaughlin
Seb Tinning
Stephen Russell
Steven Fyffe
Ross Wortley
Declan Winters
Mike Adams
David Love
Nicky Millar
Jordan Thomson
Seb Tinning
Steven Fyffe

East Region League Cup Competitions

These competitions were discontinued for 2013/14 due to the increased number of League fixtures.

Recent East (Central) Sectional League Cup Finals

Season	Winners	Runners Up	Score	Venue
2003/4	Rosyth Recreation	Thornton Hibs	2-1	Keir's Park, Hill of Beath
2004/5	Hill of Beath Hawthorn	Kircaldy YM	4-0	Ore Park, Glencraig
2005/6	Oakley United	Kelty Hearts	1-1, 4-3 pens	Recreation Park, Rosyth
2006/7	Kelty Hearts	Glenrothes	3-1	Recreation Park, Rosyth
2007/8	Hill of Beath Hawthorn	Glenrothes	2-1	Ore Park, Glencraig
2008/9	Hill of Beath Hawthorn	Glenrothes	1-1, 7-6 pens	Ore Park, Glencraig
2009/10	Glenrothes	Hill of Beath Hawthorn	1-1, 5-4 pens	Moorside Park, Dundonalc
2010/1	Hill of Beath Hawthorn	Glenrothes	2-1	Central Park, Kelty
2011/2	Hill of Beath Hawthorn	Dundonald Bluebell	4-0	Keir's Park, Hill of Beath
2012/3	Jeanfield Swifts	Kelty Hearts	1-0	Blairwood Park, Oakley

Recent East (South) Sectional League Cup Finals

Season	Winners	Runners Up	Score	Venue
2004/5	Harthill Royal	Broxburn Athletic	2-0	Prestonfield, Linlithgow
2005/6	Musselburgh Athletic	Penicuik Athletic	1-0	New Victoria Park, Newtongr
2006/7	Linlithgow Rose	Armadale Thistle	4-3	Carmuirs Park, Camelon
2007/8	Linlithgow Rose	Newtongrange Star	3-1	Prestonfield, Linlithgow
2008/9	Newtongrange Star	Camelon	1-1, 2-1 pens	Creamery Park, Bathgate
2009/10	Camelon	Linlithgow Rose	2-1	Prestonfield, Linlithgow
2010/1	Linlithgow Rose	Camelon	2-1	Creamery Park, Bathgate
2011/2	Linlithgow Rose	Newtongrange Star	3-0	Albyn Park, Broxburn
2012/3	Linlithgow Rose	Newtongrange Star	3-0	Albyn Park, Broxburn

Recent East (North) Sectional League Cup Finals

Season	Winners	Runners Up	Score	Venue
2000/1	Tayport	Dundee North End	2-0	Westfield Park, Carnoustie
2002/3	Montrose Roselea	Forfar West End	4-2	Westfield Park, Carnoustie
2003/4	Montrose Roselea	Carnoustie Panmure	3-0	Strathmore Park, Forfar
2004/5	Dundee North End	Scone Thistle	3-0	Westfield Park, Carnoustie
2005/6	Scone Thistle	Violet	4-1	Laing Park, Carnoustie
2006/7	Lochee United	Tayport	3-1	Laing Park, Carnoustie
2007/8	Lochee United	Tayport	2-2, 5-3 pens	Laing Park, Carnoustie
2008/9	Forfar West End	Lochee United	1-0	Laing Park, Carnoustie
2009/10	Montrose Roselea	Lochee United	0-0, 4-3 pens	Laing Park, Carnoustie
2010/1	Forfar West End	Tayport	2-2, 4-3 pens	Laing Park, Carnoustie
2011/2	Lochee United	Carnoustie Panmure	1-0	North End Park, Dundee
2012/3	Kirrie Thistle	Lochee United	2-1	Laing Park, Carnoustie

The new League structures, combined with a relatively mild winter, meant that some clubs were finished their fixtures very early in 2013/14 and 2014/15. Some teams in the North and South Divisions were finished by lat March / early April.

DJ Laing East of Scotland Junior Cup 2016/17

1	03/09/2016	Bathgate Thistle	Kelty Hearts	0	4	
1	03/09/2016	Blackburn United	Armadale Thistle	4	0	
1	03/09/2016	Broxburn Athletic	Dundee Violet	5	3	
1	03/09/2016	Carnoustie Panmure	Kinnoull	4	1	
1	03/09/2016	Coupar Angus	Jeanfield Swifts	0	5	
1	03/09/2016	Craigroyston	Arbroiath Victoria	1	3	
1	03/09/2016	Dalkeith Thistle	Bo'ness United	2	2	3-5p
1	03/09/2016	Dunbar United	St Andrews United	0	0	3-4p
1	03/09/2016	Dundonald Bluebell	Scone Thistle	6	1	
1	03/09/2016	Edinburgh United	Forfar West End	1	1	4-2p
1		Falkirk	Camelon	sc	wo	
1	03/09/2016	Fauldhouse United	Tranent	0	0	2-4p
1	03/09/2016	Hill of Beath Hawthorn	Arniston Rangers	1	1	5-4p
1	03/09/2016	Kennoway Star Hearts	Whitburn	0	5	
1	03/09/2016	Kirkcaldy YM	Musselburgh Athletic	0	5	
1	15/10/2016	Linlithgow Rose	Thornton Hibs	2	1	
1	03/09/2016	Livingston United	Penicuik Athletic	0	9	
1	03/09/2016	Lochee Harp	Newtongrange Star	0	6	
1	03/09/2016	Lochgelly Albert	Pumpherston	2	2	6-5p
1	03/09/2016	Lochore Welfare	Glenrothes	2	2	4-5p
1	03/09/2016	Luncarty	East Craigie	2	0	
1	03/09/2016	Newburgh	Easthouses Lily	1	2	
1	03/09/2016	Oakley United	Brechin Victoria	2	3	
1	03/09/2016	Rosyth	Kirriemuir Thistle	0	1	
1	03/09/2016	Sauchie	Haddington Athletic	2	1	
1	03/09/2016	Stoneyburn	Dundee North End	0	5	
1	03/09/2016	Tayport	Forfar Albion	4	1	
1	03/09/2016	West Calder United	Broughty Athletic	0	1	
1	03/09/2016	Lochee United	Downfield	0	2	
2	21/01/2017	Camelon	Newtongrange Star	1	4	
2	05/11/2016	Blackburn United	Crossgates Primrose	1	3	
2	07/01/2017	Carnoustie Panmure	Arbroath Vics	3	1	
2	21/01/2017	Tranent	Dundonald Bluebell	1	1	5-4p
2	07/01/2017	Penicuik Athletic	Glenrothes	3	1	
2	05/11/2016	Edinburgh United	Dundee North End	0	1	
2	05/11/2016	Blairgowrie	Luncarty	5	1	
2	10/04/2017	Downfield	Bonnyrigg Rose	1	3	
2	05/11/2016	Whitburn	Easthouses Lily	3	0	
2	01/04/2017	Linlithgow Rose	Bo'ness United	1	1	7-8p
2	18/02/2017	Broughty Athletic	Lochgelly Albert	2	0	
2	17/12/2016	Brechin Vics	Sauchie	1	4	
2	04/03/2017	Musselburgh Athletic	St Andrews United	5	1	
2	21/01/2017	Tayport	Jeanfield Swifts	2	2	3-4p
2	21/01/2017	Kirrie Thistle	Broxburn Athletic	3	3	3-4p
2	18/03/2011	Kelty Hearts	Hill of Beath Hawthorn	3	0	
3	01/04/2017	Broxburn Athletic	Broughty Athletic	3	2	
3	25/02/2017	Blairgowrie	Whitburn	0	3	
3	22/04/2017	Penicuik Athletic	Jeanfield Swifts	2	2	6-7p
3	18/11/2017	Dundee North End	Crossgates Primrose	3	2	
3	19/04/2017	Tranent	Bo'ness United	3	2	
3	22/04/2017	Sauchie	Kelty Hearts	0	3	
3	06/05/2017	Carnoustie Panmure	Bonnyrigg Rose	2	3	
3	01/04/2017	Newtongrange Star	Musselburgh Athletic	2	3	
4	17/05/2017	Bonnyrigg Rose	Kelty Hearts	0	0	5-4p
4	27/05/2017	Musselburgh	Jeanfield Swifts	9	1	
4	13/05/2017	Tranent	Broxburn Athletic	2	2	4-1p
4	06/05/2017	Whitburn	Dundee North End	2	2	3-4p
SF	07/06/2017	Musselburgh Athletic	Bonnyrigg Rose	1	3	
SF	20/05/2017	Dundee NE	Tranent	0	1	
F	10/06/2017	Tranent at Bathgate	Bonnyrigg Rose	1	1	4-1p

The East of Scotland Junior Cup is now played for by all the member clubs of the East Region - from Brechin in the North to Dunbar in the South.

Immediately prior to 2002 the East of Scotland Junior Cup was confined to Edinburgh and Lothians District clubs.

However, in earlier days the entry came from a wider area.

North Western were the first winners, in 1885/6. They defeated Hawthorn 3-2 in the Final at Drum Park, Leith. Winner4s from pre-World War One days included Alva Albion Rangers (Clacks), Wemyss (Fife) and Vale of Grange (Stirlingshire). Defeated finalists included Dundee Violet, Lochgelly Rangers, Brechin Harp and Bowhill Rovers.

EAST OF SCOTLAND CUP FINAL 2016/17

Tranent v Bonnyrigg Rose
10/6/16, at Creamery Park Bathgate, Att 800
1-1, 4-1 on penalties

Tranent Juniors: Jackson, Christie, Wojtowycz, Todd, Kerr, Smith, Miller, Hawkins, Fisher, Kane, Patterson, Manson.
Subs: Watters, Murray, Fiddler, Smeaton, J Patterson.
Bonnyrigg Rose: Andrews, Horne, Brett, Young, Moyes, Turner, Gray, McIntosh, McGachie, Nelson, Kidd. Subs: Brown, Archibald, Jamieson, Stewart, Hoskins.

Referee
Scott Lambie

Goals

0-1 38 mins Kidd (pen)
1-1 42 mins Fisher

All Time East of Scotland Cup Finals

Season	Winners	Runners Up	Score	Venue
1885/6	North Western	Hawthorn	3-2	Drum Park, Leith
1886/7	Leith Emerald	Cardinals	7-1	Olive Park, Musselburgh
1887/8	Woodburn	Leith Craighall	5-4	Drum Park, Leith
1888/9	Woodburn	Bathgate Harp	1-0	Boghall, Linlithgow
1889/90	Broxburn Athletic	Uphall Athletic	6-0	Newton Park, Bo'ness
1890/1	Hawthorn	Dalry Primrose	8-2	Powderhall, Edinburgh
1891/2	Hawthorn	Broxburn Emmet	6-5	Powderhall, Edinburgh
1892/3	Niddrie Bluebell	East Benhar Heatherbell	1-0	Bogshole Park, Bathgate
1894/5	Leith Celtic	Hawthorn	3-2	Powderhall, Edinburgh
1895/6	Hawthorn	Balmoral	6-0	Easter Road, Edinburgh
1896/7	Broxburn Athletic	Hearts of Beath	wo	
1897/8	Bonnyrigg Rose	Broxburn Athleic	1-0	Bogshole Park, Bathgate
1898/9	Leith Ivanhoe	Dundee Violet	2-1	Carolina Port, Dundee
1899/00	Niddrie Bluebell	Leith Renton	1-0	Tynecastle Park, Edinburgh
1900/1	Vale of Grange	Leith Craighall	4-3	Bogshole Park, Bathgate
1901/2	Leith Ivanhoe	Lochgelly Rangers	2-1	Brucefield, Dunfermline
1902/3	Vale of Grange	Broxburn Athletic	2-1	Volunteer Park, Armadale
1903/4	Broxburn Athletic	Brechin Harp	2-2, 4-2	Gayfield Park, Arbroath
1904/5	Vale of Grange	Lochgelly Rangers	7-1	East End Park, Dunfermline
1905/6	Alva Albion Rangers	Bowhill Thistle	1-1, 2-1	East End Park, Dunfermline
1906/7	Newtongrange Star	Bonnyrigg Rose	2-0	Mains Park, Tranent
1907/8	Alva Albion Rangers	Arniston Rangers	2-2, 3-0	Easter Road / Forthbank Park, Stirling
1908/9	Penicuik Juniors	Newtongrange Star	1-1, 1-0	Royal Gymnasium, Edinburgh
1909/10	Arniston Rangers	Bowhill Thistle	1-1, 2-0	East End Park, Dunfermline
1910/11	Penicuik Juniors	Kelty Rangers	2-0	Prestonfield, Linlithgow
1911/2	Wemyss Athletic	Penicuik Juniors	2-0	Easter Road, Edinburgh
1912/3	Arniston Rangers	Vale of Grange	1-0	Royal Gymnasium, Edinburgh
1913/4	Tranent	Inverkeithing United	2-1	Royal Gymnasium, Edinburgh
1914/5	Denbeath Star	Loanhead Mayflower	2-1	Newton Park, Bo'ness
1915/6	Loanhead Mayflower	Broxburn Athletic	4-0	Tynecastle Park, Edinburgh
1916/7	Denbeath Star	Winchburgh Violet	4-0	East End Park, Dunfermline
1917/8	Winchburgh Violet	Leith Benburb	1-0	Tynecastle Park, Edinburgh
1918/9	Winchburgh Violet	Broxburn Athletic	1-0	Easter Road, Edinburgh
1919/20	Tranent	Hearts of Beath	1-1, 3-0	Easter Road, Edinburgh
1920/1	Musselburgh Bruntonians	Tranent	1-0	Tynecastle Park, Edinburgh
1921/2	Arniston Rangers	Bonnyrigg Rose	3-1	King's Park, Dalkeith
1922/3	Arniston Rangers	West Calder	0-0, 1-0	Chancelot Park, Edinburgh / Royal Gymnasium
1923/4	Musselburgh Bruntonians	Wallyford Bluebell	2-0	Tynecastle Park, Edinburgh
1924/5	Edinburgh Emmet	West Calder	3-0	Easter Road, Edinburgh
1925/6	Newtongrange Star	Dalkeith Thistle	4-0	New Logie Green, Edinburgh
1926/7	Portobello Thistle	Duns Juniors	3-1	Easter Road, Edinburgh
1927/8	Portobello Thistle	Dalkeith Thistle	2-1	Tynecastle Park, Edinburgh
1928/9	Edinburgh Emmet	Wallyford Bluebell	1-0	Tynecastle Park, Edinburgh
1929/30	Newtongrange Star	Wallyford Bluebell	1-1, 1-0	Tynecastle Park, Edinburgh
1930/1	Tranent	Dunbar United	3-1	Tynecastle Park, Edinburgh
1931/2	Tranent	Ormiston Primrose	3-1	Tynecastle Park, Edinburgh
1932/3	Rosewell Rosedale	Tranent	4-2	Tynecastle Park, Edinburgh
1933/4	Tranent	Rosewell Rosedale	1-0	Tynecastle Park, Edinburgh
1934/5	Thorntree United	Tranent	2-0	Tynecastle Park, Edinburgh
1935/6	Tranent	West Calder United	5-1	Tynecastle Park, Edinburgh
1936/7	Musselburgh Athletic	Thorntree United	3-2	Easter Road, Edinburgh
1937/8	Tranent	Thorntree United	2-0	Easter Road, Edinburgh
1938/9	Stoneyburn	Portobello Renton	3-1	Tynecastle Park, Edinburgh
1939/40	Polkemmet	Whitburn	2-2, 4-2	Easter Road, Edinburgh
1940/1	Haddington Athletic	Polkemmet	4-1	Tynecastle Park, Edinburgh
1941/2	Bathgate Thistle	Armadale Thistle	4-3	Easter Road, Edinburgh
1942/3	Burnbank Athletic	Wishaw	2-2, 4-2	Fir Park, Motherwell
1943/4	Armadale Thistle	Bathgate Thistle	3-1	Tynecastle Park, Edinburgh
1944/5	Fauldhouse United	Burnbank Athletic	2-1	Easter Road, Edinburgh
1945/6	Fauldhouse United	Bo'ness United	2-0	Tynecastle Park, Edinburgh
1946/7	Stoneyburn	Bo'ness United	2-1	Tynecastle Park, Edinburgh
1947/8	Arniston Rangers	Haddington Athletic	1-0	Easter Road, Edinburgh
1948/9	Armadale Thistle	Stoneyburn	1-1, 3-0	Albyn Park, Broxburn
1949/50	Stoneyburn	Newtongrange Star	3-0	Tynecastle Park, Edinburgh
1950/1	Broxburn Athletic	Thorntree United	2-0	Easter Road, Edinburgh
1951/2	Bo'ness United	Arniston Rangers	2-0	Tynecastle Park, Edinburgh

1952/3	Armadale Thistle	Bathgate Thistle	3-1	Easter Road, Edinburgh
1953/4	Linlithgow Rose	Fauldhouse United	1-1, 4-0	Volunteer Park, Armadale
1954/5	Bo'ness United	Arniston Rangers	3-2	Tynecastle Park, Edinburgh
1955/6	Loanhead Mayflower	Haddington Athletic	2-1	Tynecastle Park, Edinburgh
1956/7	Haddington Athletic	Newtongrange Star	2-0	Easter Road, Edinburgh
1957/8	Newtongrange Star	Arniston Rangers	2-0	Tynecastle Park, Edinburgh
1958/9	Newtongrange Star	Musselburgh Athletic	5-3	Easter Road, Edinburgh
1959/60	Tranent	Broxburn Athletic	1-0	Tynecastle Park, Edinburgh
1960/1	Dunbar United	Bo'ness United	2-0	Easter Road, Edinburgh
1961/2	Armadale Thistle	Arniston Rangers	2-1	Tynecastle Park, Edinburgh
1962/3	Bonnyrigg Rose	Tranent	3-3, 3-1	Easter Road, Edinburgh
1963/4	Dunbar United	Bo'ness United	2-2, 2-2, 6-1	Olive Bank, Musselburgh
1964/5	Linlithgow Rose	Armadale Thistle	3-1	Tynecastle Park, Edinburgh
1965/6	Whitburn	Tranent	3-1	Easter Road, Edinburgh
1966/7	Dalkeith Thistle	Newtongrange Star	2-0	Tynecastle Park, Edinburgh
1967/8	Linlithgow Rose	Arniston Rangers	4-1	Tynecastle Park, Edinburgh
1968/9	Whitburn	Bo'ness United	1-0	Tynecastle Park, Edinburgh
1969/70	Whitburn	Newtongrange Star	1-1, 3-0	Prestonfield, Linlithgow
1970/1	Arniston Rangers	Camelon	6-2	Meadowbank Stadium, Edinburgh
1971/2	Dalkeith Thistle	Musselburgh Athletic	1-1, 1-0	Newbyres Park, Gorebridge
1972/3	Haddington Athletic	Linlithgow Rose	1-0	Tynecastle Park, Edinburgh
1973/4	Whitburn	Sauchie	2-1	Firs Park, Falkirk
1974/5	Newtongrange Star	Broxburn Athletic	2-2, 3-1	Olive Bank, Musselburgh
1975/6	Linlithgow Rose	Newtongrange Star	4-1	Tynecastle Park, Edinburgh
1976/7	Newtongrange Star	Bonnyrigg Rose	1-0	Olive Bank, Musselburgh
1977/8	Linlithgow Rose	Bonnyrigg Rose	1-1, 3-2	Newbyres Park, Gorebridge
1978/9	Tranent	Camelon	3-1	Prestonfield, Linlithgow
1979/80	Newtongrange Star	Penicuik Athletic	1-0	Newbyres Park, Gorebridge
1980/1	Arniston Rangers	Newtongrange Star	3-2	New Dunas Park, Bonnyrigg
1981/2	Newtongrange Star	Camelon	2-0	Prestonfield, Linlithgow
1982/3	Sauchie	Camelon	2-1	Prestonfield, Linlithgow
1983/4	Ormiston Primrose	Bo'ness United	1-1, 4-1	Prestonfield, Linlithgow
1984/5	Bo'ness United	Linlithgow Rose	2-2, 3-1	Newtown Park, Bo'ness
1985/6	Bonnyrigg Rose	Linlithgow Rose	3-1	Forresters Park, Tranent
1986/7	Bonnyrigg Rose	Whitburn	2-1 AET	Prestonfield, Linlithgow
1987/8	Broxburn Athletic	Linlithgow Rose	1-1, 2-1 AET	Central Park Whitburn
1988/9	Linlithgow Rose	Broxburn Athletic	3-0	Central Park, Whitburn
1989/90	Dunbar United	Whitburn	2-1	Forresters Park, Tranent
1990/1	Linlithgow Rose	Bo'ness United	4-3	Central Park, Whitburn
1991/2	Newtongrange Star	Whitburn	2-0	Newbyres Park, Gorebridge
1992/3	Linlithgow Rose	Fauldhouse United	2-0	Volunteer Park, Armadale
1993/4	Camelon	Livingston United	2-1	Prestonfield, Linlithgow
1994/5	Ormiston Primrose	Dunbar United	2-1	Newbyres Park, Gorebridge
1995/6	Linlithgow Rose	Camelon	3-0	Newtown Park, Bo'ness
1996/7	Newtongrange Star	Bo'ness United	3-, 3-1 pens	Recreation Park, Pumpherston
1997/8	Whitburn	Bonnybridge	2-0	Prestonfield, Linlithgow
1998/9	Bo'ness United	Whitburn	2-0	Prestonfield, Linlithgow
1999/00	Linlithgow Rose	Bo'ness United	2-1	Carmuirs Park, Camelon
2000/1	Linlithgow Rose	Harthill Royal	5-0	Station Park, Livingston
2001/2	Whitburn	Musselburgh Athletic	2-1	Newbyres Park, Gorebridge
2002/3	Bonnyrigg Rose	Musselburgh Athletic	5-3	Newbyres Park, Gorebridge
2003/4	Linlithgow Rose	Whitburn	1-0	Albyn Park, Broxburn
2004/5	Linlithgow Rose	Newtongrange Star	1-0	Carmuirs Park, Camelon
2005/6	Bonnyrigg Rose	Hill of Beath Hawthorn	2-1	Volunteer Park, Armadale
2006/7	Bathgate Thistle	Rosyth	3-0	Recreation Park, Rosyth
2007/8	Camelon	Bonnyrigg Rose	4-0	Prestonfield, Linlithgow
2008/9	Lochee United	Glenrothes	3-0	Canniepairt, Tayport
2009/10	Linlithgow Rose	Musselburgh Athletic	2-1	Creamery Park, Bathgate
2010/1	Newtongrange Star	Dundee North End	2-0	Central Park, Kelty
2011/2	St Andrews United	Kinnoull	2-1	Keir's Park, Hill of Beath
2012/3	Bonnyrigg Rose	Linlithgow Rose	3-0	Creamery Park, Bathgate
2013/4	Sauchie	Arniston Rangers	4-1	Prestonfield, Linlithgow
2014/5	Hill of Beath Hawthorn	Bo'ness United	0-0, 4-2p	Beechwood Park, Sauchie
2015/6	Bo'ness United	Dundonald Bluebell	5-1	Creamery Park, Bathgate
2016/7	Tranent	Bonnyrigg Rose	1-1, 4-1p	Creamery Park, Bathgate

Conservatory Converters Fife and Lothians Junior Cup 2016/17

Rd	Date	Home	Away	F	A	
1	08/10/2016	Haddington Athletic	Bonnyrigg Rose	1	2	
1	08/10/2016	Lochore Welfare	Newtongrange Star	0	6	
1	08/10/2016	Sauchie	Craigroyston	4	1	
1	08/10/2016	Linlithgow Rose	Pumpherston	4	1	
1	08/10/2016	Whitburn	Lochgelly Albert	0	1	
1	08/10/2016	Easthouses Lily	Thornton Hibs	2	4	
1	08/10/2016	Arniston Rangers	Crossgates Primrose	2	1	
1	08/10/2016	Penicuik Athletic	St Andrews United	7	3	
1	08/10/2016	Broxburn Athletic	Bathgate Thistle	1	0	
2	05/11/2016	Arniston Rangers	Musselburgh Athletic	1	2	
2	08/10/2016	Livingston	Armadale Thistle	1	5	
2	26/04/2017	Bo'ness United	Bonnyrigg Rose	0	0	5-4p
2	18/02/2017	Linlithgow Rose	Thornton Hibs	7	1	
2	08/10/2016	Dunbar United	Dalkeith Thistle	2	5	
2	08/10/2016	Fauldhouse United	West Calder United	5	0	
2	08/10/2016	Stoneyburn	Kelty Hearts	0	8	
2		Falkirk	Edinburgh United	sc	wo	
2	08/10/2016	Newburgh	Tranent	3	4	
2	08/10/2016	Blackburn United	Rosyth	3	0	
2	05/11/2016	Sauchie	Dundonald Bluebell	1	6	
2	05/11/2016	Penicuik Athletic	Camelon	2	0	
2	05/11/2016	Lochgelly Albert	Newtongrange Star	0	3	
2	05/11/2016	Kirkcaldy YM	Broxburn Athletic	1	5	
2	08/10/2016	Kennoway Star Hearts	Glenrothes	1	1	0-3p
2	08/10/2016	Hill of Beath Hawthorn	Oakley United	2	0	
3	10/05/2017	Bo'ness United	Fauldhouse United	6	1	
3	18/02/2017	Dundonald Bluebell	Musselburgh Athletic	0	1	
3	25/02/2017	Dalkeith Thistle	Tranent	2	2	3-4p
3	08/04/2017	Kelty Hearts	Hill of Beath Hawthorn	1	1	5-3p
3	01/04/2017	Penicuik Athletic	Blackburn United	1	2	
3	26/04/2017	Glenrothes	Linlithgow Rose	0	2	
3	25/02/2017	Broxburn Athletic	Newtongrange Star	2	1	
3	01/04/2017	Edinburgh United	Armadale Thistle	2	2	4-3p
4	19/04/2017	Musselburgh Athletic	Blackburn United	3	0	
4	06/05/2017	Tranent	Kelty Hearts	2	1	
4	19/04/2017	Broxburn Athletic	Edinburgh United	9	0	
4	22/05/2017	Bo'ness United	Linlithgow Rose	2	0	
SF	24/05/2017	Musselburgh Athletic	Tranent	2	2	4-5p
SF	27/05/2017	Bo'ness United	Broxburn Athletic	0	3	
F	07/06/2017	Tranent	Broxburn Athletic	1	0	
		at Newtongrange, Att 1100				

The Fife and Lothians Cup was playe for between 1934 and 1940 but then lapsed. It was revived in 1968 and ha been played for continuously since then. It is organised by the Fife and Lothians Junior Football Association, NOT the East Region of the SJFA.

FINAL TIE 2016/17 - Sponsored by Conservatory Convertors

Tranent v Broxburn Athletic
1-0, Att 1100

Tranent Juniors: Pucko, Christie, Wojtowycz, Todd, Kerr, Jamie Patterson, Miller, Hawkins, Fisher, Kayne Paterson and Watter
Subs: Smith, Murray, Manson, Fidd Smeaton.
Broxburn: Wallace, Gavin, Cole, Purves, Paterson, Linton, Scott, Mill Locke, Gribben, Anderson Subs Richards, Baptie, Downie, McNaughton. Sub: Donoghue.
Referee: Peter Stuart
Goals

1-0 90 mins Fisher

All-Time Fife and Lothians Cup Finals

Season	Winners	Runners Up	Score	Venue
1934/5	Kirkford Juniors	West Calder United	3-1	Tynecastle Park
1935/6	Bowhill Rovers	Dunbar United	3-1	Tynecastle Park
1936/7	Lochgelly Albert	Tranent	6-2	Central Park, Cowdenbeath
1937/8	Arniston Rangers	Blairhall Colliery	6-4	Central Park, Cowdenbeath
1938/9	Tranent	Armadale Thistle	3-1	Tynecastle Park
1939.40	Haddington Athletic	Tranent	4-2	Tynecastle Park
1968/9	Linlithgow Rose	Lochore Welfare	3-1	Newtown Park, Bo'ness
1969/70	Whitburn	Bo'ness United	2-0	Prestonfield, Linlithgow
1970/1	Camelon	Glenrothes	3-2	Newtown Park, Bo'ness
1971/2	Glenrothes	Armadale Thistle	4-1	Prestonfield, Linlithgow
1972/3	Linlithgow Rose	Dalkeith Thistle	2-0	Newtown Park, Bo'ness
1973/4	Linlithgow Rose	Fauldhouse United	2-1	Central Park, Whitburn
1974/5	Linlithgow Rose	Glenrothes	2-2, 4-3p	Central Park, Lochore
1975/6	Arniston Rangers	Linlithgow Rose	4-1	Newtown Park, Bo'ness
1976/7	Penicuik Athletic	Glenrothes	3-0	Central Park, Lochore
1977/8	Newtongrange Star	Glenrothes	4-2	Prestonfield, Linlithgow
1978/9	Linlithgow Rose	Broxburn Athletic	2-0	Central Park, Whitburn
1979/80	Linlithgow Rose	Newtongrange Star	2-1	Newbyres Park, Gorebridge
1980/1	Penicuik Athletic	Arniston Rangers	1-0	King's Park, Dalkeith
1981/2	Bonnyrigg Rose	Broxburn Athletic	1-0 AET	Victoria Park, Newtongrange
1982/3	Oakley United	Fauldhouse United	3-1	Warout Stadium, Glenrothes
1983/4	Linlithgow Rose	Fauldhouse United	2-1	Central Park, Whitburn
1984/5	Linlithgow Rose	Newtongrange Star	3-0	Central Park, Whitburn
1985/6	Linlithgow Rose	Newtongrange Star	2-1	Prestonfield, Linlithgow
1986/7	Whitburn	Oakley United	3-0 AET	Prestonfield, Linlithgow
1987/8	Newtongrange Star	Kelty Hearts	1-0	Prestonfield, Linlithgow
1988/9	Edinburgh United	Camelon	1-1, 3-1 pens	Prestonfield, Linlithgow
1989/90	Newtongrange Star	Bo'ness United	2-0	Prestonfield, Linlithgow
1990/1	Newtongrange Star	Linlithgow Rose	2-1 aet	Newtown Park, Bo'ness
1991/2	Whitburn	Livingston United	2-1	Albyn Park, Broxburn
1992/3	Fauldhouse United	Bathgate Thistle	1-0	Volunteer Park, Armadale
1993/4	Bo'ness United	Hill of Beath Hawthorn	2-1	Carmuirs Park, Camelon
1994/5	St Andrews United	Hill of Beath Hawthorn	4-3	Warout Stadium, Glenrothes
1995/6	Hill of Beath Hawthorn	Whitburn	1-0	Prestonfield, Linlithgow
1996/7	Bo'ness United	Bonnybridge	3-1	Carmuirs Park, Camelon
1997/8	Arniston Rangers	Haddington Athletic	1-0	New Dundas Park, Bonnyrigg
1998/9	Whitburn	Bo'ness United	3-2 aet	Prestonfield, Linlithgow
1999/00	Linlithgow Rose	Stoneyburn	4-1	Carmuirs Park, Camelon
2000/1	Linlithgow Rose	Whitburn	5-1	Carmuirs Park, Camelon
2001/2	Linlithgow Rose	Hill of Beath Hawthorn	6-5	Carmuirs Park, Camelon
2002/3	Sauchie	Glenrothes	5-3	Carmuirs Park, Camelon
2003/4	Sauchie	Linlithgow Rose	4-0	Central Park, Whitburn
2004/5	Bonnyrigg Rose	St Andrews United	1-0	Central Park, Whitburn
2005/6	Camelon	Kelty Hearts	2-1 aet	Prestonfield, Linlithgow
2006/7	Bonnyrigg Rose	Musselburgh Athletic	2-0	Prestonfield, Linlithgow
2007/8	Camelon	Hill of Beath Hawthorn	5-0	Prestonfield, Linlithgow
2008/9	Linlithgow Rose	Thornton Hibs	1-0	Keir's Park, Hill of Beath
2009/10	Bathgate Thistle	Musselburgh Athletic	1-0	New Victoria Park, Newtongrange
2010/1	Linlithgow Rose	Bo'ness United	2-1	Prestonfield, Linlithgow
2011/2	Linlithgow Rose	Broxburn Athletic	3-1	Newtown Park, Bo'ness
2012/3	Linlithgow Rose	Camelon	5-3	Creamery Park, Bathgate
2013/4	Linlithgow Rose	Bo'ness United	2-1	Newtown Park, Bo'ness
2014/5	Camelon	Sauchie	1-0	Creamery Park, Bathgate
2015/6	Penicuik Athletic	Bonnyrigg Rose	3-1	Olive Bank, Musselburgh
2016/7	Tranent	Broxburn Athletic	1-0	New Victoria Park, Newtongrange

NORTH JUNIORS

The North Region of the Scottish Junior FA was created in 1968. Prior to that there were several County and Local Associations, mainly in the North East of Scotland. An Inverness Junior League existed in the 1950s.

The North Region now encompasses teams from Inverness, through Moray, Strathspey, Banffshire, Aberdeenshire, the City of Aberdeen and as far south as Montrose. The League structure has changed several times and will do so again for 2018/19.

For 2017/18 it will be as follows:

SUPER LEAGUE (14, play 2x)
Two teams relegated
One team in relegation Play Off aginst winners of Div 1 East v Div 1 West runners-up

DIV ONE WEST (11, play 2x)
One team promoted, runners up in play off v East runners-up
Bottom four or five relegated

DIV ONE EAST (9, play 3x)
One team promoted, runners up in play off v West runners-up
Bottom four or five relegated

League Composition 2017/18

Superleague
Banchory St Ternan
Banks o' Dee
Colony Park
Culter
Dufftown
Dyce Juniors
Ellon United
Hall Russell United
Hermes
Inverness City
Maud
Montrose Roselea
Newburgh Thistle
Stonehaven

First Division East
Aberdeen University
Buchanhaven Hearts
Cruden Bay
East End
Fraserburgh United
Glentanar
Lewis United
Longside
Newmachar United
Stoneywood Parkvale
Sunnybank

First Division West
Buckie Rovers
Burghead Thistle
Deveronside
Forres Thistle
Islavale
Nairn St Ninian
New Elgin
Spey Valley United
Whitehills

The 2016/17 revealed some problems and anomalies in the League structure. Spey Valley United, winners of the West Division, refused to accept promotion to the Super League. At one stage it looked like they had folded. At the last minute they were granted permission to remain in the West Division.

Newmachar United, who had been forced from the East to the West were unhappy at this and asked to be returned to the East Division.

Montrose Roselea, newcomers for 2016/17, had played in the West Division despite it meaning much greater travelling. The rule-book used a simple line of longitude as the dividing mark and Montrose's geographical position saw them "go west".

At the 2017 AGM there was much discussion of these issues. Spey Valley United were not in attendance. Finally, a decision was taken that as from 2018/19 the Region will move to a three-league vertical structure with no East-West divide. Promotion will be mandatory if the club ground meets Super League requirements.

North Junior Super League 2016/17

	BST	BOD	BUC	COL	CUL	DEV	DUF	DYC	HRU	HER	INV	MAU	NEW	STO
Banchory St Ternan		Aug 20	Mar 25	Sep 3	Apr 25	Nov 12	Oct 29	Dec 10	Sep 17	Dec 17	Feb 18	Feb 4	Oct 22	Apr 1
		0-1	3-0	2-4	2-5	3-2	7-1	1-6	0-6	4-4	2-1	3-3	1-3	1-1
Banks o' Dee	Mar 18		Oct 8	Sep 17	Jan 7	Apr 11	Feb 18	Jan 21	Nov 26	May 20	Feb 11	Mar 15	Feb 22	Apr 18
	3-1		5-1	7-1	1-0	6-1	3-1	0-0	3-0	4-1	2-0	4-0	2-0	3-0
Buckie Rovers	Nov 5	Feb 4		Nov 19	Jan 21	Dec 10	Dec 17	Feb 25	Mar 18	Sep 3	Aug 2	Nov 26	Oct 1	Apr 22
	2-3	0-6		1-3	0-1	3-0	4-1	2-4	0-3	3-1	3-2	4-4	3-1	1-1
Colony Park	May 2	Apr 22	Apr 15		May 9	Dec 17	Oct 1	Nov 5	Feb 11	Apr 25	Oct 29	Apr 1	May 18	Jan 7
	3-3	0-1	3-0		0-1	5-2	2-1	1-3	1-1	1-2	3-1	1-3	0-3	1-2
Culter	Feb 25	Apr 8	Oct 15	Oct 8		Apr 29	Apr 1	Apr 15	May 6	Apr 18	Mar 18	May 13	Mar 11	May 2
	4-1	1-5	8-2	1-3		2-0	3-1	2-2	3-1	1-0	6-0	1-1	2-2	3-2
Deveronside	Jan 7	Feb 25	Jan 28	Mar 18	Oct 29		Oct 8	Nov 19	Feb 18	Apr 15	Dec 3	Apr 22	Jan 21	Sep 17
	0-1	2-3	1-1	0-3	2-2		4-2	0-2	1-1	2-1	2-5	1-2	2-3	0-2
Dufftown	Mar 11	Mar 25	Aug 9	Feb 4	Apr 22	May 2		Oct 15	Dec 10	Sep 17	Jan 21	Aug 20	May 6	Apr 15
	2-3	1-	2-2	4-2	2-3	3-2		1-5	1-3	0-2	1-4	2-4	3-5	3-4
Dyce	Aug 27	May 13	Sep 17	Mar 11	Feb 18	Apr 1	Dec 3		Oct 8	Nov 12	Jan 7	Oct 29	Feb 11	Feb 4
	2-1	1-1	3-0	3-1	0-0	11-0	7-0		2-0	1-2	5-2	3-1	5-0	1-1
Hall Russell United	Apr 22	Apr 15	Dec 3	Aug 9	Dec 17	Sep 10	Jan 7	Mar 25		May 16	Oct 15	Feb 25	Apr 8	May 9
	3-1	3-2	2-0	0-1	1-3	2-1	2-3	1-0		3-1	1-0	5-0	1-2	2-2
Hermes	Sep 10	Feb 28	May 6	Oct 15	Nov 26	Oct 1	Apr 8	Mar 18	Apr 29		May 13	Mar 29	Apr 11	Aug 27
	1-2	2-3	6-2	4-2	1-2	3-0	2-2	1-1	2-3		4-2	5-1	0-4	2-3
Inverness City	Oct 8	Dec 10	Apr 8	May 6	Sep 17	Feb 4	Sep 10	Apr 29	Nov 19	Apr 22		Dec 17	Nov 12	Mar 25
	3-1	0-8	2-0	3-1	0-1	5-1	2-3	2-4	1-1	1-4		2-3	3-1	0-4
Maud	May 6	Apr 29	Feb 18	Dec 3	Sep 3	Aug 9	Mar 18	Apr 8	Sep 24	May 9	Apr 15		May 2	Oct 8
	1-2	0-3	6-2	5-1	0-1	3-3	0-3	2-3	3-3	1-3	2-3		2-4	1-1
Newburgh Thistle	Apr 15	May 9	Jan 7	Dec 10	May 23	Sep 3	Apr 29	Apr 25	Oct 29	May 30	Apr 1	Sep 17		May 13
	4-0	2-3	4-3	0-2	1-4	2-2	2-3	1-2*	1-5	4-2	6-0	5-0		1-3
Stonehaven	Jan 21	May 6	Oct 29	Apr 29	Aug 16	Apr 8	Sep 3	Aug 9	Oct 1	Feb 18	Sep 24	Mar 11	Dec 17	
	9-0	2-0	5-0	2-4	4-2	3-0	4-1	1-1	2-0	1-0	7-0	1-0	1-1	

* at Dyce

	Team	Pl	HW	HD	HL	AW	AD	AL	W	D	L	F	A	Diff	Pts
1	**Banks o' Dee**	26	12	1	0	10	1	2	22	2	2	83	20	63	68
2	Dyce Juniors	26	9	3	1	8	4	1	17	7	2	77	24	53	58
3	Culter	26	8	3	2	9	2	2	17	5	4	62	34	28	56
4	Stonehaven	26	10	2	1	6	5	2	16	7	3	68	28	40	55
5	Hall Russell United	26	8	1	4	5	4	4	13	5	8	53	36	17	44
6	Newburgh Thistle	26	5	1	7	7	2	4	12	3	11	62	55	7	39
7	Colony Park (P)	26	4	2	7	7	0	6	11	2	13	49	55	-6	35
8	Hermes	26	5	2	6	5	1	7	10	3	13	56	53	3	33
9	Banchory St Ternan	26	4	3	6	5	1	7	9	4	13	49	74	-25	31
10	Inverness City	26	5	1	7	3	0	10	8	1	17	44	76	-32	25
11	Maud	26	2	3	8	4	3	6	6	6	14	48	69	-21	24
12	Dufftown	26	2	1	10	4	1	8	6	2	18	47	84	-37	20
13	*Buckie Rovers (P)*	*26*	*5*	*2*	*6*	*0*	*2*	*11*	*5*	*4*	*17*	*39*	*81*	*-42*	*19*
14	*Deveronside*	*26*	*2*	*3*	*8*	*0*	*2*	*11*	*2*	*5*	*19*	*31*	*79*	*-48*	*11*

For the second year running Banks o'Dee were the best team by quite a distance. As full SFA members they already qualify for the Scottish Cup so there will be no second North Junior participant this season. Dyce, Culter and Stonehaven were the only clubs to keep up the chase but they finished well adrift of Banbks o' Dee.

Promoted club Colony Park did very well in their first season in the Super League.

As a consequence of Spey Valley United refusing promotion there were two play-offs to settle the promotion / relegation issue. Montrose Roselea earned promotion by beating Buckie Rovers, but Dufftown retained top flight status with a win over Sunnybank.

PLAY OFF SUPER LEAGUE					
13/05/2017	Buckie Rovers	Montrose Roselea	0	5	at Colony Park
20/05/2017	Dufftown	Sunnybank	3	2	at Dufftown

North Junior Jim McPherson Trophy 2016/17

F	31/07/2016	Banks o' Dee	Islavale	3	0		at Colony Park

The Jim McPherson Trophy was introduced in 2015/16. It is an invitation Charity Trophy played for by the winners of the North Region Super League and the winners of the North Region Junior Cup.

Previous Final:

07/08/2015	Hermes	Dyce	2	2	4-3p	at East End FC

NORTH JUNIOR SUPER LEAGUE ALL TIME POSITIONS	2001-2	2002-3	2003-4	2004-5	2005-6	2006-7	2007-8	2008-9	2009-10	2010-11	2011-12	2012-13	2013-14	2014-15	2015-16	2016-17
Banchory St Ternan								5	3	6	7	10	11	10	12	9
Banks o' Dee	5	8	6	6	3	3	1	1	5	4	5	4	2	3	1	1
Buchanhaven Hearts	14								13							
Buckie Rovers																13
Colony Park																7
Cruden Bay	10	12	13											13		
Culter	2	2	1	1	1	1	3	3	2	1	4	1	1	4	5	3
Deveronside	13	14										5	6	5	10	14
Dufftown															8	12
Dyce						6	6	4	4	5	3	2	3	8	4	2
East End	6	4	11	12			9	9	14				13			
Ellon United				13	7	12	5	10	10	11	8	9	10	12	13	
FC Stoneywood	3	5	12	8	14				12	12	6	6	12	6	14	
Formartine United	1	6	7	4	2	7	13									
Forres Thistle											13					
Fraserburgh United					13					14		14				
Glentanar	12	10	3	2	9	14										
Hall Russell United									11	2	10	12	9	11	6	5
Hermes	7	11	8	9	6	9	12	7	6	3	1	3	4	1	2	8
Inverness City														7	7	10
Islavale						13										
Lads Club		9	14													
Lewis United								11	8	8	11	13				
Longside	9	3	10	5	11	8	11	6	9	13	9	11	14			
Maud				14			4	8	7	9	12	8	5	2	9	11
New Elgin													8	14		
Parkvale					12	10	14									
Stonehaven	8	7	4	11	10	4	8	14		10	2	7	7	9	3	4
Sunnybank	4	1	2	7	5	2	2	2	1	7	14					
Turriff United			5	3	8	5	7	12								
Wilsons XI / Hillhead / Bridge of Don Thistle / Newburgh Th	11	13	9	10	4	11	10	13							11	6

North Junior First Division (West) 2016/17

	BUR	FOC	FOR	ISL	MON	NAI	NEL	NMA	SVU	WHI
Burghead Thistle		Feb 4	Sep 24	Oct 15	Jan 7	Apr 1	Nov 26	Apr 22	Sep 17	Nov 19
		3-1	2-5	1-3	0-4	1-3	1-5	3-2	0-6	5-2
Fochabers	Oct 29		Feb 25	Apr 1	Sep 17	Feb 18	Aug 27	Dec 10	Nov 12	Oct 15
	0-4		0-2	0-10	1-6	0-2	3-8*	0-7	0-10	4-3
Forres Thistle	Dec 10	Oct 1		Sep 17	Mar 4	Dec 3	Oct 8	Sep 10	Aug 20	Oct 29
	6-2	9-0		2-0	0-10	0-4	5-0	3-1	0-3	4-0
Islavale	Feb 18	Aug 10	May 6		Dec 3	Sep 3	Jan 7	Jan 28	Oct 8	Nov 5
	2-2	5-3	3-0		2-3	5-1	4-0	5-1	2-4	5-1
Montrose Roselea	Mar 18	Jan 14	Jan 21	Feb 25		Oct 8	Feb 18	Oct 29	Dec 10	Feb 4
	5-0	16-0**	5-0	5-2		1-3	7-0	4-0	0-1	4-0
Nairn St Ninian	Oct 1	Sep 10	Oct 15	Dec 17	Mar 25		Nov 12	Sep 24	Oct 29	Nov 26
	4-1	11-0	4-2	3-3	1-2		1-0	1-2	4-3	9-0
New Elgin	Sep 10	Nov 5	Dec 17	Oct 29	Oct 15	Feb 4		Dec 3	Feb 11	Dec 10
	1-3	4-2	2-0	3-3	1-5	1-2		0-0	1-3	1-1
Newmachar United	May 6	Aug 6	Mar 18	Oct 1	Dec 17	Nov 5	Sep 17		Apr 1	Apr 8
	1-1	1-1	0-3	0-7	0-4	2-7	3-1		2-3	1-2
Spey Valley United	Dec 3	Sep 3	Nov 5	Mar 25	Jan 28	Feb 25	Oct 1	Oct 15		Sep 10
	3-0	6-0	2-1	3-1	3-3	3-1	4-0	4-3		9-2
Whitehills	Sep 3	Dec 3	Jan 7	Apr 15	Nov 12	Sep 17	Oct 22	Oct 8	Dec 17	
	1-3	4-1	2-1	0-5	0-8	2-3	1-1	1-0	2-3	

* at Fochabers, other home games at New Elgin

** at Links Park, Montrose FC

	Team	Pl	HW	HD	HL	AW	AD	AL	W	D	L	F	A	Diff	Pts
1	Spey Valley United	18	8	1	0	8	0	1	16	1	1	73	22	51	49
2	Montrose Roselea	18	7	0	2	8	1	0	15	1	2	93	14	79	46
3	Nairn St Ninian	18	6	1	2	7	0	2	13	1	4	64	28	36	40
4	Islavale	18	6	1	2	4	2	3	10	3	5	67	32	35	33
5	Forres Thistle	18	6	0	3	3	0	6	9	0	9	43	40	3	27
6	Burghead Thistle	18	3	0	6	3	2	4	6	2	10	32	55	-23	20
7	New Elgin	18	2	3	4	2	1	6	4	4	10	29	48	-19	16
8	Whitehills	18	3	1	5	1	1	7	4	2	12	24	67	-43	14
9	Newmachar United	18	1	2	6	2	1	6	3	3	12	26	50	-24	12
10	Fochabers	18	1	0	8	0	1	8	1	1	16	16	111	-95	4

Spey Valley United and newcomers Montrose Roselea fought it out for the Championship. In the end it was the Cromdale-based club who came out on top but they declined promotion. They cited travel difficulties - that their players did not want to go as far as Aberdeen to play their football on a regular basis.

They were allowed to turn down promotion and Montrose went up through a play-off against Buckie Rovers.

Fochabers struggled badly all season. They moved from Fochabers to New Elgin but resigned at the end of the season.

Newmachar United deserve credit for enduring a season of long-distance travel without as much as a complaint.

North Junior First Division (East) 2016/17

	AEE	AUN	BUC	CRU	ELL	FRA	GLE	LEW	LON	STO	SUN
Aberdeen East End		Oct 1	Jan 28	Apr 22	Aug 20	Apr 1	May 9	Sep 17	Oct 29	Dec 17	Sep 10
		5-4	3-0	5-0	3-4	3-0	5-0	4-0	4-0	1-1	2-1
Aberdeen University	Apr 25		Sep 17	Dec 17	Nov 12	Oct 15	Feb 10	Oct 8	Mar 24	Apr 1	Nov 5
	1-5		3-1	3-2	1-3	1-2	1-2	2-0	1-1	2-3	0-2
Buchanhaven Hearts	May 6	Apr 8		Oct 22	Feb 4	Mar 18	Oct 1	Feb 25	Dec 17	Feb 11	Apr 22
	1-2	1-2		2-0	1-1	1-0	2-1	1-4	1-1	2-3	0-0
Cruden Bay	Oct 15	Sep 10	Dec 3		Nov 5	Apr 15	May 6	Aug 20	Jan 28	Oct 1	Feb 11
	1-2	2-3	1-3		0-4	1-1	3-1	0-3	2-3	0-8	4-2
Ellon United	Dec 10	Sep 3	Oct 29	Mar 25		Apr 22	Sep 17	Dec 17	Mar 11	Jan 28	Aug 13
	3-0	2-1	2-0	4-0		1-1	2-1	2-1	1-1	4-3	0-5
Fraserburgh United	Oct 8	Dec 10	Sep 10	Apr 8	Nov 26		Jan 28	Sep 3	Apr 25	Oct 29	Oct 1
	2-1	4-2	0-1	2-2	0-3		2-3	2-1	0-4	1-2	0-1
Glentanar	Sep 24	Oct 29	Dec 10	Feb 4	Apr 15	Aug 27		Aug 9	Sep 3	Dec 3	Oct 15
	1-5	0-3	0-1	4-1	1-3	1-1		1-0	0-9	2-3	1-5
Lewis United	May 2	Dec 3	Oct 15	Apr 1	Sep 10	Feb 11	Nov 12		Oct 1	Aug 27	Nov 26
	0-2	1-0	1-1	2-0	3-6	3-4	3-0		3-3	0-0	1-1
Longside	Feb 11	Sep 24	Apr 14	Nov 12	Oct 8	Sep 16	Nov 5	Feb 4		Jan 7	Dec 10
	1-0	2-3	0-1	3-0	4-5	0-4	0-1	2-0		3-5	1-0
Stoneywood Parkvale	Aug 9	Apr 18	Mar 25	Apr 25	Oct 15	May 6	Sep 10	Dec 10	May 2		Aug 2
	1-1	4-3	5-1	1-0	2-4	2-1	3-2	1-1	0-0		1-2
Sunnybank	Apr 18	Mar 11	Oct 8	Sep 17	Dec 3	Mar 25	Dec 17	Oct 29	Apr 1	Oct 22	
	1-1	4-0	3-2	4-0	1-0	2-0	4-1	1-0	1-0	2-2	

	Team	Pl	HW	HD	HL	AW	AD	AL	W	D	L	F	A	Diff	Pts
1	**Ellon United (R)**	**20**	**7**	2	1	8	1	1	15	3	2	54	29	25	48
2	Sunnybank	20	8	2	0	5	2	3	13	4	3	42	16	26	43
3	East End	20	8	1	1	5	2	3	13	3	4	54	22	32	42
4	Stoneywood Parkvale (R)	20	5	3	2	6	3	1	11	6	3	50	32	18	39
5	Longside	20	4	0	6	3	5	2	7	5	8	38	32	6	26
6	Buchanhaven Hearts	20	3	3	4	4	1	5	7	4	9	23	32	-9	25
7	Fraserburgh United	20	3	1	6	3	3	4	6	4	10	27	35	-8	22
8	Aberdeen University	20	3	1	6	4	0	6	7	1	12	36	46	-10	22
9	Lewis United	20	3	4	3	2	1	7	5	5	10	27	33	-6	20
10	Glentanar	20	2	1	7	3	0	7	5	1	14	23	56	-33	16
11	Cruden Bay	20	2	1	7	0	1	9	2	2	16	19	60	-41	8

Ellon United bounced back at the first time of asking. Runners-up Sunnybank lost out in a play-off against Dufftown and remain in the East Division for 2017/18.

Recent finishing positions in Divisions One and Two are included below.

North Juniors First Division 2003-2013

	2003-4	2004-5	2005-6	2006-7	2007-8	2008-9	2009-10	2010-11	2011-12	2012-13
Banchory St Ternan	6	4	6	3	1					
Bishopmill United							9	14		
Buchanhaven Hearts	8	9	12	5	4	1		5	11	13
Buckie Rovers	9					12	7	13	14	
Burghead Thistle	12	11	14					12	13	11
Cruden Bay		13	8	13	13	14				
Deveronside	3	6	10				5	9	3	
Dufftown	13	12	11	10	10	13	13	11	12	
Dyce	10	7	1							
East End			5	1				10	5	2
Ellon United	2									
FC Stoneywood				11	12	4				
Formartine United						2				
Forres Thistle				7	9	8	11	2		10
Fraserburgh United	5	2		9	11	6	1		2	
Glentanar					7	11	4	3	4	4
Hall Russell United	4	10	13	12	8	5				
Hillhead / Bridge of Don Thistle							10	8	8	12
Inverness City							2	1	1	3
Islavale		3	2		6	9	12	6	9	5
Lads Club		8	7	6	3					
Lewis United	11	5	4	4	2					
Lossiemouth United						7	6	7	10	14
Maud	1		3	2						
Nairn St Ninian					14					9
New Elgin							8	4	6	1
Parkvale	7	1				10	14		7	6
Portgordon Vics										7
Stonehaven							3			
Strathspey Thistle			9	8	5	3				
Sunnybank										8
Whitehills	14									

North Juniors Second Division 2003-2013

	2003-4	2004-5	2005-6	2006-7	2007-8	2008-9	2009-10	2010-11	2011-12	2012-13
Bishopmill United	9	6	7	5	1	4			7	
Buckie Rovers			5	3	3					2
Burghead Thistle				8	5	5	1			
Colony Park									4	1
Cruden Bay							5	7	5	4
Deveronside					6	3				
Fochabers	7	3	3	1	Ab	6	3	5	9	5
Forres Thistle	3	2	2							
Inverness City						1				
Islavale	1									
Kinloss	10	9	9							
Lossiemouth United	5	7	6	4	2					
Nairn St Ninian	6	5	4	2		7	2	4	2	
New Elgin	4	1	1	6	4	2				
Newmachar United								2	3	3
Parkvale								1		
Portgordon Victoria									1	
RAF Lossiemouth	8	8	8	9	7	8	4	6	8	
Strathspey Thistle	2	4								
Whitehills		10	10	7	8	9	6	3	6	6

EAST DIVISION Since Reconstruction

	2013/14	2014/15	2015/16	2016/17
Aberdeen East End		10	4	3
Aberdeen University		8	9	8
Bridge of Don Thistle / Newburgh Th	2	1		
Buchanhaven Hearts	9	4	3	6
Colony Park	3	3	1	
Cruden Bay	1		12	11
Ellon United				1
Fraserburgh United	7	4	2	7
Glentanar	4	11	11	10
Lewis United	5	6	5	9
Longside		9	7	5
Newmachar United	10	12	8	
Parkvale / Stoneywood-Parkvale	6	2	6	4
Sunnybank	8	7	10	2

WEST DIVISION Since Reconstruction

	2013/14	2014/15	2015/16	2016/17
Buckie Rovers	7	4	1	
Burghead Thistle	4	7	9	6
Dufftown	2	1		
Fochabers	10	Ab	8	10
Forres Thistle	6	6	2	5
Grantown		2	7	
Inverness City	1			
Islavale	3	3	4	4
Lossiemouth United		9	res	
Montrose Roselea				2
Nairn St Ninian	8	5	3	3
New Elgin			6	7
Newmachar United				9
Portgordon Victoria	5	10	5	
Spey Valley (United)		8	5	1
Whitehills	9	11	Ab	8

CUP DRAWS 2017/18
The Cup draws were made at the Region's AGM.

NORTH REGIONAL CUP

Preliminary Round
Hall Russell United v Cruden Bay
Inverness City v CulterFirst Round
Sunnybank v Hermes
Hall Russell United or Cruden Bay v Inverness City or Culter
Lewis United v Dufftown
Ellon United v Stonehaven
Stoneywood Parkvale v Newmachar United
Islavale v Forres Thistle
Longside v Spey Valley United
New Elgin v Burghead Thistle
Aberdeen University v Colony Park
Buchanhaven Hearts v Nairn St Ninian
Glentanar v Buckie Rovers
Banks o' Dee v Fraserburgh United
Banchory St Ternan v Montrose Roselea
Newburgh Thistle v Whitehills
East End v Deveronside
Maud v Dyce Juniors

GRILL SECTIONAL LEAGUE CUP

Group 1
Buchanhaven Hearts
Banks o' Dee
Culter
Buckie Rovers
Dufftown

Group 2
Hermes
Nairn St Ninian
Whitehills
Dyce Juniors
Deveronside

Group 3
Forres Thistle
Newmachar United
East End
Stonehaven

Group 4
Islavale
Sunnybank
Hall Russell United
Inverness City

Group 5
Montrose Roselea
Aberdeen University
Stoneywood Parkvale
Burghead Thistle

Group 6
Spey Valley United
Lewis United
Fraserburgh United
Ellon United

Group 7
New Elgin
Colony Park
Newburgh Thistle
Maud

Group 8
Longside
Glentanar
Banchory St Ternan
Cruden Bay

North Region Juniors Playing Squads 2016/17

NB These are not necessarily comprehensive lists of players used - there will be some omissions. However, all players listed were associated with the club concerned during 2015/16.

North Juniors Super League

Banchory St Ternan
Manager: Neil Findlay
Assistant: Graeme DavidsonCoaches: Craig Stephen, Kevin Fraser
Andrew Shepherd
Callum Wilson
Coran Wilson
Craig Peter
Craig Simpson (2016 Deveronvale, Ex Buckie Thistle)
Darren Reid
Dean Colbert
Grant Munro
Greig Mackie
Jack Mitchell
Jack Pressly (2016 Culter, Ex Montrose, Banchory, Deveronvale, Rothes)
Jamie Buglass
Josh Robertson
Kieran Davidson
Lydian O'Brien
Michael bruce
Nico Berton
Riain Findlay
Sam Smith
Seamus Croll
Steve Travers
Taylor Christie

Banks o' Dee
Managers: Tommy Forbes and Sandy McNaughton (ex Stenhousemuir, Dunfermline Athletic, Queen's Park)
Aiden Sopel (2016 Peterhead OL, ex ICT)
Alan Whyte
Andy Shearer (2016 Formartine United, Ex Keith)
Craig Buchanan
Craig Duguid (2015 Formartine Utd, Ex Lewis Utd, Montrose, Aberdeen)
Darren Forbes (2012 Cove R)
Jack Henderson (2016 Banchory St T)
Jamie Lennox (2015 Cove R, ex Keith)
Jamie Watt (2016 Cove R, Ex ECU Joondalup, Stirling Lions, Cove R)
Josh Winton (2014 Hermes, Ex Montrose, Banks o Dee)
Kane Winton
Kieran Heads (2016 Deveronvale, ex Culter)
Liam McCall
Matt Hamilton
Matthew Robertson
Max Alexander
Michael Phillipson
Michael Taylor (2015 Culter, ex Cove R, Turriff Utd)

Neale Allan (2017 Huntly)
Ryan Hall
Scott Adams (2017 Peterhead OL)
Steven Jack

Buckie Rovers
Manager: David Findlay
Darren Thain
David Day
Ethan Murray
Gordon Riddoch (2016 New Elgin)
Jordan Marandola
Jordan Sutherland
Kieran Cowie
Kyle McKay
Liam wood
Marcus Flett
Michael Campbell
Michael Gauld
Michael Wood
Ross Elder
Liam Gordon
Nathan Walls
Bleu Innes
Scott Mair
Adam Scott
Scott Davidson
Russell McLaughlin
Calum Murray
Robert Scott
Niki Smith

Colony Park
Manager: Andy Roddie
Darren McGuinness
Barry Marwick
Ally Graham
Calum Reid
Kevin Bonarius
Craig Ross
Calvin Roddie
Jack Strachan
Peter Douglas
Chris Ness
Greg Dorrat
Craig Brown
Richard Davidson
James Cairns
John Farquhar
Neil Cowie
Steven Morrison
Steven Craib
Ross Durno
Jordan Clark
Stuart Mackay

Culter
Manager: Duncan Ord
Assistant: Graeme Laird
Coach:
Steve Dryburgh
Adam Wilson (2014, Sunnybank)
Allan Ogston
Andrew Anderson (2015, Ellon United)
Andrew Sim
Andrew Smith (2017 Stoneywood-Parkvale)
Benjamin McGregor (2015 Banchory St Ternan)
Bruce Dryburgh (2017 Stnoeywood Parkvale, ex Banks o' Dee)
Cameron Moultrie
Craig Reid
Derek Boylan (2016 Torry Select)
Derek McKechnie (2016 FC Stoneywood)
Frank Smyth
Gary McNamee (2015 Huntly)
Greg Smith (2016 Keith)
Jamie Cromar (2014 FC Stoneywood)
Keith Horne (2015 Banks o' Dee)
Kevin Stewart (2016 Banks o' Dee)
Liam Bain (2016 FC Stoneywood)
Nicky Gordon (2014 Dyce)
Reece Duncan (2015 East End, ex Albion BC)
Ross Buchanan (ex Dyce, Turriff United)
Ryan Robertson
Scott McArthur (ex Sunnybank, East End)
Sean Croll (Ex Stonehaven, Banks o' Dee, Keith)
Shaun Robertson (ex Ellon United)

Deveronside
Manager: John McLeay / Wayne Murdo
A MaCallum
A Taylor
Billy Blanchard
Bruce Thomson
C McDonald
Chris Strachan
Colin "Coco" Legge (2011 Deveronvale)
Damian Wojcik
Duncan Philip
Ernie Milne
Ewan Clark
Gavin Murdo (2010 Rothes)
James McLeay
Jamie McKinnon
Jody Munro
Joel Watt
John McLeay
Kev Thomson
Kieran Buchan
Kieran McCaffrey
Kyle Rae
Martin Hay
Michael McKinnon
Philip Watt (2015 Deveronvale, ex Rothes)
Ross Thompson
Stuart Gray
Wayne Murdo
Z Christie
Z Sopel

Dufftown
Manager: Steve "Pele" Paterson
Assistant: Mike Morrison
Andrew Munro
Connor Merson (2016 Ugie Youths)
Dale Wood (2015 Elgin City)
Daryl Tippings
David Mackie
Darren Mitchell
Euan Storrier (OL from Forres Mechanics)
Finlay Robertson
Gary Ewen (2016 Rothes, ex Dufftown)
James Grant
James McLaren
James Reid
James Stables (2011 Islavale, Ex Ross County, Deveronvale)
JJ Urquhart (2017 Hunbtly, ex Lossiemouth, Deveronvale, Buckie Th, Elgin C, Ross Co)
Karl Harris
Kevin Stuart
Marc Connolly
Mark Thomson (2016 Elgin C)
Michael Morrison
Michael McMullen (2017 Lossiemouth, Ex Dufftown)
Ruari Watt (2017 Rothes)
Sam Angus
Scott Bowie (2013 Rothes)
Scott Coull (2016 New Elgin, ex Elgin C)
Scott Johnston (2017 Keith, ex Dufftown)
Scott Thompson
Sean Davidson (2016 New Elgin)
Stuart Strathdee (2016 New Elgin)
Stuart Thomson (2016 Rothes)

Dyce
Manager: Mike McKenzie
Adam MacNamee (2016 Ex Huntly, Dyce)
Adam Morrison (2014 Keith, Ex Dyce BC)
Gordon Forsyth (2017 Inverurie Locos, ex Dyce)
Grant Moorhouse
Ian Leith (2016 Culter)
Jamie McAllister (2015 ex Culter, Cove R)
Liam Strachan (2016 Turriff United OL)
Magnus Barclay (2015 ex Montrose, Deveronvale, Banchory St T)
Mark Bartlett (2011 Ex Chattan Rovers, Wilsons AFC, Bon Accord City, Sunnybank)
Michael Clayton (2014 Banchory St T)
Michelle Lombardi (2015 ex Deveronvale, Ross Co, Aberdeen)
Muir Murray (ex Banks o Dee, Sunnybank, Longside)
Nicky Wozniak (2016 Turriff United OL)
Philip Low (2016 Stonehaven)
Richard Shand (2015 Culter)
Ricky Horne (2015 Dyce, Rothes)
Ryan Dick (2015 Banks o Dee, Sunnybank, Dyce, Bridge of Don Thistle)
Scott Wightman
Sean Napier (ex Dyce, Banchory St T)
Stephen Jeffrey (2017 Ex Dyce, Formartine Utd, Inverurie Locos)
Steven Bartlett (2011 Ex Buckie Th, Glentanar, Sunnybank)
Stewart McKenzie
Shaun Reid
Tom Hutchison (2014 Ex Westdyke, Peterhead, Deveronvale)
Tom Yeats (2014 Cove R)
Andy Pennycook (2016 Huntly)

Hall Russell United
Manager: John Carroll
Assistant: Ian Hay
Coaches:Davie Ingram, Derek Daun, Gordon Davidson
Andrew Davidson
Callum Innes
Cameron Milne
Christon Mackie
Craig Carroll
Craig Mackie
Elliott MacDonald
Gordon Hardie
Gordon Russell
Grant Mitchell
Greg Hay
Greg Simpson
Jack Goodwin
Jordan Cooper
Lee Cooper
Liam Cheyne
Matthew Wallace
Matthew Whitfield
Paul Esslemont
Bruno Fati
Callum Porteous
Daniel Crisp
Lewis Forbes
Lewis Wilson
Liam Morrison
Stuz Carroll (on Loan to Echt)

Hermes
Manager: Neil Dawson
Coach: Steven Watson
Lee Sweeney (2013 Sunnybank)
Grant Campbell
Scott Freeland (ex Dundee Utd, Cove R)
Lee Smith (ex Hazlehead United)
Alan McRae
Craig Macklin
Keith Wilson
Matthew Gairns
Richard Wyness
Keith Robertson
Andrew Close
Michael Dawson
Alan Fuller

Dude Love
Darren Mitchell
Ryan Nash
Ernests Pilats (ex Daugava Riga, RFS, FB Gulbene 2005, Sitka FA)
Erik Thomson
Josh Winton

Inverness City
Manager:
Alan Kerr
Alan MacPhee
Brett Mitchell
Daniel Murdoch
Darren Jarvie
Gary Miller
Graeme Stewart
Grant Beattie
Jordan MacDonald
Kelvin MacKenzie
Kevin Mackinnon
Martin Duncan
Michael Corbett
Reece Paterson
Steven Sanderson
Colin Mason
Donald Horsburgh
Gordon McNab

Maud
Manager: Mike Cramp / Chris Allsop
Martin Crisp,
Ryan Smart,
Mark Aitken,
Richard Kirk,
Grant Thomson,
Hamish Burr,
Edward Flinn,
Rhys Fyfe,
Graeme McLeman,
Steve Whyte,
James Wilson,
Gary Davidson,
Mark Lawson
Jordan Smith,
Shaun Reid,
Owen Tocher,
Kevin Simpson,
Craig Ritchie,
Sam Downie,
Lee MacDonald
Dean Still
Aaron Scully)

Newburgh Thistle
Manager: Lewis Muirhead
Assistant Manager; Justin Brown
Coach: Paul McLean
Ryan Cameron
Kevin Clark
Kieran Lawrence
Tito Silva
Liam Burnett
Mark Galashan
Matthew Tewnion
Matthew Milne
Chris Hardie
Clark Petrie
Craig Marshall
Darren Holt
Andrew Cooper
Bradley Deans
Cameron Gray
Charles Niven
David Black
Shaun Johnstone
Sam Muirhead (2016 Banks o'Dee, ex Newburgh Th)
Herbert Craik
Gavin Elphinstone

Stonehaven
Manager: Ian Esslemont
Assistant: Jim George
Adam McWilliam
Barry Smith
Craig Mackie
Danny Anderson
Darren Taylor
Fraser Stark
Gavin Robertson
Jason Coyle
Jordan Reid
Lewis Shand
Ludwik Metelski
Martin Shand
Michael Cormack
Neal McTavish
Rob Armstrong
Rhys Gray
Ryan Arbuckle
Ryan Stewart
Scott Pyper
Stephen Robertson
Steven Reid

North Juniors East Division

Aberdeen East End
Manager: Lee Youngson
Andy Youngson (2016 Aberdeen)
Callum Dunbar (2015 Ex Formartine Utd, Huntly)
Callum Youngson (2015 Ex Lewis Utd and Keith) - Left the club
Calvin Kennedy (2015 Sunnybank)
Daniel Johnstone (2011 Banks o Dee Youth) Left the club
Dean Henderson (2016 Keith)
Elliot Duff (2017 Huntly)
Glen Donald (2016 Cove R)
Graeme Wilson (2016 Ex Stonehaven, FC Stoneywood)
Jo Garrow (ex Newburgh)
Jonathan Cook (2017 Stonehaven)
Lewis Jopp (2015 Ex Lewis Utd and Keith)
Lewis Masson (2015 Seyon Koshedo (2016 Aberdeen)
Liam Todd
Mark Adam (2016 Westdyke)
Martyn Valentine (2016 Lewis Utd)
Murray Adam (2015 Ex Keith HFC, Echt) - Out on loan
Paul Rennie (2013 East End)
Phil Helson (2010 Lewis Utd) Out on loan
Randy Ross – (2016 Hermes, Out on loan)
Rhys Leiper (2015 Sunnybank)
Richard Binnie (2015 Ex Lewis Utd and Keith) Out on loan
Richie Petrie (2015 Aberdeen)
Stuart Fraser (2011 Ex Banks o Dee Youth, Cove R) Out on loan
William Beej Pauline (2016 ex Lewis Utd, Deveronvale)

Aberdeen University
Manager: Scott McKenzieAssistant: Ali Hynd
Jack McLennan
Dan McKendrick
Hamish Levein
Declan Laing
Andrew Rait
Jack Harkness
Sam McLaren
John Pearson
Paul Spence
Hamish Tubby
Andrew McKinlay
Paul Kirke
Andrew Shafik
Ahmed Maged
Craig Shanks
Ben Storie
Joseph Walker
Ciaran Ellison
Justin McBryan
Ryan Grant
Jyle Stuary
Caleb Ogwuru
Sam Toufiqe
David Akpara
Sam Caswell

Buchanhaven Hearts

Cruden Bay
Managers: Steve Scott / Kevin Coyle
Jordi Walker (2017 Turriff Utd OL)
Hamish Burr (2017 Ex Fraserburgh, Maud)
Matthew Stewart (2017 Turriff Utd OL)
Michael Ironside (2017 Turriff Utd OL)
Scott Moir (2017 Turriff Utd OL)
Neil Holland
Kevin Coyle (2017 Turriff Utd)
Scott Moir
Dean Still
Lee Lawrence
Matthew Stewart
Mark Aitken
Dale McCouaig
Daniel Smith
Scott Kelly
Cammy Fraser
Mark Foley
Jamie Masson

Ellon United
Manager: Steven Main
Dean McDonald
Fraser Tait
Lenny Johnson
Bob Morrice
Callum Tremaine
Chris Craib
David Coutts
Jack Sim
James Bain
James Seivwright
Jason Thornton
Kevin Anderson
Kyle Harker
Mark Kerr
Mike Mckinnon
Morgan Cook
Neil Irvine
Neil Main
Ross Gibbon
Scott Firth
Steven Main
Stuart Massie
Warren Robertson
Steven Benzie
Jonathan Millsom

Fraserburgh United
Manager: Roy Noble (ex Fraserburgh Link Up, Portlethen Juvs, Maud, Fraserburgh)
Craig Bruce (Ex St Combs Colts, Fraserburgh Link Up, St Combs, Longside, Cruden Bay)
Zak Conway (ex Fraserburgh Link Up, Aberdeen, Fraserburgh, Maud)
Liam Reid (ex Fraserburgh Link Up, Fraserburgh, Criden Bay, Invercairn United)
Cameron Buchan (ex Peterhead BC, Maud, Fraserburgh)
Fraser Davidson (ex Longside)
Jack Simpson (ex Fraserburgh Link Up, Fraserburgh)
Malcolm Maitland (ex Fraserburgh Link Up, Maud, Deveronvale, Fraserburgh)
John Smith (ex St Combs Ath, Mormond Thistle, Peterhead BC, Crimond, St Combs, Invercairn Utd)
Eric-John West (ex Crusaders, Frraserburgh BC, Invercairn Utd, Fraserburgh Utd, St Combs, Cruden Bay)
Bob Buchan (ex Fraserburgh Utd, Crimond, Clinton AFC)
David Devine (ex Cheers, Galleon, Clinton AFC)
Steven Whyte (ex Fraserburgh BC, Cheers, Station Hotel, Invercairn Utd, St Combs, Maud)
Ian Wheeler (ex Fraserburgh BC, Fraserburgh, Rothes, Longside)
Marco Del Testa
Reece Duncan
Neil Hay
Michael Clark

Steven Lawrence
Chalmers
Marc Noble
Daniel Reid
Bruce Paterson
Jonathan Garden
Liam Rollo

Glentanar
Manager: Graham McBeathCoach: Derek Robertson
Reece Duncan
Grant Stephen
Michael Duncan
Lewis Hamilton
Connor Hunter
Cameron Laird
Paul Orr
Hamza Ouahbi
Lee Sharp
Christopher Fairley
Kell Findlay
James Philip Flaherty
Matthew Milne
Ethan Smith
Jack Walker
Lewis Dalgleish
Sam Harrison
Adam Monk
Craig Simpson
Greg Smart
Lewis Stephen
Greg Wood

Lewis United
Player Manager: Darren Paul
Adam Davidson (ex Cove R)
Andreas Mitchell
Ben Leslie - Left the club
Caine Bacon - left the club
Callum Stewart
Calum Ritchie
Chris Hay
Clark Robertson
Colin Pirie (ex Lewis Utd, Ellon Utd, Glentanar, Sportsmans Club)
Cooper Brown (ex Huntly)
Dan Milne (ex Parkvale, Ellon Utd)
Daniel Forde (Ex New Elgin, Lossiemouth, Lads Club - Retired due to injury)
Darren Paul (ex Glentanar, Parkvale, Cove R, Crudxen Bay)
David Poupard
Dean McDonald
Garry Lothian - left the club
Gavin Elphinstone (ex Newburgh Th, East End, Parkvale)
James Bremner - left the club
Javier Bobes Bascaran
John Chalmers (ex Sportsmans Club, Ellon Utd, Glendale Youth)
Jordan Cheyne
Josh Cruickshank
Martyn Hazzard
Nathan Greig - left the club
Ross Gibson (ex Cove R)
Sean Cronin (2016 Ex Parkvale, Woodside AFC)
Sean Davidson
Shaun Goate (ex Cove R, Lewis U, Ellon U, Stoenhaven, Banks o Dee Thistle)
Tom Andrews
William Pauline (ex Whitehills, Deveronvale, Buckie Th - Left the club)

Longside
Manager: Charles West
Aidan Glennie
Bailey Simpson
Blair Fraser
Bruce Mair
Bruce Munro
Callum Davidson
Chris Cameron
Craig Findlay
Daniel Glendinning
Darren Steele
Dean Allan
Drew Marshall
Duncan Wallace
Ian Summers
Jack Heatherwick
Jake West
Jamie Ramsay
Jason Bain
Jordan Bremner
Jordan Mowat
Kyle Finnie
Liam Cameron
Liam Norris
Mark Stainton
Nathan Stuart
Neil Moir
Nicol Davidson
Paul McIntosh
Ross Mackie
Scott Michie
Sean Butcher
Sean Flett
Sean Smith
Shaun Jamieson
Stuart Kemp
Willie Filson

Stoneywood Parkvale
Manager: Alan Stables
Coaches: Grant Colligan, Ian Finnie
James Thouless
Robbie Collinson
Middleton
Bruce Dryburgh
Keller
Nathan Greig (2016 Lewis United)
Danny Robertson
Herbie Craik
James Watt
David Baillie
Ross Gibson
Andrew Smith
Sean Cronin
Stevie Gordon (2016 Newburgh Th)
Jamie Robertson
Scott McArthur (2016 Culter)
Joe Burr (2017 Huntly)
Curtis Kane
Scott Robison
Michael Middler
Dean Still (2017 Turriff United)
Jamie Cromer (2016 Culter)
Jordan Cromer (2017 Culter)
Stevie Young
Lee Adams
Brian Hay (still playing Aged 58)
Scott Goodbrand
Greg Simpson

Sunnybank
Manager: Kevin McHattie
Callum Youngson
Daniel Scott
Mike Wojcik
Ally Nicol
Scott Burnett
Jamie Abel
Sam Smith
Brian Docherty
Adam Elphinstone
Connor Kelly
Cammy Knowles
Aiden Taylor
Stuart Bathgate
Andrew Mutch
Dom Rae
Sean Cunningham
Paul Leahy
Anthony Harkin
Dean Lunan
Cameron Elphinstone
Scott Cowper
Lee Todd
Marc Lee
Alan Markey
Matthew Connell
Chris Davidson
Stuart Skinner
Jack Steven

North Juniors West Division

Burghead Thistle
Manager: Kevin Walker
Kiran Paterson
Taylor Gray
Jamie Davidson
Scott Gordon (2017 Lossiemouth)
Andrew Stewart (2017 Lossiemouth)
Steven McKenzie
Danny Williamson
Cameron More
Kyle Stewart
Finlay Nicol
Craig Smith
Blair Tulloch
Ian Wilson
Doug Wood

Fochabers
Player Manager: Bryan Henderson
John Ross (ex Lossie United)
Ian Wilson (ex Lossie United)
Tam Hearns
Mitch McGrath

Forres Thistle
Manager: Ian Campbell
Coaches: Robert McKinnon, Mark Pennie
Charlie Beck
Danny Black
Ross Campbell
Scott Campbell
Craig Daley
Lee Davidson
Matthew Davidson
Stuart Engelmann
Cameron Farquhar
Matthew Fraser
Gary Gallacher
Calum Gemmell
Aaron Hamilton
Richard Jack
Ryan McKenzie
Alistair Mackintosh
Ross MacPherson
Donald James McCulloch
John McInnes
Aaron McLellan
Daniel McLeod
Antbony Ross
Craig Snape
Craig Short
Andrew Taylor

Islavale
Manager: Kenny HendryAssistant: Kevin Collins
Coach: Roy McPherson
Gary J Morrison
Jordan Milne
Kieran Dey
David Blackhall
Scott McIntosh (2017 Rothes)
Craig Sim
Blair Moir
Aaron McPherson
Bruce Morrison
Craig Simpson
Paul Winton
Darren Stewart
Lewis Robertson
Gary Morrison
Michael Clark (2016 Huntly)
Steven Stuart
Douglas Wood (2016 Burghead Th)
Jonathan Mooty
Ricky Henderson (2017 Rothes, ex Islavale)
Scott Johnston (2016 Keith, OL)
Scott Davidson
David Christie
Stephen Todd
David Dey
Mark Hector
Oliver Kelly
Steven Reid
Kyle Mackay
Daniel Cormack
Callum McIntosh (2017 Rothes)

Montrose Roselea
Manager: Chris Simpson
Coaches: David Craig, Craig Anderson, Paul Ross (until Dec)
Calum Watson

Scott Watson
Joe Aitken
Lloyd Hester
Liam Campbell
Aaron Thomson
Kade McCormack
Ross McLeod
Ross Mitchell
Chris Milne
Liam Baillie
Michael Cruikshank
Stuart Richardson
Ryan Taylor (Freed Sep 2016 joined St Laurence Ams)
Euan Duff (Freed Sep 2016, joined Merpro)
Jordan Reoch
Callum Rae
Doan
David Beedie
Morgan Smith
Ross McLeod
Steven Greig
Kane Hester (2017 Arbroath OL)
Craig
Jack Dalgarno

Nairn St Ninian
Manager: Mike Hendry
Alistair Scott
Robert MacDonald
Charlie Fonweban
Robbie Flett
P Morganti
Jason Duncan
Scott Hendry
Ali Scott
Lee Haines
Jason Morganti
Kyle White
Scott Morrison
David Smith
Simon Hill
Jack Anderson
Gavin Chisholm
Michael Mulligan
Graeme Smith
Craig Smith
Sam Walker
Kendall
McRae

Gary Calvert
Donoghue

New Elgin
Manager: Robbie Hope (until April 2017)
Simon Lobban
Kevin Grant
Sean Petrie
Alan Turner
Brodie Allan
Mikey Paterson
Jamie Sutherland (2016 Burghead Th)
Jack McArthur
David McNamara
Grant Duguid
Grant McKnockiter
Ross Elliot (2016 Lossiemouth OL)
Stephen Dey (2016 New Elgin Welfare)
Zac Vale (2016 New Elgin Welfare)
Chris Ramage
Cameron Milne
Scott Mathieson
Jordan Whitta
Ross Elliot
Scott Coull
Ryan McPherson
Allen
Dean Stewart (2016 New Elgin Welfare)
Ingram
Kyle Paton (2016 FC Elgin, ex ICT Youths)
Callum Shand (2016 Aberlour Villa)
Ryan Thomson
Thomas Kinnaird
Cameron Milne

Newmachar United
Manager: Ian Cooper
Assistant: Brian Johnston
Callum Parley
Connor Manson
Angus Grant
Bradley Milne
Callum Saunders
Cameron Jarvie

Dawid Omernik
Josh Reynolds
Kevin Petrie
Kieran Morrison
Shane Pirie
Angus Brock
Ben Soutar
Callum Morrison
Christopher Mcdonald
Daniel Ross
David Wilson
Fraser Marcelline
Gavin Chandler
Hogan Ruddell
Keith Duncanson
Nicol Christie
Owen Shand
Richard Binnie
Sam Anderson
Sam Forsyth
Tom Riach

Spey Valley United
Manager: Fraser Tulloch (ex Strathspey Thistle, Broughty Ferry, Grantown FC) Coach: Alan Geegan (ex Clach, Dornoch, Inverness City, Muir of Ord)
Gavin Hay (scored 9 goals v Fochabers in Elginshire Cup game in January, ex Inverness Caley Thistle, Mearns United, Cromdale FC, Grantown FC)
David Ritchie (ex Clach, Napier Marist, Strathspey Thistle, Spey Valley)
D Manson
Iain Ross (ex Golspie Sutherland)
Davie Ross (ex Ross County, Elgin City, Nairn County, Strathspey Thistle)
Scott Shields (ex Ross County Youth, Clach, Grantown)
Andy Hay (ex Clydebank, Grantown)
Terry Swinton (ex Strathspey Th)
A Fraser
Paul MacDonald
Chris Tilbury (ex Grantown)

Mateus Bobrowski
Tolga Dagtas
DJ McPhee (2016 Fort William)
Andy Hay
Ricky Lee (ex Grantown)
Robert Donaldson (ex Caley Thistle, Clach, Fort William and Strathspey Thistle)
Euan Donaldson (ex Nairn county. Strathspey Thistle)
Nick Mochan (ex St Johnstone Youth, Strathspey Th)
Scott Morrison (ex Muir of Ord, Clach, Inverness City, Grantown)
David Watson (ex Nairn Co, Clach, Deveronvale)
Keith Mason
Scott Smith (ex Grantown, Strathspey Th)
Kevin Leitch (ex Grantown, Muir of Ord, Aberdeen University)
Chic Innes
Stuart Patience (es Ross Co Youth, Clach, Avoch, Alness Utd, Strathspey Th, Culbokie)
Cammy Haddow (2017 Clydebank)
Cruikshank
Clark Robertson (2017 Huntly OL)
Gary Gray (ex Grantown, Cromdale, Aberdeen Uni)

Whitehills
Manager: Watson
Stuart Smith
Deccy Smith
Taylor
Paul Mellon
Forsyth
Greig
Findlay

North Juniors Grill League Cup 2016/17

Group 1	BH	CB	IC	MR	NU
Buchanhaven Hearts		Aug-16 3-1			Aug 2 2-0
Cruden Bay			Aug 6 1-2	Aug 27 0-9	
Inverness City	Aug 20 5-0			Aug 13 1-4	
Montrose Roselea	Aug 6 0-0				Aug 20 8-0
Newmachar United		Aug 9 1-5	Aug 27 2-5		

#	Team	Pl	W	D	L	F	A	Diff	Pts
1	Montrose Roselea	4	3	1	0	21	1	20	10
2	Inverness City	4	3	0	1	13	7	6	9
3	Buchanhaven Hearts	4	2	1	1	5	6	-1	7
4	Cruden Bay	4	1	0	3	7	15	-8	3
5	Newmachar United	4	0	0	4	3	20	-17	0

Group 2	C	DEV	HRU	HER	NE
Culter		Aug 6 6-0		Aug 9 3-3	
Deveronside			Aug 13 0-5		Aug 2 3-0
Hall Russell United	Aug 2 1-1			Aug 16 1-3	
Hermes		Aug 20 0-2			Aug 6 9-0
New Elgin	Aug 13 1-10		Aug 20 0-3		

#	Team	Pl	W	D	L	F	A	Diff	Pts
1	Culter	4	2	2	0	20	5	15	8
2	Hall Russell United	4	2	1	1	10	4	6	7
3	Deveronside	4	2	0	2	5	11	-6	6
4	Hermes	4	2	1	1	15	6	9	1
5	New Elgin	4	0	0	4	1	25	-24	0

Group 3	BT	CP	DY	FOC	FOR
Burgead Thistle		Aug 20 0-2			Aug 9 0-4
Colony Park			Aug 2 0-4	Aug 13 9-0	
Dyce	Aug 6 3-0				Aug 13 2-4
Fochabers	Aug 16 1-3		Aug 20 0-12		
Forres Thistle		Aug 6 0-1		Aug 2 2-1	

#	Team	Pl	W	D	L	F	A	Diff	Pts
1	Dyce Juniors	4	3	0	1	21	4	17	9
2	Colony Park	4	3	0	1	12	4	8	9
3	Forres Thistle	4	3	0	1	10	4	6	9
4	Burghead Thistle	4	1	0	3	3	10	-7	3
5	Fochabers	4	0	0	4	2	26	-24	0

Group 4	AU	DUF	GLE	NEW	WHI
Aberdeen University					
Dufftown					Aug 2 6-0
Glentanar		Aug 6 2-3			
Newburgh Thistle		Aug 13 4-1	Aug 2 8-1		
Whitehills			Aug 13 2-0	Aug 6 0-6	

#	Team	Pl	W	D	L	F	A	Diff	Pts
1	Newburgh Thistle	3	3	0	0	18	2	16	9
2	Dufftown	3	2	0	1	10	6	4	6
3	Whitehills	3	1	0	2	2	12	-10	3
4	Glentanar	3	0	0	3	3	13	-10	0

Group 5	AEE	BOD	FU	LU	
Aberdeen East End			Aug 6 2-2		
Banks o' Dee			Aug 3 6-2	Aug 16 7-0	
Fraserburgh United	Aug 13 1-2			Aug 6 3-1	
Lewis United	Aug 2 3-3				

#	Team	Pl	W	D	L	F	A	Diff	Pts
1	Banks o' Dee	3	2	1	0	15	4	11	7
2	East End	3	1	2	0	7	6	1	5
3	Fraserburgh United	3	1	0	2	6	9	-3	3
4	Lewis United	3	0	1	2	4	13	-9	1

Group 6	BST	BUC	LON	SUN	
Banchory St Ternan		Aug 6 4-1			
Buckie Rovers			Aug 13 2-6		
Longside	Aug 2 2-1			Aug 6 3-3	
Sunnybank	Aug 9 1-2	Aug 20 2-2			

#	Team	Pl	W	D	L	F	A	Diff	Pts
1	Longside	3	2	1	0	11	6	5	7
2	Banchory St Ternan	3	2	0	1	7	4	3	6
3	Sunnybank	3	0	2	1	6	7	-1	2
4	Buckie Rovers	3	0	1	2	5	12	-7	1

Group 7	ISL	NSN	SVU	STO	
Islavale		Aug 6 1-0			
Nairn St Ninian			Aug 2 2-1	Aug 13 3-2	
Spey Valley United	Aug 13 1-2			Aug 6 3-2	
Stoneywood Parkvale	Aug 20 2-3				

#	Team	Pl	W	D	L	F	A	Diff	Pts
1	Islavale	3	3	0	0	6	3	3	9
2	Nairn St Ninian	3	2	0	1	5	4	1	6
3	Spey Valley United	3	1	0	2	5	6	-1	3
4	Stoneywood Parkvale	3	0	0	3	6	9	-3	0

Group 8	AU	ELL	MAU	STO	
Aberdeen University		Aug 9 0-1	Aug 6 0-5		
Ellon United			Aug 2 3-4	Aug 6 0-2	
Maud				Aug 13 3-1	
Stonehaven	Aug 2 6-0				

#	Team	Pl	W	D	L	F	A	Diff	Pts
1	Maud	3	2	0	1	11	5	6	6
2	Stonehaven	3	2	0	1	9	3	6	6
3	Ellon United	3	2	0	1	5	5	0	6
4	Aberdeen University	3	0	0	3	0	12	-12	0

LEAGUE CUP KO STAGES

QF	10/09/2016	Culter	Dyce	4	0	
QF	10/09/2016	Islavale	Maud	0	1	
QF	10/09/2016	Montrose Roselea	Longside	3	0	
QF	10/09/2016	Newburgh Thistle	Banks o' Dee	4	6	
SF	01/10/2016	Maud	Culter	3	0	
SF	01/10/2016	Montrose Roselea	Banks o' Dee	1	3	
F	16/10/2016	Banks O' Dee	Maud	2	0	at Dyce

Banks o' Dee won the Grill League Cup by beating Maud 2-0 at Ian Mair Park. Second half goals from Josh Winton and Jamie Lennox earned Dee the first silverware of the season and sets them up for their forthcoming Scottish Cup ties against Formartine United and Kilbirnie Ladeside. Persistent rain and a swirling wind made life difficult for both teams and the first half was a low key affair with the best chance falling to Dee's Michael Phillipson heading wide after beating Maud keeper Rhys Fyfe to Max Alexander's centre. Dee took the lead in fortuitous circumstances ten minutes into the second half as Josh Winton's 25 yard strike took a wicked deflection and looped up over Fyfe. Maud then had their best spell of the match, but failed to seriously threaten Andrew Shearer in the Dee goal and the McBookie.com Superleague champions sealed victory when Jamie Lennox beat Fyfe with a composed finish.

Recent North Sectional League Cup Finals				
Season	**Winners**	**Runners Up**	**Score**	**Venue**
1999/00	Sunnybank	Formartine United	4-3	Harlaw Park, Inverurie
2000/1	Sunnybank	Formartine United	2-0	Harlaw Park, Inverurie
2001/2	Sunnybank	Glentanar	1-0 aet	Keith Park, Aberdeen*
2002/3	Strathspey Thistle	Banks o' Dee	2-2, 4-3 pens	Keith Park, Aberdeen*
2003/4	Hermes	Glentanar	0-0, 4-3 pens	Heathryfold Park, Aberdeen
2004/5	Glentanar	Stonehaven	4-2	Heathryfold Park, Aberdeen
2005/6	Culter	Formartine United	2-0	Heathryfold Park, Aberdeen
2006/7	Turriff United	Hillhead	3-0	Heathryfold Park, Aberdeen
2007/8	Sunnybank	Culter	2-2, 5-4 pens	Hillhead Sports Centre, Aberdeen*
2008/9	Dyce	East End	0-0, 4-2 pens	Spain Park, Aberdeen
2009/10	Sunnybank	Longside	3-1	New Advocates Park, Aberdeen
2010/1	Culter	Inverness City	1-0	Merson Park, Buckie
2011/2	Maud	Inverness City	3-2	Simpson Park, Keith
2012/3	FC Stoneywood	Dyce	2-0	Hillhead Sports Centre, Aberdeen*
2013/4	Banks o' Dee	Culter	0-0, 4-2 pens	Hillhead Sports Centre, Aberdeen*
2014/5	Hermes	Maud	3-1	Davidson Park, Longside
2015/6	Dyce	Culter	3-1	Heathryfold Park, Aberdeen
2016/7	Banks o' Dee	Maud	2-0	Ian Mair Park, Dyce
* Keith Park was later renamed Hillhead Sports Centre				

Domino's Pizza North Regional Junior Cup 2016/17

P	13/08/2016	Lewis United	Buchanhaven Hearts	0	1		
P	27/08/2016	Spey Valley Unitec	Islavale	1	2		
1	24/09/2016	Dyce	Montrose Roselea	1	1	1-2p	
1	13/08/2016	Burhgead Thistle	Aberdeen University	4	1		
1	20/08/2016	Stonehaven	Fraserburgh United	0	0	4-5p	
1	10/12/2016	Maud	Islavale	2	1		
1	16/08/2016	Glentanar	Newmachar United	1	2		
1	27/08/2016	Banks o' Dee	Forres Thistle	8	0		
1	08/10/2016	Stoneywood Parkv	Cruden Bay	16	1		
1	27/08/2016	Longside	Culter	2	2	5-6p	
1	27/08/2016	Ellon United	Nairn St Ninian	4	1		
1	27/08/2016	Whitehills	Aberdeen East End	0	6		
1	01/10/2016	Banchory St Ternb	Inverness City	2	2	4-5p	
1	27/08/2016	Colony Park	Sunnybank	2	1		
1	27/08/2016	Buchanhaven Hear	Newburgh Thistle	0	3		
1	08/10/2016	Fochabers	Hermes	0	14		
1	27/08/2016	Dufftown	Buc kie Rovers	3	1		
1	27/08/2016	Deveronside	Hall Russell United	3	1		
2	05/11/2016	Deveronside	Inverness City	1	1	3-5p	
2	05/11/2016	Montrose Roselea	Fraserburgh United	2	2	5-3p	
2	05/11/2016	Stoneywood Parkv	Aberdeen East End	1	2		
2	17/12/2016	Burghead Thistle	Banks o' Dee	0	15		
2	25/03/2017	Colony Park	Newburgh Thistle	1	0		
2	12/11/2016	Dufftown	Culter	1	6		
2	18/02/2017	Ellon United	Newmachar United	5	2		
2	07/01/2017	Maud	Hermes	3	0		
3	25/03/2017	East End	Deveronside	4	2		
3	25/03/2017	Maud	Culter	3	5		
3	01/04/2017	Banks o' Dee	Ellon United	3	0		
3	08/04/2017	Montrose Roselea	Colony Park	0	0	3-4p	
SF	17/05/2017	East End	Banks o' Dee	1	0		
SF	16/05/2017	Colony Park	Culter	2	2	5-4p	
F	03/06/2017	East End	Colony Park	2	0		at Dyce

East End lifted the Dominos Pizza North Regional Cup after beating Colony Park 2-0 at Ian Mair Park. Second half goals from - man of the match - Calvin Kennedy and William Pauline secured victory for the New Advocates Park side. East End had slightly the better of a goal-less first half that saw Colony Park reduced to ten men when James Cairns was given a straight red card for a challenge around the half hour mark. East End took the lead on 55 minutes when Calvin Kennedy curled in a glorious shot from 20 yards and while they were always in the game, the ten men of Colony Park struggled to create any clear cut chances and William Pauline wrapped up victory with an angled strike five minutes from time.

Recent North Region Cup Finals				
Season	**Winners**	**Runners Up**	**Score**	**Venue**
1988/9	Bon Accord	Culter	2-1 aet	Spain Park, Aberdeen
1989/90	Culter	Stonehaven	2-1	Spain Park, Aberdeen
1990/1	Stonehaven	FC Stoneywood	2-1	Spain Park, Aberdeen
1991/2	FC Stoneywood	Aberdeen East End	3-0	Heathryfold Park, Aberdeen
1992/3	Hall Russell United	Stonehaven	3-2	Heathryfold Park, Aberdeen
1993/4	Sunnybank	FC Stoneywood	0-0, 2-0 pens	Spain Park, Aberdeen
1994/5	FC Stoneywood	Sunnybank	2-1	Spain Park, Aberdeen
1995/6	Inverurie Locos	Bon Accord	3-1	Spain Park, Aberdeen
1996/7	Sunnybank	Bon Accord	3-1	New Advocates Park, Aberdeen
1997/8	Hermes	Cruden Bay	2-1	The Meadows, Ellon
1998/9	FC Stoneywood	Stonehaven	1-0	Heathryfold Park, Aberdeen
1999/00	Culter	Formartine United	2-1	Heathryfold Park, Aberdeen
2000/1	Inverurie Locos	Forres Thistle	3-1	The Haughs, Turriff
2001/2	Sunnybank	Culter	3-0	Pittodrie Stadium, Aberdeen
2002/3	Islavale	Banks o' Dee	3-2	Pittodrie Stadium, Aberdeen
2003/4	Hermes	Aberdeen East End	2-1	Pittodrie Stadium, Aberdeen
2004/5	Islavale	Banchory St Ternan	7-1	North Lodge Park, Pitmedden
2005/6	Islavale	Longside	3-1	The Haughs, Turriff
2006/7	Turriff United	Forres Thistle	2-1	Simpson Park, Keith
2007/8	Dyce	Turriff United	2-0	Pleasure Grounds, Maud
2008/9	Dyce	Formartine United	4-1	Heathryfold Park, Aberdeen
2009/10	FC Stoneywood	Hermes	5-3	Heathryfold Park, Aberdeen
2010/1	Banks o' Dee	Sunnybank	7-1	Crombie Park, Culter
2011/2	Culter	Inverness City	2-0	Kynoch Park, Keith
2012/3	Stonehaven	Maud	3-1	Ian Mair Park, Dyce
2013/4	Culter	Banks o' Dee	0-0, 4-2 pens	Ian Mair Park, Dyce
2014/5	Hermes	Dyce	4-1	Crombie Park, Culter
2015/6	Islavale	Dyce	2-0	Colony Park, Inverurie
2016/7	Aberdeen East End	Colony Park	2-0	Ian Mair Park, Dyce

McLeman Cup 2016/17

The McLeman Cup is competed for by teams in the top division of the North Juniors.

1	28/01/2017	Culter	Inverness City	1	1	3-4p	
1	28/01/2017	Dyce	Banchory St Ternan	3	2		
1	28/01/2017	Hall Russell United	Colony Park	5	1		
1	28/01/2017	Maud	Banks o' Dee	2	3		
1	18/03/2017	Newburgh Thistle	Stonehaven	1	3		
1	25/02/2017	Hermes	Dufftown	5	2		
2	11/03/2017	Banks O' Dee	Deveronside	8	0		
2	11/03/2017	Hall Russell United	Inverness City	4	1		
2	01/04/2017	Buckie Rovers	Hermes	0	2		
2	22/04/2017	Dyce	Newburgh Thistle	2	1		
SF	02/05/2017	Banks O' Dee	Hall Russell United	2	1		
SF	02/05/2017	Hermes	Dyce	1	1	3-2p	
F	26/05/2017	Banks O' Dee	Hermes	5	1		at Sunnybank

Banks o' Dee retained the PMAC Group McLeman Cup after beating Hermes 5-1 at Heathryfold Park. Michael Phillipson put Dee ahead before Liam McCall doubled the lead from the spot in an incident that saw Fraser Strachan sent off. Jack Henderson added a third after the break and although Lee Smith pulled a goal back from the spot, further goals from Henderson and McCall wrapped up a convincing victory.

Recent McLeman Cup Finals				
Season	**Winners**	**Runners Up**	**Score**	**Venue**
1988/9	Culter	Inverurie Loco Works	2-1	Heathryfold Park
1989/90	Bon Accord	East End	1-0	Spain Park
1990/1	Banks o' Dee	Crombie Sports	1-0	Heathryfold Park
1991/2	Lewis United	Sunnybank	2-1	Spain Park
1992/3	Culter	Longside	4-3	North Lodge Park
1993/4	FC Stoneywood	Culter	3-3, 3-2 pens	Spain Park
1994/5	Stonehaven	Hermes	3-1	Heathryfold Park
1995/6	Sunnybank	Banks o' Dee	3-1	New Advocates Park
1996/7	Sunnybank	Lads Club	4-0	New Advocates Park
1997/8	Sunnybank	Formartine United	3-2	New Advocates Park
1998/9	Formartine United	Stonehaven	1-0	Denmore Park
1999/00	Sunnybank	East End	2-1	Pittodrie
2000/1	Culter	Longside	4-1	Lochside Park
2001/2	Formartine United	Culter	1-0	Heathryfold Park
2002/3	Culter	Longside	1-0	Heathryfold Park
2003/4	Glentanar	Formartine United	2-1	Lochside Park
2004/5	Culter	Sunnybank	1-0	Lochside Park
2005/6	Formartine United	Parkvale	3-0	Heathryfold Park
2006/7	Sunnybank	Stonehaven	1-1, 4-3 pens	Keith Park
2007/8	Ellon United	Sunnybank	3-2	Lochside Park
2008/9	Hermes	Banks o' Dee	1-0	New Advocates Park
2009/10	Culter	Hermes	2-1	Keith Park
2010/1	Culter	Fraserburgh United	2-1	Longside
2011/2	Stonehaven	Hermes	1-1, 5-4 pens	Keith Park
2012/3	Culter	FC Stoneywood	3-1	Pittodrie
2013/4	Culter	Maud	2-1	Colony Park
2014/5	FC Stoneywood	Hall Russell United	4-2	Heathryfold Park
2015/6	Banks o' Dee	Inverness City	3-0	Merson Park, Buckie
2016/7	Banks o' Dee	Hermes	5-1	Heathryfold Park
aka	Gordon Campbell Construction Trophy 1991-2001			
	Acorn Heating Trophy 2002-2006			
	ATR Group Cup 2006-7			

AM Property Maintenance Morrison Cup 2016/17

n recent seasons this cup has been played for by Division 1 (East) clubs.

oup 1	AU	EE	CB	FU	L	SP
erdeen University				Jan 21		Feb-18
				3-0		01-Feb
st End	Feb 25		Feb 18			
	6-0		4-0			
uden Bay	Jan 7				Feb 25	
	1-4				2-3	
aserburgh United		Jan 7	Mar 4		Feb 18	
		0-3	4-2		2-0	
ngside	Mar 17	Jan 21				
	1-0	4-0				
oneywood Parkvale		Mar 18	Jan 21	Feb 25	Apr 8	
		2-4	3-1	0-4	2-4	

#	Team	Pl	W	D	L	F	A	Diff	Pts
1	East End	5	4	0	1	17	6	11	12
2	Longside	5	4	0	1	12	6	6	12
3	Fraserburgh United	5	3	0	2	10	8	2	9
4	Aberdeen University	5	2	0	3	8	10	-2	6
5	Stoneywood Parkvale	5	2	0	3	9	14	-5	6
6	Cruden Bay	5	0	0	5	6	18	-12	0

oup 2	BH	EU	G	LU	SUN	
chanhaven Hearts		Jan 21	Apr 1		Feb 18	
		1-1	3-2		1-2	
on United				Mar 18	Feb 25	
				4-0	3-0	
entanar		Jan 7			Apr 8	
		1-7			3-2	
wis United	Jan 7		Feb 18			
	2-4		1-3			
nnybank				Jan 28		
				0-2		

#	Team	Pl	W	D	L	F	A	Diff	Pts
1	Ellon United	4	3	1	0	15	2	13	10
2	Buchanhaven Hearts	4	2	1	1	9	7	2	7
3	Glentanar	4	2	0	2	9	13	-4	6
4	Sunnybank	4	1	1	2	4	7	-3	4
5	Lewis United	4	0	1	3	3	11	-8	1

F	29/04/2017	Aberdeen East End	Buchanhaven Hearts	6	0		
F	29/04/2017	Ellon United	Longside	1	2		
	04/05/2017	Aberdeen East End	Longside	1	1	4-3p	at Ellon

East End won the AM Property Maintenance Morrison Cup after a dramatic final at The Meadows. East End led through Callum Dunbar's early second half strike and looked to be holding out until a horrendous defensive mix up allowed Longside's Bailey Simpson to scramble home an equaliser with virtually the last kick of the game. Longside missed two of their opening three penalties which gave Dunbar the chance to win it for East End but the drama continued as his spot kick was kept out by Ian Summers, but East End it won when keeper Rhys Leiper saved Longside's last penalty.

cent Morrison Cup Finals

ason	Winners	Runners Up	Score	Venue
88/9	Buchanhaven Hearts	Banks o' Dee	2-1	North Lodge Park
89/90	Longside	Turriff United	2-1	North Lodge Park
90/1	FC Stoneywood	Banks o' Dee	1-0	Heathryfold Park
91/2	Lewis United	Dyce	3-1	New Advocates Park
92/3	Lewis United	Hall Russell United	1-0	Keith Park
93/4	Hermes	Banchory St Ternan	1-0	New Advocates Park
94/5	Banchory St Ternan	Hermes	1-0	Crombie Park, Culter
95/6	Banchory St Ternan	Buchanhaven Hearts	2-1	Denmore Park
96/7	Hermes	Lewis United	2-1	Denmore Park
97/8	Cruden Bay	East End	1-1, 4-3 pens	The Meadows, Ellon
98/9	East End	Patkvale	2-1	Spain Park
99/00	Cruden Bay	Buchanhaven Hearts	4-1	Davidson Park, Longside
00/1	Lads Club	Glentanar	3-2	Ian Mair Park, Dyce
01/2	Dyce	Lewis United	2-1	Woodside
02/3	Lewis United	Parkvale	2-1	Ian Mair Park, Dyce
03/4	Fraserburgh United	Banchory St Ternan	2-1	Ian Mair Park, Dyce
04/5	Banchory St Ternan	Parkvale	2-1	Ian Mair Park, Dyce
05/6	Banchory St Ternan	Lewis United	2-1	Ian Mair Park, Dyce
06/7	East End	Maud	5-0	Ian Mair Park, Dyce
07/8	Islavale	Hall Russell United	1-0	Pleasure Park, Maud
08/9	Formartine United	Buckie Rovers	2-2, 5-4 pens	The Haughs, Turriff
09/10	Stonehaven	Inverness City	2-2, 5-4 pens	Simpson Park, Keith
10/1	Glentanar	Lossiemouth United	4-2	Pleasure Park, Maud
11/2	New Elgin	Fraserburgh United	4-4, 4-3 pens	Colony Park, Inverurie
12/3	East End	Inverness City	1-1, 5-4 pens	Simpson Park, Keith
13/14	Sunnybank	Buchanhaven Hearts	1-1, 4-3 pens	The Meadows, Ellon
14/15	Longside	Buchanhaven Hearts	3-2	Balmoor Stadium, Peterhead
16/16	Fraserburgh United	Buchanhaven Hearts	3-1	Davidson Park, Longside
16/17	Aberdeen East End	Longside	1-1, 4-3 pens	The Meadows, Ellon

til 91/2 played for by all North (East) clubs
91/2 - 2012/3 played for by tier 2 clubs
13/4- played for by all North (East) clubs

Elginshire Cup 2016/17

In recent years this Cup has been played for by Division 1 (West) clubs.

Group 1

	BT	NSN	NE	NMA	WHI
Burghead Thistle			Feb 25 3-2	Mar 4 2-1	
Nairn St Ninian	Mar 11 4-0				Jan 28 2-1
New Elgin		Mar 18 0-2			Mar 4 0-3
Newmachar United		Jan 7 3-2	Mar 25 3-3		
Whitehills	Jan 21 1-2			Feb 11 4-1	

	P	W	D	L	F	A	PTS
Nairn St Ninian	4	3	0	1	10	4	9
Burghead Thistle	4	3	0	1	7	8	9
Whitehills	4	2	0	2	9	5	6
Newmachar United	4	1	1	2	8	11	4
New Elgin	4	0	1	3	5	11	1

Group 2

	FOC	FOR	ISL	SVU
Fochabers		Jan 28 0-11	Feb 11 2-7	
Forres Thistle			Mar 11 1-4	
Islavale				Mar 18 4-3
Spey Valley United	Jan 7 17-1	Feb 18 1-1		

	P	W	D	L	F	A	PTS
Islavale	3	3	0	0	15	6	9
Spey Valley United	3	1	1	1	22	6	4
Forres Thistle	3	1	1	1	13	5	4
Fochabers	3	0	0	3	3	35	0

SF	08/04/2017	Islavale	Bughead Thistle	2	0	
SF	08/04/2017	Nairn St Ninian	Spey Valley United	5	1	
F	23/04/2017	Nairn St Ninian	Islavale	0	2	at Elgin City

Recent Elginshire Cup Finals

Season	Winners	Runners Up	Score	Venue
1988/9	Bishopmill United	Deveronside	2-0	Forest Park, Burghead
1989/90	Islavale	Deveronside	2-1	Forest Park, Burghead
1990/1	Islavale	Forres Thistle	3-1	Merson Park, Buckie
1991/2	Nairn St Ninian	RAF Kinloss	2-1	Forest Park, Burghead
1992/3	Islavale	Nairn St Ninian	3-1	Logie Park, Forres
1993/4	Kinloss	Lossiemouth United	3-2	Logie Park, Forres
1994/5	New Elgin	Strathspey Thistle	2-1	Mosset Park, Forres
1995/6	Deveronside	Islavale	1-0	Gordon Park, Portgordon
1996/7	Deveronside	Islavale	2-2 aet, 4-3 pens	Mosset Park, Forres
1997/8	Deveronside	Lossiemouth United	5-2	Logie Park, Forres
1998/9	Islavale	Bishopmill United	2-1	Logie Park, Forres
1999/00	Nairn St Ninian	Islavale	1-0	Mosset Park, Forres
2000/1	Deveronside	Whitehills	3-2	Canal Park, Banff
2001/2	Strathspey Thistle	Islavale	3-2	Mosset Park, Forres
2002/3	Forres Thistle	Islavale	1-0	Merson Park, Buckie
2003/4	New Elgin	Lossiemouth United	2-0	Mosset Park, Forres
2004/5	Forres Thistle	New Elgin	4-3 aet	Mosset Park, Forres
2005/6	New Elgin	RAF Lossiemouth	1-1	Mosset Park, Forres
2006/7	Nairn St Ninian	Fochabers	1-1, 5-3 pens	Fochabers
2007/8	Burghead Thistle		wo	
2008/9	Inverness City	Bishopmill United	3-0	Logie Park, Forres
2009/10	Burghead Thistle	Cruden Bay	1-0	Merson Park, Buckie
2010/1	Newmachar United	Nairn St Ninian	1-0	Kynoch Park, Keith
2011/2	Nairn St Ninian	Portgordon Victoria	3-0	Logie Park, Forres
2012/3	Colony Park	Buckie Rovers	1-0	Boroughbriggs, Elgin
2013/4	Forres Thistle	Buckie Rovers	3-1	Boroughbriggs, Elgin
2014/5	Buckie Rovers	Dufftown	1-1, 3-1 pens	Boroughbriggs, Elgin
2015/6	Forres Thistle	Buckie Rovers	6-2	Boroughbriggs, Elgin
2016/7	Islavale	Nairn St Ninian	2-0	Boroughbriggs, Elgin

Islavale won the Elginshire Cup beating Nairn St Ninian 2-0 in the final at Borough Briggs. Vale went in front after 12 minutes when Nairn defender Mark MacDonald put through his own goal trying to clear Lewis Robertson's centre and Keiran Dey made it two ten minutes after the break with a fine left strike from the edge of the box. MacDonald's day went from bad to worse when he was sent off for receiving a second caution ten minutes from time and although Jason Duncan came close with a header near the end, Vale held out comfortably to lift the cup.

Archibald Cup 2016/17

The Archibald Cup had been dormant for a number of years but was revived I 2015/16 to provide additional fixtures 'or the North (West) Division clubs. For 2016/17 all Division One East and West clubs were invited to enter but participation was not mandatory.

roup 1	FOR	GLE	LEW	NEW	WHI
orres Thistle		Apr 29 3-1		Apr 15 3-0	
lentanar			Mar 25 2-1		Mar 18 0-0
ewis United	Apr 8 0-3			Apr 25 1-0	
ewmachar United		Apr 18 4-5			Apr 29 4-1
'hitehills	Mar 25 2-5		Mar 11 0-3		

#	Team	Pl	W	D	L	F	A	Diff	Pts	Adj
1	Forres Thistle	4	4	0	0	14	3	11	12	0
2	Glentanar	4	2	1	1	8	8	0	7	0
3	Lewis United	4	2	0	2	5	5	0	6	0
4	Newmachar United	4	1	0	3	8	10	-2	3	0
5	Whitehills	4	0	1	3	3	12	-9	1	0

roup 2	AEE	BUR	ISL	NEW	STO
berdeen East End				Apr 8 2-0	Mar 11 3-2
urghead Thistle	Apr 15 0-3		Apr 26 3-1		
lavale	Apr 12 0-2				May 9 3-1
ew Elgin		May 2 2-3	Apr 29 0-4		
toneywood Parkvale		Apr 29 4-1		Apr 15 3-1	

#	Team	Pl	W	D	L	F	A	Diff	Pts	Adj
1	East End	4	4	0	0	10	2	8	12	0
2	Stoneywood Parkvale	4	2	0	2	10	8	2	6	0
3	Islavale	4	2	0	2	8	6	2	6	0
4	Burghead Thistle	4	2	0	2	7	10	-3	6	0
5	New Elgin	4	0	0	4	3	12	-9	0	0

roup 3	FOC	MON	NSN	SUN
ochabers				Mar 18 0-7
lontrose R	Mar 11 9-0			
aim St N	Mat 4 6-0	Apr 29 2-2		
unnybank		Apr 15 2-4	May 6 2-1	

#	Team	Pl	W	D	L	F	A	Diff	Pts	Adj
1	Montrose Roselea	3	2	1	0	15	4	11	7	0
2	Sunnybank	3	2	0	1	11	5	6	6	0
3	Nairn St Ninian	3	1	1	1	9	4	5	4	0
4	Fochabers	3	0	0	3	0	22	-22	0	0

F	13/05/2017	Forres Thistle	Sunnybank	0	4		
F	20/05/2017	Montrose Roselea	East End	3	2	Protest	
	Montrose Expelled due to playing ineligible players						
	09/06/2017	Sunnybank	East End	1	1	2-4p	at Hermes

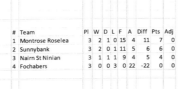

East End won the Archibald Cup beating Sunnybank 3-2 on penalties after the sides drew 1-1 at Uinconn Park. The success meant the New Advocates Park had won three trophies this season following their triumphs in the Dominos Pizza North Regional Cup and the AM Property Maintenance Morrison Cup. East End took the lead thanks to Paul Rennie's penalty and while they had the majority of the chances they couldn't add a crucial second goal and were made to pay when Daniel Scott equalized for Sunnybank to send the match to penalties, but East End prevailed thanks to a couple of fine saves from keeper Jo Garrow.

ecent Archibald Cup Finals

eason	Winners	Runners Up	Score	Venue
988/9	Bon Accord	Culter	3-1	Spain Park, Aberdeen
989/90	Culter	FC Stoneywood	1-0	Heathryfold Park, Aberdeen
990/1	FC Stoneywood	Culter	6-0	Spain Park, Aberdeen
991/2	Buchanhaven Hearts	Sunnybank	1-0	Spain Park, Aberdeen
992/3	FC Stoneywood	Crombie Sports	1-0	Spain Park, Aberdeen
993/4	Aberdeen East End	Culter	4-2	Spain Park, Aberdeen
994/5	Sunnybank	Inverurie Loco Works	2-1	Spain Park, Aberdeen
995/6	Sunnybank	FC Stoneywood	2-0	Spain Park, Aberdeen
996/7	FC Stoneywood	Culter	4-2	Spain Park, Aberdeen
997/8	Sunnybank	Inverurie Loco Works	1-0	Polo Park, Stoneywood
998/9	Formartine United	Lewis United	3-2	Hermes FC, Lochside Park
999/00	Inverurie Locos Works	FC Stoneywood	3-1	North Lodge Park, Pitmedden
000/1	FC Stoneywood	Wilsons XI	2-2, 4-2p	Spain Park, Aberdeen
015/16	Forres Thistle	Buckie Rovers	1-0	Forest Park, Burghead
016/17	Aberdeen East End	Sunnybank	1-1, 4-2p	Hermes FC, Uniconn Park

Jp to 2000/1, the Archibald Cup was contested by all North Region clubs.

GA Inter-Regional Cup 2016/17

PN	03/09/2016	Montrose Roselea	Dyce	0	1	
1S	24/09/2016	Dundee Violet	Forfar Albion	7	0	
1S	08/10/2016	Downfield	Dundee North End	3	0	
1S	08/10/2016	Scone Thistle	Jeanfield Swifts	0	2	
1S	24/09/2016	Brechin Victoria	Broughty Athletic	1	5	
1N	13/08/2016	Banchory St Ternan	Hermes	0	4	
1N	20/08/2016	Aberdeen University	Longside	1	5	
1N	20/08/2016	Culter	Whitehills	8	0	
1N	20/08/2016	Newburgh Thistle	Glentanar	3	0	
1N	03/09/2003	Buchanhaven Hearts	Forres Thistle	3	3	5-4p
1N	27/08/2016	Burghead Thistle	Maud	1	4	
1N	03/09/2003	New Elgin	Cruden Bay	2	5	
1N	03/09/2003	Newmachar United	Aberdeen East End	1	6	
1N	03/09/2003	Stoneywood Parkvale	Hall Russell United	1	4	
1N	03/09/2003	Sunnybank	Inverness City	3	1	
1N	03/12/2016	Fraserburgh United	Banks o' Dee	1	0	
1N	24/09/2016	Fochabers	Lewis United	1	8	
1N	24/09/2016	Dufftown	Colony Park	0	2	
1N	01/10/2016	Ellon United	Dyce	1	4	
1N	24/09/2016	Deveronside	Islavale	0	3	
1N	10/09/2016	Stonehaven	Buckie Rovers	5	0	
2S	05/11/2016	Downfield	Forfar West End	0	0	3-4p
2S	08/10/2016	Luncarty	Kirrie Thistle	1	3	
2S	01/10/2016	Coupar Angus	Tayport	1	3	
2S	05/11/2016	Carnoustie Panmure	Jeanfield Swifts	3	2	
2S	08/10/2016	Lochee Harp	Arbroath Victoria	8	2	
2S	08/10/2016	Dundee Violet	Kinnoull	2	1	
2S	08/10/2016	Lochee United	Dundee East Craigie	2	2	1-3p
2S	15/10/2016	Broughty Athletic	Blairgowrie	5	2	
2N	12/11/2016	Aberdeen East End	Colony Park	5	0	
2N	26/11/2016	Buchanhaven Hearts	Islavale	2	2	5-6p
2N	05/11/2016	Culter	Maud	6	3	
2N	03/12/2016	Newburgh Thistle	Longside	4	2	
2N	10/12/2016	Hermes	Cruden Bay	8	1	
2N	12/11/2016	Sunnybank	Stonehaven	4	4	2-0p
2N	17/12/2016	Fraserburgh United	Dyce	1	1	4-3p
2N	05/11/2016	Lewis United	Hall Russell United	2	6	
3	04/02/2017	Hall Russell United	Dundee Violet	0	1	
3	04/02/2017	Culter	Broughty Athletic	1	3	
3	04/02/2017	Tayport	Sunnybank	7	1	
3	04/02/2017	Fraserburgh United	Lochee Harp	1	1	2-4p
3	04/02/2017	East Craigie	Aberdeen East End	2	0	
3	04/02/2017	Carnoustie Panmure	Islavale	4	1	
3	04/02/2017	Forfar West End	Hermes	3	3	2-3p
3	18/02/2017	Kirrie Thistle	Newburgh Thistle	7	0	
4	11/03/2017	Broughty Athletic	Hermes	5	1	
4	11/03/2017	Dundee Violet	East Craigie	5	3	
4	11/03/2017	Tayport	Carnoustie Panmure	2	0	
4	11/03/2017	Kirrie Thistle	Lochee Harp	3	0	
SF	22/04/2017	Kirrie Thistle	Tayport	1	3	
SF	22/04/2017	Dundee Violet	Broughty Athletic	1	2	
F	28/05/2017	Broughty Athletic	Tayport	5	1	
		at Tannadice				

The GA Cup is contested by clubs from the North Region and the former Tayside Region. Eight clubs from the North and eight from Tayside come out of regionalised early stages to produce 8 North v Tayside ties in Round 3.

2016/17 FINAL

Broughty Athletic v Tayport
5-1

Broughty:: Ross, McCunnie, Blair, Suttie, McLellan, Winter, McConnachie, Clark, Lawson, Smart, McCord. Subs Sinclair, Adam, Cavanagh, Coulter
Tayport - Sorley, Conway, Sturrock, Sanchez, G Anderson, Alvarez (Tulleth), Mackie, Walton, Reid, Ogg, Paterson (F Anderson).

1-0	20 mins	McCord pen
2-0	58 mins	Ovenstone
3-0	60 mins	Lawson
3-1	69 mins	Tulleth (or Suttie og?)
4-1	80 mins	McLellan
5-1	83 mins	Lawson pen

Recent North / Tayside Region Cup Finals				
Season	**Winners**	**Runners Up**	**Score**	**Venue**
1988/9	Deveronside	Downfield	1-0	North End Park, Dundee
1989/90	Downfield	Banks o' Dee	2-1	Heathryfold Park, Aberdeen
1990/1	Downfield	Bon Accord	2-0	North End Park, Dundee
1991/2	Tayport	Forfar West End	2-0	North End Park, Dundee
1992/3	Forfar West End	Islavale	4-2	The Haughs, Turriff
1993/4	St Josephs	Downfield	3-1	North End Park, Dundee
1994/5	Tayport	Violet	4-2	North End Park, Dundee
1995/6	St Josephs	Downfield	2-1	North End Park, Dundee
1996/7	St Josephs	Tayport	2-1	North End Park, Dundee
1997/8	St Josephs	Dundee North End	0-0, 5-4 pens	Glenesk Park, Dundee
1998/9	Kirrie Thistle	Inverurie Locos	3-2	Heathryfold Park, Aberdeen
1999/00	Tayport	Lochee United	1-0	North End Park, Dundee
2000/1	Dundee North End	Broughty Athletic	2-2, 3-0 pens	Strathmore Park, Forfar
2001/2	Tayport	Sunnybank	5-1	Keith Park, Aberdeen
2002/3	Tayport	Dundee North End	3-0	Glenesk Park, Dundee
2003/4	Tayport	Lochee United	3-1 aet	North End Park, Dundee
2004/5	Tayport	Carnoustie Panmure	3-1	North End Park, Dundee
2005/6	Lochee United	Montrose Roselea	3-2	North End Park, Dundee
2006/7	Montrose Roselea	Forfar West End	1-1, 10-9 pens	Station Park, Forfar
2007/8	Forfar West End	Carnoustie Panmure	3-2	Westview Park, Kirriemuir
2008/9	Sunnybank	Blairgowrie	2-2, 4-3 pens	Hillhead, Aberdeen
2009/10	Sunnybank	Broughty Athletic	4-0	North End Park, Dundee
2010/1	Dundee North End	Broughty Athletic	3-2	Downfield Park, Dundee
2011/2	Jeanfield Swifts	Culter	3-0	Heathryfold Park, Aberdeen
2012/3	Jeanfield Swifts	Montrose Roselea	3-0	Whitton Park, Broughty Ferry
2013/4	Lochee United	Luncarty	1-1, 4-3 pens	Tannadice Park, Dundee
2014/5	Tayport	Dundee North End	4-1	Tannadice Park, Dundee
2015/6	Lochee United	Jeanfield Swifts	1-1, 4-2 pens	Tannadice Park, Dundee
2016/7	Broughty Athletic	Tayport	5-1	Tannadice Park, Dundee

WEST JUNIORS

The West Region has existed in its present format since 2002 when the Ayrshire and Central Regions were merged. The current League structure is as follows:

SUPER PREMIER LEAGUE (12, play 2x)
Two teams relegated
One team in relegation Play Off against third placed Super First club

SUPER FIRST LEAGUE (14, play 2x)
Two teams promoted, third in play off against third bottom in Super Premier
Four teams relegated

CENTRAL DIV ONE (15, play 2x)
Two teams promoted
Three teams relegated

AYRSHIRE LEAGUE (11, play 2x)
Two teams promoted

CENTRAL DIVISION TWO (12, play 2x)
Three teams promoted

WEST JUNIORS 2017/18				
SUPER PREMIER	**SUPER FIRST**	**AYRSHIRE**	**CENTRAL 1**	**CENTRAL 2**
Arthurlie	Camuslang Rangers	Annbank United	Benburb	Ashfield
Auchinleck Talbot	Cumbernauld United	Ardeer Thistle	Blantyre Vics	Bellshill Athletic
Beith	Darvel	Ardrossan Winton Rovers	East Kilbride Thistle	Carluke Rovers
Clydebank	Irvine Meadow	Craigmark Burntonians	Forth Wanderers	Dunipace
Cumnock	Kello Rovers	Dalry Thistle	Glasgow Perthshire	Gartcairn
Girvan	Kilsyth Rangers	Irvine Vics	Greenock	Johnstone Burgh
Glenafton Athletic	Largs Thistle	Lugar Boswell Thistle	Lesmahagow	Lanark United
Hurlford United	Larkhall Thistle	Maybole	Neilston	Newmains United
Kilbirnie Ladeside	Maryhill	Muirkirk	Port Glasgow	Royal Albert
Kilwinning Rangers	Petershill	Saltcoats Vics	Rossvale	St Anthony's
Kirkintilloch Rob Roy	Renfrew	Whitletts Vics	Shotts Bon Accord	Vale of Clyde
Pollok	Rutherglen Glencairn		St Rochs	Vale of Leven
	Shettleston		Thorniewood United	
	Troon		Wishaw	
			Yoker Athletic	

At the 2017 West Region AGM a proposal was put forward for League Reconstruction for season 2018/19. In essence this proposed a four-division vertical structure with no regionalisation. The Ayrshire and Central Divisions would disappear with all clubs involved in trans-regional divisions.

The motion was approved, as was an amendment which introduced an element of play-offs for season 2016/17. Larkhall Thistle made this proposal, arguing that otherwise there would not be much (or indeed anything) fior some clubs to play for during 2016/17.

The framework for season 2016/17 is shown on the following page.

West Region Season 2016/17—What clubs are playing for . . .

SUPER PREMIER

1 1st tier (Premiership)
2 1st tier
3 1st tier
4 1st tier
5 1st tier
6 1st tier
7 1st tier
8 1st tier
9 1st tier
10 1st tier
11 play-off v Super First Team
12 play-off v Super First Team

SUPER FIRST

1 1st tier (premiership)
2 1st tier
3 1st tier
4 1st tier
5 play-off v Super Premier Team
6 play-off v Super Premier Team
7 2nd tier (Championship)
8 2nd tier
9 2nd tier
10 2nd tier
11 2nd tier
12 2nd tier
13 play-off v Central First or ADL Team
14 play-off v Central First or ADL Team

AYRSHIRE DISTRICT LEAGUE

1 2nd tier (Championship)
2 2nd tier
3 2nd tier
4 play-off v Super First Team
5 3rd tier (League One)
6 3rd tier
7 3rd tier
8 4th tier (League Two)
9 4th tier
10 4th tier
11 4th tier

CENTRAL FIRST

1 2nd tier (Championship)
2 2nd tier
3 2nd tier
4 play-off v Super First Team
5 3rd tier (League One)
6 3rd tier
7 3rd tier
8 3rd tier
9 3rd tier
10 3rd tier
11 3rd tier
12 3rd tier
13 4th tier (League Two)
14 4th tier
15 4th tier

CENTRAL SECOND

1 3rd tier (League One)
2 3rd tier
3 3rd tier
4 4th tier (League Two)
5 4th tier
6 4th tier
7 4th tier
8 4th tier
9 4th tier
10 4th tier
11 4th tier
12 4th tier

McBookie.com West Junior Super League Premier Division 2016/17

	ART	AUC	BEI	CUM	GLE	HUR	LAD	KWG	KRR	LAR	POL	TRO
Arthurlie		Aug 27 0-4	Mar 18 1-4	Sep 17 3-1	Apr 29 1-1	Dec 3 4-5	Jan 7 4-3	May 6 3-1	Dec 10 0-2	Oct 1 4-2	Jan 28 1-6	Nov 5 3-0
Auchinleck Talbot	Sep 24 1-0		Nov 12 1-1	Oct 1 3-0	Apr 26 0-1	Oct 29 2-0	Dec 10 0-1	May 22 0-2	Mar 25 1-0	Feb 4 2-1	Mar 11 2-1	May 13 1-0
Beith	Dec 17 2-0	May 20 3-0		Aug 27 2-0	Apr 8 1-1	Apr 19 1-3	Jan 28 2-2	Apr 22 3-1	May 13 0-0	Apr 15 3-2	Oct 1 2-2	Jan 7 3-1
Cumnock	Nov 26 1-2	Apr 1 0-1	Feb 4 2-2		Jan 7 0-1	Nov 12 1-1	Jan 21 3-1	Oct 8 4-1	Sep 3 2-4	Sep 10 4-0	Dec 10 3-1	Oct 22 2-0
Glenafton Athletic	May 13 2-0	Sep 17 3-1	Oct 8 1-3	Oct 29 1-1		May 6 0-1	Mar 11 3-1	Dec 17 1-0	May 27 0-2	Mar 4 4-1	Aug 27 1-0	May 17 2-1
Hurlford United	Jan 21 0-1	Apr 29 2-2	Feb 18 2-2	Apr 22 0-6	Nov 5 2-3		Sep 17 0-0	Aug 27 2-0	Jan 7 1-1	Dec 10 0-2	Apr 15 2-0	Oct 1 4-4
Kilbirnie Ladeside	Sep 3 1-1	Mar 4 0-1	Apr 1 0-0	Nov 19 0-0	Sep 10 0-3	Dec 17 2-2		Oct 1 1-2	Nov 12 0-2	Oct 22 5-0	Jan 14 3-1	Dec 3 2-1
Kilwinning Rangers	Jan 14 1-2	Nov 5 0-1	Dec 10 3-1	Apr 15 1-1	Sep 3 1-1	Apr 8 2-2	Feb 4 1-3		Sep 10 1-2	Jan 7 0-1	May 13 1-0	Mar 4 3-0
Kirkintilloch Rob Ro	Apr 15 2-0	May 6 0-0	Nov 5 0-2	Dec 17 1-0	May 20 0-2	Oct 8 4-2	Apr 29 0-1	Dec 3 5-1		Aug 27 3-2	Sep 17 3-2	Apr 22 3-1
Largs Thistle	Nov 12 4-3	Jun 12	Jan 14 0-1	Dec 3 0-1	Apr 1 4-1	Sep 3 0-1	Feb 25 4-1	Sep 17 1-3	Jan 21 1-2		Oct 29 1-4	Nov 19 2-1
Pollok	Oct 8 2-0	Jan 7 2-0	Mar 25 2-2	Nov 5 4-0	Nov 12 1-2	Sep 10 2-2	Feb 18 1-1	Apr 1 2-3	Apr 24 1-1	Dec 17 4-1		Sep 3 3-1
Troon	Sep 10 2-3	Dec 17 0-3	Apr 29 2-4	Jan 14 2-4	Dec 10 0-1	Feb 4 2-3	Aug 27 3-1	Nov 12 2-1	Oct 29 1-0	Oct 8 3-1	Jan 21 1-0	

		P	W	D	L	F	A	GD	PTS
1	**Glenafton Athletic**	22	14	4	4	35	21	14	46
2	Kirkintilloch Rob Roy	22	13	4	5	37	21	16	43
3	Beith Juniors	22	11	9	2	44	26	18	42
4	Auchinleck Talbot (C)	22	12	4	6	26	17	9	40
5	Hurlford United	22	7	9	6	37	41	-4	30
6	Cumnock Juniors (P)	22	8	5	9	36	31	5	29
7	Arthurlie	22	9	2	11	36	47	-11	29
8	Pollok	22	7	5	10	41	33	8	26
9	Kilbirnie Ladeside	22	6	7	9	29	34	-5	25
10	Kilwinning Rangers (P)	22	7	3	12	29	38	-9	24
11	*Largs Thistle (P)*	*22*	*6*	*1*	*15*	*30*	*50*	-20	19
12	*Troon*	*22*	*5*	*1*	*16*	*28*	*49*	-21	11

Promotion / Relegation Play Off

May 31st
Kilsyth Rangers v Kilwinning Rangers
0-1

June 2nd
Kilwinning Rangers v Kilsyth Rangers
2-2

Aggregate
Kilsyth Rangers v Kilwinning Rangers
2-3

Auchinleck Talbot's domination of the West Juniors was broken as they slumped to fourth in the table. Neighbours Glenafton Athletic won the title and also lifted the Scottish Cup for a memorable double. Kirkintilloch Rob Roy, still ground sharing with Cumbernauld United, had an excellent season and finished second.

Troon were relegated by some distance with their neighbours Largs Thistle also dropping down. Kilwinning Rangers avoided making it a North Ayrshire treble by beating Kilsyth Rangers in the Play Offs.

WEST SUPER LEAGUE ALL TIME PLACES	2002-3	2003-4	2004-5	2005-6	2006-7	2007-8	2008-9	2009-10	2010-11	2011-12	2012-13	2013-14	2014-15	2015-16	2016-17
Arthurlie		2	2	10	3	7	7	2	2	7	6	9	9	9	7
Ashfield										6	10				
Auchinleck Talbot	10	8	3	1	2	4	4	3	3	3	1	1	1	1	4
Beith						5	3	1	7	5	11		6	7	3
Bellshill Athletic			6	9	9	9	9	11							
Benburb	12														
Clydebank										4	3	4	12		
Cumnock	9	4	7	5	6	10	11		9	9	9	5	11		6
Glenafton Athletic	3	5	9	8	10	6	10				4	6	4	6	1
Hurlford United												3	2	2	5
Irvine Meadow	11					2	1	4	1	1	5	2	3	12	
Johnstone Burgh	5	9	10	11											
Kilbirnie Ladeside	6	12						6	8	12		7	8	3	9
Kilsyth Rangers				7	8	12									
Kilwinning Rangers	4	1	11												10
Kirkintilloch Rob Roy							6	8	6	8	7	10		8	2
Lanark United								10	11						
Largs Thistle								7	5	11		12			11
Larkhall Thistle	7	10	5	12											
Maryhill	8	6	4	6	11										
Neilston	2	11			4	8	12								
Petershill					7	3	5	9	10	2	2	8	5	11	
Pollok	1	3	1	3	1	1	2	5	4	19	8	11		5	8
Renfrew			8	2	12										
Rutherglen Glencairn									12						
Shettleston														10	
Shotts Bon Accord				4	5	11					12		10		
Troon		7	12										7	4	12
Vale of Clyde							8	12							

West Super Premier League Playing Squads 2016/17

NB These are not comprehensive lists of players used - there will be some omissions. However, all players listed were associated with the club concerned during 2016/17.

Arthurlie
Manager: Steve Kerrigan (until December), Chris Mackie (from January)
Anton Nugent (ex Rangers, Doncaster R, Stirling Alb, E Stirling, Dumbarton, Kirnintilloch RR, Petershill, Albion R, Ashfield, Gartcairn)
Brian Turner
Chris Mackie (ex Albion R, Cumbernauld Utd, Carluke R, Shotts BA, Alloa, Forfar Ath, Dumbarton, Clydebank, Kirkntilloch RR, St Anthonys, Beith, Petershill, Bo'ness Utd)
Craig Palmer
Darren Gribben
Daryl Convery
David Morrison
Eddie McTernan
Gary Bishop
Gary Carroll
Gary Smith (ex Q Park, Motherwell, Dumbarton, Stenhousemuir, Shettleston)
Gavin Rushford
Graham Girvan (ex Rangers, Ross Co, Clyde, Arbroath, Petershill, Irvine M)
Grant Hay (ex Q Patk, E Stirling, Maryhill)
Ian Nimmo
John Gemmell
Jordan Chisholm
Jordan Leyden (ex Partick Th, E Fife)
Josh Graham
Kevin Macklin
Keiran Brannan (ex Celtic, Spartak Trnava, Arbroath, Armadale Th)
Mark Blakey
Martin Curran
Michael Fulton
Michael MacNeil
Ross Munday
Ryan Deas (ex Largs Th, Arthurlie, Pollok, Kirkintilloch RR, Irvine M)
Ryan McGregor
Scott Gair (ex St mirren, Stenhousemuir, Berwick R, Pollok, Kilbirnie L)

Auchinleck Talbot
Manager: Tommy Sloan
Assistant: Allan McLuckie, Mick McGinn
Andy Leishman (2010 Lugar BT, ex Kello R)
Brian Hewitt (2015 Dalry Th, Ex Beith, Neilston, Irvine M)
Bryan Young (2005 Ross Co)
Craig McCracken (2016 Ayr Utd)
Danny Boyle (2016 Kirkintilloch RR)
Dwayne Hislop (2012 Annbank United)
Dylan Pooler (2016 St Mirren, ex Kilmarnock)
Dylan Stevenson (2016 Morton, ex Ayr Utd, Dalry Th, Berwick R)
Gordon Pope (2014 Ayr United,

ex Dundee Utd, Montrose)
Graham Wilson (2012 Cumnock, ex Dumbarton)
James Latta (2004 Ayr Utd)
Keir Millikan (2011 Irvine M)
Klark Thompson (2016 Lugar BT)
Mark Shankland (2014 Ayr Utd, ex Albion R)
Martin McGoldrick (2010 Maryhil, ex Albion Rl)
Neil McPherson (2016 Darvel)
Ross Harvey (2016 Geelong, Ex Rangers, Brechin C, Dumbarton, Penicuik Ath, Inglewood Utd, Brisbane Force, Johnstone Burgh))
Stephen Wilson (2015 Troon)
Steven White (2016 Annbank Utd)
Willie Lyle (2012 Stenhousemuir, ex Ayr Utd, Raith R, Stranraer)

Beith
Manager: John Millar
Calum McBain (2016 Tower Hearts)
Calum Watt (ex Hurlford Utd),
Cameron Elliot,
Connor McGlinchey (ex Hamilton Acc, Berwick Rangers, Peterhead, Team Wellington, Arthurlie),
Darren Christie (ex Neilston, St Peters)
David McGowan (ex Livingston, Arbroath, Clyde, Montrose),
Euan Clarke (ex Johnbstone Burgh U21, OL to Neilston 2016/17)
Iain Fisher (ex Ayr Utd, Ardrossan Winton Rovers, Largs Thistle, Hurlford United),
Jamie Wilson (ex Hurlford Utd).
John Sheridan (ex Neilston),
Josh McArthur (ex St Mirren, Ayr Utd),
Kenny McLean (ex Hillwood BC, Morton),
Kevin MacDonald (ex Kirkintilloch RR, Irvine M, Kilbirnie L),
Mark McLaughlin (ex Arthurlie, Clyde, Hamilton Acc, Morton, Dumbarton),
Nicky Docherty (ex Drumchapel United),
Paul Frize (ex Glasgow Perthshire),
P McMenamin
Richard Burke,
Ross McPherson (ex Airdrie, Clydebank, Irvine Meadow, Queen's Park),
Stephen Grindlay (ex Celtic, Newcastle United, Grimsby Town, Dumbarton, QOS, Ayr United),
Thomas Collins (ex Queen's Park, St Mirren Youth, Total Soccer),
Tommy Martin (ex Clydebank)
S Wilson
J Bradley
J McArthur

Cumnock
Manager: John McKeown
Darren Johnstone (2015 Troon, Ex Ex Ayr Utd, Girvan, Whitletts Vics)
Keiran Wood (2016 Ayr Utd, Ex St Mirren, Stranraer)
Steven Crawford (2013 Arthurlie, Ex Ayr Utd, Hurlford Utd)
James Lundie (2012 Arthurlie, ex beith, Auchinleck T)
Paul Burns (ex QOS, Dunfermline Ath)
Stephen McKenna (ex Rangers, QOS, Airdrie)
Sean McKenzie (2017 Ayr United)
Mark Williams
Ray Montgomery (2013 Auchinleck T, ex Q Park, Stranraer, Kilbirnie L)
Keir Samson
Adam Hunter (ex Arbroath, Ayr Utd, Rangers)
Scott Anson (2016 Shettleston, ex Hamilton Accies, Kilmarnock, Montrose, Annan Ath, Bo'ness Utd, Petershill, Neilston, Cumnock)
Calum McRobbie
Andrew Muir
TJ Shirkie (ex Kilmarnock U20, Mauchline BC, Catrine Thistle)
D McMaster
Adam Forsyth (2017 Troon)
Jordan Morton
Derek Esplin (ex Eastfield, Blantyre Vics, Rutherglen Glencairn)
Josh Watt
Christopher Thomson
Fraser Bryden
Nathan Porte
Louis Kerr

Glenafton Athletic
Manager: Craig McEwan
Brian McGarrity (ex Annbank Utd, Auchinleck Talbot)
Blair Lochhead (2016 Albion R, ex Q Park)
Kyle McAusland (2016 Alloa, ex Dunfermline Ath, Ayr Utd, Brechin C, Rangers)
Andrew Hunter (2016 Bonnyton Th)
Alan Cairns (2013 ex Cumnock, St Mirren, Kilmarnock)
Craig Menzies (2011,)
Ryan McChesney (ex Glenafton Ath Youths)
Chris Meikle (2014 Harmony Row)
Ally Park (2015 Auchinleck Talbot)
David Gray (2016 BSC Glasgow, Ex Clyde, Morton, Dumbarton, Airdrie United, Renfrew, Kilbirnie L, Kilmarnock, Dundee Utd, Kitsap Pumas (USA))
Ryan Borris (2016 Ex Hurlford Utd, Kilbirnie L, Stranraer, Dumbarton, Stirling Albion, Ayr Utd, Raith R)
Daniel Orsi (2014 Ex QOS, Annan Ath)
Cameron Marlow (2016 Q Park, Ex LA Wolves, Los Angeles Galaxy, Ayr United, Lugar BT)
Darren McGill (ex Ayr Utd, Rangers)
Michael McCann (2015 Troon, Ex Annbank U, Auchinleck T, Irvine M)
Joe Andrew (2015 Clydebank, Ex Rutherglen G, Arthurlie, Alloa, Maryhill, Dundee Utd)
John Boyle (2015 Kilbirnie L, ex Arthurlie, Cumnock, Irvine M)
Chris Dallas (2016 Arthurlie, Ex Albion R, EK Thistle, Albion R)
John Carter (2017 Q Park, ex Sturry FC, Canterbury City, Gibshill, Greenock Juniors)

Hurlford United
Manager: Darren Henderson
Alistair Brown (2013 Ayr Utd, ex Hibernian, Cowdenbeath, Raith R, Stenhousemuir, Forfar Ath)
Ryan Donnelly
Darren Moffat (2016 Ross Co, ex Livingston)
Ross Brash (2016 Shotts BA, Ex Stenhoseumuir, Beith,)
Ross Robertson
Michael Kelly
Paul Byrne
Richie McKillen
Tony Marenghi
Mark Roberts
Adam Hodge
Martin Brown
Ross Fisher
Glen Mitchell
Craig Molloy (2016 Brechin C, ex St Mirren, Stirling Albion, Stenhousemuir)
Paul McKenzie
Danny Mitchell (2013 Glenafton Ath, Ex Stranraer)
Chris Murchie
Stewart Kean (2013 Stenhousemuir, ex Craigmark B, Ayr Utd, St Mirren, QOS, Morton)
Dean Agnew (2017 Kilwinning Rangers, ex Stranraer, Wigtow
Stuart McColm (2016 Annan A
Ex QOS, Threave R, Stranraer, Clyde)
Chris Robertson
Ross Chisholm (2014 Arbroath ex Hibernian, Shamrock R, Darlington, Dundee, Shumen 2010)
John Gemmell

Kilbirnie Ladeside
Manager: Steven Swift
Assistant: Mark CameronCoaches: Gavin Dunc
Billy Peacock
Adam Forde
Chris Malone
Ciaran Donnelly
Ciaran McElroy (2016 Q Park, Campsie BW, Clydebank, Petershill)
David Anderson (ex Q Park)
David Green (2016 Blantyre V ex Knightswood Juvs, Q Park, Nairn County, Clydebank, Petershill)
Edward McTernan
Gavin Duncan
Ian Gold
Ian Gray
Kieran Brannan (2015 Annan Ath, ex Dumbarton, Clyde, Albion R, Arthurlie)
Kieran Hughes (2015 Albion R Q Park, St Mirren)
Kyle Maxwell
Kyle Rafferty (2015 Arthurlie, Stranraer)
Mark Staunton (2015 Stirling Albion, ex Celtic, Charlton At Falkirk, Berwick R, E Fife, Bei Stranraer, Irvine M)
Martin Grehan
Mike O'Byrne (2015 Linlithg R, ex Dundee Utd, Dumbart Albion R, Livingston, Airdrie, Stirling Albion)
Paul Harkins
Ryan Haxton
Steven Meechan (2014 Linlithgow Rose, ex Mother Albion R, Kettering Town, Bishopmill Utd, Kirkintilloch

Kilwinning Rangers
Manager: Chris Strain Assis
Jim McLeod Coac
Stuart Wilson
Adam Strain (2015 Beith, ex Auchinleck T, Q Park)
Barry Fleeting
Ben Lewis

Bryan Boylan
Calvin Kemp
Carlo Monti (2016 Pollok, ex Celtic, Morton, Kings Park, Drumchapel Utd, Pollok, Dundee, Zebbug Rangers, Qormi)
Craig Burns
Darren McLean
Darren Moffat
Dean Agnew
Findlay Frye (2016 Pollok, ex Ardrossan WR, Kirkintilloch RR, Irvine M, Glenafton Ath)
Graeme Barbour (2016 Kirkintilloch RR, ex Dumbarton, Glenafton, Dalry Th, Renfrew, Arthurlie, Benburb)
Grant Bolton
Ian Cashmore (2011 Girvan, ex Kilwinning R, Ayr Utd, Stirling Albion, Glenafton, Stranraer, Cumnock)
Isaac Kerr
Joe Coleman
Jordan Cairney (2016 Morton, ex Ardrossan WR, E Stirling)
Lewis Morrison
Liam McGuinness
Michael Morris
Ricky Hanvey (2015 Cumnock, ex Troon, Whitletts)
Ryan Clark
Sam McCloskey (2016 Stranraer OL, ex Bonnyton Th, Stranraer, Kilbirnie L)
Tommy Maitland

Kirkintilloch Rob Roy
Manager: Stewart MaxwellAssistant: Gordon MoffatCoaches: Kevin Finlayson, John Doyle, Brian McNeil
Jordan Brown
Michael McKinven (2016 Linlithgow R)
Scott Walker (2016 Blantyre V)
Daniel McKenzie
David Barr (2014 Petershill)
Kevin Green (ex Airdrie, Albion R, Arthurlie, Blantyre V)
Craig Buchanan (2016 E Kilbride)
Luke Whelan (2015 Harmony Row)
Sean McCall (2016 Tower Hearts)
Jordan McGuire (2015 Tower Hearts)
Shaun Fraser (2016 Irvine M)
Gary McMenamin (ex Annan Ath, Cumnock)
Luke Whelan
Reece Pearson (2015 Yoker Ath)
Lee Gallacher (2015 Partick Th)
Liam Crichton (2016 Wishaw)
Chris Duff (ex CDampsie Minerva, Campsie BW)
William Sawyers (2015 Irvine M)
Kevin Watt (2014 Clyde)
Gavin Mackie (ex Cumbernauld Utd, Jeanfield Swifts, Bankfoot Ath)
Amadou Kassarate (2016 Dumbarton OL, Senegal U20 Cap)

Largs Thistle
Manager: Bryan Slavin (until Oct), Stuart "Arnie" Davidson (from Oct)
Assistant: Drew Walsh (until Oct), Kevin Struthers (from Oct)
Adam Paterson-McKeen
Alan Gilbride (ex Morton, Stenhousemuir)
Alex McWaters
Caleb Reid
Edward Walton (2011 Irvine M, ex Port Glasgow, Largs T)
Garry Fleming
Glenn Thomson (2013 Dumbarton, ex Albion R)
Iain Fisher
Jay Little
John Tennant
Kevin Struthers
Laurie McMaster
Nicholas Jamieson (2014 Morton, ex Gourock Juvs)
Creag Little (2012 Morton, Ex St Mirren)
Jaime McDonald
Ciaran Friel
Kristofer Littler
Robert Love
Bryan Slavin
Matthew Bennett
Lawrence McMahon
Matthew Ashe
James Marks
Sean Graham
Ross Lundy (2015 Saltcoats Vics, ex Q Park, Kilwinning R)
Ross Chesney

Pollok
Manager: Tony McInally
Assistant: Murdo McKinnon
Coaches: Brian Wherlan, Brian Sheldon
Michael Daly (2016 Petershill)
Grant Evans (2016 Irvine Meadow)
Paul Gallacher (2014 Queen's Park)
Tom Hanlon (2011 Shotts BA)
Del Hepburn (2015 Vale of Clyde)
Ben Lawton (2016 Pollok Juvs)
Jordan Longmuir (2014 Colville Park)
Kieran McAleenan (2013 Kirkintilloch RR)
Ross McCabe (2015 Petershill)
Gary McCann (2016 Irvine Meadow)
Allan MacKenzie (2010 Auchinleck T)
Liam Rowan (2016 Stranraer)
Mark Sideserf (2015 Irvine M)
Chris Walker (2009 Shotts BA)
Colin Williamson (2015 Cumnock)
David Winters (2014 Sauchie)
Robbie Winters
Ryan McStay

Troon
Manager: Gordon Burns (until May 2017), Jimmy Kirkwood (from June 2017)
Adam Forsyth
Alistair Semple (2015 Cumnock, ex St Mirren, Glenafton)
Scott Chatham
Chris McKnight (2015 Cumnock, ex Dalry Th)
Colin Spence (2015 Auchinleck T, ex Gretna)
Dale Keenan (2016 Stranraer, ex Celtic, Partick Th, E Fife, Ayr Utd,)
Dale Moore (2012 Ayr Utd, ex Troon)
Dean Keenan (2012 Ayr Utd, ex Clydebank, Pollok, Morton, Kirkintilloch RR)
Evan Maley
Gareth Armstrong (2012 Ayr Utd)
Gavin Collins (2013 Auchinleck T, ex Darvel)
Jordan Muir
Mark Curragh (2016 Troon U17)
Martin Fraser
Morgan Brown
Ross Barbour (2016 Stranraer, ex Hamilton Accies, Kilmarnock,, Kirkintilloch RR)
Ross McCrea
Ross Robertson
Ryan Nisbet (2016 Ayr Utd, ex Cumnock)
Zak Simpson

McBookie.com West Junior Super League First Division 2016/17

	BLA	CLY	CUM	GIR	MEA	VIC	KIL	MAR	PET	REN	RUT	SHE	SHO	YOK
Blantyre Vics		Jan 7	Aug 27	Jan 28	Oct 8	Apr 15	May 17	Sep 17	Mar 25	Apr 26	Mar 11	Apr 22	Apr 24	Feb 18
		1-4	3-3	1-6	0-1	1-2	0-3	6-1	2-8	0-0	1-2	2-1	2-3	0-0
Clydebank	Oct 1		Apr 15	May 6	Mar 11	Jan 21	Dec 17	May 13	Nov 5	Dec 3	Feb 18	May 20	Sep 3	Sep 10
	0-0		3-0	2-1	0-1	2-1	1-4	5-0	5-2	1-2	0-2	4-1	3-0	3-4
Cumbernauld United	May 24	Dec 10		Oct 1	Oct 29	Sep 10	Apr 24	May 17	Apr 8	Mar 25	May 22	Apr 26	Jan 7	Sep 3
	3-1	1-5		2-2	0-3	4-3	2-2	0-0	0-3	3-2	1-1	3-2	3-6	0-4
Girvan	Sep 10	Oct 8	Dec 17		Dec 10	Mar 11	Apr 1	May 22	Apr 22	May 20	Feb 11	Feb 18	May 13	Nov 5
	1-0	3-4	2-0		3-2	4-0	2-2	3-0	1-0	1-0	0-3	6-1	4-1	3-1
Irvine Meadow	Mar 4	Aug 27	Jan 14	Apr 15		Oct 1	Nov 12	Nov 5	Dec 17	Apr 24	Sep 10	Apr 1	Feb 4	May 13
	1-0	1-2	3-0	0-0		3-1	4-1	2-1	1-1	0-1	1-1	3-0	2-0	2-1
Irvine Victoria	Sep 3	Sep 17	Feb 18	Oct 29	Mar 18		Oct 8	Apr 29	Jan 28	Jan 7	Apr 22	Dec 10	Apr 8	Dec 3
	0-3	1-1	0-2	1-3	4-1		0-1	2-3	2-2	1-3	0-1	0-1	0-2	2-0
Kilsyth Rangers	Dec 10	Apr 22	Dec 3	Apr 29	Sep 17	May 27		Jan 7	Mar 18	Apr 15	Oct 29	Aug 27	Feb 18	Oct 1
	3-0	0-3	8-0	1-1	3-0	3-1		1-1	1-1	3-2	2-2	2-2	6-0	1-1
Maryhill	May 6	Apr 8	Apr 22	May 10	May 20	May 24	Sep 3		Dec 10	Oct 29	Apr 26	Apr 15	Oct 1	Dec 17
	2-0	3-0	3-0	0-1	2-2	3-2	2-5		2-3	1-0	1-3	1-5	1-2	2-4
Petershill	Oct 29	Apr 29	Oct 8	Jan 7	May 22	Nov 12	May 13	Aug 27		Sep 17	Apr 15	Feb 4	Apr 26	Mar 11
	4-2	1-2	1-2	1-3*	2-0	2-0	5-1	6-0		4-1	2-3	1-0	1-0	3-0
Renfrew	Dec 17	Jan 28	Nov 26	Jan 14	Sep 3	Nov 5	Sep 9	Feb 4	Apr 19		Dec 10	Oct 8	Apr 29	Apr 22
	6-1	2-1	2-3	1-0	2-2	1-0	1-2	2-2	1-1		1-1	0-1	3-0	3-3
Rutherglen Glencairn	Nov 5	Nov 12	Sep 17	Apr 8	Apr 29	Apr 1	Jan 21	Dec 3	Oct 1	Aug 27		Mar 25	Mar 18	Jan 7
	3-0	1-2	1-4	3-1	0-0	2-1	1-1	5-0	2-2	3-1		0-1	4-2	1-1
Shettleston	Nov 12	Sep 24	Nov 5	Dec 3	Jan 7	May 13	Mar 11	Apr 24	Sep 10	Mar 4	Sep 3		Jan 28	Jan 21
	1-2	1-0	3-0	2-1	1-1	3-4	0-4	0-1	2-2	3-1	1-1		1-0	2-1
Shotts Bon Accord	May 20	Mar 25	Apr 1	Aug 27	Apr 22	Dec 17	Nov 5	Apr 19	Dec 3	Mar 11	Oct 8	Sep 17		Apr 15
	0-1	0-2	1-0	1-3	2-0	3-1	0-7	0-1	0-6	0-2	3-2	1-4		0-1
Yoker Athletic	Apr 29	Feb 11	Mar 4	May 27	Apr 8	Aug 27	Apr 26	Oct 8	Jun 3	Apr 1	Nov 19	Oct 29	Dec 10	
	6-4	0-3	0-2	1-4	3-1	2-2	0-0	1-2	0-6	1-3	3-2	3-4	5-3	

* at St Anthonys

ABD

13/6/17 Cumbernauld U v Rutherglen G, 0-1, ABD 15 mins, rain

		P	W	D	L	F	A	W	PTS
1	**Girvan (P)**	*26*	*16*	*4*	*6*	*59*	*30*	29	52
2	**Clydebank**	*26*	*16*	*2*	*8*	*58*	*33*	25	50
3	*Kilsyth Rangers*	26	13	10	3	67	32	35	49
4	Petershill (R)	26	14	6	6	70	33	37	48
5	Rutherglen Glencairn	26	12	9	5	50	32	18	45
6	Irvine Meadow XI (R)	26	11	7	8	37	31	6	40
7	Shettleston (R)	26	12	4	10	43	44	-1	40
8	Renfrew (P)	26	10	6	10	43	38	5	36
9	Cumbernauld United	26	9	5	12	38	64	-26	32
10	Maryhill (P)	*26*	*9*	*4*	*13*	*35*	*60*	-25	31
11	**Yoker Athletic**	*26*	*8*	*6*	*12*	*46*	*58*	-12	30
12	**Shotts Bon Accord**	*26*	*8*	*0*	*18*	*30*	*65*	-35	24
13	**Blantyre Victoria**	*26*	*5*	*4*	*17*	*33*	*64*	-31	19
14	**Irvine Victoria (P)**	26	4	3	19	31	56	-25	15

Girvan secured a second successive promotion to take them to the Super Premier for the first time. Clydebank join them in promotion with Kilsyth Rangers missing out the Play Off.

All three relegated teams failed to bounce back at the firs attempt. Inconsistency was Petershill's main problem bu Irvine Meadow and Shettleston were well off the pace.

Irvine Vics, Shotts Bon Accord, Blantyre Victoria and Yok Athletic were relegated - Yoker will feel hard done by as their performances over the season merited better.

T SUPER FIRST DIVISION ALL TIME PLACES

	2002-3	2003-4	2004-5	2005-6	2006-7	2007-8	2008-9	2009-10	2010-11	2011-12	2012-13	2013-14	2014-15	2015-16	2016-17
bank United				10	8	9	9	9	14						
er Thistle													13		
ossan Winton Rovers										8	13			12	
urlie	1														
ield								8	1			11			
n	4	5	4	4	2							2			
shill Athletic	3	1							12					13	
ourb		11													
tyre Vics														5	13
buslang Rangers	11		10	14											
ebank						8	5	3	2					4	2
bernauld United	10	10	13						9	7	8	5	4	8	9
nock								2						1	
y Thistle								11		14					
pace				13											
Kilbride Thistle					9	7	8	6	6	11					
an					14		4	5	4	13					1
gow Perthshire											11				
afton Athletic								7	3	1					
enock												9	8	11	
ford United	9	8	6	8	11		14		10	10	1				
e Meadow		7	11		1										6
e Vics													11		14
nstone Burgh					10	14									
o Rovers											12				
rnie Ladeside			12			4	2				2				
yth Rangers		4	1				10	13		4	9	10	7	6	3
inning Rangers				7	3	3	13		11			13		3	
ntilloch Rob Roy			8	11		1							3		
ark United							3			12					
s Thistle	12			3	6	5	1				3		9	2	
hall Thistle					12										
mahagow					7	13						14			
ar Boswell T		9	7	9	13										
yhill						11									10
bole			9	12		6	6	12			10	4	6	14	
ston			5	1				14					12		
ershill	6	6	3	2											4
ok													1		
Glasgow							11								
frew	8	2				10	7	4	8	3	7	12			8
herglen Glencairn								1		6	6	7	5	7	5
coats Victoria			14												
ttleston	5	12											2		7
tts Bon Accord	7	3	2				12		7	2		3		9	12
miewood United										5	4	6	14		
on	2			5	5	12						1			
e of Clyde				6	4	2			13						
tletts Victoria								10	5	9	14				
er Athletic											5	8	10	10	11

West Super First Division Playing Squads 2016/17

NB These are not comprehensive lists of players used - there will be some omissions. However, all players listed were associated with the club concerned during 2016/17.

Blantyre Vics
Manager: John Gibson (ex Alloa, Stirling Albion, Morton)
Keiran Coleman
Gary Griffin
Sam McKenzie
Scott Law
Ross McKechnie
Ryan Lockie
Darren McLear
Jordan White
Jack Marriot
Dale Jones
Fraser Allan
Corey Pearson
Scott Law
J Craig
Dale Jones
Danny Grainger
Jordan O'Donnell
Peter Bryne
Peter McMahon
Gary Campbell
Craig Kerr
Martin McLaaughlin
Mark McHendry
Ross Smith

Clydebank
Manager: Kieran McAnespie (ex St Johnstone, Fulham etc)
Alan Frizzell
Alan Vezza
Andy Paterson
Calum Gow
Danny MacKinnon
Hashim Cole
Jamie Darroch
Jamie Lyden
Joel Kasubandi
Johnny Allan
Jordan Shelvey
Josh Lumsden
Kieran McAnespie
Mark Burbridge
Nicky Little
Peter McGill
Phil Barclay
Rab O'Neill
Robbie Halliday
Ross Cameron
Stevie Young

Cumbernauld United
Manager: John Queen (until September), George Shaw (until December), Andy Frame (from January), Assistant: John Paul McBride (from January)
Conor McArdle
Murray Loudon (ex Airdrie)
John Higgins (ex Airdrie)
Paddy McCabe

Jamie Watson
Connor O'Boyle
John Higgins
Ryan Sullivan
Joe Bunch
Tony Stevenson
Simon Eeles
Ryan Tiffoney
Scott Upton
Craig Johnston
Wallace
Scott McHaffie
Billy Robb
David Dickson
Alan Clark
Scott Murphy
Ross Foley
Mike McLaughlin
Dylan McGuigan (2017 E Stirling)
Tony Stevenson
David Hamilton
Terry Hewitt
Kieran Brown
David Buchanan
Chris Lennon
James Brown
James McGowan

Girvan
Manager: Peter Leonard
Andy Stevenson
Connor Gracie
Craig Reid
David Cunningham
David Jardine
Jack McDowall
John Frame
Marc Cameron
Mark Doolan
McCulloch
McTaggart
Michael Mossie
Michael Reilly
Robert Paterson
Ryan McCubbin
Scott Dinwoodie
Scott Irvine
Scott Johnstone
Sean Robertson
Steven McCreadie
Tony Murphy

Irvine Meadow
Manager: Gareth Turner / Michael Wardrope Coach: Neil McGowan
Andrew Cripps
Andrew Strachan
Ben Black
Ben Carson
Chris McKnight
Connor Browning
Graham Boyd
Graham Muir
Grant Weir
Greg Vernon
Ian Seymour
James Cuthbertson
Jared Willet
Joseph Young
Lee McCrea
Mark McLennan
Mark Murray
Neil McGowan
PJ Doolan
Ryan Begley
Scott Purdie
Shaun Newman
Stuart Hannah

Irvine Victoria
Manager: Stevie Wilson
Assistant: Neil Greenwood-
Coach: Graham Hamill
Eddie Ablohr
Jamie Anderson
Callum Davidson
Kieran Hollis
Graeme Longair
Kevin Adam
Scott Chesney
Cameron Hambleton
Robert Kirkland
Martin McDonald
David Adams
Jordan Craig
Andrew Hislop
Chris Lamb
Mark McRobert
Sean Mears
Darren Russell
Carlo Scaramuzza
Ryan Singleton
George Thomson
David Wilson
Paul Young

Kilsyth Rangers
Manager: Keith Hogg
Assistant: Kevin McBrideCoaches: Alan Mackin, Steven Kidd
Andy Carlin
Michgael Duke
Paul Boyle
Kevin McBride
David McWilliams
Chris Reid
Mark Tyrell
David Waters
Gary Kelly
Michael McGhee
Corey Pearson
Damon Welsh
Scott Davidson
Franny Kelly
Gary Livingstone
Paul McBride
Nicky Prentice
Keith Hogg

Maryhill
Manager:
Jack Baker
Andy Banks
Joe Beckley
Justin Begg
Paul Coyle
Jamie Docherty
Craig Ferguson
Shaun Fraser
Kieran Fury
David Green
Gordon Ion
Ross Kearns
Jordan McGrotty (ex Partick Th)
Dyman McLaughlin
Ross McLean
Lee McLelland
Paul McLernon
Kyle McQueen
Andy Monaghanm
David Murray
Allan Orr
Frankie Owens
Eddie Walton
Gareth Watson

Petershill
Co Managers: William Paterson and Paul Kelly,
Coaches: Scott Black and Terry Waters
Francis Hughes
Michael White
Steven McNeil
Ciaran Friel
Fraser McGhee
Chris Wilson
Peter Bradley
Chris Ketterer
Fraser Chisholm
Jordan Kennedy
Kevin Nicoll
Atli Jhansson
Paul Murphy
Paul Callander
Liam Finnigan
Jordan Murch
Alex Cassells
Luke Crerand
Connor Stevenson
Stuart McCann
Kevin Kelly
Ian Gold
Chris Hall
Jason Hardie
Graeme Hearton
Stephen McGladrigan

Renfrew
Managers: Martin Ferry and Colin Clark
Coach: Jimmy Quigley
Dale Burgess
Danny McLeay
Fraser Barbour
David Gordon
Anton Heffron
Kieran Healey
Bryan Mulgrew
Martin Brogan
Martin McInnes
Euan Ramsay
Lee Cochrane
Jamie Benton
Marc McDaid
Sean Fitzharris
Ross Hocknull
Adam Nisanci
Paddt O'Keefe
Colin Forbes
Scott Morton
Chris Zok
Gary McGarroch
Darren Jones
Gregor Wylie

Rutherglen Glencairn
Manager: Willie Harvey
Assistant: Joe Pryce
Coach: Alan Colquhoun
Alan Muir
Andy Neil
Anthony Dempsey
Brian Eadie
Craig McGregor
David Dunnachie
Del McNab
Dean Muir
Danny Salah
Fraser Team
Graeme Brown
Jamie Hamilton
Jamie Hunter
Jay McKay
JC Hutchison
Jordan Marshall
Mark McHendry
Rhys Donaldson
Ross McConville
Ryan Bennett
Ryan Docherty
Ryan McArdle
Sean McGuire
Stewart Hall
Tony Fraser

Shettleston
Manager: Peter Weatherson (until Dec)
Assistant: Ryan McStay
Dean Trainor
Gary Whyte
Iain Chisholm
Lewis Kinnaird
Bob Campbell
Ross Dickson
Josh Horne
Greig McDonald
Ryan Scott
Lloyd Kinnaird
Ricky McIntosh
Jordan Dalzell
Stevie Logan
Bob Campbell
Ryan McStay
Jordan Halsman
Chris Kennedy
David Telfer
Jordan Morton
Brian McEwan
Martin Welsh

Shotts Bon Accord
Manager: Kieran McGuinness
Assistant: Paul Finnigan
Ally Martin
Andy Cross
Andy Scott
Barry McGowan
Billy Struthers
B Fraser Jun.
Colin McGraw

or McMullan
r McLeod
y Burns
y McGuinness
Sutherland
Barr
n McPherson
n Eadie
e Brophy
ny Murdoch
than Lindsay
n Campbell
Russell

Kyle Banner
Liam Crichton
Mark Duffy
Max McKee
Paul Doyle
Paul Finnigan
Ryan Kennedy
Sean McKenna
Stephen Maguire
Stuart Livingstone

Yoker Athletic
Manager: Steven Reilly (ex Queen's Park, Stirling Albion, Bo'ness United etc)
Alan Cairns
Andrew Campbell
Andrew Rankin
David Crerand
David Manley
Gareth Watson
Gary Arbuckle
Gary Bissland
Greg Maitland
James Ross
Jamie Carson
Kenny Hadden
Kerr Allan
Liam Campbell
Mark Maxwell
Mark McManus
Michael Bailey
Reece McGillion
Richard Hendry
Ryan Hynes
Scott Smith
Shaun Kelly
Stuart Fyfe

McBookie.com West Junior Ayrshire League 2016/17

	ANN	ARD	AWR	CRA	DAL	DAR	KEL	LBT	MAY	MUI	SAL	WHI
Annbank United		Oct 29	Aug 27	Dec 10	Oct 1	Feb 18	May 13	Apr 15	Jan 7	Apr 19	Sep 17	Dec 3
		4-2	3-4	2-1	2-3	1-2	3-2	5-2	1-2	6-1	3-1	1-0
Ardeer Thistle	Apr 22		Jan 7	Oct 1	Feb 11	Nov 12	Jan 21	Oct 22	Sep 3	Dec 3	Nov 19	Mar 4
	0-2		1-4	2-2	0-3	1-1	2-2	5-1	0-2	4-3	1-2	4-2
Ardrossan Winton Rovers	Jan 14	Nov 4		Sep 3	Feb 18	Sep 10	Oct 1	Nov 19	Apr 1	Apr 8	Dec 17	Jan 28
	2-2	2-0		3-1	4-0	1-1	5-0	9-0	0-1	3-0	3-0	2-3
Craigmark Burntonians	Sep 10	Apr 15	Jan 21		Nov 5	Dec 17	Oct 8	Feb 18	Apr 29	Jan 7	Aug 27	Mar 11
	0-6	3-0	0-4		4-3	0-2	1-2	3-2	1-6	1-3	5-3	0-1
Dalry Thistle	Apr 29	Oct 8	Sep 17	May 6		Apr 22	Aug 27	Dec 17	May 13	Jan 21	Dec 3	Jan 7
	2-2	2-1	2-3	2-3		0-1	4-5	1-0	5-2	2-1	2-1	2-1
Darvel	Oct 8	Mar 25	Feb 4	Sep 24	Dec 10		Jan 7	Apr 1	Jan 21	Apr 29	Mar 18	Aug 27
	1-0	1-0	4-3	5-4	1-0		1-0	6-2	2-1	1-0	6-0	1-6
Kello Rovers	Dec 17	Apr 8	Feb 11	Apr 19	Nov 12	Sep 3		Oct 29	Sep 10	Sep 24	Feb 18	Apr 1
	1-0	3-1	6-1	5-2	3-6	1-1		2-1	4-2	4-1	6-2	3-2
Lugar Boswell Thistle	May 6	Aug 27	Oct 8	Dec 3	Apr 19	Oct 1	Jan 28		Nov 5	Feb 11	Jan 7	Dec 10
	0-3	0-7	0-6	1-4	2-3	2-4	1-2		4-4	1-1	3-2	1-4
Maybole	Sep 24	Dec 17	Dec 3	Oct 29	Apr 15	May 6	Dec 10	Mar 11		Aug 27	Feb 4	Apr 22
	2-3	3-0	2-4	1-0	0-3	1-3	1-2	3-3		3-2	5-1*	2-1
Muirkirk	Nov 5	Mar 11	Dec 10	May 20	Sep 3	May 13	Apr 22	Sep 10	Feb 18		Apr 1	Oct 1
	1-4	1-3	0-4	0-3	0-4	0-5	0-5	0-1	0-5		3-0	1-3
Saltcoats Victoria	Jan 21	Sep 10	Mar 11	Jan 14	Jan 28	Apr 15	Nov 5	Sep 3	Nov 12	Oct 8		Feb 25
	2-3	0-3	0-5	2-3	1-7	0-4	0-1	9-0	2-5	2-1		0-6
Whitletts Victoria	Sep 3	Feb 18	Mar 18	Nov 12	Sep 10	Nov 5	Apr 15	Jan 21	Oct 8	Dec 17	Oct 29	
	3-2	2-3	2-1	2-1	4-1	0-3	1-3	3-1	2-0	4-2	6-0	

* at Dam Park, Ayr, due to fire damage at Maybole

Two of the "less fashionab Ayrshire sides came throu secure promotion. Both cl have hard-working commit and fully deserved to go up

Saltcoats, Muirkirk and Lu were some way adrift of th rest. Prophets of doom su gest that the reconstructior from 2018/19 will hit these clubs hardest. Membershi Ayrshire Junior football has been the most stable of all regions and districts—coul this be about to change?

		P	W	D	L	F	A	W	PTS
1	**Darvel**	*22*	*18*	*3*	*1*	*56*	*23*	33	57
2	**Kello Rovers**	22	16	2	4	62	38	24	50
3	Ardrossan Winton Rovers (I	22	15	2	5	73	28	45	47
4	Whitletts Victoria	22	14	0	8	58	34	24	42
5	Annbank United	22	13	2	7	58	34	24	41
6	Dalry Thistle	22	13	1	8	57	41	16	40
7	Maybole Juniors (R)	22	11	2	9	53	43	10	35
8	Craigmark Burntonians	22	8	1	13	42	57	-15	25
9	Ardeer Thistle	22	7	3	12	40	45	-5	24
10	Saltcoats Victoria	22	3	0	19	30	81	-51	9
11	Lugar Boswell Thistle	22	2	3	17	28	86	-58	9
12	Muirkirk Juniors	22	2	1	19	21	68	-47	7

AYRSHIRE DISTRICT LEAGUE - All Time Positions

	2002-3	2003-4	2004-5	2005-6	2006-7	2007-8	2008-9	2009-10	2010-11	2011-12	2012-13	2013-14	2014-15	2015-16	2016-17
Annbank United	10	4	2							5	8	10	8	9	5
Ardeer Thistle	11	12	11	5	5	9	12	12	8	9	4	2		11	9
Ardrossan Winton Rovers	9	9	3	9	6	5	4	4	1			5	1		3
Craigmark Burntonians	8	8	7	4	7	6	9	6	12	11	11	13	10	7	8
Dalry Thistle	5	13	10	8	3	4	1		2		10	8	9	8	6
Darvel	13	7	9	12	12	11	7	9	5	10	9	6	3	3	1
Girvan			4	2		2					7	7	11	1	
Hurlford United						1		1							
Irvine Meadow				1											
Irvine Victoria	6	3	5	10	9	7	8	8	9	6	5	1		2	
Kello Rovers	4	5	6	6	8	10	6	5	11	2		11	6	6	2
Kilbirnie Ladeside				3	1										
Kilwinning Rangers								2		4	1		2		
Largs Thistle		6	1									4			
Lugar Boswell Thistle	1					8	3	3	7	7	12	3	5	5	11
Maybole	2	1			2				4	1					7
Muirkirk	3	11	8	13	11	13	10	11	10	8	12	12	12	10	12
Saltcoats Victoria	7	2		11	10	12	11	10	3	7	6	9	7	12	10
Troon							5	7	6	3	2				
Whitletts Victoria	12	10	12	7	4	3	2					3	4	4	4

West Super Ayrshire League Playing Squads 2016/17

NB These are not comprehensive lists of players used - there will be some omissions However, all players listed were associated with the club concerned during 2016/17.

Annbank United
Manager: Tam Robertson
Andrew Hainey
Colin Granger
Craig Fisher
David Ballantyne
David Richardson
David White
Grant Kirkwood
Jack Sherrie
Jai Holland
James Hilton
Jamie Ballantyne
Jamie Martin
Lee Sloan
Lyall Cameron
Luke McGowan
MacLean Simpson
Marc Fisher
Roddy Paterson
Rory Tait
Ryan Connelly
Scott Granger
Sean Robertson
Stuart Faulds

Ardeer Thistle
Manager: Derek Gemmell
Assistant: Mark McCann, Gareth Armstrong
Coach: John Colligan
Paul McCann (ex Ardrossan WR, Saltcoats Vi
Dalry Th, Kilbirnie L, Hurlford Utd, Ardeer Th

Kevin Ramsay (ex Ardeer Rovers, Cross Keys, Largs Kintyre, Stevenston Utd)
Stefan Johnstone (2016 Irvine Vics, ex Dalry Th, Ayr Utd)
Jamie Donnelly (Ex Annbank Utd, Glenafton Ath, Craigmark B, Tarbolton, Wallacetoun, Dundee Utd, Kilmarnock)
Michael Holden (ex Ardeer Th, Girvan, Hurlford Utd, Ardrossan WR, Kilwinning R, Dalry Thj, Saltcoats Vics, Largs Th)
Paul McKay (Ex Barrhead YM, Arthurlie, Eastwood Park, Knockentiber, Newton Mearns Rovers, Neilston, brother of Barrie McKay of Rangers)
Gary Nugent (ex Harmony Row, Troon, Glasgow Uni, Tower Hearts)
Jordan Bruce (2014 Ardeer Th U19, Craigmark B)
Scott Reid (2009 Rosehill Star)
Andy Thomson (Ex Edinburgh Uni)
Jack Robertson (2016 Winlinton Wolves, Ex Girdle Toll Utd, Bonnyton Thistle)
Greg Kean (ex Ardrossan Castle Rovers, Saltcoats Vics, Kilwinning SC)
Archie Sewell (2016 Stranraer)
Ryan Morrow (ex St Mirren, Dalry Th)
James Maxwell (ex Partick Th, Ardrossan Castle Rovers, Cunninghame Ams, Ardeer Th)
Lee Munro (ex Dalry Th, Saltcoats Vics, Ardeer Th, KSC Wolves)
Iain Reid (Ex QOS, Kilnbrnie L, Dalry Th, Saltcoats Vics, Redbrae Ath, Glasgow Harp, Ardrossan WR)
Calvin Smith (ex Ardrossan WR, Saltcoats Vics, Kilwinning Rangers U19)
Chris McInnes (ex Stenhousemnuir, Partick Th, Ardrossan Castle Rovers, Saltcoats Vics, Cunninghame Ams)

Ardrossan Winton Rovers
Manager: Sandy MacLeanAssistant: Colin Lindsay
Coach: Stevie O'Neill
Alan Jamieson
Adam Easdon
Andy McGregor
Bobby Colligan
Colin Stevenson
Darren Miller
David McNeil
Dylan Caddis
Gavin Sim
Harry Donaldson
John Mullen
Jordan Cairnie
Kenny Munro
Larry McMahon
Liam Caddis
Luke Irvine
Marc Davidson
Michael Lennox
Reagan Ross
Ross Kearns
Ryan Caddis
Scott Houston
Steve Lamont
Steven Tan
Tom Jamieson

Craigmark Burntonians
Manager: John Redmond
Assistant: Jonny Baillie
Coach: Ian Paterson, Steve Holland
Craig Barrett
Bryce Reid
Jamie Brotherston
Lewis Kirkwood
Mark Dyer
Mark Higgins
Martin Madden
Morgan Brown
Paul Dawson
Paul McCambley
Robbie Graham
Ryan McKay
Ryan McGubbin
Sean Hainey
Stephen McKay
Stewart Steele
William Hall
Andrew Mair
Sam McCrorie
Paul McCambley
Callum Nairn
Bryce Reid
Scott Dempster
Stephen Hopewell
Kieran Nisbet
Graham Swailes
Dylan Thirtle

Dalry Thistle
Manager: Gavin Friels
Blair Lochead
Dylan Connelly
William Slater
Greg Morrison
Christoper McKie
Scott Watson
Scott Peletier
Christoper McGowan
Andrew Brown
Chris McGowan
Shaun Lavery
Kieran McLaughlin
Marc Hood
Martin Stewart
Scott Guy
Mark Archdeacon
Scott Stenhouse
Andrew Hunter
William Boyd
Mark Archdeacon
Kyle Cumming
Jordan Stewart
Craig Marshall
Harris Beech

Darvel
Manager: Scott Clelland
David Markey
Martin Findlay
Alan Orr
Alisdair Gaw
Calum Walsh
Ian McCreadie
Mark Armour
Jamie Henderson
Jordan Ryan
Mark Gilmolur
Murray Johnston
Greg Vernon
Stewart Davidson
Kenny Paris
Fraser Gaul
Josh Caldow
Alan Moodie

Kello Rovers
Manager: Ross Wilson
Ally Smith
Craig Gordon
Declan Hill
Geoff Paterson
Graeme Ramage
Greg Miller
Jack Anderson
Kieran Pagan
Liam Fleming
Liam Weir
Mark McKenna
Martin Shaw
Robert Hampson
Ross Costello
Ross Thomson
Ross Ballantyne
Jordan Quinn
Ryan Dunsmuir
Sean Bennie
Alan Cairns
Scott Caldwell

Lugar Boswell Thistle
Manager: Derek McMurdo
Jim Wilson
McFarlane
Stuart Milligan
Jackson Stevenson
Jack Hannah
Ryan Hutchison
Ian Stewart
Stewart McGarrison
Aarton Watters
James Hart
Steven Shankland
Ronald Davis
Ryan Ross
Adam Lowe
Robbie Crolley
Craig Muir
David Clapperton
Lewis Gardiner

Maybole
Manager: Carlo Walker
Elliot Masterson
Thomas Sloan
Nathan Baird
Nicholas Warren
Stuart Peacock
Damien Bloy
Craig Brown
Alex Bell
Sam Nimmo
Gavin Scott
Fraser McMillan
Dillan Dunn
Callum Walker
Frazer Dempsey
Chris Allan

Muirkirk
Manager: George Grierson
Robbie Wilson
Craig Peck
Paul Millar
Bryce Barrie
Darren McIntyre
Lee Williamson
Chris Wilson
Stephen Campbell
Ross Ballantyne
Steven Hill
Ryan Beveridge
Jordan Burt
Mark Kiltie
Gordon Hume
Sean Murtagh

Saltcoats Victoria
Manager: Derek Frye (until February), Tam McLelland (from February)
Adam Easdon
Ally Patrick
Andrew Tremble
Angus Gault
Billy Arthur
Brett McKenzie
Callum McDade
Callum McLaughlin
Craig Breen
Chris McInnes
Chris Lyon
Chris McKie
Colin Frye
Dale Clark
Darren McMahon
David Anderson
George Bonner
Greg Thomson
Jamie Paton
Jason Kean
Jim Catterson
Joe Young
John Gallagher

Jordan Greenlees
Jordan Stewart
Kieran Hollis
Liam Harkin
Mark Ferris
Martin McDonald
Matthew Santos
McLean Simpson
Michael Hart
Murray Grayston
Paul Weaver
Paul McInnes
Raymond Milligan
Robert Park
Ryan McKie
Scott Houston
Seamus McGrady
Sean Quinn
Shaun Kirkland
Shaun Wark
Simon Johnston
Stephen Reid
Tam McLelland

Whitletts Victoria
Manager: Neil Duffy
Alistair Boyle
Ally McInnes
Aron Dorigo
Blair Anderson
Chris Black
Craig Harvey
Danny Cunningham
Darren Baird
David Mathieson
Jordan Boyd
Jordan Mullen
Josh Sloan
Kris Kerr
Louis Kerr
Niall Kennedy
Paul Cameron
Robert Kirkland
Ross Campbell
Sean Ewart
Tony Balfour

McBookie.com West Junior Central League First Division 2016/17

	BEL	BEN	CAM	FOR	GRE	JOH	LAR	LES	NEI	ROS	STR	THO	VOC	WIS
ellshill Athletic		Apr 19	Jan 28	Oct 8	Feb 11	Mar 11	Apr 15	Jan 7	May 6	Aug 27	Nov 12	May 17	Oct 22	Sep 17
		2-3	2-4	2-4	6-4	4-2	0-3	1-5	0-1	2-3	1-2	1-3	1-1	2-1
enburb	Oct 29		Dec 10	May 13	Oct 8	Dec 17	Jan 7	Apr 22	Apr 1	Feb 4	Feb 25	Sep 10	Jan 14	Mar 11
	4-4		1-9	2-2	5-2	4-0	2-3	4-0	0-2	1-1	1-2	1-3	1-1	4-1
ambuslang Range	Sep 10	Mar 4		Apr 22	Sep 3	Oct 8	Nov 5	Apr 8	Dec 3	Feb 18	Dec 17	Nov 12	Mar 25	Mar 18
	3-2	3-0		3-3	2-0	8-0	4-1	5-0	5-1	2-3	0-1	6-4	4-0	1-2
rth Wanderers	Apr 1	Apr 29	Oct 1		Mar 25	Oct 29	Sep 10	Apr 26	Apr 15	Dec 17	Mar 11	Sep 3	Nov 5	May 17
	4-2	0-4	2-8		0-3	3-2	2-3	2-1	3-0	3-3	0-2	1-3	2-4	2-0
eenock	Apr 8	Feb 18	Jan 7	Sep 17		Mar 18	Oct 29	Apr 15	Apr 22	Nov 12	Oct 1	May 22	Feb 4	Aug 27
	3-2	2-0	1-4	3-1		1-0	1-2	1-2	1-2	1-1	0-4	2-0	3-2	1-0
hnstone Burgh	Nov 5	Aug 27	Feb 11	Apr 8	Sep 10		Oct 1	Jan 21	May 13	Dec 3	Apr 29	Apr 1	Dec 10	Jan 7
	3-5	3-1	1-1	2-0	3-2		2-4	1-1	1-1	1-4	0-2	1-3	0-2	2-2
rkhall Thistle	Dec 3	Sep 17	Mar 11	Apr 19	Dec 17	Feb 18		Oct 8	Sep 3	Dec 10	May 13	Apr 26	Mar 18	Apr 22
	5-1	2-1	2-1	4-1	1-1	2-1		3-4	1-2	2-1	2-1	2-2	5-0	2-3
esmahagow	Apr 29	Dec 3	Aug 27	Mar 18	Nov 5	Sep 17	May 6		May 22	Oct 22	Apr 24	Mar 25	Feb 11	Dec 10
	2-0	4-4	2-3	3-4	0-1	3-1	0-2		2-2	0-2	0-0	2-5	1-3	1-4
eilston	Dec 10	May 17	May 20	Aug 27	May 26	Nov 12	Apr 29	Feb 18		Sep 17	Oct 8	May 24	Jan 7	Jan 21
	4-2	2-1	3-4	3-1	3-1	0-0	3-2	1-2		2-3	3-4	3-2	4-1	2-3
ossvale	Mar 4	Nov 5	May 6	May 27	Feb 25	Jan 28	Apr 8	Sep 3	Mar 18		Sep 10	Oct 1	Apr 22	Mar 25
	2-3	2-2	0-4	5-1	1-2	3-2*	4-5	1-2	4-2		0-2	1-0	3-0	1-0
Rochs	Jan 21	Sep 3	Sep 17	Dec 10	May 20	Nov 19	Mar 25	Oct 29	Apr 26	Jan 7		Mar 18	Aug 27	Apr 15
	2-0	0-3	1-0	2-3	2-2	6-1	1-1	6-2	1-0	0-3		4-2	4-0	3-3
orniewood United	Apr 22	Jan 28	Apr 29	May 6	Apr 24	May 20	Aug 27	Apr 19	Nov 5	Apr 15	Feb 18		Sep 17	Oct 8
	1-2	1-3	3-3	3-2	4-1	3-1	1-2	4-4	1-1	1-1	2-4		4-0	3-2
ale of Clyde	Sep 3	Nov 12	Nov 19	Feb 18	Apr 29	Apr 15	Apr 24	Mar 11	Sep 10	Oct 8	Jan 28	Dec 17		Oct 1
	1-0	1-2	0-4	2-2	1-1	3-1	1-2	2-2	0-1	1-1	1-0	1-1		0-0
ishaw	Feb 18	Apr 8	Oct 29	Apr 24	Jan 28	Sep 3	Nov 12	Sep 10	Dec 17	Nov 19	May 6	May 13	Dec 3	
	2-1	2-3	1-3	4-2	2-1	4-1	1-3	1-0	2-0	2-0	4-2	2-3	1-0	

BD
'11/16 Wishaw v St Rochs, 1-3, 78 mins, player injury
at St Anthonys

'10/16, Lesmahagow v Neilston, order to be replayed as referee blew for time ten minutes early
core 3-1

		P	W	D	L	F	A	GD	PTS
1	**Cambuslang Rangers (P)**	26	18	3	5	94	37	57	57
2	**Larkhall Thistle**	26	18	3	5	66	41	25	57
3	St Roch's	26	16	4	6	58	34	24	52
4	Thorniewood United	26	12	5	9	62	50	12	43
5	Rossvale	26	12	6	8	53	43	10	42
6	Wishaw Juniors	26	13	3	10	49	43	6	42
7	Neilston Juniors	26	12	4	10	48	47	1	40
8	Benburb (P)	26	10	6	10	57	54	3	36
9	Greenock Juniors (R)	26	10	5	11	41	49	-8	35
10	Forth Wanderers (P)	26	8	4	14	50	73	-23	28
11	Lesmahagow Juniors	26	7	5	14	42	63	-21	26
12	**Vale of Clyde**	26	6	8	12	28	50	-22	25
13	**Bellshill Athletic (R)**	26	6	2	18	49	72	-23	20
14	**Johnstone Burgh**	26	2	6	18	31	72	-41	12

. points awrded to Thorniewood for Vale of Clyde
playing player under false name against them
. points were deducted from Vale of Clyde for:
ielding a player under a false name v Thorniewood United (17 December)

West Central Division One Playing Squads 2016/17

NB These are not comprehensive lists of players used - there will be some omissions. However, all players listed were associated with the club concerned during 2016/17.

Bellshill Athletic
Manager: Robert Sneddon
Assistant: Reon Juskowiak
Coaches: Harry Erwin, Gerry McLaughlin, Keiran Dougan
Liam Grant
Chris Fitzpatrick
Michael Brunton
Michael Smith
Richard Kane
Reon Juskowiak
Liam McGuire
Declan brown
Chris McCormack

West Region Central Division One - All Time Positions

	2002-3	2003-4	2004-5	2005-6	2006-7	2007-8	2008-9	2009-10	2010-11	2011-12	2012-13	2013-14	2014-15	2015-16
Ashfield						3	2						14	
Bellshill Athletic										10	9	4	2	
Benburb			11			8	11			5	8	3	12	
Blantyre Victoria	12				9	10		7	13				1	
Cambuslang Rangers		1			11		5	4	5	12		11		
Carluke Rovers			12								7	5	5	12
Clydebank			2	8	2									
Cumbernauld United				5	3	5	6	1						
Dunipace		6	3		10	11		8	9	8	10	7	4	14
East Kilbride Thistle	6	5	6	2							14			
Forth Wanderers														
Glasgow Perthshire	8	12			13			10	6	1		13		
Greenock	3	3	9	10					10	3	1			
Johnstone Burgh							12		12			12		7
Kilsyth Rangers	1								1					
Kirkintilloch Rob Roy	7	2			1									
Lanark United	5	11		6	7	2					6	10	13	
Larkhall Thistle						7	8	12		6	3	6	8	6
Lesmahagow	11			1			9	11			2		6	9
Maryhill							4	13				9	3	2
Neilston									4	4	11	1		11
Port Glasgow		10			4	1		9	8	7	12			
Renfrew													7	1
Rossvale														4
Rutherglen Glencairn	2	9	8	3	5	4	1							
Shettleston			7	12					11	9	4	2		
Shotts Bon Accord								2						
St Anthonys		8	5	9	8	9	7	3	3	11	5	8	11	13
St Rochs	10					12					13			5
Thorniewood United				11			3	6	2					10
Vale of Clyde	9	7	1							14			9	8
Vale of Leven	4	4	10	7	12		10	5	7	13				
Wishaw													10	3
Yoker Athletic			4	4	6	6				2				

Chris Paton
Lee Nichol
Kyle Robertson
Conor McDonald
Andrew Cockerall
Dylan Simpson
Darren Simpson
Stephen Sweeney
Scott Simon

Benburb
Manager:
Scott Somerville
Colin McInnes
Eamonn Connor
Steve Greer
Josh Meechan
Scott Jackson
Kieran Blackwood
Sean Gallagher
Ryan Livingstone
Ryan Metcalfe
Ryan McCrone
Jamie Boyle
Scott Jarvie
Scott Hendry
Andy Wright
Sinclair Soutar

Cambuslang Rangers
Manager: Paul McColl
Assistant: Willie Dobbins
Alessandro Savarese
Alex Smith
Andrew Scanlan
Brian Welsh
Calum Nolan
Chris Faulds
Colin Boylan
Chris Gordon
Dale Simeon
Dyman Hnedry
George Scott
Hal Bohme
Iain Stewart
Jamie McLeod
Jordan Brand
Kieran Chalmers
Kris Gebbie
Liam Gormley
Mark Bishop
Mark Houston
Martin Brogan
Matt Lynch
Neil Newman
Paul McLaughlin
Robert Davidson
Robert Halliday
Ryan McKay
Ryan Scanlan
Ross Gillan
Ryan Kerr
Ryan McBeth
Stuart Davidson
Thomas Kilmartin

Forth Wanderers
Manager: Jamie McKenzie
Assistant Manager: Brian Crawford (until May 2017), Jim Dick (from May 2017 ex St Mirren, Airdrie etc)
David Cherrie
Jason Corbett (2016 Thorniewood Utd, Ex Forth W)
Gary McMullen
Warren Grenfell
Barry McGeechan
Kris Jarvie
Willie McLaren (ex Airdrie, St Johnstone etc)
Taylor Scott
Lachlan Tait
Stephen Tait
John Watson
Martin Hannaway
David Dunn (2016 Cambuslang R, Ex Clyde, Airdrie, Ayr U, Lanrk Utd, Newmains Utd)
Dillon MacDonald (2016 Mill Utd)
Martyn Meek (2016 Gartcairn, Ex Newmains, Vale of Clyde , EK Thistle)
Gerry Ward
Alan Clark
Martin Harty
Craig Gupwell
Roddy Hunter
Kevin Bradley (ex Clyde, Pollok)

Greenock
Manager: Stephen Mooney
Alan Docherty
Allan Williams
Andrew Biddulph
Andrew Irvine
Barri Stanton
Barry McLaughlin
Colin Gailey
Corey Low
Cory Hughes
Craig Brown
Daniel Orr
Darren Patton
Jamie Cunning
John Mitchell
Jonathan Donnelly
Kevin McKay
Kristofer Littler
Mark Downie
Mark Monk
Mark O'Donnell
Martin McGowan
Martin O'Donoghue
Martin Orr
Reece Williamson
Regan Williamson
Robbie Graham
Ross McWilliams
Ryan Craig
Ryan McWilliams
Scott Rodger
Sean Doherty
Simon McBryde
Stephen Dallas
Stephen Mooney
William Easton
William Fleming
William McClure

Johnstone Burgh
Co-Managers: David Brolly and Colin Smith
Kenny Wright
Steven Fitzpatrick
Connor Milne
Chris McCormick
Daniel Finnigan
Jack Herron
Jonathan McStay
Garry McCormick
Steven Brown
Stephen McGarrigle
Liam McGonnigle
Jordan Keaning
Gareth Brown
Derek Carson
Jay Elder
James Usher
Gavin Wallace
Fraser Wilson
Ian Ross
Daniel Smith
Ross Perrie
David Murray
Chris Docherty
Robbie Kelly

Larkhall Thistle
Manager: Dunky Sinclair,
Assistant: Tam McLaughlin
Moss
David Thomson
Andy Brown
Neil Reynolds
Stewart Thomson
Scott Nicholl
Josh Payne
Ryan Innes
Brian Jack
Mark Canning
Davie Reid
Graham Gracie
Matty Clarke
Hugh Kelly
Declan Doyle
Liam Mushett
Gary McStay
Mark McKeever
Paul Burns (to Lanark Utd Jan 2017)
Craig Rutherford

Lesmahagow
Manager: Robert Irving
Assistant: David Jackson
Steven Clark
Mark Fitzpatrick
John McStay
Jack Currie
Johnny Boal
Paul Woodlock
Craig Steele
Jordan Lithgow
Stewart Leishman
Paul McVey
Scott Cumming
Darren Lygate
Daryl MacDonald
Martin Maguire
Ryan Cherrie

Neilston
Co Manager: Martin Campbell and John Paul Dow:
Daniel Bamford
Grant Beattie
Robbie Cameron
Euan Clark
Sean Crumlish
Martin Curren
Allan Diack
James Digney
Stephen Docherty
David Edwards
Ralph Gamba
Ross Geddes
Robbie Graham
Fraser Gunn
Luke Hemphill
Derek Kennedy
Ruaridh Langan
Kieron Magennis
Mark McCuish
Kieran McDade
Marc McDaid
Martin McLachlan
Chris McQuade
Ian Nixon
Chris Noon
Allan Orr
John Paterson
Craig Patterson
Robert Payne
Matthew Stevenson
Danny Stoney
Robert Storrie
David Strachan
Brian Turner
Paul Young

Rossvale
Manager: Brian McGinty
Anton McDowall (ex Shotts BA, Bellshill Ath)
Kirk Forbes
Eraid Krasniqi
Jamie Donnelly
Sean Docherty
David Shaw
Gary McGrath
Gary Trussler (2016 Rossvale U19)
Hepburn
Craig Holmes
Euan Baird (2016 Arthurlie)
Ryan Spalding (2016 Rossvale U19)
David Leadbetter
Steven Tart
Dylan Clark (2016 Rossvale U19)
Phil Bannister
Steven Seaton (2016 Irvine Meadow)

St Rochs
Manager: Andy Camnron
John Paul Stark
Daniel Irvine
James McKnight
Stephen Bryson
Kieran Daw
Jordan Logan
Keiran Martin
Martin Shiels
Robert Maguire
Brian McQueen
Chrisd McFadyen
Dom Febers
Mark Mathieson
JHordan McCue
Johnny Carter
Declan Docherty
Baboucarr Musa
John Sweeney
TJ McCluskey

Shotts Bon Accord
Manager: Kieran McGuinness
Danny McGuinness
Ryan Lockie
Andy Cross
Dean Sutherland
Gavin McPherson
Max McKee
Danny Burns
Barry McGowan (2016 Bellshill Ath)
Ally Martin (2016 Kirkintilloch RR)
Jamie Brophy (2016 Bellshill Ath)
Shaun Fallon (2016 Hawick RA)
Mark Duffy (2016 THorniewood United)
Andy Scott (2016 Ex Cumnock, Wishaw)
Johnny Murdoch (2016 Kirkintilloch RR)
Andy Scott (2016 Kirkintilloch RR)

Thorniewood United
Manager: Andy Frame (until January), Gerry Bonham (from February)
Brendan Smith
Chris Jackson
John Paul McBride
Crielly
Darren Bowie
Chris Lennon
Johnny Logan
Anthony Higgins
Terry Hewitt
Alex Connell
McShane
David Hamilton
Kieron McIntyre
Stefan Law
Shane Jackson (2016 Southside AFC)
Liam Anderson
Craig Forbes
Alan Brown
Lafferty
Graeme Watson
Gary Jack
Keigan Parker
Damon Welsh
Lee Pettigrew
Andrew Sinclair
Darren Ferguson
Daryl Meikle
Ali Morgan
Derek Barnes
Damon Welsh

Vale of Clyde
Manager: Ian Currie (Until May)
Anton Franchetti
Matt Lynch (2016 Cambuslang R)
Chris Martin
Scott McManus
David Mackay
Dean Currie
Allan Kane (2016 Clyde)
Lee Morrison
Gavin Ross (ex Rutherglen Glencairn)
Kris Irvine (2016 Cumbernauld Utd, ex Celtic Youths)
Ryan Frances (ex Clyde)
Kyle Stewart
Kyle Prior
Salim Koudir-Aissa
Haydn Cochrane
Reece Glackin
Alan Kane
James McKinstry
Robert O'Donnell
Dean Currie (ex Shotts BA)

Wishaw
Manager: Chris McGroarty
Assistant: Glenn Weir
Coaches: David Lannigan, David Grant
Sandy Thomson
Ryan Lawrie
Mark Daly
Barry Eley
Chris McIntyre
Paul O'Kane
Graeme Wood
David Bannerman
Paul McGeouch
Dean Kindlan
Gerard Watt
Dan McNulty
Kevin B Grant
Michael Collinder
James Coffey
Ryan Smillie
Sean Mckenna
Ross McGeachie
Dan Kindlan
Stephen Mullen

McBookie.com West Junior Central League Second Division 2016/17

	ASH	CAR	DUN	EKT	GAR	GLA	LAN	NEW	POR	ROY	STA	VOL
Ashfield		Apr 1	Apr 24	Aug 27	Oct 8	Sep 17	Apr 22	Jan 21	Dec 10	May 6	Jan 28	Jan 7
		4-3	0-1	1-1	0-4	2-4	1-2	1-0	1-2	5-5	1-1	2-2
Carluke Rovers	Sep 10		May 6	Apr 22	Feb 4	Aug 27	Oct 8	Apr 8	Nov 5	Dec 17	Mar 18	Nov 12
	1-2		5-4	6-3	3-2	4-2	2-2	1-2	4-2	2-0	4-0	3-2
Dunipace	Apr 8	Sep 17		May 13	Apr 15	Nov 12	Apr 29	Apr 19	Feb 18	Oct 8	Dec 10	Aug 27
	2-0	1-0		2-2	1-2	0-5	0-4	4-1	3-2	4-1	1-0	2-2
East Kilbride Thistle	Apr 19	Sep 3	Mar 18		Apr 24	Oct 29	Feb 18	May 20	Apr 8	Apr 29	Apr 26	Apr 15
	3-1	3-2	1-0		1-2	2-5	1-3	1-0	0-2	1-0	4-3	0-0
Gartcairn	Apr 29	Oct 29	Sep 3	May 17		Oct 1	Sep 10	Nov 12	Mar 25	Dec 10	Jan 7	Mar 11
	1-2	6-1	3-1	0-2		2-4	5-4	3-0	2-1	1-2	1-3	2-4
Glasgow Perthshire	Feb 18	Jan 7	Jan 21	May 6	Dec 17		Dec 10	Nov 5	Sep 10	Sep 3	Oct 8	Feb 4
	5-0	5-5	0-0	0-2	4-1		3-1	4-2	0-3	6-1	3-1	4-0
Lanark United	Oct 1	Mar 11	Dec 3	Dec 17	May 6	Mar 25		Aug 27	Jan 21	Nov 5	Feb 4	Sep 17
	3-1	2-1	4-0	2-1	1-3	0-3		4-1	0-0	2-2	4-2	0-1
Newmains United	Apr 15	Apr 26	Jan 28	Oct 8	Apr 22	Mar 11	Jan 7		Apr 29	Sep 10	Sep 3	Feb 18
	0-4	0-2	1-0	2-5	0-1	0-5	2-3		0-5	0-2	2-2	1-4
Port Glasgow	Feb 11	Jan 28	Apr 1	Jan 7	Dec 3	Jan 14	Sep 3	Sep 17		Mar 11	Nov 19	Oct 8
	1-0	1-2	2-1	2-1	4-1	0-3	1-0	4-2		1-1	2-0	2-0
Royal Albert	Dec 3	Apr 24	Jan 7	Nov 12	Sep 17	Jan 28	Apr 15	May 13	Aug 27		Apr 8	Oct 29
	5-0	1-3	0-1	2-3	0-4	4-3	1-1	4-3	1-4		2-3	1-2
St Anthonys	Dec 17	Dec 3	Mar 4	Sep 17	Aug 27	Feb 25	Nov 12	Mar 25	Oct 1	Feb 18		Feb 11
	1-1	1-4	0-0	1-2	2-0	2-3	2-2	1-2	2-1	2-5		1-1
Vale of Leven	Sep 3	Mar 4	Dec 17	Mar 25	Nov 5	Dec 3	Jan 28	Oct 1	Feb 25	Jan 21	Sep 10	
	3-4	4-1	0-0	1-2	2-1	1-1	1-2	5-2	2-0	2-1	1-2	

		P	*W*	*D*	*L*	*F*	*A*	GD	*PTS*
1	**Glasgow Perthshire**	*22*	*15*	*3*	*4*	*72*	*33*	39	48
2	**Port Glasgow Juniors**	*22*	*13*	*2*	*7*	*42*	*26*	16	41
3	**East Kilbride Thistle**	22	12	3	7	41	37	4	39
4	Lanark United	22	11	5	6	46	34	12	38
5	Carluke Rovers (R)	22	12	2	8	59	49	10	38
6	Vale of Leven	22	9	6	7	40	34	6	33
7	Gartcairn Juniors	22	11	0	11	47	42	5	33
8	Dunipace Juniors (R)	22	8	5	9	28	35	-7	29
9	Ashfield	22	6	5	11	33	50	-17	23
10	Royal Albert	22	6	4	12	41	53	-12	22
11	St Anthony's (R)	22	5	6	11	32	46	-14	21
12	Newmains United	22	3	1	18	23	65	-42	10

Glasgow Perthshire were convincing league champions but the fight for the two other promotion places went to the wire. Despite a huge backlog of fixtures East Kilbride Thistle made it into third, joining Perthshire and Port Glasgow in stepping up.

Gartcain had a fine run in the Scottish Cup but that may have been a distraction from League matters.

West Central Division Two Playing Squads 2016/17

NB These are not comprehensive lists of players used - there will be some omissions. However, all players listed were associated with the club concerned during 2016/17.

Ashfield

Manager: Robert Docherty (ex Stirling Albion, St Mirren, Dumbarton etc)
Adam Nisanci
Alex Amos
Alex Donnelly
Andy Yule
Barry Rodgers
Barry Tulloch
Billy Stevenson
Chris Moulangou
Chris Wright
Conor Johnstone
Craig Murphy
Craig Murphy
Craig O'Brien
David Brown
David Cane
Jaludi Karenzi
Jordan Lynch
Kris Griffin
Kwaku Nyame
Kyle Lochhead
Mark Huggins
Lee Foggins
Martin Storey

West Region Central Division Two - All Time Positions

	2002-3	2003-4	2004-5	2005-6	2006-7	2007-8	2008-9	2009-10	2010-11	2011-12	2012-13	2013-14	2014-15	2015-16	2016-17
Ashfield	4	7	5	4	1									11	9
Baillieston	5														
Benburb				8	3			4	3					2	
Blantyre Vics		5	8	1			1			9	8	1			
Cambuslang Rangers						3					1		5	3	
Carluke Rovers	12	2		7	5	4	4	6	7	1					5
Clydebank		1													
Coltness United / Newmains United	11	13	13	W	9	Ab	10	11	12	10	11	11	11	9	12
Cumbernauld United															
Dunipace	3						2								8
East Kilbride Thistle												10	8	7	3
Forth Wanderers	6	6	10	9	7	5	8	9	11	3	9	4	7	1	
Gartcairn														5	7
Glasgow Perthshire			12	3			3						4	8	1
Greenock					4	6	7	3							
Johnstone Burgh								1		6	3		2		
Lanark United			1											6	4
Larkhall Thistle									2						
Lesmahagow		4	3						9	4					
Maryhill									6	5	2				
Port Glasgow	2		4	2								8	6	4	2
Rossvale										8	5	7	1		
Royal Albert	13	9	11	10	11	10	6	10	10	11	10	5	10	12	10
Shettleston					6	7	5	2							
St Anthonys	1														11
St Rochs		8	7	5	2		9	7	4	2		9	3		
Stonehouse Violet	10	12	6	6	10	8	Ab	Ab	5						
Thorniewood United	9	10	2		8	2									
Vale of Clyde											6	2			
Vale of Leven						1					7	6	9	10	6
Wishaw	7	11	9	11	12	9	11	8	8	7	4	3			
Yoker Athletic	8	3						5	1						
Ab = In abeyance															
W= withdrew															

Michael Giblin
Neil Schoneville
Paul Mallon
Paul Brennan
Ryan McGarry
Steven Dymock
Steven Mather
Vincent Newlands

Carluke Rovers
Manager: Colin Slater Assistant:
Andy Barr
Alisdair Graham
Charles McCole
Dale Gordon
Daniel Tobin
Darren Hamilton
Garry Gow
Gordon Bruce
Greg John Finnie
Ian Watt
Jamie Dickson
John Renwick
Jonathon Wilson
Jordan Duncan
Lerwis McDougall
Mark Haddow
Mark Weir
Peter Lynn
Reece Lowdon
Ryan Carnwath
Sam Biggart
Scott Bellew
Scott Burns
Stephen Murray
Stuart Mitchell
William Soutar

Dunipace
Manager: Gareth Alexander
Aiden Stevenson
Alan Deans
Calum Runciman
Corey Burnett
Craig Cowan
Craig Hughes
Craig Waddell
Daniel Murphy
David Grant
Dominic McGrandles (ex Steins Thistle U21)
Fowler
Gavin Sulivan
Gordon Passmore (ex Ashfield)
Greg McPherson
Gregor Dryden
Leo Williamson (Ex Steins T Stenhousemuir Youths)
Liam McMaster
Mark McLinchey
Nicholas Taylor
Paul Nash
Ross Balmer
Sean Robertson
Steven Ferguson
Steven Stewart
Liam McNally
Aarom McKenzie
Andrew Thomson
Paul Donnelly
Zak Christie
Kevin Wilson

David McFarlane

East Kilbride Thistle
Manager: Billy Campbell
Coaches: Ronnie Sanderson, Gary Johnstoner
Aaron Connolly
Adam Boyle
Alan McFadden
Andy Gibson
Barry Devine
Chris Faulds
Chris Treacey
Ciaran Johnston
Craig Duncan
Craig Hastings
Darryl McDonald
John Craig
Kieran Johnstone
Liam McLaughlin
Liam Sloan
Phil McCabe
Ross Gillan
Scott Edgar
Steven Oates
William Hastings

Gartcairn
Manager: Gerry Bonham (until december), David Greig
Aidan Bickerton
Alistair Morgan
Barry Canning
Bryn Halliwell
Callum Brady
Chris Dolan
Chris Patrick (to Whitburn Jan 2017)
Colin Marshall (ex Falkirk, Clyde, Cowdenbeath)
Craig Holmes
Dylan Whitelaw
Gary Carmichael (ex Blochairn Star)
Gary Miller (ex Bo'ness United)
Jonathan Grier
John Henderson
Joprdan Love
Josh Moore
Kevin Ross
Lee McShane (ex Blantyre Vics, Perthshire, Ashfield, Rutherglen Glencairn)
Lee Pettigrew
Liam Tuite
Martin Harty
Martin Regan
Robert McAvoy
Ryan Kennedy
Scott Murphy
Stuart Easton
Yami Misanjo (to Wishaw Jan 2017)

Glasgow Perthshire
Manager: Billy Adams (Current longest serving manager in West Juniors)
Chris Calder (2016 Rossvale)
Logan McIntyre
Bradley Rodden (2016 Possil YM)
McLaughlin
Mark Thompson (2016 Blantyre Vics)
Davie Kirkwood
Marr
Jordan Currie-Mclean
Gemmell
Craig Smith (2016 Blantyre Vics)
Ryan McGarry
Scott Forrester
Fraser Malcolm (2016 Blantyre Vics)
Andy Gibson (ex Partick Th, Stirling Albion, Stranraer)
Gerald O'Donnell
Craig Munro
Brian McLaughlin (2016 Blantyre Vics)
Lee McShane (2016 Blantyre Vics)
Marc Wilson
Ralph Gamba
Stewart Brodie (2016 Neilston)
Paul Hanlon
John Paul Craig
Willie Ferguson (2016 Blantyre Vics)

Lanark United
Manager: John Brogan (ex St johnstone, Hamilton Accies, Stirling Albion etc)
Alan Christie
Alan McCrum
Alistair Shearer
Andrew Crielly (2017 Thornie-wood United)
Andy Finnigan (ex Forth W)
Cammy Lawson
David Bannerman (2016 Wishaw OL)
David Collins
David O'Donnell
Gareth Halford (2016 Newmains Utd)
Gary Duggan (2016 Benburb)
Gordon
Gordon Murphy
Grant Ebbs
James Faughnan (2016 Wishaw OL)
Jamie Brown (2016 Alloa)
Jamie Cubis (2017 Albion Rovers)
Jordan Munn (2016 Port Glasgow)
Kerr
Kieran McGurk
Kyle Maxwell
Lee Imrie
Mark Brown (2016 Gartcairn)
Martin McGuire (2016 Shotts BA)
Martin Smith
Neil Schoneville (2016 Ashfield)
Owen Mooney
Paul Burns (2016 Larkhall Th)
Paul Hewitt
Peter O'Donnell
Ronan Kearney (2016 Alloa OL)
Ryan Hutchison
Mustafa El Zubaidi (2016 Gartcairn)
Shaun Gallagher
Stuart Annetts

Newmains United
Manager: Kevin Muirhead
Assistant: Don McKinlay
Coach: Brian Roberts
Alan Thompson
Alexander Moore (OL from Albion Rovers)
Alex White
Andy McKinlay
Cathal Tracey
Connor Cowan
Dillon McLauchlan
Gary Stewart (ex Red Road Utd, Blairdardie BC, Galston, Hibernian Youths)
Jamie Brown (ex Alloa, Rossvale, Lanark Utd)
Jamie Mitchell
Jack Heron
Jay Burns (ex Barrhead BC, Partick Th Youths)
Jay Cameron (OL from Dumbar-ton)
Kieran O'Hear
Kris Taylor
Kyle Meaney
Lee Shankie (ex Johnstone B, Neilston)
Liam Adams
Mark Cassidy
Mark O'Neill
Martin O'Keefe (ex Kilbarchan AFC)
Paul McKane
Richie Lovering
Ross Carrigan
Willie Tippen
Zander White

Port Glasgow
Manager: Craig Brown (No, not that one), Assistant: Scott Jackson
Aidan McMillan
Bradley Anderson
Craig Beaton
Craig McCormick
Darren Boyle
David McGarrigle
Dylan McLaughlin
Gary Pettigrew
Grant
Jamie McKenna
Jordan Munn
Lee Cruickshank
Mark Monk
Steven McAfee
McArthur
Craig McCormick
Graeme McClement
McGilp
Jamie McKenna
Aiden McMillan
Martin Paton
Paul Pettigrew
Paul Johnstone
Robbie Davis

Royal Albert
Manager: Jamie Nesbitt
Alan Campbell
Barry Murdoch
Chris Finn
Colin Boylan
Craig Smith
Davie Hamilton
Eddie Haley
Fraser Scott
Fraser Stobie
Fraser Sylvie
Jack Baptie
Jack Wardlaw
Jordan Rennie
Josh Anderson
Liam O'Kane
Marc Howson
Michael Anderson
Michael Neill
Scott Baillie
Scott Brennan
Scott Cunningham (ex Forth W, Albion R U20)
Scott McLachlan
Stevie Clarke

St Anthony's
Co Managers: John Doyle, Ronnie MacDonald
Adam Dougan
Aiden Lennon
Anton Conway (ex Lesmahagow)
Conor Meechan
Craig Smith
Daniel Campbell
Dean McKay
Gavin Wallace
Graeme Crawford
Grant Kelly
James Lennox (ex Clydebank, Kirkintilloch RR, neilston)
Jon Connolly
John McGowan
Kieron Maxwell (ex Arthurlie, Cumnock)
Kyle Brown
Maxi Neossi)ex Blantyre Vics, Muirkirk, St Rochs)
Michael McDowall
Michael O'Hara
Paul O'Brien
Ross Cameron
Ryan Smith
Sammy Adesola
Serge Kimbala
Thomas Miller (ex Cambuslang Rangers)
Tony Kane
Willliam Duncan

Vale of Leven
Manager:
Alex Rennie
Charles Smith (ex Carlton YM, Johnstone Burgh)
Stuart Bryson (ex Maryhill)
Adam Monaghan (ex St.Pat's FP's, Queens Park, Kilbirnie Ladeside, Dumbarton, St.Johnstone)
Brian Cameron
Matthew Devine (ex Vale U21)
Craig Cowan (ex Drymen, Vale U21)
Josh Grace (ex Kilbowie Union)
Stephen Griffen (ex Dumbarton Accies U19)
Lee McGeachie (ex Dumbarton Accies U19, Vale U21)
Antony Pilkington (ex Dumbarton Accies U19, Vale U21
Andrew Clark (ex Dumbarton)
David McNaught (ex Clyde, Dumbarton)
Andrew Campbell (ex Lomond Vale, Argyle Athletic, Renton YC)
Mark Butler
Kenny Wilson (ex Vale U21)
Lewis King (ex Vale U19, Erskine YC, Antonine FC, Dumbarton North)
Rhys Percival (ex Heleneburgh U17)
Robbie Dolan (ex Argyle Ath)
Scott Cowan (ex Drymen Utd, Vale U21)
Mark Pawsey (ex leven Valley, Vale u21)
Greg Ross (ex Dumbarton Utd, Vale U21)
Ryan Degan
Sean Stewart (ex Clydebank)
Andrew Campbell
Graeme McKenzie
Scott Morrison (ex E Stirling, Arbroath, Stirling Albion etc)
Connor Quinn
Scott Arthur (ex Ayr United, Morton, Kilbirnie Ladeside, Dalry Thistle)
Andrew Orr (ex Dumbarton)

Ardagh Ayrshire League Cup 2016/17

	AWR	B	DT	KR	LT	KL
Ardrossan Winton Rovers				Aug 17 5-2	Aug 10 3-1	
Beith	Aug 15 4-1		Aug 10 4-0		Aug 17 2-2	
Dalry Thistle	Aug 6 2-3			Aug 13 2-1		Aug 17 0-7
Kilwinning Rangers		Aug 20 1-9				Aug 10 0-2
Largs Thistle			Aug 20 3-1	Aug 6 2-2		
Kilbirnie Ladeside	Aug 20 2-0	Aug 6 1-3			Aug 13 1-1	

GROUP 1	P	W	D	L	F	A	PTS
Beith	5	4	1	0	22	5	13
Kilbirnie Ladeside	5	3	1	1	13	4	10
Ardrossan Winton Rovers	5	3	0	2	12	11	9
Largs Thistle	5	1	3	1	9	9	6
Dalry Thistle	5	1	0	4	5	18	3
Kilwinning Rangers	5	0	1	4	6	20	1

	AT	D	HU	IM	IV	SV
Ardeer Thistle			Aug 20 0-5		Aug 17 3-1	
Darvel	Aug 6 2-4		Aug 13 1-5			Aug 20 4-0
Hurlford United						Aug 17 9-1
Irvine Meadow	Aug 13 1-1	Aug 17 0-1	Aug 10 4-3		Aug 19 4-3	
Irvine Vics		Aug 10 0-1	Aug 6 0-1			
Saltcoats Vics	Aug 10 0-3			Aug 6 3-2	Aug 13 2-3	

GROUP 2	P	W	D	L	F	A	PTS
Hurlford United	5	4	0	1	23	6	12
Ardeer Thistle	5	3	1	1	11	9	10
Darvel	5	3	0	2	9	9	9
Irvine Meadow	5	2	1	2	11	11	7
Irvine Vics	5	1	0	4	7	11	3
Saltcoats Vics	5	1	0	4	6	21	3

	AU	CB	G	M	T	WV
Annbank United			Aug 10 1-4		Aug 20 2-3	
Craigmark Burntonians	Aug 6 1-3		Aug 20 1-5			Aug 10 1-3
Girvan					Aug 13 0-2	Aug 17 1-1
Maybole	Aug 17 2-6	Aug 13 2-2	Aug 6 0-1			
Troon		Aug 17 4-1		Aug 10 10-0		
Whitletts Vics	Aug 13 1-2			Aug 20 2-5	Aug 6 2-2	

GROUP 3	P	W	D	L	F	A	PTS
Troon	5	4	1	0	21	5	13
Girvan	5	3	1	1	11	5	10
Annbank United	5	3	0	2	14	11	9
Whitletts Vics	5	1	2	2	9	11	5
Maybole	5	1	1	3	9	21	4
Craigmark Burntonians	5	0	1	4	6	17	1

	AT	C	GA	KR	LBT	M
Auchinleck Talbot		Aug 15 1-1			Aug 17 2-0	
Cumnock					Aug 6 6-0	Aug 20 7-0
Glenafton Athletic	Aug 10 1-1	Aug 17 0-2				Aug 13 6-1
Kello Rovers	Aug 20 2-7	Aug 10 1-3	Aug 6 1-3			
Lugar Boswell Thistle			Aug 20 0-5	Aug 13 1-1		
Muirkirk	Aug 6 1-4			Aug 17 0-2	Aug 10 1-1	

GROUP 4	P	W	D	L	F	A	PTS
Cumnock	5	4	1	2	19	2	13
Auchinleck Talbot	5	3	2	0	15	5	11
Glenafton Athletic	5	3	1	1	15	5	10
Kello Rovers	5	1	1	3	7	14	4
Lugar Boswell Thistle	5	0	2	3	2	15	2
Muirkirk	5	0	1	4	3	20	1

QF	24/08/2018	Beith	Ardeer Thistle	8	0	
QF	24/08/2018	Hurlford United	Kilbirnie Ladeside	1	2	
QF	24/08/2018	Cumnock	Girvan	3	2	
QF	24/08/2018	Troon	Auchinleck Talbot	1	2	
SF	31/08/2016	Auchinleck Talbot	Beith	2	1	
SF	31/08/2016	Kilbirnie Ladeside	Cumnock	2	1	
F	09/10/2016	Auchinleck Talbot	Kilbirnie Ladeside	0	1	at Meadow Park

FINAL DETAILS

Kilbirnie Ladeside v Auchinleck Talbot, 1-0

Scorer - Eddie McTernan (73 mins)

Talbot – Leishman, Lyle, Pope, McGoldrick, Boyle, S Wilson, Young, White, G Wilson, McCracken, Hyslop Subs – Shankland, Milliken, Stevenson, Thomson, Pooler
Kilbirnie – Hughes, Haxton, Gold, Staunton, Rafferty, Gray, Anderson, Green, McElroy, Grehan, Brannan Subs – Forde, Donnelly, Malone, Meechan, McTernan

Recent Ayrshire Sectional League Cup Finals				
Season	**Winners**	**Runners Up**	**Score**	**Venue**
1989/90	Auchinleck Talbot	Irvine Meadow	1-1, 5-3 pens	Rugby Park, Kilmarnock
1990/1	Auchinleck Talbot	Beith	2-1	Rugby Park, Kilmarnock
1991/2	Beith	Glenafton Athletic	2-1	Rugby Park, Kilmarnock
1992/3	Auchinleck Talbot	Irvine Meadow	1-1, 4-3 pens	Winton Park, Ardrossan
1993/4	Beith	Auchinleck Talbot	0-0, 4-3 pens	Somerset Park, Ayr
1994/5	Kilbirnie Ladeside	Auchinleck Talbot	0-0, 4-2 pens	Somerset Park, Ayr
1995/6	Cumnock	Ardeer Thistle	3-1	Somerset Park, Ayr
1996/7	Cumnock	Kilwinning Rangers	1-0	Somerset Park, Ayr
1997/8	Auchinleck Talbot	Beith	2-1	Somerset Park, Ayr
1998/9	Kilwinning Rangers	Auchinleck Talbot	2-1	Somerset Park, Ayr
1999/00	Glenafton Athletic	Kilwinning Rangers	4-1	Somerset Park, Ayr
2000/1	Cumnock	Kilwinning Rangers	2-2, 5-3 pens	Somerset Park, Ayr
2001/2	Cumnock	Irvine Meadow	3-2	Somerset Park, Ayr
2002/3	Auchinleck Talbot	Irvine Meadow	3-1	Somerset Park, Ayr
2003/4	Irvine Meadow	Auchinleck Talbot	2-0	Somerset Park, Ayr
2004/5	Beith	Auchinleck Talbot	1-1, 4-2 pens	Somerset Park, Ayr
2005/6	Glenafton Athletic	Cumnock	4-3	Somerset Park, Ayr
2006/7	Auchinleck Talbot	Cumnock	2-1	Somerset Park, Ayr
2007/8	Auchinleck Talbot	Irvine Meadow	2-1	Somerset Park, Ayr
2008/9	Irvine Meadow	Lugar Boswall Thistle	3-0	Meadow Park, Irvine
2009/10	Kilbirnie Ladeside	Cumnock	3-0	Meadow Park, Irvine
2010/1	Auchinleck Talbot	Irvine Meadow	1-1, 8-7 pens	Bellsdale Park, Beith
2011/2	Auchinleck Talbot	Irvine Meadow	3-0	Bellsdale Park, Beith
2012/3	Irvine Meadow	Auchinleck Talbot	4-4, 4-2 pens	Bellsdale Park, Beith
2013/4	Cumnock	Beith	1-1, 9-8 pens	Portland Park, Troon
2014/5	Glenafton Athletic	Auchinleck Talbot	2-0	Portland Park, Troon
2015/6	Hurlford United	Troon	4-2	Meadow Park, Irvine
2016/7	Kilbirnie Ladeside	Auchinleck Talbot	1-0	Meadow Park, Irvine

Euroscot Central Sectional League Cup 2016/17

Section 1	FW	LU	LT	L	RA
Forth Wanderers		Aug 13 2-3	Aug 15 1-0		
Lanark United				Aug 20 0-2	Aug 17 1-0
Larkhall Thistle		Aug 10 3-1		Aug 13 2-1	
Lesmahagow	Aug 17 4-1				Aug 6 4-1
Royal Albert	Aug 10 2-2		Aug 20 0-5		

	P	W	D	L	F	A	PTS
Larkhall Thistle	4	3	0	1	10	3	9
Lesmahagow	4	3	0	1	11	4	9
Lanark United	4	2	0	2	5	7	6
Forth	4	1	1	2	6	9	3
Royal Albert	4	0	1	3	3	12	1

Section 2	CR	GAR	NU	SBA	W
Carluke Rovers		Aug 20 1-2		Aug 6 2-4	
Gartcairn				Aug 13 8-1	Aug 17 2-2
Newmains United	Aug 17 0-4	Aug 6 4-7			
Shotts Bon Accord			Aug 10 1-0		Aug 20 0-4
Wishaw	Aug 10 6-1		Aug 13 4-1		

	P	W	D	L	F	A	PTS
Wishaw	4	3	1	0	16	3	10
Gartcairn	4	3	1	0	19	8	10
Shotts BA	4	2	0	2	6	14	6
Carluke R	4	1	0	3	8	12	3
Newmains U	4	0	0	4	5	16	0

Section 3	BA	P	SH	SR	TU
Bellshill Athletic				Aug 20 2-5	Aug 6 0-0
Petershill	Aug 17 3-3			Aug 6 2-0	
Shettleston	Aug 10 5-4	Aug 13 2-1			
St Rochs			Aug 17 0-2		Aug 13 1-2
Thorniewood United		Aug 10 2-6	Aug 20 0-1		

	P	W	D	L	F	A	PTS
Shettleston	4	3	0	1	8	7	9
Petershill	4	2	1	1	12	7	7
Thorniewood	4	1	1	2	4	8	4
St Rochs	4	1	0	3	6	8	3
Bellshill	4	0	2	2	9	13	2

Section 4	BV	CR	EKT	RG	VOC
Blantyre Vics				Aug 17 1-2	Aug 6 2-3
Cambuslang Rangers	Aug 20 5-3			Aug 6 2-2	
East Kilbride Thistle	Aug 10 1-6	Aug 13 0-1			
Rutherglen Glencairn			Aug 20 6-0		Aug 13 2-1
Vale of Clyde		Aug 10 2-3	Aug 17 3-4		

	P	W	D	L	F	A	PTS
Rutherglen Glencairn	4	3	1	0	12	4	10
Cambuslang R	4	3	1	0	11	7	10
Blantyre V	4	1	0	3	12	11	3
Vale of Clyde	4	1	0	3	9	11	3
East Kilbride Th	4	1	0	3	5	16	3

Section 5	A	B	N	P	SA
Arthurlie				Aug 20 1-1	Aug 6 2-0
Benburb	Aug 17 4-3			Aug 6 0-2	
Neilston	Aug 13 2-0	Aug 10 2-1			
Pollok			Aug 17 5-1		Aug 10 9-0
St Anthonys		Aug 13 1-3	Aug 20 1-2		

	P	W	D	L	F	A	PTS
Pollok	4	3	1	0	17	2	10
Neilston	4	3	0	1	7	7	9
Benburb	4	2	0	2	8	8	6
Arthurlie	4	1	1	2	6	7	4
St Anthonys	4	0	0	4	2	16	0

Section 6	A	C	GP	M	YA
Ashfield		Aug 20 0-1			Aug 13 1-4
Clydebank			Aug 10 6-1		Aug 6 2-2
Glasgow Perthshire	Aug 6 2-3			Aug 13 1-5	
Maryhill	Aug 10 0-1	Aug 17 0-2			
Yoker Athletic			Aug 17 3-1	Aug 20 1-0	

	P	W	D	L	F	A	PTS
Clydebank	4	3	1	0	11	3	10
Yoker Ath	4	3	1	0	10	4	10
Ashfield	4	2	0	2	5	7	6
Maryhill	4	1	0	3	5	5	3
Glasgow Perthshire	4	0	0	4	5	17	0

Section 7	G	JB	PG	R	VOL
Greenock		Aug 17 1-1		Aug 6 3-0	
Johnstone Burgh				Aug 20 1-1	Aug 6 0-0
Port Glasgow	Aug 13 0-6	Aug 10 2-1			
Renfrew			Aug 17 1-1		Aug 13 4-0
Vale of Leven	Aug 10 2-6		Aug 20 2-3		

	P	W	D	L	F	A	PTS
Greenock	4	3	1	0	16	3	10
Port Glasgow	4	2	1	1	6	10	7
Renfrew	4	1	2	1	6	5	5
Johnstone Burgh	4	0	3	1	3	4	3
Vale of Leven	4	0	1	3	4	13	1

Section 8	CU	D	KR	KRR	R
Cumbernauld United				Aug 6 1-4	Aug 17 1-2
Dunipace	Aug 20 1-2		Aug 17 1-4	Aug 10 1-4	
Kilsyth Rangers	Aug 10 4-1				Aug 6 4-2
Kirkintilloch Rob Roy			Aug 13 2-1		Aug 20 5-2
Rossvale		Aug 13 4-0			

	P	W	D	L	F	A	PTS
Kirkintilloch RR	4	4	0	0	15	5	12
Kilsyth R	4	3	0	1	13	6	9
Rossvale	4	2	0	2	10	10	6
Cumbernauld Utd	4	1	0	3	5	11	3
Dunipace	4	0	0	4	3	14	0

QF	24/08/2018	Kirkintilloch Rob Roy	Clydebank	2	1			
QF	24/08/2018	Lesmahagow	Wishaw	1	3			
QF	24/08/2018	Rutherglen Glencairn	Pollok	1	3			
QF	24/08/2018	Shettleston	Greenock	2	0			
SF	31/08/2016	Shettleston	Wishaw	4	2			
SF	31/08/2016	Kirkintilloch Rob Roy	Pollok	2	0			
F	02/10/2016	Shettleston	Kirkintilloch Rob Roy	0	0	2-4p	at Cambuslang	646

FINAL DETAILS

Kirkintilloch Rob Roy v Shettleston 0-0, 4-2 pens, Att 646
Rob Roy: Brown, Walker, McKenzie, Green, Buchanan,. Wheelan, Duff (Sub Gallacher), Fraser, Sawyers, Watt (Sub McMenamin), Mackie (Sub Pearson). Unused subs: McGuire and Barr
Shettleston: Trainor, Chisholm, R Campbell (Sub Scott), Logan, Dickson, McDonald, Lewis Kinnaird (Sub Lloyd Kinnaird), McStay, Weatherson, McIntosh, Halsman (Sub Welsh). Subs not used Kennedy and Home
Referee: W Wilson

Recent Central Sectional League Cup Finals

Season	Winners	Runners Up	Score	Venue
1978/9	Arthurlie	East Kilbride Thistle	3-1	New Kilbowie Park, Clydebank
1979/80	Shettleston	Blantyre Vics	2-1	Fir Park, Motherwell
1980/1	Larkhall Thistle	Shotts Bon Accord	2-1	Fir Park, Motherwell
1981/2	Petershill	Blantyre Celtic	2-0	Fir Park, Motherwell
1982/3	East Kilbride Thistle	Kirkintilloch Rob Roy	2-1	Fir Park, Motherwell
1983/4	Pollok	Larkhall Thistle	1-0	Fir Park, Motherwell
1984/5	Shotts Bon Accord	Ashfield	3-0	Fir Park, Motherwell
1985/6	Yoker Athletic	Arthurlie	3-2	Fir Park, Motherwell
1986/7	Arthurlie	Pollok	2-1	Fir Park, Motherwell
1987/8	Larkhall Thistle	Pollok	2-1	Douglas Park, Hamilton
1988/9	Shotts Bon Accord	Renfrew	2-1	Fir Park, Motherwell
1989/90	Dunipace	Arthurlie	2-2, 7-6 pens	Fir Park, Motherwell
1990/1	Pollok	Arthurlie	0-0, 4-3 pens	Fir Park, Motherwell
1991/2	Rutherglen Glencairn	Arthurlie	4-1	Hannah Park, Shotts
1992/3	Pollok	Rutherglen Glencairn	3-1	Douglas Park, Hamilton
1993/4	Lesmahagow	Petershill	2-1	Kilbowie Park, Clydebank
1994/5	Petershill	Larkhall Thistle	2-1	Fir Park, Motherwell
1995/6	Blantyre Vics	Pollok	1-0	Fir Park, Motherwell
1996/7	Pollok	Shettleston	4-2	Fir Park, Motherwell
1997/8	Shotts Bon Accord	Arthurlie	0-0, 4-1 pens	Fir Park, Motherwell
1998/9	Neilston	Baillieston	5-0	Fir Park, Motherwell
1999/00	Pollok	Shotts Bon Accord	4-1	Firhill Stadium, Glasgow
2000/1	Cambuslang Rangers	Shotts Bon Accord	1-0	Firhill Stadium, Glasgow
2001/2	Bellshill Athletic	Larkhall Thistle	3-0	Firhill Stadium, Glasgow
2002/3	East Kilbride Thistle	Bellshill Athletic	2-0	Firhill Stadium, Glasgow
2003/4	Pollok	Kilsyth Rangers	1-1, 5-3 pens	Firhill Stadium, Glasgow
2004/5	Maryhill	Shotts Bon Accord	2-0	Firhill Stadium, Glasgow
2005/6	Neilston	East Kilbirde Thistle	0-0, 4-3 pens	Firhill Stadium, Glasgow
2006/7	Pollok	Clydebank	2-1	Lochburn Park, Glasgow
2007/8	Rutherglen Glencairn	Port Glasgow	2-1	Lochburn Park, Glasgow
2008/9	Arthurlie	Shotts Bon Accord	3-2	Lochburn Park, Glasgow
2009/10	Arthurlie	Shotts Bon Accord	1-0	Lochburn Park, Glasgow
2010/1	Shotts Bon Accord	Lanark United	1-0	New Southcroft, Rutherglen
2011/2	Petershill	Shotts Bon Accord	3-2	Lochburn Park, Glasgow
2012/3	Pollok	Renfrew	3-0	Lochburn Park, Glasgow
2013/4	Clydebank	Pollok	2-0	Lochburn Park, Glasgow
2014/15	Blantyre Vics	Cumbernauld United	3-3, 4-2p	Gasworks Park, Larkhall
2015/16	Petershill	Vale of Clyde	1-1, 4-2p	Somervell Park, Cambuslang
2016/7	Kirkintilloch Rob Roy	Shettleston	0-0, 4-2p	Somervell Park, Cambuslang

West of Scotland Junior Cup 2016/17

Round	Date	Home	Away	F	A	
1	15/10/2016	Ashfield	Larkhall Thistle	1	2	
1	15/10/2016	Beith	Ardeer Thistle	4	1	
1	15/10/2016	Bellshill Athletic	Petershill	1	2	
1	15/10/2016	Benburb	Glasgow Perthshire	0	0	5-4p
1	15/10/2016	Cambuslang Rangers	Auchinleck Talbot	0	3	
1	15/10/2016	Cumnock	Clydebank	4	0	
1	15/10/2016	Dalry Thistle	Pollok	0	3	
1	11/02/2017	Dunipace	Lanark United	2	5	
1	15/10/2016	Gartcairn	Cumbernauld United	2	0	
1	15/10/2016	Glenafton Athletic	Carluke Rovers	3	2	
1	15/10/2016	Greenock	Troon	0	2	
1	15/10/2016	Irvine Victoria	Rossvale	0	3	
1	15/10/2016	Johnstone Burgh	Royal Albert	1	2	
1	15/10/2016	Kello Rovers	Blantyre Victoria	1	1	2-4p
1	15/10/2016	Kilbirnie Ladeside	Forth Wanderers	4	1	
1	15/10/2016	Kilsyth Rangers	Renfrew	0	0	4-3p
1	15/10/2016	Kilwinning Rangers	Arthurlie	3	0	
1	15/10/2016	Kirkintilloch Rob Roy	East Kilbride Thistle	7	2	
1	15/10/2016	Largs Thistle	Wishaw	1	0	
1	15/10/2016	Lesmahagow	Craigmark Burntonians	1	2	
1	15/10/2016	Lugar Boswell Thistle	Maryhill	2	3	
1	15/10/2016	Maybole	Girvan	2	0	
1	15/10/2016	Newmains United	Ardrossan Winton Rovers	0	4	
1	15/10/2016	Port Glasgow	Neilston	1	1	2-3p
1	15/10/2016	Ritherglen Glencairn	Irvine Meadow	1	1	3-4p
1	15/10/2016	Saltcoats Victoria	Shotts Bon Accord	2	1	
1	15/10/2016	Shettleston	Hurlford United	3	2	
1	15/10/2016	St Rochs	Muirkirk	2	0	
1	15/10/2016	Thorniewood United	Yoker Athletic	4	2	
1	15/10/2016	Vale of Clyde	Darvel	2	3	
1	15/10/2016	Vale of Leven	Annbank United	0	3	
1	15/10/2016	Whitletts Victoria	St Anthonys	3	1	
2	11/02/2017	St Rochs	Petershill	4	0	
2	08/04/2017	Thorniewood United	Darvel	1	1	3-5p
2	11/02/2017	Largs Thistle	Beith	1	1	5-4p
2	11/02/2017	Cumnock	Kilbirnie Ladeside	6	0	
2	11/02/2017	Larkhall Thistle	Craigmark Burntonians	3	3	3-5p
2	04/03/2017	Gartcairn	Lanark United	2	1	
2	25/03/2017	Annbank United	Maryhill	2	1	
2	25/03/2017	Royal Albert	Maybole	0	2	
2	11/02/2017	Glenafton Athletic	Troon	0	3	
2	11/02/2017	Auchinleck Talbot	Whitletts Vics	1	0	
2	11/02/2017	Benburb	Kilwinning Rangers	2	4	
2	11/02/2017	Shettleston	Blantyre Victoria	0	2	
2	04/03/2017	Kirkintilloch Rob Roy	Ardrossan Winton Rovers	1	1	5-4p
		at Ardrossan				
2	11/02/2017	Rossvale	Neilston	0	1	
2	11/02/2017	Pollok	Irvine Meadow	1	0	
2	04/03/2017	Saltcoats Victoria	Kilsyth Rangers	5	7	
3	08/04/2017	Largs Thistle	Kirkintilloch Rob Roy	0	2	A
3	08/04/2017	Maybole	Auchinleck Talbot	0	2	B
3	08/04/2017	Craigmark Burntonians	Kilsyth Rangers	0	3	C
3	08/04/2017	St Rochs	Annbank United	5	1	D
3	08/04/2017	Pollok	Neilston	5	0	E
3	19/04/2017	Darvel	Kilwinning Rangers	2	0	F
3	08/04/2017	Troon	Gartcairn	1	4	G
3	08/04/2017	Cumnock	Blantyre Vics	5	2	H
4	17/05/2017	Darvel	Auchinleck Talbot	1	3	W
4	19/04/2017	Kilsyth Rangers	Gartcairn	2	0	X
4	22/04/2017	Pollok	St Rochs	3	1	Y
4	17/05/2017	Cumnock	Kirkintilloch Rob Roy	1	1	5-3p
SF	24/05/2017	Auchinleck Talbot	Cumnock	0	1	
SF	06/05/2017	Pollok	Kilsyth Rangers	2	1	
F	27/05/2017	Pollok	Cumnock	2	2	5-4p
		at Pollok Att 1027				

First Round Draw, 2017/18

Ardeer Thistle - Greenock Juniors
Arthurlie - Saltcoats Victoria
Ashfield - Rutherglen Glencairn
Auchinleck Talbot - Carluke Rovers
Benburb - Lanark United
Blantyre Victoria - Beith Juniors
Cambuslang Rangers - Muirkirk
Craigmark Burntonians - Cumbernauld United
Cumnock Juniors - Glasgow Perthshire
Dalry Thistle - Darvel
Dunipace - Gartcairn Juniors
Forth Wanderers - Thorniewood United
Glenafton Athletic - Girvan
Hurlford United - Lesmahagow Juniors
Kello Rovers - Troon Juniors
Kilsyth Rangers - Vale of Leven
Kilwinning Rangers - Irvine Meadow
Kirkintilloch Rob Roy - Irvine Victoria
Kilbirnie Ladeside - Johnstone Burgh
Largs Thistle - Bellshill Athletic
Lugar Boswell Thistle - Clydebank
Maryhill - Ardrossan Winton Rovers
Neilston - Port Glasgow Juniors
Petershill - Whitletts Victoria
Renfrew - Larkhall Thistle
Royal Albert - Pollok
St Anthony's - Annbank United
St Roch's - Newmains United
Shettleston - Rossvale
Shotts Bon Accord - East Kilbride Thistle
Vale of Clyde - Wishaw Juniors
Yoker Athletic - Maybole

FINAL DETAILS 2016/17

Pollok 2 Cumnock 2, 5-4 pens

Pollok:- Longmuir, Hanlon (15: R. Winters 77), Sideserf, Gallacher, Walker, McCabe, McCann, Williamson, D. Winters (12: McAleenan 46), Daly, MacKenzie (14: Hepburn 74
Subs not used:- 16: McLean, Gk: Lawton

Goals:- Gallacher (52), Hepburn (90 + 2)

Bookings:- Williamson (28), MacKenzie (38)

Cumnock:- Johnson, Wood, Crawford, Lundie, McKenna, Esplin, Montgomerie (12: Muir 67), Burns, Anson, Hunter, McRobbie (15: Watt 60)
Subs not used:- 14: Samson, 16: Shirkie, Gk: Kerr

Goals: McRobbie (33), Burns (89)
Bookings:- Burns (21), Esplin (89)

Recent West of Scotland Cup Finals				
Season	**Winners**	**Runners Up**	**Score**	**Venue**
1988/9	Auchinleck Talbot	Shotts Bon Accord	1-0 aet	Rugby Park, Kilmarnock
1989/90	Irvine Meadow	Larkhall Thistle	4-1	Newlandsfield, Glasgow
1990/1	Largs Thistle	Renfrew	1-0	Somervell Park, Cambuslang
1991/2	Pollok	Beith	1-0	Somervell Park, Cambuslang
1992/3	Shettleston	Lesmahagow	2-0	Somervell Park, Cambuslang
1993/4	Kilwinning Rangers	Shettleston	2-0	Somervell Park, Cambuslang
1994/5	Shettleston	Pollok	1-1, 4-2 pens	Somervell Park, Cambuslang
1995/6	Petershill	Maryhill	2-0	Somervell Park, Cambuslang
1996/7	Arthurlie	Irvine Meadow	5-0	Somervell Park, Cambuslang
1997/8	Pollok	Petershill	3-1	Somervell Park, Cambuslang
1998/9	Kilwinning Rangers	Arthurlie	2-1	Newlandsfield, Glasgow
1999/00	Pollok	Glenafton Athletic	2-1	Somervell Park, Cambuslang
2000/1	Maryhill	Pollok	1-0	Somervell Park, Cambuslang
2001/2	Benburb	Johnstone Burgh	3-2	Newlandsfield, Glasgow
2002/3	Glenafton Athletic	Bellshill Athletic	4-2	Meadow Park, Irvine
2003/4	Maryhill	Bellshill Athletic	3-1	Newlandsfield, Glasgow
2004/5	Troon	Arthurlie	4-3	Newlandsfield, Glasgow
2005/6	Glenafton Athletic	Maryhill	1-1, 4-3 pens	Newlandsfield, Glasgow
2006/7	Petershill	Kilbirnie Ladeside	2-1	Newlandsfield, Glasgow
2007/8	Kilbirnie Ladeside	Pollok	5-1	Lochburn Park, Glasgow
2008/9	Beith	Auchinleck Talbot	2-1	Newlandsfield, Glasgow
2009/10	Irvine Meadow	Kirkintilloch Rob Roy	1-0	Newlandsfield, Glasgow
2010/1	Arthurlie	Pollok	1-0	Newlandsfield, Glasgow
2011/2	Irvine Meadow	Ashfield	2-0	Newlandsfield, Glasgow
2012/3	Glenafton Athletic	Glasgow Perthshire	2-2, 4-3 pens	Newlandsfield, Glasgow
2013/14	Auchinleck Talbot	Troon	2-0	Newlandsfield, Glasgow
2014/15	Arthurlie	Kilwinning Rangers	4-2	Newlandsfield, Glasgow
2015/16	Auchinleck Talbot	Hurlford United	2-0	Newlandsfield, Glasgow
2016/17	Pollok	Cumnock	2-2, 5-4 pens	Newlandsfield, Glasgow

Ayrshire Weekly Press Ayrshire Junior Cup 2016/17

1	25/03/2017	Girvan	Lugar Boswell Thistle	4	0	
1	25/03/2017	Glenafton Athletic	Kilbirnie Ladeside	2	1	
1	25/03/2017	Hurlford United	Kilwinning Rangers	1	1	1-4p
1	01/04/2017	Troon	Ardeer Thistle	4	1	
1	25/03/2017	Irvine Meadow	Craogmark Burntonians	6	1	
1	25/03/2017	Muirkirk	Whitletts Vics	0	7	
1	25/03/2017	Cumnock	Largs Thistle	3	2	
1	25/03/2017	Kello Rovers	Ardrossan Winton Rovers	0	2	
2	03/05/2017	Girvan	Glenafton Athletic	1	0	
2	26/04/2017	Kilwinning Rangers	Darvel	3	2	
2	03/05/2017	Troon	Auchinleck Talbot	3	5	
2	06/05/2017	Beith	irvine Meadow	1	1	4-3p
2	03/05/2017	Maybole	Whitletts Vics	2	1	
2	06/05/2017	Irvine Vics	Cumnock	1	2	
2	21/04/2017	Ardrossan Winton Rov	Saltcoats Victoria	5	1	
2	03/05/2017	Dalry Thistle	Annbank United	2	3	
3	10/05/2017	Auchinleck Talbot	Ardrossan Winton Rovers	7	1	
3	10/05/2017	Maybole	Kilwinning Rangers	0	2	
3	31/05/2017	Cumnock	Girvan	4	1	
3	10/05/2017	Annbank United	Beith	2	3	
SF	07/06/2017	Kilwinning Rangers	Auchinleck Talbot	1	2	
SF	07/06/2017	Cumnock	Beith	1	1	4-2p
F	14/06/2017	Auchinleck Talbot	Cumnock	5	1	
		at Irvine Meadow, Att 943				

FINAL DETAILS 2016/17

Auchinleck Talbot v Cumnock, 5-1

Auchinleck: Leishman, S Wilson, White, Shankland, Pope, G Wilson, Hyslop (Sub Thompson), Young (Sub Stevenson), McCracken, McPherson, Latta (Sub Whyte).
Cumnock: Johnston, Wood, Muir, Crawford, McKenna, Esplin, Hunter, Burns, McRobbie, Ansc Samson. Subs Kerr, Muncie, Shirkie, McMaster

1-0	14 mins	Wilson
2-0	44 mins	Wilson
2-1	57 mins	Woods
3-1	60 mins	Wilson
4-1	65 mins	Shankland
5-1	67 mins	Shankland

Recent Ayrshire Cup Finals

Season	Winners	Runners Up	Score	Venue
1988/9	Glenafton Athletic	Dalry Thistle	3-1	Meadow Park, Irvine
1989/90	Cumnock	Saltcoats Vics	3-0	Meadow Park, Irvine
1990/1	Beith	Largs Thistle	3-2 aet	Valefield, Kilbirnie
1991/2	Beith	Irvine Meadow	3-0	Valefield, Kilbirnie
1992/3	Glenafton Athletic	Cumnock	2-1	Townhead Park, Cumnock
1993/4	Auchinleck Talbot	Irvine Meadow	2-0	Abbey Park, Kilwinning
1994/5	Kilwinning Rangers	Largs Thistle	3-1	Meadow Park, Irvine
1995/6	Auchinleck Talbot	Cumnock	3-1	Beechwood Park, Auchinleck
1996/7	Auchinleck Talbot	Kilwinning Rangers	2-1	Meadow Park, Irvine
1997/8	Kilwinning Rangers	Troon	3-2 aet	Meadow Park, Irvine
1998/9	Kilwinning Rangers	Irvine Meadow	2-1	Meadow Park, Irvine
1999/00	Kilwinning Rangers	Auchinleck Talbot	3-2	Beechwood Park, Auchinleck
2000/1	Glenafton Athletic	Kilwinning Rangers	1-0	Meadow Park, Irvine
2001/2	Kilwinning Rangers	Lugar Boswall Thistle	2-0	Blair Park, Hurlford
2002/3	Beith	Kilwinning Rangers	3-1	Meadow Park, Irvine
2003/4	Beith	Lugar Boswall Thistle	2-0	Townhead Park, Cumnock
2004/5	Auchinleck Talbot	Kilbirnie Ladeside	5-0	Rosebank Park, Lugar
2005/6	Irvine Meadow	Kilwinning Rangers	2-1	Townhead Park, Cumnock
2006/7	Irvine Meadow	Dalry Thistle	7-0	Meadow Park, Irvine
2007/8	Cumnock	Kilwinning Rangers	5-0	Townhead Park, Cumnock
2008/9	Irvine Meadow	Auchinleck Talbot	2-1	Townhead Park, Cumnock
2009/10	Cumnock	Girvan	4-3	Beechwood Park, Auchinleck
2010/1	Auchinleck Talbot	Irvine Meadow	4-0	Beechwood Park, Auchinleck
2011/2	Auchinleck Talbot	Troon	5-1	Portland Park, Troon
2012/3	Largs Thistle	Cumnock	3-0	Bellsdale Park, Beith
2013/4	Troon	Hurlford United	2-0	Beechwood Park, Auchinleck
2014/5	Hurlford United	Auchinleck Talbot	2-0	Meadow Park, Irvine
2015/6	Beith	Irvine Meadow	5-1	Abbey Park, Kilwinning
2016/7	Auchinleck Talbot	Cumnock	5-1	Meadow Park, Irvine

Central Regional Cup 2016/17

1	01/04/2017	Royal Albert	Vale of Clyde	3	2	
1	25/03/2017	Ashfield	Benburb	0	5	
		at Benburb				
1	25/03/2017	Neilston	Johnstone Burgh	1	2	
1	19/04/2017	Cumbernauld United	Pollok	1	1	2-4p
1	25/03/2017	Carluke Rovers	Bellshill Athletic	2	1	
1	08/04/2017	Shettleston	Renfrew	2	1	
1	25/03/2017	Yoker Athletic	Kilsyth Rangers	2	1	
2	22/04/2017	Dunipace	Royal Albert	3	1	
2	03/05/2017	Benburb	Thorniewood United	2	2	5-4p
2	01/04/2017	Maryhill	East Kilbridce Thistle	1	2	
2	01/04/2017	Petershill	Clydebank	2	0	
2	03/05/2017	Johnstone Burgh	Forth Wanderers	0	2	
2	03/05/2017	Port Glasgow	Pollok	0	5	
2	13/05/2017	Carluke Rovers	Rossvale	1	4	
2	03/05/2017	Newmains United	Lesmahagow	1	2	
2	01/04/2017	Gartcairn	Vale of Leven	2	0	
2	03/05/2017	Kirkintilloch Rob Roy	St Rochs	0	1	
2	01/04/2017	St Anthonys	Blantyre Vics	2	2	6-7p
2	03/05/2017	Shettleston	Rutherglen Glencairn	0	4	
2	06/05/2017	Shotts Bon Accord	Yoker Athletic	0	4	
2	01/04/2017	Greenock	Lanark United	0	3	
2	01/04/2017	Wishaw	Cambuslang Rangers	0	2	
2	01/04/2017	Larkhall Thistle	Arthurlie	2	2	3-5p
3	10/05/2017	Rutherglen Glencairn	St Rochs	1	2	
3	03/05/2017	East Kilbride Thistle	Petershill	2	4	
3	17/05/2017	Dunipace	Lesmahagow	0	1	
3	03/05/2017	Arthurlie	Gartcairn	3	0	
3	10/05/2017	Pollok	Blantyre Vics	4	1	
3	10/05/2017	Yoker Athletic	Cambuslang Rangers	4	3	
3	17/05/2017	Rossvale	Greenock	3	0	
3	20/05/2017	Forth W	Benburb	3	4	
4	20/05/2017	Rossvale	Petershill	1	5	
4	17/05/2017	Yoker Athletic	St Rochs	1	1	5-4p
4	31/05/2017	Benburb	Lesmahagow	2	2	5-4p
		Protest (upheld), game replayed				
4	17/05/2017	Arthurlie	Pollok	2	4	
4	05/06/2017	Benburb	Lesmahagow	3	0	
SF	31/05/2017	Pollok	Petershill	1	2	
SF	07/06/2017	Benburb	Yoker Athletic	1	3	
F	11/06/2017	Petershill	Yoker Athletic	2	0	
		at Cambuslang, Att 400				

FINAL DETAILS

Petershill v Yoker Athletic, 2-0

Petershill: White, Friel, Bradley, Kennedy, Murphy, Murch, McCann, Stevenson, McGladrigan, Callander, Gold. Subs Cassells, Hall, Hardie, Ketterer, McNeil

Yoker: Campbell, Bailey, Smith, Allan, Harvie, Bissland, Rankin, henry, Hynes, Roberts, Maitland. Subs Carson, Arbuckle, Campbell, Crerand, Wilson

1-0	32 mins	Callander
2-0	44 mins	McGladrigan

Recent Central District KO Cup Finals				
Season	**Winners**	**Runners Up**	**Score**	**Venue**
1988/9	Pollok	Glasgow Perthshire	2-1	Greenfield Park, Glasgo
1989/90	Vale of Clyde	Shotts Bon Accord	5-1	Newlandsfield, Glasgow
1990/1	Arthurlie	Cambuslang Rangers	3-2	Newlandsfield, Glasgow
1991/2	Petershill	Shotts Bon Accord	1-0	Newlandsfield, Glasgow
1992/3	Lesmahagow	Bellshill Athletic	3-1	Newlandsfield, Glasgow
1993/4	Shotts Bon Accord	Shettleston	0-0, 4-2 pens	Newlandsfield, Glasgow
1994/5	not completed			
1995/6	Maryhill	Pollok	1-0	Somervell Park, Cambu
1996/7	Arthurlie	Pollok	2-1 aet	Somervell Park, Cambu
1997/8	Arthurlie	Shettleston	4-0	Newlandsfield, Glasgow
1998/9	Rutherglen Glencairn	Shettleston	4-1	Newlandsfield, Glasgow
1999/00	Benburb	Shettleston	2-1	Newlandsfield, Glasgow
2000/1	Bellshill Athletic	Pollok	0-0, 3-2 pens	Somervell Park, Cambu
2001/2	Shettleston	Johnstone Burgh	4-1	Petershill Park, Glasgo
2002/3	Arthurlie	Larkhall Thistle	2-1	Petershill Park, Glasgo
2003/4	Petershill	Maryhill	2-0	Adamslie Park, Kirkintil
2004/5	Pollok	Arthurlie	2-0	Petershill Park, Glasgo
2005/6	Maryhill	Greenock	2-1	Newlandsfield, Glasgow
2006/7	Lanark United	Kirkintilloch Rob Roy	2-1	Somervell Park, Cambu
2007/8	Arthurlie	Renfrew	3-0	Dunterlie Park, Barrhea
2008/9	Pollok	Kilsyth Rangers	1-1, 4-3 pens	Newlandsfield, Glasgow
2009/10	Clydebank	Ashfield	2-0	Newlandsfield, Glasgow
2010/1	Pollok	Shotts Bon Accord	7-3	Newlandsfield, Glasgow
2011/2	Clydebank	Shotts Bon Accord	3-0	Newlandsfield, Glasgow
2012/3	Pollok	Ashfield	3-0	Newlandsfield, Glasgow
2013/4	Clydebank	Cumbernauld United	3-0	Newlandsfield, Glasgow
2014/5	Thorniewood United	Blantyre Vics	2-2, 4-3 pens	Newlandsfield, Glasgow
2015/6	Pollok	Greenock	7-1	Somervell Park, Cambu
2016/7	Petershill	Yoker Athletic	2-0	Somervell Park, Cambu

Early Season 2017/18 West Junior Fixtures

CENTRAL SECTIONAL LEAGUE CUP

06/08/2016	14:00	Arthurlie F.C.	v St. Anthony's F.C.
06/08/2016		Bellshill Athletic F.C.	v Thorniewood United F.C.
06/08/2016		Benburb F.C.	v Pollok F.C.
06/08/2016		Blantyre Victoria F.C.	v Vale of Clyde F.C.
06/08/2016		Cambuslang Rangers F.C.	v Rutherglen Glencairn F.C.
06/08/2016		Carluke Rovers F.C.	v Shotts Bon Accord F.C.
06/08/2016		Clydebank F.C.	v Yoker Athletic F.C.
06/08/2016		Cumbernauld United F.C.	v Kirkintilloch Rob Roy F.C.
06/08/2016		Forth Wanderers F.C.	v Larkhall Thistle F.C.
06/08/2016		Glasgow Perthshire F.C.	v Ashfield F.C.
06/08/2016		Greenock Juniors F.C.	v Renfrew F.C.
06/08/2016		Johnstone Burgh F.C.	v Vale of Leven F.C.
06/08/2016		Kilsyth Rangers F.C.	v Rossvale JFC
06/08/2016		Lesmahagow Juniors F.C.	v Royal Albert F.C.
06/08/2016		Newmains United Comm FC	v Gartcairn F.C.
06/08/2016		Petershill F.C.	v St. Roch's F.C.
10/08/2016	18:45	Clydebank F.C.	v Glasgow Perthshire F.C.
10/08/2016		Dunipace F.C.	v Kirkintilloch Rob Roy F.C.
10/08/2016		East Kilbride Thistle F.C.	v Blantyre Victoria F.C.
10/08/2016		Kilsyth Rangers F.C.	v Cumbernauld United F.C.
10/08/2016		Larkhall Thistle F.C.	v Lanark United F.C.
10/08/2016		Maryhill F.C.	v Ashfield F.C.
10/08/2016		Neilston Juniors F.C.	v Benburb F.C.
10/08/2016		Pollok F.C.	v St. Anthony's F.C.
10/08/2016		Port Glasgow Juniors F.C.	v Johnstone Burgh F.C.
10/08/2016		Royal Albert F.C.	v Forth Wanderers F.C.
10/08/2016		Shettleston F.C.	v Bellshill Athletic F.C.
10/08/2016		Shotts Bon Accord F.C.	v Newmains United Comm FC
10/08/2016		Thorniewood United F.C.	v Petershill F.C.
10/08/2016		Vale of Clyde F.C.	v Cambuslang Rangers F.C.
10/08/2016		Vale of Leven F.C.	v Greenock Juniors F.C.
10/08/2016		Wishaw Juniors F.C.	v Carluke Rovers F.C.
13/08/2016	14:00	Ashfield F.C.	v Yoker Athletic F.C.
13/08/2016		East Kilbride Thistle F.C.	v Cambuslang Rangers F.C.
13/08/2016		Forth Wanderers F.C.	v Lanark United F.C.
13/08/2016		Gartcairn F.C.	v Shotts Bon Accord F.C.
13/08/2016		Glasgow Perthshire F.C.	v Maryhill F.C.
13/08/2016		Kirkintilloch Rob Roy F.C.	v Kilsyth Rangers F.C.
13/08/2016		Larkhall Thistle F.C.	v Lesmahagow Juniors F.C.
13/08/2016		Neilston Juniors F.C.	v Arthurlie F.C.
13/08/2016		Port Glasgow Juniors F.C.	v Greenock Juniors F.C.
13/08/2016		Renfrew F.C.	v Vale of Leven F.C.
13/08/2016		Rossvale JFC	v Dunipace F.C.
13/08/2016		Rutherglen Glencairn F.C.	v Vale of Clyde F.C.
13/08/2016		Shettleston F.C.	v Petershill F.C.
13/08/2016		St. Anthony's F.C.	v Benburb F.C.
13/08/2016		St. Roch's F.C.	v Thorniewood United F.C.
13/08/2016		Wishaw Juniors F.C.	v Newmains United Comm FC
17/08/2016		St. Roch's F.C.	v Shettleston F.C.
17/08/2016	18:45	Benburb F.C.	v Arthurlie F.C.
17/08/2016		Blantyre Victoria F.C.	v Rutherglen Glencairn F.C.
17/08/2016		Cumbernauld United F.C.	v Rossvale JFC
17/08/2016		Dunipace F.C.	v Kilsyth Rangers F.C.
17/08/2016		Gartcairn F.C.	v Wishaw Juniors F.C.
17/08/2016		Greenock Juniors F.C.	v Johnstone Burgh F.C.
17/08/2016		Lanark United F.C.	v Royal Albert F.C.
17/08/2016		Lesmahagow Juniors F.C.	v Forth Wanderers F.C.
17/08/2016		Maryhill F.C.	v Clydebank F.C.
17/08/2016		Newmains United Comm FC	v Carluke Rovers F.C.
17/08/2016		Petershill F.C.	v Bellshill Athletic F.C.
17/08/2016		Pollok F.C.	v Neilston Juniors F.C.
17/08/2016		Renfrew F.C.	v Port Glasgow Juniors F.C.
17/08/2016		Vale of Clyde F.C.	v East Kilbride Thistle F.C.
17/08/2016		Yoker Athletic F.C.	v Glasgow Perthshire F.C.
20/08/2016	14:00	Arthurlie F.C.	v Pollok F.C.
20/08/2016		Ashfield F.C.	v Clydebank F.C.
20/08/2016		Bellshill Athletic F.C.	v St. Roch's F.C.
20/08/2016		Cambuslang Rangers F.C.	v Blantyre Victoria F.C.
20/08/2016		Carluke Rovers F.C.	v Gartcairn F.C.
20/08/2016		Dunipace F.C.	v Cumbernauld United F.C.
20/08/2016		Johnstone Burgh F.C.	v Renfrew F.C.
20/08/2016		Kirkintilloch Rob Roy F.C.	v Rossvale JFC
20/08/2016		Lanark United F.C.	v Lesmahagow Juniors F.C.
20/08/2016		Royal Albert F.C.	v Larkhall Thistle F.C.
20/08/2016		Rutherglen Glencairn F.C.	v East Kilbride Thistle F.C.
20/08/2016		Shotts Bon Accord F.C.	v Wishaw Juniors F.C.
20/08/2016		St. Anthony's F.C.	v Neilston Juniors F.C.
20/08/2016		Thorniewood United F.C.	v Shettleston F.C.
20/08/2016		Vale of Leven F.C.	v Port Glasgow Juniors F.C.
20/08/2016		Yoker Athletic F.C.	v Maryhill F.C.

AYRSHIRE SECTIONAL LEAGUE CUP

06/08/2016	14:00	Craigmark Burntonians F.C.	v Annbank United F.C.
06/08/2016		Cumnock Juniors F.C.	v Lugar Boswell Thistle F.C.
06/08/2016		Dalry Thistle F.C.	v Ardrossan Winton Rovers F.C.
06/08/2016		Darvel Juniors F.C.	v Ardeer Thistle F.C.
06/08/2016		Irvine Victoria F.C.	v Hurlford United F.C.
06/08/2016		Kello Rovers F.C.	v Glenafton Athletic F.C.
06/08/2016		Kilbirnie Ladeside F.C.	v Beith Juniors F.C.
06/08/2016		Largs Thistle F.C.	v Kilwinning Rangers F.C.
06/08/2016		Maybole Juniors F.C.	v Girvan F.C.
06/08/2016		Muirkirk Juniors F.C.	v Auchinleck Talbot F.C.
06/08/2016		Saltcoats Victoria F.C.	v Irvine Meadow XI F.C.
06/08/2016		Whitletts Victoria F.C.	v Troon F.C.
10/08/2016	18:45	Annbank United F.C.	v Girvan F.C.
10/08/2016		Ardrossan Winton Rovers F.C.	v Largs Thistle F.C.
10/08/2016		Beith Juniors F.C.	v Dalry Thistle F.C.
10/08/2016		Craigmark Burntonians F.C.	v Whitletts Victoria F.C.
10/08/2016		Glenafton Athletic F.C.	v Auchinleck Talbot F.C.
10/08/2016		Hurlford United F.C.	v Irvine Meadow XI F.C.
10/08/2016		Irvine Victoria F.C.	v Darvel Juniors F.C.
10/08/2016		Kello Rovers F.C.	v Cumnock Juniors F.C.
10/08/2016		Kilwinning Rangers F.C.	v Kilbirnie Ladeside F.C.
10/08/2016		Muirkirk Juniors F.C.	v Lugar Boswell Thistle F.C.
10/08/2016		Saltcoats Victoria F.C.	v Ardeer Thistle F.C.
10/08/2016		Troon F.C.	v Maybole Juniors F.C.
13/08/2016	14:00	Auchinleck Talbot F.C.	v Cumnock Juniors F.C.
13/08/2016		Beith Juniors F.C.	v Ardrossan Winton Rovers F.C.
13/08/2016		Dalry Thistle F.C.	v Kilwinning Rangers F.C.
13/08/2016		Darvel Juniors F.C.	v Hurlford United F.C.
13/08/2016		Girvan F.C.	v Troon F.C.
13/08/2016		Glenafton Athletic F.C.	v Muirkirk Juniors F.C.
13/08/2016		Irvine Meadow XI F.C.	v Ardeer Thistle F.C.
13/08/2016		Kilbirnie Ladeside F.C.	v Largs Thistle F.C.
13/08/2016		Lugar Boswell Thistle F.C.	v Kello Rovers F.C.
13/08/2016		Maybole Juniors F.C.	v Craigmark Burntonians F.C.
13/08/2016		Saltcoats Victoria F.C.	v Irvine Victoria F.C.
13/08/2016		Whitletts Victoria F.C.	v Annbank United F.C.
17/08/2016	18:45	Ardeer Thistle F.C.	v Irvine Victoria F.C.
17/08/2016		Ardrossan Winton Rovers F.C.	v Kilwinning Rangers F.C.
17/08/2016		Auchinleck Talbot F.C.	v Lugar Boswell Thistle F.C.
17/08/2016		Beith Juniors F.C.	v Largs Thistle F.C.
17/08/2016		Dalry Thistle F.C.	v Kilbirnie Ladeside F.C.
17/08/2016		Girvan F.C.	v Whitletts Victoria F.C.
17/08/2016		Glenafton Athletic F.C.	v Cumnock Juniors F.C.
17/08/2016		Hurlford United F.C.	v Saltcoats Victoria F.C.
17/08/2016		Irvine Meadow XI F.C.	v Darvel Juniors F.C.
17/08/2016		Maybole Juniors F.C.	v Annbank United F.C.
17/08/2016		Muirkirk Juniors F.C.	v Kello Rovers F.C.
17/08/2016		Troon F.C.	v Craigmark Burntonians F.C.
18/09/2016		Irvine Meadow XI F.C.	v Irvine Victoria F.C.
20/08/2016	14:00	Annbank United F.C.	v Troon F.C.
20/08/2016		Ardeer Thistle F.C.	v Hurlford United F.C.
20/08/2016		Craigmark Burntonians F.C.	v Girvan F.C.
20/08/2016		Cumnock Juniors F.C.	v Muirkirk Juniors F.C.
20/08/2016		Darvel Juniors F.C.	v Saltcoats Victoria F.C.
20/08/2016		Kello Rovers F.C.	v Auchinleck Talbot F.C.
20/08/2016		Kilbirnie Ladeside F.C.	v Ardrossan Winton Rovers F.C.
20/08/2016		Kilwinning Rangers F.C.	v Beith Juniors F.C.
20/08/2016		Largs Thistle F.C.	v Dalry Thistle F.C.
20/08/2016		Lugar Boswell Thistle F.C.	v Glenafton Athletic F.C.
20/08/2016		Whitletts Victoria F.C.	v Maybole Juniors F.C.

WEST SUPER PREMIER			
27/08/2016	14:00	Arthurlie F.C.	v Auchinleck Talbot F.C.
	14:00	Beith Juniors F.C.	v Cumnock Juniors F.C.
	14:00	Glenafton Athletic F.C.	v Pollok F.C.
	14:00	Hurlford United F.C.	v Kilwinning Rangers F.C.
	14:00	Kirkintilloch Rob Roy F.C.	v Largs Thistle F.C.
	14:00	Troon F.C.	v Kilbirnie Ladeside F.C.
03/09/2016	14:00	Auchinleck Talbot F.C.	v Beith Juniors F.C.
	14:00	Cumnock Juniors F.C.	v Kirkintilloch Rob Roy F.C.
	14:00	Kilbirnie Ladeside F.C.	v Arthurlie F.C.
	14:00	Kilwinning Rangers F.C.	v Glenafton Athletic F.C.
	14:00	Largs Thistle F.C.	v Hurlford United F.C.
	14:00	Pollok F.C.	v Troon F.C.
10/09/2016	14:00	Auchinleck Talbot F.C.	v Troon F.C.
	14:00	Beith Juniors F.C.	v Arthurlie F.C.
	14:00	Cumnock Juniors F.C.	v Largs Thistle F.C.
	14:00	Kilbirnie Ladeside F.C.	v Glenafton Athletic F.C.
	14:00	Kilwinning Rangers F.C.	v Kirkintilloch Rob Roy F.C.
	14:00	Pollok F.C.	v Hurlford United F.C.
17/09/2016	14:00	Arthurlie F.C.	v Cumnock Juniors F.C.
	14:00	Glenafton Athletic F.C.	v Auchinleck Talbot F.C.
	14:00	Hurlford United F.C.	v Kilbirnie Ladeside F.C.
	14:00	Kirkintilloch Rob Roy F.C.	v Pollok F.C.
	14:00	Largs Thistle F.C.	v Kilwinning Rangers F.C.

WEST SUPER FIRST			
27/08/2016	14:00	Blantyre Victoria F.C.	v Cumbernauld United F.C.
	14:00	Irvine Meadow XI F.C.	v Clydebank F.C.
	14:00	Kilsyth Rangers F.C.	v Shettleston F.C.
	14:00	Petershill F.C.	v Maryhill F.C.
	14:00	Rutherglen Glencairn F.C.	v Renfrew F.C.
	14:00	Shotts Bon Accord F.C.	v Girvan F.C.
	14:00	Yoker Athletic F.C.	v Irvine Victoria F.C.
	14:00	Clydebank F.C.	v Shotts Bon Accord F.C.
03/09/2016	14:00	Cumbernauld United F.C.	v Yoker Athletic F.C.
	14:00	Girvan F.C.	v Petershill F.C.
	14:00	Irvine Victoria F.C.	v Blantyre Victoria F.C.
	14:00	Maryhill F.C.	v Kilsyth Rangers F.C.
	14:00	Renfrew F.C.	v Irvine Meadow XI F.C.
	14:00	Shettleston F.C.	v Rutherglen Glencairn F.C.
10/09/2016	14:00	Clydebank F.C.	v Yoker Athletic F.C.
	14:00	Cumbernauld United F.C.	v Irvine Victoria F.C.
	14:00	Girvan F.C.	v Blantyre Victoria F.C.
	14:00	Irvine Meadow XI F.C.	v Rutherglen Glencairn F.C.
	14:00	Maryhill F.C.	v Shotts Bon Accord F.C.
	14:00	Renfrew F.C.	v Kilsyth Rangers F.C.
	14:00	Shettleston F.C.	v Petershill F.C.
17/09/2016	14:00	Blantyre Victoria F.C.	v Maryhill F.C.
	14:00	Irvine Victoria F.C.	v Clydebank F.C.
	14:00	Kilsyth Rangers F.C.	v Irvine Meadow XI F.C.
	14:00	Petershill F.C.	v Renfrew F.C.
	14:00	Rutherglen Glencairn F.C.	v Cumbernauld United F.C.
	14:00	Shotts Bon Accord F.C.	v Shettleston F.C.
	14:00	Yoker Athletic F.C.	v Girvan F.C.

AYRSHIRE DISTRICT			
27/08/2016	14:00	Annbank United F.C.	v Ardrossan Winton Rovers F.C.
	14:00	Craigmark Burntonians F.C.	v Saltcoats Victoria F.C.
	14:00	Dalry Thistle F.C.	v Kello Rovers F.C.
	14:00	Darvel Juniors F.C.	v Whitletts Victoria F.C.
	14:00	Lugar Boswell Thistle F.C.	v Ardeer Thistle F.C.
	14:00	Maybole Juniors F.C.	v Muirkirk Juniors F.C.
03/09/2016	14:00	Ardeer Thistle F.C.	v Maybole Juniors F.C.
	14:00	Ardrossan Winton Rovers F.C.	v Craigmark Burntonians F.C.
	14:00	Kello Rovers F.C.	v Darvel Juniors F.C.
	14:00	Muirkirk Juniors F.C.	v Dalry Thistle F.C.
	14:00	Saltcoats Victoria F.C.	v Lugar Boswell Thistle F.C.
	14:00	Whitletts Victoria F.C.	v Annbank United F.C.
10/09/2016	14:00	Ardrossan Winton Rovers F.C.	v Darvel Juniors F.C.
	14:00	Craigmark Burntonians F.C.	v Annbank United F.C.
	14:00	Kello Rovers F.C.	v Maybole Juniors F.C.
	14:00	Muirkirk Juniors F.C.	v Lugar Boswell Thistle F.C.
	14:00	Saltcoats Victoria F.C.	v Ardeer Thistle F.C.
	14:00	Whitletts Victoria F.C.	v Dalry Thistle F.C.
17/09/2016	14:00	Annbank United F.C.	v Saltcoats Victoria F.C.
	14:00	Ardeer Thistle F.C.	v Muirkirk Juniors F.C.
	14:00	Dalry Thistle F.C.	v Ardrossan Winton Rovers F.C.
	14:00	Darvel Juniors F.C.	v Craigmark Burntonians F.C.
	14:00	Lugar Boswell Thistle F.C.	v Kello Rovers F.C.
	14:00	Maybole Juniors F.C.	v Whitletts Victoria F.C.

CENTRAL DISTRICT DIVISION 1			
27/08/2016	14:00	Bellshill Athletic F.C.	v Rossvale JFC
	14:00	Greenock Juniors F.C.	v Wishaw Juniors F.C.
	14:00	Johnstone Burgh F.C.	v Benburb F.C.
	14:00	Lesmahagow Juniors F.C.	v Cambuslang Rangers F.C.
	14:00	Neilston Juniors F.C.	v Forth Wanderers F.C.
	14:00	St. Roch's F.C.	v Vale of Clyde F.C.
	14:00	Thorniewood United F.C.	v Larkhall Thistle F.C.
03/09/2016	14:00	Benburb F.C.	v St. Roch's F.C.
	14:00	Cambuslang Rangers F.C.	v Greenock Juniors F.C.
	14:00	Forth Wanderers F.C.	v Thorniewood United F.C.
	14:00	Larkhall Thistle F.C.	v Neilston Juniors F.C.
	14:00	Rossvale JFC	v Lesmahagow Juniors F.C.
	14:00	Vale of Clyde F.C.	v Bellshill Athletic F.C.
	14:00	Wishaw Juniors F.C.	v Johnstone Burgh F.C.
10/09/2016	14:00	Benburb F.C.	v Thorniewood United F.C.
	14:00	Cambuslang Rangers F.C.	v Bellshill Athletic F.C.
	14:00	Forth Wanderers F.C.	v Larkhall Thistle F.C.
	14:00	Johnstone Burgh F.C.	v Greenock Juniors F.C.
	14:00	Rossvale JFC	v St. Roch's F.C.
	14:00	Vale of Clyde F.C.	v Neilston Juniors F.C.
	14:00	Wishaw Juniors F.C.	v Lesmahagow Juniors F.C.
17/09/2016	14:00	Bellshill Athletic F.C.	v Wishaw Juniors F.C.
	14:00	Greenock Juniors F.C.	v Forth Wanderers F.C.
	14:00	Larkhall Thistle F.C.	v Benburb F.C.
	14:00	Lesmahagow Juniors F.C.	v Johnstone Burgh F.C.
	14:00	Neilston Juniors F.C.	v Rossvale JFC
	14:00	St. Roch's F.C.	v Cambuslang Rangers F.C.
	14:00	Thorniewood United F.C.	v Vale of Clyde F.C.

CENTRAL DISTRICT DIVISION 2			
27/08/2016	14:00	Ashfield F.C.	v East Kilbride Thistle F.C.
	14:00	Carluke Rovers F.C.	v Glasgow Perthshire F.C.
	14:00	Dunipace F.C.	v Vale of Leven F.C.
	14:00	Lanark United F.C.	v Newmains United Comm FC
	14:00	Royal Albert F.C.	v Port Glasgow Juniors F.C.
	14:00	St. Anthony's F.C.	v Gartcairn F.C.
03/09/2016	14:00	East Kilbride Thistle F.C.	v Carluke Rovers F.C.
	14:00	Gartcairn F.C.	v Dunipace F.C.
	14:00	Glasgow Perthshire F.C.	v Royal Albert F.C.
	14:00	Newmains United Comm FC	v St. Anthony's F.C.
	14:00	Port Glasgow Juniors F.C.	v Lanark United F.C.
	14:00	Vale of Leven F.C.	v Ashfield F.C.
10/09/2016	14:00	Carluke Rovers F.C.	v Ashfield F.C.
	14:00	East Kilbride Thistle F.C.	v Dunipace F.C.
	14:00	Gartcairn F.C.	v Lanark United F.C.
	14:00	Glasgow Perthshire F.C.	v Port Glasgow Juniors F.C.
	14:00	Newmains United Comm FC	v Royal Albert F.C.
	14:00	Vale of Leven F.C.	v St. Anthony's F.C.
17/09/2016	14:00	Ashfield F.C.	v Glasgow Perthshire F.C.
	14:00	Dunipace F.C.	v Carluke Rovers F.C.
	14:00	Lanark United F.C.	v Vale of Leven F.C.
	14:00	Port Glasgow Juniors F.C.	v Newmains United Comm FC
	14:00	Royal Albert F.C.	v Gartcairn F.C.
	14:00	St. Anthony's F.C.	v East Kilbride Thistle F.C.

sUbsequent fixtures issued on an ad hoc basis

Evening Times Champions Cup 2016/17

P	20/05/2017	Glasgow Perthshire	Darvel	1	0
SF	31/05/2017	Glasgow Perthshire	Cambuslang Rangers	4	2
SF	07/06/2017	Glenafton Athletic	Girvan	3	1
F	10/06/2017	Glenafton Athletic	Glasgow Perthshire	2	0
		at Benburb, Att 500			

FINAL DETAILS

Glenafton Athletic v Glasgow Perthshire, 2-0

1-0 3 mins Gray
2-0 72 mins Marlow

The Evening Times Trophy has been competed for since 1896/7 but in a variety of formats.

1896/7-1926/7 The trophy was the prize for the winners of the Glasgow Junior League.

1927/8-1930/1 This was the time of the "split" and the Evening Times Trophy was awarded to the overall Champions of the Scottish Intermediate League, following a play off between the winners of the East and West Divisions.

1931/2-1967/8 The trophy went to the winners of the Central League. Depending on the number of divisions there might be semi -finals or a preliminary round.

1968/9-1978/9 By now there were three Divisions A, B and C. The winners of B and C played off for the right to meet the A Division Champions. The lower league sides frequently won due to fixture congestion catching up on the A Division club.

1979/80-1981/2 The Evening Times Trophy was renamed the Evening Times Cup. It was contested for by the Central League's Division A Champions, the Sectional Cup winners, Central KO Cup winners and the McLeod Trophy winners

1982/3 to 2001/2 The 3 Central Division winners, plus the winners of the Sectional and KO League cups were entered.

2002/3 to 2011/2 Amalgamation of the Central and Ayrshire Juniors led to an expanded tournament. The five Divisional winners were joined by the West of Scotland , Ayrshire District, Central District KO, Ayrshire Sectional and Central Sectional Cups, giving a potential 10 entrants.

2012/13 - date Difficulties in fitting in dates for so many clubs meant the Cup was restricted to the 5 League Champions - it was renamed the Evening Times Champions Cup.

Clydesdale Cup 2016/17

SF	26/07/2016	Forth Wanderers	Lesmahagow	3	0	
SF	25/07/2016	Lanark United	Carluke Rovers	1	1	4-1 p
F	01/08/2016	Lanark United	Forth Wanderers	4	1	

FINAL DETAILS

Lanark United v Forth Wanderers, 4-1, H.T. 2-1
Scorers Lanark: Gallagher, Maxwell 2, McGurk, Forth: McLaren

Lanark United: Duke, Christie, Murphy, Lawson, Collins, Imrie, Maxwell, McCrum, Gallacher, Duggan, McGurk
Forth Wanderers: Cherrie, Watson, St. Tait, Gupwell, McMullen, Dick, Greenfell, Rennie, Scott, McGeechan, McLaren

Several local councils around Scotland have sponsored Cup competitions for Junior sides. The only one that seems to be extant is the Clydesdale Cup, covering the former Clydesdale District Council area in Lanarkshire. The East, North and South Ayrshire competitions continued into the 2000s before disappearing from the calendar. Midlothian Council's Andy Kelly trophy ran for a few years in the late 2000s.

Evening Times Cup Winners Cup / Champions Cup - Recent Finals				
Year	*Winners*	*Runners Up*	*Score*	*Venue*
1988/9	Arthurlie	Lesmahagow	2-1	Somervell Park, Cambuslang
1989/90	Vale of Clyde	Dunipace	1-0	Greenfield Park, Shettleston
1990/1	Cambuslang Rangers	Pollok	2-0 AET	Greenfield Park, Shettleston
1991/2	Petershill	Johnstone Burgh	3-1 AET	Somervell Park, Cambuslang
1992/3	Lesmahagow	Pollok	4-1	Somervell Park, Cambuslang
1993/4	Arthurlie	Shotts Bon Accord	3-1	Somervell Park, Cambuslang
1994/5	Arthurlie	Petershill	3-1	Newlandsfield, Pollok
1995/6	Maryhill	Blantyre Vics	3-0	Somervell Park, Cambuslang
1996/7	Maryhill	Pollok	2-1	Somervell Park, Cambuslang
1997/8	Maryhill	Greenock	5-1	Lochburn Park, Maryhill
1998/9	Dunipace	Rutherglen Glencairn	3-0	Somervell Park, Cambuslang
1999/00	Port Glasgow	Shettleston	3-1	Somervell Park, Cambuslang
2000/1	Arthurlie	Bellshill Athletic	2-0	Adamslie Park, Kirkintilloch
2001/2	Johnstone Burgh	Bellshill Athletic	3-1	Adamslie Park, Kirkintilloch
2002/3	Kilsyth Rangers	Larkhall Thistle	1-0	Petershill Park, Glasgow
2003/4	Pollok	Petershill	3-1	Lochburn Park, Maryhill
2004/5	Lanark United	Beith	2-0	Petershill Park, Glasgow
2005/6	Irvine Meadow	Maryhill	1-0	Newlandsfield, Pollok
2006/7	Pollok	Irvine Meadow	3-1	Somervell Park, Cambuslang
2007/8	Pollok	Cumnock	3-1	Lochburn Park, Maryhill
2008/9	Irvine Meadow	Pollok	1-0	Newlandsfield, Pollok
2009/10	Irvine Meadow	Kilbirnie Ladeside	4-0	Newlandsfield, Pollok
2010/11	Arthurlie	Shotts Bon Accord	1-0	Newlandsfield, Pollok
2011/2	Ashfield	Irvine Meadow	1-0	Newlandsfield, Pollok
2012/3	Auchinleck Talbot	Hurlford United	3-0	Newlandsfield, Pollok
2013/4	Auchinleck Talbot	Neilston	7-1	Newlandsfield, Pollok
2014/5	Pollok	Blantyre Vics	3-1	Newlandsfield, Pollok
2015/6	Auchinleck Talbot	Renfrew	5-2	Newlandsfield, Pollok
2016/7	Glenafton Athletic	Glasgow Perthshire	2-0	New Tinto Park, Govan

SENIOR NON LEAGUE FOOTBALL

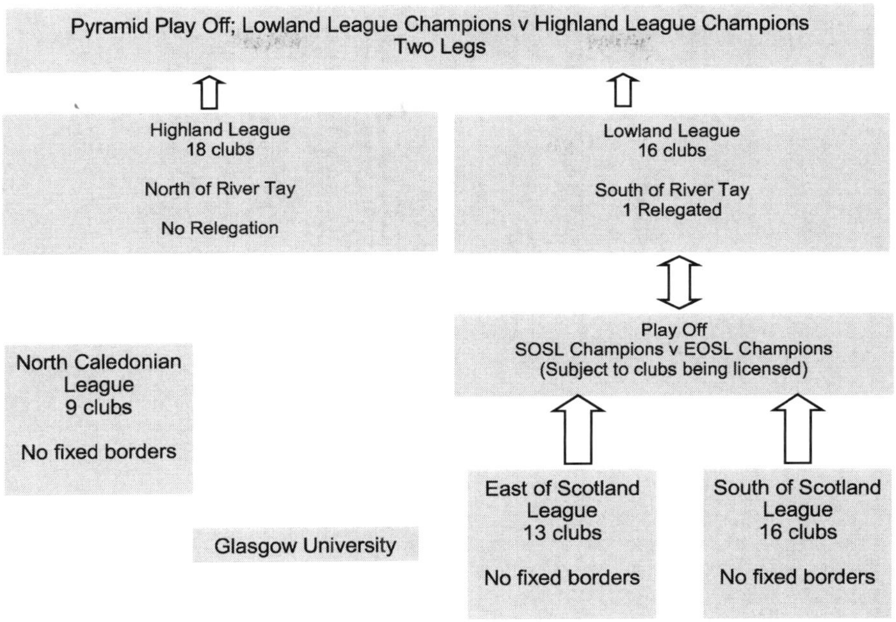

The table below shows the distribution of Senior Non League teams by Local Authority population.

	Local Authority	Pop	Teams		Local Authority	Pop	
1	City of Glasgow	596,550		17	Scottish Borders	112,900	7
2	City of Edinburgh	492,680	7	18	South Ayrshire	111,400	
3	Fife	365,000	2	19	Angus	110,600	
4	North Lanarkshire	338,000	2	20	East Dunbartonshire	104,600	
5	South Lanarkshire	314,000	1	21	East Lothian	97,500	2
6	Aberdeenshire	253,000	12	22	West Dunbartonshire	90,600	
7	Highland	221,600	14	23	Stirling	89,900	
8	City of Aberdeen	217,100		24	East Renfrewshire	89,500	
9	West Lothian	172,100		25	Argyll and Bute	89,200	
10	Renfrewshire	170,300		26	Moray	87,700	
11	Falkirk	153,300	2	27	Midlothian	81,100	1
12	Dumfries and Galloway	148,200	16	28	Inverclyde	79,800	
13	Perth and Kinross	147,800		29	Clackmannanshire	50,600	1
14	City of Dundee	144,300		30	Na h-Eileanan Siar (Western Isles)	26,200	
15	North Ayrshire	135,200		31	Shetland Islands	22,400	
16	East Ayrshire	120,200	1	32	Orkney Islands	20,100	1
	Total 69 clubs						
	Does not include Annan, Stranraer or Stirling Uni Reserves, or Tweedmouth						

Ferrari Packaging Lowland League 2016/17

	BSC	CSS	CUM	DAL	EK	ES	EDU	GAL	GRE	HAW	PRE	SEL	SPA	STIR	VOL	WHI
BSC Glasgow		Sep 9	Nov 19	Nov 12	Mar 4	Dec 31	Aug 10	Jul 30	Dec 10	Aug 13	Nov 26	Jan 28	Aug 27	Jan 7	Oct 5	Apr 22
		2-1	1-1	2-3	1-1	0-6	0-0	2-3	2-0	3-1	8-3	1-1	1-2	4-1	2-0	3-0
Civil Service Strollers	Apr 8		Dec 17	Oct 29	Mar 25	Aug 27	Mar 18	Aug 10	Apr 1	Jul 30	Oct 8	Nov 5	Sep 3	Apr 15	Mar 11	Jan 7
	3-1		1-1	4-2	1-1	3-8	2-1	3-3	1-2	0-5	3-1	5-2	2-2	1-2	2-4	0-2
Cumbernauld Colts	Feb 4	Aug 20		Jan 7	Oct 8	Mar 3	Sep 3	Apr 22	Jul 30	Nov 4	Aug 10	Feb 18	Apr 1	Dec 10	Feb 25	Mar 29
	4-3	1-0		3-0	0-2	3-3	2-0	1-1	2-3	1-1	5-0	1-2	2-0	0-3	1-3	2-1
Dalbeattie Star	Aug 20	Jan 28	Aug 6		Jan 14	Apr 15	Mar 25	Nov 19	Oct 8	Feb 11	Dec 17	Sep 10	Oct 1	Sep 3	Dec 10	Mar 15
	3-2	2-2	2-0		0-3	2-2	1-2	2-0	1-3	7-1	2-3	5-1	4-3	0-1	2-0	2-0
East Kilbride	Nov 5	Nov 16	Dec 30	Aug 10		Sep 3	Feb 18	Aug 27	Jan 7	Mar 21	Feb 11	Aug 6	Apr 15	Feb 25	Oct 29	Dec 10
	3-1	4-0	0-1	3-0		1-0	2-0	3-1	3-0	2-1	4-0	6-0	2-0	5-0	4-2	4-1
East Stirlingshire	Oct 8	Dec 10	Sep 10	Nov 5	Apr 22		Jan 7	Feb 25	Oct 1	Aug 20	Nov 19	Nov 26	Jan 29	Sep 21	Aug 6	Feb 18
	3-0	3-3	4-1	2-1	3-2		1-1	3-0	5-0	3-1	6-2	5-0	1-4	4-1	2-2	3-0
Edinburgh University	Apr 1	Aug 31	Feb 11	Aug 13	Oct 4	Jan 21		Dec 10	Aug 27	Mar 4	Apr 22	Feb 25	Feb 4	Jan 10	Nov 19	Oct 1
	1-3	0-0	2-0	0-1	0-4	0-1		0-1	3-4	2-1	4-0	3-2	0-0	1-3	1-1	2-0
Gala Fairydean Rovers	Mar 11	Mar 4	Oct 1	Feb 4	Apr 1	Dec 3	Aug 20		Apr 15	Dec 31	Sep 10	Jan 21	Nov 5	Aug 6	Nov 16	Aug 31
	2-1	3-2	2-2	2-4	1-6	1-10	1-3		1-0	5-1	3-1	1-1	3-2	1-1	4-2	2-3
Gretna 2008	Sep 3	Aug 6	Jan 14	Dec 31	Aug 31	Feb 11	Dec 17	Oct 4		Apr 8	Nov 12	Mar 25	Feb 18	Sep 17	Apr 22	Aug 20
	1-3	0-4	1-1	1-0	1-5	0-3	0-0	1-1		2-0	5-3	1-1	0-3	0-3	3-0	3-1
Hawick Royal Albert	Apr 15	Feb 18	Mar 18	Sep 17	Dec 17	Mar 25	Sep 10	Oct 8	Aug 10		Aug 27	Oct 4	Mar 11	Nov 19	Apr 18	Aug 6
	2-3	2-5	4-3	2-4	2-4	2-4	4-3	4-1	1-4		3-0	4-3	0-4	0-1	3-1	2-3
Preston Athletic	Aug 6	Dec 31	Mar 24	Oct 4	Aug 20	Apr 1	Nov 5	Jan 28	Mar 11	Dec 10		Apr 15	Jan 7	Oct 1	Aug 31	Sep 3
	1-1	3-4	0-2	1-4	0-5	1-7	0-3	3-4	1-2	2-1		3-2	0-2	4-3	0-3	0-2
Selkirk	Oct 1	Apr 22	Aug 13	Mar 4	Feb 4	Sep 17	Oct 29	Sep 3	Nov 19	Jan 7	Jul 30		Dec 10	Aug 27	Dec 31	Apr 1
	4-0	1-3	1-3	3-1	2-2	7-4	2-3	7-1	1-2	0-3	0-3		0-6	2-5	6-0	2-4
Spartans	Dec 17	Jan 14	Aug 31	Apr 22	Nov 19	Sep 24	Aug 6	Mar 25	Sep 10	Oct 29	Nov 15	Aug 20		Feb 11	Mar 4	Dec 31
	2-1	3-1	0-1	1-2	1-0	1-0	1-1	1-1	4-1	9-1	2-1	3-0		0-1	2-2	2-0
Stirling University	Aug 31	Oct 4	Dec 2	Nov 26	Sep 10	Jan 13	Oct 8	Feb 18	Jan 28	Apr 22	Mar 4	Dec 17	Jul 29		Aug 20	Mar 25
	1-1	2-1	2-2	0-0	1-3	0-2	3-1	1-0	4-2	7-2	5-3	3-3	0-3		0-4	3-0
Vale of Leithen	Mar 25	Dec 3	Aug 27	Jul 30	Oct 1	Dec 17	Apr 15	Jan 7	Nov 5	Sep 3	Feb 18	Oct 8	Aug 10	Apr 8		Apr 12
	2-6	1-2	1-2	1-1	1-2	2-4	1-0	2-3	3-1	4-3	3-1	2-1	1-6	0-1		2-1
Whitehill Welfare	Oct 29	Nov 19	Apr 15	Aug 27	Jul 30	Aug 13	Apr 8	Dec 17	May 16	Feb 4	Mar 18	Aug 10	Oct 8	Nov 5	Sep 10	
	1-5	4-0	0-3	2-2	0-3	2-5	1-3	5-3	5-1	3-1	4-1	3-1	1-0	4-2	0-2	

Abandoned
4/2/17, CSS v Gretna, player injury, 75 mins

P	Team	P	W	D	L	F	A	GD	Pts
1	**East Kilbride**	**30**	**24**	**3**	**3**	**89**	**21**	**68**	**75**
2	East Stirlingshire (R)	30	21	5	4	107	43	64	68
3	Spartans	30	17	5	8	69	30	39	56
4	University of Stirling	30	16	5	9	60	53	7	53
5	Dalbeattie Star	30	14	5	11	60	50	10	47
6	Cumbernauld Colts	30	13	8	9	51	43	8	47
7	BSC Glasgow	30	12	6	12	63	56	7	42
8	Whitehill Welfare	30	13	1	16	53	64	-11	40
9	Gretna 2008	30	12	4	14	44	65	-21	40
10	Gala Fairydean Rovers	30	11	7	12	55	77	-22	40
11	Edinburgh University	30	10	7	13	40	42	-2	37
12	Civil Service Strollers (N)	30	10	7	13	59	68	-9	37
13	Vale of Leithen	30	11	4	15	52	66	-14	37
14	Hawick Royal Albert (N)	30	8	1	21	58	93	-35	25
15	Selkirk	30	6	5	19	58	86	-28	23
16	*Preston Athletic*	*30*	*5*	*1*	*24*	*41*	*102*	*-61*	*16*

East Kilbride were runaway winners. They recruited a team of experienced players, and were rumoured to be paying wages similar to top League Two sides. The previous season they had a huge windfall from their Scottish Cup tie versus Celtic.

The top four clubs qualify to participate in the SPFL Challenge Cup for 2017/18.

Sourcing accurate stats for Lowland League scores still proved remarkably difficult. The League's own website sometimes published wrong scorelines on a Saturday evening. The BBC coverage of the League was frequently inaccurate with scorelines. Ten days after the Final match of the season had been played the Lowland League website had still not been updated with an accurate final league table.

Promotion / Relegation
The Lowland League Champions play off against the Highland League Champions in the Pyramid Play Off, played under the auspices of the SFA. The winners of that game then play the bottom team in SPFL League Two - this time under the auspices of the SPFL. East Kilbride succeeded in defeating Buckie Thistle but then lost to Cowdenbeath. Consequently they remain in the Lowland Leagvue for 2017/18.

The bottom club in the Lowland League are relegated if one or both of the winners of the East and South of Scotland Leagues are SFA licensed. In 2016/17 South Champions Edusport were licensed. East Champions Lothian Thistle were not licensed, so Edusport were promoted automatically in place of Preston Athletic.

In the event of the Highland League Champions being successful in the end of season play offs, then TWO Lowland League teams would be relegated, provided the team dropping from SPFL2 were from south of the Tay.

Membership of the Lowland League is capped at 16 and the second relegation place may be required to balance the numbers.

Lowland League - All Time Positions	2013-14	2014-15	2015-16	2016-17
BSC Glasgow		10	7	7
Civil Service Strollers				12
Cumbernauld Colts			4	6
Dalbeattie Star	3	4	9	5
East Kilbride	8	2	5	1
East Stirlingshire				2
Edinburgh City	5	1	1	
Edinburgh University		11	6	11
Gala Fairydean Rovers	10	8	11	10
Gretna 2008	7	3	10	9
Hawick Royal Albert				14
Preston Athletic	9	13	14	16
Selkirk	12	12	12	15
Spartans	1	5	2	3
Stirling University	2	6	3	4
Threave Rovers	11	14	15	
Vale of Leithen	6	9	13	13
Whitehill Welfare	4	7	8	8

Accurate attendances for Lowland League games are seldom published. From our own visits and anecdotal evidence from others, typical home gates seemed to be:

200	East Kilbride, East Stirlingshire, Gala Fairydean Rovers
100	Dalbeattie Star, Spartans, Whitehill W
70	Hawick RA
60	Civil Service Strollers, Cumbernauld Colts, Gretna, Selkirk, Vale of Leithen
50	BSC Glasgow, Edinburgh University, Preston Ath, Stirling Uni

For the Play Off Final Second Leg East Kilbride took around 300 fans with them to Cowdenbeath.

Lowland League Cup 2016/17

1	29/04/2017	Gala Fairydean Rovers	Edinburgh University	1	2	
1	29/04/2017	Vale of Leithen	Stirling University	1	3	
1	29/04/2017	Whitehill Welfare	Gretna	0	1	
1	30/04/2017	East Kilbride	Spartans	0	3	
1	29/04/2017	Civil Service Strollers	Dalbeattie Star	1	0	
1	28/04/2017	Cumbernauld Colts	BSC Glasgow	1	2	
1	29/04/2017	Selkirk	East Stirlingshire	2	3	
1	29/04/2017	Hawick Royal Albert	Preston Athletic	1	4	
2	06/05/2017	Civil Service Strollers	Preston Athletic	6	2	
2	06/05/2017	BSC Glasgow	Edinburgh University	3	2	
2	06/05/2017	Spartans	East Stirlingshire	1	0	
2	06/05/2017	Stirling University	Gretna	0	1	aet
F	13/05/2017	Civil Service Strollers	BSC Glasgow	1	2	
F	13/05/2017	Gretna	Spartans	0	3	
	21/05/2017	Spartans	BSC Glasgow	3	0	
		(played at Spartans)				

FINAL DETAILS
Spartans 3 BSC Glasgow 0, at Ainslie Park
Spartans: Carswell, Herd, Maxwell (Corbett 83), Tolmie, Greenhill, Beesley, Dishington (Hay 88), Allum (Saunderson 88), Stevenson, Brown, Townsley. Subs (Not Used) Thomson, Comrie, Gilpin.
BSC: Barr; Bowers, Bell, Niven, Keys (Toner, 74); Corrieri (Lyons, 62), Bembo (Woods, 81), Duncan, Traynor; Ferris, Jones. Subs (Not Used) Wilton, Malcolm, Nicol, Beckett

1-0	10mins Allum
2-0	69 minsTolmie
3-0	85 minsStevenson

Att 242

evious Lowland League Cup Finals

eason	Winners	Runners Up	Score	Venue
13/14	Stirling University	Preston Athletic	5-2	Netherdale, Gala
14/15	East Kilbride	Gretna 2008	3-1	Netherdale, Gala
15/16	East Kilbride	Gretna 2008	0-0, 4-2p	Netherdale, Gala
16/17	Spartans	BSC Glasgow	3-0	Ainslie Park

Lowland League Club Playing Squads 2016/17

NB These are not comprehensive lists of players used - there will be some omissions. However, all players listed were associated with the club concerned during 2016/17.

BSC Glasgow
Manager: Mark Adams (until March), Steven Swift (from March)
Aidan Ferris (ex St Mirren, Morton),
Ayden Nicol
*Arnauld Bembo (ex Slavia Prague, Threave R, Ardeer Th, Vale of Clyde),
Blair Lyons
Christian Kasongo,
Fraser Malcolm
*Gary Redpath (ex Dalbeattie Star, Annan Athletic, St Cuthbert Wanderers),
*Gerard Traynor (ex Clyde, East Kilbride),
Husnain Mansoor
Jamie Cunningham (ex East Stirlingshire, Newburgh),
*Joe Wilton,
Lewis Bell (ex Celtic U20),
Mark Dryden,
Mark Toner,
Matt Beckett (ex Dumbarton),
*Matt Niven,
Paul Keys,
Riccardo Corrieri,
*Robbie Duncan (ex Stenhousemuir, Cumbernauld Colts),
*Robert Jones,
Shaun Bowers (ex Celtic U20),
*Spencer Brown
*Stephen Barr,
Tom Woods (ex Morecambe, Lancaster City),
Vinny Newlands (ex E Kilbride, Clyde),
Rodrick Watupa
* Contracted for 2017/18

Civil Service Strollers
Manager: Alex Cunningham
Stuart Burnside (ex Edinburgh Utd, Craigroyston)
Alex Brown
Barry Milven
Blair McWhirter (ex Dunferml,ine Ath U20, Stirling University, Spartans)
Brad Rixon
Chris Milligan
Craig Newall (ex Aberdeen U17, Cowdenbeath U20)
David Churchill
David Stewart
Dean Carse (ex Hutchison Vale, Aberdeen U20, Berwick R, Bonnyrigg R, Edinburgh City)
Greg Tulloch (ex Leith Ath, Berwick R, Vale of Leithen, Craigroyston)
Haydn Crane (ex Tynecastle FC)
Ian Ballantyne
Jack Downie (ex Craigroyston, Livingston, Berwick R)
Joe Dingwall (ex Hibernian, Raith R, Arbroath, Berwick R, Dalbeattie Star, Edinburgh City, East Stirling)
Jonathan Watson
Jordan Boyle
Jordan Finnie (ex Spartans, Whitehill W, Peebles Rovers)
Lewis Kidd
Mark Law
Matty Cunningham
Michael Lee (ex Stirling Albion U20)
Paul Campbell
Paul Greenhill (ex CSS, Vale of Leithen, Craigroyston)
Robbie Laird
Russell McLean (OL from Hearts)
Scott Clapperton (ex Anderson University Trojans, Edinburgh City, Spartans)
Shaun Turnbull (ex Edinburgh City, Craigroyston, Tynecastle)
Stephen Anderson (ex Berwick Rangers, Selkirk, Peebles R)
Steven Froude

Cumbernauld Colts
Manager: Craig McKinlay / James Orr
Andy Hunter (ex Stirling Albion, Dunipace, Inverurie Locos)
Andy Selkirk (ex Albion R, Campsie BW, Clydebank, Bellshill Ath)
Andy Ward (ex Q Park, Campsie BW, East Kilbride Thistle, Glenafton Ath, Kirkintilloch RR, Rutherglen Glencairn, Cumbernauld Utd, Benburb)
Broque Watson (2017 Celtic OL)
Chris Fahey (ex Larkhall Th, Albion R, Stenhousemuir, Raith R, Glenafton Ath, Cumnock, Stranraer, Kilbirnie L). Retired at end of season 2016/17.
Connor McKenzie (ex Stirling Albion, Stebnhousemuir)
Craig Murray (ex Aberdeen, Ayr Utd, E Fife)
Daniel McFarlane
Fraser Sheridan
Gavin Lachlan (ex Q Park, Pollok, E Kilbride)
Harry Purves
Jamie Barclay
Jamie Broadfoot (ex Harestanes AFC)
Jeff Angus
John Tennant
Jonathan Black (ex Motherwell, Partick Th)
Jordan Marshall (2017 Rutherglen Glencairn)
Jordan Pirie
Kenny Giles
Lee Foggin, Freed Jan 2017 (ex Airdrie U20, Q Park U20, Blantyre Vics)
Lewis Wilson (2016 OL from Alloa)
Mark Anthony Byrne
Mark Batchelor (ex Rutherglen Glencairn)
Owen Ronald, Freed Mar 2017, (ex Q Park, Dumbarton, Berwick R, Kirkintilloch RR, Cumnock)
Richard Kirwan (ex Stirling Albion, Dunipace)
Ross Ballantyne (ex Celtic U20, Motherwell, Fauldhouse Utd, Kilwinning R, Arthurlie, E Kilbride Thistle, Rutherglen Glencairn)
Ryan Milne (ex Clyde)
Sam George (ex Rangers U17, Clyde, Q Park,)
Scott Davidson (2017 Stirling Albion, Ex Carse Th)
Sean Brown (ex Stirling Albion, Dunblane, Dunipace)
Stephen O'Neill (ex Aberdeen, Peterhead, E Fife, Montrose)

Dalbeattie Star
Player Manager: Darren Kerr- Coaches: Gary Holden, Ali Cathro, Jim Fingland, Alan Milligan
Alistair Cathro
Ally Mason(2016 Palmerston Colts)
Connor Graham (Ex Gretna, transferred to Mid Annandale)
Craig Ferguson
Craig Neill (OL to Lochar Th 2016/17)
Curtiss Wilson (ex Wigtown & Bladnoch)
Danny Dunglinson (ex Annan Ath, Thrfeave R, Gretna)
Darren Kerr (ex Threave Rovers)
David Proudlock
Dean Brotherston (OL from QOS)
Dean Fyfe (transferred to Creetown)
Fraser Morton (ex QOS, Heston R)
Graham Wright
Greig Thorburn (ex Kilmarnock, Annan Ath, Gretna)
Iain Anderson (ex Gretna)
Jack Johnston
Jack Steele (ex Dalbeattie Star, Annan Ath, Glenafton Ath)
Jake Thomson (transferred to Lochar Th)
James Baty (ex Threave R, Q Park)
Jamie McHarrie (ex Wigtown & B, Hurlford Utd)
Jesse Akubuine (OL from QOS)
Lee Wells (ex Annan Ath)
Lewis Sloan (ex QOS, Kilmarnock, Annan Ath, Stenhousemuir, Glenafton Ath)
Lewis Todd (ex Gretna, QOS)
Liam Park
Ritchie Maxwell (ex Crichton, St Cuthbert W, Dalbeattie Star, QOS)
Richard Murray (OL from QOS)
Russell Parker
Joe Slattery (ex Kilmarnock, Gretna)
Steven Degnan (ex St Cuthbert W)
Tommy Muir
Vinnie Parker (ex Gretna, Threave R)

East Kilbride
Manager: Martin Lauchlan (ex Partick Th, St Johnstone, Clyde, Stenhousemuir etc) Assistant: Carlos Girasoli, Coach: Paul Roberts (ex E Stirling, Arbroath, Stirling Albion etc)
Adam Strachan (2016 Glenafton Ath, ex Clydebank, Irvine M, Arbroath, Clyde, Dumbarton, Albion R, Ross Co, Partick Th),
Anthony Marenghi (2016 Stenhousemuir, Ex Stranraer, Ayr United),
Barry Russell (2015 Stranraer, Ex Albion Rovers, East Kilbride Thistle), Bernard Coll (2015 Q Park, ex Celtic Youths),
Craig Howie (Ex EK Youths),
David Proctor (2016 Ex Airdrieonians, FC Edmonton, ICT, Dundee United, Hibernian),
Declan Hughes (2016 Cowdenbeath, ex St Mirren),
Fabio Capuano (2016 Clyde, ex Q Park),
Jacob Kean,
Jack Smith (OL from Stenhousemuir, ex EK)
Paul Woods (Mar 2017 Q Park, joined Stranraer May 2017) – missed vital penalty v Cowdenbeath in promotion play-off shoot-out
James Brough (2015 Queen's Park, ex Weirs Rec),
Joao Victoria (2016 Arbroath, ex East Kilbride, Q Park, Giffnock North),
Kieran Gibbons (2016 Livingston, ex Aberdeen, Hamilton Accies Youth, Cowdenbeath OL),
Martin McBride (2015 Ex Q Park,

Dumbarton, Stranraer, Cowdenbeath, Albion R, Gretna, Partick Th),
Matt McGinley (2015 Buckie Th, Ex BSC Glasgow, Morton, Albion R, Rutherglen Glencairn),
Robbie Winters (2016 Pollok, Ex Muirend Ams, Dundee Utd, Aberdeen, Brann Bergen, Clyde, Ayr U, Livingston, Grindavik, Alloa, Peterhead, Albion R, Dumbarton, Rossvale, Full Scotland Cap)
Ross McNeil (2016 Cumnock, Ex Rutherglen Glencairn, Albion Rovers, Stenhousemuir),
Scott Stevenson (2016 Stirling Albion, Ex Motherwell, St Johnstone, Albion Rovers),
Sean Winter (2015 Stranraer, ex Arthurlie, East Kilbride Thistle),
Bernard Coll (ex Q Park)
Michael Hardie
Ross McNeill (ex Cumnock)
Gavin Miller (ex EK U20)
Dominic McLaren
Craig McLeish (OL from Q Park)

East Stirlingshire
Manager: John Sludden
Adam Murray (nephew of Jim McInally),
Andy Rogers (2016 Peterhead, Ex Falkirk, Dumbarton, Montrose, Ayr Utd, Stenhousemuir, E Stirling),
Connor Greene (ex Falkirk)
Connor Hogg (ex Falkirk, Stenhousemuir),
Darren Dolan (2015 Sauchie, Ex Livingston Utd, Stirling Albion, Hamilton Accies),
Dean Shaw (2016 Stenhousemuir),
Derek Ure (2016 Camelon, ex East Stirlingshire),
Drew Ramsay (2016 Cumbernauld Colts),
Dylan McGuigan (2016 Cumbernauld United, ex Hamilton Accies youths),
Gavin McMillan,
Graeme McGregor (206 Linlithgow Rose, ex Falkirk, Bolton W, Hamilton, St Mirren, E Stirling, E Fife),
Jamie Barclay (2015 Ex Stenhousemuir, Clyde, Berwick R, Falkirk, E Stirling, Scotland U21 Caps), Andy Grant (2016 Camelon, ex Bannockburn Ams),
Liam Allison (2016 Camelon, ex Stirling Uni, Blackburn Utd)
Jamie Glasgow (Ex Camelon, E Stirling, Celtic Youths)
Kris Faulds (2015 Falkirk, Ex Stenhousemuir),
Lewis Peddie (ex Stenhousemuir, Hamilton Accies),
Paul Sludden (ex Falkirk, E Fife, Stenhousemuir, Stirling University, Spartans, son of John Sludden), David Grant (2016 Camelon, Ex Stirling Albion, Berwick R),
Simon White (ex Alloa Youths),
Steven Brisbane (ex Falkirk, Broxburn Ath, E Stirling, Clyde)

Edinburgh University
Manager: Dorian Ogunro
Coaches: Tom Archer, Stuart Dearden, David MacMillan
Andrew Swinney
Callum Davidson
Callum Irvine (ex Formartine Utd, Cruden Bay)
Calum Frain
Craig McMillan (ex Edinburgh City)
Daniel Pacitti
David Smith
Ewan Ritchie
Finn Daniels-Yeoman
Fraser Thomson
Gordon Davison
Greg Swan
Jack Guthrie
Liam Hely
Luke Murray
Mark Scott (ex Stenhousemuir U20)
Mark Tait
Max Condie
Max Verkaik
Michael Ness
Nathan Evans
Paul Sutherland (ex Spartans, Gala FR)
Peter Mair (ex Spartans)
Scott McCrory-Irving
Tim Rawlinson
Bertie Collins
Rafa Calbacho
David Maskrey
Bruce Scott

Gala Fairydean Rovers
Manager: Steven Noble
Adam Watson (20126 Hibernian U20, OL),
Ben Herdman (2015 Kelso Utd),
Billy Miller (2014 Stow),
Danny Simpson.
Darren Smith (2016 Lothian Thistle HV, ex Hibernian, Airdrie Utd, Albion R, Berwick R, Kelty H, Ballingry R, Bonnyrigg R),
David Bonnar (2016 Newtongrange Star, Hearts U17, Livingston U17),
Dean McColm,
George Windram (2016 Duns, Ex Eyemouth United),
Kevin Waugh (2016 Hibernian U20 Loan),
Kieron Wright (2016 Rangers U20 OL),
Kyle Collins (2016, ex Eyemouth Utd, Gala FR),
Lee Stephen (2013 Selkirk),
Michael Fenton,
Ross Aitchison (ex Vale of Leithen, Whitehill W, Eyemouth Utd, Civil Service S)
Ryan Clapperton,
Scott Main (2016 Dalkeith Th, ex Bonnyrigg R, Raith R U20),
Sean Paliczka (2016 Newtongrange Star, ex Hibs, Raith R, Vale of Leithen, E Fife, Berwick R, Bonnyrigg R, Penicuik Ath, Gala F, Musselburgh Ath),
Shane Bonnington, Stuart Noble (2013, Ex Berwick R, Alloa, Airdrie Utd, Gala F, E Fife, Northampton Town, Fulham, Torquay United, Woking, St Johnstone),
Taylor Hope,

Gretna
Manager: Matt Henney
Aaron Kelly
Adam Meagan
Adam Telfer
Alan Inglis (ex Workington, Annan Ath, Gretna, Threave R)
Arron Bradbury
Christopher Wraighte
Connor Casey
Daniel Armstrong (ex Carlisle Utd, QOS)
Daniel Wadge (ex Annan Ath)
Daniel Wood (ex Annan Ath, Gretna)
Darren Addison
David Renyard
Dylan Neil (ex Annan Ath, Heston R, QOS)
Ellis Monaghan
Ellis Pearson (ex Carlisle Utd, Annan Ath)
Jack Brannan (ex Carlisle Utd, QOS)
Jack Dickinson (ex Carlisle Utd, QOS)
Jack Hunter
Jack Leighfield (OL from QOS)
Jake Smith
Jamie Hope
Jonathan Blake (ex Workington, Carlisle Utd, Annan Ath)
Jordan Little
Josh Simpson
Karlton Rudd
Liam Studholme
Marc Shiel
Michael Ballantyne
Owen Moxon
Robb McCartney
Sam Atkinson

Hawick Royal Albert
Manager: Dean Shanks (until February), Kevin Milne (Feb-May)
Alieu Badara Faye
Andrew Laidlaw
Andrew McKay
Blake Wales
Brian Allison (ex Falkirk, Stirling Albion)
Cameron McFarlane
Craig Robertson (ex Tynecastle FC, Berwick R)
Dale Urey
Darren Linton (ex Leith Ath, Berwick R)
Daryl Johnson (ex Dunbar Utd, Selkirk)
Fergus Lockhart
Gavin Pettigrew
Jon McInally
Josh Morris (ex Tynecastle FC, Berwick R, Vale of Leithen, Kelty Hearts)
Kris Mitchell (ex Vale of Leithen)
Kyle Rankin (ex Leith Ath)
Lewis Mitchell
Mark McEwan
Mikey Lynch (ex Motherwell U20)
Robert Boyd
Ryan Stevenson
Scott McKenzie
Shaun Spence
Stewart Crozier

Preston Athletic
Manager: Craig Nisbet (until March), Paul Riley / Jack Lynch (from April)Coaches: James Maloney, Kevin Douglas, Darryl Wilson
Bruce Callan (2016 Alba Ath, Ex Coldstream, Peebles R, Hanswell Town, Craigroyston, Civil Service S, Vale of Leithen)
Craig Innes (2016 Ormiston)
Craig Pennycuick
Danny O'Rourke
Darryl Wilson
David McLeod
David Porcher
Frazer Anderson
Gavin Stevenson
Greg Douglas
Jack Bruce
Jack Jardine
Josh Rogers
Kenny Erskine
Kenny Park
Kevin Keane (ex Whitehill Welfare, Haddington Ath)
Mark Law
Matthew Baines
Matthew Graham
Mikey Park
Neil Shave
Reece Cochrane (2016 Dunbar Utd, Ex Dunfermline Ath U20, Spartans)
Ross Colquhoun (2016 Dunbar Utd, Ex Edinburgh Utd, Tranent)
Ross Cowan (2016 Dunbar Utd, Ex Berwick R)
Scott Barclay
Scott Siegel
Sean Lawson (2016 Shortwood)
Stuart Ritchie
Sean Brown
Jamie Newman
McNaughton
Brandon Archibald
Shaun Conway
Lewis Turkington

Jason Young
Chris Inglis
Mark Smith
Jay Cochrane
McMahon
Gavin Stevenson
Fabio Neto
Robbie Carter (2016 Dalkeith Thistle OL)
Greg Binnie
Matthew Baines
Brandon Cameron

Selkirk
Manager: Gary O'Connor (Until Dec), Ian Fergus
Gregor Amos (2017 Edinburgh City, ex Falkirk, Lothian Thistle HV)
Andrew Fleming
Brydon Fairgrieve
Dale Baxter
Daniel Greig
Daniel Terry (Ex Shettleston, to Upper Annandale May 2017)
Edvinas Valatka (ex Kingstonian)
Eric Tshibango
Fraser Neave
Gary Amos
Gary McCormack (ex Tynecastle FC, Bonnyrigg Rose, Preston Ath, Dunbar United)
Gary Nicholson
Gary O'Connor
Jake Moyes
James Harley
Jay Doyle
Jordan Neill
Kerr Scott
Liam Robertson
Mark Samson
Michael Collin
Murray Christie (ex Hearts U20, Coldstream, Cowdenbeath, Musselburgh Ath)
Peter Beagley
Phil Addison
Ricky Miller (2016 Edinburgh Utd, ex East Stirling, Haddington Ath, Penicuik Ath, Musselburgh Ath, Vale of leithen, Tranent, Blackburn Utd, Stenhousemuir U20)
Ross King
Ryan Sclater (2017 Edinburgh Utd, Ex Vale of Leithen)
Ryan Scott
Scott Ritchie

Spartans
Manager: Dougie Samuel
Blair Carswell (ex Hearts U17), Ross Gilpin (ex E Stirling, Preston Ath, Vale of Leithen), Michael Herd (2014 E Stirling, ex Whitehill W, Lothian Th, Arniston R), Eddie Malone (2015 Ex Stenhousemuir, Raith R, Ayr Utd, Dundee, St Mirren, Clyde, St Johnstone), Paul Thomson (2015 Tayport, ex Dundee NE, Edinburgh Uni), Blair Tolmie (2016 Newtongrange Star, ex Hibernian, Berwick R, Arniston R, nephew of Alex Cropley), Chris Townsley (2016 E Stirlingshire, Ex Hearts Youths, Ross Co, Alloa, Spartans, Berwick R, E Stirling), Jack Beesley (2010 Edinburgh Uni), Alan Brown (2013 Whitehill W, ex Newtongrange S, Linlithgow R), Jamie Dishington (ex Spartans Youth), David Greenhill (2015 E Stirling, Ex St johnstone, Clyde, Montrose, Alloa, Berwick R), Andy Mair, Scott Maxwell (2015 Berwick R, ex E Stirling, Dalkeith Th), Brad Raiker, Craig Stevenson (2014 Lothian Th, ex Berwick R, Cowdenbeath Youth), Dan Ward (2015 Edinburgh Uni), Dean Horribine (2015 Berwick R, ex Hibernian), Keith Murray (2015 Leith Ath), Igor Gabiola (2016 Gernika, Ex Portugalete, Athletic Bilbao Youth), Broque Watson (OL from Celtic), Craig Johnston, (OL from Cowdenbeath), Craig Comrie (2016 E Stirling, Ex Falkirk, Stirling Albion), Jonny Grotlin, Harry Girdwood, Brandon Archibald

Stirling University
Manageress: Shelley Kerr (until May)
Andrew Gillen
Angus Mailer
Ben Cuff (ex Grimsby Town)
Calum Burns
Chris Geddes (ex Stirling Albion, Pumpherston, Brechin City, Forfar Athletic, Linlithgow Rose, Broxburn Ath, Central Queensland)
Daniel Ashe (ex Stirling Albion, Sauchie)
Daniel Fitzpatrick (ex Clyde)
Dominic Kane
George Leigh (ex Rochdale)
Harvey Moyes (ex Carlisle United U18, KR Reykjavik, IK Grotta)
Jack Nixon (ex St Cuthbert W, Spartans)
Jeff Duah-Kessie (ex Greenwich Borough, returned to them Aug 2016)
Kyle Faulds (ex St Mirren U20, Arbroath, Girvan, Auchinleck Talbot)
Lewis Bonar (ex Celtic U20, Falkirk U20, Stirling Albion, Peninsula Power, Shepparton South, Montrose)
Lewis Hunter
Michael Tuohy
Paul McCafferty (ex Motherwell U20)
Peiman Pahlevan (2015 Vallentuna BK, ex Vasalunds IF, IK Frej, Valsta Syri, Osteraker FK, Freed Jan 2017)
Peter Byrne
Rory MacEwan (ex Elgin City)
Ross Kellock (ex Motherwell u20)
Ryan Marshall (ex Celtic U20, Stranraer)
Thomas Jones (ex Oldham Athletic)
Tim Hughes (ex Macclesfield Town)
Michael McAnespie (ex Annan Athletic)
Matt Sheridan
Tom Cowley (ex Morecambe)
Aiden Peden (ex Burton Park Wanderers)

Vale of Leithen
Manager: Chris Anderson
Assistant Keith McLeod
Ainslie Hunter (2014 Coldstream, Ex Spartans, Arniston R)
Andrew McQueen
Ben McGregor
Blair Atkinson
Brad Raiker (OL from Spartans)
Brendan Edwards
Danny O'Donnell (ex Vale of Leithen, Spartans, Whitehill Welfare)
James Elliot (2014 Berwick R, Ex Edinburgh City)
Jamie Shiel (2016 Berwick R)
Jay Stevens
Jonny Scott-Mercer (ex Edinburgh City, Whitehill W, AC Oxgangs, Arbroath)
Keith Boyes (2016 Spartans, Ex Gala Fairydean R)
Keith McLeod (2015 ex Spartans, CSS, Alloa, Tollcross Utd. Son of Iain MacLeod, ex Berwick Rangers, Stirling Albion etc)
Kevin Motion (2016 Newtongrange Star, Ex Spartans, Stenhousemuir, Berwick R, Alloa, Forfar)
Liam McIntosh
Matt Underhill
Robbie Manson (2016 Preston Ath, Ex Heriot Watt Uni, berwick R, Spartans, Broxburn Ath)
Ross Brady (2014 Berwick R, Ex Livingston U2o)
Ross Lamb
Sean Stewart
Steven Lynch (2014 Tynecastle, Ex Leith Ath)
Tommy Paterson

Whitehill Welfare
Manager: Steven Hislop (Until Nov), David Bingham (from Nov)
Assistant: David Bingham (Until Nov), Sean McCauley (from Nov)
Aaron Moffat
Andrew Martin
Bryan Young (2013 Easthouses Lily)
Callum Brook
Callum Connolly
Charlie Adams
Charlie Denton
Ciaran Chalmers
Conan McDiarmid (2014 Musselburgh Ath, Ex Whitehill W, Lothian Thistle HV)
Connor Bryden
Connor McGregor (2015 Bo'ness Utd, Ex Lothian Thistle)
Connor Spowart
Corey Robertson (ex WW U20)
Dale O'Hara
Darren Aird
Daryl Healey
Dylan Weldon (ex WW U20)
Frankie Arthur
Harvey Swann (2016 Cowdenbeath OL)
Jack Bruce
Jamie Chapman
Jamie Laing
John Gilbertson (2016 Lotian Th HV, ex Cowdenbeath, Tynecastle, Preston Ath)
John Hall (2016 Musselburgh Ath, Ex Edinburgh City, Vale of Leithen, Whitehill W)
John Williams
John Kerr (2016 Lothian Th, Ex Preston Ath, Civil Service S, Vale of leithwen, Whitehill W)
Kerr Dodds (2013 Vale of Leithen Ex Ross County, Montrose, East Fife, Edinburgh City, Edinburgh University, Vale of Leithen, Spartans)
Kevin Keane
Lee Barrett
Liam McCabe
Liam Robertson
Liam Wishart
Mark Samson
Matthew Jameson
Matthew Palfreyman
Michael Osborne (2016 Ormiston, Ex Peebles R, Vale of Leithen, Spartans, Coldstream, Preston Ath)
Nikki Murray
Omar Ali
Robbie Dowie (ex WW U20)
Robert Bailey
Rory Rutherford
Ross Jardine
Scott Gormley (2016 Lothian Th Ex Whitehill W, Civil Service S, Vale of Leithen)
Scott McCulloch (2016 Musselburgh Ath, ex Whitehill W, Vale of Leithen , Penicuik Ath)
Scott Moffat (to Haddington At Aug 20160
Scott Russell
Sean McAuley
Steven Hislop
Steven Manson (2011 Craigroyston)
William Kidd (2017 Haddington Ath, Ex Easthouses Lily, Whiteh W, Dalkeith Th)

SFA South Region Challenge Cup 2016/17

When the Scottish Qualifying Cups (North and South) were scrapped in favour of an all-in Scottish Cup draw from 2007/8, the SFA sponsored tournaments to replace the Qualifying Cups in the fixture lists. The North Challenge Cup was dropped from the fixture list after a couple of years but the South competition carries on. It is open to all members of the Lowland, East and South of Scotland Leagues, as well as the 'odd' SFA member from the South—Glasgow University. Girvan and presumably Linlithgow Rose are also eligible but have opted not to play in the competition in recent years.

1	17/09/2016	Heriot Watt University	BSC Glasgow	2	4
1	17/09/2016	Burntisland Shipyard	Glasgow University	1	6
1	17/09/2016	Lothian Thistle HV	Ormiston	11	0
1	17/09/2016	Peebles Rovers	Edinburgh University	1	2
1	17/09/2016	Civil Service Strollers	East Kilbride	1	2
1	17/09/2016	Cumbernauld Colts	St Cuthbert Wanderers	1	0
1	17/09/2016	Gala Fairydean Rovers	Heston Rovers	4	1
1	17/09/2016	Preston Athletic	Tweedmouth Rangers	7	1
1	17/09/2016	Vale of Leithen	Creetown	6	0
2	15/10/2016	Preston Athletic	Lothian Thistle HV	1	2
2	15/10/2016	Spartans	Lochar Thistle	6	0
2	15/10/2016	Coldstream	Leith Athletic	0	3
2	15/10/2016	Abbey Vale	BSC Glasgow	1	0
2	15/10/2016	Dalbeattie Star	Wigtown & Bladnoch	2	3
2	15/10/2016	East Kilbride	Gala Fairydean Rovers	1	0
2	15/10/2016	Gretna 2008	Vale of Leithen	1	2
2	15/10/2016	Hawick Royal Albert	Cumbernauld Colts	1	3
2	15/10/2016	Mid Annandale	East Stirlingshire	0	3
2	15/10/2016	Nithsdale Wanderers	Threave Rovers	1	4
2	15/10/2016	Stirling University	Edinburgh University	1	2
2	15/10/2016	Upper Annandale	Whitehill Welfare	1	5
2	15/10/2016	Eyemouth United	Tynecastle	1	6
2	14/10/2016	Glasgow University	Dumfries YMCA	9	0
2	14/10/2016	Lochmaben	Edusport Academy	1	7
2		Newton Stewart	Duns	wo	scr
3	12/11/2016	Whitehill Welfare	Abbey Vale	5	0
3	12/11/2016	Edusport Academy	East Kilbride	0	2
3	12/11/2016	Threave Rovers	Vale of Leithen	1	0
3	12/11/2016	East Stirlingshire	Newton Stewart	9	0
3	12/11/2016	Edinburgh University	Wigtown & Bladnoch	1	0
3	12/11/2016	Leith Athletic	Cumbernauld Colts	1	4
3	12/11/2016	Tynecastle	Spartans	1	0
3	19/11/2016	Lothian Thistle HV	Glasgow University	3	0
4	11/03/2017	East Stirlingshire	Tynecastle	3	2
4	11/03/2017	Lothian Thistle HV at Spartans FC	Whitehill Welfare	2	0
4	11/03/2017	Threave Rovers	East Kilbride	1	5
4	11/03/2017	Edinburgh University	Cumbernauld Colts	0	4
SF	07/04/2017	East Stirlingshire	Cumbernauld Colts	2	3
SF	08/04/2017	East Kilbride	Lothian Thistle HV	3	1
F	28/05/2017	Cumbernauld Colts at Falkirk FC, Att 450	East Kilbride	2	4

2016/17 FINAL

East Kilbride v Cumbernauld Colts, 4-2

EK: McGinley, Stevenson, Howie, Proctor, McLaren, Winter, Mcleish, Gibbons, Strachan, Victoria (Sub Woods), McLean (Sub Hughes).
Colts: Fahey, Hunter (Sub Pirrie), Fergus, Marshall, Ward, Lachlan (Sub Kirwan), O'Neill, Murray, Brown, Broadfoot, Sheridan. Subs not used: George, Barclay, Mckenzie, Batchelor, Byrne

1-0	Winter	
2-0	36 mins	Stevenson
2-1	40 mins	Brown
3-1	45 mins	Strachan
4-1	47 mins	Victoria
4-2	62 mins	O'Neill

SOUTH CHALLENGE CUP DRAW 2017/18

1st Round
Vale of Leithen vs. Tweedmouth Rangers
Selkirk vs. Kelty Hearts
Wigtown & Bladnoch vs. Gala Fairydean Rovers
Leith Athletic vs. Heriot-Watt University
Threave Rovers vs. Abbey Vale
Lochmaben vs. Upper Annandale
Lothian Thistle HV vs. Eyemouth United
East Stirlingshire vs. Nithsdale Wanderers
Dumfries YMCA vs. Lochar Thistle
Stirling University vs. Edinburgh University
Coldstream vs. Dalbeattie Star

2nd Round
Dumfries YMCA or Lochar Thistle vs. Coldstream or Dalbeattie Star
Stirling University or Edinburgh University vs. Burntisland Shipyard
Vale of Leithen or Tweedmouth Rangers vs. Lochmaben or Upper Annandale
Whitehill Welfare vs. Creetown
BSC Glasgow vs. Bonnyton Thistle
Gretna 2008 vs. Civil Service Strollers
Peebles Rovers vs. Heston Rovers
Glasgow University vs. Hawick Royal Albert
Wigtown & Bladhoch or Gala Fairydean vs. East Stirlingshire or Nithsdale Wanderers
EduSport Academy vs. St Cuthbert Wanderers
Spartans vs. Ormiston
Threave Rovers or Abbey Vale vs. Mid Annandale
Leith Athletic or Heriot-Watt University vs. Preston Athletic
Newton Stewart vs. Selkirk or Kelty Hearts
Lothian Thistle HV or Eyemouth United vs. Tynecastle
Cumbernauld Colts vs. East Kilbride

SOUTH CHALLENGE CUP ALL-TIME FINALS					
Year	Winners	Runners Up	Score		Venue
2007/8	Annan Athletic	Edinburgh City	3-2		Netherdale
2008/9	Spartans	Edinburgh University	6-0		Meadowbank
2009/10	Spartans	Gretna 2008	3-1		Tynecastle
2010/1	Spartans	Edinburgh City	3-0		Tynecastle
2011/2	Stirling University	Duns	4-2		Netherdale
2012/3	Whitehill Welfare	Dalbeattie Star	3-1		Galabank
2013/4	East Kilbride	Dalbeattie Star	2-0		Palmerston
2014/5	BSC Glasgow	Civil Service Strollers	2-0		Ferguson Park
2015/6	Whitehill Welfare	Edinburgh City	2-2	AET, 3-2p	Peffermill
2016/7	East Kilbride	Cumbernauld Colts	4-2		Falkirk Stadium

South-East Challenge Shield 2016/17

Introduced for 20167/17, this is a match played between the winners of the Alex Jack Cup (East) and Alternate (Alba) Cup South. These are competitions for East and South of Scotland League clubs respectively, who do not have licences or who have not otherwise qualified for the Scottish FA Cup.

Saturday April 29th (at King Edward Park, Lockerbie)
Lothian Thistle HV v Lochar Thistle, 6-1, H.T 2-1
LTHV: Swain, McKenzie, Crawford, Munro, Sherlock, Hare, Brown, Muir, O'Donnell, Wringe, Devlin.
Lochar: D Martin, C Muir , Stevenson, Hogg, R Muir, Scott, McGauchie, Coates, L Martin, McMath, Miller, Subs Dempster, McDougall, Krause, White
Scorers: LTHV- Jamie Devlin 2, Tony Muir, Kevin Borwn, Sean Wringe, Scott Taylor-MacKenzie
Lochar Thistle- L Martin

EAST SENIORS

The East of Scotland League endured a difficult season having lost two clubs to the Lowland League and one to the Juniors. Lothian Thistle Hutchison Vale and Leith Athletic led the way with Tynecastle also in contention.

The League will have quite a different look for 2017/18 with two new clubs. Preston Athletic drop down from the Lowland League and Kelty Hearts, the East Junior Champions, have switched to the Senior grade.

East of Scotland League 2016/17

	BUR	COL	EYE	HER	LEI	LOT	ORM	PEE	STI	TWE	TYN
Burntisland Shipyard		Nov 5	May 13	Jan 21	Oct 8	Apr 22	Oct 15	Sep 24	Mar 25	Oct 22	Apr 1
		2-2	1-0	3-2	0-6	0-7	0-6	1-2	0-7	1-5	1-0
Coldstream	Apr 29		Sep 24	May 13	Feb 25	Sep 10	Apr 22	Jan 7	Oct 22	Oct 29	Mar 25
	3-1		2-2	2-2	0-4	0-4	2-0	1-3	2-2	4-2	0-2
Eyemouth United	Oct 1	Jan 21		Apr 22	Apr 15	Mar 25	Dec 17	Oct 29	Sep 3	Mar 11	Nov 19
	10-0	0-2		1-2	0-6	0-3	1-0	3-2	4-3	4-4	2-3
Heriot Watt University	Oct 29	Nov 19	Dec 10		Mar 11	Feb 11	Oct 1	Sep 10	Jan 7	Feb 25	Feb 18
	9-0	2-3	3-0		2-2	3-1	6-1	3-1	4-2	8-1	4-1
Leith Athletic	Feb 18	Oct 1	Nov 26	Nov 5		Jan 14	Jan 7	Dec 10	Mar 4	Sep 10	Jan 21
	9-0	8-2	5-0	2-1		0-3	3-1	7-0	2-0	6-0	5-0
Lothian Thistle HV	Dec 10	Feb 4	May 6	Mar 29	May 13		Jan 21	Feb 18	Apr 15	Nov 5	Oct 8
	6-1	7-0	8-0	3-2	3-2		8-0	1-0	2-0	1-1	3-0
Ormiston	Nov 19	Dec 10	Oct 22	Feb 4	Mar 26	Oct 29		Mar 11	Sep 24	Feb 18	Dec 3
	4-0	1-2	0-3	1-2	1-4	2-4		0-1	1-4	2-0	0-6
Peebles Rovers	Dec 17	Oct 8	Apr 1	Oct 22	Apr 8	Nov 12	Nov 5		Oct 15	Jan 21	Sep 3
	4-0	0-1	1-2	0-0	0-4	2-5	2-1		0-1	7-2	0-4
Stirling University Reserves	Mar 11	Nov 12	Feb 18	Oct 8	Sep 17	Jan 28	Apr 1	Dec 3		Oct 1	Nov 5
	6-0	3-4	4-1	1-3	1-2	3-3	3-0	3-2		8-0	0-3
Tweedmouth Rangers	Apr 15	May 5	Oct 8	Oct 15	May 2	May 10	May 13	Mar 25	Apr 29		Dec 10
	2-1	0-4	0-1	0-2	2-2	0-11	3-4	3-1	1-2		0-1
Tynecastle	Mar 15	Dec 17	May 10	Jan 28	Apr 5	Jan 7	Apr 19	Apr 29	Oct 29	Apr 22	
	4-0	6-3	4-0	5-1	2-1	0-2	3-0	3-0	2-2	7-2	

	Club	P	W	D	L	F	A	GD	Pts
1	Lothian Thistle Hutchison Vale	20	17	2	1	85	16	69	53
2	Leith Athletic	20	15	2	3	80	18	62	47
3	Tynecastle	20	14	1	5	56	26	30	43
4	Heriot Watt University	20	12	3	5	61	30	31	39
5	Coldstream	20	9	4	7	39	51	-12	31
6	Stirling University	20	9	3	8	55	36	19	30
7	Eyemouth United	20	7	2	11	34	53	-19	23
8	Peebles Rovers	20	6	1	13	28	45	-17	19
9	Ormiston	20	4	0	16	25	57	-32	12
10	Tweedmouth Rangers	20	3	3	14	28	77	-49	12
11	Burntisland Shipyard	20	3	1	16	12	94	-82	10

East of Scotland League Recent Positions

	1987/8	1988/9	1989/90	1990/1	1991/2	1992/3	1993/4	1994/5	1995/6	1996/7	1997/8	1998/9	1999/00	2000/1	2001/2	2002/3	2003/4	2004/5	2005/6	2006/7	2007/8	2008/9	2009/'0	2010/11	2011/2	2012/3	2013/4	2014/5	2015/6	2016/7
Annan Athletic	B1	A8	A1	A7	A9	B2	A5	A3	A3	A5	A4	A3	A1	A1	A3	A2	A4	2	A6	A1	A7									
Berwick Rangers Reserves	B5	B2	A7	A5																	B8			B8	B10	B4	B3			
Burntisland Shipyard																										B13	B6	B5	A13	A11
Civil Service Strollers	A4	A2	A2	A9	B7	B1	A7	A4	A10	B2	A6	A4	A7	A11	B7	B2	A7	A9	A10	A12	B4	B2	A5	A8	A7	A8	A9	A5	A3	
Coldstream	B4	B6	B1	A6	A7	A10	B7	B5	B11	B7	B3	B3	A8	A9	A9	A11	B9	B10	B6	B2	A10	A9	A11	B9	B7	B2	A8	A9	A11	A5
Craigroyston	A7	A6	A8	A8	A5	A7	A4	A5	A5	A8	A3	A7	A9	A5	A8	A6	A12	B6	B1	A9	A12	B5	B3	B6	B5	B13	A3	A8	A12	
Dalbeattie Star															B5	B3	B2	A8	A11	B1	A6	A2								
Duns																									B6	B10	B8	B3	A15	
Easthouses MW / Lily	B6	B5	B4	B1	A1	A6	A8	A9	B5	B10	B8	B1	A10	A12	B3	B10	B5	B10	A9	A7	A9	A11	B6	B5	B12	B6	B2	A2		
Edinburgh City	A6	A9	B2	A3	A6	A5	A10	B8	B11	A6	A5	A5	A6	A6	A6	A8	A2	A7	A1	A5	A4	A8	A7	A6	A5	A5				
Edinburgh University	B8	B9	B9	B9	B11	B5	B2	A8	A8	A10	B5	B7	B5	B2	A12	B10	A6	A3	A8	A4	A2	A4	A8	A5	A4	A11	A5			
Eyemouth United	B2	A4	A10	B3	B9	B10	B10	B11	B8	B11	B12	B13	B6	B7	B6	B12	B12	B12	B8	B9	B9	B10	B3	B4	B5	B10	B6		A14	A7
Gala Fairydean (Rovers)	A3	A1	A3	A1	A4	A3	A3	A2	A2	A3	A9	B8	B2	A10	A10	A4	A5	A11	B10	B4	B5	B6	B7	B4	B3	B7				
Gretna																									A6	A4				
Hawick Royal Albert	A9	B4	B7	B4	B5	B3	B9	B3	B9	B4	B9	B6	B8	B4	B12	B9	B10	B9	B11	B11	B10	B12	B12	B12	B13	B14	B7	B8	A5	
Heriot Watt University	B10	B10	B10	B10	B10	B9	B5	B4	B12	B12	B11	B11	B9	B11	B11	B6	B4	B2	A2	A11	B10	A7	A6	A12	B1	A10	A10	B2	A10	A4
Hibernian U20																											B1			
Kelso United	A5	A7	A9	B7	B4	B4	B3	B9	B10	B9	B6	B12	B3	B9	B4	B4	B1	A10	A12	B8	B7	B11	B8	B10	B8	B8	B5	B7		
Lothian Thistle (/ Hutchison Vale)									B3	B1	A7	A6	A4	A7	A7	A7	A9	A5	A3	A8	A8	A3	A3	A3	A10	A6	A1	A1	A2	A1
Manor Thistle / Edinburgh Athletic / Leith Athletic					B1	A8	A9	B7	B2	A4	A10	B10	B10	B5	B8	B5	B7	B4	B3	B6	B12	B8	B5	B2	A11		A7	A3	A1	A2
Peebles Rovers	B3	B10	A6	A10	B8	B7	B8	B10	B4	B5	B1	A8	A11	B3	B2	A12	B6	B8	B7	B7	B2	A12	B11	B7	B11	B12	B4	B1	A6	A8
Pencaitland	A10	B3	B8	B5	B6	B6	B6	B1	A6	A7	A8	A10																		
Pencaitland & Ormiston / Ormiston													B7	B11	A11	B7	B3	B7	B5	B10	B11	B9	B9	B11	B9	B11	B9	B4	A8	A9
Preston Athletic								B2	A7	A9	B4	B5	B4	B6	B1	A9	A8	A6	A7	A6	A5	A6	A9	A11	B2	A7				
Selkirk	B9	B8	B5	B6	B3	B8	B4	B6	B6	B3	B10	B9	B11	B10	B10	B8	B8	B3	B2	A10	A11	A10	A10	A10	A12	B9				
Spartans	A8	A5	A5	A4	A8	A2	A6	A7	A4	A1	A2	A2	A3	A4	A1	A3	A1	A1	A4	A2	A3	A1	A1	A1	A2	A3				
Spartans Reserves																											A6	A6	A7	
Stirling University																						B3	B1	A2	A1	A2				
Stirling University Reserves																											B2	A7	A9	A6
Threave Rovers												B4	B1	A3	A4	A5	A3													
Tollcross United / Tynecastle	B7	B7	B6	B8	B2	A9	B10	A10	B7	B8	B2	A9	A12	B8	B9	B11	B11	B11	B9	B5	B3	B1	A4	A9	A9	A12	A4	A4	A4	A3
Tweedmouth Rangers																														A10
Vale of Leithen	A2	A10	B3	B2	A3	A4	A2	A6	A9	B6	B7	B2	A5	A8	A5	A10	A11	B5	B4	B3	B6	B7	B2	A7	A8	A9				
Whitehill Welfare	A1	A3	A4	A2	A2	A1	A1	A1	A1	A2	A1	A1	A2	A2	A2	A1	A10	A4	A5	A3	A1	A5	A2	A4	A3	A1				

A = Top Division
B = Lower Division

East of Scotland Qualifying League 2016/17

Group A

	BSY	COL	EYE	LOT	ORM	PEE
Burntisland Shipyard		Aug 6 2-1	Aug 20 0-4			Aug 27 0-1
Coldstream					Aug 20 6-2	Jul 30 4-1
Eyemouth United		Aug 13 2-5		Jul 30 0-7		Aug 6 3-2
Lothian Thistle	Aug 3 7-0	Aug 27 5-1				
Ormiston	Sep 10 7-3		Aug 27 1-2	Aug 6 0-5		
Peebles Rovers				Aug 23 0-1	Aug 3 3-2	

	P	W	D	L	F	A	PTS
Lothian Thistle	5	5	0	0	25	1	15
Coldstream	5	3	0	2	17	12	9
Eyemouth United	5	3	0	2	11	15	9
Peebles Rovers	5	2	0	3	7	10	6
Ormiston	5	1	0	4	12	19	3
Burntisland SY	5	1	0	4	5	20	3

Top three teams in each section qualified for the East of Scotland League Cup.

Group B

	HWU	LTH	SU	TYN	TWE
Heriot Watt University			Aug 20 1-0	Jul 30 2-0	
Leith Athletic	Aug 2 2-0		Aug 27 3-2		
Stirling University Reserves				Aug 13 1-5	Aug 6 5-2
Tynecastle		Aug 6 2-1			Aug 20 1-2
Tweedmouth Rovers	Aug 27 2-1	Jan 28 1-9			

	P	W	D	L	F	A	PTS
Leith Athletic	4	3	0	1	15	5	9
Tynecastle	4	2	0	2	8	6	6
Heriot Watt University	4	2	0	2	4	4	6
Tweedmouth Rovers	4	2	0	2	6	16	6
Stirling University Reserves	4	1	0	3	8	11	3

East of Scotland League Cup 2016/17

KO Stages						
1	08/04/2017	Tynecastle	Eyemouth United	6	1	
1	15/04/2017	Coldstream	Heriot Watt University	1	2	
SF	12/04/2017	Lothian Thistle HV	Tynecastle	1	1	aet, 2-3p
SF	29/04/2017	Leith Athletic	Heriot Watt	2	1	
F	07/05/2017	Tynecastle	Leith Athletic	1	2	at CSS

Two section winners from the Qualifying League had byes to the Semi Final stage.

Final 2016/17

Tynecastle: McMullen, Grant, McIntyre, Ferguson, Leslie, Mitchell, Cowan (Crabbe 61), Robinson (Kelly 84), Khosrowpour, Mayer, Swanson. Subs: Cockburn, Catlin, Brkic, Greig, Muttitt.

Leith Athletic: Gordon, Black, Fee, Melvin, Lewis, Burns, McKinlay, Allan (Mason 56), Hainey, Wilkie (Craigie 89), Wilson (Tracey 29). Subs: Beaton, Combe, Ferguson, Glynn.

1-0 39 mins Khosrowpour, 1-1 61 mins Hainey, 1-2 73 mins Mason (pen)

Complete East of Scotland League Cup Finals				
Season	**Winners**	**Runners Up**	**Score**	**Venue**
1987/8	Whitehill Welfare	Spartans	1-0	Tynecastle
1988/9	Whitehill Welfare	Spartans	1-0	Easter Road
1989/90	Berwick Rangers Reserves	Gala Fairydean	2-1 aet	Netherdale
1990/1	Whitehill Welfare	Spartans	1-0	Muirhouse
1991/2	Whitehill Welfare	Manor Thistle	4-1	Muirhouse
1992/3	Edinburgh City	Civil Service Strollers	1-0	Ferguson Park
1993/4	Gala Fairydean	Whitehill Welfare	0-0, 4-2pens	Whitestone Park
1994/5	Whitehill Welfare	Civil Service Strollers	2-0	Pennypit Park
1995/6	Whitehill Welfare	Annan Athletic	3-2 aet	Netherdale
1996/7	Whitehill Welfare	Vale of Leithen	2-0	Pennypit Park
1997/8	Whitehill Welfare	Craigroyston	3-0	Pennypit Park
1998/9	Whitehill Welfare	Threave Rovers	1-1, 5-4 pens	Netherdale
1999/00	Annan Athletic	Coldstream	2-1	Netherdale
2000/1	Civil Service Strollers	Edinburgh City	3-1	Ferguson Park
2001/2	Edinburgh City	Spartans	1-0	Ferguson Park
2002/3	Whitehill Welfare	Craigroyston	2-0	Saughton Enclos
2003/4	Spartans	Edinburgh City	4-1	Saughton Enclos
2004/5	Spartans	Edinburgh City	2-0	Ferguson Park
2005/6	Heriot Watt University	Easthouses Lily	2-0	Ferguson Park
2006/7	Whitehill Welfare	Annan Athletic	1-0	Islecroft Stadium
2007/8	Spartans	Whitehill Welfare	1-0	Pennypit Park
2008/9	Dalbeattie Star	Preston Athletic	2-0	Yarrow Park
2009/10	Spartans	Lothian Thistle	2-1	St Marks Park
2010/1	Spartans	Edinburgh University	4-2	Pennypit Park
2011/2	Whitehill Welfare	Edinburgh City	2-0	St Marks Park
2012/3	Edinburgh City	Spartans	2-0	Muirhouse
2013/4	Hibernian U20	Craigroyston	4-1	Muirhouse
2014/5	Leith Athletic	Spartans EOS	2-0	St Marks Park
2015/6	Spartans EOS	Leith Athletic	2-1	St Marks Park
2016/7	Leith Athletic	Tynecastle	2-1	Muirhouse
All Time Winners				
12	Whitehill Welfare			
5	Spartans			
3	Edinburgh City			
2	Leith Athletic			
1	Berwick Rangers Reserves	Gala Fairydean	Annan Ath	Civil Service S
	Heriot Watt University	Dalbeattie Star	Hibernian U20	Spartans EOS

Alex Jack Cup 2016/17

This competition, named after former League Secretary Alex 'Sandy' Jack, is for clubs which are not full members of the Scottish Football Association, and therefore do not play in the Scottish Cup. It was introduced to

1	03/09/2016	Lothian Thistle HV	Ormiston	4	1	
1	03/09/2016	Heriot Watt University	Tweedmouth Rangers	4	1	
1	10/09/2016	Tynecastle	Eyemouth United	9	0	
SF	24/09/2016	Tynecastle	Heriot Watt University	4	2	
SF	01/10/2016	Lothian Thistle HV	Peebles Rovers	2	0	
F	23/10/2016	Tynecastle	Lothian Thistle HV	1	3	at Riccarton

Scorers: **LTHV** - Jamie Devlin, Kevin Brown, Liam O'Donnell; **Tynecastle** - Martyn Robertson
The final was played on the outdoor artificial pitch at Riccarton. Attendance was 200 approx.

Leith Athletic did not defend their trophy as they were playing in the Scottish Cup.

Complete Alex Jack Cup Finals

Season	Winners	Runners Up	Score	Venue
1988/9	Kelso United	Craigroyston	2-1	Netherdale, Galashiels
1989/90	Edinburgh City	Berwick Rangers 'A'	4-2	Ferguson Park, Rosewell
1990/1	Easthouses Lily	Pencaitland	2-1 aet	Ferguson Park, Rosewell
1991/2	Edinburgh City	Easthouses Lily	2-1	Ferguson Park, Rosewell
1992/3	Manor Thistle	Edinburgh City	1-0	Ferguson Park, Rosewell
1993/4	Craigroyston	Tollcross	1-0	Marine Drive, Edinburgh
1994/5	Preston Athletic	Craigroyston	2-0	Ferguson Park, Rosewell
1995/6	Manor Thistle	Lothian Thistle	2-0	Ferguson Park, Rosewell
1996/7	Edinburgh Athletic	Pencaitland	1-0	Ferguson Park, Rosewell
1997/8	Tollcross	Lothian Thistle	2-1 aet	Ferguson Park, Rosewell
1998/9	Easthouses Lily	Craigroyston	3-1	Ferguson Park, Rosewell
1999/00	Peebles Rovers	Easthouses Lily	1-1, 5-4 pens	Ferguson Park, Rosewell
2000/1	Lothian Thistle	Craigroyston	2-0	Ferguson Park, Rosewell
2001/2	Kelso United	Easthouses Lily	2-1	Victoria Park, Innerleithen
2002/3	Edinburgh Athletic	Lothian THistle	2-1	Ferguson Park, Rosewell
2003/4	Lothian THistle	Edinburgh Athletic	1-0	Ferguson Park, Rosewell
2004/5	Easthouses Lily	Lothian Thistle	1-1, 5-4 pens	Ferguson Park, Rosewell
2005/6	Lothian Thistle	Kelso United	2-1	Pennypit, Prestonpans
2006/7	Easthouses Lily	Tynecastle	2-0	Ferguson Park, Rosewell
2007/8	Lothian Thistle	Peebles Rovers	3-0	Victoria Park, Innerleithen
2008/9	Gretna	Tynecastle	4-2	Netherdale, Galashiels
2009/10	Leith Athletic	Eyemouth United	2-0	Pennypit, Prestonpans
2010/1	Stirling University	Lothian Thistle	8-0	Falkirk Stadium
2011/2	Stirling University	Gretna	3-0	Pennypit, Prestonpans
2012/3	Leith Athletic	Craigroyston	1-0	Ainslie Park, Edinburgh
2013/4	Leith Athletic	Lothian Thistle	2-1	Marine Drive, Edinburgh
2014/5	Leith Athletic	Peebles Rovers	4-1	Victoria Park, Innerleithen
2015/6	Leith Athletic	Eyemouth United	6-0	Home Park, Coldstream
2016/7	Lothian Thistle HV	Tynecastle	3-1	Riccarton, Edinburgh

Football Nation East of Scotland Qualifying Cup 2016/17

1	13/08/2016	Civil Service Strollers	Peebles Rovers	2	0	
1	13/08/2016	Ormiston	Stirling University	1	5	
1	13/08/2016	Gretna	East Kilbride	1	6	
1	13/08/2016	Preston Athletic	Burntisland Shipyard	3	2	
1	13/08/2016	Spartans	Gala Fairydean Rovers	5	2	
1	13/08/2016	Vale of Leithen	Heriot Watt University	1	2	
1	24/09/2016	Tweedmouth Rangers	Lothian Thistle HV	0	2	
2	30/11/2016	Lothian Thistle HV	Selkirk	3	0	
2	17/09/2016	Coldstream	Spartans	1	3	
2	17/09/2016	Whitehill Welfare	Tynecastle	2	0	
2	03/12/2016	Hawick Royal Albert	Heriot Watt University	2	1	
2	22/10/2016	Civil Service Strollers	Edinburgh University	0	3	
2		Eyemouth United	Duns	wo	scr	
2	10/11/2016	Stirling University	East Kilbride	1	2	
2	29/10/2016	Preston Athletic	Leith Athletic	1	2	
3	03/12/2016	Spartans	Leith Athletic	3	0	
3	21/01/2017	Whitehill Welfare	Hawick RA	2	3	
3	03/12/2016	Lothian Thistle HV	Eyemouth United	5	0	
3	07/12/2016	Edinburgh University	East Kilbride	2	3	
SF	22/02/2017	Hawick RA	Lothian Thistle HV	0	4	
SF	21/01/2017	East Kilbride	Spartans	1	2	
F	19/03/2017	Spartans	Lothian Thistle HV	2	1	at ORIAM

Played for by East of Scotland FA members who are NOT members of the Scottish Professional Football League.

FINAL 2016/17
Spartans v Lothian Thistle HV
19/3/16, 2-1
Att 250 (est)
At ORIAM (Indoors)

SPARTANS
1 Carswell
2 Thomson
3 Maxwell
4 Herd
5 Tolmie
6 Stevenson*
7 Beesley
9 Allum
10 Dishington+
11 Brown
19 Townsley

Subs
12 Murray
15 Gabiola* (for 6)
16 Comrie+ (for 10)
17 Mair
18 Dawson
GK Gilpin

LOTHIAN THISTLE HV
1 Swain
2 Moore
3 Crawford
4 Sherlock
5 Taylor-McKenzie
6 Hare
7 Brown
8 Muir
9 O'Donnell
10 Wringe*
11 Devlin

Subs
12 Guy* (for 10)
14 Moffat
15 Henrique
16 Simpson
17 Munro
18 Alastuey

0-1 9 mins Sherlock
1-1 52 mins Maxwell
2-1 64 mins Allum

LTHV, of the East of Scotland League, dominated the first half against Lowland League side Spartans. They led thanks to a cross-cum-shot by Sherlock which evaded the keeper and dropped into the net.

Scott Maxwell equalised for Spartans and was injured in the process - both he and the LTHV goalkeeper Swain needed lengthy treatment before continuing.

Ross Allum, signed earlier in the season from Edinburgh City, scored the winner.

This was the first Senior competitive match in Scotland played indoors. Several Scottish Junior Cup ties have been played at the Ravenscraig Indoor Stadium in Motherwell.

Recent East of Scotland Qualifying Cup Finals

Season	Winners	Runners Up	Score	Venue
1988/9	Civil Service Strollers	Spartans	3-1	Ferguson Park, Rosewell
1989/90	Spartans	Edinburgh City	3-0	Tynecastle Park, Edinburgh
1990/1	Gala Fairydean	Whitehill Welfare	1-0	Victoria Park, Innerleithen
1991/2	Whitehill Welfare	Vale of Leithen	4-0	Netherdale, Galashiels
1992/3	Manor Thistle	Kelso United	2-2, 4-2 pens	Victoria Park, Innerleithen
1993/4	Whitehill Welfare	Selkirk	2-0	Netherdale, Galashiels
1994/5	Gala Fairydean	Kelso United	2-1	Netherdale, Galashiels
1995/6	Spartans	Edinburgh City	3-1	Pennypit Park, Prestonpans
1996/7	Lothian Thistle	Whitehill Welfare	2-1	Pennypit Park, Prestonpans
1997/8	Spartans	Gala Fairydean	2-0	Victoria Park, Innerleithen
1998/9	Whitehill Welfare	Lothian Thistle	2-0	Pennypit Park, Prestonpans
1999/00	Whitehill Welfare	Coldstream	4-2	Victoria Park, Innerleithen
2000/1	Whitehill Welfare	Lothian Thistle	2-0	Pennypit Park, Prestonpans
2001/2	Spartans	Whitehill Welfare	2-1 aet	Saughton Enclosure, Edinburgh
2002/3	Edinburgh City	Edinburgh University	2-1	Pennypit Park, Prestonpans
2003/4	Preston Athletic	Edinburgh City	2-1	Saughton Enclosure, Edinburgh
2004/5	Edinburgh University	Spartans	2-1 aet	Riccarton, Currie
2005/6	Spartans	Preston Athletic	6-4	Marine Drive, Edinburgh
2006/7	Spartans	Kelso United	3-0	Riccarton, Currie
2007/8	Selkirk	Lothian Thistle	3-1	Victoria Park, Innerleithen
2008/9	Whitehill Welfare	Edinburgh City	3-2	Pennypit Park, Prestonpans
2009/10	Gretna	Vale of Leithen	2-0	Albert Park, Hawick
2010/1	Spartans	Tynecastle	2-1 aet	St Marks Park, Edinburgh
2011/2	Edinburgh City	Whitehill Welfare	3-2	Ainslie Park, Edinburgh
2012/3	Gretna	Stirling University	2-1	Albert Park, Hawick
2013/4	Whitehill Welfare	Spartans	2-2 aet, 5-4 pens	St Marks Park, Edinburgh
2014/15	Lothian Thistle	Leith Athletic	3-2aet	St Marks Park, Edinburgh
2015/16	East Kilbride	Spartans	4-1	Albyn Park, Broxburn
2016/17	Spartans	Lothian Thistle HV	2-1	ORIAM, Edinburgh

In Victorian times the East of Scotland Cup was hugely prestigious. The "big clubs", hearts, Hibs and St Bernards, were unhappy at having to enter the draw at the first stage with a growing number of smaller clubs. They withdrew from the EOSFA and only returned on condition that an East of Scotland Qualifying Cup was established. They were exempt from this competition - but faced the teams that reached the latter stages in the East of Scotland "City" Cup instead. In a sense this model endures with the finalists from the East of Scotland Qualifying Cup taking no Berwick Rangers and Edinburgh City in the City Cup Semi Finals.

King Cup 2016/17

1	18/03/2017	Heriot Watt University	Eyemouth United	6	0	
1	18/03/2017	Leith Athletic	Ormiston	8	0	
1	01/04/2017	Tweedmouth Rangers	Coldstream	2	3	
2	18/03/2017	Tynecastle	Stirling University	5	1	
2	08/04/2017	Coldstream	Burntisland Shipyard	6	0	
2		Leith Athletic	Peebles Rovers*	wo		
2	01/04/2017	Lothian Thistle HV	Heriot Watt University	3	1	
SF	03/05/2017	Lothian Thistle HV	Coldstream	5	0	
SF	25/04/2017	Leith Athletic	Tynecastle	7	2	
F	20/05/2017	Leith Athletic	Lothian Thistle HV	4	2	aet

Peebles Rovers excluded after scratching at SF stage in 2015/16

Percival King

Leith Athletic: Gordon, Black, Fee, Lowson, Melvin, Burns, Tracey, Wilkie, Hainey (Beaton 110), Allan (Ferguson 82), McKinlay (Lewis 88). Subs: Beaton, Combe, Lewis, Craigie, Mason, MacPherson.
Lothian Thistle Hutchison Vale: Swain, Moore (Sherlock 61), Taylor-MacKenzie, Crawford, Munro, Muir, Hare (Guy 75), Brown, Wringe (Hutchison 67), Devlin, O'Donnell. Subs: Mungall, Simpson, Wishart, Alastuey.

1-0	15 mins	Wilkie
1-1	21 mins	Munro
1-2	56 mins	Muir
2-2	63 mins	Black
3-2	extra time	Hainey
4-2	extra time	Ferguson

Leith played extra time with ten men and an outfield player (Neil Lowson) in goals following the sending off of regular 'keeper Iain Gordon during normal time.

Recent King Cup Finals

Season	Winners	Runners Up	Score	Venue
1989/90	Berwick Rangers Reserves	Civil Service Strollers	2-1	Rosewell
1990/1	Civil Service Strollers	Edinburgh University	3-0	Rosewell
1991/2	Vale of Leithen	Spartans	1-0	Rosewell
1992/3	Whitehill Welfare	Spartans	1-0	Muirhouse
1993/4	Whitehill Welfare	Craigroyston	3-1	Muirhouse
1994/5	Whitehill Welfare	Spartans	2-0 aet	Prestonpans
1995/6	Whitehill Welfare	Civil Service Strollers	3-0	Tynecastle Park, Hearts FC
1996/7	Craigroyston	Edinburgh Athletic	2-0	Prestonpans
1997/8	Whitehill Welfare	Civil Service Strollers	3-2	Rosewell
1998/9	Edinburgh City	Edinburgh University	3-1	Rosewell
1999/00	Edinburgh City	Whitehill Welfare	2-1	Rosewell
2000/1	Spartans	Vale of Leithen	2-0	Rosewell
2001/2	Spartans	Gala Fairydean	4-2	Prestonpans
2002/3	Spartans	Ormiston	2-0	Rosewell
2003/4	Lothian Thistle	Heriot Watt University	1-1 aet, 4-1 pens	Muirhouse
2004/5	Spartans	Edinburgh City	4-0	Muirhouse
2005/6	Spartans	Edinburgh City	6-1	Rosewell
2006/7	Edinburgh University	Lothian Thistle	2-0	Selkirk
2007/8	Spartans	Vale of Leithen	7-2	Rosewell
2008/9	Heriot Watt University	Vale of Leithen	1-0	Rosewell
2009/10	Spartans	Stirling University	2-0	Rosewell
2010/1	Spartans	Stirling University	2-1	Falkirk Stadium
2011/2	Stirling University	Spartans	2-1	Rosewell
2012/3	Spartans	Berwick Rangers Rese	3-1	St Marks Park, Edinburgh
2013/14	Edinburgh University	Whitehill Welfare	1-0	Prestonpans
2014/15	Peebles Rovers	Spartans EOS	2-0	Muirhouse
2015/16	Leith Athletic	Lothian Thistle HV	4-2 aet	Musselburgh
2016/17	Leith Athletic	Lothian Thistle HV	4-2 aet	Rosewell

East of Scotland City Cup 2016/17

The City Cup is now played between East of Scotland FA members who are SPFL members but outwith the top flight, plus the finalists of the East of Scotland Qualifying Cup. In practice this has meant, until last seasons, a single tie between Berwick Rangers and the Qualifying Cup winners. With Edinburgh City's promotion to the SPFL, Semi Finals were re-started for 2016/17.

SF	08/03/2017	Lothian Thistle HV	Berwick Rangers	2	0
SF	28/03/2017	Spartans	Edinburgh City	0	2
F	19/04/2017	Edinburgh City	Lothian Thistle HV	1	2

Final
Edinburgh City: Antell, Caddow, Donaldson, Harrison, McConnell, Cummings (Deniran 84), McFarland, Gair (Laird 64), Riordan, Guthrie, Makofo (Walker 64).
LTHV: Swain, Sherlock, Taylor-McKenzie, Crawford, Munro, Muir, Hutchison, Brown, Wringe (Mungall 67), Devlin (O'Donnell 50), Hare.
Referee: E Cairns.
Attendance: 133.

0-1 35 mins	Devlin
0-2 75 mins	Hare
1-2 82 mins	Riordan

RECENT CITY CUP FINALS

1985/6	Meadowbank Thistle	Gala Fairydean	3-1		Netherdale
1986/7	Meadowbank Thistle	Berwick Rangers	0-1		Meadowbank
1987/8	Gala Fairydean	Berwick Rangers	1-1	4-2 pens	Shielfield
1988/9	Meadowbank Thistle	Berwick Rangers	2-1		Shielfield
1989/90	Meadowbank Thistle	Berwick Rangers	1-1	5-4 pens	Meadowbank
1990/1	Berwick Rangers	Meadowbank Thistle	2-1		Shielfield
1991/2	Vale of Leithen	Whitehill Welfare	4-1		Innerleithen
1992/3	Berwick Rangers	Meadowbank Thistle	2-1		Shielfield
1993/4	Whitehill Welfare	Berwick Rangers	2-2	6-5 pens	Shielfield
1994/5	Meadowbank Thistle	Kelso United	7-1		Netherdale
1995/6	Berwick Rangers	Livingston	5-2		Almondvale
1996/7	Livingston	Whitehill Welfare	2-1		Almondvale
1997/8	Spartans	Livingston	2-1		Almondvale
1998/9	Whitehill Welfare	Lothian Thistle	5-0		Rosewell
1999/00	Whitehill Welfare	Livingston	1-0		Rosewell
2000/1	Livingston	Lothian Thistle	3-0		Rosewell
2001/2	Berwick Rangers	Spartans	2-1		Rosewell
2002/3	Berwick Rangers	Edinburgh City	3-1		Shielfield
2003/4	Preston Athletic	Berwick Rangers	3-2		Prestonpans
2004/5	Spartans	Berwick Rangers	4-1		Shielfield
2005/6	Spartans	Berwick Rangers	2-1		Shielfield
2006/7	Spartans	Berwick Rangers	3-2		Shielfield
2007/8	Berwick Rangers	Lothian Thistle	2-0		Saughton
2008/9	Berwick Rangers	Whitehill Welfare	3-1		Shielfield
2009/10	Berwick Rangers	Gretna	2-0		Shielfield
2010/11	Berwick Rangers	Spartans	2-1		Shielfield
2011/12	Berwick Rangers	Edinburgh City	2-0		Shielfield
2012/13	Gretna	Berwick Rangers	4-2		Gretna
2013/14	Whitehill Welfare	Berwick Rangers	2-1		Shielfield
2014/15	Berwick Rangers	Lothian Thistle HV	0-0	4-3p	Shielfield
2015/16	East Kilbride	Berwick Rangers	2-0		Shielfield
2016/17	Lothian Thistle HV	Edinburgh City	2-1		Meadowbank

East of Scotland Shield 2015/16 (played 2016/17)

Tuesday September 22nd (at Easter Road)
Hibernian 1 (Gullan pen) Hearts 2 (Henderson, MacDonald), H.T. 0-0, Att 466

Hibs: Martin, Donaldson, Hall, O'Conner, Porteous, Smith, Walker, Campbell, Gullan, Murray, Gallantes (Shanley 74).
Hearts: Mason, Morrison, Reid, Hamilton, Smith, Gillan, McDonald, Petrov, Leonard (Ritchie 90), Irving, Henderson.

The Annual Shield match had been held over from the previous season. The 2016/17 Final was not played.

East of Scotland League Club Playing Squads 2016/17

NB These are not comprehensive lists of players used - there will be some omissions. However, all players listed were associated with the club concerned during 2016/17

Burntisland Shipyard
Manager: Craig Winter (Until Jan), Chris Maxwell (from Feb)
Aitken
Alan Hynd
Andrew McDonald
Arran Haddow
Ben Paterson
B Jenkins
Ben Saunders
Black
Bowman
Cammy Lambie
C Drury
C Hampseed
C Hamilton
Calum McAleavey
Connor Allison
C Macwell
Daniel Butt
Daniel Roberts
Daryl Taylor
Dennis Ginc
Donald Hyslop (ex Steelend Vics)
Ewan Fotheringham
Grant Buckley
G Bowers
Josh Anderson
Kellichan
Kenneth Ford
Lee Halpin
L Thompson
Lewis McIntosh
Luke Fleming
Marc Black
Marcus Taylor
McIntosh
Nathan McKay
Paterson
Prendergast
Ryan Calder
Scott Powrie
Sean Cusick
Sean Doyle
S Murphy
S Wilson
S Stark
Thomas Hall
Watt
Yanis Iliopolous (ex Oakley United)

Coldstream
Manager: Grant Davidson, Assistant: David Brown
Alexander Simpson
Calum Watson (Signed Jan 2017, Freed Feb 2017)
Cameron Beasley
Craig Hall
Des Sutherland
Ewan Gray (2016 Hawick RA, Freed Jan 2017)
Gary Wales
Gary Windram (2017 Berwick Colts)
Grant Robinson
Hagen Steele (Freed Jan 2017)
Jack Logan (2016 Greenlaw, ex Kelso Utd)
Jake Birkett
Jason Inglis
John Crawford (Freed Jan 2017 – scored over 200 goals in 3 spells with Coldstream)
Josh Hebden
Kai Strang
Kieran Lee
Kris Dixon
Kuba Polniak (2017 Tweedmouth Rangers)
Leigh Walker (2017 Tweedmouth Rangers)
Liam Howel
Luke Dickson
Mark Johnston (2016 Vale of Leithen)
Mark Walters (2016 Berwick Rangers, ex Coldstream)
Paul Hossack
Reece Bowling (2016 Duns U16, Freed Jan 2017)
Rhys Dixon
Richard Davidson
Robin Brown
Sean Dixon

Eyemouth United
Manager: Stuart Wilson
Adam Mutch
Aiden Lauder
Alan Spiers
Alexander Martin
Andrew Patterson
Andrew Sword
Callum McLure
Connor Lough
Daniel Blackie
Ewan Wilson
Gordon McInnes
Graham Paterson
Gregg McCrudden
James Wilson (2016 Eyemouth Ams, Ex Eyemouth Utd)
Jamie Logie
Jeff Colin
John Crawford (2017 Coldstream, ex Eyemouth Utd, Dunbar Utd)
Jonathan Cowe
Joshua Waddell
Kevin Strachan
Michael Gillen
Paul Cowe
Ross Patterson (2016 Edinburgh University)
Sean Campbell

Heriot Watt University
Manager: Banji Koya
Adam Breen
Adam Woolven
Aidan Quinn
Anton Dowds
Callum Smith
Chris Donnelly
Chris Lane
Craig Saunders
Elliot Sutherland
Finn Watt
Harry Warner
Jamie Bain
Jamie Forsyth
Liam Walker
Max Allison
Michael Lynch
Neil Laurenson
Robert Service
Ryan Higgins
Scott Dargo
Scott Munro
Tom Maher

Leith Athletic
Manager: Derek Riddell (until May 2017)
Assistant: Paul McGlynn
Brodie MacKenzie
Chris Beaton
Daniel McKinlay
Gavin Kneeshaw
Grant Burns
Iain Gordon
Jack Brian
Jack Combe
James Hainey
John Ferguson
Jordan Smith
Kerr Allan
Kyle Fee
Lewis Tracey
Mark Wilkie
Neil Fairnie
Neil Lowson

Robbie Mason
Scott Wilson
Sean Melvin
Steven Glynn
Taylor Black
Rhys Craigie
Kenneth Hall
Sam Laverty
Sean McPherson
Daniel Simpson

Lothian Thistle Hutchison Vale
Manager: Raymond Carr
Adrian Shala
Alan McDonagh
Benat
Declan Moffat
Dylan Moore
Elliot Taylor
Grant Munro
James Guy
Jamie Devlin
Jamie Simpson
Jaxon Wishart
John Sherlock
Jordan Mungall
Kevin Brown
Kevin Swain
Liam O'Donnell
Luis Diego Henriques
Paul Crawford
Richie Wilkes
Ryan Fox
Scott Taylor McKenzie
Sean Wringe
Tony Muir
Willis Hare

Ormiston
Manager: Richard Weir
Aidan McMillan
Alan Morgan
Alex MacLeod
Ally Simpson
Andrew Noble
Blair Millar
Cameron Milne
Christopher Malcolm
Colin McArthur
Craig O'Neill
Dale Urey
Daryl Burdett
Daryl Johnston
David Nash
Declan Heron
Ethan Clark
Finlay Hughes
Finlay Watson
Gary Hadden
Gary Millard
Graeme Purves
Ian Little
Jack Findlay
James Livingston
John Morgan
Johnathan Edmond
Jonathan Bisset
Jonathan Malcolm
Keith Buckley
Kevin Amagou
Kevin Gordon
Kevin Smith
Liam Hunter
Liam McCathie
Mark Law
Mark Samson
Murray Lorimer
Nicky Cairns
Richard Fairnie
Richard Weir
Ross Cowan
Ross Ferguson
Ryan Collinson
Sean Lawson
Stewart Johnston
Thomas Carr
Yusif Bernawi
Zack Walker

Peebles Rovers
Manager: Ger Rossi
Assistant: Alan MacDonald
Alan McMath (ex Leithen Rovers)
Ben Brown (ex Peebles Rovers Ams)
Ben McGinley (2016 Whitehill Welfare)
Colin Smith (ex Leithen Rovers)
David Lindsay
David Lindsay (2016 Tweeddale Rovers)
Ger Rossi (ex Hibernian Youth)
Gregor Lamb (2017 Tynecastle)
James Dods (ex Peebles Ams)
James Runciman (2016 Stow)
Jamie Mackay (2016 Tweeddale Rovers)
Jason Newell
Lee Zavaroni
Michael Cockburn
Robbie Renwick (ex Livingston Youths)
Ross Forrest
Ross Lamb
Saul Schulz-Keith (2016 Tynecastle)
Sterricks

Stirling University
Coach - Frank Nuttall
Andrew Macdonald
Arron Gunn
Dale Corrin
David Beaton
David Collins
David McCaughie
Dominic Slattery
Eric Jeffrey
Greg Jacobs
Gussie Dey
Harry Ball
Jack May
James Donaldson
Joe Greig
John McNaught
Khan Mitchell
Malcolm Burgess
Mark Shiels
Matt Underhill
Sam Maclean

Tweedmouth Rangers
Manager: Mark Reid (until May 2017), John Patterson (from May 2017)
Ben Jackson
Craig Colquhoun
Craig Grieve
Craig Heugh
Craig Howard
Craig Walker
Graeme Cain
Jake Gibson
Jake Rutherford
James Turnbull
John Patterson
Jordan Ainslie
Kieran Ainslie
Kieran Cromarty
Lee Dodd
Leigh Walker
Luke Dickson
Michael Allan
Michael Antcliff
Michael Robinson
Nial Jones
Peter McAskill
Reagan Graham
Ross Moore
Rudy McLeod
Sean Dixon
Sean Simpson
Shane McGregor
Stuart Coyle

Tynecastle
Manager: Steven Vinter
Calvin Muttitt
Chris Joyce
Connor Bryden
Craig Cockburn
Dayne Robertson
Dean Crabbe
Douglas Cunnison
Jack Cowan
Louis Swanson
Mark Leslie
Martyn Robinson
Michael Catlin
Pieyam Khrosowspour
Robbie McIntyre
Ross McMullen
Ryan Ferguson
Ryan Malcolm
Sonny Swanson
Stephen Manson
Stewart Adams
Willie Mitchell

East / Lowland Under 20s

East / Lowland League Under 20s 2016/17

	BSC	CUM	EK	EC	EUNI	EDUS	HWU	LTHV	PA	SPA	TYN	UOS	WW
BSC Glasgow		Mar 20	Oct 7	Nov 18	Apr 21	Dec 2	Mar 3	May 12	Jan 13	Feb 3	Oct 21	Mar 17	Mar 31
		2-4	1-2	0-3	2-2	2-0	4-2	4-5	0-6	1-6	1-2	2-1	3-3
Cumbernauld Colts	Mar 10		Nov 11	May 1	Sep 30	Jan 27	May 5	Oct 14	Oct 28	Apr 24	Apr 3	Dec 16	Feb 10
	8-0		0-4	0-2	1-0	2-3	2-0	8-4	0-3	2-3	3-0	3-3	3-0
East Kilbride	Jan 27	Mar 28		Apr 21	Dec 2	Mar 6	May 22	Dec 16	Sep 30	Oct 26	Mar 3	Nov 18	Apr 4
	9-0	3-2		3-2	3-1	6-2	5-1	4-2	2-1	3-3	6-1	3-3	4-0
Edinburgh City	Mar 24	Sep 9	Apr 24		Oct 14	Feb 10	<ay 19	Oct 28	Mar 17	May 5	Dec 9	Jan 20	Mar 10
	5-1	1-2	1-2		2-5	5-0	0-2	1-5	4-3	1-5	2-5	1-6	1-3
Edinburgh University	Nov 25	Jan 20	May 5	Feb 3		Oct 28	Sep 23	Mar 10	Mar 24	Dec 9	May 19	Oct 7	Nov 30
	2-0	1-4	0-2	2-3		1-1	2-2	6-3	3-1	2-1	1-0	2-2	1-1
Edusport Academy	May 5	Oct 7	May 12	Oct 21	Mar 3		Jan 20	Nov 9	Nov 25	May 19	Oct 18	Feb 3	Mar 24
	2-1	2-4	1-5	3-5	0-0		1-2	2-6	0-1	1-2	2-2	1-3	1-2
Heriot Watt University	Oct 28	Dec 2	Mar 10	Dec 16	Apr 24	Sep 30		Jan 27	Feb 13	Nov 11	Mar 24	May 12	Oct 14
	3-2	3-0	0-4	2-0	3-2	3-2		4-2	3-1	2-4	4-1	1-1	3-0
Lothian Thistle HV	Dec 9	Feb 3	May 19	Mar 3	Nov 4	Mar 17	Oct 7		May 5	Sep 6	Jan 20	Oct 21	Apr 28
	3-1	0-3	0-2	3-3	3-1	6-0	1-4		5-1	4-1	3-1	2-6	2-1
Preston Athletic	Sep 2	Mar 3	Jan 20	Nov 14	Nov 18	Apr 28	Oct 21	Dec 2		Oct 7	Feb 3	Nov 4	May 12
	1-0	2-2	1-5	0-3	0-3	1-2	1-3	4-4		2-6	0-6	1-3	1-4
Spartans	Oct 14	Mar 13	Feb 10	Nov 29	May 12	Dec 16	Mar 17	Jan 13	Jan 27		Mar 21	Apr 21	Sep 30
	8-2	1-2	4-4	3-2	4-3	2-0	1-0	3-0	0-2		7-2	2-0	6-1
Tynecastle	May 2	Apr 21	Oct 28	May 12	Dec 16	Jan 13	Nov 18	Sep 30	Oct 14	Mar 10		Dec 2	Jan 27
	9-1	0-3	2-1	1-2	5-0	1-2	1-1	2-2	2-1	1-3		3-1	2-0
University of Stirling	Apr 3	May 19	Mar 24	Sep 30	May 22	Oct 14	Dec 9	Apr 7	Mar 10	Mar 6	May 5		Oct 28
	2-4	3-1	3-4	9-1	5-0	2-0	5-0	3-0	6-4	1-4	4-0		6-0
Whitehill Welfare	May 19	Oct 21	Sep 16	May 8	Mar 17	Nov 18	Feb 3	Apr 21	Dec 9	Jan 20	Nov 4	Mar 3	
	3-1	0-4	2-7	2-2	2-10	2-1	1-6	2-1	0-7	0-4	2-3	2-3	

	Club	P	W	D	L	F	A	GD	Pts
1	East Kilbride	24	20	3	1	93	33	60	63
2	The Spartans	24	18	2	4	83	38	45	56
3	University of Stirling	24	14	4	6	81	41	40	46
4	Heriot Watt University	24	14	3	7	55	43	12	45
5	Cumbernauld Colts	24	14	2	8	63	40	23	44
6	Tynecastle	24	10	3	11	52	52	0	33
7	Lothian Thistle Hutchison Vale	24	10	3	11	66	67	-1	33
8	Edinburgh University	24	8	6	10	50	50	0	30
9	Edinburgh City	24	9	2	13	52	67	-15	29
10	Whitehill Welfare	24	6	3	15	33	82	-49	21
11	Preston Athletic	24	6	2	16	45	67	-22	20
12	Edusport Academy	24	4	3	17	29	66	-37	15
13	BSC Glasgow	24	4	2	18	35	91	-56	14

Matches in this league are usually played on Feriday evenings.

Three new teams are joining for 2017/18—Bonnyton Thistle, Selkirk and Burntisland Shipyard. Burntisland will play their games at East Fife's stadium.

East / Lowland League Under 20s KO Cup Draw 2017/18

1st Round
Preston Athletic v Spartans
Edinburgh University v Mid Annandale
BSC Glasgow v Selkirk
Edusport Academy v Cumbernauld Colts
Lothian Thistle HV v Bonnyton Thistle
Whitehill Welfare v Heriot Watt University
Edinburgh City v Tynecastle
Burntisland Shipyard v Stirling University

Quarter Finals

Whitehill Welfare or Heriot Watt University v BSC Glasgow or Selkirk
Edinburgh University or Mid Annandale v Lothian Thistle HV or Bonnyton Thistle
Preston Athletic or Spartans v Burntisland Shipyard or Stirling University
Edinburgh City or Tynecastle v Edusport Academy or Cumbernauld Colts

Semi Finals

Preston Athletic or Spartans or Burntisland Shipyard or Stirling University v Whitehill Welfare or Heriot Watt University or BSC Glasgow or Selkirk
Edinburgh City or Tynecastle or Edusport Academy or Cumbernauld Colts v Edinburgh University or Mid Annandale or Lothian Thistle HV or Bonnyton Thistle

Challenge Cup is discontinued for 2017/18.

East / Lowland League Cup Under 20s 2016/17

QUALIFYING LEAGUE SECTION A

	CUM	LTHV	PA	WW	EDU
Cumbernauld Colts				Sep 2 7-1	Sep 16 3-1
Lothian Thistle HV	Aug 26 2-5			Sep 9 6-1	
Preston Athletic	Sep 6 1-4	Sep 15 1-0			
Whitehill Welfare			Aug 26 5-1		Sep 6 0-2
Edusport Academy		Sep 2 1-0	Sep 9 1-1		

QUALIFYING LEAGUE SECTION B

	BSC	EK	EDI	SPA	TYN
BSC Glasgow			Sep 5 3-3	Sep 16 2-3	
East Kilbride	Aug 26 2-1				Sep 6 5-1
Edinburgh City		Sep 12 0-6			Sep 16 3-4
Spartans		Sep 9 1-1	Aug 26 3-0		
Tynecastle	Sep 9 4-2			Sep 2 1-3	

League Cup						
SF	18/11/2016	Cumbernauld Colts	Spartans	2	0	
SF	09/12/2016	East Kilbride	Edusport Academy	5	0	
F	17/03/2017	East Kilbride	Cumbernauld Colts	1	0	at Benburb

East / Lowland League Challenge Cup Under 20s 2016/17

1 (1)	17/02/2017	Cumbernauld Colts	BSC Glasgow	1	1			
1 (1)	17/02/2017	Preston Athletic	Whitehill Welfare	3	0			
1 (1)	17/02/2017	Spartans	Edusport Academy	3	2			
1 (1)	17/02/2017	East Kilbride	Stirling University	3	1			
1 (1)	17/02/2017	Heriot Watt Universit	Edinburgh City	0	3			
1 (2)	24/02/2017	BSC Glasgow	Cumbernauld Colts	1	7		2	8
1 (2)	24/02/2017	Edinburgh City	Heriot Watt University	0	1		3	1
1 (2)	24/02/2017	Edusport Academy	Spartans	2	3		4	6
1 (2)	24/02/2017	Stirling University	East Kilbride	4	3		5	6
1 (2)	24/02/2017	Whitehill Welfare	Preston Athletic	0	8		0	11
2 (1)	24/02/2017	Tynecastle	Lothian Thistle HV	2	3			
2 (1)	31/03/2017	Cumbernauld Colts	Spartans	1	2			
2 (1)	31/03/2017	Preston Athletic	Edinburgh University	1	4			
2 (1)	31/03/2017	East Kilbride	Edinburgh City	8	0			
2 (2)	31/03/2017	Lothian Thistle HV	Tynecastle	4	3		7	5
2 (2)	07/04/2017	Edinburgh University	Preston Athletic	2	1		6	2
2 (2)	07/04/2017	Edinburgh City	East Kilbride	1	7		*1*	*15*
2 (2)	07/04/2017	Spartans	Cumbernauld Colts	1	0		*3*	*1*
SF(1)	02/05/2017	Spartans	Lothian Thistle HV	1	2			
SF(1)	03/05/2017	Edinburgh University	East Kilbride	0	3			
SF(2)	09/05/2017	Lothian Thistle HV	Spartans		wo			
SF(2)	09/05/2017	East Kilbride	Edinburgh University	4	1		7	1
F	26/05/2017	East Kilbride	Spartans	0	1			

East / Lowland League KO Cup Under 20s 2016/17

1	27/3/17	Preston Athletic	Edinburgh University	0	7	
1	27/3/17	Edusport Academy	BSC Glasgow	1	4	
1	27/3/17	Stirling University	Tynecastle	1	0	
1	04/04/2017	Spartans	Lothian Thistle HV	3	0	
1	10/04/2017	Whitehill Welfare	Edinburgh City	1	3	
2	28/04/2017	Edinburgh City	Stirling University	1	6	
2	28/04/2017	Spartans	BSC Glasgow	wo		
2	28/04/2017	East Kilbride	Cumbernauld Colts	1	1	4-3p
2	28/04/2017	Heriot Watt Universit	Edinburgh University	3	3	3-4p
SF	16/05/2017	Spartans	Stirling University	1	0	
SF	16/05/2017	East Kilbride	Edinburgh University	2	1	
F	31/05/2017	Spartans	East Kilbride	0	1	

NORTH SENIORS

The Highland League became a three-way fight between Buckie Thistle, Cove Rangers and Brora Rangers. With the Champions due to Play Off against East Kilbride for the right to meet the bottom club in the SPFL, the title race took an unexpected twist. Buckie included Callum Murray in their matchday squad for their penultimate match against Formartine United—he was an unused substitute. This was a breach of rules—the player had been on loan to Deveronvale and returned to Buckie after the transfer deadline at the end of March.

Some wild speculation ensued. Had Buckie deliberately infringed the rules to avoid having to play for promotion to the SPFL? Buckie Thistle vigorously denied any such assertion. Given the rule breach it seemed inevitable that points would be deducted from Buckie, opening the way for Cove Rangers to take the title and the Play off position.

A meeting of Highland League clubs was hastily arranged and the matter discussed. The outcome was that Buckie had broken the rules but that they would not be punished. Instead, it was acknowledged that the rules were poorly worded and should be re-written and clarified for next season.

The decision reached can be interpreted in various ways. However, the salient fact was that Buckie won the league title and advanced to meet East Killbride, to whom they lost.

Cove Rangers remained homeless but are now confident that their new home in Aberdeen will be ready early in 2017/18. Of all the Highland League clubs they are the most keen to move on to SPFL status.

Fort William flagged up a problem towards the end of the season and for a spell it looked like they might not continue. Thankfully new committee and helpers were recruited and the Claggan Park side will take their place as usual for the 2017/18 season.

Good news also from Rothes who seem to have put their off-field issues behind them. Some progress has now been made on the field of play and they were no longer the whipping boys they had been in recent seasons.

There remains no pyramid structure in the North. The Highland League is a “closed shop” and seemingly has no interest in articulating with other bodies. There is a clear disparity between the North and South of the country. In the South two clubs, Kelty Hearts and Bonnyton Thistle, have joined the Senior leagues for 2017/18. Any club from the North—Banks o’ Dee being the most likely—would be unable to do so as there is nowhere for them to go. Furthermore, if Scone Thistle or Lochee United decided to go down the Senior Route they would be forced into trying to gain membership of the Highland league, despite the distances involved.

If the SFA are serious about a Pyramid, which is highly debatable, then they should be taking a lead and demanding that the Highland League open up membership to applicant clubs, even if it meant creating a Second Division. That would be the most logical answer to the problem—creating a second tier with clubs from the North Juniors and North Caledonian Leagues.

Press & Journal Highland League 2016/17

	BRO	BUC	CLA	COV	DEV	FUTD	FMEC	FWI	FRA	H	INV	KEI	LOS	NAI	ROT	STR	TUR	WIC
Brora Rangers		Feb 4	Oct 29	Dec 3	Jan 21	Mar 25	Aug 6	Nov 12	Oct 1	Apr 8	Sep 10	Oct 8	Aug 31	Nov 19	Aug 20	Nov 26	Dec 17	Apr 12
		2-1	6-0	1-2	6-2	5-0	3-0	8-0	2-0	2-0	2-2	6-0	7-0	3-3	5-0	4-3	2-1	2-0
Buckie Thistle	Oct 5		Jul 30	Dec 24	Apr 8	Nov 12	Aug 27	Aug 13	Oct 15	Sep 17	Jan 28	Apr 1	Jan 14	Dec 10	Jan 4	Apr 22	Sep 10	Mar 18
	5-0		4-0	1-0	3-0	3-1	3-0	4-2	1-1	7-0	3-1	6-0	5-0	2-1	3-0	9-0	4-0	1-0
Clachnacuddin	Mar 18	Nov 19		Sep 14	Nov 5	Mar 22	Jan 7	Dec 23	Apr 15	Feb 18	Oct 15	Aug 6	Feb 4	Sep 3	Jan 21	Aug 27	Oct 12	Aug 20
	0-5	1-5		2-2	2-1	0-2	2-4	2-2	3-2	1-1	2-0	1-2	2-0	1-0	2-1	0-2	0-0	0-0
Cove Rangers	Aug 13	Aug 31	Mar 29		Dec 10	Sep 10	Feb 18	Jan 28	Aug 27	Aug 24	Nov 26	Jan 2	Apr 22	Oct 5	Oct 29	Sep 17	Apr 1	Oct 15
	2-1*	2-3**	3-2*		2-0*	5-1*	3-2*	7-0****	2-2**	6-0*	3-0***	3-0***	5-0$	2-1*	5-0	4-0**	0-0*	6-0*
Deveronvale	Sep 17	Oct 8	Apr 1	Aug 20		Nov 16	Mar 25	Jul 30	Feb 4	Sep 10	Apr 5	Mar 4		Nov 26	Dec 17	Nov 12	Aug 31	Jan 28
	1-2	2-9	5-1	0-2		2-3	0-2	4-2	1-2	0-2	0-3	3-2	0-0	2-2	5-0	7-2	0-1	0-2
Formartine United	Oct 15	Apr 15	Aug 13	Jan 7	Mar 18		Sep 3	Aug 27	Nov 5	Oct 5	Feb 18	Dec 7	Mar 15	Dec 24	Sep 14	Dec 10	Mar 29	Aug 6
	1-4	0-0	2-1	1-1	1-0		2-2	4-2	4-0	8-0	2-1	5-2	1-0	2-0	6-1	2-1	3-2	0-3
Forres Mechanics	Feb 15	Dec 17	Sep 10	Oct 8	Aug 13	Apr 19		Sep 17	Aug 20	Nov 12	Jul 30	Aug 31	Apr 1	Mar 22	Apr 8	Jan 18	Nov 16	Oct 5
	1-2	3-2	2-2	0-3	2-1	0-0		4-0	0-2	2-1	1-1	4-1	4-2	7-1	1-1	2-0	1-4	3-5
Fort William	Apr 15	Dec 3	Aug 31	Oct 1	Oct 22	Dec 17	Jan 21		Aug 6	Oct 29	Apr 1	Aug 20	Mar 4	Sep 14	Mar 25	Apr 12	Oct 8	Sep 10
	1-5	2-5	0-5	2-6	1-2	1-1	2-6		0-3	2-5	1-4	2-3	1-4	1-2	3-5	4-1	3-2	3-8
Fraserburgh	Jan 28	Apr 12	Nov 12	Dec 17	Oct 5	Apr 1	Dec 10	Nov 26		Apr 22	Sep 17	Oct 29	Sep 10	Aug 13	Aug 31	Jul 30	Dec 30	Feb 18
	2-0	2-5	3-3	2-2	3-0	0-1	2-3	3-2		2-0	1-0	1-3	0-4	3-3	2-1	3-0	3-0	1-1
Huntly	Sep 3	Mar 25	Oct 8	Feb 15	Jan 7	Feb 22	Apr 15	Mar 18	Sep 14		Dec 24	Oct 1	Aug 20	Nov 5	Aug 6	Oct 15	Dec 3	Dec 17
	1-6	1-0	0-2	0-8	5-2	3-3	0-3	5-1	2-4		2-1	2-1	0-0	4-6	2-1	2-2	2-4	1-5
Inverurie Locos	Jan 7	Oct 1	Mar 4	Aug 6	Sep 14	Oct 8	Mar 15		Mar 25	Aug 31		Feb 4	Dec 17	Apr 15	Dec 3	Oct 29	Aug 20	Jan 3
	2-2	1-1	4-1	2-3	2-0	1-2	4-2	3-0	1-5	2-1		3-3	2-2	1-0	6-0	3-0	0-2	1-3
Keith	Feb 18	Nov 16	Nov 26	Sep 3	Oct 15	Jul 30	Dec 23	Dec 10	Mar 18	Mar 11	Oct 22		Sep 17	Aug 27	Jan 7	Aug 13	Nov 5	Apr 15
	1-4	3-2	6-1	0-3	4-0	1-4	3-2	7-2	2-6	4-1	1-6		4-1	0-1	2-1	5-2	1-0	2-1
Lossiemouth	Dec 23	Sep 14	Oct 5	Apr 15	Sep 3	Oct 12	Nov 5	Oct 15	Jan 7	Dec 10	Aug 27	Jan 21		Mar 18	Nov 19	Feb 18	Aug 6	Feb 15
	4-1	2-5	2-3	1-6	0-2	1-3	1-2	5-0	1-2	2-2	1-0	4-1		0-0	1-2	4-1	2-0	1-2
Nairn County	Jul 30	Aug 20	Dec 30	Feb 4	Aug 6	Aug 31	Oct 12	Mar 11	Dec 3	Apr 1	Nov 12	Dec 17	Oct 29		Oct 8	Sep 10	Mar 4	Sep 17
	0-4	3-8	1-2	2-5	1-2	0-2	4-4	5-0	0-2	2-1	2-3	1-1	2-1		3-0	0-2	1-2	1-2
Rothes	Dec 10	Sep 3	Sep 17	Mar 18	Aug 27	Apr 12	Oct 15	Oct 5	Mar 11	Jan 28	Aug 13	Sep 10	Jul 30	Apr 22		Mar 15	Nov 12	Nov 5
	0-6	1-6	2-2	0-1	2-1	1-5	0-5	2-1	0-5	2-2	2-2	4-2	0-2	0-2		4-2	1-4	0-9
Strathspey Thistle	Nov 5	Aug 6	Dec 17	Jan 21	Apr 15	Aug 20	Sep 14	Sep 3	Feb 25	Mar 4	Mar 18	Dec 3	Oct 8	Jan 7	Oct 1		Mar 25	Aug 31
	0-5	2-9	1-4	1-1	0-3	1-6	1-3	0-1	0-7	0-2	1-7	0-4	1-2	2-2	0-1		0-2	0-3
Turriff United	Aug 27	Jan 7	Jan 28	Apr 12	Dec 24	Sep 17	Mar 18	Feb 18	Oct 22	Aug 13	Dec 10	Sep 14	Nov 30	Oct 15	Apr 15	Oct 5		Apr 8
	0-1	2-2	4-2	1-1	2-1	1-2	3-4	4-0	1-0	2-0	0-1	3-2	2-0	2-0	0-0	2-0		1-0
Wick Academy	Sep 14	Mar 11	Dec 10	Mar 25	Oct 1	Apr 22	Feb 4	Jan 7	Oct 8	Aug 27	Sep 3	Nov 12	Aug 13	Jan 21	Apr 1	Mar 29	Jul 30	
	1-2	1-2	3-1	2-3	2-2	2-2	2-2	2-0	0-1	4-4	1-1	3-1	1-2	1-5	1-1	3-0	2-0	

* at Inverurie
** at Huntly
*** at Banks o' Dee
**** at Lossiemouth
$ at Keith

			Home					Away					Total						
Pos		Pl	GF	GA	W	D	L	GF	GA	W	D	L	GF	GA	W	D	L	GD	Points
1	Buckie Thistle FC	34	65	6	16	1	0	65	30	10	3	4	130	36	26	4	4	94	82
2	Cove Rangers FC	34	60	12	14	2	1	49	18	11	5	1	109	30	25	7	2	79	82
3	Brora Rangers FC	34	66	14	14	2	1	50	22	12	1	4	116	36	26	3	5	80	81
4	Formartine United FC	34	44	20	12	3	2	38	27	10	4	3	82	47	22	7	5	35	73
5	Fraserburgh FC	34	33	28	8	4	5	44	20	11	2	4	77	48	19	6	9	29	63
6	Forres Mechanics FC	34	37	28	8	4	5	47	35	9	3	5	84	63	17	7	10	21	58
7	Turriff United FC	34	32	17	11	2	4	24	25	7	2	8	56	42	18	4	12	14	58
8	Wick Academy FC	34	31	29	5	6	6	44	23	10	2	5	75	52	15	8	11	23	53
9	Inverurie Loco Works FC	34	38	28	8	4	5	33	25	6	4	7	71	53	14	8	12	18	50
10	Keith FC	34	46	37	11	0	6	28	51	4	2	11	74	88	15	2	17	-14	47
11	Clachnacuddin FC	34	21	29	6	5	6	32	48	5	3	9	53	77	11	8	15	-24	41
12	Lossiemouth FC	34	32	32	6	2	9	20	38	5	3	9	52	70	11	5	18	-18	38
13	Nairn County FC	34	28	41	4	2	11	29	33	5	5	7	57	74	9	7	18	-17	34
14	Huntly FC	34	32	49	6	3	8	22	48	3	4	10	54	97	9	7	18	-43	34
15	Deveronvale FC	34	32	37	5	2	10	19	38	4	1	12	51	75	9	3	22	-24	30
16	Rothes FC	34	21	57	4	3	10	16	49	3	2	12	37	106	7	5	22	-69	26
17	Fort William FC	34	29	67	2	1	14	15	69	1	1	15	44	136	3	2	29	-92	11
18	Strathspey Thistle FC	34	10	62	0	2	15	18	58	2	1	14	28	120	2	3	29	-92	9

and League - Recent Positions

	1980-1	1981-2	1982-3	1983-4	1984-5	1985-6	1986-7	1987-8	1988-9	1989-90	1990-1	1991-2	1992-3	1993-4	1994-5	1995-6	1996-7	1997-8	1998-9
Rangers	10	5	3	7	3	16	15	12	14	14	9	14	13	10	5	8	14	11	9
ie Thistle	5	14	13	5	5	7	5	2	9	10	11	7	9	8	10	12	13	10	12
lonian	9	1	1	1	2	4	2	1	10	2	2	2	4	2					
nacuddin	4	12	8	11	12	13	16	14	16	18	16	12	7	12	13	11	5	8	6
Rangers							8	10	2	6	3	4	2	4	2	2	7	4	7
onvale	13	11	14	14	14	17	17	11	13	16	15	13	11	14	9	9	8	9	10
City	3	4	2	4	7	2	3	7	5	1	7	8	1	6	8	7	9	5	4
artine United																			
s Mechanics	16	13	11	9	4	1	6	6	6	5	4	11	17	13	11	13	12	7	8
William						12	11	17	18	13	12	16	16	16	12	14	16	15	16
erburgh	2	7	6	8	13	14	13	13	11	7	13	15	10	9	7	5	6	2	5
y	12	9	12	10	9	6	9	9	3	8	6	3	6	1	1	1	1	1	2
ess Thistle	8	8	7	6	11	8	1	4	4	4	5	10	8	15					
rie Locos																			
	1	3	4	2	1	5	4	5	7	12	14	5	12	7	4	6	2	6	3
emouth	15	16	16	16	16	15	10	16	12	9	10	6	3	5	3	3	4	12	13
County	14	15	10	12	10	9	12	18	15	15	17	18	18	17	16	16	15	16	15
head	6	2	5	3	8	3	7	3	1	3	8	9	14	11	6	4	3	3	1
County	11	6	9	13	6	10	18	8	8	11	1	1	5	3					
es	7	10	15	15	15	11	14	15	17	17	18	17	15	18	15	15	11	13	11
nspey Thistle																			
United																			
Academy															14	10	10	14	14

	1999-00	2000-1	2001-2	2002-3	2003-4	2004-5	2005-6	2006-7	2007-8	2008-9	2009-10	2010-11	2011-12	2012-13	2013-14	2014-15	2015-16	2016-17
Rangers	12	13	8	14	12	15	14	13	14	14	15	11	16	8	1	1	3	3
ie Thistle	3	3	3	4	2	6	3	3	4	6	1	1	5	12	10	10	7	1
lonian																		
nacuddin	7	4	4	7	1	7	9	9	10	11	12	15	10	5	11	11	14	11
Rangers	8	1	6	3	10	5	8	6	1	1	2	2	2	1	7	3	1	2
onvale	11	6	2	1	4	4	1	4	3	2	3	4	7	7	6	12	13	15
City	9																	
artine United											6	9	11	2	4	6	2	4
s Mechanics	6	7	10	11	8	9	4	12	8	9	5	6	1	9	9	9	11	6
William	16	14	13	15	15	13	15	15	15	15	17	18	18	18	18	13	17	17
erburgh	2	8	1	6	3	3	7	8	5	7	4	13	6	6	5	5	9	5
y	5	2	9	8	6	1	6	5	7	8	7	10	13	13	13	16	15	14
ess Thistle																		
rie Locos			7	9	7	2	2	2	6	3	10	7	4	10	2	7	6	9
	1	5	5	2	5	8	5	1	2	4	8	3	9	14	14	14	10	10
emouth	10	12	11	10	13	11	13	14	13	12	14	12	12	17	15	15	12	12
County	15	9	12	5	9	10	10	7	9	10	11	5	3	4	3	8	8	13
head	4																	
County																		
es	13	11	15	12	14	14	11	10	12	13	16	16	15	16	17	18	18	16
nspey Thistle											18	17	17	15	16	17	16	18
United											13	8	14	11	12	2	4	7
Academy	14	10	14	13	11	12	12	11	11	5	9	14	8	3	8	4	5	8

ALL TIME HIGHLAND LEAGUE CHAMPIONS

1893/4	Inverness Thistle	1935/6	Inverness Thistle	1977/8	Caledonian
1894/5	Clachnacuddin	1936/7	Buckie Thistle	1978/9	Keith
1895/6	Caledonian	1937/8	Fraserburgh	1979/80	Keith
1896/7	Clachnacuddin	1938/9	Clachnacuddin	1980/1	Keith
1897/8	Clachnacuddin	1939/40	No competition	1981/2	Caledonian
1898/9	Caledonian	1950/1	No competition	1982/3	Caledonian
1899/00	Caledonian	1941/2	No competition	1983/4	Caledonian
1900/1	Clachnacuddin	1942/3	No competition	1984/5	Keith
1901/2	Caledonian	1943/4	No competition	1985/6	Forres Mechanics
1902/3	Clachnacuddin	1944/5	No competition	1986/7	Inverness Thistle
1903/4	Clachnacuddin	1945/6	No competition	1987/8	Caledonian
1904/5	Clachnacuddin	1946/7	Peterhead	1988/9	Peterhead
1905/6	Clachnacuddin	1947/8	Clachnacuddin	1989/90	Elgin City
1906/7	Inverness Thistle	1958/9	Peterhead	1990/1	Ross County
1907/8	Clachnacuddin	1949/50	Peterhead	1991/2	Ross County
1908/9	Inverness Citadel	1950/1	Caledonian	1992/3	Trophy witheld
1909/10	Inverness Thistle	1951/2	Caledonian	1993/4	Huntly
1910/11	Caledonian	1952/3	Elgin City	1994/5	Huntly
1911/12	Clachnacuddin	1953/4	Buckie Thistle	1995/6	Huntly
1912/13	Aberdeen "A"	1954/5	Not completed	1996/7	Huntly
1913/14	Caledonian	1955/6	Elgin City	1997/8	Huntly
1914/15	Not completed	1956/7	Buckie Thistle	1998/9	Peterhead
1915/16	No competition	1957/8	Buckie Thistle	1999/00	Keith
1916/17	No competition	1958/9	Rothes	2000/1	Cove Rangers
1917/18	No competition	1959/60	Elgin City	2001/2	Fraserburgh
1918/19	No competition	1960/1	Elgin City	2002/3	Deveronvale
1919/20	Buckie Thistle	1961/2	Keith	2003/4	Clachnacuddin
1920/1	Clachnacuddin	1962/3	Elgin City	2004/5	Huntly
1921/2	Clachnacuddin	1963/4	Caledonian	2005/6	Deveronvale
1922/3	Clachnacuddin	1964/5	Elgin City	2006/7	Keith
1923/4	Clachnacuddin	1965/6	Elgin City	2007/8	Cove Rangers
1924/5	Aberdeen "A"	1966/7	Ross County	2008/9	Cove Rangers
1925/6	Caledonian	1967/8	Elgin City	2009/10	Buckie Thistle
1926/7	Buckie Thistle	1968/9	Elgin City	2010/1	Buckie Thistle
1927/8	Buckie Thistle	1969/70	Elgin City	2011/2	Forres Mechanics
1928/9	Inverness Thistle	1970/1	Caledonian	2012/3	Cove Rangers
1929/30	Huntly	1971/2	Inverness Thistle	2013/4	Brora Rangers
1930/1	Caledonian	1972/3	Inverness Thistle	2014/5	Brora Rangers
1931/2	Elgin City	1973/4	Elgin City	2015/6	Cove Rangers
1932/3	Fraserburgh	1974/5	Clachnacuddin	2016/7	Buckie Thistle
1933/4	Buckie Thistle	1975/6	Nairn County		
1934/5	Elgin City	1976/7	Caledonian		

Evening Express Aberdeenshire Cup 2016/17

Rd	Date	Home	Away	F	A		Notes
1	27/07/2016	Inverurie Locos	Formartine United	1	2		
1	27/07/2016	Turriff United	Banks o' Dee	5	1		
2	10/08/2016	Cove Rangers	Deveronvale	2	0		at Deveronva
2	10/08/2016	Formartine United	Fraserburgh	3	3	4-5p	
2	10/08/2016	Huntly	Turriff United	0	4		
2	10/08/2016	Keith	Buckie Thistle	1	5		
SF	24/08/2016	Buckie Thistle	Fraserburgh	2	1		
SF	07/09/2016	Turriff United	Cove Rangers	2	3		
F	05/11/2016	Buckie Thistle	Cove Rangers	2	2	5-4p	at Turriff

CUP FINAL DETAILS

Cove led 1-0 at half time through a Blair Yule goal. Mitch Megginson made it 2-0 for Cove in the 48th minute. Drew Copeland pulled a goal back in the 70th minute but a couple of minutes later Buckie were reduced to ten men when Dorrat was sent off. Despite this setback Buckie equalised in stoppage time through Chris Angus. Buckie's Kevin Fraser was sent off early in extra time but the nine-men dug deep to hold out for penalty kicks.

Buckie: Salmon, Cheyne (Carrol 90), Mackinnon (Macrae119), Munro, Dorrat, Low (Copeland 66), K Fraser, McLean, McLeod, Angus, Urquhart. Not used: Scott, J Fraser, Strong.

Cove: McKenzie, Redford, Milne, Yule, Watson, Kelly, Scully (Stott 81), Campbell, Megginson (Buchan 89), Smith (Park 53), Duff. Not used: McCulloch, McBain, Burnett, McCafferty.

Recent Aberdeenshire Cup Finals

Season	Winners	Runners Up	Score	Venue
1989/90	Aberdeen	Peterhead	3-0	Recreation Park, Peterhead
1990/1	Aberdeen	Huntly	1-0	Pittodrie, Aberdeen
1991/2	Huntly	Aberdeen	2-1	Christie Park, Huntly
1992/3	Aberdeen	Cove Rangers	1-0	Allan Park, Cove
1993/4	Huntly	Peterhead	1-0	Kynoch Park, Keith
1994/5	Huntly	Cove Rangers	3-0	Kynoch Park, Keith
1995/6	Huntly	Deveronvale	2-1	Kynoch Park, Keith
1996/7	Fraserburgh	Peterhead	3-2	Recreation Park, Peterhead
1997/8	Aberdeen	Deveronvale	5-1	Kynoch Park, Keith
1998/9	Peterhead	Aberdeen	3-1	Balmoor Stadium, Peterhead
1999/00	Huntly	Deveronvale	2-0	Christie Park, Huntly
2000/1	Deveronvale	Fraserburgh	2-1	Christie Park, Huntly
2001/2	Cove Rangers	Deveronvale	1-1. 5-4 pens	Christie Park, Huntly
2002/3	Aberdeen	Deveronvale	3-0	Harlaw Park, Inverurie
2003/4	Aberdeen	Inverurie Locos	4-0	Harlaw Park, Inverurie
2004/5	Aberdeen	Fraserburgh	4-1 aet	Bellslea Park, Fraserburgh
2005/6	Buckie Thistle	Deveronvale	2-2, 3-2 pens	Christie Park, Huntly
2006/7	Deveronvale	Inverurie Locos	1-0	Kynoch Park, Keith
2007/8	Buckie Thistle	Keith	1-0	Christie Park, Huntly
2008/9	Keith	Huntly	5-2	Harlaw Park, Inverurie
2009/10	Buckie Thistle	Cove Rangers	2-0	The Haughs, Turriff
2010/1	Cove Rangers	Buckie Thistle	3-0	Harlaw Park, Inverurie
2011/2	Deveronvale	Keith	5-4	Christie Park, Huntly
2012/3	Fraserburgh	Formartine United	2-2 aet, 3-1 pens	Victoria Park, Buckie
2013/4	Formartine United	Inverurie Locos	3-2	Bellslea Park, Fraserburgh
2014/5	Fraserburgh	Buckie Thistle	3-2	Kynoch Park, Keith
2015/6	Fraserburgh	Inverurie Locos	2-0	Christie Park, Huntly
2016/7	Buckie Thistle	Cove Rangers	2-2 aet, 5-4 pens	The Haughs, Turriff

ALL TIME WINNER

35 Aberdeen (1903)
20 Peterhead
13 Buckie Thistle
10 Fraserburgh
8 Deveronvale
7 Keith, Huntly
6 Victoria United
5 Orion, Aberdeen (1881)
2 Cove Rangers
1 Aberdeen Univ, Formartine United

DEWAR SHIELD

The Dewar Shield w played for regularly until the 1950s, and irregularly until the early 1980s. It was envisaged as the Championship of the Northern Counties a was contested by th winners of the Aberdeenshire, Forfarshire, Perthshi and Stirlingshire Cup The first winners we King's Park in 1898/ The last winners we St Johnstone in 1982/3.

Morrison Motors Aberdeenshire Shield 2016/17

Rd	Date	Home	Away	F	A		Notes
1	12/10/2016	Banks o' Dee	Buckie Thistle	4	2		
1	12/10/2016	Keith	Fraserburgh	0	1		
1	26/10/2016	Cove Rangers	Formartine United	2	2	2-4p	at Formartine
2	26/10/2016	Deveronvale	Inverurie Locos	0	4		
2	26/10/2016	Fraserburgh	Huntly	0	2		
2	26/10/2016	Turriff United	Aberdeen University	3	0		
2	02/11/2016	Formartine United	Banks o' Dee	2	3		
SF	09/11/2016	Inverurie Locos	Huntly	2	1		
SF	09/11/2016	Turriff United	Banks o' Dee	1	2	AET	
F	30/11/2016	Inverurie Locos	Banks o' Dee	5	2		at Huntly

Recent Aberdeenshire Shield Finals

Season	Winners	Runners Up	Score	Venue
1990/1	Cove Rangers	Fraserburgh	1-0	Peterhead
1991/2	Fraserburgh	Deveronvale	2-2, 4-3 pens	Huntly
1992/3	Buckie Thistle	Huntly	3-2	Keith
1993/4	Fraserburgh	Keith	4-2	Huntly
1994/5	Deveronvale	Cove Rangers	1-0	Keith
1995/6	Fraserburgh	Peterhead	2-1	Huntly
1996/7	Fraserburgh	Peterhead	6-3 aet	Cove
1997/8	Keith	Peterhead	3-2	Banff
1998/9	Peterhead	Keith	3-1	Keith
1999/00	Fraserburgh	Keith	2-1	Keith
2000/1	Cove Rangers	Buckie Thistle	2-1	Peterhead
2001/2	Keith	Fraserburgh	3-2	Inverurie
2002/3	Deveronvale	Inverurie Locos	3-2	Keith
2003/4	Inverurie Locos	Deveronvale	5-1	Banff
2004/5	Keith	Inverurie Locos	3-1 aet	Inverurie
2005/6	Keith	Inverurie Locos	2-1	Banff
2006/7	Keith	Fraserburgh	3-0	Inverurie
2007/8	Buckie Thistle	Inverurie Locos	3-0	Huntly
2008/9	Cove Rangers	Banks o' Dee	2-0	Pittodrie
2009/10	Peterhead	Inverurie Locos	3-0	Peterhead
2010/11	Turriff United	Aberdeen	2-0	Peterhead
2011/12	Fraserburgh	Banks o' Dee	5-0	Peterhead
2012/13	Turriff United	Cove Rangers	6-1	Inverurie
2013/14	Inverurie Locos	Turriff United	5-0	Huntly
2014/15	Turriff United	Fraserburgh	4-3	Banff
2015/16	Fraserburgh	Cove Rangers	1-0	Inverurie
2016/17	Inverurie Locos	Banks o' Dee	5-2	Huntly

Aberdeenshire Shield

The Shield is open to all Aberdeen and District FA clubs that have senior status. This includes the Highland League clubs from Aberdeenshire and Banffshire, plus Banks o' Dee and Aberdeen University - although the Senior status of the latter is debatable. Aberdeen FC are excluded from the modern version of the competition.

Originally known as the Fleming Charity Shield, the ciompetition was held from 1899 until 1929. It was resurrected in 1990 as the Aberdeenshire Shield.

The following clubs have won the Shield:

Aberdeen	12
Fraserburgh	8
Keith	5
Cove Rangers	3
Inverurie Locos	3
Turriff United	3
Bucxkie Thistle	2
Deveromnvale	2
Peterhead	2
Victoria United	2
Aberdeen "A"	2
Dundee United	1

Final Details

Inverurie Locos 5 Banks o' Dee 1 (H.T. 3-1)
Scorers
Locos: Anderson 2, Hunter 2, Bavidge
Banks: Philpson, Hall
Locos: Mathieson Rennie McLean Souter Anderson Broadhurst Leyden (Forsyth) Laing Hunter (Bavidge) McCabe Donaldson (Charlesworth) Unused subs Jeffrey Selfridge Crisp Booth
Dee: Shearer White Duguid Heads Winton (Hamilton) Henderson (McLeod) McCall Lennox Philipson Hall Alexander (Sopel) Unused subs Buchanan Stephen
Referee – Graham Beaton
Att 200

AJG Parcels North of Scotland Cup 2016/17

1	01/04/2017	Tain St Duthus	Brora Rangers	0	9		
1	19/04/2017	Rothes	Wick Academy	2	0		
1	08/04/2017	Fort William	Lossiemouth	3	3	4-1p	
1	22/04/2017	Forres Mechanics	Clachnacuddin	2	1		
1	08/04/2017	Strathspey Thistle	Nairn County	0	4		
2	29/04/2017	Fort William	Invergordon	3	0		
2	29/04/2017	Nairn County	Brora Rangers	1	3		
2	29/04/2017	Halkirk	Forres Mechanics	0	3		
2	29/04/2017	Golspie Sutherland	Rothes	0	3		
SF	06/05/2017	Brora Rangers	Forres Mechanics	4	1		
SF	06/05/2017	Rothes	Fort William	1	2		
F	20/05/2017	Brora Rangers	Fort William	4	1		at Rothes

Recent North of Scotland Cup Finals

Season	Winners	Runners Up	Score	Venue
1988/9	Elgin City	Brora Rangers	3-1	Kingsmills
1989/90	Elgin City	Inverness Thistle	0-0, 4-0 rep	Forres
1990/1	Brora Rangers	Forres Mechanics	2-1	Dingwall
1991/2	Ross County	Lossiemouth	0-0, 1-0 rep	Kingsmills
1992/3	Clachnacuddin	Inverness Thistle	4-2 aet	Caley
1993/4	Caledonian	Forres Mechanics	1-0	Kingsmills
1994/5	Lossiemouth	Fort William	4-0	Forres
1995/6	Lossiemouth	Clachnacuddin	1-0	Forres
1996/7	Lossiemouth	Forres Mechanics	4-1	Elgin
1997/8	Elgin City	Inverness CT	3-1	ICT
1998/9	Elgin City	Rothes	2-0	Forres
1999/00	Inverness CT	Lossiemouth	3-0	Forres
2000/1	Lossiemouth	Forres Mechanics	3-1	Forres
2001/2	Clachnacuddin	Inverness CT	2-0	ICT
2002/3	Lossiemouth	Rothes	3-1	Forres
2003/4	Elgin City	Inverness CT	1-0	Forres
2004/5	Forres Mechanics	Clachnacuddin	2-0	Dingwall
2005/6	Nairn County	Forres Mechanics	3-1	Clachnacuddin
2006/7	Ross County	Nairn County	3-0	Clachnacuddin
2007/8	Inverness CT	Elgin City	3-2	Forres
2008/9	Nairn County	Inverness CT	2-0	Clachnacuddin
2009/10	Inverness CT	Nairn County	3-2	Forres
2010/1	Forres Mechanics	Wick Academy	3-2	Brora
2011/2	Inverness CT	Forres Mechanics	4-3	Forres
2012/3	Nairn County	Wick Academy	2-1	Clachnacuddin
2013/4	Brora Rangers	Nairn County	3-0	Clachnacuddin
2014/5	Brora Rangers	Elgin City	3-1	Clachnacuddin
2015/6	Wick Academy	Nairn County	6-2	Brora
2016/7	Brora Rangers	Fort William	4-1	Rothes

Final Details

Brora Rangers 4 Fort William 1

Scorers - **Brora**: Morrison (9), Ross (75 and 86), Williamson (90) **Fort**: Davidson (60)

Brora: Joe Malin, James Ross, Steven Mackay, Colin Williamson, Jamie Duff, Gavin Morrison, Scott Graham, Kyle Macleod (Steven Ross), Zander Sutherland, Martin Maclean, Andrew Greig (Craig Campbell)

Breedon Aggregates Highland League Cup 2016/17

1	28/01/2017	Keith	Forres Mechanics	2	5		
1	04/02/2017	Strathspey Thistle	Formarrtine United	2	6		
2	11/02/2017	Brora Rangers	Inverurie Locos	8	0		
2	11/02/2017	Buckie Thistle	Forres Mechanics	4	4	AET	2-4p
2	15/02/2017	Clachnacuddin	Fort William	6	2		
2	11/02/2017	Cove Rangers	Lossiemouth	4	2		at Inverurie
2	22/02/2017	Deveronvale	Nairn County	1	2	AET	
2	11/02/2017	Huntly	Fraserburgh	2	1		
2	15/02/2017	Rothes	Formartine United	1	2		
2	11/02/2017	Wick Academy	Turriff United	0	1		
3	25/02/2017	Formartine United	Clachnacuddin	2	1		
3	25/02/2017	Huntly	Brora Rangers	2	3		
3	25/02/2017	Nairn County	Turriff United	1	3		
3	07/03/2017	Forres Mechanics	Cove Rangers	9	1		
SF	11/03/2017	Brora Rangers	Cove Rangers	0	1	AET	
SF	11/03/2017	Turriff United	Formartine United	0	1	AET	
F	08/04/2017	Formartine United	Cove Rangers	1	2		at Fraserburgh

FINAL DETAILS

Cove Rangers 2 Formartine United 1, Crowd 350 approx

1-0 76 mins Paul McManus
1-1 80 mins Gary Wood
2-1 90 mins Jason Brown

Cove: Stuart McKenzie, Jason Brown, Alan Redford, Blair Yule, Eric Watson, Darryn Kelly, Daniel Park, Grant Campbell, Paul McManus, Sam Burnett, Connor Scully. Subs Ryan Stott, Nicholas GFray, Matthew McDonald, Murray McCulloch, Jonny Smith, Dean Lawrie, Cameron Jarvie
Formartine: Andrew Reid, Calum Dingwall, Stuart Smith, Derek Young, Gary Wood, Graeme Rodger, Conor Gethins, Jamie Masson, Stuart Anderson, Scott Barbour, Russell McBride. Subs Scott Ferries, Jonathan Crawford, Neil Gauld, Liam Burnett, Max Berton, Paul Lawson, Ewen MacDonald

HIGHLAND LEAGUE CUP

The competition is often known as the Morganti Cup. It was first contested in 1946/7.

Past winners are:

10 times - Keith; 8 times - Buckie Thistle; 7 times - Forres Mechanics; 5 times - Peterhead, Caledonian, Elgin City, Clachnacuddin, Cove Rangers and Huntly; 4 times - Ross County; 3 times - Inverness Thistle; 2 times - Nairn County, Lossiemouth, Fraserburgh and Inverurie Locos; 1 time - Brora Rangers.

Deveronvale, Rothes, Wick Academy, Formartine United, Turriff United and Strathspey Thistle, of the current HFL members, have never won the Cup.

Recent Highland League Cup Finals				
Season	**Winners**	**Runners Up**	**Score**	**Venue**
1988/9	Keith	Caledonian	1-1, Replay3-2	Boroughbriggs, Elgin
1989/90	Peterhead	Forres Mechanics	2-1	Boroughbriggs, Elgin
1990/1	Elgin City	Cove Rangers	2-1	Kynoch Park, Keith
1991/2	Ross County	Fraserburgh	3-1	Boroughbriggs, Elgin
1992/3	Huntly	Cove Rangers	1-1, 5-4 pens	Boroughbriggs, Elgin
1993/4	Huntly	Fraserburgh	4-1	Boroughbriggs, Elgin
1994/5	Cove Rangers	Lossiemouth	2-2, 5-3 pens	Christie Park, Huntly
1995/6	Huntly	Cove Rangers	2-1 aet	Kynoch Park, Keith
1996/7	Lossiemouth	Fraserburgh	2-1	Christie Park, Huntly
1997/8	Elgin City	Cove Rangers	1-0	Christie Park, Huntly
1998/9	Forres Mechanics	Keith	1-0	Boroughbriggs, Elgin
1999/00	Cove Rangers	Elgin City	4-3	Kynoch Park, Keith
2000/1	Forres Mechanics	Deveronvale	2-1	Christie Park, Huntly
2001/2	Forres Mechanics	Deveronvale	1-1, 4-3 pens	Kynoch Park, Keith
2002/3	Keith	Deveronvale	3-2	Harlaw Park, Inverurie
2003/4	Clachnacuddin	Forres Mechanics	3-0	Kynoch Park, Keith
2004/5	Cove Rangers	Deveronvale	2-0	Kynoch Park, Keith
2005/6	Fraserburgh	Cove Rangers	4-1	Kynoch Park, Keith
2006/7	Keith	Buckie Thistle	5-0	Princess Royal Park, Banff
2007/8	Inverurie LW	Cove Rangers	3-1	Christie Park, Huntly
2008/9	Inverurie LW	Fraserburgh	2-1 aet	Kynoch Park, Keith
2009/10	Forres Mechanics	Rothes	2-0	Victoria Park, Buckie
2010/1	Nairn County	Fraserburgh	4-0	Princess Royal Park, Banff
2011/2	Buckie Thistle	Cove Rangers	2-0	Princess Royal Park, Banff
2012/3	Keith	Inverurie LW	2-1	Princess Royal Park, Banff
2013/4	Clachnacuddin	Buckie Thistle	3-3, 4-3 pens	Kynoch Park, Keith
2014/5	Cove Rangers	Wick Academy	4-0	Grant Street Park, Invernes
2015/6	Brora Rangers	Nairn County	,0-0, 5-4p	Grant Street Park, Invernes
2016/7	Cove Rangers	Formartine United	2-1	Bellslea Park, Fraserburgh

CUP DRAWS 2016/16

ABERDEENSHIRE CUP
First

Semi Final (16th September 2015):
East and West Section Winner of Tie A v Winner Tie B

Final (10th October 2015):
West Section Winner v East Section Winner.

Highland League Club Playing Squads 2016/17

NB These are not comprehensive lists of players used - there will be some omissions. However, all players listed were associated with the club concerned during 2016/17.

Brora Rangers
Manager: Grant Munro (Until Dec 2016) Ross Tokeley (from Dec)
Ally McDonald (2012 Huntly, Ex ICT, Elgin C)
Andrew Greig
Blair McLennan (2017 ICT OL)
Cameron Lisle (2016 Clach)
Colin Williamson (2014 Clach, ex ICT)
Craig Campbell (2013 Ex Alloa, Nairn Co, Elgin C, Forres M, Peterhead, Ross Co)
Dale Gillespie (2012 Nairn Co, ex ICT, Elgin C)
Daniel Cormack (2016 Clach)
Gavin Morrison (2013 ICT, Ex Elgin C, Grindavik)
Grant Munro (ex ICT, resigned as player manager Dec 2016)
James Ross (2016 Ross Co)
Jamie Duff (2016 Elgin C, ex ICT)
Joe Malin (2013 Elgin C, ex Celtic, Ross County)
John Pickles (2015 Rendall, Ex Ross Co)
Kyle McLeod (2017 Ross Co, ex Elgin C)
Martin McLean
Paul Brindle (2015 Clach, ex Muir of Ord)
Ross Munro (OL from Ross County, Dec-May)
Ross Tokeley (2013 Ross Co, ex ICT, Huntly)
Scott Graham (2017 Forres Mechanics, Ex Brora R, Nairn Co, Shepparton South)
Scott Houston (2013 Ex Nairn Co)
Scott Lisle (2016 Clach)
Steven Mackay (2012 Nairn Co, Ex Ross Co, Elgin C, Forres M, Peterhead)
Steven Ross (2016 Ex Elgin C, Ross Co, Brora R, Forrmes M, Dumbarton)
Will Counsell
Zander Sutherland (2013 Buckie Th, Ex ICT, Elgin C)
Calum McDonald (2016 Clach, Ex Ross Co, Elgin C, Stirling Uni)

Buckie Thistle
Manager: Graeme Stewart
Andy Low
Callum Murray (2016 Buckie Rovers, ex Elgin City)
Cieran MacLan (2016 Elgin City)
Chris Angus
Craig Dorrat (2016 Huntly, ex Islavale, Turriff United)
Drew Copeland
Greg Sim (2015 Turriff United, ex Banchory St Ternan, Cove R, Rothes)
Hamish Munro (2016 Formartine Utd, ex Fochabers, Forres M, Peterhead)
Iain MacRae
James Fraser
Jay Cheyne (2014 ICT, ex Buckie Th)
John MacLeod (2016 Brora R, ex Fort William)
Kai Ross
Kevin Fraser (2015 North Queensland Fury, ex ICT, Clach)
Kyle Gauld
Lewis McKinnon
Paul Napier
Robert Scott
Ross Salmon (2016 Montrose, Peterhead, Sunnybank, Forfar Ath)
Sam Urquhart (2016 Nairn Co, ex Clach, Elgin C)
Shaun Carroll (2012 Banchory St Ternan, ex ICT, Sunnybank)
Shaun Wood (2012 Buckie Rovers)
Stuart Taylor

Clachnacuddin
Manager:
Aiden MacDonald
Blair Lawrie
Colin McLean
Daniel McLennan
David McGury
Duncan Jones
Ian Penwright
James Beeston
Liam Shewan
Mark Kennedy
Martin Callum
Matthew Grant
Michael Finnie
Paul Smith
Rorie McLeod
Scott McLean
Stuart Leslie

Cove Rangers
Manager: John Sheran Assistant: Roy McBain
Stuart McKenzie (2015 Montrose, Ex Cove R, ICT Youths),
John McCaffery (2015 Montrose, Carnoustie P, E Fife, Peterhead, Dundee),
Grant Campbell (2015 Wick Acad),
Darryn Kelly (2014 Culter, ex Montrose, Elgin C, Banchory ST),
Dean Lawrie (ex Cove BC),
Harry Milne (Ex Culter),
Alan Redford (2010 Huntly),
Stirling Smith (2011 Ex Aberdeen, Peterhead, Dumbarton, Alloa),
Stuart Walker (2013 Keith, Ex Glentanar, Colony Park),
Eric Watson (2007 Tayport, Ex Montrose),
Blair Yule (2010 Montrose, Ex Dyce),
Sam Burnett (2014 Arbroath),
Stuart Duff (2014 FK Kairat Almaty, Ex Dundee Utd, Aberdeen, ICT),
Roy McBain (2013 Peterhead, ex ICT, Ross County)),
Murray McCulloch (2016 Huntly, Ex Aberdeen, Nantwich Town, Inverurie Locos, Cove R, Keith), Daniel Park (2014 Formartine Utd, ex Cove R, ICT Youths),
Ryan Stott (2016 ex Culter),
Kevin Buchan (2016 Broughty Athletic, ex Brechin City, Dundee, ICT, Peterhead, Arbroath),
Mitchell Megginson (2016 Alloa, Ex Aberdeen, Dumbarton, Raith Rovers),
Connor Scully (2012 Dee BC, Dyce OL, Banchory OL),
Jonny Smith (2013 Keith, ex Wigan Athletic U18, Aberdeen, Halifax Town, Keith, Peterhead).

Deveronvale
Manager: Steve Dolan Assistant: Mark Chisholm Coach:
Craig Stewart
Grant Pennet
James Blanchard
Scott Fraser
Steven Fraser
Ross Aitken
Lukas Krobot
Zander Jack
Kevin Adams
Lewis Dunbar
Craig Cowie
Graeme Watt
Chris Blackhall
Liam Forbes
Kevin Souter
Dan SAmith
Grant Noble
Steven Davidson
Dane Ballard
Nathan Ross
Paul Sutherland
Stuart Patterson
James McLaren
Matthew Mackie
Callum Murray

Formartine United
Manager: Kris Hunter (son of ex Fraserburgh and Buckie player Rex Hunter) / Mike Cormack
Andy Reid
Ewen MacDonald
Calum Dingwall
Craig McKeown
Stuart Smith
Johnny Crawford
Jamie Michie
Scott Henry
Stuart Anderson (2014 Brechin City, Ex Southampton, Blackpool, Ross Co, Livingston, Peterhead, Salisbury Town, Eastbourne Borough, Raith R)
Graham Rodger
Paul Lawson (rx Celtic, Ross County, Motherwell)
Neil McVittie
Calum Bagshaw
Scott Barbour (2015 Fraserburgh)
Cammy Keith
Garry Wood (2015 Montrose, Ex Elgin City, ICT, Ross Co)
Max Berton
Neil Gauld
Conor Gethins
Derek Young
Scott Ferries

Forres Mechanics
Manager: Charlie Rowley
Stuart Knight
Steven Simpson
Simon Allan
Graham Fraser
Gordon Finlayson
Graeme Grant
Connor MacIver
Jordan Wardrope

Scott Graham
Martin Groat
Drew Howard
Stuart Soane
Ross McPherson
Scott Moore
Owen Paterson
Aaron McLean
Dachi Khutashvili
Kyle Scott
Liam Baxter
John Cameron
Fraser Forbes
Lee Fraser
Brandon Hutcheson
Craig McGovern

Fort William
Manager: Ally Ewen Assistant Manager: Kevin Munro
Adam Porritt
Andreas Broomfield
Barna Tot
Conor MacPhee
Craig Mainland
Daniel Highet
Daviud Moffat
Douglas MacLennan
Farquhar MacRae
Glenn Fell
Iain Foggo
Iain MacIntyre
Iain MacLellan
Jack Lingard
Kieran Forbes
Lewis Campbell
Liam Taylor
Martin Munro
Michael Ellis
Richard Tawse
Scott Chisholm
Scott Davidson

Fraserburgh
Manager: Mark Cowie
Coaches: James Duthie, Stevie Doak, Alex Mair
Joe Barbour (ex Maud, Fraserburgh Utd)
Paul Leask (Freed Feb 17, ex Peterhead)
Russell McBride (Ex Elgin C), Freed Nov 2016
Ryan Christie (2016 Fraserburgh U20)
William West (ex Aberdeen)
Dean Cowie (ex Peterhead)
Graham Johnston
Marc Lawrence (OL from Peterhead)
Bailey Simpson (ex Fraserburgh U20)
Marc Dickson (ex Elgin C)
Bryan Hay (ex Fraserburgh U20, Fraserburgh Utd)
Jack Simpson (ex Fraserburgh U20)
Nathan Stuart (ex Fraserburgh U20)
Stuart Taylor (ex Peterhead, Turriff Utd)
Jamie Beagrie (ex Cove R, Peterhead)
Cameron Buchan (ex CRuden Bay, Longside, Maud)
Greg Buchan (2016 Deveronvale)
Liam Cameon (ex Fraserburgh U20)
Sean Douglas (ex Fraserburgh U20)
Blair Fraser (ex Fraserburgh U20)
Liam Norris (ex Fraserburgh U20)
Michael Rae (2016 Maud, ex Fraserburgh)
Marc Summers (ex Fraserburgh U20)
Paul Campbell (ex FC Stoneywood, Maud)
Aiden Combe (ex Keith U17)
Kane McCrory (ex Fraserburgh U20)
Grant Noble (Transferred to Deveronvale Sep 2016)
Jamie Ramsey (ex Longside)
Edward Flinn (2015 Ex St Johnstone Youth)
Peter Tait (ex Fraserburgh U20)
Ryan Cowie (ex Turriff United)
Scott Henry (ex Fraserburgh U20)
Jordan Bremner (ex Fraserburgh U20)
Callum Reid (ex Fraserburgh U20)
Gary Harris (2016 Deveronvale)

Huntly
Co-Managers: Douglas Baxter / Mark Gray
Stuart Grant (2016 OL to Colony Park)
Sean Webb (2016 Nairn County)
Neale Allan
Ross Still
Martin McDonald (2016 Nairn County)
Sean Croll
Alexander Thoirs
Ian Cruikshank
Dennis Wyness (2016 Buckjie Th, ex Aberdeen, ICT, Hearts)
Elliot Duff
Paul Napier (2016 Buckie Thistle, ex Elgin C, Montrose, Petrerhead)
Neale Davidson
Blair Johnston
Adam Naismith (2016 Nairn County)
Robert Duncanson (2016 Nairn County)
Cory Ritchie
Lewis Ingram
Glenn Murison
Garry McGowan (2016 Turriff United)
Joe Burr
Andrew Pennycook
Jordan Morrice
Stuart Hodge
Sean Fraser
Tom Andrews (2016 OL to Lewis United)
Christopher Hay (2016 OL to Lewis United)
Ben Leslie (2016 OL to Lewis United)
Andreas Mitchell (2016 OL to Lewis United)
Clark Robertson (2016 OL to Lewis United, then Spey Valley United)
Grant Stephen
John Urquhart

Inverurie Locos
Manager: Neil Cooper
Andy Hunter
Colin Charlesworth
Daniel Crisp
Greg Mitchell
Joe McCabe
Jordan Leyden
Marc Young
Mark Souter
Martin Laing
Michael Selfridge
Morgan Cook
Neil McLean
Ross Anderson
Ryan Broadhurst
Scott Mathieson
Stephen Jeffrey

Keith
Manager: Allan Hale Assistant: Gavin Wemyss Coach: Ewan Robb, Graeme Bain
David Dey
Ross Salmon
Greg Smith
Adam Clark
Stewart Hutcheon
Bruce Milne
Michael Ralton
Frazer Hall
Michael Dunn
Ryan Spink
Courtney Cooper
Andrew Smith
Gary McNamee
Ryan Keir
Scott Whelan
Craig McAskill
James Brownie
Bruce Raffell
Donald Fraser
Michael Ewen
Craig Cormack
Kris Duncan
Luke Barbour
Ross Salmon (2017 Buckie Thistle OL)

Lossiemouth
Manager: Ally Ewen
Stewart Black
Connor Hall
Michael Miele
Sam Milton
Greig Watson
Stephen McKenzie
Iain MacRae
Mark Smith
Bryan Bell
Kevin Flett
Chris Ross
Harry Noble
Jordan Main
Aaron Hamilton
Scott Wilson
Tony Ross
Liam Archibald
Gary MacDonald
Kevin Grant
Finlay Stables
Darren Bailey
Callûm Dunbar
Garry McDonald
Jordan McBain
Connor Macaulay
Scott Miller
Scott Matheson
Scott McIntosh
Matty Davidson
Ross Campbell
Ryan Farquhar
Ryan Green
Ross Archibald
Shawn Scott

Nairn County
Manager: Ronnie Sharp
Callum Ednie
Calum Riddell
Callum Maclean
Chris Moir
Dylan McKenzie
Dylan McLean
Craig Munro
Fraser Wilkie
Gary Kerr
Glenn Main
Gregg Main
Jack McLean
Jason Morganti
Jamie Mackay
Jordan MacRae
Kenny McKenzie
Matthew McLeod
Paul MacLeod
Reece Barton
Ross Naismith
Ryan MacLeod
Stephen Mackenzie
Wayne Mackintosh
William Barron

Rothes
Manager: Fraser Bremner (until . . .)
Ben Cullen
Blair Mcdonald
Callum Browett
Callum McIntosh
Chris Brown
Craig MacMillan
Daniel Maciver
David McNamara
Finlay Stables
Fraser Forbes
Gary Gallacher
Gordon McNab
Grant Johnston

Grant Munro
Iain Macrae
Jack Maley
James Mackay
James Mclaren
Jonathon Smith
Kayode Ezekiel
Keir Smith
Kevin Edward Duguid
Kyle Cooper
Kyle Gauld
Kay Ezekiel
Lewis Mackay
Nathan Sharp
Ruari Watt
Ryan McRitchie
Ryan Stuart
Scott Riddoch
Sean Charles Mcintosh
Sean Jennings
Sean McIntosh
Stephen Rennie
Struan Mcarthur
Scott Davidson
Ricky Henderson
Dan Smith

Strathspey Thistle
Manager: Brian Grant
Aiden Herse
Owen Cairns
Jack Maley (Transferred to Rothes Jan 17)
James McShane
Mark McKernie
Ryanm McLeod
Dominick Edwards (2016 Nairn Co U20)
Adam McLeod
Inaki Fernandino-Soto (ex Clach, Nairn Co)
Callkum Fraser
Ryan Ingram
Donald McPhee
Josh Race
Kevin McKie
Stephen McKenzie
Kenny Mair
Scott Hume
John Treasurer
James Mackay (Transferred to Rothes Jan 17)
Duncan Lamont
Stefan McRitchie (2016 Fort William)
Jack McLeod
Michael McCallum
Paul McLennan
David Aitchison
James Duncan

Turriff United
Manager: Ross Jack
Assistant: Bobby Beckwith (until Feb), Graham Roy / Ian Bruce (after Feb)
Kevin Main (ex Buckie Thistle, Lossiemouth)
Lewis Davidson (2012 Peterhead, ex Aberdeen, signed pre-contract for Fraserburgh Feb 2017)
Cammy Bowden (2010 Peterhead, ex Aberdeen)
Paul Young (2012 Peterhead, ex Huntly, signed pre-contract for Fraserburgh Feb 2017)
Nicholas Gray (2014 Banks o' Dee, ex Montrose, joined Cove R Mar 2017)
Lesez Nowosielski (2015 Montrose, Ex Odra Opole, Promien Opalenica, Ruch Zdzieszowice, GKS Belchatow, Warta Poznan, MKS Kluczbork, Poland U19 and U20 international)
Robbie Allan
James Chalmers (2013 Maud)
Chris Herd (2010 Montrose)
Allen McKenzie (2015 Elgin City, Ex Benburb, Strathspey Th)
Kenny Mair (2013 Maud)
Darren Wood (2016 Huntly, ex Buckie Th, Rothes)
Aaron Sherman (2016, ex Buckie Thistle)
Scott Moir (Transferred to Cruden Bay, Mar 2017)
David Booth (ex Huntly, Formartine Utd, Banks o' Dee, Aberdeen)
Cameron Booth
Andrezej Klezkowski (2016 Buckie Th, Ex Inverurie Locos, MKS Mazurelk, Huntly, Wigry Suwalki, Portstewart FC, Mazur Elk)
Matthew Mackie
Andrew Smith (2015 Keith)
Liam Strachan
Jordi Walker (2016 Maud Junior)
Nikolas Wozniak (OL to Dyce Juniors)
Dean Still (Transferred to Stoneywood Parkvale Mar 2017)
Antonio Vastano (2016, ex Strathspey Th, Elgin C, Spartans)
David Ross
Neale Davidson (2017 Huntly)
Ryan Bruce

Wick Academy
Manager: Gordon Connelly
Sean McCarthy (2014 Ross County)
Michael McCallum (2016 Strathspey Th OL, Ex brora R)
Danny McCarthy (2015 Ross County)
Danny Mackay (ex brora R, Castletown)
Colin MacRae (2016 Ross County)
Grant Steven (2011)
Michael "Joe" Steven (ex Brora R)
Andrew Hardwick (2016 Nairn Co, ex Glasgow Uni, Pentland Utd, Clach)
Ross Allan (2009 Ross Co)
Alan Farquhar (ex Halkirk, Brora R)
Richard Macadie (2003)
Sam Mackay (2009 Deveronvale, ex Brora R)
Gary Manson (ex Pentland Utd, Ross Co)
James Pickles (ex Rendall FC)
Andrew Mackay (2016 Strathspey Th, ex Ormlie Hotspur)
James McLean (2016 Halkirk Utd)
Michael Petrie (2016 Pentland United)
David Allan
Steven Anderson (ex Golspie Stafford, Lybster)
Marc McGregor (2015 Staxigoe United)
Gary Weir

SOUTH SENIORS

For much of the season Wigtown and Bladnoch looked unassailable at the top of the league. Their results were a model of consistency that other clubs could not match. However, at the death Wigtown hit a dramatic slump and relinquished the top spot to Edusport Academy. This meant that the team of French students were promoted to the Lowland League.

Rumours abounded that Wigtown did not want promotion. St Cuthbert had been in a similar position the previous season but failed to get their license in time. Threave Rovers had taken voluntary relegation from the Lowland League. Clearly many of the clubs from Dumfries and Galloway do not want to play at a higher level.

Edusport, on the other hand, had made their intentions clear from the start. The other clubs in the league will probably not be hugely disappointed to see them promoted. Three new teams have joined the league. Annan Athletic and Stranraer Under 20s are self-explanatory. Bonnyton Thistle, from Kilmarnock, are a different kettle of fish. They follow the model of BSC Glasgow, East Kilbride or Cumbernauld Colts—a youth team seeking to establish an adult side and climb the pyramid. The South of Scotland League had little option but to accept them but one wonders what will happen if and when a team from Dumbarton or Greenock want to make the same move.

On July 10th 2017 it was announced that Champions Wigtown and Bladnoch were going into abeyance. They cited lack of players as the reason - Wigtown had used quite a few Stranraer-based players but with the Stair Park themselves entering a team in the SOSL there simply weren't enough players to go around.

Wigtown's resignation, on the day of the Scottish Cup draw, was a big blow to South football and a reminder that the League's place as a Tier 6 Feeder League for the Pyramid really doesn't make much sense.

THE WIGTOWN IMPLOSION

30/7/16	H	Lochmaben	3	1	W
3/8/16	H	Threave Rovers	3	1	W
6/8/16	A	Abbey Vale	3	0	W
10/8/16	H	Creetown	3	0	W
17/8/16	H	Newton Stewart	2	0	W
20/8/16	A	Dumfries YMCA	6	0	W
24/8/16	H	St Cuthbert Wanderers	1	1	D
27/8/16	H	Mid Annandale	4	1	W
3/9/16	H	Newton Stewart	3	2	W
7/9/16	A	Heston Rovers	3	1	W
17/9/16	H	Nithsdale Wanderers	4	2	W
24/9/16	A	Lochmaben	3	0	W
8/10/16	A	Lochar Thistle	2	0	W
29/10/16	H	Edusport	1	0	W
5/11/16	A	Creetown	2	1	W
19/11/16	H	Dumfries YMCA	8	0	W
10/12/16	H	Upper Annandale	4	1	W
7/1/17	H	Lochar Thistle	4	3	W
14/1/17	A	Threave Rovers	3	3	D
11/2/17	H	Heston Rovers	1	0	W
18/2/17	A	St Cuthbert Wanderers	3	2	W
25/3/17	A	Upper Annandale	5	1	W
1/4/17	H	Nithsdale Wanderers	1	1	D
8/4/17	A	Edusport	0	4	L
15/4/17	A	Mid Annandale	0	3	L
22/4/17	H	Abbey Vale	2	1	W

SOUTH OF SCOTLAND CUP DRAWS 2017/18

South of Scotland Alternate (Alba Cup)

Round 1
Creetown v Upper Annandale
Dumfries YM v Nithsdale Wanderers

Round 2
Lochar Thistle v Creetown or Upper Annandale
Dumfries YM or Nithsdale Wanderers v Mid Annandale
Abbey Vale v Bonnyton Thistle
Heston Rovers v Lochmaben

Tweedie Cup

Round 1
Mid Annandale v Nithsdale Wanderers
Upper Annandale v Newton Stewart
Stranraer v Wigtown & Bladnoch
Threave Rovers v St Cuthbert Wanderers
Abbey Vale v Creetown
Bonnyton Thistle v Annan Athletic
Lochar Thistle v Dumfries YMCA
Lochmaben v Heston Rovers

Potts Cup

Round 1
Creetown v Newton Stewart
St Cuthbert Wanderers v Upper Annandale
Heston Rovers v Dumfries YMCA
Mid Annandale v Queen of the South
Stranraer v Threave Rovers
Annan Athletic v Lochar Thistle
Nithsdale Wanderers v Lochmaben
Wigtown & Bladnoch v Abbey Vale

South of Scotland League Cup

Round 1
Lochmaben v Bonnyton Thistle
St Cuthbert Wanderers v Creetown
Stranraer v Newton Stewart
Lochar Thistle v Nithsdale Wanderers
Abbey Vale v Upper Annandale
Mid Annandale v Threave Rovers
Annan Athletic v Heston Rovers
Dumfries YMCA v Wigtown & Bladnoch

Southern Counties Challenge Cup

Round 1
Nithsdale Wanderers v Lochmaben
Heston Rovers v Creetown
Dumfries YMCA v Abbey Vale
The other 13 teams were given byes.

Haig Gordon Trophy and **Cree Lodge Cup** will be drawn later.

SOUTH SENIORS

South of Scotland League 2016/17

	ABB	CRE	DUM	EDU	HES	LT	LMB	MID	NEW	NIT	STC	THR	UPP	WIG
Abbey Vale		Sep 10 5-2	Nov 5 8-2	Jul 30 0-0	Apr 26 2-3**	Apr 19 1-0**	Feb 4 3-0	Mar 4 3-2**	Apr 8 2-1**	Aug 13 6-3	Nov 19 2-2	Aug 24 2-2	Oct 29 2-2	Aug 6 0-3
Creetown	Apr 1 2-4		Aug 27 5-1	Aug 24 1-3	Jul 30 0-1	Apr 15 2-1	Feb 11 2-1	Apr 22 1-1	Aug 3 2-0	Nov 19 4-1	Oct 15 3-4	Apr 26 1-0	Dec 3 1-0	Nov 5 1-2
Dumfries YMCA	Aug 17 0-3	Dec 10 1-8		Aug 6 0-4	Oct 5 0-5	Oct 26 1-5	Aug 13 1-6	Sep 24 1-6	Mar 11 0-3	Nov 26 2-4	Nov 12 2-9	Dec 3 0-15	Aug 10 1-4	Aug 20 0-6
Edusport Academy	Oct 26 3-0	Mar 18 5-0	Mar 4 4-0		Aug 3 3-2	Feb 18 1-0	Sep 28 3-0	Oct 5 5-3	Jan 14 5-2	Dec 17 4-0	Apr 22 5-0	Apr 12 1-0	Sep 7 1-0	Apr 8 4-0
Heston Rovers	Apr 14 1-2	Jan 14 7-2	Mar 25 8-2	Jan 7 2-4		Aug 6 2-4	Aug 17 1-0	Oct 29 5-2	Aug 24 2-4	Oct 19 5-1	Oct 26 2-6	Sep 10 0-0	Apr 19 3-2	Sep 7 1-3
Lochar Thistle	Aug 10 3-2	Feb 4 3-0	Jul 30 10-0	Sep 10 2-3	Nov 5 1-3		Sep 17 0-4	Feb 25 5-1**	Oct 29 1-3	Aug 24 2-0	Aug 3 3-5	Apr 1 0-2**	Apr 21 0-0	Oct 8 0-2
Lochmaben	Sep 6 0-1	Aug 6 2-4	Aug 24 4-1	Nov 19 3-8	Apr 1 4-1	Nov 12 0-2		Sep 9 1-4	Mar 4 2-3	Aug 10 1-0	Oct 29 2-7	Feb 25 2-2	Jan 7 2-0	Sep 24 0-3
Mid Annandale	Sep 17 3-1	Aug 13 2-3	Aug 3 8-0	Feb 11 2-6	Dec 3 2-2	Aug 17 3-7	Jan 14 2-2		Mar 18 3-8	Sep 7 3-1	Aug 20 3-2	Jul 30 1-0	Apr 12 3-0	Apr 15 3-0
Newton Stewart	Dec 10 4-1	Oct 19 4-1	Sep 7 7-3	Sep 17 2-4	Oct 15 3-1	Apr 12 1-1	Oct 22 4-1	Aug 6 1-3		Jan 7 2-2	Apr 1 2-3	Aug 10 4-3	Feb 25 2-2	Aug 17 0-2
Nithsdale Wanderers	Aug 3 5-4	Oct 29 1-0	Sep 10 8-1	Nov 5 3-5	Apr 8 0-6	Feb 11 0-3	Oct 8 4-5	Nov 12 4-8	Feb 18 4-1		Dec 3 2-5	Apr 22 1-1	Aug 17 1-5	Sep 17 2-4
St Cuthbert Wanderers	Jan 7 3-2	Sep 7 9-0	Jan 14 9-0	Oct 19 3-1	Dec 17 5-1	Apr 8 4-3	Mar 11 4-0	Feb 4 5-4	Sep 24 4-3	Jul 30 4-2		Oct 5 3-1	Aug 6 2-2	Feb 18 2-3
Threave Rovers	Oct 19 2-0	Aug 17 2-1	Oct 29 3-0	Sep 24 0-0	Aug 13 5-0	Sep 7 6-0	Dec 10 2-1	Dec 17 2-2	Apr 15 3-1	Aug 6 1-3	Apr 5 3-2		Sep 17 3-0	Jan 14 3-3
Upper Annandale	Feb 11 4-4	Nov 12 4-3	Feb 4 3-3	Oct 8 2-6	Sep 24 3-4	Nov 19 2-3	Aug 3 0-2	Aug 24 3-4	Jul 30 1-3	Mar 11 1-0	Sep 3 2-7	Nov 5 1-0*		Mar 25 1-5
Wigtown & Bladnoch	Apr 22 2-1	Aug 10 3-0	Nov 19 8-0	Oct 29 1-0	Feb 11 1-0	Jan 7 4-3	Jul 30 3-1	Aug 27 4-1	Sep 3 3-2	Apr 1 1-1	Aug 24 1-1	Aug 3 3-1	Dec 10 4-1	

* at Mid Annandale
** at Dumfries HS

	P	W	D	L	F	A	GD	Pts
Edusport Academy	26	22	2	2	88	28	60	68
Wigtown and Bladnoch FC	26	21	3	2	74	29	45	66
St Cuthbert Wanderers FC	26	19	3	4	110	54	56	60
Threave Rovers FC	26	11	7	8	62	32	30	40
Mid Annandale FC	26	12	4	10	79	72	7	40
Newton Stewart FC	26	12	3	11	70	59	11	39
Heston Rovers FC	26	12	2	12	68	61	7	38
Abbey Vale FC	26	11	5	10	61	54	7	38
Lochar Thistle FC	26	11	2	13	62	52	10	35
Creetown FC	26	10	1	15	49	67	-18	31
Lochmaben FC	26	8	2	16	46	65	-19	26
Upper Annandale FC	26	5	6	15	45	69	-24	21
Nithsdale Wanderers FC	26	6	3	17	53	84	-31	21
Dumfries YMCA FC	26	0	1	25	22	163	-141	1

South of Scotland League - Recent Placings

Club	1980-1	1981-2	1982-3	1983-4	1984-5	1985-6	1986-7	1987-8	1988-9	1989-90	1990-1	1991-2	1992-3	1993-4	1994-5	1995-6	1996-7	1997-8	1998-9
Abbey Vale																			
Annan Athletic	3	2	3	1	2	4	1	3											
Annan Athletic Reserves									7	7	9		10	7	8	6	12	8	5
Blackwood Dynamoes / Crichton Royal / Crichton / Lochmaben													5	9		7	2	13	8
Creetown	8	5	9	9	3	9	10	10	5	5	11	9	12	10		12	10	4	4
Dalbeattie Star	6	3	4	2	1	1	2	5	1	3	4	3	2	5	6	10	13	6	7
Dalbeattie Star Reserves																			
Dumfries HSFP / Dumfries / Heston Rovers															4	3	5	3	2
Dumfries YMCA																			
Edusport Academy																			
Fleet Star																			
Girvan Amateurs / Girvan	7	10	10	6	8	8	8	9	8	1	7	4	9	8	7	4	9	7	12
Gretna Reserves																			
Lochar Thistle																			
Maxwelltown HSFP											1	2	7	2	3	8	8	10	3
Mid Annandale																			
Newton Stewart	10	9	5	8	7	3	6	1	4	8	5	6	8	6		13	7	12	10
Nithsdale Wanderers																			
Queen of the South Reserves													6				1		
St Cuthbert Wanderers	1	7	7	7	4	6	3	6	3	4	6	7	4	3	5	1	3	5	9
Stranraer Athletic																2	4	9	11
Stranraer Reserves	2	1	1	3	5	7	7	4			8								
Tarff Rovers	9	8	8	10	10	10	9	8			10	8	11	11	9	11	11	1	1
Threave Rovers	4	4	2	4	6	2	5	2	2	2	2	5	1	1	1	9	6	2	6
Threave Rovers Reserves																			
Upper Annandale																			
Wigtown & Bladnoch	5	6	6	5	9	5	4	7	6	6	3	1	3	4	2	5	14	11	13

Club	1999-00	2000-1	2001-2	2002-3	2003-4	2004-5	2005-6	2006-7	2007-8	2008-9	2009-10	2010-11	2011-12	2012-13	2013-14	2014-15	2015-16	2016-17
Abbey Vale			14	6	12	8	3	12	12	9	7	13	11	7	9	7	11	8
Annan Athletic																		
Annan Athletic Reserves	5	8	7	13	5	3	2	6	10	6								
Blackwood Dynamoes / Crichton Royal / Crichton / Lochmaben	7	4	12	7	16	11	11	8	1	2	5	5	8	9	5	9	4	11
Creetown	8	7	4	11	3	2	5	4	6	13	11	9	13	11	11	12	10	10
Dalbeattie Star	2	3									2	2	1	1				
Dalbeattie Star Reserves			8	14	14	13	10	9	4	7								
Dumfries HSFP / Dumfries / Heston Rovers	13	5	6	8	6	6	13	11	15	10	10	8	3	5	6	6	5	7
Dumfries YMCA																14	14	14
Edusport Academy																5	2	1
Fleet Star						10	14	14	11	14	12	11	9	12	10	8	13	
Girvan Amateurs / Girvan	11	9	2	4	7													
Gretna Reserves			9	3														
Lochar Thistle															7	4	7	9
Maxwelltown HSFP	10																	
Mid Annandale					11	9	9	13	14	11	9	7	6	10	8	10	8	5
Newton Stewart	3	10	15	15	15	14	12	10	9	12	8	6	5	6	3	2	9	6
Nithsdale Wanderers			11	9	10	7	7	2	7	8	13	12	12	8	4	13	12	13
Queen of the South Reserves		1			2													
St Cuthbert Wanderers	4	6	3	5	8	5	6	5	5	5	3	3	4	2	2	3	1	3
Stranraer Athletic	6	13	5	1	1	1	4	3	8									
Stranraer Reserves					4				3	4	6	4	7					
Tarff Rovers	1	2	1	2														
Threave Rovers						4	1	1	2	1	1	1	2	4				4
Threave Rovers Reserves	9	11	10	12	9													
Upper Annandale																11	6	12
Wigtown & Bladnoch	12	12	13	10	13	12	8	7	13	3	4	10	10	3	1	1	3	2

South of Scotland League Cup 2016/17

SOUTH OF SCOTLAND LEAGUE CUP							
1	27/08/2016	Lochar Thistle	Heston Rovers	1	5		
1	27/08/2016	Lochmaben	St Cuthbert Wanderers	1	6		
1	27/08/2016	Nithsdale Wanderers	Abbey Vale	4	4	AET 6-8p	
1	27/08/2016	Threave Rovers	Eudsport Academy	0	0	AET 5-4p	
1	27/08/2016	Upper Annandale	Newton Stewart	2	3		
2	08/10/2016	Abbey Vale	Heston Rovers	0	5		
2	08/10/2016	Creetown	Newton Stewart	1	2		
2	08/10/2016	Mid Annandale	Dumfries YMCA	5	0		
2	08/10/2016	St Cuthbert Wanderer:	Threave Rovers	2	4		
SF	19/11/2016	Newton Stewart	Heston Rovers	2	1		
SF	19/11/2016	Threave Rovers	Mid Annandale	3	1		
F	10/02/2017	Newton Stewart	Threave Rovers	0	0	AET, 4-1p	at St Cuthbert W

Wigtown & Bladnoch were excluded from the Cup for 2016/17 due to registration issue the previous year.

Recent South of Scotland League Cup Finals				
Season	**Winners**	**Runners Up**	**Score**	**Venue**
1988/9	Dalbeattie Star	Threave Rovers	3-2	2 legs
1989/90	Threave Rovers	Dalbeattie Star	3-2	2 legs
1990/1	Threave Rovers	Maxwelltown HSFP	3-2	2 legs
1991/2	Girvan Amateurs	Dalbeattie Star	6-1	2 legs
1992/3	Dalbeattie Star	Wigtown & Bladnoch	2-2, 4-3 pens	2 legs
1993/4	Threave Rovers	Wigtown & Bladnoch	4-1	2 legs
1994/5	Wigtown & Bladnoch	Annan Athletic	4-2	2 legs
1995/6	St Cuthbert Wanderers	Maxwelltown HSFP	4-3	2 legs
1996/7	QOS Reserves	Stranraer Athletic	5-3	2 legs
1997/8	Tarff Rovers	Threave Rovers	5-2	2 legs
1998/9	Tarff Rovers	QOS Reserves	5-4	2 legs
1999/00	Tarff Rovers	Threave Rovers	2-0	Kirkcowan
2000/1	Newton Stewart	St Cuthbert Wanderers	5-0	Newton Stewart
2001/2	Girvan	Stranraer Athletic	2-1	Girvan
2002/3	Crichton	Nithsdale Wanderers	4-1	Crichton
2003/4	Stranraer Athletic	Girvan	3-1	Girvan
2004/5	Annan Athletic Reserves	St Cuthbert Wanderers	5-0	Kirkcudbright
2005/6	Creetown	Stranraer Athletic	1-0	Creetown
2006/7	Threave Rovers	Crichton	2-1	Castle Douglas
2007/8	St Cuthbert Wanderers	Stranraer Reserves	4-2	Kirkcudbright
2008/9	St Cuthbert Wanderers	Crichton	1-0	Crichton
2009/10	Stranraer Reserves	St Cuthbert Wanderers	3-0	Stranraer
2010/1	Dalbeattie Star	Threave Rovers	1-0	Castle Douglas
2011/2	Dalbeattie Star	St Cuthbert Wanderers	4-1	Dalbeattie
2012/3	Dalbeattie Star	Threave Rovers	3-1	Palmerston Park
2013/4	Wigtown & Bladnoch	Lochar Thistle	5-1	Kirkcudbright
2014/5	Edusport Academy	St Cuthbert Wanderers	3-1	Lockerbie
2015/6	Edusport Academy	Mid Annandale	7-2	Palmerston Park
2016/7	Newton Stewart	Threave Rovers	0-0, 4-1p	Kirkcudbright

Potts Cup (SCFA) 2016/17

1	25/03/2017	Abbey Vale	Edusport Academy	1	3		at Dumfries HS
1	25/03/2017	Creetown	St Cuthbert Wanderers	1	3		
1	25/03/2017	Mid Annandale	Threave Rovers	5	2		
1	25/03/2017	Nithsdale Wanderers	Lochar Thistle	2	0		
1	26/04/2017	Wigtown & Bladnoch	Dumfries YMCA	6	0		
2	03/05/2017	Heston Rovers	Mid Annandale	2	3		
2	06/05/2017	Newton Stewart	Upper Annandale	3	0		
2	06/05/2017	St Cuthbert Wanderers	Nithsdale Wanderers	4	0		
2	06/05/2017	Wigtown & Bladnoch	Edusport Academy	4	1		
SF	17/05/2017	St Cuthbert Wanderers	Mid Annandale	7	2		
SF	17/05/2017	Wigtown & Bladnoch	Newton Stewart	3	4		
F	24/05/2017	St Cuthbert Wanderers	Newton Stewart	4	3	aet	at Creetown

Recent Potts Cup Finals				
Season	**Winners**	**Runners Up**	**Score**	**Venue**
1988/9	St Cuthbert Wanderers	Threave Rovers	3-2	Castle Douglas
1989/90	Wigtown & Bladnoch	St Cuthbert Wanderers	3-2	Wigtown
1990/1	Threave Rovers	Dalbeattie Star	5-0	Dalbeattie
1991/2	Dalbeattie Star	Wigtown & Bladnoch	1-0 aet	Dalbeattie
1992/3	Dalbeattie Star	Newton Stewart	4-1	Dalbeattie
1993/4	Threave Rovers	Dalbeattie Star	5-2	Dalbeattie
1994/5	Threave Rovers	Dumfries HSFP	4-2	David Keswick Centre
1995/6	Stranraer Athletic	Dumfries HSFP	2-1	Stair Park
1996/7	St Cuthbert Wanderers	Maxwelltown HSFP	2-0	Maxwelltown HS
1997/8	Tarff Rovers	Newton Stewart	3-0	Newton Stewart
1998/9	Dalbeattie Star	Dumfries HSFP	1-0	Dalbeattie
1999/00	Dalbeattie Star	Creetown	5-1	Creetown
2000/1	Season abandoned			
2001/2	Tarff Rovers	St Cuthbert Wanderers	3-1	Kirkcudbright
2002/3	Annan Athletic Reserves	Tarff Rovers	3-0	Annan
2003/4	Stranraer Athletic	Creetown	4-0	Creetown
2004/5	Stranraer Athletic	Newton Stewart	3-0	Newton Stewart
2005/6	Nithsdale Wanderers	Threave Rovers	2-0	Sanquhar
2006/7	Wigtown & Bladnoch	Crichton	3-1	Crichton
2007/8	Stranraer Reserves	Creetown	1-1, 4-1 pens	Creetown
2008/9	Wigtown & Bladnoch	St Cuthbert Wanderers	3-1	Wigtown
2009/10	Stranraer Reserves	St Cuthbert Wanderers	2-0	Kirkcudbright
2010/1	Threave Rovers	Crichton	0-0, 3-0 pens	Crichton
2011/2	Dalbeattie Star	Threave Rovers	2-0	Dalbeattie
2012/3	Wigtown & Bladnoch	Newton Stewart	2-0	Stair Park
2013/4	Heston Rovers	Newton Stewart	3-1	Kirkcudbright
2014/5	Newton Stewart	Mid Annandale	4-0	Kirkcudbright
2015/6	Lochar Thistle	Creetown	2-0	Palmerston Park
2016/7	St Cuthbert Wanderers	Newton Stewart	4-3	Creetown

ree Lodge Cup (Wigtownshire FA) 2016/17

1	01/10/2016	Heston Rovers	Abbey Vale	4	2		
1	01/10/2016	Lochar Thistle	Creetown	4	0		
1	01/10/2016	Mid Annandale	Dumfries YM	10	0		
1	01/10/2016	Newton Stewart	Threave Rovers	2	1		
1	01/10/2016	Nithsdale Wanderers	Upper Annadale	3	4		
1	01/10/2016	Wigtown & Bladnoch	St Cuthbert Wanderers	1	4		
2	05/11/2016	St Cuthbert Wanderers	Newton Stewart	5	2		
2	04/11/2016	Mid Annandale	Lochmaben	2	1		
2	16/11/2016	Edusport Academy	Lochar Thistle	4	1		
2	16/11/2016	Heston Rovers	Upper Annadale	4	0		
SF	10/12/2016	Mid Annandale	Heston Rovers	1	4		
SF	10/12/2016	St Cuthbert Wanderers	Edusport Academy	5	2		
F	24/02/2017	Heston Rovers	St Cuthbert Wanderers	2	5		at Threave

cent Cree Lodge Cup Finals

ason	Winners	Runners Up	Score	Venue
88/9	St Cuthbert Wanderers	Threave Rovers	3-1	Castle Douglas
89/90	No competition			
90/1	Annan Athletic	Stranraer Reserves	2-1	Stair Park
91/2	No competition			
92/3	Threave Rovers	Girvan	2-1	Girvan
93/4	Annan Athletic	Threave Rovers	3-0	Annan
94/5	Annan Athletic	Threave Rovers	7-1	Annan
95/6	Annan Athletic	Stranraer Athletic	3-2	Stair Park
96/7	Threave Rovers	Tarff Rovers	4-0	Castle Douglas
97/8	Tarff Rovers	Threave Rovers	1-0	Castle Douglas
98/9	Tarff Rovers	Dumfries HSFP	1-0	David Keswick Centre
99/00	Tarff Rovers	Creetown	3-1	Kirkcowan
00/1	Not completed			
01/2	Girvan	St Cuthbert Wanderers	1-0 aet	Girvan
02/3	Annan Athletic Reserves	Dumfries	3-2	Annan
03/4	Creetown	Annan Athletic Reserves	2-0	Annan
04/5	Creetown	Mid Annandale	4-0	Lockerbie
05/6	Threave Rovers	Wigtown & Bladnoch	2-1	Wigtown
06/7	Stranraer Athletic	Creetown	1-1, 8-7 pens	Stranraer High School
07/8	Crichton	St Cuthbert Wanderers	3-0	Crichton
08/9	Threave Rovers	Nithsdale Wanderers	6-2	Sanquhar
09/10	Stranraer Reserves	St Cuthbert Wanderers	1-1, 8-7 pens	Stair Park
10/1	Threave Rovers	St Cuthbert Wanderers	5-1	Kirkcudbright
11/2	Threave Rovers	St Cuthbert Wanderers	4-2	Castle Douglas
12/3	St Cuthbert Wanderers	Nithsdale Wanderers	5-2	Dalbeattie
13/4	Heston Rovers	Threave Rovers	3-2	Dalbeattie
14/5	Wigtown & Bladnoch	Edusport Academy	2-0	Annan
15/6	St Cuthbert Wanderers	Heston Rovers	5-3 aet	Dumfries High School
16/7	St Cuthbert Wanderers	Heston Rovers	5-2	Castle Douglas

Haig Gordon Memorial Trophy (SCFA) 2016/1

1	22/10/2016	Abbey Vale	Wigtown & Bladnoch	1	3		
1	22/10/2016	Creetown	Upper Annandale	0	3		
1	22/10/2016	Dumfries YMCA	St Cuthbert Wanderers	1	6		
1	22/10/2016	Edusport Academy	Threave Rovers	2	1		at QOS FC
1	22/10/2016	Mid Annandale	Lochar Thistle	0	1		
1	22/10/2016	Nithsdale Wanderers	Heston Rovers	1	6		
2	26/11/2016	Heston Rovers	Upper Annandale	2	1	AET	
2	26/11/2016	St Cuthbert Wanderers	Edusport Academy	1	2		
2	17/12/2016	Lochar Thistle	Newton Stewart	1	2		
2	17/12/2016	Wigtown & Bladnoch	Lochmaben	2	0		
SF	04/02/2017	Edusport Academy	Wigtown & Bladnoch	0	3		
SF	04/02/2017	Newton Stewart	Heston Rovers	2	3		
F	30/04/2017	Heston Rovers	Wigtown & Bladnoch	1	4		at Kirkcudbright

Recent Haig Gordon Memorial Trophy Finals				
Season	**Winners**	**Runners Up**	**Score**	**Venue**
1988/9	Dalbeattie Star	Annan Athletic	3-1	Dalbeattie
1989/90	Threave Rovers	Newton Stewart	4-3 aet	Castle Douglas
1990/1	Wigtown & Bladnoch	Dalbeattie Star	2-1	Wigtown
1991/2	Maxwelltown HSFP	Annan Athletic	1-0	Maxwelltown HS
1992/3	Annan Athletic	St Cuthbert Wanderers	5-2	Annan
1993/4	Annan Athletic	Wigtown & Bladnoch	0-0, 7-6 pens	Wigtown
1994/5	No competition			
1995/6	Annan Athletic	Dumfries HSFP	5-0	Glencaple
1996/7	Stranraer Athletic	Dumfries HSFP	0-0, 5-3 pens	Glencaple
1997/8	St Cuthbert Wanderers	Newton Stewart	4-1	Newton Stewart
1998/9	Tarff Rovers	Newton Stewart	1-1, 6-5 pens	Newton Stewart
1999/00	Tarff Rovers	St Cuthbert Wanderers	3-1	Castle Douglas
2000/1	Not completed			
2001/2	Tarff Rovers	Crichton	4-1	Crichton
2002/3	Gretna	Tarff Rovers	5-3	Kirkcowan
2003/4	Creetown	Dumfries	6-3	Glencaple
2004/5	Stranraer Athletic	Threave Rovers	1-0	Stair Park, Stranraer
2005/6	Annan Athletic	Wigtown & Bladnoch	3-2	Wigtown
2006/7	Stranraer Athletic	Mid Annandale	3-0	Lockerbie
2007/8	Annan Athletic	St Cuthbert Wanderrs	3-3, 4-1 pens	Kirkcudbright
2008/9	Nithsdale Wanderers	Creetown	5-5, 5-4 pens	Sanquhar
2009/10	St Cuthbert Wanderers	Dalbeattie Star	2-1	Kirkcudbright
2010/1	Queen of the South	Threave Rovers	2-2, 4-2 pens	Palmerston Park, Dum
2011/2	Dalbeattie Star	Threave Rovers	3-0	Dalbeattie
2012/3	Wigtown & Bladnoch	St Cuthbert Wanderers	2-1 AET	Kirkcudbright
2013/4	Wigtown & Bladnoch	Newton Stewart	2-1	Creetown
2014/5	Wigtown & Bladnoch	Newton Stewart	2-1	Creetown
2015/6	St Cuthbert Wanderers	Mid Annandale	4-3	Annan
2016/7	Wigtown & Bladnoch	Heston Rovers	4-1	Kirkcudbright

Southern Counties FA Challenge Cup 2016/17

1	03/12/2016	Abbey Vale	Lochar Thistle	4	1		
1	03/12/2016	Edusport Academy	Wigtown & Bladnoch	1	2		
1	03/12/2016	Newton Stewart	Lochmaben	6	2		
2	21/01/2017	Heston Rovers	Fleet Star	2	1		
2	21/01/2017	Nithsdale Wanderers	Mid Annandale	2	3	aet	
2	21/01/2017	St Cuthbert Wanderers	Wigtown & Bladnoch	1	2		
2	21/01/2017	Stranraer	Dumfries YMCA	5	5	aet, 3-4p	
2	21/01/2017	Threave Rovers	Newton Stewart	1	1	aet, 5-4p	
2	21/01/2017	Upper Annandale	Creetown	1	3		
2	17/02/2017	Abbey Vale	Queen of the South	0	3		at QOS
2	20/01/2017	Annan Athletic	Dalbeattie Star	1	3		
3	18/02/2017	Dumfries YMCA	Dalbeattie Star	0	5		
3	11/03/2017	Heston Rovers	Wigtown & Bladnoch	2	2	AET, 1-3p	
3	08/04/2017	Queen of the South	Creetown	5	1		
3	08/04/2017	Threave Rovers	Mid Annandale	3	4		
SF	18/04/2017	Queen of the South	Mid Annandale	6	2		
SF	19/04/2017	Wigtown & Bladnoch	Dalbeattie Star	0	4		
F	13/05/2017	Queen of the South	Dalbeattie Star	1	2		at Annan

Fleet Star's game v Heston Rovers was the only match they played this season. The club went into abeyance but had to enter the Southern Counties FA Challenge Cup in order to maintain membership. They folded at the end of the season.

Recent Southern Counties Challenge Cup Finals				
Season	**Winners**	**Runners Up**	**Score**	**Venue**
1988/9	Stranraer	Queen of the South	2-1	Palmerston Park
1989/90	Annan Athletic	Threave Rovers	1-0	Galabank
1990/1	Queen of the South	Annan Athletic	2-2, 4-3 pens	Palmerston Park
1991/2	Stranraer	Dalbeattie Star	2-1	Islecroft Stadium
1992/3	Dalbeattie Star	Annan Athletic	4-2	Islecroft Stadium
1993/4	Stranraer	Wigtown & Bladnoch	3-1	Trammondford Park
1994/5	Stranraer	Annan Athletic	3-1	Galabank
1995/6	Annan Athletic	Stranraer	4-0	Galabank
1996/7	Queen of the South	Annan Athletic	2-0	Palmerston Park
1997/8	Threave Rovers	Newton Stewart	5-1	Blairmount Park
1998/9	Annan Athletic	Stranraer Athletic	4-0	Galabank
1999/00	Queen of the South	Tarff Rovers	5-2 aet	Palmerston Park
2000/1	Not completed			
2001/2	Tarff Rovers	Annan Athletic	3-0	Ballgreen Park
2002/3	Queen of the South	Stranraer Athletic	2-0	Stranraer High School
2003/4	Queen of the South	Threave Rovers	3-1	Palmerston Park
2004/5	Gretna	Stranraer	4-3	Raydale Park
2005/6	Annan Athletic	Creetown	3-1	Galabank
2006/7	Dalbeattie Star	Stranraer Athletic	4-1	Islecroft Stadium
2007/8	Threave Rovers	Mid Annandale	4-0	Meadow Park
2008/9	Dalbeattie Star	Annan Athletic	4-1	Galabank
2009/10	St Cuthbert Wanderers	Wigtown & Bladnoch	3-1	St Marys Park
2010/1	Annan Athletic	Newton Stewart	3-2	Blairmount Park
2011/2	Dalbeattie Star	Queen of the South	8-1	Galabank
2012/3	Dalbeattie Star	Nithsdale Wanderers	6-2	Annan
2013/4	Wigtown & Bladnoch	Dalbeattie Star	2-1	St Marys Park
2014/5	Queen of the South	Wigtown & Bladnoch	3-2	Blairmount Park
2015/6	Queen of the South	St Cuthbert Wanderers	5-1	Annan
2016/7	Dalbeattie Star	Queen of the South	2-1	Annan

Tweedie Cup (Wigtownshire FA) 2016/17

1	28/01/2017	Dumfries YMCA	Creetown	0	8		
1	28/01/2017	Lochmaben	Lochar Thistle	1	2		
1	28/01/2017	Newton Stewart	Upper Annandale	4	2		
1	28/01/2017	Nithsdale Wanderers	Mid Annandale	8	6	AET	
1	03/04/2017	Abbey Vale	Threave Rovers	2	2	AET, 4-5p	at St Cuthberts
1	18/03/2017	Wigtown & Bladnoch	St Cuthbert Wanderers	0	4		at St Cuthberts
2	05/04/2017	Newton Stewart	Lochar Thistle	2	0		
2	12/04/2017	St Cuthbert Wanderers	Heston Rovers	3	0		
2	15/03/2017	Nithsdale Wanderers	Edusport Academy	1	0	AET	
2	19/04/2017	Threave Rovers	Creetown	2	1		
SF	03/05/2017	St Cuthbert Wanderers	Nithsdale Wanderers	3	4		
SF	03/05/2017	Threave Rovers	Newton Stewart	4	0		
F	19/05/2017	Nithsdale Wanderers	Threave Rovers	2	0		at Dalbeattie

Recent Tweedie Cup Finals

Season	Winners	Runners Up	Score	Venue
1988/9	No competition			
1989/90	St Cuthbert Wanderers	Threave Rovers	4-2	Kirkcudbright
1990/1	No competition			
1991/2	Newton Stewart	Wigtow & Bladnoch	1-0	Newton Stewart
1992/3	No competition			
1993/4	Maxwelltown HSFP	Dalbeattie Star	2-1	Maxwelltown HS
1994/5	No competition			
1995/6	Annan Athletic	Stranraer Athletic	3-1	Annan
1996/7	Threave Rovers	Annan Athletic	3-1	Castle Douglas
1997/8	Tarff Rovers	Annan Athletic	2-0	Annan
1998/9	Tarff Rovers	Creetown	2-2, 6-5 pens	Creetown
1999/00	Dalbattie Star	Threave Rovers	3-0	Kirkcowan
2000/1	Not completed			
2001/2	St Cuthbert Wanderers	Gretna	2-1	Kirkcudbright
2002/3	Creetown	Girvan	4-0	Creetown
2003/4	Creetown	Gretna	2-0	Creetown
2004/5	Annan Athletic	Stranraer Athletic	3-1	Annan
2005/6	Abbey Vale	Wigtow & Bladnoch	2-1	Abbey Vale
2006/7	Annan Athletic	Stranraer Athletic	6-2	Annan
2007/8	Creetown	St Cuthberts Wanderers	3-1	Creetown
2008/9	St Cuthbert Wanderers	Newton Stewart	2-0	Newton Stewart
2009/10	Crichton	Threave Rovers	3-3, 4-3 pens	Crichton
2010/1	Stranraer	Heston Rovers	6-3	Heston Rovers
2011/2	Threave Rovers	Newton Stewart	1-0	Castle Douglas
2012/3	Dalbeattie Star	Threave Rovers	2-1 AET	Annan
2013/4	Wigtown & Bladnoch	Threave Rovers	4-2 AET	Newton Stewart
2014/5	Abbey Vale	Edusport Academy	1-0	Sanquhar
2015/6	Edusport Academy	Upper Annandale	4-0	Lockerbie
2016/7	Nithsdale Wanderers	Threave Rovers	2-0	Dalbeattie

South Senior Competitions—All Time Winners

	SOS League Champions	Southern Counties Challenge Cup	Potts Cup	Haig Gordon Trophy	Cree Lodge Cup	Tweedie Cup	SOS League Cup
'1/2		5th Kirkcudbright RV					
2/3		QOS Wanderers					
3/4		5th Kirkcudbright RV					
4/5		Maxwelltown Thistle					
5/6		St Cuthbert Wanderers					
5/7		5th Kirkcudbright RV					
7/8		Dumfries					
3/9		Dumfries				Newton Stewart Athletic	
9/00		Dumfries				Stranraer	
0/1		Dumfries				Newton Stewart Athletic	
1/2		Dumfries	Maxwelltown Volunteers			Barholm Rovers	
2/3		Dumfries	Nithsdale Wanderers			Stranraer	
3/4		Nithsdale Wanderers	Maxwelltown Volunteers			Stranraer	
4/5		Maxwelltown Volunteers	Dumfries			Stranraer	
5/6		Dumfries	Nithsdale Wanderers			Newton Stewart	
/7		Nithsdale Wanderers	Dumfries			Newton Stewart	
/8		Maxwelltown Volunteers	Dumfries			Garlieston	
/9		Dalbeattie Star	Nithsdale Wanderers			Whithorn	
/10		Dumfries	Nithsdale Wanderers			Stranraer	
/11		Nithsdale Wanderers	St Cuthbert Wanderers			Stranraer	
/12		Nithsdale Wanderers	Dumfries			Home Office Rovers	
/13		Solway Star	Solway Star				
'14		Nithsdale Wanderers	Nithsdale Wanderers				
'15		5th KOSB	St Cuthbert Wanderers				
'16		No competition					
'17		No competition					
'18		No competition					
'19		No competition					
'20		Nithsdale Wanderers	Nithsdale Wanderers				
'1		QOTS	QOTS				
'2		Nithsdale Wanderers	Douglas Wanderers		Newton Stewart		
3		Nithsdale Wanderers	Nithsdale Wanderers		Whithon		
4		QOTS	Douglas Wanderers		Newton Stewart		
5		Dalbeattie Star	Dalbeattie Star		Tarff Rovers		
6		Stranraer	Stranraer		Stranraer		
7		Stranraer	Stranraer		St Cuthbert Wanderers	Newton Stewart	
8		Nithsdale Wanderers	Stranraer		Stranraer	Stranraer	
9		Mid Annandale	not completed		Newton Stewart	Stranraer	
30		St Cuthbert Wanderers	St Cuthbert Wanderers		Newton Stewart	Stranraer	
1		Dalbeattie Star	Stranraer				
2		Stranraer	Wigtown & Bladnoch				
3		Stranraer	Stranraer		Wigtown & Bladnoch		
4		Dalbeattie Star	Creetown		Stranraer		
5		QOTS	Creetown		Wigtown & Bladnoch		
6		QOTS	St Cuthbert Wanderers				
7		Stranraer	St Cuthbert Wanderers		Creetown		
8		Solway Star	No competition				
9		Stranraer	Wigtown & Bladnoch		St Cuthbert Wanderers		
40		No competition					
.		No competition					
2		No competition					
3		No competition					
4		No competition					
5		No competition					
		Nithsdale Wanderers					
'	Ayr United Reserves	Dalbeattie Star	Stranraer		Wigtown & Bladnoch		
	Ayr United Reserves	Stranraer	Wigtown & Bladnoch			Stranraer	
	Stranraer	Newton Stewart	Stranraer		Newton Stewart	St Cuthbert Wanderers	
0	Tarff Rovers	Tarff Rovers	Tarff Rovers		Stranraer "A"	Stranraer	
	Newton Stewart	Newton Stewart	Wigtown & Bladnoch			not completed	Newton Stewart
	Wigtown & Bladnoch	Tarff Rovers	Newtown Stewart			not completed	Wigtown & Bladnoch
	Tarff Rovers	St Cuthbert Wanderers	Newtown Stewart			Stranraer "A"	Wigtown & Bladnoch
	Wigtown & Bladnoch	St Cuthbert Wanderers	Tarff Rovers		Stranraer "A"	not completed	St Cuthbert Wanderers
	St Cuthbert Wanderers	Whithorn	St Cuthbert Wanderers			St Cuthbert Wanderers	Tarff Rovers
	Newton Stewart	Newton Stewart	St Cuthbert Wanderers		Stranraer "A"	not completed	Tarff Rovers
	St Cuthbert Wanderers	Stranraer	St Cuthbert Wanderers			Tarff Rovers	Stranraer "A"
	Greystone Rovers	Greystone Rovers	Greystone Rovers		Greystone Rovers	not completed	Stranraer "A"
	St Cuthbert Wanderers	Newton Stewart	Stranraer "A"			Wigtown & Bladnoch	Newton Stewart
	Stranraer Reserves	Stranraer	QOTS "A"		Stranraer "A"	Stranraer "A"	Tarff Rovers
	Stranraer Reserves	Stranraer	QOTS "A"		Threave Rovers	not completed	Tarff Rovers
	Stranraer Reserves	QOTS	Newtown Stewart		Newton Stewart	Stranraer "A"	Stranraer "A"
	Tarff Rovers	Newton Stewart	Threave Rovers			not completed	
	Tarff Rovers	Stranraer	Stranraer "A"		Newton Stewart	Threave Rovers / St Cuthbert W	
	Threave Rovers	Threave Rovers	Tarff Rovers	Tarff Rovers		not completed	
	Stranraer Reserves	QOTS	Threave Rovers	Tarff Rovers	Stranraer "A"	not completed	
	Stranraer Reserves	Stranraer	Tarff Rovers	Threave Rovers		Stranraer "A"	
	Stranraer Reserves	Tarff Rovers	Threave Rovers	Stranraer "A"		not completed	
	Threave Rovers	Stranraer	No competition	Threave Rovers		Threave Rovers	Stranraer "A"
	Stranraer Reserves	St Cuthbert Wanderers	St Cuthbert Wanderers	St Cuthbert Wanderers		not completed	St Cuthbert Wanderers

	SOS League Champions	Southern Counties Challenge Cup	Potts Cup	Haig Gordon Trophy	Cree Lodge Cup	Tweedie Cup	SOS League Cup
1970/1	St Cuthbert Wanderers	Stranraer	Stranraer "A"	Stranraer "A"		Stranraer "A"	St Cuthbert Wanderers
1971/2	Threave Rovers	QOTS	St Cuthbert Wanderers	Stranraer "A"	St Cuthbert Wanderers	not completed	Threave Rovers
1972/3	Stranraer Reserves	Tarff Rovers	Stranraer "A"	St Cuthbert Wanderers		not completed	St Cuthbert Wanderers
1973/4	Stranraer Reserves	Stranraer	Stranraer "A"	Threave Rovers		St Cuthbert Wanderers	
1974/5	Stranraer Reserves	Tarff Rovers	St Cuthbert Wanderers	Stranraer "A"	Stranraer "A"	no competition	
1975/6	Stranraer Reserves	QOTS	Stranraer "A"	Stranraer "A"		Lincluden Swifts	Girvan Amateurs
1976/7	Stranraer Reserves	Stranraer	Stranraer "A"	Stranraer "A"		not completed	Stranraer "A"
1977/8	Girvan Amateurs	Lincluden Swifts	Stranraer "A"	Dalbeattie Star		Threave Rovers	Girvan Amateurs
1978/9	Threave Rovers	Lincluden Swifts	No competition			not completed	Lincluden Swifts
1979/80	Lincluden Swifts	Threave Rovers	No competition			Annan Athletic	Lincluden Swifts
1980/1	St Cuthbert Wanderers	Threave Rovers	Threave Rovers	Threave Rovers	Dalbeattie Star	no competition	Threave Rovers
1981/2	Stranraer Reserves	QOTS	Creetown	Threave Rovers		Threave Rovers	St Cuthbert Wanderers
1982/3	Stranraer Reserves	QOTS	Dalbeattie Star	Wigtown & Bladnoch	Annan Athletic	no competition	Annan Athletic
1983/4	Annan Athletic	Newton Stewart	Stranraer "A"	Dalbeattie Star		Annan Athletic	Wigtown & Bladnoch
1984/5	Dalbeattie Star	Creetown	St Cuthbert Wanderers	Annan Athletic	Dalbeattie Star	no competition	Annan Athletic
1985/6	Dalbeattie Star	Threave Rovers	Dalbeattie Star	Stranraer "A"		Threave Rovers	Newton Stewart
1986/7	Annan Athletic	QOTS	St Cuthbert Wanderers	Annan Athletic	St Cuthbert Wanderers	no competition	Wigtown & Bladnoch
1987/8	Newton Stewart	QOTS	Newtown Stewart	Annan Athletic		Threave Rovers	Threave Rovers
1988/9	Dalbeattie Star	Stranraer	St Cuthbert Wanderers	Dalbeattie Star	St Cuthbert Wanderers	no competition	Dalbeattie Star
1989/90	Girvan	Annan Athletic	Wigtown & Bladnoch	Threave Rovers		St Cuthbert Wanderers	Threave Rovers
1990/1	Maxwelltown HSFP	QOTS	Threave Rovers	Wigtown & Bladnoch	Annan Athletic	no competition	Threave Rovers
1991/2	Wigtown & Bladnoch	Stranraer	Dalbeattie Star	Maxwelltown HSFP		Newton Stewart	Girvan
1992/3	Threave Rovers	Dalbeattie Star	Dalbeattie Star	Annan Athletic	Threave Rovers	no competition	Dalbeattie Star
1993/4	Threave Rovers	Stranraer	Threave Rovers	Annan Athletic	Annan Athletic	Maxwelltown HSFP	Threave Rovers
1994/5	Threave Rovers	Stranraer	Threave Rovers	Annan Athletic	Annan Athletic	no competition	Wigtown & Bladnoch
1995/6	St Cuthbert Wanderers	Annan Athletic	Stranraer Athletic	Annan Athletic	Annan Athletic	Annan Athletic	St Cuthbert Wanderers
1996/7	QOTS Reserves	QOTS	St Cuthbert Wanderers	Stranraer Athletic	Threave Rovers	Threave Rovers	QOS Reserves
1997/8	Tarff Rovers	Threave Rovers	Tarff Rovers	St Cuthbert Wanderers	Tarff Rovers	Tarff Rovers	Tarff Rovers
1998/9	Tarff Rovers	Annan Athletic	Dalbeattie Star	Tarff Rovers	Tarff Rovers	Tarff Rovers	Tarff Rovers
1999/00	Tarff Rovers	QOTS	Dalbeattie Star	Tarff Rovers	Tarff Rovers	Dalbeattie Star	Tarff Rovers
2000/1	Season abandoned	not completed	Season abandoned	Not completed	Not completed	not completed	Newton Stewart
2001/2	Tarff Rovers	Tarff Rovers	Tarff Rovers	Tarff Rovers	Girvan	St Cuthbert Wanderers	Girvan
2002/3	Stranraer Athletic	QOTS	Annan Athletic Reserves	Gretna	Annan Athletic Reserves	Creetown	Crichton
2003/4	Stranraer Athletic	QOTS	Stranraer Athletic	Creetown	Creetown	Creetown	Stranraer Athletic
2004/5	Stranraer Athletic	Gretna	Stranraer Athletic	Stranraer Athletic	Creetown	Annan Athletic	Annan Athletic Reserves
2005/6	Threave Rovers	Annan Athletic	Nithsdale Wanderers	Annan Athletic	Threave Rovers	Abbey Vale	Creetown
2006/7	Threave Rovers	Dalbeattie Star	Wigtown & Bladnoch	Stranraer Athletic	Stranraer Athletic	Annan Athletic	Threave Rovers
2007/8	Crichton	Threave Rovers	Stranraer Reserves	Annan Athletic	Crichton	Creetown	St Cuthbert Wanderers
2008/9	Threave Rovers	Dalbeattie Star	Wigtown & Bladnoch	Nithsdale Wanderers	Threave Rovers	St Cuthbert Wanderers	St Cuthbert Wanderers
2009/10	Threave Rovers	St Cuthbert Wanderers	Stranraer Reserves	St Cuthbert Wanderers	Stranraer Reserves	Crichton	Stranraer Reserves
2010/1	Threave Rovers	Annan Athletic	Threave Rovers	Queen of the South	Threave Rovers	Stranraer "A"	Dalbeattie Star
2011/2	Dalbeattie Star	Dalbeattie Star	Dalbeattie Star	Dalbeattie Star	Threave Rovers	Threave Rovers	Dalbeattie Star
2012/3	Dalbeattie Star	Dalbeattie Star	Wigtown & Bladnoch	Wigtown & Bladnoch	St Cuthbert Wanderers	Dalbeattie Star	Dalbeattie Star
2013/4	Wigtown & Bladnoch	Wigtown & Bladnoch	Heston Rovers	Wigtown & Bladnoch	Heston Rovers	Wigtown & Bladnoch	Wigtown & Bladnoch
2014/5	Wigtown & Bladnoch	QOTS	Newton Stewart	Wigtown & Bladnoch	Wigtown & Bladnoch	Abbey Vale	Edusport Academy
2015/6	St Cuthbert Wanderers	QOTS	Lochar Thistle	St Cuthbert Wanderers	St Cuthbert Wanderers	Edusport Academy	Edusport Academy
2016/7	Edusport Academy	Dalbeattie Star	St Cuthbert Wanderers	Wigtown & Bladnoch	St Cuthbert Wanderers	Nithsdale Wanderers	Newton Stewart

South of Scotland League Club Playing Squads 2016/17

NB These are not comprehensive lists of players used - there will be some omissions. However, all players listed were associated with the club concerned during 2016/17.

Abbey Vale
Managers: Allan Clark / Frazer Brolls
Alex Maxwell
Alisdair Mason
Allan Clark
Brodie Turner
Christopher Mellon
Clarke Chambers
Curtis Telfer
Daniel Thom
Darren Holt
David Kennedy
David Proudlock
David Ruddick
Dylan Cairnie
Ewan Brolls
Findlay Steele
Fraser Brolls
Fraser Maxwell
Frazer McClelland
Frazer Sneddon
Graeme Bell
Greig Robertson
Hayden Edgar
Jack Connelly
John MacBeth
John Wilson
Keiran Pirrie
Lee Malin
Lee True
Michael Love
Rees Brown
Ricky Baxter
Ross Kerr
Ryan Chambers
Struan Parker
Stuart Cameron
Stuart Clark
Taylor Hall

Creetown
Manager: Keith Knox
Adam Kirkwood
Aiden Cluckie
Alistair Birse
Allan McKie
Andrew Davidson
Andrew Downie
Andrew Houston
Ben Herries
Callum Murray
Craig McKie
David Byers
David Hughes
Dean Fyfe
Duncan Anderson
Fraser Anderson
Gavin Williamson
Grant Parker
Greg Jarvie
Harry Fidler
Jordan Hughes
Jordan Wilson
Keiran Marshall
Keith Knox
Kenny Allan
Mark Craig
Michael Sutherland
Robert Landers
Robert Smith
Rory Marshall
Ross Drysdale
Ross Landers
Scott Phillips
Scott Whannel
Stephen Ross
Steven Beggs
William Cloy

Dumfries YMCA
Managers: Greg Wallace / Steven Little
Aaron Cowan
Alex Carter
Alister Baird
Bjorn Kelly
Blair Crossan
Bobby Fairhurst
Chris Wood
Christopher Faulds
Craig Hope
Craig Peat
Dale Osborne
Daniel Emmerson
Danny Bryson
Duncan Wright
Elliott Harris
Euan McMorran
Graham Beckett
Greg Cameron
Greg Harkness
Greg Jardine
Greg Wallace
Ian Hiddleston
Jack Jones
Jack Stewart
Jake McMillan
James Wharton
Joe Burton
Keenan Moss
Keenan Moss
Kenneth Meader
Kieran Johnston
Kriss Lismanis
Liam Watson
Marc Zutic
Mark Wilson
Marty Bryson
Murray Campbell
Murray Coulthard
Nathan Watt
Paul Wharram
Peter Will
Robbie Service
Robert Porter
Ross Bell
Ross McCole
Samuel Rowe
Scott Robson
Sean Peat
Stefan Tate
Stuart Gall
Stuart Ramsay
Terry Traynor
Thomas Wright
Walter Jardine

Edusport Academy
Manager: Ricky Waddell
Ahmed Bouchentouf
Alexandre Lebrisse
Andrew McDonald
Bandiougou Toure
Bastien Brunet
Benjamin Ngongo
Claudio Coelho
Colin Cameron
Craig Johnston
Eric Tshimbangu
Fakataulavelua Teva
Francisco Gomes
Frederic Lacroix
Gautier Moutou
Gerrard Lunday
Granit Zejnulllahi
Gregory David
Guillaume Prevot
Hoareau Luidgi
Hoareau Luidgi
Hugo Boisseaux
Ilies Belkacem
Jason Malin
Jean-Mike Bonjotin
Jeremy Burlet-Parendel
Jeremy Djebbar
Julien Gregoire
Laurence Jeffrey
Louis Besnard
Luca Agati
Makendi Clitus
Morgan Reid
Mouenis El Afia
Moussa Tounkara
Munur Solak
Nathan Bodusseau
Nicolas Manier
Odilon Faria Da Cruz
Quentin Pereira
Regan McLaren
Richard Jacquenet
Ryan McCann
Steve Kyenge
Theo Rodrigues
Tony Ribeiro
Ugo Hussenet
Warren Neme
Yacine Boualem
Yoan Massuet
Yoann Clowez
Yves Nyami

Heston Rovers
Manager: David Bradbury
Aaron Crosbie
Ally Queen
Cammy Sinclair
Craig Adamson
Craig Campbell
Darren Monteith
David Bradbury
David McKie
Dayne Moore
Declan Tremble
Finlay Johnston
Fraser Magee
Fraser Scott
Gary Tweedie
Graeme Kilpatrick
Grant Learmont
Jai Wilson
James Struthers
Jamie Dalziel
John Kirkaldie
Jonathan Boyd
Keith Proudfoot
Kieran McKie
Kieron McCulloch
Murray Coulthard
Oliver Spence
Robson Halliday
Ross Newlands
Rowan McGill
Russell Jardine
Ryan Adamson
Sam Hughes
Sean Kevan
Shaun Handling
Stephen McDill
Stuart Alison
Stuart Douglas
Tom Smith
William Black

Lochar Thistle
Manager: Nikki White
Adam McMath
Alan Hodgson
Ben Wilson
Blair Steele
Cameron McDougall
Craig Jones
Craig McCrone
Craig Muir
Craig Neill
Darren Martin
Darren McKnight
Darren Stevenson
Dean Rea
Dylan Neill
Hamish Currie
Jake Thompson
Jamie Crosbie
Joe Jardine
Jordan Jones
Keiran Roan

Kieran Krause
Lee Martin
Mark Neill
Michael McGauchie
Nikki White
Robbie Hogg
Robbie Miller
Robert Muir
Ross Hunter
Ross Woodward
Ryan Coates
Ryan Service
Scott Woodward
Steven Scott
Tommy Goss
William Dempster

Lochmaben
Adam Henderson
Alan Maxwell
Alistair Sloan
Cameron Thorburn
Connor McCrudden
Craig Scobie
Darren Howat
Darren Johnstone
Fraser Morton
Gary White
Gavin Smith
Grant Kerr
Irving Agnew
James Walker
Josh Gilston
Laurie Maxwell
Lee Livingstone
Liam Nichol
Liam Robertson
Logan Galloway
Michael Boyd
Nathan Muir
Peter Johnstone
Robbie Collins
Robson Mackay
Russell Paisley
Russell Thomson
Ryan Gilmour
Sean Currie
Shayne Watson
Stefan Ramsay
Thomas Emmerson
Thomas Herdman

Mid Annandale
Manager: Stuart Murray / Douglas White, then Paddy Flannery
Alistair Ferguson
Andrew Dorrance
Andrew Thom
Andrew White
Barry Morton
Ben Robson
Benjamin Wagner
Callum Smith
Cammy Dean
Connor Graham
Conor Murray
Craig Murray
Darren Notman
Dean Smith
Denver Milligan
Drew Jackson
Josh Davidson
Karlton Rudd
Keith Houston
Kieran Kenny
Kyran Jackson
Levi Carrick
Matthew Copeland
Michael Henderson
Patrick Flannery
Peter Crolla
Robson McKay
Sam Copeland
Sean Dunbar
Volcan Yuldiz

Newton Stewart
Manager: John Kiltie
Aaron MacGuire
Alex Dick
Alistair Fisher
Dale Leith
Euan Drysdale
Gary Flannigan
Graeme Blain
John Kiltie
Johnny Fisher
Kyle McCutcheon
Lewis Dawson
Marc Whyte
Martyn Henry
Matthew Deazeley
Michael Wilson
Robbie Thomson
Robert Dargie
Robert Hughan
Robert Middleton
Roddy Cooksley
Rory Drysdale
Ross McCrindle
Ryan Dawson
Ryan Holmes
Ryan McKie
Scott Forrester
Taylor Kiltie
Thomas Garrett

Nithsdale Wanderers
Aidan Lang
Andrew Wallace
Ben Johnston
Brandon Wallace
Brett Lawrie
Callum Kilpatrick
Colin Bell
Dale West
Damion Finlayson
David Thomson
Declan Farrow
Dillan Wells
Dylan Irving
Dylan McLean
Ethan Weir
Finlay Lang
Gary Morrison
Gary Robertson
Graeme Park
James Grozier
James Houston
Jamie Kerr
Jordan Telfer
Kevin Roy
Kris Barbour
Kris Herries
Kris Hynd
Lee McGinley
Lewis Lang
Lewis West
Logan Hamilton
Lori Johnson
Mark McGinley
Martin Bell
Martin Milne
Mitchell Black
Niall McGarva
Patrick Lopez
Paul Lopez
Reece Griffiths
Regan Farrow
Richard Dalzell
Ross Cook
Russell Currie
Sam Harvey
Sam Simpson
Scott Fleming
Sean McKenzie
Shaun McHugh
Shaun Perry
Steven Hyslop
Stuart Bell
Stuart Bennie
Stuart Campbell

St Cuthbert Wanderers
Managers: Raymond Gordon / Craig Fraser
Andrew Donley
Ben Jaekel
Bryce Wilson
Colin Carnochan
Craig Rudd
David Kirk
Farrell O'Sullivan
Fraser Henderson
Grant Middlemiss
Gregor Patterson
Hugh Cameron
Ian Miller
Jack Loudon
Jack McMurdo
Jak Dingwall
Joe McMillan
Louie Forsyth
Nathan Cannon
Phillip Middlemiss
Raymond Gordon
Roman Soltys
Ross Hunter
Ross Wilson
Scot Alexander
Scott Milligan
Sebastian Teneggi
Zak Caldwell

Threave Rovers
Manager: Scott Wilby
Alastair Barnes
Andrew Forsyth
Ben Irving
Callum Wilson
Connor Docherty
Connor Jamieson
Connor Liddell
Conor Barnes
Corey Thomson
Craig McKeand
Dale Milligan
Daniel Graham
Greig Goodwin
Jake Gemmell
Jay McInally
Liam Gibson
Liam Patterson
Luke Hammond
Luke McMurtrie
Matthew Wilson
Paul Gray
Ross Gray
Scott Wilby
Shaun Milligan
Steven Couper
Vincent Parker

Upper Annandale
Manager: Bryan Gilfillan
Aaron Bell
Adam Uphill
Bailey White
Bryan Gilfillan
Callum Benson
Callum Williams
Cameron Grierson
Darren Dunbar
Darren Ferbie
Dean Richardson
Dion Abe Irving
Ewan Gourlay
Graham Maxwell
Grant Watson
Jamie Wylie
Joseph Usher
Josh Usher
Kieran McCrudden
Liam Robertson
Logan Dixon
Luke Proudfoot
Mark Leighfield
Michael Mendy
Michael Swan
Morgan Etchells
Neil Roddick
Peter Pagan
Richard Swan
Robbie Matthews
Ryan Johnstone
Sam Henderson
Scott Porteous
Stefan Jackson
Steven Watt

Wigtown and Bladnoch
Manager: Mickey Doygan (ex Stranraer player) Coach Ivan White
Blair Dougan
Callum Scott
Chris Chilton (ex Stranraer U17)
Iam Miller (ex Threave R)

John Lowe (ex Newton Stewart, St Cuthbert W)
Jordan Rose (ex Stranraer U17)
Justin Nicholl
Lewis Dunn (ex Dalbeattie Star)
Lewis McIntyre (ex Kilwinning R)
Lewis Richardson (ex Newton Stewart)
Mark Hoad (ex Bridge Ams)
Mark Whorlow (ex Stranraer)
Martin Flannighan
Martin McCaulay
Martyn Roddie (ex Bar 12)
Matthew Robertson (ex Creetown)
Neil Erskine
Reece Agnew
Richard Jones (ex Stranraer)
Robert Jamieson
Robert Paisley
Stuart Cluckie (ex Threave R)
Tom Garrett (ex Newton Stewart)
Tyler Rennie (ex Stranraer U17)
William White

South of Scotland League Early Season Fixtures 2017/18

Saturday, July 29
Abbey Vale – Annan Athletic
Creetown – Bonnyton Thistle
Dumfries YMCA – Heston Rovers
Mid Annandale – Wigtown and Bladnoch
Newton Stewart – Nithsdale Wanderers
Stranraer – Lochmaben
Threave Rovers – Lochar Thistle
Upper Annandale – St Cuthbert Wanderers

Wednesday, August 2 (7.30pm)
Annan Athletic – Lochar Thistle
Heston Rovers – Nithsdale Wanderers
Lochmaben – Mid Annandale
Newton Stewart – Bonnyton Thistle
St Cuthbert Wanderers – Wigtown and Bladnoch
Stranraer – Creetown
Threave Rovers – Dumfries YMCA
Upper Annandale – Abbey Vale

Saturday, August 5
Abbey Vale – Mid Annandale
Bonnyton Thistle – St Cuthbert Wanderers
Creetown – Heston Rovers
Dumfries YMCA – Newton Stewart
Lochar Thistle – Stranraer
Lochmaben – Threave Rovers
Nithsdale Wanderers – Annan Athletic
Wigtown and Bladnoch – Upper Annandale

Wednesday, August 9
Annan Athletic – Mid Annandale
Bonnyton Thistle – Stranraer
Heston Rovers – Abbey Vale
Lochar Thistle – Creetown
Lochmaben – Upper Annandale
Nithsdale Wanderers – Dumfries YMCA

Friday, August 11
Annan Athletic – Lochmaben

Saturday, August 12
Heston Rovers – Bonnyton Thistle
Lochar Thistle – Abbey Vale
Stranraer – Mid Annandale
SCFA Alba Cup

Tuesday, August 15
Lochmaben – Lochar Thistle

Wednesday, August 16
Bonnyton Thistle – Abbey Vale
Creetown – Newton Stewart
Dumfries YMCA – Annan Athletic
Mid Annandale – Upper Annandale
St Cuthbert Wanderers – Heston Rovers
Threave Rovers – Nithsdale Wanderers
Wigtown and Bladnoch – Stranraer

Friday, August 18
Annan Athletic – Heston Rovers

Saturday, August 19
Abbey Vale – Nithsdale Wanderers
Bonnyton Thistle – Wigtown and Bladnoch
Lochar Thistle – Dumfries YMCA
Lochmaben – Creetown
Newton Stewart – Mid Annandale
St Cuthbert Wanderers – Stranraer
Upper Annandale – Threave Rovers

Wednesday, August 23
Abbey Vale – Lochmaben
Creetown – Annan Athletic
Dumfries YMCA – Bonnyton Thistle
Heston Rovers – Lochar Thistle
Mid Annandale – St Cuthbert Wanderers
Nithsdale Wanderers – Upper Annandale
Stranraer – Newton Stewart
Wigtown and Bladnoch – Threave Rovers

Saturday, August 26
Bonnyton Thistle – Annan Athletic
Heston Rovers – Threave Rovers
Mid Annandale – Creetown
Newton Stewart – Lochar Thistle
Nithsdale Wanderers – Wigtown and Bladnoch
St Cuthbert Wanderers – Lochmaben
Stranraer FC – Abbey Vale
Upper Annandale – Dumfries YMCA

Wednesday, September 6
Annan Athletic – Upper Annandale
Bonnyton Thistle – Nithsdale Wanderers
Dumfries YMCA – Stranraer
Heston Rovers – Lochmaben
Mid Annandale – Lochar Thistle
Newton Stewart – Wigtown and Bladnoch
St Cuthbert Wanderers – Abbey Vale
Threave Rovers – Creetown

Saturday, September 9
South of Scotland League Cup

Wednesday, September 13
Dumfries YMCA – Wigtown and Bladnoch
Newton Stewart – Threave Rovers
St Cuthbert Wanderers – Nithsdale Wanderers

Saturday, September 16
Creetown – St Cuthbert Wanderers
Mid Annandale – Bonnyton Thistle
Newton Stewart – Annan Athletic
Stranraer – Heston Rovers
+ South Region Challenge Cup

Saturday, September 23
Abbey Vale – Dumfries YMCA
Annan Athletic – Stranraer
Heston Rovers – Mid Annandale
Lochar Thistle – St Cuthbert Wanderers
Nithsdale Wanderers – Creetown
Threave Rovers – Bonnyton Thistle
Upper Annandale – Newton Stewart
Wigtown and Bladnoch – Lochmaben

Saturday, September 30
Potts Cup

Wednesday, October 4
Annan Athletic – St Cuthbert Wanderers
Heston Rovers – Wigtown and Bladnoch
Newton Stewart – Abbey Vale
Threave Rovers – Stranraer

Saturday, October 14
Abbey Vale – Creetown
Lochar Thistle – Bonnyton Thistle
Lochmaben – Newton Stewart
Nithsdale Wanderers – Stranraer
St Cuthbert Wanderers – Dumfries YMCA
Threave Rovers – Mid Annandale
Upper Annandale – Heston Rovers
Wigtown and Bladnoch – Annan Athletic

Saturday, October 28
Tweedie Cup

Saturday, November 4
Bonnyton Thistle – Lochmaben
Creetown – Dumfries YMCA
Heston Rovers – Newton Stewart
Nithsdale Wanderers – Lochar Thistle
St Cuthbert Wanderers – Mid Annandale
Threave Rovers – Annan Athletic
Upper Annandale – Stranraer
Wigtown and Bladnoch –

Senior Non League Clubs - Highland League

Club	**Brora Rangers**
Formed	1878
Joined HL	1962
Ground	Dudgeon Park
Tel	01408 621231
Postcode	KW9 6QH
Capacity	2000
Secretary	Kevin Mackay
E Mail	brorarangersfc@highlandleague.com
Home Top 2016/17	Red
Shorts	Red
Nickname(s)	Cattachs

Club	**Buckie Thistle**
Formed	1889
Joined HL	1909
Ground	Victoria Park
Tel	01542 831946
Postcode	AB56 1BJ
Capacity	5000
Secretary	David Pirie
E Mail	buckiethistlefc@highlandleague.com
Home Top 2016/17	Green and White Hoops
Shorts	White
Nickname(s)	Jags

Club	**Clachnacuddin**
Formed	1886
Joined HL	1893 (Founder Members)
Ground	Grant Street Park
Tel	01463 718261
Postcode	IV3 8DR
Capacity	1500
Secretary	Douglas Noble
E Mail	clachnacuddinfc@highlandleague.com
Home Top 2016/17	White
Shorts	Black
Nickname(s)	Lilywhites

Club	**Cove Rangers**
Formed	1922
Joined HL	1986
Ground	2016/17 games at various venues, 2016/17
Postcode	mainly at Harlaw Park, Inverurie and Station
	Park, Forfar
Tel	
Capacity	
Secretary	Duncan Little
E Mail	coverangersfc@highlandleague.com
Home Top 2016/17	Blue and White
Shorts	Blue
Nickname(s)	Cove

Club	**Deveronvale**
Formed	1938
Joined HL	1938
Ground	Princess Royal Park, Banff
Postcode	AB45 1AZ
Tel	01261 818303
Capacity	5000
Secretary	Stewart McPherson
E Mail	deveronvalefc@highlandleague.com
Home Top 2016/17	Red with White Trim
Shorts	Red
Nickname(s)	Vale

Club	**Formartine United**
Formed	1946
Joined HL	2009
Ground	North Lodge Park, Pitmedden
Tel	01651 843266
Postcode	AB41 7PA
Capacity	2500
Secretary	Bryan Braidwood
E Mail	formartineunitedfc@highlandleague.com
Home Top 2016/17	Red and White Stripes
Shorts	White or Red
Nickname(s)	

Club	**Forres Mechanics**
Formed	1884
Joined HL	1893 (Founder Members)
Ground	Mosset Park
Postcode	IV36 1AU
Tel	01309 675096
Capacity	1500
Secretary	David McDonald
E Mail	forresmechanicsfc@highlandleague.com
Home Top 2016/17	Gold with Chocolate and White Flashes
Shorts	Gold
Nickname(s)	Can Cans

Club	**Fort William**
Formed	1984
Joined HL	1985
Ground	Claggan Park
Postcode	PH33 6TE
Tel	01397 698003
Capacity	4000
Secretary	Marie McMillan
E Mail	fortwilliamfc@highlandleague.com
Home Top 2016/17	Amber
Shorts	Black
Nickname(s)	Fort

b	**Fraserburgh**
med	1910
ned HL	1921
und	Bellslea Park
tcode	AB43 9BB
	01346 518444
acity	3000
retary	Finlay Noble
lail	fraserburghfc@highlandleague.com
ne Top 2016/17	Black and White Stripes
rts	Black
kname(s)	Broch

b	**Huntly**
med	1928
ned HL	1928
und	Christie Park
tcode	AB54 8JE
	07867 625303
acity	1800
retary	Alix Turner
lail	huntlyfc@highlandleague.com
me Top 2016/17	Black and Gold Stripes
rts	Black
kname(s)	

b	**Inverurie Locos**
med	1903
ned HL	2001
und	Harlaw Park
tcode	AB51 4SG
	01467 622168
acity	2500
retary	Billy Thomson
lail	inverurielocoworksfc@highlandleague.com
me Top 2016/17	Red with Black Band
rts	Black
kname(s)	Locos

b	**Keith**
med	1910
ned HL	1924
und	Kynoch Park
tcode	AB55 5EN
	01542 882629
acity	4000
retary	Ryan Rodger
lail	keithfc@highlandleague.com
me Top 2016/17	Maroon and Sky Blue
rts	Maroon and Sky Blue
kname(s)	Maroons

Club	**Lossiemouth**
Formed	1945
Joined HL	1946
Ground	Grant Park
Postcode	IV31 6JG
Tel	01343 813717
Capacity	2400
Secretary	Alan McIntosh
E Mail	lossiemouthfc@highlandleague.com
Home Top 2016/17	Red
Shorts	Red
Nickname(s)	Coasters

Club	**Nairn County**
Formed	1914
Joined HL	1919
Ground	Station Park
Postcode	IV12 5LT
Tel	01667 454298
Capacity	3000
Match Secretary	Donald Matheson
E Mail	nairncountyfc@highlandleague.com
Home Top 2016/17	Yellow
Shorts	Black
Nickname(s)	County

Club	**Rothes**
Formed	1938
Joined HL	1938
Ground	MacKessack Park
Postcode	AB38 7AD
Tel	01340 831972
Capacity	1731
Secretary	Andrew Simpson
E Mail	rothesfc@highlandleague.com
Home Top 2016/17	Tangerine
Shorts	Black
Nickname(s)	Speysiders

Club	**Strathspey Thistle**
Formed	1993
Joined HL	2009
Ground	Seafield Park
Postcode	PH26 3HY
Tel	01479 831233
Capacity	2000
Secretary	Malcolm Taylor
E Mail	strathspeythistlefc@highlandleague.com
Home Top 2016/17	Blue
Shorts	Blue
Nickname(s)	

Club	Turriff United
Formed	1954
Joined HL	2009
Ground	The Haughs
Postcode	AB53 4ER
Tel	01888 562169
Capacity	1200
Secretary	Morgan Greig
E Mail	turriffunitedfc@highlandleague.com
Home Top 2016/17	Blue and Red
Shorts	Blue and Red
Nickname(s)	Turra

Club	Wick Academy
Formed	1893
Joined HL	1994
Ground	Harmsworth Park
Postcode	KW1 5NH
Tel	01955 602446
Capacity	2000
Secretary	Jan Robertson
E Mail	wickacademyfc@highlandleague.com
Home Top 2016/17	Black and White Stripes
Shorts	Black
Nickname(s)	Scorries

Senior Non League Clubs - Lowland League

Club	BSC (Glasgow)
Formed	2014
Joined LL	2014
Ground	Recreation Park, Alloa (for 2017/18)
Postcode	FK10 1RY
Tel	01259 219596 (Alloa Ath FC)
E Mail	geo_fraser@hotmail.co.uk
Capacity	2500
Secretary	George Fraser
Home Top 2016/17	Yellow
Shorts	Yellow
Nickname(s)	

Club	Civil Service Strollers
Formed	1908
Joined LL	2016
Ground	Christie Innes Park (Muirhouse)
Postcode	EH4 5EJ
Tel	0131 3321175
E Mail	keith.l.stewart@bt.com
Capacity	c1000
Secretary	Keith Stewart
Home Top 2016/17	Red
Shorts	Red
Nickname(s)	Civvy

Club	Cumbernauld Colts
Formed	1969
Joined LL	2015
Ground	Broadwood Stadium
Postcode	G68 9NE
Tel	07798646110
E Mail	stewart.mckenzie@ggc.scot.nhs.uk
Capacity	7936
Secretary	Stewart McKenzie
Home Top 2016/17	Yellow
Shorts	Blue
Nickname(s)	Colts

Club	Dalbeattie Star
Formed	c1900
Joined LL	2013
Ground	Islecroft Stadium
Postcode	DG5 4HE
Tel	07860 549444 (Match Sec Mobile)
E Mail	bob@solwaypressservices.freeserve.co.uk
Capacity	c1500
Match Secretary	Robert Geddes
Home Top 2016/17	Red and Black
Shorts	Black
Nickname(s)	Star

Club	East Kilbride
Formed	2010
Joined LL	2013
Ground	K Park
Postcode	G74 2AG
Tel	01355 243000
E Mail	eastkilbride2@slfl.co.uk
Capacity	c900
Secretary	David McKenna
Home Top 2016/17	Navy and Gold Halves
Shorts	Navy
Nickname(s)	Kilby

Club	East Stirlingshire
Formed	1881
Joined LL	2016
Ground	Ochilview Park, Stenhousemuir
Postcode	FK5 4QL
Tel	01324 871171 (Club Office)
	01324 562992 (Ground - Stenhousemuir FC)
E Mail	Fceaststirlingshire@gmail.com
Capacity	3746
Secretary	Andy Williamson
Home Top 2016/17	Black and White Hoops
Shorts	Black
Nickname(s)	Shire

Club	**Edinburgh University**
Formed	1877
Joined LL	2014
Ground	East Peffermill
Postcode	EH16 5LL
Tel	0131 661 8842
E Mail	euafc@ed.ac.uk
Capacity	c1500
Secretary	Max Verkaik
Home Top 2016/17	Green
Shorts	Navy Blue
Nickname(s)	Uni

Club	**Edusport Academy**
Formed	
Joined SOSL	2014
Ground	Galabank, Annan
Postcode	DG12 5AA
Tel	07795807927
E Mail	c.ewing@edusportacademy.com
Capacity	c800
Secretary	Chris Ewing
Home Top 2016/17	Black
Shorts	Black
Nickname(s)	

Club	**Gala Fairydean Rovers**
Formed	2013
Joined LL	2013
Ground	Netherdale
Postcode	TD1 3HE
Tel	07738 615 562
E Mail	graememciver@btinternet.com
Capacity	c2500
Secretary	Graeme McIver
Home Top 2016/17	Red and Black Stripes
Shorts	White
Nickname(s)	Gala

Club	**Gretna 2008**
Formed	2008
Joined LL	2013
Ground	Raydale Park
Postcode	DG16 5AP
Tel	Sec Mobile: 07902 826124
E Mail	kevinsmith@gretnafc2008.co.uk
Capacity	c1500
Secretary	Kevin Smith
Home Top 2016/17	White and Black Hoops
Shorts	Black
Nickname(s)	

Club	**Hawick Royal Albert**
Formed	1947
Joined LL	2016
Ground	Albert Park
Postcode	TD9 8AG
Tel	01450 374231
E Mail	dpurves4@aol.com
Capacity	c2000
Secretary	Douglas Purves
Home Top 2016/17	Blue and Red
Shorts	White
Nickname(s)	Albert

Club	**Selkirk**
Formed	1880
Joined LL	2013
Ground	Yarrow Park
Postcode	TD7 5AX
Tel	07984 984572 (Sec Mob)
E Mail	selkirkfootballclub@hotmail.co.uk
Capacity	c2000
Secretary	Sheree Davidson
Home Top 2016/17	Blue
Shorts	Blue
Nickname(s)	Souters

Club	**Spartans**
Formed	1951
Joined LL	2013
Ground	Ainslie Park, Edinburgh
Postcode	EH5 2HF
Tel	0131 552 7854
E Mail	macabiteam@hotmail.com
Capacity	c2500
Secretary	John McCabe
Home Top 2016/17	White
Shorts	Red
Nickname(s)	

Club	**Vale of Leithen**
Formed	1891
Joined LL	2013
Ground	Victoria Park, Innerleithen
Postcode	EH44 6RB (approx)
Tel	Mobile: 07763 514158
E Mail	ianhaggarty11@gmail.com
Capacity	c1500
Secretary	Ian Haggarty
Home Top 2016/17	Navy Blue
Shorts	White
Nickname(s)	Vale

Club	University of Stirling
Formed	1969
Joined LL	2013
Ground	Falkirk Stadium (for 2016/17)
Postcode	FK2 9EE
Tel	Mobile: 07740 500140
E Mail	r.n.gowrie@stirling.ac.uk
Capacity	8750
Secretary	Raleigh Gowrie
Home Top 2016/17	Green
Shorts	Green
Nickname(s)	Uni

Club	Whitehill Welfare
Formed	1953
Joined LL	2013
Ground	Ferguson Park, Rosewell
Postcode	EH24 9DS
Tel	0131 440 0115
E Mail	whitehillwelfare@supanet.com
Capacity	c1500
Secretary	Andrew Renwick
Home Top 2016/17	Maroon with Sky Blue Sleeves
Shorts	White
Nickname(s)	Welfare

Senior Non League Clubs - East of Scotland League

Club	Burntisland Shipyard
Formed	1925
Joined ESL	2012
Ground	Shipyard Recreation Ground
Postcode	KY3 0JG
Tel	07867 795898 (Sec Mobile)
E Mail	abeveridge.shipyard@sky.com
Capacity	c1500
Secretary	Andrew Beveridge
Home Top 2016/17	White
Shorts	White
Nickname(s)	Shippy

Club	Coldstream
Formed	1895
Joined ESL	
Ground	Home Park
Postcode	TD12 4DT
Tel	01890 883085
E Mail	allan@integrityifa.com
Capacity	c1500
Secretary	Allan Easton
Home Top 2016/17	Blue
Shorts	Blue
Nickname(s)	Streamers

Club	Eyemouth United
Formed	1945
Joined ESL	1945
Ground	Warner Park
Postcode	TD14 5DX
Tel	Sec 07526 244 570
E Mail	tcollin71@hotmail.com
Capacity	c1000
Secretary	Tommy Collin
Home Top 2016/17	Maroon
Shorts	Maroon
Nickname(s)	Fishermen

Club	Heriot Watt University
Formed	1971
Joined ESL	1971
Ground	Riccarton Campus
Postcode	EH14 4AS
Tel	Sec 07747 616 402
E Mail	info@hwufc.org.uk
Capacity	c1000
Secretary	Alasdair Matheson
Home Top 2016/17	Yellow
Shorts	Blue
Nickname(s)	Watt

Club	Kelty Hearts
Formed	1975
Joined ESL	2017
Ground	New Central Park
Postcode	KY4 0AG
Tel	07982 725903
E Mail	keltygaz@yahoo.co.uk
Capacity	3000
Secretary	Garry Grandison
Home Top 2016/17	Maroon
Shorts	White
Nickname(s)	Hearts

Club	Leith Athletic
Formed	1996
Joined ESL	1991 (as Manor Th)
Ground	Meadowbank 3G
Postcode	EH7 6AE
Tel	Sec 07850 772 706
E Mail	tam.currie@leithathleticfc.com
Capacity	c200
Secretary	Tam Currie
Home Top 2016/17	White and Black Stripes
Shorts	Black
Nickname(s)	

ub	**Lothian Thistle Hutchison Vale**
rmed	1969
ned ESL	1995
ound	Saughton Enclosure
stcode	EH11 3BQ
	Sec 07730 256 783
Aail	tom@lothianthistlefc.co.uk
pacity	c3000
cretary	Tom Allison
me Top 2016/17	Black and Yellow
orts	White
ckname(s)	Hutchie

ub	**Ormiston**
rmed	1999
ned ESL	1999
ound	Recreation Ground (new location for 2016/17 adjacent to old pitch)
stcode	EH35 5LQ
l	0131 539 0687
Mail	tamcuthbert@blueyonder.co.uk
pacity	c2000
cretary	Tom Cuthbert
me Top 2016/17	Maroon
orts	Maroon
ckname(s)	Ormy

ub	**Peebles Rovers**
rmed	1893
ned ESL	1979 (Rejoined)
ound	Whitestone Park
stcode	EH45 8BE
l	01721 722669
Mail	mcdonaldjmac@aol.com
pacity	c1500
cretary	Allan MacDonald
me Top 2016/17	Red
orts	Red
ckname(s)	Rovers

ub	**Preston Athletic**
rmed	1945
ined LL	2013
ound	Pennypit Park
stcode	EH32 9JQ
l	01875 815221
Mail	prestonathletic@slfl.co.uk
pacity	c3000
cretary	Lesley Birrell
ome Top 2016/17	Blue / White
orts	Blue
ckname(s)	Panners

Club	**Stirling University EOS**
Formed	1969
Joined ESL	2013
Ground	Gannochy Sports Complex
Postcode	FK9 4LA
Tel	01786 466901
E Mail	harryballindsay@gmail.com
Capacity	c1000
Secretary	Harry Ball
Home Top 2016/17	Green
Shorts	Green
Nickname(s)	

Club	**Tweedmouth Rangers**
Formed	
Joined ESL	2016
Ground	Old Shielfield Park
Postcode	TD15 2EF
Tel	Sec 01289 304071
E Mail	alexander.aitchison115@btinternet.com
Capacity	c1500
Secretary	Alex Aitchison
Home Top 2016/17	Orange with white trim
Shorts	Navy Blue
Nickname(s)	

Club	**Tynecastle**
Formed	1928
Joined ESL	1987
Ground	Saughton Enclosure
Postcode	EH17 7HY
Tel	Sec 07889 931 054
E Mail	alistair@wilkielaw.co.uk
Capacity	c1000
Secretary	Alistair Wilkie
Home Top 2016/17	Maroon
Shorts	White
Nickname(s)	Tynie

Senior Non League Clubs - South of Scotland League

Club	**Abbey Vale**
Formed	1971
Joined SOSL	2001
Ground	Maryfield Park, New Abbey
Postcode	DG2 8BY
Tel	01387256004 (Sec)
E Mail	info@abbeyvalefc.co.uk
Capacity	c1000
Secretary	David Morton
Home Top 2016/17	Black / Amber
Shorts	Black
Nickname(s)	Vale

Club	**Bonnyton Thistle**
Formed	1912 (Reformed 1978)
Joined SOSL	2017
Ground	Harriet Road, Townholm, Kilmarnock
Postcode	KA3 1BB
Tel	
E Mail	
Capacity	1000
Secretary	Neil Wilson
Home Top 2016/17	Red / Black
Shorts	Black
Nickname(s)	

Club	**Creetown**
Formed	1905
Joined SOSL	1946
Ground	Castle Cary Park
Postcode	
Tel	01671820628 (Sec)
E Mail	
Capacity	c1000
Secretary	Steve Dorrans
Home Top 2016/17	Yellow
Shorts	Black
Nickname(s)	Ferrytoun

Club	**Dumfries YMCA**
Formed	
Joined SOSL	2014
Ground	Dumfries HS 3G
Postcode	DG1 1PX
Tel	01576202438 (Sec)
E Mail	
Capacity	c1000
Secretary	Blair Crossan
Home Top 2016/17	Red
Shorts	Red
Nickname(s)	YM

Club	**Heston Rovers**
Formed	1978
Joined SOSL	2008
Ground	Palmerston Park, Dumfries
Postcode	DG2 9BA
Tel	Sec 07779289748
E Mail	
Capacity	7620
Secretary	Bobby Lumsden
Home Top 2016/17	Black and White stripes
Shorts	Black
Nickname(s)	

Club	**Lochar Thistle**
Formed	
Joined SOSL	2013
Ground	Maxwelltown High School
Postcode	DG2 0EL
Tel	Sec 07828160408
E Mail	r.caskie@btinternet.com
Capacity	c1000
Secretary	Russell Caskie
Home Top 2016/17	Red and Black Stripes
Shorts	Black
Nickname(s)	

Club	**Lochmaben**
Formed	1972
Joined SOSL	1992 (as Crichton)
Ground	King Edward Park Lockerbie (for 2016/
Postcode	DG11 2BL
Tel	01387 263285 (sec)
E Mail	tparker3659@sky.com
Capacity	c1000
Secretary	Tommy Parker
Home Top 2016/17	Navy and Black
Shorts	Black
Nickname(s)	

Club	**Mid Annandale**
Formed	1959
Joined SOSL	2003
Ground	King Edward Park Lockerbie
Postcode	DG12 5DQ
Tel	Sec 01576 202757
E Mail	
Capacity	2514
Secretary	George Trudt
Home Top 2016/17	Yellow
Shorts	Black
Nickname(s)	Mids

Club	**Newton Stewart**
Formed	1884
Joined SOSL	1946
Ground	Blairmount Park, Newton Stewart
Postcode	DG8 6NU
Tel	07702871739 (Sec Mob)
E Mail	sean.1990.campbell@gmail.com
Capacity	c1000
Secretary	Sean Campbell
Home Top 2016/17	Black and White Stripes
Shorts	Black
Nickname(s)	Creesiders

Club	**Nithsdale Wanderers**
Formed	2001
Joined SOSL	2001
Ground	Lorimer Park, Sanquhar
Postcode	DG4 6DB
Tel	0165950822 (Sec)
E Mail	
Capacity	c1000
Secretary	Stephen Cook
Home Top 2016/17	Blue
Shorts	White
Nickname(s)	

Club	**St Cuthbert Wanderers**
Formed	1879
Joined SOSL	1946
Ground	St Mary's Park, Kirkcudbright
Postcode	DG6 4AW
Tel	07813 634787
E Mail	michaelmcgarrie@gmail.com
Capacity	c 1000
Secretary	Michael McGarrie
Home Top 2016/17	Blue and White Hoops
Shorts	Blue
Nickname(s)	Saints

Club	**Threave Rovers**
Formed	1953
Joined SOSL	
Ground	Meadow Park, Castle Douglas
Postcode	DG7 1DJ
Tel	01556 504536
E Mail	davy.mcmath@scottishwater.co.uk
Capacity	c1500
Secretary	David McMath
Home Top 2016/17	Black and White Stripes
Shorts	Black
Nickname(s)	

Club	**Upper Annandale**
Formed	1966
Joined SOSL	2014
Ground	Moffat Academy
Postcode	DG10 9QF
Tel	07776166835 (Sec Mob)
E Mail	
Capacity	c800
Secretary	Bob Smith
Home Top 2016/17	Black and White
Shorts	Black
Nickname(s)	

Club	**Wigtown & Bladnoch**
Formed	1888
Joined SOSL	1946
Ground	Trammondford Park, Wigtown
Postcode	DG8 9DY (approx)
Tel	07849 432008 (Sec Mob)
E Mail	sturen@btinternet.com
Capacity	c2000
Secretary	James McColm
Home Top 2016/17	Red
Shorts	Red
Nickname(s)	

NB Wigtown and Bladnoch in abeyance for 2017/18

Details for Annan Athletic and Stranraer Reserves are in the SPFL club section towards the front of this book.

Other Licensed Non League Clubs

Club	**Banks o' Dee**
Formed	1902
Ground	Spain Park, Aberdeen
Postcode	AB12 3AB
Tel	01244 893333 (Ground)
E Mail	tom.ewan@mac.com
Capacity	2300
Secretary	Thomas Ewan
Home Top 2016/17	Sky Blue and Nevy Hoops
Shorts	Blue
Nickname(s)	Rechabites
Club	**Girvan**
Formed	1947
Ground	Hamilton Park
Postcode	KA26 9HF
Tel	07759 753425
E Mail	andrewsinclair35@hotmail.com
Capacity	3000
Secretary	Andrew Sinclair
Home Top 2016/17	Azure and Black Stripes
Shorts	Black
Nickname(s)	
Club	**Glasgow University**
Formed	1877
Ground	Excelsior Stadium (for SFA matches)
Postcode	ML6 8QZ
Tel	01236 622000
E Mail	donniefergusson@aol.com
Capacity	10101
Secretary	Donald Fergusson
Home Top 2016/17	Gold
Shorts	Black
Nickname(s)	

Club	**Golspie Sutherland**
Formed	1877
Ground	King George V Park, Golspie
Postcode	KW10 6SN
Tel	07774 913946
E Mail	email@jamesurquhart.co.uk
Capacity	1000
Secretary	James Urquhart
Home Top 2016/17	Royal Blue
Shorts	Royal Blue
Nickname(s)	
Club	**Linlithgow Rose**
Formed	1889
Ground	Prestonfield
Postcode	EH49 6HF
Tel	01506 842108
E Mail	calder.william@hotmail.co.uk
Capacity	4000
Secretary	William Calder
Home Top 2016/17	Maroon
Shorts	White
Nickname(s)	Rosey-Posey, Gallant

MISCELLANEOUS FOOTBALL

North Caledonian League 2016/17

RECENT LEAGUE CHAMPIONS

1970/1	Dingwall Thistle
1971/2	Dingwall Thistle
1972/3	Alness
1973/4	Alness
1974/5	Golspie Sutherland
1975/6	Golspie Sutherland
1976/7	Invergordon
1977/8	Dingwall Thistle
1978/9	Wick Academy
1979/80	Wick Academy
1980/1	Wick Academy
1981/2	Wick Academy
1982/3	Bunillidh Thistle
1983/4	Muir of Ord
1984/5	Fort William
1985/6	Muir of Ord
1986/7	Wick Academy
1987/8	Invergordon
1988/9	Bunillidh Thistle
1989/90	Balintore
1990/1	Balintore
1991/2	Clachnacuddin Reserves
1992/3	Golspie Sutherland
1993/4	Halkirk United
1994/5	ICT Reserves
1995/6	Fearn Thistle
1996/7	Ross County Reserves
1997/8	ICT Reserves
1998/9	Golspie Sutherland
1999/00	Thurso
2000/1	Alness United
2001/2	Invergordon
2002/3	Thurso
2003/4	Golspie Sutherland
2004/5	Thurso
2005/6	Balintore
2006/7	Golspie Sutherland
2007/8	Golspie Sutherland
2008/9	Golspie Sutherland
2009/10	Thurso
2010/1	Halkirk United
2011/2	Halkirk United
2012/3	Thurso
2013/4	Halkirk United
2014/5	Golspie Sutherland
2015/6	Halkirk United

	AU	GS	HAL	IGD	IVS	O	TSD	T
Alness United		Nov 26	Sep 3	Nov 19	Dec 10	Apr 8	Oct 22	Sep 24
		4-3	0-0	2-5	0-4	2-4	3-2	0-4
Golspie Sutherland	Mar 25		Oct 22	Feb 25	Oct 29	Feb 4	Apr 8	Jan 21
	3-2		3-2	1-2	3-1	0-2	4-2	1-1
Halkirk United	Feb 4	Mar 11		Feb 18	Jan 21	Mar 4	Nov 19	Sep 9
	6-3	4-1		3-2	3-0	1-0	5-0	3-1
Invergordon	Sep 17	Oct 8	Dec 3		Feb 4	Oct 22	Sep 3	Mar 18
	2-0	5-4	1-0		3-1	1-0	3-3	1-0
Inverness Athletic	Oct 15	Mar 4	Oct 8	Sep 10		Apr 1	Dec 3	Nov 19
	10-0	3-3	1-4	1-4		1-3	1-3	1-1
Orkney	Oct 8	Mar 18	Sep 17	Jan 21	Sep 3		Dec 10	Jan 28
	5-2	4-2	2-0	2-0	2-0		1-2	1-0
Tain St Duthus	Jan 21	Sep 24	Oct 1	Mar 11	Sep 10	Oct 29		Feb 25
	1-1	0-3	3-0	0-1	4-2	1-2		1-2
Thurso	Mar 11	Dec 3	Apr 1	Dec 10	Feb 18	Nov 26	Oct 8	
	2-0	1-2	0-2	1-4	6-1	1-1	2-0	

	P	W	D	L	F	A	GD	Pts
Invergordon	14	11	1	2	34	18	16	34
Orkney FC	14	10	1	3	29	13	16	31
Halkirk United	14	9	1	4	33	17	16	28
Golspie Sutherland	14	6	2	6	33	33	0	20
Thurso	14	5	3	6	22	18	4	18
St.Duthus	14	4	2	8	22	30	-8	14
Inverness Athletic	14	2	2	10	27	39	-12	8
Alness United	14	2	2	10	19	51	-32	8

HOME GROUNDS USED

Alness United	Dalmore Park
Invergordon	Recreation Grounds
Orkney	Kirkwall Grammar School Grass
	Kirkwall Grammar School Astro
	Stromness 3G
	Dounby Playing Fields
Halkirk	Morrison Park
Inverness Athletic	Inverarnie Park
	Highland Football Academy
	Pavilion Park, Muir of Ord
Tain St Duthus	Links Playing Fields
Thurso	St Georges Park, aka The Dammies
	Naver All Weather Pitch
Golspie Sutherland	King George V Playting Fields

North Caledonian Cup							
QF	05/11/2016	Golspie Sutherland	Alness United	9	0		
QF	05/11/2016	Halkirk United	Thurso	4	1		
QF	05/11/2016	Invergordon	Inverness Athletic	8	1		
QF	30/11/2016	Lossiemouth	Tain St Duthus	2	3		
SF	26/11/2016	Halkirk United	Invergordon	1	4		
SF	17/12/2016	Golspie Sutherland	Tain St Duthus	2	1		
F	28/01/2017	Golspie Sutherland	Invergordon	2	1		at Brora
Football Times Cup							
1	10/09/2016	Orkney	Lewis & Harris	0	2		at Alness
1	10/09/2016	Shetland	Tain St Duthus	3	3	5-3 pens	at Halkirk
1	17/09/2016	Golspie Sutherland	Thurso	2	3		
QF	01/10/2016	Lossiemouth	Lewis & Harris	0	6		at Invergordon
QF	01/10/2016	Shetland	Alness United	2	2	5-3 pens	at KGV, Golspie
QF		Thurso	Inverness Athletic	wo	scr		
QF	24/09/2016	Halkirk United	Invergordon	0	2		
SF	15/10/2016	Invergordon	Shetland	2	1		at Halkirk
SF	22/10/2016	Lewis & Harris	Thurso	1	2		at Stafford Park, Golspie
F	29/10/2016	Invergordon	Thurso	2	0		at Helmsdale
Jock Mackay Cup							
1	18/02/2017	Alness United	Golspie Sutherland	4	1		
1	18/02/2017	Orkney	Shetland	2	1		
QF		Lossiemouth U20	Halkirk				
QF	04/03/2017	Invergordon	Thurso	1	2		
QF	11/04/2017	Orkney	Inverness Athletic	12	1		
QF	18/03/2017	Tain St Duthus	Alness United	3	1		
SF	25/03/2017	Orkney	Halkirk United	3	2		
SF	25/03/2017	Thurso	Tain St Duthus	1	2		
F	15/04/2017	Orkney	Tain St Duthus	1	1	2-1 pens	at Invergordon

North Caledonian League Cup Draws 2017/18

Football Times Cup:

1st Round
Elgin U20s v Lewis & Harris
Nairn U20s v St Duthus
Thurso v Shetland
Bunillidh Thistle v Golspie Sutherland
Inverness Athletic v Halkirk United

Quarter-Finals
Alness United v Nairn/St Duthus
Inverness/Halkirk v Orkney
Invergordon v Thurso/Shetland
Bunillidh/Golspie v Elgin/Lewis & Harris

Semi-Finals
Alness/Nairn/St Duthus v Bunillidh/Golspie/Elgin/L&H
Invergordon/Thurso/Sheltand v Inverness/Halkirk/Orkney

North Caledonian Cup:

1st Round
Golspie v Elgin U20s
Alness v Inverness Athletic

Quarter-Finals
Golspie/Elgin v Invergordon
Bunillidh Th v St Duthus
Halkirk U v Nairn U20s
Thurso v Alness/Inverness A

Semi-Finals
Bunillidh/St Duthus v Halkirk/Nairn
Golspie/Elgin/Invergordon v Thurso/Alness/Inverness

Jock Mackay Cup:

1st Round
Golspie v Elgin U20s
Sheltand v Thurso
Bunillidh Th v Invergordon
Inverness Ath v Halkirk U
Lewis & Harris v Nairn U20s

Quarter-Finals
St Duthus v Shetland/Thurso
Bunillidh/Invergordon v Alness
Lewis & Harris/Nairn v Inverness/Halkirk
Orkney v Golspie/Elgin

Semi-Finals
Orkney/Golspie/Elgin v Bunillidh/Invergordon/Alness
L&H/Nairn/Inverness/Halkirk v St Duthus/Shetland/Thurso

Tommy Ross Memorial Cup:

Quarter-Finals
Inverness Ath v St Duthus
Invergordon v Bunillidh Th
Golspie v Thurso
Alness U v Halkirk U

Semi-Finals
Golspie/Thurso v Inverness/St Duthus
Invergordon/Bunillidh Th v Alness/Halkirk

;enior County Cup Competitions 2016/17

ce regarded as important, these matches are now frequently unplayed. When they do take place it is often with ow-strength team line-ups. They are included here only for the sake of completeness rather than any great nificance.

ST OF SCOTLAND SHIELD 2016/17
2015/16 final was played:
dnesday 21/9/16, at Easter Road
ernian 1 (Gullan pen) Hearts 2 (Henderson, MacDonald), H.T. 0

s: Martin, Donaldson, Hall, O'Conner, Porteous, Smith, Walker, npbell, Gullan, Murray, Gallantes (Shanley 74).
arts: Mason, Morrison, Reid, Hamilton, Smith, Gillan, McDonald, ov, Leonard (Ritchie 90), Irving, Henderson.

2016/17 final was not played

E CUP 2016/17
draw for the 2016/17 competition was:
liminary Round (27/9/16)
st Fife 7 (McManus 3, O'Hara 2, Mercer, Insall)Burntisland pyard 0
st Fife: M. Hurst; S. Mercer; P. Slattery; C. Kane; R. Brown; J. all; T. Wallace; G. Naysmith; J. Austin; P. McManus; K. O'Hara. os: G. Good; K. Wilkie; M. Lamont.
ntisland Shipyard: M. Taylor; B. Saunders; L. Fleming; L. ntosh; K. Ford; D. Roberts; C. McAleavey; A. MacDonald; D. ylor; T. Hall; M. Black. Subs: G. Cusick; G. Buckley; B. Paterson; Doyle; D. Butt; N. McKay; C. Winter.

ni Finals -
8/16, Raith Rovers 1 (Trialist) Dunfermline Athletic 1 (5-4p)
. 0-1
th Rovers: Trialist, Trialist, Euan Valentine, James Berry, vid McKay (c), Trialist, Andrew Thorsen, Ryan Stevenson, Yan ei, (Trialist 13), Johnny Court, Jack Smith (Trialist 38) SUBS T USED: Trialist
nfermline: Cammy Gill, Reece Duncan, Paul Allen, Ewan ark, Conner Duthie, Evan Horne (Brandon Luke 73) Nat dderburn (Johnny Galloway 63), Lewis Spence (Ciaran Lafferty , Scott Lochhead, James Thomas (c), Trialist SUBS NOT ED: Robbie Crawford, Callum Smith, Josh Dunn(G/K)

wdenbeath v East Fife, wo-scr

al -
th Rovers v Cowdenbeath, 2-1, May 3 2017

th Rovers: Brian, Watson, Valentine, Berry, McDonald, McKay, l, Stevenson, Osei, Thorsen, Collins. Subs: McCann, Swanson, ith, Trialist Q.
wdenbeath: Donoghue, Watt, Kellichan, Thomson, Trialist 1, nbull, Denton, Key, Muirhead, Rooney, Swann. Subs: Trialist 2, lis, Trialist 3, McManus, George, Henderson.
; 47 mins Trialist (Connolly);2-0 54 mins Muirhead; 2-1 82 mins venson
h teams fielded their 20s sides and Cowdenbeath ran out entual winners, after a bizarre end to the match. With only two nutes left to play and Cowdenbeath leading 2-1, the Stark's Park odlights failed, plunging the stadium into darkness. The referee d Club officials he would allow ten minutes to get the lights back or he would abandon the match. The Raith Rovers ground staff d in vain to solve the problem in the allotted time but could not the lights back on and the referee duly asked the players to urn to their dressing rooms. However, just as the last players the pitch and most of the spectators had left the ground, the nts came on again! Both sets of players and their coaches nted to play the game to a finish and appealed to the referee to tart the game. After consulting an SFA official by telephone, he reed he could and would play the remaining two minutes. The yers then ran out again onto the pitch and played two minutes of tball in front of an almost empty stadium. There were no goals or significant incidents and after only 120 seconds of football, the referee blew his whistle to formally end the Fife Cup final. The trophy was duly presented to the victorious Cowdenbeath players.

FORFARSHIRE CUP 2016/17 Rd 1
The draw for the 2015/16 competition was:
Round One
Brechin City v Dundee United
St. Johnstone v Arbroath
Forfar Athletic v Dundee

Semi Finals
Brechin City of Dundee United v Forfar Athletic or Dundee
St. Johnstone or Arbroath v Montrose
None of the ties were played during 2015/16 but the Brechin v Dundee United match was scheduled for pre-season 2016/17.
9/7/16, Brechin City 0 Dundee United 5 (Johnson, Fraser, Spittal, Murray 2) Att 923
Brechin: Smith, C O'Neill (Sub Hill), Ford, McCormack, Rodger, Dale, Trouten, E Smith (Sub Graham). Caldwell, Jackson, Love. Subs Fusco, P O'Neill
Dundee Utd: Bell, Dillon (Sub Toshney), Dixon, C Donaldson, Spittal, Murdoch, Murray, Fraser, Telfer (Sub Coote), Johnson (Sub Obadeyi), Souttar. Subs not used Anier, Sukar, Ballantyne, Zwick.

As far as can be ascertained no draw was made for the 2016/17 competition.

RENFREWSHIRE CUP
The two Semi Finals are contested by the two finalists of the Renfrewshire Victoria Cup (for Amateurs) who meet Morton and St Mirren. The Final was usually played pre-season in the following season. Sometimes it has been played before the Semi Finals in which case it has been billed as a Friendly.

No matches were played during 2015/16 or 2016/17. The last match was the 2013/14 Final, held at the start of 2014/15.

STIRLINGSHIRE CUP 2015/16

The Final of the 2015/16 competition was not played and the competition was placed in abeyance for 2016/17.

The **Glasgow Cup** is now played as an Under 17 competition (see next page).

The **Ayrshire** and **Lanarkshire Cups** are now discontinued.

GLASGOW CUP 2016/17					
31-Aug	Partick Thistle	0	Celtic	5	
09-Sep	Queen's Park	1	Rangers	2	
30-Sep	Queen's Park	2	Partick Thistle	0	
05-Oct	Rangers	1	Celtic	1	
27-Oct	Celtic	3	Queen's Park	1	
28-Oct	Partick Thistle	0	Rangers	2	
19-Jan	Celtic	5	Partick Thistle	0	
18-Dec	Rangers	6	Queen's Park	0	
09-Dec	Partick Thistle	1	Queen's Park	4	
15-Feb	Celtic	1	Rangers	6	
22-Feb	Queen's Park	0	Celtic	1	
21-Feb	Rangers	3	Partick Thistle	1	
FINAL					
Apr-17	Celtic	2	Rangers	1	Firhill
			Att 1333		

Final table	P	W	D	L	F	A	GD	Pts
Rangers	6	5	1	0	20	4	16	16
Celtic	6	4	1	1	16	8	8	13
Queen's Park	6	2	0	4	8	13	-5	6
Partick Thistle	6	0	0	6	2	21	-19	0

Rangers:- Brian Kinnear; Jordan Houston, Danny Finlayson, Lewis Mayo, Scott Gray; Cammy Palmer (Zac Butte worth 71 mins); Billy Gilmour, Stephen Kelly (Michael Hewitt 84 mins); Dapo Mebude (Mati Zata 65 mins), Zak Rudden, Matthew Shiels. Not Used:- Nick Hogarth (Gk), Nathan Patterson, Jay Mack, Josh McPake

Celtic:- Ryan Mullen; Max Potter, Stephen Welsh, Robbie Deas, Daniel Church; Kerr McInroy, Kristi Marku (Kieran McGrath 76 mins); Keiran Can bell (David McKay 88 mins), Ewan Henderson, Tommy Caffrey (Grant Savoury HT); Jack Aitchison. Not Use Joshua Rae (Gk), Scott Robertson, Pa Kennedy, Andrew Kerr.

0-1	18 mins	Henderson
1-1	45 mins	Shiels
1-2	68 mins	Aitchison

Match was broadcast live on STV Glasgow.

RECENT GLASGOW CUP FINALS						
U17 Competition						
2007/8	Celtic	Rangers	3	1		
2008/9	Rangers	Celtic	2	1		Broadwood
2009/10	Rangers	Celtic	2	1		Broadwood
2010/11	Celtic	Rangers	1	0		Parkhead
2011/2	Rangers	Celtic	1	1	4-2p	Ibrox
2012/3	Rangers	Celtic	3	2		Firhill
2013/4	Celtic	Rangers	1	0		Parkhead
2014/5	Celtic	Rangers	2	0		Hampden
2015/6	Celtic	Rangers	4	0		Ibrox
2016/7	Celtic	Rangers	2	1		Firhill

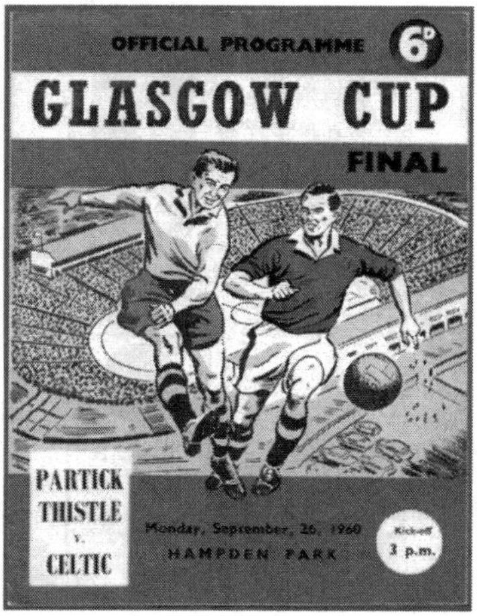

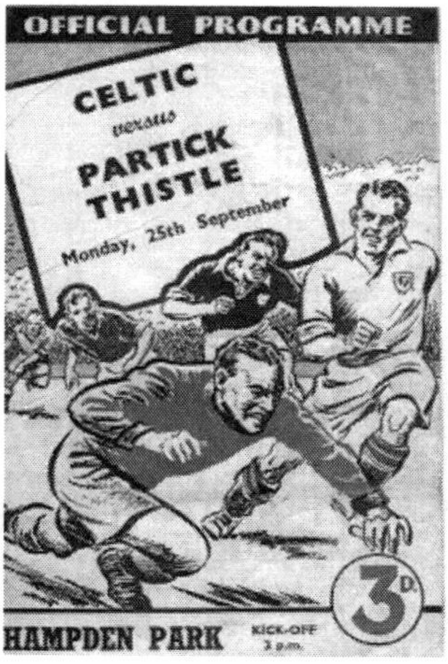

ɴiversity Football 2016/17

ver many years the biggest prize in Scottish University football was the Queen's Park Shield, competed for on 'ednesday afternoon's by the Scottish seats of learning. Nowadays the top Scottish sides compete in the various visions of the UK-wide British Universities and Colleges Sport (BUCS) tournaments. The Queen's Park Shield is ill played for but it is now a knock out competition rather than a League.

NS PREMIER NORTH

	P	W	D	L	GD	PTS	
Loughborough 1st	10	6	2	2	7	20	
Northumbria 1st	10	5	1	4	8	16	
Durham 1st	10	5	1	4	0	16	
Birmingham 1st	10	3	3	4	1	12	
Stirling 1st	10	3	2	5	-12	11	
Nottingham 1st	10	2	3	5	-4	9	

OTTISH DIVISION 1A

Stirling 2nd	10	6	2	2	4	20	
Edinburgh 1st	10	5	4	1	8	19	
Strathclyde 1st	10	4	3	3	5	15	
Robert Gordon 1st	10	3	4	3	-1	13	
Abertay 1st	10	2	4	4	-1	10	
Edinburgh Napier 1	10	0	3	7	-15	3	

OTTISH DIVISION 2A

Glasgow 1st	10	6	2	2	10	20	
St Andrews 1st	10	5	4	1	15	19	
Heriot-Watt 1st	9	4	3	2	9	15	
Aberdeen 1st	8	4	1	3	1	13	
Stirling 3rd	9	3	0	6	-8	9	
Dundee 1st	10	0	2	8	-27	2	

OTTISH DIVISION 3A

West of Scotland 1s	10	7	0	3	2	21	
Edinburgh 2nd	10	6	0	4	8	18	
Heriot-Watt 2nd	10	5	2	3	11	17	
Edinburgh 3rd	10	3	3	4	1	12	
St Andrews 2nd	10	2	3	5	-5	9	*
Glasgow Caledonia	10	2	2	6	-17	5	*

OTTISH DIVISION 4A

Strathclyde 2nd	10	6	3	1	12	21	*
Glasgow Kelvin 1st	10	7	0	3	8	21	
Glasgow 2nd	10	6	0	4	1	18	
Edinburgh 4th	10	4	1	5	-3	13	
Glasgow 3rd	10	2	2	6	-9	8	
Edinburgh Napier 2	10	1	2	7	-9	2	*

OTTISH DIVISION 4B

Aberdeen 2nd	10	9	0	1	26	27	
D&A 1st (Dundee)	10	9	0	1	47	27	
Robert Gordon 2nd	10	4	2	4	3	14	
Abertay 2nd	10	4	1	5	-12	13	
Dundee 2nd	10	2	1	7	-16	7	
Dundee 3rd	10	0	0	#	-48	0	

latches take place on Wednesday fternoons, usually from September until April. ull details are shown on the BUCS website.

SCOTTISH DIVISION 5A

1	Strathclyde 3rd	4	4	0	0	19	12	
2	Strathclyde 4th	4	2	0	2	-1	6	
3	Glasgow Caledonian 2nd	4	0	0	4	-18	0	

SCOTTISH DIVISION 5B

1	Stirling 4th	10	8	0	2	39	24	
2	Stirling 5th	10	6	2	2	9	20	*
3	Heriot-Watt 3rd	10	4	0	6	-17	12	
4	Edinburgh College 1st	10	6	0	4	16	12	*
5	Queen Margaret 1st	10	2	2	6	-18	8	
6	Edinburgh Napier 3rd	10	1	2	7	-29	5	

SCOTTISH DIVISION 5C

1	St Andrews 3rd	10	7	1	2	12	22	
2	Aberdeen 3rd	10	6	2	2	6	20	
3	D&A 2nd (Angus)	10	5	1	4	0	16	
4	St Andrews 4th	10	4	3	3	2	15	
5	Aberdeen 4th	10	2	3	5	-4	9	
6	Dundee 4th	10	1	0	9	-16	0	

SCOTTISH DIVISION 6A

1	WCS 1st	10	8	0	2	31	24	*
2	NCL 2nd (Cumbernauld)	10	6	1	3	23	19	
3	Glasgow Clyde 1st (Anniesland)	10	6	0	4	8	15	*
4	COG 1st	10	5	2	3	-4	14	*
5	D&G 1st	10	2	1	7	-16	4	*
6	Glasgow Caledonian 3rd	10	1	0	9	-42	3	

SCOTTISH DIVISION 6B

1	Edinburgh 5th (IM)	10	5	4	1	11	19	
2	Stirling 6th	10	5	3	2	5	18	
3	Heriot-Watt 4th	10	4	3	3	3	15	
4	West Lothian 1st	10	4	3	3	-2	15	
5	Edinburgh 6th (IM)	10	1	4	5	-6	7	
6	Heriot-Watt 5th	10	1	3	6	-11	6	

SCOTTISH DIVISION 6C

1	NESCOL 1st	6	5	1	0	26	16	
2	Robert Gordon 3rd	6	3	3	0	13	12	
3	UHI 1st (Moray)	6	4	0	2	-6	12	*
4	Aberdeen 5th (Medics)	6	2	1	3	-6	7	
5	St Andrews 5th	6	2	0	4	-2	6	
6	St Andrews 6th	6	1	0	5	-17	3	
7	Dundee 5th	6	1	1	4	-8	1	*

Rd	Date	Home	Away	F	A		Venue
QUEEN'S PARK SHIELD							
1	25/01/2017	Edinburgh University	Edinburgh College	wo	scr		Peffermill
1	25/01/2017	Robert Gordon University	Dundee University	0	0	2-4p	Garthdee
1	25/01/2017	Edinburgh Napier	Glasgow Kelvin	1	3		Spartans FC
1	25/01/2017	Glasgow Uni	Abertay	1	3		Garscube 3G
1	22/02/2017	Heriot Watt	Dundee & Angus Coll	wo	scr		Oriam Outdoor 4G
1	25/01/2017	West of Scotland Uni	Aberdeen	2	4		Hamilton Palace
1	25/01/2017	St Andrews	Glasgow Caledonian	4	0		Uni Sports Centre
1	25/01/2017	Strathclyde	Stirling	1	2		Stepps PF
QF	08/03/2017	Edinburgh University	Dundee University	3	1		Peffermill
QF	22/02/2017	Glasgow Kelvin	Abertay	0	10		Petershill JFC
QF	08/03/2017	Heriot Watt	Aberdeen	4	0		Oriam Grass
QF	08/03/2017	St Andrews	Stirling	1	1	4-5p	Uni Sports Centre
SF	22/03/2017	Edinburgh University	Abertay	1	2		Peffermill
SF	29/03/2017	Heriot Watt	Stirling	1	2		Oriam Outdoor 4G
F	05/04/2017	Abertay	Stirling	0	5		New Lesser Hampden
BRITISH UNIVERSITIES KO CUP (Scottish Teams Only Shown)							
1	22/02/2017	Cardiff Met	Stirling University 1st	2	0		
	Cardiff Met went on to win the trophy						
BRITISH UNIVERSITIES TROPHY (Scottish Teams Only Shown)							
1	23/11/2016	Strathclyde Uni 1st	Newcastle Uni 1st	3	2		Stepps
1	23/11/2016	Abertay 1st	UCLAN 1st	2	4		Gussie Park
1	23/11/2016	Sheffield Uni 1st	Stirling Uni 2nd	2	1		Norton
1	23/11/2016	Sheffield Hallam	Robert Gordons Uni	4	3		SHU Sports Park
1	23/11/2016	Edinburgh Napier 1st	John Moores 1st	1	0		Spartans FC
1	23/11/2016	Birmingham Uni 2nd	Edinburgh Uni 1st	2	1		Metchley 3G
2	15/02/2017	Strathclyde Uni 1st	UCLAN 1st	3	1		Stepps
2	15/02/2017	Edinburgh Napier 1st	Birmingham 2nd	2	1		Spartans FC
QF	22/02/2017	Strathclyde Uni 1st	Nottingham Trent 1st	2	0		Stepps
QF	22/02/2017	Sheffield Hallam	Edinburgh Napier 1st	3	2		SHU Sports Park
SF	01/03/2017	Strathclyde Uni 1st	Sheffield Hallam	2	2	6-5p	Stepps
F	22/03/2017	Worcester Uni 1st	Strathclyde Uni 1st	0	0	4-3p	Bath
SCOTTISH CONFERENCE CUP							
1		Heriot Watt				BYE	
1		Stirling Uni 3rd				BYE	
1	12/10/2016	Dundee Uni 3rd	Edinburgh Napier 2nd	3	3	4-2p	Riverside 3G
1	12/10/2016	Aberdeen 1st	Edinburgh 2nd	2	1		Hillhead
1	12/10/2016	Glasgow Caledonian 1st	Glasgow 3rd	2	0		Firhill Complex
1		West of Scotland 1st				BYE	
1	12/10/2016	Aberdeen 2nd	Edinburgh Uni 4th	3	1		Balgownie
1		Robert Gordon 2nd				BYE	
1		Edinburgh Uni 3rd				BYE	
1		St Andrews 1st				BYE	
1		Heriot Watt 2nd				BYE	
1	12/10/2016	Glasgow Uni 1st	Strathclyde 2nd	2	2	3-4p	Garscube 3G
1		Abertay 2nd				BYE	
1		Dundee Uni 2nd				BYE	
1		St Andrews 2nd				BYE	
1	12/10/2016	Dundee Uni 1st	Glasgow 2nd	1	3		Riverside 3G
2	02/11/2016	Heriot Watt 1st	Stirling Uni 3rd	5	3		Oriam Indoors
2	02/11/2016	Dundee Uni 3rd	St Andrews 2nd	1	4		Riverside 3G
2	02/11/2016	Glasgow Uni 2nd	Aberdeen Uni 1st	0	1		Garscube 3G
2	02/11/2016	Glasgow Caledonian 1st	West of Scotland 1st	4	1		Firhill Complex
2	02/11/2016	Anerdeen 2nd	Robert Gordon 2nd	4	1		Balgownie
2	02/11/2016	Edinburgh 3rd	St Andrews 1st	0	7		Peffermill
2	02/11/2016	Heriot Watt 2nd	Strathclyde 2nd	3	0		Oriam Indoors
2	02/11/2016	Abertay 2nd	Dundee 2nd	3	0		Gussie Park
QF	08/02/2017	Heriot Watt 1st	St Andrews 2nd	7	1		Oriam Outdoors 4G
QF	20/02/2017	Aberdeen 1st	Glasgow Caledonian 1st	0	1		Hillhead
QF	19/02/2017	Aberdeen 2nd	St Andrews 1st	3	2		Balgownie
QF	08/02/2017	Heriot Watt 2nd	Abertay 2nd	1	2		Oriam Outdoors 4G
SF	22/02/2017	Heriot Watt 1st	Glasgow Caledonian 1st	3	0		Oriam Indoors
SF	22/02/2017	Aberdeen 2nd	Abertay 2nd	1	0		Balgownie
F	22/03/2017	Heriot Watt 1st	Aberdeen 2nd	2	2	4-2p	St Andrews Uni PF

AMATEUR FOOTBALL

SCOTTISH AMATEUR FA 2016/17

OFFICE BEARERS (2016 – 2017)

HONORARY PRESIDENT
Charles R Gallacher (Lothian & Edinburgh A.F.A.)

HONORARY VICE PRESIDENT
Stuart Urquhart (Ayrshire A.F.A.)

HONORARY TREASURER
George Dingwall, (Central Scottish A.F.L.)

NATIONAL SECRETARY
Thomas McKeown MCIBS
Scottish Amateur Football Association
Hampden Park,
Glasgow
G42 9DB
(B) 0141 620 4550 (Fax) 0141 620 4551
Email: SAFA@scottish-football.com

TECHNICAL ADVISER
Stephen McLaughlin

ADMINISTRATIVE ASSISTANT
Mary Jardine

STANDING COMMITTEES (2016 - 2017)

EXECUTIVE & FINANCE COMMITTEE
C.R. Gallacher (Chairman) S. Urquhart, G. Dingwall, J.Rodgers, D. Ramage, I.Cowden, R.J. Hughes, J. Napier, G. Mair, T. Doyle

APPEALS COMMITTEE
G. Dingwall (Chairman) C.R. Gallacher, G. Farmer, L.Wallace, I. Cowden, R. Hughes, J. Locke, J. Keating

GENERAL PURPOSES COMMITTEE
S. Urquhart (Chairman) A.Martin, R. Baird, J. McKerley, I.Sommerville, A. Bryant, D. Smith, R. Marshall

INTERNATIONAL COMMITTEE
D. Ramage (Chairman) I. Sommerville
T. McKeown (National Secretary) G. Dingwall (Treasurer)

NATIONAL DISCIPLINARY COMMITTEES

NATIONAL DISCIPLINARY COMMITTEE (NORTH)
R. Hughes (Chairman), J.Napier, A.Martin,T.Latto, G Farmer, A.Denny, S.McSwiggan, M.Nicol

NATIONAL DISCIPLINARY COMMITTEE (SOUTH)
I. Cowden (Chairman), G. Mair, L.Wallace, A. Bryant R. Baird, T.Williamson, C. Denholm, D. Smith

NATIONAL DISCIPLINARY COMMITTEE (HIGHLAND)
H. Morrison (Chairman), H. Cormack, K.MacLeod D. Stuart, M. Coghill, C. Grant.

DISTRICT COMMITTEES

WESTERN DISTRICT EXECUTIVE COMMITTEE
K. Lindsay (Chairman) J. Rodgers, G. Mair, G. Robertson L.Wallace, J. Robert, J. Duncan, R. Marshall

Secretary:
J. Rodgers,
Email: rodgersj892@gmail.com

Match Secretary:
J. Robert,
Email: jradmcentral@hotmail.co.uk

EASTERN DISTRICT EXECUTIVE COMMITTEE
I. Sommerville (Chairman), D. J. Ramage, L.Walls, J. Clark, L. Robertson, K. Boyle, K. Page, G. Moore

Secretary/ Match Secretary:
D. J. Ramage,
Email: djramage@blueyonder.co.uk

NORTH OF TAY EXECUTIVE COMMITTEE
R. J. Hughes (Chairman), A. Martin, S. McSwiggan, G. Farmer, T. Latto, J. Martin, I. Leith, M. Nicol.

Secretary:
A.Martin,

Match Secretary:
G. Farmer,
Email: gordon.mafa@virginmedia.com

FIFE EXECUTIVE COMMITTEE
A. Melville (Chairman), A. Denny, C. Justice, J. Hastie, T. Doyle, J. Lessels, M. Donaldson, R. Currie

Secretary/Match Secretary:
A. Denny,
Email: archibald.denny@btinternet.com

NORTH OF SCOTLAND EXECUTIVE COMMITTEE
J. Napier, (Chairman), J McGunnigle, B. Christie, J. Irvine, D. Strath,
D. Fleming, S. Summers, G. Ross

Secretary/Match Secretary:
G. Ross,
Email: george.ross@eu.weatherford.com

SOUTH OF SCOTLAND EXECUTIVE COMMITTEE
T.Williamson (Chairman), A.McKay, D. Swan, C. Lowrie, D. Connell

Secretary/Match Secretary:
C. Lowrie,

HIGHLAND EXECUTIVE COMMITTEE
(H. Morrison - Chairman), E. Campbell, M. Coghill H. Cormack, K. MacLeod, D. Stuart, H. Morrison.

Secretary/Match Secretary:
H. Cormack,
Email: secretary@slafa.org.uk

WESTERN DISTRICT EXECUTIVE SUNDAY COMMITTEE
A. McDowall (Chairman), A. Black, A. Bryant, R. Baird, J. McFarlane, J. Smyth, C. Burton, A. Coleman

Secretary:
A. Bryant,
Email: abrymack@btinternet.com

SCOTTISH AMATEUR FA LIFE MEMBERS

The year after each name represents the year Life Membership was conferred.

J.A.Barbour, F.R.I.C.S.,8,Blairtum Drive, Burnside, Rutherglen, Glasgow G73 3RY (1976)

Jn.Robertson, 24 West Woodstock Street, Kilmarnock, Ayrshire KA1 2JH (1983)

A. C. McConnell, 38, Carrick Road, East Kilbride, Glasgow G74 4AE (1984)

G. Dingwall, 27, Owendale Avenue, Bellshill, Lanarkshire ML4 1NS (1985)

T.A.Wilkie, 5, Ancrum Place, Dundee, DD2 2JH ((1987)

G. R. Powrie, 22, St Fort Road,Wormit, Newport on Tay, Fife DD6 8LA (1987)

R. B. Boyes, 63, Sydney Place, Lockerbie, Dumfries-shire DG11 2JA (1988)

J.C.B.Muirhead, 96, St.Andrews Drive, Fraserburgh, Aberdeenshire AB4 5BG (1989)

J.McKerley,69, Parnell Street, Airdrie ML6 9EG (1991)

A.M.Smith, 104, BallerupTerrace, Whitehills, East Kilbride, Glasgow G75 0NN (1991)

J.Smith,182, Arbroath Avenue, Glasgow G52 3HH (1992)

G. Steel, 100 Links Avenue,Whitley Bay,Tyne & Wear NE26 3EH (1994)

D. F. Grant,'Hillcrest', 7 Caberston Avenue, Walkerburn, Peebleshire EH43 6B (1994)

G. Butler, 40 Netherplace Road, Newton Mearns, Glasgow G77 6DG (1995)

J. Mitchell, 33 Inglewood Crescent, Hairmyres, East Kilbride, Glasgow G75 8QD (1997)

R. Lamberton, 11 Menteith Street, Broughty Ferry, Dundee DD5 3EN (1998)

W.Twaddle,"Taugh an Achaidh", 1 Largue Farm, Largue, Huntly, Aberdeenshire AB54 6HS (1998)

K. G.Wood, 38 Whitehouse Park,Wick, Caithness KW1 4NX (1999)

T.W.Allison,31 Clermiston Place, Edinburgh EH4 7DN (2000)

A. J. Fitzgerald, 12 Riccarton Mains Road, Currie, Edinburgh EH14 5NG (2000)

K. Lindsay, 35 Harris Close, Glasgow. G77 6TU (2001)

W. D.Wilson, 6 Greenlaw Drive, Paisley PA1 3RU (2001)

J. Lyle, 1/1, 3 New Street, Kilbarchan, Johnstone, Renfrewshire PA10 2LN ((2002)

A. M. Ramsay, 91 Appin Terrace, Perth (H) (2003)

J Keating, 20 Benbecula, St Leonards, East Kilbride, Glasgow, G74 2BT (2004)

R. J. Hughes, 4 Downie Park, Dundee, DD3 8JW (2008)

J.Drewery,7 Rysland Drive, Fenwick, Ayrshire, KA3 6EY (2008)

A Mackay, Elmwood, Symington, Biggar, ML12 6JU ((2010)

H Knapp, 7 Struther Street, Larkhall, ML9 1PE (2010)

H Carswell, 78 Louden Road, Newmilns, KA16 9HG (2011)

R.W. McGechie, 42 Roseberry Avenue, South Queensferry, EH30 9JH (2012

I. McTweed M.B.I.M., D.M.S. 16 Bellfield Crescent, Barrhead, G78 1HD (201

R. Baird, 10 Conisborough Close, Cumbernauld, Glasgow, G34 9NE (2014)

J.Locke, 1 Gregory Street,Mauchline,Ayrshire, KA5 6BY (2014)

M. Mackay, 4 Dunnet Place, Thurso, Caithness (2014)

J. Napier, 7 Townhead Terrace, Kintore, Aberdeenshire AB51 0UT (2015)

T.F. Harding, 5c, 80 Glenfinnan Road, Wyndford Estate, Maryhill, Glasgow, G20 8JQ (2015)

A. Martin, 3 Godfrey Street, Barnhill, Dundee DD5 2QZ (2015)

J. McGunnigle, 47f Nelson Street, Aberdeen, AB24 5ER (2016)

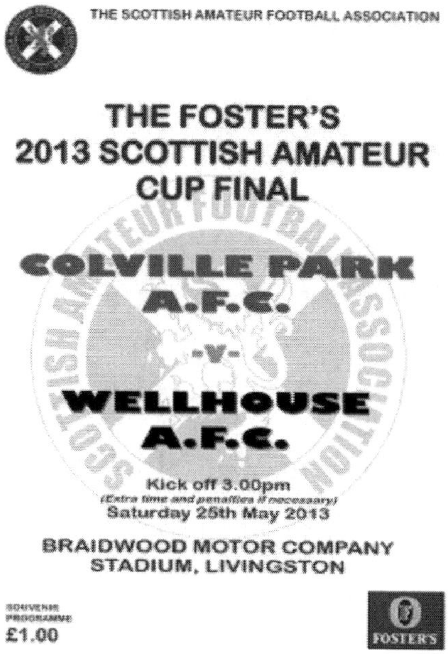

ABERDEEN SUNDAY AMATEUR FA 2016/17

Contact: Brian Derrett
Email: bderrett@oceaneering.com
Tel: 01224 486895.
www.leaguewebsite.co.uk/aberdeensundayamateurs

Games are usually played on a Sunday morning with 10.30am Kick Offs. Most matches are played at Inverdee or Hazelhead pitches., and occasionally at Sheddocksley.

For 2016/17 the League was played on a straight home / away format with no split.

Membership was 14 teams, down 1 from 2015/16.

FINAL TABLE	P	W	D	L	F	A	GD	Pts
G.B. United	26	22	2	2	112	46	66	68
Shirlaws	26	22	0	4	127	44	83	66
Malibu	26	18	3	5	105	63	42	57
Abergeldie Bar	26	16	3	7	118	61	57	51
North East Dynamo	26	16	2	8	126	69	57	50
Mither Tap Bar	26	13	2	11	135	93	42	41
Kincorth Thistle	26	12	3	11	89	87	2	39
MLK Aberdeen	26	11	4	11	83	78	5	37
M.N. United	26	10	2	14	87	101	-14	32
Inverdee AFC	26	9	5	12	69	91	-22	32
Police Scotland Aberdeen	26	4	5	17	62	126	-64	17
Granite Thistle	26	4	2	20	46	145	-99	14
Ablift	26	2	3	21	59	151	-92	12
Bon Accord Amateurs	26	4	2	20	51	114	-63	11

CUP FINALS

Jim Lumsden Cup (May 21 at Inverdee Pitches)
North East Dynamo v Shirlaws, 3-2

Gavin Robertson Cup (May 14 at Inverdee Pitches)
North East Dynamo v Mither Tap Bar, 3-2

Rotosearch Cup (May 21 at Inverdee Pitches)
Police Scotland Aberdeen v MLK Aberdeen, 1-0

The Jim Lumsden Cup is contested by all member clubs.

The Gavin Robertson and Rotosearch Cups are played from March onwards. The Robertson Cup is for teams in top half of the league at the time of the draw. The Rotosearch Cup is for teams in the lower half of the league.

ABERDEENSHIRE AMATEUR FA 2016/17

Contact: Brian Christie
Tel 01224 895851 (H) 07730 611960 (m)
E-mail - aafasecretary@hotmail.co.uk

League website: www.aberdeenshireafa.com

This is the main Saturday Amateur association for the north east of Scotland. It covers a wide area from Banffshire in the north to Kincardineshire in the southern including the city of Aberdeen. Over the years many member clubs have made the step up to the North Region Junior Leagues.

Cup Finals are usually played on Fridays or Sundays. League fixtures are played on Saturday afternoons.

Membership for 2016/17 was 82 clubs, an increase of 1 compared to 2015/16.

	PREMIER	P	W	D	L	F	A	+/-	Pts
1	Woodside	26	19	2	5	91	41	50	59
2	Sportsmans Club	26	18	5	3	69	27	42	59
3	Rothie Rovers	26	15	3	8	72	50	22	48
4	MS United	26	15	1	10	79	61	18	46
5	University	26	12	5	9	44	39	5	41
6	Westhill	26	12	4	10	60	44	16	40
7	RGU	26	12	2	12	63	57	6	38
8	Newtonhill	26	9	5	12	44	55	-11	32
9	Ellon Amateurs	26	9	3	14	54	61	-7	30
10	Echt	26	9	2	15	39	57	-18	29
11	Kincorth	26	7	7	12	46	72	-26	28
12	AC Mill	26	7	5	14	43	71	-28	26
13	Torry Amateurs	26	8	1	17	53	83	-30	25
14	Westdyke	26	5	5	16	47	86	-39	20

	DIV ONE NORTH	P	W	D	L	F	A	+/-	Pts
1	Cove Thistle	26	18	6	2	89	42	47	60
2	Old Aberdonians	26	18	2	6	73	34	39	56
3	Beacon Rangers	26	16	4	6	83	56	27	52
4	Granite City	26	15	4	7	86	49	37	49
5	St Laurence	26	12	4	10	53	54	-1	40
6	Glendale	26	11	3	12	43	59	-16	36
7	Kaimhill United	26	10	5	11	61	58	3	35
8	Nicolls Amateurs	26	10	5	11	45	61	-16	35
9	Bon Accord City	26	10	4	12	62	56	6	34
10	Bervie Caledonian	26	10	3	13	63	67	-4	33
11	Stonehaven Athletic	26	8	4	14	46	65	-19	28
12	Turriff Thistle	26	7	4	15	48	74	-26	25
13	Dyce ITC Hydraulics	26	6	3	17	46	79	-33	21
14	West End	26	3	5	18	40	84	-44	14

	DIV ONE EAST	P	W	D	L	F	A	+/-	Pts
1	Cowie Thistle	24	17	3	4	103	44	59	54
2	Banchory Amateurs	24	16	4	4	76	50	26	52
3	Alford	24	13	4	7	50	32	18	43
4	Tarves	24	13	4	7	63	49	14	43
5	Insch	24	12	4	8	58	36	22	40
6	Stoneywood East End *	24	14	6	4	55	33	22	34
7	Halliburton *	24	10	5	9	44	49	-5	32
8	Rattrays XI	24	8	7	9	45	63	-18	31
9	Ellon Thistle	24	8	4	12	33	49	-16	28
10	Cammachmore	24	6	3	15	52	72	-20	21
11	Blackburn	24	5	3	16	41	72	-31	18
12	Great Western United *	24	5	5	14	48	69	-21	17
13	Formartine United	24	3	0	21	39	89	-50	9

NEWBURGH THISTLE FC

	DIV TWO NORTH	P	W	D	L	F	A	+/-	Pts
1	Newburgh Thistle	26	21	2	3	97	27	70	65
2	Don Athletic	26	20	2	4	85	36	49	62
3	Burghmuir	26	19	4	3	84	28	56	61
4	Northern United	26	16	2	8	79	52	27	50
5	BSFC	26	15	3	8	81	48	33	48
6	Kintore	26	11	4	11	49	60	-11	37
7	FC Polska	26	11	3	12	62	78	-16	36
8	Balmedie	26	10	6	10	62	59	3	36
9	Glendale XI	26	10	2	14	66	76	-10	32
10	Huntly Amateurs	26	7	5	14	56	69	-13	26
11	Fintray Thistle	26	7	3	16	46	75	-29	24
12	Monymusk	26	5	5	16	54	93	-39	20
13	Kemnay Youth	26	4	4	18	31	77	-46	16
14	Theologians	26	2	3	21	39	113	-74	9

	DIV TWO EAST	P	W	D	L	F	A	+/-	Pts
1	Bridge of Don	26	19	3	4	73	41	32	60
2	Sheddocksley	26	17	4	5	71	36	35	55
3	Westdyce	26	16	4	6	79	36	43	52
4	Lads Club Amateurs	26	15	5	6	74	54	20	50
5	JS XI	26	12	7	7	69	52	17	43
6	Auchnagatt Barons	26	10	7	9	46	51	-5	37
7	Glentanar Reflex	26	11	2	13	59	72	-13	35
8	Torphins	26	10	3	13	57	58	-1	33
9	University Strollers	26	10	3	13	53	59	-6	33
10	Aboyne	26	10	3	13	51	65	-14	33
11	Highland Hotel	26	7	3	16	36	60	-24	24
12	Jesus House	26	6	4	16	37	63	-26	22
13	Grammar FP's	26	6	3	17	52	86	-34	21
14	Glendale Youth	26	5	5	16	48	72	-24	20

	DIV THREE	P	W	D	L	F	A	+/-	Pts
1	Faithlie United	24	20	2	2	115	25	90	62
2	Tolbooth	24	19	3	2	136	35	101	60
3	McTeagle	24	14	4	6	81	58	23	46
4	Continental	24	13	4	7	53	37	16	43
5	Postal ALC	24	12	4	8	77	51	26	40
6	Colony Park	24	10	7	7	60	50	10	37
7	University Colts	24	11	3	10	54	54	0	36
8	St Marnans	24	9	3	12	64	63	1	30
9	Feughside	24	8	4	12	58	65	-7	28
10	Ferryhill	24	6	4	14	60	86	-26	22
11	AFC Murdos	24	5	5	14	50	79	-29	20
12	Bon Accord Thistle	24	3	4	17	49	128	-79	13
13	Middlefield Wasps *	24	2	1	21	31	157	-126	1

CUP FINALS

Aberdeen FC Trophy (All Clubs), May 30 at Stonehaven JFC
Cove Thistle v Newtonhill 2-0

Association Trophy (Prem and Div 1 clubs), May 26 at Stonehaven JFC
Torry Amateurs v Cowie Thistle, 4-3

Dickie Trophy (Div 2 and 3 clubs), May 23 at Aberdeen EE JFC
Bridge of Don v Contiental, 3-2 aet

Edmond Trophy (Teams kod in Rd 1 of Aberdeen FC Trophy), Mar 26 at Stonehave
Tolbooth v Glendale XI, 3-0

Bowie Cup (Teams kod in Rd 1 of Association Trophy), May 5 at Newmachar Utd J
Formartine United v Great Western United, 3-1

Hans Fyfe Trophy (Teams kod in Rd 1 of Dickie Trophy) May 22 at Stonehaven JFC
Don Athletic v Jesus House, 9-1

Premier Trophy (Prem Division clubs), May 12 at Aberdeen EE JFC
Sportsmans Club v Woodisde, 2-0

Stephen Shield (Div 1 North clubs), April 16 at Woodside Complex
Cove Thistle v Turriff Thistle, 4-0

White Cup (Div 1 East clubs), Feb 12 at Woodside Complex
Stoneywood East End v Halliburton, 3-2

Castle Rovers Cup (Div 2 North clubs), April 30 at Woodside Complex
Newburgh Thistle v FC Polska, 3-2

Barclay Cook Cup (Div 2 East clubs), Nov 13 at Stonehaven JFC
Sheddocksley v Glendale Youth, 2-0

Chattan Rovers Trophy (Div 3 clubs), Dec 4 at Newmachar United
Tolbooth v Continental, 4-1

Ian Napier Shield (previous seasons champions from D1 N and E), Sedp 18 at Sto
AC Mill Inn v Westhill, 5-0

John Todd Trophy (Top 2 clubs in Premier Div from previous season), Oct 2 at Sur
Woodside v RGU, 6-0

FERRYHILL AFC EST. 1979

CLUBS IN MEMBERSHIP 2016/17

Club	Division	Ground	Home Colours	Change Colours
Aboyne	Two (East)	Aboyne Green	Blue	Black/White
AC Mill Inn	Premier	Mineralwell Park, Stonehaven	Red/Black	White
AFC Murdos	Three	Sheddocksley	Red/White	Blue/Yellow
Alford	One (East)	Alford Pleasure Park	Blue/Black	Yellow/Black
Auchnagatt Barons	Two (East)	Auchnagatt	White/Black	Blue/Black
Balmedie	Two (North)	Potterton	Black	Green
Banchory Amateurs	One (East)	King George V Park, Banchory	Blue	Red/Black
Beacon Rangers	One (North)	Bucksburn Academy	Red	Black
Bervie Caledonian	One (North)	Booth Park, Gourdon	Maroon	Orange/Black
Blackburn	One (East)	Blackburn Pleasure Park	Blue/White	Black/Orange
Bon Accord City	One (North)	Balgownie, Bridge of Don	Blue/Yellow	Yellow/Blue
Bon Accord Thistle	Three	Hazlehead	Red/White	Black
Bridge of Don	Two (East)	Westfield Park, Bridge of Don	Black/Blue	Red
BSFC	Two (North)	Balgownie, Bridge of Don	Blue	Red
Burghmuir	Two (North)	Strathburn Park, Inverurie	Yellow/Black	Blue
Cammachmore	One (East)	Newtonhill	Maroon	Navy
Colony Park	Three	Colony Park, Inverurie	Red/Black	White/Black
Continental	Three	Webster Park, Kingswells	Black	Blue
Cove Thistle	One (North)	Catto Park, Cove	Red	Navy
Cowie Thistle	One (East)	Glenury Park, Stonehaven	Blue/White	Black/Gold
Don Athletic	Two (North)	Westfield Park, Bridge of Don	Green/Black	White/Blue
Dyce ITC Hydraulics	One (North)	Dyce Academy	Blue/Black	Red/White
Echt	Premier	Echt Pleasure Park	Red	Blue
Ellon Amateurs	Premier	The Meadows, Ellon	Red	Blue/White
Ellon Thistle	One (East)	The Meadows, Ellon	Sky/White	Black/White
Faithlie United	Three	College Park, Fraserburgh	Orange/Black	Black/White
FC Polska	Two (North)	Inverdee	Red/Black	White/Green
Ferryhill	Three	Hazlehead	Red/Black	Blue/Black
Feughside	Three	Farquharson Park, Finzean	Red/Black	Blue
Fintray Thistle	Two (North)	Strathburn Park, Inverurie	Red/Black	Orange/Black
Formartine United	One (East)	Oldmeldrum Pleasure Park	Red/White	Black
Glendale	One (North)	Corbie Park, Maryculter	Maroon/Sky	Red/Black
Glendale XI	Two (North)	Inverdee	Maroon/Blue	Black/White
Glendale Youth	Two (East)	Hazlehead	Sky/Black	Maroon/Sky
Glentanar Reflex	Two (East)	Hazlehead	Yellow/Blue	Red
Grammar FP's	Two (East)	Rubislaw	Blue/White	Black
Granite City	One (North)	Findon Park	Orange/Black	Navy/Sky/White
Great Western United	One (East)	Kaimhill (Grass)	Blue/White/Black	Red
Halliburton	One (East)	Lawsondale, Westhill	Black	Green/Black
Highland Hotel	Two (East)	Inverdee	Red	Yellow
Huntly Amateurs	Two (North)	The Meadows, Huntly	Maroon/Sky	Red/Black
Insch	One (East)	Recreation Park, Insch	Black	Yellow/Blue
Jesus House	Two (East)	Inverdee	Red	Blue/Black
JS XI	Two (East)	Groats Road, Hazlehead	Orange	Black
Kaimhill United	One (North)	Kaimhill (Grass)	Black	Red
Kemnay Youth	Two (North)	Bogbeth Park, Kemnay	Black/White	Yellow/Blue
Kincorth	Premier	Kincorth Academy	Black	White/Black
Kintore	Two (North)	Kintore Pleasure Park	Blue	Red
Lads Club Amateurs	Two (East)	Potterton	Maroon/Sky	Green/White
McTeagle	Three	Sheddocksley	Red	Black
Middlefield Wasps	Three	Beach Park, Balmedie	Black/Red	Navy/Sky
Monymusk	Two (North)	Deer Park, Monymusk	Blue/Red	White/Red
MS United	Premier	Inverdee	Black/Green	Green/Black
Newburgh Thistle	Two (North)	Gallowhill Park, Newburgh	Black	Blue/White
Newtonhill	Premier	Newtonhill	Red/White	Blue/Black
Nicolls Amateurs	One (North)	Denmore Park, Bridge of Don	Red/Navy	Black/Yellow
Northern United	Two (North)	Inverdee	Gold/Black	Blue
Old Aberdonians	One (North)	Balgownie, Bridge of Don	Red/Black	White
Postal ALC	Three	Webster Park, Kingswells	Maroon/Sky	Blue/White
Rattrays XI	One (East)	Heathryfold	Navy	Yellow/Blue
RGU	Premier	Kaimhill (All Weather)	White/Black	Purple/Black
Rothie Rovers	Premier	Rothienorman	Yellow/Blue	Navy
Sheddocksley	Two (East)	Sheddocksley	White/Black	Red/White
Sportsmans Club	Premier	Clark Commercials Park	Red	Blue
St Laurence	One (North)	Memorial Park, Laurencekirk	Yellow/Black	Black
St Marnans	Three	McRobert Park, Aberchirder	Maroon/Sky	Sky/Maroon
Stonehaven Athletic	One (North)	Mineralwell Park, Stonehaven	Red/White/Black	Blue/White/Black
Stoneywood East End	One (East)	New Advocates Park	Gold/Black	Blue/White
Tarves	One (East)	Hillhead Park, Tarves	Black/White	Blue/White
Theologians	Two (North)	Hazlehead	Blue/White	White/Black
Tolbooth	Three	Inverdee	Black/Red	Blue/White
Torphins	Two (East)	Kincardine O'Neil Pleasure Park	Black/White	Red
Torry Amateurs	Premier	Tullos	Yellow	Blue
Turriff Thistle	One (North)	The Haughs, Turriff	Red/Blue	Blue
University	Premier	Balgownie, Bridge of Don	Red	Blue
University Colts	Three	Balgownie, Bridge of Don	Red	Yellow/Blue
University Strollers	Two (East)	Balgownie, Bridge of Don	Red	Yellow/Blue
West End	One (North)	Rubislaw	Red/Black	Purple/White
Westdyce	Two (East)	Inverdee	Red	Black/White
Westdyke	Premier	Lawsondale, Westhill	Sky/White/Black	Black
Westhill	Premier	Westdyke Leisure Centre	Blue	Black
Woodside	Premier	St Machar Academy	White	Orange/Black

ABERDEENSHIRE AFA CHAMPIONS

1947-48 Cove Rangers
1948-49 Cove Rangers
1949-50 Ellon United
1950-51 Ellon United
1951-52 Millburn FC
1952-53 Millburn FC
1953-54 Cove Rangers
1954-55 Cove Rangers
1955-56 Cove Rangers
1956-57 Cove Rangers
1957-58 Cove Rangers
1958-59 Nicoll's XI
1959-60 Cove Rangers
1960-61 Cove Rangers
1961-62 Ellon United
1962-63 Ellon United
1963-64 Bon Accord FC
1964-65 Cove Rangers
1965-66 Aboyne
1966-67 Aberdeen City Police
1967-68 Aberdeen City Police
1968-69 Aberdeen City Police
1969-70 Aberdeen City Police
1970-71 Maud
1971-72 Kemnay
1972-73 Culter
1973-74 Culter
1974-75 Culter
1975-76 Culter
1976-77 Cove Rangers
1977-78 Kemnay
1978-79 Culter
1979-80 Culter
1980-81 Culter
1981-82 Grandholm Rosslyn
1982-83 Cove Rangers
1983-84 Aberdeen Shamrock
1984-85 Cove Rangers
1985-86 Crombie Sports
1986-87 Mugiemoss Amateurs
1987-88 Longside
1988-89 Hall Russell United
1989-90 Great Western United
1990-91 Kincorth
1991-92 Kincorth
1992-93 Kincorth
1993-94 Kincorth
1994-95 Dyce
1995-96 Hilton
1996-97 Echt
1997-98 Hilton
1998-99 Hilton
1999-00 Hilton
2000-01 Echt
2001-02 Echt
2002-03 Kincorth
2003-04 Kincorth
2004-05 Sunnybank Amateurs
2005-06 Sunnybank Amateurs
2006-07 Echt
2007-08 Echt
2008-09 Cove Thistle
2009-10 Bon-Accord City
2010-11 Kincorth
2011-12 Woodside
2012-13 Sportsmans Club
2013-14 Sportsmans Club
2014-15 Cove Thistle
2015-16 RGU
2016-17 Woodside

ABERDEENSHIRE AFA TROPHY	ASSOCIATION TROPHY	BARCLAY COOK CUP	BOWIE CUP
1947-48 Cove Rangers			
1948-49 Cove Rangers			
1949-50 Cove Rangers			1949-50 Castlehill
1950-51 Ellon United			1950-51 No Competition
1951-52 Cove Rangers			1951-52 Banchory
1952-53 Cove Rangers			1952-53 Mugiemoss FC
1953-54 Cove Rangers			1953-54 Banchory
1954-55 Banchory			1954-55 No Competition
1955-56 Cove Rangers			1955-56 Formartine United
1956-57 Cleansing Department			1956-57 University
1957-58 Cove Rangers			1957-58 Cove Rangers
1958-59 Cove Rangers			1958-59 Avondale
1959-60 Banchory			1959-60 Formartine United
1960-61 Bon Accord			1960-61 Ellon United
1961-62 Cove Rangers			1961-62 Cove Rangers
1962-63 Cove Rangers			1962-63 Aboyne
1963-64 Ellon United			1963-64 University
1964-65 Cove Rangers		1964-65 Cove Rangers	1964-65 Cove Rangers
1965-66 Ellon United		1965-66 Cove Rangers	1965-66 Cove Rangers
1966-67 Aberdeen University		1966-67 Cove Thistle	1966-67 Cove Rangers
1967-68 Aberdeen City Police		1967-68 Kemnay	1967-68 Dyce Amateurs
1968-69 A.D. Club		1968-69 No Competition	1968-69 No Competition
1969-70 Aboyne		1969-70 Links Parks	1969-70 College of Education
1970-71 Maud		1970-71 Grandholm	1970-71 Dyce Amateurs
1971-72 Culter		1971-72 Alford	1971-72 Bon Accord
1972-73 Maud		1972-73 Ellon Youth	1972-73 Cove Thistle
1973-74 Culter		1973-74 Albion Rangers	1973-74 Chattan Rovers
1974-75 Cove Rangers		1974-75 Longside	1974-75 Aboyne
1975-76 Culter		1975-76 Savings Bank	1975-76 Newtonhill
1976-77 Culter		1976-77 Carlton	1976-77 Banchory
1977-78 Kemnay		1977-78 Braemar	1977-78 Maryculter
1978-79 Longside		1978-79 G.S.A.	1978-79 Commercial Thistle
1979-80 Chattan Rovers		1979-80 Cup Withheld	1979-80 Commercial Thistle
1980-81 Denmore Thistle		1980-81 Kingseat	1980-81 Aboyne
1981-82 Aboyne		1981-82 Raeden Thistle	1981-82 Grampian Police
1982-83 Cove Rangers		1982-83 Parkinson's	1982-83 Shamrock
1983-84 Cove Rangers		1983-84 McTeagle Taylor	1983-84 Marley United
1984-85 Cove Rangers		1984-85 No Competition	1984-85 No Competition
1985-86 Culter		1985-86 No Competition	1985-86 No Competition
1986-87 Culter		1986-87 Rothie Rovers	1986-87 Banchory St Ternan
1987-88 Longside		1987-88 Feughside	1987-88 Banchory St Ternan
1988-89 Kincorth		1988-89 APG McTeagle	1988-89 Potterton
1989-90 Kincorth	1989-90 Kincorth	1989-90 FC Hayloft	1989-90 Dyce Amateurs
1990-91 Hermes	1990-91 Glentanar	1990-91 Riverside	1990-91 Rattray's XI
1991-92 Kincorth	1991-92 Great Western United	1991-92 Echt	1991-92 Cults
1992-93 Kincorth	1992-93 Raeden Thistle	1992-93 RGU	1992-93 Hatton
1993-94 Hilton	1993-94 Kincorth	1993-94 AC Mill Inn	1993-94 Dyce
1994-95 Dyce	1994-95 Hatton	1994-95 Theologians	1994-95 Hilton
1995-96 Echt	1995-96 Glentanar	1995-96 Theologians	1995-96 FC Hayloft
1996-97 Hilton	1996-97 FC Hayloft	1996-97 Cults	1996-97 Glendale
1997-98 Echt	1997-98 Echt	1997-98 No Competition	1997-98 Braemar
1998-99 Echt	1998-99 Luthermuir	1998-99 Chattan Rovers	1998-99 Beacon Rangers
1999-00 Echt	1999-00 Cowie Thistle	1999-00 Cults	1999-00 Inverurie FP's
2000-01 Cowie Thistle	2000-01 Hilton	2000-01 College of Education	2000-01 Kemnay Youth
2001-02 Echt	2001-02 Echt	2001-02 Newmachar United	2001-02 Nicolls XI
2002-03 Walker Road	2002-03 Walker Road	2002-03 Newmachar United	2002-03 Sunnybank Amateurs
2003-04 Kincorth	2003-04 Aberdeen Sporting C	2003-04 Newtonhill	2003-04 Glendale
2004-05 Sunnybank Amateurs	2004-05 Stoneywood SSC	2004-05 Postal ALC	2004-05 Bridge of Don
2005-06 Echt	2005-06 Echt	2005-06 PA United	2005-06 Glentanar Reflex
2006-07 Stoneywood SSC	2006-07 Stoneywood SSC	2006-07 Blackburn	2006-07 Frigate
2007-08 Echt	2007-08 Echt	2007-08 Turriff Thistle	2007-08 Bon-Accord City
2008-09 University	2008-09 Cowie Thistle	2008-09 Luthermuir	2008-09 Glendale XI
2009-10 Bon-Accord City	2009-10 Echt	2009-10 Mearns United	2009-10 Dyce
2010-11 Woodside	2010-11 Cove Thistle	2010-11 Westhill	2010-11 Stoneywood Amateurs
2011-12 Woodside	2011-12 Cove Thistle	2011-12 Hazlehead United	2011-12 Westdyke
2012-13 Sportsmans Club	2012-13 Echt	2012-13 AC Mill Inn	2012-13 Lads Club Amateurs
2013-14 Cove Thistle	2013-14 Cowie Thistle	2013-14 JS XI	2013-14 Feughside
2014-15 Rothie Rovers	2014-15 Cove Thistle	2014-15 Bridge of Don	2014-15 Woodside
2015-16 Ellon Amateurs	2015-16 Ellon Amateurs	2015-16 Westdyce	2015-16 Dee Amateurs
2016-17 Cove Thistle	2016-17 Torry Ams	2016-17 Sheddocksley	2016-17 Formartine United Ams

STLE ROVERS CUP	CHATTAN ROVERS CUP	DICKIE TROPHY	EDMOND TROPHY	HANS FYFE TROPHY
			1954-55 Fittie Rangers	
			1955-56 Millbank	
			1956-57 Rowatt	
			1957-58 Rowatt	
			1958-59 CWD Athletic	
			1959-60 No Competition	
			1960-61 No Competition	
			1961-62 No Competition	
			1962-63 No Competition	
			1963-64 Mugiemoss Sports	
			1964-65 Lads Club	
			1965-66 Kintore	
			1966-67 Kemnay	
			1967-68 Newtonhill	
		1968-69 Aberdeen City Police	1968-69 College of Education	
		1969-70 Monymusk	1969-70 Richard's XI	1969-70 Kemnay
			1970-71 Hall Russell United	1970-71 Culter
		1971-72 Culter	1971-72 Marley United	1971-72 Kemnay
		1972-73 Kemnay	1972-73 Stonehaven	1972-73 Culter
		1973-74 Kemnay	1973-74 Stoneywood Amateurs	1973-74 Cove Rangers
	1974-75 Kemnay	1974-75 Culter	1974-75 Grampian Spurs	1974-75 Culter
	1975-76 Culter	1975-76 Culter	1975-76 Banchory St. Ternan	1975-76 Culter
	1976-77 Culter	1976-77 Longside	1976-77 Seaview Spurs	1976-77 Kemnay
	1977-78 Grampian Spurs	1977-78 Newtonhill	1977-78 Seaview Spurs	1977-78 Chattan Rovers
8-79 Glentanar	1978-79 Dyce Amateurs	1978-79 Longside	1978-79 Seaview Spurs	1978-79 Newtonhill
9-80 Turriff Amateurs	1979-80 Grandholm Rosslyn	1979-80 Chattan Rovers	1979-80 Alford	1979-80 Chattan Rovers
80-81 Parkinson's	1980-81 Longside	1980-81 Aberdeen Shamrock	1980-81 Denmore Thistle	1980-81 Culter
81-82 Bieldside	1981-82 Culter	1981-82 Grandholm Rosslyn	1981-82 Carlton	1981-82 Aberden Shamrock
82-83 Chattan Rovers	1982-83 Cove Rangers	1982-83 Longside	1982-83 Postal	1982-83 Cove Rangers
83-84 Feughside	1983-84 Cove Rangers	1983-84 Shamrock	1983-84 Kintore	1983-84 Longside
84-85 No Competition	1984-85 Crombie Sports	1984-85 Hall Russell United	1984-85 No Competition	1984-85 Crombie Sports
85-86 Beacon Rangers	1985-86 No Competition	1985-86 No Competition	1985-86 No Competition	1985-86 No Competition
86-87 Donside	1986-87 Kincorth	1986-87 Walker Road	1986-87 Potterton	1986-87 Longside
87-88 No Competition	1987-88 Braemar	1987-88 Potterton	1987-88 Kincorth	1987-88 Longside
88-89 FC Hayloft	1988-89 FC Central	1988-89 West End	1988-89 Portlethen Thistle	1988-89 Kemnay Youth
89-90 Cammachmore	1989-90 Theologians	1989-90 Grampian Police	1989-90 Blackburn	1989-90 University
90-91 Trophies International	1990-91 Albion Rangers	1990-91 Glentanar	1990-91 Hilton	1990-91 Tarves
91-92 Hilton	1991-92 Grampian CD	1991-92 Glentanar	1991-92 Cruden Bay	1991-92 Alford
92-93 Luthermuir	1992-93 Hilton	1992-93 Kincorth	1992-93 Royal Cornhill	1992-93 Grampian CD
93-94 Greentrees	1993-94 Echt	1993-94 Hatton	1993-94 Old Aberdonians	1993-94 Hilton
94-95 Old Aberdonians	1994-95 Deep Freeze	1994-95 Dyce	1994-95 Gramar FPs	1994-95 Hayloft Pearsons
95-96 Sheddocksley	1995-96 Deep Freeze	1995-96 Cove Thistle	1995-96 Frigate	1995-96 Woodside
96-97 Frigate	1996-97 Sheddocksley	1996-97 Hilton	1996-97 Great Western United	1996-97 Turriff Amateurs
97-98 Royal Cornhill	1997-98 Albion Rangers	1997-98 Skene	1997-98 No Competition	1997-98 Trophies International
98-99 Carlton	1998-99 Bankhead	1998-99 University	1998-99 Grammar FPs	1998-99 Frigate
99-00 Halliburton	1999-00 Alford	1999-00 Echt	1999-00 West End	1999-00 Grampian Police
00-01 Auchnagatt Barons	2000-01 Trophies International	2000-01 University	2000-01 Grampian Police	2000-01 Walker Road
01-02 Maryculter	2001-02 Torphins	2001-02 Glentanar Reflex	2001-02 Frigate	2001-02 Quayside Rosebowl
02-03 Woodbank	2002-03 Torry United	2002-03 Woodbank	2002-03 Frigate	2002-03 Turriff Thistle
03-04 RGU	2003-04 Millburn	2003-04 Cove Thistle	2003-04 Stoneywood SSC	2003-04 Johnshaven Athletic
04-05 No Winner	2004-05 Inverurie FPs	2004-05 Ferryhill	2004-05 Frigate	2004-05 Theologians
05-06 Postal ALC	2005-06 Kincorth Rovers	2005-06 Bervie Caledonian	2005-06 Kincorth Rovers	2005-06 Alford
06-07 Alford	2006-07 Bankhead	2006-07 Theologians	2006-07 Westdyke	2006-07 Stonehaven Athletic
07-08 Stonehaven Athletic	2007-08 Kemnay Youth	2007-08 Insch	2007-08 Bon-Accord City	2007-08 Tarves
08-09 University Colts	2008-09 Hilton	2008-09 Hilton	2008-09 Cowie Thistle	2008-09 Glendale
09-10 Hilton	2009-10 Portlethen United	2009-10 Rattrays XI	2009-10 Cowie Thistle	2009-10 Hilton
10-11 Postal ALC	2010-11 Torphins	2010-11 Rothie Rovers	2010-11 Kincorth	2010-11 Postal ALC
11-12 Ellon Thistle	2011-12 Great Northern Athleti	2011-12 Hazlehead United	2011-12 Cove Thistle	2011-12 St Laurence
12-13 Northern United	2012-13 Granite City	2012-13 Granite City	2012-13 Woodside	2012-13 Glentanar Reflex
13-14 Granite City	2013-14 Fintray Thistle	2013-14 Bankhead	2013-14 Cowie Thistle	2013-14 Granite City
14-15 Westhill	2014-15 Sheddocksley	2014-15 Sheddocksley	2014-15 Westhill	2014-15 Westhill
15-16 Newburgh Thistle	2015-16 Monymusk	2015-16 Ellon Thistle	2015-16 West End	2015-16 Glendale XI
16-17 Newburgh Thistle	2016-17 Tolbooth	2016-17 Bridge of Don	2016-17 Tolbooth	2016-17 Don Athletic

AIRDRIE & COATBRIDGE SUNDAY AMATEUR LEAGUE 2016/17

Contact: Mr A Coleman,
Email: archiec@blueyonder.comuk
Tel 07961579078
Facebook Page: Airdrie & Coatbridge Sunday AFL
www.airdrie.leaguerepublic.com

This League has spread and now includes teams from Glasgow and Renfrewshire as well as Airdrie and Coatbridge. Membership for 2016/17 was 31 teams, an increase of 11 from 2015/16. At least ten more teams were seeking to join for 2017/18.

The League's website and facebook pages provide detailed information. Matches are usually played on Sunday afternoons. Cup Finals are usually played at the Excelsior Stadium, often as "double headers".

	PREMIER DIVISION	P	W	D	L	F	A	+-	PTS
1	Bullfrog	15	14	0	1	84	13	71	42
2	Alpha Afc	15	13	0	2	51	23	28	39
3	Rollingbarrell	14	8	0	6	26	26	0	24
4	Airdrie Albion	14	7	1	6	40	28	12	22
5	Cellar Bar Colts	14	6	1	7	51	46	5	19
6	Greengairs Dynamo Afc	14	3	2	9	29	56	-27	11
7	Renfrewshire United	14	3	1	10	32	68	-36	10
8	Lochgreen Afc	14	0	1	13	23	76	-53	1

	FIRST DIVISION	P	W	D	L	F	A	+-	PTS
1	Waverley afc	18	15	1	2	91	16	75	46
2	CC Infinity	18	14	0	4	66	27	39	42
3	Eastend Utd Afc	18	13	0	5	56	31	25	39
4	Wishaw Wycombe wanderers 1997	18	12	1	5	63	35	28	37
5	Coatbridge United Afc	18	11	2	5	73	36	37	35
6	Unity Afc	18	7	1	10	43	50	-7	22
7	Airdrie Athletic Afc	18	6	0	12	45	66	-21	18
8	Redbridge Rovers Afc	18	5	1	12	38	50	-12	16
9	Clyde Thistle Afc	18	2	1	15	12	116	-104	7
10	Monklands Utd Afc	18	1	1	16	23	83	-60	4

	SECOND DIVIAION	P	W	D	L	F	A	+-	PTS
1	Baillieston Afc	24	22	0	2	145	24	121	66
2	The Burgh	24	20	1	3	102	49	53	61
3	Condorrat Weavers	24	20	0	4	138	58	80	60
4	Coltness Utd	24	18	1	5	110	42	68	55
5	Motherwell Villa Afc	24	11	1	12	76	66	10	34
6	The Well Foundation	22	9	3	10	70	68	2	30
7	Wishaw Athletic	23	9	2	12	49	75	-26	29
8	Eastend Thistle Afc	23	7	6	10	61	77	-16	27
9	Bellshill Athletic	24	8	1	15	59	82	-23	25
10	Bellshill Utd	24	7	2	15	51	89	-38	23
11	Airdrie Utd Reds	22	7	1	14	57	116	-59	22
12	Viewpark Utd	23	3	1	19	42	113	-71	10
13	Newarthill Athletic Afc	23	1	1	21	33	134	-101	4

CUP FINALS

Billy Harkness Memorial Cup Final (May 28 at Airdrieonian
The Rolling Barrell v The Burgh, 5-1

Billy Harkness Challenge Cup Final (May 28 at Airdrieonian
Bullfrog v Baillieston, 4-3

Premier League Cup Final (April 30, at Airdrieonians FC)
Airdrie Albion v Bullfrog, 2-1

First Division Cup Final (April 30th, at Airdrieonians FC)
Coatbridge United v Wishaw Wycombe Wanderers, 3-6

New Cup Final (April 27, at Airdrieonians)
Clyde Thistle v Well Foundation 2-2, 2-3p

Second Division Cup Final (April 16 at Airdrieonians FC)
Coltness United v Baillieston, 1-4

All-In Cup Final (Mar 31, at Airdrieonians FC)
Bullfrog v Airdrie Albion, 2-2, 4-2p

VENUES	
Airdrie Sports Centre	ML6 7HU
Bathgate Sports Centre	EH48 4LA
Bothwellhaugh Park, Motherwell	ML1 3RB
Broadwood Stadium	G68 9NE
Caldervale HS	ML6 8PG
Carrick Park, Gleboig	ML5 2QW
Cathedral Primary School	ML1 1DX
Central Park, Airdrie	ML6 6AS
Coltness HS	ML2 8LY
Craigneuk Parks, Airdrie	ML6 8JT
Crownpoint Stadium, Glasgow	G40 2AL
Dalziel Park, Motherwell	ML1 5RZ
Excelsior Stadium, Airdrie	ML6 8QZ
Firhill Complex, Glasgow	G20 7HH
Gartcairn Park, Airdrie	ML6 7HU
Greenfield Sports Centre, Shettleston	G32 6TP
Hamilton Palace Grounds	ML3 6EF
Keir Hardie SC, Holytown	ML1 4TP
Ladywell Road, Motherwell	ML1 3HQ
Lochend HS, Easterhouse	G34 0NZ
Matt Busby SC, Bellshill	ML4 3DP
Morar Park, Motherwell	
Petershill Park, Glasgow	G21 4DD
Ravenscraig SC, Motherwell	ML1 2TZ
Renfrew Leisure Centre	PA4 8JH
Rockburn Park, Bellshill	ML4 3EU
Seedhill Sports Centre, Paisley	PA1 1RQ
Stepford Sports Complex, Glasgow	G33 4NU
Townhead Community Centre, Coatbridge	ML5 2HT
Whifflet Park, Coatbridge	ML5 4HF
Wishaw SC	ML2 0HQ

Teams tend not to have any one fixed home venue

AYRSHIRE AMATEUR FA 2016/17

act:
cis Andrews (Match Secretary)
0734101
isandrews@live.co.uk

'/www.ayrshireafa.co.uk

Ayrshire Amateur League is one of the gest in the country both in terms of ty and membership. The League had 49 ber clubs in 2016/17, four fewer than in /16.

r West Recreation	1	Black / White	Ardeer Quarry
ssan Castle Rovers	1	Red / Black	St Matthews Acad, Ardrossan
nleck Boswell	2	Black / Gold	Merlin Park, Auchinleck
Ams	2	Black / White	Beith Astro
eld Lochan	2	Blue / Black	Riccarton Park, Kilmarnock
nlands	3	Blue / White	Annick Park, Irvine
k	P	Blue / White	Glebe Park, Maybole
e	2	Blue / Yellow	Riverside Park, Catrine
Drive	P	Blue / White	Irvine Sports Club
on	3	Orange / Black	Coylton Public Park
e	2	Blue / White	Grange Academy 3G, Kilmarnock
			Newlands Drive, Kilmarnock
hill Thistle	2	Blue / White	Crosshill Public Park, Nr Maybole
house Waverley	3	Red / Black	Lindsay Park, Crosshouse
ock AFC	1	Black / White	Broomfield Park, Cumnock
	1	Maroon / Sky	Riverside Park, Dailly
Ams	3	Blue / White	Dalry Public Park
l Vics	3	Red / Black	Jamieson Park, Newmilns
	1	Blue	Scott Ellis PF, Kilmarnock
s Athletic	P	Royal Blue	Kilwinning Sports Centre
gan United	2	Sky Blue / White	Drongan Public Park
ick Thistle	1	Royal Blue	Riccarton Park, Kilmarnock
on United	P	Red / Black	Loudon Academy, Galston
uir Thistle	1	Navy Blue	Logan Playing Field, Logan
urn MW	P	Yellow / Blue	Prestwick Academy
ord Ams	1	Red / Black	Richardson Park, Hurlford
ord Thistle	P	Yellow / Blue	Richardson Park, Hurlford
Town	2	Royal Blue / Yellow	Quarry Road, Irvine
nie	1	Amber / Black	Valefield, Kilbirnie
de Thistle	P	Royal Blue	St Matthews Acad, Ardrossan
rnock AFC	2	Blue	Dean Park, Kilmarnock
entiber	1	Royal Blue	Knockentiber Public Park
	2	Royal Blue	Bowencraig Park, Largs
			Barrfields, Largs
hline United	1	Blue / White	Beechgrove Park, Mauchline
hant	3	Red / Yellow	Kewnston Park, Minishant
blown Boswell	P	Blue / White	Goodwin Drive, Annbank
Cumnock Afton	2	Red / White	Greenhead Park, New Cumnock
Farm Loch	2	Red / White	Dean Park, Kilmarnock
tree United	2	Red / Blue	Broomfield Park, Cumnock
wick AFC	2	Blue / Black	The Oval, Prestwick
lees	P	Red / Black	Burn Park, Shortlees, Kilmarnock
arton Annick	3	White / Blue	Cocklebie Park, Stewarton
arton United	1	Red / Yellow	Stewarton Sports Centre
ngton Caledonian	3	Red / Black	Shaw Park, Symington
lton	P	Royal Blue	Tarbolton Public Park
Dundonald	1	Maroon / Sky	Marr College Playing Field, Troon
etoun AFC	1	Black / White	KGV Playing Field, Ayr
Kilbride	P	Amber / Black	Kirktonhall Glen, West Kilbride
nton Wolves	P	Old Gold / Black	Quarry Road, Irvine

PREMIER	P	W	D	L	F	A	GD	Pts
Hurlford Thistle	22	19	2	1	102	28	74	59
Glenburn MW	22	18	2	2	83	31	52	56
Dirrans Athletic	22	13	2	7	61	41	20	41
Shortlees	22	13	4	3	78	33	45	37
Kilbride Thistle	22	8	2	12	60	67	-7	29
Clark Drive	22	10	2	10	42	55	-13	26
Carrick	22	7	2	13	32	47	-15	26
West Kilbride	22	9	4	9	60	48	12	25
Galston United	22	7	3	12	44	66	-22	24
Tarbolton	22	4	5	13	39	68	-29	20
Mossblown Boswell	22	3	3	14	35	94	-59	12
Winlinton Wolves	22	3	1	18	42	98	-56	7

FIRST DIVISION	P	W	D	L	F	A	GD	Pts
Hurlford AFC	26	21	2	3	104	36	68	65
Cumnock AFC	26	20	2	4	104	35	69	62
Ardrossan Castle Rovers	26	17	1	8	61	35	26	52
Dailly	26	15	4	7	64	37	27	49
Kilbirnie	26	15	1	10	76	51	25	46
Stewarton United	26	13	5	8	70	50	20	44
Ardeer West Recreation	26	12	7	7	76	56	20	43
Mauchline United	26	9	4	13	48	66	-18	31
Glenmuir Thistle	26	9	1	16	53	90	-37	28
Knockentiber	26	7	5	14	45	61	-16	26
Troon Dundonald	26	7	3	16	47	80	-33	24
Dean AFC	26	7	2	17	43	90	-47	23
Wallacetoun AFC	26	3	5	16	46	68	-22	14
Fenwick Thistle	26	4	2	20	38	120	-82	14

SECOND DIVISION	P	W	D	L	F	A	GD	Pts
Catrine	22	17	1	4	72	21	51	52
Crosshill Thistle	22	15	3	4	53	33	20	48
Kilmarnock AFC	22	15	2	5	64	41	23	47
New Farm Loch	22	14	3	5	68	34	34	45
Largs Thistle	22	13	2	7	69	43	26	41
Craigie	22	12	2	8	60	45	15	38
Irvine Town	22	10	6	6	65	43	22	36
Beith	22	4	6	12	36	49	-13	18
Auchinleck Boswell	22	4	3	15	37	83	-46	15
Drongan United	22	3	5	14	30	58	-28	14
Bellfield Lochan AFC	22	2	4	16	26	60	-34	10
Ochiltree United	22	4	1	17	35	101	-66	10
New Cumnock Afton AFC	0	0	0	0	0	0	0	0
Prestwick AFC	0	0	0	0	0	0	0	0

THIRD DIVISION	P	W	D	L	F	A	GD	Pts
Crosshouse Waverley	21	15	3	3	65	30	35	48
Dalry Ams	21	14	3	4	67	33	34	45
Coylton	21	10	5	6	54	54	0	37
Minishant	21	9	6	6	47	41	6	36
Symington Caledonian	21	8	2	11	59	55	4	26
Darvel Victoria	21	5	2	14	43	61	-18	17
Broomlands	21	6	3	12	36	60	-24	17
Stewarton Annick	21	4	2	15	39	72	-33	2
Moorpark Thistle	0	0	0	0	0	0	0	0

	AYRSHIRE CUP	JAMES SCOTT MEMORIAL TROPHY	THISTLE BAR TROPHY
1935/6	Ayr Corinthians	(North Ayrshire)	(South Ayrshire)
1936/7	Kilmarnock Accies		
1937/8	Boswell Thistle		
1938/9	Maybole Ams		
1939/40	Glenburn Ams		
1945/6	Towholm United		
1946/7	Claremont Ams		
1947/8	Galston Ams		
1948/9	Eglinton Ams		
1949/50	Girvan Ams		
1950/1	Crosshill Thistle		Ayr British Leghion
1951/2	Star of the Sea	Eglinton Ams	Ayr British Leghion
1952/3	Dunlop Corinthians	Irvine Corinthians	Springside Ams
1953/4	Springside Ams	Eglinton Ams	Crosshill Thistle
1954/5	Crosshill Thistle	Glengarnock Thistle	Crosshill Thistle
1955/6	Star of the Sea	Shell Ams	Glenfield Welfare
1956/7	Crosshill Thistle	Shell Ams	Newmilns Ams
1957/8	Dunlop Corinthians	Star of the Sea	Minishant Ams
1958/9	Crosshill Thistle	Ardrossan Winton	Minishant Ams
1959/60	Ramblos Ams	Girdle Toll United	Crosshill Thistle
1960/1	Ayr Volants	Girdle Toll United	Barony Colliery
1961/2	Minishant Ams	Crosshouse Waverley	Crosshill Thistle
1962/3	Crosshill Thistle	Eglinton Ams	Crosshill Thistle
1963/4	Crosshill Thistle	Crosshouse Waverley	Crosshill Thistle
1964/5	Mossblown Ams	St Joseph's	Dalmellington Red Star
1965/6	Eglinton Ams	Fenwick Thistle	Dalrymple Ams
1966/7	Minishant Ams	Irviine United	Crosshill Thistle
1967/8	St Joseph's	Troon Rovers	Drongan Utd
1968/9	Knockentiber	Dirrans Ath / Fenwick Thistle	Vale of Girvan
1969/70	Eglinton Ams	Dirrans Ath	Vale of Girvan
1970/1	Crosshouse Waverley	Crosshouse Waverley	Stiebel Ams
1971/2	Dirrans Athletic	Girdle Toll United	Crosshill Thistle
1972/3	Whitletts Ams	Knockentiber	Whitletts Ams
1973/4	Newmilns Vesuvius	Winlinton Wolves	Vale of Girvan
1974/5	Knockentiber	Knockentiber	Vale of Girvan
1975/6	Crosshouse Waverley	Knockentiber	Vale of Girvan
1976/7	Crosshouse Waverley	West Kilbride	Darvel Vics
1977/8	Crosshouse Waverley	Knockentiber	Galston Ams
1978/9	Knockentiber	Crosshouse Waverley	Minishant Ams
1979/80	Crosshouse Waverley	Knockentiber	Heathside
1980/1	Knockentiber	Knockentiber	Heathside
1981/2	Darvel Vics	Ardrossan Castle Rovers	Minishant Ams
1982/3	Knockentiber	Crosshouse Waverley	Heathside
1983/4	Hysters	Knockentiber	Heathside
1984/5	Drongan Utd	Knockentiber	Drongan Utd
1985/6	Knockentiber	Crossbrae Thistle	Wallacefield
1986/7	Knockentiber	Knockentiber	Drongan Utd
1987/8	Clark Drive	Ardrossan Castle Rovers	Dalmellington Red Star
1988/9	Johnnie Walkers	Dreghorn SC	Galston United
1989/90	Clark Drive	Knockentiber	Drongan Utd
1990/1	Minishant Ams	Clark Drive	Maybole Ams
1991/2	Heathside	Johnnie Walkers	Heathside
1992/3	Shortlees	Knockentiber	Heathside
1993/4	Knockentiber	Girdle Toll United	Heathside
1994/5	Clark Drive	Knockentiber	Galston United
1995/6	West Kilbride	West Kilbride	Heathside
1996/7	Dailly Ams	Not awarded	Heathside
1997/8	Knockentiber	Bourtreehill	Heathside
1998/9	Dailly Ams	Clark Drive	Dailly Ams
1999/00	Maybole Ams	Kilwinning Ams	Mossblown
2000/1	Mossblown Ams	Clark Drive	Maybole Ams
2001/2	Maybole Ams	West Kilbride	Maybole Ams
2002/3	Galston United	Knockentiber	Hurlford Thistle
2003/4	Craigie Ams	Clark Drive	Hurlford Thistle
2004/5	Ardeer Rovers	Dean Thistle	Hurlford Thistle
2005/6	Clark Drive	Knockentiber	Broomfield Rov
2006/7	Clark Drive	Knockentiber	Broomfield Rov
2007/8	Knockentiber	Clark Drive	Hurlford Thistle
2008/9	Knockentiber	Knockentiber	Glenburn MW
2009/10	Hurlford Thistle	Clark Drive	Galston United
2010/1	Galston United	Clark Drive	Hurlford Thistle
2011/2	Hurlford Thistle	Girdle Toll United	Hurlford Thistle
2012/3	Hurlford Thistle	Stewarton United	Hurlford Thistle
2013/4	Clark Drive	Clark Drive	Hurlford Thistle
2014/5	Hurlford Thistle	Ardrossan Castle Rovers	Carrick
2015/6	Shortlees	Dirrans Athletic	Hurlford Thistle
2016/7	Hurlford Thistle	Shortlees	Hurlford Thistle

CUP FINALS

EDF Energy Ayrshire Cup, May 26 at Auchinleck Tal
Hurlford Thistle v New Farm Loch, 3-0

Thistle Bar Trophy, May 19 at Hurlford United JFC
Hurlford Thistle v Galston United, 2-0

James Scott Trophy, May 16 at Ardeer Stadium
Shortlees v Kilbride Thistle 2-1aet

Donsport Trophy, May 14 at Cumnock JFC
West Kilbride v Glenburn MW, 2-1

Eric White Trophy, Oct 16 at Kilwinning Sports Cent
Shortlees v Hurlford Thistle, 1-1, 3-2 pens

AYRSHIRE SUNDAY AF
2016/17

DIVISION 1	P	W	D	L	F	A
Charlie's Bar	14	12	1	1	58	18
AFC Whitehirst	14	8	3	3	38	22
Irvine Vics Amateurs	14	8	2	4	53	40
Bobby's Bar	14	8	0	6	50	38
Irvine No1 CSC	14	7	1	6	49	42

DIVISION 2	P	W	D	L	F	A
Elms	15	7	3	5	46	44
Kilbirnie United	15	7	3	5	46	34
Killie Athletic	15	5	2	8	51	57
Dalry Tartan	15	3	2	10	29	55
Kilmarnock Supporters FC	15	2	5	8	35	46
Castlehill Vaults	15	1	2	12	18	77

"Split" league Format Used

CUP FINALS

Go Vending Cup Final, June 2
Irvine No 1 CSC v AFC Whitehirst, 5-3

Association Cup Final, May 21
Charlie's Bar v Irvine No 1 CSC, 3-1

Wayne Bannerman Memorial trophy, May 5
Kilmarnock Supporters v Dalry Tartan, 2-0

CUP FINALS

Waddell Cup (All In), May 13 at Greenlaw
Hawick Waverley v Chirnside United, 5-4

Border Cup (Div A), Oct 29 at Greenlaw)
Chirnside United v Jed Legion, 1-0

Beveridge Cup (Div A), May 5 at Duns
Chirnside United v Greenlaw, 2-0

Vright Cup (Div B), Oct 29 at Kerfield Park, Peebles
Hawick United v Biggar United, 4-0

Valls Cup (Div B), Apr 29 at Earlston
Hawick United v Newtown, 5-4 aet

'ollie Cup (Div C), Nov 5 at Ancrum
:FC Bowholm v St Boswells, 4-2

anderson Cup (Div C), April 29 at Kelso
Duns v Lauder, 4-1

orsyth Cup, May 6 at Earlston
Hawick United v Biggar United, 1-0

BORDER AMATEUR FA

Contact: Colin Campbell
Email colinhcam@talktalk.net
Tel 01450 373840
www.bafl.leaguerepublic.com

Membership of the Border Amateur FA remained constant - 30 clubs in 2015/16 and 30 in 2016/17. For 2017/18 West Barns Star have moved to the Lothians Amateur League.

However, 5 new teams have entered for 2017/18 - Langlee Rovers (Gala), Highfields United (Berwick), Gala Fairydean Rovers Ams, Gala Thistle and Tweeddale Rovers Colts (Peebles).

order Amateur League, Placings Since 1990

	1990-1	1991-2	1992-3	1993-4	1994-5	1995-6	1996-7	1997-8	1998-9	1999-00	2000-1	2001-2	2002-3	2003-4	2004-5	2005-6	2006-7	2007-8	2008-9	2009-10	2010-11	2011-12	2012-13	2013-14	2014-15	2015-16	2016/17
botsford Albion / Melrose																							C11	C5	C10	C9	
crum	A11	B6	B1	A9	B6	B3	B10	B2	A10	A12	B8	B6	B5	B6	B2	A9	A7	A12	B8	B6	B6	B3	B1	A8	A10	B10	C9
ton	B14	C8	C6	C9	C7	C6	C4	B1	A9	A8	A7	A12	B9	B8	B3												
rwick Colts																											C6
rwick Harrow						C1	B7	B3	B3	B1	A8	A8	A9														
ggar / Biggar United																								B10	C3	C2	B5
C Bowholm																		C11	C8	C12	C5	C2	B11	C8	C9	C5	C5
imside / Chirnside United Colts	B8	C2	B9	C1	B4	B10	B11	B11	C5	C7	C9	C8	C10	C10	C11	C8	C9	C13	C4	C1	B8	B12	C5	C1	B10		
imside / Chirnside United	A2	A3	A1	A2	A1	A2	A1	A5	A7	A9	A9	A4	A3	A4	A3	A3	A5	A2	A1	A2	A6	A8	A5	A1	A7	A5	A1
ckburnspath / Dunbar Ams		C7	C4	C5	C3	C9	C8	C1	B2	A10	A10	A10	A10	A5	A8	A12											
ldstream Amateurs	B2	B7	B10	C10	C9	C3	C1	B4	B1	A5	A4	A7	A7		C7	C3	B1	A8	A12	B8	B9	B6	B9	B6	B3	B5	B3
ns Amateurs Colts																		C12									
ns Legion / Duns Ams	A1	A2	A2	A4	A2	A6	A4	A1	A1	A2	A12	B9	B7	B1	A7	A6	A2	A6	A10	A4	A1	A10	A12		C2	B9	C2
ns Legion Colts	B10	C5	C7	C2	B8	B11	B6	B9	B12	C4	C5																
lston Rhymers	B1	B1	A7	A10	B2	A3	A2	A2	A4	A4	A6	A2	A1	A9	A12	B4	B6	B10	C5	C4	B11	C8	C8	C2	B8	B8	B7
lston Rhymers Colts			C9																								
emouth Ams										C9							C6	C10	C3	B7	B4	B8	B3	B7	B6	B4	
emouth Legion	A12	B2	A8	A6	A8	A10	B12	B10	B4	B4	B3	B2	A12	B7													
emouth Legion Colts	B11	C12																									
a Hotspur	B6	B3	B6	B3	B7	B6	B3	A11	B6	B3	B4	B10	B10	B11	C8	C7	C4	B9	C2	B10	C3	C1	B8	B8	B7	B6	B9
a McQueen					C10	C4	C3	B7	B11	C8	C3	C2	B2	A7	A9	A11											
a Rovers / Gala Fairydean Rovers Reserves	A7	A6	A9	B4	B1	A1	A5	A7	A2	A1	A1	A1	A5	A1	A4	A4	A9	A3	A3	A3	A5	A4	A1	A9	A2		
a United / Athletic																		C5	C10	C2	B12	C10	C12				
don	B16	C11	C8	C6	C6	C8	C7	C9	C9	C6	C4	C7	C8	C5	C3	B5	B9	C2	B6	B1	A7		C2	B1	A3	A2	A8
enlaw	B12	C4	C12		C11	C10	C12	C5	C1	B11	C2	B8	B11	C4	C2	B8	B5	B4	B2	A8	A12	B1	A9	A6	A6	A6	A2
ick Legion	A4	A1	A3	A3	A10	B2	A3	A6	A3	A3	A11	B7	B1	A3	A5	A7	A6	A4	A4	A9	A10	A11	B10	B5	B2	A9	B4
ick Legion Rovers	B5	B4	B8	B5	B10	B12	C2	B12	C7	C5	C10	C6	C9	C8	C4	C5	C8	C3	C7	C10	C7	C11	C9	C9	C4	C8	C7
ick United	A3	A9	B5	B1	A9	B4	B8	B8	B5	B9	B6	B1	A11	A11	B4	B2	A11	B6	B1	A12	B10	B10	B4	B3	B4	B3	B1
ick United Colts	B9	C3	B7	B8	B12	C13	C10	C6	C8	C11	C8	C4	C6	C6	C5	C2	B4										
ick Waverley	A10	A5	A6	A1	A7	A4	A8	A4	A8	A7	A2	A6	A2	A6	A1	A8	A3	A10	A8	A6	A9	A3	A7	A5	A8	A8	A4
ick Youth Centre / Scrumz /Mayfield /Thistle			C10	C7	C5	C7	C11	C7	C6	C3	C7	C1	B12														
rts of Liddesdale																					C2	B2	A8	A11			
ot	A9	A7	A5	A7	A4	A8																					
Legion	A14	B9	C5	C3	B9	B7	B9	B6	B7	B2	A5	A11	B8	B4	B9	C1	B7	B5	B5	B2	A11	B9	B6	B2	A9	A3	A6
so Amateurs	B13	C10	C2	B9	C4	C12	C9	C10	C2	B8	B12																C8
so Thistle	B3	B8	B3	B6	B3	B5	B2	A9	A6	A6	A3	A9	A6	A10	A11	B10	C5	C1	B3	B11	C11	C5	C6	C3	C8	B4	B6
gholm Legion					C2	B1	A6	A3	A11	B5	B10	B4	B3	B5	B6	B1	A10	A7	A11	B5	B2	A6	A11	B4	B1	A7	A9
der	A5	A8	A10	B10	C8	C2	B4	B5	B10	B6	B7	B11	C2	B3	B8	B9	B8	C4	C6	C5	C4	C4	C4	C6	C5	C6	C3
en Rovers	B4	B10	C1	B2	A5	A5		C3	C3	C2	B1	A3	A4	A2	A6	A2	A1	A5	A2	A1	A2	A2	A3	A2	A1	A10	B10
on Hotspur																				C3	B3	B4	B7	B9	B9	B7	B8
ose																											C4
town						C11	C5	C2	B8	B12	C1	B5	B6	B10	C6	C4	C1	B3	A5	A7	A8	A9	A2	A7		C1	B2
les Ams															C9	C6	C3	B8	B10	C9		C7	C10		C7	C3	
les Rovers Reserves																					C6						
caitland													C1	B2	A2	A1	A4	A1	A6	A5	A3	A1	A4				
rk Victoria	A13	B5	B4	B7	B11	C5	C6	C8	C4	C1	B5	B3	B4	B9	B5	B6	B2	A11	B9	C6	C1	B11	B5	B11	C11	C7	C10
al Rovers	A8																										
oswells														C9	C10	C10	C10	C7	C9	C11	C8	C9	C7	C4	C6	C10	C1
[illegible]	B7	C1	B2	A5	A3	A7	A7	A8	A5	A11	B2	A5	A8	A8	A10	A10	A12	B1	A7	A11	B5	B5	B2	A3	A4	A4	A7
eddale Rovers Colts / Rovers		C9	C11	C8	C1	B8	B5	A10	A12	B7	B11	C3	C3	C1	B7	B7	B10	C6	C1	B4	B1	A5	A6	A10	B5	B1	A5
edmouth Amateurs / Berwick Legion	B15	C6	C3	C4	B5	B9	B1	A12	B9	B10	B9	B12	C7	C3	C1	B3	B3	B7	B4	B3	B7	B7		C7	C1	B2	A10
dmouth Amateurs Colts																		C8	C11	C8	C10	C6	C3				
Barns Star													C4	C2	B1	A5	A8	A9	A9	A10	A4	A7	A10	A4	A5	A1	A3
on																	C2	B2	B7	B9		C3	B12				
olm	A6	A4	A4	A8	A6	A9		C4	C10	C10	C6	C5	C5	C7	C12	C9	C7	C9	C12	C7	C9						

Divisions, Division A, B and C

MAJOR POST WAR HONOURS							
	LEAGUE CHAMPIONS	BORDER CUP	BEVERIDGE CUP	WADDELL CUP	WRIGHT CUP	WALLS CUP	COLLIE CUP
1946/7		Gala Fairydean					
1947/8	Hawick SC LNER	Gala Fairydean	Hawick Royal Albert				
1948/9	Hawick Royal Albert		Hawick Royal Albert				
1949/50	Gala Rovers	Penicuik Athletic	Lauder Leadervale				
1950/1	Gala Rovers	Peebles Rovers	Fairydean Ams				
1951/2		Peebles Rovers	Roxburgh United				
1952/3	Gala Rovers	Peebles Rovers	Lauder Leadervale				
1953/4	Gala Rovers	Vale of Leithen	Gala Rovers				
1954/5	Gala Rovers	Eyemouth United	Selkirk Parkvale Rovers				
1955/6	Greenlaw	Gala Fairydean	Gala Amateurs				
1956/7	Greenlaw		Ancrum				
1957/8	Greenlaw		Jedburgh Amateurs				
1958/9	Leithen Rovers		Leithen Rovers				
1959/60	Leithen Rovers		Leithen Rovers				
1960/1	Morebattle	Morebattle					
1961/2	Morebattle	Morebattle					
1962/3	Hawick Legion	Gala Rovers	Gala Hotspur		Gala Rovers		
1963/4	Gala Rovers	Kelso Thistle	Kelso United		Leithen Rovers		
1964/5	Hawick Legion		Gala Amateurs		Gala Ams		
1965/6	Hawick Legion	Hawick United	Gala Amateurs		Gala Rovers		
1966/7	Kelso United	Hawick Legion	Gala Rovers		Hawick Legion Rovers		
1967/8	Duns Amateurs	Gala Rovers	Duns Amateurs		Leithen Rovers		
1968/9	Hawick Legion		Kelso United		Duns Ams	Hawick United	
1969/70	Hawick Legion		Leithen Rovers				
1970/1	Kelso United	Hawick Legion	Hawick United		Hawick Utd Colts	Earlston Rhymers	
1971/2	Hawick United		Hawick United		Gala Hotspur	Gala Hotspur	Kelso United
1972/3	Gala Hotspur	Chirnside	Kelso United		Hawick Legion Rovers	Lauder	Hawick Legion
1973/4	Hawick United		Hawick United		Chirnside	Hawick Utd Colts	Hawick Utd
1974/5	Greenlaw		Leithen Rovers		Morebattle	Yetholm	
1975/6	Hawick Legion	Hawick United	Hawick United			Hawick YC	
1976/7	Leithen Rovers	Greenlaw	Hawick United	Greenlaw	Yetholm	Heriot	
1977/8	Gala Rovers		Gala Rovers	Greenlaw	Peebles Rovers	Peebles Rovers	
1978/9	Gala Hotspur	Peebles Rovers	Peebles Rovers	Greenlaw	Earlston Rhymers		
1979/80	Gala Hotspur		Gala Hotspur	Eyemouth Legion	St Abbs Thistle	Selkirk Vics	
1980/1	Gala Hotspur	Hawick YC	Hawick Legion	Hawick Legion	Kelso Legion Thistle		
1981/2	Hawick United		Hawick YC	St Abbs Thistle	Ancrum	Eyemouth Colts	
1982/3	Hawick United	Ancrum	Hawick Waverley	Spittal Rovers	Spittal Rovers	Spittal Rovers	
1983/4	Eyemouth Legion	Hawick United	Gala Hotspur		Selkirk Vics	Selkirk Vics	
1984/5	Hawick United	Hawick United	Hawick United	Earlston Rhymers	Gala Rovers	Grove	
1985/6	Hawick United	Hawick United	Hawick United	Hawick Waverley	Grove	St Abbs Thistle	
1986/7	Gala Rovers	Hawick Waverley	Selkirk Victoria	Hawick Waverley	Ancrum	Leithen Rovers	
1987/8	Eyemouth Legion	Eyemouth Legion	Hawick Legion	Gala Rovers	Heriot	Ancrum	
1988/9	Spittal Rovers	Duns Legion	Eyemouth Legion	Eyemouth Legion	Heriot	Heriot	
1989/90	Duns Legion	Hawick United	Duns Legion	Eyemouth Legion	Earlston Rhymers	Ancrum	
1990/1	Duns Legion	Hawick Legion	Selkirk Victoria	Spittal Rovers	Stow	Earlston Rhymers	
1991/2	Hawick Legion	Heriot	Eyemouth Legion	Chirnside	Chirnside Colts	Chirnside Colts	
1992/3	Chirnside	Duns Legion	Chirnside	Chirnside	Hawick United	Kelso Thistle	Leithen Rovers
1993/4	Hawick Waverley	Chirnside	Chirnside	Ancrum	Leithen Rovers	Hawick Legion Rovers	Chirnside Colts
1994/5	Chirnside	Chirnside	Chirnside	Chirnside	Gala Rovers	Gala Rovers	Coldstream Ams
1995/6	Gala Rovers	Gala Rovers	Gala Rovers	Earlston Rhymers	Kelso Thistle	Gala Hotspur	Coldstream Ams
1996/7	Chirnside	Lanmgholm Legion	Stow	Duns Legion	Gala Hotspur	Kelso Thistle	Hawick Legion Rovers
1997/8	Duns Legion	Hawick Legion	Duns Legion	Duns Legion	Berwick Harrow	Ayton	Cockburnspath
1998/9	Duns Legion	Duns Legion	Chirnside	Stow	Cockburnspath	Hawick United	Leithen Rovers
1999/00	Gala Rovers	Gala Rovers	Duns Legion	Earlston Rhymers	Jed Legion	Jed Legion	Selkirk Vics
2000/1	Gala Rovers	Chirnside	Hawick Waverley	Gala Rovers	Gala Hotspur	Gala Hotspur	Gala McQueen
2001/2	Gala Rovers	Gala Rovers	Leithen Rovers	Hawick Waverley	Eyemouth	Duns Legion	Gala McQueen
2002/3	Earlston Rhymers	Gala Rovers	Gala Rovers	Gala Rovers	Jed Legion	Hawick Legion	Pencaitland
2003/4	Gala Rovers	Kelso Thistle	Gala McQueen	Duns Ams	Duns Ams	Duns Ams	West Barns Star
2004/5	Hawick Waverley	Hawick Waverley	Chirnside	Hawick Waverley	West Barn Star	Ancrum	Gordon
2005/6	Pencaitland	Pencaitland	Pencaitland	Pencaitland	Selkirk Vics	Hawick United	Coldstream Ams
2006/7	Leithen Rovers	Chirnside	Leithen Rovers	Duns Ams	Jed Legion	Gordon	Winton
2007/8	Pencaitland	Hawick Waverley	Hawick Legion	Leithen Rovers	Stow	Greenlaw	Gordon
2008/9	Chirnside	Chirnside	Leithen Rovers	Newtown	Jed Legion	Hawick United	Tweeddale Rovers
2009/10	Leithen Rovers	Hawick Legion	Gala Rovers	Pencaitland	Gordon	Tweeddale Rovers	Linton Hotspur
2010/1	Duns Amateurs	Pencaitland	Pencaitland	Leithen Rovers	Tweeddale Rovers	Tweeddale Rovers	Selkirk Vics
2011/2	Pencaitland	Leithen Rovers	Hawick Waverley	Pencaitland	Ancrum	Ancrum	CFC Bowholm
2012/3	Gala Rovers	Pencaitland	Gala Rovers	Gala Rovers	Hawick Legion	Ancrum	Biggar
2013/4	Chirnside United	West Barns Star	Newtown	Greenlaw	Gordon	Gordon	Lauder
2014/5	Leithen Rovers	Gala Fairydean Rovers	Gala Fairydean Rovers	Stow	Eyemouth Ams	Hawick Legion	Weddmouth Ams
2015/6	West Barns Star	Gordon	Gordon	Stow	Gala Hotspur	Hawick United	Newtown
2016/7	Chirnside United	Chirnside United	Chirnside United	Hawick Waverley	Hawick United	Hawick United	CFC Bowholm

mateur FA Clubs 2016/17	Ground	Colours
	Bridgend	Yellow
Colts	Billendean / Ivinson / Old Shielfield	
	Hartree Mill / Kerfield Park	Blue / Black
	Monteith Park, Carstairs	
	King George V Park, Carnwath	
	Symington	
holm	Canonbie Playing Field	Tangerine / Black
e United	Comrades Park	Green / Black
n Amateurs	Home Park	Blue
ateurs	New Hawthorn Park	Red / Black
Rhymers	Runciman Park	Blue / White
spur	Netherdale, Galashiels	Blue / White
	Stewart Park	Black / Gold
y	WS Happer Memorial ark	Green / Black
egion	Wilton Lodge Park	Green / Black
egion Rovers	Volunteer Park 3G / Wilton Lodge	Light Blue / White
nited	Albert Park / Volunteer Park 3G	Gold / Black
Waverley	Wilton Lodge Park / Volunteer Parfk 3G	Yellow / Black
n	Elliot Park	Blue
ns	Woodside Park	
stle	Woodside Park	Black / White
n Legion	Castleholm / Scholars Park 3G	Yellow / Black
	Woodcot Pavilion	Yellow / Black
Rovers	Victoria Park / Walkerburn Rugby Club	Blue
otspur	New Moor Road / Penicuik Leisure C	Blue / White
	Penicuik 3G / Auchendinny	
	Wellington School	
	Tweedbank	Yellow / Black
	Netherdale, Galashiels	
	KGV Park	
ictoria	Yarrow Park	Blue
ells	Jenny Moore's Road	Maroon
	Stow Park	Yellow / Black
ale Rovers	Kerfield Park, Peebles	Red / White
outh Ams	Five Arches / Berwick Acad	Black / Gold
ns Star	West Barns Park	Maroon

	A LEAGUE	P	W	D	L	F	A	+/-	Pts
1	Chirnside Utd	18	15	0	3	51	30	21	45
2	Greenlaw	18	12	2	4	56	38	18	38
3	West Barns Star	18	11	1	6	61	36	25	34
4	Hawick Waverley	18	9	3	6	48	41	7	30
5	Tweeddale Rovers	18	8	2	8	35	39	-4	26
6	Jed Legion	18	7	4	7	41	36	5	25
7	Stow	18	5	3	10	34	39	-5	18
8	Gordon	18	4	3	11	37	54	-17	15
9	Langholm Legion	18	4	3	11	33	55	-22	15
10	Tweedmouth Ams	18	3	3	12	27	55	-28	12

	B LEAGUE	P	W	D	L	F	A	+/-	Pts
1	Hawick Utd	18	15	1	2	81	32	49	46
2	Newtown	18	12	2	4	67	32	35	38
3	Coldstream Ams	18	12	1	5	52	38	14	37
4	Hawick Legion	18	10	3	5	54	33	21	33
5	Biggar Utd	18	7	3	8	48	48	0	24
6	Kelso Thistle	18	5	4	9	33	49	-16	19
7	Earlston Rhymers	18	6	1	11	32	66	-34	19
8	Linton Hotspur	18	5	3	10	39	58	-19	18
9	Gala Hotspur	18	3	5	10	27	43	-16	14
10	Leithen Rovers	18	2	3	13	36	70	-34	9

	C LEAGUE	P	W	D	L	F	A	+/-	Pts
1	St.Boswells	18	14	1	3	55	39	16	43
2	Duns	18	12	3	3	65	37	28	39
3	Lauder	18	11	3	4	60	29	31	36
4	Melrose	18	8	2	8	57	61	-4	26
5	CFC Bowholm	18	7	3	8	52	38	14	24
6	Berwick Colts	18	6	4	8	48	50	-2	22
7	Hawick Legion Rovers	18	5	4	9	48	62	-14	19
8	Kelso Ams	18	6	1	11	38	60	-22	19
9	Ancrum	18	5	2	11	33	60	-27	17
10	Selkirk Victoria	18	4	1	13	37	57	-20	13

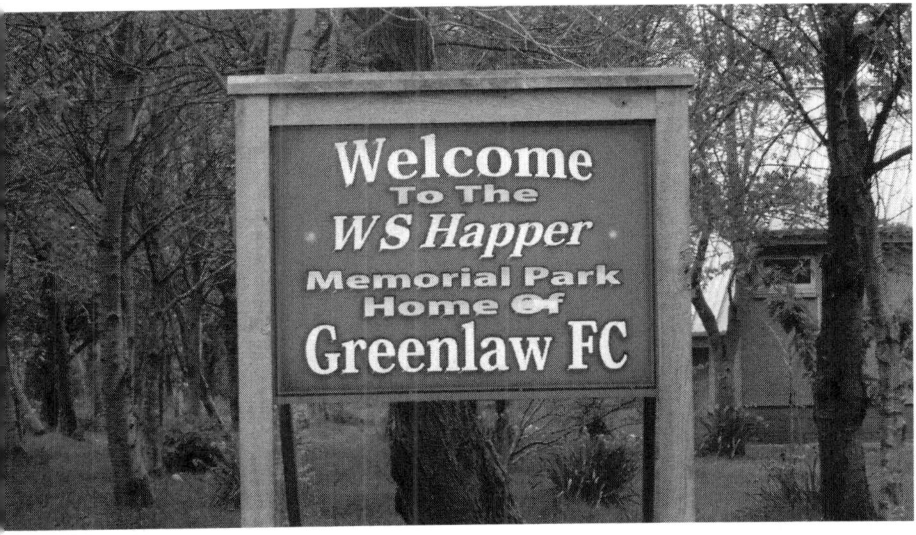

CAITHNESS AMATEUR FA 2016

The Caithness Amateur FA plays a Summer season. The Association was founded in 1927 when clubs from the Wic[k] and Thurso Leagues joined together to play for a trophy donated by Captain A J Mackay. Thurso Academicals, or Acks as they are known, won.

Contact: Andrew Lannon
Email: alannon@live.co.uk
Tel 07716 333775
www.leaguewebsite.co.uk/
caithnessamateurfootballassociation

Caithness Amateur FA 2016								
DIVISION ONE	P	W	D	L	F	A	GD	Pts
Wick Groats	14	12	1	1	54	10	44	37
Pentland United	14	9	3	2	39	20	19	30
Staxigoe United	14	7	4	3	35	25	10	22
Thurso Acks	14	4	6	4	34	30	4	18
Halkirk	14	4	5	5	23	27	-4	17
John O'Groats	14	4	1	9	22	39	-17	13
Castletown	14	2	5	7	29	43	-14	11
High Ormlie Hotspur	14	0	3	11	10	52	-42	3
DIVISION TWO	P	W	D	L	F	A	GD	Pts
Wick Thistle	16	16	0	0	82	17	65	48
FC Retro	16	12	1	3	55	27	28	37
Keiss	16	9	2	5	39	30	9	29
Thurso Pentland	16	8	2	6	50	32	18	26
Top Joes	16	8	2	6	51	44	7	26
Lybster	16	5	0	11	53	55	-2	15
Thurso Swifts	16	3	4	9	23	46	-23	13
Watten	16	3	2	11	22	59	-37	11
Francis Street Club	16	1	1	14	12	77	-65	4

League Positions Mid June 2017								
DIVISION ONE	P	W	D	L	F	A	GD	Pts
Pentland United	7	6	0	1	30	6	24	18
Wick Groats	6	6	0	0	21	1	20	18
Thurso Acks	5	4	0	1	10	7	3	12
John O'Groats	6	2	0	4	10	23	-13	6
Wick Thistle	6	1	2	3	7	17	-10	5
Staxigoe United	5	1	1	3	5	10	-5	4
Halkirk	5	0	2	3	5	10	-5	2
Castletown	6	0	1	5	7	21	-14	1
DIVISION TWO	P	W	D	L	F	A	GD	Pts
Lybster	8	7	0	1	27	9	18	21
Thurso Swifts	7	5	1	1	20	8	12	16
High Ormlie Hotspur	6	4	1	1	13	5	8	13
Top Joes	8	3	1	4	14	22	-8	10
FC Retro	8	3	0	5	11	9	2	9
Watten	7	3	0	4	13	21	-8	9
Thurso Pentland	7	2	1	4	15	18	-3	7
Keiss	7	2	1	4	11	17	-6	7
Francis Street Club	8	1	1	6	6	21	-15	4

YEAR OF FORMATION OF MAJOR CLUBS

1887	Lybster
1889	Wick Thistle
1893	Wick Groats
1897	Thurso Swifts
1898	Thurso Acks
1900	Castletown
1918	Thurso Pentland
1926	Halkirk
1927	Keiss
1948	Pentland United
1960	Wick Rovers
1980	St Francis Club
1982	John O' Groats
1983	Top Joes

League Play Off						
26/08/2016	Castleton	FC Retro	3	2		at Halkirk
CUP FINALS						
David Allan Shield						
20/08/2016	Thurso Acks	High Ormlie Hotspur	3	0		
Steven Cup						
12/08/2016	Wick Thistle	Top Joes	3	2		at Naver AW, Th
Eain McIntosh Cup						
23/07/2016	Staxigoe United	John o' Groats	3	0		at Halkirk
Archer Shield						
09/07/2016	Caithness	Orkney	1	1	4-5 pens	at The Dammes,
Colin McLeod Memorial Cup						
11/06/2016	Wick Groats	Staxigoe United	3	1	AET	at Back Park, Cas

HOME GROUNDS		
Castletown	Back Park	Naver All Weather, Thurso
FC Retro	Lower Bignold, Wick	
Francis Street Club	Upper Bignold, Wick	
Halkirk	Recreation Park	
High Ormilie Hotspur	Ormilie, Thurso	
John o' Groats	John o' Groats	
Keiss	Keiss	
Lybster	Lybster	
Pentland United	Ham Park, Dunnet	
Staxigoe United	Lower Bignold, Wick	Upper Bignold, Wick
Thurso Acks	The Dammies, Thurso	
Thurso Pentland	The Dammies	
Thurso Swifts	Naver All Weather	
Top Joes	Ormilie, Thurso	
Watten	Watten	
Wick Groats	Upper Bignold, Wick	Back Park, Castletown
Wick Thistle	Upper Bignold	

CALEDONIAN AMATEUR LEAGUE 2016/17

Contact: Ian Cowden,
Email johncowden@ntlworld.com
Tel 0141 576 8507
www.caledonianafa.org.uk

Membership for 2016/17 was 33 clubs, down 1 from 2015/16.

	PREMIER	P	W	D	L	F	A	GD	PTS	
1	Dalziel (C)	22	16	5	1	68	26	42	53	
2	Giffnock North	22	14	2	6	46	34	12	44	
3	Thorn Ath	22	13	4	5	66	40	26	43	
4	Dumbarton	22	13	4	5	51	29	22	43	
5	Doune Castle	22	8	5	9	41	44	-2	29	
6	Glasgow Harp	22	9	3	10	52	54	-2	30	
7	Gartcosh Utd	22	8	3	11	39	50	-11	27	
8	Strathclyde Uni	22	8	5	9	45	50	-5	23	(-6)
9	Milton	22	5	5	12	40	63	-23	20	
10	Cumbernauld C	22	7	2	12	32	44	-12	19	(-4)
11	Bearsden	22	5	3	14	29	55	-26	18	
12	St Mungo's	22	3	5	14	35	56	-21	14	

	DIVISION 1A	P	W	D	L	F	A	GD	PTS	
1	Westerlands	20	14	1	3	81	24	57	49	(+6)
2	Stenhousemuir	19	13	0	4	58	29	29	45	(+6)
3	Larkhall Th	19	12	4	3	91	30	61	40	
4	Eaglesham	20	12	1	7	56	33	23	37	
5	Cambusbarron	20	11	3	6	67	31	36	36	
6	Rhu	20	8	3	6	46	35	11	33	(+6)
7	Hamilton	20	7	4	9	72	42	30	25	
8	Woodhall Th	20	7	1	10	42	46	-4	22	
9	Weirs	20	4	5	10	47	49	-2	13	(-4)
10	Rothesay	20	3	2	16	43	73	-30	11	
11	Viewfield	20	0	0	18	9	220	-211	-3	(-3)

	DIVISION 1B	P	W	D	L	F	A	GD	PTS	
1	Broomhouse (C)	18	14	2	1	59	16	43	47	(+3)
2	Glasgow Uni	18	13	1	4	59	26	33	40	
3	EKYM	18	12	2	4	71	33	38	38	
4	Finnart	18	12	0	6	40	24	16	36	
5	Cambria	17	10	2	5	49	21	28	32	
6	Baillieston Jnr	18	9	2	7	46	47	-1	25	(-4)
7	Milngavie	18	4	2	12	42	60	-18	14	
8	Balmore	18	3	1	14	19	57	-38	10	
9	Symington	17	2	1	13	29	76	-47	7	
10	Corkerhill	18	2	1	15	23	72	-51	7	

CUP FINALS

Presidents Cup, June 2nd at Clyde FC
Larkhall v Westerlands, 2-1

Challenge Cup Final, May 19, AT Clyde FC
Dalziel v Glasgow Harp, 6-1

Douglas Smith League Cup, April 7, at Clyde FC
Dumbarton v Thorn, 1-0

LEAGUE PLAY OFFS

Division 1 Runners-Up Play Off
Glasgow Uni v Stenhousemuir, 2-1

Premier Division Play-Off
Cumbernauld Colts v Glasgow University, 3-1

Division 1 Winners Play Off
Westerlands v Broomhouse, 0-1

CALEDONIAN LEAGUE CHAMPIONS	
1983/4	Drumchapel Ams
	Queen's Park Hampden XI
1984/5	Bannockburn
1985/6	Muirend
1986/7	Stanley
1987/8	Stanley
1988/9	Queen's Park Hampden XI
1989/90	Liberton Cropley
1990/1	Stanley
1991/2	Dalziel HSFP
1992/3	Milngavie Wanderers
1993/4	Dalziel HSFP
1994/5	Dalziel HSFP
1995/6	Dalziel HSFP
1996/7	Bannockburn
1997/8	Dalziel HSFP
1998/9	Milton Ams
1999/00	Bannockburn
2000/1	Bannockburn
2001/2	Drumchapel Ams
2002/3	Netherton
2003/4	Coatbridge CC
2004/5	Bannockburn
2005/6	Dumbarton Academy FP
2006/7	Bannockburn
2007/8	Bannockburn
2008/9	Bannockburn
2009/10	Strathclyde University
2010/1	Bannockburn
2011/2	Glasgow Harp
2012/3	Giffnock North
2013/4	Glasgow Harp
2014/5	Doune Castle
2015/6	Doune Castle
2016/7	Dalziel HSFP

	Club Directory 2016/17 Member Club	Match Secretary	Contact Tel : No	Ground Postcode	Ground Name
1	Baillieston Junior AFC	William Andrews	07943 712410	ML5 2HT	St Ambrose HS, Coatbridge
2	Balmore AFC	Alan Crawford	7918185501	ML8 5HA/ML1 5RZ	Public Park, Law
3	Bearsden AFC	Jim Gettie	07912 731784	G61 4BP	Thorn Park, Bearsden
4	Broomhouse AFC	Russell Cairns	07812 049783	G32 6TP	Greenfield Football Centre, Shettleston
5	Cambria AFC	Ross Wilson	7837401650	G33 6ND	Strathclyde University Sports Ground
6	Cambusbarron Rovers AFC	Gary Grahamslaw	07590 913525	FK7 9LP	Mill Road Park, Cambusbarron
7	Corkerhill AFC	Alan McNaught	07910 378963	G52 1RR	Nethercraigs Sports Ground, Glasgow
8	Cumbernauld Colts AFC	Fiona McKenzie	07749 381652	G68 9NE	Broadwood Stadium, Cumbernauld
9	Dalziel HSFP AFC	Peter Langford	07952 320930	ML1 5RZ	Dalziel Park, Motherwell
10	Doune Castle AFC	William Docherty	07825 290666	FK16 6DH	Public Park, Doune
11	Dumbarton Acad FP AFC	John O`Neill	07970 806742	G82 2BL	Meadow Road, Dumbarton
12	Eaglesham AFC	Alan Kyle	07710 464 397	G77 6DT	Crookfur Park, Newton Mearns
13	East Kilbride YM AFC	Billy Hamilton	07551 994599	ML3 6BY	Ballerup Sports Ground, East Kilbride
14	Finnart AFC	Stuart McKechnie	07793 381035	G40 1HB	Glasgow Green Football Centre
15	Gartcosh United AFC	Stuart Hegarty	7837529142	G69 8AO	Gartcosh
16	Giffnock North AAC	Andrew Davies	07801 052576	G46 6HU	Giffnock North AAC, East Renfrewshire
17	Glasgow Harp AFC	Michael O`Neill	07947 691830	G64 2NE	Allan Glen's Grounds, Bishopbriggs
18	Glasgow University FC	Donald Fergusson	07789 545439	ML6 8QZ	New Broomfield Park, Airdrie
19	Hamilton FP AFC	Euan Gray	07889 886595	ML3 6BY	Bents Sports Ground, Hamilton
20	Larkhall Thistle AFC	Ian Pattie	07899 844706	ML9 1	Gasworks Park, Larkhall
21	Milngavie Wanderers AFC	David McCleary	07904 8188345	G62 7LN	Cloberfield, Milngavie
22	Milton AFC	Craig Anderson	07342 965600	FK7 0EN	Bluebellwood Park, Bannockburn
23	Rhu AFC	Bobby Dunn	07912 312535	G84 8RX	Ardconnel Park, Rhu
24	Rothesay Brandane AFC	Neil Whitelaw	07715 406912	PA20 9BS	Rothesay Stadium, Isle of Bute
25	St.Mungo`s AFC	Raymond Barrett	07500 865784	G64 2PZ	Loretto Playing Fields, Bishopbriggs
26	Stenhousemuir Community	Steven Thomson	07909 221562	FK5 3BL	Larbert High School, Stenhousemuir
27	Strathclyde University AFC	Martyn Stevenson	07967 076480	G33 6ND	Strathclyde University Sports Ground
28	Symington Tinto AFC	Douglas McMillan	07798 755200	ML12 6LL	Symington, South Lanarkshire
29	Thorn Athletic AFC	Derrick McMillan	07957 665180	PA5 0LD	Thomas Shanks Park, Johnstone
30	Viewfield Rovers AFC	Ali McMaster	07775 578795	PA12 4DE	Viewfield Park, Lochwinnoch
31	Weirs Recreation AFC	Martin Guthrie	07754 549056	G43 2HA	Albert Park, Glasgow
32	Westerlands AFC	Gerry O`Hare	07843 097572	G20 0SP	Glasgow University Sports Ground, Garscube
33	Woodhall Thistle	David France	07486 606178	ML1 2TZ	Ravenscraig, Motherwell

CALEDONIAN LEAGUE - ALL TIME MEMBERSHIP

	83/4	84/5	85/6	86/7	87/8	88/9	89/90	90/1	91/2	92/3	93/4	94/5	95/6	96/7	97/8	98/9	99/0	00/1	01/2	02/3	03/4	04/5	05/6	06/7	07/8	08/9	09/10	10/1	11/2	12/3	13/4	14/5	15/6	16/7
Baillieston Juniors																																	X	X
Balmore																				X	X	X	X	X	X	X	X	X	X	X	X	X	X	X
Bannockburn	X	X	X	X	X	X	X	X	X	X	X	X	X	X	X	X	X	X	X	X	X	X	X	X	X	X	X	X						
Barr & Stroud / Netherton	X	X	X	X	X	X	X	X	X	X	X	X	X	X	X	X	X	X	X	X	X	X	X	X										
Bearsden																							X			X	X	X	X	X	X	X	X	X
Bo'ness Amateurs		X	X	X	X	X	X	X	X	X	X	X	X	X	X	X	X	X																
Broomhouse																																X	X	X
Cambria																														X	X	X	X	X
Cambusbarron Rovers	X	X	X	X	X	X	X	X	X	X	X	X	X	X	X	X	X	X	X	X	X	X	X	X	X	X	X	X	X	X	X	X	X	X
Castlemilk																																X	X	
Coatbridge CC		X	X	X	X	X	X	X	X	X	X	X	X	X	X	X	X	X	X	X	X	X	X	X										
Corkerhill																																	X	X
Cumbernauld Colts																															X	X	X	X
Dalziel HSFP								X	X	X	X	X	X	X	X	X	X	X	X	X	X	X	X	X	X	X	X	X	X	X	X	X	X	X
Doune Castle																					X	X	X	X	X	X	X	X	X	X	X	X	X	X
Drumchapel Ams	X	X	X	X	X	X	X	X	X	X	X	X	X	X	X	X	X	X	X	X	X	X	X	X	X									
Dreumchapel FP																												X	X	X	X	X	X	
Dumbarton Academy FP																X	X	X	X	X	X	X	X	X	X	X	X	X	X	X	X	X	X	X
Eaglesham																																	X	X
East Kilbride YM													X	X	X	X	X	X	X	X	X	X	X	X	X	X	X	X	X	X	X	X	X	X
EKFC Whitehills																														X	X			
Erskine Thistle																						X	X	X										
Finnart																																		X
Gartcosh United																									X	X	X	X	X	X	X	X	X	X
Giffnock North	X	X	X	X	X	X	X	X	X	X	X	X	X	X	X	X	X	X	X	X	X	X	X	X	X	X	X	X	X	X	X	X	X	X
Glasgow Harp																					X	X	X	X	X	X	X	X	X	X	X	X	X	X
Glasgow University	X	X	X	X	X	X	X	X	X	X	X	X	X	X	X	X	X	X	X	X	X	X	X	X	X	X	X	X	X	X	X	X	X	X
Hamilton Academy FP																	X	X	X	X	X	X	X	X	X	X	X	X	X	X	X	X	X	X
Jordanhill College	X	X	X	X																														
Larkhall Thistle Ams																																	X	X
Liberton Cropley						X	X	X	X	X	X	X																						
Links United													X	X	X	X	X	X	X	X	X	X	X	X	X	X	X							
Lothian Thistle									X	X	X	X																						
Milngavie Wanderers						X	X	X	X	X	X	X	X	X	X	X	X	X	X	X	X	X	X	X	X	X	X	X	X	X	X	X	X	X
Milton Amateurs								X	X	X	X	X	X	X	X	X	X	X	X	X	X	X	X	X	X	X	X	X	X	X	X	X	X	X
Morriston YMCA		X	X	X	X	X	X	X	X	X	X	X	X	X	X																			
Muirend	X	X	X	X	X	X	X	X	X	X	X	X	X	X	X	X	X	X	X	X	X	X	X	X	X	X								
Muirhead																									X									
Myre																																X		
Newton Mearns Rovers																						X	X	X		X	X	X	X					
Overtown Thistle																																X	X	
Pencaitland		X	X																															
Queen's Park Hampden XI	X	X	X	X	X	X	X	X	X	X	X																							
Rannoch																																X	X	
Rhu					X	X	X	X	X	X	X	X	X	X	X	X	X	X	X	X	X	X	X	X	X	X	X	X	X	X	X	X	X	X
Rothesay Brandane																						X	X	X	X	X	X	X	X	X	X	X	X	X
St Mungos FP	X	X	X	X	X	X	X	X	X	X	X	X	X	X	X	X	X	X	X	X	X	X	X	X	X	X	X	X	X	X	X	X	X	X
Stanley	X	X	X	X	X	X	X	X	X	X	X	X	X	X	X																			
Stenhousemuir Comm																																		X
Stirling University	X		X	X	X		X	X	X	X	X	X	X	X	X	X	X	X	X	X	X	X	X	X	X	X	X	X	X	X				
Strathclyde Police	X	X	X	X	X	X	X	X	X	X	X	X	X	X	X	X	X	X	X	X	X													
Strathclyde University																									X	X	X	X	X	X	X	X	X	X
Symington Tinto					X	X	X	X	X	X	X	X	X	X	X	X	X	X	X	X	X	X	X	X	X	X	X	X	X	X	X	X	X	X
Thorn Athletic																																	X	X
Viewfield Rovers	X	X	X	X	X	X	X	X	X	X	X	X	X	X	X	X	X	X	X	X	X	X	X	X		X	X	X	X	X	X	X	X	X
Weir Recreation	X	X	X	X	X	X	X	X	X	X	X	X	X	X	X	X	X	X	X	X	X	X	X	X	X	X	X	X	X	X	X	X	X	X
Westerlands	X	X	X	X	X	X	X	X	X	X	X	X	X	X	X	X	X	X	X	X	X	X	X	X	X	X	X	X	X	X	X	X	X	X
Woodhall																																		X

CARLUKE AND DISTRICT SUNDAY AMATEUR LEAGUE

ɿis League folded at the end of 2015/16. The majority of teams moved to the Airdrie and Coatbridge Sunday ɿmateur League.

CENTRAL SCOTTISH AMATEUR LEAGUE 2016/17

ɔntact: Mr George Dingwall
nail: georgedingwall@outlook.com
el: 01698 749044
ww.centralscottishafl.co.uk

ɿis is generally agreed to be the strongest league in terms of quality. Membership declined from 33 in 2015/16 to for 2016/17.

ɔr 2017/18 six new clubs were accepted into membership: Tullibody Community, Polmont Community, Shettleston ıniors AFC, Gartcosh Ulited, Craigneuk and Drumchapel Ams Strollers.

REMIER DIVISION	P	W	D	L	F	A	GD	Pts
ɔlville Park	18	14	3	1	50	11	39	45
: Patricks FP	18	10	5	3	40	21	19	35
astfield	18	10	2	6	41	32	9	32
ast Kilbride	18	8	5	5	38	33	5	29
arestanes	18	7	2	9	44	50	-6	23
annockburn	18	5	7	6	35	40	-5	22
ambusnethan Talbot	18	5	7	6	29	40	-11	22
rumchapel	18	5	4	9	28	33	-5	19
reenock HSFP	18	4	3	11	28	47	-19	15
ampsie Minerva	18	2	2	14	24	50	-26	8

IVISION 1A	P	W	D	L	F	A	GD	Pts
ɔuthside	18	15	2	1	64	19	45	47
unblane Thistle	18	14	1	3	56	18	38	43
ossil YMCA	18	10	2	6	62	38	24	32
BW Waterside	18	9	3	6	51	43	8	30
antyre Celtic	18	9	2	7	47	38	9	29
ilsyth Ams#	18	7	3	8	36	40	-4	24
lydebank AFC	18	6	3	9	32	46	-14	21
C Clydebank	18	5	2	11	31	56	-25	17
⁄ill United	18	3	1	14	30	69	-39	10
tedfast	18	2	1	15	27	69	-42	7

IVISION 1B	P	W	D	L	F	A	GD	Pts
ourock Athletuc	16	14	0	2	58	24	34	42
ridgewater	16	12	3	1	62	21	41	39
tirling City	16	9	3	4	53	36	17	30
teins Thistle	16	8	1	7	42	44	-2	25
Vishaw HSFP	16	7	2	7	39	39	0	23
arrowhill Athletic	16	7	1	8	37	38	-1	22
ddington Anvil	16	4	3	9	20	42	-22	15
SC Glasgow	16	2	4	10	25	46	-21	10
rthurlie	16	0	1	15	20	66	-46	1

CUP FINALS

Bunrigh Trophy, Jan 13 at New Lesser Hampden
Possil YMCA v Southside, 2-1

Cinema Cup, June 2 at Kilsyth Rangers
Stirling City v East Kilbride 6-2

M and M Trophy, June 7 at Kilsyth Rangers
Colville Park v St Patricks FP, 2-0

PLAY OFF

Premier Division
Dunblane Thistle v Campsie Minerva, 1-2
Campsie Minerva v Bridgewater, 2-0
Bridgewater v Dunblane Thistle, 0-5

Campsie	6 pts
Dunblane	3pts
Bridgewater	0 pts

CENTRAL SCOTTISH AFL	CLUB DIRECTORY 2016/17
	Ground 1 is the registered home park. Others listed may be
CLUB	***used if Ground 1 is unplayable / unavailable***
Arthurlie United AFC	1. West of Scotland Uni, Thornly Park Campus, Paisley
H Sky Blue / Navy / White	2. Kingston Park, Neilston, (when only 1 game playing)
A Navy Blue	3. Cowan Park, Barrhead
Bannockburn AFC	1. Ladywell Park, Bruce Street, Bannockburn
H Maroon and White	2. Forthbank Park 3G, Peak Leisure Facility, Stirling
A Sky Blue and White	3. Bannockburn HS 3G, St Ninians Road, Bannockburn
Blantyre Celtic AFC	1. Jock Steins Complex 3G, Hillhouse Road, Hamilton
H Green and White	2. Stonefield Park, Glasgow Road, Blantyre
A All Green	3. Matt Busby Sports Centre 3G, Main Street, Bellshill*
Bridgewater AFC	
H	1. Palace of Arts, Bellahouston
A	
BSC Glasgow	
H Yellow / Blue	1. Scotstoun Showground 3G
A	
Cambusnethan Talbot AFC	1. Dalziel Parks, Hagen Drive, Motherwell
H All red	2. Dalziel Parks 4G, Hagen Drive,Motherwell
A Black or Yellow	
Campsie Minerva AFC	1. High Park, Lennoxtown
H All red	2. Ferguson Park, Lennoxtown
A Blue	3. Milton Battlefield, Campsie Rd, Milton of Campsie
	4. Kilsyth 3G, Garrell Road, Kilsyth
	5. Loretto Playing Fields, Cole Road, Glasgow
Clydebank AFC	1. Colquhoun Park, Bearsden, Glasgow
H Black and Red	
A	
Colville Park AFC	1. Colville Park Country Club, Motherwell
H Navy Blue	2. Ravenscraig Regional Sports Centre, Wishaw (3G)
A Light Blue	3. Dalziel Park, Hagen Drive, Motherwell (4G)
Drumchapel AFC	1. Glenhead Park, Duntocher*
H Red and Black	2. Science Park, Maryhill Road, Glasgow
A Green and Black	3. Clydebank High School 3G, Kilbowie Road, Clydebank.
Dunblane Thistle	1. Stirling University, Airthey Road, Stirling
H Navy & Maroon	2. Wallace H.S., Airthey Road, Stirling
A Black	
East Kilbride AFC	1. Murray Public Parks, East Kilbride
H Red and Blue	2. Ballerup Public Parks, East Kilbride
A Yellow and Navy	3. Kirktonholme Public Parks, East Kilbride
Eastfield AFC	1. Ravenswood, Dowanfield Road, Cumbernauld*
H Navy / Gold	2. Broadwood Stadium, Cumbernauld (3G)
A White	
FC Clydebank	1. Colquhoun Park, Bearsden, Glasgow
H	2. Thorn Park, Bearsden
A	

Garrowhill Athletic AFC	1. Lochend Community High School, Easterh
H Black & White	2. Bannerman High School (3G)
A Red & White	
Gourock Athletic AFC	1. Gourock Playing Fields, George Road, Gou
H Red	2. Gourock Playing Field 3G, George Road, G
A Black	3. Battery Park, Eldon Street, Greenock
Greenock HSFP AFC	1. Battery Park, Eldon Street, Greenock
H Blue & White Hoops	2. Inverclyde Academy 3G, Greenock
A All Black or All White	3. Battery Park 3G, Eldon Street, Greenock*
Harestanes AFC	1. Merkland Park, Kirkintilloch
H Red & Navy	2. Tintock Park, Kirkintilloch, (changing Merk
A Yellow & Navy	3. Huntershill Park, Bishopbriggs
	4. Waterside Park, Kirkintilloch
Kilsyth AFC	1. Kilsyth Sportsfield, Garrell Road, Kilsyth*
H Green & Black	2. Croy Community (3G), Croy
A Blue & White	3. Duncansfield Park, Kilsyth Rangers JFC*
Mill United AFC	1. Fairhill Park, Mill Road, Hamilton. ML3 8HZ
H Red & Black Stripes	2. Palace Grounds, Hamilton. ML3 0FD
A Blue & Black Stripes	3. Stonefield Park, Glasgow Road, Blantyre. G
Possil YM AFC	1. St Monica's Club, Milton
H Red & Black	2. John Paul Academy 3G
A Black	
St Patricks FP AFC	1. Posties Park, Woodyard Road, Dumbarton
H Green & White	2. Dumbarton Common, Elm Road, Dumbarto
A All Yellow	
Southside AFC	1. New Tinto Park, Govan*
H	
A	
Stedfast AFC	1. Temple Parks, Anniesland, Glasgow
H Royal Blue / Amber	2. John Paul Academy (3G)
A Black & Orange	
Steins Thistle AFC	1. Allandale Park, Allandale
H Dark Blue	2.Oak Road, Cumbernauld.
A Red & Black	
Stirling City AFC	1. Kings Park, Park Avenue, Stirling
H Red	2. Forthbank Stadium 4G, Stirling. FK7 7UJ
A Blue	3. Wallace H.S., Airthey Road, Stirling
Uddingston Anvil AFC	1. Tannochside 3G pitch, Douglas Street, Tann
H Red	2. Hamilton Palace Sports Grounds, Hamilton
A Black	3. Porterswell Playing Fields, Uddingston
Waterside CBW	1. Luggie Park, Waterside Road, Kirkintilloch
H Sky Blue	2. Waterside Park, Kirkintilloch
A Navy Blue	3. Kirkintilloch High School 3G
Wishaw HSFP AFC	1. King George V Parks, Wishaw
H Yellow & Blue	2. Wishaw Sports Centre, Wishaw (4G)*
A Blue & Black	3. Coltness High School, Wishaw (4G)
* Current or former Junior grounds	

AFL HONOURS

	LEAGUE CHAMPS	DIV 1 CHAMPS	CINEMA CUP	MCAVOY McINTYRE	BUNRIGH TROPHY	ROBERT WHYTE
38/89	Knightswood Afc	Tower Hearts Afc	Bankhall Villa Afc	Bankhall Villa Afc	St Benedict's Afc	
39/90	Bankhall Villa Afc	Hillwood Afc	Knightswood Afc	Dumbarton Academy Fp Afc	Cumbernauld Thistle Afc	
30/91	Bankhall Villa Afc	Denny Westpark Afc	St. Benedicts Afc	Cardross Rock Afc	Knightswood Afc	
31/92	St. Benedict's Afc	IBM Afc	Dumbarton Academy Fp Afc	Gartcosh Utd	Vale Of Clyde Afc	
32/93	Cardross Rock Afc	Bellshill Ymca Afc	Cardross Rock Afc	Cardross Rock Afc	Bellshill Ymca Afc	
33/94	Cardross Rock Afc	Renfrew Ymca Afc	Bankhall Villa Afc	Gartcosh Utd	High Blantyre Utd Afc	
34/95	Bellshill Ymca Afc	Colville Park Afc	BP Afc	Colville Park Afc	Bellshill Ymca Afc	
35/96	Bankhall Villa Afc	Wellhouse Afc	Bellshill Carousel Afc	Cardross Rock Afc	Wellhouse Afc	
36/97	Killermont Afc	Shettleston Afc	St Benedict's Afc	Vale Of Clyde Afc	Fauldhouse Afc	
37/98	Harestanes Afc	Balmore Afc	BP Afc	Bellshill Ymca Afc	Vale Of Clyde Afc	
38/99	Balmore Afc	Motherwell Mw Afc	Motherwell Mw Afc	St Benedict's Afc	Harestanes Afc	
39/00	Harestanes Afc	Aberforth Rangers Afc	Balmore Afc	Plains Afc	Balmore Afc	
00/01	Harestanes Afc	Spartans Afc	Aberforth Rangers Afc	Harestanes Afc	Aberforth Rangers Afc	
01/02	Balmore Afc	Motherwell Mw Afc	Harestanes Afc	Brightons Afc	Drumchapel Utd Afc	
02/03	Harestanes Afc	Tullibody Afc	Colville Park Afc	Harestanes Afc	Harestanes Afc	
03/04	Kilsyth Afc	Motherwell Mw Afc	Blantyre Afc	Aberforth Rangers Afc	The Spartansafc	Redbrae Afc
04/05	Drumchapel Utd Afc	Mearns Afc	Harestanes Afc	The Spartans Afc	Drumchapel Utd Afc	
05/06	Redbrae Afc	Colville Park Afc		Kilsyth Afc	Motherwell Mw Afc	Waterside Afc
06/07	Colville Park Afc	Buchanan Thistle Afc	Drumchapel Utd Afc	Colville Park Afc	Harestanes Afc	Eastfield Utd Afc
07/08	Drumchapel Utd Afc	Eddlewood Afc	Drumchapel Utd Afc	The Spartans Afc	Colville Park Afc	Uddingston Afc
08/09	Drumchapel Utd Afc	St Patricks Fp Afc	Harestanes Afc	The Spartans Afc	Eddlewood Afc	Stedfast Afc
09/10	Drumchapel Utd Afc	Pollok Afc	Drumchapel Utd Afc	Steins Thistle Afc	Colville Park Afc	Wishaw Hsfp Afc
10/11	Drumchapel Utd Afc	Ashvale Victoria Afc	Drumchapel Utd Afc	Harestanes Afc	Drumchapel Utd Afc	Ashvale Victoria Afc
11/12	Colville Park Afc	Bannockburn Afc	Drumchapel Utd Afc	Drumchapel Utd Afc	Drumchapel Utd Afc	Drumchapel Afc
12/13	Colville Park Afc	Drumchapel Afc	Bannockburn Afc	Bannockburn Afc	Colville Park Afc	Drumchapel Afc
13/14	Bannockburn Afc	Aikenhead Thistle Afc	Colville Park Afc	Wellhouse Afc	Wellhouse Afc	Blantyre Celtic Afc
14/15	Harestanes Afc		Greenock HSFP	East Kilbride	Drumchapel Ams	Steins Thistle
15/16	Colville Park Afc		Campsie Minerva Afc	East Kilbride	Greenock HSFP	Garrowhill Thistle
16/17	Colville Park Afc		Stirling City AFC	Colville Park Afc	Possil YMCA	

AGUE COMPOSITION 2017/18

REMIER	DIV 1A	DIV1B
annockburn	Bridgewater	Arthurlie
ambusnethan Talbot	Clydebank	Blantyre Celtic
ampsie Minerva	Garrowhill Thistle	Craigneuk
olville Park Electric	Kilsyth	Drumchapel Ams Strollers
rumchapel Amateurs	Mill United	East Kilbride
unmblane Thistle	Polmont Community	FC Clydebank
astfield	Possil YM	Gartcosh United
ourock Athletic	Steins Thistle	Shettleston Juniors
reenock HSFP	Stirling City	St Cadocs Mearns
arestanes	Tullibody Community	Stedfast
outhside	Uddingston Anvil	Wishaw HSFP
Patricks FP		

DUMFRIES SUNDAY AMATEUR FA 2016/17

Contact: Richard Irving
Email: totti14@btinternet.com
Tel 01387261592
www.sundayamateurs.wix.com

Membership dropped from 20 in 2015/16 to 18 in 2016/17.

PREMIER DIVISION	P	W	D	L	F	A	GD	Pts
Moffat Thistle 2010	18	13	2	3	59	27	32	41
Hole in the Wa	18	10	6	2	77	32	45	36
Nithside	18	10	4	4	58	48	10	34
Normandy Star	18	9	5	4	71	34	37	32
Palmerston Colts	18	8	2	8	60	46	14	26
Morton Youth	18	7	4	7	60	57	3	25
Annan Town	18	7	4	7	49	49	0	25
Scaur	18	5	5	8	60	61	-1	20
Kelloholm Arms	18	3	0	15	23	112	-89	9
Queens Bar	18	1	2	15	35	86	-51	5

FIRST DIVISION	P	W	D	L	F	A	GD	Pts
Five Arches Bombers	21	20	1	0	140	26	114	61
Dumfries Athletic	21	12	3	6	73	55	18	39
FC Annan	21	12	1	8	91	59	32	37
Summerhill	21	10	2	9	62	55	7	32
Park Thistle	21	10	2	9	67	67	0	32
Loreburn Thistle*	21	6	1	14	51	110	-59	16 (
Ruthwell Rovers	21	3	4	14	48	90	-42	13
Black Bull Rovers	21	3	2	16	49	119	-70	11

CUP FINALS

Houliston Cup Final, May 28 at Holm Park
Nithside v Normany Star, 4-2

Heathhall Garden Centre Trophy,
May 21, at QOS FC
Normandy Star v Five Arches Bombers, 5-1

Harkness Plumbing and Heating Trophy Final,
Feb 3 at David Keswick Centre
Nithside v Palmerston Colts, 3-2

Doonhamer Bistro League Cup,
Oct 28 at Marchmount 3G
Hole I' the Way v Palmerston Colts, 3-2

CLUB DIRECTORY	Founded	Contact	Colours	Home Grounds	
Annan Town	2011	Garry Jackson 07733296678	White / Red	Everholm, Annan	
Black Bull Rovers		Kenneth Smith 07849349438	Black	King Edward Park, Lockerbie	
Dumfries Athletic	2008	Iain Cruickshank 07523568799	Navy / Yellow	Jock's Loaning, Dumfries	Maryfield, Dumf
FC Annan	2014	Matthew Rogerson 07801860882	Yellow / Black	Everholm, Annan	Galabank, Annan
Five Arches Bombers		Jake Brown 07775504196	Yellow / Blue	Holm Park, Dumfries	Jock's Loaning, D
Hole in the Wa		Craig McCallay 07799896787	Yellow / Black	Holm Park, Dumfries	
Kelloholm Arms	2014	David McCron 07939997331	Navy	Hillview	
Loreburn Thistle	2008	Martin Dyer 07482 206548	Navy / Yellow	Marchmount, Dumfries	Jock's Loaning, D
Moffat Thistle 2010	2010	Mike Wilson 07717317940	Yellow / Black	Beattock Park, Beattock	
Morton Youth	2013	Billy Gracie 07973 178918	Black / Gold	Jock's Loaning, Dumfries	
Nithside	2009	Dean Livingstone 07934482381	Blue	Jock's Loaning. Dumfries	
Normandy Star	2008	David Nish 07809516526	Red	Holm Park, Dumfries	Hospital Park, Du
Palmerston Colts	2008	Ross Corbett 07519 836921	Royal Blue	Palmerston Park, Dumfries	
Park Thistle	2013	Steven Studholme 07572 509581	White / Black / Red	Kingholm, Dumfries	Holm Park, Dumf
Queens Bar	2009	Ali Cronie 07803 534542	Blue / White	Holm Park, Dumfries	
Ruthwell Rovers		Paul Otway 07595417618	Navy / Yellow	Clarencefield Park, Clarencefield	
Scaur		Colin Bell 07795261627	Sky Blue / Navy	Gladstone Park, Penpont	
Summerhill	2013	Corrie Kirkpatrick 07748635598	Blue / Yellow	Jock's Loaning. Dumfries	

DUNDEE SATURDAY MORNING AMATEUR LEAGUE 2016/17

Contact: Ian Leith
E Mail dsmfl@hotmail.co.uk
Tel 01382 861554
www.dsmfl3.wixsite.com/dsmfl

Facebook Page: Dundee Saturday Morning Football League

Matches are played on various council pitches around Dundee. The university pitches at Riverside are heavily used, as are Fairmuir, Drumgeith Lochee and Dawson Park. Teams do not have specific home grounds.

Membership in 2016/17 was 34, up from 31.

CUP FINALS
Adamson Cup, Sep 14, at Violet JFC
Hilltown Hotspurs v DC Athletic, 2-1
George McArthur Cup, June 2 at Violet JFC
FC Kettledrum v Charleston AFC
Premier League Cup Final, May 17 at Violet
Hilltown Hotspur v DUSC, 7-1
Division 1 League Cup Final, May 10 at Violet JFC
Fintry Rovers v FC Kettledrum, 4-2
Division 2 League Cup Final, May 3 at Violet JFC
FC Menzieshill v Cairdy Thistle, 3-0
Shaun Kelly Cup Final, June 3 at North End JFC
Riverside CSC v Hilltown Hotspur, 2-1

PREMIER DIVISION		P	W	D	L	GD	PTS
1	Hilltown Hotspur	15	12	2	1	46	38
2	DUMS	16	10	4	2	24	34
3	Docs Hibernia	15	11	1	3	23	34
4	DC Athletic	15	10	1	4	22	31
5	Riverside CSC	16	9	1	6	8	28
6	DUSC	17	5	1	11	-15	16
7	Hawkhill Athletic	17	5	1	11	-25	16
8	Dryburgh CC	15	4	2	9	-20	14
9	AC Harleys	16	4	0	12	-32	12
10	Cannon Fodder	16	2	1	13	-31	7
11	AFC Ambassador	0	0	0	0	0	0
12	Lochee Celtic	0	0	0	0	0	0
FIRST DIVISION							
1	FC Kettledrum	14	12	2	0	55	38
2	Park Tool	18	12	1	5	28	37
3	Fintry Rovers	16	10	1	5	20	31
4	Ferry Mechanics	16	8	4	4	14	28
5	Club 83	18	9	1	8	5	28
6	Monifieth Hurricanes	17	9	0	8	9	27
7	Coldside Athletic	17	8	1	8	7	25
8	DK Raiders	17	4	1	12	-52	13
9	Lochee	16	3	1	12	-21	10
10	Wellbeat	17	2	0	15	-65	6
11	Clarks Cowboys	0	0	0	9	0	0
SECOND DIVISION							
1	Stobswell	16	16	0	0	88	48
2	FC Menzieshill	18	13	0	5	59	39
3	Cairdy Thistle	18	11	1	6	29	34
4	Charleston	18	11	0	7	20	33
5	RNL Dundee	18	11	0	7	10	33
6	Stobswell Athletic	17	7	0	10	-12	21
7	Dundee City	18	6	0	12	-40	18
8	Fife Thistle	17	4	2	11	-37	14
9	Sidlaw Albion	16	2	3	11	-64	9
10	Dundee Central	18	2	2	14	-53	8
11	Harlequins	0	0	0	9	0	0

DUNDEE SUNDAY AMATEUR FA 2016/17

Contact: Allan Ramsey
Email: alanramsey2706@hotmail.com
Tel: 01382 509158

Only 7 teams contested the League, and with only 4 seeking to continue for 2017/18 this League has now folded.

	P	W	D	L	Pts
Dundee Argyle	10	10	0	0	30
Annfield	13	9	0	4	27
Tayport	10	7	0	3	21
Dundee Social	10	7	0	3	21
Osnaburg	13	5	0	8	15
Charlies Accies	18	2	1	15	7
FC Polonia Dundee	10	1	1	8	4

CUP FINALS

Chairmans Cup Final,Apr 2 at Tayport JFC
Tayport v Dundee Argyle, 0-4

Association Cup Final, May 27
Dundee Argyle v Dundee Social, w-l

EAST OF SCOTLAND CHURCHES 2016/17

Contact: Mr Ian Midwinter
Email ianmidwinter@salvationarmy.org.uk
Tel 07949742115
www.escfa.leaguerepublic.com

At one time Churches football was an important grade in its own right—running alongside the Amateurs, Welfare and Juveniles. Nowadays Churches football is confined to a couple of Leagues, one in Edinburgh and one in Glasgow.

Games are normally played at 10am on a Saturday morning. Many of the Edinburgh-based clubs use the Gyle Playing Fields or Saughton Park. Cowan AFC sometimes used Meadowmill.

1	Loanhead Parish Loanhead Parish	17	16	1	0	82	9	73	49
2	Morningside United FC	18	15	1	2	68	26	42	46
3	Fairmilehead	17	14	1	2	91	27	64	43
4	The Standard	18	10	2	6	49	38	11	32
5	Gorgie United	18	7	2	9	48	57	-9	23
6	Cabrera MC	18	6	2	10	35	61	-26	20
7	Cowan AFC	18	5	2	11	26	72	-46	17
8	Corstorphine Timbers	18	5	1	12	33	57	-24	16
9	Ladywell BCFC	18	4	2	12	40	71	-31	14
10	Shandon SK	18	0	0	18	0	54	-54	0

CUP FINALS
Norrie Wilson Cup, May 26 at Dalkeith Thistle JFC
Loanhead Parish v Fairmilehead, 1-1 aet, l-w on pens
Association Cup, May 6 at Dalkeith Thistle JFC
Fairmilehead v Niddrie Community Church, 2-1

EDINBURGH & DISTRICT SUNDAY A.F.A.

This League folded at the end of 2015/16. Some cluibs switched to the Lothian and Edinburgh Amateurs Sunday Section.

FIFE AMATEUR FOOTBALL ASSOCIATION 2016/17

Contact: Archie Denny
Email: Archibald.denny@btinternet.com
Tel:01383 730932
www.fifefootball.co.uk

The Fife Amateur FA was formed in the 1980s by the amalgamation of the Kirkcaldy & District AFA and the East Fife AFA. It operated alongside the Kingdom Caledonian FA, covering the same area. A merger had been suggested on many occasions - in 2017 it was agreed and a new Association will operate in 2017/18. This will be known as the Kingdom of Fife Amateur Football Association.

CUP FINALS
Peter Omand Cup, June 2 at Star
Denbeath v Glenrothes Strollers, 6-0
Taylor Sullivan Cup, June 9 at Kelty Hearts JFC
AM Soccer v Hearts of Beath, 1-2
Ron Brindley Memorial Prem Division Cup, May 12 at Star
Auchtermuchty Bellevue v AM Soccer, 2-1
Wallace Wright Championship Cup, May 5 at Dundonald Bluebell JFC
Burntisland United v Fife Thistle, 3-2
Division 1 League Cup, April 28 at Dundonald Bluebell JFC
Glenrothes Strollers v Kirkland Villa, 4-0
Tom McIntyre Cup, June 16 at Kelty Hearts JFC
Kirkcaldy v Hearts of Beath

PREMIERSHIP	P	W	D	L	F	A	GD	PTS
Pitenweem Rovers	18	11	4	3	48	21	27	37
Auchtermuchty Bellevue	18	10	4	4	32	24	8	34
AM Soccer	17	9	2	6	40	29	11	29
Hearts of Beath	17	8	4	5	45	32	13	28
Fossoway	18	8	4	6	32	35	-3	28
Denbeath	18	7	4	8	36	38	-2	25
Kingdom Athletic	18	7	4	8	30	36	-6	25
Methilhill Strollers	18	5	3	10	30	41	-11	18
Kirkcaldy AFC	18	4	4	10	26	42	-16	16
Kirkcaldy YMCA AFC	18	1	5	12	24	50	-26	8
Valleyfield AFC	0	0	0	0	0	0	0	0

CHAMPIONSHIP	P	W	D	L	F	A	GD	PTS
FC Bayside	17	14	1	2	59	27	32	43
Rosyth ZAFC	18	13	2	3	49	28	21	41
Burntisland United	17	11	2	4	54	34	20	35
Lomond Victoria	18	9	5	4	52	44	8	32
St Monans Swallows	18	10	1	7	46	36	10	31
Fife Thistle	18	6	3	9	50	54	-4	21
St Andrews University	18	5	2	11	27	35	-8	17
Rosebank Rangers	18	4	5	9	36	51	-15	17
Leslie Hearts	18	5	2	11	34	50	-16	17
Freuchie	18	0	1	17	22	70	-48	1

DIVISION ONE	P	W	D	L	F	A	GD	PTS
Glenrothes Strollers	14	12	0	2	53	18	35	36
Klinglassie	15	10	1	4	32	26	6	31
Kelty Hearts AFC	14	9	2	3	45	25	20	29
Kirkland Villa	15	9	0	6	49	32	17	27
Kinross Colts	16	7	1	8	41	40	1	22
Kirkcaldy Rovers	15	6	1	8	54	53	1	19
AM Soccer Reserves	16	5	4	7	35	42	-7	19
St Andrews Amateurs	15	4	3	8	38	45	-7	15
Glenrothes Athletic	16	0	0	16	17	83	-66	0

FIFE SUNDAY AMATEUR FOOTBALL LEAGUE 2016/17

Contact: Craig Lindsay
Email: fife 528@hotmail.co.uk
Tel: 01337 831049
Www.freewebs.com/fifesundayamateurfootballleague

remier League

os	Team	P	W	D	L	F	A	W	D	L	F	A	GD	Pts	
1	Lauders AFC Champions	18	6	2	1	45	8	8	1	0	39	8	68	45	Townhill Park, Dunfermline
2	Jokers AFC Runners Up	18	6	0	3	20	13	7	0	2	40	10	37	39	St Leonards, Dunfermline
3	Minto Lounge AFC	18	6	1	2	19	18	6	0	3	32	16	17	37	Moore Park, Lochgelly
4	Lochore Castle AFC	18	6	0	3	33	14	4	3	2	25	23	21	33	Dallas Doyle Park, Ballingry
5	Eddys Bar AFC	18	6	0	3	40	27	2	1	6	16	32	-3	25	Beveridge Park, Kirkcaldy
6	Crystal Barcelona AFC	18	4	1	4	29	33	3	2	4	25	24	-3	24	Village Park, Halbeath
7	Templehall Tavern AFC	18	3	2	4	37	23	3	1	5	29	30	13	21	Beveridge Park, Kirkcaldy
8	Torleys AFC	18	3	3	3	22	28	2	1	6	19	35	-22	19	Moore Park, Lochgelly
9	Dunfermline United AFC	18	1	0	8	17	36	3	1	5	16	23	-26	13	Rex Park, Dunfermline
10	CISWO AFC	18	1	1	7	19	47	0	0	9	6	80	-102	4	Dovecot Park, Glenrothes
11	Brucefield AFC	0	0	0	0	0	0	0	0	0	0	0	0	0	Rex Park, Dunfermline
12	Kennoway AFC	0	0	0	0	0	0	0	0	0	0	0	0	0	Cotlands Park, Kennoway

nd Division

os	Team	P	W	D	L	F	A	W	D	L	F	A	GD	Pts	
1	McPhails AFC Champions	26	13	0	0	70	19	11	1	1	60	22	89	73	KGV Park, Leven
2	Maltings AFC Runners Up	26	11	0	2	55	29	11	1	1	49	20	55	67	Rob Roy Park, Culross
3	Crown Inn AFC -1pt	26	7	2	4	37	34	9	1	3	48	29	22	50	KGV Park, Leven
4	Carousel United AFC	26	7	1	5	38	37	7	1	5	44	46	-1	44	Kinghorn
5	Styx AFC	26	7	1	5	39	34	6	1	6	47	29	23	41	Randolph Park, Kirkcaldy
6	Coadys AFC	26	7	1	5	45	39	5	2	6	40	33	13	39	St Leonards, Dunfermline
7	Glenrothes Rovers AFC	26	7	1	5	40	41	4	2	7	29	32	-4	36	Warout Parks, Glenrothes
8	Sky AFC	26	3	3	7	36	40	7	2	4	40	33	3	35	Dalgety Bay SC n/ Duloch Park, Dunfermline
9	Steadings AFC	26	6	1	6	27	31	5	0	8	35	40	-9	34	Randolph Park, Kirkcaldy
10	The Bruce Arms	26	5	2	6	46	48	5	0	8	38	44	-8	32	Limekilns
11	Athletico Rosyth AFC -1pt	26	4	3	6	29	32	4	3	6	35	41	-9	29	Rosyth Institute
12	Novar Rovers AFC	26	3	1	9	38	67	5	0	8	38	53	-44	25	Kinghorn
13	FC Ingolstadt Kdy	26	4	0	9	25	45	3	1	9	32	56	-44	22	Beveridge Park, Kirkcaldy
14	Victoria Rovers AFC	26	0	0	13	16	64	0	1	12	25	63	-86	1	Randolp Park, Kirkcaldy

CENT HONOURS

	Premier League	Division 2	Division 3	Fife Cup	JS Anderson Cup	League Cup
06/7	Bogarts	Wishart Abbey	Wemyss Central	The Yard, Glenrothes	Royal Scot	Sun Tavern
07/8	White Heather	Wemyss Central	Station Buffet	Gilvenbank	Bowhill	Bogarts
08/9	Bogarts	Prinlaws	Lochore Castle	Bogarts	Bogarts	Prinlaws
09/10	Railway Tavern	Burns Tavern	Jokers	Jokers	Lang Toun Thistle	Railway Tavern
10/11	St Clair Tavern	Lochore Castle	Crystal Barcelona	Railway Tavern	Dunfermline Thistle	Railway Tavern
11/12	Railway Tavern	Dunfermline Thistle	Crown Inn	Railway Tavern	Railway Tavern	Railway Tavern
12/13	Railway Tavern	Crown Inn	King's Arms	Brucefield	Railway Tavern	Railway Tavern
13/14	Rosyth	Minto Lounge	Bayview Bar	Rosyth	Bayview Bar	Society
14/15	Brucefield	Auld Hoose	Jokers	FC Brig	Auld Hoose	Auld Hoose
15/16	FC Brig	Kennoway		FC Brig	FC Brig	Crystal Barcelona
16/17	Lauders	McPhails		Lauders	Styx	Lauders

CUP FINALS
Summer Cup, May 31 at Dallas Doyle
Eddy's Bar v Templehall Tavern , 2-1
JS Anderson Cup, May 7 at Glenrothes JFC
Styx v Jokers, 6-3
CISWO Fife Sunday Trophy, May 21 at Gelnrothes JFC
Lauders v Athletico Rosyth, 4-1
League Cup, April 27 at Glenrothers JFC
Maltings v Lauders, 0-2

GLASGOW & DISTRICT SATURDAY MORNING A.F.L. 2016/17

Contact: Gordon A Fergusson, Email: gdsml1986@hotmail.co.uk
Tel: 0141 965 7371

http://www.leaguewebsite.co.uk/gdsml

Membership dropped from 27 clubs in 2015/16 to 23 in 2016/17.

CUP FINALS
GDSM League Cup, May 27 at Benburb JFC
Blairdardie United v Blantyre, 6-0
William Drummond Cup, May 6 at Dalziel Park
Red Star v Abronhill Intrans, 2-1 aet
Vince McGlinchey Cup, April 1 at Dalziel Park
Milngavie BC v Crosslands 3-2

PREMIER DIVISION	P	W	D	L	F	A	GD	Pts	Ground
Blairdardie Utd	20	14	3	3	72	32	40	45	Donald Dewar Centre, Glasgow
AFC Columba	20	12	2	6	66	45	21	38	St Ambrose HS, Coatbridge
Red Star	20	10	2	8	58	48	10	32	Lochend SC, Easterhouse
Crosslands	20	9	5	6	48	38	10	32	Glasgow Club, Milton
Bellahouston	20	9	3	8	53	58	-5	30	Nethercraigs, Glasgow
Finnieston Park	20	8	3	9	46	45	1	27	Stepford Centre, Glasgow
Renfrew FC	20	6	5	9	42	48	-6	23	KGV Parks, Renfrew
Bishopton AFC	20	7	2	11	34	56	-22	23	Top Park Pitches, Bishopton
Milngavie BC	20	6	4	10	39	50	-11	22	Thorn Park, Bearsden
Glasgow Caledonian	20	4	8	8	42	61	-19	20	Netherton Parks, Glasgow
Glasgow Islay	20	3	7	10	35	54	-19	16	Lochend SC, Easterhouse

DIVISION ONE	P	W	D	L	F	A	GD	Pts	
Abronhill Intrans	22	17	4	1	83	40	43	55	Ravenswood Pitches, Cumbernauld
FC Drumchapel	21	16	2	3	99	41	58	50	Donald Dewar Centre, Glasgow
Hamilton Wanderers	22	12	3	7	62	45	17	39	Meikle Earnock Poark, Hamilton
Blantyre AFC	22	11	5	6	75	41	34	38	
Kings Park Rovers	22	10	4	8	52	49	3	34	
Braehead AFC	22	9	3	10	56	62	-6	30	KGV Parks, Renfrew
Parklife	22	9	2	11	55	55	0	29	Colquhoun Park, Bearsden
Bridgend Amateurs	21	8	4	9	46	51	-5	28	Gartferry Park, Moodiesburn
Kilpatrick	22	8	3	11	51	52	-1	27	Mountblow Pitches, Clydebank
Strathclyde University	22	6	3	13	33	46	-13	21	Strathclyde Uni Grounds, Glasgow
AC Milanda	22	7	0	15	40	72	-32	21	Stepford Centre, Glasgow
Glenavon Thistle	22	1	1	20	30	128	-98	4	

GLASGOW COLLEGES A.F.A. 2016/17

Contact: Donnie Brooks,
Email: donnie_brooks2003@hotail.com
Tel 0141 578 9961

http://www.glasgowcollegesfa.co.uk/

Membership dropped from 32 in 2015/16 to 30 in 2016/17.
Matches are played on Saturday mornings, usually with a 9.45 or 10am Kick Off.

Hampden AFC occasionally use the pitch at Cathkin Park, former home of Third Lanark.

CUP FINALS
CTB Cup, May 27 at Petershill JFC
Albion v Lomond Vale
Association Cup Final, May 20 at Petershill JFC
St Davids v Maryhill Thistle, 2-2, 5-4 pens
League Cup Final, May 13 at Petershill JFC
Glasgow Island v Albion 2-1
Jim Harvey Cup Final, May 6 at Petershill JFC
Maryhill Thistle v Singer 2-1
Challenge Cup Final, April 29 at Petershill JFC
Singer v Central, 5-3

Latest Available Tables												
PREMIER DIVISION									**Home Grounds Used**			
Maryhill Thistle	20	18	1	1	69	33	36	55	Firhill Complex			
Gryffe Thistle	20	12	4	4	70	37	33	40	Springburn Astro	Nethercraigs		
Glasgow Islands	19	13	1	5	50	38	12	40	Drumoyne Complex			
Saint Davids	19	11	1	7	67	49	18	34	Palace of Arts 3G	Drumoyne 3G		
Albion	20	12	1	7	83	56	27	37	Milton Astro	Donald Dewar		
Clydeside Athletic	20	9	3	8	61	54	7	30	Springburn Astro			
Muirton	19	9	0	10	57	38	19	27	Scotstoun Showground 3G			
Hampden	20	7	0	13	51	56	-5	21	Cathkin Park			
Rosehill United	20	5	3	12	53	86	-41	18	Donald Dewar Centre Grass	Glasgow Green 3G	Greenfield Astro	
Clyde Valley Rovers	20	4	0	16	28	66	-38	12	Nethercraigs	Nether Pollok		
MSM	18	0	2	17	16	84	-68	2	Whifflet Park, Coatbridge			
DIVISION ONE												
Singer	15	13	0	2	80	25	55	39	St Peter the Apostle HS			
Central	15	11	2	2	68	23	45	35	Toryglen			
Newlands	17	10	2	5	52	37	15	32	Nether Pollok	Muirend	Huntly Park	Toryglen
Southside United	17	7	2	9	45	40	5	23	Castlemilk HS			
Cambuslang United	16	6	5	5	38	38	0	23	Nether Pollok	Stepford Complex		
JCS	17	6	4	7	39	48	-9	22	John Brown's Grounds, Clydebank			
porto	18	8	1	11	38	61	-23	19	Greenfield Grass			
Glasgow Medics	17	6	1	10	38	65	-27	19	Nether Pollok	Peterson Park		
Glasgow Ansar	18	6	2	11	40	67	-27	17	Greenfield Grass	Glasgow Green		
omond Vale	18	3	3	12	33	67	-34	12	Argyle Park, Alexandria			
IVISION TWO												
okomotive Glasgow	16	10	4	2	63	29	34	34	Nether Pollok			
C Innter	16	10	1	5	47	34	13	31	Blairdardie	Nertherton		
rown Athletic	16	9	1	6	60	48	12	28	Stepford Complex			
Vest Stone	16	8	2	6	53	52	1	26	Priory Park, Blantyre			
reater Glasgow	16	7	4	5	46	34	12	25	Glasgow Green 3G			
rskine Town	16	5	5	6	32	37	-5	20	Park Mains HS			
iver Nevis	16	5	2	9	27	40	-13	17	Scotstoun Showground 3G	Milton Grass		
lympique Energetik	16	4	2	10	33	54	-21	14	Hamilton Palace			
nsar YFC	16	3	1	12	30	63	-33	10	Renfrew SC			

GREATER GLASGOW PREMIER A.F.L. 2016/17

Contact: Paul Gunn (Match Secretary)
Telephone:
[H] 01418837436
[M] 07917712850
http://www.greaterglasgow.co.uk

CUP FINALS

Spring Cup, May 29 at Cambuslang Rangers JFC
Craigneuk v Cambria, 2-1

Bobby Thomson Challenge Cup, May 19 at Cambuslang Rangers JFC
Craigneuk v Glasgow University "B", 2-0

Presidents League Cup, May 17 at Cambuslang Rangers JFC
Newton Vale v Eaglesham, 3-1

DIVISION ONE	**P**	**W**	**D**	**L**	**F**	**A**	**GD**	**Pts**	**HOME GROUND**
Robslee AFC	18	13	0	5	59	37	22	39	Huntly Park, Giffnock
Erskine AFC	18	12	0	6	52	31	21	36	Erskine
Strathclyde University AFC	18	10	1	7	41	41	0	31	Strathclyde Uni Playing Fields, Stepps
Craigneuk AFC	18	8	6	4	44	29	15	30	Muirhouse Park, Motherwell
Dynamo East Kilbride AFC	18	8	3	7	39	45	-6	27	John Wright Sports Centre
St. Mungo's AFC	18	7	4	7	37	32	5	25	Loretto PF, Bishopbriggs
Calderglen AFC	18	6	4	8	36	42	-6	22	Lochwinnoch
Cambria AFC	18	6	3	9	41	42	-1	21	Strathclyde Uni Playing Fields, Stepps
St. Patrick's FP AFC	18	5	1	12	25	42	-17	16	Dumbarton Common
Renfrew Thistle AFC	18	3	2	13	34	67	-33	11	KGV Parks, Renfrew
Baillieston Thistle AFC	0	0	0	0	0	0	0	0	Lochend HS, Easterhouse
Kilbarchan Thistle AFC	0	0	0	0	0	0	0	0	Kilbarchan

DIVISION TWO	P	W	D	L	F	A	GD	Pts	
Eaglesham AFC	18	13	1	4	52	29	23	40	Eaglesham Public Park
Newton Vale	18	11	4	3	59	31	28	37	Glasgow Green
Eastwood Parkmount 'A' AFC	18	11	3	4	42	24	18	36	Bogton Playing Fields
Glasgow University 'A' AFC	18	10	4	4	54	34	20	34	Garscube
GSC Jordanhill AFC	18	8	4	6	50	37	13	28	Jordanhill Campus
Springburn Thistle AFC	18	8	2	8	45	43	2	26	Springburn Astro
Westerlands 'A' AFC	18	7	0	11	35	49	-14	21	Greenfield Football Centre
East Kilbride Y.M. AFC	18	5	3	10	39	51	-12	18	Kirktonholme Park
Ashvale Victoria AFC	18	4	4	10	35	52	-17	16	
E.K.R.R. AFC	18	0	1	17	22	83	-61	1	Brancumhall, East Kilbride
Dumbarton Harp Celtic AFC	0	0	0	0	0	0	0	0	
Weir Recreation AFC	0	0	0	0	0	0	0	0	Albert Park, Glasgow

DIVISION THREE	P	W	D	L	F	A	Pts		
Third Lanark AFC	20	16	3	1	91	29	62	51	Fullartion Park (Vale of Clyde JFC)
Crookston Castle AFC	20	14	2	4	89	36	53	44	
Carbrain AFC	20	12	3	5	72	37	35	39	Ravenswood, Cumbernauld
Glasgow University 'B' AFC	20	12	3	5	44	35	9	39	Garscube
FC Baillieston	20	10	2	8	64	58	6	32	
John Street AFC	20	8	3	9	58	64	-6	27	Glasgow Green
Rannoch 'A' AFC	20	5	3	12	30	49	-19	18	KGV Park, Bearsden
North Kelvin Sports AFC	20	5	3	12	46	79	-33	18	
Eastwood Parkmount 'B' AFC	20	5	2	13	37	62	-25	17	Bogton Playing Fields
Westerlands 'B' AFC	20	5	2	13	41	72	-31	17	Glasgow Green
Colquhoun Utd AFC	20	3	4	13	41	92	-51	13	Colquhoun Park, Bearsden

INVERNESS & DISTRICT A.F.A. 2016 and 2017

Contact: Ruaridh Morrison
Email: idfasec@gmail.com
Tel: 07732 106679

Season runs from April to October. Many games are played at the Bught Parks in Inverness.

Final Tables for 2016 Season

PREMIER	P	W	D	L	PTS
Avoch	16	13	2	1	41
ANM Ace	16	12	1	3	37
Hilton	16	10	2	4	32
Merkinch	16	7	3	7	24
Ardersier	16	7	1	8	22
Police	16	7	1	8	22
Culbokie	16	5	2	9	17
ICM Electrical	16	2	2	12	8
North Kessock	16	2	0	14	6

FIRST	P	W	D	L	PTS
Loch Ness	14	10	1	3	31
Tomatin	14	9	3	2	30
Inverness Thistle	14	8	0	6	24
Innes Cl	14	7	2	5	23
NMM Sam's	14	6	1	7	19
Inverness Central	14	4	4	6	16
Cairngorm Windows	14	3	1	10	10
Caley Club	14	2	2	10	8

SECOND	P	W	D	L	PTS
Maryburgh	14	10	4	0	34
IRN Security	14	10	2	2	32
White House	14	10	0	4	30
Culloden Moor	14	5	3	6	18
Pockets	14	6	0	8	18
Polonia	14	4	3	7	15
Hill Rovers	14	4	2	8	14
So Bar	14	0	0	14	0

CUP FINALS

Premier League Cup, Aug 13 at Culloden
Hilton v Ardersier, 7-0

Div 1 / 2 Cup
Tomatin v Maryburgh, l-w

Association (All In) Cup Sep 3 at Caley Stadium
ANM Ace v Police, 1-4

2017 Member Clubs and Divisions:

Premier League	1st Division	2nd Division
ANM Ace	Culloden Moor Inn	Balloan
Ardersier	ICM Electrical	Belmac
Avoch	Innes Cl	Cairngorm Windows
Culbokie	Inverness Central	Contin
Inverness Thistle	IRN Security	Dog House Rovers
Loch Ness	Maryburgh	Drakies
Merkinch	NMM Sams	Ferrybache
Police	North Kessock	Hill Rovers
Tomatin	Sobar	Polonia

KINGDOM CALEDONIAN A.F.A. 2016/17

Contact: Mr James M Mitchell, 2 Newton Place, Rosyth, Dunfermline, KY11 2LX
Email jjlpsmitch@aol.com
Tel 01383 414339

http://www.leaguewebsite.co.uk/kingdomcaledonianafa

Once again at the end of 2015/16 there were suggestions that the Kingdom Caledonian and Fife Amateur FA might merge.

In the early 1980s there were two Amateur Asociations in Fife, the Kirkcaldy and District and the North East Fife. A number of the more ambitions sides broke away and formed the Kingdom Caledonian League.

Later the K and D and the NEF merged top form the Fife Amateur Football Association.

From 2017/18 the KCAFA and FAFA have merged therefore this is the Final League table for the KCFA..

	P	W	D	L	F	A	GD	PTS
Bowhill Rovers	20	17	0	3	78	25	53	51
Aberdour	20	16	2	2	70	17	53	50
Leven United	20	15	1	4	72	27	45	46
Greig Park Rangers	20	12	2	6	58	35	23	38
Cupar Hearts	20	12	1	7	72	33	39	37
Strathmiglo United	20	11	0	9	66	46	20	33
Lumphinnans United	20	10	1	9	69	42	27	31
Kinross	20	7	1	12	45	66	-21	22
Balgonie Scotia 1896	20	2	1	17	31	76	-45	7
Glenrothes AFC	20	2	1	17	28	105	-77	7
Falkland	20	1	0	19	14	131	-117	3

CUP FINALS
Challenge Cup Final. June 16 at Kelty hearts JFC
Leven United v Greig Park Rangers, 2-0
Fence and Deck Cup Final, May 27 at Dundonald Bluebell JFC
Leven United v Bowhill Rovers, 4-3
Bridgeview Joinery Cup Final, June 23 at Star
Kinross v Leven United
League Cup Final, June 3 at Dundonald Bluebell
Bowhill Rovers v Leven United, 1-3

CLUB DIRECTORY		
Aberdour	Red / Black	Hawkcraig Park, Aber
Balgonie Scotia	Blue / Black	KGV Park, Coaltown o
Bowhill Rovers	Blue	Wallsgreen Park, Bow
Cupar Hearts	Maroon / Sky Blue	Duffus Park, Cupar
Glenrothes AFC	Tangerine	Gilvenbank, Glenroth
Greig Park Rangers		Greig Park, Windygat
Kettle United	Tangerine / Black	Kingskettle
Kinross AFC	Purple / White	The Myre, Kinross
Leven United	Blue	KGV Park, Leven
Lumphinnans United	Red	Ochilview Park, Lump
Strathmiglo United	Red / Black / White	Strathmiglo Park

LEWIS & HARRIS A.F.A. 2016

Contact: Allan MacLeod,
Email: allanmacleod1967@btinternet.com
Tel: 01851 810660

www.lhfa.org.uk

		P	W	D	L	F	A	GD	PTS
1	Lochs	14	12	1	1	44	11	33	37
2	Point	14	11	1	2	46	12	34	34
3	Westside	14	9	2	3	39	22	17	29
4	Carloway	14	7	0	7	30	25	5	21
5	Aths	14	4	1	9	26	41	-15	13
6	Ness	14	4	0	10	18	47	-29	12
7	Back	14	3	1	10	16	25	-9	10
8	United	14	3	0	11	14	50	-36	9

CUP FINALS
Moldova Cup, Sep 3 at Goathill Park
Carloway v Lochs, 1-3
Acres Boys Club Cup April 29 at Goathill Park
Carloway v Westside, 4-3 AET
Jock Stein Cup, June 10 at Goathill Park
Point v Westside, 3-1
Coop Cup, July 23 at Garrabost
Westside v Iochdar Saints 2-1
Eilean Fhrraoich Cup
Carloway v Lochs, 1-0 at Creagan Dubh (Lochs)

LEWIS AND HARRIS LEAGUE HONOURS			
Year	Champions	Runners-up	Third place
1980	Ness	Point	Stornoway Ro
1981	Point	Ness	Stornoway At
1982	Ness	Stornoway Athletic	Tolsta
1983	Harris	Point	Ness
1984	Ness	Back	Stornoway At
1985	Ness	Point	Stornoway At
1986	Ness	Point	Stornoway At
1987	Ness	Stornoway Athletic	Lochs
1988	Stornoway Athletic	Ness	Lochs
1989	Ness	Lochs	Stornoway At
1990	Ness	Stornoway Athletic	Stornoway Ro
1991	Ness	Stornoway Athletic	Lochs
1992	Ness	Point	Stornoway At
1993	Point	Ness	Harris
1994	Ness	Back	Point
1995	Lochs	Back	Ness
1996	Point	Ness	Harris
1997	Point	Stornoway Athletic	Harris
1998	Point	Stornoway Athletic	Harris
1999	Ness	Point	Harris
2000	Back	Harris	Point
2001	Harris	Ness	Lochs
2002	Point	Harris	Back
2003	Lochs	Back	Point
2004	Point	Back	Lochs
2005	Lochs	Stornoway Athletic	Back
2006	Stornoway Athletic	Lochs	Point
2007	Lochs	Back	Stornoway At
2008	Lochs	Back	Carloway
2009	Lochs	Back	Carloway
2010	Lochs	Back	West Side
2011	Back	Carloway	West Side
2012	Stornoway Athletic	Back	Lochs
2013	Carloway	Stornoway Athletic	West Side
2014	Westside	Lochs	Carloway
2015	Lochs	Point	West Side
2016	Lochs	Point	West Side

LOTHIAN & EDINBURGH A.F.A. 2016/17

Contact: David J Ramage,
Email: djramage@blueyonder.co.uk
Tel 0131 538 3222

www.leafa.co.uk

Premier Division						
Sandys	18	14	3	1	45	
Tollcross Th	18	12	4	2	40	
Danderhall Miners AFC	18	9	4	5	31	
Edinburgh Rose	18	8	3	7	27	
Linlithgow Th	18	7	4	7	25	
Edin University	18	7	4	7	25	
East Linton	18	5	2	11	17	
Musselburgh Ams	18	2	9	7	15	
Fernieside	18	2	8	8	14	
The Spartans	18	2	3	13	9	
Championship						
Craigshill Th	16	13	2	1	41	
St Bernards	16	10	1	5	31	
Barca-Milton 97	16	9	4	3	31	
Clermiston Star	16	6	4	6	22	
Redhall Star	16	6	4	6	22	
Lochend	16	6	2	8	20	
Hermiston Vale	16	4	4	8	16	
New'hall Leith Vics	16	3	3	10	12	
Armadale Th	16	2	2	12	8	
Lothian West						
Salvesen FC	16	16	0	0	48	
Shotts Th	16	9	1	6	28	
North Merchiston Vale	16	8	2	6	26	
Edinburgh Harps	16	8	2	6	26	
Balerno Ath	16	6	5	5	23	
B of S Strollers	16	5	4	7	19	
Queensferry Ath	16	5	3	8	18	
Craigroyston CYFC	16	5	1	10	16	
Ratho Ath	16	0	2	14	2	
Lothian East						
Edin South Vics	18	16	0	2	48	
Tranent Ams	18	10	4	4	34	
Waverley Ath	18	10	3	5	33	
Pencaitland FC	18	8	2	8	26	
Redpath Albion	18	7	3	8	24	
Musselburgh Windsor	18	7	3	8	21	(-3)
Heriot Watt	18	5	3	10	18	
Edinburgh South Ams	18	5	3	10	18	
Pathhead	18	4	6	8	18	
Salters Ath	18	3	3	12	12	

Edinburgh West					
Fauldhouse Ams	16	14	0	2	42
Blackridge Vale of Craig	16	10	2	4	32
Carnwath Ams	16	10	1	5	31
East Calder Utd	16	9	1	6	28
Edinburgh Star	16	7	3	6	24
Armadale Rose	16	7	2	7	23
Inter Edinburgh	16	6	3	7	21
Edinburgh City	16	3	0	13	9
Sporting Icapb	16	0	0	16	0
Edinburgh East					
North Edinburgh Wdrs	18	11	3	4	36
Edin Uni Colts	18	11	3	4	36
Dunedin Ath	18	10	5	3	35
Portobello Th	18	10	3	5	33
C S Strollers	18	9	3	6	30
Lauriston Th	18	7	1	10	22
Cavalry Park	18	6	3	9	21
Haddington Ath	18	5	1	12	16
Edinburgh Th	18	4	4	10	16
Edina Hibs	18	4	0	14	12
SUNDAY SECTION					
Sunday Morning Division 1					
West End Utd	18	17	1	0	52
Tranent Ath	18	12	1	5	37
Broxburn AFC	18	10	3	5	33
Partizan FC	18	7	0	11	21
Stables FC	18	6	2	10	20
Burgh Vale	18	4	2	12	14
Roseburn Th	18	2	1	15	7
Sunday Morning Division 2					
Edin Caledonian	18	17	1	0	52
Vittoria Group AFC	18	15	1	2	46
Macmerry Miners Ath	18	12	2	4	38
Pumpherston Th	18	9	2	7	29
Gotham City	18	9	2	7	29
Meadowbank Wed	18	6	4	8	22
Dalkeith Ath	18	6	1	11	19
Joppa Utd	18	6	0	12	18
South Edinburgh	18	3	1	14	10
Oxgangs Trinity	18	0	0	18	0

SUNDAY AFTERNOON					
Premier Division					
Meadowbank FC	6	5	1	0	16
Westside AFC	6	2	2	2	8
C S Strollers	6	2	1	3	7
Craigentinny AFC	6	0	2	4	2
Division 1					
Duddingston Ath	12	11	0	1	33
Edinburgh East	12	8	2	2	26
Whitehackle FC	12	7	2	3	23
Armadale Th	12	4	2	6	14
AC Midlothian	12	4	0	8	12
Bathgate Th	12	2	1	9	7
Corstorphine Dynamo	12	2	1	9	7
Division 2					
St Bernards	18	14	0	4	42
Hibeernian FC	18	12	2	4	38
Port O'Leith	18	11	4	3	37
Rivals AFC	18	11	1	6	34
Thornybank Th	18	9	3	6	30
Lochend Star	18	9	1	8	28
Edinburgh City	18	8	2	8	26
Harro Star	18	6	1	11	19
Longstone Utd	18	2	0	16	6
Pentland Th	18	1	0	17	3

CUP FINALS

Saturday Section

Champions Cup
Edinburgh South Vics v St Bernards, 1-0

Logan Cup (All Clubs) May 26 at Spartans
Tollcross Thistle v Tranent Ams, 6-0

Centenary Cup (All Clubs) May 24 at Paties Road
Clermiston Star v Linlithgow Thistle, 2-2 w-l pens

Miller Cup (Consolation Cup for Logan Cup)
Edinburgh University v Portobello Thistle, 2-0

Challenge Cup (Prem and Champ teams)
Craigshill Thistle v East Linton, 6-1

Ian McDonald Cup (Lothian East and West clubs)
Edinburgh South Vics v Pencaitland, 2-1

Anderson Cup (Edinburgh East and West clubs)
Fauldhouse Ams v Carnwath Ams, 6-0

Rex Gallacher Cup (Championship)
St Bernards v Clermiston Star, 2-1

Blaikie Cup (Prem Div 1) May 13 at Spartans
Linlithgow Thistle v Edinburgh University, 2-1

Cairns Cup (Premier 2)
Linlithgow Thistle v Edinburgh University

Victory Cup (Lothian West)
Salvesen v Edinburgh Harps 3-2

Ronnie Travers Memorial Cup (Lothian East)
Edinburgh South Vics v Pencaitland, 6-3

Dunedin Cup (Edinburgh West)
Fauldhouse Ams v Blackridge Vale of Craig

Robertson Cup (Edinburgh East)
Portobello Thistle v Civil Service Strollers

Stead and Simpson Cup (Supplemenary) May 20 at Spartans
Sandy v Fernieside, 2-1, l-w on pens

Sunday Section

Presidents Cup (All Clubs) May 19 at Newtongrange Star
Meadowbank v Civil Service Strollers, 3-1

Edinburgh Cup (Consolation for Pres Cup), May 7 at Newtongrange Star
Westside v Craigentinny, 1-0

IME Premier Div Cup, May 14 at Newtongrange Star
Meadowbank v Civil Service Strollers, 3-1

Association Div 1 League Cup, April 30 at Newtongrange Star
Duddington Athletic v Armadale Thistle, 1-0

Colin Campbell Div 2 League Cup May 7 at Newtongrange Star
St Bernards v Lochend Star 1-1, 4-2 pens

Morning Div 1 League Cup
West End United v Broxburn 3-2

Morning Div 2 League Cup
Edinburgh Caledonian v Meadowbank Wed, 1-0

LEAFA - SATURDAY SECTION

NB - Grounds listed are most often used by these clubs but matches can be scheduled elsewhere

Club	Ground		
Armadale Thistle Amateurs	Wood Park, Armadale		
Balerno Athletic	Currie		
Bank of Scotland Strollers	Broughton HS 3G, Edinburgh	Meggetland	The Gyle, Edinburgh
Barca Milton 97	The Jewel, Edinburgh		
Bathgate Thistle	Bathgate Sports Centre, Bathgate		
Blackridge Vale of Craig	Public Park, Westrigg	Armadale Academy 3G	
Cavalry Park	Duddingston, Edinburgh		
Civil Service Strollers Reserves	Marine Drive, Edinburgh		
Clermiston Star	Clermiston Park, Edinburgh		
Craigroyston CYFC	Craigie Park, Edinburgh		
Craigshill Thistle	Craigswood, Livingston		
Danderhall Miners	Danderhall Recreation Park		
Dunbar Athletic	Hall Hill Centre, Dunbar		
Dunedin Athletic	Royal High School 3G, Edinburgh		
East Linton	Memorial Park, East Linton		
Edinburgh Harps	Meggetland, Edinburgh		
Edinburgh Rose	Duddingston, Edinburgh	Peffermill, Edinburgh	
Edinburgh South Ams	The Inch, Edinburgh		
Edinburgh South Vics	Saughton 3G, Edinburgh		
Edinburgh Star	The Gyle, Edinburgh		
Edinburgh United Alba	Paties Road, Edinburgh		
Edinburgh University	Peffermill, Edinburgh		
FC Oceana	Seafield, Edinburgh		
Fernieside	Peffermill, Edinburgh		
Forth Community Ams	Recreation Park, Forth		
Gilmerton	Jack Kane Centre, Edinburgh		
Haddington Athletic Ams	Whittinghame Drive 3G, Haddington		
Heriot Watt	Riccarton, Edinburgh		
Hermiston Vale	The Gyle, Edinburgh		
nter Edinburgh	The Gyle, Edinburgh		
.anark AFC	Monteith Park, Carstairs		
Lauriston Thistle	East Pilton, Edinburgh		
.inlithgow Thistle	Kettilstoun Mains, Linlithgow		
.ochend	Seafield, Edinburgh		
Mayfield & Easthouses	Easthouses		
Musselburgh Amateurs	Pinkie St Peters, Musselburgh		
Musselburgh Windsor	Whitecraig		
Newcraighall Leith Vics	Newcraighall Park, Edinburgh		
North Edinburgh Wanderers	West Pilton, Edinburgh	Broughton HS 3G, Edinburgh	
North Merchiston Vale	Harrison Park, Edinburgh		
'athead	Meadowmill	Callander Park, Pathead	
encaitland	Park View		
'enicuik Athletic Ams	Auchendinny	Penicuik Playing Fields	
'olbeth United	Limefield Park, Polbeth		
Queensferry Athletic	Queensferry Rec Centre, South Queensferry		
'atho Athletic	Ratho Public Park		
edhall Star	Redhall Park		
'edpath Albion	Leith Academy 3G, Leith		
alters Athletic	Millerhill Park		
alvesen FC	Forrester HS 3G, Edinburgh		
andys	Castleview Centre, Edinburgh		
hotts Thistle	Calderhead High School, Shotts		
hotts Victoria	Calderhead High School, Shotts		
outh Gyle	The Gyle, Edinburgh		
porting ICAPB	Saughton 3G, Edinburgh		
Bernards	Royal High School, Edinburgh		
he Spartans	Ainslie Park, Edinburgh		
ollcross Thistle	Saughton 3G, Edinburgh		
anent Ams	Polson Park, Tranent		
phall Station	Craigswood, Livingston		
ctoria Loco	Saughton 3G, Edinburgh		
averley Athletic	Birkenside		
'est Edinburgh United	The Gyle, Edinburgh		

PREVIOUS LEAGUE WINNERS			
Year	**Premier**		
1998/1999	Queensferry		
1999/2000	Manfort		
2000/2001	Liberton Royal Mail		
2001/2002	AVU		
2002/2003	Craigmillar Th/Manfort		
2003/2004	Manfort		
2003/2004	Uphall Station		
2004/2005	Uphall Station		
2005/2006	Uphall Station		
2006/2007	Blackridge		
2007/2008	Uphall Station		
2008/2009	Preston Ath		
Year	**Premier Division 1**	**Championship**	
2009/2010	Uphall Station	Loanhead MW	
2010/2011	Dalkeith MW	Edinburgh South Vics	
2011/2012	Sandys	Heriot Vale	
2012/2013	Sandys	Fernieside	
2013/2014	Heriot Vale	Lochend FC	
2014/2015	Newcraighall Leith Vics	Linlithgow Thistle	
2015/2016	Edinburgh Rose	Danderhall MW	
2016/2017	Sandys	Craigshill Thistle	
Year	**Lothian West**	**Lothian Edinburgh**	**Lothian East**
1998/1999	Melbourne Th	Liberton WBM	NCB
1999/2000	Tower	AFC Bingham	Tranent
2000/2001	Oscars	Tynecastle Star	Drummohr
2001/2002	Uphall Station	Craigmillar Th	Danderhall MW
2002/2003	Blackridge	Park Vale Utd	Edin University
2003/2004	Addiewell Hearts	Spartans	Drummohr
2004/2005	Bo'ness Fisons	Sandys	Penicuik Utd
2005/2006	St Bernards	Broughton	Musselburgh
2006/2007	West Pilton Albion	Seaforth Highlanders	Liberton AVU
2007/2008	Armadale Ath	Redhall Star	Preston Ath
2008/2009	Granton Vale	Whitson Star	Dalkeith MW
2002/2003	Blackridge	Park Vale Utd	Edin University
2003/2004	Addiewell Hearts	Spartans	Drummohr
2004/2005	Bo'ness Fisons	Sandys	Penicuik Utd
2005/2006	St Bernards	Broughton	Musselburgh
2006/2007	West Pilton Albion	Seaforth Highlanders	Liberton AVU
2007/2008	Armadale Ath	Redhall Star	Preston Ath
2008/2009	Granton Vale	Whitson Star	Dalkeith MW
2009/2010	Linlithgow Th		Edinburgh South Vics
2010/2011	Tollcross Th		Edinburgh Rose
2011/2012	LBC Lochend		East Linton
2012/2013	Whitburn Bluebell		Mayfield & Easthouses
2013/2014	South Gyle		Newtongrange Star A
2014/2015	Shotts Victoria		North Berwick
2015/2016	Craigshill Thistle		St Bernards
2016/2017	Salvesen FC		Edinburgh South Vics
Year	**Edinburgh West**	**Edinburgh East**	**Central**
1998/1999	Oscars	Whitson Star	
1999/2000	Balerno Ath	Danderhall MW	
2000/2001	Blackridge	Scottish Widows	
2001/2002	Cadlee Star	Mayfield	
2002/2003	Cabrera Ath	Tranent	Argyle
2003/2004	West Pilton Albion	Birkenside	Argyle
2004/2005	Queensferry	Arniston	
2005/2006	Liberton AVU	Prestonpans Ath	
2006/2007	Redhall Star	Breck Hermitage Albion	
2007/2008	Gorgie Hearts	Lochend Ams	Watt Star
2008/2009	Linlithgow Th	Edin South Vics	Sandys
2009/2010	Livingston AFC	Haddington Ath	
2010/2011	Balerno Ath	Tranent Juniors	
2011/2012	Cramond FC	Mayfield & Easthouses	
2012/2013	Blackridge Vale of Craig	Inverleith FC	
2013/2014	Shotts Victoria	Pencaitland FC	Redhall Star
2014/2015	Craigshill Thistle	Clermiston Star	Craigroyston CYFC
2015/2016	Shotts Thistle	Edinburgh South Vics	
2016/2017	Fauldhouse Ams	North Edinburgh Wand	

MIDLANDS A.F.A.
2016/17

Contact: Alistair Martin,
Email: ally1martin@btinternet.com
Tel 0o1382 447903

http://www.midlandsafa.co.uk/

Membership in this league dropped markedly from 2015/16 to 2016/17, from 57 to 41.

CUP FINALS

Bremner Cup, May 20
Menzieshill v Douglas, 2-3

Fairfield Sports & Leisure Cup, Oct 22
Menzieshill v Menzieshill Rovers, 3-1

Ferrari's Shield, May 27
Tayside Fire Brigade v Broughty United, 3-2

Buckman Mackie Trophy, May 24
menzieshill v Tayside Fire Brigade, 5-1

Gray Trophy, May 31
Douglas v St James Athletic, 2-0

Alliance Cup May 17
Broughty United v Arbroath HSFP A, 2-1

Lunan Trophy, Oct 15
Logie Harp v Portcullis, 4-3

Mel Ross Trophy, May 3
Morgan Acad FCP v Carnoustie Panmure YM A, 2-1

Wallace Trophy, May 6
Portcullis v Arbroath HSFP B, 3-2

George Buckman Premier Division table

	Team	Pl	W	D	L	F	A	Diff	Pts
1	Menzieshill AFC	21	20	0	1	89	30	59	60
2	Menzieshill Rovers	21	15	3	3	77	26	51	48
3	Carnoustie Panmure YM	21	13	2	6	58	34	24	41
4	Broughty Utd	21	12	2	7	62	49	13	38
5	Morgan Academy FP	21	11	3	7	60	51	9	36
6	Tayside Fire Brigade	20	10	3	7	59	44	15	33
7	Barnhill	21	9	3	9	41	41	0	30
8	Logie Harp	20	8	4	8	44	56	-12	28
9	Portcullis AFC	20	7	3	10	44	41	3	24
10	Merpro	20	6	4	10	44	44	0	22
11	Newport	20	6	3	11	73	69	4	21
12	Invergowrie	20	7	0	13	36	73	-37	21
13	Douglas Athletic	20	6	2	12	41	69	-28	20
14	NCR	20	5	1	14	48	70	-22	16
15	Kirriemuir Thistle AFC	20	1	1	18	29	108	-79	4

Drain Doctor Division 1 table

	Team	Pl	W	D	L	F	A	Diff	Pts
1	Douglas Amateurs	15	12	2	1	73	21	52	38
2	Fintry Athletic	15	11	0	4	49	34	15	33
3	Lowson Utd	15	9	2	4	38	20	18	29
4	St James Athletic	15	9	2	4	38	32	6	29
5	Arbroath Harp	14	8	0	6	35	36	-1	24
6	Finavon AFC	15	6	2	7	40	32	8	20
7	Forfar West End AFC	14	6	2	6	36	43	-7	20
8	Arbroath HSFP	15	5	2	8	30	41	-11	17
9	Wellbank AFC	14	4	1	9	31	45	-14	13
10	Bank Street Athletic	14	2	1	11	27	46	-19	7
11	Monifieth Tayside	14	1	0	13	17	64	-47	3

Alliance Championship table

	Team	Pl	W	D	L	F	A	Diff	Pts
1	Broughty Utd	21	17	3	1	91	29	62	54
2	Carnoustie Panmure YM B	21	14	4	3	76	31	45	46
3	Carnoustie Panmure YM A	21	14	2	5	71	28	43	44
4	Morgan Academy FP	21	12	4	5	71	48	23	40
5	Menzieshill Rovers	20	10	5	5	72	58	14	35
6	Tayside Fire Brigade	21	10	3	8	67	65	2	33
7	Portcullis AFC	20	9	4	7	38	46	-8	31
8	Logie Harp	20	9	1	10	37	47	-10	28
9	Arbroath HSFP A	21	8	3	10	50	51	-1	27
10	Barnhill	21	8	2	11	42	49	-7	26
11	St James Athletic	21	8	1	12	60	63	-3	25
12	Newport	20	7	3	10	56	72	-16	24
13	Arbroath HSFP B	20	3	3	14	31	81	-50	12
14	Invergowrie	20	3	1	16	29	63	-34	10
15	Monifieth Tayside	20	2	1	17	27	87	-60	7

	League Champions
1926/27	Aeros
1927/28	YM Anchorage
1928/29	Grove Academy FP
1929/30	Aeros
1930/31	Aeros
1931/32	Clifton Thistle
1932/33	RAF Leuchars
1933/34	YM Anchorage
1934/35	YM Anchorage
1935/36	YM Anchorage
1936/37	YM Anchorage
1937/38	YM Anchorage
1938/39	YM Anchorage
1939/40	YM Anchorage
1946/47	YM Anchorage
1947/48	YM Anchorage
1948/49	YM Anchorage
1949/50	YM Anchorage
1950/51	YM Anchorage
1951/52	YM Anchorage
1952/53	YM Anchorage
1953/54	Invergowrie
1954/55	YM Anchorage
1955/56	Wormit
1956/57	Wormit
1957/58	YM Anchorage
1958/59	YM Anchorage
1959/60	NCR
1960/61	NCR
1961/62	NCR
1962/63	NCR
1963/64	NCR
1964/65	NCR
1965/66	NCR
1966/67	NCR
1967/68	NCR
1968/69	NCR
1969/70	Broughty United
1970/71	NCR
1971/72	Broughty United
1972/73	Lawside FP
1973/74	Broughty United
1974/75	Broughty United
1975/76	Auchterhouse
1976/77	Auchterhouse
1977/78	Auchterhouse
1978/79	SMT
1979/80	Harris Academy FP
1980/81	Harris Academy FP
1981/82	Tayport
1982/83	Harris Academy FP
1983/84	Kingsway TC
1984/85	Harris Academy FP
1985/86	Riverside Ath
1986/87	Riverside Ath
1987/88	Lawside FP
1988/89	Riverside Ath
1989/90	Riverside Ath
1990/91	Riverside Ath
1991/92	Riverside Ath
1992/93	Lawside FP
1993/94	NCR
1994/95	Barnhill
1995/96	Riverside Ath
1996/97	Riverside Ath
1997/98	NCR
1998/99	Riverside Ath
1999/00	Riverside Ath
2000/1	Riverside Ath
2001/2	SS Peter & Paul
2002/3	Riverside Ath
2003/4	Riverside Ath
2004/5	Riverside Ath
2005/6	Riverside Ath
2006/7	Riverside Ath
2007/8	SS Peter & Paul
2008/9	Riverside Ath
2009/10	Riverside Ath
2010/11	Bank Street Ath
2011/12	Bank Street Ath
2012/13	St James
2013/14	Riverside Ath
2014/15	St James
2015/16	Carnoustie Panmure '
2016/17	Menzieshill AFC

	Gray Trophy	Lunan Trophy
1948/49		YM Anchorage
1949/50		YM Anchorage
1950/51	Tayport Violet	YM Anchorage
1951/52	Tayport Violet	YM Anchorage
1952/53	Alyth Violet	YM Anchorage
1953/54	Wormit	YM Anchorage
1954/55	Invergowrie	YM Anchorage
1955/56	RAF Leuchars	Bullionfield
1956/57	YM Anchorage	Bullionfield
1957/58	YM Anchorage	YM Anchorage
1958/59	Wormit Ams	Grays United
1959/60	Morgan Acad FP	YM Anchorage
1960/61	Grays Utd	Morgan Acad FP
1961/62	Longforgan	Grays United
1962/63	No competition	No competition
1963/64	NCR	NCR
1964/65	NCR	NCR
1965/66	NCR	Grove Academy FP
1966/67	No competition	Grove Academy FP
1967/68	Lawside Academy FP	NCR
1968/69	Lawside Academy FP	Longforgan
1969/70	NCR	NCR
1970/71	Lawside Academy FP	Wormit Ams
1971/72	Grove Ams	Broughty United
1972/73	SMT	Timex
1973/74	Broughty United	Carnoustie YM
1974/75	NCR	St James
1975/76	Auchterhouse	NCR
1976/77	SMT	Carnoustie YM B
1977/78	Tayport Ams	Timex
1978/79	SMT	Carnoustie YM A
1979/80	Timex	Broughty United
1980/81	Harris Academy FP	Harris Academy FP
1981/82	Timex	Kingsway TC
1982/83	Harris Academy FP	Kingsway TC
1983/84	Kingsway TC	Kingsway TC
1984/85	Kingsway TC	Harris Academy FP
1985/86	Riverside Ath	NCR
1986/87	Lawside Academy FP	YMCA
1987/88	NCR	Riverside Ath
1988/89	Riverside Ath	DCFE
1989/90	Riverside Ath	Riverside Ath
1990/91	Timex	Kingsway Ath
1991/92	Kingsway Athletic	Riverside Ath
1992/93	Letham LC	NCR
1993/94	Dundee YMCA	NCR
1994/95	Dundee YMCA	Riverside Ath
1995/96	Broughty United	Arbroath Harp
1996/97	Letham LC	Inchture Ath
1997/98	Fintry Thistle	Riverside Ath
1998/99	Dee Club	Riverside Ath
1999/00	Arbroath HSFP	Barnhill
2000/1	Arbroath HSFP	NCR B
2001/2	Dee Club	NCR B
2002/3	Carnoustie YM	Broughty United
2003/4	Invergowrie	NCR
2004/5	Dundee Shamrock	Carnoustie YM
2005/6	Morgan Acad FP	NCR
2006/7	Arbroath HSFP	NCR
2007/8	Menzieshill Athletic	Barnhill
2008/9	Bank Street Ath	Broughty United
2009/10	SS Peter and Paul	Barnhill
2010/11	Newport	Carnoustie YM B
2011/12	Dundee College	Broughty United B
2012/13	Dundee City	Invergowrie
2013/14	Lowson United	Tayside Fire Brigade
2014/15	Portcullis	St James
2015/16	Morgan Acad FP	Arbroath HSFP A
2016/17	Douglas AFC	Logie Harp

Carne Trophy
NCR
YMCA
Broughty Hearts
Harris Academy FP
Craigiebank
Auchterhouse
6th BB
Tayport Ams
Lawside Academy FP
Monifieth
Tayport Ams
YM Anchorage
YMCA
Carnoustie YM
Kingsway TC
SMT
Kelso
Arbroath HSFP
Barnhill
Lochee BC
Kelso
Timex
Kelso
YM Anchorage
Arbroath HSFP
PO Phones
Riverside Athletic
Carnoustie YM
YM Anchorage
Broughty Ex-Service
Hillside BC
St Francis
Broughty East End
Broughty United
Kingsway Athletic
Letham Lads Club
Harris Academy FP
Fintry Thistle
Douglas Ams
Whitfield Labour Club
Lochee United
Carnoustie YM / HS
Lowson United
Dundee Shamrock
Fintry Thistle
Carnoustie YM
Invergowrie
Dundee University
Arfbroath Harp
St James
Portcullis
Douglas Sports Club
FC Claypotts
Caird Park
Monifieth Tayside
Inchture Ath
Monfiieth Tayside
Menzieshill
Mid Craigie
Bank Street Ath
No competition

	Buckman Mackie Trophy	Fairfield S and L Trophy	Mel Ross Trophy	Wallace Trophy
1990/91	Lawside Academy	Riverside Athletic		
1991/92	Lawside Academy	Riverside Athletic		
1992/93	Tayside Fire Brigade	Tayside Fire Brigade		
1993/94	NCR	Riverside Athletic		
1994/95	SS Peter & Paul	Tayside Fire Brigade		
1995/96	Riverside Athletic	Barnhill		Auchterhouse Admiral
1996/97	Douglas Ams	Riverside Athletic		St James
1997/98	Lawside Academy	Logie Harp		Monifieth Tayside
1998/99	Riverside Athletic	Tayside Fire Brigade	Logie Harp	Dundee Shamrock
1999/00	Barnhill	Dundee College	Harris Acad FP	Harris Academy FP
2000/1	Riverside Athletic	Arbroath Ams	Dundee College	Arbroath Ams
2001/2	Riverside Athletic	Riverside Athletic	Carnouistie YM	Carnoustie YM
2002/3	Riverside Athletic	Riverside Athletic	Harris Acad FP	Cup witheld
2003/4	SS Peter & Paul	Riverside Athletic	Arbroath HSFP	Morgan Acad FP
2004/5	Riverside Athletic	Riverside Athletic	NCR	Dundee University
2005/6	Riverside Athletic	SS Peter and Paul	Dundee College	Dundee University
2006/7	Carnoustie YM	Riverside Athletic	Invergowrie	Carnoustie YM B
2007/8	Riverside Athletic	Riverside Athletic	Carnouistie YM B	Harris Academy FP
2008/9	Invergowrie	Riverside Athletic	Riverside Ath	Michelin Ath
2009/10	St James	Bank Street Ath	Carnoustie YM A	Morgan Acad FP
2010/11	Bank Street Athletic	Carnoustie YM	Broughty United A	Arbroath HSFP A
2011/12	NCR	Bank Street Ath	Broughty United B	Arbroath CSC A
2012/13	NCR	St James	Carnoustie YM A	St James
2013/14	Riverside Athletic	St James	Arbroath HSFP A	Monifieth Tayside
2014/15	St James	St James	NCR	Riverside Ath
2015/16	Menzieshill Rovers	Riverside Athletic	Riverside Ath	St James
2016/17	Menzieshill AFC	Menzieshill AFC	Morgan Acad FP	Portcullis

NORTH WEST SUTHERLAND A.F.A. 2016

Contact: Hugh Morrison,
Email: info@orcadiadurness.com
Tel 01971 511336
http://www.nwsafa.co.uk
Facebook page: nwsafa

FINAL TABLE

	P	W	D	L	F	A	GD	PTS
Lairg	18	13	3	2	79	34	45	42
Brora	18	13	3	2	79	35	44	42
Lochinver	18	9	4	5	64	40	24	31
Helmsdale	18	9	0	9	51	57	-6	27
Golspie	18	7	4	7	48	39	9	25
Embo	18	7	3	8	34	52	-18	24
Melvich	18	6	3	9	55	52	3	21
Kinlochbervie	18	6	3	9	48	86	-38	21
Dornoch	18	5	2	11	59	54	5	17
Tongue	18	2	1	15	36	104	-68	7

Polla Cup
24/9/16, Lairg v Brora, 3-2
Played for by two highest scoring teams
Mackay Cup
17/9/16, Melvich v Golsipe, 1-1
Melvich won on penalties

.
2017 League Membership

Brora Wanderers
Dornoch City
Durness (league games only, no Cup ties)
Embo
Golspie Stafford
Helmsdale United
Kinlochbervie (KLB)
Lairg Rovers
Lochinver
Melvich
Tongue United

NORTH & SOUTH LANARKSHIRE A.F.A. 2016/17

Contact: Craig Denholm
Email: nslafa.2008@yahoo.co.uk
Tel: 07919 161077

www.nslafa-est2008.com

FINAL TABLE

	P	W	D	L	F	A	GD
Wishaw Wycombe Wanderers	22	18	2	2	88	20	68
Blantyre (RGM) AFC	23	16	2	5	95	41	54
Carluke Hearts	19	15	1	3	70	19	51
Eddlewood	21	12	2	7	65	42	23
FC Dal Riata	24	11	1	12	60	57	3
Mill United	21	9	6	6	65	34	31
Lanarkshire Forest	23	10	2	11	60	54	6
Springhill	24	9	4	11	52	72	-20
Holytown Colts Youth	22	8	4	10	42	66	-24
Motherwell Bridgeworks	25	6	5	14	42	82	-40
East Kilbride	21	3	3	15	29	60	-31
Strathclyde Thistle	20	3	1	16	26	115	-89
North Motherwell	7	2	1	4	14	24	-10
Clydesdale	7	1	0	6	10	29	-19

CUP FINALS

Lanarkshire Cup, May 26 at Airdrieonians FC
Wishaw Wycombe Wanderers v Carluke Hearts, 2-1

John Ross Cup, May 19 at Airdrieonians FC
Carluke Hearts v Eddlewood, 1-0

Freddy Davis Memorial League Cup, May 12 at Airdrieonians
Wishaw Wycombe Wanderers v Lanarkshire Forest, 7-2

ORKNEY A.F.A.
2016 AND 2017

Contact: Bryn Loggenberg
Email: bryn.loggenberg@gogglemail.com
Tel 01856 761897

www.oafa.leaguerepublic.com

www.facebook.com/pages/Orkney-Amateur-Football-Association-Results

LEAGUE COMPOSITION 2017

A Division

Dounby Athletic
Firth
Kirkwall Hotspurs
Kirkwall Rovers
Kirkwall Thorfinn
Rendall
St Andrews
Stromness Athletic

B Division

Burray
Harray
Holm
Isles United
Kirkwall Aacdemicals
Kirkwall Wanderers
South Ronaldsay

"A" League

		P	W	D	L	F	A	GD	PTS
1	Thorfinn	14	12	1	1	53	10	43	37
2	Hotspurs	14	11	1	2	36	13	23	34
3	Stromness	14	8	3	3	39	12	27	27
4	Rovers	14	7	1	6	47	24	23	22
5	Dounby	14	5	3	6	18	22	-4	18
6	Rendall	14	6	0	8	22	31	-9	18
7	Firth	14	2	1	11	25	67	-42	7
8	Isles United	14	0	0	14	11	72	-61	0

"B League"

		P	W	D	L	F	A	GD	PTS
1	St Andrews	13	9	3	1	48	24	24	30
2	Harray	13	8	3	2	46	25	21	27
3	Accies	12	8	1	3	33	25	8	25
4	South Ronaldsay	12	7	0	5	27	17	10	21
5	Burray	12	3	1	8	29	31	-2	10
6	Holm	12	2	0	10	25	58	-33	6
7	Wanderers	12	1	2	9	16	44	-28	5

Reserve League

		P	W	D	L	F	A	GD	PTS
1	Rovers Reserves	14	12	1	1	47	19	28	37
2	Stromness Reserve	14	10	3	1	42	14	28	33
3	Thorfinn Reserves	14	8	4	2	47	14	33	28
4	Hotspurs Reserves	14	7	0	7	38	35	3	21
5	Rendall Reserves	14	6	1	7	44	14	30	19
6	Dounby Reserves	14	4	1	9	27	35	-8	13
7	Firth Reserves	14	3	0	11	17	76	-59	9
8	Isles United Reserv	14	1	0	13	12	67	-55	3

Junior League

		P	W	D	L	F	A	GD	PTS
1	East United Juniors	5	4	1	0	20	8	12	13
2	Dounby Juniors	6	3	0	3	7	13	-6	9
3	Thorfinn Juniors	5	2	1	2	14	9	5	7
4	Stromness Juniors	4	0	0	4	4	15	-11	0

CUP FINALS

Oxy Cup (29/4/16)
Harray v South Ronaldsay, 1-1, 7-6 pens

Isaac Newlands Cup (28/4/16)
Stromness v Thorfinn, 1-1, 4-1p

Orcadian Parish Cup (13/8/16)
Stromness v Rendall, 2-0

Heddle Cup (9/9/16)
Rendall v Stromness, 1-1, 3-2p

Thomson Cup (10/9/16)
St Andrews v South Ronaldsay, 5-2

Reid Cup (11/9/16)
Stromness Reserves v Rovers Reserves, 1-1, 5-4p

Craigmyle Cup (16/9/16)
Thorfinn v Hotspurs, 3-0

Ferry Inn Thornley Binders Cup (4/9/16)
Stromness v Birsay, 2-0

Dr Gordon Cup (7/9/16)
East United Juniors v Thorfinn Juniors, 9-1

Jolly Cup (13/9/16)
Stromness v Thorfinn, 1-0

PAISLEY & DISTRICT A.F.A.
2016/17

Contact: Jackie Loughlin,
Email: jackiefbs@yahoo.co.uk
Tel 01505 346474

http://www.leaguewebsite.co.uk/pdafa

USUAL HOME GROUNDS	
Arden AFC	
Beith Meadowside AFC	Bellsdale Astro, Beith
Boswell AFC	Rosshall Academy, Glasgow
Brucehill United AFC	
Ferguslie Star AFC	
Fordbank Star AFC	Thomas Shanks Park, Johnstone
Glasgow Deaf AFC	Glasgow Green Football centre
Glenburn AFC	
Glenvale AFC	Ferguslie SC, Paisley
Glynhill Moorcroft AFC	KGV Parks, Renfrew
Langcraigs AFC	Lochfield (The Marshes)
Linwood Thistle AFC	On-X Linwood
New Meadow AFC	Glasgow Green Football centre
Paisley Caledonia AFC	
Stanley Athletic AFC	Ralston Sports Centre, Paisley
Tannahill AFC	St James PF, Paisley
Westcliff AFC	

PREMIER DIVISION	P	W	D	L	Pts
Glynhill Moorcroft AFC	21	17	1	3	49
Glenburn AFC	21	13	1	6	43
Glenvale AFC	21	13	4	4	43
Stanley Athletic AFC	21	11	1	9	37
Fordbank Star AFC	21	11	1	8	34
Langcraigs AFC	21	9	1	11	28
Boswell AFC	21	4	0	17	12
Glasgow Deaf AFC	21	0	1	20	1
Ferguslie Star AFC	0	0	0	0	0
Linwood Thistle AFC	0	0	0	0	0

DIVISION ONE	P	W	D	L	Pts
Westcliff AFC	20	15	2	3	47
Arden AFC	20	14	1	4	46
New Meadow AFC	20	12	3	5	39
Paisley Caledonia AFC	20	8	2	9	26
Tannahill AFC	20	4	1	14	16
Beith Meadowside AFC	20	0	1	18	1
Brucehill United AFC	0	0	0	0	0

CUP FINALS

Fleming Cup, May 26 at Johnstone Burgh JFC
Glenvale v Glynhill Moorcroft, 2-1

Jimmy Muir Memorial Cup, May 24 at Johnstone Burgh JFC
Glenburn v Glenvale, 2-1

McLean / Lothian Cup, May 19 at Johnstone Burgh JFC
Glynhill Moorcroft v Boswell, 3-1

CIBA Cup, May 5 at Johnstone Burgh
Westcliff v Tannahill, 7-0

PERTHSHIRE A.F.A.
2016/17

Contact : League Secretary position vacant
www.leaguewebsite.co.uk/pafa

IER DIVISION	P	W	D	L	F	A	GD	Pts	Usual Home Ground
AM	18	18	0	0	110	13	97	54	Seven Acres, Perth
ORAL UTD	18	10	2	2	39	31	8	44	Davie Park, Blairgowrie (Outside Pitch)
OF EARN	18	10	3	5	33	29	4	33	Market Park, Crieff*
IELD SWIFTS	18	9	2	7	50	58	-8	29	Riverside Park, North Muirton
HNS	18	8	2	8	55	47	8	26	North Inch, Perth
ITY	18	7	1	7	38	40	-2	22	Huntingtower Park, Ruthvenfield
TERARDER PRIMROSE	18	6	4	7	38	47	-9	22	Public Park, Auchterarder*
IE	18	5	5	8	37	48	-11	20	South Inch, Perth* / St Johnstone Astro
ELTON	18	1	2	14	23	76	-53	5	Recreation Park, Burrelton
NLUIG	18	1	1	15	26	61	-35	4	Recreation Park, Ballinluig
ION ONE	P	W	D	L	F	A	GD	Pts	
GE OF EARN	17	14	1	2	45	14	31	43	Victory Park, bridge of Earn
rtyAsc	17	13	1	3	51	23	28	40	Brownlands Park, Luncarty
DALBANE	16	10	2	4	40	24	16	32	Home Street, Aberfeldy
OSSIE/CALEDONIAN	16	9	2	5	45	35	10	29	Kinrossie Park
HISTLE	16	7	2	7	39	46	-7	23	Victory Park, bridge of Earn
AR ANGUS	16	3	4	9	28	38	-10	13	Largan Park, Coupar Angus
GETON UTD	16	3	4	9	33	50	-17	13	South Inch, Perth*
RAY	16	3	2	11	24	50	-26	11	Davie Park, Blairgowrie (Outside Pitch)
H	16	2	0	14	15	41	-26	6	Diamond Jubilee Park, Alyth*
ION TWO	P	W	D	L	F	A	GD	Pts	
NS	18	16	2	0	80	10	70	50	Lindsay Park, Kettins
TEAM	18	12	3	3	49	18	31	39	South Inch, Perth*
AM COMMUNITY FC	18	11	0	7	71	45	26	33	Seven Acres, Perth
OF ATHOLL	18	10	3	5	42	36	6	33	Recreation Ground, Pitlochry*
THEARN GROVE	18	9	0	9	44	54	-10	27	Braidhaugh Park, crieff
CRIEFF	18	8	1	9	65	55	10	25	
FHILL	18	7	1	10	34	49	-15	22	Guildtown Park, Hall Road
KELD & BIRNAM	18	5	0	13	36	57	-21	15	Dunkeld Park*
THISTLE	18	3	2	13	27	61	-34	11	Davie Park (Outside), Blairgowrie
LE	18	3	0	15	29	92	-63	9	Meigle Village Park

CUP FINALS

Atholl Cup, May 4
Breadalbane v Dunkeld and Birnam, 2-1

North Perthshire Cup, May 13
Breadalbane v Ballinluig, 3-2

Consolation Cup, May 20 at Scone Thistle JFC
Kettins v St Johns, 4-2

Birks Cup, April 29 at Aberfeldy
Vale of Atholl v Ballinluig, 4-1

Ashleigh Cup, May 18 at Luncarty JFC
Letham v Bridge of Earn, 4-0

Smith League Cup, May 23 at Kinnoull JFC
Letham v Auchterarder Primrose, 4-1

Perthshire Cup, May 11 at Luncarty JFC
Letham v Auchterarder Primrose, 7-0

Perth and District Cup, May 9 at Kinnoull JFC
Letham v Jeanfield Swifts, 6-1

SCOTTISH AMATEUR FOOTBALL LEAGUE 2016/17

Contact: Mr Mike McLean,
Email: scotaflsec@yahoo.co.uk
Tel 07778 744651

www.safl.co.uk/

	PREMIER DIVISION	P	W	D	L	F	A	GD	PTS	usual Home Ground
1	St. Joseph's FP	18	15	1	2	68	24	44	46	William Street, Duntocher
2	Oban Saints	17	11	1	5	55	30	25	34	Glencruitten, Oban
3	Goldenhill	18	11	0	7	46	27	19	33	Clydebank HS
4	East Kilbride FC	18	10	3	5	42	27	15	33	K-Park
5	Shawlands FP	18	7	2	9	31	35	-4	23	Nether Pollok PF, Glasgow
6	Motherwell Thistle	18	6	4	8	38	51	-13	22	Muirhouse PF, Motherwell
7	Inverclyde	17	6	2	9	37	45	-8	20	Battery Park, Gourock
8	Drumchapel Colts	18	4	4	9	29	55	-26	19	Glenhead Park, Duntocher
9	Campbeltown Pupils	18	4	2	11	31	51	-20	14	Kintyre Park, Campbeltown
10	Ferguslie Star	18	4	1	13	34	66	-32	13	Ferguslie SC, Paisley

	PREMIER ONE	P	W	D	L	F	A	GD	PTS	
1	Alba Thistle	18	14	2	2	59	24	35	44	Seedhill Park, Paisley
2	EKRR	18	12	3	3	59	24	35	39	the Murray, East Kilbride
3	Hillington	18	10	4	4	45	36	9	34	Penilee Comm centre, Glasgow
4	Rutherglen	18	8	4	6	57	48	9	28	Burnhill SC, Rutherglen
5	Dunoon	17	7	5	5	45	45	0	26	Dunoon Stadium
6	Kings Park Rangers	18	6	5	7	38	35	3	23	Glasgow Green
7	Neilston	18	4	5	9	33	45	-12	17	Kingston PF, Neilston
8	Rosehill Star	18	5	2	11	25	48	-23	17	Nether Pollok PF, Glasgow
9	Duncanrig FP	18	3	4	11	23	50	-27	13	Ballerup Arena, EK
10	Easthall Star	17	1	4	12	34	63	-29	7	Stepford Complex, Glasgow

	PREMIER 2A	P	W	D	L	F	A	GD	PTS	
1	Rossvale	16	12	2	2	54	16	38	38	Huntershill PF, Bishopbriggs
2	East Kilbride YMCA	16	11	0	5	42	25	17	33	East Kilbride Stadium
3	Lochgilphead Red Star	16	10	2	4	51	16	35	32	Ropework Park, Lochgilphead
4	Houston	16	9	4	3	41	28	13	31	Linwood On-X Centre
5	Broomhill	16	8	0	8	39	47	-8	24	Battery Park, Greenock
6	Millbeg	16	6	1	9	29	57	-28	19	Lochend Comm centre, Easterhouse
7	Castlemilk	16	3	4	9	34	47	-13	13	Barlia SC, Castlemilk
8	Port Glasgow OBU	16	3	2	11	33	48	-15	11	Parklea PF, Port Glasgow
9	Carlton YMCA	16	2	1	13	24	63	-39	7	Kibble Complex, Paisley

	PREMIER 2B	P	W	D	L	F	A	GD	PTS	
1	Arkleston	16	12	2	2	55	19	36	38	Cowan Park, Barrhead
2	Claremont	16	11	1	4	37	25	12	34	Ballerup Rec centre, EK
3	Port Glasgow	16	9	2	5	47	30	17	29	Parklea PF, Port Glasgow
4	Paisley	16	8	2	6	38	28	10	26	Seedhill, Paisley
5	Duntocher	16	8	0	8	40	32	8	24	Mountblow, Glasgow
6	FC Argyle	16	5	4	7	51	46	5	19	Argyle Park, Alexandria
7	East End United	16	6	1	9	31	40	-9	19	Notre Dame HS, Greenock
8	Busby	16	5	2	9	28	47	-19	17	overlea PF, Clarkston
9	Tarbert	16	1	0	15	16	76	-60	3	Cil Andreis, Tarbert

CUP FINALS

Coronation Cup, May 31 at Vale of Clyde JFC
Ferguslie Star v Motherwell Thistle, 2-1

Jimmy Marshall Cup, May 26 at Vale of Clyde JFC
Easthall Star v Oban Saints, 2-2 3-2 pens

Hall Cup, May 25
East Kilbride YMCA v Rossvale, 1-0 at Vale of Clude JFC

Centenary Cup, May 12 at Valeof Clyde JFC
St Josephs FP v Alba Thistle, 2-2, 8-7 pens

SCOTTISH POLICE A.F.A.
2016/17

	P	W	D	L	F	A	GD	Pts
Dunbartonshire	8	6	0	2	35	12	23	18
Renfrewshire	7	4	1	2	17	21	-4	13
Glasgow North	6	4	0	2	20	16	4	12
Glasgow South	7	2	0	5	7	19	-12	6
Glasgow Central	8	1	1	6	15	26	-11	4

Competitive Police football has declined markedly in recent years. Reduced levels of staffing have made non-essential time off much more difficult.

CUP FINALS

Colquhoun Shield, May 11
Dunbartonshire v Glasgow South, 7-0

Challenge Cup, May 18
Dunbartonshire v Tayside, 5-0

Scottish Cup
Tayside v Renfrewshire P-P
Match postponed due to heightened security levels following terror attacks in England

SHETLAND A.F.A.
2016

Contact: Brydon Robertson,
Email: shetlandfa@yahoo.co.uk
Tel 01806 566239

http://www.shetlandfootball.co.uk/

League A	P	W	D	L	F	A	GD	PTS
Spurs	14	11	1	2	55	21	34	34
Whitedale	14	8	2	4	37	36	1	26
Thistle	14	8	0	6	35	28	7	24
Celtic	14	6	1	7	32	32	0	19
Ness Utd	14	5	3	6	23	26	-3	18
Delting	14	4	5	5	28	31	-3	17
Whalsay	14	5	1	8	25	29	-4	16
Scalloway	14	2	1	11	26	58	-32	7

League B	P	W	D	L	F	A	GD	PTS
North Isles FC	14	10	1	3	48	18	30	31
Spurs	14	9	2	3	53	42	11	29
Delting	14	9	1	4	59	33	26	28
Thistle	14	6	3	5	35	32	3	21
Ness Utd	14	6	2	6	43	47	-4	20
Scalloway	14	4	3	7	25	39	-14	15
Whalsay	14	4	1	9	26	37	-11	13
Celtic	14	1	1	12	17	58	-41	4

Works League	P	W	D	L	F	A	GD	PTS
Services	14	11	1	2	61	18	43	34
West Side Rebels	13	9	1	3	45	29	16	28
Ness C	13	7	2	4	35	21	14	23
Wast Linga Ramblers	13	6	1	6	47	37	10	19
Baroc Revolution	13	6	0	7	27	36	-9	18
Bressay	14	6	0	8	26	49	-23	18
Wrultizers	14	3	1	10	29	42	-13	10
Banks	14	3	0	11	23	61	-38	9

CUP FINALS

H Williamson & Sons Fraser Cup (24/8/16)
Spurs v Whalsay, 6-2

Highland Fuels Cup (20/4/16)
Spurs v Delting, 2-0

Simpson & Ward Manson Cup (3/7/16)
Spurs v Celtic, 2-0

Simpson & Ward Madrid Cup (15/6/16)
Celtic v Whalsay, 4-1

GTS County Shield (27/9/16)
Thistle v Celtic, 2-1 AET

Bloomfield Cup (B League) (11/9/16)
Spurs v Delting, 1-0

Joint Cup (23/7/16)
North Isles v Ness United , 5-5, 3-0 pens

Works League Association Cup (27/8/16)
Services v West Side Rebels, 3-3, 4-3 pens

Works League DITT Cup (25/6/16)
Services v West Side Rebels , 3-3 AET, 4-2 pens

REPRESENTATIVE GAMES

Football Times Cup						
10/09/2016	1	A	Tain St Duthus	3	3	5-3p
01/10/2016	QF	N	Alness	2	2	5-3p
15/10/2016	SF	A	Invergordon	1	2	
Jock Mackay Cup						
20/02/2016	1	A	Halkirk United	P	P	scr
18/02/2017	1	A	Orkney	2	1	
Inter-County						
30/07/2016		A	Orkney	2	3	
Island Games (in Gotland)						
25/06/2017		N	Saaremaa			
26/06/2017		N	Guernsey			
27/06/2017		N	Aland islands			
Friendly						
16/07/2016		A	Formartine United	2	3	
25/03/2017		N	Western Isles	3	1	at Ross County FC

Club	Home Pitches	Division
Celtic	Clickimin South / Gilbertson / Seafield	A
Ness United	Cunnisburgh / Boddam	A
Whalsay	Harbison / Seafield	A
Spurs	Gilbertson Park / Seafield	A
Thistle	Seafield / Gilbertson / Clicikin South	A
Scalloway	Hamnavoe / Fraser Park	A
Delting	Brae Grass Pitch / Fraser Park	A
Whitedale	Strom	A
Thistle	Clickimin South / Gilbertson / Seafield	B
Whitedale	Strom	B
Ness Utd	Cunnisburgh	B
Whalsay	Harbison	B
Celtic	Gilbertson Park / Seafield / Clickimin South	B
Delting	Brae Grass Pitch	B
Yell FC	Unst / Mid Yell	B
Spurs	Gilbertson Park / Clickimin South / Seafield	B
Scalloway	Fraser Park / Hamnavoe	B
Banks	Gilbertson Park / Seafield	W
Services	Clickimin South / Gilbertson	W
Dynamo Chernobyl	Clickimin South / Gilbertson / Seafield	W
Baroc Revolution	Clickimin South	W
West Side Rebels	Aith	W
Bressay	Bressay	W
Wrultizers	Brae Grass Pitch	W
Ness C	Cunnisburgh / Sandwick	W
Wast Linga Ramblers	Harbison	W

SHETLAND FOOTBALL ASSOCIATION

SHETLAND
SELECT
V
ABERDEEN
FC SELECT

INVITATION MATCH TO CELEBRATE 100 YEARS
OF ASSOCIATION FOOTBALL IN SHETLAND

at GILBERTSON PARK, LERWICK

on SATURDAY, 1st AUGUST, 1987

Kick-off 2 pm

Admission:
Adults £1
Children & OAPs 50p

PROGRAMME 50p

Current Shetland Squad,

Managed by Niall Bristow and Kevin Main;

Goalkeepers: Grant Wood (Spurs), Iain Devonald (Delting) & Saul Swanson (Thistle).

Defenders: Richard Arthur (Whalsay), Shane Jamieson (Celtic), Joel Bradley (Celtic), Robert Smith (Celtic), Andrew Flett (Spurs), Piotr Drozdowski (Whitedale), Josie Kay (Spurs), Ryan Grant (Celtic) & Jack Clubb (Celtic).

Midfielders: Leighton Flaws (C) (Delting), Connor Regan (Celtic), Calvin Leask (Thistle), James Farmer (Ness), James Aitken (Celtic), Magnus Thompson (Whalsay), John Allan (Scalloway), Sam Maver (Spurs), Stuart Copland (Thistle) & Bobby Scott (Whitedale).

Forwards: Greg Tulloch (Whitedale), Gary Sutherland (Delting) & David Murray (Whalsay).

SKYE & LOCHALSH A.F.A. 2016

Contact: Heckie McCormack
Email: secretary@slafa.org.uk
Tel 01478 613427

www.slafa.org.uk/

	Club	P	W	D	L	F	A	GD	Pts
1	Portree Junio	16	16	0	0	85	20	65	48
2	Kyleakin	16	12	1	3	69	28	41	37
3	Sleat & Strath	16	10	2	4	86	31	55	32
4	NW Skye	16	6	2	8	46	47	-1	20
5	GA United	16	5	4	7	50	50	0	19
6	Portree	16	5	3	8	44	51	-7	18
7	Plockton	16	5	1	10	35	59	-24	16
8	Glenelg	16	4	3	9	28	66	-38	15
9	Kyle	16	0	2	14	10	101	-91	2

CUP FINALS

GF McRae Cup (17/6/16)
Kyleakin v Portree Juniors, 2-0
At Kyleakin

Ross Cup (6/8/16)
Sleat & Strathnaver v Portree, 4-1
at Broadford

Clan Donald Cup (17/9/16)
Portree v GA United, 5-1
at Kyleakin

Ewan MacRae Cup (17/9/16)
Kyleakin v Portree Juniors, 4-2
at Kyleakin

2017 TABLE, Mid June

	Club	P	W	D	L	F	A	GD	Pts
1	Kyleakin	7	6	0	1	24	10	14	18
2	Portree Juniors	6	5	1	0	30	9	21	16
3	Sleat & Strath	7	4	0	3	27	14	13	12
4	GA United	7	4	0	3	31	24	7	12
5	NW Skye	7	2	1	4	17	20	-3	7
6	Kyle	6	2	0	4	9	24	-15	6
7	Glenelg	7	2	0	5	10	27	-17	6
8	Portree	7	1	0	6	12	32	-20	3

STEWARTRY SUNDAY A.F.A. 2016

Contact: Brian Mellon,
Email: robertmellon41@btinternet.com
Tel 01557 500233

Summer season

Latest Published Table	P	W	D	L	F	A	GD	Pts
Morton Thistle Afc	9	7	0	2	46	12	34	21
Glenkens	8	5	1	2	34	22	12	16
Galloway	10	5	1	4	28	23	5	16
Twynholm	8	3	0	5	23	30	-7	9
The Bay	8	2	2	4	15	26	-11	8
The Swan	6	2	1	3	15	16	-1	7
Sams Bar	9	2	1	6	12	44	-32	7

CUP FINALS

Telfer Cup, July 29, at Newton Stewart FC
Galloway Wanderers v Morton Thistle, 2-1

League Cup Final, July 22 at Colliston Park, Dalbeattie
Galloway Wanderers v Morton Thistle, 4-3

Exclusive Security Cup, May 27 at Colliston Park, Dalbeattie
Glenkens v Morton Thistle

Harris Cup, July 1 at Colliston Park, Dalbeattie
Kirkcudbright Bay Hotel v Swan Inn, 1-5

Lockhart Trophy, August 7

Baines Cup, August 5

HOME GROUNDS

Galloway Wanderers	Trammondford Park, Wigtown
Glenkens	Market Row, Crocketford
Morton Thistle	Jock's Loaning, Dumfries
Sam's Bar	Market Row, Crocketford
The Bay	Gartshore Park, Kirkcudbright
The Swan	Stranraer Academy
Twynholm	Gartshore Park, Kirkcudbright

STIRLING & DISTRICT A.F.A.
201617

Contact: Alan Upton (Match Sec)
Email: alanupton@btinternet.com
Tel: 01236874692 (M) 07872593238
www.leaguewebsite.co.uk/sdafa

PREMIER DIVISION	P	W	D	L	Pts	Normal Home Ground		
Callander Thistle	14	10	2	2	32	McLaren HS, Callander		
Bonnybridge YFP	14	7	3	4	24	Duncan Stewart Memorial Park*		
Grangemouth Rovers	14	7	3	4	24	Zetland Park, Grangemouth		
Polmont Community	14	7	1	6	19	Meadowbank Park, Polmont		
Linlithgow Rose Community FC	14	5	2	7	17	Xcite Linlithgow		
Bo'ness Cadora	14	4	2	8	14	Douglas Park, Bo'ness		
Barrhill AFC	14	3	3	8	12	Twechar Rec Centre		
Stirling University	14	4	2	8	11	Stirling University		
DIVISION 1A	P	W	D	L	Pts			
Loganlea United	16	15	0	1	45	New Murrayfield, Blackburn*	Recreation Park, Addiewell*	
Pennies	16	12	1	3	37	Victoria Park, Falkirk		
Tillicoultry AFC	16	10	1	5	31	Dumyat Centre, Menstrie	Johnston Park, Alva	
Maddiston AFC	16	10	0	6	30	Maddiston Welfare Ground		
Beechwood Albion	16	9	1	6	28	Stirling University	Beechwood Park, Stirling	
Kincardine	16	6	1	9	19	Burnside Park, Kincardine*		
Stirling Colts	16	4	0	12	12	Stirling University		
Denny Ams.	16	3	2	11	11	Top Castle Park, Denny		
Glenvale AFC	16	0	0	16	0	Ravenswood, Cumbernauld*		
DIVISION 1B	P	W	D	L	Pts			
Tullibody Community AFC	20	18	0	2	54	Lornshill Academy 3G	Beechwood Park, Sauchie*	Tullibody Civic Centre
Fallin AFC	20	17	0	3	51	Alva Academy 3G	Paterson Playing Fields, Fallin	
Syngenta	20	13	2	5	41	Little Kerse, Grangemouth		
Camelon Albion	20	10	2	8	32	Easter Carmuirs		
MLS Leeds	20	9	2	9	29	St Ambrose HS, Coatbridge		
Campsie FC	20	8	3	9	27	Battlefield Park, Milton of Campsie		
Clackmannan Community	20	8	2	10	23	KGV Park, Clackmannan*		
Westfield Colts	20	6	1	13	19	Westfield Park, Cumbernauld		
Riverside AFC	20	6	3	11	18	Wallace HS, Stirling		
Stirling B.C.	20	3	3	14	12	Haws Park, Bridge of Allan		
Drumpellier Thistle	20	1	4	15	7	Ravenswood, Cumbernauld*	Lomond Grove, Cumbernauld	
DIVISION 2	P	W	D	L	Pts			
Greentree	20	16	2	2	50	Creamery Park, Bathgate*	Bathgate SC	
AFC Chryston	20	15	2	3	47	Carrick Park, Glenboig*		
Carronshore Athletic	20	14	2	4	44	Sunnyside PF, Falkirk	Glensburgh, Grangemouth	Little Kerse, Grangemout
Dunblane Soccer Club	20	13	1	6	40	Dunblane HS		
AFC Carbrain	20	8	5	7	29	Oak Road, Cumbernauld		
Gormac Thistle	20	8	2	10	26	Airdrie SC		
Harestanes United	20	7	1	12	22	Tintock Park, Kirkintilloch		
Dollar Glen	20	6	3	11	21	Dumyat Centre, Menstrie		
Mill Inn	20	5	1	14	13	Victoria Park, Falkirk		
Stirling Amateurs	20	3	3	14	12	Broom Road, Stirling		
Forth Thistle	20	3	2	15	11	Wallace HS, Stirling		
* Current or former Junior ground								

CUP FINALS

Mathieson Cup, July 9 at Stenhousemuir FC
Tullibody Commuinity v Pennies

David McKinnon Memorial Trophy, June 2 at Stenhousemuir FC
Syngenta v Tullibody Community, 3-2

JF Colley Cup, May 19 at Stenhousemuir FC
Fallin v Loganlea United, 3-2

Robertson Trophy (Premier), Sep 16 at D Stewart Mem Park
Bonnybridge YFP v Grangemouth Rovers, 3-1

Taylor Trophy (Div 1A)

Cameron Craig Trophy (Div 1B), Nov 25 at Stenhousemuir FC
Fallin v Tullibody Community, 3-2

Drysdale Trophy, Oct 7 at Stenhousemuir FC
AFC Chryston v Greentree, 2-1 AET

STRANRAER & DISTRICT A.F.L. 2016/17

This Association appears to have ceased playing in May 2016.

STRATHCLYDE EVANGELICAL CHURCHES A.F.L. 2016/17

Contact: Mr David Findlay, 24 Maxwood Place, Irvine, KA11 1QG
Email: dafindlay@virgin.net
Tel 0141 618 5955

http://www.churchesleague.com Saturday Morning, 10 am KOs

CUP FINALS

Fraser Trophy, May 27 at Airdrieonians FC
Avendale v Machan United, 2-0

Atholl Cup Final (Div 1), May 20 at Airdrieonians
UCA v GMAFC, 3-1

Atholl Cup (Prem), May 20 at Airdrieonians
Avendale v Machan United, 3-2

Atholl Cup (Div 2), May 27 at Airdrieonians
Coatdyke v Mearns, 2-1

PREMIER DIVISION	P	W	D	L	F	A	GD	Pts
Greenbank BB	20	18	2	0	79	24	55	56
Avendale	18	14	0	4	78	35	43	42
Motherwell King's	20	13	2	5	77	50	27	41
Machan United	16	10	2	4	47	37	10	32
Cartsbridge Evangelical	20	10	2	8	58	52	6	32
Anniesland	20	8	3	9	56	60	-4	27
Parkhead Tollcross United	20	8	1	11	34	53	-19	25
Houston and Killellan	19	6	1	12	51	60	-9	19
Law Parish	20	5	2	13	42	78	-36	17
Port Glasgow Juniors CSC	19	3	3	13	43	56	-13	12
West Glasgow	20	2	0	18	35	95	-60	6

	DIVISION 1	P	W	D	L	F	A	GD	Pts
1	GMAFC (St Francis)	20	16	1	3	71	24	47	49
2	United Churches of Ayr	20	16	1	3	55	19	36	49
3	Cumbernauld Colts (Kilsyth Utd)	20	15	3	2	49	24	25	48
4	St Silas	20	12	2	6	59	47	12	38
5	C7	20	9	3	8	40	51	-11	30
6	West Hamilton	20	8	1	11	39	54	-15	25
7	Glasgow Vineyard	20	7	2	11	43	51	-8	23
8	Inverclyde Nazarene	20	6	3	11	39	62	-23	21
9	Glasgow Free Churches	20	7	0	13	43	76	-33	21
10	Woodhill	20	6	0	14	28	58	-30	18
11	Irvine Nazarene	20	0	0	20	0	0	0	0

	DIVISION 2	P	W	D	L	F	A	GD	Pts
1	Auchenfoyle	22	17	3	2	112	33	79	54
2	Lenzie Union	22	16	2	4	80	35	45	50
3	Coatdyke Congregational	22	14	6	2	63	28	35	48
4	Kings Park Baptist Football Club	22	10	3	9	58	68	-10	33
5	St. Ninian's	22	10	2	10	86	78	8	32
6	Mearns Churches	22	9	4	9	50	48	2	31
7	Croftfoot Parish	22	8	4	10	56	81	-25	28
8	Re:Hope	22	7	3	12	52	57	-5	24
9	Fullarton Irvine	22	5	9	8	42	50	-8	24
10	Chalmers	22	6	5	11	47	61	-14	23
11	Glasgow Elim	22	6	4	12	47	82	-35	22
12	Greenbank Church of Scotland	22	0	3	19	36	108	-72	3

CLUB GROUNDS	
Club	Ground
Anniesland	Garscube Complex, Maryhill Road, Glasgow, G20 0SP
Auchenfoyle	Parklea Playing Fields, Port Glasgow
Avendale	Tileworks Sports Ground, Union Street, Stonehouse, ML9 3LF
C7	Lochinch Police Club, Pollock Park, Glasgow, G41 4AR
Cartsbridge Evangelical	Muirend Playing Fields, Braemar Court, Glasgow G44 3HQ
Chalmers	Ashgilhead Road, Ashgill, Lanarkshire, ML9 3FJ
Coatdyke Congregational	Caldervale High School, Airdrie, Lanarkshire, ML6 8PG
Croftfoot Parish	Toryglen Football Centre, Glasgow, G42 0BY (3G Surface)
Cumbernauld Colts (Kilsyth Utd)	Kilsyth Sportsfield, Kilsyth, G65 9JX
Fullarton Irvine	Recreation Park (aka Quarry Road), Irvine, KA12 0PZ
Glasgow Elim	
Glasgow Free Churches	Ballerup Pavilion
Glasgow Vineyard	Greenfield 3G
GMAFC (St Francis)	Inverclyde Academy, Greenock, PA16 0FB (3G Surface)
Greenbank BB	Muirend Playing Fields, Braemar Court, Glasgow G44 3HQ
Greenbank Church of Scotland	Muirend Playing Fields, Braemar Court, Glasgow G44 3HQ
Houston and Killellan	King George V Playing Fields, Renfrew, PA4 0SA
Inverclyde Nazarene	Parklea Playing Fields, Port Glasgow, PA14 6TR
Irvine Nazarene	Recreation Park (aka Quarry Road), Irvine, KA12 0PZ
Kings Park Baptist Football Club	Eaglesham Pavillion
Law Parish	Law Public Parks, Lawhill Road, Law ML8 5HA
Lenzie Union	Whitegates, Lenzie
Machan United	Birkenshaw Park, Larkhall, ML9 2TP
Mearns Churches	Crookfur Playing Fields, Newton Mearns, G77 6DT
Motherwell King's	Keir Hardie Sports Centre Holytown (3g)
Parkhead Tollcross United	Greenfield Playing Fields, Shettleston, G32 6TP
Port Glasgow Juniors CSC	Battery Park, Greenock, PA16 7QG
Re:Hope	
St Silas	Blairdardie Pitches, Drumchapel, G15 6JP
St. Ninian's	Lochinch Police Club, Pollock Park, Glasgow, G41 4AR
United Churches of Ayr	King George V (KG5), Mosside Road, Ayr, KA8 9ET
West Glasgow	Garscube Complex, Maryhill Road, Glasgow, G20 0SP
West Hamilton	Dalserf Primary School, Ashgill, ML9 3FJ
Woodhill	

STRATHCLYDE SATURDAY MORNING A.F.L. 2016/17

Contact:
Match Secretary: Craig Burton,
Flat 0/2, 52 Finnart Street, Glasgow G40 4BZ
07449 556676
ssmaflreg1@btinternet.com

www.ssmafl.co.uk/

CUP FINALS
Challenge Cup
Plains v Cambusnethan Talbot, 3-1
Presidents Cup
Petershall Villa v Quayside Thistle, 3-1
Strathclyde Cup
Blochairn Star v Petershall Villa, 5-2
Chairmans Cup
Hillwood v Plains, 4-1

EMIER DIVISION	P	W	D	L	F	A	PTS
ıecastle	24	20	0	4	108	32	60
awbridge	24	18	1	5	78	37	55
st Dunbartonshire	24	14	2	8	67	47	44
chairn Star	24	12	6	6	77	40	42
ngal Lancers	24	11	6	7	56	56	39
FC Ravenscraig	24	9	5	10	67	69	32
ndlaw	24	8	6	10	57	62	30
ryhill Black Star	24	8	4	12	62	69	28
nfrew	24	7	4	13	42	69	25
Airdrie	24	7	3	14	45	74	24
mbusnethan Talbot	24	6	5	13	46	76	19
derglen	24	6	4	14	39	74	18
MSA	24	5	1	18	54	93	13
VISION 1A							
asgow South	21	16	4	1	55	21	52
ctoria Criftfoot	21	12	5	4	57	34	41
lwood	21	14	4	3	81	34	40
kintilloch Thistle	21	10	3	8	56	52	33
hill United	21	7	5	9	43	46	27
rshaw	21	4	4	13	31	59	16
dgeton Vale	21	3	3	15	36	61	12
anhattan Blacks	21	1	5	15	35	85	8

DIVISION 1B							
East Kilbride Thistle	18	13	2	3	66	25	41
Holytown Colts	18	13	1	4	80	32	40
Port Glasgow United	18	13	1	4	72	36	40
Tantallon Victoria	18	10	3	5	48	37	33
Bargeddie Ams	18	8	3	7	47	46	27
Westercommon Star	18	7		8	66	52	24
Plains	18	8	1	9	52	54	19
Chaplains	18	4	2	12	37	75	14
Moorlands	18	4	0	14	32	74	12
EK Accies	18	2	0	15	25	92	3
DIVISION 1C							
UB United	18	14	1	3	69	38	43
Kelvinbridge	18	11	4	3	48	29	37
Carluke	18	9	3	6	60	41	30
Quayside Thistle	18	10	1	7	58	43	28
Petershall Villa	18	9	0	9	52	54	27
Port Glasgow Celtic	18	7	2	9	46	53	23
Barony of Blackhall	18	6	4	8	35	42	22
Southside White Cart	18	7	0	11	37	47	21
DTI	18	4	5	9	40	48	17
Gartcairn	18	2	2	14	36	85	8

ATHCLYDE SATURDAY MORNING AMATEUR FA - MAJOR HONOURS

	Premier Lge	Division 1 / 1A	Division 2 / 1B	Division 2 B / 1C	Strathclyde Cup	Tommy Marshall Trophy	League Cup	Presidents Cup
8/9	Ellsworth	Giffnock	Morton		Ellsworth	Lorne Star	Ellsworth	
9/90	Parkhead	Levern	Tynecastle		Giffnock	Airdrie Caldervale B	Parkhead	
0/1	Parkhead	Minstrels			Levern	Lorne Star	Parkhead	
1/2	Lorne Star	Levernbank			Airdrie Caldervale	Dalmarnock	Airdrie Caldervale	
2/3	GDC	Northill			Airdrie Caldervale	Springburn	Levern	
3/4	Levern	Rutherglen PO			Rutherglen PO	Soputhside	Kelvin	
4/5	Rutherglen PO	St Ambrose			Rutherglen PO	Levern	St Ambrose	
5/6	GDC	Tynecastle			St Ambrose	Provan Thistle	Forest	
6/7	St Ambrose	Patrick Thistle			Levern	Patrick Thistle	Levern	
7/8	Patrick Thistle	Windlaw			Patrick Thistle	Bellgrove	Patrick Thistle	
8/9	Levern	Cowder Vaults			Cowder Vaults	Levern	Levern	
9/00	Levern	Portcullis			Cambusglen	Forest	Greenhill Dynamo	
0/1	Levern	Reidvale			Kilpatrick Thistle	Windlaw	Levern	
1/2	Windlaw	Telecom			Windlaw	Greenhills Dynamo	Shawbridge	
2/3	Windlaw	Blochairn Star			Windlaw	Greenhills Dynamo	Windlaw	
3/4	Blochairn Star	Vale United			Greenhills Dynamo	Kilpatrick Thistle	Vale United	
4/5	Vale United	Greenbank United	Bridgeton United		Shawbridge	Vale United	Windlaw	
5/6	Windlaw	Dunbreac	NC United		Tynecastlle	Greenbank United	Lochend United	
6/7	Blochairn Star	Clydebank United	Kelvinbank Star		Clydebank United	Blochairn Star	Windlaw	
7/8	Blochairn Star	NC United	SCYP		Clydebank United	Trade Team	AS Airdrie	
8/9	Tynecastle	SCYP	ICC		Greenhills Dynamo	Blochairn Star	SCYP	
9/10	Greenhills Dynamo	ICC	Whitefield Rovers		SCYP	East Kilbride Accies	Greenhill Dynamo	
0/1	Tynecastle	Whitefield Rovers	Seafar Villa		AS Airdrie	St Marys	Seafar Villa	
1/2	Blochairn Star	Victoria Croftfoot	Dennistoun Vale		Tynecastle	Dennistoun Vale	Whitefield Rovers	
2/3	Blochairn Star	Dennistoun Vale	Kilbride Villa	Seafar Villa	Dennistoun Vale	ICC	Whitefield Rovers	
3/4	Whitefield Rovers	Blochairn Star B	Whifflet Athletic	Hutchesontown	Whitefield Rovers	Tynecastle	Blochairn Star	
4/5	Tynecastle	Maryhill Black Dtar	Southside		Dennistoun Vale	Motherwell FC Trust	Southside	Dennistoun Vale
5/6	Blochairn Star	SEMSA	Westercommon		Tynecastle	Firhill United	Maryhill Black Star	Bengal Lancers
6/7	Tynecastle	Glasgow South	East Kilbride Th	UB United	Blochairn Star	Hillwood	Plains	Petershall Villa

SUNDAY CENTRAL A.F.L.
2016/17

Contact: Alison Black,
Email: alisonjohnny.ab@googlemail.com
Tel: 07447 401529

CUP FINALS

Health Rewards League Cup Final, May 26 at Benburb
Eastfield Star v Castlemilk Dynamo

Arrow Cars Cup

Presidents Cup, May 7 at Benburb
Sporting Pumas v Carluke Thistle, 5-3

Harleys Skybar Cup, May 12 at Benburb
Haldane United v Overlee Partizans, 1-4

PREMIER DIVISION	**P**	**W**	**D**	**L**	**F**	**A**	**GD**	**Pts**	**Usual Home Ground**
Overlee Partizans	18	15	1	2	85	25	60	46	Overlee PF, Clarkston
Northend	18	13	3	2	39	18	21	42	Palace of Arts, Bellahouston, Glasgow
Castlemilk Dynamo	18	13	2	3	60	36	24	41	Barlia Football Centre, Glasgow
Haghill	18	10	3	5	57	37	20	33	Glasgow Club, Haghill, Glasgow
Hillview	18	8	1	9	50	51	-1	25	Donald Dewar SC, Garscadden
Haldane United	18	9	2	7	53	42	11	23	Vale of Leven Acad, Alexandria
Calderside	18	4	3	11	53	63	-10	15	Priory Park, Blantyre
Springhall Spartans	18	4	1	13	48	82	-34	13	Peter Brownlie Pavilion, Cambuslang
Fernhill United	18	3	1	14	32	94	-62	7	Toryglen, Glasgow
The Treble 2	18	2	1	15	26	55	-29	4	Crownpoint, Glasgow

DIVISION ONE	P	W	D	L	F	A	GD	Pts	
Brunswick	24	20	3	1	120	38	82	63	Easter Carmuirs, Camelon
Eastfield Star	24	19	2	3	93	37	56	59	Glasgow Green
Albion	24	17	3	4	105	49	56	54	Springburn Football Centre, Glasgow
Castlemilk United	24	12	5	7	60	55	5	41	Peter Brownlie Pavilion, Cambuslang
Glasgow Rovers	24	12	2	10	74	72	2	38	Greenfield Football centre, Glasgow
Gartferry	24	11	1	12	69	70	-1	34	Oak Road, Cumbernauld
Kirkintilloch Rob Roy	24	9	5	10	59	65	-6	32	St Patricks PF, Kilsyth
Polonia Glasgow	24	9	4	11	86	71	15	31	Crownpoint, Glasgow
Rosehill Thistle	24	6	7	11	64	71	-7	25	John Paul Acad, Glasgow
Rutherglen Rovers	24	6	3	15	50	102	-52	21	
Strathclyde	24	6	4	14	59	74	-15	19	Toryglen, Glasgow
Eastend Tower	24	4	3	17	53	113	-60	15	Greenfield SC, Shettleston
Lanarkshire Forrest	24	2	4	18	51	126	-75	10	Bent Recreation Ground, Hamilton

DIVISION TWO A	P	W	D	L	F	A	GD	Pts	
Sporting Pumas	14	12	2	0	73	23	50	38	
Crownpoint United	14	10	3	1	74	23	51	33	Crownpoint, Glasgow
Carluke Thistle	14	8	4	2	68	25	43	28	
Gorbals United	14	6	0	8	36	40	-4	18	Glasgow Green
Red Staars Baagrade	14	5	2	7	30	50	-20	17	Glasgow Club, Milton
Glasgow Irish	14	5	1	8	40	40	0	16	
Cambuslang Football Academy	14	4	0	10	35	64	-29	12	
Shawfield Wednesday	14	0	0	14	10	101	-91	0	Crownpoint, Glasgow

DIVISION TWO B	P	W	D	L	F	A	GD	Pts	
Sauchie	16	13	2	1	51	20	31	41	Fairfield Park, Sauchie
PFD	16	11	0	5	55	38	17	33	Clydebank HS
Carluke Victoria	16	8	4	4	45	37	8	28	Crawforddyke Park, Carluke
Budhill United	16	8	0	8	49	47	2	24	Palace of Arts, Bellahouston, Glasgow
Lanarkshire	16	6	2	8	39	36	3	20	Matt Busby Centre, Bellshill
Hamilton FP Colts	16	6	2	8	36	39	-3	20	Hamilton Palace
Bengal Lancers AFC	16	6	2	8	45	52	-7	20	Glasgow Club, Milton
Provanmill Thistle	16	4	1	11	36	46	-10	13	John Paul Acad, Glasgow
Newmains United	16	2	3	11	21	62	-41	9	Keir Hardie SC, Holytown

DIVISION TWO C	P	W	D	L	F	A	GD	Pts	
Ferniegair Rose	25	21	2	2	157	42	115	65	Daisy Parks, Motherwell
New Stevenson United	25	19	2	4	103	40	63	59	Dalziel Park, Motherwell
Bardykes Rovers 2016	25	18	1	6	110	47	63	55	Hamilton Palace
Eastend Rovers	25	16	4	5	117	51	66	52	Lochend CHS, Easterhouse
Townhead Thistle	25	14	4	7	108	56	52	45	St Andrews HS, Coatbridge
Glasgow Rangers	25	14	2	9	108	62	46	44	Glasgow Green
Glasgow City Academy	26	13	3	10	87	72	15	42	Glasgow Club, Drumoyne
South Lanarkshire Ravens	25	12	2	11	91	75	16	38	Ballerup Sports Centre, E Kilbride
Broadwood Clyde	25	12	1	12	72	66	6	37	Ravenswood, Cumbernauld
Glasgow Athletic	26	8	1	17	63	108	-45	25	Glasgow Green
Rosehill Thorns	25	6	4	15	51	89	-38	22	Glasgow Green
Croftfoot	25	5	3	17	39	117	-78	17	Donald Dewar Centre, Garscadden
Strathclyde West	25	3	0	22	35	203	-168	9	John Paul Acad, Glasgow
Kilsyth Rovers	25	0	1	24	17	130	-113	1	St Patricks PF, Kilsyth

UIST AND BARRA A.F.A. 2016

Contact: Roddy F MacIsaac,
Tel 01870 602081
Email: rfmcisaac@ginetig.com

The same 6 teams are competing in 2017.

Final Table 2016	P	W	D	L	F	A	PTS	
Barra	15	11	2	2	62	28	34	35
Iochdar Saints	15	11	0	4	69	26	43	33
Southend	15	8	2	5	37	41	-4	26
North Uist United	15	5	0	10	26	49	-23	15
Benbecula	15	4	1	10	46	61	-15	13
Eriskay	15	3	1	11	23	58	-35	10

CUP FINALS

Billy MacNeil Summer Cup Final (24/9/16)
Barra v Benbecula, 6-3
at Liniclate School

Coop Cup (23/7/16)
West Side v Iochdar Saints, 2-1
This cup is contested by clubs from the Lewis, Harris, Barra and Uist Leagues.

WEST LOTHIAN SUNDAY A.F.L. 2016/17

ontact: Robert McLean, Email: wlsaflsecretary@btinternet.com
el: 01508 432191

ww.westlothian.leaguerepublic.com

EMIER DIVISION	P	W	D	L	F	A	GD	PTS
rvester	12	12	0	0	56	15	41	36
kehead	12	10	0	2	49	17	32	30
aigshill	12	5	2	5	36	34	2	17
ackburn	12	5	2	5	29	37	-8	17
'ness	12	3	2	7	32	45	-13	11
wtown	12	2	2	8	28	36	-8	8
rron Valley	12	1	0	11	23	69	-46	3

'ISION ONE	P	W	D	L	F	A	GD	PTS
nfourhill	11	10	0	1	67	15	52	30
ngston CFC	14	10	0	4	65	31	34	30
nside	12	9	1	2	46	21	25	28
North	11	8	0	3	68	21	47	24
Calder	11	8	0	3	55	22	33	24
ss 108	11	6	1	4	27	23	4	19
st Lothian Albior	13	5	1	7	38	75	-37	16
nadale	14	4	2	8	30	81	-51	14
nland Park	10	4	1	5	22	29	-7	13
ngston Star	13	3	0	10	41	56	-15	9
adowpark	12	1	2	9	25	53	-28	5
nville Thistle	12	0	0	12	15	72	-57	0

CUP FINALS

Energywise Cup Final, Sunday May 21 at Whitburn JFC
Harvester v Newtown 5-0

Premier Division Cup Final, May 7 at Whitburn JFC
Harvester v Newtown 2-0

WEST AYRSHIRE SUNDAY A.F.L.

The West Ayrshire Sunday AFL was dissolved at the end of 2015/16. A new Ayrshire Sunday AFA was formed.

WEST OF SCOTLAND A.F.L. 2016/17

Contact: Garry Watson, Email
garrywatson82@googlemail.com
Tel: 07473 506835

http://www.leaguewebsite.co.uk/
westofscotlandamateurfootballleague

Founded in 1898, the West of Scotland Amateur League folded at the end of 2016/17.

	P	W	D	L	F	A	GD	Pts
Newshot	15	13	1	1	47	14	33	40
South Lochaber Thistle	15	10	1	4	45	23	22	31
Cardross	15	5	3	7	35	44	-9	18
Carradale	15	5	0	10	32	34	-2	15
Helensburgh	15	5	0	10	21	46	-25	15
Bellaire	15	3	3	9	21	41	-20	12
United Glasgow	0	0	0	0	0	0	0	0

CUP FINALS

Challenge Shield, May 20
South Lochaber Thistle v Newshot, 2-2, 6-5 pens

Thomson Trophy, June 17 at Shettleston
South Lochaber Thistle v Cardross 3-1

League Cup, May 13
Newshot v Cardross, 1-0

SCOTTISH AMATEUR CUP WINNERS

1909/10	John Neilson FP	(Paisley)
1910/11	Edinburgh Civil Service	
1911/12	Queen's Park Hampden XI	
1912/13	Leith Amateurs	
1913/14	Cameronians	(Stirling)
1919/20	Queen's Park Hampden XI	
1920/21	Edinburgh Civil Service	
1921/22	Greenock HSFP	
1922/23	Falkirk Amateurs	
1923/24	Moorpark	(Renfrew)
1924/25	Coldstream	
1925/26	Murrayfield Amateurs	(Edinburgh)
1926/27	Glasgow University	
1927/28	Queen's Park Hampden XI	
1928/29	Murrayfield Amateurs	(Edinburgh)
1929/30	Murrayfield Amateurs	(Edinburgh)
1930/31	Murrayfield Amateurs	(Edinburgh)
1931/32	Glasgow Corporation Transport	
1932/33	Queen's Park Hampden XI	
1933/34	Queen's Park Hampden XI	
1934/35	Camphill Secondary FP	(Paisley)
1935/36	Queen's Park Hampden XI	
1936/37	Gogarburn	(Edinburgh)
1937/38	Coats	(Paisley)
1938/39	Murrayfield Amateurs	(Edinburgh)
1945/46	Craigton Athletic	(Glasgow)
1946/47	Queen's Park Hampden XI	
1947/48	Mearns	
1948/49	Greenock HSFP	
1949/50	Queen's Park Hampden XI	
1950/51	Queen's Park Hampden XI	
1951/52	Port Glasgow Hibernian	
1952/53	Mearns	
1953/54	Royal Technical College	(Glasgow)
1954/55	Eglinton Ams	(Glasgow)
1955/56	Milanda	(Glasgow)
1956/57	Giffnock North	
1957/58	Weir Recreation	(Glasgow)
1958/59	Crosshill Athletic	(Glasgow)
1959/60	Minishant	
1960/61	Glenavon	
1961/62	Bearsden Ams	
1962/63	Queen's Park Hampden XI	
1963/64	Queen's Park Hampden XI	
1964/65	NCR	(Dundee)
1965/66	Jordanhill TC	(Glasgow)
1966/67	Rhu	
1967/68	Cambusbarron Rovers	
1968/69	Cambusbarron Rovers	
1969/70	Douglas	
1970/71	Dumbarton Academy FP	
1971/72	Douglas	
1972/73	Knockentiber	
1973/74	Douglas	
1974/75	Star Hearts	
1975/76	Colville Park	(Mothewell)
1976/77	Morriston YMCa	(Cambuslang)
1977/78	Cambusbarron Rovers	
1978/79	Crosshouse Waverley	
1979/80	Newarthill Hearts	
1980/81	Knockentiber	
1981/82	Avon Villa	(Hamilton)
1982/83	Strathclyde Police	
1983/84	Pencaitland	
1984/85	Drongan United	
1985/86	Coatbridge CC	
1986/87	Bannockburn	
1987/88	Coatbridge CC	
1988/89	Norton House	(Leven)
1989/90	St Patricks FP	(Dumbarton)
1990/91	Bannockburn	
1991/92	Heathside	
1992/93	Bankhall Villa	
1993/94	Bannockburn	
1994/95	Heathside	
1995/96	Bellshill YMCA	
1996/97	Knockentiber	
1997/98	Dalziel HSFP	(Motherwell)
1998/99	St Patricks FP	(Dumbarton)
1999/00	Liberton Royal Mail	(Edinburgh)
2000/1	Dalziel HSFP	(Motherwell)
2001/2	Harestanes	(Kirkintilloch)
2002/3	Harestanes	(Kirkintilloch)
2003/4	Viewfield Rovers	(Lochwinnoch)
2004/5	Drumchapel	
2005/6	St Patricks FP	(Dumbarton)
2006/7	Drumchapel United	
2007/8	Eddlewood	(Hamilton)
2008/9	Queen's Park Hampden XI	
2009/10	Eddlewood	(Hamilton)
2010/11	Wishaw HSFP	
2011/12	Hurlford Thistle	
2012/13	Wellhouse	(Glasgow)
2013/14	Hurlford Thistle	
2014/15	Harestanes	(Kirkintilloch)
2015/16	Colville Park	(Motherwell)
2016/17	Colville Park	(Motherwell)

SCOTTISH AMATEUR CUP 2016/17

1W	03/09/2016	Barony of Blackall AFC (SSMAFL)	v	Millbeg AFC (SAFL)	3	3
1W	03/09/2016	Blantyre Celtic AFC (CSAFL)	v	Baillieston Thistle AFC (GGPAFL)	2	1
1W	03/09/2016	Bridgeton Vale AFC (SSMAFL)	v	Erskine Town AFC (GCAFA)	0	1
1W	03/09/2016	Caldergien AFC (GGPAFL)	v	Glenburn Athletic AFC (P&DAFA)	4	3
1W	03/09/2016	Caldergien AFC (SSMAFL)	v	Renfrew Thistle AFC (GGPAFL)	3	0
1W	03/09/2016	Colquhoun United AFC (GGPAFL)	v	Ashvale Victoria AFC (GGPAFL)	7	4
1W	03/09/2016	Dalziel HSFP AFC (Cale)	v	Crosshouse Waverley AFC (AYR)	6	0
1W	03/09/2016	East Kilbride YM AFC (Cale)	v	Larkhall Thistle AFC (Cale)	2	2
1W	03/09/2016	Electric AFC (CSAFL)	v	Arthurlie AFC (CSAFL)	1	1
1W	03/09/2016	Finnart AFC (Cale)	v	Oban Saints AFC (SAFL)	1	3
1W	03/09/2016	Finnieston Park AFC (G&DSMAFL)	v	New Cumnock Afton AFC (AYR)	2	1
1W	03/09/2016	Galston United AFC (AYR)	v	Eastwood Park Mount 'A' AFC (GGPAFL)	0	2
1W	03/09/2016	Hillington AFC (SAFL)	v	Castlemilk BC AFC (SAFL)	5	1
1W	03/09/2016	Holytown Colts AFC (SSMAFL)	v	New Farm Loch AFC (AYR)	3	4
1W	03/09/2016	Kelvinbridge AFC (SSMAFL)	v	Carradale AFC (WoS)	5	2
1W	03/09/2016	Mill United AFC (NSLAFA)	v	Wishaw High School FP's AFC (CSAFL)	1	0
1W	03/09/2016	Minishant AFC (AYR)	v	St. Patricks AFC (CSAFL)	0	11
1W	03/09/2016	Moorlands AFC (SSMAFL)	v	Holytown Colts Youth AFC (NSLAFA)	2	2
1W	03/09/2016	North Kelvin Sports AFC (GGPAFL)	v	Kirkintilloch Thistle AFC (SSMAFL)	2	6
1W	03/09/2016	Ochiltree United AFC (AYR)	v	Campsie AFC (S&DAFA)	1	2
1W	03/09/2016	Parkhead Tollcross United AFC (SECAFL)	v	Milton AFC (Cale)	2	2
1W	03/09/2016	Port Glasgow AFC (SAFL)	v	FC Clydebank (CSAFL)	3	3
1W	03/09/2016	Port Glasgow United AFC (SSMAFL)	v	Petershall Villa AFC (SSMAFL)	3	0
1W	03/09/2016	Rosehill Star AFC (SAFL)	v	Invac AFC (G&DSMAFL)	2	2
1W	03/09/2016	St. David's AFC (GCAFA)	v	Stas AFC (G&DSMAFL)	0	0
1W	03/09/2016	St. Mungo's AFC (GGPAFL)	v	East Kilbride AFC (SAFL)	1	2
1W	03/09/2016	Stanley Athletic AFC (P&DAFA)	v	Chaplins AFC (SSMAFL)	3	2
1W	03/09/2016	Strathclyde University AFC (GGPAFL)	v	Glenmuir Thistle AFC (AYR)	2	1
1W	03/09/2016	Thorn Athletic AFC (Cale)	v	AFC Chryston (S&DAFA)	4	0
1W	03/09/2016	Tynecastle AFC (SSMAFL)	v	Glenburn Miners Welfare AFC (AYR)	5	1
1W	03/09/2016	UCS AFC (GCAFA)	v	Blochairn Star AFC (SSMAFL)	1	6
1W	03/09/2016	Victoria Croftfoot AFC (SSMAFL)	v	Kilsyth AFC (CSAFL)	3	4
1E	03/09/2016	Armadale Thistle AFC (LEAFA)	v	Edinburgh Star AFC (LEAFA)	3	1
1E	03/09/2016	Bathgate Thistle AFC (LEAFA)	v	Burntisland United AFC (FAFA)	0	1
1E	03/09/2016	Beechwood Albion AFC (S&DAFA)	v	Hearts of Beath AFC (FAFA)	3	0
1E	03/09/2016	Craigshill Thistle AFC (LEAFA)	v	Steins Thistle AFC (CSAFL)	9	1
1E	03/09/2016	Cupar Hearts AFC (KCAFA)	v	Edinburgh Thistle AFC (LEAFA)	6	0
1E	03/09/2016	Inter Edinburgh AFC (LEAFA)	v	Fossoway AFC (FAFA)	2	6
1E		Kettle United AFC (KCAFA)	v	Doune Castle AFC (Cale)	scr	wo
1E	03/09/2016	Leslie Hearts AFC (FAFA)	v	Glenrothes Strollers AFC (FAFA)	5	2
1E	03/09/2016	Linlithgow Rose CFC AFC (S&DAFA)	v	Musselburgh Windsor AFC (LEAFA)	2	2
1E	03/09/2016	Lomond Victoria AFC (FAFA)	v	Stirling University AFC (S&DAFA)	1	1
1E	03/09/2016	Rosebank Rangers AFC (FAFA)	v	Redpath Albion AFC (LEAFA)	4	3
1E	03/09/2016	Spartans AFC (LEAFA)	v	Newcraighall Leith Victoria AFC (LEAFA)	1	2
1E	03/09/2016	St. Monans Swallows (FAFA)	v	Dunblane Thistle AFC (CSAFL)	1	8
1E	03/09/2016	Tillicoultry AFC (S&DAFA)	v	Bank of Scotland Strollers AFC (LEAFA)	2	0
1E	03/09/2016	Tweeddale Rovers AFC (BAFA)	v	Lochend AFC (LEAFA)	1	3
1NOT	03/09/2016	Alyth AFC (PAFA)	v	Ferry Mechanics AFC (DSMAFL)	1	0
1NOT	03/09/2016	Fair City AFC (PAFA)	v	St. Johns AFC (PAFA)	3	1
1NOT		FC Boukir (DSMAFL)	v	Newport AFC (MAFA)	scr	wo
1NOT	03/09/2016	Fintry Rovers AFC (DSMAFL)	v	Polteam Perth AFC (PAFA)	1	2
1NOT	03/09/2016	Forfar West End AFC (MAFA)	v	Kettins AFC (PAFA)	1	2
1NOT	03/09/2016	Kirriemuir Thistle AFC (MAFA)	v	FC Kettledrum (DSMAFL)	1	6
1NOT	03/09/2016	Rattray AFC (PAFA)	v	Coldside Athletic AFC (DSMAFL)	1	5
1NOT	03/09/2016	Wellbank AFC (MAFA)	v	Wolfhill AFC (PAFA)	1	2
1N	27/08/2016	B.S. AFC (AAFA)	v	Cammachmore AFC (AAFA)	2	4
1N		CBC Hilton AFC (AAFA)	v	Highland Hotel AFC (AAFA)	scr	wo
1N	03/09/2016	Colony Park AFC (AAFA)	v	Kemnay Youth AFC (AAFA)	4	1
1N		Glendale XI AFC (AAFA)	v	Dee AFC (AAFA)	wo	scr
1N	03/09/2016	Glendale Youth AFC (AAFA)	v	McTeagle AFC (AAFA)	5	2
1N	03/09/2016	Woodside AFC (AAFA)	v	Stonehaven Athletic AFC (AAFA)	4	0

1R	17/09/2016	Millbeg		Barony of Blackhall	3	2	
1R	09/09/2016	Larkhall Thistle		East Kilbride YM	2	3	
1R	10/09/2016	Arthurlie		Electric	4	1	
1R	10/09/2016	Holytown Colts Youth		Moorlands	4	3	
1R	09/09/2016	Milton		Parkhead Tollcross United	3	2	
1R	09/09/2016	FC Clydebank		Port Glasgow	2	0	
1R	10/09/2016	Invac		Rosehill Star	2	1	
1R	17/09/2016	Stas		St David's	2	1	
1R	10/09/2016	Musselburgh Windsor		Linlithgow Rose CFC	0	2	
1R	10/09/2016	Stirling University		Lomond Victoria	3	2	Appeal ?
		WEST					
2W	01/10/2016	AFC Carbrain (S&DAFA)	v	Condorrat (S&DAFA)	6	1	
2W	01/10/2016	AFC Columba (G&DSMAFL)	v	Kilmarnock Ams (AYR)	9	4	
2W		AFC Manhattan Blacks (SSMAFL)	v	St Mungo's (Cale)			P
2W	01/10/2016	Anniesland (SECAFL)	v	Motherwell Thistle (SAFL)	1	8	
2W	01/10/2016	Ardeer West Recreation (AYR)	v	FC Argyle (SAFL)	0	0	
2W	01/10/2016	Arden (P&DAFA)	v	Kings Park Rangers (SAFL)	1	3	
2W	01/10/2016	Arkleston Barrhead (SAFL)	v	Port Glasgow United (SSMAFL)	6	0	
2W		Ashvale Victoria (CSAFL)	v	Finnieston Park (G&DSMAFL)	scr	wo	
2W	01/10/2016	Baillieston Juniors (Cale)	v	Glasgow Caledonian (G&DSMAFL)	7	0	
2W	01/10/2016	Balmore (Cale)	v	West Stone (GCAFA)	7	0	
2W	01/10/2016	Barrhill (S&DAFA)	v	Bannockburn (CSAFL)	1	6	
2W	01/10/2016	Beith Ams (AYR)	v	Rossvale (SAFL)	4	1	
2W	01/10/2016	Bellaire (WoS)	v	Mill United (NSLAFA)	1	2	
2W	01/10/2016	Bellfield Lochan (AYR)	v	FC Baillieston (GGPAFL)	0	1	
2W	01/10/2016	Bengal Lancers (SSMAFL)	v	Giffnock North AAC (Cale)	1	5	
2W	01/10/2016	Blairdardie United (G&DSMAFL)	v	Albion (GCAFA)	3	3	
2W	01/10/2016	Blantyre RGM (NSLAFA)	v	Kelvinbridge (SSMAFL)	3	2	
2W		Blantyre Soccer Academy	v	Renfrew Ams (SSMAFL)	scr	wo	
2W	01/10/2016	Blochairn Star (SSMAFL)	v	Coatdyke Congregational (SECAFL)	3	1	
2W	01/10/2016	Boswell (P&DAFA)	v	DTI (SSMAFL)	2	3	
2W	08/10/2016	Bridgend (G&DSMAFL)	v	Renfrew Ams (G&DSMAFL)	2	2	
2W		Bridgewater (CSAFL)	v	Motherwell Community Trust (SSMAFL)	wo	scr	
2W	08/10/2016	Broomlands (AYR)	v	Campbeltown Pupils (SAFL)	2	3	
2W	01/10/2016	Calderglen (GGPAFL)	v	Hampden (GCAFA)	3	3	
2W	08/10/2016	Calderglen (SSMAFL)	v	Broomhouse (Cale)	0	6	
2W	08/10/2016	Cambusnethan Talbot Community (CSAFL)	v	Easthall Star (SAFL)	8	2	
2W	01/10/2016	Campsie (S&DAFA)	v	Campsie Black Watch Waterside (CSAFL)	2	5	
2W	01/10/2016	Catrine (AYR)	v	Cumnock Ams (AYR)	2	3	
2W	08/10/2016	Central Albion (S&DAFA)	v	GSC Jordanhill (GGPAFL)	0	11	
2W	08/10/2016	Clydeside Athletic (GCAFA)	v	Hurlford Thistle (AYR)	0	2	
2W	01/10/2016	Colquhoun United (GGPAFL)	v	Red Star (G&DSMAFL)	2	1	
2W	01/10/2016	Colville Park (CSAFL)	v	Gormac Thistle (S&DAFA)	6	0	
2W	01/10/2016	Craigie (AYR)	v	Machan United (SECAFL)	5	2	
2W	01/10/2016	Craigneuk (GGPAFL)	v	Mill United (CSAFL)	4	1	
2W		Cumbernauld Athletic (S&DAFA)	v	Rannoch (GGPAFL	scr	scr	
2W	01/10/2016	Cumbernauld Colts (Cale)	v	Westerlands (Cale)	2	2	
2W	01/10/2016	Dalry (AYR)	v	Eaglesham (Cale)	1	2	
2W	08/10/2016	Darvel Victoria (AYR)	v	Wallacetoun (AYR)	0	3	
2W	01/10/2016	Dirrans Athletic (AYR)	v	Drumpellier Thistle (S&DAFA)	6	0	
2W	08/10/2016	Drumchapel Ams (CSAFL)	v	Ardrossan Castle Rovers (AYR)	5	1	
2W	01/10/2016	Drumchapel Colts (SAFL)	v	Crown Athletic (GCAFA)	16	2	
2W		Drumchapel United (CSAFL)	v	Southside Star (SSMAFL)	scr	wo	
2W	08/10/2016	Dumbarton Academy FP (Cale)	v	Cambria (Cale)	1	2	
2W	08/10/2016	Dumbarton Harp Celtic (GGPAFL)	v	Dean (AYR)	3	1	
2W	08/10/2016	Duncanrig (SAFL)	v	Possil YM (CSAFL)	0	4	
2W	01/10/2016	East Dunbartonshire (SSMAFL)	v	Busby (SAFL)	4	2	
2W	01/10/2016	East Kilbride (CSAFL)	v	Croftfoot Parish Church (SECAFL)	6	0	
2W	08/10/2016	East Kilbride Rolls Royce (SAFL)	v	BSC Glasgow (CSAFL)	4	1	
2W	01/10/2016	East Kilbride Thistle (SSMAFL)	v	Kings (SECAFL)	2	4	
2W	01/10/2016	Eastfield (CSAFL)	v	Langcraigs (P&DAFA)	8	2	
2W	01/10/2016	Eddlewood (NSLAFA)	v	Carton YMCA (SAFL)	5	1	
2W		Edenvale (GGPAFL)	v	Greater Glasgow (GCAFA)	scr	wo	
2W	01/10/2016	FC Clydebank (CSAFL)	v	St Silas (SECAFL)	3	0	
2W	01/10/2016	FC Dal Riata (NSLAFA)	v	Maryhill Blackstar (SSMAFL)	1	4	
2W	01/10/2016	FC Drumchapel (G&DSMAFL)	v	East Kilbride YM (GGPAFL)	7	2	
2W	01/10/2016	Ferguslie Star (SAFL)	v	Bargeddie (SSMAFL)	12	0	
2W	08/10/2016	Fordbank Star (P&DAFA)	v	Rutherglen (SAFL)	0	10	
2W	01/10/2016	Garrowhill Thistle (CSAFL)	v	Paisley Ams (SAFL)	5	1	
2W	15/10/2016	Gartcosh United (Cale)	v	South Lochaber Thistle (WoS)	2	0	
2W	01/10/2016	Glasgow Harp (Cale)	v	Broomhill (SAFL)	1	1	
2W	01/10/2016	Glasgow South (SSMAFL)	v	Houston United (SAFL)	3	1	
2W	01/10/2016	Glasgow University (Cale)	v	Glencoats (P&DAFA)	10	0	
2W	08/10/2016	Glenvale (S&DAFA)	v	Woodhall Thistle (Cale)	3	6	

2W		Glenwood Thistle (SSMAFL)	v	United Glasgow (WoS)	scr	wo	
2W	01/10/2016	Goldenhill (SAFL)	v	Carluke Hearts (NSLAFA)	4	4	
2W	01/10/2016	Gourock Thistle (CSAFL)	v	Eastend (SAFL)	6	2	
2W	01/10/2016	Greenock HSFP (CSAFL)	v	Tantallon Victoria (SSMAFL)	10	1	
2W	01/10/2016	Gryffe Thistle (GCAFA)	v	Crookston Castle (GGPAFL)	2	1	
2W	01/10/2016	Helensburgh (WoS)	v	Robslee (GGPAFL)	2	3	
2W	01/10/2016	Hillington (SAFL)	v	Erskine Town (GCAFA)	13	0	
2W	01/10/2016	Holytown Celtic Youth (NSLAFA)	v	Clydebanks Ams (CSAFL)	0	0	
2W	01/10/2016	Invac (G&DSMAFL)	v	Fenwick Thistle (AYR)	2	1	
2W		Inverclyde (SAFL)	v	Cambuslang Football Academy (CSAFL)	wo	scr	
2W	01/10/2016	Irvine Town (AYR)	v	Dennistoun Vale (SSMAFL)	0	4	
2W		Kilbarchan Thistle (GGPAFL)	v	Kirkintilloch Thistle (SSMAFL)	scr	wo	
2W	01/10/2016	Kilbirnie (AYR)	v	Eastwood Park Mount "B" (GGPAFL)	6	0	
2W		Kilbowie Union (SAFL)	v	Westercommon Star (SSMAFL)	scr	wo	
2W	01/10/2016	Kilbride Thistle (AYR)	v	Duntocher Hibs (SAFL)	4	1	
2W	01/10/2016	Kilsyth Ams (CSAFL)	v	Dalziel HSFP (Cale)	0	3	
2W	01/10/2016	Knockentiber (AYR)	v	Coylton (AYR)	7	1	
2W	01/10/2016	Lanarkshire Forrest (NSLAFA)	v	Alba Thistle (SAFL)	3	4	
2W	01/10/2016	Law Parish (SECAFL)	v	St Joseph's (SAFL)	1	7	
2W	01/10/2016	Linwood Thistle (P&DAFA)	v	Hamilton FPs (Cale)	2	2	
2W		Mauchline United (AYR)	v	Eastwood Park Mount 'A' (GGPAFL)	scr	wo	
2W	08/10/2016	Millbeg (SAFL)	v	Crosshill Thistle (AYR)	3	1	
2W		Millerston United (SAFL)	v	Moorpark Thistle (AYR)	wo	scr	
2W	01/10/2016	Milngavie (G&DSMAFL)	v	Stedfast (CSAFL)	2	1	
2W	01/10/2016	Milngavie Wanderers (Cale)	v	Glasgow Deaf Athletic (P&DAFA)	A	A	
2W		Milton (Cale)	v	Weir Recreation (Cale)	wo	scr	
2W		Milton of Colquhoun (SAFL)	v	Dynamo East Kilbride (GGPAFL)	scr	wo	
2W	01/10/2016	MLS Leeds United (S&DAFA)	v	Postal United (CSAFL)	3	6	
2W	01/10/2016	Mossblown Boswell (AYR)	v	John Street (GGPAFL)	0	0	
2W	01/10/2016	Muirton (GCAFA)	v	Clark Drive (AYR)	2	2	
2W	01/10/2016	New Farm Loch (AYR)	v	Newlands (GCAFA)	3	2	
2W	01/10/2016	New Meadow (P&DAFA)	v	Haldane United (CSAFL)	1	12	
2W		Newshot (WoS)	v	Rosneath (WoS)	wo	scr	
2W	01/10/2016	North Motherwell (NSLAFA)	v	Stewarton Annick (AYR)	7	0	
2W		Oban Saints (SAFL)	v	Bishopton (G&DSMAFL)	wo	scr	
2W	01/10/2016	Plains (SSMAFL)	v	Third Lanark (GGPAFL)	0	3	
2W	08/10/2016	Port Glasgow Celtic (SSMAFL)	v	Beith Meadowside (P&DAFA)	15	1	
2W	08/10/2016	Port Glasgow OBU (SAFL)	v	East Kilbride (SAFL)	1	4	
2W		Prestwick (AYR)	v	Braehead (G&DSMAFL)	scr	wo	
2W	01/10/2016	Quayside Thistle (SSMAFL)	v	Claremont (SAFL)	3	2	
2W		Rannoch (Cale)	v	Clyde Valley Rovers (GCAFA)	scr	WO	
2W		Redbrae Athletic (S&DAFA)	v	Erskine (GGPAFL)	scr	WO	
2W	08/10/2016	Rhu (Cale)	v	Harestanes (CSAFL)	1	6	
2W	01/10/2016	River Nevis (GCAFA)	v	AS Airdrie (SSMAFL)	1	5	
2W	01/10/2016	Rosehill United (GCAFA)	v	Corkerhill (Cale)	5	1	
2W	01/10/2016	Rothesay Brandane (Cale)	v	Lochgilphead Red Star (SAFL)	1	2	
2W	01/10/2016	Shawbridge (SSMAFL)	v	Campsie Minerva (CSAFL)	1	5	
2W	01/10/2016	Shawlands FP (SAFL)	v	Harestanes United (S&DAFA)	3	0	
2W	01/10/2016	Shortlees (AYR)	v	Glasgow Island (GCAFA)	7	1	
2W	01/10/2016	Southside (CSAFL)	v	Symington Caledonian (AYR)	10	0	
2W	01/10/2016	Southside Accies (G&DSMAFL)	v	Semsa (SSMAFL)	3	8	
2W	01/10/2016	Southside United (GCAFA)	v	Carbrain (GGPAFL)	2	4	
2W	22/10/2016	Springhill (NSLAFA)	v	Southside Whitecart (SSMAFL)	1	3	
2W	01/10/2016	Stanley Athletic (P&DADA)	v	Dunoon (SAFL)	4	0	
2W	01/10/2016	Stas (G&DSMAFL)	v	Clydesdale (NSLAFA)	6	2	
2W	01/10/2016	Stewarton United (AYR)	v	Blantyre Celtic (CSAFL)	2	5	
2W	08/10/2016	Strathaven Dynamo (SAFL)	v	St Patrick's (CSAFL)	1	12	
2W		Strathclyde Thistle (NSLAFA)	v	Chapelhall (NSLAFL)	wo	scr	
2W	01/10/2016	Strathclyde University (Cale)	v	Mearns (CSAFL)	2	4	
2W	01/10/2016	Strathclyde University (GGPAFL)	v	Thorn Athletic (Cale)	1	5	
2W	08/10/2016	Tannahill (P&DAFA)	v	Motherwell Bridgeworks (NSLAFA)	2	1	
2W		Tarbert (SAFL)	v	AFC Ravenscraig (SSMAFL)			P
2W	01/10/2016	Tarbolton (AYR)	v	Gartcairn (SSMAFL)	11	0	
2W	01/10/2016	Troon Dundonald (AYR)	v	Singer (GCAFA)	2	2	
2W	01/10/2016	Tynecastle (SSMAFL)	v	Bearsden (Cale)	4	0	
2W	01/10/2016	UB United (SSMAFL)	v	Maryhill Thistle (GCAFA)	1	4	
2W	01/10/2016	Uddingston Anvil (CSAFL)	v	East Kilbride YM (Cale)	1	2	
2W	01/10/2016	Carrick (AYR)	v	Lanarkshire United (NSLAFL)	16	0	
2W		Viewfield Rovers (Cale)	v	Hurlford Ams (AYR)	scr	wo	
2W	01/10/2016	Weir Recreation (GGPAFL)	v	Largs Thistle Ams (AYR)	3	4	
2W	01/10/2016	West Kilbride (AYR)	v	Cambusnethan Talbot Community (SSMAFL)	1	3	
2W	01/10/2016	Westcliff (P&DAFA)	v	Wishaw Wycombe Wanderers (NSLAFA)	0	15	
2W	01/10/2016	Westerlands 'B' (GGPAFL)	v	Arthurlie Ams (CSAFL)	3	7	
2W	01/10/2016	Windlaw (SSMAFL)	v	Neilston Ams (SAFL)	3	1	
2W	08/10/2016	Winlinton Wolves (AYR)	v	Newton Vale (GGPAFL)	1	4	

		EAST				
2E	01/10/2016	AM Soccer (FAFA)	v	Bo'ness Cadora (S&DAFA)	5	0
2E	01/10/2016	Armadale Rose (LEAFA)	v	Kirkcaldy YMCA (FAFA)	1	2
2E	01/10/2016	Bowhill Rovers KCAFA)	v	North Edinburgh Wanderers (LEAFA)	11	1
2E	01/10/2016	Burntisland United (FAFA)	v	Linton Hotspur (BAFA)	6	2
2E	01/10/2016	Callander Thistle (S&DAFA)	v	AM Soccer Reserves (FAFA)	5	5
2E	01/10/2016	Cavalry Park SC (LEAFA)	v	Falkland KCAFA)	4	2
2E	01/10/2016	Civil Service Strollers Ams (LEAFA)	v	Fossoway (FAFA)	4	6
2E	01/10/2016	Clackmannan Community (S&DAFA)	v	Edinburgh Rose (LEAFA)	2	4
2E	01/10/2016	Craigroyston CYFC (LEAFA)	v	Carronshore Athletic (S&DAFA)	0	2
2E	01/10/2016	Danderhall Miners (LEAFA)	v	Pencaitland (LEAFA)	5	3
2E	01/10/2016	Denbeath (FAFA)	v	Greenlaw (BAFA)	2	1
2E	01/10/2016	Denny (S&DAFA)	v	Musselburgh (LEAFA)	1	3
2E	01/10/2016	Dollar Glen (S&DAFA)	v	St Andrews (FAFA)	3	4
2E	01/10/2016	Doune Castle (S&DAFA)	v	Freuchie (FAFA)	2	1
2E	01/10/2016	Dunblane Soccer (S&DAFA)	v	Strathmiglo United KCAFA)	2	6
2E	01/10/2016	Dunblane Thistle (CSAFL)	v	East Calder United (LEAFA)	3	2
2E	01/10/2016	East Linton (LEAFA)	v	Valleyfield (FAFA)	3	2
2E	01/10/2016	Edina Hibs (LEAFA)	v	Symington Tinto (Cale)	2	5
2E	01/10/2016	Edinburgh City Ams (LEAFA)	v	Fife Thistle (FAFA)	0	2
2E	01/10/2016	Edinburgh Harps (LEAFA)	v	Stirling Colts (S&DAFA)	4	3
2E	01/10/2016	Edinburgh South Vics (LEAFA)	v	Sporting ICAPB (LEAFA)	9	1
2E	01/10/2016	Edinburgh University (LEAFA)	v	Syngenta (S&DAFA)	1	2
2E	01/10/2016	Forth Thistle (S&DAFA)	v	Tillicoultry (S&DAFA)	0	6
2E	01/10/2016	Grangemouth Rovers (S&DAFA)	v	Greentree (S&DAFA)	4	2
2E		Greenhill (S&DAFA)	v	Lochend (LEAFA)	scr	wo
2E	01/10/2016	Hermiston Vale (LEAFA)	v	Camelon Albion (S&DAFA)	0	4
2E		Hutchison Vale (LEAFA)	v	Polmont Cmmunity (S&DAFA)	scr	wo
2E	01/10/2016	Kelty Hearts (FAFA)	v	Dunedin Athletic (LEAFA)	4	3
2E	01/10/2016	Kinross Colts (FAFA)	v	Gordon (BAFA)	6	3
2E	01/10/2016	Kirkcaldy (D)	v	Fallin (S&DAFA)	2	4
2E	01/10/2016	Kirkcaldy Rovers (FAFA)	v	Waverley Athletic (LEAFA)	2	2
2E	01/10/2016	Lanark (LEAFA)	v	Cupar Hearts KCAFA)	0	9
2E	01/10/2016	Laurieston Lions (S&DAFA)	v	Glenrothes KCAFA)	2	4
2E	01/10/2016	Leslie Hearts (FAFA)	v	Doune Castle (Cale)	1	5
2E	01/10/2016	Leven United KCAFA)	v	Greig Park Rangers KCAFA)	3	0
2E	01/10/2016	Linlithgow Thistle (LEAFA)	v	Kinglassie (FAFA)	10	0
2E	01/10/2016	Loganlea United (S&DAFA)	v	Kirkland Villa (FAFA)	7	2
2E		Lumphinnans United	v	Eastvale KCAFA)	wo	scr
2E	01/10/2016	Maddiston (S&DAFA)	v	Craigshill Thistle (LEAFA)	1	6
2E	01/10/2016	Methilhill Strollers (FAFA)	v	Kincardine (S&DAFA)	2	5
2E	01/10/2016	Newcraighall Leith Victoria (LEAFA)	v	Balgonie Scotia 1896 KCAFA)	3	3
2E	01/10/2016	North Merchiston Vale (LEAFA)	v	Clermiston Star (LEAFA)	4	5
2E	01/10/2016	Pathhead (LEAFA)	v	Beechwood Albion (S&DAFA)	3	4
2E	01/10/2016	Pennies (S&DAFA)	v	Armadale Thistle Ams (LEAFA)	3	0
2E	01/10/2016	Pittenweem Rovers (FAFA)	v	Tullibody Community (S&DAFA)	1	2
2E	01/10/2016	Portobello Thistle (LEAFA)	v	Stow (BAFA)	2	1
2E	01/10/2016	Queensferry Athletic (LEAFA)	v	Linlithgow Rose CFC (S&DAFA)	1	1
2E	01/10/2016	Redhall Star (LEAFA)	v	Bonnybridge YFP (S&DAFA)	1	2
2E	01/10/2016	Riverside (S&DAFA)	v	Heriot Watt University (LEAFA)	2	0
2E	01/10/2016	Rossebank Rangers (FAFA)	v	Balerno Athletic (LEAFA)	1	2
2E	01/10/2016	Rosyth (FAFA)	v	Hawick United (BAFA)	1	2
2E	01/10/2016	Salters Athletic (LEAFA)	v	Glenrothes Athletic (FAFA)	12	3
2E	01/10/2016	Salvesen (LEAFA)	v	Shotts Thistle (LEAFA)	4	1
2E	01/10/2016	Sandys (LEAFA)	v	FC Bayside (FAFA)	6	1
2E	08/10/2016	Slamannan (S&DAFA)	v	Kinross KCAFA)	2	0
2E	01/10/2016	St Bernards (LEAFA)	v	Aberdour SDC KCAFA)	3	2
2E	01/10/2016	Stenhousemuir Community (Cale)	v	Haddington Athletic Ams (LEAFA)	5	1
2E	01/10/2016	Stirling Ams (S&DAFA)	v	Cambusbarron Rovers (Cale)	0	6
2E	01/10/2016	Stirling Boys Club (S&DAFA)	v	Barca Milton 97 (LEAFA)	3	5
2E	08/10/2016	Lomond Victoria (FAFA)	v	Kingdom Athletic (FAFA)	1	1
2E		Sunnyside Thistle (S&DAFA)	v	Fauldhouse (LEAFA)	scr	wo
2E	01/10/2016	Tollcross Thistle (LEAFA)	v	Auchtermuchty Bellvue (FAFA)	4	0
2E	01/10/2016	Tranent (LEAFA)	v	Mill Inn (S&DAFA)	6	2
		NORTH OF TAY				
2NOT	01/10/2016	Arbroath Harp (MAFA)	v	Douglas (MAFA)	1	7
2NOT	01/10/2016	Arbroath HSFP (MAFA)	v	Carnoustie Panmure YM (MAFA)	2	5
2NOT	01/10/2016	Auchterarder Primrose (PAFA)	v	Morgan FP (MAFA)	1	1
2NOT	01/10/2016	Ballinluig (PAFA)	v	Jeanfield Swifts Ams (PAFA)	1	2
2NOT	01/10/2016	Balmoral United (PAFA)	v	Finavon (MAFA)	2	2
2NOT	01/10/2016	Blair Thistle (PAFA)	v	Monifeith Tayside (MAFA)	1	5
2NOT	01/10/2016	Burrelton Rovers (PAFA)	v	Breadalbane (PAFA)	1	0
2NOT	01/10/2016	Cannon Fodder (DSMAFL)	v	Fintry Athletic (MAFA)	0	9
2NOT	01/10/2016	Coldside Athletic (DSMAFL)	v	Tayside Fire Brigade (MAFA)	0	6
2NOT	01/10/2016	Coupar Angus Ams (PAFA)	v	Broughty United (MAFA)	1	0
2NOT	01/10/2016	Craigie (PAFA)	v	Bridge of Earn (PAFA)	1	3
2NOT	01/10/2016	Dunkeld & Birnham (PAFA)	v	Menzieshill (MAFA)	3	16
2NOT	01/10/2016	FC Kettledrum (DSMAFL)	v	Barnhill (MAFA)	3	2
2NOT	01/10/2016	Hilltown Hotspurs (DSMAFL)	v	Alyth (PAFA)	2	0
2NOT	01/10/2016	Kettins (PAFA)	v	Tay Thistle (PAFA)	9	1

2NOT	01/10/2016	Kinrossie Caledonian (PAFA)	v	Parktool Athletic (DSMAFL)	4	2	
2NOT	01/10/2016	Letham (PAFA)	v	Brechin City Ams (MAFA)	10	2	
2NOT	01/10/2016	Letham Community (PAFA)	v	Stobswell Athletic (DSMAFL)	2	1	
2NOT	01/10/2016	Lochee (DSMAFL)	v	Invergowrie (MAFA)	2	5	
2NOT	01/10/2016	Logie Harp (MAFA)	v	Douglas Athletic (MAFA)	1	1	
2NOT	01/10/2016	Lowson United (MAFA)	v	Newport (MAFA)	1	2	
2NOT	01/10/2016	Meigle Victoria (PAFA)	v	Vale of Atholl (PAFA)	0	12	
2NOT		Menzieshill Rovers (MAFA) w/o-scr	v	Riverside Athletic (MAFA)	wo	scr	
2NOT	01/10/2016	Merpro (MAFA)	v	Bridgeton United (PAFA)	7	0	
2NOT	01/10/2016	Moncrieff (PAFA)	v	AC Harleys (DSMAFL)	3	1	
2NOT	01/10/2016	NCR (MAFA)	v	Luncarty ASC (PAFA)	4	4	
2NOT	01/10/2016	Portcullis (MAFA)	v	Fair City (PAFA)	6	2	
2NOT	01/10/2016	St James Athletic (MAFA)	v	Polteam Perth (PAFA)	3	3	
2NOT	01/10/2016	Vale of Earn (PAFA)	v	Strathearn Grove (PAFA)	2	4	
2NOT	01/10/2016	Wolfhill (PAFA)	v	Dundee Hamlet (MAFA)	5	4	
		NORTH					
2N	01/10/2016	Aboyne (AAFA)	v	Glendale (AAFA)	0	3	
2N	01/10/2016	AC Mill Inn (AAFA)	v	Cammachmore (AAFA)	0	4	
2N	01/10/2016	AFC Murdos (AAFA)	v	Glendale XI (AAFA)	2	4	
2N	01/10/2016	Auchnagatt Barons (AAFA)	v	Tarves (AAFA)	0	9	
2N	01/10/2016	Beacon Rangers (AAFA)	v	Echt (AAFA)	5	4	
2N	01/10/2016	Bervie Caledonian (AAFA)	v	Monymusk (AAFA)	4	0	
2N	01/10/2016	Bon Accord Thistle (AAFA)	v	Alford (AAFA)	0	13	
2N	01/10/2016	Burghmuir (AAFA)	v	M S United (AAFA)	1	2	
2N	01/10/2016	Colony Park Ams (AAFA)	v	Northern United (AAFA)	3	4	
2N	01/10/2016	Cowie Thistle (AAFA)	v	Westdyke (AAFA)	1	4	
2N	01/10/2016	Ellon (AAFA)	v	Bridge of Don (AAFA)	4	1	
2N	01/10/2016	Faithlie United (AAFA)	v	Newburgh Thistle (AAFA)	1	3	
2N	01/10/2016	Formartine United Ams (AAFA)	v	Fintray Thistle (AAFA)	2	0	
2N	01/10/2016	Glendale Youth (AAFA)	v	Stoneywood East End (AAFA)	0	2	
2N	01/10/2016	Glentanar Reflex (AAFA)	v	Huntly Ams (AAFA)	3	6	
2N	01/10/2016	Highland Hotel (AAFA)	v	Tolbooth (AAFA)	1	3	
2N	01/10/2016	Insch (AAFA)	v	Balmedie (AAFA)	0	1	
2N	01/10/2016	Kaimhill United (AAFA)	v	Dyce ITC Hydraulics (AAFA)	2	3	
2N	01/10/2016	Old Aberdonians (AAFA)	v	Grammar FP (AAFA)	7	0	
2N	01/10/2016	Rothie Rovers (AAFA)	v	Theologians NE (AAFA)	7	0	
2N	01/10/2016	St Laurence (AAFA)	v	Kintore (AAFA)	7	2	
2N	01/10/2016	Westdyce (AAFA)	v	Rattrays XI (AAFA)	2	1	
2N	01/10/2016	Woodside (AAFA)	v	Torphins (AAFA)	7	0	
2R	08/10/2016	Milngavie Wanders (CAL)	v	Glasgow Deaf United (P&DAFA)	4	1	
2R	08/10/2016	FC Argyle (SAFL)	v	Ardeer West Recreation (AYR)	1	2	
2R	08/10/2016	Albion (GCAFA)	v	Blairdardie United (G&DSMAFL)	1	2	
2R	08/10/2016	Hampden (GCAFA)	v	Calderglen (GGPAFL)	2	1	
2R	08/10/2016	Westerlands (Cale)	v	Cumbernauld Colts (Cale)	3	1	
2R	08/10/2016	Carluke Hearts (NSLAFA)	v	Goldenhill (SAFL)	6	4	
2R	08/10/2016	Clydebanks Ams (CSAFL)	v	Holytown Celtic Youth (NSLAFA)	2	1	AET
2R	08/10/2016	Hamilton FPs (Cale)	v	Linwood Thistle (P&DAFA)	6	1	
2R	08/10/2016	John Street (GGPAFL)	v	Mossblown Boswell (AYR)	3	5	
2R	08/10/2016	Clark Drive (AYR)	v	Muirton (GCAFA)	4	1	
2R	08/10/2016	Singer (GCAFA)	v	Troon Dundonald (AYR)	4	1	
2R	08/10/2016	Broomhill (SAFL)	v	Glasgow Harp (Cale)	1	7	
2R	08/10/2016	AM Soccer Reserves (FAFA)	v	Callander Thistle (S&DAFA)	0	1	
2R	08/10/2016	Balgonie Scotia (KCAFA)	v	Newcraighall Leith Victoria (LEAFA)	1	1	AET, 4-2p
2R	08/10/2016	Linlithgow Rose CFC (S&DAFA)	v	Queensferry Athletic (LEAFA)	6	0	
2R	08/10/2016	Waverley Athletic (LEAFA)	v	Callander Thistle (S&DAFA)	5	2	
2R	08/10/2016	Morgan FP (MAFA)	v	Auchterarder Primrose (PAFA)	4	1	
2R	08/10/2016	Finavon (MAFA)	v	Balmoral United (PAFA)	1	1	AET, 4-5p
2R	08/10/2016	Douglas Athletic (MAFA)	v	Logie Harp (MAFA)	3	4	
2R	08/10/2016	Luncartyu ASC (PAFA)	v	NCR (MAFA)	7	0	
2R	08/10/2016	Polteam Perth (PAFA)	v	St James Athletic (MAFA)	0	2	
2R	15/10/2016	Renfrew Ams (G&DSMAFL)	v	Bridgend (G&DSMAFL)	1	2	
2R	15/10/2016	Kingdom Athletic (FAFA)	v	Lomond Vics (FAFA)	2	3	
3		Shortlees		Dennistoun Vale	wo	scr	
3	05/11/2016	Glasgow South (SSMAFL)	v	EKRR (SAFL)	2	2	
3	05/11/2016	East Kilbride YM (Cale)	v	Blairdardie United (G&DSMAFL))	3	3	
3	05/11/2016	Carrick (AYR)	v	Balgonie Scotia 1896	6	1	
3	05/11/2016	Possil YM (CSAFL) v	v	Cambusbarron Rovers (Cale)	5	3	
3	05/11/2016	Eaglesham (Cale) v	v	Dunblane Thistle (CSAFL)	2	2	
3	05/11/2016	Portobello Thistle (LEAFA)	v	Tolbooth (AAFA)	4	1	
3	05/11/2016	Symington Tinto (Cale)	v	Tillicoultry (S&DAFA)	1	2	
3	19/11/2016	M.S. United (AAFA)	v	Blantyre Celtic (CSAFL)	2	2	
3	05/11/2016	Fauldhouse (LEAFA)	v	Tranent (LEAFA)	3	4	
3	05/11/2016	Danderhall Miners (LEAFA)	v	Balmoral United (PAFA)	4	0	
3	05/11/2016	Menzieshill Rovers (MAFA)	v	Hilltown Hotspurs (DSMAFL)	3	2	

3	05/11/2016	Drumchapel Colts (SAFL)	v	Southside Star (SSMAFL)	16	2
3	12/11/2016	Formartine United (AAFA)	v	Clermiston Star (LEAFA)	1	7
3	05/11/2016	Tollcross Thistle (LEAFA)	v	Beacon Rangers (AAFA)	5	1
3	05/11/2016	Westdyke (AAFA)	v	Musselburgh (LEAFA)	3	1
3	05/11/2016	Slamannan (S&DAFA)	v	Woodside (AAFA)	0	5
3	05/11/2016	Cambusnethan Talbot Community (SSMAFL)	v	Kirkintilloch Thistle (SSMAFL)	3	2
3	05/11/2016	Broomhouse (Cale)	v	Hawick United (BAFA)	6	1
3	05/11/2016	Riverside (S&DAFA)	v	Old Aberdonians (AAFA)	2	3
3	05/11/2016	Cupar Hearts (KCAFA)	v	Largs Thistle (AYR)	4	3
3	05/11/2016	Sandys (LEAFA)	v	Bonnybridge YFP (S&DAFA)	4	3
3	05/11/2016	FC Clydebank (CSAFL)	v	Oban Saints (SAFL)	1	3
3	05/11/2016	Third Lanark (GGPAFL)	v	St. Joseph's (SAFL)	2	2
3	12/11/2016	Huntly (AAFA)	v	Cambusnethan Talbot Community (CSAFL)	1	6
3		Invac (G&DSMAFL)	v	Millerston United (SAFL)	WO	SCR
3	05/11/2016	Harestanes (CSAFL)	v	Colville Park (CSAFL)	1	2
3	05/11/2016	Giffnock North AAC (Cale)	v	East Dunbartonshire (SSMAFL)	5	0
3	05/11/2016	Strathearn Grove (PAFA)	v	Newburgh Thistle (AAFA)	3	3
3		Strathmiglo United (KCAFA)	v	Postal United (CSAFL)	wo	scr
3	05/11/2016	Fintry Athletic (MAFA)	v	Alba Thistle (SAFL)	0	4
3	05/11/2016	Beith (AYR)	v	Edinburgh South Vics (LEAFA)	1	3
3	05/11/2016	Renfrew (SSMAFL)	v	Knockentiber (AYR)	1	1
3	05/11/2016	Syngenta (S&DAFA)	v	Menzieshill (MAFA)	1	2
3	19/11/2016	Carronshore Athletic (S&DAFA)	v	Carnoustie Panmure YM (MAFA)	0	3
3	05/11/2016	Craigshill Thistle (LEAFA)	v	Maryhill Thistle (GCAFA)	3	3
3	05/11/2016	Gryffe Thistle (GCAFA)	v	Eastwood Park Mount 'A' (GGPAFL)	4	0
3	05/11/2016	Tullibody Community (S&DAFA)	v	Gartcosh United (Cale)	2	2
3	05/11/2016	Fife Thistle (FAFA)	v	Stenhousemuir Community (Cale)	0	6
3	05/11/2016	Rosehill United (GCAFA)	v	Mearns (CSAFL)	1	1
3	05/11/2016	Finnieston Park (G&DSMAFL)	v	Glasgow Harp (Cale)	2	6
3	05/11/2016	Newton Vale (GGPAFL)	v	Quayside Thistle (SSMAFL)	0	2
3	05/11/2016	Newshot (WoS)	v	Wishaw Wycombe Wanderers (NSLAFA)	0	2
3	05/11/2016	Inverclyde (SAFL)	v	Windlaw (SSMAFL)	6	2
3	05/11/2016	Luncarty ASC (PAFA)	v	Stirling City (CSAFL)	3	5
3	05/11/2016	Tayside Fire Brigade (MAFA)	v	Ferguslie Star (SAFL)	3	4
3	12/11/2016	Bowhill Rovers (KCAFA)	v	Milton (Cale)	2	0
3	05/11/2016	Coupar Angus (PAFA)	v	Milngavie Wanderers (Cale)	2	1
3	05/11/2016	Callander Thistle (S&DAFA)	v	Kelty Hearts (FAFA)	9	1
3	05/11/2016	Douglas (MAFA)	v	Balmore (Cale)	3	2
3	05/11/2016	Kincardine (S&DAFA)	v	Portcullis (MAFA)	4	5
3	05/11/2016	Bridge of Earn (PAFA)	v	Stas (G&DSMAFL)	0	1
3	05/11/2016	Kinross Colts (FAFA)	v	Newport (MAFA)	3	7
3		East Linton (LEAFA)	v	Rannoch (GGPAFL)	wo	scr
3	05/11/2016	Millbeg (SAFL)	v	Hampden (GCAFA)	2	3
3	05/11/2016	Southside Whitecart (SSMAFL)	v	Gourock Athletic (CSAFL)	0	12
3	05/11/2016	Denbeath (FAFA)	v	FC Drumchapel (G&DSMAFL)	5	1
3	05/11/2016	Dyce ITC Hydraulics (AAFA)	v	Blantyre RGM (NSLAFA)	0	0
3	05/11/2016	Doune Castle (Cale)	v	Rothie Rovers (AAFA)	5	1
3	05/11/2016	Singer CFC (GCAFA)	v	Carluke Hearts (NSLAFA)	2	1
3	12/11/2016	Colquhoun United (GGPAFL)	v	Woodhall Thistle (Cale)	1	6
3	05/11/2016	Doune Castle (S&DAFA)	v	Kilbirnie (AYR)	0	5
3	05/11/2016	63 Bridgend (G&DSMAFL)	v	East Kilbride (CSAFL)	1	5
3	05/11/2016	St Mungo's (Cale)	v	St. Andrews (FAFA)	9	2
3		Blochairn Star (SSMAFL)	v	Campbeltown Pupils (SAFL)	wo	scr
3	05/11/2016	Pennies (S&DAFA)	v	Vale of Atholl (PAFA)	9	0
3	05/11/2016	Maryhill Blackstar (SSMAFL)	v	Westercommon Star (SSMAFL)	3	3
3	05/11/2016	North Motherwell (NSLAFA)	v	Jeanfield Swifts (PAFA)	4	2
3	05/11/2016	Glendale (AAFA)	v	Dirrans Athletic (AYR)	2	2
3	05/11/2016	Lumphinnans United (KCAFA)	v	Erskine (GGPAFL)	3	1
3	05/11/2016	Wallacetoun (AYR)	v	Bridgewater (CSAFL)	1	2
3	26/11/2016	Balmedie (AAFA)	v	Glendale XI (AAFA)	0	2
3	05/11/2016	Semsa (SSMAFL) v	v	Lomond Victoria (FAFA)	3	1
3	05/11/2016	Port Glasgow Celtic (SSMAFL))	v	Bervie Caledonian (AAFA)	1	3
3	05/11/2016	Braehead (G&DSMAFL)	v	FC Kettledrum (DSMAFL)	2	2
3	19/11/2016	Westdyce (AAFA)	v	Firhill United (SSMAFL)	5	3
3	05/11/2016	New Farm Loch (AYR)	v	FC Baillieston (GGPAFL)	3	1
3	05/11/2016	Cavalry Park SC (LEAFA)	v	Kettins (PAFA)	2	4
3	05/11/2016	Hurlford (AYR)	v	Waverley Athletic (LEAFA)	5	2
3	05/11/2016	Kinrossie Caledonian (PAFA)	v	Dunoon (SAFL)	1	8
3	05/11/2016	Shawlands FP (SAFL)	v	Loganlea United (S&DAFA)	1	1
3	05/11/2016	Cammachmore (AAFA)	v	Burrelton Rovers (PAFA)	7	1
3	05/11/2016	Camelon Albion (S&DAFA)	v	Dynamo East Kilbride (GGPAFL)	1	1
3	05/11/2016	Arkleston Barrhead (SAFL)	v	Rutherglen (SAFL)	4	1
3	05/11/2016	Stoneywood East End (AAFA)	v	Invergowrie (MAFA)	5	3
3	05/11/2016	United Glasgow (WoS)	v	Linlithgow Rose CFC (S&DAFA}	0	9
3	05/11/2016	Glenrothes (KCAFA)	v	Grangemouth Rovers (S&DAFA)	1	1
3	05/11/2016	Dalziel HSFP (Cale)	v	St James Athletic (MAFA)	2	0
3	05/11/2016	Morgan FP (MAFA)	v	Letham (PAFA)	3	6
3	05/11/2016	Thorn Athletic (Cale)	v	Tynecastle (SSMAFL)	2	1
3	05/11/2016	Garrowhill Thistle (CSAFL)	v	Ardeer West Recreation (AYR)	2	2
3	05/11/2016	Greenock HSFP (CSAF L)	v	Letham Community (PAFA)	7	1
3	05/11/2016	Merpro (MAFA)	v	Greater Glasgow (GCAFA)	4	3

3	05/11/2016	Bannockburn (CSAFL)	v	Camspie Minerva (CSAFL)	1	0
3	05/11/2016	Robslee (GGPAFL)	v	Logie Harp (MAFA)	1	5
3	05/11/2016	Cumnock (AYR) v	v	St. Bernards (LEAFA)	2	4
3	05/11/2016	Monifieth Tayside (MAFA)	v	Westerlands (Cale)	0	3
3	05/11/2016	Clyde Valley Rovers (GCAFA)	v	Cambria (Cale)	0	0
3	05/11/2016	Hamilton FPs (Cale)	v	Kings Park Rangers (SAFL)	4	1
3	05/11/2016	Baillieston Juniors (Cale)	v	Ravenscraig (SSMAFL)	5	2
3	05/11/2016	Lochend (LEAFA)	v	Linlithgow Thistle (LEAFA)	1	2
3	05/11/2016	AM Soccer (FAFA)	v	Hurlford Thistle (AYR)	0	5
3	05/11/2016	Leven United (KCAFA)	v	Motherwell Thistle (SAFL)	2	1
3	05/11/2016	Moncrieff (PAFA)	v	Beechwood Albion (S&DAFA)	2	4
3	05/11/2016	Tannahill (P&DAFA)	v	Milngavie (G&DSMAFL)	0	4
3	05/11/2016	Hillington (SAFL)	v	Northern United (AAFA)	10	0
3	05/11/2016	Campsie Blackwatch Waterside (CSAFL)	v	Kilbride Thistle (AYR)	3	4
3	05/11/2016	Tarbolton (AYR) v	v	Alford (AAFA)	3	3
3	05/11/2016	East Kilbride (SAFL)	v	Craigneuk (GGPAFL)	1	1
3	05/11/2016	Mill United (NSLAFA)	v	BSC Jordanhill (GGPAFL)	1	1
3	05/11/2016	Dumbarton Harp Celtic (GGPAFL)	v	Fossoway (FAFA)	0	3
3	05/11/2016	Edinburgh Harps (LEAFA)	v	Polmont Community (8&DAFA)	0	5
3	05/11/2016	DTI (SSMAFL)	v	Clark Drive (AYR)	0	2
3	05/11/2016	AS Airdrie (SSMAFL)	v	Salvesen (LEAFA)	3	8
3	05/11/2016	Clydebank (CSAFL)	v	Glasgow University (Cale)	0	0
3	12/11/2016	Ellon (AAFA)	v	Arthurlie (CSAFL)	5	1
3	05/11/2016	Kirkcaldy YMCA (FAFA)	v	Salters Athletic (LEAFA)	5	3
3	05/11/2016	Balerno Athletic (LEAFA)	v	Lochgilphead Red Star (SAFL)	3	1
3	12/11/2016	St. Laurence (AAFA)	v	Columba (G&DSMAFL)	2	0
3	05/11/2016	Tarves (AAFA)	v	Eddlewood (NSLAFA)	3	4
3	05/11/2016	Edinburgh Rose (LEAFA)	v	Southside (CSAFL)	2	3
3	05/11/2016	Eastfield (CSAFL)	v	Wolfhill (PAFA)	10	0
3	05/11/2016	Drumchapel Al (I (CSAFL)	v	Craigie (AYR)	7	0
3	05/11/2016	St Patrick's (CSAFL)	v	AFC Carbrain (8&DAFA)	5	0
3	05/11/2016	Kings (SECAFL) v	v	Fallin (S&DAFA)	3	5
3	05/11/2016	Strathclyde Thistle (NSLAFA) v	v	Burntisland United (FAFA)	1	6
3	05/11/2016	Carbrain (GGPAFL) v	v	Barca Milton 97 (LEAFA)	2	5
3		Haldane United (CSAFL))	v	Mossblown Boswell (AYR	wo	scr
3R	12/11/2016	East Kilbride Rolls-Royce (SAFL)	v	Glasgow South (SSMAFL)	3	1
3R	12/11/2016	Blairdardie United (G&DSMAFL)	v	East Kilbride YM (Cale)	2	3
3R	12/11/2016	Dunblane Thistle (CSAFL)	v	Eaglesham (Cale)	3	1
3R	12/11/2016	St. Joseph's (SAFL)	v	Third Lanark (GGPAFL)	5	2
3R	19/11/2016	Newburgh Thistle (AAFA)	v	Strathearn Grove (PAFA)	7	0
3R	12/11/2016	Knockentiber (AYR)	v	Renfrew (SSMAFL)	1	3
3R	12/11/2016	Maryhill Thistle (GCAFA)	v	Craigshill Thistle (LEAFA)	0	4
3R	12/11/2016	Gartcosh United (Cale)	v	Tullibody Community (S&DAFA)	3	4
3R	12/11/2016	Mearns (CSAFL)	v	Rosehill United (GCAFA)	4	6
3R	12/11/2016	Blantyre RGM (NSLAFA)	v	Dyce ITC Hydraulics (AAFA)	0	1
3R	12/11/2016	Westercommon Star (SSMAFL)	v	Maryhill Blackstar (SSMAFL)	2	3
3R	12/11/2016	Dirrans Athletic (AYR)	v	Glendale (AAFA)	4	1
3R	12/11/2016	FC Kettledrum (DSMAFL)	v	Braehead (G&DSMAFL)	4	2
3R	12/11/2016	Loganlea United (S&DAFA)	v	Shawlands FP (SAFL)	2	0
3R	19/11/2016	Dynamo East Kilbride (GGPAFL)	v	Camelon Albion (S&DAFA)	2	2
3R	12/11/2016	Grangemouth Rovers (S&DAFA)	v	Glenrothes (KCAFA)	2	0
3R	12/11/2016	Ardeer West Recreation (AYR)	v	Garrowhill Thistle (CSAFL)	1	2
3R	12/11/2016	Cambria (Cale)	v	Clyde Valley Rovers (GCAFA)	7	1
3R	12/11/2016	Alford (AAFA)	v	Tarbolton (AYR)	1	2
3R	12/11/2016	Craigneuk (GGPAFL)	v	East Kilbride (SAFL)	5	1
3R	12/11/2016	GSC Jordanhill (GGPAFL)	v	Mill United (NSLAFA)	2	0
3R	12/11/2016	Glasgow University (Cale)	v	Clydebank (CSAFL)	3	1
3R	03/12/2016	Blantyre Celtic (CSAL)	v	MS United (AAFA)	3	0
4	03/12/2016	Dunoon (SAFL)	v	Baillieston Juniors (Cale)	3	3
4	03/12/2016	Cambusnethan Talbot Community (CSAFL)	v	GSC Jordanhill (GGPAFL)	3	2
4	03/12/2016	Menzieshill (MAFA)	v	Thorn Athletic (Cale)	1	2
4	03/12/2016	Stoneywood East End (AAFA)	v	Drumchapel Ams (CSAFL)	1	0
4	03/12/2016	Hampden (GCAFA)	v	St. Mungo's (Cale)	2	2
4	03/12/2016	Menzieshill Rovers (MAFA)	v	Hurlford Thistle (AYR)	0	4
4	03/12/2016	Eastfield (CSAFL)	v	Coupar Angus Ams (PAFA)	9	0
4	03/12/2016	Barca Milton 97 (LEAFA)	v	Bervie Caledonian (AAFA)	5	2
4	03/12/2016	Gourock Athletic (CSAFL)	v	Stirling City (CSAFL)	0	4
4	03/12/2016	Clermiston Star (LEAFA)	v	Logie Harp (MAFA)	2	2
4	03/12/2016	Singer CFC (GCAFA)	v	Southside (CSAFL)	1	7
4	03/12/2016	Pennies (S&DAFA)	v	Hillington (SAFL)	5	1
4	03/12/2016	New Farm Loch (AYR)	v	Bowhill Rovers	1	2
4	03/12/2016	Tillicoultry (S&DAFA)	v	Kilbride Thistle (AYR)	1	2
4	03/12/2016	Dalziel HSFP (Cale)	v	East Kilbride YM	3	2
4	03/12/2016	Alba Thistle (SAFL)	v	Possil YM (CSAFL)	2	1
4	03/12/2016	Fallin (S&DAFA)	v	Dirrans Athletic (AYR)	0	4
4	03/12/2016	Garrowhill Thistle (CSAFL)	v	Cambusnethan Talbot Community (SSMAFL)	5	0

4	03/12/2016	Tullibody Community (S&DAFA)	v	Clark Drive (AYR)	5	2	
4	03/12/2016	FC Kettledrum (DSMAFL)	v	Ferguslie Star (SAFL)	5	4	
4	03/12/2016	Haldane United (CSAFL)	v	Inverclyde (SAFL)	4	2	
4	03/12/2016	Cupar Hearts (KCAFA)	v	Glasgow University (Cale)	4	4	
4	03/12/2016	Fossoway (FAFA)	v	Woodside (AAFA)	2	2	
4	03/12/2016	Tollcross Thistle (LEAFA)	v	Callander Thistle (S&DAFA)	6	2	
4		Invac (G&DSMAFL)	v	St Joseph's (SAFL)	scr	wo	
4	03/12/2016	Carronshore Athletic (S&DADA)	v	Dunblane Thistle (CSAFL)	2	2	
4	03/12/2016	Westdyke (AAFA)	v	Gryffe Thistle (GCAFA)	2	1	
4	03/12/2016	Woodhall Thistle (Cale)	v	Letham (PAFA)	1	5	
4	03/12/2016	Kilbirnie (AYR)	v	Newburgh Thistle (AAFA)	4	0	
4	03/12/2016	Salvesen (LEAFA)	v	Oban Saints (SAFL)	0	2	
4	03/12/2016	Sandys (LEAFA)	v	Ellon (AAFA)	5	1	
4	03/12/2016	St Laurence (AAFA)	v	St. Patricks (CSAFL)	3	2	
4	10/12/2016	Blantyre Celtic (CSAFL)	v	Quayside Thistle (SSMAFL)	6	1	
4	03/12/2016	Doune Castle (Cale)	v	Wishaw Wycombe Wanderers (NSLAFA)	2	1	
4	03/12/2016	Portcullis (MAFA)	v	Drumchapel Colts (SAFL)	1	2	
4	03/12/2016	Semsa (SSMAFL)	v	Cammachmore (AAFA)	1	3	
4	03/12/2016	Edinburgh South Vics (LEAFA)	v	Linlithgow Thistle (LEAFA)			ABD
4	03/12/2016	Westerlands (Cale)	v	Broomhouse (Cale)	1	1	
4	03/12/2016	Craigshill Thistle (LEAFA)	v	Maryhill Black Star	6	1	
4	03/12/2016	Portobello Thistle (LEAFA)	v	Burntisland United (FAFA)	1	3	
4	03/12/2016	North Motherwell (NSLAFA)	v	East Linton (LEAFA)	1	6	
4	03/12/2016	Dyce ITC Hydraulics (AAFA)	v	Tarbolton (AAFA)	1	4	
4	03/12/2016	Douglas (MAFA)	v	Bridgewater (CSAFL)	3	1	
4	03/12/2016	Hurlford Ams (AYR)	v	Tranent Ams (LEAFA)	3	2	
4	03/12/2016	Craigneuk (GGPAFL)	v	Leven United (KCAFA)	2	8	
4	03/12/2016	Shortlees (AYR)	v	Glasgow Harp (Cale)	2	3	
4	03/12/2016	Eddlewood (NSLAFA)	v	Merpro (MAFA)	2	1	
4	03/12/2016	Greenock HSFP (CSAFL)	v	East Kilbride Ams (CSAFL)	1	1	
4	03/12/2016	Cambria (Cale)	v	Dynamo East Kilbride (GGPA)	5	2	
4	03/12/2016	Beechwood Albion (S&DAFA)	v	Danderhall Miners (LEAFA)	1	3	
4	03/12/2016	Kirkcaldy YMCA (FAFA)	v	Carrick (AYR)	3	1	
4	03/12/2016	Newport (MAFA)	v	Stenhousemuir Community (Cale)	1	4	
4	03/12/2016	Blochairn Star (SSMAFL)	v	Stas (G&DSMAFL)	2	2	
4	03/12/2016	East Kilbride Rolls Royce (SAFL)	v	Polmont Community (S&DAFA)	0	0	
4	03/12/2016	Strathmiglo United (KCAFA)	v	Westdyce (AAFA)	1	1	
4	03/12/2016	Arkleston Barrhead (SAFL)	v	St. Bernards (LEAFA)	7	1	
4	03/12/2016	Balerno Athletic (LEAFA)	v	Bannockburn (CSAFL)	2	6	
4	03/12/2016	Loganlea United (S&DAFA)	v	Glendale XI (AAFA)	8	1	
4	03/12/2016	Kettins (PAFA)	v	Rosehill United (GCAFA)	2	1	
4	03/12/2016	Giffnock North AAC (Cale)	v	Old Aberdonians (AAFA)	6	3	
4	03/12/2016	Grangemouth Rovers (S&DAFA)	v	Linlithgow Rose CFC (S&DAFA)	2	0	
4	03/12/2016	Milngavie (G&DSMAFL)	v	Denbeath (FAFA)	4	2	
4	02/12/2016	Renfrew Ams (SSMAFL)	v	Colville Park (CSAFL)	0	4	
4	03/12/2016	Hamilton FP (Cale)	v	Lumphinnans United (KCAFA)	0	0	
4R	10/12/2016	Baillieston Juniors (Cale)	v	Dunoon (SAFL)	5	1	
4R	10/12/2016	Broomhouse (Cale)	v	Westerlands (Cale)	3	1	
4R	10/12/2016	Dunblane Thistle (CSAFL)	v	Carnoustie Panmure (MAFA)	3	2	
4R	10/12/2016	East Kilbride Ams (CSAFL)	v	Greenock HSFP (CSAFL)	0	2	
4R	10/12/2016	Glasgow University (Cale)	v	Cupar Hearts (KCAFA)	1	2	
4R	10/12/2016	Logie Harp (MAFA)	v	Clermiston Star (LEAFA)	4	2	
4R	10/12/2016	Lumphinnans United (KCAFA)	v	Hamilton FP (Cale)	1	2	
4R	10/12/2016	Polmont Community (S&DAFA)	v	East Kilbride Rolls Royce (SAFL)	3	1	
4R	10/12/2016	Stas (G&DSMAL)	v	Blochairn Star (SSMAFL)	1	0	
4R	10/12/2016	St Mungo's (Cale)	v	Hampden (GCAFA)	3	2	
4R	10/12/2016	Westdyce (AAFA)	v	Strathmiglo United	2	0	
4R	10/12/2016	Woodside (AAFA)	v	Fossoway (FAFA)	3	0	
5	07/01/2017	Alba Thistle (SAFL)	v	Craigshill Thistle (LEAFA)	1	4	
5	07/01/2017	Arkleston Barrhead (SAFL)	v	St Laurence (AAFA)	0	3	
5	07/01/2017	Baillieston Juniors (Cale)	v	Dunblane Thistle (CSAFL)	0	2	
5	07/01/2017	Barca Milton 97 (LEAFA)	v	Stoneywood East End (AAFA)	1	0	
5	07/01/2017	Cambria (Cale)	v	Southside (CSAFL)	1	5	
5	07/01/2017	Cammachmore (AAFA)	v	Kilbride Thistle (AYR)	0	1	
5	07/01/2017	Dalziel HSFP (Cale)	v	Hurlford Thistle (AYR)	0	2	
5	07/01/2017	Danderhall Miners (LEAFA)	v	Hamilton FP (Cale)	1	2	
5	07/01/2017	Dirrans Athletic (AYR)	v	Tarbolton (AAFA)	0	4	
5	07/01/2017	Douglas (MAFA)	v	Haldane United (CSAFL)	4	1	
5	07/01/2017	Drumchapel Colts (SAFL)	v	Colville Park (CSAFL)	0	6	
5	07/01/2017	Greenock HSFP (CSAFL)	v	Doune Castle (Cale)	1	1	
5	07/01/2017	Eddlewood (NSLAFA)	v	FC Kettledrum (DSMAFL)	3	3	
5	21/01/2017	Garrowhill Thistle (CSAFL)	v	Polmont Community (S&DAFA)	4	3	
5	07/01/2017	Glasgow Harp (Cale)	v	Stenhousemuir Community (Cale)	1	3	
5	07/01/2017	Cupar Hearts (KCAFA)	v	East Linton (LEAFA)	2	0	
5	07/01/2017	Grangemouth Rovers (S&DAFA)	v	Sandys (LEAFA)	1	1	
5	07/01/2017	Hurlford Ams (AYR)	v	Stirling City (CSAFL)	4	1	
5	07/01/2017	Kettins (PAFA)	v	Bowhill Rovers (KCAFA)	1	5	
5	07/01/2017	Kirkcaldy YMCA (FAFA)	v	Eastfield (CSAFL)	1	3	
5	07/01/2017	Letham (PAFA)	v	Tollcross Thistle (LEAFA)	3	3	
5	07/01/2017	Leven United (KCAFA)	v	St Josephs (SAFL)	1	1	
5	07/01/2017	Loganlea United (S&DAFA)	v	Giffnock Borth AAC (Cale)	0	1	

5	07/01/2017	Logie Harp (MAFA)	v	Pennies (S&DAFA)	0	6	
5	07/01/2017	Milngavie (G&DSMAFL)	v	Bannockburn (CSAFL)	1	7	
5	07/01/2017	Oban Saints (SAFL)	v	Westdyce (AAFA)	5	1	
5	07/01/2017	Stas (G&DSMAL)	v	St Mungo's (Cale)	0	3	
5	21/01/2017	Thorn Athletic (Cale)	v	Burntisland United (FAFA)	6	1	
5	07/01/2017	Tullibody Community (S&DAFA)	v	Kilbirnie (Ayr)	4	1	
5	07/01/2017	Westdyke (AAFA)	v	Broomhouse (Cvale)	1	3	
5	07/01/2017	Woodside (AAFA)	v	Blantyre Celtic (CSAFL)	1	0	
5		Cambusnethan Talbot (CSAFL)	v	Edinburgh South Vics (LEAFA)	wo		
				or Linlithgow Thistle (LEAFA)			
5R	14/01/2017	Sandys (LEAFA)	v	Grangemouth Rovers (S&DAFA)	2	1	
5R	14/01/2017	Tollcross Thistle (LEAFA)	v	Letham (PAFA)	0	4	
5R	21/01/2017	Doune Castle (Cale)	v	Greenock HSFP (CSAFL)	4	1	
5R	21/01/2017	FC Kettledrum (DSMAFL)	v	Eddlewood (NSLAFA)	1	2	PROTEST
5R	21/01/2017	St Josephs (SAFL)	v	Leven United	4	0	
6	04/02/2017	Hurlford Thistle	v	Hamilton FP	4	2	
6	04/02/2017	Dunblane Thistle	v	Hurlford Ams	4	3	
6	04/02/2017	St Josephs	v	Southside	0	0	
6	04/02/2017	Colville Park	v	Woodside	5	1	
6	04/02/2017	Letham	v	Kilbride Thistle	3	0	
6	11/02/2017	Garrowhill Thistle	v	Eastfield	1	4	
6	04/02/2017	Douglas	v	Bannockburn	1	3	
6		Eddlewood	v	Thorn Athletic		wo	
6	04/02/2017	Craigshill Thistle	v	Sandys	2	0	
6	11/02/2017	Pennies	v	Bowhill Rovers	0	1	
6	04/02/2017	Cambusnethan Talbot Community	v	Doune Castle	5	3	
6	11/02/2017	Giffnock North AAC	v	Stenhousemuir Community	1	0	
6	04/02/2017	Tarbolton	v	Oban Saints	1	3	
6	04/02/2017	Tullibody Community	v	Cupar Hearts	2	1	
6	11/02/2017	St Mungos	v	Barca Milton	0	1	
6	04/02/2017	Broomhouse	v	St Laurence	3	1	
6R	11/02/2017	Southside	v	St Josephs	3	1	
7	04/03/2017	Bannockburn	v	Tullibody Community	6	1	
7	04/03/2017	Broomhouse	v	Hurlford Thistle (AYR)	0	1	
7	04/03/2017	Cambusnethan Talbot Community	v	Barca Milton 97	1	5	
7	04/03/2017	Colville Park	v	Thorn Athletic	6	1	
7	04/03/2017	Craigshill Thistle	v	Dunblane Thistle (CSAFL)	1	1	
7	04/03/2017	Eastfield	v	Bowhill Rovers	2	2	
7	11/03/2017	Giffnock North AAC	v	Southside	0	3	
7	04/03/2017	Letham	v	Oban Saints	1	1	
7R	11/03/2017	Dunblane Thistle	v	Craigshill Thistle	0	2	
7R	11/03/2017	Bowhill Rovers	v	Eastfield	3	2	
7R	11/03/2017	Oban Saints	v	Letham	4	3	
8	25/03/2017	Bannockburn	v	Colville Park	1	3	
8	25/03/2017	Hurlford Thistle	v	Bowhill Rovers	0	3	
8	25/03/2017	Barca Milton 97	v	Oban Saints	0	2	
8	25/03/2017	Craigshill Thistle	v	Southside	1	1	
8R	08/04/2017	Southside	v	Craigshill Thistle	4	1	
SF	15/04/2017	Colville Park	v	Oban Saints	3	1	at Hamilton
SF	28/04/2017	Southside	v	Bowhill Rovers	1	0	at Hamilton
F	28/05/2017	Colville Park	v	Southside	1	0	at Hampden

SCOTTISH AMATEUR FA DISTRICT CUPS 2016/17

AND AMATEUR CUP 2016

Date	Home	Away	F	A	
23/04/2016	Portree	ICM Electrical	2	4	
23/04/2016	IRN Security	Tomatin	0	0	AET, 7-6 p
23/04/2016	Avoch	Hill Rovers	9	0	
23/04/2016	Polonia	NMM Sams	2	8	
14/05/2016	North Kessock	Ardersier	2	6	
07/05/2016	Avoch	ICM Electrical	3	1	
14/05/2016	Culbokie	Pockets Inverness	10	1	
14/05/2016	Sleat & Strathnaver	Maryburgh	2	3	
04/06/2016	Portree Juniors	Inverness Thistle	5	3	
13/05/2016	ANM Ace	Hilton	2	5	
14/05/2016	Merkinch	Culloden	3	1	
14/05/2016	NMM Sams	Kyleakin	0	1	
13/05/2016	Police	Caley Club	7	1	
14/05/2016	Innes GI	GA United	3	3	aet 6-5p
14/05/2016	IRN Security	Lochness	1	3	
14/05/2016	Stromness	Firth	3	0	
03/05/2016	Kirkwall Rovers	Dounby Athletic	5	3	
14/05/2016	Kirkwall Thorfinn	Isles United	10	0	
14/05/2016	St Andrews	Rendall	1	5	
14/05/2016	Kirkwall Hotspurs	Kirkwall Accies	4	0	
20/05/2016	Point	Ness	1	1	
14/05/2016	Benbecula	Lochs	0	1	
14/05/2016	Stornoway Athletic	Southend	4	1	
13/05/2016	Back	Carloway	1	0	
21/05/2016	Westside	Iochdar Saints	1	2	
23/04/2016	Tongue United	Thurso Swifts	2	1	aet
23/04/2016	Watten	Staxigoe United	0	3	
14/05/2016	Golspie Stafford	John o' Groats	2	4	
14/05/2016	Helmsdale United	Francis Street Club	3	2	
14/05/2016	Castletown	Halkirk	2	4	
14/05/2016	Lybster	Keiss	2	3	
14/05/2016	Lochinver	Brora Wanderers	4	2	
14/05/2016	Tongue United	Thurso Pentland	2	1	
14/05/2016	Lairg Rovers	Staxigoe United	3	2	
14/05/2016	Wick Groats	FC Retro	5	0	
14/05/2016	High Ormlie Hotspur	Wick Thistle	1	2	
14/05/2016	Top Joes	Dornoch City	2	3	
14/05/2016	Thurso Academicals	Pentland United	1	3	
28/05/2016	Culbokie	Pentland United	1	3	
30/05/2016	Avoch	Tongue United	7	0	
04/06/2016	Castletown	Stornoway Athletic	2	0	at Culbokie
04/06/2016	Keiss	Point	0	5	at Avoch
04/06/2016	Kirkwall Thorfinn	Kyleakin	7	0	at Golspie
04/06/2016	Lairg Rovers	Rendall	3	2	
04/06/2016	Lochinver	Kirkwall Rovers	7	3	
04/06/2016	John O' groats	Kirkwall Hotspurs	3	1	
04/06/2016	Dornoch City	Wick Groats	1	6	
04/06/2016	Ardersier	Back	4	4	???
04/06/2016	Innes GI	Hilton	1	6	
04/06/2016	Lochs	Merkinch	7	0	
04/06/2016	Maryburgh	Helmsdale United	4	0	
04/06/2016	Police	Loch Ness	1	4	
11/06/2016	Stromness	Portree Juniors	4	1	at Golspie
18/06/2016	Wick Thistle	Iochdar Saints	scr	wo	
25/06/2016	Loch Ness	Stromness Athletic	1	0	
25/06/2016	Back	Iochdar Saints	1	3	
25/06/2016	Hilton	Point	3	0	
25/06/2016	John O' groats	Lochs	0	3	at Culbokie
25/06/2016	Avoch	Lochinver	3	2	
25/06/2016	Castletown	Wick Groats	0	5	
25/06/2016	Maryburgh	Pentland United	3	3	aet 5-3p
09/07/2016	Kirkwall Thorfinn	Lairg Rovers	8	1	
16/07/2016	Iochdar Saints	Kirkwall Thorfinn	1	4	at Maryburgh
16/07/2016	Avoch	Hilton	4	2	
16/07/2016	Lochs	Loch Ness	1	0	
16/07/2016	Wick Groats	Maryburgh	3	0	
06/08/2016	Lochs	Wick Groats	0	1	at Golspie
06/08/2016	Avoch	Kirkwall Thorfinn	1	2	at Halkirk
27/08/2016	Wick Groats	Kirkwall Thorfinn	0	0	aet 4-2p
	at Brora Rangers FC				

SOUTH OF SCOTLAND AMATEUR CUP

Rd	Home	Away	F	A	
1	Avendale	Linton Hotspur	7	0	
1	Kelso Thistle	Jed Legion	0	2	
1	Larkhall Thistle	Pathhead	6	5	AET
1	Newtown	West Barns Star	3	5	
1	Pencaitland	Musselburgh Windsor	5	1	
2	Avendale	Melrose	5	0	
2	Danderhall MW	Haddington Athletic	8	1	
2	Dunbar Athletic	Tweeddale Rovers	0	4	
2	East Linton	Earlston Rhymers	6	2	
2	Hawick Legion	Jed Legion	3	2	
2	Hawick United	Carluke Hearts	3	5	
2	Hawick Waverley	Biggar United	6	3	
2	Lanark	Carnwath	2	7	
2	Larkhall Thistle	Greenlaw	1	4	
2	Law Parish	Lauder	4	3	aet
2	Machan United	Symington Tinto	4	3	
2	Pencaitland	Chirnside United	3	5	
2	Selkirk Victoria	Shotts Thistle	0	12	
2	Springhill	Coldstream AFC	5	2	
2	Tranent AFC	Gordon	3	4	
2	West Barns Star	Peebles AFC	wo	scr	
3	Carnwath	Tweeddale Rovers	2	3	
3	East Linton	Machan United	0	2	
3	Gordon	Avendale	2	3	
3	Greenlaw	Hawick Legion	2	1	
3	Law Parish	Springhill	2	2	aet 4-5p
3	Shotts Thistle	Hawick Waverley	4	5	aet
3	West Barns Star	Chirnside United	0	2	
3	Carluke Hearts	Danderhall MW	0	2	
4	Avendale	Chirnside United	4	1	
4	Hawick Waverley	Springhill	5	0	
4	Machan United	Tweeddale Rovers	3	4	
4	Greenlaw	Danderhall MW	0	6	
SF	Hawick Waverley	Avendale	2	2	3-1p
	at Carluke				
SF	Tweeddale Rovers	Danderhall MW	0	2	
	at Easthouses				
F	Hawick Waverley	Danderhall MW	1	4	aet
	at Hamilton	Att 183			

FIFE AMATEUR CUP					
Rd	Home	Away	F	A	
1	AM Soccer Reserves	Kirkcaldy Rovers	2	3	
1	Glenrothes	Newport	1	2	
1	Leslie Hearts	Balgonie Scotia	3	2	
1	AM Soccer Reserves	Greig Park Rangers	1	3	
1	Bowhill Rovers	Glenrothes Athletic	13	1	
1	Hearts of Beath	Kelty Hearts	12	0	
1	Kingdom Athletic	Fossoway	1	3	
1	Strathmiglo United	Cupar Hearts	1	3	
2	Bowhill Rovers	Pittenweem Rovers	6	3	
2	Denbeath	Lumphinnans United	1	4	
2	Fossoway	Kirkland Villa	4	0	
2	Freuchie	Falkland	3	2	
2	Kinglassie	Kirkcaldy Rovers	2	3	
2	Methilhill Strollers	Leven United	1	2	
2	FC Bayside	Leslie Hearts	4	2	
2	Auchtrmuchty Bellevue	Fife Thistle	6	1	
2	Kirkcaldy AFC	Lomond Victoria	4	1	
2	Rosebank Rangers	Greig Park Rangers	1	5	
2	Rosyth AFC	Aberdour SDC	1	4	
2	St Andrews AFC	Hearts of Beath	2	5	
2	Glenrothes Strollers	Burntisland United	2	1	aet
2	Kinross Colts	Newport	2	7	
2	Cupar Hearts	St Monans Swallows	3	0	
2	Valleyfield	Kirkcaldy YMCA	scr	wo	
3	Aberdour SDC	Glenrothes Strollers	3	2	
3	Bowhill Rovers	Hearts of Beath	7	3	
3	Cupar Hearts	Auchtermuchty Bellevue	1	2	aet
3	FC Bayside	Newport	7	7	aet, 3-4p
3	Kirkcaldy AFC	Lumphinnans United	1	2	
3	Kirkcaldy YMCA	Kirkcaldy Rovers	6	1	
3	Leven United	Fossoway	4	1	
3	Greig Park Rangers	Freuchie	7	0	
4	Aberdour SDC	Kirkcaldy YMCA	2	1	
4	Bowhill Rovers	Newport	7	2	
4	Leven United	Auchtermuchty Bellevue	9	2	
4	Lumphinnans United	Greig Park Rangers	1	4	
SF	Aberdour SDC	Greig Park Rangers	1	2	
	at Glenrothes				
SF	Bowhill Rovers	Leven United	1	2	aet
	at Glenrothes				
F	Leven United	Greig Park Rangers	2	2	5-4p
	at Kelty Hearts				

NORTH OF TAY AMATEUR CUP					
Rd	Home	Away	F	A	
1	Arbroath HSFP	FC Kettledrum	3	4	
1	Barnhill	Dryburgh Athletic Community	7	1	
1	Broughty Athletic	Portcullis	1	0	
1	Craigie	Kettins	5	2	
1	DC Athletic	Kirriemuir Thistle	5	1	
1	Doc's Hibernia	Jeanfield Swifts	9	0	
1	Letham	Coupar Angus	2	1	
1	Lochee Celtic	Coldside Athletic	0	4	
1	Monifieth Tayside	Menzieshill Rovers	0	4	
1	Tayside Fire Brigader	Ballinluig	9	2	
1	Vale of Atholl	Merpro	2	7	AET
1	Balmoral United	Blair Thistle	13	1	
1	Cannon Fodder	Logie Harp	1	8	
1	Dundee Uni Med Students	Carnoustie YM Panmuir	0	1	
1	Lowson United	Ambassador	7	0	
1	Monifieth Hurricans	Vale of Earn	0	4	
1	St James Athletic	Tay Thistle	7	5	
2	AC Harleys	Vale of Earn	3	5	AET
2	Douglas	Menzieshill Rovers	2		
2	Letham	Finavon	6		
2	Menzieshill	Wellbank	13		
2	St John's	Broughty United	3		
2	Coldside Athletic	DC Athletic	0		
2	Letham Community	FC Kettledrum	5		
2	Balmoral United	Brechin City	7		
2	Breadalbane	Moncrieff	6		
2	Bridge of Earn	Doc's Hibernia	1		
2	Burrelton Rovers	Fair City	1		
2	Craigie	Hilltown Hotspurs	1		
2	Douglas Athletic	FC Menzieshill	3		
2	Dunkeld & Birnam	Barnhill	1		
2	Ferry Mechanics	Polteam Perth	2		
2	Forfar West End	Fintry Athletic	2		
2	Invergowrie	Hawkhill Athletic	7		
2	Kinrossie Caledonian	Stobswell Athletic	7		
2	Lochee	Auchterarder Primrose	0		
2	Meigle Victoria	Kinross	2		
2	NCR	Luncarty	1		
2	Rattray	Riverside CSC	0		
2	St James Athletic	Stobswell Athletic	6		
2	Tayside Fire Brigade	Bank Street Athletic	8		
2	Merpro	Strathearn Grove	5		
2	Carnoustie YM Panmuir	Dundee United SC	5		
2	Logie Harp	Lowson United	1		
2	Brigeton Athletic	Morgan Academy FP	scr		
2	Clark's Cowboys	Arbroath Harp	scr		
2	Club 83	Wolfhill	wo		
2	Dundee Hamlet	Alyth	scr		
2	Fife Royals	Fintry Rovers	scr		
3	Fair City	FC Kettledrum	7		
3	Alyth	Balmoral United	0		
3	Barnhill	Fintry Athletic	2		
3	FC Menzieshill	DC Athletic	3		
3	Invergowrie	Merpro	1		
3	Kinrossie Caledonian	Polteam Perth	5		
3	NCR	Menzieshill AFC	1		
3	Riverside CSC	Breadalbane	4		
3	St James Athletic	Broughty United	2		
3	Tayside Fire Brigade	Bridge of Earn	2		
3	Vale of Earn	Hilltown Hotspurs	1		
3	Kinross	Carnoustie YM Panmuir	1		
3	Auchterarder Primrose	Morgan Academy FP	2		
3	Fintry Rovers	Arbroath Harp	2		
3	Letham AFC	Club 83	12		
3	Lowson United	Douglas AFC	0		
4	Arbroath Harp	Riverside CSC	1		
4	Bridge of Earn	Menzieshill AFC	1		
4	Broughty United	FC Menzieshill	1		
4	Carnoustie YM Panmuir	Douglas AFC	2		
4	Fair City	Merpro	1		
4	Fintry Athletic	Balmoral United	2		
4	Letham Ams	Morgan Academy FP	4		
4	Hilltown Hotspur	Kinrossie Caledonian	5		
5	Balmoral United	Hilltown Hotspurs	2		
5	Douglas	FC Menzieshill	9		
5	Letham	Fair City	12		
5	Riverside CSC	Menzieshill	3		
SF	Douglas	Riverside CSC	3		
	at Violet				
SF	Hilltown Hotspur	Letham	1		
	at Kinnoull				
F	Douglas	Letham	1		
	at Forfar Athletic				

EST OF SCOTLAND AMATEUR CUP

Rd	Home	Away	F	A	
1	Blochairn Star	Castlemilk BC	3	2	
1	Braehead	Cartsbridge Evangelical Church	1	3	
1	Broomhouse	Ardeer West Recreation	4	0	
1	Campsie Black Watch Waterside	Tynecastle AFC	5	1	
1	Coatdyke Congregational	East Kilbride Thistle AFC	1	10	
1	Crosshouse Waverley	Greater Glasgow	4	0	
1	East End	Gartcairn AFC	5	0	
1	East Kilbride AFC	Carlton YMCA	7	0	
1	Ferguslie Star	Possil YM	0	8	
1	Finnieston Park	Craigneuk	1	1	
1	Garrowhill Thistle	Motherwell Thistle	1	3	
1	Gartcosh United	Broomlands	4	0	
1	Glenburn MW	Catrine	4	0	
1	Gryffe Thistle	Crosshill Thistle	4	3	
1	Harestanes	Cdrumchapel Colts	6	1	
1	Invac	Carluke	3	4	
1	John Street	Milton AFC	2	11	
1	Maryhill Black Star	Giffnock North	0	8	
1	Port Glasgow	Dalry	3	1	
1	Postal United	Motherwell Bridgeworks	5	0	
1	Red Star	Hampden AFC	1	2	
1	Rossvale	AFC Carbrain	3	3	
1	Southside	Stewarton United	3	1	
	Stedfast	Holytown Colts	3	1	
1	Strathclyde University (GGPAFL)	Albion AFC	1	4	
	Strathclyde University Cal	Blantyre RGM	1	1	
	Symington Caledonian	West Stone	1	5	
	Windlaw	Crown Athletic	7	1	
	Woodhall Thistle	MLS Leeds United	7	0	
	Shawlands FP	Langcraigs	7	2	
	Southside Whitecart	Millbeg	5	2	
	Haldane	Cambria	1	2	
	Cumbernauld Athletic	Kelvinbridge	scr	wo	
	Shawbridge	Blantyre Soccer Academy	wo	scr	
	Tarbolton	Anniesland	scr	wo	
	AFC Ravenscraig	Newshot	2	1	
	Alba Thistle	Lanarkshire Forrest	2	1	
	Albion	East Kilbride AFC	1	13	
	Ardrossan Castle Rovers	Renfrew Thistle	7	1	
	Arleston Barrhead	Craigie	5	1	
	Arthurlie AFC	BSC Glasgow AFC	2	2	
	Auchinleck Boswell	Broomhill	2	1	
	Bannockburn AFC	Shawlands FP	4	1	
	Bargeddie	Mearns Churches	3	0	
	Belleaire	St Mungo's	1	6	
	Bellfield Lochan	Dirrans Athletic	0	4	
	Bengal Lancers	Baillieston Juniors	4	3	AET
	Blairdardie United	Moorlands	7	1	
	Blochairn Star	Eaglesham	2	1	
	Boswell	new Meadow	0	3	
	Bridgeton Vale	St Patrick's FP	2	2	
	Busby	Wishaw HS FP	1	4	
	alderglen AFC (GGPAFL)	Balmore	1	1	AET, 4-2p
	ambusnethan Talbot Community	Cumbernauld Colts AFC	2	3	AET
	ambusnethan Talbot Community	Ferguslie Star	1	2	
	ampsie AFC	Arden	7	1	
	ampsie Black Watch Waterside	Blantyre AFC	1	0	
	arbrain	Kilbride Thistle	3	4	
	arrick	Postal United	5	0	
	lyde Valley Rovers	Campsie Minerva	1	4	
	lydebank AFC	Irvine Town	4	3	
	lydesdale	Drumchapel AFC	0	5	
	lydeside Athletic	Carluke AFC	4	3	
	orkerhill	Clark Drive	2	5	
	oylton	AS Airdrie	4	8	
	rosshouse Waverley	Eastwood Parkmount "B"	3	2	
	rongan United	Eastwood Parkmount "A"	2	1	
	umbarton Harp Celtic AFC	King's Park Rangers	2	3	
	ast Dunbartonshire	Barrhill	0	2	
	ast End	Briodgewater	0	5	
	ast Kilbride Thistle AFC	Weir Recreation	1	1	AET, 9-8p
	ast Kilbride YM	Goldenhill	1	5	
	sthall Star	Glasgow University	2	3	
	dlewood AFC	Hillington	3	2	
	RR	Semsa	4	0	
	Argyle	Rutherglen AFC	3	2	
	Baillieston	Cardross	2	4	AET
	Clydebank	New Farm Loch	1	2	
2	Fenwick Thistle	Rosehill United	3	2	AET
2	Finnart	Croftfoot Parish	4	1	
2	Firhill United	Southside Whitecart	4	4	AET, 3-1p
2	Fordbank Star	Campbeltown Pupils	3	2	
2	Glasgow Island	Dalziel HSFP	2	8	
2	Glynhill Moorcroft	Eastfield	1	5	
2	Gormac Thistle	Glasgow Harp	2	5	
2	Gourock Athletic	Beith	3	2	
2	GSC Jordanhill	South Lochaber Thistle	4	3	
2	Hamilton Wanderers	New Cumnock Afton	4	2	
2	Hampden AFC	Glenmuir Thistle	7	2	
2	Harestanes	Giffnock North	2	1	AET
2	Helensburgh	Beith Meadowside	11	0	
2	Hurlford AFC	Glenvale (P&DAFA)	1	1	AET, 2-4p
2	Hurlford Thistle	Colquhoun United	11	1	
2	Kelvinbridge	Glenvale (S&DAFA)	4	1	
2	Kilbirnie AFC	Port Glasgow OBU	11	0	
2	Kilmarnock AFC	Mossblown Boswell	3	2	
2	Kirkintilloch Thistle	Broomhouse	1	4	
2	Knockentiber	Crookston Castle	4	2	
2	Largs Thistle AFC	Bearsden	4	2	AET
2	Linwood Thistle	Kings	1	4	
2	Lochgilphead Red Star	Inverclyde	7	0	
2	Mauchline United	Wishaw Wycombe Wanderers	1	2	
2	Muirton	Strathclyde University	1	4	
2	Newton Vale	Renfrew Thistle	2	1	
2	North Kelvin Sports	Westercommon Star	1	2	
2	North Motherwell	Gartcosh United	1	1	AET, 3-4p
2	Ochiltree United	United Clydebank Supporters	0	2	
2	Petershill Villa	Oban Saints	0	8	
2	Port Glasgow AFC	Mill United	4	2	
2	Port Glasgow Cewltic	Claremont	2	4	
2	Port Glasgow United	Electric	2	3	
2	Possil YM	Darvel Victoria	10	1	
2	Quayside Thistle	Lomond Vale	2	4	AET
2	Rannock	Stedfast	3	2	
2	Robslee	AFC Chryston	2	1	
2	Rosehill Star	West Kilbride	2	3	AET
2	Rossvale	Cumnock	1	2	
2	Rothesay Brandane	Hamilton FP	0	3	
2	Shawbridge	Mill United (CSAFL)	3	1	
2	Shortlees	FC Dal Riata	12	1	
2	Singer	Barony of Blackhall	4	3	AET
2	Southside AFC	Anniesland	3	0	
2	Southside Star	Finnieston Park	4	2	
2	St David's	Colville Park	1	7	
2	St Joseph's	Carradale	8	0	
2	St Patrick's FP	Dean	8	0	
2	St Silas	Paisley Caledonian	2	3	
2	Stanley Athletic	Greenock HSFP	0	6	
2	Stewarton Annick	Galston United	3	4	
2	Strathaven Dynamo	Milngavie Wanderers	3	7	
2	Tannahill	Erskine	0	3	
2	Tarbet	Dailly	0	2	
2	Third Lanark	Maryhill Thistle	2	1	
2	Thorn Athletic	Paisley AFC	5	3	AET
2	UB United	Kilsyth AFC	5	4	
2	United Churches of Ayr	East Kilbride AFC	0	4	
2	Victoria Croftfoot	Plains	5	7	
2	Viewfield Rovers	Blantyre Celtic	0	13	
2	Wallacetoun	Dumbarton Academy FP	2	5	
2	Westcliff	Bridgend	1	2	
2	Westerlands "B"	Dunoon	2	3	
2	Westerlands AFC	River Nevis	5	1	
2	Windlaw	Milton AFC	2	5	
2	Winlinton Wolves	Cartsbridge Evangelical Church	7	2	
2	Woodhall Thistle	Glenburn Athletic	3	1	
2	Southside Accies	Neilston	2	4	
2	Calderglen AFC (SSMAFL)	Troon Dundonald	scr	wo	
2	Chapelhall	Condorrat	scr	wo	
2	Dennistoun Vale	Holytown Colts Youth	scr	wo	
2	Duntocher Hibs	Kilbowie Union	wo	scr	
2	Erskine Town	Rhu	scr	wo	
2	Gryffe Thistle	Ashvale Victoria	wo	scr	
2	Kilbarchan Thistle	Harestanes United	scr	wo	
2	Lanarkshire United	Milngavie	scr	wo	
2	Millerston Thistle	Glenburn MW	scr	wo	
2	Minishant	Moorpark Thistle	wo	scr	
2	Motherwell Thistle	Redbrae Athletic	wo	scr	
2	Rosneath	United Glasgow	scr	wo	

2	Uddingston Anvil	Prestwick	wo	scr	
2	Weir Recreation	Milton of Colquhoun	wo	scr	
2	West Stone	Duncanrig	scr	wo	
3	Barrhill AFC	Helensburgh AFC	4	3	
3	Broomhouse	East Kilbirde AFC	0	4	
3	Claremont	Arkleston Barrhead	3	1	
3	Clark Drive	West Kilbiride	1	2	
3	Clydeside Athletic	Calderglen AFC	2	1	
3	Colville Park	Westerlands	5	1	
3	Condorrat	Blochairn Star	0	10	
3	Cumbernauld Colts	Uddingston Anvil	5	4	
3	Cumnock AFC	Knockentiber AFC	2	0	
3	Daily AFC	Bridgewater AFC	2	6	
3	Duntocher Hibs AFC	Dumbarton Academy FP	1	2	
3	FC Argyle	Newton Vale	1	4	
3	Ferguslie Star	Westercommon Star	6	1	
3	Finnart	Bridgend AFC	4	0	
3	Glenburn MW	Dunoon AFC	5	4	
3	Greenock HSFP	AS Airdrie	2	1	
3	GSC Jordanhill	United Clydebank Supporters	5	3	
3	Harestanes	Eddlewood	3	1	
3	Kilbirnie AFC	Clydebank	1	3	
3	Kings ASFC	Ardrossan Castle Rovers	1	7	
3	Kings Park Rangers	Hampden AFC	0	4	
3	Largs Thistle AFC	Carrick	2	0	
3	Milton AFC	Lochgilphead Red Star	3	6	
3	Minishant	Kelvinbridge	1	5	
3	Motherwell Thistle	Campsie BW Waterside	1	2	
3	Neilston AFC	Possil YM	2	3	
3	New Meadow	Electric	2	0	
3	Paisley Caledonian	Crosshouse Waverley	1	2	
3	Plains	Gryffe Thistle	2	1	
3	Rannoch	Drongan United	2	0	
3	Shawbridge	Duncanrig	6	0	
3	Singer	Strathclyde University	3	6	aet
3	Southside	Harestanes United	5	0	
3	St Josephs	Glenvale	7	1	
3	St Mungos	Port GlasgowAFC	4	3	
3	Third Lanark	AFC Ravenscraig	2	3	
3	Troon Dundonald	Bengal Lancers	3	2	
3	United Glasgow AFC	Dirrans Athletic	1	9	
3	Wishaw Wycombe Wanderers	Hurlford Thistle	1	3	
3	Woodhall Thistle	Bargeddie	5	2	
3	Bannockburn AFC	Gartcosh United	2	0	
3	Campsie Minerva	East Kilbride Thistle AFC	5	2	
3	Erskine AFC	East Kilbride AFC	3	4	
3	Firhill United	BSC Glasgow AFC	3	0	
3	Glasgow Harp AFC	Rhu AFC	5	0	
3	Lomond Vale	Milngavie AFC	1	2	aet
3	Robslee	Shortlees	1	14	
3	St Patricks FPs	UB United	2	5	
3	Cardross	Fordbank Star	4	2	
3	Hamilton Wanderers	Holytown Colts	3	4	
3	Winlinton Wolves	Wishaw HSFP	0	5	
3	Alba Thistle	Drumchapel AFC	2	0	
3	Campsie	Cambria	1	6	
3	Fenwick Thistle	East Kilbride YM	1	7	
3	Kilmarnock AFC	Gourock Athletic	0	4	
3	Milngavie Wanderers	New Farm Loch	4	3	aet
3	St Patricks FPs (CSAFL)	Blairdardie	1	1	
3	Blantyre Celtic	Goldenhill	2	3	
3	Glasgow University	East Kilbride Rolls Royce	0	3	
3	Hamilton FP	Galston United	1	0	
3	Eastfield	Dalziel HSFP	2	1	aet
3	Oban Saints	Auchinleck Boswell	wo	scr	
3	Thorn Athletic	Southside Star	wo	scr	
3	Weir Recreation	Kilbride Thistle	scr	wo	
4	Bridgewater	Kilbride Thistle	4	0	
4	Campsie BW Waterside	AFC Ravenscraig	4	1	
4	Campsie Minerva	Cardross	11	2	
4	Crosshouse Waverley	Troon Dundonald	0	4	
4	Ferguslie Star	Harestanes United	1	3	
4	Glasgow Harp AFC	Strathclyde University	3	1	
4	GSC Jordanhill	Ardrossan Castle Rovers	2	4	
4	Kelvinbridge	Dumbarton Academy FP	1	2	
4	Lochgilphead Red Star	Claremont	2	1	
4	Milngavie Wanderers	Clydebank	1	2	
4	Plains	Clydeside Athletic	2	4	
4	Rannoch	Colville Park	0	4	
4	Shawbridge AFC	Barrhill	1	2	

4	Shortlees	Holytown Colts Youth	7	1	
4	Southside	Finnart	2	0	
4	St Josephs	Glenburn MW	3	1	
4	West Kilbride	New Meadow	6	1	
4	Wishaw HSFP	Woodhall Thistle	3	1	aet
4	Bannockburn AFC	Gourock Athletic	2	3	
4	Blochairn Star	Possil YM	7	3	
4	Cambria	Largs Thistle	5	2	
4	East Kilbride (SAFL)	Alba Thistle	4	2	aet
4	East Kilbride AFC (CSAFL)	Oban Saints	1	0	
4	Firhill United	St Patricks FPs (CSAFL)	1	2	
4	Greenock HSFP	UB United	11	1	
4	Milngavie Wanderers	East Kilbride YM	4	1	
4	Newton Vale	Dirrans Athletic	1	3	aet
4	St Mungos AFC	Cumnock AFC	1	3	
4	Cumbernauld Colts	Hamilton FP	4	1	
4	Hurlford Thistle	Goldenhill	3	2	
4	Eastfield	Hampden AFC	2	0	
4	East Kilbride Rolls Royce	Thorn Athletic	0	2	
5	Barrhill AFC	Greenock HSFP	2	7	
5	Clydebank AFC	Hurlford Thistle	0	3	
5	Colville Park	St Josephs	2	1	
5	Southside AFC	Cumbernauld Colts AFC	5	1	
5	Thorn Athletic	Harestanes	2	4	ae
5	Eastfield	Blochairn Star	2	2	ae
5	Ardrossan Castle Rovers	West Kilbride	1	3	
5	Campsie Minerva	Shortlees	2	0	
5	Clydeside Athletic	East Kilbride	0	3	
5	Dirrans Athletic	Glasgow Harp	4	3	
5	Dumbarton Academy FP	Bridgewater AFC	2	1	
5	East Kilbride (CSAFL)	Cumnock	4	2	
5	Lochgilphead Red Star	Cambria	1	4	
5	Milngavie Wanderers	Wishaw HSFP	1	2	
5	St Patricks FP	Gourock Athletic	5	5AET,	
5	Troon Dundonald	Camsie Blackwatch Waterside	0	5	
6	Campsie Minerva	Dirrans Athletic	3	0	
6	Dumbarton Academy FP	St Patrick's FP	1	2	
6	East Kilbride (CSAFL)	Campsie Blackwatch Waterside	7	2	
6	East Kilbride (SAFL)	Harestanes AFC	3	2	
6	Greenock HSFP	Hurlford Thistle	1	3	
6	Southside	West Kilbride	3	2	
6	Wishaw HSFP	Colville Park	scr	wo	
6	Cambria	Eastfield	5	3	a
7	Colville Park	East Kilbride (CSAFL)	2	0	
7	Hurlford Thistle	Southside	2	2	a
7	St Patrick's FP	Campsie Minerva	3	2	
7	Cambria	East Kilbride (SAFL)	1	0	
SF	Southside	St Patrick's FP	2	0	
	at Hamilton	Att 321			
SF	Colville Park	Cambria	0	1	
	at Hamilton	Att 308			
F	Southside	Cambria	0	1	
	at Hamilton	Att 525			

EAST OF SCOTLAND AMATEUR CUP

Rd	Home	Away	F	A
1	Bank of Scotland Strollers	Armadale Rose	1	5
1	Barca Milton 97	Heriot Watt University	5	2
1	Bo'ness Cadora	Edinburgh City	7	0
1	Bonnybridge YFP	Kincardine	1	0
1	Cavalry Park	Fauldhouse	1	0
1	Central Albion	Sporting ICAPB	1	2
1	Clermiston Star	Stirling Colts	6	1
1	Denny AFC	Slamannan AFC	1	3
1	Dunedin Athletic	Craigroyston CYFC	2	3
1	Edinburgh Harp	Beechwood Albion	0	2
1	Greentree	Waverley Athletic	6	2
1	Inter Edinburgh	Civil Service Strollers	5	0

1	Laurieston	Linlithgow Thistle	0	14	
1	Maddiston	Ferneiside	3	2	
1	Mill Inn	Forth Thistle	3	2	
1	Riverside	North Merchiston Vale	2	3	
1	Salvesen	Laurieston Thistle	12	0	
1	Spartans	Camelon Albion	1	3	
1	St Bernards	Redhall Star	2	0	
1	Tullibody Community	Stirling AFC	8	0	
1	Stirling City	Stenhousemuir Community	2	3	
1	Craigshill Thistle	Polmont Community	5	2	
1	Doune Castle (S&D)	Portobello Thistle	0	2	
1	Grangemouth Rovers	Pennies	0	6	
1	Edinburgh South	Sunnyside Thistle	wo	scr	
1	Greenhill	Fallin	scr	wo	
2	Bathgate Thistle	Edina Hibs	2	1	
2	Clackmannan Community	Beechwood Albion	3	4	
2	Dollar Glen	Callander Thistle	2	3	
2	Dunblane Soccer Club	Carronshore Athletic	1	1	AET, 4-5p
2	East Calder United	Musselburgh AFC	3	1	
2	Edinburgh South Vics	Greentree	3	1	
2	Edinburgh Star	Clermiston Star	3	2	
2	Hermiston Vale	Stirling Universityt	5	0	
2	Inter Edinburgh	Armadale Rose	3	4	
2	Linlithgow Thistle	Edinburgh Rose	3	1	
2	Lochend	Craigroyston CYFC	6	0	
2	Maddiston	Edinburgh Thistle	1	0	
2	Mill Inn	Syngenta	0	5	
2	Newcraighall Leith Vics	Edinburgh University	2	1	
2	North Edinburgh Wanderers	Doune Castle (Cal)	3	8	
2	Salters Athletic	St Bernards	4	5	
2	Salvesen	Dunblane Thistle	2	1	
2	Slamannan Albion	Redpath Albion	0	1	
2	Sporting ICAPB	Cambusbarron Rovers	2	11	
2	Stirling Boys Club	Drumpellier Thistle	2	3	
2	Stirling City	Stenhousemuir Community	2	3	
2	Tollcross Thistle	Edinburgh South	3	0	
2	Bo'ness Cadora	North Merchiston Vale	4	3	
2	Bonnybridge YFP	Armadale Thistle	3	1	
2	Camelon Albion	Tillicoultry	3	0	
2	Craigshill Thistle	Tullibody Community	5	1	
2	Fallin	Linlithgow Rose Community	4	2	AET
2	Portobello Thistle	Balerno Athletic	1	0	
2	Steins Thistle	Cavalry Park	4	0	
2	Westfield Colts	Loganlea United	0	8	
2	Blackridge Vale of Craig	Pennies	0	2	
2	Hutchison Vale	Barca Milton 97	scr	wo	
3	Salvesen	Pennies	4	1	
3	Tollcross Thistle	Camelon Albion	3	2	
3	Armadale Rose	Stenhousemuir Community	0	9	
3	Bathgate Thistle	Hermiston Vale	0	2	
3	Bo'ness Cadora	Newcraighall Leith Vics	4	2	
3	Callander Thistle	Beechwood Albion	3	0	
3	Cambusbarron Rovers	Maddiston	3	3	9-8p
3	Barca Milton 67	Carronshore Athletic	5	2	
3	Craigshill Thistle	Linlithgow Thistle	3	2	
3	Doune Cstle (Cal)	Fallin	3	2	
3	East Calder United	Bonnybridge YFP	2	4	
3	Edinburgh Star	Redpath Albion	4	2	
3	Lochend	Portobello Thistle	6	0	
3	Loganlea United	Edinburgh South Vics	1	2	
3	St Bernards	Steins Thistle	3	4	
3	Syngenta	Drumpellier Thistle	5	1	
4	Barca Milton 67	Edinburgh South Vics	1	2	
4	Bonnybridge YFP	Cambusbarron Rovers	3	2	
4	Craigshill Thistle	Bo'ness Cadora	3	0	
4	Salvesens	Callander Thistle	4	1	
4	Stenhousemuir Community	Edinburgh Star	3	2	
4	Syngenta	Hermiston Vale	3	1	
4	Tollcross Thistle	Steins Thistle	6	0	
4	Lochend	Doune Castle	4	3	
5	Edinburgh South Vics	Tollcross Thistle	1	3	
5	Syngenta	Salvesen	2	3	
5	Lochend	Craigshill Thistle	1	7	
5	Bonnybridge YFP	Stenhousemuir Community	1	2	
SF	Craigshill Thistle	Salvesen	2	3	
	at Blackburn Utd				
SF	Stenhousemuir Community	Tollcross Thistle	2	3	
	at Spartans FC				
F	Tollcross Thistle	Salvesen	3	4	
	at Livingston FC				

NORTH OF SCOTLAND AMATEUR CUP

Rd	Home	Away	F	A	
1	Balmedie	Burghmuir	1	3	
1	Fintray Thistle	Echt	0	8	
1	Newtonhill	McTeagle	9	2	
1	Nicolls	Kintore	1	3	
2	Auchnagatt Barons	Banchory	3	5	
2	Beacon Rangers	BS	2	1	
2	Dyce ITC Hydraulics	West End	1	2	
2	Huntly	Bervie Caledonian	3	6	AET
2	Monymusk	Glendale XI	2	4	AET
2	Rothie Rovers	Ellon Thistle	4	2	
2	Sportsmans Club	AC Mill Inn	3	2	AET
2	Aboyne	Tarves	0	5	
2	Alford	MS United	2	2	AET, 5-4p
2	Blackburn	Rattrays XI	4	3	AET
2	Bon Accord City	Westdyke	1	5	
2	Bon Accord Thistle	Great Western United	1	9	
2	Burghmuir	Glendale Youth	7	3	
2	Cammachmore	Formartine United	3	2	
2	Colony Park	Cove Thistle	2	6	
2	Cowie Thistle	Westdyce	6	1	
2	Echt	JS XI	3	2	
2	Glendale	Kincorth	4	2	
2	Halliburton	Faithlie United	2	1	
2	Highland Hotel	University	0	1	
2	Kaimhill United	Insch	0	6	
2	Kemnay Youth	Torphins	0	1	
2	Lads Club	Robert Gordon University	0	5	
2	Newburgh Thistle	Glenmtanar Reflex	3	1	
2	St Laurence	Ellon Thistle	3	2	
2	Stoneywood east End	Feughside	6	2	AET
2	Theologians NE	Kintore	3	4	
2	Torry	Postal ALC	5	2	
2	Westhill	Tolbooth	3	0	
2	Woodside	Newtonhill	6	2	
2	AFC Murdo's	Stonehaven Athletic	sc	wo	
2	Granite City	Turriff Thistle	w	scr	
3	Beacon Rangers	Cove Thistle	4	2	AET
3	Cammachmore	Bervie Caledonian	2	5	
3	Westhill	Westdyke	2	1	AET
3	Woodside	Glendale	3	1	
3	Robert Gordon Univers	Torry	1	3	
3	St Laurence	Torphins	7	0	
3	Stonehaven Athletic	Stoneywood East End	0	3	
3	Alford	Rothie Rovers	0	3	
3	Blackburn	Insch	2	5	
3	Burghmuir	Banchory	3	2	
3	Echt	University	2	1	
3	Great Western United	Kintore	6	2	
3	Halliburton	Granite City	1	3	
3	Tarves	West End	6	2	AET
3	Cowie Thistle	Newburgh Thistle	0	4	
3	Glendale XI	Sportsmans Club	3	4	
4	Echt	Woodside	1	3	
4	Granite City	Great Western United	5	3	
4	Newburgh Thistle	Burghmuir	6	1	
4	Rothie Rovers	Stoneywood East End	4	3	
4	Sportsmans Club	Bervie Caledonian	4	4	AET, 3-4p
4	St Laurence	Torry Amateurs	2	2	AET, 1-3p
4	Tarves	Beacon Rangers	2	0	
4	Westhill	Insch	5	2	AET
5	Bervie Caledonian	Woodside	1	3	
5	Granite City	Newburgh Thistle	0	1	
5	Westhill	Rothie Rovers	3	0	
5	Tarves	Torry	2	3	
SF	Torry	Newburgh Thistle	2	4	aet
	at Newburgh				
SF	Westhill	Woodside	2	4	
	at Newburgh				
F	Newburgh Thistle	Woodside	5	2	
	at Formartine Utd				

SCOTTISH SUNDAY AMATEUR TROPHY 2016/17

1W	Airdrie United Reds AFC (A&CAFL) 2-1 Townhead Thistle AFC (SCAFL)
1W	Annan Town AFC (Dumfries Sunday AFL) 2-1 Redbridge Rovers AFC (A&CAFL)
1W	Baillieston Boys Club AFC (A&CAFL) 10-0 AFC Whitehirst (ASAFA)
1W	Bobby's Bar AFC (ASAFA) 2-6 Normandy Star AFC (Dumfries Sunday AFL)
1W	Broadwood Clyde AFC (SCAFL) 0-3 Polonia Glasgow AFC (SCAFL)
1W	Cambuslang Football Academy AFC (SCAFL) 1-1 Eastend Tower AFC (SCAFL) (4-2 pens)
1W	Carluke Thistle AFC (SCAFL) 7-4 Kirkintilloch Rob Roy AFC (SCAFL)
1W	Carluke Victoria AFC (SCAFL) 1-6 Bullfrog AFC (A&CAFL)
1W	Castlemilk Dynamo AFC (SCAFL) 16-0 Killie Athletic AFC (ASAFA)
1W	Cellar Bar Colts AFC (A&CAFL) 1-6 Crownpoint United AFC (SCAFL)
1W	Charlie's Bar AFC (ASAFA) 6-0 Bellshill Athletic AFC (A&CAFL)
1W	Clyde Thistle AFC (A&CAFL) wo-scr Cranhill United AFC (SCAFL)
1W	Coatbridge Cumbernauld Infinity AFC (A&CAFL) 5-3 Airdrie Athletic AFC (A&CAFL)
1W	Coatbridge United AFC (A&CAFL) 10-0 Budhill United AFC (SCAFL)
1W	Croftfoot AFC (SCAFL) 1-2 PFD AFC (SCAFL)
1W	Eastend United AFC (A&CAFL) 5-4 South Lanarkshire Ravens AFC (SCAFL)
1W	Eastfield Star AFC (SCAFL) 6-5 Alpha AFC (A&CAFL)
1W	EKYM AFC (SCAFL) wo-scr Burnbank AFC (A&CAFL)
1W	Forgewood AFC (A&CAFL) 6-3 FC Annan (Dumfries Sunday AFL)
1W	Glasgow City Academy AFC (SCAFL) 3-7 Gorbals United AFC (SCAFL)
1W	Glasgow Rovers AFC (SCAFL) wo-scr Smiths Albion AFC (A&CAFL)
1W	Haldane United AFC (SCAFL) 3-2 Airdrie Albion AFC (A&CAFL)
1W	Hole in the Wa AFC (Dumfries Sunday AFL) 8-3 Dalry Tartan AFC (ASAFA)
1W	Irvine No.1 CSC AFC (ASAFA) 1-5 Haghill AFC (SCAFL)
1W	Irvine Victoria AFC (ASAFA) 6-6 Brunswick AFC (SCAFL), 4-5 pens
1W	Kilbirnie United AFC (ASAFA) 1-5 Albion AFC (SCAFL)
1W	Kilmarnock Supporters AFC (ASAFA) 9-0 Kelloholm Arms AFC (Dumfries Sunday AFL)
1W	Lanarkshire AFC (SCAFL) 3-5 AFC Coltness United (A&CAFL)
1W	Lochgreen AFC (A&CAFL) 6-2 Burgh AFC (A&CAFL)
1W	Loreburn Thistle AFC (Dumfries Sunday AFL) 2-5 Moffat Thistle 2010 AFC (Dumfries Sunday AFL)
1W	Morton Youth AFC (Dumfries Sunday AFL) 1-7 Springhall Spartans AFC (SCAFL)
1W	New Stevenston United AFC (SCAFL) 8-0 Glasgow Athletic AFC (SCAFL)
1W	Newarthill Athletic AFC (A&CAFL) 3-7 Greengairs Dynamo AFC (A&CAFL)
1W	Newmains United AFC (SCAFL) 0-2 Hillview AFC (SCAFL)
1W	Northend AFC (SCAFL) 5-3 Five Arches Bombers AFC (Dumfries Sunday AFL)
1W	Queens Bar AFC (Dumfries Sunday AFL) 1-4 Condorrat Weavers AFC (A&CAFL)
1W	Red Stars Baagrade AFC (SCAFL) 2-4 Bellshill United AFC (A&CAFL)
1W	Ruthwell Rovers AFC (Dumfries Sunday AFL) wo-scr Bourtreehill AFC (ASAFA)
1W	Sauchie AFC (SCAFL) 3-2 Palmerston Colts AFC (Dumfries Sunday AFL)
1W	Scaur AFC (Dumfries Sunday AFL) 4-5 Lanarkshire Forrest AFC (SCAFL)
1W	Shawfield Wednesday AFC (SCAFL) 0-14 Overlees Partizans AFC (SCAFL)
1W	Shotts Albion AFC (A&CAFL) 7-0 Castlehill Vaults AFC (ASAFA)
1W	Sporting Pumas AFC (SCAFL) 4-0 Fernhill United AFC (SCAFL)
1W	Summerhill AFC (Dumfries Sunday AFL) 3-4 Galloway Wanderers AFC (SSAFA)
1W	The Craft AFC (ASAFA) 5-0 Glasgow Rangers AFC (SCAFL)
1W	Treble Two AFC (SCAFL) P-P Rosehill Thistle AFC (SCAFL)
1W	Unity AFC (A&CAFL) 2-4 Elms AFC (ASAFA)
1W	Waverley AFC (A&CAFL) 7-0 Eastend Thistle AFC (A&CAFL)
1W	Wishaw Athletic AFC (A&CAFL) 3-3 Dumfries Athletic AFC (Dumfries Sunday AFL) (6-5 pens)
1W	13 byes
1E	AC Midlothian AFC (LEAFA Sunday) 3-3 Pumpherston Thistle AFC (LEAFA Sunday) (4-5 pens)
1E	Armadale United AFC (WLSAFL) 2-3 Dunalba AFC (LEAFA Sunday)
1E	Blackburn Allstars AFC (WLSAFL) scr-wo Westquarter AFC (FVAFA)
1E	Blairhall Village Bar AFC (FVAFA) 7-1 FC Braes 04 (WLSAFL)
1E	Bo'ness AFC (WLSAFL) 2-1 Lochore Castle AFC (FSAFL)
1E	Bo'ness Athletic AFC (FVAFA) 8-4 St. Bernards AFC (LEAFA Sunday)
1E	Broxburn AFC (LEAFA Sunday) 4-3 Newtongrange Star Academy AFC (LEAFA Sunday)
1E	Burnside Athletic AFC (WLSAFL) 2-4 Jokers AFC (FSAFL)
1E	Carron Valley AFC (WLSAFL) 5-2 Crystal Barcelona AFC (FSAFL)

1E	Civil Service Strollers AFC (LEAFA Sunday) wo-scr Rosewell Miners AFC (LEAFA Sunday)
1E	Club Livingston AFC (WLSAFL) 3-3 Brucefield AFC (FSAFL) (5-4 pens)
1E	Corstrophine Dynamo AFC (LEAFA Sunday) 3-3 Styx AFC (FSAFL) (10-9 pens)
1E	Craigshill Thistle AFC (WLSAFL) 5-0 Crown Inn AFC (FSAFL)
1E	Duddingston Athletic AFC (LEAFA Sunday) 7-3 Meadowbank Wednesday AFC (LEAFA Sunday)
1E	East Calder United AFC (WLSAFL) 1-0 Armadale Thistle AFC (LEAFA Sunday)
1E	Eddy's Bar AFC (FSAFL) 2-2 Lauders AFC (FSAFL) (2-3 pens)
1E	Edinburgh Caledonian AFC (LEAFA Sunday) 5-1 Dalkeith Athletic AFC (LEAFA Sunday)
1E	Grangemouth United AFC (FVAFA) 1-1 Dunfermline United AFC (FSAFL) (5-4 pens)
1E	Horseshoe Bar AFC (FVAFA) 1-9 Harvester AFC (WLSAFL)
1E	Kennoway AFC (FSAFL) 3-3 Livingston Community AFC (WLSAFL) (3-1 pens)
1E	Krossbar AFC (WLSAFL) 0-8 Blackburn United AFC (WLSAFL)
1E	Limekilns AFC (FSAFL) 1-3 Royal Penicuik AFC (LEAFA Sunday)
1E	Livingston North AFC (WLSAFL) 3-1 Brunswick United AFC (FVAFA)
1E	Lochend Star AFC (LEAFA Sunday) 6-2 Livingston Star AFC (WLSAFL)
1E	Longstone United AFC (LEAFA Sunday) 1-4 Templehall Tavern AFC (FSAFL)
1E	Macmerry Miners Atheltic AFC (LEAFA Sunday) 5-1 Burgh Vale AFC (LEAFA Sunday)
1E	Maltings AFC (FSAFL) 5-1 FC ingolstadt Kirkcaldy (FSAFL)
1E	McPhails AFC (FSAFL) 0-4 Meadowbank AFC (LEAFA Sunday)
1E	Meadowpark Thistle Community AFC (WLSAFL) 1-6 Dykehead AFC (WLSAFL)
1E	Minto Lounge AFC (FSAFL) 5-1 Partizan AFC (LEAFA Sunday)
1E	Mitchells AFC (LEAFA Sunday) 4-0 North Merchiston AFC (LEAFA Sunday)
1E	Polton Inn AFC (LEAFA Sunday) 2-3 Coadys AFC (FSAFL)
1E	Rivals AFC (LEAFA Sunday) 0-1 Hibeernian AFC (LEAFA Sunday)
1E	Roseburn Thistle AFC (LEAFA Sunday) 2-6 Novar Rovers AFC (FSAFL)
1E	Roslin Da Vinci AFC (LEAFA Sunday) 2-7 Vittoria Group AFC (LEAFA Sunday)
1E	Salters Athletic AFC (LEAFA Sunday) 5-2 Athetico Central AFC (FSAFL)
1E	Thornybank Thistle AFC (LEAFA Sunday) 0-11 Dalkeith Thistle AFC (LEAFA Sunday)
1E	Torbothie Rose AFC (WLSAFL) 17-1 Pentland Thistle AFC (LEAFA Sunday)
1E	Torleys AFC (FSAFL) 1-6 Raploch Hearts AFC (FVAFA)
1E	Tranent Athletic AFC (LEAFA Sunday) 3-4 Highland Park AFC (WLSAFL)
1E	West Lothian Albion AFC (WLSAFL) 5-3 Royal Oak AFC (FVAFA)
1E	Westside AFC (LEAFA Sunday) 3-0 West End United AFC (LEAFA Sunday)
1E	Whitehackle AFC (LEAFA Sunday) 2-2 Craigentinny AFC (LEAFA Sunday) (2-4 pens)
1E	15 byes
1NT	Dundee Argyle AFC (DSAFA) 10-3 Annfield AFC (DSAFA)
1NT	Dundee Social Club AFC (DSAFA) 7-2 Charlie Accies AFC (DSAFA)
1NT	Kirkton Athletic AFC (DSAFA) scr-wo FC Polonia Dundee (DSAFA)
1NT	1 bye
1N	MN United AFC (ASAFL) 2-2 GB United AFC (ASAFL) (4-5 pens)
1N	3 byes
2	AFC Coltness United (A&CAFL) 2-4 Coatbridge United (A&CAFL)
2	Airdrie United Reds (A&CAFL) 6-1 Ruthwell Rovers (Dumfries Sunday AFL)
2	Bathville Thistle (WLSAFL) 1-13 Baillieston Boys Club (A&CAFL)
2	Bellshill United (A&CAFL) 7-4 Galloway Wanderers (SSAFA)
2	Blackburn United (WLSAFL) w/o-scr Forgewood (A&CAFL)
2	Blairhall Village Bar (FVAFA) 0-2 Crownpoint United (SCAFL)
2	Bo'ness (WLSAFL) 2-4 Brunswick (SCAFL)
2	Bo'ness Athletic (FVAFA) 1-1 Grangemouth United (FVAFA) (7-6 pens)
2	Broxburn (LEAFA Sunday) 2-6 Bullfrog (A&CAFL)
2	Cambuslang Football Academy (SCAFL) w/o-scr EKYM (SCAFL)
2	Carron Valley (WLSAFL) 6-2 Castlemilk United (SCAFL)
2	Civil Service Strollers (LEAFA Sunday) 0-3 Haldane United (SCAFL)
2	Coatbridge Cumbernauld Infinity (A&CAFL) 9-1 Clyde Thistle (A&CAFL)
2	Craigentinny (LEAFA Sunday) 4-2 Glenrothes Rovers (FSAFL)
2	Craigshill Thistle (WLSAFL) P-P Livingston North (WLSAFL)
2	Dalkeith Thistle (LEAFA Sunday) 4-2 Bardykes Rovers 2016 (SCAFL)
2	Direct Savings (WLSAFL) scr-w/o Rosehill Thorns (SCAFL)
2	Duddingston Athletic (LEAFA Sunday) 3-` Inverdee (ASAFL)
2	Dundee Argyle (DSAFA) 2-1 Northend (SCAFL)
2	Dykehead (WLSAFL) 5-0 Cross 108 (WLSAFL)
2	Eastfield Star (SCAFL) 1-9 Overlee Partizans (SCAFL)
2	Edinburgh Caledonian (LEAFA Sunday) 4-1 Victoria Rovers (FSAFL)
2	Edinburgh City (LEAFA Sunday) 3-5 Jokers (FSAFL)

2	Elms (ASAFA) w/o-scr Paisley Star (SCAFL)
2	FC Polonia Dundee (DSAFA) 2-4 Glasgow Rovers (SCAFL)
2	GB United (ASAFL) 3-5 Charlie's Bar (ASAFA)
2	Gorbals United (SCAFL) 3-3 Club Livingston (WLSAFL) (11-10 pens)
2	Harvester (WLSAFL) 7-0 Calderside (SCAFL)
2	Highland Park (WLSAFL) 3-7 Westquarter (FVAFA)
2	Hole in the Wa (Dumfries Sunday AFL) 3-1 Corstrophine Dynamo (LEAFA Sunday)
2	Kennoway (FSAFL) 5-1 Westside (LEAFA Sunday)
2	Kilmarnock Supporters (ASAFA) 4-1 Kilwinning Sunday (ASAFA)
2	Kilsyth Rovers (SCAFL) 1-11 Dundee Social Club (DSAFA)
2	Kincardine Colts (FVAFA) 8-2 Bon Accord (ASAFL)
2	Lanarkshire Forrest (SCAFL) 2-4 Annan Town (Dumfries Sunday AFL)
2	Lauders (FSAFL) 4-1 Edinburgh East (LEAFA Sunday)
2	Lochend Star (LEAFA Sunday) 2-3 Normandy Star (Dumfries Sunday AFL)
2	Lochgreen (A&CAFL) 3-4 Raploch Hearts (FVAFA)
2	Macmerry Miners Athletic (LEAFA Sunday) 2-3 East Calder United (WLSAFL)
2	Maltings (FSAFL) 2-2 The Craft (ASAFA) (7-6 pens)
2	Meadowbank (LEAFA Sunday) 5-0 Eastend United (A&CAFL)
2	Moffat Thistle 2010 (Dumfries Sunday AFL) 3-3 Coadys (FSAFL) (4-3 pens)
2	Motherwell Villa (A&CAFL) 2-3 Whitburn Newton (WLSAFL)
2	Novar Rovers (FSAFL) 4-5 Sporting Pumas (SCAFL)
2	Ochil (FVAFA) 3-10 Greengairs Dynamo (A&CAFL)
2	PFD (SCAFL) 5-0 Park Thistle (Dumfries Sunday AFL)
2	Polonia Glasgow (SCAFL) 2-8 Hillview (SCAFL)
2	Pumpherston Thistle (LEAFA Sunday) 0-7 Minto Lounge (FSAFL)
2	Rolling Barrel (A&CAFL) 10-0 Hibeernian (LEAFA Sunday)
2	Rutherglen Rovers (SCAFL) 0-8 Haghill (SCAFL)
2	Salters Athletic (LEAFA Sunday) 5-3 Gartferry (SCAFL)
2	Sauchie (SCAFL) v Carousel United (FSAFL)
2	Shotts Albion (A&CAFL) 1-7 Castlemilk Dynamo (SCAFL)
2	Sky (FSAFL) 6-3 Mitchells (LEAFA Sunday)
2	Springhall Spartans (SCAFL) 6-2 Albion (SCAFL)
2	Steadings (FSAFL) 5-3 Well Foundation (A&CAFL)
2	Tayport (DSAFA) P-P Stables (LEAFA Sunday)
2	Templehall Tavern (FSAFL) 3-4 Carluke Thistle (SCAFL)
2	Torbothie Rose (WLSAFL)7-3 Royal Penicuik (LEAFA Sunday)
2	Treble Two (SCAFL) 4-1 Dunalba (LEAFA Sunday)
2	Vittoria Group (LEAFA Sunday) 4-1 MLK Aberdeen (ASAFL)
2	Waverley (A&CAFL) 5-1 Condorrat Weavers (A&CAFL)
2	West Lothian Albion (WLSAFL) 1-6 New Stevenston United (SCAFL)
2	Wishaw Athletic (A&CAFL) 2-4 Tamfourhill United (WLSAFL)
3	Sporting Pumas (SCAFL) 5-3 Vittoria Group (LEAFA Sunday)
3	Dykehead (WLSAFL) 5-0 Carron Valley (WLSAFL)
3	Coatbridge United (A&CAFL) 3-1 Cambuslang Football Academy (SCAFL)
3	Torbothie Rose (WLSAFL) 5-1 East Calder United (WLSAFL)
3	PFD (SCAFL) 2-4 Baillieston Boys Club (A&CAFL)
3	Whitburn Newtown (WLSAFL) 7-0 Bellshill United (A&CAFL)
3	Greengairs Dynamo (A&CAFL) 6-2 Bo'ness Athletic (FVAFA)
3	Westquarter (FVAFA) 4-1 Maltings (FSAFL)
3	Rosehill Thorns (SCAFL) 3-4 Normandy Star (Dumfries Sunday AFL)
3	Haldane United (SCAFL) 3-7 Haghill (SCAFL)
3	Meadowbank (LEAFA Sunday) 4-2 Duddingston Athletic (LEAFA Sunday)
3	Bullfrog (A&CAFL) 6-2 Rolling Barrel (A&CAFL)
3	Blackburn United (WLSAFL) 3-1 Salters Athletic (LEAFA Sunday)
3	Gorbals United (SCAFL) 3-3 Edinburgh Caledonian (LEAFA Sunday), 4-2 pens
3	Harvester (WLSAFL) 4-1 Minto Lounge (FSAFL)
3	Tamfourhill United (WLSAFL) 4-1 Carluke Thistle (SCAFL)
3	Raploch Hearts (FVAFA) 7-1 Coatbridge Cumbernauld Infinity (A&CAFL)
3	Sky (FSAFL) 2-2 Springhall Spartans (SCAFL), 3-5 pems
3	Dundee Social Club (DSAFA) 3-2 Charlie's Bar (ASAFA)
3	Kilmarnock Supporters (ASAFA) 1-4 Waverley (A&CAFL)
3	Hole in the Wa' (Dumfries Sunday AFL) 1-2 Airdrie United Reds (A&CAFL)
3	Hillview (SCAFL) 7-1 Crownpoint United (SCAFL)
3	Glasgow Rovers (SCAFL) 1-3 Moffat Thistle 2010 (Dumfries Sunday AFL)

3	Steadings (FSAFL) 1-1 Kincardine Colts (FVAFA), 7-6 pens
3	Treble Two (SCAFL) 1-1 Tayport (DSAFA), 1-4 pens
3	Craigentinny (LEAFA Sunday) VOID Westside (LEAFA Sunday)
3	Castlemilk Dynamo (SCAFL) 0-2 Dundee Argyle (DSAFA)
3	Overlee Partizans (SCAFL) 5-2 Jokers (FSAFL)
3	Carousel United (FSAFL) 0-6 Dalkeith Thistle (LEAFA Sunday)
3	Lauders (FSAFL) 11-0 Elms (ASAFA)
3	Craigshill Thistle (WLSAFL) 1-1 New Stevenston United (SCAFL), 4-3 pens
3	Annan Town (Dumfries Sunday AFL) 2-4 Brunswick (SCAFL)
4	Airdrie United Reds AFC (A&CAFL) 2-6 Tamfourhill United AFC (WLSAFL)
4	Baillieston Boys Club AFC (A&CAFL) 1-3 Coatbridge United AFC (A&CAFL)
4	Dalkeith Thistle AFC (LEAFA Sunday) wo-scr Hillview AFC (SCAFL)
4	Gorbals United AFC (SCAFL) 0-4 Waverley AFC (A&CAFL)
4	Greengairs Dynamo AFC (A&CAFL) 4-7 Westquarter AFC (FVAFA)
4	Haghill AFC (SCAFL) 1-2 Dykehead AFC (WLSAFL)
4	Harvester AFC (WLSAFL) 5-2 Springhall Spartans AFC (SCAFL)
4	Lauders AFC (FSAFL) 4-2 Moffat Thistle 2010 AFC (Dumfries Sunday AFL)
4	Meadowbank AFC (LEAFA Sunday) 0-1 Dundee Argyle AFC (DSAFA)
4	Overlee Partizans AFC (SCAFL) 4-1 Bullfrog AFC (A&CAFL)
4	Raploch Hearts AFC (FVAFA) 4-3 Normandy Star AFC (Dumfries Sunday AFL)
4	Sporting Pumas AFC (SCAFL) 3-3 Whitburn Newtown AFC (WLSAFL), 4-2 pens
4	Tayport (DSAFA) 2-2 Craigshill Thistle (WLSAFL), 4-3 pens
4	Torbothie Rose AFC (WLSAFL) 3-0 Steadings AFC (FSAFL)
4	Brunswick AFC (SCAFL) BYE
4	Dundee Social Club AFC (DSAFA) 0-0 Blackburn United AFC (WLSAFL), 1-3 pens
5	Blackburn United 1-4 Overlee Partizans
5	Lauders 2-2 Sporting Pumas, 3-5 pens
5	Dundee Argyle 3-2 Brunswick
5	Dalkeith Thistle 2-2 Coatbridge United, 4-3 pens
5	Waverley 3-1 Tamfourhill United
5	Torbothie Rose 1-5 Harvester
5	Raploch Hearts 4-1 Tayport
5	Dykehead 3-2 Westquarter
6	Raploch Hearts 2-3 Harvester
6	Dalkeith Thistle 2-2 Sporting Pumas, 5-4 pens
6	Waverley 0-3 Dykehead
6	Overlee Partizans 1-4 Dundee Argyle
SF	Dykehead 2-2 Dundee Argyle, 3-2 pens at Airdrieonians FC
SF	Dalkeith Thistle 1-6 Harvester, at Stenhousemir FC
F	Dykehead 0-4 Harvester, April 30th, at Livingston FC

SCOTTISH AMATEUR FA - PREVIOUS CUP WINNERS

	West	East	North of Tay	Fife
1923/24	Moorpark Ams			
1924/25	Greenock HSFP			
1925/26	Moorpark Ams			
1926/27	Whitehall Athletic			
1927/28	Castings Ams			
1928/29	Greenock HSFP		YMCA Anchorage	
1929/30	Greenock HSFP		Hillcrest	
1930/31	Pointhouse		Aeros (Leuchars)	
1931/32	Glasgow University		Woodside Rangers	Burntisland Shipyard
1932/33	Queen's Park		Pittenweem Rangers	Bishopshire Swifts
1933/34	Mavor's XI		YMCA Anchorage	Glencraig Victoria
1934/35	Camphill Sec School FP		Pittenweem Rovers	St Andrews University
1935/36	Glasgow Corporation Transport		St Monance Swifts	Crail
1936/37	Greenock HSFP		Pittenweem Rovers	Pittenweem Rovers
1937/38	Coats Ams		RAF Leuchars	Freuchie Rovers
1938/39	Cartha Athletic		Harris Academy FP	Pittenweem Rovers
1945/46	Queen's Park		Lochee Ams	Burntisland Shipyard
1946/47	Queen's Park		YMCA Anchorage	Gallatown
1947/48	Rothesay Brandane	Edinburgh University	Ashdale	Milton Violet
1948/49	Laidlaw Ams	Civil Service Strollers	YMCA Anchorage	Victoria Swifts
1949/50	Queen's Park	Torphichen Ams	YMCA Anchorage	Boreland
1950/51	Govan Ams	Eastern Ams	YMCA Anchorage	Ladybank Violet
1951/52	Gartsherrie United	Dalkeith Ams	YMCA Anchorage	Ladybank Violet
1952/53	Babcock & Wilcox	Cobbinshaw Rovers	Kinrossie	Boreland
1953/54	Albion Motors	Cobbinshaw Rovers	Windsor	Thornton Loco
1954/55	Albion Motors	Cobbinshaw Rovers	Invergowrie	Thornton Loco
1955/56	Queen's Park	Lorwood AFC	YMCA Anchorage	Boreland
1956/57	Shell Amateurs	Pathead AFC	Windsor	Thornton Loco
1957/58	Muirend Ams	Orphan Hospital AFC	YMCA Anchorage	St Andrews University
1958/59	Kilmacolm AFC	Lorwood AFC	YMCA Anchorage	Cupar YM
1959/60	Crosshill Thistle	Pathead AFC	Ballinluig	Westwood Wanderers
1960/61	Queen's Park	Grangemouth Refinery	NCR	Nairn Star
1961/62	Glenavon	Winchburgh Albion	NCR	Westwood Wanderers
1962/63	Lincluden Swifts	West Lothian Steel Foundry	Ballinluig	Nairn Star
1963/64	Fenwick Thistle	Lorwood AFC	NCR	St Monance Swallows
1964/65	Lincluden Swifts	Edinburgh Albion	NCR	St Monance Swallows
1965/66	Minishant	Blackrodge Welfare	Withheld	Cambusbarron Rovers
1966/67	Vale of Girvan	Lorwood AFC	NCR	Cambusbarron Rovers
1967/68	Vale of Girvan	Lorwood AFC	Westgrove Albion	Star Hearts
1968/69	Bishopton AFC	Lorwood AFC	NCR	Star Hearts
1969/70	Fenwick Thistle	Bilston AFC	Broughty United	Star Hearts
1970/71	Douglas Ams	Cambusbarron Rovers	Newtyle Hearts	Star Hearts
1971/72	Morriston YMCA	Pathead AFC	Errol	St Monance Swallows
1972/73	Clyde United	Links United	Hillside BC	Methil United
1973/74	Knockentiber	Whitson Star	Auchterhouse	Star Hearts
1974/75	Morriston YMCA	Whitson Star	Auchterhouse	Star Hearts
1975/76	Nithsdale	Bilston MW	Auchterhouse	Star Hearts

	West	East	North of Tay	Fife
976/77	Weir Recreation	Pencaitland	Auchterhouse	Hill of Beath Hawthorn
77/78	Morriston YMCA	Pencaitland	Auchterhouse	Windygates
978/79	Newarthill Hearts	Pencaitland	Riverside Athletic	Star Hearts
979/80	Muirend Ams	Windsor AFC	Harris Academy FP	Windygates
80/81	Cambusbarron Rovers	Telman Star	SMT	Norton House
81/82	Westerlands	Bilston Colliery	Harris Academy FP	Strathmiglo United
82/83	Bannockburn Ams	Milton Ams	Fintry	Star Hearts
83/84	Initial Star	Cropley AFC	Harris Academy FP	Norton House
84/85	Hyster	Bilston Cropley	Harris Academy FP	Ballingry Rovers
85/86	Muirend Ams	Bilston Cropley	Riverside Athletic	Strathmiglo United
86/87	Drumchapel AFC	Lothian Thistle	Lawside FP	Norton House
87/88	Coatbridge CC	Liberton Cropley	Lawside FP	Hill of Beath Ramblers
88/89	Knightswood AFC	Telman Star	Riverside Athletic	Norton House
89/90	Clark Drive	Liberton Cropley	Riverside Athletic	Burntisland Shipyard
90/91	Bellshill YMCA	Fallin MW	Riverside Athletic	Star Hearts
91/92	Clark Drive	Bentswood Inn	Kingsway Athletic	Burntisland Shipyard
92/93	Milngavie Wanderers	Craigmillar AFC	Lawside FP	Norton House
93/94	Heathside	Cambusbarron Rovers	Alyth	Benarty
94/95	Dalziel HSFP	Fallin MW	SS Peter and Paul	Benarty
95/96	Dalziel HSFP	Cambusbarron Rovers	Riverside Athletic	Kettle United
96/97	Knockentiber	AVU	Riverside Athletic	Burntisland Shipyard
97/98	Newmilns Vesuvius	Fallin MW	Fair City Athletic	Lomond Victoria
98/99	West Kilbride	Royburn AFC	Riverside Athletic	Leven United
9/00	Dalziel HSFP	Manfort AFC	Fair City Athletic	Norton House
0/1	Bannockburn Ams	Spartans	Riverside Athletic	Norton House
1/2	Bannockburn Ams	Aberforth Rangers	Fair City Athletic	Norton House
2/3	Drumchapel AFC	Aberforth Rangers	Fair City Athletic	Norton House
3/4	Wellhouse AFC	Tullibody	Tayside Fire Brigade	Valleyfield
4/5	Drumchapel United	Falkirk Amateurs	Riverside Athletic	Kettle United
5/6	Drumchapel United	Stenhouse Athletic	Riverside Athletic	Kirkland
6/7	St Patricks FPs	Doune Castle	NCR	Cupar Hearts
7/8	Drumchapel United	Links United	Carnoustie YMCA	Cupar Hearts
8/9	Bannockburn Ams	Cambusbarron Rovers	Vale of Earn	Strathmiglo United
9/10	Harestanes	Bluebell	Breadalbane	Cupar Hearts
0/11	Drumchapel United	Falkirk Amateurs	Riverside Athletic	Cupar Hearts
1/12	Dumbarton Academy FP	Doune Castle	Burrelton Rovers	Kennoway
2/13	Colville Park	Edinburgh Rose	Arbroath CSC	Leven United
3/14	Hurlford Thistle	Steins Thistle	St James	Bowhill Rovers
4/15	Greenock HSFP	Steins Thistle	St James	Pittenweem Rovers
5/16	Shortlees	Craigshill Thistle	Menzieshill	Pittenweem Rovers

	North of S	South	Highland	Sunday Trophy
1949/50	Dyce			
1950/51	Aberdeen University			
1951/52	Invercairn United	Eyemouth Swifts		
1952/53	Millburn	Peebles YMCA		
1953/54	Cove Rangers	Gala Rovers		
1954/55	Invercairn United	Greenlaw		
1955/56	Fraserburgh Toolworks	Greenlaw		
1956/57	Fraserburgh Toolworks	Gordon Westruther		
1957/58	Fraserburgh Toolworks	Broughton United		
1958/59	Aberdeen University	Selkirk Thistle		
1959/60	Formartine United	Gordon Westruther		
1960/61	Bon Accord	Tweeddale Rovers		
1961/62	Old Meldrum	Morebattle		
1962/63	Bon Accord	Gala Rovers		
1963/64	Aberdeen Dockers	Gala Rovers		
1964/65	Ellon United	Gala Ams		
1965/66	Bon Accord	Tweeddale Rovers		
1966/67	Cove Rangers	Tweeddale Rovers		
1967/68	Aberdeen University	Tweeddale Rovers		
1968/69	Kemnay	Symington		
1969/70	Maud	Lauder		
1970/71	Culter	Symington		
1971/72	Kemnay	Hawick United		
1972/73	Culter	Kelso United		
1973/74	Kemnay	Tweeddale Rovers		
1974/75	Culter	Tweeddale Rovers		
1975/76	Culter	Tweeddale Rovers		
1976/77	Banchory	Dunbar Blue Circle		
1977/78	Newtonhall	Dunbar Blue Circle	Blackmuir	
1978/79	Kemnay	Lanark Thistle	South Ronaldsay	Liberton Cropley
1979/80	Chatton Rovers	Lanark Thistle	Thurso Pentland	GJs
1980/81	Mugiemoss	Shotts MD	Thurso Pentland	Elphinston / Hillburn
1981/82	Shamrock	Monteith	Halkirk	Cambridge United
1982/83	Cove Rangers	Monteith	Thurso Pentland	Duncraig
1983/84	Longside	Tweeddale Rovers	Ness	Cambridge United
1984/85	Shamrock	Douglas Thistle	Halkirk	CISWO
1985/86	Chatton Rovers	Monteith	Maryburgh	Cambridge United
1986/87	Culter	Hawick Legion	Pentland United	Househill
1987/88	Kemnay Youth	Maxwelltown HSFP	Kirkwall Thorfinn	Dolphin
1988/89	Kincorth	Chirnside	Dingwall Thistle	Linden 30 Club
1989/90	Glentanar	Rigside	Marybugh	Cambridge United
1990/91	Great Western United	Monteith	Ness	St Lawrence
1991/92	Kincorth	Duns Legion	Ness	FJR
1992/93	Wilsons XI	Shotts YM	Pentland United	Jolly Farmer
1993/94	Hilton	Monteith	Point	Gauntlet
1994/95	Echt	Shotts YM	Ness	Tower
1995/96	Echt	Kirk United	Dingwall Thistle	Finnart
1996/97	Hilton	Duns Legion	Kirkwall Rovers	Finnart
1997/98	Hilton	Duns Legion	Pentland United	Cathkin

	North of S	South	Highland	Sunday Trophy
1998/99	Hilton	Upper Annandale	Contin	Railway Hotel
1999/00	Wilsons XI	Coldstream	Pentland United	Finnart
2000/1	Echt	Symington Tinto	Wick Thistle	Centaur
2001/2	Great Western United	Kirkconnel	Pentland United	The Braes
2002/3	Mintlaw	Symington Tinto	Lochs	Cavendish
2003/4	Aberdeen SC	Monteith	Back	Harvester
2004/5	Mintlaw	Chirnside	Lochs	Cavendish
2005/6	Dyce	Hawick W	Avoch	Rowantree
2006/7	Echt	Leithen Rovers	Avoch	Finnart
2007/8	Cove Thistle	Gala Rovers	Pentland United	Finnart
2008/9	Hazlehead United	Chirnside	Kirkwall THorfinn	Gantry
2009/10	Sportsmans Club	Newtongrange Star A	Pentland United	Finnart
2010/11	Kincorth	Leithen Rovers	Avoch	Tower
2011/12	Cove Thistle	Leithen Rovers	Avoch	Finnart
2012/13	Cove Thistle	Pencaitland	Wick Groats	Rutherglen Vogue
2013/14	Cove Thistle	Leithen Rovers	Wick Groats	Harvester
2014/15	Cove Thistle	Shotts Victoria	Avoch	Cranhill United
2015/16	Cove Thistle	Danderhall MW	Wick Groats	Dundee Argyle

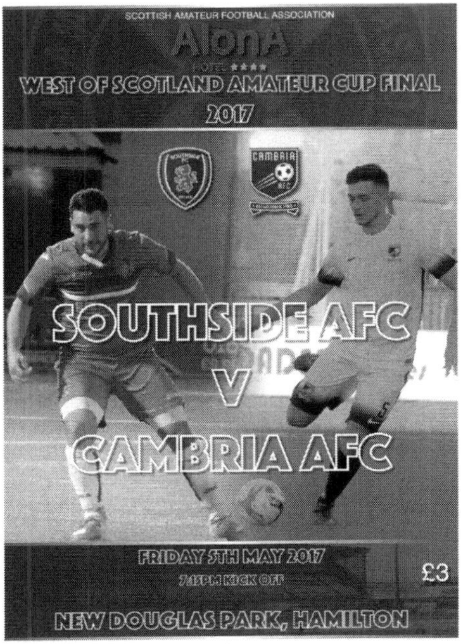

WELFARE FOOTBALL

WINTER SEASON 2016/17

GREENOCK WELFARE F.A.

Team	P	W	L	D	F	A	GD	PTS
Maukenhil	14	14	0	0	97	21	76	42
BayHomes	14	9	4	1	70	39	31	28
Blackthorn	12	6	5	1	42	33	9	19
Whinhill	12	6	6	0	40	45	-5	18
Larkfield	12	3	9	0	31	69	-38	9
Thistle	14	0	14	0	30	103	-73	0

McShane Builders Cup

Team	P	W	L	D	F	A	GD	PTS
Whinhill	2	1	0	1	14	5	9	4
Maukenhil	1	0	0	1	4	4	0	1
Larkfield	1	0	1	0	1	10	-9	0

Team	P	W	L	D	F	A	GD	PTS
Blackthorn	2	1	1	0	12	6	6	3
BayHomes	1	1	0	0	5	3	2	3
Thistle	1	0	1	0	1	9	-8	0

FINAL at Battery Park, 21/5/17
Whinhill v Maukenhill, 3-3, Whinhill on pens

RidgeDoc Cup

Team	P	W	L	D	F	A	GD	PTS
Whinhill	2	1	0	1	4	3	1	4
Thistle	2	1	1	0	6	4	2	3
BayHomes	2	0	1	1	4	7	-3	1

Team	P	W	L	D	F	A	GD	PTS
Maukenhil	2	2	0	0	11	1	10	6
Blackthorn	2	1	1	0	2	5	-3	3
Larkfield	2	0	2	0	2	9	-7	0

FINAL at Barrfields, Largs, 20/11/16
Maukenhill v Whinhill, 6-0

One of the few remaining Winter Leagues, the Greenocxk Welfare has struggled to get new teams to join in recent years. Matches are played, usually in Greenock, Gourock or Port Glasgow, on Sunday afternoons.

MONTROSE AND DISTRICT WELFARE F.A.

This is the most stable of the Sunday / Winter Welfare Leagues. Some clubs have roots back in the old Kincardineshire Junior League. Matches are usually played on Sunday Mornings, 10.45 ko.

www.leaguewebsite.co.uk/montrosewelfare

	P	W	D	L	F	A	GD	Pts	USUAL HOME GROUND	CUP FINALS
Johnshaven FC	20	18	2	0	89	22	67	56	Johnshaven Park*	
Hillside FC	20	17	0	3	95	34	61	51	Hillside Park*	Matrix Cup, April 17, at Broomfield Pitch 1
Golf Inn	20	16	1	3	114	32	82	49	Broomfield Park Pitch 1	Lochside United v Hillside 2-0
St Cyrus FC	20	12	0	8	62	54	8	36	St Cyrus Park*	
Lochside United	20	10	3	7	87	45	42	33	Broomfield Park Pitch 2	Charlie Wallace Trophy
MCT	20	8	3	9	73	62	11	27	Broomfield Park, Pitch 3	
The Old Bolag	20	8	1	11	55	54	1	25	Brechin Park	
Millgate	20	7	2	11	57	52	5	23	Hercules Den, Arbroath	Neil Taylor Memorial Cup, May 14 at Hillside
Northern Vaults	20	4	2	14	47	81	-34	14	Balwyllo	Hillside v The Old Bolag
Neptune Bar	20	2	0	18	41	118	-77	6	Marykirk*	
Star Bar	20	1	0	19	18	184	-166	3	Broomfield Park Pitch 2	
									* Former Kincardineshire Junior League venue	

SUMMER SEASON 2016

FORRES AND NAIRN WELFARE F.A. 2016

	P	W	D	L	F	A	GD	Pts
Elgin Thistle	18	15	0	3	105	27	78	45
Kinloss Sappers	18	15	0	3	77	19	58	45
FC Elgin	18	13	1	4	58	36	22	40
Uncle Bobs	18	10	1	7	48	43	5	31
Jackos	18	9	0	9	61	38	23	27
Carisbrooke	18	7	1	10	46	54	-8	22
Carlton	18	6	1	11	39	76	-37	19
Mosset Tavern	18	5	2	11	36	73	-37	17
Nairn United	18	3	2	13	32	84	-52	11
Catalans	18	2	2	14	29	81	-52	8

Play Off
Elgin Thistle v Kinloss Sappers, Home win

CUP FINALS

Bridgemill Ally Ross Rosebowl (12/6/16)
Kinloss Sapper v Jackos, 5-4
at Riverside Park, Nairn

M and D Toyota Mackintosh Rosebowl (25/9/16)
Elgin Thistle v Uncle Bobs, 1-0
at Elgin City FC

Penta Welfare League Cup (17/7/16)
Kinloss Sappers v Elgin Thistle, 8-4
at Forres Thistle JFC

FORTH AND ENDRICK WELFARE F.A. 2016

Compared to most of the others, the Forth and Endrick Welfare Association is settled and thriving. Matches are mainly played on Saturday evenings between teams representing the small towns and villages in the area between Stirling and Loch Lomond. Cup ties are often played on Sundays, with fixtures on midweek evenings as well.

www.facebook.com/pages/Forth-Endrick-Football-League

League Table	P	W	D	L	F	A	PTS
Balfron Rovers	22	19	0	3	88	15	57
Killearn	22	15	3	4	70	32	48
Drymen United	22	14	4	4	79	33	46
Buchlyvie Unitec	22	11	4	7	59	48	37
Blanefield Thistl	20	11	3	6	67	36	36
Gartocharn	22	10	4	8	66	46	34
Gargunnock	21	9	4	8	68	59	31
Aberfoyle Rob R	22	9	2	11	56	67	29
Deanston	22	8	1	13	65	76	25
Thornhill	22	5	3	14	54	79	18
Kippen	20	2	1	17	23	96	7
Fintry	21	1	1	19	15	123	4

Telfer Cup Tables

Forth Section

Buchlyvie Unitea	10	6	2	2	34	22	20
Aberfoyle Rob R	10	6	2	2	32	24	20
Deanston	10	5	0	5	37	33	15
Gargunnock	10	4	3	3	42	32	15
Thornhill	10	3	2	5	28	34	11
Kippen	10	1	1	8	13	41	4

Endrick Section

Balfron Rovers	10	8	0	2	42	9	24
Drymen United	10	5	3	2	30	11	18
Killearn	10	5	3	2	20	13	18
Blanefield Thistl	10	4	3	3	25	14	15
Gartocharn	10	2	3	5	21	32	9
Fintry	10	0	1	9	4	61	1

Semi Finals
Buchlyvie United v Drymen United, 2-2 aet, Drymen won pn pens
Balfron Rovers v Aberfoyle Rob Roy, 4-1

Final (28/8/16, at Thornhill)
Drymen United v Balfron Rovers, 2-3

CUP FINALS

McGregor Ferguson Trophy
Gartocharn v Blanefield Thistle, 1-0
10/06/2016

Margaret White Trophy
Balfron Rovers v Drymen United, 3-2
16/7/16, at Blanefield

Cameron Cup
Balfron Rovers v Gartocharn, 3-2
11/9/16, at Drymen

MORAY WELFARE F.A. 2016

PREMIER LEAGUE	P	W	D	L	F	A	GD	Pts
Aberlour Villa	18	14	2	2	71	31	40	44
FC Fochabers	18	13	1	4	92	41	51	40
Buckie United	18	9	4	5	52	45	7	31
Burghead United	18	8	2	8	47	46	1	26
Cullen	18	7	4	7	66	62	4	25
Hopeman	18	7	4	7	48	55	-7	25
Portsoy	18	6	2	10	29	52	-23	20
Rothes Amatuers	18	5	3	10	45	55	-10	18
RAF Lossiemouth	18	4	2	12	45	63	-18	14
Bishopmill Villa	18	4	2	12	45	90	-45	14

FIRST DIVISION	P	W	D	L	F	A	GD	Pts
Ugie Youths	14	12	1	1	51	15	36	37
New Elgin Welfare	14	9	4	1	63	19	44	31
Bishopmill Rovers	14	10	1	3	64	22	42	31
Banff Rovers	14	8	2	4	55	33	22	26
Tomintoul	14	4	1	9	28	32	-4	13
Elgin Athletic	14	4	1	9	19	41	-22	13
Lhanbryde Caley	14	1	2	11	19	55	-36	5
Mosstodloch	14	1	2	11	20	102	-82	5

CUP FINALS

Mike Simpson Cup
FC Fochabers v Ugie Youths, 7-1
18/9/16, at Elgin City FC

Tewnion Cup
FC Fochabers v Buckie United, 6-0
09/09/2016, at Keith FC

LOCHABER WELFARE F.A. 2016

Teams taking part:	CUP FINALS
Ballachulish	
Caol United	Duthie Cup, Aug 14 at Lochaber HS
Mallaig	Mallaig v Tekkerslovakia, 8-0
Nevis Range	
Tekkerslovakia	Uisdean MacDonald Cup, Aug 10 at Lochaber HS
	Mallaig v Nevis Range, 4-1
	John Baird Cup Final, June 27 at Lochaber HS
	Mallaig v Tekkerslovakia, 6-4

The 2016 season was beset with problems. Teams withdrew during the season and others failed to fulfil fixtures. It wuld appear that the League season was abandoned but the Cups were played to a finish.

However, the Association was not functioning in 2017.

CAMPBELTOWN & DISTRICT AFL

Very difficult to obtain information
Teams definitely competing in 2015 were:
Campbeltown Loyal Rangers SA
Meadows

LEWIS & HARRIS WELFARE AFL 2016

AKA Communities League.
Teams competing 2016:

Hotel Hebrides	Rally Park, Tarbert.
Ness	Fivepenny.
Rangers Club	Smith Avenue (grass) OR Sgoil Nan Loch (Lochs F C).
Sea Angling	Smith Avenue (grass).
Stornoway	Smith Avenue (grass).
Tolsta	Coll Centre (Back FC).

Games played Mondays & Wednesdays (18/04 - 06/08) dependant on pitch availability

NORTH EAST SCOTLAND WELFARE F.A. 2016

om season 2014 the North East Scotland and Buchan Welfare Leagues opted to merge eating a two division format under the name North East Scotland Welfare FA.

PREMIER DIVISION

#	Team	Pl	W	D	L	F	A	Diff	Pts	Adj
1	Clinton Thistle	18	13	3	2	65	20	45	42	0
2	Bellslea	18	12	4	2	57	28	29	40	0
3	Balmoor	18	9	4	5	50	39	11	31	0
4	New Pitsligo	18	8	6	4	35	22	13	30	0
5	Invercairn United	18	9	3	6	51	43	8	30	0
6	Mintlaw FC	18	7	2	9	41	37	4	23	0
7	Faithlie United	18	6	4	8	40	41	-1	22	0
8	Panasonic	18	5	2	11	38	72	-34	17	0
9	St Combs	18	4	3	11	37	60	-23	15	0
10	Elizabethan Link U	18	1	1	16	16	68	-52	4	0

FIRST DIVISION

#	Team	Pl	W	D	L	F	A	Diff	Pts	Adj
1	Mormond Thistle	21	19	2	0	82	17	65	59	0
2	New Deer	21	16	0	5	86	40	46	48	0
3	Buchanhaven FC	21	9	1	11	55	53	2	31	3
4	Ardallie	21	10	3	8	52	58	-6	30	-3
5	Peterhead United	21	9	0	12	85	71	14	27	0
6	Longside Thistle	21	6	2	13	54	68	-14	20	0
7	Methlick	21	5	2	14	33	83	-50	17	0
8	Cuminestown	21	3	4	14	30	87	-57	13	0

CUP FINALS

Ardallie Cup, 23/9/16
Mormond Thistle v New Deer, 5-3

Brucklay Cup, 10/6/16
Mormond Thistle v Cuminestown, 2-1

Gordon Leak Memorial Cup, 3/6/16
Invercairn United v Clinton Thistle, 0-1

Cuminestown Shield, 15/7/16
Ardallie v Cuminestown

Terry Sutton Memorial Cup, 8/7/16
Balmoor v Invercairn United, 4-3

Ship Inn League Cup, 12/8/16
Invercairn United v Clinton Thistle

Soccerworld Cup, 25/8/16
Bellslea v Mintlaw, 3-2

Victoria Coaches Cup, 30/9/16, at Fraserburgh FC
Bellslea v Clinton Thistle, 2-1

Mormond August, 5/8/16
New Deer v Longside Thistle, 6-3

ROSS-SHIRE WELFARE F.A. 2016

16 table	P	W	D	L	F	A	PTS	**USUAL HOME GROUND**	**CUP FINALS**
in Thistle	12	1	1	0	77	9	34	Links Park, Tain	
ontin	12	10	1	1	51	12	31	Munro Park, Contin	*Pattison Cup, Aug 6 at Tain Links*
ness United	11	7	0	4	61	16	21	Academy Park, Alness	Contin v Tain Thistle, 2-1
vegordon SC	12	5	0	7	32	45	15	Recreation Grounds, Invergordon	
alintore	12	4	1	7	22	44	13	Lower Seaboard Park, Balintore	*Highland Heatsave Seaboard Cup Final*
rtrose Union	11	1	2	8	13	37	5	KGV Park, Fortrose	July 16 at Balintore
stern Rose	12	0	1	11	18	111	1	Portmahomack	Tain Thistle v Contin, 6-1
rmer Members:									*Coronation Cup, June 25 at Dingwall*
ness Athletic								Academy Park, Alness	Alness United v Contin, 1-0
ack Rock Rovers								Culcairn Park, Evanton	
omarty FC								Victoria Park, Cromarty	*Cordiner Cup, June 4 at Inver*
ngwall FC								Jubilee Park Dingwall	Tain Thistle v Balintore, 3-1
ngwall Vertex								Jubilee Park Dingwall	
ornoch City								The Meadows, Dornoch	*Merrythought Cup Final, May 13 at Fortrose*
ver								The Bay, Inver	Tain Thistle v Alness United, 2-0
oss-shire Club								Jubilee Park Dingwall	
utor Inn								Recreation Grounds, Invergordon	

STRATHSPEY AND BADENOCH WELFARE F.A.

	P	W	D	L	F	A	GD	Pts
Grantown Utd	12	10	1	1	59	13	46	31
Aviemore Thistle	12	8	3	1	44	21	23	27
Tomatin Utd	12	3	4	5	34	55	-21	13
Cromdale	12	3	0	9	25	50	-25	9
Boat of Garten Ospre	12	0	4	8	31	54	-23	4

CUP FINALS

Revack Cup (13/5/16, at Aviemore)
Aviemore Thistle v Grantown United, 3-2

McCook Cup (3/6/16, at Aviemore)
Garntown United v Cromdale, 5-1

Stuart Cup (24/7/16, at Tomatin)
Aviemore Thistle v Cromdale, 4-3 AET

MacLean Cup (15/7/16, at Nethy Bridge)
Aviemore Thistle v Grantown United, 5-4 AET

Dalvey Cup (5/8/16 at Cromdale)
Cromdale v Grantown United, 4-2

MID DEESIDE SUMMER WELFARE F.A. 2016

1938	Aboyne	1976	Banchory Swifts
1939	Not Known	1977	Charleston Rovers
1940	No Competition	1978	Charleston Rovers
1941	No Competition	1979	Charleston Rovers
1942	No Competition	1980	Banchory Swifts
1943	No Competition	1981	Banchory Swifts
1944	No Competition	1982	Banchory Swifts
1945	No Competition	1983	Charleston Rovers
1946	Banchory	1984	Charleston Rovers
1947	Banchory	1985	Charleston Rovers
1948	Banchory	1986	Banchory Swifts
1949	Banchory	1987	Banchory Swifts
1950	Banchory	1988	Banchory Swifts
1951	Lumphanan	1989	Banchory Swifts
1952	Banchory Swifts	1990	Charleston Rovers
1953	Banchory Swifts	1991	Banchory Swifts
1954	Lumphanan	1992	Banchory United
1955	Lumphanan	1993	Parkers
1956	Lumphanan	1994	Lumphanan
1957	Banchory Swifts	1995	Kincardine O'Neil
1958	Charleston Rovers	1996	Kincardine O'Neil
1959	Lumphanan	1997	Kincardine O'Neil
1960	Lumphanan	1998	Ballater
1961	Lumphanan	1999	Banchory Stoats
1962	Lumphanan	2000	Banchory Youth
1963	Lumphanan	2001	Ballater
1964	Lumphanan	2002	Ballater
1965	Lumphanan	2003	Kincardine O'Neil
1966	Lumphanan	2004	Banchory Youth
1967	Lumphanan	2005	Banchory Youth
1968	Lumphanan	2006	Banchory Youth
1969	Lumphanan	2007	Banchory Thistle
1970	Lumphanan	2008	Banchory Thistle
1971	Lumphanan	2009	Banchory Youth
1972	Kincardine O'Neil	2010	Lumphanan
1973	Lumphanan	2011	Banchory Thistle (Pla
1974	Lumphanan	2012	No Competition
1975	Banchory Swifts (Playoff)	2013	No Competition

	P	W	D	L	F	A	GD	PTS
Banchory Thistle	7	6	1	0	20	6	14	19
Drumosk and Durris	7	6	0	1	23	15	8	18
Tarland	7	5	0	2	22	16	6	15
Laurencekirk West E	7	3	2	2	30	10	20	11
Alford	7	3	1	3	19	15	4	7
Ballater	7	1	1	5	13	32	-19	4
Lumphanan	7	1	1	5	6	27	-21	4
Charleston Rovers	7	0	0	7	3	15	-12	0

CUP FINALS

Sandison Cup (3/6/16 at Lumphanan)
Banchory Thistle v Alford 3-1

Kynoch Cup (6/7/16 at Ballater)
Ballater v Lumphanan, 3-1
Contested by four bottom sides

Littlejohn Trophy (1/7/16 at Banchory)
Laurencekirk West End v Banchory Thistle, 2-0

Gilbert Trophy (8/7/16 at Banchory)
Drumoak and Durris v Banchory Thistle
Contested by 4 top sides

DONALD McNAIR Scottish Cup 2016/17

With the declining numbers of teams participating in welfare football, only one Scottish Cup was played rather than a Saturday and a Sunday version. Ties were played from January until May, accommodating both Summer and Winter clubs as required.

Rd	H	A	F	A	
1	Neptune Bar	Inbverclyde Thistle	3	3	l-w pens
1	Johnshaven	Mosstodloch	W	scr	
1	Larkfield	Invercairn United	0	6	
1	Clinton Thistl	Elgin Athletic	4	1	
1	Golf Inn	Buchanhaven	5	1	
1	St Combs	Peterhead United	3	6	
1	Whinhill	Northern Valuts	w	scr	
1	Cuminestowr	New Deer	3	2	
1	Jhopeman	Hillside	4	0	
1	St Cyrus	Blackthorn Rovers	3	2	
1	Elizabethan L	Panasonic	1	3	
1	Lochside Unit	BYE			
1	Balmoor	BYE			
1	Bellslea	BYE			
1	Maukinhill Ur	BYE			
1	Mormond Thi	BYE			
2	Lochside Unit	Cuminestown	4	2	
2	Hopeman	Panasonic	1	2	
2	Invercairn Un	Golf Inn	3	2	
2	Bellslea	Johnshaven	2	0	
2	Inverclyde Th	Whinhill	0	3	
2	Mormond Thi	Balmoor	3	2	
2	St Cyrus	Clinton Thistle	4	2	
2	Maukinhill Ur	Peterhead United	w	scr	
3	Panasonic	Lochside United	5	3	
3	St Cyrus	Bellslea	2	2	l-w pens
3	Invercairn Un	Maukinhill United	8	2	
3	Whinhill	Mormond Thistle	2	3	
SF	Panasonic	Bellslea	2	4	
SF	Mormond Thi	Invercairn United	0	2	
F	Bellslea	Invercairn United	0	1	

	Templeton Cup / Donald McNair Cup	Daily Record Cup / Jack Bryson Cup
1919/20	Beardmore Mossend	
1920/21	Coats Juniors	
1921/22	Coats Juniors	
1922/23	Coats Juniors	
1923/24	Cleansing	
1924/25	Coats Juniors	
1925/26	Clark Anchor	
1926/27	Coats Juniors	
1927/28	Phoenix	
1928/29	Seafield	
1929/30	Westfield	Renton Thistle
1930/31	Hydepark Loco Works	St Martins Guild
1931/32	Anniesland	Camelot Welfare
1932/33	Napier House	Withheld
1933/34	Napier House	Shawfield Chemicals
1934/35	St Pauls	Shawfield Chemicals
1935/36	Templeton Albert	Smith & McLean
1936/37	Templeton Albert	Carwadric
1937/38	Kelvindale	Kerse
1938/39	Clyde Alloy	Scotia
1939/40		Vulcan
1940/41		Queen's Society
1941/42		Forth and Clyde
1942/43		Ardnance
1943/44		Scottish Cables
1944/45		Phoenix
1945/46	Harland & Wolff Ordnance	RNAS
1946/47	Milton Welfare	Carron Primrose
1947/48	ICI Welfare	Cadder Welfare
1948/49	Loco	Seafield Athletic
1949/50	Singers	Germiston Works
1950/51	Dalmarnock Power	Dalmarnock Power
1951/52	Singers Athletic	Templeton Albert
1952/53	Templeton Albert	Provan Gas / Ferranti Thistle
1953/54	Dalmarnock Power	Singer Athletic
1954/55	Rolls Royce (Hillington)	Rolls Royce (Hillington)
1955/56	Metro Vics	Howdens Athletic
1956/57	Singers	British Legion Polmont
1957/58	Rolls Royce (Hillington)	St Bernards
1958/59	Clyde Trust	St Bernards
1959/60	Dalmarnock Power	Clyde Trust
1960/61	J and T Boyds	Shanks Welfare
1961/62	Dalmarnock Power	Quay United
1962/63	Burroughs (Cumbernauld)	Grangemouth Dockers
1963/64	Grangemouth Dockers	Shanks Welfare
1964/65	Grangemouth Dockers	Quay United
1965/66	Clyde Port Authority	Grangemouth Dockers

	Templeton Cup / Donald McNair Cup	Daily Record Cup / Jack Bryson Cup
1966/67	British Hydro Chemicals	Shanks Welfare
1967/68	Rolls Royce (Hillington)	Brown Land Boilers
1968/69	British Aluminium	Shanks Welfare
1969/70	British Aluminium	Hoods
1970/71	Waverly Thistle	British Aluminium
1971/72	Winchburgh	Waverly Thistle
1972/73	Waverly Thistle	Dukes Head
1973/74	Plean Welfare	Waverly Thistle
1974/75	Tennents Caledonia	Tennents Caledonina
1975/76	200 FC	Tennents
1976/77	Singers	Clyde Blowers
1977/78	Singers	Singers
1978/79	Grangemouth Dockers	Singers
1979/80	Tennents	GSL
1980/81	East Stirlingshire Social Club	200 FC
1981/82	John Brown Engineering	Tennents
1982/83	200 FC	Malvern Star
1983/84	Malvern Star	Possil
1984/85	Withheld	Westquarter Violet
1985/86	Springfield	Commercial
1986/87	Glen Star	Westquarter Violet
1987/88	Westquarter Violet	Withheld
1988/89	Gordon Athletic	Tennents
1989/90	Robert Rae FC	Westquarter Violet
1990/91	Concord Metals	John Brown Engineering
1991/92	Withheld	Robert Rae
1992/93	Aldbury	Kelty Villa
1993/94	Aldbury	Aldbury
1994/95	John Brown Engineering	Jamestown
1995/96	Templeton Albert	Valley Bar
1996/97	Summerhill	Summerhill
1997/98	St Peters	Summerhill
1998/99	Rosyth Ex Service Club	St Ninians
1999/00	Peppes	Valley Bar
2000/1	St Peters	Tullibody WMC
2001/2	Calton Athletic	Kelty Villa
2002/3	Clydeshore	Peppes
2003/4	Invercairn United	Jokers
2004/5	Lauders FC	Oakwood
2005/6	Valley Bar	Braehead
2006/7	Blairhall	St Ninians Borestone
2007/8	Linlithgow Rose B	Star Inn
2008/9	Oakwood	Valley Bar
2009/10	Peppes	Oakwood
2010/11	Oakwood	Blairhall
2011/12	Castleview	Treetops
2012/13	Horseshoe	MISC
2013/14	Bank	Maukenhill United
2014/15	Clinton Thistle	Dollar Glen
2015/16	Invercairn United	

UNOFFICIAL FOOTBALL

ISLE OF ARRAN LEAGUE 2016

A five-team Summer League operates on Arran.

North End Thistle play in Lochranza . South End are based in Whiting Bay. Shiskine's home ground is in Blackwaterfoot. Lamlash and Brodick complete the League. Important games are sometimes played at Ormidale Park, Brodick, which is also the home ground of Arran RUFC.

League Table 2016

	P	W	D	L	F	A	PTS			
Brodick	8	8	0	0	59	10	24			Arran Cup Final
Lamlash	7	5	0	2	36	8	12			Aug 20 at Whiting Bay
Southend	8	4	0	4	29	26	12			Brodick v Lamlash, 4-1
Shiskine	8	2	0	6	19	36	6			
North End	7	0	0	7	7	70	0			

ISLAY FOOTBALL LEAGUE 2016

The following three teams were involved in the 2016 Summer League and Cup competitions:

Kilchoman FC
Bowmore FC
Port Ellen FC

Most games are played at Port Mor, just south of the village of Port Charlotte.

The Islay Cup Final was held on June 5 2016. Port Ellen beat Kilchoman 5-3 at Port Mor.

The McTaggart Cup Final on May 18th was contested by the same two teams, Port Ellen won 5-4 on penalties after a 4-4 draw.

The Logan Cup Final on May 8 ended Port Ellen 3 Kilchoman 1.

The Bramble Cup Final on April 27 finished Port Ellen 3 Kilchoman 2

The Dewar Cup Final on March 20 ended Kilchoman 5 Port Ellen 3.

YOUTH FOOTBALL

This grade of football might best be termed as "Age Group Football". The Scottish Youth FA organises national cups for teams at age groups up to Under 21. The SYFA is a comparatively recent creation, having bene formed in 1999 to rationalise the various age group football associations that existed.

The Scottish Juvenile FA dated back to Victorian times. In 1921 it split into two organisations - the Scottish Juvenile FA (First Class Juveniles) and the Scottish Secondary Juvenile FA. The difference was age groups - First Class Juveniles went up to "Under 27" and Secondary Juveniles to "Under 21".

Other age group football existed, organised by the Scottish Amateur FA, the Boys Brigade, the Churches FA and the Boys Guilds, amongst others.

By the 1980s much had changed. The First Class Juveniles were confined mainly to the Dundee area. The Scottish Juvenile FA began to run Under 21 and other age group competitions as well as Under 27s. The Secondary Juveniles became the Association of Scottish Youth Football Clubs and were dominant in the Edinburgh area, the Forth Valley and Ayrshire.

There was much confusion about different rules, eligibility and so on. It made eminent sense to bring all age group under one umbrella and this was achieved in 1999 through the creation of the Scottish Juvenile FA.

The Scottish Juvenile Cup (Under 27s) was a very prestigious tournament in its heyday and winners are shown below. Several teams progressed to the Junior grade after success in the Juveniles:

1899-00	Granton Oak Vale
1900-01	Dumbarton Corinthians
1901-02	Airdriehill Shamrock
1902-03	Vale of Garnock Strollers
1903-04	Orbiston Star
1904-05	Burnbank Oakvale
1905-06	Dunipace Juveniles
1906-07	Benvue
1907-08	Anderston Benburb
1908-09	Motherwell Hearts
1909-10	Fern Thistle
1910-11	Fern Thistle
1911-12	Govan Hibernian
1912-13	Clydebank Corinthians
1913-14	Old Kilpatrick
1914-15	Old Kilpatrick
1915-16	Parkhead White Rose
1916-17	Blantyre Caledonian
1917-18	Mosshill United
1918-19	Cadzow St Anne's
1919-20	Parkhead White Rose
1920-21	Vale of Bannock
1921-22	Bridgeton Waverley
1922-23	Bridgeton Waverley
1923-24	Bridgeton Waverley
1924-25	Regent Star
1925-26	Springburn United
1926-27	Greenhead Thistle
1927-28	Niddrie Thistle
1928-29	Cowie
1929-30	Blairhall
1930-31	Blairhall
1931-32	St Mungo
1932-33	Shieldhill Thistle
1933-34	Park United
1934-35	Holytown United
1935-36	Holytown United
1936-37	Cleland St Mary's
1937-38	Partick Dolphins
1938-39	St Mungo
1939-40	Park United
1940-41	Mossend Boys Guild
1941-42	Mossend Boys Guild
1942-43	Lumphinnans Wanderers
1943-44	Thorniewood United
1944-45	Dundonald Bluebell
1945-46	Dundonald Bluebell
1946-47	Kilbowie Union
1947-48	Banknock United
1948-49	St Mungo
1949-50	Coylton
1950-51	Kirkmuirhill
1951-52	Sauchie
1952-53	Cowie
1953-54	Cowie
1954-55	Germiston Star
1955-56	Burnbank Swifts
1956-57	Sauchie
1957-58	Sauchie
1958-59	Burnbank Swifts
1959-60	Sauchie
1960-61	Burnbank Swifts
1961-62	Lochend Hearts
1962-63	Tradeston Holmlea
1963-64	Rosebery
1964-65	Lochee Renton
1965-66	Glencairn
1966-67	Lochee Renton
1967-68	Maryfield United
1968-69	Provanside Hibernian
1969-70	Burnbank Swifts
1970-71	Germiston Star
1971-72	Inverurie Locos 'A'
1972-73	Germiston Star
1973-74	Coatbridge
1974-75	Mount Ellen
1975-76	Newburgh
1976-77	Fairfield
1977-78	ALC Spurs
1978-79	Fairfield
1979-80	Woodacon
1980-81	Newburgh
1981-82	Stanley
1982-83	Scone Thistle
1983-84	Dee Club
1984-85	Blue Star BC
1985-86	Royals
1986-87	Royals
1987-88	Dundee United SC
1988-89	Dundee United SC
1989-90	Royals
1990-91	Fintry

Scottish Youth FA Cup 2004s (Under 12) 2016/17

P	Whitburn FCA	Leith Athletic FC	0	12	
P	St Bernards BC Midlothian Strollers	Broxburnb Athletic Colts Reds	6	5	
P	Dunbar United Colts	Lochend YFC	3	4	
P	Murieton United CFC Reds	broxburn Athletic Colts	1	10	
P	Edinburgh South CFC Reds	Penicuik Athletic YFC Reds	12	2	
P	Bonnyrigg Rose	Armadale CFC United	3	5	
P	Gala Fairydean Rovers JFC	Bathgate Thistle CFC Blues	1	0	
P	Broxburn Athletic Colts United	Portobello CFA	0	11	
P	KSC United	Valspar FC	12	0	
P	Dreghorn FC	Irvine Meadow	3	9	
P	Syngenta Grange	Milton	3	5	
P	North Glasgow Celtic	East Kilbride FC	6	3	
P	FC Kirkwood	Dunbeth FC	3	7	
P	Riverside FC	Seafar Villa Cumbernauld FC	0	12	
P	West Park United	Jerviston FC	0	5	
P	Holytown Colts YC	Newmains Hammers	12	0	
P	Wishaw Wycombe Wanderers	Gairdoch United FC	0	4	
P	Drumsagard FAC	Clyde FC School of Football	10	2	
P	Dundee West FC	Dryburgh Athletic	1	3	
P	St davids YFC	Crieff Juniors	8	0	
P	Maryfield United	Burntisland Shipyard	1	3	
P	Krrie Thistle Youths	Fairmuir BC	3	4	
P	Jeanfield Swifts	Arbroath CSC	0	2	
P	Templehall United	Breadalbane Strathtay YFC	12	1	
P	Mugiemoss	Glentanar CFC	0	12	
P	Banks o' Dee Albion	Colony Colts FC	12	0	
P	Deveronvale	Portlethen SC	1	4	
P	Arthurlie Juniors FC Blaze	Barrhead YFC	0	12	
P	Broomhill SC (PJ and D)	Glenvale AFC	3	2	
P	East Kilbride Caledonian THistle	Rangers SABC	7	1	
P	Hillwood BC	Giffnock SC Whites	5	1	
P	East Kilbride Burgh United	Houston United	1	10	
P	Kilpatrick FC	Pollok United Soccer Academy (East Ren)	2	1	
P	Port Glasgow BC Black	St Mirren YFC	1	0	
1	Gala Fairydean Rovers JFC	Musselburgh Youngstars	7	3	
1	Broxburn Athletic Colts	Armadale Thistle SC	1	0	
1	Spartans FC Youth Reds	Murieston United Blue	4	0	
1	Kirkfield United	Currie Star	1	0	
1	Portobello CFA Thistle	St Bernards BC Midlothian Strollers	4	2	
1	Longniddry Villa Colts	Spartans FC Whites	1	7	
1	Penicuik Athletic YFC Blues	Arniston Rangers	12	0	
1	Polbeth United	AC Oxgangs	3	7	
1	Craigroyston BC	Tynecastle FC	0	12	
1	North Berwick Colts	Leith Athletic FC	0	12	
1	Lochend YFC	East Calder Colts	10	1	
1	Musselburgh Windsor FC	Edinburgh South AFC	11	0	
1	Armadale CFC United	Broxburn Athletic Colts Whites	12	1	
1	Bathgate Thistle CFC Rovers	Lochend YFC Colts	1	0	
1	Gullane Athletic AFC	Edinburgh South CFC Reds	5	3	
1	Earlston Rhymers YFC	Edinburgh City Mbu's	9	0	
1	Cramond FC	Star A CYP	1	0	
1	Eyemouth United FC Juniors	Hutchison Vale Hornets	1	6	aet
1	Leith Athletic FC Colts	Beechwood	12	0	
1	Currie FC	Tranent Colts	1	3	
1	Livingston FC BC	Hutchison Vale Colts	1	2	
1	Penicuik Athletic YFC	St Bernards BC Midlothian Strollers	0	12	
1	Bonnyrigg Rose FC Whites	Blackburn United CYFC	1	0	
1	Spartans FC Youth	Armadale CFC United / Rovers	12	0	
1	Hutchison Vale FC	Livingston FC BC Lions	11	0	
1	Musselburgh Windsor FC Blue	Dalkeith Thistle CFC	0	6	
1	Longniddry Villa	Whitburn FCA Wolves	10	2	
1	Portobello CFA	Currie Star FC Colts	1	0	
1	Kirkliston & South Queensferry	Linlithgow Rose CFC Maroon	8	1	
1	Redhall Star YFC	Linlithgow Rose CFC	1	4	
1	Edinburgh City FC Gair's	Mid Calder Colts	1	0	
1	Bathgate Thistle CFC	Haddington Athletic CFC	1	0	
1	Irvine Victoria Thistle & Rovers	Cumnock Juniors YFC	8	2	
1	Crosshouse BC	Heston Rovers	2	0	
1	Valspar United	Winlinton Wolves	2	7	
1	Stewarton Annick FC	Mid Annandale AFC	5	0	
1	Dean Thistle	Coylton FC	0	5	
1	KSC Boys	Irvine Meadow	0	7	
1	Galston YFC	Townhead United	7	3	
1	Troon Thistle YFC	Caledonian YC	5	8	
1	KSC United	Ayr Boswell BC	10	0	
1	Prestwick Community FC	Tass Thistle	1	3	
1	Arbroath LC	Broughty United YFC	0	3	
1	St David's YFC	Riverside CSC	8	0	
1	Bridge of Earn	Dryburgh United	1	2	

1	East Fife Junior Supporters Club	St Andrews Colts FC	2	4	
1	Forfar BC	Duloch Juniors	5	1	
1	Arbroath CSC	Fairmuir BC	2	12	
1	Montrose Youth	Monifieth Athletic	6	1	
1	Dundee Celtic BC	Dundee United SC	7	4	
1	Burntisland Shipyard	Lumphinnans United	2	1	
1	Douglas YFC	Letham SC Whites	3	5	aet
1	Templehall United	Letham SC Tangerines	1	0	
1	Brechin City YFC	AM Soccer Club	2	7	
1	Blue Brazil BC	Ferry Athletic	9	2	
1	Kirkcaldy Inter	Scone Thistle	10	2	
1	Pitfour FC	Kennoway United	7	1	
1	Letham SC Sky Blues	Inverkeithing Hillfield Swifts East Fife	5	4	
1	Lenzie YC	Stenhousemuir FC	8	6	
1	West Park United (CSFDA)	Bellshill BC	0	1	
1	Cumbernauld Colts FC	Carbrain BC Claret	2	3	
1	Falkirk FC Community Foundation CSFDA	Notre Dame Soccer Academy	9	3	
1	North Glasgow Celtic	Rossvale FC	2	3	aet
1	Motherwell FC Community Trust	Kilsyth Athletic	3	4	
1	Gartcairn Football Academy	Cambuslang FC	7	2	
1	Gairdoch United FC	Mossend FC	4	1	
1	Dunipace Juniors FC	Steins Thistle	1	3	
1	Larkhall Thistle AFC Blue	Larkhall Thistle AFC White	1	0	
1	Rossvale FC Inter	AC Rovers FC	7	2	
1	East Kilbride FC Blue	Bo'ness United CFC	1	6	
1	Asfield FC Athletic	Seafar Villa Cumbernauld FC	8	0	
1	Dumbarton Riverside FC	Syngenta Juveniles	1	12	
1	Wasp Community Club	Alloa Rovers	4	2	
1	Biggar United Juniors	Claremont AFC	3	4	
1	Milan FC	Cumbernauld Colts FC Blues	0	1	
1	Holytown Colts YC	Lenzie YC Sky	12	0	
1	Stirling United FC	Renton Craigandro	0	11	
1	Aston Villa BC	Clarkston BC	0	5	
1	Jimmy Johnstone Academy	Bargeddie Colts	6	2	
1	Carbrain BC Sky	Oban Saints	0	1	
1	Maddiston Minis	Jerviston FC	5	1	
1	North Motherwell BC	Milton Blacks	0	12	
1	Blantyre Soccer Academy	Eddlewood BC	1	3	
1	Bellshill Athletic FC	Dunblane Soccer Club	4	0	
1	Sauchie Juniors FC	Mill United	0	12	
1	Rosebank United	Strathendrick FC	12	2	
1	Ashfield FC United	Milngavie FC	9	1	
1	Milton Rovers YFC	Milton	3	0	
1	Dumbarton United	Bannockburn Amateurs	4	6	
1	Albion Rovers In The Community	Stirling Albion Junior Academy	0	12	
1	Dunbeth FC	Auchterarder Juniors	6	7	
1	Falkirk Football Community Foundation	EDFC	0	9	
1	Jim Baxter Memorial	Falkirk Community Foundation White	1	6	
1	Condorrat BC	Drumsagard Football Academy Club	1	11	
1	Portlethen SC	Aberdon	12	0	
1	Banks o' Dee Albion	Westdyke CC	0	3	
1	Formartine United Youth	Fraserburgh Link-Up YFC	4	2	
1	Northstar CFC	Colony Park FC	4	2	
1	Banchory Boys FC	Westdyke CC Thistle	4	0	
1	Newmachar United FC	Portlethen SC United	10	2	
1	Lewis United Youth	Middlefield Wasps	6	1	
1	Thistle Youth FC	Dyce BC	2	10	
1	Glentanar Community FC	Huntly FC	1	0	
1	Stonehaven Youth FC madrid	West End FC Reds	12	1	
1	Barrhead YFC	Palace Park BC	4	2	
1	Giffnock North BC Athletic	Southside Star	1	9	
1	Johnstone Burgh BC	Baljaffray FC	2	3	
1	Westerton United FC	Klilpatrick FC	5	4	
1	East Kilbride Caledonian THistle	Port Glasgow BC Black	3	2	
1	Hillwood BC	Castlemilk BC	1	0	
1	Langcraigs FC Blues	Renfrew FC	3	10	
1	St Cadocs YC	St Peters FC	0	12	
1	Giffnock North BC United	Thorn Athletic	6	2	
1	Houston United	Ashfield FC Albion	12	0	
1	Erskine YFC	Giffnock SC Blacks	4	1	
1	Clyde FC Community	Ashfield FC Albion	0	12	
1	Hillwood BC Thistle	Hampden Weir Recreation AFC	0	12	
1	Kelvindale Thistle	Park Palace BC C	1	12	
1	Giffnock SC Reds	Broomhill SC (PJ&D)	2	1	
1	Rangers Girls	Port Glasgow BC Orange	2	3	
1	Ferguslie Star Youth	Giffnock North BC Thistle	2	8	
1	renfrew FC Blue	St Cadocs YC Saints	0	11	
1	The Celtic BC	Hampden BC Red	2	0	
1	East Kilbride Caledonian Thistle Reds	Finnart BC	3	1	
1	Thistle Weir	Morton Community	10	1	

1	Parkmoor FC	Drumchapel Amateurs	1	0	
1	Moorlands FC	St Cadocs YC United	2	5	
1	Giffnock North BC Rovers	Port Glasgow Juniors CSC	7	1	
2	Tynecastle FC	AC Oxgangs	4	0	
2	Leith Athletic FC Colts	Portobello CFA	1	5	
2	Hutchison Vale Colts	Kirkfield United	3	0	
2	Spartans FC Youth Reds	Kirkliston & South Queensferry	7	0	
2	Spartans FC Youth	Tranent Colts	7	0	
2	Gala Fairydean Rovers JFC	Bonnyrigg Rose FC Whites	4	0	
2	Musselburgh Windsor FC	St Bernards BC Midlothian	4	3	
2	Cramond FC	Gullane Athletic AFC	9	1	
2	Broxburn Athletic Colts	Leith Athletic FC	4	7	
2	Bathgate Thistle CFC	Dalkeith Thistle CFC	0	7	
2	Portobello Community Football Academy Thistle	Lochend YFC	3	3	aet 2-3p
2	Edinburgh City Gairs	Linlithgow Rose CFC	1	10	
2	Hutchison Vale Hornets	Bathgate Thistle CFC Rovers	6	2	
2	Longniddry Villa	Earlston Rhymers YFC	5	0	
2	Hutchison Vale FC	Armadale CFC United	12	1	
2	Spartans FC Whites	Penicuik Athletic YFC Blues	5	2	
2	Mill United	Maddiston Minis	4	3	
2	Carbrain BC Claret	Rosebank United	10	0	
2	Drumsagard FAC	Milton Blacks	4	2	
2	Clarkston BC	Wasp Community Club	3	1	
2	Ashfield FC United	Rossbale FC Inter	5	2	
2	Rossvale FC	Holytown Colts YC	2	4	
2	Jimmy Johnstone Academy	EDFC	5	3	
2	Gartcairn Football Academy	Auchterarder Juniors	4	0	
2	Bo'ness United CFC	Stirling Albion Junior Academy	2	5	
2	Larkhall Thistle AFC Blue	Lenzie YC Sky	11	2	
2	Milton Rovers YFC	Ashfield FC Athletic	3	4	aet
2	Kilsyth Athletic FC	Claremont AFC	2	0	
2	Steins Thistle	Bannockburn Amateurs	7	0	
2	Eddlewood BC	Oban Saints	5	1	
2	Falkirk FC Foundation White	Renton Craigandro	1	3	
2	Syngenta Juveniles	Bellshill Athletic	12	0	
2	Cumbernauld Colts FC Blues	Falkirk Community Foundation CSFDA	6	3	
2	Gairdoch United FC	Bellshill BC	6	0	
2	Forfar BC	Pitfour FC	2	5	
2	Blue Brazil BC	Dryburgh Athletic	12	2	
2	Broughty United YFC	Montrose Youth	2	4	
2	Burntisland Shipyard	St Andrews Colts FC	6	1	
2	Kirkcaldy Inter	Templehall United	2	5	
2	Letham SC Whites	Fairmuir BC	0	12	
2	AM Soccer Club	Letham SC Sky Blues	5	2	
2	St Davids YFC	Dundee Celtic Boys	5	3	aet
2	Glentanar Community FC	Dyce BC	0	9	
2	Stonehaven YFC madrid	Lewis United Youth	2	5	
2	Banchory Boys FC	Portlethen SC	1	2	
2	Northstar CFC	newmachar United FC	12	1	
2	Westdyke CC	Formartine United FC	6	1	
2	Crosshouse BC	Irvine Meadow	6	1	
2	Caledonian YC	Galston YFC	1	2	
2	Irvine Victoria Thistle & Rovers	Winlinton Wolves	12	2	
2	Tass Thistle	Stewarton Annick	3	1	
2	KSC United	Coylton FC	5	4	
2	Baljaffray FC	The Celtic BC	0	4	
2	East Kilbride Caledonian Thistle	Palace Park BC	1	5	
2	Barrhead YFC	Renfrew FC	0	2	
2	Westerton United FC	Ashfield FC	3	2	
2	Southside Star	Thistle Weir	9	2	
2	St Peters FC	East Kilbride Caledonian Thistle Reds	12	1	
2	Giffnock North BC United	St Cadocs YC United	7	0	
2	Giffnock SC Reds	Port Glasgow BC Orange	7	2	
2	Hillwood BC	Parkmoor FC	8	3	
2	Hampden Weir Recreation AFC	Giffnock North BC Roversw	12	0	
2	Houston United	St Cadocs YC Saints	4	7	
2	Erskine YFC	Giffnock North BC Thistle	6	3	
3	Erskine YFC	St Cadocs YC Saints	4	2	
3	Clarkston BC	Fairmuir BC	3	3	at 5-4p
3	Hillwood BC	Spartans FC Whites	0	5	
3	Montrose Youth	Tynecastle FC	1	3	
3	St Davids YFC	Hutchison Vale Colts	2	1	
3	Northstar CFC	Westerton United	3	1	
3	Renton Craigandro	Eddlewood BC	3	1	
3	Stirling Albion Junior Academy	Lochend YFC	3	2	aet
3	Galston YFC	Mill United	2	0	
3	Spartans FC Youth	KSC United	9	2	GP Comn
3	Irvine Victoria Thistle & Rovers	Cramond FC	12	1	
3	Dyce BC	Crosshouse BC	4	2	
3	Musselburgh Windsor	Pitfour FC	4	3	

3	Palace Park BC C	Blue Brazil BC	3	5	
3	Ashfield FC United	Linlithgow Rose CFC	0	0	aet 4-5p
3	Tass Thistle	Drumsagard Football Academy Club	2	7	
3	Spartans FC Youth Reds	Kilsyth Athletic	0	12	
3	Dalkeith Thistle CFC	Templehall United	1	8	
3	Hampden Weir Recreation AFC	Cumbernauld Colts FC Blues	8	0	
3	Leith Athletic	Syngenta Juveniles	3	3	aet 2-4p
3	Portobello Community Football Academy	Gartcairn Football Academy	2	1	
3	Westdyke CC	The Celtic BC	7	1	
3	Holytown Colts YC	Giffnock SC Reds	1	2	
3	Southside Star	Hutchison Vale FC	0	6	
3	Larkhall Thistle AFC Blue	Ashfield FC Athletic	3	1	
3	Longniddry Villa	Carbrain BC Claret	4	7	
3	Gala Fairydean Rovers JFC	Steins Thistle	3	1	
3	Hutchison Vale Hornets	St Peters FC	0	9	
3	AM Soccer Club	Jimmy Johnstone Academy	1	1	aet 3-4p
3	Lewis United Youth	Portlethen SC	3	3	aet 5t-2p
3	Gairdoch United FC	Renfrew FC	4	2	
3	Giffnock North BC United	Burntisland Shipyard	8	0	
4	Northstar CFC	Carbrain BC Claret	0	3	
4	Hutchison Vale FC	Westdyke CC	5	1	
4	Drumsagard FAC	Stirling Albion Junior Academy	6	2	
4	Templehall United	Linlithgow Rose CFC	0	4	
4	Clarkston BC	St Peters FC	0	7	
4	Larkhall Thistle AFC Blue	Spartans FC Whites	3	0	
4	Gairdoch United FC	Galston YFC	3	3	aet 3-1p
4	Renton Craigandro	Tynecastle FC	0	3	
4	Jimmy Johnstone Academy	Syngenta Juveniles	1	7	
4	Musselburgh Windsor	Irvine Victoria Thistle & Rovers	2	1	
4	Giffnock North BC United	Hampden Weir Recreation AFC	2	1	
4	St David's YFC	Portobello CFA	0	3	
4	Kilsyth Athletic FC	Erskine YFC	11	2	
4	Spartans FC Youth	Dyce BC	0	1	
4	Giffnock SC Reds	Gala Fairydean Rovers JFC	4	2	
4	Blue Brazil BC	Lewis United Youth	4	1	
5	Carbrain BC Claret	Hutchison Vale FC	2	0	
5	Musselburgh Windsor FC	Giffnock North BC United	0	5	
5	Syngenta Juveniles	Tynecastle FC	6	1	
5	Larkhall Thistle AFC Blue	Kilsyth Athletic	4	1	aet
5	Linlithgow Rose CFC	Portobello CFA	0	2	
5	Dyce BC	Blue Brazil BC	0	1	
5	Giffnock SC Reds	Drumsagard Football Academy Club	6	7	aet
5	St Peters	Gairdoch United FC	6	0	
6	Sygenta Juveniles	Drumsagard Football Academy Club	7	1	
6	Blue Brazil BC	St Peters FC	0	2	
6	Portobello CFA	Giffnock North BC United	4	2	
6	Larkhall Thistle AFC Blue	Carbrain BC Claret	4	2	
SF	Portobello CA	Syngenta Juveniles	4	5	
	at Haddington Ath				
SF	St Peters	Larkhall Thistle AFC Blue	2	0	
	at Benburb FC				
F	Syngenta Juveniles	St Peters FC	4	6	
	at Airdrie				

Scottish Youth FA Cup 2003s (Under 13) 2016/17

P	Newtongrange Star Youth Dev Acad	Linlithgow Rose CFC	8	7	
P	Spartans FC Youth Whites	Craigshill Thistle Reds	2	1	
P	Currie FC	Lochend YFC	0	4	
P	Edinburgh City	Musselburgh Youngstars Blues	6	0	
P	Portobello CFA	Polbeth United	12	0	
P	Glenburn MW	Knockroon Thistle YFC	5	0	
P	Troon Thistle YFC	Rowallan SC	6	5	aet
P	Jerviston FC	Milton Reds	4	1	
P	Alpha BC	Claremont AFC	1	7	
P	Westfield Colts	Lenzie YC	0	8	
P	Monifieth Athletic	Broughty United YFC Panthers	3	1	
P	Real Fife Yellows	Forfar BC	0	5	
P	Dundee Thistle	Hearts of Beath Juniors	6	2	
P	Breadalbane Strathtay YFC	Letham SC Tangerines	6	1	
P	Ellon Meadows FC	West End FC United	8	2	
P	Fraserburgh Link Up YFC	Newtonhill BC	2	4	
P	Oban Saints	Hillwood BC	2	1	
P	Glenvale AFC	Drumsagard Football Acad Club	1	2	
P	Rossvale FC United	Giffnock SC Black	4	1	
P	East End United BC	Alba Thistle	9	0	
P	Tass Thistle	St Cadocs YC	5	0	
P	Bishopton Juniors FC	Milngavie FC	0	3	
1	Kirkfield United	Bathgate Thistle CFC	2	0	
1	Blackburn United Community YFC	Leith Athletic	0	12	
1	Longniddry Villa Blues	Beechwood	3	3	aet 4-2p
1	Edinburgh South FC Blues	Broxburn AC United	1	12	
1	Bathgate Dynamo	Gala Fairydean Rovers JFC	5	1	
1	Peebles	Edinburgh South FC Reds	4	2	
1	St Bernards BC Midlothian Blues	Musselburgh Youngstars Blues	0	1	
1	Longniddry Villa	Portobello CFA	6	0	
1	Arniston Rangers	Armadale CFC Orange	9	4	
1	Shotts YMCA	Kirkfield United White	1	7	
1	Broxburn Athletic Colts Diamonds	Tranent Colts	12	1	
1	Spartans FC Youth Whites	Edinburgh South CFC	7	2	
1	Newtongrange Star YDA	Bonnyrigg Rose Cobras	4	2	
1	Edinburgh City Blacks	Lochend YFC	6	0	
1	Craigroyston BC	Broxburn Athletic Colts	4	3	
1	Edinburgh City Jaguars	Salvesen CFC	0	1	
1	Musselburgh Windsor	Leith Athletic FC Colts	4	1	
1	Bonnyrigg Rose	Murieston Blues	2	1	
1	Kirkliston & South Queensferry	East Calder Colts	12	0	
1	Spartans FC Youth Whites	Cramond	5	5	aet 1-3p
1	Cavalry Park	Hutchison Vale	0	12	
1	Spartans FC Youth Reds	Musselburgh Windsor FC Blue	5	2	aet
1	Mid Calder Colts	Dunbar United Colts	4	5	
1	Star A CYP	St Bernards BC Midlothian	0	1	
1	Currie Star	Edinburgh City	0	1	
1	Armadale Falcons	Tynecastle	0	12	
1	Crosshouse BC	Greystone Athletic	1	0	
1	Cunninghame YFC	Heston Rovers	5	4	aet
1	Irvine Meadow	Valspar FC	4	1	
1	Caledonian YC Thistle	Dalrymple Thistle	1	12	
1	Troon Thistle YFC Titans	prestwick CFC	8	2	
1	Galston YFC	Girvan Juniors	3	1	
1	Ayr Boswell	Greystone Rovers AFC YFA	5	1	
1	Ayr Boswell BC Colts	Bonnyton Thistle	0	1	
1	Hurlford United YFC	KSC Barca Bulls	1	12	
1	Gleburn MW	Bellfield Royals	1	3	
1	East Kilbride FC Gold	Sauchie Juniors	9	1	
1	Clyde FC School of Football	Condorrat BC	12	0	
1	East Kil bride YC	newmains Harriers	4	2	
1	Dunblane Soccer Club	Strathendrick	9	1	
1	Falkirk Football Community Foundation	Gartcairn Football Academy	5	2	
1	Dalziel BC Blacks	Mossend FC	0	12	
1	Rossvale FC Athletic	Blantyre Soccer Academy Gold	5	1	
1	Scotland BC 2003	Rozsebank United	6	0	
1	Stenhousemuir	Stirling Albion Junior Academy	3	8	
1	Bridgend BC	Claremont AFC	3	2	aet
1	Wishaw Wycombe Wanderers	Seafar Villa Cumbernauld	6	1	
1	East End Thistle	Airdrie United	1	4	
1	Jim Baxter Memorial	Dalziel BC	1	10	
1	Bonnybridge YFC	Cumbernauld Colts	1	12	
1	Milton Rovers YFC	Falkirk Football Community Foundation Navy Blue Foxes	12	1	
1	Bellshill Athletic	Moorlands	4	3	
1	Hamilton Academical BC	Cumbernauld Colts FC Blues	12	0	
1	Milton	Stonehouse BC	7	0	
1	Stenhousemuir BC	Strathaven Dynamo	10	0	
1	Dunbeth	Calderbraes	12	0	
1	Campsie	Blantyre Soccer Academy Black	3	8	

1	Syngenta Juveniles	Alba BC	5	0	
1	Dunipace Juniors	Rossvale FC Munich	3	1	
1	East Kilbride Caledonian Thistle	East Stirlingshire Galaxy	7	2	
1	Cowie United	Falkirk Football Community Foundation Blue	0	12	
1	Mill United Black	Gairdoch United	2	3	
1	Jerviston FC	Carbrian BC	7	3	
1	Syngenta Grange	AC United	0	11	
1	West Park Gold	Kildrum United	9	0	
1	North Motherwell BC	Lenzie YC	4	2	
1	Holytown Colts YC	East Kilbride Burgh United	8	0	
1	Cleland BC	West Park United	8	1	
1	East Fife YA	Scone Thistle	4	4	aet 1-3p
1	Aberdour SDC	Dundee West	0	5	
1	Breadalbane Strathtay YFC	Montrose Youth	4	0	
1	Rothes Juniors	Glenrothes Strollers	0	1	
1	Elgin Star	DFC Wanderers	5	1	
1	Fairmuir BC	Forfar BC	7	3	
1	Letham SC Whites	Pitfour BC	0	11	
1	Inverkeithing Hillfield Swifts Whites	Dundee United SC	5	0	
1	Crossgates Primrose Juniors	jeanfield Swifts	0	9	
1	Dundee Thistle	Ferry Athletic	1	4	
1	East Fife YA Gold	Kennoway United	0	9	
1	Douglas Lads Club	AM Soccer Club	3	6	
1	Bridge of Earn	Blue Brazil BC	5	10	
1	Blairgowrie YFC	Errol	9	3	
1	Arbroath Lads Club	Kettle United	7	0	
1	Monifieth Athletic	Crossford	11	1	
1	Real Fife Yellows	Brechin City Youths	4	2	
1	Riverside CSC	Broughty United YFC Panthers	1	4	
1	Crieff Juniors	Divit Soccer Team	10	2	
1	Duloch Juniors	Carnoustie Panmure YFC	4	3	
1	Insch & District FC	Newtonhill BC	1	4	
1	Donside Juvenile	Colony Colts	4	2	
1	Stoenhaven YFC	Dyce BC	1	6	
1	West End	FDS	3	0	
1	Colony Park	Banks o' Dee Albion	0	3	
1	newmachar United	West End FC Reds	0	3	
1	Deveronvale	Glentanar Community FC	6	3	
1	Banchory Boys	Westdyke Community Club	6	1	
1	Kintore United	Ellon Meadows	5	7	aet
1	Formartine United Youth	Dee BC	12	0	
1	Byron Milan	CBC Hilton	0	12	
1	Peterhead BC Jags	Lewis United Youth	4	5	aet
1	Ardencaple BC	West End Soccer Glasgow	12	2	
1	Busby Amateur FC	Pollok United Soccer Academy	0	6	
1	Drumchapel United	Broomhill SC PJ&D	0	1	
1	Drumchapel Amateurs	Johnstone Burgh BC	1	8	
1	Oban Saints	Drumsagard Football Acad Club	1	4	
1	Milngavie	Rossvale FC United	2	1	
1	Giffnock SC PJ&D	Finnart BC	0	2	
1	Largs Thistle	Westerton United White	10	0	
1	Hillwood BC Thistle	Clyde FC Community	2	6	
1	Linwood Rangers YC	St Cadocs YC United	7	3	
1	Rutherglen Glencairn JFC	Stamperland FC Juniors	9	1	
1	The Celtic Boys Club	Rangers Girls	10	0	
1	Budhill Football Academy	Bridgewater BC	4	1	
1	Barrhead YFC	Barrhead YFC Sky Blues	2	0	
1	East End United BC	Westerton United White	4	1	
1	Tass Thistle	Glenvale AFC Whites	9	0	
1	Houston United	Gourock YAC	3	3	aet 5-4p
1	Langcraigs FC	Dumbarton United	2	4	
1	Erskine YFC United	Kilpatrick FC	0	7	
1	Wetercommon Star	KSC Thistle	3	12	
1	Rutherglen Glencairn JFC Red	Pollok United Soccer Academy	6	2	
1	St Peters FC	Everton BC	8	0	
1	Park Villa BC	Baljaffray FC	0	3	
1	Carolside SC	Port Glasgow Juniors CSC	3	5	
1	Renton Craigandro	Port Glasgow BC	5	3	
1	Erskine YFC United	Mill United White	6	1	
1	Broomhill SC	Stamperland FC PJ&D	1	6	
1	Giffnock SC Red	Haldane United	2	6	
2	Musselburgh Youngstars	Longniddry Villa	1	5	
2	Salvesen CFC	Spartans FC Youth Reds	0	12	
2	Craigroyston BC	Kirkliston & South Queensferry	1	6	
2	Peebles FC	Edinburgh City	9	0	
2	Longniddry Villa Blues	Arniston Rangers	3	4	
2	Edinburgh City Blacks	Musselburgh Windsor FC Blue	3	0	
2	Hutchison Vale FC	Bonnyrigg Rose	12	1	
2	St Bernards BC Midlothian Blues	Kirkfield United White	1	0	
2	Broxburn Athletic Colts Diamonds	Dunbar United Colts	1	0	

2	Cramond FC	Tynecastle FC	0	1	
2	Broxburn AC United	Kirkfield United	1	0	
2	Newtongrange Star YDA	Leith Athletic	0	12	
2	Spartans FC Youth	Bathgate Dynamo FC	3	0	
2	Breadalbane Strathtay YFC	Real Fife	5	1	
2	Glenrothes Strollers	Crieff Juniors	10	2	
2	Elgin Star	Blairgowrie YFC	9	2	
2	Monifieth Athletic	Blue Brazil BC	1	6	
2	Duloch Juniors	Pitfour FC	3	5	
2	Jeanfield Swifts	Ferry Athletic	1	3	
2	Fairmuir BC	Broughty United YFC	5	2	aet
2	Inverkeithing Hillfield Swifts Whites	Scone Thistle	8	1	
2	Arbroath Lads Club	AM Soccer Club	3	2	
2	Kennoway United	Dundee West	3	1	
2	Deveronvale	Newtonhill BC	6	0	
2	West End FC	CBC Hilton	0	3	
2	Donside Juvenile	Lewis United Youth	1	12	
2	Banks o' Dee Albion	Ellon Meadows	12	0	
2	Formartine United Youth	West End FC Reds	1	3	
2	Banchory Boys	Dyce BC	0	7	
2	Cunninghame YFC	Irvine Meadow	4	5	
2	Bonnyton Thistle	KSC Barca Bulls	3	4	
2	Dalrymple Thistle	Bell field Royals	3	4	
2	Troon Thistle YFC	Ayr Boswell FC	3	5	
2	Crosshouse BC	Galston Youth	9	0	
2	Holytown Colts YC	North Motherwell BC	2	1	
2	Gairdoch United FC	Hamilton Academical BC	0	7	
2	Milton	Dunblane Soccer Club	9	0	
2	AC United	Rossvale FC Athletic	3	5	
2	Syngenta Juveniles	Cleland BC	3	4	
2	Clyde FC School of Football	Mossend FC	6	7	
2	Milton Rovers YFC	Stirling Albion Junior Academy	5	0	
2	Scotland BC 2003 Red	East Kilbride FC Gold	1	1	aet 3-2p
2	Airdrie United	East Kilbride Caledonian Thistle	7	1	
2	Blantyre Soccer Academy Black	Wishaw Wycombe Wanderers	6	2	
2	Stenhousemuir BC	Falkirk Football Community Foundation	7	0	
2	Cumbernauld Colts FC	Bellshill Athletic	2	1	
2	Bridgend BC	West Park Gold	4	1	
2	East Klilbride YC	Jerviston FC	2	6	
2	Falkirk Football Community Foundation Blue	Dalziel BC	3	1	
2	Dunbeth FC	Dunipace Juniors	5	1	
2	Ardencaple BC	Tass Thistle	3	6	
2	Johnstone Burgh BC	Haldane United AFC	1	0	
2	Broomhill SC (PJ&D)	Kirkpatrick FC	3	4	
2	Pollok United Soccer Academy	Rutherglen Glencairn JFC	3	0	
2	Finnart BC	Baljaffray FC	4	0	
2	Renton Craigandro	Stamperland FC (PJ&D)	4	9	
2	Largs Thistle	Dumbarton United	57	0	
2	Milngavie FC	St Peters FC	1	4	
2	Drumsagard Football Academy Club	KSC Thistle	3	1	
2	Clyde FC Community	Budhill Football Academy	3	4	
2	Port Glasgow Juniors CSC	Erskine YFC Reds	2	5	
2	Linwood Rangers YC	Rutherglen Glencairn JFC Red	0	4	
2	The Celtic Boys Club	Houston United	5	4	
2	Barrhead YFC	East End United BC	8	3	
3	CBC Hilton	Mossend FC	4	2	
3	Blue Brazil BC	Fairmuir BC	5	4	
3	Leith Athletic	Spartans FC Youth Reds	5	1	
3	Rossvale FC Athletic	Pitfour FC	3	2	aet
3	Arniston Rangers	Crosshouse BC	2	3	
3	Airdrie United	West End FC Reds	3	1	aet
3	Tynecastle FC	Bellfield Royals	0	3	
3	Pollok United Soccer Academy	Irvine Meadow	1	3	
3	Budhill Football Academy	Tass Thistle	1	12	
3	Cumbernauld Colts FC	Edinburgh City Blacks	2	3	
3	Breadalbane Strathtay YFC	Johnstone Burgh BC	1	4	
3	Largs Thistle	Dyce BC	0	8	
3	Kennoway United	Hamilton Academical BC	2	5	aet
3	Deveronvale	Banks o' Dee Albion	0	11	
3	Bridgend BC	Hutchison Vale FC	2	6	
3	St Bernards BC Midlothian	Ferry Athletic	5	2	
3	The Celtic Boys Club	Inverkeithing Hillfield Swifts Whites	1	2	
3	Elgin Star	Longniddry Villa	2	1	
3	KSC Barca Bulls	Glenrothes Strollers	0	4	
3	Broxburn AC United	Milton Rovers YFC	0	9	
3	Erskine YFC Reds	Falkirk Football Community Foundation Blue	2	4	
3	Stamperland FC PJ&D	Broxburn Athletic Colts Diamonds	4	0	
3	Milton	Dunbeth FC	2	4	
3	Holytown Colts YC	Drumsagard Football Acad Club	3	7	
3	Kirkliston & South Queensferry	Peebles	1	4	

3	Jerviston FC	Barrhead YFC	1	12	
3	Finnart BC	Lewis United Youth	5	3	
3	Kilpatrick FC	Spartans FC Youth	2	3	aet
3	Stenhousemuir BC	Ayr Boswell FC	4	1	
3	Scotland BC Red	Blantyre Soccer Academy Black	3	4	
3	Rutherglen Glencairn JFC	Arbroath Lads Club	4	4	aet 2-4p
3	St Peters FC	Cleland BC	5	0	
4	Finnart BC	Crosshouse BC	5	0	
4	Johnstone Burgh BC	Tass Thistle	0	6	
4	Stamperland FC PJ&D	Edinburgh City Blacks	1	0	
4	Spartans FC Youth	Elgin Star	3	4	
4	Barrhead YFC	Milton Rovers YFC	11	1	
4	Airdrie United	Leith Athletic	0	5	
4	Glenrothes Strollers	Blue Brazil BC	3	4	aet
4	Dumsagard Football Academy Club	Peebles FC	3	1	
4	Stenhousemuir BC	Falkirk Football Community Foundation Blue	5	2	
4	CBC Hilton	St Bernards BC Midlothian	7	0	
4	Irvine Meadow	Arbroath Lads Club	3	6	
4	Banks o' Dee Albion	Blantyre Soccer Academy Black	4	1	
4	Hamilton Academical BC	Hutchison Vale FC	0	1	
4	St Peters FC	Dyce BC	0	3	
4	Bellfield Royals	Inverkeithing Hillfield Swifts Whites	3	3	aet 5-4p
4	Dunbeth FC	Rossvale FC Athletic	5	2	
5	Stenhousemuir BC	Stamperland FC (PJ&D)	3	0	
5	Barrhead YFC	Arbroath Lads Club	6	0	
5	Elgin Star	Finnart BC	0	2	
5	Dunbeth FC	Drumsagard Football Acad Club	4	7	
5	Blue Brazil BC	Leith Athletic	1	4	
5	Dyce BC	Bellfield Royals	3	2	
5	Hutchison Vale FC	CBC Hilton	6	0	
5	Tass Thistle	Banks o' Dee Albion	1	6	
6	Dyce BC	Leith Athletic	0	3	
6	Barrhead YFC	Stenhousemuir BC	3	3	4-2p
6	Banks o' Dee Albion	Hutchison Vale	1	0	aet
6	Finnart BC	Drumsagard Football Acad Club	1	2	
SF	Banks o' Dee Albion	Drumsagard Football Acad Club	3	1	
	at Hillhead, Aberdeen				
SF	Barrhead YFC	Leith Athletic	3	1	
	at Arthurlie JFC				
F	Banks o' Dee Albion	Barrhead YFC	1	4	
	at Airdrie				

Scottish Youth FA Cup 2002s (Under 14) 2016/17

P	East End Thistle	Scotstoun Athletic FC	3	0	
P	Riverside CSC	Kirrie Thistle Youths	1	0	
P	LKB United	Fairmuir BC	0	7	
P	Deveronvale Colts	Colony Colts FC	3	5	
P	Cove BC	Donside Juvenile FC	1	3	
P	Byron Swifts	Longside BC	2	5	
1	West Calder United	Hutchison Vale	0	12	
1	Broxburn Athletic Colts Whites	Bathgate Thistle CFC	2	2	aet 4-2p
1	Musselburgh Athletic	Salvesen CFC	10	0	
1	Bonnyrigg Rose FC Pumas	Craigroyston BC	3	1	
1	Bonnyrigg Rose FC Reds	Tynecastle FC Colts	1	5	
1	Currie Star Colts	Portobello CFA	0	10	
1	Murieston United	leith Athletic FC Colts	12	0	
1	Dunbar United Colts	Blackburn United CYFC	12	0	
1	Edinburgh South FC Colts	Gairdoch United Black	2	1	
1	Edinburgh City Reds	Hutchison Vale Colts	0	9	
1	Linlithgow Rose FC Maroon	Edinburgh City	0	3	
1	Pumpherston United	Cavalry Park	2	3	
1	Armadale Falcons	FC Coasters	0	3	
1	Bonnyrigg Rose FC Colts	Bonnyrigg Rose	8	3	
1	Spartans FC Youth Colts	Edinburgh South	4	1	
1	Musselburgh Windsor	Earlston Rhymers YFC	12	0	
1	Gala Fairydean Rovers JFC Borders	Gala Fairydean Rovers JFC	1	11	
1	Spartans FC Youth	Currie Star	7	2	
1	Linlithgow Rose CFC	Armadale Thistle	0	12	
1	Armadale CFC Galaxy	Spartans FC Youth Reds	0	4	
1	Livingston FC BC	Haddington Athletic CFC Sky Blues	5	1	
1	Peebles FC	Livingston CFC	11	1	
1	Tynecatle FC	North Berwick Colts (Black)	4	0	
1	Ayr Boswell BC Colts	St Cuthbert Wanderers (Blue)	3	2	
1	Glenburn MW	Prestwick CFC	2	3	
1	KSC Kilwinning Thistle	AC Irvine	1	1	aet 2-3p
1	Bonnyton Thistle	Greystone Rovers AFC YFA	3	2	
1	Largs Colts	Patna FC Juniors	12	0	
1	Galston YFC	Ayrshire Rosebank United	6	4	
1	Crosshouse BC	KSC Barca	2	8	
1	Mid Annandale AFC	Valspar FC	1	10	
1	Ayr Thistle	Caledonian YC United	1	0	
1	Beveridge Lions	Rothes Juniors	6	3	
1	Carnoustie Panmure YFC	Riverside CFC	0	3	
1	Scone Thistle	St Andrews Colts	3	2	
1	Brechin City YFC	Dryburgh Athletic CC Maroons	2	5	
1	Valleyfield Colts	St Murdoch's	6	2	
1	West Fife United	Letham SC Tangerines	0	10	
1	Dundee Celtic BC	Dryburgh Athletic	0	5	
1	Montrose Youth	Bayside FC	6	0	
1	AM Soccer Club	Dundee West	1	0	
1	Forfar West End	Glenrothes Strollers	2	8	
1	Dundee Thistle	Jeanfield Swifts Reds	1	7	
1	Pitreavie Pumas	Blue Brazil	3	4	aet
1	Lumphinnans United	Monifeith Athletyic	4	3	
1	Broughty United YFC	Greig Park	2	7	
1	Templehall United	Glenrothes Strollers Colts	9	5	
1	Fairmuir BC	Dundee United SC	1	0	
1	Jeanfield Swifts Black	Cupar Soccer Sevens	9	0	
1	Inverkeithing Hillfield Swifts Colts	Ferry Athletic	1	7	
1	Beveridge Lions Blues	Inverkeithing Hillfield Swifts	1	9	
1	Breadalbane Strathtay YFC	Lochgelly Albert Colts	0	12	
1	Racing Kinross Colts	Blairgowrie & Rattray CFC	4	9	
1	Forfar BC	Lomond Colts United	3	2	
1	Logie Harp	Benarty Astros	2	0	
1	Elgin Star	Lincraig FC	4	2	
1	Glen Thistle	Moorlands BC	1	4	
1	Carluke United	Kilsyth Athletic	0	12	
1	Kirkshaws Colts	Dumbarton United	4	5	
1	Clyde FC School of Football	Drumchapel United	0	4	
1	Syngenta Juveniles	Strathaven Dynamo	12	1	
1	Mossend FC	Calder Thistle	6	2	
1	East Kilbride Caledonian Thistle	Mill United Colts	0	5	
1	Cumbernauld Colts	Dunipace Juniors	1	2	
1	Central Boys Football Academy	Oban Saints	2	5	
1	Blantyre Soccer Academy Gold	Stirling Albion Junior Academy	3	5	
1	newmains Hammers	Ardencaple BC	0	1	
1	Motherwell FC Community Trust	Wishaw Wycombe Wanderers	6	3	
1	Cowie United	Wolves FC	1	4	
1	Holytown Colts	Seafar Villa Cumbernauld	10	1	
1	AC Rovers	Eastend Colts	1	7	
1	Milton	The Celtic BC	1	3	
1	East Kilbride Rolls Royce Youth	Rangers SABC	4	3	

1	East Kilbride Burgh Colts	North Kelvin United	0	10	
1	East Kilbride FC Reds	Claremont AFC	0	4	
1	Busby Amateur	Bargeddie Colts	0	4	
1	Campsie FC	Blantyre Soccer Academy Black	2	7	
1	Wasp Community Club	Mill United Colts	0	1	
1	West Park United (Navy)	Jerviston FC	1	6	
1	Milngavie FC	Coatshill FC	8	2	
1	Bo'ness United CFC	East Stirlingshire Galaxy	0	2	
1	Kildrum United	Kirkfield United	9	2	
1	Lenzie YC	Westerton United FC Whites	6	3	
1	Dunblane Soccer Club	Craigpark Colts	0	7	
1	Yelt Farm BC	Torrance	4	2	
1	Drumsagard Football Academy	east End Thistle	4	1	
1	Campbeltown Pupils Youths	Albion Rovers FC BC	1	2	
1	EDFC	Hampden Weir Recreation AFC	0	4	
1	Stirling City	Milan FC	5	1	
1	Clyde FC Community	Jimmy Johnstone Academy	0	12	
1	Strathendrick	Dumbarton United	1	4	
1	Greenock United	Bonnynridge YFC	4	3	aet
1	Aston Villa BC	Garnkirk United	4	2	
1	Stenhousemuir FC	Milton Rovers YC	11	1	
1	Formartine United Youth	Middlefield Wasps	1	4	
1	Banchory Boys	Northstar CFC	12	1	
1	Fraserburgh Link Up YFC Falcons	Ellon Meradows	1	0	
1	Banks o' Dee Albion	Colony Colts FC	12	0	
1	Glentanar Community	Stonehaven YFC	8	1	
1	Lewis United Youth	Stonehaven United	1	0	
1	Culter United	Dyce BC	6	1	
1	Colony Park	Huntly FC	1	0	
1	Deveronvale Colts	newmachar United	4	1	
1	Culter Cobras	Portlethen SC	3	4	
1	Longside BC	Donside Juvenile FC	0	3	
1	Kintore United	Greyhope Boys	6	4	
1	Airdrieoniains FC BC	Park Villa BC	1	4	
1	Paisley FC	East Kilbride FC Blue	0	1	
1	Barrhead YFC	Hampden BC Reds	4	1	
1	St Cadocs YC United	Arthurlie Juniors	1	0	
1	Baljaffray FC Inter	St Cadocs YC	1	3	
1	Broomhill SC PJ&D	Linwood Rangers YC	4	5	aet 5-4p
1	St Andrews BC Reds	Giffnock SC Black	5	2	
1	St Andrews BC	Carolside SC	1	0	
1	PFD United	Erskine YFC	0	7	
1	Port Glasgow BC	Glasgow East BC	0	1	
1	Port Glasgow Juniors CSC	Harmony Row YC	0	1	
1	Renfrew Victoria YFC	Glenvale AFC	3	2	
1	Rossvale Fc Thistle	Erskine YFC Athletic	6	2	
1	Hillwood BC	Rossvale FC Rovers	5	1	
1	Linwood Rangers YC Reds	Johnstone Burgh BC	2	8	
1	Everton BC	Gleniffer Thistle	12	0	
1	Giffnock SC	Baljaffray FC United	4	5	
1	St Convals	St Mirren YFC	11	2	
1	Giffnock SC Reds	St Mirren YFC North	0	12	
2	Hutchison Vale	Tynecastle FC Colts	12	0	
2	Broxburn Athletic Colts Whites	Musselburgh Athletic	3	2	
2	Musselburgh Athletic Whites	Armadale Thistle	4	2	
2	Bonnyrigg Rose FC Colts	Spartans FC Youth	3	4	
2	Cavalry Park	FC Coasters	2	3	
2	Portobello Community Football Academy	Spartans FC Youth Colts	0	2	
2	Hutchison Vale FC Colts	Bonnyrigg Rose FC Pumas	9	0	
2	Edinburgh South FC Colts	Musselburgh Windsor	0	5	
2	Peebles FC	Dunbar United Colts	1	1	aet 4-5p
2	Tynecatle FC	Spartans FC Youth Reds	12	-	
2	Livingston FC BC	Edinburgh City	3	3	aet 5-6p
2	Murieston United	Gala Fairydean Rovers JFC	4	2	
2	Lochgelly Albert Colts	Scone Thistle	6	1	
2	Ferry Athletic	Inverkeithing Hillfield Swifts		wo	
2	Letham SC Tangerines	Templehall United	5	2	
2	Forfar BC	Dryburgh Community Club Maroons	4	0	
2	Logie Harp	AM Soccer Club	1	2	
2	Beveridge Lions	Elgin Star	8	0	
2	Jeanfield Swifts Red	Blue Brazil	1	10	
2	Blairgowrie & Rattray CFC	Greig Park	4	5	
2	Fairmuir BC	Valleyfield Colts	9	0	
2	Jeanfield Swifts Black	Lumphinnans United	7	0	
2	Glenrothes Strollers	Riverside CSC	5	1	
2	Dryburgh Athletic	Montrose Youth	7	1	
2	Portlethen SC	Colony Park	0	5	
2	Kintore United	Culter United	1	4	
2	Lewis United Youth	Banchory Boys	3	1	
2	Banks o' Dee Albion	Fraserburgh Link Up YFC Falcons	4	0	

2	Donside Juvenile FC	Glentanar CFC	3	1	
2	Middlefield Wasps	Deveronvale	4	0	
2	Largs Colts	Ayr Boswell BC	3	2	
2	Galston YFC	Prestwick CFC	6	1	
2	Bonnyton Thistle	Valspar FC	7	6	
2	KSC Barca	Cumnock Juniors YFC	2	3	
2	AC Irvine	Ayr Thistle	11	0	
2	Craigpark Colts	Dumbarton United Black	3	1	
2	Yett Farm BC	Stenhosuemuir FC	1	6	
2	East Kilbride Rolls Royce Youth	Drumchapel United	8	1	
2	Mill United	East Stirlingshire Galaxy	1	2	
2	Dunipace Juniors	Claremont AFC	2	1	
2	Moorlands BC	The Celtic BC	0	10	
2	Holytown Colts	Kilsyth Athletic	3	5	
2	Aston Villa BC	Jerviston FC	0	9	
2	Ardencaple BC	Blantyre Soccer Academy Black	0	12	
2	Jimmy Johnstone Academy	Mossend FC	3	0	
2	Mill United Colts	Albion Rovers FC BC	3	5	
2	Syngenta Juveniles	Eastend Colts	5	2	
2	Dumbarton United	Motherwell FC Community Trust	3	7	
2	Oban Saints	Milngavie FC	2	1	aet
2	Wolves FC	Stirling Albion Junior Academy	10	0	
2	Drumsagard Football Academy	North Kelvin United	8	1	
2	Kildrum United	Stirling City FC	1	9	
2	Lenzie YC	Hampden Weir Recreation AFC	1	4	
2	Greenock United	Bargeddie Colts	0	9	
2	Park Villa BC	St Cadocs YC	12	0	
2	Saltire FC	East Kilbride FC Blue	1	12	
2	Rossvale Fc Thistle	Barrhead YFC	5	1	
2	Broomhill SC PJ&D	Linwood Rangers YC	3	1	aet
2	PFD United	Gleniffer Thistle	5	0	
2	Giffnock SC Black	St Mirren YFC	1	7	
2	St Cadocs YC United	Hillwood BC	2	6	
2	St Andrews BC	Giffnock SC Red	3	1	
2	Glasgow East BC	Giffnock SC	3	4	
2	Harmony Row	Glenvale AFC	0	2	
3	Cumnock Juniors YFC	East Kilbride FC Blue	0	4	
3	Hillwood BC	Drumsagard Football Academy			
3	Dunbar United Colts	AM Soccer Club	2	4	aet
3	Spartans FC Youth Colts	Wolves FC	6	3	
3	FC Coasters	Tynecastle FC	1	4	
3	Syngenta Juveniles	Largs Colts	5	0	
3	Beveridge Lions	Edinburgh City	2	3	
3	Musselburgh Windsor	EK Rolls Royce Youth	4	2	
3	Craigpark Colts	Murieston United	2	3	
3	Glenvale AFC	Stenhousemuir FC	5	0	
3	Blantyre Soccer Academy Black	Dunipace Juniors	7	0	
3	Banks o' Dee Albion	Park Villa BC	1	5	
3	St Andrews BC	Kilsyth Athletic	3	5	
3	East Stirlingshire Galaxy	Culter United	2	6	
3	Greig Park	Glenrothes Strollers	3	2	
3	Stirling City	Albion Rovers FC BC	5	1	
3	St Mirren YFC	Broomhill SC PJ&D	1	6	
3	Giffnock SC	Jeanfield Swifts Black	5	1	
3	Hutchison Vale	Spartans FC Youth	1	2	
3	Hutchison Vale FC Colts	Broxburn Athletic Colts Whites	2	3	
3	Inverkeithing Hillfield Swifts	Lewis United Youth	1	0	
3	Jimmy Johnstone Academy	Motherwell FC Community Trust	4	2	aet
3	Jerviston FC	Galston YFC	4	3	
3	Fairmuir BC	Rossvale FC Thistle	2	3	aet
3	AC Irvine	Musselburgh Athletic Whites	7	2	
3	Forfar BC	PFD United	1	2	
3	Blue Brazil	Colony Park FC	3	2	
3	Middlefield Wasps	Dryburgh Athletic	1	2	
3	Donside Juvenile FC	Hampden Weir Recreation AFC	1	0	
3	Bonnyton Thistle	Letham SC Tangerines	4	0	
3	The Celtic BC	Lochgelly Albert Colts	7	1	
3	Bargeddie Colts	Oban Saints	0	1	
4	Drumsagard Football Academy	Murieston United	2	6	
4	Broxburn Athletic Colts Whites	PFD United	0	3	
4	Glenvale AFC	Kilsyth Athletic	2	0	
4	Oban Saints	Donside Juvenile FC	2	0	
4	Spartans FC Youth Colts	Stirling City FC	0	7	
4	Jerviston FC	Blantyre Soccer Academy Black	1	1	aet 4-5p
4	Broomhill SC PJ&D	Blue Brazil	3	3	aet 5-4p
4	The Celtic BC	Jimmy Johnstone Academy	1	4	
4	Giffnock SC	Rossvale FC Thistle	5	1	
4	Greig Park	Bonnyton Thistle	0	2	
4	Musselburgh Windsor FC	Park Villa BC	1	4	
4	Tynecatle FC	Edinburgh City	12	0	

4	AC Irvine	AM Soccer Club	3	1	
4	Spartans FC Youth	Culter United	3	1	
4	East Kilbride FC Blue	Syngenta Juveniles	1	0	
4	Dryburgh Athletic	Inverkeithing Hillfield Swifts	2	1	aet
5	Dryburgh Athletic	Tynecastle FC	0	4	
5	Blantyre Soccer Academy Black	Murieston United	3	1	
5	East Kilbride FC Blue	Stirling City FC	9	0	
5	Glenvale AFC	Bonnyton Thistle	5	1	
5	Oban Saints	Jimmy Johnstone Academy	0	7	
5	PFD United	Park Villa BC	0	1	
5	Spartans FC Youth	AC Irvine	4	0	
5	Broomhill SC PJ&D	Giffnock SC	3	2	
6	Broomhill SC PJ&D	Glenvale AFC	1	5	
6	Park Villa BC	Jimmy Johnstone Academy	0	2	
6	Tynecatle FC	Spartans FC Youth	0	1	
6	Blantyre Soccer Academy Black	East Kilbride FC Blue	2	0	
SF	Jimmy Johnstone Academy	Spartans FC Youth	2	2	3-4p
	at St Rochs JFC				
SF	Blantyre Soccer Academy Black	Glenvale AFC	0	3	
	at Pollok JFC				
F	Glenvale AFC	Spartans FC Youth	0	0	2-4p
	at Airdrie				

Scottish Youth FA Cup 2001s (Under 15) 2016/17

1	Murieston United CFC Reds	Tynecastle FC	0	12	
1	Gorebridge United YFC	Armadale Falcons	5	1	
1	Leith Athletic	Spartans FC Youth	2	3	
1	Fauldhgouse Foves Whites	Peebles FC	1	0	
1	Dalkeith Thistle CFC	North Berwick Colts	6	3	
1	Blackburn United Community YFC	Kirkliston & South Queensferry	2	4	aet
1	Linlithgow Rose CFC	Longniddy Villa	0	8	
1	Longniddry Villa Colts	Leith Athletic FC Colts	4	6	
1	Tynecastle FC Colts	Forth Athletic	0	6	
1	Inverkeithing Hillfield Swifts	Edinburgh City Real	2	5	
1	Edinburgh City	Currie FC	7	0	
1	Tranbent Colts	Duns Juniors	3	5	
1	Huitchison Vale Fc Colts	Blackhall Athletic	3	2	
1	Dunbar United Colts	Currie Star BC	2	3	
1	Gairdoch United	Musselburgh Youngstars	3	4	aet
1	Gartcairn Football Academy	Spartans FC Whites	11	0	
1	Bathgate Thistle CFC	Harvey Juveniles	4	1	
1	Murieston United CFC Blues	Spartans FC Reds	6	2	
1	Edinburgh City Whites	Broxburn Athletic Colts	3	4	
1	Broxburn Athletic Colts Badgers	Linlithgow Rose CFC Maroons	5	1	
1	Currie Star Colts	East Calder Colts	2	1	
1	Hutchison Vale	Easthouses FC	1	0	aet
1	Polbeth United Dynamos	Gala Fairydean Rovers JFC	2	1	
1	East Stirlingshire	Grangemouth BC	3	1	
1	Greystone Athletic	Crosshouse Boys Club Athletic	0	12	
1	Bellfield Royals	Bonnyton Thistle	4	1	
1	Valspar FC	Tass Thistle United	0	7	
1	Hurlford BC	Irvine Meadow	2	1	
1	KSC Rovers	Auchinleck Talbot BC	5	3	
1	Largs Thistle	Glemburn MW BC	3	2	
1	Hurlford United YFC	Cumnock Juniors YFC	3	6	aet
1	Irvine Vic toria YFC	Caledonian YC	1	5	
1	Milton Rovers YFC	East Kilbride Burgh United	4	3	
1	Seafar Villa Cumbernauld	Rangers SABC	1	4	
1	Drumsagard Football Academy Club Blues	Newmains BC	9	1	
1	Milngavie FC	Clyde Valley FC	1	0	
1	Cumbernauld Colts	Bonnybridge YFC	8	1	
1	Wasp Community Club	Coatshill FC	3	1	
1	East Kilbride YC	Rossvale Fc United	0	2	
1	Cameron Thistle	Rossvale Fc United	0	12	
1	Port Glasgow BC	Clydebank FC	0	12	
1	Oban Saints	Drumsgard Football Academy Club	0	2	
1	North Kelvin United	Strathaven Dynamo	1	7	
1	Wishaw Wycombe Wanderers	Central Boys Football Academy	4	3	
1	Bellshill Athletic	Stirling City	9	0	
1	Lenzie YC	Cumbernauld Colts FC Blues	2	0	
1	Jerviston FC	Mossend FC	4	1	
1	Blantyre BC Yellow	Grange FC	1	7	
1	Bargeddie Colts	Tullibody Hearts	4	2	

1	Larkhall Thistle AFC	East Kilbride RR	3	4	
1	Aston Villa BC	Claremont AFC	2	4	
1	EDFC United	Milton	1	6	
1	Calderbraes BC	Stenhousemuir FC	3	6	
1	Syngenta Juveniles	Helensburgh FC	12	0	
1	Sefar Villa Cumbernauld FC Reds	Gartsherrie BC	0	4	
1	Loch Lomond FC	Dumbarton United	1	12	
1	Westerton United	Armadale Falcons Calcio	0	3	
1	Dunblane Soccer Club United	Rosebank United	11	0	
1	Kelty Hearts	AM Soccer Club	5	5	aet 3-4p
1	Pitfour FC	Rosyth FC	5	2	
1	Carnoustie Panmure	Monifieth Athletic	1	3	
1	Brechin City Youths	East Craigie Swifts	1	3	
1	Arbroath CSC	Jeanfield Blacks	12	2	
1	Montrose Youth	Kirrie Thistle Youths	0	6	
1	Glenrothes Athletic	Riverside CSC	7	1	
1	Luncarty FC	St Andrews Colts	1	6	
1	Rosyth FC Fury	Ferry Athletic	3	1	
1	Thornton Locos	Elgin Star	5	0	
1	Fairmuir BC	Klirkcaldy Eagles	9	0	
1	Kinrossie Scone Thistle	Kennoway United	6	0	
1	East Fife YA	Forfar West End	1	0	
1	Lochgelly Albert Colts Blacks	Dundee Celtic Boys	5	1	
1	Arbroath Lads Club	Bayside FC	4	3	
1	Westdyke CC Thistle	Longside BC	9	0	
1	Cove BC	Lewis United Youth	1	2	
1	Culter BC	Banchory Boys	3	2	
1	Colony Park	Deveronvale	9	1	
1	Huntly FC	Peterhead BC	3	6	aet
1	Ellon Meadows	Fraserburgh Link Up Cubs	3	6	
1	Banks o' Dee Albion	Middlefield Wasps	11	0	
1	Westdyke CC Thistle	Stonehaven Youth	11	0	
1	Glentanar Community	CBC Hilton	5	2	
1	Colony Colts	Formartine United Youth	1	3	
1	The Celtic BC	Clyde FC Community	1	2	
1	Cantera FC	Barrhead YFC	8	2	
1	Giffnock North BC	Giffnock SC Milan	6	0	
1	Hillwood BC	St Peters FC	0	10	
1	Broomhill BC (GK)	East Kilbride FC Blue	1	3	
1	Gourock YAC	Olm Athletic	3	6	
1	Pollok United Socer Scademy	Broomhill SC Thistle	0	9	
1	Glenvale AFC	Stamperland FC Juniors	1	2	
1	St Cadocs Youth Club Thistle	Stamperland FC	2	4	
1	Stonelaw BC	St Cadocs YC United	2	9	
1	St Mirren BC	Paisley City	1	0	
1	Renfrew Victoria YFC	Erskine YFC	1	2	aet
1	Linwood Rangers YC	Cantera FC Reds	2	11	
1	Harmony Row YC	Olm United	1	0	
1	Broomhill SC	Houston FC	12	0	
1	Clydebank United BFC	Ardencaple BC	1	0	
1	Antonine FC	Cambuslang Football Academy	3	4	
2	Dalkeith Thistle CFC	Kirkliston & South Queensferry	1	2	
2	Edinburgh City	Leith Athletic FC Colts	3	2	aet
2	East Stirlingshire	Forth Athletic	0	1	
2	Murieston United CFC Blues	Salvesen CFC Reds	9	0	
2	Gartcairn Football Academy	Gorebridge United YFC	1	0	
2	Duns Juniors	Spartans FC Youth	2	9	
2	Fauldhouse Foxes White	Penicuik Athletic YFC Reds	3	2	
2	Kirkfield United	Musselburgh Youngstars	0	1	
2	Salvesen CFC	AC Oxgangs	2	0	
2	Broxburn Athletic Colts	Polbeth United Dynamos	8	0	
2	Portobello CFA	Longniddry Villa	3	0	
2	Hutchison Vale FC Colts	Broxburn Athletic Colts Badgers	3	4	
2	Bathgate Thistle CFC	Currie Star BC	1	0	
2	Currie Star Colts	Tynecastle FC	1	8	
2	Hutchison Vale	Edinburgh City Real	3	4	
2	East Fife YA	Rosyth FC (Fury)	3	4	aet
2	East Craigie Swifts	AM Soccer Club	2	1	
2	St Andrews Colts	Lochgelly Albert Colts Blacks	1	8	
2	Kirrie Thistle Youths	Arbroath CSC	3	3	aet 4-3p
2	Pitfour FC	Glenrothes Athletic	0	12	
2	Monifieth Athletic	Forfar BC	4	3	
2	Arbroath Lads Club	Thornton Locos	9	1	
2	Fairmuir BC	Kinrossie Scone Thistle	5	3	
2	Dryburgh Athletic	Dundee United SC	2	1	
2	Blue Brazil	Glenrothes Strollers Colts	12	0	
2	Formartine United Youth Reds	Peterhead BC	2	7	
2	Westdyke CC Thistle	Culter BC	1	2	aet
2	Colony Park	Formartine United Youth	1	0	
2	Banks o' Dee Albion	Glentanar CFC	7	1	

2	Fraserburgh Link Up Cubs	Westdyke CC	1	2	
2	Lewis United Youth	FDS BC	10	2	
2	AC Rovers	Riverside FC Athletic	3	1	
2	Milan FC	Russell Latapy	5	1	
2	Bargeddie Colts	Milngavie FC	7	2	
2	Syngenta Juveniles	Armadale Falcons Calcio	1	0	
2	Rossvale FC	Claremont AFC	8	0	
2	Milton Rovers YFC	Grange FC	5	2	
2	Lenzie YC	Rangers SABC	1	7	
2	Kirkintilloch Rob Roy	Gartsherrie BC	7	2	
2	Strathaven Dynamo	Stenhousemuir FC	0	10	
2	Baljaffray FC	Wasp Community Club	2	3	
2	Rossvale FC United	Mill United	1	2	
2	Cumbernauld Colts	Jerviston FC	2	5	
2	Drumsagard Football Academy Club Blues	Wishaw Wycombe Wanderers	1	5	
2	Clydebank FC	Dumbarton United	6	1	
2	Bellshill Athletic	Drumsagard Fooball Academy Club	1	6	
2	Strathendrick	EK Rolls Royce	4	5	
2	Dunblane Soccer Club United	Dalziel BC	2	5	
2	Motherwell FC Com munity trust	Westwood Rovers	1	0	
2	Dunblane Soccer Club City	Milton	0	4	
2	Cumnock Juniors YFC	Crosshouse Boys Club Athletic	1	11	
2	Hurlford BC	Largs Thistle	4	2	
2	Prestwick CFC	Tass Thistle United	2	1	
2	KSC Rovers	Caledonian YC	4	0	
2	Bellfield Royals	Greystone United	10	3	
2	Cantera FC	St Mirren BC	3	0	aet
2	Clyde FC Community	Harmony Row	5	4	
2	Giffnock North BC	Cambuslang Football Academy	1	1	aet 4-3p
2	Rutherglen Glencairn JFC	Stamperland FC	1	2	
2	Broomhill SC	Broomhill SC Thistle	2	1	
2	Clydebank United BFC	St Cadocs YC United	2	1	
2	Stamperland FC Juniors	Olm Athletic	1	10	
2	St Peters FC	Cantera FC Reds	1	4	
2	East Kilbride FC Blue	Erskine YFC	7	0	
3	Broxburn Athletic Colts Badgers	Kirkintilloch Rob Roy	0	5	
3	Syngenta Juveniles	EK Rolls Royce	11	1	
3	Broomhill SC	Fairmuir BC	12	1	
3	Bargeddie Colts	Rossvale	2	6	
3	Hurlford BC	Clyde FC Community	4	3	
3	Giffnock North BC	Glenrothes Athletic	1	5	
3	KSC Rovers	Gartcairn Football Academy	2	3	
3	Stamperland FC	Forth Athletic	2	3	
3	Rangers SABC	AC Rovers	2	1	
3	Mill United	Colony Park	4	1	
3	Milton	Stenhousemuir FC	4	2	
3	Lochgelly Albert Colts Blacks	Crosshouse Boys Club Athletic	0	2	
3	Banks o' Dee Albion	East Kilbride FC Blue	3	5	aet
3	Milan FC	Prestwick CFC	1	5	
3	Dalziel BC	Arbroath Lads Club	1	2	
3	Spartans FC Youth	Cantera FC	2	3	aet
3	East Craigie Swifts	Culter BC	7	0	
3	Edinburgh City Real	Monifieth Athletic	10	1	
3	Murieston United CFC Blues	Blue Brazil	0	8	
3	Clydebank United BFC	Jerviston FC	2	2	aet 6-5p
3	Dryburgh Athletic	Wasp Community Club	1	0	
3	Clydebank FC	Bellfield Royals	4	0	
3	Kirrie Thistle Youths	Milton Rovers YFC	1	1	aet 6-7p
3	Lewis United Youth	Edinburgh City	1	0	
3	Musselburgh Youngstars	Fauldhouse Foxes White	1	0	
3	Peterhead BC	Cantera FC Reds		2	7
3	Salvesen CFC	Broxburn Athletic Colts	0	4	
3	Portobello CFA	Bathgate Thistle	4	0	
3	Wishaw Wycombe Wanderers	Motherwell FC Community Trust	6	0	
3	Tynecastle FC	Olm Athletic	6	0	
3	Drumsagard Football Academy Club	Westdyke CC	0	1	
3	Kirkliston & South Queensferry	Rosyth FC (Fury)	2	6	
4	Glenrothes Athletic	Dryburgh Athletic	10	1	
4	Rangers SABC	Westdyke CC	3	1	
4	East Kilbride FC Blue	Prestwick CFC	7	1	
4	Blue Brazil	Milton	3	3	aet 2-3p
4	Gartcairn Football Academy	Broxburn Athletic Colts	3	1	
4	Forth Athletic	Clydebank United	1	4	
4	Lewis United Youth	Wishaw Wycombe Wanderers	3	0	
4	Crosshouse Boys Club Athletic	Kirkintilloch Rob Roy	1	1	aet 5-4p
4	Hurlford BC	Cantera FC Reds	2	3	
4	Rosyth FC Fury	Clydebank FC	0	2	
4	Broomhill SC	Arbroath Lads Club	6	1	
4	Musselburgh Youngstars	Mill United	1	2	
4	Syngenta Juveniles	Tynecastle FC	1	4	

4	Portobello CFA	Cantera FC	2	1	aet
4	East Craigie Swifts	Edinburgh City Real	3	1	
4	Milton Rovers YFC	Rossvale FC	3	1	
5	Tynecastle FC	Milton Rovers YFC	6	0	
5	Mill United	Clydebank United BFC	0	3	
5	Rangers SABC	Crosshouse Boys Club Athletic	3	0	
5	Milton	Portobello Community FA	1	2	
5	Glenrothes Athletic	Clydebank FC	7	3	
5	Broomhill SC	Cantera FC Reds	0	1	
5	East Kilbride FC Blue	East Craigie Swifts	1	2	aet
5	Lewis United Youth	Gartcairn Football Academy	3	2	
6	Cantera FC	Lewis United Youth	0	1	
6	Glenrothes Athletic	Rangers SABC	1	2	
6	East Craigie Swifts	Tynecastle FC	1	1	2-4p
6	Portobello CFA	Clydebank United BFC	4	0	
SF	Rangers SABC	Lewis United Youth	0	1	
	at St Anthonys JFC				
SF	Portobello CFA	Tynecastle FC	0	2	
	at Newtongrange Star				
F	Lewis United Youth	Tynecastle FC	1	7	
	at Airdrie FC				

Scottish Youth FA Cup 2000s (Under 16) 2016/17

1	Livingston FC BC	Broxburn Athletic Colts	3	6	
1	Kirkfield Wallace	Polbeth United Colts	5	3	
1	Linlithgow Rose CFC Maroon	Cramond FC Blues	0	2	aet
1	Murieston United Blues	Musselburgh Youngstars	8	6	aet
1	Linlithgow Rose CFC Maroon	St Bernards FC Midlothian	3	1	
1	Blackburn United Community Youth	Dalkeith Thistle CFC	1	2	aet
1	Peebles FC	Whitehill Welfare	3	2	
1	Victoria FC	Musselburgh Windsor Blues	2	0	
1	Currie Star	Spartans FC Reds	2	9	
1	Glenafton BC	Valspar FC	0	12	
1	Irvine Thistle	Ayr Boswell BC	2	6	
1	Bonnyton Thistle	Carrick Colts	2	6	
1	Troon Thistle	Mid Annandale AFC	1	3	
1	Milton	East Kilbride YM	1	0	
1	Newton	Cambuslang FC	1	0	
1	Ek Rolls Royce	Riverside FC	2	7	
1	Muirton AFC	Falkirk Community Foundation	4	1	aet
1	Finnart BC	Larkhall Thistle AFC	1	0	
1	Kelvindale Thistle	East Kilbride Burgh United	2	4	
1	Gartcairn Youth Academy	Carmuirs Colts	1	2	
1	Burnmhead Colts	New Stevenston FC	5	1	
1	Dunipace JFC	Syngenta Juveniles	1	7	
1	AM Alloa Athletic 1	The Celtic BC	0	1	
1	Ferry Athletic	Aberdour SDC	7	1	
1	Glenrothes Strollers	Bayside FC Colts	10	0	
1	Kelty Hearts Colts	Kirkcaldy Eagles Barca	1	0	
1	NCR Youths	Forfar West End	5	0	
1	Eastvale	Elgin Star 2000	3	3	aet, 3-1p
1	Abernethy YC	Fairmuir BC	0	3	
1	Turriff United YFC	ALC Athletic	2	3	
1	Banchory Boys	Cove BC	0	7	
1	Colony Park	Fraserburgh Link Up	5	1	
1	Kemnay FC	Culter BC	0	3	
1	Hermes Youth	Banks o' Dee Albion	1	9	
1	Colony Colts	Peyterhead BC	3	2	aet
1	Barrhead YFC	Cantera FC	6	1	
1	Beith Juniors	Stamperland FC Juniors	5	6	
1	Dumbarton United	St Peters FC	7	1	
1	Renfrew Victoria	EDFC Rovers	6	1	
1	PFD United	Haldane United	0	1	
1	Linwood Rangers	Erskine YFC	9	1	
1	Hillwood BC	Broomhill SC (United)	0	4	
1	Glasgow East BC	Glenbrae Colts	4	1	
2	Cramond FC	Currie FC	7	2	
2	AC Oxgangs	Murieston United Blues	1	4	
2	Broxburn Athletic Colts	Cramond FC Blues	6	0	
2	Edina Hibs	Spartans FC Blues	1	0	
2	Kirkfield Wallace	Blackhall Athletic	1	1	aet 2-4p
2	Musselburgh Windsor	Dalkeith Thistle CFC	1	2	

2	Bonnyrigg Rose	Leith Athletic	4	1	
2	M urieton United Red	Hutchison Vale	0	9	
2	Gala Fairydean Rover4s	Tynecastle FC Colts	0	6	
2	Peebles FC	Shotts Victoria	0	8	
2	Spartans FC Reds	Fauldhouse United	2	7	
2	Linlithgow Rose CFC	Victoria FC	5	0	
2	Tynecastle FC	Edinburgh City	7	3	
2	Fairmuir BC	Pitfour FC	10	3	
2	Kelty Hearts Colts	Ferry Athletic	2	7	
2	Eastvale	Bankfoot FC	5	3	
2	Lochgelly Albert Colts	Letham SC Tangerines	10	3	
2	Glenrothes Strollers	NCR Youths	5	0	
2	Montrose Youth	Arbroath Lads Club	1	0	
2	Douglas YFC	Rothes Juniors FC	2	8	
2	Banks o' Dee Albion	Colony Colts	12	0	
2	ALC Athletic	Middlefield Wasps SC	4	2	
2	Culter BC	Cove BC	6	1	
2	Westdyke Community Club	Ellon Meadows	0	2	
2	Newmachar United	South End BC	3	2	
2	Formartine United Youth	Glentanar BC	2	5	
2	Colony Park FC	Portlethen SC	4	0	
2	Clyde FC Youth	Mossend FC	1	0	
2	Milton	Jerviston FC	2	1	
2	Jim Baxter Memorial FC	Camelon Thistle Jeveniles	0	1	
2	Blantyre BC	Finnart BC	0	1	
2	East Kilbride FC	Wishaw Wycombe Wanderers	11	0	
2	East Kilbride FC Reds	Cumbernauld Colts	3	0	
2	Strathaven Dynamo	Burnhead Colts	1	10	
2	Dunblane Soccer Club	Drumchapel Amateurs	0	10	
2	East Kilbride FC Blue	Motherwell FC Community Trust Claret	0	8	
2	Newton	Muirton AFC	2	4	
2	Bo'ness United Community FC	Dalziel BC	0	4	
2	East Kilbride Burgh United	East End Thistle	5	0	
2	The Celtic BC	Stenhousemuir FC	5	5	aet 3-2p
2	Blantyre Victoria	Carmuirs Colts	3	2	
2	Syngenta Juveniles	Bannockburn Amateurs	8	1	
2	Calderbraes BC	Mill United BC	3	1	
2	Riverside FC	Aston Villa BC	6	4	
2	Carrick Colts	Mid Annandale AFC	4	1	
2	Crosshouse BC	St Cuthbert Wanderers	12	1	
2	Stewarton Annick	Coylton FC	1	2	
2	Greystone Rovers AFC Youth Football Academy	Ayr Boswell BC	0	6	
2	Valspar FC	Nithsdale YFC	8	2	
2	KSC Garnock	prestwick CFC	1	0	
2	Broomhill SC (United)	Drumchapel United	7	0	
2	Broomhill SC Blue	Renfrew FC	0	1	
2	Glasgow East BC	Giffnock SC Caledonia	1	2	
2	Stamperland FC	Dumbarton Riverside FC	0	1	
2	Rutherglen Glencairn JFC	Broomhill BC (GK)	3	4	
2	Hamilton Accies	Linwood Rangers YC	1	1	aet 5-4p
2	Harmony Row YC	Baljaffray FC	3	1	
2	Barrhead YFC	Peterhead Youths	1	7	
2	St Andrews BC	Ardencaple BC	8	0	
2	Giffnock SC Thistle	Dumbarton United	4	1	
2	Stamperland FC Juniors	Gleniffer Thistle BC	5	4	aet
2	Renfrew Victoria YFC	Houston United	11	1	
2	Rossvale FC	Westerton United	7	4	
2	East End Athletic	Haldane United	4	2	
3	Culter BC	Lochgelly Albert Colts	0	1	
3	KSC Garnock	Stamperland FC Juniors	1	2	
3	ALC Athletic	Dalziel BC	1	2	
3	Camelon Thistle Juveniles	Hutchison Vale	1	6	
3	Colony Park	Ferry Athletic	4	5	
3	Rossvale FC	Dumbarton Riverside FC	6	1	
3	Clyde FC Youth	Burnhead Colts	3	6	
3	Calderbraes BC	Carrick Colts	5	4	
3	Linlithgow Rose CFC	The Celtic BC	1	3	
3	Giffnock SC Caledonia	Bonnyrigg Rose FC	5	4	
3	Riverside FC	East Kilbride Burgh United	5	2	
3	Shotts Victoria	Muirton AFC	3	0	
3	Valspar FC	Cramond FC	11	1	
3	Motherwell FC Community Trust Claret	Ellon Meadows	4	1	
3	Ayr Boswell BC	East Kilbride FC Reds	3	3	aet 3-5p
3	Tynecastle FC	Blackhall Athletic	12	0	
3	Newmachar United	Broomhill BC (GK)	0	3	
3	Giffnock SC Thistle	Glentanar BC	8	0	
3	Syngenta Juveniles	Renfrew Victoria YFC	9	1	
3	East End Athletic	Renfrew FC	0	1	
3	Dalkeith Thistle CFC	East Kilbirde FC	1	3	
3	St Andrews BC	Broxburn Athletic Colts	2	1	

3	Peterhead Youths	Broomhill SC (United)	2	3	
3	Harmony Row YC	Glenrothes Strollers	3	0	
3	Crosshouse BC	Hamilton Accies	4	5	
3	Fairmuir BC	Fauldhouse United	0	3	
3	Eastvale	Edina Hibs	1	0	
3	Drumchapel Amateurs	Rothes Juniors FC	2	4	
3	Finnart BC	Montrose Youth	6	1	
3	Blantyre Victoria	Tynecastle FC Colts	3	2	
3	Banks o' Dee Albion	Murieston United Blues	12	0	
3	Coylton FC	Milton	2	2	aet 4-5p
4	Hamilton Accies	St Andrews BC	4	3	
4	Calderbraes BC	Burnhead Colts	1	2	
4	Harmony Row YC	Milton	6	0	
4	Syngenta Juveniles	East Kilbride FC Reds	3	1	
4	Fauldhouse United	Banks o' Dee Albion	0	2	
4	Giffnock SC	Finnart BC	7	1	
4	Motherwell FC Community Trust Claret	Hutchison Vale	2	1	
4	Tynecastle FC	Renfrew FC	4	0	
4	Eastvale	Dalziel BC	1	4	
4	Rothes Juniors FC	Rossvale FC	2	2	aet 7-6p
4	The Celtic BC	Broomhill SC (United)	2	0	
4	Ferry Athletic	Shotts Victoria	0	3	
4	Blantyre Victoria	Riverside FC	2	7	
4	Giffnock SC Caledonia	Valspar FC	4	5	
4	Broomhill BC	East Kilbride FC Reds	2	12	
4	Lochgelly Albert Colts	Stamperland FC Juniors	6	5	aet
5	Riverside FC	Hamilton Accies	1	2	
5	Lochgelly Albert Colts	Giffnock SC Thistle	1	2	
5	Dalziel BC	Tynecastle FC	0	2	
5	Rothes Juniors FC	Syngenta Juveniles	1	3	
5	Motherwell FC Community Trust Claret	East Kilbride FC Reds	1	3	
5	Burnhead Colts	Shotts Victoria	2	3	
5	Banks o' Dee Albion	The Celtic BC	5	2	
5	Harmony Row YC	Valspar FC	5	2	
6	Tynecastle FC	Harmony Row	0	2	
6	Syngenta Juveniles	East Kilbride FC	2	1	
6	Shotts Victoria	Giffnock SC Thistle	2	3	aet
6	Hamilton Accies	Banks o' Dee Albion	1	4	
SF	Syngenta Juveniles	Harmony Row	2	1	
	at Falkirk FC				
SF	Banks o' Dee Albion	Giffnock SC Thistle	3	1	
	at Culter JFC				
F	Syngenta Juveniles	Banks o' Dee Albion	1	2	
	at Airdrie				

Scottish Youth FA Cup 1998s (Under 18) 2016/17

1	Bonnyrigg Rose	Livingston CFC	1	0	
1	Falkirk Grahamston	Dalkeith Thistle CFC	4	0	
1	Loanhead MW YFC Blues	Penicuik Athletic YFC Blues	3	2	
1	Syngenta Juveniles	Tynecastle FC	1	3	
1	Polbeth United	Hutchison Vale	1	10	
1	Craigshill Thistle	Dunbar United Colts	2	5	
1	Leith Athletic	Airdrie United	1	4	
1	Lurieston United Blue	Leith Athletic Fc Whites	4	0	
1	Edinburgh City Blacks	Spartans FC Reds	0	8	
1	Troon FC	Bellfield BC	6	1	
1	Stewarton Annick	Girvan Youth FC	1	0	aet
1	Whitletts Victoria	Glenafton Athletic	3	1	
1	Cumnock Enterprise FC	Glenburn MW	1	0	
1	Drumsagard Football Academy	Jerviston FC	2	2	aet, 4-3p
1	Cumbernauld United Juniors	Campsie FC	4	1	
1	Claremont ASFC	Hamilton Accies BC	0	12	
1	Carbrain BC Clarets	Knightswood FC	1	8	
1	Larkhall Thistle AFC	East Kilbride Thistle YC	5	0	
1	Milton FVDA	East End Thistle	0	1	

1	Finnart BC	Alva Swifts YFC	3	4	aet
1	Cumbernauld Colts	Wishaw Wycombe Wanderers	0	2	
1	Riverside FC	Carbrain BC Sjys	5	3	
1	Townhill FC	Tayport United	2	0	
1	Monifieth Athletic	West Fife Albion	0	4	
1	St James Youth	Stanley Socca	0	8	
1	Aberdour SDC	Rothes Juniors	2	3	
1	Dundee United SC	Ferry Athletic Yellows	0	4	
1	Burentisland Shipyard	Balgonie Scotia	5	0	
1	Craigie Thistle	Coupar Angus	1	2	
1	Monifieth Athletic Crown	Dundee West	1	4	
1	Banks o' Dee Albion	Huntly FC	1	0	
1	Banchory Boys	Culter BC	1	7	
1	West End FC	Formartine United Youth	0	9	
1	Port Glasgow Juniors CSC	Moorlands BC	0	12	
1	Drumchapel United	Ardencaple BC	12	0	
1	Hillwood BC	Antonine FC	4	0	
1	Tass Thistle	Renfrew FC Blue	1	0	
1	Giffnock SC lazio	Rutherglen Glencairn JFC	1	2	
1	Beith Juniors	Cardonald Thistle	1	0	
1	Baljaffray FC	Gourock YAC	3	6	
1	Port Glasgow BC	Maryhill Juniors	5	5	aet 2-4p
1	Eastwood Juveniles Fc Rovers	Arthurlie Juniors	3	2	
2	Tynecastle FC	Edinburgh City	3	1	
2	Linlithgow Rose CFC	AC Oxgangs	0	4	
2	AC Oxgangs	Spartans FC Reds	0	1	
2	Broxburn Athletic Colts Badgers	Loanhead Miners YFC	0	1	
2	Loanhead Miners Youth FC Blues	ockenzie Star	1	4	
2	Musselburgh Windsor FC	Hutchison Vale	2	1	
2	Bonnyrigg Rose FC	Falkirk Grahamston FC	1	2	aet
2	Musselburgh Youngstars	Dunbar United Colts	3	1	
2	Cavalry Park	Murieston United Blue	1	3	
2	Beechwood FC	Broxburn Athletic Colts	0	1	
2	Gartciarn Football Academy	Airdrfie United	0	1	
2	Preston Athletic	Edinburgh South CFC	0	5	
2	Dryburgh Athletic	Crossgates Primrose JFC	5	3	
2	St Andrews Colts	West Fife Albion	0	1	
2	Eastvale	Kelty Hearts Colts Development	1	2	
2	Kennoway United	Ferry Athletic Yellows	1	5	
2	Coupar Angus	Townhill FC	1	7	
2	Brechin City YFC	Forfar West End	0	2	
2	Rosyth FC (Cairneyhill)	Scone Thistle	6	0	
2	Carnoustie Panmure BC	Burntisland Shipyard	5	7	
2	Dundee West FC	Kirkcaldy FC	10	2	
2	Kirrie Thistle Youths	Jeanfield Swifts	4	5	aet
2	Rothes Juniors	Stanley Socca	7	1	
2	Cove BC	Culter Rovers	12	0	
2	Echt BC	Formartine United Youth	3	1	
2	Culter BC	Fraserburgh Link Up FC	1	0	
2	Stoneywood BC	Stonehaven YFC	1	3	
2	Northstar CFC	Inverurie Locos	1	2	
2	Banks o' Dee Albion	Ellon Meadows	8	2	
2	Dee BC	Turriff United YFC	0	12	
2	Cumnock Enterprise FC	Troon FC	3	4	
2	Stewarton Annick	Whitletts Victoria	4	8	
2	Valspar FC	Bonnyton Thistle	6	7	
2	DC Bishopbriggs Youth	Larkhall Thistle AFC	0	1	
2	Condorrat BC	Sauchie Juniors FC	4	3	aet
2	East Kilbride Burgh United	Steins Thistle	2	1	
2	East Kilbride Hotspur	Dunblane Soccer Club	12	1	
2	Alva Swifts YFC	Cumbernauld United Juniors	2	3	
2	Riverside FC	Stenhousemuir FC	6	2	
2	East End Thistle	Cowie United	6	0	
2	Blantyre BC Yellow	Blantyre BC	1	6	
2	Pollok United Soccer Academy	Steins Thistle	5	3	
2	Hamilton Accies BC	Dalziel BC	3	0	
2	Coltswood Athletic	Mill United BC Colts	5	2	
2	East Kilbride FC Reds	Wishaw Wycombe Wanderers	scr	wo	
2	Milton FVDA	Mossend FC	5	2	
2	Braehead FC	Knightswood FC	4	3	
2	Drumsagard Football Academy	Seafar Villa Cumbernauld Blue	1	0	
2	Giffnock SC Rtoma	Drumchapel United	0	6	
2	Eastwood Juveniles Fc Rovers	Glasgow East BC	7	1	
2	Girdle Toll YFC	Beith JFC	1	5	
2	Moorlands BC	Giffnock SC Milan	4	0	
2	Cameron Thistle	Erskine YFC	1	4	
2	Milngavie FC	Maryhill Juniors	5	4	
2	Eastwood Juveniles Fc Rovers	Barrhead YFC	9	0	
2	East Kilbride Thistle AFC Academy	Tass Thistle	1	2	
2	Ritherglen Glencairn JFC	Whitacres Community Academy	12	0	

2	Arthurlie Juniors	KSC Royals	3	2	
2	Pirie Park YFC	Gourock YAC	3	2	
2	St Cadocs YC United	Hatmony Row YC	3	6	
2	Barrhead YFC Whites	Gleniffer Thistle BC	1	0	
2	Dumbarton United Yellow	Hillwood BC	2	4	
2	Glenvale AFC	Broomhill BC (GK)	3	2	
2	Clydebank FC	Renfrew FC Blue	12	2	
3	Stonehaven YFC	Hamilton Accies BC	0	2	
3	Falkirk Grahamston	Beith JFC	0	3	
3	Erskine YFC 1	Larkhall Thistle AFC	6	0	
3	Coltswood Athletic	Edinburgh South CFC	5	0	
3	Townhill FC	Troon FC	5	0	
3	Rutherglen Glencairn JFC	Cockenzie Star	3	1	
3	Spartans FC Reds	Clydebank FC	1	2	
3	Wishaw Wycombe Wanderers	Burntisland Shipyard	2	3	
3	Glenvale AFC	Murieston United Blue	4	1	
3	Whitletts Victoria	Dryburgh Athletic	5	2	
3	Culter BC	Musselburgh Youngsters	2	1	
3	Drumchapel United	Kelty Hearts Colts Development	3	1	ABD
3	Cumbernauld United Juniors	Blantyre BC	2	0	aet
3	Broxburn Athletic Colts	Dundee West	6	3	
3	Milton	Arthurlie Juniors	0	1	aet
3	Ferry Athletic Yellows	Harmony Row YC	2	3	
3	Turriff United YFC	Musselburgh Windsor	2	2	aet 7-8p
3	Riverside FC	Tynecastle FC	4	5	aet
3	Condorrat BC	Loanhead Miners YFC	2	3	
3	Inverurie Locos	Jeanfield Swifts	5	1	
3	Rosyth FC (Cairneyhill)	East Kilbride Burgh United	0	1	
3	East Kilbride Hotspur	Banks o' Dee Albion	0	4	
3	East End Thistle	Moorlands BC	1	12	
3	Eastwood Juveniles Fc Rovers	Tass Thistle	7	2	
3	West Fife Albion	Barrhead YFC Whites	1	0	
3	Echt BC	Cove BC	0	7	
3	Pollok United Soccer Academy	Forfar West End	3	1	
3	Braehead FC	Bonnyton Thistle	0	6	
3	Airdrie United	Drumsagard Football Academy Cl	6	1	
3	Rothes Juniors	Eastwood Juveniles	2	1	
3	AC Oxgangs	Pirie Park YFC	5	6	aet
3	Hillwood BC	Milngavie	5	0	
4	Harmony Row YC	Loanhead Miners YFC	5	2	
4	Broxburn Athletic Colts	Inverurie Locos	0	0	aet 3-0p
4	Bonnyton Thistle FC	Erskine YFC	0	1	
4	Moorlands BC	Culter BC	6	2	
4	Hillwood BC	Banks o' Dee Albion	4	2	
4	Rothes Juniors	Glenvale AFC	1	2	
4	Rutherglen Glencairn JFC	Coltswood Athletic	4	2	
4	Townhill FC	West Fife Albion	6	0	
4	Burntisland Shipyard	Whitletts Victoria	4	0	
4	Arthurlie Juniors	Clydebank FC	0	3	
4	Airdrie United	Hamilton Accies BC	3	1	
4	Cove BC	Pirrie Park YFC	2	1	
4	Pollok United Soccer Academy	Pollok United Soccer Academy	0	1	
4	Tynecastle FC	Cumbernauld United Juniors	3	1	
4	Beith Juniors	East Kilbride Burgh United	2	1	
4	Eastwood Juveniles Fc Rovers	Musselburgh Windsor	2	4	
5	Musselburgh Windsor FC	Hamilton Accies BC	3	1	aet
5	Burntisland Shipyard	Pollok United Soccer Academy	1	2	
5	Beith Juniors	Glenvale AFC	7	5	aet
5	Rutherglen Glencairn JFC	Clydebank FC	0	2	
5	Hillwood BC	Broxburn Athletic Colts	3	2	
5	Townhill FC	Harmony Row YC	2	3	
5	Moorlands BC	Tynecastle FC	5	0	
5	Erskine YFC 1	Airdrie United	3	4	
6	Pollok United	Clydebank FC	0	3	
6	Musselburgh Windsor FC	Hillwood BC	0	2	
6	Beith Juniors	Harmony Row YC	2	1	
6	Moorlands BC	Airdrie United	0	1	
SI	Airdrie United	Hillwood BC	2	1	
	at Blackburn Utd				
SI	Clydebank FC	Beith JFC	6	1	
	at Petershill JFC				
F	Airdrie United	Clydebank FC	1	3	
	at Airdrie FC				

Scottish Youth FA Cup 1995s (Under 21) 2016/17

					Rep		
1	Thorniewood United	St Andrews BC	4	4	4	0	
1	Busby Amateurs	Leith Athletic	0	9			
1	Arsenal BC (Glasgow)	Bonnyrigg Rose	3	3	4	1	
1	St Peters Juveniles Giffnock North	Tower Hearts	1	5			
1	Bishopton Juniors	East Kilbride Thistle YC	0	1			
1	Vale of Leven	Harmony Row YC	1	4			
1	Rossvale	Langcraigs	6	0			
1	Linlithgow Thistle	Renfrewshire Thistle	5	2			
1	Pollok Juveniles	Rutherglen Glencairn JFC	1	8			
1	Kilpatrick FC	Craigroyston BC	2	1			
1	St Mungo	Renfrew FC Blue	3	1			
1	Ardgowan Thistle	Dalkeith Thistle CFC	3	3	2	3	
1	Easthouses FC	Glentyan Thistle	3	2			
1	Arthurlie Juniors Whites	West Calder United	1	0			
1	Whitletts Victoria	Craigshill Thistle	12	0			
1	Campsie FC	Milngavie	1	4			
2	Murieston United	Steins Thistle	0	6			
2	Tossvale	Bonnyton Thistle	3	4			
2	Tower Hearts	Musselburgh Windsor	6	0			
2	Harmony Row	Linlithgow Thistle	2	0			
2	Erskine YFC	Kirkintilloch Rob Roy	2	3			
2	Drumchapel Amateurs	Arsenal BC (Glasgow)	2	2	?	?	
2	Bonnyrigg Rose Athletic "A"	Milngavie FC	1	3			
2	Easthouses FC	Barrhead YFC	0	5			
2	Arthurlie Juniors Whites	Ritherglen Glencairn JFC	1	8			
2	Leith Athletic	Thorniewood United	3	0			
2	Antonine FC	Newcraighall Leith Victoria AFC	5	2			
2	Ashfield FC	Whitletts Victoria	0	4			
2	Aston Villa BC	Wesyt Park United	0	8			
2	Johnstone Burgh BC	Kilpatrick FC	6	1			
2	St Mungo	Dalkeith Thistle CFC	6	0			
2	Newtongrange Star Youth Development Academy	East Kilbride Thistle YC	7	1			
3	Arsenal BC (Glasgow)	Johnstone Burgh BC	1	2			
3	Kirkintilloch Rob Roy	Harmony Row YC	1	3			
3	West Park United	Rutherglen Glencairn JFC	2	2	2	3	
3	Leith Athletic	Newtongrange Star YDA	9	0			
3	Tower Hearts	Bonnyton Thistle	3	0			
3	Barrhead YFC	Steins Thistle	2	0			
3	Milngavie FC	St Mungo	0	3			
3	Whitletts Victoria	Antonine FC	0	8			
4	Harmony Row	Barrhead YFC	0	1			
4	St Mungo	Rutherglen Glencairn JFC	1	3			
4	Johnstone Burgh BC	Tower Hearts	1	1	2	2	6-7p
4	Leith Athletic	Antonine FC	1	2			
SF	Barrhead YFC	Antonine FC	3	0			
	at Neilston JFC						
SF	Tower Hearts	Rutherglen Glencairn JFC	0	1			
	at Benburb JFC						
F	Barrhead YFC	Rutherglen Glencairn JFC	1	2			
	at Airdrie FC						

SCHOOLS FOOTBALL

The Scottish Schools FA runs National Cup competitions for Boys and Girls in age groups from Under 13 through to Und 18. The early rounds are regionalised. Entrants range from the Nicolson Institute from the Western Isles, to schools in t Borders and Dumfries & Galloway. Some private schools enter, as well as local authority schools. Readers from outwit Scotland should note that the terminology of a school name (e.g. HS or Academy) gives no indication of its status.

HS = HS, GS = Grammar School, Acad = Academy, Sec = Secondary

Scottish Schools Under 18 Shield 2016/17

1	Aberdeen Grammar v. Gordonstoun School 5-1
1	All Saints Sec. v. Jordanhill School
1	Balfron HS v. St.Margaret's HS 3-2
1	Beath HS v. Harris Ac. 1-0
1	Braes HS v. Taylor HS 1-0
1	Braidhurst HS v. Cumbernauld Ac. 1-0
1	Broughton HS v. Stewart's Melville College 1-6
1	Calderglen HS v. Strathaven Ac. 5-2
1	Clydebank HS v. Woodfarm HS
1	Clydeview Ac. v. Glasgow Gaelic School
1	Crieff HS v. Webster's HS
1	Currie HS v. Lasswade HS 0-1
1	Eastwood HS v. High School of Glasgow
1	Firrhill HS v. Musselburgh Grammar 1-4
1	Gleniffer HS v. Cathkin HS 3-2
1	Gracemount HS v. St.Kentigern's Ac.
1	Grange Ac. v. Duncanrig Sec. 2-4
1	Greenfaulds HS v. Our Lady's HS Motherwell
1	Greenwood Ac. v. St.Matthew's Ac.
1	Hamilton College v. Girvan Ac.
1	Hermitage Ac. v. St.Ninian's HS Giffnock 0-3
1	Hyndland Sec. v. Barrhead HS 1-2
1	Johnstone HS v. Bannerman HS
1	Newbattle HS v. Portobello HS 1-4
1	Notre Dame HS v. Our Lady & St.Patrick's HS
1	Oban HS v. Paisley Grammar 1-0
1	Penicuik HS v. Peebles HS
1	Perth Grammar v. St.Andrew's HS Kirkcaldy 1-1 (7-6 pens)
1	Perth HS v. Carnoustie HS
1	Preston Lodge HS v. St.Margaret's Ac. 3-9
1	St.Joseph's College v. Largs Ac. 1-1 (6-5 pens)
1	St.Mungo's Ac. v. Holyrood Sec. 0-1
1	St.Mungo's HS v. Coatbridge HS 5-1
1	St.Paul's Ac. v. Blairgowrie HS
1	Stirling HS v. Graeme HS
1	Stonelaw HS v. Boclair Ac.
1	Trinity HS Rutherglen v. Linwood HS 1-0
1	Turnbull HS v. Cardinal Newman HS 3-1
1	Viewforth HS v. Bell Baxter HS
1	Wallace HS v. Our Lady's HS Cumbernauld
1	Whitburn Ac. v. Holy Rood HS 1-0
1	Williamwood HS v. Douglas Ac.
2	Alloa Ac. v. St.Modan's HS 0-7
2	Arbroath HS v. Perth HS 1-7
2	Ardrossan Ac. v. Uddingston Grammar 1-3
2	Auchinleck Ac. v. St.Joseph's College 0-2
2	Balwearie HS v. St.Columba's HS Dunfermline 4-0
2	Banff Ac. v. Banchory Ac. 0-2
2	Bannerman HS v. Holyrood Sec. 3-5
2	Barrhead HS v. Notre Dame HS 4-7
2	Beath HS v. Madras College 8-2
2	Bell Baxter HS v. St.John's HS 1-2
2	Blairgowrie HS v. Dunfermline HS 0-9
2	Braes HS v. Dunblane HS 0-2
2	Braidhurst HS v. Airdrie Ac. 5-2
2	Dalkeith HS v. North Berwick HS 0-2
2	Denny HS v. St.Ninian's HS Kirkintilloch 0-2
2	Dingwall Ac. v. Nicolson Institute 3-0
2	Douglas Ac. v. St.Ninian's HS Giffnock 1-6
2	Douglas Ewart HS v. Lanark Grammar 1-2
2	Dumbarton Ac. v. St.Peter the Apostle HS 2-1
2	Dunoon Grammar v. All Saints Sec. 1-7
2	Eastwood HS v. Hutcheson's Grammar 4-1
2	Ellon Ac. v. Millburn Ac. 0-2
2	Falkirk HS v. Bishopbriggs Ac. 0-5
2	Forfar Ac. v. Crieff HS 9-1
2	Fraserburgh Ac. v. Aberdeen Grammar 4-3
2	George Heriot's School v. Ross HS 0-2
2	George Watson's College v. Lasswade HS 0-2
2	Girvan Ac. v. Duncanrig Sec. 4-0
2	Gleniffer HS v. St.Andrew's Sec. 9-1
2	Glenwood HS v. Perth Grammar 4-5
2	Grangemouth HS v. Wallace HS 0-4
2	Greenwood Ac. v. Dumfries HS 2-0
2	Grove Ac. v. Auchmuty HS 3-4
2	Gryffe HS v. Inverclyde Ac. 1-2
2	Holy Cross HS v. St.Andrew's & St.Bride's HS 1-5
2	Inverkeithing HS v. Queen Anne HS 2-2 (5-4 pens)
2	Inverness HS v. Inverurie Ac. 0-2
2	James Young HS v. Boroughmuir HS 1-1 (5-6 pens)
2	John Paul Ac. v. Clydeview Ac. 2-0
2	Kincorth Ac. v. Alford Ac. 1-3
2	Larbert HS v. Chryston HS 2-2 (7-8 pens)
2	Lenzie Ac. v. Glasgow Ac. 2-0
2	Levenmouth Ac. v. Glenrothes HS 2-5
2	Lockerbie Ac. v. Carluke HS 0-2
2	McLaren HS v. Balfron HS 3-8
2	Mearns Castle HS v. Clydebank HS 4-3
2	Meldrum Ac. v. Cults Ac. 0-2
2	Monifieth HS v. Kirkcaldy HS 2-0
2	Montrose Ac. v. Brechin HS 5-2
2	Oban HS v. Lourdes Sec. 1-6
2	Park Mains HS v. St.Margaret Mary's Sec. 2-0
2	Peebles HS v. Stewart's Melville College 2-6
2	St.Aidan's HS v. St.Mungo's HS 1-6
2	St.Aloysius College v. Trinity HS Rutherglen 3-3 (3-4 pens)
2	St.Ambrose HS v. Coltness HS 3-2
2	St.Kentigern's Ac. v. Portobello HS 0-0 (7-6p)
2	St.Margaret's Ac. v. Whitburn Ac. 9-2

2	St.Thomas Aquinas Sec. v. St.Columba's HS Gourock 0-6
2	Stirling HS v. St.Maurice's HS 0-3
2	Stonelaw HS v. Bearsden Ac. 4-3
2	Stranraer Ac. v. Calderglen HS 0-6
2	Thurso HS v. Aboyne Ac. 2-0
2	Turnbull HS v. Our Lady's HS Motherwell 3-0
2	West Calder HS v. Musselburgh Grammar 2-5
3	Alford Ac. v. Cults Ac. 0-6
3	Balfron HS v. Turnbull HS 0-3
3	Braidhurst HS v. St.Ninian's HS Kirkintilloch 8-1
3	Calderglen HS v. Carluke HS 1-1
3	Dingwall Ac. v. Millburn Ac. 0-2
3	Dumbarton Ac. v. All Saints Sec. 3-3
3	Dunblane HS v. St.Mungo's HS 9-2
3	Eastwood HS v. Bearsden Acad 4-1
3	Gleniffer HS v. Mearns Castle HS 5-1
3	Glenrothes HS v. Perth Grammar 3-6
3	Holyrood Sec. v. Park Mains HS 5-3
3	Inverkeithing HS v. Dunfermline HS 1-9
3	Inverurie Ac. v. Banchory Ac. 3-3
3	John Paul Ac. v. Trinity HS Rutherglen 1-5
3	Lanark Grammar v. Greenwood Ac. 5-2
3	Lourdes Sec. v. Inverclyde Ac. 3-0
3	Monifieth HS v. Forfar Ac. 4-0
3	Montrose Ac. v. Auchmuty HS 3-0
3	Musselburgh Grammar v. Ross HS 0-2
3	North Berwick HS v. Lasswade HS 4-5
3	Perth HS v. Balwearie HS 4-1
3	St.Ambrose HS v. Chryston HS 1-0
3	St.Andrew's & St.Bride's HS v. St.Joseph's College 1-4
3	St.Columba's HS Gourock v. Lenzie Ac. 0-1
3	St.John's HS v. Beath HS 2-3
3	St.Kentigern's Ac. v. Stewart's Melville College 1-8
3	St.Margaret's Ac. or Whitburn Ac. v. Boroughmuir HS
3	St.Maurice's HS v. Wallace HS 1-6
3	St.Modan's HS v. Bishopbriggs Ac.4-3
3	St.Ninian's HS Giffnock v. Notre Dame HS 9-0
3	Thurso HS v. Fraserburgh Ac. 3-0
3	Uddingston Grammar v. Girvan Ac. 1-2
4	Boroughmuir HS v St Modans HS 0-2
4	Calderglen HS v Dumbvarton Azcad 5-0
4	Dunblane HS v Braidhurst HS 2-2
4	Eastwood HS v Lanark GS 5-0
4	Holyrood Sec v Girvan Acad 4-2
4	Lasswade HS v Stewart's Melville Coll 2-3
4	Millburn Acad v Dunfermline HS 0-1
4	Monifieth HS v Inverurie Acad 1-2
4	Montrose Acad v Thurso HS 2-2
4	Perth GS v Beath HS 3-1
4	Perth HS v Cults Acad 3-2
4	St Josephs Coll v Gleniffer HS 1-5
4	St Ninians HS Giffnock v Lourdes RC Sec 6-1
4	Trinity RC HS v Lenzie Acad 4-1
4	Turnbull HS v Ross HS 5-3
4	Wallace HS v St Ambrose HS 2-0
5	Eastwood HS v Trinity RC HS
5	Holyrood Sec v Wallace HS 1-6
5	Inverurie Acad v Calderglen HS 0-8
5	Perth GS v St Ninians HS Giffnock 1-7
5	Perth HS v Dunfermline HS 0-3
5	St Modans HS v Gleniffer HS 2-1
5	Stewart's Melville Coll v Turnbull HS 0-2
5	Thurso HS v Braidhurst HS 0-3
6	St.Ninian's HS Giffnock v. Turnbull HS 4-0
6	Eastwood HS v. Dunfermline HS 2-0
6	St.Modan's HS v. Calderglen HS 1-0
6	Braidhurst HS v. Wallace HS 0-0 (3-2 pens)
SF	Eastwood HS v. St.Ninian's HS Giffnock 2-2 (5-4 pens)
	(Tues 28 Mar, Renfrew FC, 3.30)
SF	St.Modan's HS v. Braidhurst HS 1-1 (3-4 pens)
	(Wed 29 Mar, Airdrieonians FC, 5.00)
F	Eastwood HS v Braidhurst HS 1-2 (
	Thu May 4 at Hampden Park)

Scottish Schools Under 16 Shield 2016/17

1	Auchinleck Ac. v. Stranraer Ac. 1-6
1	Balwearie HS v. Webster's HS 0-1
1	Banff Ac. v. Nicolson Institute 0-1
1	Barrhead HS v. All Saints Sec. 4-0
1	Bell Baxter HS v. Forfar Ac. 0-2
1	Boroughmuir HS v. George Watson's College 2-4
1	Braidhurst HS v. Our Lady's HS Cumbernauld 1-0
1	Broughton HS v. Hawick HS 6-1
1	Cathkin HS v. Trinity HS Rutherglen 0-2
1	Coatbridge HS v. St.Maurice's HS 1-3
1	Coltness HS v. Bishopbriggs Ac. 0-2
1	Craigmount HS v. Galashiels Ac. 4-1
1	Dingwall Ac. v. Aboyne Ac. 1-0
1	Dumbarton Ac. v. Knightswood Sec. 1-5
1	Dumfries HS v. Hamilton College 8-0
1	Dunfermline HS v. Lochgelly HS 9-2
1	Dunoon Grammar v. Mearns Castle HS 2-3
1	George Heriot's School v. Gracemount HS 5-1
1	Glenwood HS v. Levenmouth Ac. 0-4
1	Grange Ac. v. St.Matthew's Ac. 1-0
1	Greenfaulds HS v. Taylor HS 4-6
1	Gryffe HS v. John Paul Ac. 0-1
1	Harris Ac. v. Kirkcaldy HS
1	Holy Rood HS v. Lasswade HS 0-1
1	Holyrood Sec. v. Boclair Ac. 2-1
1	Largs Ac. v. Greenwood Ac. 1-0
1	Lourdes Sec. v. St.Columba's HS Gourock 1-0
1	Montrose Ac. v. Grove Ac. 1-9
1	Oban HS v. Johnstone HS 1-0
1	Our Lady's HS Motherwell v. St.Ninian's HS Kirkintilloch 6-2
1	Preston Lodge HS v. Peebles HS 4-1
1	Queen Anne HS v. Madras College
1	St.Andrew's Sec. v. Williamwood HS 5-3
1	St.Joseph's College v. St.Andrew's & St.Bride's HS 0-1
1	St.Mungo's Ac. v. Gleniffer HS 1-0
1	St.Ninian's HS Giffnock v. Hyndland Sec. 8-0
1	St.Peter the Apostle HS v. Glasgow Gaelic School 6-3
1	St.Thomas Aquinas Sec. v. St.Margaret Mary's Sec. 9-1
1	Stirling HS v. Cardinal Newman HS 3-4
1	Stonelaw HS v. Douglas Ac. 0-1
1	Trinity Ac. v. Royal HS 1-7
1	Turnbull HS v. St.Ambrose HS 2-0
1	West Calder HS v. Portobello HS 0-1
2	Airdrie Ac. v. Turnbull HS 3-0
2	Arbroath HS v. Levenmouth Ac.3-2
2	Banchory Ac. v. Webster's HS 0-2
2	Beath HS v. Dingwall Ac. 0-2
2	Braidhurst HS v. St.Maurice's HS 6-2
2	Cardinal Newman HS v. Taylor HS 3-2
2	Clydeview Ac. v. Eastbank Ac. 2-0
2	Dumfries HS v. Stranraer Ac. 6-1
2	Duncanrig Sec. v. Lanark Grammar 0-3
2	Falkirk HS v. Bishopbriggs Ac. 0-3
2	George Watson's College v. Preston Lodge HS 2-6
2	Hermitage Ac. v. Douglas Ac.
2	Irvine Royal Ac. v. Grange Ac. 0-2
2	Kirkcaldy HS v. Dunfermline HS 0-9
2	Lasswade HS v. Broughton HS 1-1 (4-3 pens)
2	Lenzie Ac. v. Barrhead HS 4-3
2	Lourdes Sec. v. John Paul Ac. 5-1
2	Mearns Castle HS v. Bannerman HS 2-0
2	Mintlaw Ac. v. Grove Ac. 4-2
2	Musselburgh Grammar v. George Heriot's School 3-5
2	Nicolson Institute v. St.John's HS 4-1
2	Oban HS v. Holyrood Sec. 0-5
2	Our Lady's HS Motherwell v. St.Mungo's HS 2-0
2	Park Mains HS v. Knightswood Sec. 2-4
2	Perth HS v. Forfar Ac. 0-2
2	Portobello HS v. Craigmount HS 1-3

2	Queen Anne HS v. Monifieth HS 2-0
2	St.Andrew's & St.Bride's HS v. Largs Ac. 2-5
2	St.Andrew's Sec. v. St.Peter the Apostle HS 3-6
2	St.Margaret's Ac. v. Royal HS 2-5
2	St.Mungo's Ac. v. St.Ninian's HS Giffnock 0-7
2	St.Thomas Aquinas Sec. v. Trinity HS Rutherglen 1-4
3	Bishopbriggs Ac. v. Preston Lodge HS 1-2
3	Braidhurst HS v. Royal HS 3-1
3	Craigmount HS v. Cardinal Newman HS 4-1
3	Dingwall Ac. v. Arbroath HS 4-6
3	Dumfries HS v. St.Ninian's HS Giffnock 1-5
3	Dunfermline HS v. Mintlaw Ac. 8-0
3	Forfar Ac. v. Nicolson Institute 4-2
3	Holyrood Sec. v. Lourdes Sec. 3-0
3	Lanark Grammar v. Knightswood Sec. 9-0
3	Largs Ac. v. Lenzie Ac. 3-3
3	Lasswade HS v. Airdrie Ac. 1-0
3	Mearns Castle HS v. Douglas Ac. 2-0
3	Our Lady's HS Motherwell v. George Heriot's School 1-4
3	Queen Anne HS v. Webster's HS 4-1
3	St.Peter the Apostle HS v. Clydeview Ac. 0-3
3	Trinity HS Rutherglen v. Grange Ac. 3-2
4	Braidhurst HS v Arbroath HS 6-0
4	Craigmount HS v George Heriots School
4	Dunfermline HS v Mearns Castle HS 4-1
4	Forfar Acad v Clydesview Acad 1-9
4	Lanark GS v St Ninians HS Giffnock 1-5
4	Lasswade HS v Lenzie Acad 1-1
4	Queen Anne HS v Preston Lodge HS
4	Trinity RC HS v Holyrood Sec 6-1
5	Clydeview Ac. v. Craigmount HS 3-1
5	St.Ninian's HS Giffnock v. Braidhurst HS 2-3
5	Lasswade HS v. Dunfermline HS 1-2
5	Queen Anne HS v. Trinity HS Rutherglen 1-1 (5-4 pens)
SF	Braidhurst HS v. Clydeview Ac. 2-2 (4-3 pens)
	(Tues 28 Mar, Cambuslang Rangers, 5.30)
SF	Dunfermline HS v. Queen Anne HS 1-1 (2-4 pens)
	(Fri 24 Mar, Kelty Hearts, 1.30)
F	Braidhurst HS v. Queen Anne HS 2-1
	(Thur 27 Apr, Edinburgh University, Peffermill, 7.00)

Scottish Schools Under 15 Shield 2015/16

1	Falkirk HS v. Coltness HS 1-0
1	St.Andrew's & St.Bride's HS v. Prestwick Ac. 1-0
1	St.Maurice's HS v. Denny HS 0-1
2	Aberdeen Grammar v. Alford Ac. 6-1
2	Arbroath HS v. Madras College 1-2
2	Ardrossan Ac. v. Irvine Royal Ac. 2-0
2	Balfron HS v. Turnbull HS 1-3
2	Balwearie HS v. Woodmill HS 3-1
2	Banchory Ac. v. Nicolson Institute 3-3 (4-3 pens)
2	Banff Ac. bye
2	Bannerman HS v. Bearsden Ac. 3-1
2	Bathgate Ac. v. Preston Lodge HS 4-1
2	Blairgowrie HS v. St.John's HS 5-2
2	Boroughmuir HS v. St.Kentigern's Ac. 2-2 (4-3 pens)
2	Braidhurst HS v. McLaren HS 2-1
2	Campbeltown Grammar v. John Paul Ac. 3-3 (6-5 pens)
2	Craigmount HS v. Deans CHS 7-4
2	Crieff HS v. Perth HS 4-2
2	Cults Ac. v. Meldrum Ac. 2-0

2	Currie HS v. Ross HS 1-4
2	Denny HS v. Our Lady's HS Motherwell 3-3 (6-5 pens)
2	Dumfries HS v. Largs Ac. 4-3
2	Duncanrig Sec. v. Auchinleck Ac. 4-4 (2-4 pens)
2	Dunfermline HS v. Grove Ac. 0-6
2	Dunoon Grammar v. All Saints Sec. 1-9
2	Firrhill HS v. Musselburgh Grammar 4-0
2	Forfar Ac. v. Inverkeithing HS 2-2 (4-2 pens)
2	Fraserburgh Ac. bye
2	Girvan Ac. v. Stranraer Ac. 0-9
2	Glenrothes HS v. Queen Anne HS 2-4
2	Glenwood HS v. Beath HS 1-1 (4-2 pens)
2	Graeme HS v. Bishopbriggs Ac. 1-6
2	Greenfaulds HS v. Alloa Ac. 4-2
2	Greenwood Ac. v. St.Joseph's College 1-2
2	Gryffe HS v. Lenzie Ac. 7-2
2	Hawick HS v. Linlithgow Ac. 2-0
2	Holy Rood HS v. Broughton HS 2-0
2	Holyrood Sec. v. Knightswood Sec. 2-4
2	Inverurie Ac. v. Thurso HS 3-0
2	James Young HS v. Lasswade HS 2-1
2	Johnstone HS bye
2	Jordanhill School v. Notre Dame HS 1-1 (5-3 pens)
2	Larbert HS v. St.Ninian's HS Kirkintilloch 2-2 (0-3p)
2	Levenmouth Ac. v. Auchmuty HS 3-1
2	Lochgelly HS v. Carnoustie HS 3-3 (5-4 pens)
2	Lourdes Sec. v. Cathkin HS 2-3
2	Mearns Castle HS v. Gleniffer HS 6-0
2	Monifieth HS v. Bell Baxter HS 3-3 (5-3 pens)
2	Newbattle HS v. Gracemount HS 4-1
2	North Berwick HS bye
2	Our Lady & St.Patrick's HS v. St.Peter the Apostle HS 0-2
2	Our Lady's HS Cumbernauld v. Chryston HS 0-2
2	Paisley Grammar v. Hyndland Sec. 2-0
2	Portobello HS v. Dalkeith HS 2-0
2	Queensferry HS v. West Calder HS 5-0
2	St.Ambrose HS v. Grangemouth HS 6-0
2	St.Andrew's & St.Bride's HS v. Calderglen HS 6-1
2	St.Andrew's HS Coatbridge v. Braes HS 2-0
2	St.Andrew's Sec. v. Eastwood HS 2-0
2	St.Columba's HS Dunfermline v. Kirkcaldy HS 1-0
2	St.Matthew's Ac. v. Holy Cross HS 0-2
2	St.Mungo's HS v. Taylor HS 1-6
2	St.Ninian's HS Giffnock v. Oban HS 9-0
2	Stirling HS v. Falkirk HS 1-1 (3-2 pens)
2	Strathaven Ac. v. Grange Ac. 0-2
2	Wallace HS v. St.Modan's HS 2-0
2	Williamwood HS v. Hermitage Ac. 3-0
3	All Saints Sec. v. Mearns Castle HS 1-1
3	Ardrossan Ac. v. Stranraer Ac. 2-5
3	Auchinleck Ac. v. Holy Cross HS 0-3
3	Balwearie HS v. St.Columba's HS Dunfermline 1-1
3	Banff Ac. v. Aberdeen Grammar 4-6
3	Bannerman HS v. Campbeltown Grammar 2-3
3	Bathgate Ac. v. James Young HS 2-8
3	Chryston HS v. Greenfaulds HS 0-2
3	Craigmount HS v. Firrhill HS 3-0
3	Dumfries HS v. St.Joseph's College 3-0
3	Fraserburgh Ac. v. Cults Ac. 2-1
3	Grange Ac. v. St.Andrew's & St.Bride's HS 1-7
3	Grove Ac. v. Lochgelly HS 2-2
3	Gryffe HS v Jordanhill School 6-1
3	Hawick HS v. Newbattle HS 1-9
3	Holy Rood HS v. Boroughmuir HS 3-3
3	Inverurie Ac. v. Banchory Ac. 2-2
3	Johnstone HS v. Williamwood HS 2-3
3	Knightswood Sec. v. St.Ninian's HS Giffnock 1-9
3	Larbert HS or St.Ninian's HS Kirkintilloch v. Denny HS
3	Levenmouth Ac. v Glenwood HS 3-3
3	Madras College v. Blairgowrie HS 4-1
3	Monifieth HS v. Forfar Ac. 1-1
3	North Berwick HS v. Queensferry HS 2-2
3	Paisley Grammar v. St.Peter the Apostle HS 1-2
3	Queen Anne HS v. Crieff HS 4-1
3	Ross HS v. Portobello HS 3-2
3	St.Ambrose HS v. Braidhurst HS 0-1
3	St.Andrew's Sec. v. Cathkin HS 7-1
3	Stirling HS v. St.Andrew's HS Coatbridge 0-4
3	Taylor HS v. Bishopbriggs Ac. 2-1
3	Wallace HS v. Turnbull HS 2-4

4	Campbeltown GS v Williamwood HS 0-2
4	Dumfries HS v St Peter The Apostle HS 2-1
4	Grennfaulds HS v Meanrs Castle HS
4	Holycross RC HS v Gryffe HS 1-5
4	Holyrood HS v Taylor HS
4	James Young HS v Newbattle HS 3-9
4	Lochgelly HS v Monifieth HS 1-3
4	Madras Coll v Inverurie Acad 1-5
4	Queen Anne HS v Aberdeen GS 5-4
4	Queensferry HS v Craigmount HS 2-4
4	St Andrews HS Coatbridge v Ross HS 1-4
4	St Andrews Sec vSt Andrews and St Brides HS 2-4
4	St Columbas HS v Glenwood HS 7-1
4	St Ninians HS Giffnock v Stranraer Acad 6-1
4	St Ninians HS v Braidhurst HS 101 (4-1p)
4	Turnbull RC HS v Fraserburgh Acad 1-1
5	Turnbull HS v. St.Ninian's HS Giffnock 2-4
5	Queen Anne HS v. Ross HS 3-2
5	St.Columba's HS Dunfermline v. Monifieth HS 4-2
5	Mearns Castle HS v. St.Ninian's HS Kirkintilloch 1-2
5	Williamwood HS v. Dumfries HS 2-4
5	Inverurie Ac. v. St.Andrew's & St.Bride's HS 5-1
5	Gryffe HS v. Holy Rood HS 1-0
5	Newbattle HS v. Craigmount HS 3-3 (4-5 pens)
6	St.Ninian's HS Giffnock v. St.Ninian's HS Kirkintilloch 1-3
6	Dumfries HS v. St.Columba's HS Dunfermline 5-1
6	Craigmount HS v. Inverurie Ac. 1-0
6	Queen Anne HS v. Gryffe HS 0-3
SF	umfries HS v. St.Ninian's HS Kirkintilloch 2-1
	(Wed 10 May, Palmerston, 5.30)
SF	Craigmount HS v. Gryffe HS 2-5
	(Tues 9 May, Fauldhouse United, 6.45)
F	Dumfries HS v. Gryffe HS
	(Thur 8 June, Airdrieonians FC, 7.45)

Scottish Schools Under 14 Shield 2016/17

1	Boclair Ac. v. Dumbarton Ac. 2-1
1	Hermitage Ac. v. Lourdes Sec. 3-2
1	St.Peter the Apostle HS v. St.Margaret Mary's Sec. 1-0
1	Hyndland Sec. v. Springburn Ac. 7-0
1	Our Lady & St.Patrick's HS v. Woodfarm HS 5-0
1	St.Columba's HS Gourock v. Lenzie Ac. 0-1
1	Johnstone HS v. Mearns Castle HS 4-1
1	Lanark Grammar v. Sanquhar Ac. 9-0
1	Carluke HS v. Ardrossan Ac. 3-0
1	St.Andrew's & St.Bride's HS v. Grange Ac. 3-3 (2-4 pens)
1	Greenwood Ac. v. Dumfries HS 2-4
1	Hamilton College v. Stranraer Ac. 0-1
1	Coatbridge HS v. St.Ambrose HS 2-5
1	St.Margaret's HS v. Balfron HS 1-0
1	St.Maurice's HS v. Taylor HS 2-4
1	Newbattle HS v. Currie HS 2-2 (4-2 pens)
1	Monifieth HS v. Auchmuty HS
1	Harris Ac. v. Queen Anne HS 0-1
1	Woodmill HS v. St.Paul's Ac. 9-2
1	Carnoustie HS v. Madras College 1-4
1	Viewforth HS v. Balwearie HS 1-2
1	Arbroath HS v. Kirkcaldy HS 0-1
1	St.Columba's HS Dunfermline v. Grove Ac. 6-6 (5-3 pens)
2	Boclair Ac. v. Our Lady & St.Patrick's HS
2	Paisley Grammar v. St.Mungo's Ac. 2-2 (5-4 pens)
2	John Paul Ac. v. Holyrood Sec. 3-4
2	St.Andrew's Ac. v. Barrhead HS 1-3
2	St.Ninian's HS Giffnock v. Notre Dame HS
2	Douglas Ac. v. Lenzie Ac.
2	Eastbank Ac. v. Gryffe HS 0-2
2	Bannerman HS v. Williamwood HS 0-2
2	Glasgow Gaelic School v. Bearsden Ac. 0-8
2	Dunoon Grammar v. Hyndland Sec. 1-7
2	Cathkin HS v. Eastwood HS 2-2 (4-3 pens)
2	Johnstone HS v. Gleniffer HS 2-0
2	Jordanhill School v. St.Andrew's Sec. 3-2
2	St.Peter the Apostle HS v. Park Mains HS
2	Hermitage Ac. v. St.Thomas Aquinas Sec.
2	Oban HS v. Linwood HS 9-0
2	Uddingston Grammar v. Carluke HS
2	Stranraer Ac. v. Lockerbie Ac.
2	Grange Ac. v. Auchinleck Ac.
2	Duncanrig Sec. v. St.Matthew's Ac. 3-2
2	Lanark Grammar v. Strathaven Ac.
2	Dumfries Ac. v. Holy Cross HS 2-9
2	Largs Ac. v. Hamilton Grammar
2	Dumfries HS v. Irvine Royal Ac. 2-0
2	St.Mungo's HS v. Turnbull HS 8-2
2	Airdrie Ac. v. Braes HS 3-4
2	Bishopbriggs Ac. v. St.Aidan's HS 4-9
2	Larbert HS v. Our Lady's HS Cumbernauld 1-2
2	Wallace HS v. St.Margaret's HS 6-0
2	Falkirk HS v. Coltness HS
2	Our Lady's HS Motherwell v. Stirling HS 2-0
2	Denny HS v. St.Andrew's HS Coatbridge 7-0
2	St.Ninian's HS Kirkintilloch v. Braidhurst HS
2	Greenfaulds HS v. St.Modan's HS
2	Cardinal Newman HS v. Graeme HS 1-4
2	Taylor HS v. St.Ambrose HS 4-5
2	West Calder HS v. Newbattle HS 3-9
2	North Berwick HS v. Portobello HS 1-4
2	Queensferry HS v. Penicuik HS 1-3
2	Dalkeith HS v. Broughton HS 0-3
2	George Heriot's School v. Ross HS 1-9
2	Beeslack HS v. Craigmount HS 2-3
2	Boroughmuir HS v. Hawick HS 7-0
2	Firrhill HS v. Musselburgh Grammar
2	James Gillespie's HS v. Stewart's Melville College 1-9
2	Broxburn Ac. v. Peebles HS 2-1
2	St.Margaret's Ac. v. Lasswade HS 2-1
2	Gracemount HS v. Preston Lodge HS
2	Bell Baxter HS v. Glenwood HS 6-4
2	Monifieth HS or Auchmuty HS v. Woodmill HS
2	Madras College v. Glenrothes HS 2-0
2	Beath HS v. Balwearie HS 0-2
2	Queen Anne HS v. Levenmouth Ac. 3-0
2	St.Columba's HS Dunfermline v. Kirkcaldy HS
2	Inverkeithing HS v. Perth HS 3-3 (4-5 pens)
2	Dunfermline HS v. St.John's HS 1-8
2	Fraserburgh Ac. v. Harlaw Ac. 0-7
2	Banchory Ac. v. Banff Ac. 2-9
2	Cults Ac. v. Kirkwall HS 9-1
2	Inverness HS v. Aberdeen Grammar
2	Dingwall Ac. v. Nicolson Institute 2-3
2	Inverurie Ac. v. Kincorth Ac.
2	Aboyne Ac. v. Mintlaw Ac.
2	Ellon Ac. bye
3	St.Peter the Apostle HS v. Bearsden Ac. 2-2 (3-5 pens)
3	Paisley Grammar v. Lenzie Ac. 3-0
3	Gryffe HS v. Jordanhill School 4-3
3	Boclair Ac. v. Johnstone HS 0-5
3	Oban HS v. Hermitage Ac. 3-3 (4-5 pens)
3	Williamwood HS v. Cathkin HS 0-3
3	Holyrood Sec. v. St.Ninian's HS Giffnock 2-3
3	Hyndland Sec. v. Barrhead HS 2-7
3	Dumfries HS v. Lanark Grammar 2-3
3	Hamilton Grammar v. Holy Cross HS 1-5
3	Carluke HS v. Grange Ac. 2-8
3	Stranraer Ac. v. Duncanrig Sec. 3-2
3	Wallace HS v. Braidhurst HS 1-2
3	Denny HS v. Braes HS 0-4
3	St.Modan's HS v. St.Ambrose HS 5-3
3	Graeme HS v. Our Lady's HS Cumbernauld 3-4
3	Our Lady's HS Motherwell v. Falkirk HS 3-0
3	St.Mungo's HS v. St.Aidan's HS 3-0

3	Newbattle HS v. Ross HS 2-9
3	Penicuik HS v. Firrhill HS 2-4
3	Craigmount HS v. Broxburn Ac. 1-2
3	Preston Lodge HS v. Boroughmuir HS 9-0
3	Portobello HS v. Broughton HS 2-4
3	Stewart's Melville College v. St.Margaret's Ac. 3-0
3	Balwearie HS v. St.Columba's HS Dunfermline 0-5
3	Madras College v. St.John's HS 1-8
3	Perth HS v. Woodmill HS 2-2 (5-6 pens)
3	Queen Anne HS v. Bell Baxter HS 6-2
3	Mintlaw Ac. v. Harlaw Ac. 0-5
3	Cults Ac. v. Kincorth Ac. 9-0
3	Ellon Ac. v. Nicolson Institute 0-1
3	Banff Ac. v. Aberdeen Grammar 9-3
4	Stranraer Ac. v. Cathkin HS 1-6
4	Barrhead HS v. Bearsden Ac. 1-5
4	Gryffe HS v. Hermitage Ac. 9-1
4	Grange Ac. v. Johnstone HS 1-1 (5-4 pens)
4	St.Ninian's HS Giffnock v. Holy Cross HS 4-3
4	Paisley Grammar v. Lanark Grammar 3-2
4	Our Lady's HS Cumbernauld v. Braidhurst HS 0-5
4	Ross HS v. Firrhill HS 6-2
4	St.Mungo's HS v. Braes HS 3-4
4	Stewart's Melville College v. Broxburn Ac. 4-2
4	Broughton HS v. Preston Lodge HS 2-3
4	Our Lady's HS Motherwell v. St.Modan's HS 2-0
4	St.Columba's HS Dunfermline v. St.John's HS 0-5
4	Queen Anne HS v. Banff Ac. 9-1
4	Harlaw Ac. v. Nicolson Institute 3-1
4	Cults Ac. v. Woodmill HS 4-2
5	Cults Ac. v. Cathkin HS 4-0
5	Queen Anne HS v. Ross HS 4-3
5	Our Lady's HS Motherwell v. Harlaw Ac. 0-8
5	Preston Lodge HS v. Braes HS 6-3
5	Bearsden Ac. v. St.Ninian's HS Giffnock 0-2
5	St.John's HS v. Gryffe HS 7-4
5	Grange Ac. v. Braidhurst HS 3-1
5	Stewart's Melville College v. Paisley Grammar 2-2 (8-9 pens)
6	Cults Ac. v. Preston Lodge HS 8-4
6	Paisley Grammar v. St.John's HS 1-7
6	St.Ninian's HS Giffnock v. Harlaw Ac. 5-4
6	Queen Anne HS v. Grange Ac. 2-1
SF	St.Ninian's HS Giffnock v. Cults Ac. 3-2
	(Wed 10 May, Tayport Juniors. 6.00)
SF	St.John's HS v. Queen Anne HS 2-3
	(Tues 9 May, Jeanfield Swifts, Perth, 6.30)
F	St.Ninian's HS Giffnock v. Queen Anne HS 2-1
	(June 6 at Spartans FC)

Scottish Schools Under 13 Shield 2016/17

1	Perth HS v. Grove Ac. 4-3
1	Fraserburgh Ac. v. Inverness HS 1-0
1	Banff Ac. v. Kincorth Ac. 0-1
2	John Paul Ac. v. Notre Dame HS
2	Trinity HS Rutherglen v. Our Lady & St.Patrick's HS 2-8
2	Woodfarm HS v. Bannerman HS 3-2
2	Lourdes Sec. v. Cathkin HS 7-2
2	Johnstone HS v. St.Mungo's Ac.
2	Jordanhill School v. Gryffe HS 1-9
2	St.Ninian's HS Giffnock v. Oban HS 9-0
2	Dunoon Grammar v. Bearsden Ac. 1-9
2	Eastwood HS v. St.Andrew's Sec.
2	Hermitage Ac. v. Boclair Ac. 1-4
2	Gleniffer HS v. Springburn Ac. 9-1
2	All Saints Sec. v. Paisley Grammar 2-0
2	Stonelaw HS v. Holyrood Sec. 1-7
2	Mearns Castle HS v. St.Andrew's Ac. 2-3
2	Williamwood HS v. Lenzie Ac.
2	St.Peter the Apostle HS v. Castlemilk HS 2-0
2	Grange Ac. v. Duncanrig Sec. 9-4
2	St.Joseph's College v. Auchinleck Ac.
2	Dumfries Ac. v. Hamilton Grammar 1-7
2	Carluke HS v. St.Matthew's Ac. 7-0
2	Greenwood Ac. v. Dumfries HS 2-6
2	Irvine Royal Ac. v. Holy Cross HS 2-8
2	St.Andrew's & St.Bride's HS v. Ardrossan Ac. 8-0
2	Stranraer Ac. v. Lanark Grammar 5-1
2	St.Modan's HS v. St.Aidan's HS
2	Taylor HS v. Falkirk HS 2-0
2	Balfron HS v. Braidhurst HS 0-9
2	St.Ninian's HS Kirkintilloch v. St.Mungo's HS 5-0
2	Chryston HS v. Wallace HS 2-2 (1-4 pens)
2	St.Margaret's HS v. Our Lady's HS Cumbernauld 0-1
2	Turnbull HS v. Graeme HS 0-5
2	Coltness HS v. Larbert HS
2	Our Lady's HS Motherwell v. Airdrie Ac. 2-2 (4-5 pens)
2	St.Ambrose HS v. Coatbridge HS 7-2
2	Greenfaulds HS v. St.Andrew's HS Coatbridge
2	Bishopbriggs Ac. v. Denny HS 0-5
2	Alloa Ac. v. St.Maurice's HS 0-9
2	Grangemouth HS bye
2	Broughton HS v. Boroughmuir HS 7-3
2	Holy Rood HS v. Newbattle HS 6-2
2	Musselburgh Grammar v. Firrhill HS
2	Lasswade HS v. Hawick HS 9-0
2	Craigmount HS v. Portobello HS 0-7
2	James Young HS v. Queensferry HS 2-0
2	Linlithgow Ac. v. Dalkeith HS 1-0
2	St.Margaret's Ac. v. Currie HS 4-2
2	James Gillespie's HS v. Ross HS 1-6
2	Preston Lodge HS v. Bathgate Ac. 3-4
2	Gracemount HS bye
2	St.Kentigern's Ac. bye
2	Carnoustie HS v. Balwearie HS 1-7
2	Webster's HS v. Glenrothes HS 9-0
2	Montrose Ac. v. Beath HS 3-6
2	Perth HS v. Arbroath HS 9-3
2	Woodmill HS v. Monifieth HS 9-1
2	Glenwood HS v. Viewforth HS 3-2
2	Auchmuty HS v. Kirkcaldy HS 0-9
2	Crieff HS v. Inverkeithing HS 0-9
2	Queen Anne HS v. St.John's HS 7-2
2	Madras College v. St.Andrew's HS Kirkcaldy 8-0
2	Fraserburgh Ac. v. Portlethen Ac. 2-4
2	Banchory Ac. v. Cults Ac. 4-0
2	Kincorth Ac. v. Inverurie Ac.
2	Nicolson Institute v. Aberdeen Grammar 2-1
3	All Saints Sec. v. Lourdes Sec. 0-9
3	St.Peter the Apostle HS v. Boclair Ac. 3-1

3	Our Lady & St.Patrick's HS v. Bearsden Ac. 4-1
3	St.Andrew's Ac. v. Gryffe HS 4-3
3	St.Ninian's HS Giffnock v. Notre Dame HS 9-0
3	Gleniffer HS v. Woodfarm HS 6-2
3	Holyrood Sec. v. Williamwood HS 2-2 (3-4 pens)
3	St.Mungo's Ac. v. St.Andrew's Sec. 0-3
3	Holy Cross HS v. Hamilton Grammar 5-1
3	Grange Ac. v. Auchinleck Ac. 3-0
3	St.Andrew's & St.Bride's HS v. Dumfries HS 1-3
3	Carluke HS v. Stranraer Ac. 2-0
3	Larbert HS v. Greenfaulds HS 2-6
3	Braidhurst HS v. St.Maurice's HS 6-1
3	Graeme HS v. Wallace HS 8-2
3	Grangemouth HS v. St.Ninian's HS Kirkintilloch 5-3
3	St.Ambrose HS v. Denny HS 0-4
3	Airdrie Ac. v. St.Modan's HS 1-2
3	Taylor HS v. Our Lady's HS Cumbernauld 1-6
3	St.Kentigern's Ac. v. Linlithgow Ac. 0-9
3	Holy Rood HS v. Portobello HS 2-9
3	Broughton HS v. James Young HS 5-0
3	Bathgate Ac. v. St.Margaret's Ac. 3-2
3	Ross HS v. Firrhill HS 3-0
3	Lasswade HS v. Gracemount HS 3-0
3	Webster's HS v. Woodmill HS 7-1
3	Madras College v. Glenwood HS 9-0
3	Portlethen Ac. v. Kirkcaldy HS 0-5
3	Beath HS v. Banchory Ac. 7-6
3	Perth HS v. Nicolson Institute 3-2
3	Inverkeithing HS v. Inverurie Ac. 8-0
3	Balwearie HS v. Queen Anne HS 6-0
4	Carluke HS v. Gleniffer HS 0-7
4	St.Andrew's Sec. v. Lourdes Sec. 1-7
4	Our Lady & St.Patrick's HS v. St.Ninian's HS Giffnock 2-5
4	Dumfries HS v. St.Andrew's Ac. 3-1
4	Williamwood HS v. Grange Ac. 1-1 (3-2 pens)
4	St.Peter the Apostle HS v. Holy Cross HS 3-3 (4-3 pens)
4	Grangemouth HS v. Greenfaulds HS 1-0
4	Our Lady's HS Cumbernauld v. Linlithgow Ac. 2-2 (4-3 pens)
4	St.Modan's HS v. Lasswade HS 1-4
4	Ross HS v. Portobello HS 4-7
4	Bathgate Ac. v. Broughton HS 7-7 (3-4 pens)
4	Denny HS v. Graeme HS 2-3
4	Braidhurst HS v. Webster's HS 5-2
4	Kirkcaldy HS v. Balwearie HS 6-0
4	Beath HS v. Inverkeithing HS 5-0
4	Perth HS v. Madras College 5-3
5	Perth HS v. Gleniffer HS 2-2 (5-4 pens)
5	Lourdes Sec. v. Williamwood HS 7-2
5	Kirkcaldy HS v. Our Lady's HS Cumbernauld 4-2
5	Braidhurst HS v. St.Ninian's HS Giffnock 7-6
5	Graeme HS v. Beath HS 3-4
5	Dumfries HS v. Grangemouth HS 4-0
5	Broughton HS v. Lasswade HS 3-5
5	Portobello HS v. St.Peter the Apostle HS 9-1
6	Perth HS v. Lasswade HS 1-5
6	Kirkcaldy HS v. Dumfries HS 6-3
6	Lourdes Sec. v. Beath HS 2-1
6	Portobello HS v. Braidhurst HS 5-3
SF	Lourdes Sec. v. Lasswade HS 0-0 (5-4 pens)
	(Tues 28 Mar, Broxburn Athletic, 3.30)
SF	Portobello HS v. Kirkcaldy HS 1-2
	(Fri 24 Mar, Kelty Hearts, 5.30)
F	Lourdes Sec. v. Kirkcaldy HS 3-0
	(Wed 3 May, Ochilview, 7.30)

Scottish Schools Under 18 Girls Shield 2016/17

Rd	
1	St.Andrew's Ac. v. St.Matthew's Ac. 1-0
1	Stranraer Ac. v. Greenwood Ac.
1	St.Andrew's Sec. v. Duncanrig Sec.
1	Park Mains HS v. Auchinleck Ac. 9-4
1	St.Peter the Apostle HS v. Lanark Grammar
1	Cardinal Newman HS v. Cumbernauld Ac. 0-3
1	Denny HS v. Bathgate Ac. 2-4
1	Falkirk HS v. Bishopbriggs Ac.
1	Boroughmuir HS v. Lasswade HS
1	Galashiels Ac. v. Braidhurst HS 0-1
1	Linlithgow Ac. v. St.Mungo's HS 3-3 (2-3 pens)
1	Cults Ac. v. Aboyne Ac. 4-0
1	St.John's HS v. Forfar Ac. 2-2 (2-3 pens)
1	Crieff HS v. Monifieth HS 2-6
1	St.Paul's Ac. v. Bell Baxter HS 1-4
1	Kincorth Ac. v. Montrose Ac. 2-0
1	Grove Ac. v. Beath HS
1	Nicolson Institute v. Banff Ac. 1-0
1	Ellon Ac. v. Perth Ac. 2-7
2	Dunoon Grammar v. Castlemilk HS 0-2
2	St.Matthew's Ac. v. Clydebank HS 2-0
2	Williamwood HS v. Stranraer Ac. 2-0
2	St.Peter the Apostle HS v. St.Andrew's Sec. 4-1
2	Eastbank Ac. v. Bannerman HS 5-6
2	Park Mains HS v. St.Ninian's HS Giffnock 0-2
2	Our Lady's HS Motherwell v. James Young HS 2-5
2	Cumbernauld Ac. v. Bishopbriggs Ac. 2-4
2	St.Mungo's HS v. Braidhurst HS 9-0
2	George Heriot's School v. Bathgate Ac. 1-6
2	Wallace HS v. St.Margaret's Ac. 2-8
2	Lasswade HS v. Graeme HS 1-5
2	Cults Ac. v. Forfar Ac. 0-4
2	Bell Baxter HS v. Beath HS 1-9
2	Nicolson Institute v. Monifieth HS 2-0
2	Perth Ac. v. Kincorth Ac. 7-3
3	Williamwood HS v. Bannerman HS 0-3
3	Castlemilk HS v. St.Peter the Apostle HS 0-9
3	St.Ninian's HS Giffnock v. St.Matthew's Ac. 0-3
3	Bishopbriggs Ac. v. St.Margaret's Ac. 1-9
3	Perth Ac. v. Bathgate Ac. 1-7
3	St.Mungo's HS v. Nicolson Institute 2-1
3	Beath HS v. James Young HS 7-1
3	Forfar Ac. v. Graeme HS 4-5
4	St.Matthew's Ac. v. Bannerman HS 3-0
4	Bathgate Ac. v. Beath HS 6-2
4	Graeme HS v. St.Peter the Apostle HS 2-3
4	St.Margaret's Ac. v. St.Mungo's HS 1-3
SF	St.Mungo's HS v. St.Matthew's Ac. 2-0
	(Wed 26 Apr, Hamilton Palace, 4.00)
SF	St.Peter the Apostle HS v. Bathgate Ac. 2-0
	(Tues 2 May, Toryglen)
F	St.Mungo's HS v. St.Peter the Apostle HS 3-4
	(Tues 23 May, Ochilview, 7.30)

Scottish Schools Under 15 Girls Shield 2016/17

1	Irvine Royal Ac. v. St.Andrew's Sec.
1	Our Lady & St.Patrick's HS v. Dunoon Grammar
1	Hermitage Ac. v. Stranraer Ac. 1-0
1	Greenwood Ac. v. St.Peter the Apostle HS
1	Lenzie Ac. v. Williamwood HS
1	Denny HS v. Penicuik HS 0-1
1	Preston Lodge HS v. Larbert HS 2-0
1	George Heriot's School v. Boroughmuir HS
1	Hawick HS v. James Gillespie's HS 0-1
1	St.Mungo's HS v. Musselburgh Grammar
1	Banff Ac. v. Arbroath HS
1	Fraserburgh Ac. v. Meldrum Ac.
1	Mintlaw Ac. v. Woodmill HS
1	Monifieth HS v. Alford Ac. 4-1
1	Beath HS v. Madras College
1	St.John's HS v. Montrose Ac. 0-1
1	Crieff HS v. Webster's HS 0-9
2	Bannerman HS v. Hermitage Ac. 0-2
2	St.Andrew's Sec. v. St.Ninian's HS Giffnock 0-2
2	Mearns Castle HS v. Williamwood HS 2-0
2	Gleniffer HS v. Greenwood Ac. 2-0
2	Duncanrig Sec. v. Our Lady & St.Patrick's HS 0-1
2	Dumfries HS v. Lourdes Sec. 1-9
2	Musselburgh Grammar v. Lasswade HS 0-7
2	James Gillespie's HS v. Preston Lodge HS 2-2 (1-3 pens)
2	Broxburn Ac. v. Greenfaulds HS 6-0
2	Boroughmuir HS v. Penicuik HS 0-2
2	Meldrum Ac. v. Glenrothes HS 2-0
2	Webster's HS v. Nicolson Institute 2-0
2	Banff Ac. v. Montrose Ac. 2-0
2	Cults Ac. v. Inverurie Ac. 9-1
2	Madras College v. Aboyne Ac. 2-0
2	Monifieth HS v. Mintlaw Ac. 0-2
3	Mearns Castle HS v. Our Lady & St.Patrick's HS 3-0
3	Hermitage Ac. v. Gleniffer HS 3-0
3	Lourdes Sec. v. St.Ninian's HS Giffnock 5-1
3	Preston Lodge HS v. Meldrum Ac. 3-0
3	Mintlaw Ac. v. Penicuik HS 2-3
3	Broxburn Ac. v. Madras College 9-0
3	Cults Ac. v. Lasswade HS 6-1
3	Banff Ac. v. Webster's HS 6-1
4	Lourdes Sec. v. Mearns Castle HS 4-0
4	Preston Lodge HS v. Broxburn Ac. 4-9
4	Banff Ac. v. Hermitage Ac. 8-0
4	Penicuik HS v. Cults Ac. 5-2
SF	Broxburn Ac. v. Lourdes Sec. 6-2
	(Fri 28 Apr, Hamilton Palace, 2..00)
SF	Banff Ac. v. Penicuik HS 4-0
	(Mon 24 Apr, Station Park, Forfar, 2.00)
F	Broxburn Ac. v. Banff Ac. 3-1
	(Tues 30 May, Station Park, Forfar, 6.00)

Scottish Schools Under 13 Boys Plate 2016/17

1	Greenwood Ac. v. Springburn Ac. 1-0
1	Eastwood HS v. Jordanhill School 1-4
1	Lanark Grammar v. Dunoon Grammar 1-0
1	Castlemilk HS v. Bannerman HS 0-1
1	Lenzie Ac. v. Trinity HS Rutherglen 2-2 (5-4 pens)
1	Duncanrig Sec. v. Stonelaw HS 1-0
1	Hermitage Ac. v. John Paul Ac. 9-0
1	Oban HS v. Ardrossan Ac. 5-9
1	Paisley Grammar bye
1	Irvine Royal Ac. bye
1	Falkirk HS v. Coatbridge HS 5-2
1	Alloa Ac. v. Balfron HS 0-1
1	St.Margaret's HS v. Bishopbriggs Ac. 3-1
1	Musselburgh Grammar v. St.Mungo's HS 5-1
1	Chryston HS v. St.Aidan's HS 7-0
1	James Young HS v. Hawick HS 4-1
1	Dalkeith HS v. Newbattle HS 2-3
1	Our Lady's HS Motherwell v. Queensferry HS 1-0
1	Preston Lodge HS v. Turnbull HS 1-3
1	Taylor HS v. Coltness HS 1-0
1	St.Kentigern's Ac. v. St.Andrew's HS Coatbridge 1-7
1	Boroughmuir HS bye
1	James Gillespie's HS bye
1	Currie HS bye
1	Viewforth HS v. Carnoustie HS 1-0
1	Glenrothes HS v. Banff Ac. 1-0
1	Grove Ac. v. St.Andrew's HS Kirkcaldy 1-0
1	Fraserburgh Ac. v. Inverness HS 1-0
1	Montrose Ac. v. Crieff HS 1-0
1	Auchmuty HS bye
1	St.John's HS bye
1	Arbroath HS bye
2	Lenzie Ac. v. Jordanhill School 1-1 (3-2 pens)
2	Lanark Grammar v. Bannerman HS 2-1
2	Ardrossan Ac. v. Greenwood Ac. 0-4
2	Irvine Royal Ac. v. Duncanrig Sec. 1-3
2	Paisley Grammar v. Hermitage Ac. 0-2
2	Balfron HS v. James Gillespie's HS 2-5
2	Our Lady's HS Motherwell v. Chryston HS 0-2
2	Falkirk HS v. Boroughmuir HS 1-6
2	Musselburgh Grammar v. St.Andrew's HS Coatbridge 2-0
2	Currie HS v. St.Margaret's HS 1-6
2	Taylor HS v. Newbattle HS 2-0
2	James Young HS v. Turnbull HS 0-2
2	Glenrothes HS v. Arbroath HS 2-0
2	Auchmuty HS v. Grove Ac. 0-2
2	Fraserburgh Ac. v. St.John's HS 3-1
2	Montrose Ac. v. Viewforth HS 5-3
3	Glenrothes HS v. Chryston HS 3-2
3	Duncanrig Sec. v. Greenwood Ac. 1-1 (7-6 pens)
3	Montrose Ac. v. Lenzie Ac. 4-5
3	St.Margaret's HS v. Grove Ac. 2-2 (3-4 pens)
3	Taylor HS v. Lanark Grammar 2-1
3	Fraserburgh Ac. v. James Gillespie's HS 7-2
3	Hermitage Ac. v. Boroughmuir HS 3-6
3	Musselburgh Grammar v. Turnbull HS 0-4
4	Grove Ac. v. Glenrothes HS 9-0
4	Boroughmuir HS v. Lenzie Ac. 6-0
4	Taylor HS v. Fraserburgh Ac. 4-3
4	Duncanrig Sec. v. Turnbull HS 2-1
SF	Grove Ac. v. Taylor HS 1-3
	(Mon 15 May, Spartans FC, Edinburgh, 3.00)
SF	Duncanrig Sec. v. Boroughmuir HS 1-0
	(Fri 19 May, Broxburn Athletic, 3.00)
F	Taylor HS v. Duncanrig Sec. 0-1
	(Thur 8 June, Airdrieonians FC, 6.00)

Scottish Schools Under 14 Boys Plate 2016/17

P	Stirling HS v. North Berwick HS 2-8
P	Taylor HS v. St.Ninian's HS Kirkintilloch 1-0
1	St.Columba's HS Gourock v. Bannerman HS 1-0
1	Park Mains HS v. Strathaven Ac. 0-1
1	Eastwood HS v. Irvine Royal Ac. 1-0
1	Linwood HS v. Glasgow Gaelic School 0-1
1	Auchinleck Ac. v. St.Thomas Aquinas Sec. 0-1
1	Largs Ac. v. Dumbarton Ac. 1-0
1	John Paul Ac. v. St.Andrew's Sec. 0-1
1	Woodfarm HS v. Williamwood HS 2-1
1	St.Andrew's Ac. v. Notre Dame HS 0-1
1	Greenwood Ac. v. Ardrossan Ac. 3-0
1	Springburn Ac. v. Gleniffer HS 1-0
1	Dunoon Grammar v. St.Andrew's & St.Bride's HS 1-5
1	Coltness HS v. Bishopbriggs Ac. 1-0
1	Musselburgh Grammar v. Peebles HS 0-9
1	Larbert HS v. Queensferry HS 3-5
1	Airdrie Ac. v. Greenfaulds HS 1-0
1	St.Maurice's HS v. James Gillespie's HS 4-1
1	Balfron HS v. Taylor HS 5-8
1	Hawick HS v. Currie HS 1-0
1	Cardinal Newman HS v. George Heriot's School 4-2
1	Dalkeith HS v. Lasswade HS 0-1
1	St.Andrew's HS Coatbridge v. North Berwick HS 0-1
1	Turnbull HS v. St.Margaret's HS 0-6
1	Coatbridge HS v. Beeslack HS 3-9
1	Ellon Ac. v. Kirkwall Grammar 2-2 (3-5 pens)
1	Dunfermline HS v. Inverurie Ac. 7-0
1	Grove Ac. v. Arbroath HS 4-1
1	Glenrothes HS v. Fraserburgh Ac. 0-3
1	Banchory Ac. v. Harris Ac. 1-0
1	Glenwood HS v. Carnoustie HS 1-0
1	Inverkeithing HS v. Viewforth HS 8-1
1	Auchmuty HS v. Beath HS 3-5
2	Eastwood HS v. Largs Ac. 2-0
2	Springburn Ac. v. St.Thomas Aquinas Sec. 2-0
2	Woodfarm HS v. St.Andrew's Sec. 1-2
2	Notre Dame HS v. St.Andrew's & St.Bride's HS 0-5
2	Glasgow Gaelic School v. St.Columba's HS Gourock 0-2
2	Strathaven Ac. v. Greenwood Ac. 2-0
2	Beeslack HS v. Airdrie Ac. 0-6
2	Queensferry HS v. Hawick HS 2-0
2	Lasswade HS v. St.Maurice's HS 1-4
2	Peebles HS v. Coltness HS 2-0
2	Taylor HS v. Cardinal Newman HS 4-0
2	North Berwick HS v. St.Margaret's HS 3-5
2	Inverkeithing HS v. Beath HS 2-0
2	Kirkwall Grammar v. Grove Ac. 2-0
2	Fraserburgh Ac. v. Banchory Ac. 3-9
2	Glenwood HS v. Dunfermline HS 1-8
3	Strathaven Ac. v. St.Andrew's & St.Bride's HS 0-9
3	Taylor HS v. Springburn Ac. 3-0
3	Peebles HS v. Queensferry HS 4-3
3	St.Andrew's Sec. v. Airdrie Ac. 3-4
3	St.Margaret's HS v. St.Columba's HS Gourock 3-0
3	Banchory Ac. v. Eastwood HS 0-2
3	St.Maurice's HS v. Kirkwall Grammar 7-1
3	Dunfermline HS v. Inverkeithing HS 6-0
4	St.Andrew's & St.Bride's HS v. Dunfermline HS 4-1
4	Peebles HS v. Airdrie Ac. 2-4
4	Eastwood HS v. Taylor HS 2-0
4	St.Margaret's HS v. St.Maurice's HS 4-3
SF	St.Andrew's & St.Bride's HS v. St.Margaret's HS 4-2
	(Mon 24 Apr, Cambuslang Rangers, 6.30)
SF	Airdrie Ac. v. Eastwood HS 8-1
	(Thur 11 May, Cambuslang Rangers, 6.30)
F	St.Andrew's & St.Bride's HS v. **Airdrie Ac.** 1-2
	(Thur 25 May, Cambuslang Rangers, 7.00)

Scottish Schools Under 18 National Trophy 2016/17

Group 1	P	W	D	L	F	A	Pts	
Aberdeen	2	2	0	0	5	2	6	Angus 1 Aberdeenshire 5
Aberdeenshire	2	1	0	1	6	4	3	Aberdeenshire 1 Aberdeen 3
Angus	2	0	0	2	2	7	0	Aberdeen 2 Angus 1

Group 2	P	W	D	L	F	A	Pts	
Dundee	3	2	1	0	10	6	7	North of Scotland 1 Dundee 4
Fife	3	1	1	1	10	7	4	Fife 2 Independent Schools 3
North of Scotland	3	1	0	2	7	10	3	Dundee 3 Fife 3 (Penalty shoot-out 6-7)
Independent Schools	3	1	0	2	6	10	3	North of Scotland 5 Independent Schools 1
								Fife 5 North of Scotland 1
								Independent Schools 2 Dundee 3

Group 3	P	W	D	L	F	A	Pts	
Lanarkshire	3	2	0	1	8	4	6	Lanarkshire 4 West Lothian 2
West Lothian	3	2	0	1	12	9	6	Forth Valley 2 Ayrshire 0
Forth Valley	3	2	0	1	7	4	6	Lanarkshire 0 Forth Valley 2
Ayrshire	3	0	0	3	2	12	0	West Lothian 6 Ayrshire 2
								Ayrshire 0 Lanarkshire 4
								West Lothian 4 Forth Valley 3

Group 4	P	W	D	L	F	A	Pts	
Paisley	3	2	1	0	9	4	7	Dumfries & Galloway 0 Paisley 2
Lothian	3	2	1	0	12	8	7	Lothian 3 Glasgow 0
Glasgow	3	1	0	2	7	7	3	Dumfries & Galloway 5 Lothian 6
Dumfries & Galloway	3	0	0	3	5	14	0	Paisley 4 Glasgow 1
								Glasgow 6 Dumfries & Galloway 0
								Paisley 3 Lothian 3 (Penalty shoot-out 5-3)

QF	Lanarkshire 2 Fife 5
QF	Dundee 3 West Lothian 3 (3-4 pens)
QF	Paisley 9 Aberdeenshire 1
QF	Aberdeen 2 Lothian 8
SF	Lothian 3 Fife 1
SF	West Lothian 3 Paisley 2
F	Lothian 1 West Lothian 0 (Wed 26 Apr, Spartans FC, Edinburgh, 7.30)

Scottish Schools Under 15 National Trophy 2016/17

Group 1	P	W	D	L	F	A	Pts	
Aberdeen	2	2	0	0	8	3	6	Angus 1 Aberdeenshire 7
Aberdeenshire	2	1	0	1	8	5	3	Aberdeenshire 1 Aberdeen 4
Angus	2	0	0	2	3	11	0	Aberdeen 4 Angus 2

Group 2	P	W	D	L	F	A	Pts	
North of Scotland	2	1	1	0	5	2	4	North of Scotland 2 Dundee 2 (Penalty shoot-out 6-5)
Dundee	2	1	1	0	3	2	4	Dundee 1 Fife 0
Fife	2	0	0	2	0	4	0	Fife 0 North of Scotland 3

Group 3	P	W	D	L	F	A	Pts	
								Lanarkshire 1 West Lothian 1 (Penalty shoot-out 5-4)
Forth Valley	3	2	1	0	8	5	7	Forth Valley 3 Ayrshire 1
Ayrshire	3	1	1	1	5	4	4	Lanarkshire 2 Forth Valley 2 (Penalty shoot-out 2-4)
Lanarkshire	3	0	3	0	4	4	3	West Lothian 0 Ayrshire 3
West Lothian	3	0	1	2	3	7	1	Ayrshire 1 Lanarkshire 1 (Penalty shoot-out 4-3)
								West Lothian 2 Forth Valley 3

Group 4	P	W	D	L	F	A	Pts	
								Dumfries & Galloway 2 Paisley 4
Paisley	3	3	0	0	11	2	9	Edinburgh 0 Glasgow 1
Glasgow	3	2	0	1	7	4	6	Dumfries & Galloway 3 Edinburgh 2
Dumfries & Galloway	3	1	0	2	6	12	3	Paisley 3 Glasgow 0
Edinburgh	3	0	0	3	2	8	0	Glasgow 6 Dumfries & Galloway 1
								Paisley 4 Edinburgh 0

QF	Aberdeen 5 Dundee 1
QF	Paisley 5 Ayrshire 3
QF	North of Scotland 2 Glasgow 2 (4-5 pens)
QF	Forth Valley 5 Aberdeenshire 1
SF	Glasgow 1 Forth Valley 4
SF	Paisley 8 Aberdeen 3
F	Forth Valley 1 Paisley 4
	(Wed 19 Apr, Forthbank, Stirling Albion FC, 7.00)

Scottish Schools Under 18 Shield Winners

1904	Paisley Grammar
1905	Morrison's Academy, Crieff
1906	Hutcheson's Grammar, Glasgow
1907	Hutcheson's Grammar, Glasgow
1908	Hutcheson's Grammar, Glasgow
1909	Allan Glen's School, Glasgow
1910	Hamilton Academy
1911	Falkirk High School
1912	Whitehill Secondary School, Glasgow
1913	John Street Secondary School, Glasgow
1914	Clydebank High School
1915	St.Mungo's Academy, Glasgow
1916	St.Mungo's Academy, Glasgow
1917	Dumbarton Academy
1918	Queen's Park Secondary School, Glasgow
1919	Hamilton Academy
1920	Hamilton Academy
1921	St.Mungo's Academy, Glasgow
1922	Allan Glen's School, Glasgow
1923	St.Mungo's Academy, Glasgow
1924	Irvine Royal Academy
1925	Hamilton Academy
1926	Hamilton Academy
1927	St.Aloysius' College, Glasgow
1928	St.Mungo's Academy, Glasgow
1929	Falkirk High School
1930	Hamilton Academy
1931	Greenock High School
1932	Clydebank High School
1933	Whitehill Secondary School, Glasgow
1934	Queen's Park Secondary School, Glasgow
1935	Govan Secondary School, Glasgow
1936	Dalziel High School, Motherwell
1937	St.Mungo's Academy, Glasgow
1938	Our Lady's High School, Motherwell
1939	Dalziel High School, Motherwell
1940	Dalziel High School, Motherwell
1941	St.Mungo's Academy, Glasgow
1942	Our Lady's High School, Motherwell
1943	Our Lady's High School, Motherwell
1944	Dumbarton Academy
1945	Falkirk High School
1946	Falkirk High School
1947	Queen's Park Secondary School, Glasgow
1948	St.Mungo's Academy, Glasgow
1949	Our Lady's High School, Motherwell
1950	Our Lady's High School, Motherwell
1951	Wishaw High School
1952	Hamilton Academy
1953	Irvine Royal Academy
1954	St.Gerard's Secondary School, Glasgow
1955	Bellahouston Academy, Glasgow
1956	Dumfries Academy
1957	Not Awarded
1958	Bellahouston Academy, Glasgow
1959	Lanark Grammar School
1960	Our Lady's High School, Motherwell
1961	St.Mungo's Academy, Glasgow
1962	Holyrood Secondary School, Glasgow
1963	Hamilton Academy
1964	Dalziel High School, Motherwell
1965	St.Patrick's High School, Coatbridge
1966	Liberton Secondary School, Edinburgh
1967	Airdrie Academy
1968	Liberton Secondary School, Edinburgh
1969	Cumnock Academy
1970	Dalziel High School, Motherwell
1971	Our Lady's High School, Motherwell
1972	Dalziel High School, Motherwell
1973	Holy Cross High School, Hamilton
1974	St.Patrick's High School, Coatbridge
1975	Holy Cross High School, Hamilton
1976	Harris Academy, Dundee
1977	Holy Cross High School, Hamilton
1978	Ardrossan Academy
1979	St.Roch's Secondary School, Glasgow
1980	Coatbridge High School
1981	Dumfries Academy / Kirkcaldy High - jointwinners
1982	Holyrood Secondary School, Glasgow
1983	St.Columba's High School, Gourock
1984	Dumfries Academy
1985	St.Bride's High School, East Kilbride
1986	Braidhurst High School, Motherwell
1987	Holyrood Secondary School, Glasgow
1988	Holyrood Secondary School, Glasgow
1989	Kyle Academy, Ayr
1990	St.Mungo's Academy, Glasgow
1991	Columba High School, Coatbridge
1992	Cardinal Newman High School, Bellshill
1993	Brannock High School, Newarthill
1994	Dingwall Academy
1995	Aberdeen Grammar School
1996	Lornshill Academy, Alloa
1997	Renfrew High School
1998	Larbert High School
1999	Uddingston Grammar School
2000	Our Lady's High School, Motherwell
2001	Perth High School
2002	St.Augustine's High School, Edinburgh
2003	Craigmount High School, Edinburgh
2004	Johnstone High School
2005	Inverkeithing High School
2006	Knightswood Secondary School, Glasgow
2007	Knightswood Secondary School, Glasgow
2008	Our Lady's High School, Cumbernauld
2009	Bishopbriggs Academy
2010	Largs Academy
2011	Larbert High School
2012	St.Mungo's High School, Falkirk
2013	Bishopbriggs Academy
2014	St.Ambrose High School, Coatbridge
2015	Penicuik High School
2016	St John's HS, Dundee
2017	Braidhurst HS, Motherwell

Scottish Schools Under 16 Shield Winners

1922	Queen's Park Secondary School, Glasgow
1923	Queen's Park Secondary School, Glasgow
1924	Whitehill Secondary School, Glasgow
1925	Uddingston Secondary School
1926	Wishaw High School
1927	Clydebank High School
1928	Queen's Park Secondary School, Glasgow
1929	Dumbarton Academy
1930	Greenock High School
1931	Queen's Park Secondary School, Glasgow
1932	Wishaw High School
1933	John Street Secondary School, Glasgow
1934	St.Aloysius' College, Glasgow
1935	Clydebank High School
1936	Queen's Park Secondary School, Glasgow
1937	Queen's Park Secondary School, Glasgow
1938	Dalziel High School, Motherwell
1939	St.Mungo's Academy, Glasgow
1940	Falkirk Technical
1941	Falkirk High School
1942	Wishaw High School
1943	St.Mungo's Academy, Glasgow
1944	Falkirk High School
1945	Coatbridge Technical
1946	Shawlands Secondary School, Glasgow
1947	St.John's Grammar School, Hamilton
1948	Our Lady's High School, Motherwell
1949	Carrickvale Secondary School, Edinburgh
1950	Larkhall Academy
1951	St.Anthony's Secondary School, Edinburgh
1952	St.Gerard's Secondary School, Glasgow
1953	Our Lady's High School, Motherwell
1954	Larbert High School
1955	St.Gerard's Secondary School, Glasgow
1956	Musselburgh Grammar School
1957	St.Patrick's High School, Dumbarton
1958	Tynecastle Secondary School, Edinburgh
1959	St.Mary's Secondary School, Bathgate
1960	St.Mungo's Academy, Glasgow
1961	Bo'ness Academy
1962	Camphill Secondary School, Paisley
1963	John Street Secondary School, Glasgow
1964	Camphill Sec., Paisley / St.Michael's College, Irvine*
1965	Liberton Secondary School, Edinburgh
1966	Dalkeith High School
1967	St.Pius Secondary School, Glasgow
1968	Lawside Academy, Dundee
1969	St.Anthony's Secondary School, Edinburgh
1970	Kingsridge Secondary School, Glasgow
1971	Bathgate Academy
1972	CaldervaleHigh School, Airdrie
1973	Douglas Academy, Milngavie
1974	Our Lady's High School, Motherwell
1975	Graeme High School, Falkirk
1976	All Saints Secondary School, Glasgow
1977	Whitburn Academy
1978	Trinity High School, Cambuslang
1979	Holy Cross High School, Hamilton
1980	Cardinal Newman High School, Bellshill
1981	St.Ambrose High School, Coatbridge
1982	St.Aelred's High School, Paisley
1983	St.Modan's High School, Stirling
1984	Linwood High School
1985	St.Andrew's Academy, Saltcoats
1986	St.Ninian's High School, Kirkintilloch
1987	St.Ambrose High School, Coatbridge
1988	Larbert High School
1989	St.Patrick's High School, Dumbarton
1990	Trinity High School, Cambuslang
1991	Cardinal Newman High School, Bellshill
1992	St.Ambrose High School, Coatbridge
1993	Cardinal Newman High School, Bellshill
1994	St.Margaret's High School, Airdrie
1995	Lasswade High School, Bonnyrigg
1996	Holyrood Secondary School, Glasgow
1997	Our Lady & St.Patrick's High School, Dumbarton
1998	John Ogilvie High School, Hamilton
1999	Bearsden Academy
2000	St.Andrew's Secondary School, Glasgow
2001	Our Lady & St.Patrick's High School, Dumbarton
2002	Johnstone High School
2003	St.Aidan's High School, Wishaw
2004	Oban High School
2005	Bellahouston Academy, Glasgow
2006	Auchinleck Academy
2007	Mintlaw Academy
2008	St.Margaret's High School, Airdrie
2009	Dumfries Academy
2010	St.Peter the Apostle High School, Clydebank
2011	Holyrood Secondary School, Glasgow
2012	Springburn Academy, Glasgow
2013	St.Margaret's High School, Airdrie
2014	Holyrood Secondary School, Glasgow
2015	Boclair Academy, Bearsden
2016	St Ninian's HS, Giffnock
2017	Braidhurst HS, Motherwell

Under 15 Shield		Under 14 Shield		Under 13 Shield		Girls U18 Shield		Girls U15 Shield	
1957	Crookston Castle Secondary School, Glasgow								
1958	Clydebank High School								
1959	Onslow Secondary School, Glasgow								
1960	Penilee Secondary School, Glasgow								
1961	Our Lady's High School, Motherwell								
1962	Graeme High School, Falkirk								
1963	St.Mungo's Academy, Glasgow								
1964	St.Mungo's Academy, Glasgow								
1965	Holy Cross High School, Hamilton								
1966	Liberton Secondary School, Edinburgh								
1967	St.Margaret Mary's Secondary School, Glasgow								
1968	St.Anthony's Secondary School, Edinburgh								
1969	Broxburn Academy								
1970	Crookston Castle Secondary School, Glasgow								
1971	Caldervale High School, Airdrie								
1972	Camphill High School, Paisley								
1973	Holy Cross High School, Hamilton								
1974	Graeme High School, Falkirk								
1975	All Saints Secondary School, Glasgow								
1976	Holy Cross High School, Hamilton								
1977	St.Ambrose High School, Coatbridge								
1978	Larbert High School								
1979	Cardinal Newman High School, Bellshill								
1980	Liberton High School, Edinburgh	1980	St.Andrew's High School, Kirkcaldy						
1981	James Hamilton Academy, Kilmarnock	1981	Holyrood Secondary School, Glasgow						
1982	Gracemount High School, Edinburgh	1982	St.Bride's High School, East Kilbride						
1983	Kincorth Academy, Aberdeen	1983	Holyrood Secondary School, Glasgow						
1984	Lesmahagow High School	1984	Bellshill Academy						
1985	Braidhurst High School, Motherwell	1985	St.Patrick's High School, Dumbarton						
1986	Cathkin High School, Cambuslang	1986	Caldervale High School, Airdrie						
1987	St.Patrick's High School, Dumbarton	1987	Cathkin High School, Cambuslang						
1988	St.Patrick's High School, Coatbridge	1988	Queensferry High School						
1989	Auchmuty High School, Glenrothes	1989	Lasswade High School, Bonnyrigg						
1990	Taylor High School, New Stevenston	1990	Beath High School, Cowdenbeath						
1991	Dalkeith High School	1991	Holyrood Secondary School, Glasgow						
1992	King's Park Secondary School, Glasgow	1992	Uddingston Grammar						
1993	Madras College, St.Andrews	1993	Holy Cross High School, Hamilton						
1994	St.Columba's High School, Dunfermline	1994	Holyrood Secondary School, Glasgow						
1995	Holyrood Secondary School, Glasgow	1995	Lourdes Secondary School, Glasgow						
1996	Lourdes Secondary School, Glasgow	1996	John Ogilvie High School, Hamilton						
1997	John Ogilvie High School, Blantyre	1997	Holy Cross High School, Hamilton						
1998	St.Margaret's High School, Airdrie	1998	St.Patrick's High School, Coatbridge	1998	Musselburgh Grammar School			1998	Torry Academy, Aberdeen
1999	Whitburn Academy	1999	Our Lady & St.Patrick's High School, Dumbarton	1999	Queen Anne High School, Dunfermline	1999	Kirkland High School, Leven	1999	St.Augustine's High School, Edinburgh
2000	Holyrood Secondary School, Glasgow	2000	Johnstone High School	2000	Holy Cross High School, Hamilton	2000	Kirkland High School, Leven	2000	Inverurie Academy
2001	Johnstone High School	2001	Holy Cross High School, Hamilton	2001	Craigmount High School, Edinburgh	2001	Kirkland High School, Leven	2001	St.Augustine's High School, Edinburgh
2002	Holy Cross High School, Hamilton	2002	Aberdeen Grammar School	2002	St.Aidan's High School, Wishaw	2002	St.Augustine's High School, Edinburgh	2002	St.Andrew's Secondary School, Glasgow
2003	Oban High School	2003	Our Lady & St.Patrick's High School, Dumbarton	2003	St.Machar Academy, Aberdeen	2003	St.Augustine's High School, Edinburgh	2003	Perth High School
2004	Ardrossan Academy	2004	Greenwood Academy, Irvine	2004	Currie High School	2004	St.Andrew's Academy, Paisley	2004	Mintlaw Academy
2005	St.Ambrose High School, Coatbridge	2005	Harris Academy, Dundee	2005	Craigmount High School, Edinburgh	2005	St.Augustine's High School, Edinburgh	2005	Mintlaw Academy
2006	Greenwood Academy, Irvine	2006	Peterhead Academy	2006	Holyrood Secondary School, Glasgow	2006	Mintlaw Academy	2006	Mintlaw Academy
2007	Nicolson Institute, Stornoway	2007	St.Andrew's & St.Bride's High School, East Kilbride	2007	St.Andrew's & St.Bride's High School, East Kilbride	2007	Mintlaw Academy	2007	Perth Grammar School
2008	Dumfries Academy	2008	St.Andrew's & St.Bride's High School, East Kilbride	2008	Hazlehead Academy, Aberdeen	2008	Mintlaw Academy	2008	Calderglen High School, East Kilbride
2009	Bishopbriggs Academy	2009	St.Ambrose High School, Coatbridge	2009	Lockerbie Academy	2009	Mintlaw Academy	2009	Arbroath High School
2010	St.Ambrose High School, Coatbridge	2010	Portlethen Academy	2010	Braidhurst High School, Motherwell	2010	Mintlaw Academy	2010	Webster's High School, Kirriemuir
2011	Musselburgh Grammar School	2011	St.Peter the Apostle High School, Clydebank	2011	Paisley Grammar School	2011	St.Mungo's High School, Falkirk	2011	Hawick High School
2012	Dunfermline High School	2012	St.Andrew's High School, Coatbridge	2012	Braidhurst High School, Motherwell	2012	St.Mungo's High School, Falkirk	2012	Nicolson Institute, Stornoway
2013	Bannerman High School, Glasgow	2013	Braidhurst High School, Motherwell	2013	Broughton High School, Edinburgh	2013	Boroughmuir High School, Edinburgh	2013	Woodmill High School, Dunfermline
2014	Braidhurst High School, Motherwell	2014	St.Ninian's High School, Giffnock	2014	Broughton High School, Edinburgh	2014	Nicolson Institute, Stornoway	2014	Lasswade High School, Bonnyrigg
2015	Braidhurst High School, Motherwell	2015	Grange Academy, Kilmarnock	2015	Broughton High School, Edinburgh	2015	Graeme High School, Falkirk	2015	St.John's High School, Dundee
2016	Broughton HS, Edinburgh	2016	St Ninian's High School, Giffnock	2016	Graeme HS, Falkirk	2016	Lasswade HS, Bonnyrigg	2016	Lasswade HS, Bonnyrigg
2017	Gryffe HS, Houston	2017	St Ninian's High School, Giffnock	2017	Lourdes Sec, Glasgow	2017	St Peter the Apostle HS, Glasgow	2017	Broxburn Academy

Dumfries & Galloway Schools 2016/17

CUP FINALS
Hunter Shield (U15)
Dumfries HS v Stranraer Academy, 1-2
Under 14 Small Schools Cup
Moffat Academy v Sanquhar Academy, 1-2
Under 16 Small Schools Cup
Maxwelltown HS v Moffat Academy, 3-2
Gordon Cup (U13)
Dumfries HS v Lockerbie Academy, 5-2
JH Lorraine Trophy (U18)
Lockerbie Academy v Stranraer Academy, 2-0

LEAGUES

Results were difficult to track down. Schools participating were:

Large Schools			Small Schools	
U16	U14	U13	U18	U15
Annan Academy	St Josephs College	Annan Academy	Castle Douglas HS	Langholm Academy
Dumfries HS	Douglas Ewart HS	Dumfries HS	Maxwelltown HS	Maxwelltown HS
Douglas Ewart HS	Dumfries Academy	Wallace Hall Academy	Dalbeattie HS	Sanquhar Academy
Dumfries Academy	Wallace Hall Academy	Lockerbie Academy	Sanquhar Academy	Moffat Academy
Wallace Hall Academy	Lockerbie Academy	Stranraer Academy	Langholm Academy	Castle Douglas HS
Lockerbie Academy	Stranraer Academy			Dalbeattie HS
Stranraer Academy				

Forth Valley Schools 2016/17

LEAGUES

Results were difficult to track down. Schools participating were:

Senior East	Senior West	Under 15 East	Under 15 West	Under 14 East	Under 14 West	Under 13 East	Under 13 West
Grangmouth HS	Balfron HS	Alloa Academy	Alva Academy	Denny HS	Dunblane HS	Braes HS	Balfron HS
Braes HS	Lornshill Academy	Grangemouth HS	Bannock burn H	Larbert HS	Stirling HS	Falkirk HS	Bannockburn HS
Alva Academy	Stirling HS	Denny HS	Dunblane HS	Graeme HS	Lornshill Academy	Grangemouth HS	Lornshill Academy
Larbert HS	Dunblane HS	Larbert HS	Stirling HS	St Mungos HS	Balfron HS	Bo'ness Academy	Alloa Avcademy
Falkirk HS	Wallace HS	Falkirk HS	Lornshill Acade	Bo'ness Academy	St Modans HS	Larbert HS	Dunblane HS
Alloa Academy	St Modans HS	Braes HS	Balfron HS	Braes HS	Wallace HS	Denny HS	Stirling HS
St Mungos HS	McLaren HS	Graeme HS	Wallace HS		Alva Academy	St Mungos HS	St Modans HS
Graeme HS		St Mungos HS	St Modans HS			Graeme HS	Wallace HS

Independent Schools 2015/16

UNDER 18 NORTH	P	W	D	L	F	A	GD	Pts
High School of Dundee	6	6	0	0	40	5	35	18
Dollar	6	3	2	1	14	11	3	11
Albyn School	6	3	0	3	11	9	2	9
Gordonstoun	6	2	1	3	19	22	-3	7
Glenalmond	6	2	1	3	17	26	-9	7
Strathallan	5	2	0	3	11	19	-8	6
St Leonards	5	0	0	5	4	24	-20	0

UNDER 18 EAST	P	W	D	L	F	A	GD	Pts
Stewart's Melville 'A'	6	6	0	0	25	3	22	18
George Heriot's School	6	5	0	1	23	9	14	15
Merchiston Castle School	6	3	1	2	16	10	6	10
George Watson's College	6	3	1	2	17	12	5	10
Fettes College	6	2	0	4	8	15	-7	6
Stewart's Melville 'B'	6	0	1	5	5	22	-17	1
Clifton Hall School	6	0	1	5	3	26	-23	1

UNDER 18 SWEST	P	W	D	L	F	A	GD	Pts
St Aloysius College	4	3	0	1	16	4	12	9
Jordanhill School	4	3	0	1	13	5	8	9
Hutchesons Grammar	4	2	1	1	9	8	1	7
High School of Glasgow	4	1	0	3	6	16	-10	3
Glasgow Academy	4	0	1	3	10	21	-11	1

Aberdeen Schools 2016/17

EN FINAL TROPHY SECTION A (U13)

	P	W	D	L	Pts
nmar U13	6	6	0	0	18
aw U13	7	5	0	2	15
lethen U13	6	5	0	1	15
orth U13	5	2	0	3	6
n U13	7	1	0	6	3
: U13	3	1	0	2	3
nachar U13	3	1	0	2	3
y U13	5	0	0	5	0

EN FINAL TROPHY SECTION B (U13)

	P	W	D	L	Pts
s U13	6	5	0	1	15
ehead U13	6	5	0	1	15
ksburn U13	6	4	0	2	12
achar U13	5	3	0	2	9
hfield U13	5	1	0	4	3
ert Gordon's U13	5	1	0	4	3
ge of Don U13	5	0	0	5	0

INTERNATIONAL DIVISION 1 (U13)

	P	W	D	L	Pts
ehead U13	6	4	1	1	13
lethen U13	6	4	1	1	13
ksburn U13	6	4	0	2	12
s U13	6	3	0	3	9
achar U13	6	3	0	3	9
aw U13	6	1	1	4	4
nmar U13	6	0	1	5	1

INTERNATIONAL DIVISION 2 (U13)

	P	W	D	L	Pts
ert Gordon's U13	4	4	0	0	12
hfield U13	4	2	1	1	7
nachar U13	4	2	1	1	7
orth U13	4	1	0	3	3
y U13	4	0	0	4	0

RTSMANS TROPHY SECTION A (U14)

	P	W	D	L	Pts
s U14	4	4	0	0	12
orth U14	5	4	0	1	12
ert Gordon's U14	4	2	0	2	6
nmar U14	3	0	0	3	0
school U14	1	0	0	1	0
lachar U14	3	0	0	3	0

RTSMANS TROPHY SECTION B (U14)

	P	W	D	L	Pts
aw U14	5	5	0	0	15
ksburn U14	5	3	1	1	10
: U14	5	3	0	2	9
yn U14	5	2	1	2	7
ge of Don U14	5	0	1	4	1
nachar U14	5	0	1	4	1

CUP FINALS

Green Final Trophy (U13), 25/3/17, atg Albyn PF
Portlethen U13 v Cults U13, 2-1

NE Scotland Esso Trophy, Mar 17 at Aberdeen SV
Hazleshead U13 v Portlethen U13, 2-2, 4-3p

CNR INTERNATIONAL LEAGUE PLAY OF (U13), April 19 at Countesswells
Hazlehead v Portlethen

SPORTSMANS TROPHY. Mar 22 at Dyce Acad
14 v Haelaw U14, 3-1

NE Scotland AFC Trophy (U14), Mar 24 at Aberdeen SV
Harlaw v Dyce, 4-3 AET

Gerrard Trophy (U15), Mar 20 at Northfiueld Acad
Hazlehead U15 v Bucksburn U15, 8-1

Presidents Trophy (U18), Mar 28 at Albyn PF
Cults v Bucksburn, 2-1

JM Low Trophy (U18), Mar 29 at Ellon United JFC
Alford v Fraserburgh, 1-2

CNR INTERNATIONAL DIVISION 1 (U14)	P	W	D	L	Pts
Cults U14	5	5	0	0	15
Harlaw U14	5	4	0	1	12
Dyce U14	5	2	1	2	7
Kincorth U14	4	1	1	2	4
Bucksburn U14	4	1	0	3	3
Robert Gordon's U14	5	0	0	5	0

CNR INTERNATIONAL DIVISION 2 (U14)	P	W	D	L	Pts
Albyn U14	2	1	0	1	3
Grammar U14	1	1	0	0	3
International School U14	1	0	0	1	0

CNR INTERNATIONAL U15	P	W	D	L	Pts
Hazlehead U15	7	6	1	0	19
Cults U15	7	5	0	2	15
Oldmachar U15	7	4	0	3	12
Grammar U15	6	3	1	2	10
St Machar U15	7	3	1	3	10
Bucksburn U15	7	2	0	5	6
Westhill U15	6	2	0	4	6
Albyn U15	7	0	1	6	1

CNR INTERNATIONAL U16	P	W	D	L	Pts
Torry U16	3	3	0	0	9
Bucksburn U16	2	1	0	1	3
Northfield U16	1	0	0	1	0
Westhill U16	2	0	0	2	0

PRESIDENTS TROPHY SECTION A (U18)	P	W	D	L	Pts
Grammar U18	5	5	0	0	15
Kincorth U18	5	3	1	1	10
Portlethen U18	6	3	1	2	10
Harlaw U18	4	3	0	1	9
Hazlehead U18	4	1	0	3	3
Albyn U18	4	0	0	4	0
Northfield U18	4	0	0	4	0

PRESIDENTS TROPHY SECTION B (U18)	P	W	D	L	Pts
Cults U18	3	3	0	0	9
Bucksburn U18	3	2	0	1	6
Bridge of Don U18	3	1	0	2	3
Torry U18	3	0	0	3	0

NORTH EAST SCOTLAND TROPHY (U13)

Rd 1	Bridge of Don Acad	Cults Acad	0	4	
Rd 1	Harlaw Acad	Bucksburn Acad	3	4	
Rd 1	Ellon Acad	Robert Gordons College	w	l	
Rd 1	Albyn School	Meldrum Acad	6	5	
Rd 1	Aberdeen GS	Inverurie Acad	9	2	
Rd 2	Kincorth Acad	Banff Acadf	4	0	
Rd 2	Bucksburn Acad	Portlethen Acad	4	6	
Rd 2	Mearns Acad	Ellon Acad	1	2	
Rd 2	Hazlehead HS	Old Machar Acad	2	0	
Rd 2	Fraserburgh Acad	Torry Acad	10	0	
Rd 2	Albyn School	St Machar Acad	A	A	
Rd 2	Banchory Acad	Cults Acad	1	1	AET, 3-4p
Rd 2	Northfield Acad	Aberdeen GS	2	7	
QF	St Machar Acad	Aberdeen GS	3	3	AET, 3-4p
QF	Kincorth Ascad	Portlethen Acad	2	7	
QF	Ellon Acad	Hazlehead HS	0	3	
QF	Cults Acad	Fraserburgh Acad	2	2	AET, 2-4p
SF	Hazlehead HS	Fraserburgh Acad	3	2	
SF	Aberdeen GS	Portlethen Acad	0	3	
F	Portlethen Acad	Hazlehead HS	2	2	AET, 3-4p

NORTH EAST SCOTLAND TROPHY (U14)

Rd 1	Albyn School	Bridge of Don Acad	7	4	
Rd 1	Banchory Acad	Bucksburn Acad	2	6	
Rd 1	Ellon Acad	Turriff Acad	10	2	
Rd 1	International School	Meldrum Acad	4	1	
Rd 1	St Machar Acad	Fraserburgh Acad	3	8	
Rd 1	Inverurie Acad	Aberdeen GS			
Rd 2	Robert Gordons Coll	Albyn School	A	A	
Rd 2	Cults Acad	The Gordon Schools	10	0	
Rd 2	Old Meldrum Acad	Ellon Acad	3	2	
Rd 2	Bucksburn Acad	Dyce Acad	4	9	
Rd 2	International School	Harlaw Acad	0	8	
Rd 2	Mearns Acad	Kincorth Acad	6	7	AET, 4-2p
Rd 2	Fraserburgh Acad	Inverurie Acad	8	8	
Rd 2	Banff Acad	Hazlehead HS	w	l	
QF	Harlaw Acad	Cults Acad	5	1	
QF	Hazlehead HS	Dyce Acad	A	A	
QF	Kincorth Ascad	Ellon Acad	1	2	4-5p
QF	Fraserburgh Acad	Albyn School	2	2	
SF	Albyn School	Dyce Acad	0	5	
SF	Harlaw Acad	Ellon Acad	6	0	AET
F	Dyce Acad	Harlaw Acad	3	4	

GERRARD TROPHY (u15)

Rd 1	Aberdeen GS	Westhill Acad	5	0
QF	Cults Acad	Hazlehead HS	1	3
QF	Aberdeen GS	Albyn School	6	3
QF	Old Machar Acad	St Machar Acad	4	3
QF	Torry Acad	Bucksburn Acad	A	A
SF	Old Machar Acad	Hazlehead HS	1	8
SF	Bucksburn Acad	Aberdeen GS	1	0
F	Bucksburn Acad	Hazlehead HS	1	8

JM LOW TROPHY (U18)

Rd 1	Albyn School	Fraserburgh Acad	0	7	AET, 9-10 pen
Rd 1	Ellon Acad	International School	11	1	
Rd 1	Aberdeen GS	Turriff Acad	w	l	
Rd 1	Inverurie Acad	Cults Acad	2	2	
Rd 1	Portlethen Acad	Bucksburn Acad	4	0	
Rd 1	Bridge of Don Acad	Alford Acad	0	6	
Rd 2	Cults Acad	Bucksburn Acad	4	1	
Rd 2	Northfield Acad	Hazlehead HS	4	3	
Rd 2	Alford Acad	Meldrum Acad	2	0	AET, 4-5p
Rd 2	Banchory Acad	Banff Acad	6	1	
Rd 2	Fraserburgh Acad	Aberdeen GS	4	3	
Rd 2	The Gordon Schools	Mearns Acad	5	5	
Rd 2	Torry Acad	Ellon Acad	1	10	
Rd 2	Kincorth Acad	Harlaw Acad	2	4	
QF	Banchory Acad	Cults Acad	4	3	
QF	Northfield Acad	Mearns Acad	4	10	
QF	Harlaw Acad	Fraserburgh Acad	1	2	
QF	Alford Acad	Ellon Acad	3	2	
SF	Alford Acad	Mearns Acad	2	1	
SF	Banchory Acad	Fraserburgh Acad	2	7	
F	Fraserburgh Acad	Alford Acad	2	1	

Dundee Schools 2016/17

DSA / ARAB TRUST PRIMARY LEAGUES					
SMALL SCHOOLS LEAGUE	P	W	D	L	PTS
St Vincent's	7	6	1	0	20
St Ninian's	7	6	0	1	19
Gowriehill	5	2	2	1	11
Rosebank	7	2	1	4	11
St Fergus	4	2	0	2	8
St Cklement's	6	1	0	3	6
Ardler	4	0	0	4	4
St Pius	4	0	0	4	4
Sidlaw View	0	0	0	0	0

SECTION A	P	W	D	L	PTS
St Mary's	7	7	0	0	21
Dens Road	6	1	1	4	9
Birkhill	3	2	0	1	7
Mill of Mains	3	2	0	1	7
St Luk'es & St Matthew's	4	1	1	2	7
Longhaugh	4	0	1	3	5
Camperdown	2	0	1	1	3
Rowantree	1	0	0	1	1

SECTION C	P	W	D	L	PTS
Fintry	7	7	0	0	21
SS Peter and Paul	7	4	0	3	15
St Andrew's	5	4	0	1	13
Hillside	6	3	0	3	11
St Joseph's	4	3	0	1	10
Craigiebarns	6	2	0	4	9
Glebelands	6	1	0	5	7
Ballumbie	7	0	0	7	7

SECTION D					
Barnhill	7	7	0	0	21
Forthill	7	6	0	1	19
Ancrum Road	7	5	0	2	17
Eastern	7	4	0	3	15
Downfield	7	2	0	5	11
Claypotts Castle	6	2	0	4	10
Craigowl	7	1	0	6	9
Clepington	6	0	0	6	6

DSA UNDER 13 LEAGUE	P	W	D	L	PTS
Grove Acad	5	5	0	0	15
St John's HS	5	2	1	2	10
Harris Acad	3	2	1	0	8
Braeview Acad	2	1	1	0	5
Morgan Acad	4	0	0	4	4
Monifieth HS	2	0	1	1	3
Baldragon Acad	2	0	0	2	2
St Paul's HS	1	0	0	1	1

DSA UNDER 13 CHAMPIONS LEAGUE	P	W	D	L	PTS
Harris Acad	2	2	0	0	6
St John's HS	1	0	0	1	1
Grove Acad	1	0	0	1	1

DSA UNDER 14 LEAGUE	P	W	D	L	PTS
St Paul's HS	6	3	1	2	13
St John;s HS	3	3	0	0	9
Grove Acad	3	2	0	1	7
Monifieth HS	3	1	1	1	6
Garris Acad	2	0	0	2	2
Morgan Acad	2	0	0	2	2
Craigie HS	1	0	0	1	1

DSA UNDER 14 CHAMPIONS LEAGUE	P	W	D	L	PTS
St John's HS	2	2	0	0	6
St Paul's HS	1	1	0	1	4
Grove Acad	2	0	0	2	2

ARAB TRUST U15 LEAGUE	P	W	D	L	PTS
Baldragon Ascad	4	3	1	0	11
Grove Acad	4	2	2	0	10
Harris Acad	5	2	1	2	10
Monifieth HS	5	1	2	2	9
Morgan Acad	4	1	1	2	7
St John's HS	4	0	1	3	5

ARAB TRUST U15 CHAMPIONS LEAGUE	P	W	D	L	PTS
Baldragon Acad	2	1	1	0	5
Harris Acad	2	0	2	0	4
Monifieth HS	3	0	1	2	4
Grove Acad	1	1	0	0	3

ARAB TRUST U16 LEAGUE	P	W	D	L	PTS
Grove Acad	4	4	0	0	13
Braeview Acad	3	2	0	1	7
St John's HS	2	2	0	0	6
Craigie HS	4	0	0	4	4
Morgan Acad	2	0	0	2	2
Monifieth HS	1	0	0	1	1

DSA / ARAB TRUST SENIOR LEAGUE	P	W	D	L	PTS
Baldragon Acad	4	2	0	2	8
Grove HS	3	2	0	1	7
St John's HS	2	2	0	0	7
Harris Acad	2	2	0	0	7
Morgan Acad	4	1	0	3	6
Craigie HS	3	1	0	2	5
Monfoeth HS	1	0	0	1	1
St Paul's HS	1	0	0	1	1

DSA / ARAB TRUST SENIOR CHAMPION!	P	W	D	L	PTS
St John's HS	1	1	0	0	3
Grove Acad	1	0	0	1	1

U15 GIRLS SEVENS LEAGUE	P	W	D	L	PTS
St John's HS	5	4	1	0	14
Morgan Acad	5	4	1	0	14
Craigie HS	5	3	2	2	11
Harris Acad	5	2	3	3	9
St Paul's HS	5	1	4	4	7
Baldragon Acad	5	0	5	5	5

SENIOR GIRLS SEVENS LEAGUE	P	W	D	L	PTS
St John's HS	9	8	1	0	26
Baldragon Acad	9	5	2	2	21
Harris Acad	9	4	1	4	18
Braeview Acad	9	3	2	4	17
St Paul's HS	9	2	1	6	14
Morgan Acad	9	0	3	6	12
Craigie HS	4	3	0	1	10
Grove Acad	4	1	0	3	6

ANGUS LEAGUE DIVISION ONE	P	W	D	L	PTS
Websters HS	6	5	0	1	16
Arbroath HS	6	5	0	1	16
Montrose Acad	7	3	1	3	14
Mearns Acad	5	3	1	1	13
Forfar Acad	7	3	0	4	13
Monifieth HS	6	2	0	4	10
Carnoustie HS	4	2	0	2	8
Arbroath Acad	7	0	0	7	7

CUP FINALS

Urquhart Trophy (U14) May 2 at Dens Park
St John's HS v Monifieth HS, 6-0

Senior Sports Cup (U15), at Dens Park
Monfieth HS v Grove Acad, 2-1

Under 15 Angus Cup, May 30 at Forfar
Monifieth HS v Arbroath HS, 4-2

Under 13 Logie Cup, June 7 at Broughty Athletic JFC
Grove Acad v Harris Acad, 3-0

George Grant Mem Trophy (U17), June 7 at Broughty Athletic JFC
St John's HS v Graove Acad, 3-0

U16 Dundee United Cup, at Broughty Athletic JFC
Grove Acad v Craigie HS, 9-0

Senior U18 Johnston Trophy, at Broughty Athletic JFC
St John's HS v Grove Acad, 2-1

Linton Cup, June 14 at Elliot Road
St Joseph's v Ancrum Road, 1-0

Thomson Cup, June 14 at Elliot Road
Fintry v Craigiebarns, 5-0

Burgess Cup, June 14 at Elliot Road
Barnshill v Forthill, 3-0

Cameron Cup, June 16 at Elliot Road
St Andrew's v Downfield, 7-4

Junior Sports Cup, June 16 at Elliot Road
Barnshill v St Joseph's, 3-0

Robert Caira Mem Trophy (U16), June 20 at Forfar Athletic
Grove v St John's, 6-0

Angus Trophy Small Schools Cup Final, June 12 at Elliot Road
Gowriehill v St Fergus, 3-1

Faitrade Football Rock Cup Final, June 12 at Elliot Road
St Andrew's v St Josephs's 2-1

Glasgow Schools 2016/17

SENIOR U18	
Div 1A	
Clydebank HS	7
Hyndland Sec	7
Drumchapel HS	2
Glasgow Acad	0
Div 1B	
Lourdes Sec	12
Cleveden HS	6
John Paul Acad	6
Whithill Sec	0
Div 1C	
Holyrood Sec	6
St Thomas Aquinus	5
Hutchesons GS	1
Ballhouston Acad	0
Div 1D	
Bearsden Acad	12
King's Park HS	8
All Saints Sec	4
Vale of Leven Acad	0
Div 1E	
Bishopbriggs HS	3
St Andrews HS	1
Dumbarton Acad	0
Div 1F	
Bannerman HS	4
Our Lady & St Pauls	4
Rosshall HS	0
Div 1G	
St Peters	7
Stonelaw Acad	6
Hermitage Acad	6

UNDER 16	
Div 2A	Pts
Knightswood Sec	9
Hermitage Acad	2
Bishopbriggs HS	1
Division 2B	
St Thomas Aquinus	6
St Paul's Sec	2
Dumbarton Acad	0
Division 2C	
St Mungo's Acad	0
Stonelaw HS	0
Hillpark Sec	0
Division 2D	
St Peter's	11
Clydebank HS	7
Hyndland Sec	6
Lourdes Sdec	0
Division 2E	9
Bannerman HS	6
St Andrews HS	5
Holyrood Sec	0
John Paul Acad	

UNDER 15	
Div 3A	
Bishopbriggs HS	10
Hermitage Acad	8
Bearsden Acad	6
Div 3B	
All Saints Sec	8
John Paul Acad	2
Hillpark Sec	2
Div 3C	
Bannerman HS	8
Lourdes Sec	6
Vale of Leven Acad	2
Div 3D	
St Peter's	9
St Andrews HS	2
Rosshall	0

UNDER 14	
Div 4A	
Bearsden Acad	10
St Thomas Aquinus	10
Hermitage Acad	4
Div 4B	
St Andrew's Sec	3
Bishopbriggs HS	1
Glasgow Gaelic	0
Div 4C	
John Paul Acad	5
St Peter the Apostle	3
King's Park Sec	0
Div 4D	
Jordanhill Sec	8
St Mungo's Ascad	6
Hillhead HS	2
Div 4E	
Our Ladt and St Pauls	6
Knightswood Sec	4
Holyrood Sec	2
Div 4F	
Hyndeland Sec	12
Bannerman HS	8
St Margaret Marys	4
Div 4G	
Vale of Leven Acad	9
Lourdes Sec	2
Springburn Acad	1

UNDER 13	
Div 5A	
Lourdes Sec	12
St Peter the Apostle	11
St Mungo's HS	3
John Paul Acad	2
Div 5B	
Bishopbriggs Sec	13
Bearsden Acad	13
Vale of Leven Acad	4
Eastbank Acad	2
Div 5C	
Holyrood Sec	13
Our Lady and St Pauls	10
St Andrews Sec	7
All Saints Sec	2
Div 5D	
Stonelaw HS	9
Bannerman HS	5
Hermitage Acad	6
Kinghtswood Sec	0

PLAY OFFS			
Div 1			
Rd 1	OLSP v King's Park	1-2	
QF	Bearsden v Hyndland	3-0	
	Holyrood v Bishopbriggs	2-0	
	Hermitage v King's Park	2-1	
	Lourdes v Bannerman	4-3	
SF	Bearsden v Holyrood	w-l	
	Hermitage v Lourdes	0-3	
F (May 17)	at New Lesser Hampden		
	Bearsden v Lourdes	0-5	
Div 2			
QF	Knightswood v Holyrood	4-3	
	St Thomas Aquinus v Hermitage	wo-scr	
	St Peter the Apostle v St Paul's	5-2	
	Bannerman HS v Clydebank	2-3	
SF	Knightswood v St Thomas Aq	2-2	w-l pens
	St Peter the Apostle v Clydebank	2-1	
F (May 13)	at Loretto PF		
	Knightswood v St Peter's	1-0	
Div 3			
QF	Bishopbriggs v Lourdes	1-1	l-w pens
	All Saints v Hermitage	2-0	
	St Peter the Apostle v John Paul Acad	2-1	
	Bannerman v St Andrew's	0-4	
SF	Lourdes v All Saints	2-3	
	St Peter the Ap v St Andrew's	3-2	
F (May 16)	at Auchenhowie		
	All Saints v St Peter the Ap	2-6	
Div 4			
Rd 1	St Peter's v St Thomas Aq	2-1	
QF	Bearsden v OLSP	3-0	
	John Paul Acad v Hyndland	1-0	
	St Andrew's v St Peter's	3-5	
	Jordanhill v Vale of Leven	1-1	w-l pens
SF	Bearsen v John Paul Acad	0-3	
	St Peter's v Jordanhill	2-2	w-l pens
F (May 13)	St Peter's v John Paul Acad	1-0	
Div 5			
QF	Stonelaw v Lourdes	1-5	
	Bishopnriggs v OLSP	3-4	
	St Peter's v Hermitage	4-0	
	Holyrood v Bearsden	9-1	
SF	Lourdes v OLSP	4-3	
	St Peter's v Holyrood	1-4	
F (May 13)	Holyrood v Lourdes	2-1	

CUP FINALS
U18 Cameronian Cup, May 22 at Celtic Park
Bishopbriggs HS v St Andrew's Sec 5-1
U16 RS McColl Cup (May 6 at Loretto PF)
Knightswood v St Thomas Aquinus, 2-0
U15 Glasgow Cup, May 9 at Auchenhowie
St Peter the Apostle v All Saints, 4-2
U14 Crookston Cup
Holyrood Sec v Jordanhill, 4-1
U13 Castle Cup
Lourdes v OLSP, 2-1

	PREVIOUS WINNERS				
	Cameronian Cup (U18)	RS McColl Cup (U16)	Glasgow Cup (U15)	Crookston Cup (U14)	Castle Cup (U13)
1959	St Mungo's Academy				
1960	Holyrood Secondary				
1961	Whitehill Secondary				
1962	Lourdes Secondary				
1963	St Mungo's Academy	Shawlands Academy			
1964	Whitehill Secondary	Holyrood Secondary			
1965	Holyrood Secondary	St Augustine;s			
1966	St Augustine's	Albert Secondary			
1967	Whitehill Secondary	Bellahouston Academy			
1968	Bellarmine Secondary	Eastbank Academy		St Mungo's Acad	
1969	Holyrood Secondary	St Mungo's Academy		Duncanrig Secondary	St Mungo's Academy
1970	St Mungo's Academy	St Mungo's Academy		St Ninian's HS	Grange Secondary
1971	St Mungo's Academy	Duncanrig Secondary		St Augustines	Lourdes Secondary
1972	Whitehill Secondary	Grange Secondary		North Kelvinside	Kingsridge Secondary
1973	North Kelvinside	Lourdes Secondary		Holyrood Secondary	St Bonaventure;s Secondary
1974	St Pius Secondary	St Gregory's Secondary		Penilee Secondary	Penilee Secondary
1975	St Pius Secondary	Kingsridge Secondary		All Saints Secondary	St Leonard's Secondary
1976	No competition	Clydebank HS		St Leonards Secondary	St Gregory's Secondary
1977	Holyrood Secondary	St Columba of Iona		Cranhill Secondary	John Bosco Secondary
1978	Holyrood Secondary	St Gregory's Secondary		All Saints Secondary	St Rochs Secondary
1979	Holyrood Secondary	St Margaret Marys		Glenwood Secondary	Trinity HS
1980	Holyrood Secondary	St Columba of Iona		St Augustines	St Pius Secondary
1981	Holyrood Secondary	St Andrews High		St Andrews HS	Grange Secondary
1982	Holyrood Secondary	St Margaret Marys		Holyrood Secondary	St Leonard's Secondary
1983	Holyrood Secondary	Holyrood Secondary		St Pius Secondary	Holyrood Secondary
1984	Lourdes Secondary	Thomas Muir HS		Holyrood Secondary	All Saints Secondary
1985	St Ninian's HS	Turnbull HS		Whitehill Secondary	Holyrood Secondary
1986	No competition	No competition		No competition	No competition
1987	Paisley Grammar	No competition		St Ninian's HS	Cathkin HS
1988	Holyrood Secondary	No competition		St Margaret Marys Sec	Clydebank HS
1989	St Patrick's HS Dumbarton	No competition		Turnbull HS	St Patrick's HS
1990	St Patrick's HS Dumbarton	No competition		Holyrood Secondary	Holyrood Secondary
1991	St Patrick's HS Dumbarton	No competition		St Columba's HS	Trinity HS
1992	St Ninian's HS	No competition	Eastbank Academy	King's Park Secondary	Cathkin HS
1993	Our Lady & St Pats	No competition	Holyrood Secondary	Cathkin HS	King's Park Secondary
1994	Cleveden Sec	No competition	Our Lady & St Pats HS	Our Lady & St Pats	King's Park Secondary
1995	Cathkin HS	No competition	Our Lady & St Pats HS	Holyrood Secondary	Holyrood Secondary
1996	Holyrood Secondary	No competition	Lourdes Secondary	Castlemilk HS	Holyrood Secondary
1997	Hillpark Secondary	No competition	Our Lady & St Pats HS	Our Lady & St Pats	St Leonard's Secondary
1998	Bearsden Acad	Our Lady & St Pats	Our Lady & St Pats HS	Holyrood Secondary	Our Lady & St Pats HS
1999	St Andrew's Secondary	Cleveden Secondary	Holyrood Secondary	Our Lady & St Pats	No competition
2000	Our Lady & St Pats	All Saints Sec	St Andrews Secondary	Holyrood Secondary	No competition
2001	Our Lady & St Pats	Holyrood Secondary	St Rochs Secondary	St Columba's HS	No competition
2002	Bearsden Acad	Our Lady & St Pats	St Columba's HS	Holyrood Secondary	No competition
2003	All Saints Secondary	St Columba's	Lourdes Secondary	Holyrood Secondary	No competition
2004	St Columba's HS	All Saints Sec	Bellahouston Acad	Lochend Community HS	No competition
2005	Knightswood Sec	Our Lady & St Pats	Cathkin HS	Holyrood Secondary	No competition
2006	Knightswood Sec	Hillpark Sec	Hillhead HS	Our Lady & St Pats	No competition
2007	St Ninian's HS	Bishopbriggs Acvademy	Our Lady & St Pats HS	Jordanhill School	No competition
2008	St Margaret Marys Sec	Bishopbriggs Acvademy	Bearsden Acad	Bannerman HS	Holyrood Secondary
2009	St Peter the Apostle HS	Hermitage Academy	Eastbank Academy	Holyrood Secondary	All Saints Secondary
2010	St Peter the Apostle HS	St Peter the Apostle	Holyrood Secondary	St Paul's HS	Bearsden Academy
2011	Holyrood Secondary	Holyrood Secondary	St Paul's HS	St Peter the Apostle	Bishopbriggs Academy
2012	Bannerman HS	St Peter the Apostle	St Peter the Apostle	All Saints Secondary	Bishopbriggs Academy
2013	Hermitage Acad	St Peter the Apostle	All Saints Secondary	St Peter the Apostle	Holyrood Secondary
2014	Bishopbriggs Acad	Lourdes Secondary	Holyrood Secondary	Holyrood Secondary	Holyrood Secondary
2015	Hermitage Acad	Lourdes Secondary	St Peter the Apostle	Holyrood Secondary	Bearsden Academy
2016	Bishopbriggs Acad	Lourdes Secondary	St Peter the Apostle	Holyrood Secondary	Bearsden Academy
2017	Bishopbriggs Acad	Knightsxwood Sec	St Peter the Apostle	Holyrood Secondary	Lourdes Secondary

LEAGUE CHAMPIONS	
Senior	
1905	Allan Glen's School
1906	Paisley GS
1907	Hutcheson's GS
1908	Hutcheson's GS
1909	Ballhouston Acad
1910	North Kelvinside Sec
1911	St Aloysius
1912	Paisley GS
1913	Allan Glen's School
1914	Allan Glen's School
1915	Clydebank HS
1916	Clydebank HS
1917	Dumbarton Acad
1918	Queen's Park Sec
1919	Hamilton Acad
1920	Dumbarton Acad
1921	Allan Glen's School
1922	St Mungo's Acad
1923	St Mungo's Acad
1924	St Mungo's Acad
1925	Dumbarton Acad
1926	St Mungo's Acad
1927	Coatbridge HS
1928	Queen's Park Sec
1929	Queen's Park Sec
1930	Hamilton Acad
1931	John Street Secondary
1932	Queen's Park Sec
1933	Hamilton Acad
1934	St Mungo's Acad
1935	Hamilton Acad
1936	St Aloysius
1937	Rutherglen Acad
1938	St Mungo's Acad
1939	St Mungo's Acad
1940	Queen's Park Sec
1941	Falkirk HS
1942	Queen's Park Sec
1943	Dumbarton Acad
1944	Queen's Park Sec
1945	King's Park Sec
1946	St Mungo's Acad
1947	St Mungo's Acad
1948	St Mungo's Acad
1949	St Mungo's Acad
1950	
1951	Govan HS
1952	Govan HS
1953	St Mungo's Acad
1954	St Mungo's Acad
1955	Greenock Acad
1956	Bellahouston Acad
1957	St Mungo's Acad
1958	St Gerard's Sec
1959	Falkirk HS
1960	St Augustine's HS
1961	St Augustine's HS
1962	Lourdes Sec
1963	St Mungo's Acad
1964	St Patrick's HS, Dumbarton
1965	Holyrood Sec
1966	Eastwood HS
1967	John Neilson Institute
1968	Holyrood Sec
1969	St Mungo's Acad
1970	St Mungo's Acad
1971	St Mungo's Acad
1972	St Mungo's Acad
1973	St Mungo's Acad
1974	St Mungo's Acad
1975	St Pius Sec
1976	Eastwood HS
1977	Smithycroft Sec
1978	Eastwood HS
1979	Bearsdsen Acad
1980	Bearsdsen Acad
1981	St Thomas Aquinus
1982	Trinity HS
1983	Braidfield HS
1984	Lourdes Sec
1985	Clydebank HS
1986	Penilee Sec
1987	Whitehill Sec
1988	Holyrood Sec
1989	St Patrick's HS, Dumbarton
1990	St Patrick's HS, Dumbarton
1991	Vale of Leven Acad
1992	Holyrood Sec
1993	Bearsdsen Acad
1994	King's Park Sec
1995	Drumchapel HS
1996	Holyrood Sec
1997	Our Lady and St P
1998	Bellarmine Sec
1999	Bearsden Acad
2000	Our Lady and St P
2001	St Margaret Mary
2002	St Andrew's Sec
2003	Our Lady and St P
2004	Hillpark Sec
2005	
2006	Castlemilk HS
2007	Bishopbriggs Acad
2008	St Ninian's HS
2009	Our Lady and St P
2010	Our Lady and St P
2011	St Peter the Apostle
2012	St Peter the Apostle
2013	St Peter the Apostle
2014	Knightswood Sec
2015	Bishopbriggs Acad
2016	St Peter the Apostle

Lothians Schools 2016/17

Senior	P	W	D	L	F	A	GD	Pts
Ross HS, Tranent	13	11	1	1	62	20	42	34
Lasswade HS	13	9	3	1	38	20	18	30
Firrhill HS, Edinburgh	14	9	3	2	41	24	17	30
Musselburgh GS	13	9	2	2	52	19	33	29
James Young HS, Livingston	11	8	0	3	22	16	6	24
Boroughmuir HS, Edinburgh	14	7	2	5	37	21	16	23
North Berwick HS	10	7	0	3	30	21	9	21
Preston Lodge HS, Prestonpans	13	7	0	6	29	30	-1	21
James Gillespie's HS, Edin burgh	13	5	3	5	30	27	3	18
Royal HS, Edinburgh	13	4	3	6	35	26	9	15
George Heriots School	12	4	3	5	23	39	-16	15
St Augustine's HS Edinburgh	11	4	2	5	29	23	6	14
George Watson's College, Edinburgh	13	4	1	8	15	37	-22	13
Holyrood HS, Edinburgh	11	4	0	7	24	28	-4	12
Balerno HS	11	4	0	7	17	29	-12	12
St Thomas Aquinas, Edinburgh	14	3	3	8	23	45	-22	12
Newbattle HS	11	3	1	7	20	29	-9	10
Broughton HS, Edinburgh	13	2	0	#	11	42	-31	6
Craigroyston HS, Edinburgh	12	0	1	#	10	52	-42	1

Senior Championship Post Split	P	W	D	L	F	A	GD	Pts
Ross HS, Tranent	9	7	1	1	6	7	-1	22
Musselburgh GS	9	6	1	2	13	4	9	19
Lasswade HS	9	5	3	1	3	3	0	18
James Young HS, Livingston	8	6	0	2	4	6	-2	18
Firrhill HS, Edinburgh	8	4	2	2	10	5	5	14
Boroughmuir HS, Edinburgh	9	3	1	5	6	4	2	10
Preston Lodge HS, Prestonpans	9	3	0	4	0	0	0	9
Royal HS, Edinburgh	9	2	2	5	5	13	-8	8
Holyrood HS, Edinburgh	9	2	0	7	3	6	-3	6
George Watson's College, Edinburgh	9	1	0	8	0	2	-2	3

Senior Plate Post Split	P	W	D	L	F	A	GD	Pts
North Berwick HS	8	8	0	0	12	4	8	24
James Gillespie's HS, Edinburgh	8	5	1	0	3	2	1	16
St Augustine's HS, Edinburgh	8	4	1	3	8	1	7	13
Balerno HS	8	4	0	1	5	3	2	12
St Thomas Aquinas, Edinburgh	8	3	2	3	0	0	0	11
George Heriots School	7	3	2	2	1	6	-5	11
Newbattle HS	7	2	1	4	8	1	7	7
Broughton HS, Edinburgh	8	2	0	6	1	10	-9	6
Craigroyston HS, Edinburgh	8	0	1	7	4	15	-11	1

Under 16	P	W	D	L	F	A	GD	Pts
Portobello HS	11	9	1	1	21	9	12	28
Royal HS, Edinburgh	11	7	2	2	55	21	34	23
Broughton HS, Edinburgh	10	7	1	2	45	11	34	22
Preston Lodge HS, Prestonpans	11	7	1	3	33	20	13	22
Balerno HS	11	6	2	3	38	26	12	20
Newbattle HS	11	6	0	5	42	32	10	18
Lasswade HS	11	4	2	5	28	19	9	14
Boroughmuir HS, Edinburgh	11	4	1	6	25	36	-11	13
Firrhill HS, Edinburgh	11	3	1	7	9	52	-43	10
Dunbar GS	10	4	0	6	21	38	-17	9
James Gillespie's HS	11	2	1	8	20	43	-23	7
Trinity Acad	11	0	0	#	9	39	-30	3

East / Midlothian Under 14	P	W	D	L	F	A	GD	Pts
Ross HS, Tranent	10	8	1	1	56	23	33	25
Preston Lodge HS, Prestonpans	10	7	2	1	36	18	18	23
Lasswade HS	10	5	2	3	25	18	7	17
Newbattle HS	10	5	1	4	46	39	7	16
Dunbar GS	10	2	0	8	13	33	-20	6
St David's HS, Dalkeith	6	1	0	5	8	26	-18	3
Musselburgh GS	6	0	0	6	8	35	-27	0

East / Midlothian U13	P	W	D	L	F	A	GD	Pts
Lasswade HS	10	9	0	1	59	13	46	27
Ross HS, Tranent	10	9	0	1	45	10	35	27
Musselburgh GS	8	3	1	4	13	19	-6	10
Preston Lodge	8	3	1	4	23	33	-10	10
Newbattle HS	9	1	0	8	8	46	-38	3
Dunbar GS	7	0	0	7	9	36	-27	0

Edinburgh U13 A	P	W	D	L	Pts
Portobello HS	13	10	3	0	33
Firrhill HS, Edinburgh	12	8	0	4	24
Boroughmuir HS, Edinburgh	12	6	4	2	22
Royal HS, Edinburgh	13	7	0	6	21
Craigmount HS	8	5	1	2	16
Broughton HS, Edinburgh	14	4	1	9	13
Holyrood HS	11	2	1	8	7
James Gillespie's HS	13	1	0	#	3

Edinburgh U13 B	P	W	D	L	Pts
Leith Acad	9	9	0	0	27
Currie HS	10	7	0	3	21
St Thomas Aquinas	9	4	0	5	12
Queensferry HS	8	3	0	5	9
Balerno HS	8	2	0	6	6
Tynecastle HS	6	0	0	6	0

Edinburgh U14 (1)	P	W	D	L	Pts
Queensferry HS	10	8	1	1	25
Broughton HS, Edinburgh	10	7	2	1	23
Portobello HS	10	5	3	2	18
Craigmount HS	10	4	2	4	14
Royal HS, Edinburgh	10	2	0	8	6
James Gillespie's HS	10	0	0	#	0

Edinburgh U14 (2)	P	W	D	L	Pts
Forrester HS	10	9	1	0	28
Currie HSD	10	5	1	4	16
Firrhill HS, Edinburgh	7	5	0	2	15
Leith Acad	9	3	0	6	9
Boroughmuir HS, Edinburgh	10	2	0	8	6
St Thomas Aquinas	8	2	0	6	6

Edinburgh U15 (1)	P	W	D	L	Pts
Lasswade HS	10	8	0	2	24
Portobello HS	10	7	1	2	22
Craigmount HS	8	4	1	3	13
Leith Acad	9	2	2	5	8
Boroughmuir HS, Edinburgh	9	2	1	6	7
Queensferry HBS	10	2	1	7	7

Edinburgh U15 (2)	P	W	D	L	Pts
Gracemount HS	10	10	0	0	30
Currie HS	11	5	1	5	16
Firrhill HS, Edinburgh	8	5	0	3	15
Holyrood HS	8	3	1	4	10
Balerno HS	9	3	0	6	9
Royal HS, Edinburgh	11	2	0	9	6
Tynecastle HS	5	2	0	3	6

Lothians Senior Cup (May 19 at Spartans)

Leith Academy v Musselburgh GS, 2-2, w-l on pens

	SENIOR LEAGUE WINNERS	SENIOR CUP WINNERS
1966	Liberton HS	Norton Park Sec
1967	Liberton HS	Norton Park Sec
1968	Liberton HS	Dalkeith HS
1969	Liberton HS	Tynecastle HS
1970	Liberton HS	Liberton HS
1971	Liberton HS	Dalkeith HS
1972	Liberton HS	Musselburgh GS
1973	Firhill HS	Liberton HS
1974	Boroughmuir HS	Boroughmuir HS
1975	Liberton HS	St Augustine's HS
1976	Liberton HS	Liberton HS
1977	Bathgate Acad	Bathgate Ascad
1978	Liberton HS	St Augustine's HS
1979	St Augustine's HS	Craigmount HS
1980	Liberton HS	Liberton HS
1981	Liberton HS	St David's HS, Dalkeith
1982	Musselburgh GS	Musselburgh GS
1983	St Augustine's HS	St Augustine's HS
1984	St Kentigern's Acad	St Augustine's HS
1985	St Kentigern's Acad	St Kentigern's Acad
1986	No competition	No competition
1987	No competition	No competition
1988	Portoberllo HS	Tynecastle HS
1989	Dalkeith HS	Queensferry HS
1990	Royal HS	Liberton HS
1991	Musselburgh GS	Musselburgh GS
1992	Queensferry HS	Queensferry HS
1993	Portoberllo HS	Portobello HS
1994	Boroughmuir HS	Liberton HS
1995	Lasswade HS	Musselburgh GS
1996	Lasswade HS	Lasswade HS
1997	St David's HS Dalkeith	Bo'ness Acad
1998	Firhill HS	Craigmount HS
1999	Balerno HS	Broughton HS
2000	Craigmount HS	Leith Acad
2001	St Augustine's HS	St Augustine's HS
2002	St Augustine's HS	St Augustine's HS
2003	St Augustine's HS	Leith Acad
2004	Queensferry HS	Liberton HS
2005	St Augustine's HS	Queensferry HS
2006	Portobello HS	Portobello HS
2007	Firhill HS	Firhill HS
2008	Craigmount HS	Craigmount HS
2009	St David's HS Dalkeith	Queensferry HS
2010	Craigmount HS	Queensferry HS
2011	Newbattle HS	Balerno HS
2012	St David's HS Dalkeith	Newbattle HS
2013	Holyrood HS	Linlithgow Acad
2014	Musselburgh GS	Currie HS
2015	Newbattle HS	Penicuik HS
2016	Dalkeith HS	Royal HS
2017	Ross HS	Leith Acad

Paisley & District Schools 2016/17

Under 13	P	W	D	L	F	A	+/-	Pts
St Ninians High	7	7	0	0	51	7	44	21
Williamwood High	10	6	2	2	47	22	25	20
St Andrews Academy	10	6	2	2	41	19	22	20
Woodfarm High	6	2	0	4	15	20	-5	6
Eastwood High	7	1	1	5	13	42	-29	4
St Lukes High	4	1	0	3	8	27	-19	3
Castlehead High	8	0	1	7	19	57	-38	1

UNDER 14A	P	W	D	L	F	A	+/-	Pts
St Ninians High	7	7	0	0	48	9	39	21
St Lukes High	9	6	0	3	31	15	16	18
Mearns Castle High	6	4	1	1	24	18	6	13
Williamwood High	6	2	0	4	16	24	-8	6
Eastwood High	9	1	2	6	10	37	-27	5
Barrhead High	7	0	1	6	4	30	-26	1

UNDER 14B	P	W	D	L	F	A	+/-	Pts
Castlehead High	9	8	0	1	52	26	26	24
St Andrews Academy	7	4	2	1	40	24	16	14
Trinity High	8	3	0	5	23	40	-17	9
St Benedicts High	8	2	2	4	28	41	-13	8
Renfrew High	6	1	2	3	30	32	-2	5
Gleniffer High	4	0	0	4	7	17	-10	0

UNDER 15A	P	W	D	L	F	A	+/-	Pts
St Ninians High	7	7	0	0	39	4	35	21
Williamwood High	8	6	0	2	36	12	24	18
Woodfarm High	8	3	0	5	15	30	-15	9
Gleniffer High	4	2	0	2	13	8	5	6
St Benedicts High	6	1	0	5	5	34	-29	3
Trinity High	5	0	0	5	1	21	-20	0

UNDER 15B	P	W	D	L	F	A	+/-	Pts
Clydeview Academy	7	6	1	0	51	6	45	19
Renfrew High	9	5	3	1	39	17	22	18
Gryffe High	7	3	2	2	30	36	-6	11
St Columbas High	6	0	2	4	14	35	-21	2
St Stephens High	2	0	0	2	0	4	-4	0
Linwood High	5	0	0	5	11	47	-36	0

UNDER 16A	P	W	D	L	F	A	+/-	Pts
St Ninians High	5	5	0	0	35	0	35	15
St Lukes High	6	3	0	3	14	30	-16	9
Williamwood High	5	2	0	3	13	24	-11	6
Eastwood High	1	1	0	0	4	0	4	3
Mearns Castle High	5	0	0	5	6	18	-12	0

UNDER 16B	P	W	D	L	F	A	+/-	Pts
Johnstone High	9	7	1	1	43	17	26	22
Renfrew High	8	3	3	2	22	28	-6	12
St Benedicts High	7	3	2	2	14	16	-2	11
St Andrews Academy	5	3	0	2	24	13	11	9
Glennifer High	7	0	4	3	16	32	-16	4
Barrhead High	6	0	0	6	8	21	-13	0

Under 18	P	W	D	L	F	A	+/-	Pts
Gryffe High	8	7	1	0	33	13	20	22
Glennifer High	7	5	1	1	26	13	13	16
Castlehead High	5	2	0	3	11	17	-6	6
Renfrew High	6	0	1	5	5	17	-12	1
Linwood High	6	0	1	5	12	27	-15	1

Fife Schools 2016/17

POS	SENIOR DIV A	P	W	D	L	F	A	+-	PTS
1	Beath HS U18	7	6	1	0	25	8	17	19
2	Bell Baxter HS U18	7	5	0	2	24	11	13	15
3	Levenmouth Academy U18	7	4	0	3	21	13	8	12
4	Kirkcaldy HS U18	7	4	0	3	19	16	3	12
5	Glenrothes HS U18	7	3	0	4	16	23	-7	9
6	Madras College U18	7	2	2	3	15	17	-2	8
7	Waid Academy U18	7	2	1	4	12	19	-7	7
8	Lochgelly HS U18	7	0	0	7	2	27	-25	0

POS	SENIOR DIV B	P	W	D	L	F	A	+-	PTS
1	Balwearie HS U18	8	8	0	0	40	10	30	24
2	Dunfermline HS U18	8	7	0	1	30	8	22	21
3	Auchmuty HS U18	8	5	1	2	27	18	9	16
4	Glenwood HS U18	8	4	1	3	17	12	5	13
5	Queen Anne HS U18	8	3	2	3	24	15	9	11
6	St Columba's HS U18	8	3	2	3	16	21	-5	11
7	Viewforth HS U18	8	2	0	6	10	38	-28	6
8	Inverkeithing HS U18	8	1	0	7	10	27	-17	3
9	St Andrews HS U18	8	0	0	8	2	27	-25	0

POS	UNDER 15A	P	W	D	L	F	A	+-	PTS
1	Woodmill HS U15	5	5	0	0	21	2	19	15
2	Lochgelly HS U15	5	3	1	1	12	7	5	10
3	Bell Baxter HS U15	5	3	0	2	17	10	7	9
4	Beath HS U15	5	1	2	2	10	12	-2	5
5	Glenrothes HS U15	5	1	0	4	7	23	-16	3
6	Kirkcaldy HS U15	5	0	1	4	5	18	-13	1

POS	UNDER 15 B	P	W	D	L	F	A	+-	PTS
1	Dunfermline HS U15	5	4	1	0	12	5	7	13
2	Levenmouth Academy U15	5	3	1	1	13	3	10	10
3	Queen Anne HS U15	5	2	3	0	19	5	14	9
4	Glenwood HS U15	5	2	0	3	7	19	-12	6
5	Balwearie HS U15	5	1	1	3	5	9	-4	4
6	Auchmuty HS U15	5	0	0	5	0	15	-15	0

POS	UNDER 14A	P	W	D	L	F	A	+-	PTS
1	Woodmill HS U14	6	6	0	0	36	1	35	18
2	Madras College U14	6	4	0	2	16	8	8	12
3	Levenmouth Academy U14	6	3	1	2	17	16	1	10
4	Beath HS U14	6	3	1	2	9	17	-8	10
5	Bell Baxter HS U14	6	3	0	3	19	28	-9	9
6	Glenrothes HS U14	6	1	0	5	12	23	-11	3
7	Kirkcaldy HS U14	6	0	0	6	3	19	-16	0

POS	UNDER 14B	P	W	D	L	F	A	+-	PTS
1	Queen Anne HS U14	5	5	0	0	37	3	34	15
2	Inverkeithing HS U14	5	4	0	1	33	12	21	12
3	Auchmuty HS U14	5	3	0	2	23	19	4	9
4	Balwearie HS U14	5	2	0	3	23	26	-3	6
5	Glenwood HS U14	5	1	0	4	7	33	-26	3
6	Viewforth HS U14	5	0	0	5	4	34	-30	0

POS	OPEN GIRLS A	P	W	D	L	F	A	+-	PTS
1	Beath HS Girls	6	5	0	1	29	3	26	15
2	Waid Academy Girls	6	5	0	1	25	8	17	15
3	Kirkcaldy HS Girls	6	4	0	2	33	15	18	12
4	Bell Baxter HS Girls	6	4	0	2	17	16	1	12
5	Woodmill HS Girls	6	2	0	4	21	17	4	6
6	Levenmouth Academy Girls	6	1	0	5	8	53	-45	3
7	Madras College Girls	6	0	0	6	12	33	-21	0

POS	OPEN GIRLS B	P	W	D	L	F	A	+-	PTS
1	Queen Anne HS Girls	5	4	0	1	23	4	19	12
2	Balwearie HS Girls	5	4	0	1	25	14	11	12
3	St Andrews HS Girls	5	3	0	2	32	24	8	9
4	St Columbas HS Girls	5	2	1	2	24	28	-4	7
5	Auchmuty HS Girls	5	1	0	4	14	38	-24	3
6	Glenrothes HS Girls	5	0	1	4	0	10	-10	1

CUP FINALS

Senior (U18), April 19 at Kelty Hearts
Beath HS v Balwearie HS, 2-1

Under 16 Cup, May 3 at Kelty Hearts
Queen Anne HS v Belle Baxter HS 3-1

Under 15 Cup, April 25 at Kelty Hearts
Balwearie HS v Queen Anne HS, 3-1

Under 14 Cup, April 17 at Kelty Hearts
Queen Anne HS v Inverkeithing HS, 4-2

LEAGUE PLAY OFF FINALS

Under 14
Woodmill HS v Queen Anne HS, 1-3

Under 15
Woodmill HS v Dunfermline HS, 2-2, 5-4 pens

Senior
Dunfermline HS v Balwearie HS, 2-1

Girls
Balwearie HS v Beath HS, 2-1

Ayrshire Schools 2016/17

UNDER 13 LEAGUE A	P	W	D	L	F	A	GD	Pts
Kilwinning Academy	4	3	0	1	19	10	9	9
Garnock Academy	4	2	1	1	22	10	12	7
St Matthew's Academy	4	1	2	1	12	11	1	5
Irvine Royal Academy	4	1	1	2	14	22	-8	4
Largs Academy	4	1	0	3	6	20	-14	3

UNDER 13 LEAGUE B	P	W	D	L	F	A	GD	Pts
Greenwood Academy	5	3	1	1	23	11	12	10
Grange Academy	3	3	0	0	22	3	19	9
Auchinleck Academy	4	2	1	1	12	8	4	7
James Hamilton Academy	4	2	0	2	21	11	10	6
Loudoun Academy	5	2	0	3	17	13	4	6
Stewarton Academy	5	0	0	5	3	52	-49	0

UNDER 13 LEAGUE C	P	W	D	L	F	A	GD	Pts
Prestwick Academy	10	8	2	0	51	13	38	26
Belmont Academy	10	7	1	2	42	14	28	22
Marr College	10	5	2	3	31	28	3	17
Kyle Academy	9	2	0	7	14	35	-21	6
Queen Margaret Academy	8	1	1	6	8	41	-33	4
Cumnock Academy	7	1	0	6	10	25	-15	3

UNDER 14 LEAGUE A	P	W	D	L	F	A	GD	Pts
St Matthew's Academy	4	3	1	0	19	3	16	10
Kilwinning Academy	4	2	2	0	21	7	14	8
Garnock Academy	3	1	0	2	9	21	-12	3
Largs Academy	2	0	1	1	2	4	-2	1
Ardrossan Academy	3	0	0	3	4	20	-16	0

UNDER 14 LEAGUE B	P	W	D	L	F	A	GD	Pts
Kilmarnock Academy	2	2	0	0	3	1	2	6
Stewarton Academy	2	1	0	1	4	3	1	3
Loudoun Academy	2	0	0	2	3	6	-3	0

UNDER 14 LEAGUE C	P	W	D	L	F	A	GD	Pts
James Hamilton Academy	3	3	0	0	24	9	15	9
Auchinleck Academy	2	1	0	1	5	4	1	3
St Joseph's Academy	3	1	0	2	10	14	-4	3
Ayr Academy	2	0	0	2	5	17	-12	0

UNDER 15 LEAGUE A	P	W	D	L	F	A	GD	Pts
Largs Academy	3	2	1	0	8	4	4	7
Garnock Academy	3	1	1	1	12	7	5	4
Ardrossan Academy	3	1	1	1	6	4	2	4
Kilwinning Academy	3	0	1	2	3	14	-11	1

UNDER 15 LEAGUE B	P	W	D	L	F	A	GD	Pts
Loudoun Academy	4	4	0	0	30	5	25	12
Stewarton Academy	5	3	0	2	12	8	4	9
Greenwood Academy	4	2	0	2	15	10	5	6
Irvine Royal Academy	5	2	0	3	12	32	-20	6
Grange Academy	3	1	0	2	4	10	-6	3
Auchinleck Academy	3	0	0	3	4	12	-8	0

UNDER 18 LEAGUE A	P	W	D	L	F	A	GD	Pts
Auchenharvie Academy	3	2	1	0	8	5	3	7
Largs Academy	3	1	1	1	11	3	8	4
St Matthew's Academy	3	1	1	1	5	5	0	4
Ardrossan Academy	3	0	1	2	3	14	-11	1

UNDER 18 LEAGUE B	P	W	D	L	F	A	GD	Pts
Marr College	3	3	0	0	25	7	18	9
Prestwick Academy	3	2	0	1	13	6	7	6
Belmont Academy	3	1	0	2	13	10	3	3
Ayr Academy	3	0	0	3	2	30	-28	0

UNDER 18 LEAGUE C	P	W	D	L	F	A	GD	Pts
Grange Academy	2	1	1	0	6	4	2	4
Greenwood Academy	2	1	0	1	8	4	4	3
Kilwinning Academy	2	0	1	1	2	8	-6	1

UNDER 18 LEAGUE D	P	W	D	L	F	A	GD	Pts
Queen Margaret Academy	3	2	1	0	13	3	10	7
Kyle Academy	3	1	1	1	12	6	6	4
Cumnock Academy	2	0	2	0	4	4	0	2
Auchinleck Academy	2	0	0	2	0	16	-16	0

UNDER 18 GIRLS	P	W	D	L	F	A	GD	Pts
Auchinleck Academy	0	0	0	0	0	0	0	0
Garnock Academy	0	0	0	0	0	0	0	0
Greenwood Academy	0	0	0	0	0	0	0	0
St Matthew's Academy	0	0	0	0	0	0	0	0

CUP FINALS

Under 18 League Cup, May 3 at Whitletts Vics
Marr College v Queen Margaret Academy, 5-1

Under 14 Ayrshire Cup, May 17 at Whitletts Vics
St Matthews Academy v Kilmarnocn Academy, 3-3, 4-2p

Under 15 Ayrshire Cup, May 3 at Whiutletts Vics
Marr College v Largs Academy, 6-3

Under 13 Ayrshire Cup, May 17 at Wshitletts Vics
Prestwick Academy v Belmont Academy, 3-2

SCOTTISH SCHOOLS FA

President's Committee

Joe HARKINS (President)

Andy English (Vice President)

JOHN C. WATSON
General Secretary
OFFICE: Hampden Park, Glasgow, G42 9AZ
Tel: 0141 620 4570
Fax: 0141 620 4571

ALEX B. McMENEMY
Treasurer

W. LES DONALDSON
International Teams Secretary

ALASTAIR T. BORTHWICK
Assistant General Secretary

PETER CLARK
Assistant General Secretary

GRENVILLE DAWSON
Assistant General Secretary

DAVID GILCHRIST
Assistant General Secretary

RONNIE HAMILTON
Assistant General Secretary

J. STEWART TAYLOR
Assistant General Secretary and Child Protection Officer

JOHN GOLD
S.F.A. Council Member

BILL BARCLAY
President 2015-2017

ROBERT M. DOCHERTY
Honorary Vice President

ROD HOUSTON
Honorary Vice President

GORDON PATE
Honorary Vice President

Council

NORTH

DUNCAN MASSIE, H. STEWART NEILSON, ALAN WATKINSON , WALTER CRAIG

EAST

STUART CLARK, GARY CUNNINGHAM, KENNY FINDLAY , JUNE BOUAOIN, ALLAN GALLAZZI

SOUTH EAST
GEORGE LAING , IAN R. SMITH, JOHN FRAME, KRISTOFER YARDLEY

WEST

ROBERT ALLAN, IAN BURNS , GILLIAN DUFFY, MARK FERRIER, STEWART McLACHLAN, LEE GIBSON

CENTRAL

JIM BETTLEY, SCOTT DOUGLAS, DAVID ECCLES , CRAIG JOHNSTONE, CLARE SMITH, JAMIE BAXTER

SOUTH WEST

MICHAEL DOWNIE , STEPHEN GILMOUR , IAIN PROUDFOOT , DAVID THOMSON , ALAN SLOSS

CO-OPTED MEMBERS

AMANDA ALLAN
GORDON CATHRO
ALASTAIR MacPHERSON
GERRY O'HARE
NEIL W SLOAN

REPRESENTATIVES ON S.S.F.

G. PATE : R. HAMILTON

DISTRICT ASSOCIATIONS

NORTH

ABERDEEN AND DISTRICT
Secretary : Craig Cowie
Portlethen Ac., Bruntland Road, Aberdeenshire AB12 4QL
Email: assfasecretary@gmail.com
Colours : Seniors All Red, U15 Red/White/Red

ABERDEENSHIRE
Secretary and Treasurer : John M. Peterson
Email: mintlaw.aca@aberdeenshire.gov.uk
Colours : Gold Tops / Black Shorts / Gold Socks

ELGIN CITY FC FOOTBALL 4s & SOCCER 7s
Secretary : Craigh Stewart
Elgin City FC, Borough Briggs Road, Elgin IV30 1AP
Email: community@elgincity.com

NORTH OF SCOTLAND
Secretary : Alexander Mezals
Email: Alexander.mezals@btinternet.com
Colours : Seniors Green & Black, U15 Yellow & Black

EAST

ANGUS
Secretary and Treasurer : Steven Bell
Email: bells@angus.gov.uk
Colours : Secondary Sky Blue / Black & Red,
Primary Green or Sky Blue

DUNDEE
Secretary : Grenville Dawson
Email: grenvilledawson@googlemail.com
Colours : Seniors Navy & Red, U15 Black,
Primary Yellow & Blue : Green & Black

FIFE
Secretary : Kristy Scott
Levenmouth Ac., Methilhaven Road, Buckhaven, KY8 1EA
Email: Kristy.Scott@fife.gov.uk
Colours : Light Blue

PERTH AND KINROSS
Secretary and Treasurer : Stuart Clark
Email: stuartmclark@hotmail.co.uk
Colours : Blue

SOUTH EAST

EDINBURGH
Secretary : David Ramsay
Email: dramsay2013@gmail.com
Colours : White Shirts, Black Shorts

EDINBURGH (PRIMARY)
Secretary : Chris Roberts
Forrester HS, Broomhouse Road, Edinburgh EH12 9AE
Email: chris.roberts@ea.edin.sch.uk
Colours : White & Black / Red & Black

LOTHIAN
Secretary : William Barclay
Email: lsfa49@gmail.com
Colours : Sky Blue & Yellow

EAST & MIDLOTHIAN
Secretary & Treasurer : John Frame
Email: jframe@mgfl.net
Colours : Sky Blue

WEST LOTHIAN
Secretary and Treasurer : Nicholas Torsney (Snr)
Email: ntorsney@yahoo.com
Colours : Blue / White

SCOTTISH INDEPENDENT SCHOOLS' F.A. (SISFA)
Secretary : George A. Laing
Email georgealaing@btinternet.com
Colours : Maroon

WEST

GLASGOW
General Secretary - Ian Burns
Email: ianburns726@hotmail.com
Colours : Black & White

PAISLEY AND DISTRICT
Secretary : Robert Allan
Email: gw07allanrobert3@glow.sch.uk
Colours : Black / White / Red

NB For Representative Games contact David Gilchrist - Inverclyde Academy

CENTRAL

FORTH VALLEY
Secretary : J. Stewart Taylor
Email: coachstaylor@aol.com
Colours : Seniors Yellow / Royal, U15 Sky / Navy

NORTH LANARKSHIRE
Secretary & Treasurer : Alistair T. Borthwick
Email a.borthwick2@ntlworld.com
Colours : Red or Yellow/Black/ Yellow

SOUTH WEST

AYRSHIRE
Secretary : Stephen Gilmour
Tel: 01292 262302 (School)
Email: stephen.gilmour@south-ayrshire.gov.uk
Colours : Red with Black Shorts

AYR & DISTRICT (Primary)
Secretary : Michael Halbert
Monkton Primary School, Station Road, Monkton KA9 2RH
Email: michael.halbert@south-ayrshire.gov.uk
Colours : Blue Shirts White Shorts

EAST AYRSHIRE (Primary)
Secretary : Mark Hyslop
Email: markhyslop1@hotmail.com
Colours : Sky Blue and White

SOUTH LANARKSHIRE
Secretary & Treasurer : Alistair T. Borthwick
Email a.borthwick2@ntlworld.com
Colours : Red or Yellow/Black/Yellow

HAMILTON (Primary)
Secretary & Treasurer : Sandra Cushnie
Email sandracushnie@talktalk.net

DUMFRIES AND GALLOWAY
Secretary : Iain Proudfoot
Email rj.proudfoot53@btinternet.com
Colours : Navy Blue / White

Membership - Schools in **BOLD** were current members (SSFA website, Feb 2017). There appeared to have been a "cull", perhaps of those with unpaid subs? Most of those NOT in bold participate in SSFA competitions.

ABERDEEN GRAMMAR SCHOOL
ABOYNE ACADEMY
AIRDRIE ACADEMY
AITH JUNIOR HS (Shetland)
ALBYN SCHOOL (Aberdeen)
ALFORD ACADEMY
ALLOA ACADEMY
ALL SAINTS SECONDARY SCHOOL (Glasgow)
ALNESS ACADEMY
ALVA ACADEMY
ANDERSON HS (Lerwick, Shetland)
ANNAN ACADEMY
ARBROATH ACADEMY
ARBROATH HS
ARDROSSAN ACADEMY
ARMADALE ACADEMY
ARRAN HS
AUCHENHARVIE ACADEMY (Stevenston)
AUCHINLECK ACADEMY
AUCHMUTY HS (Glenrothes)
AYR ACADEMY

BALDRAGON ACADEMY (Dundee)
BALERNO HS (Edinburgh)
BALFRON HS
BALTASOUND JUNIOR HS (Unst, Shetland)
BALWEARIE HS (Kirkcaldy)
BANCHORY ACADEMY
BANFF ACADEMY
BANNERMAN HS (Glasgow)
BANNOCKBURN HS
BARRHEAD HS
BATHGATE ACADEMY
BEARSDEN ACADEMY
BEATH HS (Cowdenbeath)
BEESLACK HS (Penicuik)
BELLAHOUSTON ACADEMY (Glasgow)
BELL BAXTER HS (Cupar)
BELLSHILL ACADEMY
BELMONT ACADEMY (Ayr)
BELMONT HOUSE SCHOOL (Newton

Mearns)
BERWICKSHIRE HS (Duns)
BIGGAR HS
BISHOPBRIGGS ACADEMY
BLAIRGOWRIE HS
BOCLAIR ACADEMY (Bearsden)
BO'NESS ACADEMY
BOROUGHMUIR HS (Edinburgh)
BRAES HS (Falkirk)
BRAEVIEW ACADEMY (Dundee)
BRAIDHURST HS (Motherwell)
BRANNOCK HS (Motherwell)
BREADALBANE ACADEMY (Aberfeldy)
BRECHIN HS
BRIDGE of DON ACADEMY (Aberdeen)
BROUGHTON HS (Edinburgh)
BROXBURN ACADEMY
BUCKIE HS
BUCKSBURN ACADEMY (Aberdeen)

CALDERGLEN HS (East Kilbride)
CALDERHEAD HS (Shotts)
CALDERSIDE HS (Blantyre)
CALDERVALE HS (Airdrie)
CAMPBELTOWN GRAMMAR SCHOOL
CARDINAL NEWMAN HS (Bellshill)
CARLUKE HS
CARNOUSTIE HS
CARRICK ACADEMY (Maybole)
CASTLEBAY COMMUNITY SCHOOL (Barra)
CASTLEBRAE COMMUNITY
HS (Edinburgh)
CASTLE DOUGLAS HS
CASTLEHEAD HS (Paisley)
CASTLEMILK HS (Glasgow)
CATHKIN HS (Cambuslang)
CHARLESTON ACADEMY (Inverness)
CHRYSTON HS (Glasgow)
CLEVEDEN SECONDARY
SCHOOL (Glasgow)
CLIFTON HALL SCHOOL (Newbridge)
CLYDEBANK HS
CLYDE VALLEY HS (Wishaw)
CLYDEVIEW ACADEMY (Gourock)
COATBRIDGE HS
COLTNESS HS (Wishaw)
COMMUNITY SCHOOL OF AUCHTERARDER
CRAIGIE HS (Dundee)
CRAIGMOUNT HS (Edinburgh)
CRAIGROYSTON COMMUNITY
HS (Edinburgh)
CRIEFF HS
CULLODEN ACADEMY (Inverness)
CULTS ACADEMY (Aberdeen)
UMBERNAULD ACADEMY
UMNOCK ACADEMY
URRIE COMMUNITY HS (Edinburgh)

ALBEATTIE HS
ALKEITH HS
ALZIEL HS (Motherwell)
EANS COMMUNITY HS (Livingston)
ENNY HS
INGWALL ACADEMY
OLLAR ACADEMY
ORNOCH ACADEMY
OUGLAS ACADEMY (Milngavie)
OUGLAS EWART HS (Newton Stewart)
RUMCHAPEL HS (Glasgow)
UMBARTON ACADEMY
UMFRIES ACADEMY
MFRIES HS
UNBAR GRAMMAR SCHOOL
NBLANE HS
UNCANRIG SECONDARY SCHOOL (East
bride)
UNFERMLINE HS

DUNOON GRAMMAR SCHOOL
DYCE ACADEMY (Aberdeen)

EARLSTON HS
EASTBANK ACADEMY (Glasgow)
EASTWOOD HS (Newton Mearns)
EDINBURGH ACADEMY
ELGIN ACADEMY
ELGIN HS
ELLON ACADEMY
EYEMOUTH HS

FALKIRK HS
FERNHILL SCHOOL (Rutherglen)
FIRRHILL HS (Edinburgh)
FORFAR ACADEMY
FORRES ACADEMY
FORRESTER HS (Edinburgh)
FORTROSE ACADEMY
FRASERBURGH ACADEMY

GAIRLOCH HS
GALASHIELS ACADEMY
GARNOCK ACADEMY (Kilbirnie)
GEORGE HERIOT'S
SCHOOL (Edinburgh)
GEORGE WATSON'S
COLLEGE (Edinburgh)
GIRVAN ACADEMY
GLASGOW ACADEMY
GLASGOW GAELIC SCHOOL
GLENIFFER HS (Paisley)
GLENROTHES HS
GLENWOOD HS (Glenrothes)
GOLSPIE HS
GORDON SCHOOLS (Huntly)
GORDONSTOUN SCHOOL (Elgin)
GOVAN HS (Glasgow)
GRACEMOUNT HS (Edinburgh)
GRAEME HS (Falkirk)
GRANGE ACADEMY (Kilmarnock)
GRANGEMOUTH HS
GRANTOWN GRAMMAR SCHOOL
GREENFAULDS HS (Cumbernauld)
GREENWOOD ACADEMY (Irvine)
GROVE ACADEMY (Broughty Ferry,
Dundee)
GRYFFE HS (Houston)

HAMILTON COLLEGE
HAMILTON GRAMMAR
HARLAW ACADEMY (Aberdeen)
HARRIS ACADEMY (Dundee)
HAWICK HS
HAZLEHEAD ACADEMY (Aberdeen)
HERMITAGE ACADEMY (Helensburgh)
HS OF DUNDEE
HS OF GLASGOW
HILLHEAD HS (Glasgow)
HILLPARK SECONDARY
SCHOOL (Glasgow)
HOLY CROSS HS (Hamilton)
HOLY ROOD HS (Edinburgh)
HOLYROOD SECONDARY
SCHOOL (Glasgow)
HUTCHESONS' GRAMMAR
SCHOOL (Glasgow)
HYNDLAND SECONDARY
SCHOOL (Glasgow)

INVERALMOND COMMUNITY
HS (Livingston)
INVERCLYDE ACADEMY (Greenock)
INVERGORDON ACADEMY

INVERKEITHING HS
INVERNESS HS
INVERNESS ROYAL ACADEMY
INVERURIE ACADEMY
IRVINE ROYAL ACADEMY
ISLAY HS

JAMES GILLESPIE'S
HS (Edinburgh)
JAMES HAMILTON
ACADEMY (Kilmarnock)
JAMES YOUNG HS (Livingston)
JEDBURGH GRAMMAR SCHOOL
JOHN PAUL ACADEMY (Glasgow)
JOHNSTONE HS
JORDANHILL SCHOOL (Glasgow)

KEITH GRAMMAR SCHOOL
KELSO HS
KEMNAY ACADEMY
KIBBLE SCHOOL
KILMARNOCK ACADEMY
KILSYTH ACADEMY
KILWINNING ACADEMY
KINCORTH ACADEMY (Aberdeen)
KING'S PARK SECONDARY
SCHOOL (Glasgow)
KINGUSSIE HS
KINLOCHLEVEN HS
KINROSS HS
KIRKCALDY HS
KIRKCUDBRIGHT ACADEMY
KIRKINTILLOCH HS
KIRKWALL GRAMMAR SCHOOL
KNIGHTSWOOD SECONDARY
SCHOOL (Glasgow)
KNOX ACADEMY (Haddington)
KYLE ACADEMY (Ayr)

LANARK GRAMMAR SCHOOL
LANGHOLM ACADEMY
LARBERT HS
LARGS ACADEMY
LARKHALL ACADEMY
LASSWADE HS (Bonnyrigg)
LEITH ACADEMY (Edinburgh)
LENZIE ACADEMY
LESMAHAGOW HS
LEVENMOUTH
ACADEMY (Buckhaven)
LIBERTON HS (Edinburgh)
LINLITHGOW ACADEMY
LINWOOD HS
LOCHABER HS (Fort William)
LOCHEND COMMUNITY
HS (Glasgow)
LOCHGELLY HS
LOCHGILPHEAD HS
LOCKERBIE ACADEMY
LORNSHILL ACADEMY (Alloa)
LOSSIEMOUTH HS
LOUDOUN ACADEMY (Galston)
LOURDES SECONDARY
SCHOOL (Glasgow)

MACKIE ACADEMY (Stonehaven)
MADRAS COLLEGE (St.Andrews)
MARR COLLEGE (Troon)
MARY ERSKINE SCHOOL,
THE (Edinburgh)
MAXWELLTOWN HS (Dumfries)
McLAREN HS (Callander)
MEARNS ACADEMY (Laurencekirk)
MEARNS CASTLE HS (Newton
Mearns)

MELDRUM ACADEMY
MERCHISTON CASTLE (Edinburgh)
MILLBURN ACADEMY (Inverness)
MILNE'S HS (Fochabers)
MINTLAW ACADEMY
MOFFAT ACADEMY
MONIFIETH HS
MONTROSE ACADEMY
MORGAN ACADEMY (Dundee)
MUSSELBURGH GRAMMAR SCHOOL

NAIRN ACADEMY
NEWBATTLE COMMUNITY HS (Dalkeith)
NICOLSON INSTITUTE, THE (Stornoway, Western Isles)
NORTH BERWICK HS
NORTHFIELD ACADEMY (Aberdeen)
NOTRE DAME HS (Greenock)

OBAN HS
OLDMACHAR ACADEMY (Bridge of Don, Aberdeen)
OUR LADY & ST. PATRICK'S HS (Dumbarton)
OUR LADY'S HS (Cumbernauld)
OUR LADY'S HS (Motherwell)

PAISLEY GRAMMAR SCHOOL
PARK MAINS HS (Erskine)
PEEBLES HS
PENICUIK HS
PERTH ACADEMY
PERTH GRAMMAR SCHOOL
PERTH HS
PETERHEAD ACADEMY
PITLOCHRY HS
PORTLETHEN ACADEMY
PORTOBELLO HS (Edinburgh)
PORTREE HS
PRESTON LODGE HS (Prestonpans)
PRESTWICK ACADEMY

QUEEN ANNE HS (Dunfermline)
QUEEN MARGARET ACADEMY (Ayr)
QUEEN VICTORIA SCHOOL (Dunblane)
QUEENSFERRY HS (South Queensferry)

RENFREW HS
ROBERT GORDON'S COLLEGE (Aberdeen)
ROSSHALL ACADEMY (Glasgow)
ROSS HS (Tranent)
ROTHESAY ACADEMY
ROYAL HS (Edinburgh)

SANQUHAR ACADEMY
SELKIRK HS
SGOIL A'BHAC (Back, Lewis, Western Isles)
SGOIL LIONACLEIT (Benbecula, Western Isles)
SHAWLANDS ACADEMY (Glasgow)
SMITHYCROFT SECONDARY SCHOOL (Glasgow)
SPEYSIDE HS (Aberlour)
SPRINGBURN ACADEMY (Glasgow)
ST. AIDAN'S HS (Wishaw)
ST. ALOYSIUS COLLEGE (Glasgow)
ST. AMBROSE HS (Coatbridge)
ST. ANDREW'S ACADEMY (Paisley)
ST. ANDREW'S AND ST. BRIDE'S HS (East Kilbride)
ST. ANDREW'S HS (Coatbridge)
ST. ANDREW'S HS (Kirkcaldy)
ST. ANDREW'S SECONDARY SCHOOL (Glasgow)
ST. AUGUSTINE'S HS (Edinburgh)
ST. BENEDICT'S HS (Linwood)
ST. COLUMBA'S HS (Dunfermline)
ST. COLUMBA'S HS (Gourock)
ST. COLUMBA'S SCHOOL (Kilmacolm)
ST. DAVID'S HS (Dalkeith)
ST. JOHN OGILVIE HS (Hamilton)
ST. JOHN'S ACADEMY (Perth)
ST. JOHN'S HS (Dundee)
ST. JOSEPH'S ACADEMY (Kilmarnock)
ST. JOSEPH'S COLLEGE (Dumfries)
ST. KENTIGERN'S ACADEMY (Blackburn, West Lothian)
ST. LEONARDS SCHOOL (St.Andrews)
ST. LUKE'S HS (Barrhead)
ST. MACHAR ACADEMY (Aberdeen)
ST. MARGARET MARY'S SECONDARY SCHOOL (Glasgow)
ST. MARGARET'S ACADEMY (Livingston)
ST. MARGARET'S HS (Airdrie)
ST. MATTHEW'S ACADEMY (Saltcoats)
ST. MAURICE'S HS (Cumbernauld)
ST. MODAN'S HS (Stirling)
ST. MUNGO'S ACADEMY (Glasgow)
ST. MUNGO'S HS (Falkirk)
ST. NINIAN'S HS (Giffnock)
ST. NINIAN'S HS (Kirkintilloch)
ST. PAUL'S ACADEMY (Dundee)
ST. PAUL'S HS (Glasgow)
ST. PETER THE APOSTLE HS (Clydebank)
ST. ROCH'S SECONDARY SCHOOL (Glasgow)
ST. STEPHEN'S HS (Port Glasgow)
ST. THOMAS AQUINAS SECONDARY SCHOOL (Glasgow)
ST. THOMAS OF AQUIN'S HS (Edinburgh)
STEWARTON ACADEMY
STEWART'S MELVILLE COLLEGE (Edinburgh)
STIRLING HS
STONELAW HS (Rutherglen)
STRANRAER ACADEMY
STRATHAVEN ACADEMY
STROMNESS ACADEMY

TAIN ROYAL ACADEMY
TARBERT ACADEMY
TAYLOR HS (New Stevenston)
THURSO HS
TORRY ACADEMY (Aberdeen)
TRINITY ACADEMY (Edinburgh)
TRINITY HS (Renfrew)
TRINITY HS (Rutherglen)
TURNBULL HS (Bishopbriggs)
TURRIFF ACADEMY
TYNECASTLE HS (Edinburgh)

UDDINGSTON GRAMMAR SCHOOL
ULLAPOOL HS

VALE OF LEVEN ACADEMY (Alexandria)
VIEWFORTH HS (Kirkcaldy)

WAID ACADEMY (Anstruther)
WALLACE HALL ACADEMY (Thornhill)
WALLACE HS (Stirling)
WEBSTER'S HS (Kirriemuir)
WEST CALDER HS
WESTER HAILES EDUCATION CENTRE (Edinburgh)
WESTHILL ACADEMY
WHITBURN ACADEMY
WHITEHILL SECONDARY SCHOOL (Glasgow)
WICK HS
WILLIAMWOOD HS (Clarkston)
WOODFARM HS (Thornliebank)
WOODMILL HS (Dunfermline)

WOMEN'S FOOTBALL

SCOTTISH WOMEN'S PREMIER LEAGUE ONE 2016

	ABE	CEL	FOR	GLA	HIB	RAN	SPA	STIR	Home Ground (s)
Aberdeen		May 15	May 18	Jun 26	Mar 20	Apr 24	May 22	Aug 14	Sunnybank
		0-1	0-2	0-1	0-0	1-2	4-0	0-1	
		Oct 30	Sep 25		Sep 11	Oct 9			
		0-3	1-0		0-2	0-6			
Celtic	Aug 21		Mar 13	May 29	Jul 31	Apr 13	May 1	Jun 26	K Park
	5-0		4-0	2-3	1-2	5-1	6-0	2-0	
			Aug 28			Sep 25	Oct 23		
			5-0			3-1	1-0		
Forfar Farmington	Jun 19	May 22		Apr 24	Apr 17	Aug 14	May 29	May 15	Station Park
	0-3	2-3		2-4	1-3	0-2	0-3	2-0	
				Oct 9	Oct 23		Sep 11	Oct 30	
				0-3	1-2		0-1	0-1	
Glasgow City	Apr 17	Mar 20	Jul 31		May 1	Oct 30	Jun 19	May 23	Excelsior
	1-0	1-0	8-0		2-0	5-3	0-3	8-1	
	Oct 7	Sep 11			Oct 23	Aug 21			
	7-0	5-0			3-1	7-0			
Hibernian	May 29	Apr 24	Jun 26	Aug 14		Mar 13	May 15	Jun 22	Broxburn
	8-0	3-2	3-0	0-4		3-1	4-0	5-0	Easter Road
		Oct 9				Aug 28	Oct 30	Sep 25	
		3-0				9-0	5-1	5-0	
Rangers	Jul 31	Jun 19	May 1	May 15	May 22		Apr 17	Mar 20	Benburb
	2-0	1-2	3-1	0-3	0-6		1-0	4-1	
			Oct 23				Oct 23	Sep 11	
			3-0				5-4	0-5	
Spartans	Mar 13	Aug 14	Mar 20	Apr 20	Aug 21	Jun 26		Apr 24	Ainslie Park
	2-1	0-2	3-1	0-8	1-6	1-0		3-1	
	Aug 28			Sep 35				Oct 9	
	0-3			0-1				0-3	
Stirling University	May 1	Apr 17	Aug 21	Mar 13	Jun 19	May 29	Jul 31		Gannochy
	1-3	2-1	1-0	0-1	0-3	1-0	2-2		
	Oct 23	Oct 2		Aug 28					
	2-1	3-4		0-3					

	P	W	D	L	GD	PTS
Glasgow City	21	20	0	1	66	60
Hibernian	21	17	1	3	59	52
Celtic	21	13	0	8	20	39
Stirling University	21	9	1	11	-17	28
Rangers	21	9	0	12	-22	27
Spartans	21	7	1	13	-30	22
Aberdeen	21	5	1	15	-29	16
Forfar Farmington	21	2	0	19	-47	6

SCOTTISH WOMEN'S PREMIER LEAGUE TWO 2016

	BUC	GLA	HAM	HEA	HUT	INV	JEA	QP	Home Ground
Buchan Girls		Jun 19	Aug 21	Mar 13	May 29	Apr 17	Jul 31	May 1	Maud
		1-5	1-2	2-2	3-3	5-0	1-4	4-3	
				Aug 28		Oct 2		UNP	
				1-1		5-2		3-0	
Glasgow Girls	Apr 3		Jun 26	Aug 14	Mar 13	Apr 24	May 15	May 29	Budhill Park
	3-1		2-1	0-2	1-3	2-1	3-2	3-0	
	Sep 25				Aug 28	Oct 9	Oct 30		
	4-1				4-0	11-0	3-2		
Hamilton Accies	May 15	Apr 17		Apr 24	Aug 14	May 22	Mar 20	Jun 19	NDP
	5-2	2-0		1-3	5-2	11-0	4-0	5-1	
	Oct 30			Oct 9			Sep 11		
	3-1			3-1			6-0		
Hearts	May 22	May 1	Jul 31		May 15	Mar 20	Jun 19	Apr 17	Dalkeith Thistle JFC
	4-1	0-2	1-0		1-1	7-0	2-1	5-0	
		Oct 23			Oct 30	Sep 11		Oct 2	
		1-1			3-0	7-0		6-0	
Hutchison Vale	Mar 20	May 22	May 1	Aug 21		Jun 19	Apr 17	Jul 31	Saughton Enclosure
	0-3*	0-2	2-1	1-0		6-0	0-0	11-1	
	Sep 11	Oct 23	Oct 23						
	0-3	3-2	0-6						
Inverness City	Jun 26	Jul 31	Mar 13	May 29	Apr 3		May 15	Aug 21	Millburn Academy
	2-1	0-2	3-5	1-10	1-1		0-3	5-1	
			Aug 28		Sep 25		Oct 23		
			1-6		0-5		2-7		
Jeanfield Swifts	Apr 24	Aug 21	May 29	Apr 3	Jun 26	Aug 14		Mar 13	McDiarmid Park Astro
	5-2	0-2	2-3	1-4	2-4	6-1		5-1	
	Oct 9			Sep 25				Aug 28	
	4-3			0-1				9-0	
Queen's Park	Aug 14	Mar 20	Apr 3	Jun 26	Apr 24	May 15	May 22		Lesser Hampden
	4-2	0-1	1-10	1-7	1-3	4-3	0-13		
		Sep 11	Sep 25		Oct 9	Oct 30			
		0-6	0-4		0-9	4-2			

	P	W	D	L	GD	PTS
Hamilton Accies	21	17	0	4	62	51
Hearts	21	15	4	2	55	49
Glasgow Girls	21	16	1	4	38	49
Hutchison Vale	21	9	4	8	10	31
Jeanfield Swifts	21	9	1	11	25	28
Buchan Ladies	21	6	3	12	-12	21
Queen's Park	21	3	0	18	-93	9
Inverness City	21	2	1	18	-85	7

SCOTTISH CLUBS - RECORD IN EUROPEAN CUPS

GLASGOW CITY'S EUROPEAN HISTORY

2005/6	UEFA Womens Cup	Q1	N	Athletic Bilbao	SPA	2	6
2005/6	UEFA Womens Cup	Q1	A	SV Saestum	NET	0	7
2005/6	UEFA Womens Cup	Q1	N	KFC Paide Wezemaal	BEL	1	5
2008/9	UEFA Womens Cup	Q1	N	AZ 67 Alkmaar	NET	1	1
2008/9	UEFA Womens Cup	Q1	A	KFC Masinac Nis	SER	4	0
2008/9	UEFA Womens Cup	Q1	N	Narta Chisinau	MOL	11	0
2008/9	UEFA Womens Cup	Q2	A	Roa IL	NOR	1	6
2008/9	UEFA Womens Cup	Q2	N	Zvezda 2005 Perm	RUS	0	1
2008/9	UEFA Womens Cup	Q2	N	1FFC Frankfurt	GER	1	3
2009/10	UEFA Womens CL	Q	N	Bayern Munchen	GER	2	5
2009/10	UEFA Womens CL	Q	A	Gintra Universitetas	LIT	2	0
2009/10	UEFA Womens CL	Q	N	Norchi Dinamoeli	GEO	9	0
2010/11	UEFA Womens CL	Q	A	Crusaders Newtonabbey	NIR	8	0
2010/11	UEFA Womens CL	Q	N	Slovan Bratislava	SVK	4	0
2010/11	UEFA Womens CL	Q	N	Duisburg	GER	0	4
2011/12	UEFA Womens CL	Q	A	Spartak Subotica	SER	4	0
2011/12	UEFA Womens CL	Q	N	Mosta	MAL	8	0
2011/12	UEFA Womens CL	Q	N	KI Klaksvik	FAR	5	0
2011/12	UEFA Womens CL	1	H*	Valur	ICE	1	1
2011/12	UEFA Womens CL	1	A	Valur	ICE	3	0
2011/12	UEFA Womens CL	2	A	Turbine Potsdam	GER	0	10
2011/12	UEFA Womens CL	2	H*	Turbine Potsdam	GER	0	7
2012/13	UEFA Womens CL	Q	N	ZNK Osijek	BOS	3	2
2012/13	UEFA Womens CL	Q	N	FC Noroc	MOL	11	0
2012/13	UEFA Womens CL	Q	A	PK-35 Vantaa	FIN	1	1
2012/13	UEFA Womens CL	1	H*	Fortuna Hjorring	DEN	1	2
2012/13	UEFA Womens CL	1	A	Fortuna Hjorring	DEN	0	0
2013/14	UEFA Womens CL	Q	N	Osijek	BOS	7	0
2013/14	UEFA Womens CL	Q	N	Birkirkara	MAL	9	0
2013/14	UEFA Womens CL	Q	A	FC Twente Enschede	NET	2	0
2013/14	UEFA Womens CL	1	A	Standard Liege	BEL	2	2
2013/14	UEFA Womens CL	1	H*	Standard Liege	BEL	3	1
2013/14	UEFA Womens CL	2	A	Arsenal	ENG	0	3
2013/14	UEFA Womens CL	2	H*	Arsenal	ENGT	2	3
2014/15	UEFA Womens CL	Q	H	FK Union Nove Zamky	RUS	5	0
2014/15	UEFA Womens CL	Q	H**	Glentoran	NIR	1	0
2014/15	UEFA Womens CL	Q	H**	WFC Zhbytlobud Kharkiv	UKR	4	0
2014/15	UEFA Womens CL	1	A	KKPK Medyk Konin	POL	0	2
2014/15	UEFA Womens CL	1	H**	KKPK Medyk Konin	POL	3	0
2014/15	UEFA Womens CL	2	A	FC Zurich Frauen	SWI	1	2
2014/15	UEFA Womens CL	2	H**	FC Zurich Frauen	SWI	4	2
2014/15	UEFA Womens CL	3	H**	Paris St Germain	FRA	0	2
2014/15	UEFA Womens CL	3	A	Paris St Germain	FRA	0	5
2015/16	UEFA Womens CL	1	A	Chelsea	ENG	0	1
2015/16	UEFA Womens CL	1	H**	Chelsea	ENG	0	3
2016/17	UEFA Womens CL	1	A	Eskilstuna United	SWE	0	1
2016/17	UEFA Womens CL	1	H**	Eskilstuna United	SWE	1	2

* at Petershill

** at Airdrie

HIBERNIAN LADIES EUROPEAN HISTORY

2004/5	UEFA Womens Cup	Q1	N	ZNK Maksimir	CRO	5	0
2004/5	UEFA Womens Cup	Q1	A	KFC Rapid Wezemal	BEL	3	2
2004/5	UEFA Womens Cup	Q1	N	XFK Masinac Klassik Nis	SER	1	4
2006/7	UEFA Womens Cup	Q1	H*	RCD Espanyol	SPA	1	4
2006/7	UEFA Womens Cup	Q1	H*	KI Klaksvik	FAR	2	1
2006/7	UEFA Womens Cup	Q1	H*	Juvisy FCF	FRA	0	6
2007/8	UEFA Womens Cup	Q1	A	Neulengbach	AUS	3	4
2007/8	UEFA Womens Cup	Q1	N	Gol Czestechowa	POL	4	1
2007/8	UEFA Womens Cup	Q1	N	Mayo Ladies League	ROI	8	0
2016/17	UEFA Womens CL	1	**	Bayern Munchen	GER	0	6
2016/17	UEFA Womens CL	1	A	Bayern Munchen	GER	1	4

* at Livingston

** at Easter Road

UEFA WOMEN'S CHAMPIONS LEAGUE 2016/17

Round of 32 1st Leg,
October 5th, Hibernian 0 Bayern Munich 6
Att 2551 (record for women's club match in Scotland)
at Easter Road
H: Fife, Williamson (Sub Brownlie), Hunter, Robertson, Arnot, Smith, McLauchlan, Graham, J Murray, Cornet (Sub Small), Harrison (Sub Ewens). Unused subs Michie, Heron, Notley, Jeffries

Round of 32, 1st Leg
October 6th, Eskilstuna United 1 Glasgow City 0
Att 3987
At Tunavallen, Eskilstuna
GC: Fay, McCarthy, Lauder, Love, Rosen, Shine (Sub Crilly), Docherty, Keenan, Ross, brown, Cuthbert. Unused subs: McMurchie, Boyce, McCulloch, Kerr, B Hay, Clachers

Round of 32 2nd Leg,
October 12th, Bayern Munchen 4 Hibernian 1
Att 320
at Stadion an der Grunwalder Strasse, Munich
H: Fife, Williamson, Hunter, Robertson, Arnot, Smith (Sub Michie), McLauchlan, Graham, J Murray, Harrison (Sub Ewens), Brownlie.
Scorer: Harrison

October 13th, Glasgow City 1 Eskilstuna United 2
Att 728
At Excelsior Stadium, Airdrie
GC: Fay, McCarthy, Lauder, Love, Shine, Docherty, Keenan (Sub McMurchie), Ross, Brown, Crilly, Cuthbert (Sub B Hay)
Unused subs: Rosen, Boyce, McCulloch, Kerr, Clachers
Scorer: Crilly

SCOTTISH WOMEN'S LEAGUE DIVISION 1(N) 2016

	AB	CEN	DEEL	DEEV	DUND	DUNF	EAS	FFC	FALKL	FOR	STO	TAY	Home Grounds
Aberdeen Reserves		Oct 30	Jun 19	Aug 28	Apr 3	May 22	Mar 13	Sep 18	Oct 2	Oct 23	Aug 14	May 1	Garthdee
		1-1	8-1	2-0	6-0	1-5	0-3	4-0	7-2	0-1	4-2	8-0	
Central Girls	Jun 26		Oct 16	PPD	Aug 28	Oct 2	Aug 14	Apr 3	May 1	May 22	Jun 19	Sep 18	Alloa FC
	1-0		0-3		5-2	1-2	0-3	3-0	3-0	5-4	8-4	4-4	
Dee Ladies	Oct 23	Jun 5		Apr 24	Mar 13	May 1	Jun 26	Aug 28	Sep 18	Oct 23	May 22	Apr 3	Nicol Park, Portlethen
	8-3	2-4		3-1	7-1	3-6	0-3	3-3	4-3	3-0	3-1	2-0	
Dee Vale	Mar 27	Jun 12	Aug 14		May 1	Jun 19	Sep 11	Oct 2	PPD	Oct 30	Sep 18	May 29	Lawsondale
	0-5	5-5	4-1		5-5	1-10	0-7	3-6		2-7	5-3	0-7	
Dundee City	Sep 11	Mar 27	Aug 21	Sep 25		Oct 30	Apr 10	May 22	Jun 19	Mar 6	Oct 2	Oct 23	Charlotte Street
	0-12	2-4*	1-4	1-4		4-1	2-7	2-3	1-3	1-2	4-2	5-2	
Dunfermline Athletic	Oct 9	May 15	Sep 25	Oct 23	Jun 26		Jun 5	Aug 14	Aug 28	Apr 10	Apr 3	Mar 13	Humbug Park, Crossgates
	3-0	7-0	2-0	7-1	9-2		2-6	4-2	4-3	5-1	4-1	1-0	Kinross SC
East Fife	Aug 21	Mar 6	Oct 30	Apr 3	Sep 18	Oct 16		May 1	May 22	Jun 19	Aug 28	PPD	KGV Park, Leven
	7-0	5-1	3-1	8-2	9-0	4-2		2-0	8-1	6-0	9-1		Stratheden, Cupar
Falkirk FC	Apr 10	Nov 1	Mar 27	May 15	Nov 6	Mar 6	Sep 25		Oct 30	Aug 21	Oct 23	Jun 19	Falkirk Stadium
	2-2	2-2	2-1	2-0	6-2	3-5	0-4		4-0	2-3	7-0	2-1	
Falkirk Ladies	May 15	Sep 25	Apr 10	Jun 5	Oct 23	Mar 27	Oct 9	Jun 26		Sep 11	Mar 13	Aug 14	Dunipace JFC
	1-5	2-7	2-0	4-3	4-4	1-1	2-4	3-1		3-5	2-1*	4-2	Stirling Uni
Forfar Farming Develo	Jun 5	PPD	May 15	Jun 26	Aug 14	Sep 18	Oct 23	Mar 13	Apr 3		May 1	Aug 28	Station Park
	3-9		2-2	0-3	4-3	3-1	1-3	6-1	6-2*		4-2	2-2	Whitehills PS, Forfar
Stonehaven	Mar 6	Oct 23	Oct 9	Apr 10	May 15	Sdep 11	Mar 27	Jun 5	Aug 21	Sep 25		Jun 26	Mineralwell Park
	1-2	3-6	2-6	1-2*	2-5	4-2	1-6	5-8	7-1	1-9		0-5	
Tayside Ladies	Sep 25	Apr 10	Sep 11	Oct 9	Jun 5	Aug 21	May 15	Oct 23	Mar 6	Mar 27	Oct 30		St Paul's Academy
	1-0	2-2	1-6	4-4	2-1	0-7	1-6	0-3	7-1	2-2	2-8		

SCOTTISH WOMEN'S LEAGUE DIVISION 1(S) 2016

	BOR	CEL	CLA	CUM	FCK	GLA	HEA	HIB	MOT	RAN	SPA	WES	Home Grounds
Boroughmuir		Oct 19		Mar 23	Mar 27	Oct 16	Oct 30	May 22	Aug 21	Sep 18	Jun 19	Oct 2	Meggetland
		1-3		0-1	5-1	1-6	3-3	1-4	0-6	0-3	6-1	0-2	
Celtic Academy	Apr 3			Oct 30	Aug 21	May 22	Jun 19	Oct 2	Mar 6	Aug 28	Oct 16	May 1	Lennoxtown
	4-1			0-0	1-4	5-0	8-0	2-2	2-3	0-1	2-0	2-0	K Park
Claremont													
Cumbernauld	Aug 14	Jun 26			Jun 19	Sep 18	Oct 2	Apr 3	Jun 5	May 22	May 1	Aug 28	Broadwood
	5-0	0-0			2-3	0-1	8-1	2-2	1-3	3-1	11-1	3-1	
FC Kilmarnock	Aug 28	Mar 13		Oct 23		Oct 2	Oct 16	May 1	Oct 30	Aug 14	May 22	Sep 18	Rugby Park
	2-2	0-2		3-3		3-1	6-1	1-7	2-3	1-1	7-0	3-2	
Glasgow City II	Jun 23	Nov 3		Apr 10	May 15		Sep 11	Aug 14	Sep 25	Mar 13	Mar 27	Jun 26	Petershill Park
	4-4	1-0		2-2	0-3		8-4	0-3	1-8	0-1	4-2	4-1	
Hearts Development	Aug 7	Oct 23		May 15	Jun 5	Apr 3		Aug 28	Oct 9	May 1	Sep 18	Mar 13	Tranent JFC
	2-0	0-3		1-8	3-10	1-3		0-13	0-13	1-5	0-5	0-6	
Hibernian Developme	Oct 9	May 15		Sep 11	Sep 25	Mar 6	Mar 27		Apr 10	Oct 30	Aug 21	Oct 23	HTC, Ormiston
	4-0	0-1		4-1	2-0	2-4	5-1		1-2	3-1	5-0	3-1	
Motherwell	Mar 13	Aug 14		Oct 16	Jun 26	May 1	May 22	Sep 18		Jun 19	Oct 2	Apr 3	Ravenscraig
	4-3	6-2		8-2	7-1	1-2	9-0	1-2		3-2	12-0	3-1	
Rangers II	Apr 10	Mar 27		Oct 9	Mar 6	Aug 21	Sep 25	Jun 26	Oct 23		Sep 11	Jun 5	Benburb JFC
	6-2*	2-3**		4-1	1-4	2-1	7-2	3-2	1-1		9-0	5-1	Nethercraigs
Spartans Reserves	Oct 23	Jun 5		Sep 25	Oct 9	Aug 28	Apr 10	Mar 13	May 15	Apr 3		Aug 14	Ainslie Park
	1-2	0-1		1-5	1-2	0-5	1-2	0-5	0-10	1-5		4-1	
Westerlands	May 15	Sep 25		Mar 27	Apr 10	Oct 30	Aug 21	Jun 19	Sep 11	Oct 16	Mar 6		Garscube
	3-0	0-4		1-5	0-3	4-7	7-0	0-6	2-3	3-6	3-1		

WFL DIVISION ONE (N)

	P	W	D	L	GD	PTS
ast Fife	22	22	0	0	99	66
unfermline Athletic	22	16	1	5	49	49
entral Girls Academy	22	12	5	5	15	41
berdeen Reserves	22	12	2	8	36	38
orfar Farmington Dev	22	11	3	8	4	36
ee Ladies	22	11	2	9	11	35
alkirk FC	22	10	3	9	4	33
ee Vale	22	6	3	13	-43	21
ayside Ladies	22	5	5	12	-26	20
alkirk Ladies	22	6	2	14	-43	20
tonehaven	22	4	0	18	-46	12
undee City	22	3	2	17	-60	11

SWFL DIVISION ONE (S)

	P	W	D	L	GD	PTS
Motherwell	20	16	1	3	78	49
Hibernian Development	20	14	2	4	54	44
Celtic Academy	20	13	3	4	29	42
Rangers Development	20	12	2	6	25	38
FC Kilmarnock	20	11	3	6	15	36
Glasgow City II	20	11	2	7	7	35
Cumbernauld Colts	20	9	5	6	26	32
Westerlands	20	6	0	14	-16	18
Boroughmuir	20	3	3	14	-34	12
Hearts Development	20	2	1	17	-106	7
Spartans Reserves	20	2	0	18	-78	6

SCOTTISH WOMEN'S LEAGUE DIVISION TWO NORTH 2016

	BUC	DEV	ELG	FOR	GRA	KEM	ROS	TUR	
Buchan Youth		Aug 14	May 22	Aug 28	Jun 5	Apr 10	Mar 13	May 8	Kessock Park, Fraserburgh
		3-3	1-3	6-2	1-3	1-1	4-2*	1-1	
			Oct 30			Oct 16	Sep 25	Oct 23	
			2-1			4-1	3-1	5-4	
Deveronvale	Apr 3		Mar 13	Jun 5	Jun 26	May 22	May 1	PPD	Banff Academy
	2-2		2-1	2-1	1-4	6-0	2-2		Portsoy
	Oct 9		Sep 25			Oct 30	Oct 23		
	2-0		2-2			7-1	5-0		
Elgin City	Sep 11	Jun 19		Aug 14	May 1	Mar 27	Aug 21	Mar 6	Pinefield
	2-0	3-3		12-0	0-3	4-1	5-0	4-2	
					Oct 23	Oct 2		Sep 18	
					0-7	5-0		6-0	
Forfar Farmington III	May 1	Mar 6	Apr 3		Aug 21	Jun 19	Jun 26	Sep 11	Station Park
	3-2	1-2	1-3		0-15	2-6	4-2	2-2	Market Muir
	Oct 23	Sep 18	Oct 9						
	1-3	2-7	2-1						
Granite City	May 15	Apr 17	Aug 28	Apr 10		Aug 14	Sep 11	Jun 19	Garthdee
	3-0	9-0	9-1	6-1		7-1	11-0	7-1	
	Sep 18	Oct 2		Oct 16					
	7-1	7-1		2-0					
Kemnay	Aug 21	Sep 11	Jun 26	Mar 13	Apr 3		Sep 18	May 1	Bogbeth Park
	1-2	1-6	0-4	2-2	2-5		4-1	0-1	
				Sep 25	Oct 9			Oct 23	
				1-3	0-8			3-1	
Ross County	Jun 19	Aug 28	Apr 10	Mar 27	May 22	Mar 6		Aug 14	Conon
	0-5	2-3	2-3	3-0	1-6	4-1		2-3	
			Oct 16	Oct 2	Oct 30	Jun 5			
			2-3	4-3	5-7	5-1			
Turriff United	Jun 26	May 29	Jun 5	May 22	Mar 13	Aug 28	Apr 3		The Haughs
	4-7	3-5	1-5	4-3	1-2	2-5	6-1*		
		Oct 16		Oct 30	Sep 25		Oct 9		
		0-1		5-3	0-3		2-0		

	P	W	D	L	GD	P
Granite City	21	21	0	0	114	6
Deveronvale	21	13	5	3	25	4
Elgin City	21	13	2	6	28	4
Buchan Youth	21	10	4	7	7	3
Turriff United	21	7	2	12	-23	2
Forfar Farmington III	21	4	2	15	-54	1
Ross County	21	4	1	16	-44	1
Kemnay	21	3	2	16	-53	1

SCOTTISH WOMEN'S LEAGUE DIVISION TWO CENTRAL 2016

	BLA	CUM	EAS	MOT	PAR	STR	STE	WES	
Blackburn United		Sep 11	Aug 21	Jun 19	Aug 14	May 1	Mar 27	Mar 6	New Murrayfield Park
		16-0	10-1	5-2	4-4	3-0	4-1	5-1	
						Oct 23	Oct 2	Sep 18	
						8-0	6-1	3-4	
Cumbernauld Colts Yellow	May 22		Mar 13	Oct 9	Aug 28	Jun 5	Apr 10	Mar 27	Broadwood
	0-16		0-6	0-3	0-7	0-4	0-5	1-9	
	Oct 30		Sep 25				Oct 16	Oct 23	
	0-12		1-2				0-5	0-2	
East Kilbride Girls	Apr 10	Jun 19		Aug 28	Mar 27	May 22	Mar 6	Aug 14	The Murray
	1-4	6-1		1-8	1-7	1-3	2-3	0-6	
	Oct 16				Nov 6	Oct 30	Jun 5		
	0-13				0-6	1-1	1-1		
Motherwell Development	Mar 13	Apr 3	May 1		Jun 5	Jun 26	May 22	Aug 21	Coltness HS
	1-0	6-0	5-0		0-4	0-3	2-1	4-2	Daisy Park, Wishaw
	Sep 25	Aug 14	Oct 23				Oct 30		
	0-1	2-0	12-0				5-0		
Partick Thistle	Apr 3	May 1	Jun 26	Mar 6		Aug 21	Jun 19	Sep 11	Lochinch
	3-2	14-0	3-0	5-0		1-0	8-1	3-2	
	Oct 9	Oct 23		Sep 18					
	1-2	10-0		6-3					
St Rochs	Aug 28	Mar 6	Sep 11	Jun 16	Apr 10		Aug 14	Sep 4	James McGrory Park
	0-1	2-0	3-1	0-0	0-2		1-0	1-3	
		Sep 18		Oct 2	Oct 16				
		5-0		2-1	1-5				
Stenhousemuir	Jun 26	Aug 21	Sep 18	Sep 25	Mar 13	Apr 3		May 1	Ochilview
	2-1	0-1	0-2	0-5	1-3	0-1		0-3	
				Sep 11		Oct 9		Oct 23	
				0-4		3-0		0-2	
Westerlands B	Jun 5	Jun 26	Apr 3	Apr 10	May 22	Mar 13	Aug 28		Garscube
	3-2	9-1	3-2	1-3	1-5	2-2	6-2		
			Oct 9	Oct 16	Oct 30	Sep 25			
			8-0	6-0	4-2	2-0			

	P	W	D	L	GD
Partick Thistle	21	18	1	2	85
Blackburn United	21	15	1	5	93
Westerlands B	21	15	1	5	43
Motherwell Dev	21	11	2	8	12
St Rochs	21	9	3	9	-5
Stenhousemuir	21	6	0	15	-2
East Kilbride	21	4	2	15	-6
Cumbernauld Colts	21	1	0	20	-1

SCOTTISH WOMEN'S LEAGUE DIVISION TWO SOUTH WEST 2016

	AYR	BIS	DUM	FCK	POL	REN	STRA	UNI	
Ayr United		Jun 26	Jun 5		Apr 10	Mar 13	Apr 3	May 22	Prestwick Oval
		4-1	5-1		3-1	0-10	5-0	2-1	
					Oct 16	Sep 25	Oct 9	Oc t 30	
					1-0	3-4	10-1	10-2	
Bishopton	Mar 27		May 31		Aug 14	Jun 5	Mar 13	Aug 28	Donald Dewar Centre
	0-3		1-3		2-2	0-3	4-0*	4-2	
	Oct 2		Oct 30				Sep 25		
	2-5		1-2				5-1		
Dumbarton United	Mar 6	Sep 11			Jun 19	May 1	Nov 6	Aug 14	Posties Park
	2-2	3-2			19-0	2-4	3-1	13-0	
						Oct 23			
						0-11			
FC Kilmarnock II									
Pollok United	Aug 21	May 29	Mar 13				May 1	Jun 5	Nethercraigs
	5-5	3-4	9-5				3-5	0-4	
		Oct 9	Sep 25				Oct 23		
		8-2	4-3				14-0		
Renfrew	Jun 19	Mar 6	Aug 28		Mar 27		Sep 11	Apr 10	New Western Park
	6-0	3-0	4-2		10-0		20-0	9-0	
		Sep 18			Oct 2			Oct 16	
		7-0			10-2			8-0	
Stranraer	Aug 14	Jun 19	Apr 10		Aug 28	May 22		Mar 27	stranraer Academy
	0-7	1-2	0-3		2-2	1-11		0-3	Rephad
			Oct 16			Oct 30		Oct 2	
			3-5			1-16		0-3	
United Glasgow	Sep 11	May 1	Apr 3		Mar 6	Aug 21	Jun 26		Scotstoun 3G
	0-5	2-6	3-3		2-6	0-6	2-0		
		Oct 23	Oct 9		Sep 18				
		0-4	2-4		2-3				

	P	W	D	L	GD	PTS
Renfrew	18	18	0	0	134	54
Ayr United	18	12	2	4	31	38
Dumbarton United	18	9	2	7	18	29
Bischopton CFL	18	8	1	9	-6	25
Pollok United	18	6	3	9	-20	21
United Glasgow	18	4	1	13	-55	13
Stranraer	18	1	1	16	-102	4

SCOTTISH WOMEN'S LEAGUE DIVISION TWO EAST 2016

	BAY	DUND	DUNF	EAS	EDCAL	EDSOU	HUT	RAI	SET	
Bayside		Aug 28	May 1	Aug 14	Apr 3	May 13	Sep 18	Jun 19	Oct 23	Dalgety Bay SC
		2-4	3-0	7-2	0-2	8-0	5-0	1-3	5-2	
Dundee United	Mar 27		Mar 6	Apr 10	Jun 5	Sep 25	Oct 23	Sep 11	Aug 21	GA Arena
	3-2		5-0	12-1	1-0	28-0	9-0	6-0	13-0	
Dunfermline Ath Developm	Sep 25	Aug 14		Oct 9	Mar 13	Jun 19	Aug 28	May 22	Apr 10	Kinross HS
	0-3	0-6		1-3	1-1	3-0	1-5	0-3	4-7	Humbug Park, Crossgates
East Fife Violet	Mar 6	Sep 18	Jun 5		May 1	Apr 3	Oct 23	Aug 21	Oct 23	Stratheden Hospital
	0-6	0-12	5-2		1-2	6-1	2-3	1-3	4-2	KGV Park
Edinburgh Caledonia	Sep 11	Oct 9	Aug 21	Sep 25		May 22	Mar 6	Apr 10	Mar 27	Peffermill
	1-2	0-6	5-0	0-2		14-0	4-2	1-3	7-1	
Edinburgh South	Aug 21	May 1	Oct 23	Sep 11	Oct 2		Jun 5	Mar 27	Mar 6	The Inch
	0-16	0-13	4-3	0-10	1-14		4-2	1-2	0-2	
Hutchison Vale Dev	Apr 10	Jul 31	Mar 27	May 22	Aug 14	Oct 9			Sep 11	Meadowbank
	1-7	0-4	4-3	1-2	0-6	7-0			4-2	Saughton
Raith Rovers	Oct 23	Apr 3	Oct 23	Mar 13	Sep 18	Aug 28	May 1		Jun 5	Dalgety Bay SC
	2-2	1-7	10-1	4-1	2-1	12-0	6-0		8-1	
Seton Ladies	May 22	Mar 13	Sep 18	Jun 19	Aug 28	Aug 14	Apr 3	Oct 9		Meadowmill
	4-3	1-12	2-3	7-4	1-3	7-2	0-6	0-5		KGV, Port Seton

	P	W	D	L	GD	PTS
Dundee United	16	16	0	0	134	48
Raith Rovers	16	13	1	2	44	40
Bayside	16	10	1	5	48	31
Edinburgh Caledonian	16	9	1	6	36	28
East Fife Violet	16	7	0	9	-19	21
Hutchison Vale	16	6	0	10	-21	18
Seton	16	5	0	11	-45	15
Dunfermline Zath Dev	16	2	1	13	-43	7
Edinburgh South	16	2	0	14	-134	6

SCOTTISH WOMEN'S FOOTBALL HISTORICAL DATA

Scottish Women's Premier League

	Champ	RU
2002/3	Kilmarnock Ladies	Hibernian
2003/4	Hibernian	Glasgow City
2004/5	Glasgow City	Hibernian
2005/6	Hibernian	Glasgow City
2006/7	Hibernian	Glasgow City
2007/8	Glasgow City	Hibernian
2008/9	Glasgow City	Spartans
2009	Glasgow City	Celtic
2010	Glasgow City	Celtic
2011	Glasgow City	Spartans
2012	Glasgow City	Forfar Farmington
2013	Glasgow City	Hibernian
2014	Glasgow City	Rangers
2015	Glasgow City	Hibernian
2016	Glasgow City	Hibernian

Scottish Womens Premier League Cup Final

2002/3	Kilmarnock	Glasgow City	2	0	
2003/4	Kilmarnock	Glasgow City	3	1	
2004/5	Hibernian	Raith Rovers	6	1	
2005/6	Kilmarnock	Glasgow City	3	2	
2006/7	Edinburgh Ladies	Hibernian	4	1	
2007/8	Hibernian	Queen's Park	4	0	
2008/9	Glasgow City	Spartans	3	0	
2009	Glasgow City	Hibernian	3	1	
2010	Celtic	Spartans	4	1	
2011	Hibernian	Spartans	5	2	
2012	Glasgow City	Spartans	5	1	
2013	Glasgow City	Spartans	5	0	
2014	Glasgow City	Hibernian	3	0	
2015	Glasgow City	Hibernian	2	1	aet
2016	Hibernian	Glasgow City	2	1	

Scottish Women's Cup Final

1995/6	Cove Rangers	Aberdeen	5	1	
1996/7	Cove Rangers	Ayr United	5	4	
1997/8	Cumbernauld United	Giuliano	3	1	
1998/9	Cumbernauld United	Ayr United	1	0	
1999/00	Stenhousemuir	Clyde	9	0	
2000/1	Kilmarnock	Ayr United	3	3	3-2p
2001/2	Kilmarnock	Glasgow City	5	0	
2002/3	Hibernian	Kilmarnock	2	2	5-4p
2003/4	Glasgow City	Queen's Park	3	0	
2004/5	Hibernian	Cove Rangers	8	0	
2005/6	Glasgow City	Aberdeen	5	1	
2006/7	Hibernian	Glasgow City	5	1	
2007/8	Hibernian	Celtic	3	1	AET
2008/9	Glasgow City	Rangers	5	0	
2010	Hibernian	Rangers	2	1	
2011	Glasgow City	Hibernian	3	0	
2012	Glasgow City	Forfar Farmington	1	0	
2013	Glasgow City	Hibernian	1	0	
2014	Glasgow City	Spartans	5	0	
2015	Glasgow City	Hibernian	3	0	
2016	Hibernian	Glasgow City	1	1	AET, 6-5p

SSE SCOTTISH WOMEN'S CUP 2016

SCOTTISH CUP					
1	17/04/2016 Elgin City	Raith Rovers	2	3	
1	08/05/2016 Ross County	Stranraer	2	1	
1	08/05/2016 Dundee City	Granite City	1	2	
1	08/05/2016 Kemnay	St Rochs	0	2	
1	08/05/2016 Boroughmuir Thistle	FC Kilmarnock	3	2	
1	08/05/2016 East Kilbride Girls	Edinburgh South	5	2	
1	08/05/2016 Tayside	Dee Ladies	1	3	
1	08/05/2016 United Glasgow	Stenhousemnuir	1	2	
1	08/05/2016 Caithness	Dunfermline Athletic	2	16	
1	08/05/2016 Blackburn United	Dundee United	0	5	
1	08/05/2016 Renfrew	Cumbernauld Colts	4	3	
1	08/05/2016 Stonehaven	East Fife	1	9	
1	08/05/2016 Westerlands	Bayside	8	1	
1	08/05/2016 Motherwell	Central Girls Football Acad	12	0	
1	22/05/2016 Bishopton FCL	Dee Vale	0	1	
2	09/06/2016 Dee Vale	Granite City	1	5	
2	12/06/2016 Dunfermline Athletic	Dumbarton United	7	0	
2	12/06/2016 Glasgow City	East Kilbride Girls	26	0	
2	12/06/2016 Spartans	Hamilton Accies	0	0	
2	12/06/2016 Buchan Ladies	Forfar Farmington	3	5	
2	12/06/2016 Dee Ladies	Raith Rovers	3	4	
2	12/06/2016 Hearts	St Rochs	3	0	
2	12/06/2016 Hibernian	Boroughmuir Thistle	11	0	
2	12/06/2016 Jeanfield Swifts	Ross County	18	0	
2	12/06/2016 Rangers	East Fife	7	0	
2	12/06/2016 Stirling University	Westerlands	10	0	
2	12/06/2016 Renfrew	Queen's Park	5	0	
2	12/06/2016 Motherwell	Glasgow Girls	1	4	
2	12/06/2016 Hutchison Vale	Edinburgh Caledonia	5	0	
2	12/06/2016 Celtic	Aberdeen	7	0	
2	12/06/2016 Dundee United	Stenhousemuir	8	0	
3	07/08/2016 Granite City	Hutchison Vale	3	8	
3	07/08/2016 Hibernian	Renfrew	19	0	
3	07/08/2016 Celtic	Forfar Farmington	3	1	
3	07/08/2016 Dunfermline Athletic	Glasgow Girls	0	4	
3	07/08/2016 Hearts	Hamilton Accies	3	0	
3	07/08/2016 Rangers	Glasgow City	1	3	
3	07/08/2016 Dundee United	Stirling University	1	6	
3	07/08/2016 Jeanfield Swifts	Raith Rovers	6	1	
4	04/09/2016 Hibernian	Celtic	3	1	
4	04/09/2016 Stirling University	Glasgow City	0	4	
4	04/09/2016 Jeanfield Swifts	Glasgow Girls	3	5	
4	18/09/2016 Hearts	Hutchison Vale	3	3	w-l pens
SF	18/10/2016 Hearts	Hibernian	0	5	at Spartans
SF	18/10/2016 Glasgow Girls	Glasgow City	0	9	at Spartans
	06/11/2016 Hibernian	Glasgow City	1	1	6-5p
	at Hamilton	Att 857			

CUP FINAL DETAILS

Hibernian Ladies 1 Glasgow City 1, H.T. 1-0

Scorers
Hibernian: Robertson
Glasgow City: Lauder

Hibernian Ladies: Fife, Williamson (Small, 72), Hunter, Robertson, Arnot, Smith, McLauchlan (Michie, 120), Graham, Murray, Harrison (Ewens, 89), Brownlie. **Unused substitutes**: Jefferies, Russell, Notley, Leishman.
Glasgow City: Fay, McMurchie, McCarthy (McCulloch, 77), Lauder, Love, Rosen (Crilly, 45), Shine, Docherty, Ross (Kerr, 84), Brown, Cuthbert. **Unused substitutes:** Clachers, Hay, Keenan, Boyce.

Referee: Lorraine Clark

SCOTTISH WOMEN'S LEAGUE CUPS 2016

SWPL Cup					
1	28/02/2016	Glasgow Girls	Hutchison Vale	3	1
1	28/02/2016	Aberdeen	Jeanfield Swifts	5	0
1	28/02/2016	Spartans	Stirling University	5	1
1	28/02/2016	Hearts	Forfar Farmington	0	3
1	28/02/2016	Buchan Ladies	Queen's Park	7	1
1	28/02/2016	Celtic	Hibernian	0	1
1	28/02/2016	Glasgow City	Inverness City	14	0
1	28/02/2016	Rangers	Hamilton Accies	5	1
2	27/03/2016	Forfar Farmington	Hibernian	0	6
2	27/03/2016	Aberdeen	Spartans	5	1
2	27/03/2016	Glasgow City	Glasgow Girls	10	0
2	27/03/2016	Rangers	Buchan Ladies	5	0
SF	08/05/2016	Rangers	Hibernian	1	4
SF	08/05/2016	Aberdeen	Glasgow City	0	1
F	15/06/2016	Hibernian	Glasgow City	2	1
		at Spartans			

SWFL Division 1 Cup					
1	28/02/2016	Rangers	Hibernian Dev	1	4
1	28/02/2016	Spartans Reserves	Falkirk Ladies	4	1
1	28/02/2016	Hearts Dev	Tayside Ladies	4	0
1	20/03/2016	Dee Vale	Cumbernauld Colts	2	10
1	28/02/2016	Stonehaven	Forfar Farmington Dev	7	1
1	28/02/2016	East Fife	Glasgow City Dev	2	1
1	28/02/2016	FC Kilmarnock	Dunfermline Athletic	6	3
1	28/02/2016	Falkirk FC	Dee Ladies	4	3
2	20/03/2016	Boroughmuir Th	Celtic Academy	0	3
2	20/03/2016	Central Girls Acad	Stonehaven	7	1
2	20/03/2016	Dundee City	Motherwell	1	5
2	20/03/2016	East Fife	Cumbernauld Colts	3	0
2	20/03/2016	FC Kilmarnock	Aberdeen Dev	6	0
2	20/03/2016	Hibernian Dev	Spartans Reserves	2	1
2	20/03/2016	Westerlands	Hearts Dev	3	0
2		Falkirk FC	Bye		
3	24/04/2016	Falkirk FC	East Fife	1	7
3	24/04/2016	Hibernian Dev	FC Kilmarnock	4	1
3	24/04/2016	Central Girls Acad	Celtic Academy	0	5
3	24/04/2016	Motherwell	Westerlands	7	1
SF	29/05/2016	Motherwell	Hibernian Dev	0	4
SF	29/05/2016	Celtic Academy	East Fife	2	3
F	22/06/2016	Hibernian Dev	East Fife	2	1
	at Spartans				

SWFL Division 2 Cup						
P	28/02/2016	Edinburgh Caled	Motherwell Dev	4	0	
P	28/02/2016	Ross County Ladies	Blackburn United	0	2	
1	20/03/2016	St Rochs	Partick Thistle	2	1	
1	20/03/2016	Hutchison Vale Dev	Stenhousemuir	1	2	
1	20/03/2016	Ayr United	East Fife Violet	3	0	
1	20/03/2016	Buchan Youth	Raith Rovers	0	9	
1	20/03/2016	Cumbernauld Colts	Kemnay			
1	20/03/2016	Elgin City	Forfar Farmington Ladies	6	0	
1	20/03/2016	Stranraer	Edinburgh South	3	0	
1	20/03/2016	Bayside	Seton	6	1	
1	20/03/2016	Bishopton CFL	Renfrew	0	10	
1	20/03/2016	Blackburn United	East Kilbride Girls	4	1	
1	20/03/2016	Dumbarton United	Pollok United	12	1	
1	27/03/2016	Turriff United	Granite City	0	6	
1	20/03/2016	United Glasgow	Edinburgh Caledonia	0	5	
1	20/03/2016	Westerlands B	Deveronvale	17	0	
2	24/04/2016	Ayr United	Stranraer	3	0	
2	24/04/2016	Edinburgh Caled	St Rochs	0	1	
2	24/04/2016	Raith Rovers	Cumbernauld Colts Dev	9	2	
2	24/04/2016	Elgin City	Dumbarton United	4	1	
2	24/04/2016	Renfrew	Granite City	8	0	
2	24/04/2016	Westerlands B	Blackburn United	4	3	
2	24/04/2016	Stenhousemuir	Dundee United	0	7	
2	24/04/2016	Dunfermline Dev	Bayside	0	2	
3	15/05/2016	Elgin City	St Rochs	0	1	
3	15/05/2016	Renfrew	Dundee United	2	4	
3	15/05/2016	Westerlands B	Raith Rovers	5	0	
3	15/05/2016	Dunfermline Dev	Ayr United	0	0	3-
SF	29/05/2016	Westerlands B	Dunfermline Dev	2	3	
SF	29/05/2016	St Rochs	Dundee United	1	4	
F	23/06/2016	Dunfermline Dev	Dundee United	0	9	
	at Spartans					

SCOTTISH GIRL'S YOUTH LEAGUES 2016

GEMMA FAY UNDER 17S		P	W	D	L	GD	PTS
1	Central Girls	18	15	2	1	65	47
2	Celtic 17s	18	14	1	3	49	43
3	Hamilton	20	11	2	7	-10	35
4	Glasgow City	18	11	2	5	21	35
5	Kilmarnock	20	10	4	6	16	34
6	Rangers	18	10	1	7	27	31
7	Rutherglen Girls	20	5	4	11	-29	19
8	Motherwell	18	6	1	11	-24	19
9	Glasgow Girls FC	20	5	3	12	-19	18
10	Morton	20	3	5	12	-41	14
11	Kilwinning	20	2	1	17	-55	7

EAST REGION UNDER 17S

1	Jeanfield Swifts Girls U17s	15	11	2	2	32	35
2	Forfar Farmington	15	9	1	5	21	28
3	Dunfermline	15	7	3	5	-3	24
4	East Fife	15	7	2	6	0	23
5	Dryburgh Athletic	15	4	3	8	-7	15
6	Montrose	15	1	1	13	-43	4

SOUTH EAST UNDER 17S

1	Hibernian	15	15	0	0	63	45
2	Spartans	15	9	1	5	6	28
3	Boroughmuir Thistle	15	7	3	5	-1	24
4	Hearts	15	7	2	6	19	23
5	Linlithgow Rose	15	3	2	10	-14	11
6	Murieston Utd	15	0	0	15	-73	0
7	Bonnyrigg Rose	0	0	0	0	0	0

RACHEL CORSIE UNDER 16S

1	Aberdeen Ladies - 16's	13	12	1	0	76	37
2	Deveronvale Girls	14	10	2	2	50	32
3	Westdyke 16s	13	10	1	2	49	31
4	Westdyke Thistle	14	5	1	8	-25	16
5	Stonehaven Girls	14	4	2	8	-24	14
6	Aberdeen FC Ladies 15s	14	4	2	8	-34	14
7	Westdyke Girls	14	3	1	10	-54	10
8	Buchan Girls	14	1	2	11	-38	5
9	Buckie Thistle Girls	0	0	0	0	0	0

EAST REGION UNDER 15S

1	Jeanfield Swifts	16	16	0	0	107	48
2	East Fife	16	12	1	3	70	37
3	Raith Rovers	16	12	0	4	16	36
4	Dryburgh Girls u15s	16	10	1	5	23	31
5	Letham	16	6	1	9	-8	19
6	Dunfermline Athletic	16	5	0	11	-16	15
7	Forfar Flyers	16	4	2	10	-45	14
8	Monifieth U15	16	4	1	11	-53	13
9	Montrose	16	0	0	16	-94	0

JENNY BEATTIE UNDER 15S

1	Kilmarnock	6	6	0	0	31	18
2	Clark Drive	7	5	1	1	26	16
3	Kilwinning	7	5	1	1	23	16
4	Morton Girls	6	2	1	3	-5	7
5	Ayr United	7	2	1	4	2	7
6	Gleniffer Thistle 15s	7	1	2	4	-20	5
7	Erskine Girls	7	1	0	6	-31	3
8	Port Glasgow Juniors CSC	5	1	0	4	-26	3

KIM LITTLE UNDER 15S

1	Celtic 15s	6	5	0	1	12	15
2	Rangers	6	4	0	2	6	12
3	Glasgow City U14's	6	3	0	3	4	9
4	Motherwell Girls U15s	0	0	0	0	0	0
5	Glasgow City - Glasgow City	6	0	0	6	-22	0

LEANNE ROSS UNDER 15S

1	Celtic 14s	6	6	0	0	34	18
2	Central Girls	6	4	0	2	18	12
3	Kilmarnock	6	4	0	2	10	12
4	Hamilton	6	3	0	3	7	9
5	Cumbernauld Colts	6	2	0	4	-10	6
6	QOS Girls	6	2	0	4	-18	6
7	Stenhousemuir	6	0	0	6	-41	0

SOUTH EAST UNDER 15S

1	Hibernian	19	18	1	0	123	55
2	Hearts	19	17	1	1	84	52
3	Boroughmuir Thistle	19	13	2	4	26	41
4	Murieston Utd	19	9	1	9	-18	28
5	Bonnyrigg Rose Girls	19	8	2	9	-3	26
6	Hutchison Vale	19	7	4	8	-18	25
7	Musselburgh Windsor	19	7	3	9	-10	24
8	Broxburn Athletic	19	5	4	10	-28	19
9	Hibernian U13	10	3	1	6	-5	10
10	Spartans	19	2	3	14	-57	9
11	Penicuik Athletic	0	0	0	0	0	0
12	Blackhall Athletic	19	0	0	19	-94	0

KIM LITTLE UNDER 15RS LEAGUE TWO

1	Celtic 15s	7	6	1	0	22	19
2	Glasgow City U14's	7	5	2	0	29	17
3	Rangers	7	5	1	1	11	16
4	Celtic 14s	7	4	0	3	3	12
5	Kilmarnock	7	3	0	4	-9	9
6	Central Girls	7	2	0	5	-11	6
7	Kilwinning	7	1	0	6	-18	3
8	Motherwell Girls U15s	7	0	0	7	-27	0

CENTRAL AND SOUTH WEST UNDER 15S

1	Cumbernauld Colts	7	6	1	0	21	19
2	Morton Girls	5	3	1	1	14	10
3	Clark Drive	5	3	0	2	3	9
4	QOS Girls	6	3	0	3	0	9
5	Stenhousemuir	7	2	1	4	-12	7
6	Hamilton	4	2	0	1	8	6
7	Gleniffer Thistle 15s	6	1	1	4	-12	4
8	Ayr United	5	0	0	5	-22	0

CENTRAL SOUTH WEST U13

1	Motherwell Girls Claret	12	11	1	0	72	34
2	Tullibody13s	12	10	1	1	67	31
3	Hamilton Whites	11	7	0	4	41	21
4	Queen of the South	11	3	0	8	-38	9
5	Motherwell Girls U13s Amber	12	3	0	9	-51	9
6	Central Girls U/13's	10	2	0	8	-38	6
7	Wishaw Wycombe Wanderers	10	2	0	8	-53	6
8	Gartcairn FA A	0	0	0	0	0	0
9	Gartcairn FA K	0	0	0	0	0	0

EAST UNDER 13S FIFE LEAGUE							
1	Bayside 13s	10	10	0	0	78	30
2	Dunfermline 13s	10	9	0	1	59	27
3	Glenrothes Strollers	10	7	1	2	42	22
4	East Fife	10	7	1	2	38	22
5	Bayside 12s	10	5	0	5	9	15
6	Raith Rovers 13s	10	5	0	5	0	15
7	Dunfermline 12s	10	4	0	6	-20	12
8	Bayside Blaze	10	3	0	7	-27	9
9	Cowdenbeath United Girls Reds	10	3	0	7	-35	9
10	East Fife Violet	10	0	1	9	-66	1
11	Cowdenbeath United Girls Blues	10	0	1	9	-78	1
12	Lomond Colts	0	0	0	0	0	0

EAST U13 TAYSIDE LEAGUE 1							
1	DUSC 13s	7	7	0	0	47	21
2	Dryburgh Athletic 13s	7	6	0	1	23	18
3	Forfar Farmington Foxes	7	4	1	2	11	13
4	DUSC Terrors	7	4	0	3	22	12
5	Scone Thistle	7	3	0	4	12	9
6	Forfar Farmington Stars	7	2	0	5	-34	6
7	Letham	7	0	2	5	-30	2
8	Dundee West	7	0	1	6	-51	1

EAST UNDER 13S TAYSIDE LEAGUE 2							
1	Forfar Farmington Falcons	7	7	0	0	58	21
2	Jeanfield Swifts	7	6	0	1	28	18
3	Letham	7	5	0	2	17	15
4	Dryburgh Athletic u12s	7	4	0	3	1	12
5	Monifieth Fire	7	3	0	4	8	9
6	Monifieth Reds	7	2	0	5	-27	6
7	Dundee Sporting Club 13s	7	1	0	6	-32	3
8	Montrose	7	0	0	7	-53	0

AGE GROUP SCOTTISH CUP FINALS

Under 17s, 22/10/16 (at Toryglen)
Central Girls v Rangers, 1-3

Under 15s, 22/10/16 (at Toryglen)
Aberdeen v Celtic, 0-5

Under 13s, 22/10/16 (at Toryglen)
Bayside v Hibernian, 3-1

EILISH MCSORLEY U13							
1	Kilmarnock Ladies U13 Blues	20	20	0	0	116	60
2	Rutherglen Girls	18	17	0	1	101	51
3	Clark Drive	20	16	0	4	82	48
4	Ayr United Football Academy	20	12	0	8	-9	36
5	EKFC GIRLS	20	11	1	8	8	34
6	East Kilbride Girls 13s	16	8	1	7	15	25
7	Hamilton Reds	17	6	0	11	-61	18
8	Kilwinning - KSC Girls u13	17	5	2	10	-12	17
9	Kilbirnie	21	3	2	16	-56	11
10	Kilmarnock Whites	14	3	0	11	-43	9
11	Glenburn MWFC Girls Under 13's	10	3	0	7	-45	9
12	Clark Drive Girls white	7	2	0	5	-21	6
13	Tass Thistle girls	22	1	2	19	-75	5

JO LOVE U13							
1	Central Girls Albion U/13	12	9	3	0	56	30
2	Bedlay CFC U13's	13	8	2	3	38	26
3	West Park Utd	12	6	3	3	17	21
4	Morton Girls u12s	12	4	3	5	0	15
5	Port Glasgow	12	4	2	6	-6	14
6	Cumbernauld Colts Blue	11	4	2	5	-3	14
7	Clydebank Girls U13s	12	4	1	7	-20	13
8	Tullibody U12s	11	4	1	6	-25	13
9	Milton Girls	11	3	3	5	-20	12
10	Drumchapel United	10	1	2	7	-37	5
11	Stenhousemuir Girls U13s	0	0	0	0	0	0

WEST CENTRAL JANE ROSS U13							
1	Central Girls U/13's	22	22	0	0	142	66
2	Glasgow Girls FC	22	19	0	3	102	57
3	Celtic 13s	22	18	0	4	96	54
4	St Mirren YFC	22	15	0	7	42	45
5	Pollok United	22	12	3	7	14	39
6	Cumbernauld Colts	22	9	4	9	-12	31
7	Giffnock SC Blacks	22	8	3	11	-35	27
8	Giffnock SC Reds	22	7	3	12	-25	24
9	Morton Girls	22	5	5	12	-60	20
10	Gleniffer Thistle	22	4	1	17	-93	13
11	Port Glasgow	22	1	3	18	-82	6
12	Erskine Youth	22	0	2	20	-89	2

Stadia / Grounds Update

SPFL

ABERDEEN
Aberdeen have been keen to quit Pittodrie for over a decade. Further development of the site is deemed impractical due to the constrictions on space. Until May 2016 Aberdeen hoped to develop a new stadium at Loriston, south of the city, and a training ground at Balgownie, to the north of the city. These plans were dropped in order to pursue an application for a new facility at Kingsford, on the western edge of Aberdeen close to the newly-built city by-pass. A planning application was submitted in January 2017. A decision on the £50 million pound development was due in June but was delayed until October 2017, as the Council asked for more information. Objectors have raised issues about disruption to wildlife, parking, traffic and anti-social behaviour. If planning permission is granted in October 2017 Aberdeen FC are confident they can complete the project in time for season 2020/21.

CELTIC
Celtic introduced a safe-standing area in the North East corner of the ground for 2016/17. It proved popular with the support and seems to have greatly improved the matchday atmosphere. The area holds 2,600 spectators and cost £500,000 to construct. Other clubs would like to replicate the scheme but will have to wait until Celtic's trial is assessed.

CLYDE
In August 2016 Clyde signed a lease which will allow them to stay at Broadwood Stadium for five years. However, at the time the club stated that they were pursuing three other locations for a potential new base. Clyde refused to name the other options but they were thought to include a site near Rutherglen and one in East Kilbride. However, as 2016/17 progressed it seemed less and less likely that any move or plan was imminent. The likelihood is that Clyde will remain at Broadwood until at least 2021.

COWDENBEATH
Any prospect of a new ground for Cowdenbeath seems to have disappeared. The club remain tenants at Central Park. The Central Fife Times summarised Cowdenbeath's situation as follows:
Cowdenbeath FC 2007, over £200,000 in the Bank, owning Central Park, the Stock Cars pay rent of £35,000 per year, weekly market pays rent of £15,000 per year, circus, shows, other events generate extra cash, Cowdenbeath FC pays no rent, the club benefits from its own bar and catering income plus also some of this from stock cars.
Contrast this with Cowdenbeath FC 2015, Cowdenbeath has little by way of cash reserves and no bank support. Cowden don't own the ground and pays a rent of £20,000 per year. Stock Cars pay the club nothing. Weekly market pays the club nothing. Circus/shows/other events pay nothing. Catering - Cowden receives a small fee per outlet. Bar is not very often in use. Loss of ownership of ground alone has cost CFC at least £70,000 per annum".
Clearly the club cannot finance any move away from their charming but somewhat outdated home ground.

DUMBARTON
The club are hoping to leave their current stadium and build a new ground at Young's Farm on the Renton Road. a planning application was submitted in June 2017. Plans submitted by Dumbarton's parent company Brabco to West Dunbartonshire Council are understood to include a 4,000-capacity ground, comprising a 3,000-seater stand and terracing, a training base, community-use pitches, offices and a residential development, costing £13.5 million. However, later in June 2017 the West of Scotland Archaeology Service raised concerns regarding the proposals for Young's Farm as the site could have been an area where Robert the Bruce once lived. They are urging West Dunbartonshire Council to stop the club building until an archaeological evaluation is carried out and they have confirmed whether the historical link is there or not.

DUNDEE
In February 2017 Dundee owner John Nelms announced that eh hoped the club would quit Dens Park for a new home at Camperdown Park. He labelled Dens Park "a 19th century building" and revealed his hopes of "potentially playing games at a new facility". Nelms and fellow owner Tim Keyes recently purchased 29 acres of land in Camperdown Park, where their application will be based. When talking about the possibility of a move on from Dens, Nelms said: "We're also aware that we're trying to give a 21st-century entertainment product in a 19th-century building. It's not new news that Tim and I have bought 29 acres next to the ice rink in Camperdown Park and we will be putting in a land use application shortly that we hope really enhances Dundee Football Club."

EAST FIFE
A planned move away from New Bayview has been abandoned. Instead the club have put down an

artificial playing surface during the 2017 close-season.

EDINBURGH CITY
City have agreed a three-year deal to groundshare with Spartans from 2017 until the end of 2019/20. To bring the ground up to SPFL standards new turnstile blocks are being built, using antique turnstiles salvaged from the old stand at Tynecastle. There will be 4 entrance gates adjacent to the club house and 2 behind the goal at the Pilton end. Apparently spectators will be restricted to the grandstand and the areas immediately adjacent to it for SPFL fixtures. The upstairs café will be closed to the public with catering available from the downstairs servery.

HEARTS
The old Main Stand at Tynecastle Park was demolished at the end of the 2016/17 season. A new Main Stand will be ready by September 2017. Costing £12 million, the new stand will seat 7290 and will take the capacity of Tynecastle to more than 20,000. From 2017/18 the whole of the Roseburn Stand will again be available for away supporters when the demand arises.

MORTON
The Cappielow club spent £120,000 on new turnstiles during the Summer of 2017. These will scan tickets and will theoretically double the rate at which fans can enter the ground.

RAITH ROVERS
Rovers will lay an artificial playing surface at Stark's Park for 2018/19.

RANGERS
Rangers undertook an extensive programme of refurbishment to Ibrox Stadium during the Summer of 2017.

HIGHLAND LEAGUE

CLACHNACUDDIN
Clach had hoped to lay an artificial pitch at Grant Street Park and enter a ground-sharing arrangement with Inverness City JFC. Funding issues mean that the project is at least delayed, if not cancelled.

COVE RANGERS
After a couple of years of apparent inactivity, things are finally moving with Cove Rangers. Their old ground at Allan Park was demolished late in 2016. Work began on building a new £5 million stadium at Calder Park, Nigg. This will be known as the Balmoral Stadium following a sponsorship deal with Aberdeen-based Balmoral Group. The ground will have a 312-seat stand and an artificial pitch. Cone expected it to be ready early in 2017/18 but not in time for the start of the season.

LOWLAND LEAGUE

BSC GLASGOW
It seems likely that BSC Glasgow will continue to ground share at Alloa, with a deal in place until the end of 2017/18. However, the club were rumoured to be looking for a move to Petershill Park for either 2017/18 or 2018/19.

DALBEATTIE STAR
Floodlights were installed at the Islecroft Stadium during 2016/17 and have already been used on several occasions.

EAST KILBRIDE
During the Summer of 2017 a new 300-capacity standing enclosure was built at the pavilion end of the K-Park, taking the capacity to around 900. Separately, East Kilbride Community Trust (EKCT) have lodged a blueprint for a phased 4000-seater development in Hurlawcrook Road, Langlands which would see "The East Kilbride Community Stadium" operational by late 2018 and completed in its entirety by 2020. The first stage of the development would see a synthetic 4G football pitch laid in the first quarter of 2018 and phase two, the erection of a main stand with 2430 seats and perimeter fencing, is earmarked for completion in the fourth quarter of 2018. Following that, EKCT propose to build a South-West Stand with 780 seats by late 2019 and a North-East stand, also comprising approximately 780 seats, by the end of 2020. The stadium will play host to East Kilbride Football Club matches and other teams from the town, similar to the current operation at K-Park in Calderglen Country Park, which is also operated by EKCT. As well as catering for football, the stadium will house a gym, a boxing ring, sports hall, a function suite and office space. The function suite would be available for community use and private parties outwith matchdays, where it will be used as a corporate lounge.

EAST STIRLINGSHIRE
During the latter part of 2016/17 it was strongly rumoured that Shire would be leaving Ochilview to either ground-

share with Falkirk or use Grangemouth Stadium. It is understood that the rental cost at Ochilview was prohibitive. A deal was eventually done which sees Shire remain at Ochilview, presumably at a lower rental cost.

GRETNA
The large temporary stand behind the goal at Gretna is now out of bounds for safety reasons. It is sad to see the decline in facilities at Raydale Park. In 2002, when they joined the Scottish league, the ground was well-appointed and smart with adequate cover and seating. Vaulting ambition did not serve them well and the ground is shadow of what it once was.

SELKIRK
Floodlights were expected to be installed at Yarrow Park during 2017/`8.

STIRLING UNIVERSITY
The Students will continue to groundshare with Falkirk in 2017/18.

WHITEHILL WELFARE
Whitehill had hoped to be in a position to announce plans for an artificial pitch and floodlights at Ferguson Park. However, their application for funding to Sport Scotland was knocked back on the grounds that there was already sufficient provision in the area. The club will now have to decide whether to try and fund the development themselves.

EAST OF SCOTLAND LEAGUE

KELTY HEARTS
League newcomers Kelty have transformed their ground over the past 2 years and they are not finished yet. So far they have laid an artificial pitch, installed floodlights, built two new covered enclosures, new terracing, a children's astroturf play-area, upgraded the changing rooms and extended the sponsors / social club facilities. By the Summer of 2018 the ground will also have a 300 seater grandstand.

LEITH ATHLETIC
Leith will start the season on the 3G pitch at Meadowbank. At the time of writing it was not clear whether they would be able to remain there all season. The redevelopment of Meadowbank will eventually see the site cleared but the 3G pitch may not be affected until 2018/19.

LOTHIAN THISTLE HUTCHISON VALE
Towards the end of 2016/17 preparatory work began for some ground improvements at Saughton Enclosure. An area of covered terracing will be built and a new portacabin will be in place next to the pavilion. This will provide spectator facilities and a kitchen / servery.

ORMISTON
From the start of 2017/18 Ormiston will be playing on their new pitch, adjacent to the old one. Work on the new pavilion, being built on the old pitch, started in May 2017.

TWEEDMOUTH RANGERS
Based at Old Shielfield, the club were admitted to the East of Scotland League in 2016 on the understanding that they would build facilities at the ground by the end of 2017/18. At present the players change in the Berwick Rangers changing rooms and stay on the pitch at half time. There are no spectator facilities at all. By the end of 2016/17 no work was underway and no planning application had been submitted.

TYNECASTLE
It was rumoured that Tynecastle were thinking of moving back to Fernieside for 2017/18. However, the rum ours appeared to be without foundation with the club staying at Saughton Enclosure in the meantime.

JUNIOR FOOTBALL

AUCHINLECK TALBOT
Talbot have built a new kitchen / servery area during the Summer of 2017. The new building will also include a club shop.

BANKS O' DEE
Two new covered enclosures were added to the "far" side of Spain Park during 2016/17. These provide much-needed shelter as the design of the existing grandstand did little to protect fans from the elements.

BELLSHILL ATHLETIC
Bellshill have given their new home at Rockburn Park a new-century feel – 19th century, that is. Duckboards

have been installed around part of the pitch, which is roped off rather than railed. Joking apart, all credit to Bellshill for moving back to their home town and making the most of their limited site. Apparently the club have a 5-year lease on the ground.

BO'NESS UNITED
The Newtown Park Association are still looking towards installing an artificial pitch and floodlights at the ground.

BROUGHTY ATHLETIC
Broughty are part of the Dundee East Community Sports Club. In December 2016 DECSC plans were approved for a complete redevelopment of Whitton Park. A new artificial pitch will be laid and floodlights installed. A new community use building on the west side of the ground will include a 300-seater grandstand. There is no definite time-scale for the development.

CAMBUSLANG RANGERS
After several years of work the concrete terracing at the former "Hoover" end of Somervell Park has been completed.

CLYDEBANK / YOKER ATHLETIC
In September 2016 West Dunbartonshire Council gave their approval to plans to redevelop Holm Park, Yoker. The plans include an artificial pitch, floodlights and much improved community and spectator facilities. It was expected that work would begin sometime during 2017/18 with both clubs requiring to groundshare for a spell. Clydebank were rumoured to have done a deal with Renfrew to lodge there for the duration of the work. This development appears to end speculation that Clydebank would be looking for a new home of their own.

DALKEITH THISTLE
The character of King's Park has been altered (not for the better) by the removal of many of the tall trees that surrounded the ground.

DEVERONSIDE
The North Junior clubs have now moved in to their new ground at the Myrus Sports Centre in Macduff. It has an artificial pitch, floodlights and a small seated grandstand.

EASTHOUSES LILY
During 2016/17 the club opened their new grandstand which completed a systematic programme of ground improvements at Newbattle.

HILL OF BEATH HAWTHORN
A new first aid / medical room was built at Keir's Park during the Summer of 2017.

INVERNESS CITY
Confusion abounds regarding the future of the Inverness Junior club. It seems that their current home at Lister Park (part of the Bught Park) was only ever provided as a temporary compromise by the local Council and they will be forced out at some point during 2017/18. Plans to groundshare with Clachnacuddin have fallen through because of difficulties in finding the funding for a new artificial surface at Grant Street Park.

KENNOWAY STAR HEARTS
KSH have signalled their intention to quit Treaton Park at the end of 2017/18. They will move to New Bayview Stadium in Methil which had an artificial pitch put down during the Summer of 2017. The Junior club intend to have their own portacabin facilities within the ground for changing and hospitality. They will form a new Amateur side who will continue to use Treaton Park , at least until the present lease runs out in a few year's time.

KILWINNING RANGERS
Kilwinning have been gradually improving facilities at Abbey Park to give the ground a more unitary feeling. New catering facilities and a covered enclosure have been developed to replace some of the assortment of portakabins.

KIRKCALDY YM
Denfield Park has been the target for vandals during 2016/17. Two separate incidents of fire-raising saw the clubs' hospitality and storage facilities destroyed.

KIRKINTILLOCH ROB ROY
Final plans for Rob Roy's new ground were finally submitted during the Summer of 2017. The club were trying to motivate local people to support the scheme, declaring that the club would probably fold if the plans were not approved. A decision was expected during the Autumn. The new development will be in Donaldson Street, immediately south of the Forth and Clyde Canal. The plans include an artificial pitch and a substantial grandstand. In the meantime Rob Roy continue to ground share with Cumbernauld United.

LINLITHGOW ROSE
The floodlighting system at Prestonfield was dismantled during 2016/17. The club intend to install a new and more powerful set during 2017/18.

LOCHEE HARP
Harp played their final match at Beechwood Park at the end of 2016/17. The club will move to new purpose-built facility more or less across King's Cross Road from their existing ground. The new Community Hub will also host the St Francis Boxing Club, also made homeless by the development of Beechwood for a new car show-room.

MAYBOLE
The changing rooms at the Ladywell Stadium were damage din an arson attack during 2016/17, causing the club to play a number of matches away from their usual home.

MUSSELBURGH ATHLETIC
The stone wall adjoining the Olive Bank ground was demolished after structural surveys of walls on school premises throughout the area. It has been tastefully replaced and the ground has lost none of its charm.

NEILSTON
There have been no further developments regarding the proposed new stadium in Neilston.

PUMPHERSTON
The roof has been rem oved from the old covered enclosure at Recreation Park. The intention is to replace it with a new, more weather-proof, cladding.

ROSSVALE
The club were ready to move to their own new ground at Huntershill for the start of the 2017/18 season. The project was not without problems and the ground will be basic but more than enough for their needs.

ROSYTH
Rosyth were forced to play several home games away from Recreation Park during 2016/17. The council-owned ground has been sold to a developer and the club are on zero notice to quit. There is no electricity supply to the ground and the club generator broke down which led to postponements and rearrangements. The plan is for the club to move to new facility at the Fleet Grounds. As of the Summer of 2017 no new work had been done there but the existing artificial pitch looked suitable for Junior football. It has a railed off spectator area down one side and is not far from the changing rooms – it is certainly as good as, if not better than, the ground currently used by Gartcairn.

ST ROCHS
The go-ahead Glasgow club have done a lot of work to modernise the terrracing on the north-west side of the ground. Compared to a few years ago James McGrory Park is now an excellent venue - a testament to what can be achieved with a hard-working and ambitious committee, open to new ideas and input.

WHITBURN
If you had asked me 15 years ago which Junior club would be least likely to build a grandstand I might have answered Whitburn. They refused entry to the new Super League because it meant travelling outwith the Lothians and they epitomised everything about the old-guard of Junior football. Seats? Out of the question. Well, the Summer of 2017 saw a new prefabricated grandstand installed at Central Park, next to the new pavilion and adjacent to the Social Club.

YOKER ATHLETIC
See entry for Clydebank.

OBITUARIES

Sandy Anderson Born 20 February 1930, Died July 2016
Sandy Anderson, a Scot, came to the town as a PE instructor for the army at Shoebury Garrison. He had been playing for Newburgh Juniors in Fife, close to his home town of Auchtermuchty. SOPuthend pipped Cowdenbeath for his signature. The Shrimpers fullback holds the record for the number of league games played for the club of 452 League games and 31 in the cup, between 1950 and 1963. He then played for Folkestone in the Southern league.

Lee Bertie, Born 1977, Died 2017
Lee was forced to give up playing for Broughty Athletic in 2015 when he was diagnosed with Motor Neurone Disease. He had also been a regular player with Lochee United and was much liked on the Tayside Junior circuit. He continued to work in IT following his diagnosis and campaigned to raise funds for MND research.

Jimmy Campbell Born 1935, Died December 19 2015
Joined Montrose in 1958 from Lanarkshire Junior side Royal Albert. Went on to play 100 games for the Links Park side before leaving at the end of 1961/2.

Ronnie Cant Born October 6 1953, Died June 8th 2017
Former Queen's Park goalkeeper and Coach Ronnie Cant passed away suddenly in June 2017. He joined Queen's Park in 1979 from Largs Thistle. After playing a few first team games he was released but returned to serve the club for 15 years as goalkeeping coach.

Derek Carr Born 1936, Died August 2016
Carr played for Crook Town at Wembley in the 1959 FA Amateur Cup Final having previously turned out for Belford of the North Northumberland League. Upon his demob from the RAF he signed for Berwick Rangers and was a consistent player for them over 18 months from January 1960 until April 1961.

Ian ClarkBorn April 13 1961, Died March24 2016
Made a few apperances for Berwick Rangers during 1982/3 but is better known for long service to Coldstream, Hawick Royal Albert, kelso United, Gala Fairydean and Duns.

Rob Clark, Died May 5 2017
Rob was Secretary of Newtongrange Star for many years and one of the real stalwarts who keep football going at grass roots level. His canny style saw Star pull themselves up from a difficult spell to regain their place in the Super League. Away from football he worked for Scottish Power and was a well-known figure in the Scouting movement.

Alan Mathieson Cousin Born 7 March 1938, Died 20 September 2016
At the age of 16, Cousin played rugby in the mornings and football in the afternoons, for Alloa Y.M.C.A. He was noticed within a year of helping out the Central Scottish side and played for Scotland Under 16s, where as a Centre Forward, he was in the side that beat England 8-1. Scouts from various clubs sought his skills, but it was Dundee manager Willie Thornton who succeeded in signing him. Cousin made his debut when first team regular George Merchant was injured and one month later, he scored his first goal for Dundee. The match was a 5-1 friendly victory against Manchester United, who had just become the English champions. After establishing a first-team place, Cousin attended St. Andrews University to study Greek and Latin for an Arts Degree, whilst combining this with his early professional footballing career. Cousin was Dundee's top goalscorer three years in a row from 1958 to 1960. He played in attack for Dundee alongside Alan Gilzean as Dundee won the Scottish League championship in 1962 and then reached the semi-final of the European Cup in the following season. Cousin played in every match of the championship-winning season. Cousin was dubbed the 'King of the double shuffle' [6] because of his ability to repeatedly outwit opposing players, by stepping over the ball. He was inducted into the Dundee F.C. Hall Of Fame in a tribute dinner in 2011, to salute his contribution to football at the club. He later played for Hibs. Alan was never booked or sent off throughout his career. He was always a part-time player, combining football with his teaching career – he finished up as Depute Rector of Lornshill Academy in Alloa. His brother Jim was also a professional footballer and teacher, His sons forged spectacular careers away from football - Martin, as a professional classical musician, and Michael, Professor of neuronal cell biology at Edinburgh University.

Ian Cowan, Born 27 November 1944, Died 8 November 2016
"Cowboy" was a Falkirk boy who had been outstanding as a schoolboy player and he progressed to play for his local team Camelon Juniors. He was called up by Falkirk and played five league matches, He was released back to the Junior ranks and joined Rutherglen Glencairn. It didn't take long for young Cowan to show his talent, and he joined up at Partick Thistle for the 1962/63 season.His dashing wing play earned him plenty of plaudits and he had over three seasons with Thistle before a move to Perth. From St Johnstone, he moved back to Falkirk then to Dunfermline for a fee of £3,000. His next club was Southend United but Ian failed to settle at Roots Hall and his career was starting to drift. He had a spell in Belgium with KV Oostende and then in Hong

Kong before ending his senior career with Albion Rovers in 1972/73. Ian ended up playing for Whitburn Juniors. In later life, he was a regular attender at Falkirk games. His son Stevie was also a player with Stirling Albion and numerous Junior clubs.

Ken Currie Born 3 September 1925, Died 22 March 2017
Born and bred in Thornton, Ken Currie's football career saw him progress through Buckhaven High School and the Wemyss Area Select before joining Bayview Youth Club. Along with his brother Willie, Ken was a member of the team which lifted the Scottish Juvenile Cup in 1942. At the end of that season Currie joined hearts as a 17 year-old. Ken broke into the Hearts' team during the war-time North Eastern League in 1943/44 and was still there when normal service resumed in 1946. He went on to make 59 appearances for Hearts, scoring 15 goals. Finding it hard to get a regular game, a fee of £1,500 took him to Third Lanark in 1951, looking for rirst team football. Things weren't so successful there and he played just six times, scoring once, before moving on to Raith Rovers in February 1953. He was released at the end of the season without playing a competitive match but was picked up by Dunfermline. A chartered accountant by profession, Ken made 24 appearances for the Pars during 1953/54, scoring seven goals. He concluded his senior career by scoring in his one league match for Stranraer. Ken died aged 91 in a Care Home in Glenrothes.

Joe Davis Born 22 May 1941, Died August 5 2016
Full back Joe David graduated from Shettleston Juniors to Third Lanark in 1961. Consistent displays prompted Jock Stein to sign hiom for Hibs and he went on to set a club record for consecutive appearances, being ever-present for four seasons in a row. He wasl also deadly from the penalty spot, scoring 43 goals for the Easter Road side. In 1969 he moved to Carlisle United for whom he made 72 Football league appearances. On leaving football he managed a hotel in Ayrshire then worked as a sales representative.

Dennis Devlin, Born 26/11/47, Died 8/4/16
Dennis played in goals for Falkirk from season 1966/67-1971/72. He passed away on April 8th after suffering a heart attack. He hadn't been in good health for a while and was in a care home. His early football career saw him play for Holy Cross Academy and the famous Edina Hibs side. Dennis was in good company with players like Jimmy O'Rourke and Pat Stanton. Dennis joined Falkirk from Morton for a fee of £3,000. Season 1967/68 was his best in senior football during which time he made 28 appearances in the league for the Bairns. He left the club at the end of season 1972/73 and retired from senior football. Dennis joined the Fire Service and worked with the Lothians and Borders Fire Service for over 30 years. Initially based at Sighthill, he spent most of his career at the McDonald Road Station.

Dick Donnelly Born September 11 1941, Died July 21 2016
Born in Lochee in Dundee Charles Richard Donnelly was educated at the city's Harris Academy before serving his time as an apprentice hot metal worker in the case room at the DC Thomson offices in Bank Street, Dundee. He played in goal for Junior football club Carnoustie Panmure before attracting the attention of the seniors, signing for East Fife. He made 107 appearances for the Methil club between 1960 and 1964 before moving on to Brechin City and Arbroath – and in later years would fondly recall the occasion when, in a game for the Glebe Park outfit, he suffered a broken collar bone that, in the days before substitutes meant a switch from tending goal to taking up position on the wing where, remarkably, he managed to score a goal. A keen sportsman – he also played golf, table tennis and cricket as a fast bowler. Indeed, had it not been for the call of journalism he may well have excelled on the cricket pitch after hanging up his goalkeeping gloves. He started work doing match reports for The Courier in the late 1960s. He was soon full-time as a football writer on The People's Journal before joining the staff of the Scottish Sunday Express, covering the east coast all the way from Edinburgh to Aberdeen. He also turned to radio – and quickly established himself as one of the most recognisable voices on the airwaves. Dick Donnelly was the voice of football on Radio Tay (where he graduated to sports editor) with his sports desk bulletins as well as commentaries on matches. Famously lampooned by Only An Excuse, reporting "from a dreich and dismal Dens Park", he later ran a media agency in Dundee covering all aspects of local football.

Kenneth Drummond, Born 1942, Died May 7 2017
Kenny was Club President at Letham Amateurs for many years an a real stalwart of Perthshire football. He and three friends established Letham in 1960. His passion for grassroots football that led to his dream to have a 3G pitch at Seven Acres in the Letham district of Perth.

Cammy Duncan (Born August 4th 1965, Died Mat 2 2017)
Born in Shotts, Goalkeeper Cammy Duncan began his career at Sunderland, making a single league appearance before returning to Scotland with Motherwell. He had lengthy spells at Fir Park and with Ayr United and Partick Thistle before ending his career with Albion Rovers. Cammy died aged 51 as a result of cancer.

Bill Durie, Born September 26 1930, Died September 14 2016
A plasterer to trade, Billy Durie was a stalwart of the Lothians Junior football world. He played for Thorntree United and Newtongrange Star, then served Bonnyrigg Rose as Manager, Coach and Physio. He was Manager of Rose when they lifted the Scottish Junior Cup for the first time in 1966. In retirement he continued to follow the club, home and away, until the week of his death. He was survived by Janet, his wife of 63 years. As a

mark of respect Bonnyrigg printed his name and dates of birth / death on their strips for the remainder of the 2016/17 season. BBC Scotland featured his grandson and wife in a feature late in 2016, available here:
http://www.bbc.co.uk/sport/football/37758175

Ugo Ehiogu Born November 3 1972, Died April 21 2017
Former England defender Ehiogu died of a cardiac arrest at Tottenham Hotspur's training ground on April 21st 2017. Towards the end of his career, in 2007/8, Ehiogu had a short spell with Rangers, most notably scoring with a spectacular overhead kick for the only goal of a game against Celtic. He was best known for his long spells with Aston Villa and Middlesbrough and won 4 England caps.

Susan Ferries
Born 6 August 1944, Died May 19 2016
A star in the Stewarton Thistle team that dominated Women's football in Scotland during the 1970s – Susan also represented Scotland in official and unofficial matches.

Robert Adam Fraser Born 5/10/24, Died May 10 2016
Bert Fraser was a Junior internationalist whilst with Dundee Anchorage. He them moved to Lochee Harp before signing for Celtic in 1948. After just one first team game he was released, playing for Hearts, Northwich Victoria, Brechin City, Montrose and St Johnstone. His senior career ended in 1955 and two years later he emigrated to Canada, settling in Ottawa, where he died.

Donald Fraser, Died September 2016, Aged 59
Donnie Fraser was a popular Director of Inverness Caledonian Thistle. As well as his work with ICT, Helensburgh-born Fraser was well-known as managing director of Korrie Mechanical and Plumbing, a major employer in Inverness.

Tommy Gemmell Born October 16 1943, Died March 2nd 2017
No player symbolised the "glory days" of the late 1960s in Scottish football in the way that Tommy Gemmell did. He was one of a new generation of attacking full-backs, tenacious in defence but flamboyant in attack. Not only did he score Celtic's equaliser as they won the European Cup in 1967, he remains one of a select few to have scored in two European Cup Finals thanks to his goal against Feyenoord in 1970. Gemmell's character was just right for a Scottish football hero – hugely talented, but with a wild streak. His assault on West Germany's Helmut Haller in Hamburg in 1969 remains a classic Scottish football moment. Gemmell had joined Celtic in 1961 from Coltness United in the Juniors. He took some stick in his early days as a Protestant playing for Celtic but along with Jock Stein and Billy McNeill, amongst others, did much to help Celtic move on from a rather narrow-minded approach that held the club back. Jock Stein eventually became frustrated with Gemmell's individuality and he was sold to Nottingham Forest in 1971. That move didn't work out and after a short spell in th3e USA he returned to Scotland with Dundee. He enjoyed a renaissance as a player, winning the League Cup in 1973, and then as Manager at Dens Park. Later he had two spells as Manager of Albion Rovers whilst pursuing a career in insurance sales. His haul of honours was impressive – 18 caps for Scotland, 6 League Championships, 3 Scottish Cups, 5 League Cups and a European Cup. Gemmell was inducted to the Scottish football Hall of Fame in 2006.

Jim Gillespie, Born July 13 1947, Died November 25 2016
Jim Gillespie was born in the village of Chapelhall in Airdrie on 13th July 1947, and played for his Primary School team at Chapelhall and then for Airdrie High School. Jim was signed on part-time terms by Carlisle United as a teenager but the travelling proved too much and he left after only one season. Reinstated to the junior ranks with Whitburn, he was so successful that he gained Scottish junior international caps and by January 1967 he was back in the senior game with East Stirlingshire. A year later he stepped up to the First Division with Raith Rovers. A year later he joined Dunfermline. A quiet man, his new team-mates gave him the nickname "Soames" after a character in the BBC Television series "The Forsyte Saga" who didn`t say very much. He made his European debut in the 3-2 win against Anderlecht in the Fairs Cup (Dunfermline had earlier lost 1-0 in Belgium and went out on the away goals rule). Jim was released at the end of 1973/4 after playing 96 times for the Pars and scoring nine goals. He spent 1974/75 with Alloa Athletic before taking up a coaching position with Raith Rovers, where he worked alongside his former Athletic team-mate Alex Kinninmonth.
In the early 1980s Jim worked under Andy Rolland at Cowdenbeath, his last post in senior football. Outside of football Jim took on a job in electrical wholesale with Ross Electrical before moving on in the same business, becoming Regional Director for Scotland with Rexel Senate.

Giles Gillett Born 27/3/28, Died 4/3/16,
Made his senior debut for Leith Athletic in November 1950 after failing to make the grade at Middlesbrough. Later played for Montrose before returning to Teeside to work and to turn out for the ICI Works team.

Gerry Gow Born 29 May 1952, Died 10 October 2016
Gerry joined Bristol City direct from school in Drumchapel as a 15 year old. He made 375 appearances for them in The Football League. Gow made his debut for Bristol City in 1970 at the age of 17. He was a member of the side which achieved promotion in 1976 to the First Division. He left Bristol City aged 28 following the team's relegation to the Second Division in 1980. After his time at Bristol City he played for Manchester City, appearing in the 1981 FA Cup Final, and Rotherham United before transferring to Burnley in August 1983. He then moved to Yeovil Town where he was player manager for a time and then managed Weymouth. He settled in Portland after that. Bristol City granted Gow a retrospective testimonial in 2012, when a Legends team played against a Manchester City Legends side. He won one cap for the Scotland Under 23 side, playing against England at Newcastle in 1974. Gerry Gow is mentioned in the song 'This One's for Now' by the band Half Man Half Biscuit on their album *Urge For Offal*. He died of cancer on 10 October 2016 at the age of 64.

Bobby Grant Born 25/9/40, Died February 2017
Bobby joined Rangers from Ormiston Primrose in 1959 and played one first team game for the Ibrox club. He then had a season with St Johnstone without establishing himself as a regular. On his debut for Saints he scored the only goal in a 1-0 win over Celtic at Parkhead. He them oved to England playing for Leyton orient, Carlisle United, Cheltenham Town, Chelmsford City and Gloucester City. By the late 1960s he was back in Scotland playing for Newtongrange Star. He had another crack at senior football with Stirling Albion, scoring 5 goals for them in 1969/70. He continued to play Junior football into the 1980s with Pumpherston, Polkemmet, Whitburn and Livingston United. Bobby moved to Spain in later life and died in a care home there. His son Roddy was a top player in Scotland in the 1980s and 1990s with a host of clubs.

Matt Gray Norn July 11 1936, Died September 2016
Matt played and scored as a trialist for Stirling Albion in 1957 but signed for Third Lanark. He proved to be a prolific striker at Cathkin Park and was transferred to Manchester City in 1963 for a fee of £30,000. He had been part time at Third Lanark, working as an engineer for Babcock and Wilcox in Renfrew. He played 101 first team games for City and scored 23 goals. He later moved to South Africa playing for Port Elizabeth City, Highlands Park and Johannesburg Corinthians. He returned to Glasgow and worked for many years for a freight company at Glasgow Airport.

Billy Greig Died July 2016
Billy was a stalwart for Selkirk during the 1950's, ably filling the left back position. On his retirement from the game was also heavily involved in youth football in the town.

David Herd Born 15 April 1934, Died 1 October 2016
Herd was born in Hamilton, Lanarkshire but grew up in Manchester as his father Alex was playing for Manchester City and later Stockport County where Herd Jr. began his career. He made his debut on the final day of the 1950–51 season. Herd did well enough to attract the attention of Arsenal, who signed him for £10,000 in 1954. Herd made his Arsenal debut on 19 February 1955 against Leicester City. Herd was initially a fringe player, playing just eight games in his first two seasons at the club, before making his breakthrough in 1956–57, scoring 18 goals in 28 games that season. From then on he was an established goalscorer, being the club's top goalscorer for four seasons straight, from 1956–57 through to 1960–61. he moved to Manchester United in July 1961 for £35,000. He scored 145 career goals in 265 appearances (including one substitute appearance), an average of 0.54 goals per game and is currently 13th on the all-time club goalscorers list. He left Manchester United in July 1968 for Stoke City on a free transfer In December 1970 Herd signed for Shay Brennan at Waterford. Herd won five caps in total for Scotland between 1958 and 1961, scoring three goals, After retiring from playing, he had a stint managing Lincoln City between 1971 and 1972.

Arthur Hughes, Born 23/11/27, Died 31/10/15
Had been on the books of both Nottingham clubs before making his senior debut for GrimsbyTown. Scored 11 goals in 25 games for them then moved on to Gillingham. Born in Linlithgow, her settled in Kent and ended his playing days with Dover and Ashford Town, them managed Chatham Town.

Roger Hynd Born February 2nd 1942, Died February 18th 2017
A talented defender, there is some irony that Hynd is best remembered for a match he played at centre forward. Rangers selected him in that position for the 1967 European Cup Winners Cup Final in Nurnberg, which they lost 0-1 to Bayern Munich. Born in Falkirk, Hynd was part of a footballing dynasty. His mother jean was the sister of Bill and Bob Shankly so it was inevitable that Hynd would forge a career in the game. Hynd signed for Rangers as a youngster and trained to be a PE Teacher at Jordanhill College. In almost ten years at Ibrox Hynd was almost always part of the first team squad but seldom a first pick. He moved on to Crystal Palace in 1969 for a £25,000 fee , joining up at Selhurst Park just after Palace were promoted to the top flight of English football. Five successful years at Birmingham City followed, then a loan spell at Oxford and a further 100 games at Walsall. Hynd was appointed manager at Motherwell in 1977 but after a great start results turned and he quit to concentrate on his teaching career. He did have a

spell as coach and interim manager at St Johnstone on a part-time basis. He had taught at Shawlands Academy during his Rangers days, and later worked at Garrion Academy and Lanark Grammar School.

Peter Hutton Died May 2017, Aged 63
Fife Junior football was shocked by the sudden death of Peter Hutton. As a 16 year old he had trials with Liverpool but signed youth forms for Rangers. A broken leg ended his playing career but he went into management, notably with Newburgh, St Andrews United, Dundonald Bluebell and Lochore Welfare.

Bobby Jeffrey Born November 7 1942, Died May 20 2017
Born in Airdrie, Bobby played Junior with Coltness United. He went to Celtic and played 8 first team games and won Scotland Under 23 recognition. Unable to win a regular place at Parkhead he moved to Airdrieonians in 1963. That move didn't really work out and Bobby moved South to play for Rhyl, Pwlhelli & District, Altrincham and Colwyn Bay. In 1966/7 he was back in Scotland with Stranraer. At the end of that season he trialed for Cambridge City but wasn't signed – however he settled in Cambridge. He was landlord at The Rock and The Old Spring pubs in Cambridge, and later caretaker at The Manor Secondary School, also in Cambridge. In later years he worked at Downing College, part of Cambridge University. Locally Bobby played for N.C.I. (New Chesterton Institute) in the Cambridgeshire League in the late 60's/early 70's. His son Andrew was an apprentice at Leicester City and also played for Cambridge City, Cambridge United and Histon.

John Aitken (Ian) King Born Loanhead May 27 1937, Died July 24 2016
King was playing for Arniston Rangers when he was spotted by Leicester City in 1957. He played in two FA Cup Finals for Leicester, and won a league Cup winners medal. He then joined Charlton Athletic and later became player manager of Burton Albion, On leaving football he worked in the transport industry.

Johnny Little, Born 8 July 1930, Died 18 January 2017
Rangers Hall of Fame Legend Johnny Little passed away at the age of 86. Johnny, a left back defender, began his career with Queen's Park and joined Rangers in 1951. He made a total of 327 appearances and his only goal for the club came in a 1–1 draw with Hamilton Academical in March 1954. Born in Calgary, Canada on 8 July 1930, he moved with his family to Scotland at an early age, to Millport on the Isle of Cumbrae where his parents opened a fruit and vegetable shop. He made his competitive debut for the Club in a Scottish League Cup game against East Fife on 11 August 1951, and was an ever-present in the Rangers Team during the 1950s. During his time at Ibrox he won two League championships and two Scottish Cups. He left Rangers at the end of the 1961-62 season, moving to Morton, where he finished his career. Johnny was capped once for Scotland against Sweden in 1953. Away from the world of football John Little was a much respected PE teacher at Crookston Castle Secondary on the south-side of Glasgow, at St Columba's in Greenock and at the Sacred Heart Secondary in Paisley. In later years he lived with his wife Anne in Largs.

William Logie Born Montreal 1933, Died Stirling June 20 2016
Although born in Canada, Logie was brought up in Stirling. He signed for Cambuslang Rangers as a youngster and then for Glasgow Rangers. Never really a regular at Ibrox, he earned the distinction of being the first British player sent off in a European tie. Had short spells with Aberdeen, Arbroath, Brechin City and Alloa before concentrating on his trade as a joiner.

Dick Lowrie Born July 7 1943, Died 2017
Dick was playing for St Rochs when he was spotted by Brentford – he signed up at griffin Park in 1961. However, he failed to make the breakthrough in England and returned to Scotland with Morton. Again he was restricted to second team football and he finally made is senior debut for Stenhousemuir in 1964. Dick went on to play over 100 games for the Warriors before going back to the Juniors with Petershill and Cambuslang Rangers. He won two Scottish Junior Cup medals with Cambuslang. Away from football he worked for the Inland Revenue.

John Lumsden Born 15/12/60, Died 22/4/16
Made a good impression with east Fife in 1979/80 and eaned a transfer to Stoke City. He never got a first team chance at the Victoria Ground and drifted out of football.

Lord Lyall of Kinnordy, Died January 10th 2017, Aged 77.
Forfar Athletic's Honorary Patron and lifelong supporter, the Right Honourable Lord Lyell of Kinnordy, passed away in Ninewells Hospital in January 2017. He had been missing from the Station Park scene in the latter part of 2016 through illness but had been reported to be recovering well. Born in 1939, Charles inherited the title of the third Baron of Kinnordy in 1943 when his father also Charles was posthumously awarded the Victoria Cross in the Second World War. He had overseen the running of the family estates both locally and south of the border for many years, prior to handing over to his cousin a couple of years back. He was an active member of the House of Lords since 1960. He was one of the ninety-two elected hereditary peers that remain in the House of Lords after the passing of the House of Lords Act of 1999, and sat on the Conservative benches. The titles became extinct on his death in 2017. Unmarried, football

played a great part in his life. He had supported the 'Loons' since childhood and was also a keen fan of Everton and a frequent visitor to Goodison Park. Lord Lyell was thrilled when the then Chairman Sam Smith invited him to become Honorary Patron of Forfar Athletic in the early eighties and he was one of the speakers proposing the toast to the guests at the club's Centenary Dinner in November of 1984. Twenty five years later he was also instrumental through his contacts on Merseyside in getting Everton to send a team up to Forfar, totally free of charge to celebrate the 'Loons' 125th Anniversary. He also for over three decades had sponsored the club's final match of the league campaign, always bringing with him on the day much appreciated gifts for many including even the match officials!

Stuart Markland Born February 12 1948, Died March 31 2017
Markland began as a centre forward with Penicuik Athletic from whom he stepped up to Berwick Rangers in 1967. Dundee United spotted his potential as a defender and took him to Tannadice a year later. Over the next few years he played more than 150 first team games for United. He moved to Montrose in 1972 and played there for six years before moving to Australia, signing for Sydney Olympic. Markland returned to Links Park in 1980 amd then went back to Penicuik Athletic. He was employed in the building trade and contracted an asbestos-related illness which led to him being confined to a wheelchair and losing a leg.

James McAnerney Born March 20 1935, Died Mied March 14 2017
Jim learned his football with Dundee St Josephs in the Tayside Juniors. He moved south to join his brother Tom on the books at Sheffield Wednesday in 1952. Later on he moved to Plymouth Argyle, Watford and Bradford City, playing more than 300 senior games. Tommy Docherty made him Assistant Manager at Rotherham and he took over from the Doc as Manager in December 1968. He was in charge at Millmoor for five years and later coached at Leeds United and Sheffield United. Jim was also manager of Scarborough for a spell before they joined the Football League. Away from football he ran a machine tool hire business.

James Bell McCabe Born May 27 1951, Died July 6 2016
Jim McCabe was a talented attacking player at Motherwell, notable for his long hair. He starred in the Texaco Cup in the early 1970s but never really fulfilled his early potential. In 1975 he moved on to Stranraer and then to Albion Rovers. His career was cut short by an ankle injury in 1978.

Sam McCulloch, Died January 23 2017, Aged 57
Auchinleck Talbot klegend Sam is best remembered for being their goal hero in their 1-0 win over Newtongrange Star in the 1991 Scottish Cup final. He bagged the only goal of the game when he buried a header at Brockville in May 1991. Defender Sam was a focal point of the great Talbot team of the late 80's and early 90's that went on to dominate junior football. Auchinleck Talbot club secretary, Henry Dumigan said: "Sam was a big part of Talbot's success in to the early 1990's. He was a colossus of a man. He typified what Talbot were all about at the time. Passion and desire. I can't speak highly enough about Sam." From New Cumnock, Sam signed for Cumnock Amateurs before joining Talbot. He also had a brief spell at Glenafton before heading back to Beechwood Park. Fans of both Auchinleck and Glenafton dedicated their clash in the 2017 Scottish Junior Cup Final to Sam. A minute's applause was held in the fifth minute of the Junior Cup final in reference to his shirt number. Sam played 2 Scottish league games as a trialist for Queen of the South in 1984/5.

Tommy McCulloch, Born March 1 1934, Died December 10 2016
Born in Glasgow, the son of Joseph (a delivery driver with The Daily Record) and Johanna McCulloch, the young Tommy was educated at Queen's Park Secondary School on the south-side of Glasgow. He signed for Junior club Bridgeton Waverley in July 1956 and played one game at senior level with Dumbarton before joining Clyde in the summer of 1957. He won the 1958 Scottish Cup in his first season with the club, keeping a clean sheet in the final against Hibernian. McCulloch was one of Clyde's greatest servants, and spent 15 years with the club, making 475 appearances in all competitions. He left Clyde in 1972, and joined Hamilton Academical for a year, before retiring. He played a total of 491 games in his 16-year career. He regularly attended Clyde functions, and was presented with a bottle of whisky in the 2007–08 Clyde player of the year event, to commemorate the 50th anniversary of the 1958 Scottish Cup win. He was inducted into the inaugural Clyde FC Hall of Fame in 2011. McCulloch was always a part-time professional while with Clyde – an electrician by trade, he worked with the Turner Group where he met his future wife Helen MacNeill from Mull. He later worked as an auto electrician with the GPO, as a BT engineer and in the planning department before taking early retirement at the age of 58.

Kieran McDade, Died August 16th 2016, Aged 13
Alloa Athletic youth player and Celtic-fan Kieran died on the training pitch with Dunbeth FC in his native Coatbridge. Celtic Striker Leigh Griffiths held up a shirt with RIP Kieran and the number 13 on it after scoring against Aberdeen the following week. The goal came in the 13th minute of the game as supporters prepared to stage a minute's applause for Kieran McDade.

David McDonald, Died March 2017
David was a stalwart supporter of Fort William FC and contributed in many ways to the club, as match day

reporter and announcer, historian and social media coordinator. He also had a spell as Vice Chairman and his energy and enthusiasm helped the club through some difficult times.

Ian McGregor Norn December 9 1936, Died July 20 2016
Joined Raith Rovers in 1957 from Edinburgh Juvenile football. He never really became a regular in four years at Stark's Park, nor in one season he spent at Cowdenbeath thereafter.

Jackie McInally, Born 21 November 1936, Died 8 July 2016
An "Honest Man" of Ayr, McInally attended the town's Newton Park School, leaving to take up a plumbing apprenticeship. He completed his national service with the Royal Scots Greys, and his football apprenticeship with Kello Rovers, Minishant Amateurs and Crosshill Thistle. He joined Kilmarnock in 1959. McInally was a regular starter from joining up at Kilmarnock. He made his debut against Stirling Albion, in the League Cup, in August 1959, the first of 297 appearances for the club, which garnered 127 goals. One of these goals is the stuff of Rugby Park folklore. It came on 22 September, 1964, when Killie entertained Eintracht Frankfurt in the Inter-Cities Fairs Cup, seeking to overturn a 3-0 first leg deficit. McInally scored the decisive fifth goal as Killie won 5-1, after first going 0-4 behind on aggregate. He made one appearance for the Scottish League, against Scotland in the International Trial match, at Celtic Park, in January, 1961. The peak of his career came when Killie won the Scottish League in 1965. He continued to play for Killie until December, 1967 – coming off the bench for his only substitute appearance on December 2, before moving to Motherwell in a £5000 transfer. He spent six years at Fir Park, before moving to play out one final season at Hamilton prior to retiring in 1975, after more than 400 senior appearances. Post-football, he and Avril, his wife of 55 years, ran a couple of shops; Jackie also worked for a time at the Hyster fork lift factory in Irvine, before having a lengthy spell as manager of a paint wholesaler's in Kilmarnock His snon, Alan, was a prominent player for Celtic, Scotland and Bayern Munich, as well as a tv pundit. Away from football Jackie was an excellent golfer, at one time playing off a handicap of three at Prestwick St Cuthbert's.

James McIntosh Died October 2 2016, Aged 80
Jimmy was a full-back who learned his football in his native Forres, playing for both Thistle and Mechanics. He was transferred to Falkirk in 1954. Initially he was a part-time player, serving his apprenticeship as a plumber. He was awarded Under 23 caps by Scotland and represented the British Army. He was in the frame for a full Scotland Cap in 1958, playing in trials, but was not selected for the World Cup in Sweden. Jimmy played over 200 games for Falkirk, including the Scottish Cup Final win in 1957, and was being linked with Nottingham Forest when a knee injury brought his top-level career to a premature halt. In 1963 he re-turned to Forres Mechanics as player manager and bought the Eagle public house. Later he moved back to the Falkirk area where he was also landlord of various pubs including The Carronbridge Inn, The Ellwyn, The Three Kings, The Whiteside, The Dutch Inn and The Hollybank.

Mike McKenna
A talented outside left, Mike stepped up to Ayr United in 1951 from Bathgate Thistle. He played 93 first team games for Ayr before being freed in 1956. He then had spells with Berwick Rangers, Keith and Montrose before a short spell at St Johnstone Mike played for Stenhousemuir in 1958/9 then had a spell in Ireland with Bangor.

George McKimmie 19th July 1951, Died October 19 2016 in South Africa
Dundonian George was a defender as a schoolboy but was moved into the forward line after joining local junior club Dundee Violet. He quickly attracted senior attention after scoring fifteen goals in as many matches and was training regularly with Dundee. But in the late 1960s, Dunfermline Athletic was on the crest of a wave and McKimmie joined the Pars. He made his first-team debut on 2nd October 1968 in the European Cup-Winners` Cup tie against Apoel in Cyprus, aged just 17. He came
The following month, in what was only his fourth appearance for the first team, he replaced Barrie Mitchell in the second leg of the European Cup-Winners' Cup semi-final against Slovan Bratislava. How many players have played in a major European semi-final aged 17? George's career stalled somewhat and he was freed at the end of the70/1 season. He and his young family emigrated to South Africa where he joined Highlands Park. He soon gave up football and decided to take on an apprenticeship as a fitter. He moved from Johan-nesburg to Vanderbijlpark to work in the ISCOR steel factory there.

David MacLaren, Born: Auchterarder, 12 June, 1934. Died: Castlemaine, Victoria, Australia, 6 December, 2016, aged 82.
Dave Maclaren, was a member of an on-going goalkeeping dynasty. He was never more than a journeyman goalkeeper, but, he enjoyed success far away from his native Perthshire. Dave's elder brothers: Jim, who played for Chester City, Carlisle United and Berwick Rangers, Roy, who played for St. Johnstone, Bury and Sheffield Wednesday and Monty, who played for Liverpool, were all goalkeepers, so, the young Dave fol-lowed in their footsteps. While completing his National Service as a radar technician in the Royal Air Force, Dave represented Hong Kong, and helped Penang State win the Malaysia Cup. He also attracted the atten-tion of Chelsea, to whom he was attached as an amateur, before he returned to Scotland and joined Dundee as a professional. He was unable to oust future Scotland great Bill Brown from the 'Dee goalkeeper's shirt, so he went south, to Leicester City, where he helped them win the Second Division (now the Championship) title in 1956-57. He held his place in the First Division, until replaced by a youngster named Gordon Banks,

whom City had signed from Chesterfield, in 1959-60. Maclaren was then sold to Plymouth Argyle, spending five seasons at Home Park and helping the Pilgrims to their highest ever league position, fifth in the Second Division, in 1962. From there it was back to the Midlands, to Wolves, then to Southampton.
After some 300 senior games in his career, he moved on, spending 18 months with Worcester City, before beginning his coaching career back at Wolves, while big brother Roy was coaching just down the road at Aston Villa. Maclaren then decided to go globe-trotting, back to Malaysia, where he had enjoyed his time in the R.A.F. He became National Coach and guided Malaysia to the 1972 Olympic Games in Munich. This success got him head hunted, by Sydney City, so, off he went to Australia.
He spent six seasons in then joined Greek ex pats side Hellas as coach.

George McLeod Born Inverness November 30 1932, Died Luton September 5 2016
George played for Brora Rangers and Clachnacuddin before being signed by Luton Town in 1955. However, it was at Brentford between 1958 and 1964 that the skilful winger made his name, playing playing nearly 250 games for the Bees. After a single season with QPR George moved to South Africa to play for Port Elizabeth City, and then to the United States. He eventually returned to and settled in Befordshire where he ran a pub.

Charlie McNeil, Born March 11 1963, Died Dedcember 11 2016
Fallin-based Charlie played for Stirling Albion between 1980 and 1985, earning a reputation as a "supersub". A product of Grangemouth International BC, he later played for Kilsyth Rangers and Fallin Amateurs.

Aggie Moffat, Died April 13 2017
Scottish football has had many stalwarts behind the scenes who never hit the headlines. One such was Aggie Moffat, often described as St Johnstone's "tea lady" but that was just one of her many duties. Originally from Ballingry in Fife, she did the laundry and prepared lunches for the players at Muirton and McDiarmid Park. Aggie's fifteen minutes of fame came in 1991. She took umbrage with then-Rangers Manager Graeme Souness over the state of the away dressing room. After the game ended 1-1, the former Scotland international was livid with his side and took out his frustrations on a kettle. On the confrontation, Aggie said years later: "That row grew arms and legs. It's all water under the bridge now – but I still wouldn't speak to the man." She retired from her work at McDiarmid Park in 2007. Years later, Souness admitted the clash with Aggie persuaded him to quit Scottish football and head back to Liverpool. He said: "What pushed it over the edge for me was when I became involved in an incident with a tea lady at St Johnstone. I ended up arguing in the boardroom with the club chairman (Geoff Brown) and I'm one step away from... you know ... I asked myself what was I doing? This lady wasn't scared of me!"

Billy Milsom, Died December 2016
Billy had been involved with Royal Albert Juniors for over 30 years in various positions from match secretary to physio/ His support and dedication helped the club survive at times when the future looked grave.

Paul Morrison, Died February 2017 Aged 42
Highland League and Junior stalwart Paul Morrison was diagnosed with cancer early in 2017. Scottish football heroes showed their support for Mr Morrison by turning out for a charity match at Spain Park in Aberdeen on February 12. The Aberdeen and Scotland Legends XI took on a select team which was made up of Mr Morrison's team-mates from his career to raise money for cancer charities along with a sold-out sportsman's dinner. The 42-year-old also played for Stonehaven, Banchory, Cove Rangers, Lewis United, Culter and Arbroath. Away from football Paul was a firefighter.

Eric Murray Born December 12 1941, Died November 7 2016
Eric played over 200 games for Kilmarnock and was an ever-present in the season they won the Scottish League Championship, 1964/5. At the time he was described as a right-half – probably a holding midfield player in modern parlance. In 1968 he moved to St Mirren. He later worked as a newspaper circulation representative and as a bookmaker.

Matthew Murray Born December 26 1929, Died April 28 2016
Learned his skills on the wing for Queen's Park and moved to Kilmarnock in 1952. Matt played over 100 times for the Rugby Park side before moving no to Ayr United and St Mirren. By 1958 he was at Barrow, then at Carlisle United. Brought the curtain down on his senior career with Morton in 1960/1.

Max Murray Born 7 November 1935, Died 5 September 2016
Murray was born in Falkirk and began his career at Queen's Park, before moving to Rangers in 1955. His scoring debut came on the 13 August 1955 in a Scottish League Cup match against Falkirk which the club won 5–0. He had a very successful spell at Rangers, winning two Scottish league championships and finishing top scorer three times in a row. He amassed 121 goals in just 154 games and on 24 October 1956 he scored Rangers' first ever goal in European competition, an equaliser in a European Cup first round match against OGC Nice at Ibrox, a match Rangers won 2–1 He left Rangers in 1962 for West Bromwich Albion, but he only lasted a season in English football before he moved back to Scotland. He had a couple of years with Third Lanark scoring 17 goals in 61 games before moving across the city to sign for Clyde

where six games in Season 1965-66 yielded two more goals. He later played in Northern Ireland with Distillery followed before Murray retiring. In later years he was a successful businessman, working as a brewery sales manager in Edinburgh.

Derek Neilson, Born 23 January 1959, Died May 26 2017
Neilson began his career with Dundee United but left the club without making a first team appearance after loan spells with East Stirlingshire and Meadowbank Thistle. Neilson then joined Brechin City and was a regular between the goalposts for the Glebe Park club for seven seasons from 1980 to 1987. He saw out his final years in the senior game with Berwick Rangers before moving to the juniors with Armadale Thistle in 1993. A keen Hibernian fan, Derek held a season ticket with the Hibees and could still be seen regularly in the stands at Easter Road until his final weeks.

Louis Nicholls, Died November 2016
A stalwart committee member at Coldstream FC over many years – the club were saddened to learn of his death.

David Nicol Born May 2 1936, Died June 29 2016
David was signed by Falkirk in 1953 as a winger from Airth Castle Rovers but was quicvkly converted to a full back. Mostly a reserve throughout eight years as a senior, he totalled 10 first team games with the Bairns, Cowdenbeath, Airdrieonians and Stirling Albion. He worked as a mining engineer.

Albert Edward O'Hara Born October 28 1935, Died October 2016
Eddie O'Hara was capped by Scotland Schools and played for Shettleston Juniors as a youngster. He signed for Falkirk in 1955, playing over 100 games during the next three seasons. A key player in the 1957 Cup winning side for Falkirk, he signed for Everton in 1958 along with team mate Alex Parker. He went on to play for Rotherham United and Morton but had his best spell with Barnsley from 1962 until 1965, scoring 36 times in 127 League games. He later moved to South Africa where he played for Bloemfontein City, Westview Appolon and Port Elizabeth City. His bother George O'Hara played for Dundee and Queen of the South.

Stephane Paille, Born June 27 1965, Died June 27 2017
Born in Scionzier, Rhône-Alpes, Paille started out with Sochaux, with whom he played for 7 seasons between 1982 and 1989. He helped the Montbéliard side reach the 1987–88 Coupe de France final, and was voted French Player of the Year at that season's end. He also earned eight caps for France between 1986 and 1989, scoring a single goal. After leaving Sochaux for Montpellier HSC in 1989, whom he joined with close friend Eric Cantona, he spent no more than 2 seasons at the same club during the next 9 years. He joined Girondins de Bordeaux in December 1989, then FC Porto in the summer of 1990. Following a two-year spell at SM Caen between 1991 and 1993, he returned to Bordeaux for a single season. In 1994, he joined Olympique Lyonnais, then moved to Swiss side Servette Geneva in 1995. After one season he returned to France with FC Mulhouse. In September 1995 Paille retired after failing a drugs test due to cannabis use. He told L'Equipe this was due to serious personal problems. He joined Heart of Midlothian in 1996. He was released by the Edinburgh club in May 1997 after failing a drugs test due to his use of Dinintel, a highly-addictive amphetamine-based diet pill. Paille then returned to first club Sochaux, where he held a coaching position for three years between 1999 and 2002. He gained his first managerial role when he was appointed head coach of Besançon RC but left in 2004. He was briefly head coach at Racing Club Paris in 2005, before coaching Angers 2005/6. He died on 27 June 2017, his 52nd birthday.

George Peebles, Born 22 January 1936, Died 16 October 2016
George Peebles, died after a lengthy battle against Parkinson's Disease and dementia. He was one of the heroes of Dunfermline Atheltic's remarkable Scottish Cup win in 1961. That Cup-winner's medal was the only major honour he won during his career, while the closest he got to international recognition was listing as a reserve for a Scotland Under-23 team. That Cup victory catapulted Dunfermline into regular European competition throughout the 1960s, and Peebles played a full part in such games. Falkirk was the first club to spot his talents, playing for local Stirling Secondary Juvenile team Gowanhill. The Brockville club put him on a provisional signing form, and arranged for him to move up to the junior ranks with Dunipace. However, he sustained a knee injury and his provisional signing was cancelled. The Pars, however, had been watching him and quickly pounced – learning Rangers and Stirling Albion were also showing interest. In just over a decade at East End Park he played 431 games, the fourth-highest total for a Pars' player, including one run of 130 in succession. He scored 85 goals – 7th in the Dunfermline top-scoring list, including a hat-trick against Raith Rovers in a 6-0 Fife Derby win. In April, 1966 he joined hometown team Stirling Albion He played over 100 games them before, in 1971, he hung-up his boots to become Reserve Team Coach, under Bob Shankly. He moved-up to become Assistant Manager to Alex Smith, and, when Smith moved on to St Mirren, in December 1986, Peebles took over as manager, holding the reins until March 1988, when he resigned. Away from football Peebles ran a painting and decorating business in Stirling..

Daniel Prodan Born 23 March 1972, Died 16 November 2016
Prodan's link with Scottish football was a three-year spell at Rangers when he never played a single first team game. Rangers paid £2.2 million to Atletico Madrid, but Prodan had a serious knee injury. Rangers' doctor, Stewart Hillis, later revealed that no medical had been conducted, and the transfer was rushed to completion on the strength of falsified documents; the Glasgow club threatened to sue Atlético Madrid, but backed down and released the player in January 2001. He won 54 Romanian caps whilst with Steaua Bucharest and Atletico Madrid. After his time at Rangers he played a few games for lesser clubs in his native land. He died aged 44 of a heart attack.

David Provan, Born 11 March 1941, Died 26 November 2016
Born in Falkirk, Provan played for Bonnyvale Star Provan was a product of the Rangers youth team and played as a full back. He made his debut on 27 December 1958, in a league match away to Third Lanark which Rangers won 3-2. He helped the club win a domestic treble in 1963–4 and played in the 1967 European Cup Winners' Cup Final, which Rangers lost 1–0 to Bayern Munich. Provan is one of the players elected to Rangers' Hall of Fame and he played 262 competitive games for the club, scoring 11 goals. He left the club in June 1970 and joined English club Crystal Palace, although he was not there for long, making only two senior appearances in total before moving on in March 1971, to Plymouth Argyle. He stayed at Plymouth for five seasons and made over 100 appearances. Provan subsequently played for St Mirren where he finished his senior career in 1975 and began his coaching career under then-manager Alex Ferguson. Davie Provan opted not to follow Ferguson when the call from Aberdeen came in the summer of 1978 – but he returned to Ibrox the following season as chief scout and youth coach under his former teammate John Greig, a position he held until the manager's resignation in 1983. He was reserve team coach at Partick Thistle under manager Bertie Auld for a time, then in 1987 he was appointed Albion Rovers manager. He was at Cliftonhill from 1987 to 1991, leading the club to the Scottish Football League Second Division title in 1988–9. He later worked as an SFA Development Officer in Greenock.

Gordon Ritchie, Died January 2017
Gordon served on the committee of Pollok Football Club for over fifty years, including a spell as President and a great many years as club Secretary. Gordon also served as Secretary of the Pollok FC Social Club.

Douglas Rodgers (Died May 2017, Aged 76)
Clachnacuddin lost one of their greatest ever servants with the death of Dougie Rodgers. He was botn into a Clach family – hios father George played for Chelsea before serving Clach in the 1930s.Dougie's nephew, Alex Chisholm, was Chairman of the club when Dougie passed away. Dougie was an electrician to trade working in Inverness and he played as a defender for the club in the 1960s and was one of the most committed and popular players in the team of that period. After his playing days, he became a committee member, a director and ultimately, following in the footsteps of his father, George, he became chairman Clach's centenary year in 1986.

George Ross Born 15/4/23, Died 7/5/16
Born in Inverness, he joined Preston straight from school and went on to play over 400 games for the Deepdale club. He won the FA Youth Cup with them in 1960 and played in the 1964 FA Cup Final. Later played for Southport and in the USA for Washington Diplomats. After leaving football he worked for British Aerospace.

Margaret Ross Died December 16, 2016, Aged 66
Margaret was a popular Director of Dunfermline Athletic FC. In recent years she had provided sterling service to the Pars Supporters Trust and the DAFC Board

Tommy Ross, Born February 27 1946, Died May 19 2017
The scorer of the fastest hat-trick in football, Tommy Ross, died at the age of 71. Ross set the Guinness World Record by scoring three goals in 90 seconds as an 18-year-old while playing for Ross County against Nairn County in 1964. The previous record had been set by a Gillingham player in the 1950s. He scored 44 goals during the 1964-65 season. His form attracted attention from a number of clubs on both sides of the border, including Cardiff City, Millwall, Newcastle and Aberdeen before he moved to Peterborough United in 1965. He then played for York City, Wigan Athletic and Rossendale United before returning to Scotland to play for Brora Rangers in the 1970s. He was later Manager of Tain St Duthus in the North Caledonian League. As well as playing for Brora Rangers, Mr Ross started a construction company with his brothers John and James. He later worked at North Sea oil and gas industry yards in Nigg and Ardersier in the Highlands, and for a car sales company in Inverness. Ross also worked as a youth scout for Tottenham Hotspur, based in the north.

Billy Simpson Born December 12th 1929, Died January 27 2017
Simpson signed for Rangers from Linfield for a sum of £11,500 in 1950. He spent nine years (1950–59) at

Rangers making 239 appearances and scoring 163 goals. He won three championship medals and a Scottish Cup winners medal with Rangers to add to the two Irish League and two Irish Cups he won with Linfield. He left Ibrox in 1959 and spent the last couple of years of his career with Stirling Albion, Partick Thistle and (then non-league) Oxford United. Most notably, Billy Simpson scored twice in the "Ne'erday" Old Firm Derby at Ibrox, in a famous 3-1 victory, immortalised in the song 'A Trip to Ibrox'. In recognition of his service to that club, Simpson has been made a member of the Rangers F.C. Hall of Fame. Simpson made his debut for Northern Ireland in 1951 against Wales, scoring in the process. He represented his country twelve times in total between 1951 and 1958, scoring 5 goals. He was selected in Northern Ireland's squad for the 1958 FIFA World Cup in Sweden but a late injury ensured he did not play at all during the finals.

Jock Skinner (Died July 2016)
Ex President and Main Sponsor of Montrose Roselea, Jock Skinner passed away after a long illness. He spent almost 30 years with the club as they rose from also-rans to a Premier League club. He was owner of the Neptune Bar, long-time sponsor of Montrose Roselea.

John Smith Born 1930, Died August 3rd 2016
John was capped for Junior Scotland with Ardeer Thistle. He signed for Stirling Albion in 1949 and went on to play 155 League games for them, scoring 25 goals. He then switched to Dumbarton where his impressive scoring form continued. In 1959 he joined Tonbridge of the Southern League, topping the scoring charts there as well. Injury brought his career to an end but he remained as Manager of Tonbridge into the 1970s. After his playing career was over he worked in the motor trade.

Eric Stevenson, Born December 25 1942, Died May 18 2017
Stevenson was best known for his ten years of service to Hibernian in the 1960s when he chalked up nearly 400 appearances, mainly on the left wing. Eric had actually been signed by Hearts on a pro-form before he was old enough. The Tynecastle club put the form "in the drawer" and were fined when the misdemeanour was uncovered. Stevenson's mercurial skills may have impressed managers such as Jock Stein and Bob Shankly but they found little favour with Eddie Turnbull when he took over at Hibs. Stevenson was released and ran down his career with a single season at Ayr United. Although born in Eastfield near Harthill, he was brought up in Bonnyrigg in a Hibs-supporting family. After retiring from football he concentrated on his newsagents and licensed grocery business in Bonnyrigg. His biography, *Hibs Through and Through*, published in 2012 is one of the most considered and interesting of its genre.

Robert Stewart Born 3 January 1962, Died 20 August 2016
Rab Stewart's senior career began at Dunfermline for whom he famously scored at Ibrox in a Cup tie that Second Division Dunfermline led 1-0 with ten minutes to go. From Dunfermline he joined Motherwell and then Falkirk. He later played for Queen of the South. Small for a striker, he had a knack of finding space to get efforts in on goal. Away from football he worked as an NHS dental technician.

Thomas McNee Sutherland Born May 3 1931, Died July 23 2016
Tom Sutherland was a decent footballer with Airth Castle Rovers and Glasgow University and played for Scotland Schhols in 1948. He signed for Rangers later that year but never made the first team. He also had a spell with Falkirk before concentrating on an academic career. He moved to the USA and became Professor of Animal genetic at Colorado State University. In 1983 he was Dean of Agriculture and Food Science at Beirut University. In June 1985 he was taken hostage by Islamic gunmen. He spent 2353 days in captivity efore being released on the same day as Terry Waite. He returned to his old job at Colorado University and later won a lawsuit against the Iranian government. The $35 million compensation that he received was use to set up a charity, the Sutherland Family Foundation.

George Taylor Born 1930, Died February 2017
Taylor was a regular in defence for the Scotland Amateur international team in the late 1960s. he played for Hounslow Town, captaining them in the 1962 Amateur Cup Final at Wembley. He later became Manager of Hounslow Town.

John Telfer, Died April 14 2017
John Telfer, who played left back or left half, made his first team debut for Ayr United in January, 1957, after signing from Douglas Water Thistle. The team were relegated that season but the following campaign, swept to the Second Division title, scoring 115 league goals and other 24 in cups which remains a club record. Early in his Ayr United career, John approached manager Jacky Cox to see if he could get him a job in Ayr. A plumbing job was arranged. John Telfer settled in Ayr for the rest of his days and eventually established a business in his name. You will still see the John Telfer vans in and around Ayr. As an Ayr United player, he was obsessed with fitness. Living in Tryfield Place, he stayed literally in the shadow of Somerset

Park and took advantage of this to get immersed in extra training sessions.

Ernest Till, Died November 2016, Aged 97
A midfielder, Ernie represented Raith Rovers from 1938 until 1951 making 229 appearances either side of the Second World War after signing from Crossgates Primrose in September 1938. Edinburgh-born Ernie was brought up in Lawnmarket area of Edinburgh and told of his happy childhood, where his early football beginnings were of playing football "up the closes" and around back areas of the Lawnmarket houses. After playing amateur football in the Lothian Leagues, he moved to play with Bo'ness Cadora, forerunners of the current junior side Bo'ness United. He then moved to play with Crossgates Primrose. Although he had offers to take trials with both Hearts and Hamilton, Ernie decided to sign for Raith Rovers. War interrupted his football career, but before being called up for service in 1940 Ernie played as a guest for Hibernian, which with a laugh he described as hurting as he was always a Hearts supporter. He also played at Tynecastle for a Scotland select against the Empire Army XI. After the war, he was Raith's captain for a period and he was in the side that won the B Division in 1948-49. He left to join Arbroath in November 1951 and eventually finished his playing career with Leith Athletic.

Luke Wallace Died 24/6/16
Drumchapel Amateurs and Partick Thistle youth player Luke Wallace died 1 week after being stabbed at a lane near Bannerman High School in Baillieston. A 16-year-old appeared in court charged with his murder.

Tom Wardrop Born 1931, Died September 14 2016
An inside left, Tom joined East Fife in 1957 from Loanhead Mayflower. He played 1 League game for the Bayview side and later turned out for Duns in the East of Scotland League.

Robert Wilson Died August 2016
Robert was a former Director of hearts and the first Chairman of the Scottish Premier League when it was set up in 1998. Latterly he suffered from Motor Neurone Disease but he was instrumental in the fans buy-out that saw hearts saved from oblivion a few years ago.

Shaun Woodburn, Died January 1st 2017
Shaun was a talented defender playing for Bonnyrigg Rose, Whitehill Welfare and Newtongrange Star for more than ten years. He chose to take a "season out" in 2016/17 because of his young family but intended to be back playing in 2017/18. Shaun died on a New Year's night out in Leith. Three men were later charged with his murder. Shaun ws a fanatical Hibs supporters and a Charity Match was played in his honour during May between Leith Athletic and a Hibernian Legends XI.

Alexander Young Born 3 February 1937, Died 27 February 2017
Alex Young was a Scottish international footballer. He played as a creative forward for Heart of Midlothian and Everton. He won league championship and cup titles with both clubs where he was also a regular goal scorer. Young later played for Glentoran and Stockport County. Internationally he played for the Scottish League and the Scotland national football team. In football folklore he has become known as 'The Golden Vision'. He was born in Loanhead, Midlothian, and played as a youngster for Newtongrange Star. Revered by the fans at both Goodison and Tynecastle, Young featured in a Ken Loach docu-drama made in 1968, called The Golden Vision. His skills deserved greater international recognition than the 8 caps he was awarded – but he was up against players like Jimmy Johnstone and Willie Henderson for a Scotland place. Young was included in the Football League's "100 Legends of the 20th Century" in 1999,[23] and in August 2001 Everton gave him a testimonial at Goodison Park, which over 20,000 fans attended.[6] He was also named as a member of Gwladys Street's Hall of Fame. After retiring from football he settled in Penicuik and ran an upholstery business. His son Jason was also a professional footballer with

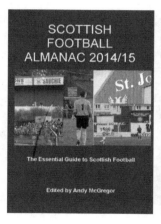

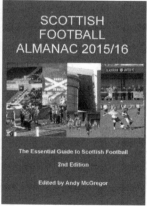

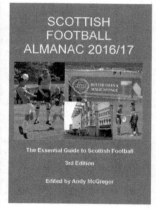